THIRD EDITION

Educational Psychology

A Realistic Approach

Thomas L. Good □ Jere E. Brophy

University of Missouri, Columbia

Michigan State University

Longman
New York & London

To our wives, Suzi and Arlene,
and our children,
Heather, Jeff, Kate, Molly, and Cheri and Joe.

Executive Editor: Raymond O'Connell
Developmental Editor: Naomi Silverman
Production Editor: Barbara A. Chernow
Text Design: Joan Greenfield
Art Director & Cover Design: Laura Ierardi
Photo Research: Leora Kahn
Production Supervisor: Eduardo Castillo
Compositor: Maryland Composition Co., Inc.
Printer and Binder: Alpine Press

(Title/Edition) Educational Psychology: A Realistic Approach, 3rd ed.

Library of Congress Cataloging-in-Publication Data

Good, Thomas L., 1943–
Educational psychology.

Bibliography: p.
Includes index.
1. Educational psychology. I. Brophy, Jere E.
II. Title.
LB1051.G593 1986 370.15 85-19920
ISBN 0-582-28560-7

Photos: p. 24, © George Bellerose, Stock Boston; pp. 26, 38, 39, © Erika Stone; p. 40, © Jean-Claude Legeune, Stock Boston; p. 42, © Elizabeth Homlin, Stock Boston; p. 45, © Joel Gordon, Joel Gordon Photography; p. 55, © Yves De Braine, Stock Boston; p. 57, © Elizabeth Crews, Stock Boston; p. 62, © Susan Lapides, Design Conceptions; p. 65, © David Hurn, Magnum Photos, Inc.; p. 68, © Elizabeth Hamlin, Stock Boston; p. 84, © J. Holland, Stock Boston; p. 95, © Nancy Hays, Monkmeyer Press Photo; p. 97, © Fred Ward, Black Star; p. 103, © Nancy Hays, Monkmeyer Press Photo; p. 107, © Erika Stone; pp. 108, 112, 146, Joel Gordon, Joel Gordon Photography; p. 156, © Susan Lapides, Design Conceptions; p. 167, © Erika Stone; pp. 185, 193, © Donald Dietz, Stock Boston; p. 211, © Marion Bernstein, Erika Stone; p. 241, © Susan Lapides, Design Conceptions; p. 260, © James McInnis, Erika Stone; p. 273, © Marcia Weinstein, Erika Stone; p. 282, © Bill Grimes, Leo de Wys, Inc.; p. 327, © Erika Stone, New York; p. 336, © Billy Grimes, Leo de Wys, Inc.; p. 349, © Peter Vandermark, Stock Boston; p. 372, © Burt Glinn and David Hurn, Magnum Photos, Inc.; p. 376, © Marcia Weinstein, Erika Stone; p. 387, © Erika Stone; p. 408, © Marcia Weinstein, Erika Stone; p. 420, © Jean-Claude Legeune, Stock Boston; pp. 431, 436, © Bill Grimes, Leo de Wys, Inc.; p. 451, © Elizabeth Crews, Stock Boston; p. 453, © Erich Hartmann and David Hurn, Magnum Photos, Inc.; p. 458, © Guy Le Querrec and David Hurn, Magnum Photos, Inc.; p. 459, © Marcia Weinstein, Erika Stone; p. 462, © Peter Vandermark, Stock Boston; p. 490, Burt Glinn and David Hurn, Magnum Photos, Inc.; pp. 502, 523, © Susan Lapides,

Design Conceptions; p. 527, © Joel Gordon, Joel Gordon Photography; p. 540 © Elizabeth Hamlin, Stock Boston; pp. 554, 556, © James McInnis, Erika Stone, New York; p. 559, © Marcia Weinstein, Erika Stone; p. 566, © Peter Vandermark, Stock Boston; p. 581, © Marion Bernstein, Erika Stone; p. 594, © Erika Stone; p. 599, © Susan Lapides, Design Conceptions; p. 604, © Monkmeyer Press Photo; p. 609, © Bill Grimes, Leo de Wys, Inc.; p. 622, © Marcia Weinstein, Erika Stone; p. 631, © Marion Bernstein, Erika Stone; p. 653, © Joel Gordon, Joel Gordon Photography; p. 654, © Frank Siteman, Stock Boston; p. 687, © James McInnis, Erika Stone; p. 700, © Erika Stone; p. 703, © Marcia Weinstein, Erika Stone; p. 725, © Susan Lapides, Design Conceptions; pp. 736, 740, © Susan Lapides, Design Conceptions; p. 763, © Bill Grimes, Leo de Sys, Inc.; p. 787, © Christopher Morrow, Stock Boston. Photo, p. 796, © Marcia Weinstein, Erika Stone. Figures & Tables: Fig. 8.1, page 202, © M. C. Escher heirs % Condon Art-Beam-Holland. Figures Tables 11.1, 11.2, 11.3, pp. 303, 309, 310, from *Principles of Instructional Design,* 2/e, by Robert M. Gagne and Leslie J. Briggs. Copyright © 1979 by Holt, Rinehart & Winston. Reprinted by permission of CBS College Publishing. Table 12.3, pp. 342–44, from Anderson, L., Evertson, C., and Brophy, J. (1982). *Principles of Small-Group Instruction in Elementary Reading.* East Lansing, MI: Institute for Research on Teaching, Michigan State University (Occasional Paper No. 58). Table 12.4, p. 347, adapted from T. Good and C. Power, "Designing Successful Classroom Environments for Different Types of Students." *Journal of Curriculum Studies* 8 (1976): 45–60. Copyright © 1976. Fig. 15.2, p. 428, from B. Weiner, "A theory of motivation for some classroom experiences." *Journal of Educational Psychology, 71* (1979), p. 18. Copyright © 1979 The American Psychological Association. Reprinted by permission of the author. Table 18.2, p. 531, from E. Buskin and R. Hess (1980). "Does affective education work: A review of seven programs." *Journal of School Psychology* 18 (1). New York: Human Sciences Press, Inc., 72 Fifth Avenue, New York, NY 10011. Copyright © 1980. Human Sciences Press, Inc. Table 20.1, p. 588, from C. M. Evartson, E. T. Emmer, J. P. Sanford, and B. S. Clements (1983). "Improving Classroom Management: An Experiment in Elementary School Classrooms." *Elementary School Journal* 84 (2). Copyright © 1983. Reprinted by permission of the University of Chicago Press. Fig. 24.1, p. 684, from Guilford, J. (1959). "Three Faces of Intellect." *American Psychologist* 14, 469–479. Copyright © 1959 by The American Psychological Assocation. Reprinted by permission of the publisher and author. Fig. 26.1, p. 728, from *Measurement and Evaluation in Education and Psychology,* 2/e, by William A. Mehrens and Irvin J. Lehman. Copyright © 1978 by Holt, Rinehart & Winston. Reprinted by permission of CBS College Publishing. Table 28.5, p. 775, from John A. Green, *Teacher-Made Tests,* 2/e (New York: Harper & Row, 1975). Copyright © 1963, 1975 by John A. Green. (After "Safety Rules for the Safe Operation of Power Woodworking Tools," Frank Pexton Lumber Co., Denver, CO., pp. 8–9). Reprinted by permission of Harper & Row, Publishers, Inc. Table 28.6, page 776, from John A. Green, *Teacher-Made Tests,* 2nd edition (New York: Harper & Row, 1975). Copyright © 1963, 1975 by John A. Green. (After *Measuring Educational Achievement,* by William J. Michels and R. Ray Karnes, McGraw-Hill, 1950). Reprinted by permission of Harper & Row, Publishers, Inc. Case Studies, pp. 781–84, adapted with permission of the publisher from "The American Revolution and Its Meaning," pp. 106–116 of A NEW HISTORY OF THE UNITED STATES; AN INQUIRY APPROACH, Bartlett, Fenton, Fowler and Mandelbaum. A book in the Holt Social Studies Curriculum, General Editor, Edwin Fenton. Copyright © 1969 by Holt, Rinehart & Winston.

Contents

Preface

This text is designed for first educational psychology courses at the college level. It provides eclectic, balanced coverage of the theories and basic concepts of educational psychology, integrates them with applications, and offers concrete advice. Appropriate instruction makes a difference in the efficiency of learning in all types of instructional settings. The purpose of this book is to improve instruction by helping teachers to understand the realities of teaching, to understand and organize relevant psychological theory, and to become competent at tasks instructors perform.

Most educational psychology texts emphasize topics or theories of educational psychology in isolation from one another and from the tasks of teaching. While prospective teachers and instructors need to master psychological concepts and principles, the key to successful teaching is the *integration* of concepts into *teaching strategies* that are responsive to the learning needs of particular groups of students.

The text is written from a decision-making perspective. Stress is placed upon the need to interpret psychological concepts so that they apply to specific learning settings. Teaching involves more than general decision making or the isolated application of principles. Successful teaching requires a fundamental understanding of how students learn and develop, the ability to use this appreciation to coordinate knowledge and skills in a specific context.

The book is organized around applications designed to enable readers to become decision makers who can stimulate student learning. It is research oriented, but with an eclectic attitude to theory and the latest research. No single approach can solve all the problems teachers confront, but an integration of ideas drawn from a variety of viewpoints can provide the basis for planning instruction.

Our stress is on teaching. Our aim is to prepare students for their future jobs. Therefore, while our approach to both learning and teaching is optimistic and humanistic, we want our readers to be realistic in recognizing problems, constraints, and limitations in students, in classes, and in themselves. Through this *realistic approach*, studnets are prepared to face the challenges and rewards of teaching others.

Teaching Features

The book includes a number of features designed to enhance student learning:

Case Studies: provocative, true-to-life classroom dilemmas or problems in other settings which accompany each chapter, add a special applied dimension.

Questions and Problems: The thought-provoking questions at the end of each chapter can be used for class discussion, assignments, or independent study.

Objectives: Each chapter begins with a brief list of objectives that describe what the student will be able to do after mastering the material.

Chapter Outlines: These open each chapter and allow students to familiarize themselves with upcoming content and to organize the material for examinations.

Marginal Notes: These make it easy for students to locate and go back to material.

Ancillaries

The *Study Guide* contains questions, with an answer key, for reviewing and mastering each chapter, along with independent projects involving student observation and experimentation. The accompanying *Instructor's Manual* will be helpful to instructors in planning their curricula. The manual contains over a thousand test items, all new, arranged in test sets and unit exams for flexible use, together with ideas for lectures and demonstrations, Study Guide Feedback Sheets, and general resources and a film guide.

Acknowledgments

We gratefully acknowledge the support provided by the Center for Research in Social Behavior, University of Missouri at Columbia, and the Institute for Research on Teaching, Michigan State University. We also want to thank several individuals who generously helped us prepare the manuscript: Diane Chappell, Gail Hinkel, and June Smith. Special thanks is given to Gail Hinkel, who read a draft of the manuscript and who offered insightful editorial advice.

Many staff members at Longman, Inc. have provided professional assistance to the development of the book, and we gratefully acknowledge their capable help. We would like to especially thank Naomi Silverman who provided special professional assistance with every aspect of the textbook.

Part One

Introduction

Jane Lawton, a junior at State University majoring in Secondary Education, had wanted to be a teacher since she was a junior high school student. Finally she had the opportunity to take teaching methods courses. Until now she had taken a range of arts and sciences courses—courses that she generally found interesting and important. She was excited that now she had the chance to combine her knowledge of content and teaching processes. She was worried, however, because she had received a phone call from her mother earlier that day informing her that both she and Jane's father were very ill with the flu and it was important for Jane to come home. Jane wondered how she could approach Harry Shelton, the professor who taught her Foundations of Education course, and how she could tell him she needed to miss the first course examination that was scheduled that day. Would he think she was conning him? She had a good grade now, and she didn't want to jeopardize that. However, she wondered what she would do if she were in that situation as a teacher. She thought, "Is it fair to extend extra time to some students but not to all; how does a teacher go about making exceptions?"

Bill Bowers was a twelfth-grade Chemistry teacher at Newton High School. As he listened to Hank Sherman discuss an experiment, he wondered why Joe Rogers had difficulty in answering the question that he had just asked him. A few days ago Joe knew the material and Bill was puzzled as to why Joe did not retain the information. As he continued listening to Hank, he noticed that two students in the back of the room had started a conversation. He wondered if he should say anything to them to bring them back to the class discussion, but he decided not to do so because the conversation "appeared" like it would be a short one, and Bill did not want to disrupt the entire class. As he continued to listen to Hank's response, Bill wondered what follow-up question he should ask, whether or not he had spent too much time in the lecture/discussion phase of the lesson, and if the class should begin laboratory work.

Ruth Mentor, a fifth-grade teacher at Casis Elementary School, noticed that Robbie Baker was extremely inattentive and doing poorly on her assignments since she had moved to the back of the room a couple of weeks ago. Ruth wondered if Robbie's poor performance was due to the fact that she had been moved away from her best friend for excessive talking, or perhaps because she was having trouble attending that far away from the teacher. Did Robbie need the extra structure and contact with the teacher that she had gotten when she was in the front of the room? Perhaps Robbie couldn't see the board or hear well from the back of the room. Ruth started to think about what she would do next in order to determine which of these possibilities was most likely. She was concerned about Robbie and wanted to get her back on track.

Tim Coleman was a seventh-grade math teacher at Jennings Junior High. He was teaching one of his favorite topics—converting base 10 to other number systems. This week he had been showing students how to convert a base 10 number system to base 2 and then to base 8. However, he was disturbed by the fact that most of the students seemed to be extremely bored with the material and assignments. He kept getting questions like, "Why do we have to study this stuff? We'll never use this in a million years." He lamented the fact that he had not been able to convey to the students the importance of the work that he was presenting.

Carolyn Lanier listened as Alice and Dick, two of her star pupils, complained after class about the exam that she had handed back that day. Alice said irritably, "That test was totally unfair. We spent 80 percent of our time the past three weeks on topics that were not covered on the exam. The material on which we spent only 20 percent of class time made up virtually the entire test! That's not a test, that's a guessing game!"

As we state in this chapter, teaching involves making many decisions and making them quickly. Some contend that teachers make more decisions, under worse conditions, than any other managers in society. Teaching is complex because it demands the ability to carefully analyze rapidly changing social and instructional interactions and to respond to a variety of issues simultaneously. Furthermore, successful teaching requires that teachers have a thorough understanding of human development, learning theory, instructional theory, motivational theory, and classroom management theory, as well as knowledge of how to assess student learning.

The vignettes here present dilemmas that teachers have to deal with in the classroom. For example, instructors must determine the extent to which social factors affecting students should be taken into consideration when making decisions about course requirements. Teachers must be fair to all students while at the same time being especially responsive to unique needs of individual students. For instance, the issue that Harry Shelton faces involves a type of decision teachers have to make every day.

To reiterate, as the Bill Bowers example shows, teachers must make many rapid decisions if they are going to be effective in the classroom. Teachers who are well organized, who know their subject matter, and who plan ahead (proactively understand what they are trying to do in the classroom) are more likely to be successful than teachers who lack the prerequisites for effective decision making.

As the example involving Ruth Mentor and her student Robbie indicates, teachers often have to make subtle inferences about whether student difficulties are caused by developmental factors, motivational factors, or instructional factors. The first step in solving a problem is understanding the cause of a student's difficulty. Teachers who have better subject-matter backgrounds and who know how students learn and develop will have a fuller range of tools with which to assess student problems.

The Tim Coleman and Carolyn Lanier examples illustrate two enduring problems of classroom teaching. If teachers are to be successful they have to motivate students so that students are involved in and actively trying to learn assigned material. Teachers must develop evaluation systems that accurately and objectively measure student ability. These vignettes represent only a few of the issues that successful classroom teachers will have to deal with.

We believe that teachers can have a major, positive influence on the way students learn and develop. Some teachers are vital forces; others have only minor impact on their students. Teachers who have an impact on students' lives have a genuine interest in students and the ability to express that interest, know their subject matter, and possess detailed information about instructional processes and the ways students learn and develop. In this chapter, we will explore the knowledge and conceptual skills that are emphasized in this textbook. You will see that educational psychology can provide an important framework for looking at learners, the learning process, and the learning situation. The content of educational psychology—including an understanding of students' development and personality, the learning process, the psychology of teaching methods, classroom management, classroom motivation, and evaluation—offers important tools that can be utilized to become an effective classroom teacher.

Chapter 1

Classrooms, Teachers, Instruction, and Educational Psychology

CHAPTER OUTLINE

OBJECTIVES

When you have mastered the material in this chapter you will be able to

1. List the component skills of teaching and explain how the study of educational psychology can help one become a successful instructor
2. Describe the relationship between theories and hypotheses, and between teaching and decision making
3. Describe the general model of teacher decision making, using a practical example
4. Describe the common aspects of classrooms, noted by Doyle and Jackson, that teachers must deal with, and explain how these common features shape the task of teaching
5. Describe Shavelson's model of teachers' preinstructional decisions
6. Distinguish successful versus less successful teachers on the basis of their expectations and attitudes toward students
7. Describe how the classroom environment, its routines, and the role expectations for teachers and students constrain teacher decision making
8. Describe ways that group pressure affects individual student performance

Teachers Make Decisions

Jan Reisch moved nervously across the room as she conducted a discussion with her American studies class. She was irritated because the discussion wasn't going particularly well and she felt that few of the students had read the material. She was also upset and distracted by the minor but constant misbehavior of a few students. She gradually became angrier—she could feel the back of her neck stiffen and her palms become moist. Finally, she reacted: "Ralph Jordan, give Terri her pencil back and get in your seat now! You've been fooling around for the last two weeks! I've had it! For the next two afternoons, I want you to report to detention period."

At the end of class, Ralph came to her desk and said politely, but with confidence, "Look, I'm sorry about being out of my seat playing with Terri. I know I've been a pain recently. I've had problems at home for the past few weeks and . . . well, I don't want to talk about it." He hesitated a moment and then said, "I'm genuinely sorry and I'll shape up. Last Thursday I started to work at the grocery store on Main Street and I need to be there after school. I really need the job. Can we work something else out?"

Should Jan stick with her statement so as not to undermine her credibility with students? Should she compromise? (She could give Ralph a couple of days to rearrange his schedule with his employer.) If she cancels the punishment or provides a substitute, should she say anything to the class?

Bill Bower looked at the test results of his fifth graders on the social studies unit. Half the class had less than 60 percent correct—a miserable performance. He asked himself, "Should I reteach this unit? It's an important one. Should I go on? It's getting late in the year and I've only covered half the text. At this rate they won't be ready to do sixth-grade work. Maybe I should go on but assign some type of homework review."

Should Bill Bower reteach the unit? If he assigns homework, but students still do relatively poorly, what then? Is the "sixth-grade curriculum" a relevant restriction on a fifth-grade teacher?

John Dalton paused and tried to think of a way he could rephrase a question in order to help Helen answer. He felt that she really knew the material. However, Helen and two other students, Rick and Jeannie, were so shy that it was difficult to determine whether they didn't respond because they didn't know the answer or because they lacked confidence. Should John Dalton ask Helen, Rick, and Jeannie easier questions than he asks other students? Or will asking them easier questions increase their embarrassment? If they don't answer his first question, should he ask additional questions until they give a response? Would such persistence only deepen the insecurity that these students feel in public response situations?

As these vignettes indicate, teaching requires making countless decisions, some of which need to be made on the spot. Teachers need to make decisions about what to teach, how to present information to students, and how to determine whether or not students understand and can apply important concepts. This is just as true for teaching in nonclassroom situations as it is for classroom teaching. Successful teachers use principles of educational psychology to make appropriate decisions.

Educators and Decision Making

Decision-making needs

Anyone who attempts to instruct others (e.g., parents teaching children, instructors teaching managerial trainees) can benefit from knowledge of educational psychology and decision-making models. For example, a nutrition educator needs to determine the amount of information to present in one training session, and the sequence in which to present it, as well as to determine what material students can master through self-study and what requires detailed explanation. Nutrition educators, as do all educators, need to define their goals and to determine criteria for meeting those goals. In this chapter the examples of decision making focus on classroom teaching. However, keep in mind that the decision making model is applicable to all instructional settings and teaching roles.

Educational Psychology and Instructional Decision Making

What is educational psychology?

Educational psychology provides a framework for looking at the student, the learning process, and the learning situation. The study of educational psychology includes the following areas:

- ☐ Educational objectives
- ☐ Student development and personality
- ☐ The learning process
- ☐ The psychology of teaching methods (selecting, organizing, motivating, and presenting)
- ☐ Classroom management (preventing and reacting to student behavior problems, obtaining student cooperation)
- ☐ Evaluation of results—have educational goals been realized?

Dembo and Hillman (1976) believe that good teaching requires mastery of three areas: (1) knowledge and conceptual skills (the content of educational psychology); (2) teaching skills; and (3) decision-making skills. Our goal in this book is to provide a format for integrating these three areas.

Other educational psychologists also have emphasized that good teaching is a blend of technical knowledge and interpersonal skills. Ausubel, Montemayor, and Svajian (1977) state that among the many characteristics effective teachers must have are the technical skills of selecting, organizing, and interpreting sequences of instruction, as well as the ability to be fair, patient, and sympathetic while managing learning activities. In essence, effective instructors combine teaching skills with the belief that the method of instruction can make a difference in learning. They are able to effectively apply the principles drawn from the study of learning, motivation, development, and teaching.

Why Emphasize Decision Making?

Importance of decision making

We stress a decision-making approach to teaching because we believe that there are no simple prescriptions for classroom success. Research yields valuable concepts and ways of looking at classrooms. However, it does not yield answers.

Action zone concept

A good example of the need to use classroom research findings as tools and concepts—ways of looking at events—rather than as answers can be seen in Adams and Biddle's (1970) discussion of the "action zone." They found that students who sat in the action zone (the middle front-row seats and the seats extending directly up the middle aisle) receive more opportunities to participate in class than do other students. Adams and Biddle's action zone concept is important as a tool for analyzing classroom participation patterns. However, if interpreted too literally, this study might suggest that teachers or classroom observers should concentrate their attention on what takes place on the front row and on the middle aisle of the classroom.

More recently, Alhajri (1981) studied 32 classrooms and found only one with an action zone that matched the pattern Adams and Biddle described. However, Alhajri found many classrooms in which a different kind of action zone was present. If observers had been monitoring these classes for only one type of action zone, they may not have perceived the action zones that were present, but that took a different form.

Goals of this Book

In this book we stress that theoretical principles and research findings provide a basis for planning and implementing instruction. However, teachers have to act as independent decision makers and apply these general concepts and principles carefully, keeping their particular students and their own goals in mind. This book provides information and introduces concepts that teachers can use to develop solutions to problems such as those Jan Reisch, Bill Bower, and John Dalton faced, and to make the types of decisions demanded of teachers or those who plan instructional activities.

We see this text and the field of educational psychology generally as the systematization of information and concepts that help a classroom teacher become more aware of classroom behavior, and to better interpret the significance of such behavior (e.g., to understand the motivation that is associated with it), as well as to help plan purposeful strategies for bringing about desired changes in students.

As Rosenholtz and Smylie (1984) noted, one of the hoped for goals of those who enter teaching is to develop skills that will be important, positive influences on students' academic and social growth. This book will assist you in the development of attitudes and behavior in yourself that will allow you to help students in your class.

Goals of this Chapter

In this chapter we introduce a model, a way of looking at classroom decision making that illustrates the fact that teachers who make good decisions (and who are willing to correct poor ones) do the most to foster student motivation and learning. After presenting a decision-making model, we discuss a few problems that almost all teachers will face and must solve if they are to make good decisions within the contexts in which they teach. Finally, we discuss some of the special problems that beginning teachers face.

Teacher Planning—The First Step in Decision Making

Teaching plans and theories

McDonald (1965) stated that any teaching plan is: (1) a guide for action; (2) a set of decisions; and (3) a small theory about how to produce learning. Although the word "theory" is aversive to many people (typically because they incorrectly interpret "theoretical" to mean "impractical"), we all use personal theories (systematic sets of beliefs about what we should do) to make decisions. For example, we all have theories about how to maximize our chances of making a good impression in a conversation. Some of us believe that listening is the best strategy; others prefer to take the initiative. Our theory, whether or not we have made it explicit to ourselves, predicts our behavior in a conversation with a new acquaintance.

Gage (1963, pp. 94–95) presents the view that "all of us are theorists" this way: "They differ not in whether they use theory, but in the degree to which they are aware of the theory they use. The choice facing the man in the street and the research worker alike is not whether to theorize but whether to articulate his theory, to make it explicit, to get it out in the open where he can examine it. Implicit theories . . . are used by all of us in our everyday affairs."

Common beliefs and assumptions

Many beliefs and assumptions that are common among teachers turn out to be myths when subjected to systematic study. For example, the popular view that frequent teacher praise of student performance facilitates student achievement has been shown to be false. Selective praise is useful, but excessive praise may interfere with student learning. Also, in general, the timing and quality of praise is more important than its frequency (see Brophy, 1981). Such complexities, even about seemingly obvious matters, illustrate why teachers must continually think and make decisions. Research does not yield simple answers like "praise is always good."

A major goal of educational psychologists is to make explicit assumptions about the conditions that facilitate learning and to collect data that verify or refute these assumptions. Some readers probably raised a puzzled eyebrow upon reading the previous sentence. They prefer the facts—"Just tell me what works; that's all I want to know." Unfortunately, if we were to restrict ourselves to a discussion of what always works, we would end the book here. No teaching strategy or plan will work for all students, all goals, or all settings. However, some teaching behaviors have a high probability of bringing about a desired response. For example, correcting a minor disturbance in the classroom nonverbally (with perhaps a shake of the head) is usually, but not always, more economical and less disruptive than a verbal strategy. Similarly, preventing behavioral problems is easier than correcting students after misbehavior has occurred (Doyle, 1985). The study of educational psychology provides a way of formulating hypotheses about effective classroom teaching.

Hypotheses

A hypothesis is simply an intelligent guess based on all available information. Decisions are based on hypotheses about what will work. The more integrated information we have, the more confident we can be. The less information we have, the greater the risk that our strategy will fail. For example, one may hypothesize that an attractive stranger is "datable" because there is no ring on the "key" finger. However, many married people do not wear wedding rings because they are lost, or are too small, or are irritating to the skin.

Teaching decisions and goals

Teaching strategies operate in the same way. Often one must make a decision ("Will my students integrate ideas better if I require them to prepare for a formal exam or if I assign a take-home exam on this new topic that I am teaching for the first time?") using only minimal knowledge, such as in the ring example in the previous paragraph. At other times decisions are made based on considerable knowledge—research, past experience with previous students—but still with the risk that the strategy will not work. If we are explicit about our teaching goals and the type of behavior that we will accept as evidence that students are making satisfactory progress, we can identify poor hypotheses and change teaching plans.

A Model for Decision Making

Instructional goals

Figure 1.1 presents a model for decision making. As the model suggests, intelligent decision making begins with a clear statement of instructional goals. If a teacher does not have clear goals and their relative importance in mind, it is impossible to make optimal use of classroom time and resources. However, it is impossible for teachers to be explicit about all decisions that they make, especially beginning teachers. For example, a new third-grade teacher who observed in a first-grade classroom during an early field experience course and who student taught in a sixth-grade classroom, faces many start-up issues—how much structure do nine-year-olds need, what are the key mathematics objectives at this grade level and how can they be presented in an interesting fashion? Important but less immediate issues may have to undergo analysis at a later time (e.g., an examination of the correspondence between the textbook and the standardized testing program).

Also, teaching is sufficiently complex that teachers can never gather all the information they would like to have or make decisions in a leisurely fashion. Teachers often have time to ask only three or four students to respond and thus must make inferences about the extent to which all students are ready to learn from the next instructional demonstration. For lack

Figure 1.1 A Model of Teacher Decision Making

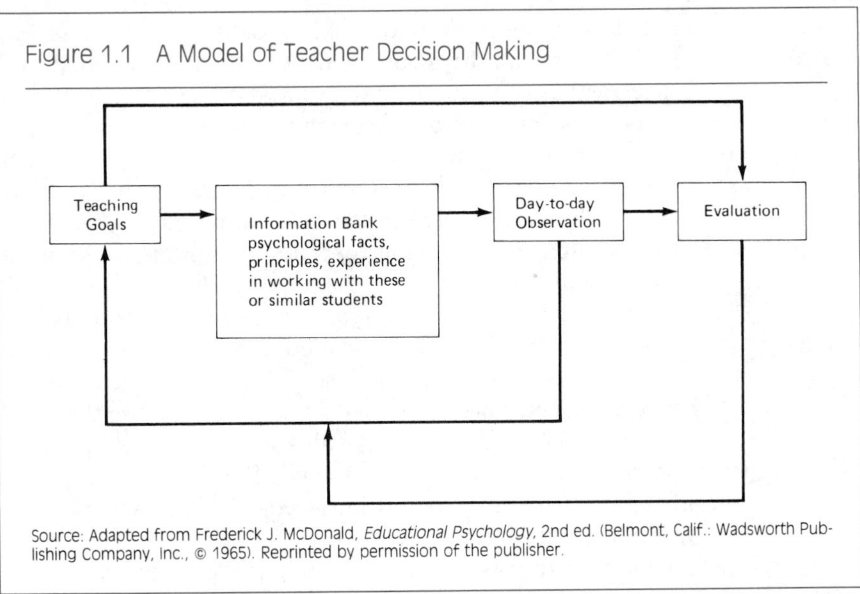

Source: Adapted from Frederick J. McDonald, *Educational Psychology*, 2nd ed. (Belmont, Calif.: Wadsworth Publishing Company, Inc., © 1965). Reprinted by permission of the publisher.

of time, teachers must depend on routines, heuristics, and other simplification strategies for processing information (Bromme and Brophy, 1983). Later in the chapter we illustrate other factors that hinder the ability of the teacher to act as a decision maker. However, despite these problems, successful teachers behave in a deliberate, reflective way whenever possible.

Decision Making: An Example

Assume that Ted Wilson, a high school speech teacher, wants his students to develop the ability to make skillful extemporaneous speeches. This is his ultimate goal. But when should Ted teach this skill—early or late in the year? How can he decide (make a hypothesis)?

To make this decision, Ted will have to specify the other goals he has in mind. Let us assume that Ted is concerned with the following learner goals: the ability to introduce a speaker; to deliver a formal, informative speech; to deliver a formal, persuasive speech; to make an extemporaneous speech; to lead a committee discussion; and to conduct interviews.

Goal statements

Next, Ted needs to define his goal statements more explicitly. What does he mean by "the ability to introduce a speaker"? Does he mean that the student will be able to deliver with ease a brief introduction that someone else has written, or that the student will be able to write and deliver appropriate introductions for different types of audiences—for example, for audiences whose preconceived notions of the speaker are either hostile, neutral, or supportive?

Scheduling class work

After defining what he wants to accomplish, Ted will be in a better position to estimate the time it will take to fulfill each goal. If Ted determines that the students' ability to deliver a formal, informative speech is his most important goal, then he probably should introduce informative speeches relatively early in the year. This will enable each student to present several speeches of this type during the year and to make better use of student-instructor feedback to enhance learning. In contrast, if interview technique is relatively unimportant, he may want to schedule it toward the end of the year, where it can be eliminated if some units take more time than anticipated. Obviously, if less important material is presented first, this option is excluded.

Pretesting

After stating goals clearly, teachers may want to evaluate their students immediately. This is often called pretesting, since the evaluation or test precedes instruction. In Ted's speech class this might mean having everyone make a one-minute, ungraded presentation before the class. Even from brief performances, Ted can gain valuable information about the general ability of the class and make guesses about how fast he can proceed in the course. Furthermore, he can gain knowledge about those students who are likely to make excellent presentations, and can use this information profitably when he arranges the order of student presentations on the first assignment. Information obtained from a preliminary evaluation, whether from a written test or an oral performance, supplements the general information that teachers possess. Hence, a teacher's familiarity with pacing, review, distributed practice, reward, modeling, and anxiety can be combined with knowledge about specific students' skills in order to make reasonable assumptions about conditions that will optimize instruction for the class and for each individual.

Decision Making Is a Continuing Process

Though preliminary evaluation is often very useful, teachers can start by making instructional decisions based on their understanding of general learning principles, instructional methodology, and knowledge acquired from past experience with students. However, whether teachers begin by pretesting or by using professional judgment, they must evaluate the wisdom of their initial decisions regularly. Teachers can do this by using the feedback (student comments, observation of student behavior) from day-to-day teaching activities and from formal evaluation (classroom tests, themes). Hence, a teacher may legitimately change some of the goals in the class as new information is gathered.

Student feedback

Student feedback often changes teachers' goals. For example, teachers may see that some students have already mastered certain objectives, so they can replace these objectives with new ones. For instance, in Ted's case effectively introducing a speaker was a skill mastered more quickly than Ted anticipated. Conversely, teachers may realize that some of their instructional aspirations will be impossible to reach.

The system we describe here is an active, dynamic one. Teachers make plans based upon their professional judgment, the philosophy and policies of the schools in which they teach, and the characteristics of students in their classrooms. Once objectives are set, effective teachers actively monitor student progress and alter instructional decisions as necessary.

Instructional objectives

The starting point and the general schedule for a course are influenced not only by the relative importance of various instructional objectives, but also by their logical sequencing. For example, it is necessary to determine whether some of these objectives involve skills that must be mastered before one can successfully pursue another objective. It would be counterproductive in a mathematics course to teach division prior to teaching subtraction.

In Ted's speech class, the simplest task for the student to master is the introduction of a speaker. This task contains key elements common to all other tasks—assumption of leadership role, public utterances, and so on. And it has several features that make it manageable for many students; it is highly structured, brief, and few memory or timing skills are needed. In general, the limited scope of the task, its minimal anxiety-arousal properties, and the high probability that students can complete it successfully combine to make it a good first presentation.

Task analysis

Task analysis, the attempt to find necessary starting and connecting points in sequencing instruction, is an important activity. In this particular example, with relatively mature high school students, Ted could probably start with any of the goals. There is no critical starting point in this instructional sequence, as there often is with younger students or with more sequentially organized subject matter. However, some arrangements are more efficient than others.

In addition to goal and task analysis, information about students' general aptitudes, interests, and other learner characteristics such as achievement motivation and anxiety is essential to effective instructional decisions. If most of the students in Ted's class are capable, he may decide to start the course with fairly difficult and challenging assignments, and plan to move along at a rapid pace. If his students are poorly motivated and untalented, he may decide to cover fewer skills and slow the pace of the course so that students can review key skills frequently. He may also spend some of the instructional time in game-like activities to maintain student interest. Or if the class has a wide range of abilities, he may choose other strategies. Concepts of intelligence (e.g., Sternberg, 1984) and motivation (e.g., Ames & Ames, 1984, 1985) are useful in making instructional decisions.

The decision-making model presented in Figure 1.1 is a general one. It is possible to develop more specific models about different types of decisions that teachers make. Figure 1.2, based on Shavelson's (1978, 1983) work, illustrates how teachers make preinstructional decisions. This figure helps to clarify some of the factors involved when teachers plan instruction.

Cues

As Shavelson (1978) notes, teachers possess much information, or cues, about students. This information comes from sources such as previous class performance, informal observation, standardized test scores, and reports from other teachers. Teachers make judgments about what students can do, what they are interested in, and so forth. This information can influence instructional planning positively if teachers use it appropriately.

Figure 1.2 Some Factors Contributing to Teachers' Preinstructional Decisions

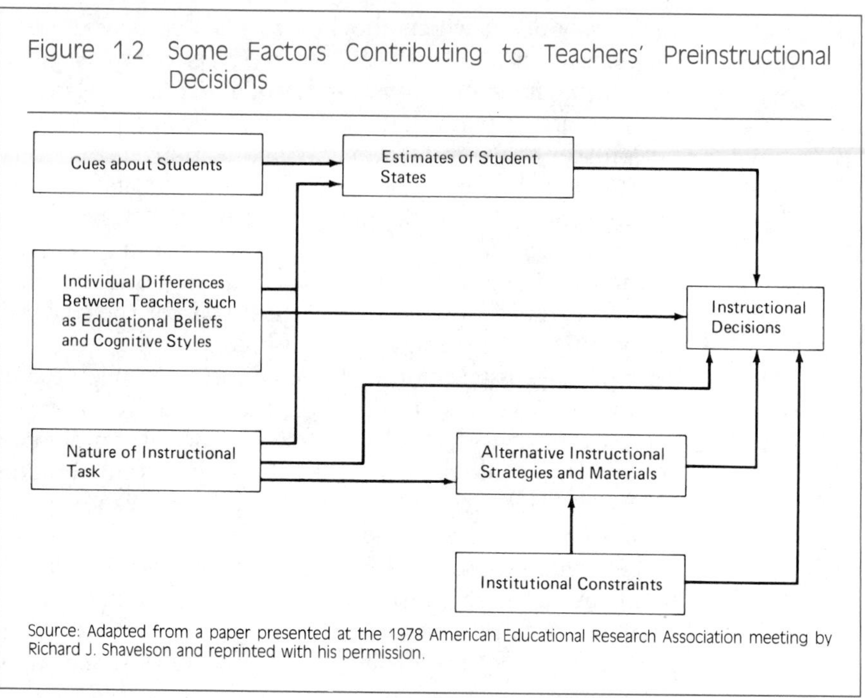

Source: Adapted from a paper presented at the 1978 American Educational Research Association meeting by Richard J. Shavelson and reprinted with his permission.

Teachers also have personal beliefs about instruction that vary widely (Clark & Peterson, 1985) and can affect instructional decisions, such as what to teach, in many ways. What teachers think about the purpose of education also influences their instructional decisions. Teachers interested in affective goals (how students *feel* about content, themselves, and others) are likely to consider different instructional strategies than teachers who are more interested in cognitive goals (subject matter knowledge). Teachers who emphasize affective goals may group students frequently and allow them to work cooperatively (Slavin, 1984; Slavin et al., 1985). In contrast, teachers who want to maximize cognitive growth may individualize the curriculum and encourage students to learn at a rapid pace.

Teaching goals

Shavelson's (1978) model suggests that the nature of instructional tasks is another source of influence on instructional decisions. The fact that a particular text or curriculum is available may make some instructional strategies more appropriate or likely than other strategies. Curriculum packages may also tend to make some student cues more important than others. We believe that teachers who are aware of how they make decisions and who consciously monitor progress toward their goals will be more effective than teachers who operate with vague theories.

Teachers Constantly Make Hypotheses

Teachers make broad strategy decisions as well as decisions about the sequence of instructional activities. Research tells us that teachers have to make complex decisions rapidly and under adverse conditions (Clark & Peterson, 1985). Consider a few of the decisions Ted will have to make. When his students make their first presentation, should the focus be on the entire skill (speaker introduction), or is it better for the students to do only a part of the task (for example, deliver an effective opening sentence that avoids a trite phrase)? When the students complete their speeches, should they get public or private feedback? Should the feedback be from peers as well as from the teacher? Should the teacher systematize the feedback either verbally or by providing a form, or should it be spontaneous? Can too much feedback—even if positive—interfere with learning? When students make good presentations early in the year, should they receive praise or just matter-of-fact, noncommital feedback? Or, should the teacher express mild disappointment and encourage the students to try harder?

Day-to-day decision making

The decisions discussed so far are ones that teachers can make prior to instruction and student performance. However, many decisions have to be made on a day-to-day basis. Five students are talking quietly but persistently in the middle of the room as George, a student in Ted's speech class, shakily delivers his first extemporaneous speech. Should Ted stop the disturbance, reassure George, and then allow him to continue? Or should Ted wait until the speech is over? In another situation, several students are not participating in the feedback discussions that follow each presentation. Should Ted ask these students to outline speeches as they listen to them? Should he call on reluctant students directly rather than allow participation in the discussion to be voluntary?

Now assume that students are performing a new speech skill and that the first two students do poorly. Ted suspects that the students have misunderstood the assignment. Should he continue with the next three student presentations planned that day? What other options does he have?

Another day, Ted decides to allow students, for variety, to analyze presentations in small groups. However, the groups engage in little substantive exchange. Should he continue with the small groups, perhaps after giving more instructions about what he expects? What information does he need to make the decision?

The psychological concepts presented in this text are useful tools for assessing classroom behavior and are helpful in making on-the-spot decisions. If teachers can see and analyze problems in an instructional sequence, they can make appropriate modifications immediately or the next day rather than delaying until they collect evaluative information.

Examination of assumptions

Effective teachers must be aware of the implicit assumptions they hold with regard to how learners make progress and they must periodically reexamine these assumptions. To accept a strategy as "the truth" regardless of its effect on learning is blind faith, not careful thinking and creative adaptation. Indeed, a procedure that has worked for five consecutive classes may prove to be ineffective for the sixth class. Teaching experience and insight into the teaching-learning process provide a base for making intelligent decisions about the design of instruction, but it is equally important that the teacher examine day-to-day instructional processes to be sure that learners are making progress. Research on teacher planning states that most teachers do not monitor their day-to-day activities in terms of general instructional goals (Clark & Yinger, 1979).

Appropriate Expectations

To function as decision makers, teachers must believe that they can make a difference—that they can be effective in the classroom. Teaching skills and knowledge are important, but if a teacher is not motivated to use them consistently, little will be accomplished.

Effective teachers

Brophy and Evertson (1976) provide an interesting description of how relatively effective and ineffective teachers see themselves. They report that the most pervasive differences between teachers who enabled students to make good learning gains and less effective teachers were in the teachers' basic role definitions. Successful teachers saw teaching as an interesting and worthwhile challenge that they approached by assuming personal responsibility for the learning of their students. These teachers saw problems, but believed that the problems could be overcome, and were therefore motivated to search for solutions.

Less successful teachers saw teaching as merely a dull job. They were likely to respond to problems by giving up because they did not assume personal responsibility for students' learning. Such teachers discussed problems as if they were too serious to be solved, and their behavior often guaranteed that the problems would remain unsolved. These teachers did not believe they could make a difference, and therefore they did not. Positive expectations alone are not sufficient to ensure teaching success, but without them no teacher will be effective in the classroom.

Brophy and Evertson also observed that teachers who reported a sense of inner control and personal responsibility clearly reflected this in their classroom behavior. More successful teachers were prepared to work with slow students, helping them to overcome failure by reteaching and providing extra practice.

Realistic attitudes

Successful teachers held realistic attitudes toward students. They liked them and enjoyed interpersonal interaction with them, but basically they saw students as learners. Less successful teachers tended to fall into one of two groups, both of which represented extreme reactions to students. One group romanticized students as warm and wonderful. These teachers concentrated on their personal relationships with students, often to the point of failing to manage the classroom effectively or to meet the students' instructional needs. Such teachers' expectations were unrealistic, and their behavior, despite its warmth, was inappropriate because it met their own needs rather than the needs of their students. The second group of unsuccessful teachers was disillusioned and bitter, looking upon their students as enemies.

Successful teachers see themselves as diagnosticians and problem solvers rather than as parent-substitutes or disciplinarians. Their goal is to design educational environments that work. Their basic task is to help students learn, and not to accept classroom problems and student limitations as unchangeable. This requires facing problems and working toward their resolution. Other researchers have also found that teachers' self-perceptions (Can I teach? Can I make a difference?) as well as their attitudes toward students' learning capacities can affect classroom learning (Gibson & Dembo, 1984; Ashton & Webb, 1985).

Factors That Restrict Teacher Decision Making

We stated that teachers who have teaching skill, knowledge of the learning process, and a "can do" attitude can make a major impact upon learners. However, teachers do not always make decisions independently. Many decisions are heavily influenced by the behavior of previous teachers, or by parents, students' peers, and school policies. For example, Schwille et al. (1983) show that teachers' views of what to teach in an elementary school mathematics course is influenced not only by what they believe to be important but also by what is required by district or school policies.

Assumptions about students

Some instructional decisions are not made in a conscious, deliberate way, often because teachers simply do not see a problem. One teacher may view a pupil as a pleasant, capable, hard-working student and another teacher might perceptively see that this student is anxious and excessively dependent on teachers, performing capably because she is a compulsive worker and socially withdrawn, seldom engaging in conversations with peers. If teachers are unaware of problems like these, the decisions they make about handling such students will be less than optimal. Careful monitoring of one's teaching behavior and periodic reexamination of assumptions about individual students or instructional strategies help to reduce errors and to minimize their effects.

Unexamined ideas

Teachers frequently make decisions on the basis of enthusiastic allegiance to an idea that has never been carefully examined. For instance, the open school, where students presumably have more opportunity to select and evaluate learning tasks, became an all-embracing answer to some educators who didn't see that such an environment might be more compatible with the needs of selected students. To other teachers, the self-contained classroom with instruction from one teacher and an emphasis on basic skills is the universal solution. These teachers don't see that some students could be stifled by too much structure. However, there is growing evidence that the quality of classroom organizational structure—the way it is implemented—is much more important than the form (Cuban, 1983; Good, 1983; Marshall & Weinstein, 1984).

Now we turn to a discussion of some of the factors that make it hard for teachers to be active decision makers. These factors operate in most classrooms, although the form of a problem may differ from classroom to classroom.

Schools Are Busy Places

Limited time

The fact that learning typically takes place in a classroom setting imposes real constraints on what can and cannot be accomplished. Whether teachers instruct the whole class, divide the class into three or four groups, or allow individuals to work on their own projects, teachers have limited time for one-to-one contact with students. This necessarily involves decisions about which students to interact with and under what circumstances.

Teachers are best viewed as managers making executive decisions in a fast-paced environment (Berliner, 1982). As managers, teachers have a difficult but "doable" job. We believe, though, that teachers must make more decisions more quickly and under worse conditions than do any other managers in American society.

Philip Jackson, in his book *Life in Classrooms* (1968), provides a taste of what school is like in the following passage:

> School is a place where tests are failed and passed, where amusing things happen, where new insights are stumbled upon, and skills acquired. But it is also a place in which people sit, and listen, and wait, and raise their hands, and pass out paper, and stand in line, and sharpen pencils. School is where we encounter both friends and foes, where imagination is unleashed and misunderstanding brought to ground. But it is also a place in which yawns are stifled and initials scratched on desktops, where milk money is collected and recess lines are formed. Both aspects of school life, the celebrated and the unnoticed, are familiar to all of us, but the latter, if only because of its characteristic neglect, seems to deserve more attention than it has received to date from those who are interested in education. (pp. 4–5)

Limited resources

Jackson reminds us that classrooms guarantee that there will be crowds, as well as frequent and pervasive evaluations. The fact that there are large groups of students under one teacher's direction means that pupils will share limited resources. Hence, the life of an individual student will be filled with interruption, delay, denial, distraction, and boredom. No matter how teachers behave or what characteristics they possess, they have to deal with these inherent characteristics of classrooms that have an important impact on the quality of their decisions.

Jackson (1968) reports that teachers commonly engage in as many as a thousand interpersonal exchanges each day. When teachers talk with individual students they must do so with only partial attention, because they must also monitor the class and respond to general problems at the same time. Because teachers are involved in numerous interactions with the class as a whole as well as with individual students, it is not surprising that some students become better known to teachers than others. Furthermore, when teachers respond immediately to students' questions and behavior, they are responding partly on the basis of what they have just witnessed and partly on the basis of their previous interactions with these students and the general expectations they hold for them.

Thus teachers may interpret an ambiguous student expression such as a puzzled look as evidence of thinking when it appears on the face of a high achiever, but as evidence of confusion on the face of a low achiever. The decision is rapid and has immediate consequences—the teacher pauses and waits for the "thinking" student to answer, but asks another student to help the "confused" peer. Teachers may or may not interpret a student's expression correctly or they may give up too soon on a particular student because they must make rapid, if not instantaneous, decisions. Because it is impossible for teachers to correctly interpret in a short span of time everything that occurs, they must learn to observe selectively and to monitor key aspects of their interaction with students.

Teachers not only have to explain concepts and demonstrate skills, they also have to monitor students for apparent understanding, and provide feedback to their responses. Furthermore, they must do this within a classroom context where they maintain pupil attention, respond to interruptions, and move through the plan of activities at an appropriate pace. Consequently, teachers' interactive decision making usually cannot involve deliberation about alternative courses of action in any great detail. There is no time for that. Instead, like other skilled individuals required to make expert decisions in complex situations, teachers build up systematic routines and rely on heuristics (implicit rules that people use, without conscious awareness) in order to reduce the complexity of the classroom (Bromme & Brophy, 1983; Shavelson & Stern, 1981).

We show in this text that routines include not only standardized methods of proactively organizing and delivering instruction, but also standardized methods of reacting to common problems. In subsequent chapters we provide detailed information about developing routines for classroom management, classroom planning, and for evaluating student performance. In addition to relying on routines, teachers also use heuristics to make sense of their environment and to make decisions in complex situations (Tversky & Kahneman, 1974; Bromme & Brophy, 1983). Our intent is to provide you with formal definitions and research findings, to help you develop a clinical sensitivity to classrooms, and to effectively apply your knowledge to classroom decision making.

Schools Are Familiar, Stable Places

Despite the complexity of classrooms there are some enduring aspects of schools that allow for stable predictions and thus make it possible to develop routines and shared assumptions that allow teachers to act as decision makers. Still, despite the seemingly predictable set of classroom events, there are always surprises that teachers must cope with. Teachers must necessarily deal with both the predictable and problematic.

Jackson (1968) describes the familiarity and stability of the classroom scene in the following statement:

> Even the odors of the classroom are fairly standardized. Schools may use different brands of wax and cleaning fluid, but they all seem to contain similar ingredients, a sort of universal smell which creates an aromatic background that permeates the entire building. Added to this, in each classroom, is the slightly acrid scent of chalk dust and the faint hint of fresh wood from the pencil shavings. In some rooms, especially at lunch time,

there is the familiar odor of orange peels and peanut butter sandwiches, a blend that mingles in the late afternoon (following recess) with the delicate pungency of children's perspiration. If a person stumbled into a classroom blindfolded, his nose alone, if he used it carefully, would tell him where he was. . . .

Not only is the classroom a relatively stable physical environment, it also provides a fairly constant social context. Behind the same old desks sit the same old students, in front of the familiar blackboard stands the familiar teacher. (p. 7)

Classroom features

Doyle (1985) also agrees that classroom settings have important stable features that students and teachers need to accommodate.

1. *Multidimensionality:* Many different tasks and events exist in the classroom. Records and schedules must be kept, and work must be monitored, collected, and evaluated. A single event can have multiple consequences. Waiting a few seconds for one student to answer a question may positively affect that student's motivation but negatively influence the interest of another student who would like to respond. At the same time it may slow the pace of the lesson for the rest of the class.
2. *Simultaneity:* This refers to the fact that many things happen at the same time in classrooms. During a discussion a teacher not only listens and helps improve students' answers, but also monitors students who do not respond for signs of comprehension and tries to keep the lesson moving at a good pace.
3. *Immediacy:* The pace of classroom events is rapid. Sieber (1979) found that teachers evaluated pupil conduct in public on the average of 15.89 times per hour, or 87 times a day, or an estimated 16,000 times a year.
4. *Unpredictable and public classroom climate:* As Doyle notes, things often go in ways that are unanticipated. Furthermore, much of what happens to a student is seen by many other students as well. Clearly, students can infer how the teacher feels about certain students by the way the teacher interacts with them in class.
5. *History:* Doyle also states that after a class has met for several weeks or months, common norms and understandings are apt to develop. Emmer, Evertson, and Anderson (1980) show how events that happen early in the year sometimes influence how classrooms function the rest of the year. To a student teacher or observer, some classes appear easy to manage; however, events that took place earlier in the school year may explain why things run smoothly at the time of observation.

Although many classrooms now have nontraditional physical arrangements such as group discussion corners, independent study cubicles, learning stations, and microcomputer and word processing corners, classrooms even in such open or individualized settings remains quite stable for a variety of reasons. The same students use the committee table together. Individual study comes at the same time each day. Class routines remain the same.

To the extent that students have had shared educational experiences in

Predictability

Student expectations

the past, expectations and restraints for the forthcoming year become narrower and more predictable. For instance, Suzi and Arlene represented the homeroom on student council last year, so it is highly likely that one or both of these students will be nominated or selected this year. Bob is expected to complain about homework, and Terri will probably push the teacher for information about what will be covered on tests. Bill and Alice will have their hands up 90 percent of the time when the teacher asks a question. Mary and Jim will rarely raise their hands and will seldom respond if the teacher calls on them.

Similarly, if teachers have taught long enough in a particular school, students will bring expectations about them to the class. "She'll read mystery stories to the students who don't go to music." "Chemistry lab exercises don't mean anything." "Don't sweat it, he only grades on tests, and they're straight from the book." Such preconceptions no doubt make it either easier or more difficult to start the year, depending on whether incoming classes view teachers positively or negatively. Teachers who have poor reputations may have students who overreact or react inappropriately to their ambiguous expressions or statements.

Thus, students who have spent thousands of hours sitting in classrooms will have general expectations about what should take place in the room. They also have a general knowledge of how well they perform various classroom activities, and they know whether they enjoy doing them. Such expectations about school life and personal performance can only be changed by systematic effort.

By middle childhood (ages nine through twelve), most students have developed relatively stable views of themselves and often reject information that presents or describes them as better or worse than they believe themselves to be. Also, students usually share classrooms with classmates who remember "the way they were," reminding them of past failures and successes. Teachers must therefore deal with individuals and their problems in a group context.

Pressure on Students to "Look Good"

Group life affects the performance of individual students. Groups exert pressure on an individual to play a role (attentive participant, class clown, class rebel), and group pressure makes it more difficult for a teacher to have a sustained, open dialogue with individual students. The presence of others, whether strangers or friends, is sufficient to alter behavior.

For instance, students have ingenious strategies for preventing teachers from finding out that they do not really know material. Consider this excerpt from an article by Shepard (1973):

> Me and Schwartz and Woczniewski sat so far back in the classroom that the blackboard was only a vague rumor to us. Miss Shields was a shifting figure in the haze on the distant horizon, her voice a faint but ominous drone punctuated by squeaking chalk. Within a short time I became adept at reading the inflection, if not the content, of those far-off sounds, sensing instantly when danger was looming. Danger meant simply

> being called on. Kids in the front of the classroom didn't know the meaning of danger. Ace test takers, they loved nothing more than to display their immense knowledge by waving their hands frantically even before questions were asked. Today, when I think of the classrooms of my youth, I see a forest of waving hands between me and the teacher. They were the smartasses who went on to become corporation presidents, TV talk-show guests and owners of cabin cruisers. . . .
>
> I made it a point to wear bland-colored clothes, the better to blend into the background. I learned to weave my body from side to side, dropping a shoulder here, shifting my neck a few degrees to the right there, with the crucial object in mind of always keeping a line of kids between me and the teacher's eagle eye.
>
> For those rare but inevitable occasions—say, during a chicken-pox epidemic—when the ranks in the rows ahead were too thin to provide adequate cover, I practiced the vacant-eyeball ploy, which has since become a popular device for junior executives the world over who cannot afford to be nailed by their seniors in sales conferences and other perilous situations. The vacant eyeball appears to be looking attentively but, in fact, sees nothing. It is a blank mirror of anonymity. I learned early in the game that if they don't catch your eye, they don't call on you. Combined with a fixed facial expression of deadpan alertness—neither too deadpan nor too alert—this technique has been known to render its practitioner virtually invisible. (p. 144)

Holt (1964) and Covington (1984) both describe a number of self-defeating strategies that students engage in to prevent them from looking bad in the classroom. In particular, Holt suggests that many dependent students read the teacher like a traffic light. They begin their answers slowly and softly. If the teacher smiles, nods, or in any way indicates approval, the answers become more animated (louder, quicker) and more relaxed. If the teacher nonverbally signals dissatisfaction the student shifts into his or her "thinking act" and the game begins—a furrowed brow, and a remark like "Let me think about that" followed by "No, what I meant to say . . . ," resulting in a beaming teacher.

Student strategies

Obviously there are countless games and strategies that students learn to play, and no doubt you can recall many of these from your own experience. We suspect that most of you who took a language course in high school or college will recall that occasionally you did not do all of the required translation. At such times you may have tried to be called on to read one of the first five or so paragraphs that you did translate by tactics such as waving your hand energetically, feigning sleep, or staring out the window, depending on the teacher. Your desire to look good to peers and teachers, and possibly your wish for good grades, were sufficiently strong to produce such behavior. Or perhaps, conversely, your wish not to look bad by saying "I don't know, I didn't do the translation," motivated the behavior.

Such strategies for camouflaging lack of knowledge often work, largely because the interactions occur in a group setting. Pressure to "perform for the group," as perceived by individual students, leads many students to adopt strategies that are ultimately self-defeating, or at least ineffective. The strategies work temporarily because the teacher either feels the pressure to move on or is personally embarrassed by students' failure to respond. In the long run, however, students profit little from such activities because they are not learning the material.

Others have written about the pressure to look good in social settings. Goffman (1959) provides an interesting and classical description of this pressure in his book, *The Presentation of Self in Everyday Life*. Recent research has focused on *attributional egotism*—the motive to take credit for success and to deny blame for failure in order to enhance self-esteem (see Snyder, Stephan, & Rosenfield, 1978). Social pressure such as being compared with peers may encourage students to spend a lot of time in impression management—projecting the image of listening to the teacher—and in general developing self-defeating behavior patterns such as learned helplessness.

Impression management

In an interesting ethnographic study, Spencer-Hall (1976) shows that some students are better impression managers than others. She contends that students' different rates of misbehavior are not as important in cuing teacher evaluations of students as are their styles of misbehavior. Many students are able to maintain favorable evaluations from teachers and peers alike by being careful to misbehave in ways that escape teacher attention.

External Pressures on Decision Making

There are also external sources of influence that impose constraints on teachers' decisions and shape or help to determine what happens in the classroom. Hall and Spencer-Hall (1980) studied the effects of school administrations, community groups, and government agencies on expectations for what takes place in schools. They report an instance in which the media had an interesting impact on a community's expectations for its schools. Because of newspaper coverage of low student performance on basic skills tests, local administrators and school board members were subjected to community pressures that reflected a concern that children were not performing up to standard. As a result, the administration went through a series of negotiations that included reinterpretation of the meaning of test scores. Such negotiations led the administration to implement classroom programs that placed greater emphasis on basic skills. Hence, public expectations, touched off in this instance by newspaper reports, can and do influence classroom functioning.

School environments

The school environment is also an important determinant of what teachers are able to accomplish. Clearly, some schools produce higher achievement than other schools with comparable student populations and resources (Rutter, 1983; Purkey & Smith, 1985). Furthermore, some principals are more supportive and active leaders than others (McDonnell, 1985). Hence, in a very real sense, it may be easier to teach in some schools than in others. If, for example, most teachers in a school support its curriculum standards, it is easier for beginning teachers to maintain standards of excellence than it would be if they taught in schools where most teachers simply kept students busy.

Interaction among teachers creates a better learning environment.

Teachers' role in academic achievement

Because so many factors (e.g., parents, school administrators, students' previous experiences in earlier grades, crowded schools) can limit what teachers accomplish, some may wonder if teachers really play a role in students' learning of academic material. Even serious and responsible scholars have questioned whether or not teachers make an important difference in student performance (see Coleman et al., 1966; Heath & Nielson, 1974). Research within the last 15 years (reviewed by Brophy & Good, 1985) made it clear that teachers at all levels do have significant effects, either positive or negative, on student achievement. Shulman (1983) contends that individual teachers, through their knowledge and practice, are the critical determinants of successful school programs. Although there are constraints, teachers are not simply the product of bureaucratic and external pressure; they are active agents—thinking professionals who can have important effects on student learning (Feiman-Nemser & Floden, 1985).

Patricia Graham, a former director of the National Institute of Education, has written, "Family, media, and peer influences, taken together, may be more important than schooling in determining a student's values and chances to succeed later in life. A variety of evidence has accumulated, however, to support the position that the classroom teacher is the most powerful single factor affecting academic achievement" (p. 28). It is because of such data that we, like many other educators (e.g., Shavelson, 1978; Shulman & Elstein, 1975; Shulman & Sykes, 1983), emphasize an active decision-making approach to teaching.

Getting Started

Unfortunately, some teachers never become active decision makers or effective instructors. Some fail because they do not have adequate knowledge of the content they teach. Although it is obvious, it is important to stress that if teachers do not understand the concepts they teach, their explanations to the class are not likely to help students learn.

More teachers fail to fulfill their potential, especially in elementary schools, not because they do not know the subject matter, but because they do not understand students or classrooms. Leinhardt and Smith (1984) distinguish between action system knowledge and subject matter knowledge. *Subject matter knowledge* includes the specific information necessary to present content. *Action system knowledge* refers to skills for planning the lesson, making decisions about lesson pace, explaining material clearly, and responding to individual differences in how students learn.

Action system knowledge

This book deals with action system knowledge rather than subject matter knowledge. Systematic study of it will help you to understand how students learn and develop, how classrooms can be managed, and how to present information, concepts, and learning assignments effectively. This information will complement the subject matter knowledge you gain in other courses by providing you with a knowledge of educational psychology—action system knowledge that will help you to become a successful teacher.

Teachers who possess both action system knowledge and subject matter knowledge will be more effective than teachers who are deficient in one of these areas. Simply put, knowledge of mathematics is a necessary but not a sufficient condition to be an effective mathematics teacher. Even with both kinds of knowledge, however, some teachers may fail because they do not apply the knowledge they possess. Such teachers may have inappropriately low expectations for students' ability to learn or for their own ability to teach. Or, they may not be active decision makers. Lacking an integrated set of theories and belief systems to provide a personal framework for informed decision making, such teachers do not have effective strategies for organizing information from the rapid occurrence of numerous classroom events.

Beginning teachers

Beginning teachers have an especially difficult task because, in addition to the enduring demands of teaching, they have to worry about concerns such as whether the students will like them, will they follow their directions, and will they themselves actually enjoy teaching. They will also have to concern themselves with preparing for new lessons and developing new tests while trying to apply action system knowledge in the classroom.

Secondary teachers will have to get to know as many as 180 students quickly, and elementary school teachers will have to prepare different lessons for the entire day. Teachers must also implement different teaching formats and utilize various activities. Yinger (1977) reports on one teacher who used 53 different activities during a 12-week period, including tasks such as book reports, creative writing, cooking, newspaper assignments, spelling bees, field trips, and reading groups.

We believe it is difficult for new teachers to be active decision makers unless they want to be and are willing to work to develop the necessary skills. In classrooms, it is easy to be overwhelmed by the rapid pace and become simply *reactive* to classroom events. To be *proactive*, it will be important for you to think actively about how to apply the ideas presented in this book as you read them, as you observe classes, and during your student teaching experience.

Student teaching experiences

Student teachers' classroom behavior is influenced by their cooperating teachers (Good & Brophy, 1984). Even though student teachers may not approve of the styles their cooperating teachers use, they practice the cooperating teachers' style so often in hopes of getting a good grade that it becomes second nature to them and resurfaces later when they have their own classrooms. Many cooperating teachers encourage student teachers to develop their own styles, so the pressure to conform is not a problem. However, some cooperating teachers believe that their role is to help student teachers teach as they do. Furthermore, during the first year of teaching, a new teacher may encounter peer teachers with strong preferences.

The best way to become an active teacher is to develop an explicit theory of teaching. You must also master subject matter content in your teaching field, understand and apply the concepts presented in this text, and develop an explicit approach to teaching (e.g., know when you will group pupils for instruction and when you will teach the entire class, know the bases for your decisions and how to collect evidence to determine their validity).

Student teachers need to establish their own style and relationships with students.

Unfortunately, many student teachers are not encouraged to think analytically and to discuss why they make certain decisions. Furthermore, action system knowledge is not utilized during discussions between cooperating teachers and student teachers. In a large-scale study of student teaching, Griffin et al. (1983) found that during supervisory interactions there was little attention paid to developing a knowledge base that would help student teachers subsequently when they had their own classrooms. Supervisory interactions focused in large measure on immediate, specific issues and a "let's see if this works" style of offering suggestions. Unfortunately, a rationale for practice typically was not provided and there were few references to learning theory, child development, instructional models, etc.

Griffin et al. (1983) note that supervisory interactions were dominated by the cooperating teacher, who selected the topics for conversation and controlled how those topics were discussed. Conversations usually focused on a particular classroom at a particular time; they seldom considered alternate ways to understand and respond to classroom events.

Some cooperating teachers enjoy discussing why they make decisions and how they evaluate them. Other cooperating teachers function differently. However, you as a student teacher can be analytical even if your cooperating teacher is not. Think about an instructional day, consider the motivational structures that the teacher used, such as how lessons were introduced or ended, and the types of feedback that were given, and speculate about their effects on various students. On another day, think about the management system in the classroom—what type of alerting and accountability systems were used and was the structure too tight or too loose for specific students? By using the vocabulary and concepts in this text, you can become a more active observer of classroom events—the first step in becoming an active classroom decision maker.

SUMMARY

Teachers can have a major, positive influence on the way students learn and develop. Some teachers are vital forces; others make only minor differences in how students learn and develop. Teachers who make an impact on students' lives communicate a genuine interest in their students, know their subject matter, and possess detailed information about instructional processes and the way students learn and develop. In this chapter we have presented a decision-making model because we believe that there are no simple answers to successful teaching.

In this book we stress that theoretical principles and research findings provide a basis for planning and implementing instruction. However, teachers have to act as independent decision makers and apply these general concepts and principles with their particular students and their own expected goals in mind. We introduced a model, a way of looking at classroom decision making, that illustrates the fact that teachers who make good decisions and who are willing to correct poor ones foster student motivation and learning.

Effective teachers see their roles as positive and worthwhile, while ineffective teachers see teaching as a dull job. Effective teachers exhibit inner control, personal responsibility, realistic attitudes, and a problem-solving orientation.

Factors that restrict a teacher's decision-making ability are lack of awareness of student problems, allegiance to unworkable ideas, limited resources, and lack of systematic feedback about the effects of their instructional behavior. Also, both student and teacher expectations, coupled with the self-defeating strategies that some students adopt, can interfere with learning. In spite of these difficulties, however, evidence supports the conclusion that the teacher is the most powerful, single factor affecting academic achievement.

Educational psychology provides a framework for looking at the learner, the learning process, and the learning situation. Educational psychology includes an understanding of educational objectives, student development and personality, the learning process, the psychology of teaching methods, classroom management, and evaluation procedures.

We believe that students who actively and systematically attempt to apply educational psychology in their preservice and inservice teaching will have a better base for understanding students and for designing appropriate instructional experiences. To be successful in the classroom, a teacher requires subject knowledge and conceptual skills (the content of educational psychology) as well as teaching and decision-making skills. Our goal in this book is to provide a format for integrating these three areas to help you to become an effective classroom instructor.

QUESTIONS AND PROBLEMS

1. What are your own theories of teaching? Are they firm or tentative? On what are they based? Be explicit. Think about a particular lesson for a certain group of students. What five things would you need to do to be successful? Why did you pick these five things?
2. What does it mean to say that some classroom decisions "aren't made"? To what extent do some things happen in a classroom without teacher intent or awareness? What sorts of things?
3. Considering the complexities of teaching, shouldn't we provide you with a few

clear, prescriptive guidelines rather than urge you to master a broad range of concepts and skills to draw on later when you are teaching and making decisions under pressure?

4. Think about the teachers you have had. How many would you describe as effective? Why were they effective? Were they equally effective for all students?
5. What sort of "front" have you presented to your teachers in the past? Have you in some instances tried to cover-up your real ideas? Why?
6. How does classroom teaching differ from teaching patients about the effects of a pending operation and how they can help their own recovery by performing certain exercises?

CASE STUDIES

Disturbing First Encounter. Tim is upset because the university supervisor has told him that his newly assigned cooperating teacher, Mr. Wilson, had given his previous semester's student teacher a "D" and was an abrasive man. Tim anxiously knocks on the door and shivers as Mr. Wilson says loudly, "Come in! " As Tim slithers in he says "Oh! You must be my new aide from the university! I thought you'd have been here fifteen minutes ago!" What would you do if you were Tim?

Rick Strikes Out. Rick felt like a fool. "Why didn't I read the assignment more carefully?" he asked himself. Last night, to get ready for his first teaching experience, he had spent a lot of time preparing his ten-minute introduction and had spent two hours working on discussion questions. But the lesson hadn't gone as planned. His ninth graders didn't seem to want to talk. And so, foolishly, he later thought, he asked for questions. He fielded the first three or four questions poorly. Finally, one student said with irritation, "I still can't understand what took place in the experiment or why the experiment was important." Rick simply couldn't think; his mind went blank. After a full minute of awkward silence he threw the question back to the class. Weakly, he asked, "Can anybody help . . . (pause) . . . I'm sorry, I forgot your name. . . ." What should Rick do now? What should he do the next day?

Jim Begins. Jim Miller, a recent college graduate, will teach chemistry for the first time at Bayside High School, in a medium-sized city of 30,000 in the Midwest. Bayside is a large school and the only high school in town, so a full range of student abilities is represented there. However, chemistry is a subject that only the college-bound students take. What are some of the major teaching decisions that Jim must make immediately? List ten to fifteen.

A Challenge for Nancy. Nancy Litton has never taught reading before. She is both stimulated and frightened by the challenge of teaching first graders. Unfortunately, she did her student teaching in a third grade classroom during the spring. She has therefore not had the opportunity to observe first-grade reading instruction, nor has she seen a teacher start the school year. It's a week before the year begins. What would you do if you were Nancy? What information would you try to obtain? What are some of the major decisions Nancy must make?

Part Two

Development

Tommy was the shortest third grader in the class. Although his mother and father had told him that he was going to get bigger and the doctor told him during his last visit that he was going to be a tall adult, Tommy wanted to be tall right now. He felt bad about how short he was, and students sometimes made fun of him because of his height.

Ruth, a fifth grader, was the first girl in her class to show signs of physical maturity. In one sense she was pleased, but in another sense she was frightened and felt alone. She wished that she had someone to talk to about her emerging physical self.

Alan was a tenth grader who was beginning to feel uneasy about himself and his academic progress. His grades were acceptable, but he didn't know what he wanted to do when he left high school or what career he wanted to pursue. His friends were beginning to talk about the colleges they would attend.

Jane Burton was disturbed by the fact that many of her classmates, seniors in an advanced chemistry course, were cheating on classroom assignments and exams. Morally, she felt that their behavior was outrageous, but yet she did not want to "rat" on them. She wished that more students had concerns about academic standards and honesty.

Jane Thorton, a sophomore in college, enjoyed courses in which she could develop her own learning assignments and do independent research. She liked to study problems analytically, particularly social issues. She not only enjoyed defining problems and conducting research, but she also enjoyed structuring and finding new problems in her sociology and psychology courses. She found her emerging interest in independent thinking and scholarship instructive, because as recently as her junior year in high school, she was still looking for adults and other peers to define what she should think about. In the past three years, however, she had developed a strong preference for independent work and the skills for pursuing it.

This unit is about human development. No doubt you or your friends had experiences such as those described in the vignettes just listed. Some of us matured early, some of us matured late. And some of us developed at an average rate throughout our school years. As we grow and mature, our development creates new opportunities and skills, but it also creates new conflicts that we have to deal with successfully.

Teachers are in a unique position to help many young adults deal successfully with developmental issues. As we see in the chapters in this section, developmental concerns vary widely from age to age, and the concerns that a second-grade teacher must address are quite different from those that an eighth-grade teacher must deal with. In these chapters we hope to provide basic information that will help you to deal successfully with students of all ages.

Several types of development are covered in this section: Chapter 2 covers physical development; Chapter 3 presents the basic principles and theories of cognitive development; Chapter 4 places these principles and theories in the context of education; and Chapter 5 deals with social development, including the application of moral development theory in programs designed to increase prosocial behavior. These chapters are intended to help you understand and respond to developmental issues that affect classroom life. To make this point more clearly, let's consider a particular experience that occurs regularly in schools and illustrate how an understanding of development is useful in responding to students.

I pledge allegiance to the flag of the United States of America, and to the republic for which it stands, one nation, under God, indivisible, with liberty and justice for all.

The pledge of allegiance to the flag of the United States is probably very familiar because it is basic to our American culture. In fact, you may have simply skimmed over the pledge once you realized what it was. If so, go back and look again as you think about these questions:

☐ Do you understand what all the words and phrases mean?
☐ Do you understand the connotations—all of the other things implied in these brief statements?
☐ Have you ever thought about either of the above questions? Do you notice anything in the pledge that you never noticed before? (Take some time to think about these questions.)

You probably know the pledge of allegiance by heart and have recited it many times. Yet until now there was something you had not noticed before. What does this mean?

For example, you may be aware that the pledge of allegiance to the flag is not a statement to the banner as such, but is in fact a loyalty oath to the nation. If you think about it, you can see that a loyalty oath to the United States does not require any mention of the flag. Furthermore, the meaning of the pledge remains the same, even if the design of the flag should change, as it did when new states entered the Union.

From the point of view of developmental psychologists you are in what Swiss psychologist Jean Piaget calls the stage of formal operations. This means, among other things, that you are capable of understanding and thinking about the purely abstract aspects of concepts and knowledge. A fourth grader, on the other hand, would have difficulty with some of the vocabulary on the pledge, especially with understanding it. Would a fourth grader interpret these statements as you did or be able to follow this discussion? The answer to both of these questions is clearly "No." You as an adult understand the pledge of allegiance in a much more conceptual and abstract way than fourth graders would. Their ability to understand and respond to statements is limited to familiar, concrete experiences, although, within these limits, the interpretation is quite logical.

Even if memorized perfectly, saying the pledge of allegiance is likely to be a relatively meaningless experience for a first grader. It will be associated with standing and holding the right hand over the heart while reciting the pledge in the presence of the flag. The child will have a general idea that the words relate to the flag, but not to the country, although he or she will probably not have much understanding of what the words mean.

This example illustrates some of the insights that developmental psychologists can offer to help us understand students. By studying systematic changes that occur in children as they get older, and by noting the kinds of limitations that apply when children have not yet acquired abilities or insights asssociated with higher stages of development, psychologists help us to understand children of different ages and levels of development by enabling us to see things from their perspectives. This ability is essential if we are to meaningfully interact with children and interpret their difficulties when they do not understand something that an adult would understand with ease. It also enables us to correct children when they develop mistaken ideas that are logical, given their point of view, but incorrect because they have not learned to take into account certain things that make a difference.

In the four chapters in this section we will elaborate on children's stages of development in relation to their ability to learn and to be taught.

Chapter 2

Physical Development

OBJECTIVES

When you have mastered the material in this chapter you will be able to

1. Differentiate the terms growth and development in the context of physical changes during childhood and adolescence
2. Describe Epstein's work on brain growth stages
3. Describe the work done by Lenneberg and others on cerebral lateralization and relate the controversy that surrounds the educational implications of such work
4. Describe the universal sequence of human growth and the importance of nutrition and exercise for physical growth and development
5. Define Sheldon's body types and explain the research relating body types to personality and development
6. List the important preadolescent growth and development characteristics and tell how teachers and school environments should accommodate these characteristics
7. Explain how boys and girls differ in physical development during preadolescence
8. Explain the physical causes of the preadolescent growth spurt and discuss environmental factors that affect it
9. Discuss adolescent sexual maturation and the differential effects of early versus late maturation on both boys and girls

To deal with students effectively, it is helpful to know where they have been and where they are likely to be going, not just where they are now. This requires a developmental perspective, a concern with changes occurring over time. Traditionally, psychologists interested in development discuss three aspects of such changes: sequence, the order in which changes occur; rate, the speed with which changes occur; and form, the shape or appearance of the developing entity at any point in time.

Developmental perspective

True developmental sequences are fixed and universal. A always precedes B, which always precedes C, and so on. One cannot get from A to C without first going through stage B. Many of these sequences involve physical growth and development under the control of genetics and maturation. However, as we shall see in the next three chapters, universal sequences have been proposed for aspects of psychological development as well.

Growth versus development

It is useful to distinguish "growth" from "development" when discussing physical changes. Growth usually refers to increases in height, weight, or other aspects of physical size. Development is a broader term than growth and refers both to the mind and to the emotions, not just the body. Basically, development is an orderly progression to increasingly higher levels of differentiation or organization.

Development can occur when no growth is taking place. This is most obvious in infancy and early childhood, where, for example, children of similar age and size can differ considerably in their ability to ride a tricycle or use a pencil. The reason is often that differences in rates of maturation of the nervous system produce differences in the ability to control, and especially to coordinate, different parts of the body. In such cases, children lacking the physical maturation needed to succeed at these types of tasks are unlikely to improve their skills until this maturation takes place, even if they have lots of instruction and time to practice. Similar, but less extreme, developmental immaturities plague certain students through much of childhood and even into adolescence. For example, hyperactive students may have difficulty concentrating or inhibiting physical movement and students with poor coordination may embarrass themselves in gym class or on the playground.

Differentiation

Most physical development involving differentiation of new parts occurs in the early weeks following conception, as the fertilized egg, starting as a single cell, continually reproduces itself and at the same time differentiates into the nervous system and sense organs, the digestive system, the circulatory system, and so on. At birth, almost all parts are differentiated, except for the myelin sheaths that cover and protect nerve cells in the brain. These sheaths, which apparently help speed up neural transmission and thus make the brain more efficient, continue to develop for at least the first few years after birth. By the time children start school, though, they are essentially fully differentiated, and physical development during the school years consists of simple growth and progress toward higher levels of organization and coordination of existing body parts.

Brain Development Theories

Epstein and Brain Growth Stages

Brain growth stages

Even though brain development seems to be complete by early childhood, some feel that theorized brain growth or changes in brain functioning affect children's intellectual development and performance at school. Epstein (1978), for example, points out that the brain increases about 35 percent in weight after age two due to more extension and branching of the axons and dendrites that extend outward from brain cells and connect them with other cells, to extension of the myelin sheaths along axons, and to increases in arterial blood supply to the brain. He suggests that these forms of brain growth affect intellectual functioning, and that such growth takes place in well-defined spurts rather than continuously occurring throughout childhood. Epstein feels that notable brain growth occurs between the ages of three to ten months, two to four years, six to eight years, 10 to 12 or 13 years, and 14 to 16 or 17 years, and that brain growth is rapid during these spurts but minimal in between spurts.

These ages, Epstein feels, correspond closely to the stages in intellectual development that have been identified by Piaget (1983) and others (mentioned further in Chapter 3). He draws educational implications from these ideas by suggesting that children should be presented with greater intellectual challenges and stimulated to develop their thinking to higher levels during these periods of rapid brain growth, but should be allowed to consolidate their gains and be presented with less demanding challenges between these growth periods. This could mean that a great deal of new and demanding input should be included in the first- and second-grade curricula (corresponding to the growth-spurt period spanning ages six to eight), but that much less demanding curricula would be developed for grades three and four (corresponding to the in-between period spanning ages eight to ten).

Epstein's ideas are intriguing, and they have at least some face validity since the age ranges that he identifies as having rapid brain growth do correspond roughly to the age ranges at which psychologists have observed noteworthy advances in intellectual functioning. However, three major obstacles would have to be overcome before educators would feel compelled to act on Epstein's ideas. First, and most fundamentally, Epstein's theories are not accepted among biological scientists. It has long been known that there is little or no relationship between brain weight and brain functioning, and there is little biological evidence to support Epstein's notions about spurts in brain growth. Second, the ages that Epstein assigns to the growth spurt periods are admittedly approximate, so that a great many children could be ahead or behind by a year or more. Thus, even if Epstein's notions about brain growth spurts should turn out to be correct, changing the school curriculum along the lines he suggests might yield no significant improvement in the percentages of students for whom curriculum demands are well matched to present readiness. Third, brain growth could just as well be an effect as a cause of advances in intellectual functioning—perhaps the increased range and sophistication of intellectual activities that occur with development stimulate brain growth, rather than vice versa. If this is the case, changes in rates of brain growth would have no educational implications at all.

Despite these problems, some educators are developing teacher training programs and an approach to curriculum called cognitive level matching based on Epstein's ideas. The best known of these programs is the one sponsored by the Shoreham-Wading River School District in Shoreham, New York (Brooks, Fusco, & Grennon, 1983; Mechanic, Daugherty, & Arden-Smith, 1982).

Lenneberg and Cerebral Lateralization

Brain lateralization theories

The cerebrum of the human brain (the "gray matter" that controls higher level intellectual functioning) is subdivided into left and right hemispheres. The hemispheres appear to have equal potential; if one hemisphere is severely injured, the other hemisphere usually takes over the functions that the first hemisphere controlled. However, the hemispheres tend to develop specialized functioning in most people. Loosely speaking, the left hemisphere controls verbal functioning and the linear, logical thinking associated with verbalization. In contrast, the right hemisphere controls the visual/spatial imagery and the intuitive, holistic thinking that is associated with perception or discovery rather than logical reasoning. This hemispheric specialization is called *cerebral lateralization* and is evident from infancy (Kinsbourne & Hiscock, 1978).

Nevertheless, some writers have theorized that delayed or incomplete lateralization causes learning disabilities. Thus, periodically there are claims that learning disabilities are frequently seen among left-handed children or children with mixed patterns (such as those who prefer the right hand and right foot but use the left eye for sighting). Lenneberg (1967) argued that language is progressively lateralized to the left hemisphere as the child develops to maturity, and that aphasias and other language disabilities are associated with disturbances in these brain lateralization tendencies. Lenneberg's ideas about brain lateralization are interesting but not well supported by biological data (Carter, Hohenegger, & Satz, 1982; Kinsbourne & Hiscock, 1978). Furthermore, it is not clear what, if any, educational implications would follow from Lenneberg's ideas about language development even if they were shown to be true.

Other writers, however, have drawn implications for education based on brain lateralization theories. Wittrock (1978), for example, feels that reading instruction that includes encouraging students to visualize and use imagery should be more effective than instruction restricted to purely verbal approaches, because it will allow children to use processes controlled by both of their brain hemispheres rather than only processes controlled by the left hemisphere. Others, noting that children from higher socioeconomic status homes tend to have more efficient left hemisphere functioning than children from lower socioeconomic status homes (Waber et al., 1984), have suggested that "right brain" approaches to instruction are especially important for teaching lower socioeconomic status children. Still others, equating right brain functioning with creativity and certain forms of problem solving, suggest that schools need to emphasize creativity and problem solving in order to develop the functioning efficiency of the right hemisphere of the brain (Bogen, 1977).

These and other brain lateralization theories go far beyond the biological data available and essentially amount to speculation. However, the educational implications drawn from such theories may be sound even though the research available is not conclusive. That is, whether or not there are meaningful linkages between classroom curriculum and instruction and biological brain growth and functioning, there are good reasons (to be detailed in later chapters) for advocating that students be taught using multiple methods rather than only one, as well as for advocating that they receive opportunities to develop their problem-solving and creative-thinking abilities in addition to receiving systematic instruction in academic facts and concepts. In summary, then, although there has been interesting speculation about spurts in brain growth and about hemispheric lateralization of brain functioning, clear linkages between these hypothesized brain activities and implications for classroom instruction remain to be demonstrated.

General Developmental Trends

Human growth patterns exhibit rapid growth in the first two years of life, slower but noticeable growth over the next eight to twelve years, followed by a second period of rapid growth during adolescence, and a fairly rapid tapering off thereafter. Within these larger sequences, growth typically occurs in spurts. There may be noticeable growth occurring over a period of a few months, followed by no noticeable growth for the next six months to a year (Tanner, 1970).

Growth spurts

Much development, however, occurs between growth spurts, especially consolidation of previously learned skills through practice with the newer, larger body, as well as exploration of activities possible for the first time. Growth spurts often create a certain awkwardness, since children and adolescents must learn to adjust to new arm lengths, leg lengths, and their new size in general when performing activities requiring complex physical coordination. They may suffer temporary difficulties or embarrassment because they have become clumsy at doing things that had been easy for them earlier.

The timing of growth spurts, and the course of physical growth in general, is controlled by secretions of growth hormone from the pituitary gland,

which in turn are ultimately controlled by the genes inherited at conception. Thus an individual's rate of growth and ultimate size are not influenced significantly by, for example, consuming health foods or large quantities of vitamins, or by doing calisthenics or stretching exercises. Some of these factors may affect physical appearance or muscle tone, but they do not stimulate actual growth.

Nutrition and Exercise

Improper diet can adversely affect performance in school.

Good nutrition and plenty of exercise are important for children. Most children get plenty of exercise in their normal daily activities, so this factor should ordinarily not be of concern to elementary teachers. As the years go by, however, certain students will develop sedentary habits, some even to the point that the only real exercise they get may be in physical education classes. Teachers can help by encouraging these students to become more interested in sports and recreation activities (e.g., hiking, cycling, swimming) that they can sustain on their own when they leave school.

Nutrition is likely to be a problem for some students at any grade level and in any kind of school. Reports indicate that perhaps as many as 30 percent of the children growing up in the United States today do not receive adequate nutrition. Most are from lower income families, but an increasing percentage are children from economically advantaged homes where the parents lack the knowledge or interest to insure adequate nutrition by monitoring their children's food intake. Many of these children have unbalanced diets because they get too many carbohydrates and fats and not enough protein, vitamins, and essential minerals (Brozek, 1978).

Inadequate nutrition can adversely affect physical growth and development (Bogin & MacVean, 1983) and, by lowering energy and alertness levels, can interfere with progress at school (McKay et al., 1978). Teachers should be aware of this factor, because listlessness in the classroom can be the result of poor nutrition rather than motivational problems (Barrett, Radke-Yarrow, & Klein, 1982). This underscores the value of school breakfast and lunch programs, and of teaching students about nutrition and health.

Body Types

Increases in height and general size follow cycles or growth curves (Tanner, 1970) that are genetically programmed for each individual. Assuming adequate nutrition and exercise, these inherited growth patterns will determine the timing and duration of increases in body size. Some individuals will be very close to average for their sex and ethnic group throughout development; others will be taller than average for much of childhood but end up shorter than average as adults. Some will show relatively even growth throughout childhood and others will shoot up every couple of years with little observable growth in between. The number and variety of growth curves make it impossible to predict future growth patterns or ultimate adult stature for specific individuals without collecting expensive and detailed information about rates of bone ossification (the gradual calcification of living bone tissue, which hardens the bone but also slows and eventually stops its growth). One can make an educated guess if information about parental growth patterns is available, especially when a child seems to be modeling after a parent of the same sex, but even here there are plenty of exceptions. Thus, as a general rule, it is inaccurate to assume that relative stature in childhood will be maintained into adulthood.

Personality stereotypes

Height is only one aspect of body type, and perhaps not even the most important one for determining self-image and self-satisfaction. Following Sheldon (1942), psychologists often differentiate between *ectomorphs* (lean, elongated bodies), *mesomorphs* (muscular, athletic bodies), and *endomorphs* (heavy-set, fleshy bodies). Sheldon held that these general constitutional factors are inherited and thus stable, although they can be temporarily masked by growth spurts and either minimized or exaggerated by exercise and nutrition. Sheldon also believed that these body types were regularly associated with a variety of personality features: ectomorphs are preoccupied with their brains and nervous systems and thus are intellectual, artistic, and sensitive; mesomorphs are preoccupied with bone and muscle and thus are athletic and action oriented, as well as sociable, outgoing, and popular; and endomorphs are preoccupied with their digestive systems and thus are oriented toward food and drink rather than thought or action, and are slothful and phlegmatic. These stereotypes did not originate with Sheldon; they go back a long time in folklore and fiction. Sheldon merely added the biologically based theory, explaining that body types were inherited and that they determined the correlated personality characteristics (McCandless & Coop, 1979).

Although the same age, these classmates have matured physically at different rates.

This theory has a certain face validity, because we all know individuals who fit the stereotypes. However, systematic research has not supported Sheldon's notions of inherited predispositions toward distinct body types or causal relationships between body types and personality characteristics. Even though his ideas seem to fit certain individuals, they do not hold up as general rules (Hall & Lindzey, 1970).

Yet body types can influence development, both directly and indirectly (Clausen, 1975; Hurlock, 1964). Directly, physical development at a given age determines what a child can or cannot do. Those who cannot compete on equal terms with their peers may be excluded from games and sports, and be discriminated against in other ways as well. Indirectly, physical development influences attitudes toward self and others. In extreme cases the result can be a vicious cycle of self-fulfilling prophecy effects, in which failures produce defeatist attitudes that in turn produce more failures. This is especially likely when a child has difficulty with what Havighurst (1972) calls *developmental tasks*—tasks that arise at a certain period of development and, if mastered, lead to success on later tasks, but if failed, lead to unhappiness in the individual, disapproval by others, and difficulty with later

Developmental tasks

To perform developmental tasks, students must learn to concentrate and to manipulate equipment.

tasks. For students at school, developmental tasks that can be affected by physical factors include not only games and sports in the gym or the playground, but tasks that affect performance, such as the inability to sustain concentrated attention and/or inhibit physical movement, as well as specific learning tasks, like the ability to grasp and control writing instruments, manipulate equipment in a chemistry experiment, or produce the sustained fine motor control required to cut out an intricate design pattern or dissect a frog.

Factors influencing self-concept

Failures in any of these activities that are due to, or even just blamed on, physical inadequacies may lead not only to temporary and specific failure perceptions (I can't do this task now), but to generalized and stable self-concepts of inadequacy (I can't do this kind of task, and I never will be able to). Once formed, such attitudes are likely to hamper performance on similar tasks in the future. Task concentration will be interrupted frequently by defeatist feelings (I can't do this, I'm going to fail, everyone is laughing at me, I look foolish), often to the point that giving up and accepting another failure becomes easier than prolonging the anxiety and pain. Chances for mastering the task may also be reduced by teachers or peers who classify the individual as unable to handle a specific task, and thus do not even give him or her the opportunity to try. This can occur either out of indifference (He can't do it, so why bother) or out of humanitarian concern (I don't want to put her on the spot or embarrass her). Either way, such exclusion will enhance the failing student's problem, unless it is accompanied by other methods of providing the student with opportunities to practice the problem task.

Effects of physical development factors on general self-concept are most likely felt by mesomorphs (especially those who are attractive as well as athletic) and endomorphs (especially those whose body type is exaggerated by too little exercise and too many calories). Students who are attractive and athletic tend to be more popular with both adults and peers, to be better adjusted psychologically and to be social leaders (Staffieri, 1967; Hartup, 1970; Tuddenham, 1951; McCandless & Coop, 1979; Lerner & Lerner, 1977). They are likely to receive preferential treatment, partly because others favor them, often unconsciously, and partly because their well-developed social skills make them adept at getting what they want from others.

Unattractive students, especially if they are obese, are likely to be rejected by adults and peers, and ultimately by themselves. Some may even compound this by withdrawing from social interaction and overeating even more than before (Krogman, 1953). Even where this does not occur, the degree of social rejection they suffer from peers may deprive them of important social experience and thus place them at a disadvantage in dealing with others (Bruch, 1958). Students like these need not only sympathy but encouragement and help from their teachers—encouragement to help them combat defeatism and sustain the will to try to overcome the problem, and help in the form of specific suggestions about reforming eating habits, coping with gibes and taunts, and initiating new friendships or changing the nature of existing social relationships.

Physical Development in Preadolescent Children

Physical development factors are of importance primarily to teachers working with preschool or early primary children and to teachers working with adolescents. Some young children will have difficulty doing school assignments involving the use of writing instruments because of slow maturation or lack of practice in holding and using tools for printing, writing, or drawing. Sometimes the problem is easy to observe and correct, such as for the child who grasps a pencil by enclosing an entire fist around it, or holds it correctly but grasps it several inches above the paper instead of only an inch or two above. However, pencil work and related activities are laborious for some children even when they hold the pencil correctly. These children will need practice over a considerable time. So will children who have difficulty with certain gym activities because of unfamiliarity or lack of coordination, as well as children who are too short or otherwise physically unsuited to the equipment involved in an activity.

Unique characteristics of young children

Young children also have unique characteristics that schools need to take into account. They exercise more often and more vigorously and seem to need more activity than older children do; they usually require more sleep and sometimes even a midday nap; and they require more frequent but smaller meals. It should be kept in mind that our sleeping and eating customs are arbitrary and that school practices place students in an artificial environment in which certain rules exist because they are necessary for group living but are unnatural for young children with limited attention spans and lots of energy for physical movement and activities.

Most of the educational implications of physical development seem ob-

Classrooms for preadolescents are often designed to meet their physical and emotional needs.

vious, yet physical problems that can be easily corrected are often observed. Examples include the following:

- ☐ Seats that are too small or too large for particular students or even for an entire class
- ☐ Failure to provide for the needs of left-handed students
- ☐ Adult-size furniture and storage facilities in classrooms for young children, forcing children to depend on the teacher for things that they could handle themselves if needed materials were within their reach
- ☐ Poor seating patterns or other aspects of physical layout that cause problems, such as visual obstructions that prevent the teacher from monitoring what is going on in certain parts of the room or poorly planned traffic patterns that cause unnecessary bumping and jostling
- ☐ Chalkboards and drinking fountains placed too high for young children to use, and wall decorations or bulletin boards placed too high for them to read

In addition to planning the arrangement of the classroom to meet students' physical needs, maintaining awareness of problems that arise with individual differences can help teachers meet students' emotional needs.

Individual differences in growth

Probably most important is teacher awareness of the great range of individual differences in rates and forms of physical growth. This will help teachers to accept the individuality of all students and enable them to provide useful information and reassurance to those who feel ashamed or inferior because they are different from their classmates. Teachers should also understand the special eating and sleeping needs of their students, and the extra nutritional needs of students who are undergoing growth spurts. Preschool and kindergarten classrooms should probably be equipped with cots or some other method of allowing children who need to nap to do so. In addition, children at this age should get a snack in the middle of the morning if they do not eat an early lunch.

Preadolescent Growth

Once past the first few grades of school, most students settle into a growth pattern that is slow and stable until preadolescence. During these years, physical growth and development are not major factors affecting teachers and schools, except for such fundamental considerations as provision of appropriately sized desks or chairs. Physical growth and development become important again at preadolescence, when the growth spurt and the development of primary and secondary sexual characteristics introduce many new dimensions into the lives of the students.

Sex Differences in Physical Development

In general, physical maturation occurs earlier in girls than in boys, and girls mature earlier at adolescence (see Figures 2.1 and 2.2). Thus, at any given point in childhood, girls are likely to be slightly ahead of boys in progression toward ultimate adult characteristics and in ability to control, and especially to inhibit, physical activity. However, most boys are developing toward an ultimately larger physical stature, so that differences between the sexes in height and weight tend to favor boys from birth until age ten or eleven. At this point girls begin to enter the adolescent growth spurt and thus, as a group, become taller and heavier than boys for a few years (Maccoby & Jacklin, 1974; Faust, 1977).

Throughout development, but especially after puberty, girls accumulate more fat than boys, as is apparent in the typical female physique (Thompson, 1954). The sex differences in weight after maturity are due to the heavier bones and muscles of boys rather than to greater fat accumulation. Differences between the sexes in motor development are minimal, although boys generally have greater size and strength and girls often have somewhat better fine motor development, especially finger coordination. These factors, in combination with culturally determined differences in sex-role socialization—what children are taught about how males and females are expected to act—make for sex differences in the patterns of abilities developed to any particular level of proficiency. Boys are usually superior to girls in skills requiring strength or speed/power combinations such as in

Sex-role socialization

Figure 2.1 Typical Individual Growth Curve Rates for Height in Boys and Girls

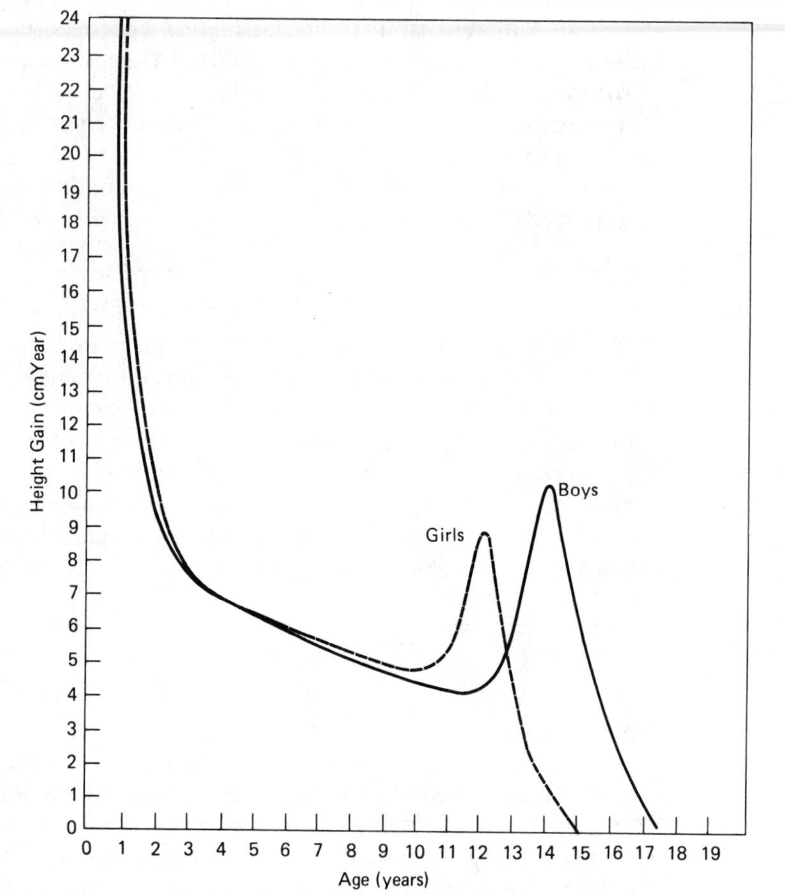

Source: From ADOLESCENTS, 2/e, by Boyd R. McCandless and Richard H. Coop, p. 28. Copyright © 1979 by Holt, Rinehart, and Winston. Reprinted by permission of CBS College Publishing.

large-muscle sports, and girls are usually superior to boys in skills involving fine motor coordination such as art and crafts, sewing, or playing musical instruments. Many of these differences can be expected to diminish or even disappear as sex-role socialization practices change.

In general, sex should not be a factor in determining individual children's opportunities for physical activities, including those that formerly were restricted to the opposite sex. Development that occurs subsequent to this initial exposure should depend on individual talents and interests rather than on sex.

Talent and interest, not sex, are the appropriate factors in selecting sports activities for students.

Figure 2.2 Typical Individual Height-attained Curves for Boys and Girls

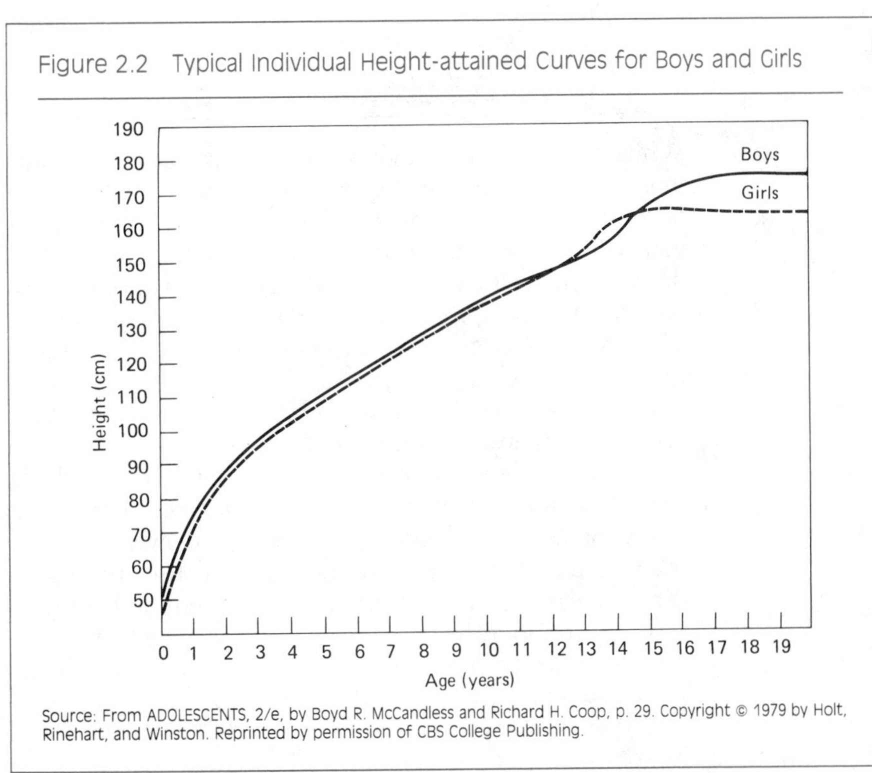

Source: From ADOLESCENTS, 2/e, by Boyd R. McCandless and Richard H. Coop, p. 29. Copyright © 1979 by Holt, Rinehart, and Winston. Reprinted by permission of CBS College Publishing.

Preadolescence: The Growth Spurt

Transition from childhood to mature physical status occurs over a period of several years. During preadolescence (the year or two prior to maturation of the sex organs), the pituitary gland begins increasing its production of growth hormones, causing a period of rapid growth that is quite noticeable for a year or two and continues at a reduced pace thereafter for several more years (Tanner, 1970; Faust, 1977; Stolz & Stolz, 1951).

Like other aspects of physical growth curves, the timing and duration of the preadolescent growth spurt are ultimately controlled by the genes. However, they are affected by nutrition, climate, and other environmental factors as well. Healthy, well-nourished children mature earlier than less advantaged children, urban children earlier than rural children, and children living in temperate climates earlier than those living in tropic or arctic zones (Tanner, 1970). Children with endomorphic or mesomorphic builds are likely to mature earlier than ectomorphs, so that in the junior high school years the former types may be not only bigger but also much more developed in the trunk areas, whereas the latter may seem to be all arms and legs. Late-maturing children often grow at a rapid rate once they do begin a growth spurt and can show gains of three to four inches and twenty-five to thirty pounds in just a few months.

Adolescence: Sexual Maturation

While the pituitary gland is secreting increased amounts of growth hormone, the gonads (ovaries in females and testes in males) are beginning to secrete hormones that stimulate the development of the sex organs. The gonads have been in existence all along but remained relatively inactive until puberty, when, following the general plan of physical maturation laid down in the genes, they begin secreting much greater quantities of hormone. The result is growth of the primary sex characteristics and development of the secondary characteristics.

Primary sex characteristics

Growth of the primary sex characteristics occurs externally, and thus visibly, in males, but internally in females. The testes not only secrete hormone but show a growth spurt, and soon afterwards the penis begins to grow, first in length and then in circumference (Ford & Beach, 1951). The growth spurt of the ovaries in females is followed shortly by menarche, the onset of menstruation, as well as by growth of the uterus and the rest of the female reproductive system. Development of this reproductive apparatus takes several months, so an adolescent girl might not be able to support a pregnancy for perhaps a year after menarche, even though her ovaries are producing eggs (Montagu, 1959).

Secondary sex characteristics

These developments of primary sex characteristics are soon accompanied by secondary sex characteristics. These include growth of hair on the face and body, change to a lower voice pitch, development of breasts in the female, and general changes in body contour that occur as the child gradually takes on the adult male or female form.

Children mature a year or two earlier now than they did in the past, because of industrialization, improvements in health and nutrition, and other environmental factors (Bullough, 1981; Tanner, 1970). Biologists refer to this as the secular trend, to indicate that it is a worldwide trend toward change in a genetically based phenomenon even though it has occurred without changes in the genes themselves. The trend may be continuing (Muuss, 1970), although there is little evidence of change in the last 40 years (Eichhorn, 1980).

The average age of puberty for girls is now about twelve with anywhere from ten to sixteen years of age falling within the normal range. For boys the average age is fourteen, with anywhere between twelve and eighteen years old within the normal range (Tanner, 1973). Physical maturation is a major life event that brings not only physical changes but also emotional consequences that may affect self-concept and social relationships (Petersen & Taylor, 1980).

Early Maturation

Students who mature early are likely to become socially dominant within their peer groups (Savin-Williams, 1979), although at the same time they may begin to have more problems than their peers have with adults. Conflicts with parents increase early in the pubertal cycle (Steinberg, 1981), and teachers sometimes see early maturers as bad influences on classmates because they begin to show some of the resistance to authority that is characteristic to most adolescents, especially boys. In general though early maturation is an advantage for boys. The early-maturing boy is more likely to be considered and treated as a mature individual, to be popular and a leader among his peers (Jones, 1957), and to be high in academic achievement and have greater educational and occupational aspirations (Duke et al., 1982).

Social adjustment

Research by Mussen and Jones (1957) on stories that teenage boys made up in response to projective test stimuli illustrates some of the psychological differences between early- and late-maturing teenagers. The stories of the early-maturing boys revealed independence, self-confidence, and the ability to take a mature or adultlike role in interpersonal relationships. In contrast, the stories of the late-maturing boys revealed frequent feelings of inadequacy, dependency, and low status with respect to parents and peers. Thus, during the junior high and especially the high school years, early-maturing boys will have many advantages in social adjustment and peer group relationships.

Early maturation is more of a mixed blessing for girls. Because girls generally mature earlier than boys anyway, the girls maturing the earliest are going to be the earliest-maturing students of either sex in the school. This may cause them confusion or concern, especially if they have negative expectations (Clark & Ruble, 1978). They may need reassurance and support, and perhaps specific suggestions about such matters as bras, feminine hygiene, and coping with the questions and comments of classmates.

Early-maturing girls are more likely than other girls to react negatively to menarche, which may stimulate ambivalent or confused emotions and associated pain or distress. This is especially likely in girls who are unprepared or who have been led to develop negative expectations (Ruble & Brooks-Gunn, 1982). Many girls become self-conscious, embarrassed, or secretive at first (Koff, Rierdan, & Jacobson, 1981), although menarche also has positive connotations associated with maturity and deepening of female identity, and negative reactions are usually mild and temporary (Greif & Ulman, 1982; Brooks-Gunn & Peterson, 1983).

In high school, early maturers, especially boys whose growth spurts started and ended early, may become upset to find their friends passing them in height, weight, and general physical development. Many who were star athletes in their early adolescence, partly because of early maturation, find two or three years later that they are smaller and less skilled than the average individual. For those who are deeply ego-involved in athletics, this will be a serious blow requiring some informal counseling. Similarly, some girls who realize that they have stopped growing may be dissatisfied with their height or body proportions, and may need help in learning to accept themselves as they are.

Late Maturation

Students who are notably late in maturing are likely to suffer anxiety and embarrassment, or perhaps worse. They need information and reassurance that there are wide individual differences in the onset and duration of maturation, and that they will mature and eventually equal or surpass most of their classmates, despite their late starts. Late maturation is especially likely to be a problem with boys, because as a group they mature later than girls. In a ninth-grade class, for example, it is typical for all of the girls to have at least begun the maturation process, and for most of the boys to have done so. The few late-maturing boys who look, and perhaps act, like "little kids" are likely to suffer teasing or rejection by their peers. These boys will need information and support if they are to be prevented from becoming deeply depressed by their temporary status, or from turning to questionable or negative forms of adjustment, such as seeking attention by becoming the class clown. Late-maturing girls are less likely to suffer intense peer problems, but they may have severe fears or doubts about their normality. If most or all of their friends have begun to mature, they may think that they never will.

Negative forms of adjustment

Most counseling and guidance concerning self-concept problems can and should be done privately, because attempts to handle situations publicly would embarrass the students and perhaps worsen the situation. In private, however, a teacher or counselor can often be helpful by providing information or reassurance to students who need it.

SUMMARY

A developmental perspective involves concern with changes occurring over time, especially in sequence, rate, and form. True developmental sequences are fixed and universal. In physical development, the sequence involves rapid growth in the first two years, slower but noticeable growth for the next eight to twelve years, followed by a second period of rapid growth in adolescence, and a fairly rapid tapering off thereafter. Growth spurts of a few months' duration occur within these larger sequences. The timing of such spurts, and the course of physical development generally, is under the control of pituitary growth hormones which in turn are genetically controlled. Normal nutrition and exercise are crucial to physical development. However, reports indicate that as many as 30 percent of American children are poorly nourished. Listlessness and poor school achievement can result, along with adverse influences on growth and development.

Individual growth curves determine timing and duration of increases in body size. Body types, although not clearly related to psychological variables, can influence developmental task achievement, self-concepts, and social acceptance. Young children may have difficulties with school tasks because of their lack of size, strength, coordination, or familiarity with tasks or equipment. They also need more sleep, more frequent meals, and more opportunity for exercise than older children or adults. However, there is a wide range of individual differences within any group, and each child should be dealt with individually.

Physical maturation occurs earlier in girls than in boys, especially from ten or eleven years old until thirteen or fourteen, when girls tend to be taller and heavier than boys. Gonads begin secreting greater quantities of hormone at puberty, resulting in the growth of primary sex characteristics and the development of secondary sex characteristics. Unusually early or late maturation may cause adjustment problems requiring reassurance and support from adults.

QUESTIONS AND PROBLEMS

1. Summarize research on body types and growth curves. What are the implications of this work, if any, for classroom teachers?
2. Summarize what is known about the physical development of boys and girls. Comment on differential rates of physical development. What implications does this knowledge have for classroom teachers?
3. Describe the following three terms associated with development: sequence, rate, and form.
4. Differentiate growth from development. What is the difference?
5. Discuss Epstein's work on brain growth and how it may affect children's intellectual development in general and performance in school specifically. How much research supports these contentions?
6. Discuss in your own terms the meaning of cerebral lateralization. Specifically, what activities are controlled by the left and right hemispheres?
7. Discuss some of the educational implications of brain lateralization (right brain-left brain). Why do the authors of this textbook argue that the implications of brain lateralization research for classroom instruction remain to be demonstrated?
8. To what extent does body type (ectomorph, mesomorph, and endomorph) influence students' intellectual and social adaptations in school?

9. As a teacher, would you expect most students in a second-grade classroom to look and behave alike? As a teacher in an eighth-grade classroom, would you expect most of the students to be similar in physical development? Would there be more variation in development within second- or eighth-grade classrooms? In general would you expect girls to be taller or shorter than boys at these two grade levels?
10. To what extent does maturation influence students' behavior in school? What are the differential costs for boys and girls of late or early maturation?
11. Suppose that one of your less physically attractive students starts to be called "Pruneface" or "Frankenstein." Should you try to do anything about this? If so, what?
12. In gym class, two of your students are poorly coordinated and slow to react, and thus repeatedly fail to "make the play" during volleyball games. Frustrated and embarrassed, they ask to be excused from further participation in volleyball. What should you tell them?
13. Should schools try to control what or how much students eat at lunch? If so, how? If not, why not?
14. What is a reasonable length of time to expect first graders to sustain concentrated attention to a lesson? Fourth graders? Tenth graders?
15. Suppose that sex education with your homeroom class is one of your teaching duties. Would you handle it differently in an inner-city school than in a suburban school? What would you do if you disagreed with part of the mandated sex-education curriculum?

CASE STUDIES

Sharon the Outsider. "Sharon, your ideas are funny, you're funny, and you're incredibly fat," said Jane (with finality). "Yeah," Mary added. "Your dumb ideas just waste our time. We have to finish the group lab project this period. You just sit there and keep your fat lip closed."

Ms. Fillmore, the biology teacher, overheard Mary's and Jane's remarks and had heard similar ones from other students during the past few weeks. What, if anything, should she say to Jane, Mary, or Sharon about this particular instance? What, if anything, should she do for Sharon generally? (Sharon is a reasonably bright but obese high school sophomore who comes from a lower-class home.)

Jim the Umpire. Jim Moore was a third-grade student at Benton Elementary School. Although Jim was obese and poorly coordinated, he loved sports, especially baseball. He followed major league games with great interest and whenever he could he tried to play baseball. However, he had very few skills and students often laughed at him and blamed him for the team's failure to win. He often dropped the ball in the outfield and was seldom successful as a batter. Mr. Wilson, Jim's teacher, wanted Jim to become more knowledgeable about the game and have the opportunity to practice skills, but without actually competing in the games. He decided to let Jim umpire during recess and lunch games so that he could be spared from critical feedback about his playing. He also planned to work with Jim after school a couple of times a week to help him develop his athletic skills for playing softball. How adequate is this plan for helping Jim to accept his physical problems? What else should the classroom teacher do? Are there any mistakes that the teacher appears to be making at this point?

Too Good to Be True. Ruth was an attractive fifth-grade student at Lewis and Clark Elementary School. She was extremely talented and was the top student in mathematics in her fifth-grade class. Her peers looked up to her and she was often chosen to be homeroom representative or classroom president. For the last two months Ruth had been unhappy at school despite all of her obvious "successes." She was the first student in her class to show signs of sexual maturity and she was extremely uncomfortable with the way she looked and felt. Ms. Kline, her teacher, had noticed her growing unhappiness. What should Ms. Kline do at this point, if anything?

Tina: The Aspiring Basketball Player. Tina, a sixth-grade student, was despondent because of her failure to make the sixth-grade basketball team. She could shoot and dribble as well as any of the other students. However, she was the shortest girl in her class. In the fourth grade she was as tall as everybody else but now everyone was bigger. Since she had failed to make the team two weeks earlier, she had become shy and withdrawn. She characteristically avoided playing with others in the classroom and stayed by herself for most activities. How important is height in determining self-image for the average student and for Tina in particular? If you were Tina's teacher, what would you say to her?

Chapter 3

Basics of Cognitive Development

CHAPTER OUTLINE

OBJECTIVES

When you have mastered the material in this chapter you will be able to

1. Define and distinguish the concepts of maturation and readiness
2. Explain how Piaget's view of learning differs from the behaviorist view of learning
3. Define scheme and discuss the adaptation-equilibration process of cognitive growth
4. Explain how thought and behavior in the preoperational period differ from the sensorimotor period
5. Define operational thought and the key characteristics of concrete versus formal operational thinking
6. Discuss Piaget's versus American psychologists' views on teaching readiness and cover the recent data assessing the extent to which cognitive development can be speeded up
7. Discuss the implications of Piaget's theory for deciding what should be taught in school and how it should be taught

In Chapter 2 we saw that physical changes occurring over time include both growth and development. In this chapter we discuss the writings of Jean Piaget, who demonstrated that children's mental abilities undergo similar development as they get older.

Before Piaget, intellectual development in children was considered to be essentially a growth process: children's minds were thought to be the same as those of adults, only smaller, and they were thought to gradually expand as knowledge and experience accumulated. Piaget and other stage theorists reject this notion that intellectual development is a smooth, gradual process in which each new concept or item of knowledge is just another brick added to the structure. Instead, they believe that children develop through a series of qualitatively distinct stages, where each stage represents a new level of organization of knowledge. When children reach a new stage they have a different kind of knowledge, not just more of the same kind of knowledge, than before. These stages are illustrated graphically in Figure 3.1.

Maturation and Readiness

A stage concept of development usually includes both the concepts of maturation and readiness. This is easiest to understand by using physical development as an example. Infants cannot learn to walk until the maturation of essential biological structures takes place. Gesell and Thompson (1929) demonstrated this by studying a number of physical skills in identical twins. One member of each pair of twins was given special training and practice in acquiring a skill such as climbing stairs while the other twin was not. The purpose was to see if this special instruction and practice could speed up development. In most cases it could not. The special help did not seem

Figure 3.1 Schematic Representation of Stages in Physical and Psychological Development

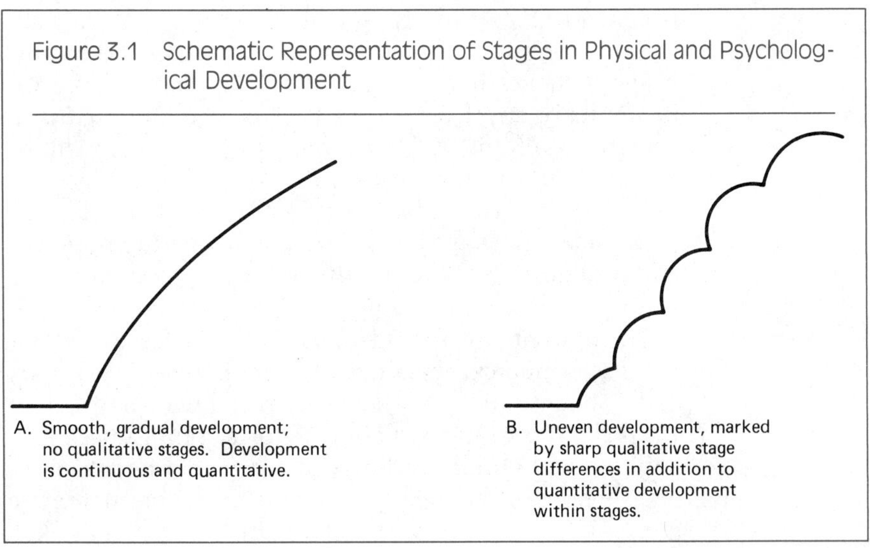

A. Smooth, gradual development; no qualitative stages. Development is continuous and quantitative.

B. Uneven development, marked by sharp qualitative stage differences in addition to quantitative development within stages.

to do any good until the time that the ability being taught could develop naturally. Furthermore, once this point was reached, the twin who had not been given any special help quickly caught up with the other. Thus, development of most physical skills in infants and toddlers depends heavily on maturation.

Readiness

The implication of these studies is that one should not try to teach children a skill until they develop readiness—until they have the biological capability of learning it with relative ease. The concept of readiness was later expanded to include cognition and interest as well as ability. If children of a certain age do not have the prerequisite knowledge to learn a skill, or are not interested, one shouldn't try to teach it to them until later when both the knowledge and interest have developed.

Piaget's theory encompasses the notion of readiness but, unlike readiness to develop physical skills, cognitive readiness was not seen as determined primarily by biological maturation, although this may have a role in early cognitive development. Piaget views the mind of the child as a structure that evolves through successively higher levels of organization and integration. At any particular stage the child will be oriented toward information that is moderately novel—new enough to be interesting but familiar enough to be comprehensible (Ginsburg & Opper, 1979). Children lack interest (at least for now) in further exploration of topics with which they are already overly familiar, and they will also lack both interest in and readiness for information that is too far beyond their present ability to comprehend.

Qualitative versus quantitative development

Not everyone agrees with Piaget on these points. Learning theorists, for example, usually reject the notion of qualitative stages in intellectual development and construe learning as a step-by-step, quantitative process. If readiness does not exist, they feel it can be created by moving through successive approximations from where the learners are to where you want them to go. Even Jerome Bruner (1966), an American psychologist who is similar to Piaget in his general orientation and ideas about development, is more optimistic about what can be accomplished through instruction. Bruner believes that almost any subject matter or content can be taught to a child of any age to at least some degree, if the instructor presents the content in a form and at a difficulty level appropriate to the child's level of cognitive development.

We will return to this matter after considering Piaget's ideas at length. In the meantime, you can check your existing notions about maturation and readiness by answering the following questions:

1. At what age should children begin formal schooling built around academic curricula having specific objectives?
2. Should children who seem very bright and cognitively "ready" be allowed to start school early or to skip grades?
3. Should children who appear dull and not ready be held back from school or retained in the same grade for another year?
4. Many people believe that children learn best by exploring and making

discoveries on their own rather than by having information organized and presented to them by someone else. However, this does not seem to be a very efficient way to learn, and it does not work well with young children learning the tool skills of reading, writing, and arithmetic. These skills are learned much more efficiently in teacher-structured lessons (Good, 1979). Besides, learning by discovery goes on outside of school all the time. With this information in mind, should schools bother at all with learning by discovery?

5. Children become more differentiated with age. By adolescence it is clear that many students will be capable of success at college but that others will have to work hard just to graduate from high school. Also, the bright, college-bound students tend to socialize together, as do the working-class-oriented students (Coleman, 1961). Should schools simply adapt to these student preferences and segregate them into separate paths so that they see very little of one another, or should they try to promote contact through heterogeneous grouping in at least some subject areas?

Piaget's Theory

Jean Piaget (1983) was a Swiss psychologist who until his death in 1980 was the guiding force in developmental psychology from birth through adolescence, concentrating on cognitive development. In his lifetime he produced a staggering number of books and articles in his field. For a long time Piaget's work was disparaged by American psychologists because it seemed unscientific; much of his initial work on infant behavior was based on observations of his own three children in their natural surroundings. He

Although he wrote little specifically about education, Jean Piaget has had a lasting influence on educational methods.

did not work in a laboratory setting, he used homemade methods rather than established scientific instruments (Voyat, 1982), and he did not always report his procedures fully enough to allow others to replicate them. Nevertheless, most of his ideas have been supported by the investigations of others, including many who set out to disprove them.

Piaget considered himself to be a philosopher interested in epistemology, or the philosophy of knowledge. He saw his experimental work as a means of gaining information about how knowledge is acquired, not as a goal in itself. He was aware of the psychological and educational implications of his work, but he persisted, for more than fifty years, in focusing primarily on epistemological questions (Piaget, 1973).

He made few specific statements about the implications of his work for educational theory or practice, believing that this should be done by individuals more directly involved in these fields. Readers should bear this in mind, because discussions of "Piagetian psychology as it applies to education" are mostly interpretations by others. Any curriculum or idea labeled as "Piagetian" is an interpretation based on Piaget's work and not a direct statement from Piaget himself (Ginsburg & Opper, 1979). For what he did say, see Piaget (1970) and Hooper and DeFrain (1980).

Physical Action as the Basis for Cognitive Development

Piaget was one of the first psychologists to recognize explicitly that humans are born as active, exploratory, information-processing organisms. These ideas make his theory popular with the advocates of discovery learning and related approaches that stress "innate" curiosity and exploration drives. Piaget stressed that people are constantly striving to adapt to their environment, and this requires learning to comprehend and control it. He saw the adaptive mechanisms that people generate as being more important and fundamental than the external stimuli and reinforcements stressed by behaviorists.

Learning and physical actions

Piaget viewed acquisition of concepts and behavioral skills as internally motivated and actively directed, not merely "elicited" by external cues. Learning is rooted in physical actions. We observe and conceptualize our own behavior, so that *what we learn is what we do.* In the process we learn what stimuli we can use to do certain things, and what the different outcomes will be if we do those things. However, for Piaget, it is not so much that stimuli elicit our responses as that our own activity engenders a search for relevant stimuli. Thus, consequences are important, not because they motivate or reinforce, but because they provide feedback about the effects of our activity.

Manipulation of stimuli

Consider children learning to ride bicycles. Behaviorists would stress both the bicycle itself and the input it provides when one tries to ride it as stimuli that elicit responses. Responses that are successful lead to positive reinforcement (successfully riding the bicycle), and thus are retained, practiced, and perfected. Responses that are unsuccessful are punished (the child falls

For Piaget, learning is rooted in developing and perfecting physical skills.

down, or at least has difficulty maintaining balance and forward motion), and are suppressed. As practice continues, associations build up that help the child recognize meaningful stimulus events, respond in a systematic way, and achieve increasing efficiency. The ability to ride a bike, then, is elicited in raw form and then shaped into smooth efficiency through practice and reinforcement.

Piaget would say that the child's present interests focus attention on certain aspects of the stimulus situation (the bicycle as opposed to other things in the environment, and specifically those aspects of the bicycle that are relevant to learning how to ride it, rather than simply looking at it or turning it upside down and spinning the wheels). Having selected these stimuli, a child then would manipulate them by pumping the pedals, moving the handlebars, and so on, and get feedback concerning the results of these actions. The feedback would be used in making corrections to increase efficiency. The child would continually monitor bike-riding activities and their effects, develop knowledge about what to do and avoid, and become increasingly efficient at doing the things that work best. Piaget would see the child as actively controlling the situation rather than passively responding to stimulation and reinforcement. He would see the bike as primarily a prop for the child to use in perfecting skills, not as a stimulus that somehow "elicits" responses. Finally, he would stress the role of consequences for providing feedback relevant for adaptive responding, and deemphasize their function as rewards or punishments. Behaviorists would see the child as learning how to respond to the bike, while Piaget would say that the child is learning what to do with a bike.

Schemes

Piaget's basic unit of cognition, speech, and behavior is the *scheme*. The term is roughly comparable to behavioristic concepts like "habit" or "response." It can apply to purely cognitive concepts though, and has the connotations of active information processing. For some purposes it is useful to distinguish between different kinds of schemes. Sensorimotor schemes, or behavioral schemes, refer to behavioral knowledge and skills such as walking, turning doorknobs, or opening bottles; cognitive schemes refer to concepts, images, and thinking and reasoning ability such as understanding the differences between plants and animals, being able to envision a triangle, or reasoning from causes to effects; and verbal schemes refer to word meanings and communication skills such as associating names with their physical referents or mastering basic grammar and syntax.

Piaget used the term "scheme" loosely, and the resulting flexibility is an asset. He spoke of specific schemes such as an infant's grasping scheme—coordination of the sensorimotor abilities required to reach out and grasp an object—but also used the term to refer to a complex body of knowledge or skills, such as the ability to reason deductively. Most of the schemes of the newborn infant are simple reflexes, but new schemes begin to appear quickly, and existing schemes become coordinated into larger schemes.

Organization versus acquisition of schemes

Although in one sense the grasping scheme is an isolated and specific sensorimotor scheme, it also involves coordination of several previously acquired schemes, such as the abilities to discriminate focal objects from background in visual perception, fix visual attention on a single object, distinguish objects that can be grasped from those that cannot, and coordinate eye and hand to reach out smoothly and grasp an object without knocking it over or missing it. Piaget placed at least as much stress on the organization of schemes into more complex ones as he did on the acquisition of individual schemes.

Adaptation

Adaptation is seen by Piaget as part of the human condition—a continuous process of interacting with the environment and learning to predict and control it to some degree. Adaptation experiences lead to the development of new schemes, initially through trial and error exploration, but more and more through systematic experimentation as schemes begin to accumulate. Each new discovery is a revelation to the child who makes it, even though it might be commonplace to adults. Knowledge about self, the immediate physical and social environment, and the world generally is literally *constructed* as the child gains experience, resolves some apparent contradictions (all daddies are men, but all men are not daddies), and coordinates isolated schemes into clusters and ultimately into a stable, internally consistent cognitive structure.

Accommodation

Piaget felt that there are two fundamental adaptational mechanisms involved in every action: accommodation and assimilation. Accommodation involves changing in response to environmental demands. It includes both acquisition of entirely new schemes and adaptation of previously learned schemes to fit the precise demands of new stimuli or situations. Extensive accommodation is necessary when we encounter a situation involving adaptational demands that we are not prepared to meet with existing schemes, such as when an appliance stops working for no apparent reason or when we have a novel experience that seems to contradict all of our previous experiences. The accommodation required will involve invention of new schemes (appliance troubleshooting) or noteworthy differentiation of existing schemes to take into account the new input. In resolving the apparent contradictions implied by a novel event, we transform our earlier limited ideas into a more sophisticated set that includes explanations of how both sets of events can be true.

At least some degree of accommodation is involved in every activity. For example, we all know how to use a lock and key, but some accommodation is involved any time we perform the action. This is most apparent with locks we open for the first time, but it also applies to such everyday events as unlocking the doors to our cars or homes. The same locks and keys are involved, but slight adaptations (accommodations) must be made to adjust for whether or not we have the key right side up, how far away from the lock we are standing, or the problems of coping with bent keys or frozen locks.

Assimilation

Assimilation, roughly equivalent to the behavioristic term "transfer," is the process by which a particular stimulus or situation is handled immediately and automatically, using schemes that have already been established. Thus familiar everyday activities mostly involve assimilation, although some minor accommodation is also demanded—we walk "automatically," however we must make accommodations when we encounter obstacles, staircases, corners, or slippery surfaces.

Theoretically, all behavior includes both assimilation and accommodation. Situations that are entirely foreign to previous experience (existing schemes) presumably would produce panic or behavioral paralysis, since we would have no adaptation mechanisms to call on. Such situations rarely exist in practice, however, because virtually any situation is partially assimilable to existing schemes, allowing systematic and to some degree predictable responses to be made. For example, consider the behavior of people on the "Candid Camera" television show when confronted with talking mailboxes and other "impossible" situations. Conversely, even the most overlearned responses require at least some accommodation, because no two situations are ever exactly the same.

Consider your signature, for example. In Piaget's terminology, you respond to situations calling for your signature by assimilating them into your "signature-signing" scheme. You have recorded your signature so often that it probably is the most overlearned and recognizable of all your writing schemes. Nevertheless, no two signatures are ever exactly the same, because each separate signing differs from the others in small ways, and minor accommodations to these differences are required. This is why Piaget referred to assimilation and accommodation as universals, or *functional invariants*. They exist in every behavior, large or small, new or familiar.

Functional invariants

Piaget saw scheme development as universal in sequence, somewhat variable in rate, and highly variable in form. Differences in rate and form are attributed to four factors (Ginsburg & Opper, 1979): (1) maturation; (2) individual experience (the specific environment that an individual grows up in, and the stimulation and experiences that he or she encounters "accidentally" rather than because of the other three factors); (3) social transmission (formal and informal socialization and education); and (4) equilibration (internal self-direction and regulation).

Scheme development differences

The equilibration principle demonstrates Piaget's emphasis on humans as intrinsically active and exploratory in attempting to impose order, stability, and meaning on experience. It postulates that people sense disequilibrium, such as curiosity, the desire to explore, or the need to resolve some conflict or problem regularly, and that this sense of disequilibrium causes them to engage in adaptational behavior. At any point in development, a person's schemes are related (assimilated) to one another in a unique way to form the person's cognitive structure. This existing cognitive

Disequilibrium

structure interacts with the specific possibilities and demands presented by the environment in order to determine behavior in particular situations.

Certain aspects of the situation will be irrelevant to the person (completely foreign to existing schemes) and thus not even partially assimilable. Other aspects will be so familiar that they can be almost completely assimilated into existing schemes. Finally, some aspects will be partially assimilable and these will induce disequilibrium. These moderately novel aspects will motivate adaptational or exploratory behaviors that involve accommodation.

The resulting accommodation will require the development of new schemes or the extension of existing ones, and will continue until the originally motivating sense of disequilibrium has dissipated and been replaced by boredom. At this point the person will shift attention to some other aspect of the situation that also involves sufficient disequilibrium to motivate adaptational activity. If nothing in the situation has this potential, the person will be motivated to leave the situation and find one that does.

This pattern is easy to observe in infants and toddlers. Placed next to a variety of toys, a toddler will inspect the toys and then select one for play. Different toddlers will select different toys, according to their unique interests. In Piagetian terms, these interests are defined by the match between the toy and the toddler's present cognitive structure. The toy that induces the most disequilibrium will be the one the toddler chooses. Following selection, the toddler will play with the toy for some time, perhaps repeating the same operations, but becoming noticeably more skillful. This will continue long past the point where adults would have shifted attention to something else, because the activity to the child is still new and interesting. Eventually, though, the infant will either start a new activity with the same toy or put the toy aside.

Motivation to explore

As another example, consider your own self-guided exploration. If you develop an interest in a new kind of music or in a different form of recreation, it probably will be familiar enough for you to relate to, but different enough to make it interesting and enjoyable. For a time this may lead to indulging the opportunity to listen to the music or participate in the activity at every spare moment. However, interest will eventually subside as the novelty wears off and new interests emerge. Piaget would say that you reached a state of equilibrium with regard to the new interest and are now ready to turn your attention to something that induces a new sense of disequilibrium, or motivation to explore.

Equilibration principle

The equilibration principle is used not only for conceptualizing momentary or short-term relationships between motivation and behavior, but also for conceptualizing trends occurring over longer periods of time. In particular, the equilibration principle predicts that, as people develop, their attention and interest will focus on progressively more complex aspects of their environment. Thus, in stating that people seek to maintain a state of equilibrium with their environments, Piaget did not mean that they keep returning to a fixed steady state. Because new and more sophisticated schemes develop all the time, people operate from continually more complex cognitive structures when seeking equilibrium with their environments. Therefore, since the principle of equilibration refers to the cognitive structure as a whole and not just to individual schemes, the amount and level of integration of knowledge needed to maintain a 10-year-old at a state of equilibrium is much greater than that required to maintain a five-year-old at equilibrium. Furthermore, the equilibration principle implies that people are always interested in extending the knowledge base they presently possess, so that they will prefer learning new things or new ways to conceptualize or manipulate familiar things over continued application of familiar schemes to familiar things (Moessinger, 1978; Block, 1982).

Piaget's Four Developmental Periods

Piaget used four primary concepts to describe how humans interact with and adapt to their environments. He saw humans as approaching situations with cognitive structures composed of interrelated *schemes*, *assimilating* certain aspects into existing schemes, but also being forced to *accommodate* existing schemes to take into account new or unique situational factors. This continuing, universal interaction with the environment is under the control of the *equilibration* principle, at least in situations where individuals are free to do as they wish. The sequence of scheme acquisition is universal, but the rates at which schemes develop, and the forms they take, depend on individual differences in maturation, environmental experiences, and social transmission, in addition to unique equilibration factors. Scheme development proceeds through four qualitatively distinct stages.

The Sensorimotor Period

During this period, the first eighteen months of life, scheme development is concentrated heavily in the sensorimotor area. The infant develops and coordinates a great variety of behavior skills, but development of verbal and cognitive schemes tends to be minimal and poorly coordinated.

The Preoperational Period

During these years, from about eighteen months until about age seven, toddlers and young children internalize their sensorimotor schemes (behavioral skills) in the form of cognitive schemes (imagery, thought). For example, instead of relying on laborious trial and error when working a puzzle or trying to construct something from blocks according to a model, children begin to guide themselves with imagery based on memories of previous behavior in the same situation.

As the development of imagery and the ability to retain images in memory progress, learning becomes much more cumulative. This reduces dependence on immediate perception and concrete experience, and makes possible more systematic reasoning and problem solving. Children not only

In the preoperational period of development, experience and some imagery take the place of mere trial and error.

can learn through discovery in the immediate situation, they also can relate situational factors to previously developed schemes retained in memory by visualizing activities without carrying them out.

Preoperational children can "think ahead" during a sequential task like block building or copying letters, whereas previously they had to try everything behaviorally and made many errors. Yet preoperational logic is notably egocentric and unstable. It is egocentric because children of this age have not yet developed the ability to see things from other people's perspectives. They act as if everyone else thinks exactly the way they do, knows exactly what they mean, and so on. Furthermore, they often seem not to notice or be bothered by indications that their assumptions are incorrect (Vygotsky, 1962; Flavell, Botkin, Fry, Wright, & Jarvis, 1968; Miller, Brownell, & Zukier, 1977).

Scheme instability

Schemes are unstable during this stage because children have not yet learned to distinguish invariant and universal aspects of the environment from aspects that are specific to particular situations and relatively unimportant. They are easily confused by *conservation* problems, problems that require them to "conserve" invariant aspects of objects in their minds, and to avoid becoming confused by manipulations of unimportant characteristics. For example, many children will say that a ball of clay contains more or less clay after it has been rolled into a "hot dog" shape when nothing has actually been added or taken away, and most will assume that a tall container filled with water has more water than a shorter container filled with water, even though the tall one may be a test tube and the short one may be a drinking glass or even a pitcher.

The Concrete Operations Period

Starting at around age seven and continuing to about age twelve, children become "operational." Their cognitive schemes, especially their thinking and problem-solving skills, become organized into concrete operations—mental representations of potential actions.

Classification skills

One set of concrete operations involves *classification skills*. Consider class-inclusion problems, where children are questioned about the different ways that objects can be classified (McCabe et al., 1982). For example a collection of toy chairs, tables, cars, and trucks, can be divided into these four groups, but also can be divided into the two larger groups of furniture and vehicles. Preoperational children will have difficulty distinguishing between these two levels of classification, especially if asked questions such as "Are there more trucks or more vehicles?" that require them to consider both classes simultaneously (Piaget & Inhelder, 1964).

Children whose classification skills have become operational can handle such questions, because concrete operations are reversible. Thus, these children can reverse combinations of smaller classes into larger ones (the vehicles can be redivided into separate groups of cars and trucks), as well as divisions of larger classes into smaller ones (the vehicles can be reassembled into a single group). Furthermore, they can perform these operations mentally, without having to move the objects around.

Conservation concepts

As these children move into and through the concrete operational years they gradually attain conservation concepts. Around ages six to seven, they attain conservation of substance (realizing that the amount of substance does not change if you divide it into subparts), length (realizing that the length of a wire or piece of string does not change if you cut it into parts or bend it into a curved shape), and continuous quantity (realizing that pouring liquid from one container to another does not change the amount of liquid). At about seven years of age, children attain conservation of number (realizing that the number of objects does not change if they are placed close together or spread far apart) and area (realizing that the total area covered by a piece of paper will not change if the paper is cut into pieces or if the pieces are rearranged into new shapes). Somewhere between ages 9 and 12, children attain conservation of weight (realizing that a piece of clay weighs the same regardless of the shape one forms it into). Finally, at around ages 11 or 12, children attain conservation of volume (realizing that a single piece of clay that has been reformed into various shapes will occupy the same volume when immersed in a liquid).

Seriation

Among the concrete operations that develop is *seriation*—the ability to place a group of objects in order from least to most in length, width, weight, or some other common property. Younger children tend to proceed laboriously on seriation tasks because they have to make paired comparisons and because they are confused by misleading cues from properties other than the property of interest. For example, if asked to order objects from lightest to heaviest, they may begin to confuse size and weight so that they misplace objects that are large but light, or small but heavy. Concrete operational children are much less prone to such confusion; they are able to see the "big picture" and thus to place groups of 10 or 12 objects in serial order easily without having to compare each separate object with each of the others.

Negation

Another concrete operation is *negation*—the recognition that an action can be negated or reversed so that events will return to the state they were in before the original action was taken. In a liquid volume conservation task, for example, preoperational children recognize that identical pitchers contain the same amounts of water when equally filled, but they become confused if the contents of one pitcher are poured into several glasses ("Is there more water in the remaining pitcher, or in all these glasses?"). Children who have mastered the concrete operation of negation immediately recognize that the amounts must be the same, because if you pour the contents of the glasses back into the pitcher, you will have the original contents of the pitcher.

Identity

Other concrete operations can also be illustrated with this same example. One is *identity*—recognition that physical substances retain their volume or quantity even if moved around, divided into parts, or otherwise transformed in appearance, so long as nothing is added or taken away. Children using the operation of identity will say that the amounts are the same because it's the same quantity of water—it was moved but none was added or removed.

Compensation

Another concrete operation that will help children comprehend this problem, at least in part, is called *compensation* or *reciprocity*—recognition that a change in one dimension is balanced by a compensating or reciprocal change in another dimension. Operational children will note that the filled pitcher is larger and thus holds more water than a glass holds, but that there are several glasses.

Higher levels of equilibrium

Concrete operations not only allow children to solve specific problems, they also constitute generalized learning-to-learn skills and logical reasoning abilities that help them make sense of a great many of their experiences. Consequently, concrete operations are important components of school readiness (Arlin, 1981). Once children become operational in their thinking, they move more systematically to higher levels of equilibrium. Their schemes, especially cognitive schemes representing their understanding of which aspects of the world are universal and invariant, and which are subject to situational changes, become more dependable, stable, and integrated, eventually forming a single cognitive structure. The elements, or schemes within the structure become coordinated and mutually supportive, so that they become available for systematic and consistently logical application to problem solving (accommodation).

Upon reaching this point, children think logically in the same way that adults do, although they cannot yet handle purely abstract material. This is the period of concrete operations because, although children now recognize invariant versus variant aspects of the environment and are capable of logical reasoning, they still depend on direct, concrete experiences, or

In the formal operations period of development, the student consolidates the ability to think in abstract terms.

at least the ability to imagine such experiences vividly, to provide "props" for thinking and reasoning. They cannot yet deal with abstract content that does not lend itself to concrete presentations, except to memorize verbal statements that they do not really understand.

The Formal Operations Period

The period of formal operations begins at about age twelve and gradually consolidates over the next several years (Inhelder & Piaget, 1958). Much is involved in this transformation, but the hallmark is the development of the ability to think in symbolic terms and comprehend content meaningfully without requiring physical objects or even imagery based on past experience with such objects. Formal operations are the logical and mathematical concepts and rules of inference used in advanced conceptualization and reasoning, including reasoning about abstract content that is difficult or impossible to represent concretely, or about events that are theoretically possible but have never occurred in reality.

Binary operations

In describing formal operations, Piaget made reference to the binary operations stressed in propositional logic and the "INRC group" stressed in algebra. Binary operations are the logical operations that can be applied to problems involving two propositions, each of which may be either true or false. People who possess well functioning formal operations can generate all of the logical combinations that may apply to the relationship between these propositions. These combinations yield a total of 16 possible outcomes, which can yield statements of affirmation, negation, denial, equivalence, conjunction, implication, reciprocal implication, conclusion, and so on.

INRC operations

The *INRC group* includes more formal and algebraic versions of the reversibility schemes first attained in concrete form in the previous period. In observing and thinking about transformations, such as those that occur during a conservation task, for example, the individual with well-functioning INRC operations can follow all of the changes that occur without becoming confused or losing track of the qualitative and quantitative properties of the material, and can mentally reverse the entire process if necessary. To accomplish this, the individual must understand the structural possibilities of identity (I), negation (N), reciprocity (R), and correlativity (C). In a conservation of matter task, for example, a person would realize that the material is the same material regardless of changes in its shape (identity), that increases in length are compensated for by decreases in width (reciprocity), that thinness is related to length and fatness is related to weight (correlativity), and that the whole process can be reversed in order to undo any of the changes made (Bybee & Sund, 1982). Furthermore, in contrast to the concrete operational child who could deal with only one or two of these relationships at a time and only in connection with observation or vivid memory of demonstrations involving actual objects, the formal operational child has a more abstract and better integrated understanding of these logical and algebraic relationships that enables him or her to think rapidly yet comprehensively and without dependence on concrete props.

Development of well-functioning formal operations apparently occurs only among individuals whose cognitive structures have been well developed and integrated at the level of concrete operational thought. Evidence of formal operations is lacking altogether in certain societies, especially those without formal educational systems (Luria, 1976; Dasen, 1972; Riegel, 1973), at least when measured with the usual Piagetian methods that involve probing the person's understanding of the actions of a pendulum (what factors affect its frequency of oscillation?) or the bending of rods (is the degree to which a rod will bend when a weight is placed on it dependent on its composition, length, thickness, cross-sectional form, or some combination of these factors?). Those that criticize the use of these experiments in undeveloped societies point out that they assume knowledge of Western classical sciences, and suggest that evidence of formal operational thinking might appear if the individuals in these societies were questioned about things that were familiar to them (Brislin, 1983; Glick, 1975; Modgil & Modgil, 1982; Laboratory of Comparative Human Cognition, 1983). This is possible, but so far has not been demonstrated convincingly.

In any case, it is clear that even within our society only certain individuals, perhaps a minority, develop well-functioning formal operations (Crain, 1980; Capon & Kuhn, 1979; Killian, 1979; Neimark, 1975, 1979; Jackson, 1965; Towler & Wheatley, 1971). Their schemes are coordinated to the point where they can be expressed in purely symbolic form as abstract, logical or mathematical principles that can be used without reference to concrete objects or imagery. This level of cognitive development is necessary to understand advanced concepts in philosophy, mathematics, and science, as well as many of the concepts taught in college courses in any subject matter. Among college students, formal operations are more developed with reference to content related to one's major subject than to other content (DeLisi and Staudt, 1980), and students with more developed formal operations tend to take more math and science courses and to do better in them, compared to students with equal ACT scores but less developed formal operations (Commons, Miller, and Kuhn, 1982). There are small but statistically significant differences favoring males over females in formal operations (Meehan, 1984), possibly due to sex differences in course enrollments in science and mathematics (Peskin, 1980).

Problem finding stage of cognitive development

Even though most people do not attain well-functioning formal operations in every aspect of their thinking, some developmental psychologists argue that the concept of formal operations needs to be differentiated or elaborated to take into account cognitive development that occurs beyond the adolescent years (Commons, Richards, and Kuhn, 1982; Long, McCrary, and Ackerman, 1980). For example, Arlin (1975) argues that there is a fifth stage of cognitive development that occurs in adulthood. Arlin describes this as a problem-finding stage that builds on the problem-solving abilities associated with attainment of Piaget's stage of formal operations. People who attain this stage not only can solve problems but can

Table 3.1 Average Ages When Selected Mathematical Concepts Develop*

Concept	Late Preoperational Period (4–7) ages	Concrete Operational Period (7–9) ages	Concrete Operational Period (9–11) ages	Period of Formal Operations (11–15) ages
Topological space	X			
Classification	X X			
Seriation	X X			
Number conservation	X X			
Length conservation	X X			
Area conservation	X X			
Closure	X X			
Addition of classes	X X	X		
Multiplication of numbers	X X	X		
Euclidean space	X X	X		
Multiple classification	X X	X X		
Identity	X X	X X		
Commutativity	X X	X X		
Associativity	X X	X X	X	
Distributivity	X X	X X	X X	
Space	X X	X X	X X	X X
Time	X X	X X	X X	X X
Movement, velocity	X X	X X	X X	X X
Volume	X X	X X	X X	X X
Measurement	X X	X X	X X	X X
Functions	X X	X X	X X	X X
Proportion	X X	X X	X X	X X
Deduction/induction				X X
Formal logic				X X
Probability				X X
Proofs				X X

* The initial steps in the construction of many of these concepts can be traced back to the sensorimotor period.

From Barry Wadsworth, *Piaget for the Classroom Teacher* (Longman, 1978).

infer implications and think creatively and divergently about the objects of their thought. Riegel (1973) has made a similar proposal concerning a fifth stage of cognitive development that occurs during adulthood.

Others have suggested that more differentiation is needed early in the stage to distinguish preadolescents who are just developing the ability to think abstractly about concrete objects and events from older students who are already capable of sustained logical reasoning on abstract or hypothetical issues. We prefer to subdivide the period of formal operations into two stages, or at least to refer to preadolescents just entering the stage as *transitional* students rather than as students who have attained formal operations.

Table 3.1 shows the typical ages and stages at which certain mathematical concepts develop.

Implications for Education

Because Piaget had so much to say about how children learn and yet so little to say about how to instruct them in classrooms, his work has inspired varied and sometimes even contradictory approaches to education that are claimed to be "Piagetian" or "based on Piaget" by their designers (Kuhn, 1979; Hooper & DeFrain, 1980; Siegel, Brodzinsky & Golinkoff, 1981). Some early interpreters, stressing Piaget's research on children learning through natural interaction with their environment and his emphasis on the importance of self-regulated learning under the equilibration principle, seemed almost hostile to the notion of instructing children rather than allowing them to learn on their own. This idea that it is inappropriate to teach children at all has faded, but among Piagetians who stress self-regulated learning as a key concept, the emphasis remains on discovery learning as the preferred approach to education. In this view, teachers should minimize group instruction involving attempts to get students to respond to a set curriculum taught in a prescribed sequence. Instead they should emphasize discovery learning through active manipulation of concrete materials. Here, the teacher is more oriented toward instructing individuals than groups, and responding to students' initiatives or evidence of readiness for learning experiences than toward teaching them more routinely (Ginsburg & Opper, 1979; Wadsworth, 1978).

Discovery learning

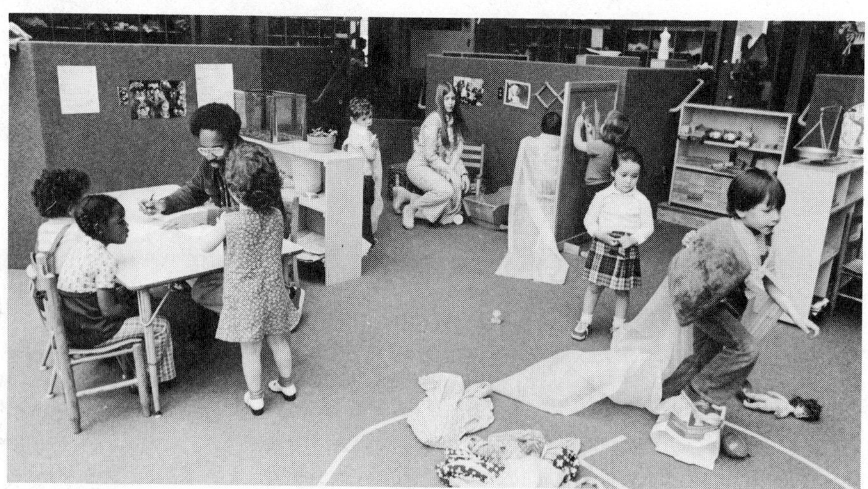

Piagetians encourage students to learn through self-discovery and play.

Piagetian research and theorizing are certainly compatible with these ideas. However, his writings about how children learn in natural play situations are essentially silent concerning the issues of what and how children should learn at school. Perhaps they can be applied to preschool and kindergarten classrooms with small student-teacher ratios, but discovery learning does not appear feasible for elementary and secondary school classrooms. Also, there are limits as to how seriously teachers can take concepts such as readiness or developmental stages. Duckworth (1979), a writer generally sympathetic to the Piagetian approach, notes that overemphasis on the need for self-regulated learning in "applying Piaget" creates a dilemma for teachers, who may be lead to feel that "either we're too early and they can't learn it or we're too late and they know it already."

Application of Piagetian theories to the classroom

Some would-be appliers of Piaget took the opposite approach and began experimenting with building Piagetian tasks into the curriculum and teaching students to conserve, to solve class inclusion problems, and so on. This approach was contrary to the spirit of Piaget's work, although it was based on the notion that if conservation, class inclusion, and other key concepts and operations that he had discovered were truly universal and basic to intellectual functioning, direct instruction in these concepts and operations might enhance or at least accelerate cognitive development. Unfortunately, but not unexpectedly, such instruction did not have such generalized effects.

More recently, attempts to apply Piaget's ideas to education have placed more emphasis on his ideas about how children learn, rather than on his stages of development. Hooper and DeFrain (1980), after reviewing several Piagetian-based programs, suggest the following principles for application of Piaget's theory in the classroom: (1) Teachers should attend to the processes, and not just the products or outcomes of students' thinking. They shouldn't concentrate just on getting corrrect answers; they should make sure that the students really understand the concepts or operations involved. (2) Teachers should appreciate the value that play and exploration/manipulation opportunities have for developing cognitive schemes, especially in the early grades. (3) Teachers should be aware that children learn a great deal from interacting with one another socially, and in particular from debating and attempting to resolve conflicting views. (4) Teachers should remember that learning that occurs through active exploration and discovery is more likely to be retained and to be meaningful than learning that occurs through more passive response to the teacher's initiatives.

The problem of the match

Unless teachers are willing to rely completely on discovery learning, they will have to find ways to solve what Hunt (1961) has called "the problem of the match." That is, they will have to find ways to keep the level and variety of input matched to students' schemes in such a way that disequilibrium (and thus their motivation to learn) is maximized. Presenting material that is too easy or familiar will be inefficient, because it will be boring and the student will already know most of it. Material that is too difficult will be more frustrating because students will not be able to assimilate it. Material that lacks interest value will be inefficient because students will not be motivated to explore it actively.

Underestimation of children's knowledge

These notions appear to be sound as general principles, but they are difficult to apply to particular situations. For one thing, it appears that Piaget systematically underestimated both the degree of knowledge that children at particular ages possess and the degree to which their existing knowledge can be extended with relative ease. For example, Piaget's findings concerning conservation of number could be taken to imply that preoperational children do not have useful quantitative knowledge. However, research on children's understanding of number indicates that even two- and three-year-olds possess notions of quantity and the ability to compare quantities even before they can count, and that older preoperational children not only can count but possess a variety of accurate and useful number concepts even though they do not yet qualify as conservers on conservation of numbers tasks (Briars & Siegler, 1984; Gelman, 1980; Gelman & Gallistel, 1978). Furthermore, counting and related number concepts and operations may be more basic to children's development of knowledge about numbers than ability to succeed on Piagetian tasks is (Clements, 1984; Fuson, Secada, & Hall, 1983).

In addition to these ambiguities about precisely when children would be ready for instruction in particular concepts, there are ambiguities about precisely what is meant by matching input to students' present needs. Early Piagetian interpreters tended to assume that such matching meant presenting students with tasks that called for application of schemes and operations associated with their present stage of cognitive development. Later, however, other interpreters began to speak of *plus-one matching*—presenting students with tasks that call for application of schemes or operations associated with the stage of development one level higher than their present stage. The idea here is that matching input to the existing level of development will merely provide for additional exercise of already well-developed schemes and operations, whereas plus-one matching will stimulate the development of schemes and operations that are just now emerging in the student. Vygotsky (1962; 1978) advances a similar notion in arguing that instruction should concentrate on the student's *zone of proximal development*—on areas of knowledge and skill that the student will not master spontaneously if left to his or her own devices, but will be able to master with relative ease if given instruction and assistance.

Plus-one matching

Critics of the Piagetian approach reject what they see as overemphasis on the need for spontaneous and self-regulated learning. For example, they note that motivation to learn a particular thing may not exist at the moment but might be stimulated easily by the teacher. Similarly, they note that "readiness" is simply a term for particular prerequisite knowledge and interests that may be possible to stimulate easily through systematic intervention. In other words, such critics stress teaching readiness rather than waiting for it to occur spontaneously.

Teaching Readiness

The issues just discussed led to a controversy between a group of psychologists, mainly American, who were interested in training nonconservers to conserve, and Piaget and his collaborators (Kuhn, 1974). The "conservation trainers" used brief treatments in attempts to bring about conceptual advances that Piaget believed would require years of broad-based natural experience as a prerequisite. Their data seemed to show that children could learn such concepts much earlier than Piaget had claimed.

Criteria for concept acquisition

However, Piaget and his colleagues (Inhelder, Sinclair, & Bovet, 1974) were unsatisfied with these findings because they believed that the criteria for concept acquisition were not strict enough, and because they doubted that the new learning would generalize to natural situations. The American studies were usually restricted to verbal questioning of the children, and "correct" answers were accepted as evidence that the child had acquired a concept being taught, such as the ability to conserve. Piaget and his colleagues required not merely correct verbalization but the ability to withstand challenges designed to confuse children who did not have a firm grasp of the new concept. They believed that true conservers not only knew that something was true, but that it was necessarily true—that it could not be otherwise. In support of their position, Piaget and his colleagues found that many newly "acquired" concepts could not withstand this kind of probing. When children were required not only to produce the correct verbal responses but to indicate understanding with corresponding physical actions as well, and especially when they were confronted with counterarguments, many became confused, backed down, or reverted to lower-level concepts. Typically, these children were the ones who showed the least evidence of readiness to achieve the concept in question before the training began.

More recent work indicates that apparently genuine, generalizable gains can be induced by such methods as confronting conservers and nonconservers with each other's beliefs and requiring them to come to agreement (Botvin & Murray, 1975; Russell, 1982), or asking children to pretend that their beliefs are opposite to the real ones (Murray, Ames, & Botvin, 1977). Others have also succeeded with more traditional approaches involving instruction in rules, provision of feedback, or exposure to models (Brainerd, 1977).

Research on attempts to teach preadolescents to use formal operations has produced the same pattern of mixed and controversial findings as the "conservation training" studies (Greenbowe et al., 1981; Nagy & Griffiths, 1982). Taken together, the Swiss and American work suggests that cognitive development is more open to meaningful stimulation through instruction than Piaget thought, but that Piaget was correct in stating that there are limits on what can be accomplished with a given child, and on whether it will be worth the effort involved (Murray, 1978). In any case, this controversy involved differences not only in beliefs about what is possible, but also in beliefs about what a particular cognitive achievement means.

Figurative versus operative knowledge

Piaget typically dismissed much of the "learning" produced in the American experiments as superficial and "merely verbal" because he felt there was a distinction between figurative and operative knowledge. Operative knowledge comes from actions, specifically those used to deal with or change the environment. These actions can be either overt (physical) or internal (mental). For Piaget, operative knowledge is the most basic kind of knowledge; it is knowledge about what we can do and how to do it. On the other hand, figurative knowledge involves taking in some kind of representation or reproduction of the environment without actually changing it or operating on it. Mainly this involves perceptions or mental images of things observed in the environment, although it also includes imitations of the actions of other persons or things; simply copying without operating on the input. Figurative knowledge is subject to egocentrism and all of the other distortions of perception and comprehension that children show, and it may or may not be meaningful to children. It is meaningful only to the

Figure 3.2 Figurative Knowledge Without Operative Knowledge

Dr. Judith Lanier of Michigan State University composed the following exercise on "traxoline" to illustrate what happens when we present (and require application of) knowledge only at the figurative level.

TRAXOLINE

It is very important that you learn about traxoline. Traxoline is a new form of zionter. It is montilled in Ceristanna. The Ceristannians gristerlate large amounts of fevon and then bracter it to quasel traxoline. Traxoline may well be one of our most lukized snezlaus in the future because of our zionter lescelidge.

Please answer the following questions in complete sentences and in your best handwriting.

1. What is traxoline?
2. Where is traxoline montilled?
3. How is traxoline quaselled?
4. Why is it important to know about traxoline?

If this example seems too farfetched, consider the next one, putting yourself in the place of a 10-year-old from Luckenbach, Texas.

Pittsburgh, "Heart of the Nation," is known for its steel production. It is located in southwestern Pennsylvania, where the Allegheny and Monongahela rivers join to form the Ohio. Iron ore, especially hematite, magnetite, and taconite, is first concentrated and then purified, using limestone as a flux to combine with impurities and float the resulting slag to the top of the melted iron in the blast furnace. Then, pig iron from the blast furnace is combined with scrap iron and various additives, annealed or tempered through heat treatment, and formed into steel ingots ready for shipment to finishing mills.

Questions

1. What is Pittsburgh's nickname, and what is the reason for it?
2. In steel production, what is the function of a flux?
3. What types of iron ore are commonly used in Pittsburgh's steel industry?
4. What happens to the ingots of annealed or tempered steel?

This second example *should* look familiar, because it is representative of the kinds of exercises included all too frequently in the social studies curricula used in elementary schools. Note that students can answer each question correctly without learning anything at all, at least not anything beyond isolated and relatively meaningless figurative knowledge.

extent that children have operative knowledge about the input as well (see Figure 3.2).

Readiness

These developmental considerations lead to the issue of readiness. To a student of cognitive development who observes and describes changes in children according to their age, readiness emerges slowly over time. However, to a teacher or other individual attempting to induce change through systematic intervention, readiness is something to teach if it is not already present. Within the limits of learner capacity, a learner who is not ready to master a given concept or skill can be made ready to master it through systematic, sequential, successive approximations; in other words, through teaching readiness. It will be important, however, to make sure that each stage in the sequence toward the ultimate objective is thoroughly mastered, because only then will the learner be able to use the skill as a tool for moving on to a higher level (Ferguson, 1954; 1956).

Teaching readiness and approaching terminal objectives through successive approximations involving intermediate objectives are theoretically possible as long as the whole sequence of events is within the learner's capacity. But is the enterprise worth pursuing in the first place? Often it is, because teaching both the intervening readiness skills and the ultimate learning objective is relatively easy and painless. However, if readiness can be taught only with continuous and highly concentrated effort that requires maximal motivation and application on the part of the learner, it may be best to teach other things in the meantime and wait for the learner to develop greater readiness naturally.

Providing Concrete Props for Learning

Piaget's work shows why concrete objects, diagrams, charts, and other visual aids facilitate learning, and why learning requires active response rather than passive watching and listening. If what we learn is what we do, then we must actually practice something, acting it out in behavior or at least formulating it actively in our own words if we are going to acquire it as a set of related schemes. Just watching and listening alone will result in "merely verbal" learning.

The importance of concrete objects resides in the fact that reliance on such props occurs naturally and thus is both more familiar and easier to assimilate than learning that does not involve them. These props bridge the gap between the known and the unknown, increasing the degree to which new material is relatively assimilable. Piaget's work suggests that everything is learned most easily and thoroughly if mastered in the order in which discovery learning would occur naturally. Sensorimotor schemes would precede cognitive schemes, and concrete experience would precede formal analysis and abstraction. For example, in science classes laboratory demonstrations illustrate, and literally make meaningful, the abstract principles being taught.

Other implications concern what can and should be taught at different developmental levels. Children may have difficulty with certain kinds of new learning if they have not yet developed the schemes necessary to comprehend the new information, even though most of their peers have developed these schemes. Instruction is unlikely to be succesful until the necessary schemes develop, either spontaneously or in response to instruction (Renner et al., 1976). Successful teachers present material in a variety of ways, so that it becomes meaningful to a group of students who differ in levels of cognitive development.

School Curricula and Methods

Briefly, Piaget's developmental work suggests the following about matching school experiences to existing cognitive development. First, children in the sensorimotor period and early in the preoperational period learn primarily through play and exploration, and their learning is concentrated in the area of sensorimotor schemes. They have difficulty comprehending even simple conceptual material, such as the school curriculum if it is presented verbally without opportunity for activity and concrete experiences, and they cannot comprehend material at the level of formal operations in any real sense. The way to optimize cognitive development in these early years is to provide a rich, stimulating environment that encourages learning through exploration. Attempts to teach conceptual material that call on schemes that would not appear naturally for several years are not likely to succeed, except in producing "merely verbal" learning. However, few environmentalists accept this implication.

Matching presentation to schemes

In the late preoperational and early concrete operational stages, children can benefit increasingly from more systematic and even formal instruction, although the content and modes of presentation must be matched to their existing schemes. Teachers must avoid objectives involving schemes that will not appear for several years or that assume a degree of mastery and coordination that is not yet available to the child. For example, children know the concept of animal and can name many different animals; the same is true for concepts such as people, vehicles, or furniture. However, attempts to teach these conceptual relationships systematically are not likely to succeed. Children at these ages can learn a great deal about many things, particularly about concrete objects they can manipulate and explore for themselves. They also learn words and memorize things easily, although they will not understand the meanings of the words if the conceptual level is beyond their grasp (i.e., if figurative knowledge is not integrated with operative knowledge).

Instruction versus discovery

We believe that this last implication does not necessarily contradict the kinds of school practice, traditional in the early grades, that proponents of so-called Piagetian approaches have criticized. While highly motivated children who are learning by discovery will probably benefit more than learners being instructed under less ideal conditions, certain things, especially certain forms of knowledge that are initially figurative, are much more easily learned from instruction than by discovery. The list is debatable, but it almost certainly includes such fundamental skills as reading, writing, and arithmetic.

Critics often charge that these subjects are taught with too much emphasis on rote memorization of letters, sounds, spelling, and computation tables, and too much practice of printing, writing, and computation to the point of mastery and beyond. They call for more attention to the conceptual (cognitive) aspects of these subject-matter areas, and less attention to the behavioral (sensorimotor) aspects. However, our own interpretation of Piaget suggests different conclusions.

Children in the early grades are still in the preoperational stage or are early in the concrete operational stage, with the exception of a small percentage of extremely bright youngsters. Consequently, activities that stress sensorimotor schemes and active practice to mastery are more suited to their existing cognitive structures than learning that places greater stress on cognitive schemes and integrative concepts. This appears to be the main problem with teaching the "new math," for example.

In short, although Piagetian theory and research generally favor discovery learning, they can also be interpreted as being compatible with the traditional procedure of teaching the fundamental skills of reading, writing, and arithmetic by methods that stress rote memorization and practice rather than discovery and conceptualization. These tool skills must be mastered to the point of overlearning and eventually must be coordinated with one another before they can be used efficiently to learn about subject matter and to solve problems that require efficient concrete operations (Greeno, 1978).

Mastery of tool skills

The traditional school curriculum seems fairly well matched to natural levels of cognitive development. Typically, school grades that correspond to the period of concrete operations involve more systematic and conceptual learning than do the first few grades, but they avoid highly abstract subject matter and emphasize concrete objects, specific examples, or other aids that help students understand the material. Attempts to go beyond this by introducing material at the level of purely formal operations typically fail, except with the brightest students, who usually acquire formal operations considerably earlier than the average.

Finally, beginning around junior high school and continuing through high school and beyond, the school curriculum concentrates increasingly on more abstract subject matter. For example, elementary school history stresses names, dates, places, and events, and usually is built around simple and romanticized stories featuring a central hero who is easy for children to identify with. In contrast, history courses in high school, and particularly in college, dispense with most of these "childish" personalizations and concentrate on more conceptual matters such as the political, social, or economic reasons for historical events, and the interrelationships between them.

Abstract subject matter

Remember, all students operate with some type of logic, although their logic may differ from that used by most adults. Teachers must be able to recognize the general developmental levels and particular logical systems

Logical systems of students

used by their students if they are to diagnose learning difficulties accurately and communicate meaningfully. All teachers, but especially those in grades two and three when children start to become operational, and in the junior high school grades when some students begin to acquire formal operations, must be prepared for a great range in developmental levels as well as in IQ. Many third graders will be preoperational in their logic, with all of the egocentricism and other childish limitations that this implies. Others will be firmly into the concrete operational stage, capable of reasoning logically as long as they do not have to deal with abstract concepts. All students in junior high classes will be logical in their thinking, but only some will be able to deal with abstract material meaningfully (Cox & Matz, 1982). Some of those who cannot do so are generally bright students with high IQs. These students probably will do well with abstract concepts later, when the necessary development has taken place, but they may have difficulty with such material before that stage.

Furthermore, even those who do show formal operational thinking in certain tasks may not do so in other tasks with which they are less familiar. Martorano (1977) measured formal operations with white, middle-class girls who had IQs between 100 and 120 using ten different tasks. Even in this group, only about 20 percent of the eighth graders and about 60 percent of the tenth graders were scored for formal operations on Piaget's "pendulum" and "rods" problems. Across the set of ten tasks, the percentages of students scored for formal operations ranged from 0 to 60 percent in sixth graders, 0 to 85 percent in eighth graders, 5 to 95 percent in tenth graders, and 15 to 90 percent in twelfth graders. Thus, ability to think abstractly depends not only on age and general cognitive development, but also on specific knowledge and experience with particular intellectual content.

Use of ability to think abstractly

Finally, it should be noted that developing the ability to think abstractly doesn't mean that one always or even often uses that ability. As with other stage phenomena, attaining the period of formal operations does not imply that previous modes of thinking are lost. On the contrary, they persist, and in fact constitute the bulk of the cognitive structure. Even the average professor will use formal operational thinking only in certain situations, most obviously when theorizing in his or her own area of specialization. When trying to comprehend politics or the stock market, and especially when trying to fix an appliance or automobile, he or she may have to make do with primarily concrete operational or even sensorimotor schemes.

SUMMARY

Piaget and other *stage theorists* believe that children develop according to qualitatively distinct stages, each of which represents a new level or coordination of knowledge. Both maturation and readiness are involved in this process, which differs from the learning theorists' emphasis on a step-by-step quantitative process of acquiring knowledge.

Piaget stressed physical action and experience with the environment in learning, but differed from behaviorists in his emphasis on learner purposes. He believed that the scheme is the basic unit of cognition, speech, and behavior. The constant process of adaptation, supported by the mechanisms of assimilation and accommodation, modifies existing schemes in keeping with new information. The principle of equilibration motivates such adaptational behavior.

Piaget divided development into four basic periods: (1) *sensorimotor* (birth to eighteen months); (2) *preoperational* (eighteen months to seven years); (3) *concrete operations* (seven to twelve years); and (4) *formal operations* (twelve years and beyond). Scheme development in the sensorimotor stage is concentrated heavily in the sensorimotor area, while the preoperational stage brings expansion of those schemes into the areas of thought and imagery. During the period of concrete operations, children add classification skills, reversibility of operations, negation, identity, and reciprocity. Finally, the ability to use symbols, abstractions, and propositions contrary to fact develops during the period of formal operations.

QUESTIONS AND PROBLEMS

1. When individuals talk about "teaching readiness," what do they mean? What are the issues associated with teaching readiness?
2. Until recently, many educators felt that children's minds were the same as those of adults, but smaller, and that they gradually expanded as knowledge and experience accumulated. Based upon the work of Piaget, modern educators now believe that children go through a series of qualitatively distinct stages as they develop cognitively. What implications does this view of children's cognitive development have for classroom teachers, specifically, for the types of learning activities and the content that students can be assigned?
3. To what extent do you believe the following statement: "If children of a certain age do not have important knowledge needed to learn about some topic, or are not interested in learning about the topic, don't try to teach it to them until later, when they have developed the knowledge and interest"? Why do you believe or not believe this and what evidence can you cite to support your position?
4. Did Piaget apply his beliefs about development and learning to educational issues?
5. What is a scheme? Differentiate, in your own words, the following types of schemes: sensorimotor, cognitive, and verbal.
6. Define the equilibration principle and discuss its importance in Piaget's developmental theory.
7. In what ways does problem finding differ from problem solving? Why do some writers contend that problem finding represents a fifth stage of cognitive development?
8. According to Hooper and DeFrain (1980), what important general principles can be derived from Piaget's work?
9. Define the terms "plus-one matching" and "zone of proximal development." What are the implications of these concepts for classroom practice?
10. Notice that we have accepted differences in learner capacity (both stage differences in individuals and general individual differences among those at the same Piagetian stage) as real. Do you? What does this imply with respect to

nature-nurture issues such as tracking, special education, IQ testing, and so on?

11. Do you agree with Piaget and others that at least some stage differences are truly qualitative? Why, or why not? How would you apply this as a teacher?
12. Piagetian theory and research strongly suggest that natural learning does not proceed according to logical and hierarchically arranged sequences. Instead, children presumably learn according to equilibration motives. How does this affect the structuring of curricula?
13. Some see Piaget's equilibration principle as excess baggage that introduces hypothesized murky internal events without need or reason. Others see it as an accurate insight into human nature. Do you accept it? Note that if you do, you reject the idea of a completely deterministic psychology, even in theory. Why, or why do you not, accept it?
14. What aspects of poetry and science can be meaningfully taught to first graders? Fourth graders? Tenth graders? Which of these aspects should be taught?

CASE STUDIES

Ms. Herbert and a Heat Wave. Ms. Herbert worked with her slowest second-grade reading group. She and the children perspired because it was a hot day in September and the room, located in an urban inner-city school, had no air conditioner. The children and Ms. Herbert had to strain to focus their interest on the reading task, as opposed to their personal discomfort. During the fifteen-minute lesson two of the boys raised several questions that were touched off by the story but not directly related to it. Jim, for example, asked, "Does anybody's father in this room work on a farm like the guy in the story?" Tim asked, "Can you really ride a horse? What do they eat?" Invariably, Ms. Herbert made minimum responses to these and similar questions and kept the children "on task." What principles of human development did Ms. Herbert ignore? Specifically, how could you improve the situation?

Successful Practice. Millie Mohatt was an enthusiastic seventh-grade general math teacher. She believed that students could learn and that she could teach them. She went very slowly through the curriculum so that students repeatedly experienced success on class assignments. Characteristically, all students worked every seatwork problem correctly, and their homework was about 95 percent correct. Students seemed to enjoy the opportunity to continue to practice things that they could do well. To what extent do you agree with Millie's teaching techniques? What suggestions might you make about improving her approach? How do plus-one matching and zone of proximal development apply to her teaching strategy?

Mr. Flaker and Book Science. Jim Flaker was a second-grade teacher who enjoyed presenting science to his students and spent considerable time at it. He felt that many teachers in the primary grades neglected science, and that this was unfortunate. Though some teachers spend only 10 to 15 minutes two or three times a week on science, Jim spent 45 minutes every day. He often described famous scientists to the students, and how and why they did experiments. Jim also liked to talk about great discoveries that had been made and the general process of science. He spent some time discussing future research, including the things we might have in the year 2050 that presently are not available. However, Jim did not like to actually *do* experiments with the students, because the class was hard to control and things would break. What principles of human development is Jim Flaker ignoring? What advice might you have for him in terms of improving his science instruction?

Supervisor on the Spot. Marge Guffy, the English coordinator for the school district, had just observed an eighth-grade general English lesson that Kim Anderson taught. At the end of the lesson, Marge says quietly to Kim, "Kim, that was generally a very good English lesson, but you taught this lesson as though the students were second graders!" Kim thoughtfully replied, "Well, I'm not sure I agree with you. What do I need to do differently?" In general, based upon your knowledge of developmental theory, what is the difference between teaching second graders and eighth graders? What sorts of differences in teaching and learning activities ought to be present in the classroom?

Chapter 4

Cognitive Development and Education

CHAPTER OUTLINE

OBJECTIVES

When you have mastered the material in this chapter you will be able to

1. Discuss what and how a teacher should teach in grades 1 through 3 versus grades 4 through 6, as well as secondary students, to insure meaningful learning
2. Explain what is meant when a child "becomes operational"
3. Distinguish the thinking characteristics of concrete versus formal operational students and the types of instruction appropriate to these two periods
4. Explain what the structural aspect of language is and how it develops via the language acquisition device (LAD)
5. Discuss the problems that occur in one's functional use of language
6. Discuss how Vygotsky and Piaget view the interaction of language and thinking
7. Give practical advice concerning the teaching of students who use nonstandard English

Piaget's theories are basic to understanding how the human mind develops by gradually constructing knowledge about the world from the feedback received during interactions with it. These theories underlie much of what will be presented in this chapter on the implications of developmental phenomena for schools and teachers. However, information given is based on developmental psychology in general and not just Piaget, representing a consensus of theorists including almost everyone but extreme environmentalists, not just those who place strong emphasis on developmental stages.

The Preoperational Years

Children show the capacity for operational thinking at five or six, but they usually don't become functionally operational (the ability to use operational thinking most of the time) until they are at least a year or two older. For educational purposes, we can say that the preoperational period extends until about third grade for most children, and beyond this for some. The two general kinds of learning that seem most appropriate during these years are exploration and manipulation of concrete objects, and rote verbal learning and physical practice of letters, numbers, sounds, words, arithmetical computations, and printing and writing skills. Most of these skills are learned in relative isolation, because children at this developmental level are much more skilled at acquiring isolated knowledge or skills than at making connections between experiences or coming to understand integrative concepts. There is relatively little transfer from one learning situation to another. Children at this level can learn from verbal presentations, but the teacher cannot just lecture, assuming that they will understand everything they hear.

Children at these ages depend on the teacher for direct instruction. They require demonstration, instruction, elicitation of responses to see if they understand the concepts, correction as necessary, and continued practice to the point of overlearning once they grasp the basic concept (Brophy & Evertson, 1976; Miller & Dyer, 1975; Rosenshine, 1976; Stallings, 1975; Brophy & Good, 1985). Other implications from research on learning in the early grades are presented in the following sections.

Difficulty with Purely Verbal Instruction

Importance of good work sheets

Good demonstrations and visual aids are required to provide children with a concrete model to watch and to imitate. They can learn relatively easily if taught this way, but have difficulty following purely verbal instruction. If tasks are complex, they should be broken into subtasks that children can master and practice in sequences that gradually grow longer until the ultimate task is learned. Follow-up assignments should contain models for imitation and other aids to learning that can help overcome short attention spans and difficulty in following purely verbal instructions. The most successful work sheets for insuring that children practice tasks properly and get good feedback contain numerous nonverbal learning aids that help them understand the instructions. These learning aids include space and lines to help keep separate things separate; arrows, boxes, and lines to indicate where responses should be placed, and where to go next; and division of assignments into modular units that can be presented, corrected, and discussed separately.

Eliciting and Monitoring Responses

It is vital to elicit and monitor responses in order to see whether children really do understand the material. Once they understand, they can successfully practice on their own. However, if they are confused, their practice will involve the repetition of errors.

Practice to the point of overlearning is necessary to insure that skills are mastered, not only for their own sake, but for further use in solving higher-order problems. It is essential to students' future school success for teachers in the early grades to make sure that they master the fundamentals of reading, writing, and arithmetic. If this requires extra practice, such practice should be provided, even at the expense of enrichment activities or other aspects of the curriculum.

Mastery of fundamentals

Teachers in subject areas other than basic skills should emphasize familiar content or else make the strange familiar by using concrete props or other media. Actual objects are best, but substitutes such as films or pictures also have positive value. These aids to learning are extremely important for young children because of the gaps in their vocabularies and difficulties in following purely verbal presentations. In a literal sense, such props help insure that the students understand what the teacher is talking about (Renner, et al., 1976).

It is necessary to make sure that children understand because they tend to give the impression that they are following a lesson even when they are not, because they know this is expected of them. If asked whether they understand, they almost always say that they do rather than admit confusion. This is partly from a desire to tell adults what they think adults want to hear, and partly due to difficulties in expressive communication that make it much easier for a child simply to nod than to attempt to express the nature and reasons for misunderstanding. Consequently, not only is apparent attention a poor indicant of actual understanding, so are simple questions that can be answered with a yes or a no answer, and simple choice responses that ask the child to indicate which of two or three alternatives is correct. In these situations, children can come up with the right answer by guessing. To find out whether or not they really understand, the teacher needs to ask questions that require them to demonstrate mastery of the concept or skill in a clear, unambiguous way (Nagy & Griffiths, 1982). If a behavioral skill is involved, this means having them perform the skill, observing them to see that they are using the proper process and achieving the desired outcomes, and correcting them if they are not. Where verbal

Demonstration of mastery of a concept

learning is involved, questions beginning with "what," "who," "when," "where," or "how many" will require the children to produce correct answers from memory, or to figure them out. Correct responses to such tests are much more likely to demonstrate true understanding of the concept than correct answers to yes-no or either-or questions, because the former offer much lower odds of success through sheer guesswork (Blank, 1973).

Throughout the early grades, it is important to elicit responses from each individual student, even during lessons. Teachers working with older students usually can sample by monitoring students at varying ability levels to get a reasonably accurate picture of where the class stands. With young children, learning patterns in a given lesson are unique and ability to learn from watching and listening to others, rather than from making responses themselves, is limited, so eliciting responses and providing corrective feedback to each individual student are essential (Brophy & Evertson, 1976; Anderson, Evertson, & Brophy, 1979).

In general, the difficulty that preoperational children have in dealing with complex or abstract content makes it unwise to try to teach them such content systematically, even though this sometimes seems to be an attractive alternative to those who see drilling in the "three Rs" as painful drudgery, even though children do not mind it. Curricula that stress mastery of the three Rs are more appropriate for, and successful with, children in the early grades than curricula that stress high-level or complex concepts. This has been shown in research on differences in teaching styles among teachers who were all using relatively traditional curricula (Stallings, 1975; Soar & Soar, 1972), and also in the difficulties that certain curricula, such as the new math in general and math systems meant for individual use in particular, have encountered in the early grades (American Institute for Research, 1976).

Mastery of the three Rs

These curricula are organized quite logically from the adult perspective, but children don't learn that way. Too many curricula assume that young children have developed learning-to-learn skills and independent, self-guided learning abilities that few have actually demonstrated. Because these fundamental assumptions are incorrect, the programs do not work very well. Only the brightest children tend to profit from them; others do much better when taught more directly by their teachers.

Even when teachers instruct their students directly, it is important that they stay with familiar and observable events, or at least with models, heroes, or events that are easily assimilated into the children's existing schemes. Attempts to discuss things totally outside the children's experience will fail. So will attempts to present content at levels too sophisticated for their present developmental status. It is easy to poke fun at the oversimplified and romanticized history and social science taught in the early grades, but these curricula are suited to specific developmental levels. Children can learn history if it is presented in a simplified manner that stresses facts over integrative concepts and perhaps contains romanticized portrayals of faultless heroes overcoming totally evil villians. However, they can't follow presentations of the same material presented from an adult perspective. To

Teaching at appropriate developmental level

see what we mean, try to picture a six- or seven-year-old sitting in on a college course in American history that stresses the political and economic reasons for events and de-emphasizes heroes and "stories." This child would probably not learn much history in such a class. Nevertheless, certain curriculum packages intended for young children are grossly inappropriate for precisely these reasons, and much teaching by well-intentioned teachers who try to go beyond "isolated facts" to teach conceptual understanding is misdirected and unsuccessful.

This does not mean that teachers should be unaware of such things as learning-to-learn skills, independent work skills, integrative concepts, or conceptual understanding (how to read for understanding; how to evaluate information and integrate it with input from elsewhere; how to budget time and plan activities to accomplish complex tasks). It does mean that these concepts and skills cannot be assumed. They develop slowly during the preoperational years and early during the concrete operational years. Children move gradually into these kinds of learning as they become operational and more responsive to the student role. As they begin to master tool skills, they begin to read for pleasure and knowledge, not just to practice reading, and they begin to use math skills for solving problems of personal interest, such as computing batting averages or money transactions. When children reach this point they are ready for instruction in new subject areas, using methods that rely on the tool skills.

It does little good to try to teach children at conceptual levels beyond their present grasp. However, teachers can develop readiness through modeling—teachers can make integrative or abstract statements about material being taught mostly at lower levels of analysis. Not all children will un-

Reading is the most important skill a teacher can impart.

Building readiness

derstand such statements, but some will. The effect on the ones that don't will be to build future readiness for deliberate conceptual instruction, such as on the properties of geometric forms, the laws of physics, the formal properties of classical poetry or drama, and so on.

The Central Importance of Reading Ability

The best way to compensate for a home environment that has not prepared a child for success in school is to make the child a functional reader. Of all things teachers can do for young children, this is the most important, at least in the realm of curriculum and instruction. Children who learn to read functionally can always make up for lost time in other areas by reading on their own, but children who never learn to read functionally are going to have difficulty in reading and other subjects for the rest of their school years. This will hamper their school performance and probably limit their options in later life. A great deal of information about effective reading instruction is now available (Anderson et al., 1985).

Becoming Operational

Children make the transition to regular, functional use of concrete operational thinking during the early grades—the brightest ones at about age six, but most not until about age eight, and many later. Because this transition is of major concern, it is worth considering at length the factors responsible for it.

Piaget stressed three stages to becoming operational: (1) developing the ability to discriminate between invariant and variant aspects of the environment; (2) coordinating separate schemes into larger ones, and ultimately into concrete operations and a unified cognitive structure; and (3) achieving the ability to reason forward from causes to effects and backward from effects to causes (reversibility). Probably the key stage is to master a large number of schemes and coordinate them into a coherent structure.

Motivational forces, which Piaget called *equilibration*, cause children to become more active in seeking information, particularly by asking questions and, when they are able to, by reading. Adults familiar with specific children will note that much of this information seeking involves attempts to fill gaps and resolve discrepancies so as to render the existing cognitive structure comprehensive and internally consistent. For the first time, children become notably aware of such gaps and inconsistencies. They want to clear up confusion between such concepts as husband and father, or cities, states, and nations, and they want more information about such matters as death, what parents do at work, or what differentiates humans, animals, plants, and inanimate objects.

Researchers studying learning in children have noted a distinct change in responses to certain experimental situations, which coincides with the general process of becoming operational. We have already mentioned the

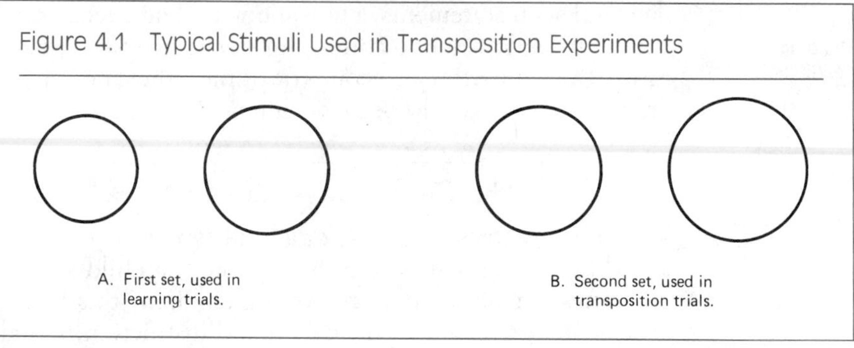

Figure 4.1 Typical Stimuli Used in Transposition Experiments

Transposition problems

changes in responses to conservation problems and other tasks used by Piaget. Another example occurs in what are called transposition problems (see Figure 4.1). In a typical example, children are taught to discriminate between a smaller and a larger circle by rewarding them for choosing the larger circle. This is usually learned quickly and easily when the correct choice is rewarded each time. Then a new set is introduced, in which the smaller circle is identical to the one that was larger and formerly the correct choice. Many investigations have revealed that animals and young children in the sensorimotor or preoperational stages respond to these new stimuli by picking the circle that is now the smaller one that is identical to the one that was correct in the previous trials. However, children who are clearly in the concrete operational stage, as well as older children and adults, typically respond by picking the larger circle, even though they have not seen it before (Stevenson, 1970).

These and other results indicate that sensorimotor and preoperational children tend to respond to the specific, observable, concrete features of stimuli, and to retain what they learn in isolation without much assimilation to other schemes. Individuals at higher levels of cognitive development are less "stimulus bound" by concrete observables and more likely to attend to the more formal, conceptual, and invariant properties of stimuli, thus approaching problems with concrete or formal operational logic. They assimilate—transfer previous learning—in approaching such problems, relating the new input to existing schemes rather than responding as if the input were completely new.

In contrast to young children who respond to the circle test as if the problem is "find the one exactly like the other one," operational children generate hypotheses, such as "the relevant principle here is to find the larger one." Young children primarily accommodate to the immediate situation; older individuals primarily assimilate the immediate situation into existing cognitive structures. This leads to a different definition of the task, and consequently a different mode of responding.

Task identification

In addition to results indicating the way different levels of cognitive development can affect learning, researchers studying these and other learning problems that show developmental differences also have found that coordination of cognitive schemes with verbal schemes (language) is an important factor in becoming operational. This is discussed later in this chapter, in the "Thought and Language" section.

The Period of Concrete Operations

In the process of becoming operational, children usually begin to ask many and varied questions. It is helpful if teachers recognize what is happening, enjoy the process rather than become irritated by it, be patient in letting children take the time to try to express themselves clearly enough to indicate what they want to know, and avoid embarrassing them by laughing at childish mistakes. The process of learning to think in words and to use words in the service of thinking is facilitated by question sequences that require the students to express themselves verbally. Without being so obvious as to put children on the spot, teachers should both expect and foster verbal communication of concerns and questions, and should patiently encourage children to elaborate or rephrase questions that are too cryptic or ambiguous to allow a meaningful response. This will socialize the children to express their needs verbally and at the same time give them practice in doing so.

Understanding and integrative concepts

As children move further into the phase of concrete operations and show evidence of ability in inductive and deductive logical reasoning, teachers can place more emphasis on understanding and integrative concepts. Children now can do more verbalizing, self-monitoring, and can work independently on complex projects. However, all of this must be kept within the concrete operational level. Attempts to teach highly abstract content using purely verbal methods will fail altogether or produce only "merely verbal" or superficial learning.

Children in the middle grades can work out elaborate mathematics or scientific problems and experiments if they can carry out the operations physically or at least approximate them in drawings or sketches. They also can respond meaningfully to questions about the reasons for historical events or events occurring in a story read during class, if these reasons were made clear in the presentation or involve situations that the children can understand by putting themselves in the place of the characters in the story. However, the material must be familiar enough for them to deal with meaningfully if they are to understand it in any real sense.

For example, when learning about the discovery of America, children in the middle grades can relate to the fear Columbus's crew had about falling off the edge of the earth, to the concept of mutiny and the reasons why mutiny was a real possibility, and, with the help of a globe, to the reasons why the men thought they had reached India. They can also relate similarly to lessons on modern space exploration or adventures into the unknown, such as the explorations of the North and South Poles. They will get more out of such lessons if teachers personalize them with objects and pictures, stimulating the imagination, especially by having them try to put themselves

Personalization of material

in the places of people they are talking about, and relating the material to familiar and observable events.

Impersonal events involving large numbers of people are more easily understood if personalized and presented as adventures involving a single hero or a small number of specific people. Personalized treatment of exploratory adventures that stresses the individuality of the explorers or astronauts involved also helps make the material more interesting. Motives are more easily understood if confined to motivational systems that children can comprehend. For example, complex political and economic rivalries are best presented to children as contests between individuals or countries, because they can relate to the motivations involved in trying to win a contest. The same events would seem a mystery to them if presented at an abstract level that described the same economic or political rivalry in an impersonal way and used terms such as "spheres of influence," "import-export ratio," and "expansionist doctrine." These are all abstractions that require formal operations to be understood in a meaningful way.

The Period of Formal Operations

Beginning around the eighth grade, some students will be able to handle largely abstract material if they are entering the formal operations stage. However, several cautions should be noted. First, many students, and depending on the school, perhaps a majority of the students, will never develop formal operations to the point that they can be used with efficiency in thinking and problem solving. They may memorize the formulas in algebra, for example, but never really understand them or get to the point where they can use them to solve problems.

Second, even for students with very efficient formal operations, learning is almost always easier if it is aided by imagery, diagrams, examples, or other forms of presentation that involve concrete operations. The fact that students can use purely formal operations does not mean that they should have to rely on them, especially in high school, when only a small percentage will be capable of doing so. It is more accurate to assume that college students can handle purely abstract material (Lawson, 1975), particularly in courses such as advanced mathematics or philosophy, but even at this level it is unwise to make the material any more difficult than necessary if the goal is to promote the greatest amount of learning by the greatest number of students.

Assessing degree of formal operations

Teachers can assess the degree of formal operational thinking in their students by determining the degree to which they can induce general principles when allowed to perform scientific experiments such as determining why a pendulum oscillates at different rates, or by asking them to define concepts such as independence or justice. Certain students will be able to produce formal responses ("length is inversely related to rate of oscillation," "justice is a condition in which all parties involved in something get the treatment they deserve"), but others will only be able to cope with the questions at a concrete level ("the short ones move the most," "justice is when a crook goes to jail but an innocent person is set free").

The Use of Integrative Concepts

To the extent that students do possess formal operations, it is now possible to present bodies of knowledge in logical sequences involving articulation of the general principles involved and then moving toward specifics, stressing deductive logic. In other words, material can now be organized and presented systematically and learning can be facilitated through the use of integrative concepts that promote conceptual understanding and general assimilation, something that was not possible previously.

In earlier stages this integrated level of knowledge was the last to develop, occurring only after students had mastered isolated facts and skills and then gradually assimilated them into increasingly larger schemes. The process can be reversed for students who have developed truly efficient formal operations. Instead of having to start with specifics and end up with general principles, it becomes possible to instruct by presenting the general principles first, as a way to promote learning by using organizational concepts to structure the content. In fact, this is how most highly abstract bodies of knowledge are taught, particularly those that are inherently organized in a logical way such as logic, mathematics, or science courses, (see Chapter 8).

Formal knowledge versus concrete experience

Formal knowledge, however, is no substitute for concrete experience. Just as a physicist who can explain why a paper airplane can fly cannot necessarily construct a good paper airplane, a student who passes an abstract, pencil-and-paper-only chemistry test cannot necessarily conduct laboratory demonstrations efficiently or do worthwhile chemical research. Teachers who expect their students to be able to apply knowledge and not just master abstract principles will have to provide application opportunities. Typically, confusion about abstract principles is only one problem encountered during such applications. Students will often have problems because they know the principle but do not understand how to apply it in a specific instance, such as how to apply a theorem to an algebra problem, or because they lack concrete knowledge or experience, such as using a protractor to measure angles.

Ability to integrate knowledge

In fact, a major challenge facing teachers at any level, but especially as instruction begins to rely on formal operations, is finding ways to get students to see the whole picture—to put it all together. Integrating knowledge and skills and applying them to problem solving are much more complex and difficult to teach than communicating the essence of a single concept, even a very abstract one. Thus, even at the high school level and beyond, we must remember Piaget's discovery that what we learn is what we do. Opportunities for concrete experience and for practice of skills to mastery levels remain important for learning at any age, and essential for skillful application. Knowledge must be operative, not just figurative.

Thought and Language

Piaget laid great stress on thought, cognitive schemes, and relatively little on language, verbal schemes. He viewed language as little more than a means for communicating thought. Others, however, place much more stress on language and its importance relative to thought (Piattelli-Palmarini, 1980; Zivin, 1979). This issue has notable implications for education, which depends heavily on language to communicate concepts and skills and sometimes is conducted as if thought and language were identical, even though there are important differences. Clarity about these differences can help teachers distinguish between students who "have the concept" and those who have "merely verbal" learning.

Structural and Functional Aspects of Language

Language development can be separated into structural and functional aspects. Structural aspects deal with learning the elements of sentences, or grammar, and how these elements are combined to form meaningful phrases and sentences that conform to the structural requirements of the language, or syntax. Functional aspects concern the ability to use language to communicate, think, and solve problems. Much confusion has resulted from failure to distinguish between these two aspects of language, because different factors are involved in determining their development.

Innate Language-Acquisition Device

Traditionally, learning theorists explained language development with concepts such as exposure (modeling), repetition, and reinforcement. Children were believed to learn to speak one language rather than another, and to speak it with particular vocabularies and idioms, because they imitated and were reinforced for imitating the language spoken in their homes and neighborhoods.

Chomsky on language

Chomsky (1965) rejected this explanation. He argued that reinforcement cannot explain why or how children regularly generate new sentences they have never spoken or even heard before, and he presented convincing data and arguments showing that structural aspects of language are learned spontaneously. He postulates an innate language-acquisition device (LAD), unique to and present in all humans, that enables us to learn language simply by being exposed to it. By "learning" a language, we mean learning not only its vocabulary words, but also its structure. Chomsky's view, like Piaget's, can be characterized as nativist; he is saying that the ability to generate language according to grammatical rules is inherent in the human brain. No systematic instruction or reinforcement is required. Language can be learned through systematic instruction, of course, but Chomsky's point is that typically it is not.

This can be illustrated in many ways, but perhaps the most convincing are analyses of the errors that children spontaneously make in learning language. Except for errors caused by certain pronunciation difficulties common to young children ("aminal, aksed"), most of their linguistic errors are "logical." That is, they conform to the general rules implicit in the structure of the language, and errors result because certain linguistic conventions do not follow the typical rule. For example, it is common for children to say "they goed to the store" instead of "they went to the store." This error is perfectly understandable. In fact, it indicates that, although they are using it inappropriately in this case, the children have mastered not only specific words but the general rule that past-tense verbs are formulated by adding a "d" sound to the present-tense verb (open-opened, lift-lifted). All kinds of linguistic rules concerning language structure are learned and used regularly, although seldom formulated verbally. Children "just know" the rules.

Linguistic conventions

Analysis of the kinds of errors that rarely occur, if ever, is also instructive. In contrast to common errors that involve using rules that usually apply but do not happen to pertain in a specific instance, errors that involve violations of syntax—that is, violations of the basic structure of grammatical sentences in a language—hardly ever occur. Thus children might say "they goed to the store," "them went to the store," or "they gone to the store," but not "store to the they went," or "went they the store to." English sentence structure has an implicit "subject-then verb-then object" rule for such sentences. Children know and use this rule regularly, even though they cannot express it verbally. Even deaf children use the same patterns when they begin to generate sentences (Bellugi & Klima, 1972). These and other data illustrate what Chomsky means in stating that language is learned spontaneously and involves an innate language-acquisition device.

Syntax

Chomsky appears correct in his assertions, but only for the structural aspects of language. A complete language structure is not sufficient, although it may be necessary, to insure good language functioning—the ability to use language to communicate and solve problems efficiently (Niemark & Santa, 1975; Pozner & Saltz, 1974). Language development is affected by environmental input, not just the operation of an innate LAD (Nelson, 1977; Whitehurst, 1977).

Functional Aspects of Language

Studies of the functional aspects of language indicate that people differ considerably in the degree to which they can use language to communicate, think, and solve problems. Difficulties often reflect poor language development, but sometimes individuals who possess relevant language do not use it in situations where it would be helpful for them. This is observable in persons of any age, although most attention has been given to the problem as it appears around the time that children become operational.

Investigators studying transposition problems, such as the one given earlier requiring the ability to pick the larger circle, not the one exactly the same as the larger one in the first part of the problem, found that verbalization is associated with the tendency to respond at a higher developmental level. Particularly interesting results have been obtained with children between five and seven years old who have what Kendler and Kendler (1962) have termed "mediational deficiencies." These children possess all the verbal and cognitive schemes necessary to conceptualize and respond to the problem in the more developmentally sophisticated way, but nevertheless do not do so.

Mediational deficiencies

Mediational Deficiencies in the Functional Use of Language

The Kendlers use the term mediational deficiency to refer to situations in which children verbalize concerning a problem, but their verbalizations do not result in a higher-level response (for instance, they do not pick the larger circle in the above mentioned problem). Since thoughts apparently are mediated by language at this age (children should be able to think by literally talking to themselves, if they have the relevant cognitive and verbal schemes), and since children are known to possess and use the necessary language, those who use it but fail to conceptualize and respond to the problem at the higher level of development are considered to have a mediational deficiency. For some reason, their language does not succeed in "carrying" their thought processes. They verbalize the problem correctly, but then respond incorrectly, contrary to their own verbalizations. This phenomenon is rare, but it happens. Piaget would say that instances like these are just more examples of situations where children have "merely verbal" learning without corresponding understanding—cognitive schemes coordinated with the relevant verbal schemes.

Production Deficiency

Other investigators have noted a similar but more frequent problem termed production deficiency (Flavell, Beach, & Chinsky, 1966). The phenomenon was originally noted in studies of memory in children, but has since been applied to many other learning problems as well. Like transposition problems, the memory problems studied by these investigators could be approached with either a lower-level or a higher-level solution strategy. A typical problem might involve memorizing a list of words such as "apple, cow, lamp, peach, horse, table, pear, chair, pig." Preoperational children typically try to learn such lists through rote memory, learning the words in order and failing to see any connections between them. Operational children and adults tend to recognize that there are three fruits, three items of furniture, and three animals on the list, and they use this information to aid them in memorizing the items. In fact, if it is not necessary for them to repeat the words in order, they usually reorder them according to these conceptual clusters. In any case, individuals who perceive and use these relationships master the task much more quickly than those who do not.

Children, or adults, in some cases, with production deficiency are those who possess all the necessary concepts and language and who understand the relationships among the subsets, but do not use this information in approaching the problem. Instead, they approach it through rote memory methods like those used by young children. Flavell and his colleagues prefer the term "production deficiency" to "mediational deficiency," because it is rare for children who verbalize the problem to fail to use the higher level of response. Typically, the problem is not that language does not mediate thought processes; it is that the relevant language and thought processes are not produced in the situation, and thus are not used.

The Flavell interpretation appears correct for the most part, although the Kendlers and others have demonstrated that mediational deficiency does exist. The educational implications of both lines of research are the same: it is important to see that children master fundamental verbal and cognitive schemes that can be used as tool skills or learning-to-learn skills in approaching other kinds of problems. Such mastery is necessary to insure that the schemes will be available for immediate assimilation of new information and situations. (Production deficiency apparently occurs because the relevant schemes, while learned to some degree, are either not well enough mastered individually or not well enough coordinated with other schemes to allow the person to use them for solving problems.) Consider algebra, for example. If you know it thoroughly, you can use it to solve problems in everyday life that lend themselves to algebraic formulation. If you studied algebra but did not learn it thoroughly, however, you couldn't apply it beyond the concrete problems presented in class.

The Interaction between Language and Thought

These considerations return us to the general problem of thought and language and to the distinction between structural and functional aspects of language. By now it should be clear that thought and language interact in complex ways that are not completely understood, and that possession of language at the structural level does not guarantee the ability to use it for functional purposes.

Much interesting speculation has been offered concerning the relationship between thought and language. Piaget represents one extreme, deemphasizing language and clearly subordinating it to thought (cognitive schemes). He saw language primarily as a vehicle for expressing thoughts, and did not assign much importance to it as a precursor or cause of thought. At the other extreme are certain linguists and psycholinguists who believe that language is at least as important as thought, and maybe more important. Some still endorse the so-called Whorfian hypothesis, named after Benjamin Whorf (1956). In its most simplified and extreme form, the *Whorfian hypothesis* states that language structures thought, rather than vice versa, as Piaget would claim. Ironically, Whorf himself never stated or accepted the hypothesis in this extreme form. However, many other individuals accept and propound it even today.

Whorfian hypothesis

It is true that language and thought interact, although it does not seem to be true that language structures thought. Instead, it appears, as Ferguson (1956) has stated, that cultures tend to focus attention on certain aspects of the environment because of their importance for general adaptation or cultural traditions. This, in turn, leads both to a relatively rich conceptual understanding of these salient aspects of the environment and to a proliferation of language, particularly vocabulary, relating to these aspects. The most typical example is the Eskimos, who have many different words referring to different kinds of snow, whereas most individuals in warmer climates have only the single noun, "snow," perhaps modified by adjectives such as "soft" or "fluffy." However, skiers and others who have reason to be interested in the more specific aspects of snow have developed specialized terminologies that facilitate communication about the aspects of interest. Thus a proliferation of discriminations about any aspect of the environment is likely to be associated with a rich vocabularly related to it, although, in our opinion, it is going too far to say that language causes thought.

Independence of thought and language development

The complex relationships between thought and language probably have been expressed best by Vygotsky (1962), a Russian psychologist interested in developmental phenomena much like those that interested Piaget. Vygotsky notes that, in the sensorimotor and early preoperational stages, thought and language develop independently of each other. Thought, as Piaget stated, mostly involves nonverbal sensorimotor and cognitive schemes. Although children think,they do so in intuitive ways that do not involve expressing perceptions and conceptions in language and using language to think about problems. They do have language, however, and it develops all along, parallel to but not in direct conjunction with thought. Language develops primarily as a way to express personal needs, emotions, and feelings. It functions as a method of communication rather than as a vehicle for thought during these early years.

However, as part of the general pattern of developmental changes that occur when children become operational, thought and language become related, or in Piaget's terms, cognitive and verbal schemes become coordinated. As this process continues, children are increasingly able to express thought in language, to use language to communicate conceptual material, and to think and solve problems verbally. Apparently because of this, they also make the transition between lower and higher forms of response to problems and overcome mediational and production deficiencies. In short, as children become operational, there is a confluence of several developmental factors that makes for qualitative changes in their cognitive structures and in the ways that these structures function, particularly in new situations requiring accommodation or problem solving.

Vygotsky's formulation of the relationship between thought and language makes more sense to us than the formulations of those who see one of these abilities as more important than the other, or who do not give sufficient attention to the ways in which they interact and support each other. Furthermore, Kohlberg, Yeager, and Hjertholm (1967) have produced data that, along with Vygotsky's own, support his contentions. Their findings deal with what Piaget called egocentric speech—overt utterances that chil-

Egocentric speech

As children develop, they use language to think out loud about their activities.

dren emit in the presence of listeners that resemble ordinary social speech but do not require response or even attention from the listeners.

Piaget minimized the importance of egocentric speech, seeing it as just more evidence that young children are egocentric. However, Vygotsky and other more recent investigators have noted developmental changes in the rates and types of egocentric speech that occur as children become operational. Among children who are clearly preoperational, egocentric speech tends to be social and immature, similar to the kinds of speech that Vygotsky saw as essentially unrelated to thought in young children. It involves verbalizations about feelings and emotions, events important in the child's life, the child's family and possessions, and so on. Usually it has little direct bearing on what the child is doing at the moment.

Inner speech

As children become more operational, their egocentric speech gradually changes from the social speech typical of earlier years to what Vygotsky called "inner speech." Inner speech is roughly equivalent to verbalized thought, the kind of verbalization we make to ourselves when we are thinking. Such inner speech would often be incomprehensible to someone else. It would have to be translated into social speech that took into account the needs of the listener by transforming a mixture of verbalized and nonverbal thought processes into a coherent verbal explanation or communication. Thus children playing in a sandbox who at earlier ages might have been chattering about unrelated matters gradually begin to talk about the sand castles they are building. As this process continues, they increasingly seem to be talking to themselves. Their egocentric speech becomes less social and more like inner speech, and also more focused on the task at hand. They literally are thinking out loud about how to solve problems in building the castle or about what they are going to do when they finish the part they are working on. Later, this kind of inner speech becomes virtually unintelligible, because most of the thinking is done silently. The child may utter only a few words or phrases aloud, or perhaps mutter unintelligibly.

Taken together, the results of many studies suggest that egocentric speech is quite functional, and that these changes that occur during the course of becoming operational are part of the process of linking thought and language (Frauenglass & Diaz, 1985; Zivin, 1979). Children apparently think out loud for the same reasons they count on their fingers: it is a temporary "crutch" or learning aid that helps them make the transition between two different modes of functioning. When they no longer need to verbalize out loud, they begin to mutter and eventually to think silently.

Actually, the process never completely ends. Most adults find it helpful to think out loud occasionally by talking to themselves when wrestling with a complex problem. Thus egocentric speech is functional throughout life.

In summary, thought and language develop separately for the most part until children begin to become operational at around age six or seven. Verbal and cognitive schemes then become assimilated to one another and coordinated into more powerful and differentiated schemes that ultimately become learning-to-learn strategies, concrete operational logic, and other information-processing anad problem-solving skills.

Language and the School

Linguists and psycholinguists have been convincing in showing that children acquire structural aspects of language spontaneously merely by being exposed to it, so there is little that schools can or should do about this aspect of language. However, teachers can promote development of the ability to use language functionally for communication and problem solving. Children should learn that they will be expected to verbalize their thoughts, and should be treated with patience and encouragement as they struggle to do so.

Use of Local Dialect

Many children learn so-called "black English" or other nonstandard English dialects instead of the standard English that forms the basis for school curricula. These dialects are structurally complete languages with grammatical rules of their own, and not merely immature forms of standard English such as those spoken by young children (Burling, 1973; Labov, 1972). Dialect speakers may have difficulty with certain lessons that assume that students speak standard English. For example, children who pronounce the words "pour," "more," and "sew" as if they all rhyme with one another may have difficulty with lessons based on rhyming, and children who tend to drop the "t" sound in past tense verbs such as saying "pass" instead of "passed" may have trouble with lessons where one must distinguish between present and past tense verb forms.

There is considerable disagreement about how teachers should handle students who speak nonstandard dialects. Advice ranges from insisting on standard English and attempting to correct every deviation from it to attempting to modify curriculum and instruction so that students can be taught in the local dialect rather than in standard English.

Experiments performed where children were taught in nonstandard English dialects suggest that this is not a good idea, although there is agreement that teachers should *accept* local dialects rather than punish children or make them feel inferior because they use them. The ideal seems to be acceptance of whatever dialect the child uses to communicate, with emphasis on helping the child to succeed in communicating (Harber & Bryen, 1976).

Developmental errors versus specialized errors

Familiarity with language development is useful in helping teachers to distinguish common errors that occur in the normal course of development and disappear of their own accord from specialized errors that are associated with a subcultural dialect or a unique problem in language learning. Developmental errors that come and go on their own should be ignored, although the teacher should provide the appropriate model when speaking to the child. This should be done without interrupting the natural flow of conversation. Thus if a child should say "He goed out," the teacher should respond with "Yes, he went out, and then what did he do?" The teacher should model correct language and not interrupt the flow of interaction to correct the child or do anything to make the child feel ashamed or inadequate.

Basis for changing dialect

Changing Students' Language

When nonstandard English involves a dialect or some other usage that is not simply a developmental phenomenon, there is agreement that teachers should provide good language models, but little agreement on whether or not teachers should attempt to correct the language used by the students. If the dialect is prevalent in the neighborhood, there is probably little point in attempting to change it.

Because of his heavy Texas dialect, many experts criticized Lyndon Johnson's performance as a public speaker.

If a dialect is likely to pose a serious problem for students later by interfering with their abilities to cope successfully with school or, more probably, reducing their opportunities to get jobs, there may be some basis for attempting to change it. It seems pointless to do this in the early years, when students are not mature enough to understand the reasons for changes or are unlikely to be able to make them consistently even if they tried, assuming they are regularly exposed to the dialect in their home or neighborhood. However, students in high school and beyond who speak a dialect that might hinder future social or occupational success, and any students who have difficulty expressing themselves through verbal communication, should be encouraged to work on the problem.

In dealing with students at this level of development and maturity, it is usually most efficient to approach the subject directly, finding out the degree to which the student is aware of the nonstandard speech or difficulties in communication and the degree to which he or she sees this as a problem and wants to change it. Even though most adults speak with dialects and accents learned in their youth, these aspects of language are relatively easy to change if one makes a conscious effort to do so. The "standard" speech of radio and television announcers provides a good example here. These individuals come from all parts of the country and all ethnic and racial groups, yet they speak in a remarkably homogeneous manner. At the moment, several of the most prominent network newscasters are southerners, although few would guess this from hearing them.

Use of dialect in the classroom

Teachers familiar with local lingo and dialect need to decide for themselves whether they want them used in the classroom. Sometimes this helps promote solidarity with the group and establish credibility and acceptability—but only when the teacher is credible in using the local language. Teacher attempts to use such language that come off as forced or phony are likely to undermine rather than reinforce credibility. Thus teachers should use such language only when they feel comfortable with it. Students expect teachers to use "teacher language," so failure to use local lingo will not cause any particular problems. However, the ability to use local lingo successfully might be a useful addition to the teacher's repertoire of classroom skills.

SUMMARY

During the preoperational years, children deal best with exploration and manipulation of concrete objects and with rote verbal learning and physical practice of letters, numbers, sounds, words, computation, and writing skills. They have difficulty with purely verbal instruction and require demonstrations and visual aids to provide concrete models. Practice is essential at this stage, as is feedback concerning adequacy of responses. Curricula that stress overlearning of the three Rs are more appropriate than those stressing high-level or complex concepts. Teacher modeling of good examples, especially in language, and student mastery of reading will contribute to later academic success.

Piaget stresses three central aspects of becoming operational: (1) discrimination of variant from invariant environmental features; (2) coordination and integration of separate schemes into a unified cognitive structure; and (3) achieving the ability to reverse operations. Children learn to deal with transposition problems through the gradual process of assimilating immediate situations into existing cognitive structures.

Teachers dealing with children in the stage of concrete operations should emphasize understanding and integrative concepts. Children also thrive on "personalized" material. Beginning in about the eighth grade, some students will be able to cope with abstract material if they have developed formal operations, but many never reach that point. And even those who do will profit from imagery, diagrams, and examples, so concrete experience is always appropriate.

Piaget placed great stress on thought and relatively little on language, but the structural and functional aspects of language require attention because of their importance in dealing with school tasks. Chomsky believes that a language-acquisition device (LAD) provides for spontaneous learning of language. Whorf advanced the hypothesis that language structures thought, which is the opposite of Piaget's view. Vygotsky noted that in early stages language and thought seem to develop independently of each other, but that later, egocentric speech gives way to inner speech which supports thought processes.

QUESTIONS AND PROBLEMS

1. Assume you are teaching in an inner-city high school and that many of your students have heavy foreign accents. You fear that their accents will reduce their chances for employment, but you don't want to embarrass or offend students by calling unnecessary attention to their speech. What would you do, if anything? If you were a first-grade teacher in the same school district, would your approach to the problem be any different? Why or why not?
2. Why are "yes or no" and simple choice questions poor ways to assess student learning? In contrast, why are "what," "who," "when," "where," or "how many" questions more appropriate?
3. Why can teachers who work with older students monitor students' learning simply by asking a few questions in the classroom, whereas teachers of younger children have to ask all students to respond?
4. Why does it do little good to try to teach children at conceptual levels beyond their present ones? What special guidelines should be observed when teaching preoperational children? What distinctive materials and specific teaching requirements do these children need that older children do not?
5. Based on your reading of this textbook, cite the most important thing you believe teachers can do to facilitate the intellectual development of children.
6. What three central aspects of becoming operational in thinking did Piaget stress?
7. Read and think about the following statement from this chapter: "Young children primarily accommodate to the immediate situation; older individuals primarily assimilate the immediate situation into existing cognitive structures." What does this sentence mean and how might it affect your behavior when teaching second-grade students versus eighth-grade students?
8. At what developmental stage will students most benefit from learning broad integrative concepts? What students are least likely to benefit from the use of integrative concepts?
9. Differentiate the structural and functional aspects of language.
10. Describe the meaning and implication of the following statement that appears in this chapter: "If you know it thoroughly, you can use it to solve problems in everyday life that lend themselves to algebraic formulation. If you studied algebra but did not learn it thoroughly, however, you couldn't apply it beyond the concrete problems presented in class."
11. What is egocentric speech and what is its function? In what ways did Piaget and Vygotsky differ in their beliefs about the importance of egocentric speech? In general, which position is supported more consistently by recent research?
12. In most respects, Piaget's theories mesh well with those of Bruner and proponents of discovery learning. However, Piagetian theories imply that young children cannot understand abstract ideas meaningfully, and also that they may not possess cognitive abilities assumed by discovery-learning approaches. What does this mean? How might you find out?

13. Suppose a teacher was bored with repetition and practice of the same old basic skills to the point that he or she wanted to move on for personal relief and stimulation, even though many children had not mastered these skills yet. Should this teacher be in the classroom? Why, or why not? If a teacher is to be effective, doesn't classroom routine have to be personally stimulating and rewarding to some minimal degree?
14. Most teachers find bright and creative (but compliant) students very stimulating and enjoyable, but not slow, dull students, even if they are friendly and obedient. This reaction is natural and understandable, but it has ominous implications about fairness and impartiality. Do you feel this way? How will you handle your slow students?
15. Why is it important, especially with younger students, to frequently elicit some kind of response or performance? Can this be done effectively when teaching humanities or social studies? If so, how? If not, why not?
16. Suppose you teach an elementary class in which some students have well-functioning concrete operations but many do not (or, suppose you teach a secondary class in which some students have well-functioning formal operations but most do not). What organizational and instructional strategies could you use to make sure that most instruction is meaningful to all of your students?

CASE STUDIES

Appropriate Teaching. Jim Roberts was working with a group of fifth-grade students who were assigned to read a selection from James Michener's *Centennial*. Responding to a student's answer, Jim said: "Yes, Jane, that is another critically important point. His willingness to stake himself to the ground and to fight to the death is a revealing dimension. Well, now, we've noted twelve important events on the board. How can we use these to generalize about his basic character traits? What kind of man was he?"

Describe the type of teaching Jim Roberts is engaging in. If he were teaching the same material to tenth-grade students, how might he approach the task differently?

Sam Not Turned On. Sam Baker, a tenth-grade student at Longfellow High School, achieves at an average level. On his last report card he received three Cs and two Bs, but most teachers suspect that he can do better than he does for two reasons. First, his measured IQ has regularly exceeded 120 on a variety of tests he has taken during his school history. Second, his performance on classroom exams is uneven. Typically, Sam answers some questions in excellent fashion, but other responses are below average. He appears to "absorb" topics he is interested in, and to comprehend the material he takes the time to read.

Sam is in the college-preparatory program, although he has no vocational plans and only a vague commitment to college. His father is a manager of a large chain grocery store in town and his mother is a first-grade teacher. An only child without regular friends, Sam's only interests are hunting with his dad on occasional weekends and reading about hunting in general and guns in particular. How could Sam's existing interests be used and eventually broadened in the following school subjects: history, Spanish, physics, and geometry?

Hard to Tell. Jane Prawat was a first-grade teacher at Thorton Bay High School. She enjoyed teaching and especially enjoyed teaching reading. She tried to involve students in thinking about what they were reading as well as simply looking at words and learning strategies to decode meaning. She spent considerable time talking to students about the words that they would see in the stories, and after reading the stories with the children she asked them a number of questions. The following activity is typical of those that occurred after a reading session. Ms. Prawat, with great interest and enthusiasm, asked: "Did you believe that Mr. Martin would ever let the cats go back to Timmy?" All children in the group nod their heads approvingly. One or two say "Yes" audibly. With continuing interest Ms. Prawat asked, "Do you think Tim was glad to see the kittens when they got home?" Again, students nod affirmatively following her question. Then she asks, "Do you think the kittens were glad to see him?" The students shake their heads, yes. What suggestions do you have for improving Ms. Prawat's teaching? What principles of development might be applied to improve the teaching discussed in this episode?

Going Beyond the Information Given. Jan Brooke was in her third year of teaching at Astoria Middle School. She enjoyed working with the eighth-grade students and tried to get them to think about the social studies that they were studying. She especially enjoyed having students challenge the conclusions authors reached and think of alternative ways in which key historical figures' behavior might be explained. She particularly liked her students to examine economic motivation as well as individual and social motivation. She constantly reminded students that most accounts of history they were reading were written from an individual's framework and did not take into consideration general economic and social factors. Some students thoroughly enjoyed this course and other students thought it was simply a lot of hot air. Based upon your knowledge of development, how might you account for these differences in students' reactions to the class? How could the teacher alter some aspects of the class in order to help *all* students think more fully about the material and concepts that they were reading?

Chapter 5

Social and Personal Development

CHAPTER OUTLINE

OBJECTIVES

When you have mastered the material in this chapter you will be able to

1. Discuss the relative importance of social learning (environmental) factors versus inherited (biological) factors in social development
2. Explain each of Erikson's eight stages of the human life cycle
3. List and discuss the characteristics of the ideal parent in terms of childrearing
4. Explain ways that elementary, middle school, and high school teachers can assist students to cope successfully with their developmental crises
5. Discuss strategies a teacher might use to help students build positive self-concepts
6. Explain how children reason about moral issues at each of Kohlberg's six stages of moral judgment
7. Critically evaluate the usefulness of Kohlberg's theory for teachers who wish to teach moral reasoning and moral behavior in school

Most of the personal qualities and social traits that individuals develop result from conditioning by social expectations and reinforcement, and from modeling by significant others in their lives, especially their parents. Certain individual differences exist at birth, however.

Arousal level

One of these differences is arousal level. Some infants are alert and physically active much of the time, exploring the environment and reacting to stimulation. Other infants sleep much of the time, and even when awake are mostly quiet and relatively unresponsive. These individual differences in infancy tend to persist, and to correlate with differences in arousal level and behavior observed later (Thomas & Chess, 1970).

Certain sex differences tend to be observable in many children from birth. Boys tend to be relatively more active, initiatory, aggressive, and oriented toward physical manipulation of objects in the environment. Girls are more apt to observe environmental events than to manipulate objects, and they do more watching, listening, and verbalizing. They also tend to be more physically mature—their body parts, and especially the neurophysiological control mechanisms that operate the body parts, tend to be more advanced and to function more efficiently. Again, these differences are observable at birth and tend to persist throughout childhood (Huston, 1983; Maccoby & Jacklin, 1974).

Early predispositions and environmental influences

These early predispositions interact with environmental influences. For example, an active and initiatory child who has siblings or peers available may spend much time in boisterous rough-and-tumble play, but one who does not have playmates readily available may spend a lot of time actively exploring the physical environment. Physically active children raised in an atmosphere of hostility and violence are likely to become predisposed to fighting and bullying (Huesmann et al., 1984; Patterson & Stouthamer-Loeber, 1984; Steinmetz, 1977), but the same type of children raised in warmer and more humanistic environments tend to become active and assertive, but nonaggressive, peer leaders (Maccoby & Martin, 1983; Rohner & Nielsen, 1978; Staub, 1979). Thus, even where biological predispositions toward personal and social traits exist, environmental influences interact with these predispositions to affect behavior.

As children become aware of sex differences, they develop a preference for playmates of their own sex.

However, there are very few biological predispositions even though there are family resemblances for everything from food preferences (Rozin, Fallon, & Mandell, 1984) to political philosophies (Boshier & Thom, 1973). Most personal and social traits are almost entirely the products of environmental rather than genetic influences (Ahern et al., 1982). These traits include such things as cooperative, competitive, or individualistic motives and activity preferences; personal interests; status as a peer leader, follower, or isolate; and a great variety of personal traits such as optimism versus pessimism, sociability, or styles of solving problems and coping with frustrations. These traits are developed in response to the influences of significant others, initially the parents and other family members, but later the teachers and peers encountered at school and the modeling and social expectations communicated through television and other media. All of these socializing influences involve the modeling of behavior that can be imitated and the projection of social expectations that tell developing children how they are supposed to act and what they are supposed to value, strive for, and even feel.

Although many socialization influences are unique to certain families and to the children within these families, there are broad influences that can be expected to affect all children in a given society, at least to some degree. Prominent among these are age and sex roles—the norms for personal qualities and behavior that tell children what is expected of boys or girls and for children at a particular age level. Children stress both age and sex in defining themselves and their peers, and most of them seem highly motivated to learn about and to strive to fulfill the role expectations they believe apply to themselves (Bradbard & Endsley, 1983; Kohlberg, 1966; Masters et al., 1979). That is, once a little girl comes to understand that she is a girl (this usually occurs between ages two and three), she is likely to begin observing intensively and asking questions to learn more about what being a girl means and about the implications for clothing and grooming, toy and game preferences, and personal mannerisms and interests. The same thing happens to boys. In the short run, this leads to preoccupation with sex differences, development of preference for playmates of one's own sex, and temporary separation and occasionally even alienation from the opposite sex. This builds to a peak sometime in mid-childhood, typically around eight years old in brighter and more socially mature children, but somewhat later for other children (Kohlberg & Zigler, 1967), and then recedes.

Age and sex roles

The role of heredity in producing sex differences in cognitive functioning and social behavior is still debated (Brooks-Gunn & Matthews, 1979; Parsons, 1980; Wittig & Petersen, 1979). After an exhaustive review, Maccoby and Jacklin (1974) concluded that all behavioral differences other than those involving aggression probably result from socialization factors rather than from heredity. Others argue a greater genetic role. Like other nature-nurture controversies, this one is unlikely to be resolved with available data, because findings are inconsistent and open to conflicting interpretations.

Heredity and behavioral differences

Several writers caution against exaggerating sex differences, noting that such differences are quite small, both in absolute terms and in comparison with individual differences within the two sexes (Hyde, 1981, 1984; Plomin & Foch, 1981). This point is well taken, especially because these already small sex differences have become even smaller in recent years due to changes in sex-role socialization. In addition, several authors suggest that the term "sex differences" be reserved for biological differences and that the term "gender differences" or "gender role differences" be used in describing culturally prescribed male and female roles and the concepts and behaviors associated with them (Bem, 1981; Unger, 1979).

Gender differences

Whether or not heredity contributes to sex or gender differences, it is clear that socialization factors do. People treat male and female infants differently from birth, regardless of their behavior, and this differential treatment continues throughout life. Such treatment tells children how

Socialization factors and gender differences

males and females are expected to act, and most people tend to conform, for the most part, to these expectations.

Children may even condition their parents to treat them in particular ways (Bell, 1971; Osofsky, 1976; Shaffer, 1977). Many girls, for example, resist the restrictions and dependency built into the traditional female role, and succeed in defeating most pressures to conform to it.

Socialization influences

Personal and social development in other areas follows a similar process. That is, behavioral predispositions and notions about oneself are acquired through socialization influences. These influences are usually quite consistent at first because they are confined to the immediate family. However, as children encounter peers, the media, and other sources of influence, new possibilities begin to appear and contradictions and conflicting demands become more of a problem. Children who have adapted easily to reasonably consistent socialization pressures and have had these pressures reinforced rather than contradicted by the increasing variety of influences they encounter as they get older are likely to become well adjusted in the sense that their personal traits and behavior are satisfactory to them and to other significant people in their lives (Kagan & Moss, 1962). However, children who have been unable or unwilling to adapt to consistent socialization pressures or who have been confused by inconsistent pressures are likely to have adjustment problems.

Several distinct stages can be identified in the development from a relatively undifferentiated infant without much "personality" to a well-defined individual with many stable traits and predictable personal qualities and behaviors. The first theory to delineate such stages was that of Freud in his famous writings about the oral, anal, phallic, oedipal, latency, and genital stages of psychosexual development. These stages will not be discussed in detail here because they can be found in any introductory psychology book (see McConnell, 1974), and because they are subsumed by the more recent psychoanalytic stage theory of Erikson (1968).

Erikson's Stage Theory

Erikson identifies eight stages in the human life cycle (see Table 5.1), six of which occur before or during schooling, including college. Each stage involves a central developmental crisis. Development during and after that stage presumably will be facilitated or impaired, depending on the degree to which the individual is successful in coping with the crisis.

Trust versus Mistrust

The central crisis of infancy (corresponding to Freud's oral stage) is the issue of trust versus mistrust. It is a universal human experience to spend the first year or so of life totally dependent on others for food and general care. Erikson believes that fundamental dispositions toward others are

Table 5.1 Erikson's Eight Stages of the Human Life Cycle

Stage	Ages	Central Conflict	Primary Implications for Optimal Development
1.	Infancy	Trust vs. mistrust	Developing general security, optimism, and trust in others (based on consistent experiences involving satisfaction of basic needs).
2.	Toddlerhood	Autonomy vs. shame and doubt	Developing a sense of autonomy and confident self-reliance, taking setbacks in stride (based on consistent experiences involving encouragement and limit setting without rejection or blame).
3.	Early childhood	Initiative vs. guilt	Developing initiative in exploring and manipulating the environment (based on consistent experiences of tolerance, encouragement, and reinforcement).
4.	Middle childhood	Industry vs. inferiority	Enjoyment and mastery of the developmental tasks of childhood, in and out of school (based on consistent experiences of success and recognition of progress).
5.	Adolescence	Identity vs. identity confusion	Achievement of a stable and satisfying sense of identity and direction (based on consistent personal experiences involving success and satisfaction combined with social acceptance and recognition).
6.	Young adulthood	Intimacy vs. isolation	Development of the ability to maintain intimate personal relationships (based on personal openness and confidence complemented by consistently rewarding experiences with intimate others).
7.	Adulthood	Generativity vs. stagnation	Satisfaction of personal and familial needs supplemented by development of interest in the welfare of others and of the world in general (based on achievement of a secure and rewarding personal life and a freedom from pressures which limit one to self-preoccupation).
8.	Aging	Integrity vs. despair	Recognizing and adjusting to aging and the prospect of death with a sense of satisfaction about the past and readiness about the future (based on consistent success in prior stages which provides a real basis for satisfaction in having led a full and good life and for accepting death without morbid fears or feelings of failure).

Source: Constructed from the information contained in, Erikson, E. (1968). *Identity: Youth and Crisis.* New York: Norton.

formed by experiences during this dependent stage. If the infant's needs are met reasonably well, a positive orientation toward and trust in others is likely to develop. If caretakers are inadequate or inconsistent in meeting basic needs, infants may develop insecurity and a fundamental mistrust of others, laying the groundwork for later paranoid ideas and a general attitude of "the world is a jungle; you have to get yours before somebody else gets

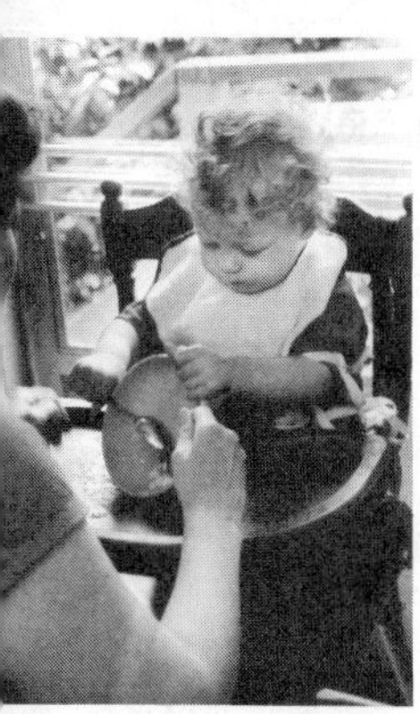

Infants who are well cared for physically and emotionally usually develop trust in others.

it or tries to take it away from you." In general, people who trust others are happier, better adjusted, and better liked than those who lack trust in others (Rotter, 1980).

Whether or not the first year of life has special importance, it seems clear that children whose needs are met by loving and reliable adults are likely to be secure, happy, trustful, and sociable toward others, and that children who suffer because apathetic or unreliable adults do not meet their basic needs or meet them inconsistently will be insecure and mistrustful.

Autonomy versus Shame and Doubt

Erikson's next stage centers on the crisis of autonomy versus shame and doubt (roughly paralleling Freud's anal stage). The universal human experience involved here is the transition from being treated as a helpless infant to being treated as a child capable of exercising some self-control, and therefore expected to conform to certain rules. Freud termed this the anal stage because conflict often appears when parents attempt to toilet train their children. However, toilet training is just one example of the more general crisis that results from adjusting to the fact that adults are for the first time imposing rules and expectations for self-control and self-denial.

Parental demands

If such socialization is carried out with proper timing and appropriate methods, children are likely to adjust to it smoothly and without losing their sense of personal autonomy. If parents make too many demands and especially if they make them too early, and if they use inadvisable socialization methods such as threats or punishment to enforce these demands, children may lose their sense of personal autonomy and begin to feel completely dependent on and under the control of adults. Furthermore, assuming that children want to please adults by meeting their expectations, failure to do so is likely to result in feelings of shame and in the development of doubt about their own capabilities and control over themselves. This sets the stage for later difficulties in areas such as self-concept and impulse control.

Initiative versus Guilt

Erikson's next stage revolves around the crisis of initiative versus guilt. Freud called this the phallic stage, believing that boys of four or five years of age tend to show off their bodies generally and their penises in particular. More broadly, the universal human experience associated with this stage is the development of an interest in one's self and one's capabilities, including an interest in showing these off to parents and interested others.

Children treated with warmth and support during this stage are likely to develop confidence and the general sense of security and well-being necessary to take the initiative in trying out new things and "showing off." In contrast, if these activities lead to punitive overreactions, children may develop a feeling of guilt, initially about the specific instances but perhaps ultimately about initiatives in general. The result of this treatment may be

Inhibition

generalized inhibition and fear of taking the initiative. A child may become obsessed with fear of failure rather than concentrating on goal-seeking and anticipation of success. People who develop such motivational systems minimize initiatives in general and try to avoid situations where their success can be judged by objective criteria.

Sullivan emphasizes the development of "chumships," particularly among girls, as students move from childhood to adolescence.

Industry versus Inferiority

Erikson's next stage resolves around the crisis of industry versus inferiority. It corresponds roughly to Freud's latency stage, and to Piaget's concrete operational period. Freud stressed the reduction of interest in sexual activities after resolution of the Oedipus complex as the hallmark of the latency stage, but Erikson stresses the universal experience of moving out from family and home into the neighborhood, the peer group, and the school.

These changes stimulate children by presenting new roles and related role expectations that children usually are motivated to try to fulfill successfully (Havighurst, 1972). In the peer group this means learning to cooperate, share, and generally get along with others, as well as to master the various skills involved in childhood play. In school it means socialization to the role of pupil and mastery of school tasks. Students who have had a good start at home attack these tasks and role expectations with relish, or, to use Erikson's term, with a sense of industry. Success results in more success and more motivation, setting off a chain of positive self-fulfilling prophecy effects. Conversely, if children should fail in meeting these expectations (either fail objectively or feel that they failed because they did not do as well as their friends), they may develop a sense of inferiority and low self-esteem, leading eventually to negative expectations and undesirable self-fulfilling prophecy effects.

Development of personal relationships

Sullivan (1953), Thornburg (1982), and others suggest that the transitional years between childhood and adolescence (roughly ages 11 through 13) constitute a stage in their own right, at least with respect to social development. Sullivan stresses the transition from playing with large groups, where the emphasis is on the activity, toward formation of close "chumships" with individuals, where the emphasis is on developing a more intimate personal relationship. He believes that such chumships are important facilitators of social development and personal development generally. Research suggests that friendships tend to be intimate during these years, especially among girls, and that early adolescents are likely to act prosocially toward their friends and attempt to achieve mutually satisfying outcomes of equality in situations where younger or older individuals might go their own way or compete (Berndt, 1982). Also, preadolescents who are involved in such chumship relationships are more likely than their peers to display high levels of altruism and the ability to put themselves in the place of others and take their perspectives (McGuire & Weisz, 1982).

Thornburg (1982) notes that ages 11 through 14 signal a shift from same sex to both sexes to opposite sex peer relationships, and from socializing primarily in a natural environment like one's own home or neighborhood to socializing in a contrived environment like a shopping center or a movie theater. At school, these years signal a shift from identification with teachers as authority figures to identification with peers and a degree of resentment of, or even resistance to, exercise of authority.

Identity versus Identity Confusion

In adolescence, Erikson speaks of the crisis of identity versus identity confusion, or role diffusion. Again Freud confined himself primarily to sexual considerations in talking about the genital stage, but Erikson speaks of the identity crisis that most adolescents experience to some degree. A complex set of factors is involved, but the basic one is that adolescents become cognitively developed to the point where they begin to really understand concepts that they have been accepting all along at the verbal level without really knowing the meaning of the words (such as beliefs, attitudes, value systems, morality, and so on).

As adolescents attain formal operations and greater understanding of both cognitive content and the people and world around them, they begin to see that some of the beliefs and values to which they have been exposed conflict with each other. Preaching and practice sometimes do not coincide in the words and actions of parents, teachers, or other socialization agents.

Belief conflicts

Many young persons become depressed or romantically idealistic about the fact that numerous values are honored more in theory than in practice, so they not only seek values they can accept, but go out of their way to practice them systematically in their lives. Included in this assessment of values are questions of personal identity (Who am I?, What do I want from life?, What kind of person should I be?, What kind of occupational, social, and sexual roles should I play?).

Adolescents who solve these dilemmas with reasonable ease tend to adjust smoothly to changes in role and status and to move into adult occupational, spousal, and parental roles without much difficulty. However many become confused about who they are and where they are going, and it may be several years before they "find themselves." They may have a more or less continual undercurrent of dissatisfaction with their lives, and a feeling of confusion that can cause difficulties in motivation, an inability to concentrate on studies, and general problems of personal adjustment in and out of school.

Marcia and Schiedel (Marcia, 1980; Schiedel & Marcia, 1985) elaborated on Erikson's concept of the identity crisis by developing ways to measure it operationally. They studied the degree to which adolescents experienced crises and made commitments in five areas; occupation, religion, political philosophy, sex-role attitudes, and beliefs about personal sexuality. Based on responses to interview questions about these topics, they classified young people into four identity status categories: identity achievement (individuals who have passed through a period of exploration and have made self-chosen commitments; moratorium (persons who are currently in crisis and have not yet made firm commitments; foreclosures (persons whose commitments generally mirror parental positions and who therefore have

Identity status categories

not yet experienced a crisis involving serious questioning of those positions; and identity diffusions (persons who, whether or not they have experienced crises, currently lack commitments and are not especially concerned about their lack of direction).

These four identity status categories are not always related to other variables in ways that would be predicted by Erikson's theory (Coté & Levine, 1983), but they have proven useful in conceptualizing and measuring progress toward achieving identity. Archer (1982) studied sixth-, eighth-, tenth-, and twelfth-grade students and found that identity status increased significantly with each increase in grade level, although it is worth noting that the diffusion and foreclosure statuses were evident at all grade levels. Thus, even by twelfth grade, only a minority of students reached the identity achievement level. Furthermore, identity achievement status varied with content area. When identity achievement status was attained, it was most likely to be in the vocational choice or religious beliefs content area. Moratorium status was also seen most frequently with respect to vocational choice, whereas foreclosure status was most frequent with sex-role preferences and identity diffusion status was most frequent with political philosophies. In general, the most extensive advances in identity formation occur during the college years rather than the high school years (Waterman, 1982).

Intimacy versus Isolation

Erikson's next stage, intimacy versus isolation, refers to the crisis faced in late adolescence or young adulthood when a person has developed to the point that intimate relationships, particularly an intimate relationship with a single member of the opposite sex, become viable and desirable. Individuals who have weathered previous stages successfully will enter this crisis trusting others, feeling a sense of autonomy, willing to take initiatives, having high self-esteem and confidence in their abilities, and being reasonably sure about who they are and what they want. These factors will make it easy for them to initiate and maintain truly intimate relationships, sharing everything about themselves with their partners.

In contrast, individuals who have had problems in previous stages, particularly those who show mistrust of others, low self-esteem, and fear of taking initiatives, are less likely to be ready to establish intimate relationships, even if good opportunities should come along. Those who want such relationships, but lack the confidence and skills needed to establish them, are likely to feel a deep sense of frustrated isolation and loneliness.

Intimacy statuses

Marcia and his colleagues (Orlofsky, Marcia, & Lesser, 1973) have elaborated and operationalized Erikson's intimacy stage. They assigned individuals to one of five intimacy statuses based on three general criteria: presence or absence of close relationships with male and female friends; presence or absence of an enduring, committed sexual relationship; and depth versus superficiality of peer relationships. The five intimacy statuses based on these criteria are: isolate (living in an interpersonal void with only casual acquaintances); stereotyped (being pleasant and friendly, but shallow and conventional in personal relationships); pseudointimate (similar to the stereotyped except being involved in a relatively permanent sexual relationship that is defined more by conventional roles than by sharing of deep feelings or self-disclosure); preintimate (having a close, open relationship with others based on mutuality and understanding, yet being ambivalent about sexual commitment in an enduring relationship); intimate (similar to the preintimate except having a committed, long-term, sexual relationship).

Research indicates that people whose interview responses place them in higher intimacy categories know their friends better and can predict their partner's responses to a personality or attitude inventory better (Orlofsky, 1976), are more self-disclosing in their interactions with other people, and are better able to conceptualize and articulate their emotional experiences (Orlofsky & Ginsburg, 1981). Furthermore, research supports Erikson's stage notions concerning the relationship between identity and intimacy, indicating that persons typically achieve high status on identity measures before they attain high status on intimacy (Fitch & Adams, 1983; Kacerguis & Adams, 1980; Schiedel & Marcia, 1985). These findings are clearer for males than for females, however, and it is not uncommon for some women to deal successfully with intimacy issues prior to resolving identity issues. These sex differences are believed due to differences in gender role socialization that orient females toward interpersonal relationships and thus toward dealing with both identity and intimacy issues throughout the adolescent and early adult years. On the other hand, males are oriented more toward intrapersonal soul-searching and thus towards a preoccupation with identity issues and their resolution during the adolescent years, followed by attention to intimacy issues in the young adult years.

Generativity versus Stagnation and Integrity versus Despair

Erikson's final two stages deal with development in adulthood and old age and are not directly relevant to most teachers. The crisis of generativity versus stagnation refers to the degree to which married persons feel capable of having and raising children successfully, and the advantages and disadvantages that result if the crisis is or is not met successfully. The final stage, integrity versus despair, refers to the degree to which aging persons adjust to the impending reality of death. Those who do so positively look back on their lives with satisfaction, feeling that they have been generally successful, happy, and useful. They are resigned to death without morbid fear or unrealistic denial. Individuals who do not solve this crisis successfully develop these concerns about death, or at least feel that their lives have been failures because they never amounted to anything.

Socialization

Universal human experiences define stages and force adjustments by individuals, but success in responding to crises depends on the quality of the socialization that children receive, particularly the quality of parenting in the home. A great volume of information about parental behaviors and the results that they produce in children is available, much of it collected during the last twenty years (Baumrind, 1971; Brophy, 1977; Henderson, 1981; Hess, 1970; Hoffman, 1970; Maccoby, 1980; Maccoby & Martin, 1983; Martin, 1975). The following adult attributes are mentioned consistently in this literature as being vital for fostering optimal development in children:

Children benefit most from parents who accept them as individuals and communicate this with warmth and affection.

1. Having basic acceptance of the child as an individual. This is what Rogers (1951) calls unconditional positive regard.
2. Communicating this acceptance through warm, affectionate interactions.
3. Having an approach to socialization that recognizes that the task is primarily one of education rather than control or "discipline."
4. Articulating and enforcing clear rules and limits as needed, but with input from the child and with flexibility for change as appropriate.
5. Presenting expectations and demands in ways that communicate respect for and concern about the child, as opposed to arbitrarily "laying down the law."
6. Offering explanations giving the rationales for demands and expectations made.
7. Stressing "golden rule" morality and regard for the effects of one's actions on oneself and others in these rationales, as opposed to stressing fear of punishment or appealing to essentially empty logic, by statements such as "good children don't do that."
8. Practicing as well as preaching the value systems articulated.
9. Continually projecting positive expectations and attitudes in interactions with the child. Treating the child as if he or she already is, or at least is in the process of becoming, the kind of person that the parents value.
10. Understanding and having tolerance for individual differences between parents and children and between children and other children, so that children are encouraged to capitalize on their strengths and follow their interests, rather than feeling pressured into becoming something else.
11. Leaving children emotionally free to question and assess values during the adolescent identity crisis, even though it is important that parents preach and practice a humanistic value system in socializing their children. Values should not be presented in such a way that children are made to feel guilty to think about them or question them.

Socialization in the Classroom

Erikson's stage theory helps alert teachers to major sources of conflict for students at varying levels of development. Students in the early grades are likely to be struggling with the crises of initiative versus guilt and industry versus inferiority. Teachers who are sensitive to these problems can help inhibited and guilt-ridden children by encouraging them and showing them that they are free to explore, satisfy their curiosity, ask questions, make suggestions, and take initiatives. Furthermore, they can reassure such children that mistakes and ventures that work out poorly are normal and expected, not causes for shame or guilt.

Encouraging emerging abilities

Children obsessed with their standing relative to peers can be helped over time to switch their orientation from comparisons with peers to comparisons with themselves, thus attending more to their cumulative gains and emerging abilities than to their failures to outperform classmates. Children who are doing well in such competition but who are becoming egotistical and elitist might also profit from such socialization. In any case, many children need to learn that trying one's best is more important than winning, and that the satisfaction of doing a job well through care and persistence is real and valuable, regardless of what others might accomplish. Children also need to know that all individuals are unique, possessing contrasting patterns of strengths and weaknesses. Everyone has something to offer someone else, as long as an atmosphere of friendliness and cooperation is established.

Dealing with reality

In dealing with feelings of inferiority, shame, guilt, or low self-esteem, it is important for teachers to be realistic rather than well meaning but condescending with students. Students know how they are doing relative to their classmates no matter how teachers might try to disguise differences in ability or progress. There is no point in trying to deny reality, or to distract children from failures that concern them by switching the conversation to something else. To a child, this is like saying "So what if you are stupid; I like you anyway." A student's poor performance needs to be faced squarely and realistically, but in a supportive way. If the problem is the student's own fault, if he or she is, for example, not listening or doing the work, this should be pointed out firmly but gently. If the problem is one of relative ability, it is important to stress absolute progress, that is, to compare the student's current and past performance. This, not progress relative to classmates, is what really counts.

When children have become deeply depressed to the point where they insist that they cannot learn, either in general or in a particular subject area, teachers should vigorously reject this claim, but in ways that provide support and realistic reasons for expecting change in the future. Empty reassurances will not help. Instead, schedule an individual goal-setting conference, geared to produce a specific plan like assigning some extra work and making arrangements to see that the student gets tutorial help.

Adolescent Identity Crises

Teachers working with junior high school and older students will need to help them cope with the crises of identity versus role diffusion and, perhaps, intimacy versus isolation. The identity crisis is so pervasive among American adolescents that virtually every teacher will have to deal with it in some form. Teachers who relish a socialization role and foster close relationships with students will have opportunities to deal with this crisis in depth, and, perhaps for a time become the primary source of realistic information and feedback for some students. Teachers are frequently of enormous help when they make a good career suggestion to a student because most adolescents are confused about career options.

Developing Positive Self-Concepts

Importance of positive feedback

Teachers can help students build high self-esteem and positive self-concepts by communicating positive expectations and attitudes, and offering positive feedback. The most obvious area for this kind of socialization is the students' perceptions of their own academic skills and progress rates. Teachers can help students perceive that they can learn when they project positive expectations for a student's success, minimize competitiveness and comparisons among fellow students, and maximize an individual student's attention to his or her own progress. This is no minor matter, because many students are thoroughly convinced that they cannot learn (Ames & Felker, 1979), and achieving genuine change in these perceptions may be a long, slow process.

Positive self-concepts can be developed in other areas if teachers are perceptive and willing to involve themselves in matters not directly related to instruction. Helping students cope with developmental crises has already been discussed. Other opportunities for assisting students with difficulties in self-concept include helping them to become aware of and develop their strong points (Hauserman, Miller, & Bond, 1976), to gain confidence and improve in areas of weakness, and to accept limitations that cannot be changed. Some students may also need guidance in accepting their sex or their physical attributes, and in developing empathy ("How do you think Jenny feels when you say that to her?), social awareness ("What do you think the other girls think about you when you put Jenny down?"), role-taking skills ("Let's act it out. I'm Jenny, and I say, 'What are you doing?' Now, what should you say?"), or insights into self and others ("Why do you think you treat Jenny this way, when you're pleasant and friendly with everyone else?"). (Eisenberg, Lennon, & Roth, 1983; Rushton & Sorrentino, 1981; Smith, 1982).

Dealing with frustration

Students also must learn to cope with frustrations by facing up to them and striving to overcome them rather than by trying to deny them or by responding with hostility or childish regression. Teachers can promote good group relations by helping isolates to become accepted group members, and by teaching bullies or other hostile students to value friendships and learn to cope with their frustrations in positive ways rather than by taking them out on others.

Unaccustomed roles

It should be noted that well-established self-concepts based on long-standing status in peer groups are not easily changed, and that attempts to help by thrusting individuals into unaccustomed roles may cause discomfort, even if the roles are attractive. This was shown by Klinger and McNelly (1976), who studied boy scout troops in which most of the members had already established themselves as leaders or followers. The boys were asked to compete in teams of four against teams from other scout troops, under circumstances in which the role of captain of the team involved considerable importance, power, and responsibility. If each group of four boys had been allowed to select its own captain, the boy who had the highest existing leadership status in the troop probably would have been picked. However, the experimenters assigned the role of captain arbitrarily so that some were the same boys who would have been elected anyway, but others were boys accustomed to low or follower status. The boys were then observed and interviewed to see how they were affected by their participation in the games. As expected, the boys who were already leaders functioned effectively as team captains and enjoyed the experience, but the boys accustomed to low status roles who were thrust into the role of captain did not. Some of them even became withdrawn or anxious.

Changing self-concepts

The findings in the study conducted by Klinger and McNelly show how powerful self-concepts are and how they are resistant to change through short-term or artificial interventions. Teachers can help bring about real changes in students' self-concepts, but this will probably require producing gradual changes not only in self-perceptions, but also in the personal characteristics and behavior on which they are based.

Altering undesirable self-concepts

This is also true when dealing with students who have developed a stable but undesirable concept of themselves as tough, hard, or evil. Certain children are labeled this way consistently enough by their parents and others in their environment that they come to accept and even try to live up to the label. Altering this kind of self-concept takes time, but it can be done through the same kind of consistent projection of positive expectations leading to self-fulfilling prophecy effects. It is important for teachers to reject and combat students' negative self-images and project images of them as persons who are basically good and well-meaning and who will do the right thing when they understand the situation fully. Students treated this way consistently can be expected to acquire and begin to try to live up to more positive self-concepts (Grusec, Kuczynski, Rushton, & Simutis, 1978; Lepper, 1973; Miller, Brickman, & Bolen, 1975).

Aiding rejected and isolated students

To help rejected or isolated students, teachers may have to work with the peer group as well as with the students themselves. It is well established that self-concept is influenced heavily by the reactions of one's immediate peers and reference groups (Coppersmith, 1967; Rogers, Smith, & Coleman, 1978). Private conferences with peers, or at least with the more mature and understanding ones, might lead to better treatment of rejected students, especially those being rejected for reasons not based on their own inappropriate conduct. Peer relationships may also be improved by introducing cooperative activities, especially activities in which each participant has a necessary and unique role to play so that he or she cannot be slighted or ignored by the others (Lucker, Rosenfield, Sikes, & Aronson, 1976).

Teachers do not have nearly as many opportunities as parents have to influence students because they see students for only a limited time, and their interactions are somewhat limited and structured by the teacher and student roles. Even so, teachers who accept the task and work at it can have significant socialization effects on classes of students, and on individual students with whom they form special relationships.

Felker (1974) suggests the following five principles for teachers who want to foster healthy self-concepts in their students:

Working with adolescents

1. Praise yourselves to set a model for self-reinforcement for accomplishments
2. Help students to evaluate themselves realistically
3. Teach students to set reasonable goals
4. Teach students to praise themselves
5. Teach students to praise others

In combination, these principles will help students learn to recognize, value, and take pride in realistically defined accomplishments. Felker adds additional suggestions for teachers working with adolescents. One is to allow them to make choices and be able to accept the consequences, but within a supportive relationship. A second suggestion is to help them cope with adolescence by explaining what is happening to them in terms of physical, social, and emotional development. A third is to help them see and accept the fact that few decisions involve easy, clear choices or perfect solutions, so that compromise is an appropriate and not merely a necessary solution. For more about self-concept development, see Harter (1983), Damon and Hart (1982), or Lynch, Norem-Hebeisen, and Gergen (1981).

Moral Development

Children do not become truly moral individuals, capable of guiding their own behavior by a set of stable ethical principles, until they enter the concrete operational period sometime during the early elementary grades. This is the same period that theologians refer to as the "age of reason," indicating an intuitive recognition that children enter into a new level of cognitive development at this time.

Piaget (1932) was one of the first to study the changes in level of moral reasoning that accompany changes in cognitive development. He noted that as children overcome egocentrism and develop the cognitive abilities necessary to put themselves in the place of others, they begin to understand concepts such as fairness and reciprocity that underlie "golden rule" morality.

Kohlberg's Stage Theory

Kohlberg (1969) elaborated on Piaget's ideas and developed a stage theory of the development of moral judgment. In various formulations over the years he has used different terminology and even varying numbers of stages (Kohlberg, 1978, 1981; Kohlberg, Levine, & Hewer, 1983). Typically, however, he discusses three general levels of moral thinking, with two stages at each level (see Table 5.2).

Preconventional morality

Individuals at the preconventional level of morality do not yet possess an organized system of moral concepts from which to operate. Stage 1 individuals (mostly young children) are highly egocentric, concerned about their own interests but not about the interests of others. If they don't do whatever they feel like doing, it is because they fear punishment rather than because they are acting out of a sense of duty or a desire to live up to some ideal. Stage 2 individuals also lack generalized moral notions and are concerned primarily with themselves, although they will enter into limited reciprocity agreements of a "you scratch my back and I'll scratch yours" nature. Most Stage 2 persons also are developing children, but some older children and adults (particularly psychopaths and criminals) never get beyond this stage.

Conventional morality

Persons who reveal conventional levels of moral thinking accept and internalize the moral socialization they receive from their families and from society generally. Children at Stage 3 identify strongly with their parents and other adult authority figures and strive to please them by doing what they want. Older persons who are still characterized by Stage 3 thinking display more adult forms of these same moral notions. Rather than use more general and abstract moral concepts, these people think in terms of doing their duty, living up to expectations, and displaying virtues. Individuals who develop from Stage 3 to Stage 4 change from a moral orientation based on pleasing others and being thought of favorably to a more generalized orientation that considers laws and social expectations as means toward the end of maintaining the social system as a whole. Stage 4 persons are impressed with the need for order and for all persons to fulfill duties and obligations. However, they often carry their emphasis on the need to uphold the law to extremes. For example, exceeding the speed limit would be seen as wrong even in emergencies because it is against the law. Stage 4 conventional morality is seen in many adults who display a "law and order" mentality when thinking about social issues.

Most middle- and upper-elementary students, and a great many high school students, show predominantly conventional morality (Stages 3 or 4) in their moral reasoning. In fact, their responses to moral issues do not involve much genuine reasoning at all, in the sense of thinking through a problem situation carefully and arriving at their own considered judgments. Instead, they merely repeat moral norms that they acquired as young children and have learned to verbalize when it seems appropriate (It's wrong to steal. We should all share). Typically, young children commit these

Table 5.2 Kohlberg's Six Stages in the Development of Moral Judgment

Level I: Preconventional Morality

Stage 1: Heteronomous Morality. Obedience based on fear of punishment. Egocentric point of view, difficulty in appreciating the viewpoints or interests of others. No real conscience or sense of morality yet, but behavior can be controlled through reinforcement, especially fear of punishment.

Stage 2. Individualism, instrumental purpose, and exchange. Still primarily egocentric and concerned with own interests, but aware that others have their interests that they try to pursue. Generally concentrates on meeting own needs and letting others do the same, but when necessary will help meet others' needs in order to get one's own needs met. In this case, what is right is what is seen as fair or what amounts to an equal exchange.

Level II: Conventional Morality

Stage 3. Mutual interpersonal expectations, relationships, and interpersonal conformity. Good boy-good girl orientation: Try to please authority figures and live up to expectations for one's role as son, daughter, sibling, friend, etc. Concern about being good by practicing the "golden rule," showing concern about others, and displaying virtues such as trust and loyalty.

Stage 4. Social system and conscience. Moral ideals become more generalized, and motivation to live up to them shifts from concern about the reactions of immediate others to a sense of duty to respect authority and maintain the social order. Awareness of the individual's responsibility to keep the system as a whole going by following its rules and meeting its defined obligations. Belief that laws are to be upheld except in extreme cases where they conflict with other fixed social duties.

Level III. Postconventional (or Principled) Morality

Stage 5. Social contract or utility and individual rights. A sense of duty and obligation to fulfill the social contract still prevails, but with recognition that laws are means to ends rather than ends in themselves, and that laws should be written to obtain the greatest good for the greatest number. Awareness that certain values and rights should take precedence over social arrangements and contracts. Recognition that the moral and the legal points of view are different and sometimes conflict; confusion about what is right when such conflict occurs.

Stage 6. Universal ethical principles. Belief in and sense of personal commitment to universal moral principles (justice, equality of human rights, respect for the dignity of humans as individual persons). Particular laws or social agreements are usually considered valid and followed because they rest on these principles, but the principles take precedence when there is conflict between what is legal and what is right.

moral norms to memory with little or no thought about their meanings and implications, even though they repeat them many times. For these children, such moral norms are not so much principles for guided living as merely "verbal learning" that is displayed in appropriate situations and then forgotten until a similar situation is encountered again.

Ausubel and Sullivan (1970) have written extensively about young children who identify closely with their parents as satellites of the parents. They discuss the consequences of different forms of desatellization as the children move out of the home and away from parental influence. Children who desatellize smoothly and gradually and who move from generally facilitative homes tend not only to verbalize the value systems that their parents teach them, but to use them to guide their own behavior. Ultimately, these value systems are internalized and become the basis for self-control. Children who have problems in satellization or desatellization processes because of inadequate parents may learn to verbalize the value systems they are taught, but they are less likely to develop truly internal controls or use these value systems to guide behavior.

Satellization and desatellization

This process is compounded at adolescence, when value systems get called into question as formal operations begin to develop and the adolescent identity crisis occurs. For the first time, adolescents begin to think about the meanings of the value systems they have been taught, and to evaluate them objectively. Those who have limited intellectual capacities, or who have what Ausubel calls satellization or desatellization problems, do relatively little serious thinking about value systems. As a result, they remain fixated at the conventional level, or even at the preconventional level, of morality, so that their moral judgments are developmentally immature, and their value systems mostly empty verbalizations that do not control behavior. In contrast, children who have developed formal operations and spent time carefully evaluating their value systems make important developmental advances in moral thinking and reasoning. They switch from merely verbalizing without doing much thinking to consciously deliberating and adopting values, sometimes the same ones they were taught, sometimes not. To the extent that children adopt values consciously, they are likely to use values to guide behavior.

Value systems

Persons who attain the postconventional level of moral thinking develop more abstract and better integrated moral concepts. Moving beyond the emphasis on social conventions and law and order seen at Stage 4, Stage 5 individuals begin to view laws more flexibly, seeing them as devices that the community agrees on to enable people to live in harmony. Stage 5 persons realize that laws can be changed if they are not meeting the needs of society, and they also have some appreciation of the notion that certain basic values such as liberty, justice, and the pursuit of happiness might take precedence over the law itself. However, Stage 5 individuals confine attempts to change laws to orderly, democratic activities. They would stop short of advocating civil disobedience or other behavior that they would see as illegal and disruptive of society.

Postconventional morality

Individuals who reach Stage 6 have clear conceptions of abstract universal principles like fairness, justice, and individual human dignity that transcend the law. Kohlberg has had difficulty defining this state in ways that differentiate it clearly from Stage 5 and feels that few persons ever reach this stage. The examples that he does give tend to be persons who are known not only as moral teachers, but as individuals who are willing to stand up and if necessary suffer for their beliefs (e.g., Socrates, Jesus, Ghandi, Martin Luther King, Jr.).

Increasing Moral Judgment Levels

It would seem that Kohlberg's stage theory of moral development could have immediate applications for the classroom, particularly if it were possible to promote or even to speed up progress through the stages. However, this has not been the case. There have been problems, including some with the theories and methods that Kohlberg has produced. For example, Stages 5 and 6 are difficult to distinguish clearly, and Rest (1974), Hoffman (1977), and others in the field criticize the methods Kohlberg uses to measure moral judgment. Yet a study by Kuhn (1976) indicates reasonably good long-term stability across a period of a year for moral judgment levels in children five through eight years old. Of 50 children interviewed, 32 showed an increase in moral judgment levels across this time period, 13 did not change, and only five declined. These figures are comparable to those that have appeared for conservation and other aspects of purely cognitive development, and for attempts to place children in Piagetian stages. Other studies also support Kohlberg's stages (Colby et al., 1983; Davison, Robbins, & Swanson, 1978; Nisan & Kohlberg, 1982; Page, 1981; Parikh, 1980; Rest, Davison, & Robbins, 1978; Snarey, Reimer, & Kohlberg, 1985; Walker, 1980; White, Bushnell, & Regnemer, 1978). In general, then, Kohlberg's stage theory of moral development has face validity (since most people find it sensible and helpful) as well as considerable empirical support.

Kohlberg's theory has also been critiqued from a feminist perspective. Gilligan (1982) notes that all of the subjects whose reponses to moral dilemmas were used to develop the original theory were male. She further asserts that men and women speak different but equally valid moral languages: men speak more of rights and women speak more of responsibilities. Gilligan argues that men are more likely to view moral dilemmas as bargaining games or conflicts, or rights between players who rationally pursue their own self-interests, whereas women tend to stress resolutions that involve concern, care, continued attachment, responsibility, sacrifice, and avoiding hurting anyone else. Men are seen as searching for abstract principles and a method that can be applied to any moral dilemma, and women as concentrating on particular situations, relationships, and people.

Sex differences in moral thinking

Gilligan's ideas about sex differences in moral thinking reflect traditional differences in gender-role socialization in our society, and they are valid for most people. Furthermore, to the extent that such differences appear in people's responses to moral dilemmas, they would tend to cause conventional women to be scored at Stage 3 but conventional men to be scored at Stage 4, and they would make men more likely than women to score at Stage 5. Thus, it could be argued that Kohlberg's scoring scheme is biased against women. This was of major concern for a brief period, but recent research shows that Kohlberg's measurement methods and scoring schemes do not yield reliable sex differences in moral judgment stages (Gibbs, Arnold, & Burkhart, 1984; Walker, 1984). Gilligan's ideas about sex differences in general orientation toward moral dilemmas appear to have some validity, especially the notion that women are more responsibility-oriented, but these differences apparently do not lead to sex differences in moral judgment as measured by Kohlberg's methods.

Application of Kohlberg's theory

Kohlberg's ideas have been applied in educational programs designed to increase children's moral judgment levels. Such programs have been generally successful (Damon & Killen, 1982; Enright et al., 1983; Jensen & Murray, 1978; Lockwood, 1978; Mosher, 1980; Norcini & Snyder, 1983). Typically, they involve presenting students with moral dilemmas like those that Kohlberg used to measure moral reasoning:

> Joe's father promised he could go to camp if he earned the $50.00 to pay for it, but he changed his mind and asked Joe to give him the money he had earned. Joe lied and said that he had only earned $10.00 and went to camp using the other $40.00 he had made. Before he went, he told his younger brother Alex about the money and about lying to his father. Should Alex tell their father?

These moral dilemmas do not allow a simple response that is clearly right or wrong. They produce a variety of responses, and similar solutions can be reached via many different chains of moral reasoning that can be scored according to Kohlberg's six stages. For example, a Stage 1 response might state that Alex should tell the father because if the father finds out that Alex knew and didn't tell, he might punish Alex as well as Joe. A Stage 3 response would stress that fathers and sons should be good to each other and treat each other well, so Alex should tell his father because this is what a good son would do. A Stage 5 response would note that Alex has no legal obligation, but does have a moral obligation to be open and truthful in his dealings with others, including his father, even though the father didn't keep his earlier promise to Joe. Failure to tell the father here would constitute sharing in Joe's lie and thus would be immoral, because it would violate one of the implicit social contracts that underlie an orderly and effective society. Note that all three of these responses involve the same conclusion about what Alex should do, but differ in the level of moral reasoning that underlies the decision.

Plus-one matching principle

Teachers attempting to use discussion of moral dilemmas to promote development of moral reasoning are usually encouraged to use the plus-one matching principle. This principle assumes that children functioning at any particular level of moral reasoning will be most likely to understand and respond well to moral reasoning that is one level above where they presently are. The discrepancy between this level and their present reasoning will introduce cognitive conflict that presumably will cause them to think more about the problem than they might otherwise, and thereby to develop higher levels of moral reasoning. Programs based on the plus-one matching principle are usually effective (Enright et al., 1983; Mosher, 1980; Norcini & Snyder, 1983; Walker, 1983), although one study (Walker, 1982) found that plus-two reasoning was just as effective as plus-one reasoning for raising moral judgment levels. Whether or not the plus-one matching principle really is the key, it is clear that some moral development programs successfully raise children's levels of moral judgment, especially when discussion of moral dilemmas is supplemented by exercises in empathy training, peer counseling, role playing, listening, and communication. Even so, most changes have occurred at Stage 2 or Stage 3 levels, with less positive results at the higher ranges (Lockwood, 1978).

Values clarification approach

The values clarification approach developed by Raths, Harmin, and Simon (1966) is somewhat more affective and less cognitive than the moral reasoning approach to moral education in the classroom. The idea is to help children to see the connection between their opinions and behavior and their underlying values, and to clarify those values by becoming more aware of them and sharpening their definitions. These authors believe that values must be recognized and freely chosen if we are to expect people to act on them consistently, so the values clarification approach concentrates on identifying these values and encouraging children to think about them rather than on trying to promote particular moral ideas as preferable to others. This approach has been less successful than the moral reasoning approach in documenting significant changes in school children (Lockwood, 1978), but it retains its appeal for many people. Readers interested in further details about these two approaches are referred to *Moral Education . . . It Comes with the Territory* (Purpel & Ryan, 1976) and to various issues of the *Journal of Moral Education.*

Moral Judgment, Moral Affect, and Moral Behavior

Moral reasoning and behavior

Most teachers will not be satisfied to concentrate only on increasing levels of moral judgment because, as noted earlier, moral reasoning does not always control behavior. In fact, moral development research generally reveals low correlations between: (1) levels of moral reasoning as measured by the methods of Piaget, Kohlberg, or Rest (1974); (2) quality and intensity of moral affect (feelings of satisfaction following good deeds or guilt following misdeeds); and (3) measures of moral behavior (prosocial, cooperative interpersonal conduct versus antisocial or otherwise objectionable behavior).

Early studies suggested almost no correlation at all between measures of moral judgment and measures of moral behavior, but more recent studies have revealed moderate relationships, at least at the extremes of the moral judgment scale. That is, individuals who score particularly low in moral judgment are especially likely to be involved in disruptive behavior at school (Bear & Richards, 1981; Geiger & Turiel, 1983) and to be involved in juvenile delinquency problems outside of school (Fleetwood & Parish, 1976; Hains & Miller, 1980; Wright, 1978). Individuals who score at Stage 5 tend to be especially likely to engage in principled moral behavior, such as helping a stranger who appeared to be having a bad trip on drugs (McNamee, 1978) or working actively to bring about social justice (Blasi, 1980). It is interesting to note that the parents of students who score at Stage 5 tend to use inductive techniques, stressing the harmful consequences of inappropriate behavior on others, whereas the parents of individuals who score at Stages 1 or 2 tend to use power assertive techniques, displaying frequent threats and punishment (Hoffman, 1979; Olejnik, 1980; Eisikovits & Sagi, 1982). Thus, there is some basis for believing that programs that increase moral judgment will also increase moral behavior, although it also seems likely that comprehensive programs aimed at all facets of moral development will be more effective than programs restricted to just one of them.

Aiding in moral development

In general, teachers can promote moral development by both modeling and articulating humanistic Golden Rule behavior. The kind of socialization that will be most successful in facilitating moral development in the classroom is the same kind that is successful in the home: a truly educational socialization provides guidelines and limits for the student, offering explanations of why these are appropriate, as opposed to using threats and punishments giving minimal explanation. It also is helpful to discuss behavioral codes with students, although this should focus on the positive, stressing idealized personal and interpersonal conduct and the reasons why it is valued. Degeneration of the discussion into an exercise in establishing punishment for violations will only reinforce the tendencies to persist in an authority-maintaining level of morality (Kohlberg's Stage 4), and will minimize the likelihood of advancement to higher stages.

SUMMARY

Although most personal and social traits are learned, certain elements such as arousal level, sex-linked traits, and physical characteristics interact with environmental influences in specific ways. The influences of biology and environment are topics of great interest to developmental theorists. Erikson, for example, built on Freud's theory to develop a theory of psychosocial development that integrates states of development and social experiences to describe conflicts and adaptations that are likely to occur at given points in the developmental sequence. Successful accommodations lead to optimal progressions toward mature functioning, while failure leads to fixation and arrestment.

Self-concept theorists emphasize the importance of positive attitudes and expectations in promoting success and satisfaction in life. They note the stability of both positive and negative self-concepts, their resistance to artificial change, and their influences on various aspects of human behavior.

Piaget and Kohlberg have been especially active in the area of moral development and moral judgment. Kohlberg has identified six stages of moral judgment that can be considered in three levels corresponding to Piaget's preoperational, concrete operational, and formal operational stages. Progression from concrete adherence to specific rules based on fear of punishment, through concrete morality, to abstract consideration of the general welfare using universal principles, brings socialization opportunities that teachers should carefully consider.

QUESTIONS AND PROBLEMS

1. How do individuals develop unique personal qualities and social characteristics? If children are born with certain biological predispositions (e.g., high

energy levels), do environmental influences make much difference in determining how an individual will develop? Why or why not?

2. Discuss these two stages of Erikson's developmental theory: industry versus inferiority and identity versus identity confusion. In what ways can classroom teachers help students move through these stages?
3. The authors present eleven adult attributes that are frequently cited as being associated with optimal development in children. Reexamine these eleven factors and identify the three or four that are most important. Why do you feel this way? Can you defend your answer? Compare your list with the list of another student and discuss the differences, if any, between the two lists.
4. How can teachers deal with students' feelings of inferiority, shame, guilt, or low self-esteem?
5. Recall the study by Klinger and McNelly that was described in this chapter. Why is it that some boy scouts did not want to be leaders?
6. Define desatellization. What is the value of this concept in assessing adolescents' development?
7. Discuss the difference between conventional morality and postconventional morality as defined by Kohlberg. If you were dealing with a student who was not obeying classroom rules, would the student's level of morality make any difference in how you interacted with him or her? Explain your reasoning.
8. School success usually is basic to the industry versus inferiority stage and to self-concept generally. What can you do to help students who overreact to school experiences by becoming depressed or withdrawn due to persistent failure or who are becoming insufferable egotists due to constant success (remember, the latter students need help, too)?
9. Almost everyone scoffs at psychoanalytic stage theories, yet they are regularly drawn upon for "explanations." Why?
10. Consider Kohlberg's moral development stages. Can you think of implications for teachers? For example, should teachers respond differently to the same misbehavior if the culprits differ significantly in level of moral development? List some implications. What effect might different teacher responses to the same behavior have on other students in the room?
11. Sex roles often get in the way of successful instruction. What might a teacher say or do when certain male students try to withdraw from literature or poetry lessons, or when certain female students try to withdraw from math or science lessons?
12. In general, there are orderly relationships between the types of modeling and socialization children are exposed to and the types of personal traits they develop. Yet, siblings from the same families are sometimes very different from one another. Also, some individuals manage to emerge well adjusted from poor backgrounds, and others emerge poorly adjusted from apparently loving and advantaged backgrounds. How can these exceptions be explained?

CASE STUDIES

Active Alice. Alice Plice is a very active sixth-grader—to put it nicely. She is always first in line due to her combined speed and physical ability and her willingness to give a shove or two, she always has something to say about everything, and she has the only voice that distinguishes itself from the general playground hubbub.

Alice, despite her "gusto" for living, drives people away from her and is quite lonely. Her teacher plans to design situations that curb Alice's excessive outbursts, as well as to provide a basis for her to develop better peer relationships. One way is to involve Alice in small group work from time to time with the same four or five students. What other principles might be applicable?

Dependent Dan. Dan, a seventh-grader at Hill Junior High, behaves anxiously in Mrs. Connor's English class. He watches her intently when she presents material and constantly nods his head in agreement as she talks. He double-checks every assignment with her, asking if he is proceeding with it correctly. Dan is an attractive bright boy with an IQ of 130. Mrs. Connor knows of no reason for his anxiety in her class, but Dan is obviously very dependent on her and desperately needs to have her approval and good will. In what ways could Mrs. Connor approach the problem? What types of tasks should she assign him, and how should she interact with him?

Quick Hands Jan. Jan, a third-grader from an affluent home, has started to "borrow" classroom supplies like her teacher's scissors and jars of paste. Mrs. Murphy notices one of her classroom rulers sticking out of Jan's open bag. Looking more closely but without touching the bag, Mrs. Murphy sees a number of classroom supplies in Jan's bag. Later that day, during afternoon recess, Mrs. Murphy asks Jan to stay in to discuss the incident. What should she say or ask Jan? Write three or four responses that Jan might make. How would Jan's response reflect her stage of development? How will Mrs. Murphy respond to Jan if she determines that Jan is at a preoperational stage of development versus a concrete operational stage?

Sticky Hands Luke. Luke, a tenth-grader from an affluent home, has started to "borrow" various supplies, including school property as well as supplies belonging to other students. During recess he pilfers supplies from the chemistry room or the industrial education room, depending upon which teacher happens to be gone during recess. One day Mr. Thornton, who teaches industrial education at Riverside High School, catches Luke as he is putting several cans of enamel into his gym bag. Mr. Thornton knows that materials have been disappearing over the past several weeks, but this is the first time he has proof that Luke has been taking materials. What should he say to Luke? How should Luke be treated in comparison to Jan, the third-grader? To what extent should teachers consider a student's chronological age and stage of moral development when they react to social problems like stealing?

Invidious Social Comparisons: Life in the Fast Lane. Jim Slink was a sophomore at Eastside High School. Jim had always been a talented student who progressed rapidly in virtually every school subject he studied. However, this year, he was doing terribly in honors physics. Partly because of his concern about his lack of progress in this subject, his grades in other subjects were beginning to suffer as well. One day he stayed after school to discuss his problems with his physics teacher. Jim whined, "I've never been in a class like this before. Everybody is so good and develops insights into the materials much more quickly than I can. The other day three fourths of the students had finished their experiments before I could even figure out what to do." If you were the teacher, what could you say or do to help Jim view himself realistically but positively?

Part Three

Learning

Mr. Simpson makes sure that his algebra students know their equations. He introduces each new equation with clear and detailed explanations in class, demonstrates their application by working out several computation problems using the overhead projector, and assigns the students a great many more computation problems as seatwork or homework exercises to insure that they master the material. As a result, most of his students learn to solve equations with speed and accuracy. Yet Mr. Simpson is not pleased because he finds that as soon as he moves away from computation problems by giving his students word problems that can be solved with the use of the equations they are learning, their performance breaks down. Many students act completely confused, and most of the rest are able to solve problems only by guessing at possible formula applications. Very few of the students do what Mr. Simpson expected most of them to do—read and think about the problem, formulate it in algebraic terms, and then solve it using appropriate equations. Why might this be?

Mrs. Abbott and Mrs. Costello both teach American history. They use the same texts and similar brief assignments to cover the same material with similar students. The only significant difference is that Mrs. Abbott grades according to performance on weekly quizzes and on a mid-term covering the first half of the course and a final covering the second half, whereas Mrs. Costello grades according to performance on a single final exam that covers the entire course and a term paper based on research about an important historical figure. Given these differences in grading, what differences would you expect between the two classes of students in the amount and distribution of study time devoted to American history? And how much they will remember about American history several years later? What attitudinal differences toward history as a subject do you feel these students will have and will they have the desire to take additional history courses in the future?

Ms. Brinks was very pleased with her science unit on force, gravity, vectors, and related concepts. She felt comfortable teaching it, the students seemed to enjoy and understand the material, and the class as a whole did very well on the unit test. Therefore, she was jolted to discover how poorly they performed on a seemingly easy item on the final exam several weeks later. She had asked, "If you released a 2,000 pound safe and a canteloupe at the same time from the top of the Leaning Tower of Pisa, which would hit the ground first, if either would hit first?" She had expected that nearly everyone would remember the basic principles that they seemingly had learned so well, and therefore would say that the two objects would fall at the same rate and hit the ground at the same time. What had happened to all of that seemingly clear understanding that the students displayed on the unit test?

Mrs. McGuffy is patient and encouraging with her low reading group, but she is discouraged with the progress of most of the students in it. They have a general understanding of basic word attack skills, but their ability to "put it all together" and read is painfully slow and uncertain. Some are "word callers" who handle most individual words correctly but don't keep track of the meaning of the words as they read, so that they don't get the meaning from their reading unless they repeat it several times. Others are even worse off, still struggling to blend sounds into words, let alone words into sentences. Yet, all of these students understand letter-sound relationships (phonics) and are familiar with the basic processes of sounding out syllables, blending these syllables into words, and combining words into sentences in order to get the meaning. So why don't they read with more efficiency and better comprehension?

Mr. Anderson is unhappy with the newly adopted social studies text that he is using for the first time this term. The text is newer and more visually attractive than the old one was, and readability formulas suggest that it should be easier to understand as well. Yet, student performance on early assignments and tests has been poor, and students are complaining about the text. Some students are only able to say that they don't like it or that it's "boring," but the more articulate students have noted that "It doesn't explain clearly—you can read it again and again and still not know what it is trying to say," and "It's hard to take notes—you can't figure out what the main points are." Mr. Anderson suspects that these students' comments are largely correct because the content covered in both the new and the old text are similar so the difference must be in how the content is presented. What do you think that Mr. Anderson will find when he compares the two texts to identify the reasons for the problems with the new text? Given that the new text has been officially adopted and may be used for some time, what can Mr. Anderson do to counter its deficiencies and help the students learn the material more successfully?

These brief vignettes illustrate just a few of the many principles of human learning discussed in the next four chapters. Mr. Simpson's problem illustrates the need for curriculum alignment: Logical relationships between the objectives of instruction, the content taught, the practice and application exercises used to develop the learning, and the evaluation methods used to assess mastery. Mr. Simpson's instructional objectives implicitly included not only the ability to solve equations in computation problems but the ability to transfer and apply learning about equations to the solution of practical problems represented in words. However, Mr. Simpson failed to teach for transfer or application. His instruction included good explanations and demonstrations of how to solve computation problems, but he never modeled the process of applying knowledge about equations to solution of practical problems. Nor did he provide his students with sufficient opportunities for guided practice to enable them to discover such applications. Thus, their figurative knowledge was not converted into operative knowledge.

Mrs. Abbott and Mrs. Costello illustrate that differences in assignments and assessment procedures will produce differences in student study patterns and thus differences in what students learn and retain. Mrs. Abbott's methods are likely to cause her students to retain most of the main ideas taught in the course, because the students will both study small subsets of the material for weekly quizzes and review larger subsets for the two major exams. In contrast, many of Mrs. Costello's students probably will do little studying early in the term and then "cram" for the final exam, with the result that most of the material will soon be forgotten. However, Mrs. Costello's students will learn a great deal about the individual they select as the focus of their term papers and will gain practice in research skills and the ability to integrate information from various sources, skills that won't be developed in Mrs. Abbott's class.

Ms. Brinks is discovering that instruction usually involves conceptual change rather than infusion of information into a vacuum. Students often bring a great deal of prior knowledge (schemas) to a learning situation and this prior knowledge establishes a framework within which new input is interpreted. When the prior knowledge brought to bear is accurate, the results are desirable and produce more efficient learning. However, when the prior knowledge includes misconceptions, the result may be distortion or even rejection of the new learning. This is especially likely when the misconceptions are well anchored in personal experience and thus stubbornly resistant to change (such as Ms. Brinks's students' belief that heavy objects fall faster than lighter objects). When teaching concepts that conflict with such misconceptions, teachers must not only teach the new information clearly but also make their students aware of and willing to part with their misconceptions.

Mrs. McGuffy's low group readers illustrate the fact that there are severe limitations on short-term working memory capacity. If a particular set of tasks takes up the entire available capacity, there will be no capacity left over for additional tasks. In the case of these beginning readers, most working memory capacity is needed for processing syllables and blending them into words, so that little is left over for making sense of the meaning at the sentence level. As basic word processing becomes more automatic and thus less demanding on working memory, more of this limited capacity will become available for sentence level processing.

Mr. Anderson's students' problems with the new textbook illustrate how learning efficiency is affected not only by the nature and inherent difficulty level of the content, but by the clarity and organization of the presentation. "Considerate" texts make learning easier by organizing and sequencing the content in a logical way, presenting it in clear language, highlighting structural features, signaling transitions between sections, calling attention to main ideas, and so on. The same is true of "considerate" lectures, presentations, and demonstrations. Since the new text is not considerate in this sense, Mr. Anderson will need to supplement it by distributing content outlines, lists of key terms, and other study aids that will help students to organize and retain the material.

Because educational institutions are established in the first place to foster learning, it seems obvious that issues surrounding learning should be basic to courses in educational psychology and should be of focal interest to individuals taking such courses. Yet, the importance of learning and related topics often goes unappreciated by teachers. Preservice teachers are often so concerned about classroom management and student motivation that they do not devote much thought to what to teach and how to teach it. Even many inservice teachers are prone to leave these issues to curriculum developers. Thus, research on teacher planning reveals that most teachers concentrate on procedures such as preparing to work through the lesson following the instructions in the manual without much thought about purposes such as making sure that they understand what knowledge or skills the lesson is intended to develop and how to assess whether or not these purposes have been achieved. Furthermore, research on teachers' thinking and decision making during the actual teaching of lessons suggests that most teachers are not well prepared to deal with the problems that arise when lessons do not go smoothly. They are not prepared to make quick and accurate diagnoses of the reasons for these problems, let alone to respond to them effectively on the spot. Even if they have good personal knowledge of their subject matter, they may not have equally good knowledge of *how to teach* the subject matter, and in particular, how to teach the content at hand to this group of students under the present circumstances. Eventually, most teachers realize that curriculum developers cannot insure success but can only provide materials and suggestions for teachers to use. Teachers must be prepared to carry the content to their students personally rather than to depend on texts to do so, especially with younger students and with slower students of any age.

This preparation begins with fundamental understanding of student learning processes, which are the focus of the next four chapters. Chapter 6 provides an overview. It defines and differentiates learning from several related but different concepts, identifies different types and levels of learning and the different forms of instruction that are associated with them, and illustrates how this information is needed for establishing instructional objectives and planning instruction, practice, application, and evaluation activities that are consistent with those objectives.

The next three chapters review theory and research on human learning, organizing the material according to the three major paradigms that have dominated work in this area. Chapter 7 covers the behavioristic tradition beginning with early research on the conditioning of animal behavior, continuing through Skinner's operant conditioning and Bandura's social learning theory, and culminating with contemporary applications such as programmed instruction, computerized instruction, and instructional applications of modeling and cognitive behavior modification.

Chapter 8 describes the cognitive structuralist approach to learning, which stresses the importance of arranging conditions so that learners can understand input as an organized body of meaningful concepts and information rather than as a seemingly random list of things to memorize. Bruner's ideas about arranging conditions to encourage learners to discover key concepts and relationships for themselves are covered in this chapter, as are Ausubel's ideas about organizing and sequencing expository instruction to maximize meaningful reception learning.

Chapter 9 concludes Part III by describing information about learning contributed by theorists who are interested in how humans attend to subsets of the input that is available at any particular time, process this limited input in short-term memory, encode it for storage in long-term memory, and retrieve it for use later. These theorists stress that learning is an active process that involves making sense of new input by interpreting it within previously developed schemas, and they stress the importance of teaching learners to process information in active ways by making rote learning more meaningful and meaningful learning more deliberate and systematic.

Chapter 6

Introduction to the Psychology of Learning

OBJECTIVES

When you have mastered the material in this chapter you will be able to

1. Define learning accurately and distinguish it from related concepts
2. Distinguish figurative knowledge from operative knowledge, intentional learning from incidental learning, rote learning from meaningful learning, and reception learning from discovery learning
3. Classify different learning objectives according to the Bloom taxonomy
4. Classify different levels of learning according to the Gagné hierarchy and different types of learning according to the Gagné and Briggs typology
5. State the different learning conditions required to accomplish different types of learning objectives
6. Formulate learning objectives that operationalize curricular roles accurately and function as effective guides to the planning of instruction, practice, and evaluation

This is the first of four chapters on the broad topic of the psychology of learning. In this chapter we will define learning, identify different types of learning, and show how this information is used to establish learning objectives when planning instruction.

Definition of Learning

Learning must be defined carefully to differentiate it from related concepts such as thinking, behavior, development, or change. Wittrock (1977) defines it this way: "Learning is the term we use to describe the processes involved in changing through experience. It is the process of acquiring relatively permanent change in understanding, attitude, knowledge, information, ability, and skill through experience" (p. ix).

Defined this way, learning is an internal, cognitive event that cannot be equated with observable performance. It is true that learning produces changes in capacity for performance, and that we must observe changes in performance in order to infer that learning has occurred. It is also true that certain kinds of learning, especially motor learning, are refined through practice. Nevertheless, the performance potential acquired through learning is not the same as its reproduction or application in any particular performance situation. Furthermore, relationships between prior learning and subsequent performance are imperfect at best. The absence of a particular behavior does not mean that the person does not know anything about it, and the disappearance of a behavior observed in the past does not mean that it has been forgotten or that the ability to perform it has been lost. Nor does particular performance necessarily reflect the learning that we may associate with it (sometimes success is due to luck or guesswork rather than knowledge).

Learning and change

Learning involves change, but only some kinds of changes qualify as learning. Because learning involves relatively permanent change, it does not include temporary situational phenomena such as random behavioral variation or the effects of drugs or fatigue. Also, because learning refers to change produced by experience, it does not include change produced by other factors such as physical growth, maturation, or senility.

Development versus learning

Learning is more difficult to differentiate from development. Traditionally, learning was seen as primarily dependent on the environment, whereas development was seen as partly dependent on internal maturation. Also, learning psychologists typically studied problems involving manipulation of the environment (particularly reinforcement contingencies), while developmental psychologists tried to identify progressive age differences and universals across individuals and cultures. However, these differences have become blurred in recent years. Learning psychologists (Weinstein & Mayer, 1985; Anderson, 1984; Corno & Rohrkemper, 1985) have begun to emphasize active information processing and other activities that occur within learners in addition to events that occur in the environment, and developmental psychologists (Palincsar & Brown, 1984) have begun to study environmentally induced changes that involve little or no biological maturation. Thus, at present, the differences are more in the emphasis and methods of study than in substance. We have presented the information generated by these two major approaches to psychology in separate sections in order to make it easier for you to learn, but the two kinds of information are complementary, and you will need to draw on both in thinking about students and their instructional needs.

Thinking versus learning

Finally, learning is not the same as thinking, although these two processes are closely linked and mutually supportive. Thinking is a broad term that refers to the exercise or application of cognitive skills like posing and attempting to answer questions, searching memory, processing information, and evaluating potential solutions to problems. When applied in routine fashion to familiar content, thinking is mere exercise of already learned cognitive skills, analogous to the exercise of physical skills. However, thinking can produce learning. This occurs routinely when the cognitive skills involved in thinking are used to process new input, and it also occurs when reflection on prior experience yields new insights. The latter kind of learning occurs frequently and is of considerable importance, which is why we define learning as change induced through experience (which includes inner reflection) rather than defining it more restrictively as change induced through encounters with the external environment. Although all learning is ultimately traceable at least in part to environmental events, only a portion of our learning involves adaptation to events occurring in the immediate external environment. Other portions, which assume more and more importance with age, involve either reflecting on past experiences or manipulating abstract concepts that we have never encountered in concrete form in the external environment.

In summary, learning is a relatively permanent change in capacity for performance, acquired through experience. The experience may involve overt interaction with the external environment, but it also will involve and sometimes will be confined to covert cognitive processes.

Qualitative Distinctions

A great many theories of learning and ideas about instruction have been proposed. For the most part, these are simply different and complementary rather than contradictory, because they were developed with different kinds of learning and instruction in mind. There is no single theory or brief list of principles that fits all learning situations equally well. Thus, it will be important for you to be able to recognize different kinds of learning situations so as to be able to apply appropriate concepts and strategies to them. To help you do so, we will now present several qualitative distinctions and then cover popular typologies that have proven useful for conceptualizing learning and instruction.

Developmental Stages

One way of classifying different types of learning has already been discussed in the previous section on development—classifying according to the different information processing skills or cognitive operations that develop with age. Thus, Piaget (1970) speaks of sensorimotor, concrete, and formal operational thinking. Similarly, Bruner (1964) speaks of learning as involving enactive, iconic, or symbolic knowledge (see Chapter 8). Klausmeier (1976) and others have also developed classification schemes that reflect developmental phenomena. These schemes help us to appreciate the qualitative changes that can occur in knowledge about particular topics (movement from concrete toward increasingly abstract knowledge, and from isolated toward increasingly integrated knowledge), and they remind us that learning experiences are likely to be more meaningful when they involve opportunities to actively manipulate concrete stimuli than when they are confined to verbal communication of abstract content.

"Knowledge That" versus "Knowledge How"

Figurative versus operative knowledge

In Chapter 3 we covered Piaget's concepts of figurative and operative knowledge. Figurative knowledge (also called declarative knowledge, propositional knowledge, or theoretical knowledge) is "knowledge that." It is intellectual knowledge of facts and principles. Operative knowledge (also called procedural knowledge or practical knowledge) is "knowledge how." It is the ability to perform tasks and solve problems. Ideally, an individual possesses both these kinds of knowledge and is able to use them in an integrated, mutually supportive fashion in solving problems. Often, however, just one of these forms of knowledge predominates. For example, most baseball pitchers talented enough to throw a major league curve ball do not have well articulated figurative knowledge of the principles of physics that explain why a curve ball curves, and most physicists who possess this figurative knowledge are nevertheless unable to throw a major league curve ball. One frequent criticism of schooling is that too much of what is taught is confined to figurative knowledge that never becomes very meaningful or useful to the students because they do not get enough opportunities to link it to operative knowledge developed through application exercises. Such criticisms have led, for example, to the inclusion of laboratory experiences in science and foreign language classes.

Intentional versus Incidental Learning

Intentional learning is consciously goal directed—a person intends to learn certain things and deliberately sets out to do so. Incidental learning is learning that occurs without deliberate intention. Much incidental learning occurs when the person is in a relatively passive state, responding to the environment but not actively pursuing specific goals. For example, if you are a typical American, you have watched hundreds of television shows dealing with crime and law enforcement, and have done so primarily to be entertained rather than to develop knowledge. Yet, in the process you have learned the meanings of many specialized terms used in police stations and courtrooms, and you probably could "read" prisoners their rights or swear in witnesses using what you remember from seeing these activities modeled by actors. Less incidental learning occurs during times when people are actively seeking to learn, because most of their attention is focused on the material to be learned intentionally. Even so, some incidental learning occurs under focused intentional learning conditions. In classrooms, for example, students incidentally learn a great deal about the mannerisms and personal attributes of instructors, even though the students are concentrating on intentional learning of the content of the course.

Rote versus Meaningful Learning

Discussions of the rote/meaningful dimension and the reception/discovery dimension are among the many important contributions of David Ausubel to the psychology of learning (Ausubel & Robinson, 1969). Both dimensions refer to situations in which learners are attempting to learn facts, concepts, or other meaningful information. The rote/discovery dimension refers to the learner's approach to the task. To the extent that learners merely attempt to memorize the new information without relating it to their existing knowledge, they are engaging in rote learning. To the extent that they attempt to retain the idea by relating it to what they already know and thereby making sense of it, they are engaging in meaningful learning. Meaningful learning is retained longer than rote learning (material memorized for a test through "cramming" is soon forgotten), and it is much more efficient since a few general principles can accommodate a great many specific applications. Consequently, it is important for teachers to learn to present information in ways that make it meaningful to their students, and to teach students the strategies for engaging in meaningful learning. Many students overuse inefficient rote memorizing strategies because they have never been taught to use meaningful learning strategies.

Reception versus Discovery Learning

The reception/discovery dimension refers to the means by which the knowlege is made available to learners. In reception learning, this knowledge is presented to learners in its final form, typically through expository instruction that states the information and then elaborates or provides examples. In discovery learning, learners are exposed to experiences and guidance designed to lead them to discover the target information or principle. Discovery learning in school involves instruction in the sense that a planned series of questions or experiences is used to guide the learners toward the target discovery, but the instructor does not present the target information to the learners in its final form, except perhaps to summarize and elaborate on it after the learners have discovered it for themselves. Like the rote versus meaningful distinction, the reception versus discovery distinction refers to a continuous dimension that varies by degrees. Combination forms involving varying degrees of reception and discovery learning occur in between the extremes of pure reception learning at one end of the dimension and pure discovery learning at the other end.

Ausubel has performed an important service by showing that these two dimensions (rote/meaningful and reception/discovery) are separate, and that although meaningful learning is generally superior to rote learning, discovery learning is not necessarily superior to reception learning. It is true that discovery learning is active by definition and is likely to produce long lasting, meaningful knowledge when successful. It is also true, however, that discovery learning is time consuming and otherwise inefficient, and that it can become confusing or frustrating if not handled carefully. Thus, discovery learning is more appropriate for some objectives than for others, and even when appropriate, it involves moving students through a well-planned series of structured experiences rather than merely exposing them to the content in some haphazard way and hoping that they will discover the target learning.

Expository instruction

Just as discovery learning is not necessarily effective, reception learning is not necessarily ineffective. Expository instruction (lectures, demonstrations, and other organized information presentations) designed to produce reception learning is often stereotyped (by people who confuse the rote/meaningful dimension with the reception/discovery dimension of learning) as producing only parrot-like repetition or rote memorization of isolated facts. In fact, expository teaching designed to produce meaningful reception learning is often an efficient and otherwise appropriate method of instruction. It is especially useful for conveying well articulated and organized bodies of knowledge, and consequently it is the primary method of instruction (partly through teacher lectures but mostly through texts) used in schools once students master basic tool skills (i.e., starting around the fourth grade and increasingly thereafter). Expository instruction and reception learning can be ineffective, of course, if addressed to inappropriate content (isolated facts without general organizing principles) or if overused to the point that instruction concentrates on knowledge and comprehension objectives to the exclusion of higher level cognitive objectives. In subsequent chapters, we will discuss when to use each approach effectively.

Learning Typologies

In addition to these qualitative distinctions, learning theorists have proposed typologies that distinguish several different types of learning according to differences in what is being learned. Two of the best known and most useful of these typologies are the taxonomy of cognitive objectives published by Bloom et al. (1956) and the classifications and learning hierarchies published by Gagné (1977) and Gagné and Briggs (1979).

Bloom's Taxonomy

Recognizing the potential value of a classification scheme that would define different kinds of learning objectives and identify them with standardized terminology, a group of educational psychology and measurement experts surveyed taxonomies existing in the early 1950s and sought to develop a common scheme. The most immediate and influential result of their work was a taxonomy of educational objectives in the cognitive domain (Bloom et al., 1956), which is often called "Bloom's taxonomy" for short. Other taxonomies were published later for objectives in the affective (Krathwohl, Bloom, & Masia, 1964) and psychomotor (Harrow, 1972) domains, but these have not influenced developers of curriculum and instruction as much as the taxonomy of cognitive objectives has.

Major categories in Bloom's taxonomy

The six major categories in Bloom's taxonomy are shown in Table 6.1 (Bloom et al., 1956 also list numerous subcategories within these six major categories). Educators find this taxonomy useful because it includes most of the goals stressed by schools and describes them in commonly used language, although educators in mathematics and science may prefer the term "problem solving" to the term "analysis," which is used more in the humanities.

Imperfections in theory

Like most taxonomies, this one can be criticized on several grounds. First, the boundary between comprehension and application is fuzzy, so that certain academic activities could seemingly be placed in either category (Ausubel & Robinson, 1969). Second, although the categories are intended to be sequenced from low to high in cognitive level, this sequencing has been questioned on the basis of both logical considerations (Furst, 1981) and empirical data (Kunen, Cohen, & Solman, 1981; Seddon, 1978). In particular, many writers believe that synthesis, rather than evaluation, should be placed at the highest level. Third, the notion of cognitive level as reflected in the taxonomy is sometimes confused with the notion of difficulty level of a task or question. In fact, these concepts are independent. A "low level" knowledge item (name Henry the Eighth's fourth wife) is extremely difficult if you don't know the answer or how to get it, and yet you may be able to respond to "high level" synthesis or evaluation tasks (evaluate the theory that all wars ultimately result from economic causes) with some degree of success even if you have little organized knowledge about the topic.

Despite these imperfections, Bloom's taxonomy is very useful to keep in mind when planning or assessing instruction. Implicitly at least, we as a society want many aspects of the school curriculum taught so that effective learning occurs at all six of the levels in the taxonomy. Yet, critical analyses of curriculum and instruction typically reveal that very high percentages of textbook content, practice exercises, and classroom activities focus on the knowledge and comprehension levels, with little attention to higher levels (Freeman et al., 1983; Gall, 1970; Trachtenberg, 1974). The same is true of the tests used to assess learning. The lesson here is obvious: To the extent that we expect students to master learning objectives that go beyond the

Table 6.1 Outline of Bloom's Taxonomy of Educational Objectives in the Cognitive Domain

Category	General Description of Category	Illustrative Items
I. Knowledge (a) of *Specifics* (terminology, facts) (b) of *Ways and Means of Dealing with Specifics* (conventions, classifications, criteria, methodology) (c) of *Universals and Abstractions* (principles, generalizations, theories)	*Recall* of specifics and universals, methods, and processes, pattern, structure of setting. Knowledge objectives emphasize most the psychological processes of *remembering*.	About what proportion of the population of Canada is living in cities? 1. 10% 2. 20% 3. 40% 4. 50% 5. 60% (Knowledge of specific fact) The volume of a given mass of gas varies directly as the ______ and inversely as the ______. 1. pressure and temperature 2. temperature and pressure 3. atomic weight and pressure 4. temperature and atomic weight (Knowledge of principles and generalizations)
II. Comprehension (a) Translation (b) Interpretation (c) Extrapolation	Lowest level of understanding of what is communicated. Can use idea being communicated without necessarily being able to relate it to other ideas or see all its implications.	Four less than three times a certain number equals eight. In algebra this may be expressed as: 1. $4 - 3X = 8$ 3. $3X - 4 = 8$ 2. $4X - 3 = 8$ 4. $4 + 3X = 8$ (Translation)*
III. Application	The use of abstractions in particular and concrete situations.	Two basic laws governing an electrical circuit are: Voltage = (Current) × (Resistance) Power = (Voltage) × (Current) If an electric iron develops greater resistance (rust, etc.) its power will: 1. increase 2. remain the same 3. decrease

IV. Analysis (a) of *Elements* (b) of *Relationships* (c) of *Organizational Principles*	Breakdown of a communication into its constituent parts, such that relative hierarchy of ideas is made clearer and/or the relations between the ideas expressed are made clear.	The given figure represents a hoop of 28 in. diameter. If the hoop is rolling without slipping in the indicated direction, how many inches has point *A* moved horizontally when the hoop has finished half a turn? ($\pi = 22/7$) (Analysis of Relationships)*
V. Synthesis (a) Production of a unique communication (b) Production of a plan (c) Derivation of a set of abstract relations	Putting together of parts to form a whole; analyzing and combining pieces in such a way as to constitute a pattern or structure not clearly there before.	Without adding all items, find the sum of: $\frac{1}{1 \times 2} + \frac{1}{2 \times 3} + \frac{1}{3 \times 4} + \frac{1}{4 \times 5} \cdots \frac{1}{98 \times 99} + \frac{1}{99 \times 100}$ *
IV. Evaluation (a) *Judgments in terms of internal criteria* (b) *Judgments in terms of external evidence*	Making judgments about the value of material and methods for given purposes. Judging extent to which material and methods satisfy given criteria.	The ability to indicate logical fallacies in arguments (Internal Evidence) Ability to compare a work with highest known standards in its field. (External Criteria)

* Illustrative items from Avital and Shettleworth (1968).

Source: Adapted from B. S. Bloom (ed.), *Taxonomy of Educational Objectives: The Classification of Educational Goals, Book 1: Cognitive Domain.* White Plains, NY: Longman, 1985. Reprinted by permission of Longman Inc.

knowledge and comprehension levels, we will need to provide those students with instruction and practice/application opportunities geared to these higher cognitive levels, and to see that objectives at these levels are given sufficient attention in our assessment programs.

Gagné's Learning Varieties and Hierarchies

Besides the Bloom taxonomy, the best known systems for classifying types of learning are those developed by Robert Gagné and published either on his own (Gagné, 1972, 1977, 1984) or in collaboration with Leslie Briggs (Gagné & Briggs, 1979).

The Gagné Learning Hierarchy. Gagné began with a behavioristic orientation toward work in the experimental psychology of learning, but with interests in the different types of learning and their relationships to one another. This led him to develop typologies called learning hierarchies, in which learning tasks were identified and arranged in sequences from the simplest to the most complex. His first learning hierarchy (Gagné, 1970) contained eight categories, but he later simplified these to the following seven (Gagné, 1977):

Learning hierarchies

1. *Signal learning*—Learning a general, diffuse response to a signal (learning to stop socializing and prepare for class when the bell rings; responding with fear when being overtaken by a police car with flashing lights).
2. *Stimulus-response learning*—Learning to make a precise response to a discriminated stimulus (to pronounce words on sight, to call people by their names, to produce and use the particular key needed to open a particular lock).
3. *Chaining*—Learning to link two or more previously learned stimulus-response connections (sounding out the individual letters in a word and then blending these sounds to form the word itself; combining letters to form words when writing).
4. *Verbal association*—Learning to link combinations of words as stimuli with other words as responses (recognizing whole words on sight when reading; translating foreign words and phrases into English).
5. *Discrimination learning*—Distinguishing among members of a set of similar stimuli so as to respond to each appropriately and individually (identify different breeds of dog; rely on context to identify the intended usage of words that have several meanings when listening to an oral presentation; use the proper versions of homonyms when writing).
6. *Concept learning*—Learning to identify individual objects, events, or ideas as members of a common general class (identify the subjects and predicates of sentences; understand and be able to identify instances of concepts such as "peninsula," "prime number," or "solvent").

7. *Rule learning*—Learning general rules or principles with sufficient understanding to be able to recognize their applications to particular situations or to be able to use them to solve problems (using the rules of English grammar and composition when writing prose; using basic mathematical principles to reduce or enlarge recipes or to determine how much paint or fertilizer to purchase).

Gagné's learning hierarchy uses more specialized terms than the Bloom taxonomy, and it makes finer distinctions among types of learning placed at the low and middle levels of the Bloom taxonomy. On the other hand, it makes fewer distinctions at the higher levels. Consequently, Gagné's scheme is more suited to the simple and relatively isolated types of learning taught in the primary grades than to the organized bodies of knowledge taught in higher grades.

The Gagné and Briggs Typology. As Gagné's interests shifted toward the education and training applications of the psychology of learning, his approach to classification became broader in scope and more concentrated on higher levels of learning. In addition, he shifted from a focus on what is learned toward a focus on the capabilities that learners acquire. Gagné and Briggs (1979) identified five major types of learning:

Learning capabilities

1. *Attitudes*—Internal states that influence learners' personal action choices.
2. *Motor skills*—Organized movements of the skeletal muscles that learners use to accomplish purposeful actions.
3. *Information*—Facts and organized knowledge about the world stored in learners' memories.
4. *Intellectual skills*—Skills that permit learners to carry out symbol-based procedures (these are subdivided into discriminations, concrete concepts, defined concepts, rules, and higher order rules).
5. *Cognitive strategies*—Strategies that learners bring to bear on their own cognitive processing in order to control their thinking or learning or to originate novel solutions to problems.

These varieties of learning capability are shown in Table 6.2, which also includes examples of each type as well as action verbs that apply when these capabilities are translated into performance.

The Gagné and Briggs scheme is comparable to the Bloom taxonomy in that it defines several categories of cognitive learning, identifies them with common terms, and is useful in planning or assessing instruction. Although there is some overlap, the two systems are largely complementary (in particular, the Gagné and Briggs system distinguishes among several types of learning that are included within the comprehension and application levels of the Bloom system, but the highest levels of the Bloom system are not addressed in the Gagné and Briggs system). Consequently, analyses of instruction that draw on both systems are likely to be more complete and informative than analyses that use only one.

Table 6.2 Standard Verbs to Describe Human Capabilities, with Examples of Phrases Incorporating Action Verbs

Capability	Capability Verb	Example (Action Verb in Italics)
Intellectual skill discrimination	DISCRIMINATES	Discriminates, by *matching* French sounds of "*u*" and "*ou*"
Concrete concept	IDENTIFIES	Identifies, by *naming*, the root, leaf, and stem of representative plants
Defined concept	CLASSIFIES	Classifies, by using a *definition*, the concept "family"
Rule	DEMONSTRATES	Demonstrates, by *solving* verbally stated examples, the addition of positive and negative numbers
Higher-order rule (problem solving)	GENERATES	Generates, by *synthesizing* applicable rules, a paragraph describing a person's actions in a situation of fear
Cognitive strategy	ORIGINATES	Originates a solution to the reduction of air pollution, by *applying model* of gaseous diffusion
Information	STATES	States orally the major issues in the presidential campaign of 1932
Motor skill	EXECUTES	Executes *backing* a car into driveway
Attitude	CHOOSES	Chooses *playing golf* as a leisure activity

Source: From *Principles of Instructional Design*, 2/e, by Robert M. Gagne and Leslie J. Briggs. Copyright © 1979 by Holt, Rinehart and Winston. Reprinted by permission of CBS College Publishing.

Internal and external conditions

Conditions of Learning. Gagné (1977) and Gagné and Briggs (1979) not only present systems for classifying different kinds of learning but also offer guidelines about the different types of instruction that each type of learning requires. In particular, they speak of the conditions of learning that must be established for each type of learning to occur. These include both internal and external conditions. Internal conditions refer to events occurring within the learner, especially recall and activation of previously learned information, concepts, or skills that the new learning must build on. External conditions refer to events in the environment, particularly instructional events that activate and support learning processes. The conditions of learning are different for each type of learning.

Attitude Learning. Attitudes are affective or emotional responses—preferences, likes and dislikes, approach or avoidance tendencies. Gagné and Briggs believe that attitudes are acquired primarily through exposure to respected models who exhibit the attitudes, rather than through more typical instructional procedures. However, they do note that attitudes can also be stimulated through persuasive communication (if the learner accepts rather than resists the message) and can be conditioned through experience by rewarding or punishing events (people who enjoy early success at activities such as playing musical instruments or solving mathematical problems may believe that they have talent for these activities and come to enjoy them, but people who encounter early frustration may conclude that they lack talent and come to dislike them).

Attitude learning clearly deserves to be classified as a form of learning, because it does involve relatively permanent changes acquired through experience. It also assumes knowledge of relevant information and concepts. Even so, we cannot teach an attitude the way we would teach the concept of a triangle. We can try to stimulate attitudes indirectly through modeling, persuasion, or manipulation of incentives, but we cannot produce them directly through instruction because they involve elements of emotional involvement and personal commitment that can come only from the learners themselves.

These are important qualitative differences between attitude learning and other forms of learning. Because attitudes are developed through general socialization mechanisms rather than taught directly through instruction, most of what we have to say about shaping students' attitudes will appear in sections on classroom management and student motivation rather than in sections on learning and instruction.

Motor Learning. Motor learning is the object of instruction in various physical skills. Motor skills are the primary focus of some classes (art, music, physical education, machine shop), and they assume importance in certain academic activities as well (handwriting, illustrating, handling laboratory equipment). It is possible to develop motor skills intuitively through experience, and to sustain them in the form of what Piaget (1970) calls sensorimotor schemes. However, such skills are likely to be learned more efficiently if learners are provided with modeling that they can imitate and with verbal instructions and visual imagery that they can use to guide their performance in addition to opportunities to practice and receive corrective feedback.

Importance of practice

Practice is critical to the development and maintenance of motor skills. Although it is true that a skill such as roller skating that is practiced until it is thoroughly mastered will be retained indefinitely and can be recovered to some degree with relative ease even when it has not been used in years, it is also true that continuous practice is needed to maintain motor skills at high levels of proficiency. This is why professional musicians, dancers, and athletes practice continuously, with attention to fundamentals as well as to higher level accomplishments.

Motor skills, which are the focus of some classes, are best learned through imitation and practice.

To be useful to learners, practice must provide feedback. Motor skill practice induces both internal and external feedback (Adams, 1977). Learners who attend to physical sensations, body images, and other forms of psychomotor feedback can learn to recognize and benefit from those internal sources of information. Baseball or tennis players, for example, can learn to recognize when they are executing a swing successfully so as to meet the ball with the "sweet spot" of the bat or racquet. Sometimes they even utter expletives or sounds of satisfaction as they do so. In addition to this internal feedback, motor skill performance may produce external feedback conveyed through environmental events. One form of external feedback is knowledge of results of their actions that learners can observe for themselves (the flight of the ball as it leaves the bat or the tennis racquet). External feedback can also be supplied through opportunities to observe videotapes of the performance, to get feedback from an instructor, or to compare products of the performance with ideal examples (i.e., to compare a page of printing or a product produced in the wood shop with the model being emulated).

Verbal information

Verbal information can assist motor performance, as the popularity and usefulness of "how to" books attest. However, verbal instructions, and even diagrams or checklists of tips, do not always communicate the desired motor image. We may know that we are supposed to "bend your knees and shift your weight as you swing," and yet we bend our knees too far or shift our weight too soon. Thus, the opportunity to observe models perform motor skills properly may be much more valuable than even a great deal of verbal instruction. This is especially true if the models verbalize their thinking as they perform the activity, thus allowing us to monitor the self-talk that guides behavior in addition to observing the behavior itself.

Bad habit prevention

Feedback presented to the learner is also likely to be more helpful if presented in the same cognitive form that the learner is using than if it is restricted to verbal description (Bruner, 1966). In teaching a golf swing, for example, instructors should not merely model and describe proper form, but also position the learners' bodies properly and physically guide them through proper executions of the swing.

In teaching motor skills, it is especially important to prevent bad habits from developing. Unless they are taught to follow basic principles and use good form, learners may develop motor skills that are functional to some extent but yet inefficient or potentially counterproductive. For example, one of the authors learned to skate "the hard way" as a child and did not find out until well into adulthood upon receiving instruction from an expert that he could achieve better body balance and more speed, and yet use less effort, by capitalizing on principles of good skating form. Meanwhile, the other author learned to write using an unusual slant that wastes half of his paper supply and annoys typists who find it hard to follow. Finally, although the recent upsurge of interest in physical fitness is generally a good thing, it has also led to an upsurge in injuries from running or participating in vigorous activities. Many of these injuries occur because the person uses poor form that unnecessarily stresses some part of the body that then becomes vulnerable to injury. Here again, instruction in good form with attention to eliminating bad habits could minimize this problem.

Information Learning. Superficially, the learning of verbally encoded information is straightforward. If learners know the language in which the information is expressed, and if the message itself is clearly formulated, learners should be able to understand it by relating it to the network of concepts, vocabulary, and verbally articulated experience they have accumulated. In practice, however, things are more complicated. First, the message may or may not be noted or registered when first encountered. Second, even if registered at that time, the message may not be understood exactly as it was intended by the communicator, and its meaning may be transformed over time.

People pick up a great deal of information every day with relative ease. This is especially true in this age of modern communications and in information-rich environments such as schools. Although most students need instruction in how to acquire and retain information through consciously directed learning efforts, the main task facing teachers is directing students' attention to particular information—the information included in the formal school curriculum—and helping them to assimilate and retain it.

Importance of good presentation

This process begins by cueing student attention to relevant information, preferably by stimulating their interest or curiosity. It is also important to see that the students can understand the information in a meaningful fashion by relating it to their existing knowledge. If the message contains undefined terms or makes reference to concepts or events that are unknown to the students, they will not be able to understand and retain it as meaningful information, although they may memorize it long enough to regurgitate it on a test. Finally, even if all of the messages in any particular collection of information are clear and meaningful to the learners, there will be limits on how much information they can retain. More of the information will be remembered when it is presented in an organized fashion and in ways that stimulate students to process it actively and encode it in their own words, such as by including questions on the information that require students to articulate their knowledge of it.

Intellectual Skill Learning. Gagné and Briggs believe that most of the intellectual skills taught in academic classes fall into the following five categories (ordered from simple to complex): discriminations, concrete concepts, defined concepts, rules, and higher-order rules.

Discriminations

Discriminations are capabilities for detecting whether physical stimuli are the same or different, and for responding differently to stimuli that differ on one or more dimensions. Discrimination learning is especially important in early reading and writing, when students must learn to respond differently to different letters that have similar components (b, d, p, q) and to the capital and small versions of the same letter (P, p). Discrimination learning also assumes importance occasionally at higher grade levels such as by hearing subtle sound discriminations in foreign languages that are not made in English, or by noting subtle but important differences in otherwise similar algebraic equations or chemical formulas.

Discriminations are typically taught using the principles of contiguity, feedback, and repetition. That is, the stimuli to be compared are presented either simultaneously (two objects, side by side), or when that is not possible, in rapid succession (one sound followed closely by another sound). This close contiguity between two stimuli facilitates comparison of them. Following presentation of the stimuli, learners are asked to state whether they are the same or different, and their responses are given immediate feedback. Such practice opportunities are repeated until the discrimination is mastered thoroughly.

Concrete concepts

Concrete concepts are capabilities for recognizing that two or more stimuli belong to a class that share a common characteristic or property (red color, round shape, etc.). Once learners "have the concept" of red, for example, they can correctly identify red objects, even though these objects may differ drastically in size, shape, or function.

Concrete concepts are taught by presenting a variety of stimuli that all share the defining attributes of the concept, and pointing out these attributes to learners. In teaching the concept of "apple," for example, one would present apples or pictures of apples that differed in size, shape, and color, noting that all of these were apples. Then, learners would be asked to discriminate apples from nonapples, beginning with easy discriminations of nonexamples that have nothing in common with apples and moving gradually toward the most difficult nonexamples of, say, cherries or pears. Sometimes it is easier to show nonexamples first before introducing positive examples of the concept. In any case, presentation of examples and nonexamples continues until learners can both identify all positive examples (even those that are atypical in appearance, such as caramel apples on sticks) as members of the class and discriminate these from nonexamples (even nonexamples such as pears that share a great many characteristics with typical examples).

Defined concepts

Defined concepts are capabilities for demonstrating the meanings of particular classes of objects, events, or relations. Unlike concrete concepts, which are based on physical attributes that one can point to directly, defined concepts are based on formal definitions (examples: rectangle, iambic pentameter, potential energy, adverb). In the case of defined concepts, learners who "have the concept" not only can state the definition but can show that they understand it by using the term in appropriate contexts in ways that indicate that they assign the appropriate meaning to it.

The terms used to identify defined concepts are often used in less formalized ways to refer to concrete objects or events. The use of the term in everyday language may facilitate learning of the defined concept—for example, hearing various three-sided objects and pictures called "triangles" facilitates understanding of the geometrical definition of a triangle as a three-sided plane figure. Colloquial language can also be confusing, however. In geometry, for example, a point is a specified location in an abstractly defined space, not a dot made with a pencil or the sharpened end of some physical object that "comes to a point." When acquiring defined concepts, students must learn to use them with precision and to avoid meanings or connotations that apply to their colloquial use but not to their formal use.

Defined concepts are typically taught by first stating their definitions and then, as with concrete concepts, by presenting examples and nonexamples. The examples and nonexamples usually must be described verbally rather than shown, however, so that the meaningfulness and ultimate success of the instruction is heavily dependent on learners' familiarity with the vocabulary and concepts used. Where a term is commonly used with colloquial meanings that differ from what is implied by the defined concept, it will be important to make the learners aware of this fact and help them to discriminate the defined concept from related informal concepts.

Rules

Rules have been learned when individuals can repond with regularity in dealing with classes of relationship among classes of objects or events. Much human activity is rule-governed behavior in which general principles are being applied to specific situations. We follow the rules of English grammar, for example, when speaking or writing. This is true, for the most part, even of people who have not received formal instruction in English grammar and who could not verbalize the rules that they follow when they speak or write.

We can, however, receive formal instruction in rules and then learn to apply them in specific situations. In fact, this is the rationale for instructing students in principles of science, mathematics, literary composition, historical analysis, and other academic disciplines. The ability to use defined concepts is one example of rule learning, in this case, the ability to follow a classifying rule. Other rules deal with such relationships as equal to, similar to, greater or less than, or sequential position. As with defined concepts, the ability to state a rule accurately does not necessarily mean that it is understood. Evidence of rule mastery must include demonstrated ability to apply the rule correctly in appropriate contexts.

Rules are usually taught through verbal instruction. Ordinarily this would include a statement of the rule followed by guided practice. Gagné and

Briggs (1979) illustrate rule teaching using as an example the rule for pronouncing words that end in a single consonant followed by a final "e." "The teacher may say, 'Notice that the letter *a* has a long sound when followed by a consonant, in a word that ends in *e*. This is true in words that you know like *made, pale, fate*. When the word does not end in *e*, the letter *a* has a short sound, as in *mad, pal, fat*. Now tell me how to pronounce these words which you may not have seen before: *Dade, pate, kale*.'" (pp. 68–69). The information given to the students prior to asking them to pronounce the new words helps them to remember concepts related to the rule (consonant, short and long sounds) and to arrange these related concepts in appropriate order (consonants followed by a final "e" versus consonants not followed by a final "e").

Higher-order rules

Higher-order rules are invented by learners in order to solve problems that are new to them. Once they invent the rule, they can store it in memory and use it again to solve other problems. Higher-order rules are so called because they are constructed by combining two or more simpler rules that the learner has available to bring to bear on the problem.

Gagné and Briggs (1979) illustrate this process with the following example:

> Suppose that a small car has been parked near a low brick fence, and is discovered to have a flat tire on one of its front wheels. No jack is available, but there is a ten-foot two-by-four, and a piece of sturdy rope. Can the front of the car be raised? In this situation, a possible solution might be found by using the two-by-four as a lever, the wall as a fulcrum, and the rope to secure the end of the lever when the car is in a raised position. (p. 69)

Such a solution would involve "putting together" rules that the learner knows but has never applied to such a problem before: A rule about application of force (to lift the car), a rule about use of a fulcrum (including the recognition that the wall is capable of bearing the estimated weight), and a rule about using leverage to lift weights that cannot be lifted by hand (including recognition that the two-by-four could be used as a lever).

In contrast to the previously described intellectual skills that can be taught directly through expository instruction, the discovery of higher-order rules must be stimulated indirectly by presenting learners with problem-solving situations. The instructor designs or selects the problem-solving situation so that it is suited to the learners (i.e., it presents a problem that the learners cannot solve directly using any of the rules they have been taught already, but that they can solve by combining the rules that they do know into a higher-order rule). In addition, the instructor may want to stimulate or guide discovery by posing a series of questions that will help learners to formulate the problem clearly or to realize that certain familiar rules are applicable to it. The instructor does not, however, "put it all together" for the learners by articulating the higher-order rule directly or teaching it in expository fashion. Thus, higher-order rule learning is discovery learning or problem solving.

Cognitive Strategy Learning. Cognitive strategies refer to the internal control processes by which learners monitor and regulate their thinking and problem solving. When learners have mastered cognitive strategies, they can approach problem solving in self-consciously deliberate and systematic ways that include what have variously been described as "metacognitive awareness skills," "learning to learn skills," "generalized thinking and problem-solving skills," and "cognitive strategies." These strategies, when present, are most evident when learners are confronted with highly novel problems that they must first formulate and then try to solve in some systematic way. To the extent that cognitive strategies are involved in this activity, learners will guide their thinking and behavior with verbally articulated "self-talk" that includes generating relevant questions about the problem, formulating answers to those questions, and organizing the available information into a systematic plan to follow in working out a solution. This activity may also include "internal dialogues" in which learners describe, comment on, review, and criticize their own problem-solving efforts in order to draw conclusions about the appropriateness of the strategies they have been using and to formulate plans for what to do next. In any case, this subjective monitoring and evaluation is directed toward learners' own thinking and problem-solving efforts. This is what makes cognitive strategies different from the intellectual skills described above, which are directed toward manipulation of input from the environment rather than toward control of one's own cognitive activity.

Creation of favorable conditions

Gagné and Briggs believe that cognitive strategies cannot be taught directly or even stimulated in direct ways through guided discovery methods. Instead, they believe that, other than making sure that learners are armed with prerequisite information and intellectual skills, teachers can only create "favorable conditions" for allowing learners to develop cognitive strategies by frequently providing them with opportunities to think creatively or solve novel problems. Other writers, however, believe that cognitive strategy development can be stimulated more directly through modeling, especially modeling in which the model "thinks out loud" to allow the learners to see how he or she generates and uses cognitive strategies in a particular situation (Palincsar & Brown, 1984; Weinstein & Mayer, 1985).

Learning Hierarchies and Task Analysis. In developing his classification systems, Gagné has attempted not only to identify different types of learning, but also to identify hierarchical relationships that exist between the different types. Where a true learning hierarchy exists, the different types can be ordered from simple to complex in such a way that each new type combines or in some way builds on simpler types. The Gagné (1977) typology discussed earlier in this chapter is considered to be a hierarchy in this sense, and so is the intellectual skills section of the Gagné and Briggs (1979) typology shown in Table 6.2. Note that Gagné and Briggs postulate hierarchical relationships only among the subtypes of intellectual skills. That is, their five major categories of learning (attitudes, motor skills, information, intellectual skills, and cognitive strategies) are considered qualitatively different from one another, representing separate domains. However, the five subcategories of intellectual skills all represent the same domain (intellectual skills) and are seen as forming a hierarchy with higher-order rules at the top, followed next by rules and defined concepts (both of these are considered equivalent in the hierarchy), then by concrete concepts, and finally by discriminations. This is because in order to discover a higher-order rule, learners must know various prerequisite rules and defined concepts. Similarly, rules specify relationships between concepts, so knowledge of these concepts is prerequisite to learning of the rules. Similarly, defined concepts often have concrete concepts as referents. Finally, before a concept can be learned, one must be able to make discriminations between critical attributes.

Dunn (1984) characterizes the Gagné hierarchies as incomplete because some intellectual skills are probably left out but are correct as far as they go, since the hypothesized hierarchical relationships between the different skills are apparently correct. He goes on to show that although these hierarchies are used mostly for developing instruction in science and mathematics, they are also applicable to other school subjects such as social studies or driver education, and even to conceptualization of such skills as "knowing when to hold 'em, and knowing when to fold 'em" in poker.

Task analysis procedures

Gagné has shown how information about learning hierarchies can be used for task analysis, which is his term for the process of analyzing learning tasks systematically in order to identify their component parts and decide what needs to be taught and in what order. Curriculum designers and instructional developers routinely rely on task analysis procedures in their work, and classroom teachers will find it useful not only for designing their own lessons but also for preparing to teach lessons using published materials. Lessons often fail because they assume that students have certain prerequisite knowledge or skills that they do not actually have. Lesson preparation that includes task analysis designed to identify these potential problems and formulate ways to deal with them by providing on-the-spot instruction can transform potential lesson failures into mere rough spots. Furthermore, it will leave the teacher in good position to plan remedial instruction for students who need it.

Figure 6.1 shows a learning hierarchy produced by analyzing the prerequisite subtasks involved in oral reading (decoding) of printed text. This scheme would be useful for diagnosing the particular errors that students were making in their oral reading. For example, one student might be mispronouncing certain syllables, while another might be pronouncing individual syllables correctly but failing to blend them properly. Both students may need remedial instruction in subskills before they can be expected to decode successfully, but the first student will need remedial instruction in one set of subskills while the second student will need instruction in a different set.

There is no single correct way to conduct task analyses and identify learning hierarchies, because the number of component parts that could be

Figure 6.1 A Learning Hierarchy for a Basic Reading Skill ("Decoding")

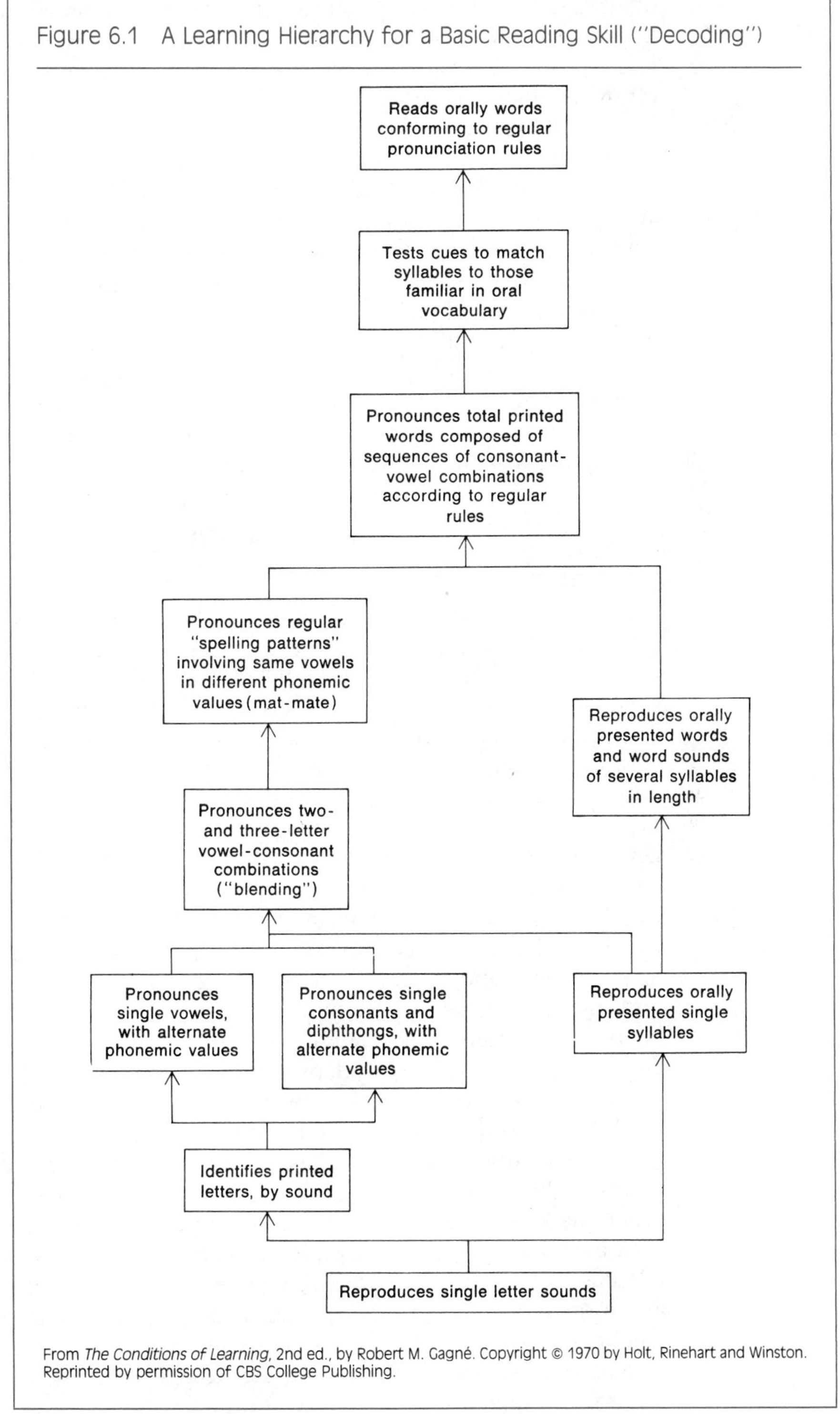

From *The Conditions of Learning*, 2nd ed., by Robert M. Gagné. Copyright © 1970 by Holt, Rinehart and Winston. Reprinted by permission of CBS College Publishing.

identified is theoretically infinite. However, it is usually easy to identify component parts that correspond to learning objectives taught previously, and to identify ways to move students from where they are now toward ultimate objectives by proceeding systematically through the identified learning hierarchy.

Preparation for instruction

Task analysis will be treated in more detail in Chapter 11. For now, bear in mind that wise teachers prepare for instruction not only by thinking about their own teaching goals but also by putting themselves in their students' places by analyzing the assumptions and demands built into the tasks that they assign. It may be that the instructions are confusing or ambiguous, that the examples are poor, or that the task calls for use of some concept or skill that the students may not possess. Teachers who make themselves aware of these problems can prevent needless confusion and frustration by changing or improving on these assignments or by providing more clarity, better examples, or needed preparatory instruction when presenting the assignments to the students.

Instructional Objectives

Educational institutions are established to achieve certain goals. In the case of the public schools, these goals are very general and often vague (e.g., to provide students with the knowledge and skills they need to function effectively as citizens in our society). Training in military and industrial settings has more specific goals such as to teach students to function effectively as fighter pilots or auto mechanics, but even these goals do not provide much guidance about what should be taught or how to teach it. Before these general educational goals can be accomplished, curriculum developers must develop, and instructors must implement, instructional sequences designed to begin where the learners are at entry level and move them gradually toward the ultimate goals. In general, then, academic activities and the teacher and student behaviors associated with them are means toward ends rather than ends in themselves, although it is easy to lose sight of this fact once you settle into "the daily grind." Education is likely to be more coherent and effective to the extent that curriculum developers, teachers, and students remain aware of the purposes of activities and of how they relate to one another and fit within the big picture.

Formulation of objectives

One way to do this is to formulate and use instructional objectives in planning instructional sequences. Clear objectives provide guidance to teachers about what to teach and how to teach it, about what students should have learned and how to evaluate it, and about what kinds of feedback to give to students. They also provide guidance to students about what to study and how to study it. These benefits are most likely to accrue when attention is focused on the students, rather than on the content to be taught, in formulating instructional objectives. That is, instructional objectives are best formulated by stating what students should be able to do following completion of the instruction.

This approach to formulation and use of instructional objectives was popularized by Mager (1962). He adopted a behavioristic approach to the topic, stressing that instructional objectives should be stated with reference to specific behaviors that can be observed and measured. Thus, he argued that objective statements such as "the student will understand two-digit subtraction" should be avoided in favor of statements such as "the student will be able to solve 50 two-digit problems in eight minutes, with no more than one error." Specifically, Mager argued that instructional objectives should include three key elements:

1. Clear specification of the target behavior (solve two-digit subtraction problems correctly).
2. Specification of the conditions under which this behavior will be demonstrated (a 50-item test).
3. Specification of the criteria for acceptable performance (completion of the 50 problems within eight minutes with no more than one error).

Behavioral objectives approach

Even though Mager used the term "instructional objectives" in the title of his book, his emphasis on stating objectives in precise and measurable behavioral terms led to the popularizing of the term behavioral objectives, which soon became associated not only with Mager but with a particular approach to curriculum planning and control. In its most extreme form, the behavioral objectives approach involved expressing the entire curriculum as behavioral objectives, sequencing these objectives in some sensible way, and developing materials and methods for both instruction and evaluation of each objective. The worst versions were unwieldy and overly rigid, confronting teachers with hundreds of objectives to be taught in a given order using particular materials and following prescribed practices. In other situations, teachers continued to use the curricula they were using, but were pressured to justify all of their instructional activities by stating behavioral objectives for them, even when the objectives were more cognitive or affective (enjoyment, appreciation) than behavioral. Sometimes, teachers were required to drop activities that could not be so "justified." Consequently, the term "behavioral objectives" carries negative connotations for many educators.

For this reason, and also because we do not believe that all instructional objectives can or should be stated strictly according to Mager's criteria, we will not use the term "behavioral objectives." However, we will use the terms "instructional objectives" or simply "objectives."

Specific statements of learning outcomes

Gronlund (1985) distinguishes between general instructional objectives and more specific statements of intended learning outcomes. He recommends that general objectives be stated using verb forms that communicate what students will be expected to be able to do on completion of instruction but that are general enough to encompass a domain of student performance that would include many more specific activities. He recommends eight to twelve general instructional objectives for an entire course, and perhaps two to four general objectives for a brief unit. General objectives for a science course, for example, might include knowing the meanings of terms,

In a laboratory class, students understand laboratory procedures and have the skills necessary for performing experiments and analyzing results.

knowing specific facts, knowing laboratory procedures, understanding concepts and principles, applying concepts and principles to new situations, demonstrating skills and abilities needed to conduct an experiment, interpreting data in scientific reports, and displaying a scientific attitude.

In planning particular activities, more specific objectives would be developed within these general ones. The general science objective "knows laboratory procedures," for example, might be broken down into subobjectives such as selecting appropriate equipment for a given experiment, assembling the equipment correctly, manipulating it appropriately, measuring accurately with measuring devices, following safety rules, and cleaning and returning the equipment properly. Similarly, a general language arts objective such as "writes effective compositions" might be broken into subobjectives such as expressing ideas clearly; relating ideas to the main thesis; developing the thesis in an organized way; writing well structured, relevant paragraphs; using correct grammar; and minimizing spelling errors.

We believe that attention to such objectives should be an important part of instructional planning. As long as it is not carried to extremes, the process of formulating instructional objectives and using them to guide the development and evaluation of instruction is likely to have the beneficial effects mentioned above. This is shown in the following example.

Using Instructional Objectives: An Example

Mrs. Wolfe is a junior high school physical education teacher who plans to teach a six-week unit on basketball. How can she use this time most effectively? Which knowledge and skill objectives should she concentrate on as the "core curriculum," and which should be touched on only briefly or not at all? There are no simple "right answers" to these questions. A range of objectives and associated activities might be appropriate for Mrs. Wolfe's students, depending on their presently existing knowledge and skill levels and on how basketball instruction fits into the larger program of physical education at the school as seen by Mrs. Wolfe and the other physical education teachers.

Given these considerations and her knowledge about what is reasonable to accomplish in a six-week unit, Mrs. Wolfe will have to formulate instructional objectives that address one or more of the three major domains of learning: 1) *affective objectives* (stimulate appreciation for the game by emphasizing teamwork, sharing, coordinated body movement, and general aspects of play); 2) *cognitive objectives* (develop the students' knowledge of rules, infractions, and concepts underlying strategies for offensive and defensive play); and 3) *psychomotor objectives* (teach the students to dribble, pass, shoot, and rebound). Mrs. Wolfe's selection of objectives for her unit will determine what activities will be included and how much time will be allocated to each. These decisions will also determine what Mrs. Wolfe should stress in evaluating the effectiveness of her instruction (i.e., evaluation should concentrate on assessing student attainment of the unit's objectives, and not on matters that were not taught at all or were only mentioned in passing).

For example, to the extent that Mrs. Wolfe decides to emphasize cognitive objectives, she will need to provide the students with topic outlines and textual material, to deliver lectures and present slides or films, to conduct recitation and discussion lessons, and to administer written tests. In contrast, to the extent that she wishes to emphasize psychomotor objectives, she will need to explain and demonstrate skills, observe and provide feedback to students as they practice these skills in the gym, provide opportunities for students to blend and apply these skills during drills and controlled scrimmages, and possibly evaluate skill development using performance checklists or other methods of observing and rating the quality of physical skill performance.

Mrs. Wolfe probably will want to include both cognitive and psychomotor objectives in her basketball unit, integrating them as much as possible. In teaching a jump shot, for example, she would provide the students with information about when and how to use the shot, with verbal description of procedures to follow or steps to go through in executing the shot, and with modeling accompanied by verbalization of the self-talk, visual-motor imagery, or kinesthetic feedback that can be used to guide the shot during its execution. However, if she wants her students to become skilled jump shooters, she will have to go beyond this figurative knowledge and give them opportunities to develop operative knowledge by practicing jump shooting both in skill drills and in game situations. Furthermore, if she wants to assess whether her objective has been met, she will need to assess actual jump shooting under specified conditions, and not merely assess whether students can label a picture of a jump shot correctly or answer essay questions about jump shooting technique.

Attention to instructional objectives

In the process of expressing her general goal (teaching basketball) in terms of specific instructional objectives, Mrs. Wolfe will develop clarity about her own values and priorities—what she thinks students, or at least these particular students, should learn about basketball. These may be quite different from the priorities of another teacher assigned to the same course, even one who is ostensibly teaching the same things. For example, two teachers may agree to concentrate on psychomotor skills during a basketball unit, but one may stress general body skills like running, jumping, or pivoting while the other may stress ball skills like passing, dribbling, or shooting. Thus, attention to instructional objectives helps teachers become aware of similarities and differences that may exist in the same course as it is taught in different sections. Such information is important for curriculum control (making sure that objectives considered essential are covered adequately in each section), and discussion of differences helps to broaden teachers' perspectives on how instruction at their grade level and subject matter can be approached.

Once a list of instructional objectives is drawn up, the teacher can assess it for feasibility and consider its implications for the nature and sequencing of instructional activities to be included within the unit. Often it will be necessary to compromise by reducing the number of objectives to be addressed or by addressing certain objectives in less depth than had been planned originally. Mrs. Wolfe, for example, may decide that her students will need to know about basic rule infractions so that they can avoid them in playing the game, but that they will not need to know the referees' signals associated with various infractions. Similarly, she may decide that she has time to cover both jump shots and hook shots, but only if she sticks to the basic forms and only teaches the students to shoot directly at the basket. Another teacher in the same situation might decide to ignore hook shots and concentrate on jump shots, but to teach several variations on basic jump shooting form and to teach the students to use the backboard in addition to shooting directly for the basket. Each teacher's choices can be supported with a sensible rationale, but each involves trade-offs—learning some things at the expense of others. However, because both teachers are clear about their respective objectives, both are likely to achieve them. The same could not be said of teachers who teach haphazardly or who try to cram so much into the unit that nothing is covered in sufficient depth.

Guidelines for Using Instructional Objectives

Learning situations are likely to be most effective when most of the learning is intentional—when you as the teacher know what you want to accomplish and how you intend to accomplish it, and your students know what is expected of them. This is especially true when planning includes attention to the steps that students must go through in the process of moving toward the ultimate objectives and not merely attention to what the teacher will do. In planning this kind of instruction, and even in implementing instruction using plans and materials developed by others, it is useful to formulate instructional objectives and use these to guide both instruction and evaluation. In doing so, keep in mind the following three general principles.

General principles

1. *State a few major objectives rather than a great many trivial ones for a given unit.* Concentrate on the objectives that represent new advances over previous learning or terminal objectives that come at the ends of curricular strands or sequences. Where appropriate, identify learning hierarchies and perform task analyses, and provide instruction and practice on whatever subskills need work before smooth performance of the ultimate target skill will become possible. However, keep in mind that you are building toward the ultimate target skill, which will need to be taught, practiced, and evaluated in its final form. Don't lose the forest for the trees.
2. *Don't be unnecessarily behavioral or precise in formulating objectives.* For psychomotor objectives and for many of the cognitive objectives taught in the early grades, it is possible and usually desirable to express objectives in specific behavioral terms as advocated by Mager (1962). However, for affective objectives and for higher level cognitive objectives that do not translate directly into behavioral skills, it may be appropriate to formulate instructional objectives in less behavioral terms. Even so, however, try to be as specific as possible in formulating such objectives, and to formulate them in terms of changes in the students that will occur as a result of instruction, rather than in terms of content coverage or other teacher behavior. The objectives should be stated specifically enough so that both you and the students can easily determine whether or not they have been reached.
3. *Don't be overly rigid in using objectives to guide instruction.* Research on teacher planning (Clark & Peterson, 1985) suggests that most teachers do not pay nearly enough attention to instructional objectives when planning instruction—teachers tend to read the teacher's manual that comes with the curriculum in order to learn how the lesson is to be conducted, giving little thought to the purpose of the lesson or to how it might be adapted if it doesn't succeed. This same research also shows, however, that among teachers who do pay attention to objectives, some respond to them in an overly rigid manner. These teachers develop lesson plans that are admirably specific and detailed, but then they implement these plans so rigidly that they are unable or unwilling to adapt the plans when events dictate or to respond to unanticipated student questions or comments. Wise teachers formulate and use instructional objectives to guide instruction, but they are flexible enough to deviate from their plans when unanticipated problems occur or when they have a chance to take advantage of a "teachable moment" by following up on a relevant student question or comment.

SUMMARY

Learning is the process of acquiring relatively permanent change in understanding, attitude, knowledge, information, ability, and skill through experience. It is a change in capacity for performance that must be distinguished from performance itself and from development, thinking, and various situational phenomena. There are different kinds of learning. Common qualitative distinctions include the developmental stages suggested by Piaget and others, figurative ("knowledge that") versus operative ("knowledge how"), intentional versus incidental learning, rote versus meaningful learning, and reception versus discovery learning.

The Bloom taxonomy distinguishes between knowledge, comprehension, application, analysis, synthesis, and evaluation objectives. Gagné's learning hierarchy distinguishes between signal learning, stimulus-response learning, chaining, verbal association, discrimination learning, concept learning, and rule learning. Gagné and Briggs distinguish between five major types of learning—attitudes, motor skills, information, intellectual skills, and cognitive strategies—and further divide intellectual skills into discriminations, concrete concepts, defined concepts, rules, and higher-order rules.

Gagné and Briggs also present guidelines concerning the different conditions of learning required for each of the types of learning that they distinguish. Attitudes are learned primarily through exposure to models, persuasive communication, or conditioning. Motor learning is stimulated through modeling, verbal instructions combined with visual imagery, and practice with feedback. Information learning is stimulated by presenting the input in an organized fashion and helping students to relate it to their existing knowledge, process it actively, and encode in their own words.

Discriminations are taught using the principles of contiguity, feedback, and repetition. Concrete concepts are taught by presenting a variety of stimuli that all share the defining attributes of the concept and pointing out these attributes to the learners, and then having them discriminate examples from nonexamples of the concept. Defined concepts are taught by stating their definitions and then presenting examples and nonexamples. Rules are taught through rule statements followed by guided practice in applying the rule to specific examples. Higher-order rules cannot be taught directly, but their discovery can be stimulated by presenting learners with problem-solving situations that require them to invent such higher-order rules. Gagné and Briggs do not believe that cognitive strategies can be either taught or stimulated directly, although they believe that teachers can encourage students to develop such strategies by giving them frequent opportunities to think creatively and solve novel problems. Other writers believe that cognitive strategy development can be stimulated more directly through modeling of the self-talk that occurs when cognitive strategies are applied to particular situations.

Gagné and Briggs hold that the five categories of intellectual skills form a hierarchy with higher-order rules at the top, followed by rules and defined concepts, then by concrete concepts, and finally by discriminations. They suggest using information about such learning hierarchies for conducting task analyses to identify the component parts of tasks and decide what needs to be taught and in what order.

Instructional planning begins with formulation of clear instructional objectives. Objectives are best formulated by stating what students should be able to do following completion of the instruction. By formulating objectives in terms of student performance rather than merely in terms of what is to be taught, instructional planners not only provide guidance to teachers about what to teach and how to teach it, but also provide guidance to teachers about how to evaluate the effects of instruction and guidance to students about where to focus their learning efforts. The authors believe that teachers should formulate instructional objectives to guide their planning and teaching, although they suggest that teachers state only a few major objectives rather than a great many trivial ones, that they do not attempt to be unnecessarily behavioral or precise in stating those objectives, and that they not be overly rigid in confining their instructional activities to those that are related directly to the objectives. Planning should allow for enough flexibility to take advantage of unanticipated teachable moments.

QUESTIONS AND PROBLEMS

1. In your own terms, differentiate between learning, development, and thinking. Why are these distinctions and terms important? How might they influence the decisions you make as a teacher?
2. Distinguish between figurative and operative knowledge. Which is more difficult to achieve? Why? Which is more important? Why? Think about the courses that you took as a college freshman. Were most of the outcomes of instruction in those courses figurative or operative? How do you account for this?
3. What are the important differences between the Bloom and the Gagné taxonomies? Think about the teaching situation that you want to be in. Which of these two taxonomies would be more useful to you? Why?
4. Examine a test that you have taken at some point during your college career. Try to determine, for each question, the level it represents in the Bloom and the Gagné taxonomies. How difficult is it to classify the questions? How useful does the classification appear to be in summarizing the knowledge emphasis of the test?
5. Read the questions that appeared at the end of Chapters 2, 3, 4, and 5 in this text. How would you characterize these questions?
6. In some classrooms, teachers emphasize a great deal of drill. In mathematics classes, for example, students may spend 60 to 70 percent of the period practicing number facts. However, this material often has to be retaught the following year. How can you account for this? What is the role of practice in retaining information? What are the conditions for appropriate or successful practice?
7. How would you apply the material presented on motor learning in this chapter if you were teaching someone the basics of ice skating? How would you apply it if you were teaching free-style ice skating?
8. What is the appropriate role of instructional objectives in effective instruction? Reread the objectives that we presented at the beginning of this chapter. How effective were these objectives for conveying the important content that was presented in the chapter? If you were writing objectives for the chapter, what changes would you make in those that were presented?
9. Why is there a need for distinction between covert learning and overt performance?

CASE STUDIES

What's the Big Idea? Miss Ditto and Miss Freehand both devote considerable attention to the topic of main idea in their language arts instruction. Each introduced it in a lesson that described the process of organizing lengthy texts into sections and paragraphs and suggested that each paragraph should have a single main idea. The two teachers differed considerably, however, in the nature of the activities they assigned during the subsequent weeks as practice and application follow-ups to the main idea lesson. Miss Ditto emphasized seatwork assignments calling for students to identify the main idea sentence in a paragraph. She began by passing out pages full of short, disconnected paragraphs and having students underline the main idea sentence. Later, she assigned them increasingly longer sections of connected text to read, and had them copy the main idea sentence or state the main idea of a paragraph in their own words if they believed that no single sentence captured it adequately. For variety, she occasionally distributed several pages of uninterrupted connected text and assigned the students to mark the places where new paragraphs should begin. In contrast, Miss Freehand followed up on the main idea lesson mostly in her writing assignments. She assigned several compositions each week, and in addition to giving guidelines for the type of composition, the desired length, and so on, she reminded the students that the compositions should be divided into paragraphs such that each paragraph was built around a main idea. Sometimes she had the students underline the main idea in each of their paragraphs.

Given these differences in approach, how would you characterize what Miss Ditto's and Miss Freehand's students are learning about main idea using concepts presented in this chapter? In particular, how would their learning compare in terms of figurative versus operative knowledge, and how would it be classified according to the Bloom taxonomy and to the Gagné and Briggs typology? What does this suggest about the relative effectiveness of these two approaches?

Everything You Always Wanted to Know About Apple Pie. Merry Cook is a home economics teacher who offers a "carbo cooking" course as a high school elective. The course centers on cooking and baking treats and desserts, but Merry wants to make sure that it includes appropriate cognitive content—chemical composition and nutritional value of foods, changes induced by cooking and trade-offs involved in various cooking methods, trade-offs involved in serving at various temperatures, etc. One of the activities that she plans to include in the course is to have the students work in small groups preparing and baking apple pies. What might she include in one or more lessons on this topic if she were to set out to include at least one worthwhile objective that would be classified at each of the six levels of the Bloom taxonomy and each of the nine types of learning described in the Gagné and Briggs typology (counting each of the five types of intellectual skill as separate types)? If she were to ask your help in drawing up such a list of objectives, what would you suggest? Keep in mind that each objective should be worthwhile in its own right and should fit together with the other objectives to form a coherent sequence of instruction.

Chapter 7

The Behavioral Approach to Learning

CHAPTER OUTLINE

OBJECTIVES

When you have mastered the material in this chapter you will be able to

1. Describe the behaviorist approach to learning and differentiate it from other approaches
2. Define the key concepts in the classical conditioning paradigm (unconditioned stimulus, unconditioned response, conditioned stimulus, conditioned response), and describe the role of contiguity and repetition in the classical conditioning process
3. Describe Thorndike's work on instrumental conditioning and explain how it differs from work by Pavlov, Watson, and others on classical conditioning
4. Explain the law of exercise and the law of effect
5. Describe the key findings of the functionalists concerning learning curves, overlearning, and massed versus distributed practice
6. Define the key concepts associated with Skinner's operant conditioning (positive reinforcement, negative reinforcement, extinction, punishment, behavioral shaping, reinforcement schedules), and explain how operant conditioning differs from classical conditioning and instrumental conditioning
7. State the similarities and differences between Skinnerian approaches to operant conditioning of animals in the laboratory and Skinnerian approaches to instructing students in classrooms

8. Define the key concepts associated with the work of Bandura and other social learning theorists (modeling, imitation, vicarious learning)
9. Describe the similarities and differences between modeling as used in traditional behavioristic approaches to instruction and the combination of modeling with verbalized self-instruction as used in cognitive behavior modification approaches
10. Define the key concepts used in programmed instruction (modules, frames, linear versus branched programming, self-pacing, learner control), and explain the basic principles of programmed instruction used in Keller's PSI system and other individualized learning systems developed for use in the schools

Behaviorists versus other learning theorists

In this chapter, we describe the concepts and information developed by learning theorists known as behaviorists. Behaviorists approach the study of learning by concentrating on overt behaviors that can be observed and measured. They seek to discover general laws that apply across species and can be used to predict and control behavior. Behavior itself is seen as determined by events external to the learner—by stimuli that elicit or cue particular behavior and by reinforcement that maintains these stimulus-response relationships. Behaviorists recognize, of course, that learning is mediated by perceptions, thoughts, and other covert processes, and some behaviorists refer to such processes in their theorizing. However, even these cognitively oriented behaviorists prefer to minimize their reliance on hypothetical constructs that must be inferred rather than observed directly. This is a major difference between behaviorists and other learning theorists (discussed in the next two chapters) who stress cognitive structures or information processing.

Behaviorism was the first of the major approaches to the study of learning to become well established as a paradigm. It developed and spread early in the twentieth century in Europe and especially in the United States, where it became the dominant approach not only to the study of learning but to psychology in general. It remained so until the 1950s, when other approaches began to gain in popularity. Behaviorism is still a highly respected and influential tradition, although it no longer is as predominant as it once was and most modern behaviorists are much more cognitive in orientation than their forebears were. The tradition retains its emphasis on developing theory, using that theory to predict behavior, and then conducting carefully controlled experiments to test these predictions.

Over the years, behaviorists have developed a great many theoretical principles, as well as associated instructional techniques. Some of these principles and techniques are designed to induce learning (i.e., to cause learners to develop new stimulus-response associations or to add to their behavioral repertoires). These instructional applications of behaviorism are discussed in this chapter. Behaviorism has also produced principles and techniques designed to control behavior (i.e., to increase or decrease the frequencies of already-learned behaviors). These applications of behaviorism are more relevant to the topic of classroom management than to the topic of learning and so are discussed in Chapter 21.

Pavlov and Classical Conditioning

Contiguity

Going back at least as far as to Aristotle, it has been observed that much learning involves recognizing associations between stimuli or events (i.e., the sight of lightning is regularly followed by the sound of thunder). The key to recognition of these associations is contiguity—the associated items regularly occur together, either simultaneously or in rapid succession. If encounters with associated events are salient enough (i.e., a brilliant flash of lightning followed by a loud clap of thunder), or if we happen to be paying close attention for some reason, we may learn the association in one trial. Usually, however, associations develop gradually through a combination of contiguity and repetition—repeated encounters with the associated items make us more and more aware of the fact that they are associated. We become conditioned to expect the associated stimuli to occur together.

When stimulus events regularly occur in close temporal contiguity, the appearance of the first event in the sequence eventually becomes a signal that the other event(s) will follow. When one event always precedes the other(s) it may be perceived as the cause, and not merely a signal for the appearance of the other(s). This is sometimes misleading, because the first in a series of two or more associations does not necessarily cause what follows. Some cause-and-effect relationships are hard to see because the contiguity principle is not operating. For example, it is easy for people to associate pain and skin swelling with bee stings, because the pain follows immediately after the sting, and the swelling sets in shortly thereafter. In contrast, the discovery of the linkage between mosquito bites and malaria had to be accomplished without contiguity clues. Only a fraction of people bitten by mosquitoes develop malaria. This minimized the likelihood that the association between mosquito bites and malaria would be recognized on the basis of mere exposure to the pattern, no matter how often the pattern was repeated. Despite these complexities, however, contiguity and repetition are basic to the learning of associations through conditioning.

Learning through conditioning experiments

Early in the twentieth century, Russian physiologist Ivan Pavlov (1927) conducted controlled experiments on learning through conditioning. At first, his observations on the topic were incidental to his physiological research on the digestive system (for which he won the Nobel Prize in 1904), but eventually he began to study conditioning in its own right.

Unconditioned stimuli and unconditioned response

Pavlov had been studying the salivation response (the automatic increase in salivation that occurs during feeding and helps promote digestion) by presenting dogs with food under controlled conditions. The salivation response is a genetically programmed reflex action in which an unconditioned stimulus (the taste of food in the mouth) automatically elicits an unconditioned response (salivation). Other reflex actions such as blinking in response to a puff of air directed at the face or the "startle response" to an unexpected loud noise also involve unconditioned responses to unconditioned stimuli. In each case, the stimulus automatically elicits the response; no process of conditioning or learning is involved.

In the process of conducting his experiments, Pavlov noticed that his dogs sometimes salivated in anticipation of feeding. The mere sight of food, or even the entrance of a laboratory assistant into the room signalling that feeding was about to occur, could elicit the salivation response, well before the food actually entered the dog's mouth. Repeated experiences with events that signalled the advent of food had conditioned the dogs to salivate in response to these events, prior to presentation of the food itself.

In a series of experiments, Pavlov showed that any neutral stimulus (one that produced no particular response from the dogs) could become a con-

Ivan Pavlov, the discoverer of the conditioned reflex.

ditioned stimulus for the salivation response if it were routinely presented immediately prior to the unconditioned stimulus (food). For example, if Pavlov repeatedly sounded a bell right before presenting food, the dog would soon begin to salivate at the sound of that bell. Once this occurred, the bell had become a conditioned stimulus capable of producing salivation as a conditioned response (the salivation response was essentially the same in either situation, but Pavlov referred to it as an unconditioned response when it was elicited by food but as a conditioned response when it was elicited by some conditioned stimulus). Further experimentation identified the following principles:

- ☐ *Extinction*—A conditioned response that had been built up by repeatedly presenting the conditioned stimulus (bell) followed by the unconditioned stimulus (food) could be extinguished by continuing to present the conditioned stimulus but no longer following it with the unconditioned stimulus. If Pavlov stopped presenting food after sounding the bell, the dog would continue to salivate at the sound of the bell for a time, but would gradually stop doing so.
- ☐ *Spontaneous recovery*—Conditioned responses that are extinguished are not lost permanently. They recover, at least to some degree, over time. Thus, if Pavlov first established salivation as a conditioned response to a bell, then extinguished this response, then allowed several days to elapse, and then sounded the bell again, the dog would salivate. This "spontaneously recovered" conditioned response would soon extinguish again, however, unless Pavlov resumed presenting the food following the sound of the bell.
- ☐ *Generalization*—Once conditioned responses became established, they could be elicited by a range of stimuli that were similar to the original conditioned stimulus. Thus, dogs trained with a particular bell would salivate not only when they heard that bell but also when

they heard other bells or sounds that resembled bell tones. The conditioned response generalized to a range of conditioned stimuli.

- ☐ *Discrimination*—The dogs could also learn to discriminate between similar stimuli if these stimuli were paired with different outcomes. Thus, if Pavlov regularly presented food following one bell tone but did not present food following a second bell tone, the dog would learn to salivate in response to the first tone but not the second.
- ☐ *Higher-order conditioning*—Conditioned responses could be chained together. Once a particular bell tone was well established as a conditioned stimulus, it became possible to establish something else (such as a flash of light) as a conditioned stimulus by routinely presenting the light followed by the bell. Soon the dog would begin to salivate at the sight of the light flash without waiting for the bell (let alone the food).

Classical conditioning

The type of conditioning studied by Pavlov is known as Pavlovian or classical conditioning because it was first described in a series of classic experiments. Narrowly defined, classical conditioning refers only to situations in which genetically programmed reflex actions become elicited by conditioned stimuli in addition to the unconditioned stimuli that normally elicit them. However, the term "classical conditioning" is sometimes used more broadly to refer to stimulus substitution learning, signal learning, and any other learning in which contiguity and repetition in presentation of stimuli are used to induce learners to generalize an existing stimulus-response connection to some new stimulus. This kind of conditioning can be used in teaching vocabulary, for example, by showing pictures paired with the printed names of the objects pictured, or by showing Spanish words followed by their English equivalents.

John B. Watson

Although early behaviorists embraced Pavlov's ideas, Pavlov himself did not consider himself a behaviorist or even a psychologist. The term "behaviorism" was coined by John B. Watson (1913, 1914), who argued that psychologists should focus on overt, measurable behaviors and avoid "unscientific" theorizing about thoughts, intentions, or other subjective experiences. Watson viewed the scientific study of behavior not only as an appropriate model for psychology but also as a method for perfecting the human condition. Watson (1924) saw the potential childrearing applications of Pavlov's demonstration that initially neutral stimuli can acquire the power to elicit conditioned responses. This led him to make his famous boast that:

> Give me a dozen healthy infants, well formed, and my own special world to bring them up in, and I'll guarantee to take any one at random and train him to become any type of specialist I might select—doctor, lawyer, artist, merchant-chief and yes, even beg-

garman and thief, regardless of his talents, penchants, tendencies, abilities, vocations, or race of his ancestry. (p. 82)

Neither Watson nor anyone else has ever demonstrated such power, although even today some behaviorists believe that we already know enough about shaping behavior by manipulating the environment to enable us to optimize human development (e.g., Greer, 1983).

Classical conditioning processes in human emotional development

Watson demonstrated the importance of classical conditioning processes in human emotional development by conditioning the responses of an infant named Albert to a white rat (Watson & Rayner, 1920). Watson knew that Albert feared sudden loud noises (such noises apparently were unconditioned stimuli for Albert), so he created a loud noise by banging a steel bar with a hammer whenever Albert touched a white rat. Soon Albert began to respond with fear and avoidance when the rat was presented, even though he had shown no such fear previously. This fear response also generalized to other small animals (a rabbit and a dog) and to a sealskin coat and a bearded Santa Claus mask, although not for long.

Watson's work with Albert was more like a pilot study with mixed results than a definite experiment. However, it has since become one of the most publicized studies in the history of psychology, and accounts of it are often embellished to suggest that the conditioned fear responses were much more long lasting and widespread than they really were, or that Watson went on to extinguish the fear response and develop positive responses by pairing the appearance of the white rat with delivery of rewards. Watson himself was responsible for some of these distortions, because he overstated his findings in his own subsequent writings (Harris, 1979; Samelson, 1980). Some embellishment would probably have occurred anyway, however, simply because the predicament of "Little Albert" had all the makings of a great story with potential for sensationalism, identification with a character (Watson for those interested in manipulating others for good or ill, Albert for those who fear such manipulation), and illustration of sweeping generalizations (i.e., about the potential benefits or dangers of behaviorism). In any case, Watson became famous for this and other research on infants, and he went on to write an infant care manual (Watson, 1928) that was highly influential into the 1940s. (Dr. Benjamin Spocks' early writings advocating permissive childrearing were in part a reaction to the regimentation advocated by Watson.)

From today's perspective, Watson can be pictured as an extremist given to unsubstantiated boasting and conducting ethically questionable research on infants. However, he does deserve credit for his theoretical contributions to behaviorism and for demonstrating the role of conditioning processes in the development of generalized emotional responses (fears, phobias, prejudices) to particular classes of stimuli. Within the school setting, conditioning acquired through a series of early experiences or even a single traumatic experience is usually the reason why certain students dread making public speeches or attending gym class.

Edward L. Thorndike

Although early behaviorists continued to study animals rather than humans, they began to supplement classical conditioning research by studying adaptive behavior (not just instinctive reflexes) under somewhat more natural, although still controlled, conditions. For example, E. L. Thorndike (1913) studied what came to be called instrumental conditioning by placing animals in problem-solving situations. For example, a hungry cat might be put in a cage where it could see food but could not reach it without escaping from the cage. The cat could escape by working a latch, but it would have to discover this for itself. Typically, the first few escapes would be accidental—the cat would happen to make the right response in the process of clawing or scratching around. However, the principle of contiguity was in effect: The cage would open immediately after the "correct" response had been made. After several repetitions, this essentially random activity evolved into "scientific" trial and error behavior. The cat had learned that there was a "trick" to getting out of the cage, concentrated on performing this "trick" properly, and became more and more efficient at doing so. Ultimately, the cat would be able to perform the "correct" response immediately on being placed in the cage.

Instrumental conditioning

Such experiments were said to involve "instrumental" conditioning because the animals learned behavior that was instrumental in helping them to reach their goals. These studies extended Pavlov's work on classical conditioning by showing that environmental manipulations could produce entirely new conditioned responses. Cats that learned to escape their cages were not acting reflexively by making unconditioned responses; instead, they were discovering and refining new responses adapted to novel stimulus situations.

Based on these experiments, Thorndike postulated "laws" of learning. The best known of these were the laws of exercise and effect. According to the law of exercise, repetition of a conditioned response would strengthen the bond between the stimulus situation and the response. This was Thorndike's version of "practice makes perfect." The law of effect was his version of the pleasure-pain principle, or the principle of reinforcement and punishment. It held that responses followed by pleasure would be strengthened, and responses followed by pain would be weakened. The more frequently a response was rewarded (100 percent of the time would be optimal), the more it would be strengthened.

Laws of exercise and effect

Although both of these principles were largely correct, each had to be modified in view of later findings. The law of exercise had to be modified to take into account the need for variation in responding and for feedback about the effects of responses. Exercise alone, without feedback (knowledge of results) and without systematic testing of alternative forms of response, does not necessarily improve performance. However, when the practice does include systematic response variation combined with feedback, performance tends to improve until peak efficiency is reached. The law of effect holds in general, but had to be modified to allow for certain exceptions. There are special situations where what would usually be considered pleasurable consequences do not motivate performance or where what usually would be considered painful consequences do not suppress it.

Mental discipline

In addition to his contribution to the psychology of learning, Thorndike was influential for his attacks on "faculty psychology" and the "mental discipline" approach to education. Influenced by philosophers and classical scholars, educators traditionally had stressed the idea that courses in science, mathematics, languages, and classical literature not only were of value in their own right, but had a special and more generalized value for "training the mind." Exposure to these subjects presumably provided mental discipline that made people more perceptive and incisive in their thinking, whereas practical subjects such as business, agriculture, or home economics presumably did not have these effects. Thorndike (1924) disproved this theory by showing that there was no evidence of special mental faculties that could be "disciplined" in the time-honored way, and no evidence that classical subjects were any more valuable than practical subjects for stimulating general intellectual development. The mental discipline approach to education declined rapidly after Thorndike's attack, and the school curriculum began to include more practical subjects. Thorndike's conclusions hold up as well today as when he stated them: there still is no evidence that particular subject matter has generalized "mind broadening" effects. However, there is some reason to believe that training in study skills and information processing strategies will improve students' abilities to learn efficiently (see Chapters 9 and 10).

Functionalism

While Thorndike was developing his general laws of learning, other behaviorally oriented investigators were developing information about factors that influence learning in particular situations. These investigators were known as functionalists because their experiments were designed to show that performance in particular situations "is a function" of some determining factor (i.e., to show that specified changes in the determining factor will produce predictable changes in performance). Functionalists produced several principles and techniques that became part of the behavioristic approach to the study of learning.

Learning curves

Functionalists preferred to describe levels of performance in quantitative terms (number of seconds required for an animal to run a maze or escape from a cage) and to express improvements in performance over repeated trials by using graphic depictions. These graphs typically resembled "flattened" S-shaped curves and eventually became known as learning curves. Learning curves typically revealed: 1) little progress in early trials (because the animal was exploring the situation through trial and error, and had not yet discovered the "trick" to solving it); then, 2) a sharp rise in the curve indicating rapid improvement in performance (because the animal had discovered the "trick" and had become more efficient at performing it); and 3) an eventual leveling off (because the animal reached its performance peak of maximum efficiency). Most of the learning studied by early behaviorists produced such learning curves when depicted graphically, although some curves rose quite steeply (because the animal made rapid progress in moving toward peak performance once it discovered the "trick"), whereas others rose more slowly and were spread over many more trials (because the animal made only slow, gradual progress toward peak performance).

As long as performance continues to improve with each new block of trials, learning is occurring (the curve continues to rise). Once the peak level of performance is attained, however, further trials no longer produce improvement (the curve levels off and becomes a horizontal line). The point at which continued practice no longer produces improvement is known as the point of overlearning, and skills practiced up to and beyond this point are said to be practiced to overlearning. Functionalists discovered that skills practiced to overlearning tend to be retained indefinitely and to be recovered with relative ease when they have not been used in years, whereas skills that are partially mastered but not to the point of overlearning tend to deteriorate quickly. If you did a lot of skating or cycling as a child, you will be able to perform these skills competently now with little or no practice, even though you may not have skated or cycled in years. However, if you were exposed to these skills only briefly and never really mastered them, you would have to start over virtually from scratch in order to master them now.

Overlearning

Functionalists discovered that progress in learning depended not merely on the amount of time or number of trials available for practice, but on how this practice was distributed. Massed practice is concentrated into just one or a small number of lengthy sessions spaced close together in time. In contrast, distributed practice involves a large number of shorter sessions, spaced further apart. Massed practice is more efficient for certain simple, isolated skills that can be mastered to overlearning with relative ease. Distributed practice is more efficient for most types of learning, however, including most of what is taught in school. This is why curricula are divided into brief lessons and assignments and that each address a limited range of content and frequently involve review of content addressed previously. This is also why frequent drills and quizzes are important, and why a progressive series of tests spaced throughout the term usually produces more learning than a single final exam at the end of the term. (You may have noticed in your own studies that last minute "cramming" followed by massive forgetting often results when the course grade is based on a single final exam.)

Massed versus distributed practice

The Role of Practice in the Classroom

Practice is one of the most important yet least appreciated aspects of learning in classrooms. Little or no practice may be needed for simple or isolated behaviors like verbalizing the names of objects or pronouncing words, but practice becomes more important as learning becomes more complex. Prolonged practice is needed for polishing skills such as reading, writing, or performing computations, as well as for learning to apply general or abstract principles such as laboratory applications of scientific principles, using mathematical or statistical principles to solve problems, or conversing in a new language.

Need for overlearning

As a general rule, basic skills need to be practiced to the point of overlearning if they are to become available for efficient functional use when we need to apply them. This is why drills, quizzes, review activities, and other forms of distributed practice are so important.

Need for immediate feedback

To be useful, such practice must involve not only opportunities to exercise skills but opportunities to receive feedback, preferably immediate feedback. So-called self-teaching or self-correcting curriculum materials make use of this principle by presenting learners with tasks that can be completed successfully in one and only one way. Here, correct response leads to immediate feedback and reinforcement in the form of success, and incorrect responses are extinguished. Much of the equipment used in Montessori schools is designed this way, as are many educational toys. For example, toys called "shape sorters" require children to place blocks or pegs into holes that correspond to their shapes. Each block or peg will fit into only one hole. The same general principles are used in form boards, puzzles, and a variety of tasks involving matching and discrimination. Programmed instructional materials also use these principles, even though the learning and performance involved are more cognitive.

Usually, though, teachers will assign seatwork and other practice activities that do not have such immediate feedback and self-correction features built in, so it will be necessary to provide feedback to the students personally or to arrange for them to get it by consulting answer keys, comparing their work with ideal models, or providing feedback to one another. Ideally, students will be monitored during their practice and provided with immediate feedback that they can use on the spot to correct misunderstandings or tendencies to make particular kinds of errors. If the feedback is delayed several days and limited to a grade and a few remarks written on a returned assignment, it may be too little and too late to do much good. In fact, for students who were confused about what to do and how to do it in the first place, the "practice" may have been counterproductive. That is, if the students were operating from misconceptions or using erroneous response patterns, repetition of this level of functioning without proper monitoring and correction would only deepen the misconceptions and reinforce the erroneous response patterns. Thus, successful skill practice involves teacher monitoring and provision of feedback sufficient to enable the students to understand what to do and how to do it, so that the practice involves making smoother, more efficient, and more automatic those skills that are already established at rudimentary levels, and not trying to establish such skills through trial and error.

Skinner and Operant Conditioning

We have described how behaviorism evolved from (1) Pavlov's early experiments on the classical conditioning of salivation responses through Watson's emphasis on conditioning as a mechanism for socializing human development; (2) Thorndike's emphasis on studying instrumental behavior in more naturalistic situations; and (3) the functionalists' emphasis on graphic depiction of performance change and on demonstrating how factors external to learners influence their learning. As these trends took root, it became clear that behaviorism offered not merely a method of studying learning scientifically, but a method of developing principles and techniques for producing learning and controlling behavior by manipulating the environment. The theory and research of B. F. Skinner and his colleagues on operant conditioning was the most influential of these developments.

Skinner used the term operant conditioning because he preferred to study operant behaviors—voluntary behaviors used in operating on the environment. This distinguished his work from classical conditioning research that dealt with what he called respondent behaviors (involuntary reflex actions). Thus, Skinner's operant conditioning is much closer to the instrumental conditioning studied by Thorndike than to the classical conditioning studied by Pavlov. However, unlike Thorndike and others who merely recorded animals' behavior when placed in particular environments and allowed to discover "tricks" for responding to them, Skinner preferred to assume a more active role by manipulating the environment in order to shape the animal's behavior in desired directions.

Contingent Reinforcement

The primary mechanism for accomplishing such behavioral shaping was contingent reinforcement: Skinner demonstrated that he could increase the frequency of any particular operant behavior by rewarding the animal for performing that behavior. Delivery of reinforcement was made contingent on performance of the behavior, so that the animal had to perform the behavior in order to get the reward.

Skinner's work on contingent reinforcement was in many respects a reformulation and application of Thorndike's law of effect. However, there were two important differences. First, Skinner used contingent reinforcement in an active way in order to shape behavior so as to speed up and refine the learning process; he did not merely wait for animals to learn through exploration and discovery. Second, Skinner avoided one of the problems associated with the law of effect by defining reinforcers in terms of their situational effects on behavior (thus avoiding the problem that even consequences generally thought of as rewarding are not experienced as rewarding by everyone in every situation). Skinner defined a reinforcer as any consequence that increases the frequency of some operant behavior when made contingent on the performance of that behavior. This definition is circular, but it has proven extremely useful.

Conditioning Mechanisms

Operant conditioning is accomplished through the following four basic mechanisms:

- ☐ *Positive reinforcement or reward*—Responses that are rewarded are likely to be repeated (good grades as reinforcement for careful study).
- ☐ *Negative reinforcement*—Responses that allow escape from painful or undesirable situations are likely to be repeated (exemption from a major test as reinforcement for good performance on quizzes).
- ☐ *Extinction or nonreinforcement*—Responses that are not reinforced are unlikely to be repeated (ignoring students who call out answers without first raising their hands and being recognized should extinguish this tendency to call out).
- ☐ *Punishment*—Responses that bring painful or undesirable consequences will be suppressed, although the behavioral potential will remain and the responses may reappear if reinforcement contingencies should change (penalizing students who call out answers by withdrawing privileges should cause these students to suppress their calling out behavior).

Behavioral Shaping

Skinner's work became well known not only because of the clarity and forcefulness of his arguments, but also because he captured the public imagination by showing that operant conditioning principles could be used to teach animals to do things that they would never learn through natural experience, such as teaching pigeons to dance or play pingpong. He accomplished this through behavioral shaping in which successive approximations of the ultimate target behavior were reinforced until the animal learned to produce the target behavior itself.

Teaching a pigeon to "dance," for example, might begin with reinforcement (delivery of a food pellet) following any lifting of the left leg. Once the pigeon learned to lift the left leg in order to earn a food pellet, the reinforcement contingency would be changed so that, for example, the pigeon now had to first lift the left leg and then replace it on the floor again before being reinforced. When this sequence was learned, reinforcement contingencies would change again, so that the pigeon would first have to go through the sequence with the left leg and then repeat it with the right leg. At this point, the pigeon would have developed a hopping sequence that resembled dancing, and this "dancing" could be extended into a "routine" through additional shaping.

Behavioral chaining

A great range of other behaviors could also be shaped in this manner. Assuming that a target behavior was in the animal's present or potential repertoire, it could be produced by initially reinforcing a partial or primitive version and then systematically reinforcing successive approximations to the final form. If some combination or sequence of behaviors were desired, one could teach the first step, then the second, and so on. This process is called behavioral chaining, or simply chaining.

Discrimination Training

Stimulus control

Skinner found that contingent reinforcement could be used not only to shape behavior but also to bring the behavior under stimulus control by applying the principles of contiguity and repetition. Just as Pavlov had shown that a conditioned stimulus could become a signal for the appearance of an unconditioned stimulus, Skinner showed that a conditioned stimulus could become a signal for the availability of contingent reinforcement. For example, if he reinforced a pigeon's dancing behavior only during times when a particular light source was turned on, the pigeon would learn to dance when the light was on but not when the light was off. At this point, the light would be a discriminative stimulus, or cue, for the dancing behavior, which would be under stimulus control; it would occur when the light was present but not when the light was absent.

Stimulus discrimination

Contingent reinforcement principles could be used to develop stimulus discrimination—a pigeon could learn to dance only in the presence of a particular type of light source. Here, only the "right" light source would function as a discriminative stimulus to cue the dancing behavior. Other light sources would be neutral stimuli without special significance.

Response discrimination

These same principles could also produce response discrimination—a pigeon could learn to dance when cued by one light source but to press a lever when cued by a different light source. The pigeon could learn that a particular situation, in this case, being placed in a specially designed experimental cage that came to be called a "Skinner box," provided a range of stimuli, including some that were neutral and of no special significance but others that functioned as cues indicating the need to produce particular responses in order to earn expected reinforcements.

Much of what is taught in school involves discrimination training. Students must learn not only to distinguish between relevant stimuli, but also to respond appropriately to each—a plus sign requires addition operations and a "times" sign cues multiplication operations.

In the classroom, cuing can be accomplished through direct statements like "Watch what happens when I add acid to the test tube," as well as through remarks like "I wonder what will happen when I push this button. Oh, look!" Cuing can also be accomplished through pointing, holding objects up for viewing, telling students where to look in the room or in their books, or asking questions that will cause them to process information and find the appropriate stimulus. Attention should be directed through cuing whenever students may be confused about where to look or what to listen to.

Partial Reinforcement Schedules

Operant responses are established more rapidly when the target behavior is reinforced immediately each time it occurs and not just some of the time.

Prior to Skinner's work on schedules of reinforcement (Ferster & Skinner, 1957), it was also assumed that a 100 percent reinforcement schedule (reinforcing the target response every time that it occurs in the presence of the controlling cue stimulus) would maximize the strength and persistence of the response. This assumption had to be changed when Skinner showed that once responses were established, they could be maintained as well or better through partial reinforcement schedules than through 100 percent reinforcement schedules.

Interval and ratio schedules

Partial reinforcement schedules include interval schedules and ratio schedules, and each of these can be either fixed or variable. In fixed interval schedules, the target response is reinforced only after a fixed interval of time (such as 60 seconds) has elapsed since the last reinforced response. In variable interval schedules, opportunities to earn reinforcement are also scheduled according to the time elapsed since the previous delivery of reinforcement, but the time intervals vary (randomly or according to some predetermined scheme) within set limits. For example, the time intervals between opportunities for reinforcement might vary randomly between one second and 120 seconds.

Ratio schedules

Ratio schedules are based on the number of target responses that have occurred rather than the time that has elapsed since the previous reinforced response. In fixed ratio schedules, a fixed percentage of the target responses made are reinforced. For example, every tenth appearance of the target response may be reinforced. In variable ratio schedules, opportunities to earn reinforcement are also scheduled according to the number of responses that have occurred since the previous reinforcement, but the number of response repetitions required varies within set limits. For example, opportunity for reinforcement may recur following anywhere from two through fifty repetitions of the target response.

Response rates

Different schedules of partial reinforcement have different effects on response rate. Under fixed schedules, where reinforcement delivery is predictable, learners adjust their behavior accordingly. When they know that a fixed time interval must elapse before the next reinforcement opportunity, they will simply wait or do something else while the time elapses, and then begin producing the target response around the time that the next reinforcement is due. Under fixed ratio schedules they learn that a fixed amount of work is required to earn reinforcement, so they tend to repeat the target behavior rapidly and forcefully at times when they particularly desire the reinforcement, but not at all or with less frequency and vigor when they become satiated with reinforcement. Variable interval and especially variable ratio schedules produce steadier and more persistent rates of response, because learners know that their efforts will pay off eventually even though they cannot predict when. For example, you may have noticed that you tend to "keep up" by maintaining a steady study schedule in courses where unannounced quizzes are expected (variable schedule), but to concentrate your studying in the days prior to exams in courses where a fixed exam schedule is being followed.

Skinner showed that an established response will persist much longer in the absence of reinforcement when it has been maintained by a partial reinforcement schedule than by a 100 percent reinforcement schedule. This finding not only had important theoretical implications, but also suggested that the use of operant conditioning principles for maintaining established behaviors might be much more feasible and cost effective than previously suspected since one would only have to reinforce the target behavior occasionally rather than every time that it occurred.

Maintaining responses

Skinner also showed that the power of partial reinforcement schedules for maintaining responses was quite remarkable: A response that would extinguish quickly following termination of a 100 percent reinforcement schedule might be sustained through thousands of unreinforced repetitions using a variable ratio schedule. Furthermore, these findings appear to hold up as well for humans as for animals. For example, you may be in the habit of purchasing snacks from a particular vending machine. In effect, you are on a 100 percent reinforcement schedule because each time you put money into the machine and pull a lever, you get reinforced with the desired snack. However, this behavior would extinguish quickly, probably in just one trial, if the machine retained your money but did not deliver the snack, and it would not reappear until the machine had been fixed or replaced. Contrast this with your response to slot machines. If you are like most people, you will continue to put your money into these machines even though pulling the lever yields no payoff most of the time, because you know that the machine will pay off eventually. Such response persistence is sustained through a variable ratio schedule of reinforcement. State lotteries and most other gambling devices operate, in effect, on the same principle.

Fading

Skinner discovered that responses maintained through 100 percent reinforcement schedules could be switched to partial reinforcement schedules through a process called fading. Like shaping, fading is accomplished through successive approximations. To introduce an interval schedule, one would initially delay just a second or two before delivering reinforcement, and then gradually extend this interval as the learner became accustomed to waiting. To introduce a ratio schedule, one would occasionally skip a response or two before reinforcing, and then gradually reduce the reinforcement rate as the learner became more accustomed to having to repeat the response several times before being reinforced. Once begun in this manner, fading procedures would continue until the desired schedule of reinforcement was established (typically, this would be the lowest rate of reinforcement that would still be effective in maintaining the response at the desired rate).

Skinner and Education

Like Watson in earlier times, Skinner has become famous not only for his advocacy of behaviorism as the appropriate approach to psychology (Skinner, 1974), but also because of his belief in its value as a method for perfecting the human condition. He not only designed the Skinner Box for research on animals, but also designed a special "air crib" that allowed him to keep one of his daughters in a controlled environment (soundproof, with constant temperature and humidity) for much of the time during her infancy. He also wrote *Walden Two* (Skinner, 1948), his fictional depiction of a Utopian community in which reinforcement principles were used to maintain interpersonal cooperation and individual labor in the service of the common good. In this vision, credits accumulated through work were exchanged for reinforcement in the form of basic necessities of living as well as opportunities for recreation or pleasure. Those willing to undertake the least desirable jobs could accumulate the most credits in the least time.

Skinner remains a pure behaviorist who excludes subjective experience from his theorizing and prefers to discuss the manipulation of behavior through stimulation and reinforcement. He believes that we are controlled by our reinforcement histories to the extent that our notions of freedom and self-determination are mere illusions (Skinner, 1971). However, his ideas about using reinforcement principles to perfect the human condition are essentially humanistic in that they are designed to minimize suffering, meet basic needs, and maximize the quality of life for everyone. Nevertheless, many people find his approach too cold and impersonal, and some fear that its manipulative aspects would lead to the sort of totalitarian "Big Brotherism" depicted by George Orwell in *1984*.

Reinforcement principles

Operant conditioning

Skinner (1968) argues that operant conditioning principles can and should be used in schools, and many of his students and associates have applied his ideas to the development of technologies for classroom management and instruction. Teaching machines, programmed instruction, and later, computer-assisted instruction are among the technologies developed at least in part on the basis of Skinner's ideas.

Skinner's principles for teaching academic content to students are essentially the same ones he uses in the laboratory for teaching animals: Elicit desirable responses in the presence of discriminative stimuli or cues and reinforce these responses immediately; continue cuing and reinforcing until the responses become well established; shape gradually through successive approximations of the ultimate target behavior if necessary; and fade reinforcement once the established stimulus-response connection can be maintained without it. There are two major differences, however, between conditioning animals and instructing students. First, because students can understand and respond to language, it is possible to cue desired responses directly by calling for them, without having to shape them gradually through reinforcement. Thus, classroom instruction is more efficient than animal conditioning, and it emphasizes eliciting responses through cuing at least as much as reinforcing those responses after they are elicited. Second, responses are reinforced primarily through feedback or knowledge of results; there is less need for food or other material rewards. In fact, material rewards are likely to be more intrusive or distracting than helpful in normal classroom situations.

Conditioning animals versus instructing students

Skinnerian approach to instruction

In summary, the Skinnerian approach to instruction involves building stimulus-response associations by cuing learners as to the nature of the response desired and then providing immediate feedback about the correctness of the response elicited, so that correct responses are reinforced and incorrect responses are extinguished. Where relevant, instructional programs are sequenced to move learners through successive approximations toward the ultimate target responses. If applied properly, these principles should produce learning that is not only efficient according to "cold" criteria such as number of trials required to reach criterion, but also desirable according to humanistic criteria. That is, the very process of learning should be more enjoyable to the learners because they get to respond actively rather than having to remain passive, because their responses yield immediate feedback, because they can move along at their own pace, and because the emphasis is on producing success experiences through reward. Explanations and examples of how these principles are used in programmed instruction approaches are given near the end of the chapter.

Social Learning Theory

Although Skinner and other purists continue to believe that behaviorism can get along without reference to cognitive information processing or subjective experience, most behaviorists have integrated at least some of these covert processes into their theorizing. This is especially true of behaviorists who study human learning that occurs in social situations. Much of human social learning does not seem to be explainable without reference to the covert mental activities of the learner.

Imitation of models

Humans learn to speak their native language, to know when and how to use tools and equipment, and to behave appropriately in a wide variety of social situations, among other things, mostly by imitating the behavior of others. Sometimes quite complex sequences of behavior are displayed following just a single observation of a model, without any deliberate cuing or behavioral shaping having occurred. Similarly, the situational specificity of various social behaviors usually develops rapidly and seemingly effortlessly, without need for the discrimination training that is required in the animal laboratory. For example, we learn to interact with friends one way in a library, another way at a party, and yet another way at a formal meeting. Such phenomena underscore the distinction between learning and performance and appear to require theorizing about learning that is qualitatively different from operant conditioning—learning that occurs before learners even begin to make overt behavioral responses, let alone to have those responses reinforced.

Sometimes, behavioral capacities acquired through observation of models are not acted out in behavior for considerable time periods, sometimes even for years, following their acquisition. For example, when preparing a lesson on a particular topic, teachers may use the same general instructional approach and content emphasis that were used with them when they were

Delayed imitation

students at the grade level they now teach. Such delayed imitation phenomena suggest that human behavior is mediated by cognitive processes and not merely learned as isolated stimulus-response associations.

Vicarious learning

We can learn not only by imitating the overt behavior of others, but also by observing how others are affected by events that occur in their lives. By putting ourselves in their place, or in other words, by identifying with them, we experience their thoughts and emotions vicariously. For example, much of what we know about human interpersonal relationships and the emotions that accompany them has been learned from books, articles, movies or television programs about real or fictional people and their experiences. A great deal of procedural knowledge about how to manipulate instruments or solve problems is also developed vicariously by watching models explore and discover. Even without benefit of explanation or thinking aloud by the models, we can learn vicariously by identifying with them and noting the nature and outcomes of the strategies that they try out.

To accommodate phenomena such as observational learning, delayed imitation, and vicarious learning, social learning theorists have broadened behaviorism to include attention to cognition and emotion in addition to behavior. Learning is seen as a cognitively mediated capacity for performance rather than identified with performance itself. Such learning can be acquired merely through observation of models, and it includes stimulus-response-reinforcement linkages, not just information about behavioral possibilities. That is, we learn not only about potential responses, but about the situations in which those responses may be relevant, the stimuli that may cue them, and the consequences that they are likely to bring about. Such learning is *mediated* through cognitive processes such as focusing of attention, encoding of input, and retention of this input in long term memory.

Bandura and Modeling

Albert Bandura (1977) is a leading social learning theorist whose ideas are important for thinking not only about classroom learning and instruction, but also about classroom motivation and management (as will be explained in later chapters). Bandura believes that human behavior must be described in terms of reciprocal interaction between cognitive, behavioral, and environmental determinants, and not just in terms of shaping through reinforcement. Reinforcement remains important, but human mediation capacities make it unnecessary to wait for a chain of responses to occur before being able to use it. Instead, one can use modeling or verbal explanation to inform learners about the consequences of producing the desired behavior, and thus cause them to begin to produce such behavior. Here, reinforcement has effects even before it occurs, because the learners anticipate its delivery and adjust their behavior accordingly. Such reinforcement effects initially occur through learner mediation of cognitive input rather than through delivery of consequences to learner behavior.

Bandura and other social learning theorists also leave room for learner

Learner mediation of stimulus input

mediation of stimulus input. It is commonly observed that different people will respond differently to the same situation. For example, if you and two friends were to visit a teacher's classroom together and discuss the teacher's effectiveness, you might find considerable disagreement because of differences in what each of you paid attention to. One of you might have concentrated on the efficiency of classroom management, another on the teacher's rapport with the students, and the third on the clarity of the teacher's explanations.

Nominal versus functional stimulus

Such phenomena have led social learning theorists to distinguish between the nominal stimulus (the stimulus situation as it can be described in terms of its observable and measurable characteristics) and the functional stimulus (the stimulus situation as observed and interpreted by the learner). When trying to understand learning that occurs in complex environments, and especially when trying to understand why different individuals learn different things from "the same" experience, one needs to identify the functional stimulus that cues each learner's response. When teaching, one needs to see that students attend to the right things (i.e., to see that each student's functional stimulus is the one that the student should focus on, and not something else). Modeling and verbal explanation can be used to enhance the salience and distinctiveness of cues, and thus to focus students' attention.

Learning through modeling

Bandura has done a great deal of research on learning induced through modeling. At first, this form of learning was called imitation because learners were exposed to filmed models who performed a series of discrete behaviors acted out in exaggerated fashion, and then were observed to see how much they imitated these models by duplicating their behavior exactly when placed in the same situation. For example, children would watch a model "take out" frustration against an inflated rubber Bobo doll, and then would be observed to see if they responded to the same frustration in the same way. Even in these early experiments on simple behaviors, and especially in later experiments involving more complex behaviors, it became clear that learners seldom imitated models by duplicating their behavior precisely in step-by-step fashion. Instead, cued by the model's behavior, they developed general notions about how to respond in the situation but then acted on these notions in their own ways. In the Bobo doll example, what the children learned from observing the model was not a specific sequence of behaviors (first punch the doll with the right hand, then kick the doll with the right foot, etc.). Instead, it was a general principle (take out frustration by attacking the Bobo doll) that could be implemented in a variety of ways (various combinations of the aggressive responses that had been modeled, along with other forms of aggression that were not shown in the film).

Because the term imitation is somewhat misleading, Bandura proposes that the term modeling be used to refer to learning that occurs as a result of observing models. Much human learning occurs through modeling, including much of what we learn about coping with everyday situations. For example, most adults typically behave much as their parents did when they respond to frustration, discipline their own children, or perform household repairs. This is often why certain adults are calm and analytical in the face of frustration while others are hysterical or resigned, why some are forgiving in disciplinary situations while others are punitive, and why some are skillful in handling household repairs while others are inept.

Modeling in classroom learning

Modeling is responsible for a great deal of classroom learning as well. Three general types of such modeling can be identified. First, simply through their presence and behavior, teachers are role models for their students. In this capacity, they are continuously supplying students with information about what and how to think not only about the academic curriculum, but about social, political, and personal life style issues. To the extent that this modeling is appropriate, and especially to the extent that it is done systematically, it can be a significant factor in socializing students' attitudes, beliefs, and behavior. The other two uses of modeling in the classroom are more specifically instructional. One of these occurs when teachers model creative thinking, problem solving, and other higher level cognitive skills. These general skills cannot be taught directly in step-by-step fashion, but teachers can stimulate their development indirectly through modeling. The third use of modeling does involve step-by-step demonstrations of procedures. This kind of modeling, traditionally called "demonstrating" by teachers, is often the most efficient way to teach motor skills and low-level cognitive skills, because students can observe the skill performance and then imitate it directly.

Cognitive Behavior Modification

We have described how both Watson and Skinner developed behaviorism not merely as an approach to theory and research but as a source of principles and technologies for improving the human condition. This tradition has continued, so that many contemporary behaviorists concentrate on developing solutions for various social problems and on applying behavioristic principles in settings such as schools, hospitals, or prisons.

Behavior modification is the general term we use for these activities. It means using techniques based on behavioristic principles to shape and control behavior. Just as behavioristic theorizing ranges from the pure behaviorism of Skinner to the more cognitive approach represented by Bandura, so do the approaches taken to behavior modification. A popular "conservative" approach is called applied behavior analysis, which is based on Skinner's ideas and concentrates on using reinforcement principles to bring behavior under stimulus control. Examples of this approach can be found in the *Journal of Applied Behavior Analysis.* More "liberal" approaches combine Skinnerian concepts with concepts developed by social learning theorists, and combine reinforcement techniques with techniques drawn from pedagogy, instructional psychology, psychotherapy, and other sources. These more recently developed approaches are sometimes called cognitive behavior modification to distinguish them from more traditional behavior modification approaches. Although behavior modification techniques are designed primarily for controlling behavior (Pressley, Reynolds, Stark, & Gettinger, 1983), they also have useful applications to instruction. This is especially true of cognitive behavior modification techniques.

Controlling one's own behavior

As described by Meichenbaum (1977), cognitive behavior modification techniques are designed to develop in learners the capacity for controlling their own behavior through goal setting, planning, self-instruction, self-monitoring, and self-reinforcement. These techniques feature modeling combined with verbalized self-instruction, in which models not only perform tasks but "think out loud" as they do so, enabling learners to see how the models use self-talk to guide their behavior by searching for relevant cues, developing ideas about how to respond, monitoring the effectiveness of these responses, and so on.

Meichenbaum and Goodman (1971) used these techniques to train a group of boys to respond thoughtfully and analytically, rather than impulsively, to matching-to-sample tasks. Such tasks, which occur frequently in seatwork assignments in the elementary grades, require students to inspect a sample stimulus and then identify its duplicate among a set of alternative choices (the alternatives are all similar to the sample, but only one is identical to it). The boys trained in this study had been doing poorly on such tasks because they impulsively selected the first choice that looked right, rather than taking time to study all of the choices and to make sure that they had selected the correct one. In this experiment, the models used exaggerated gestures and motions to make it clear that they were comparing each alternative choice to the stimulus before reaching a final decision. As they did so, they maintained a running monologue by verbalizing such thoughts as "Let's see, I'm going to have to compare each of these to make sure that I don't get the wrong one by mistake. How about this one here? Is this ear the same? How about the other ear? Wait a minute, that's not the same. This one has a round ear, and that one has a long ear. . . ." This approach was effective in improving the boys' performance on such tasks, even though other approaches like urging the boys to slow down and take their time were not effective.

Modeling combined with verbalized self-instruction

The combination of modeling with verbalized self-instruction is a powerful instructional technique, especially when teaching complex processes that are guided by covert self-talk that remains hidden from learners unless the teacher shares it with them (Leon & Pepe, 1983; Fox & Kendall, 1983; Meichenbaum & Asarnow, 1979; Sarason & Sarason, 1981). Students will not learn much from hearing a teacher identify the main ideas in a series of paragraphs or watching the teacher solve mathematics problems on the board or perform experiments in the laboratory if these "demonstrations" do not include verbalization of the thinking that guides the observable actions. When teachers do share this thinking, however, students not only can understand what the teacher is doing and why he or she is doing it, but can learn the general approach used in solving the problem and then apply it later in working on their own. The latter advantage makes modeling combined with verbalized self-instruction more effective than traditional lecture/demonstration methods for most instructional purposes. This is because such first person modeling provides students with an integrated, within-context demonstration of how to approach and solve the problem. This is easier for them to retain and use than general information presented in third person language or even a set of instructions presented in second person language ("First you do this, then you do this. . . .") that must first be internalized and then translated into first person language and used to guide behavior. We will say more about modeling as an instructional technique in subsequent chapters. For now, bear in mind that if a picture is worth a thousand words, an integrated demonstration of complex problem solving that includes verbalized self-talk is probably worth several thousand words of less direct lecturing about the topic.

Educational Technology

In addition to generating principles that teachers can use during lectures, discussions, and other traditional forms of classroom instruction, educational psychologists have developed technological innovations designed to enhance teacher-led instruction or replace it with instruction delivered from some other source. Most of the early innovations in educational technology were invented by behaviorists and based on behavioristic principles.

Teaching Machines

The notion of a teaching machine originated with Pressey (1932), who discussed principles for designing such machines and described several that he had invented. These were simple self-teaching devices that presented

Teachers can use a number of specialized machines to aid student learning.

learners with questions, required them to respond in some way, and then allowed them to check the correctness of their answers by turning a knob, opening a slot, or performing some other operation that would reveal the answer to them. Pressey's ideas generated some interest at the time, but nothing much came of them until more than 20 years later when Skinner (1954, 1958) and others began to tout teaching machines as practical alternatives to traditional schooling. As interest developed, it soon became clear that the "machine" aspects of such instruction (knobs, viewing windows, etc.) were not essential to its success. Instead, the key elements were design principles such as sequencing the instruction, providing corrective feedback, and programming for consistent success (Kulhavy, 1977). Consequently, interest in mechanization and gimmicks waned, except as motivational devices built into educational toys and computer programs, and most educational technologists began to focus on what became known as programmed instruction.

Programmed Instruction

Instructional programming involves designing instruction (following the procedures described in Chapter 11) to move learners systematically in small steps from "entry level" of performance to the target objective. Typically, programs are prepared so as to be self-contained and ready for independent

Table 7.1 A Set of Frames Designed to Teach a Third- or Fourth-Grade Pupil to Spell the Word Manufacture

1. Manufacture means to make or build. *Chair factories manufacture chairs.* Copy the word here:

   □ □ □ □ □ □ □ □ □ □ □

2. Part of the word is like part of the word **factory**. Both parts come from an old word meaning *make* or *build.*

   m a n u □ □ □ □ u r e

3. Part of the word is like part of the word **manual**. Both parts come from an old word for *hand.* Many things used to be made by hand.

   □ □ □ □ f a c t u r e

4. The same letter goes in both spaces:

   m □ n u f □ c t u r e

5. The same letter goes in both spaces:

   m a n □ f a c t □ r e

6. **Chair factories □ □ □ □ □ □ □ □ □ □ □ chairs**.

Table 7.2 Part of a Program in High School Physics

Sentence to be completed	Word to be supplied
1. The important parts of a flashlight are the battery and the bulb. When we "turn on" a flashlight, we close a switch that connects the battery with the ______.	bulb
2. When we turn on a flashlight, an electric current flows through the fine wire in the ______ and causes it to grow hot.	bulb
3. When the hot wire glows brightly, we say that it gives off or sends out heat and ______.	light
4. The fine wire in the bulb is called a filament. The bulb "lights up" when the filament is heated by the passage of a(n) ______ current.	electric
5. When a weak battery produces little current, the fine wire, or ______, does not get very hot.	filament
6. A filament which is *less* hot sends out or gives off ______ light.	less
7. "Emit" means "send out." The amount of light sent out, or "emitted," by a filament depends on how ______ the filament is.	hot
8. The higher the temperature of the filament the ______ the light emitted by it.	brighter, stronger

The machine presents one item at a time. The student completes the item and then uncovers the corresponding word or phrase shown at the right.

use by individual learners who have the appropriate entry characteristics (i.e., learners whose knowledge of the topic is such that the program will be neither too easy nor too difficult for them). Programs are divided into segments called modules that can be mastered easily in a short time. Modules are divided into small steps called frames that build up knowledge in step-by-step fashion. Examples are shown in Tables 7.1 and 7.2.

Frames

Programs reflect careful task analysis. Frames are sequenced so that material is presented in a logical order and prerequisite knowledge or skills are taught prior to teaching higher level objectives. Each frame presents any review or repetition considered necessary, and then introduces the next step in the chain of learning. This may be a new term or concept, a check on mastery of previously introduced concepts requiring the learner to make a discrimination or inference, or a change from a focus on mastery of information to a focus on requiring the learner to generalize or apply the information. The frame ends with the requirement that the learner make some kind of active response, such as underlining the correct answer or filling in a blank.

Fading of cues

Correct responses lead to reinforcement in the form of positive feedback. Extended praise statements may be frequent early in the program, but these soon evolve into simple feedback statements with just occasional praise (i.e., reinforcement is faded). There is also a fading of cues (also called a vanishing of prompts)—frames placed early in a sequence provide learners with most if not all of the information they need in order to answer the question correctly, but frames placed later in the sequence provide less information and require learners to supply or draw inferences from information presented earlier. For example, a module may begin with presentation of and questions about a fully labeled map, then begin to ask questions about a version of the map that has some of the parts missing, and then progress to asking questions without showing any map at all.

Linear and branched programming

Program sequencing may be linear or branched. Linear programming is designed to move learners through a single fixed sequence of objectives. It is used when there is reason to believe that the same program will be effective in enabling different learners to achieve the target objective with few if any errors and no need for individualized remediation. If errors should occur, learners are recycled back to earlier points in the program. Branched programs are designed to meet learners' individual needs. Learners are instructed to skip certain modules when performance on pretest frames indicates that they have already mastered the material taught in those modules. Also, when learners fail to master certain modules even after being recycled through them, they are first "branched" into special modules that provide remedial instruction and then returned to the main program.

Self-pacing

Programmed instruction is said to be self-paced or under learner control. Students progress quickly through material that they already know or can master easily, but they spend more time on, and review more frequently, any material that they find difficult. Errors are private, and feedback is immediate and constructive. In branched programs, persistent errors lead to different or more thorough remedial instruction, and not merely to repetition of the instruction that has not worked so far. Programmed instruction requires learners to attend actively to the information presented and respond thoughtfully to the questions asked, but it also reinforces these learning efforts by providing learners with the opportunity to respond overtly, to receive immediate feedback from their responses, to achieve consistent success, and to progress at their own pace.

Variations in programmed instruction

Most programmed instruction is packaged for use by learners working privately. However, other variations have developed. Some are methods that allow more teacher-student interaction while retaining the advantages of programmed instruction. Others are designed to emphasize particular learning modalities for students who need special stimulation. Still other adaptations are meant for students who do not yet have the independent work skills or functional reading ability needed to use more traditional programs. The latter programs use tape recorders, earphones, and other auditory equipment. Reading is minimized by using recorded information and instructions, but active responding is retained by using worksheets on which the students record their responses when instructed to do so. Typically, the recorded message will instruct them to respond, give them time to do so, and then provide feedback.

Limitations

These programs typically are not as successful as reading-based programs because they lack the advantages of self-pacing and flexibility in providing individualized instruction. If students make too many errors, the only option available in many cases is to have them repeat the same program. This can cause them to memorize correct responses without achieving an understanding of the material. Even if alternate programs are available to provide more intensive remedial instruction, they cannot be brought to bear immediately except when the learning is accomplished through expensive computerized methods. Usually, the best that teachers can do is to monitor student performance, identify problems that particular students are having, and then channel these students into individualized remedial work.

Research on Programmed Instruction. The ideas underlying programmed instruction have high face validity, and much programmed instruction has been successful. Nevertheless, research on programmed instruction has produced confusing findings that call into question some of the ideas that seem most intuitively obvious (Schramm, 1964).

For example, learning by students using carefully sequenced programs has been compared with learning by students using the same programs after they had been mixed randomly or even presented in reverse order. Many such studies reported no group difference in what was learned. Analyses of these data, along with some subsequent research, suggest that the studies that yielded no difference were studies in which the learners were relatively sophisticated (college students) and the programs were brief and easy to learn. Under these circumstances, poor sequencing did not make enough of a difference to impair learning. However, when learners are less skilled and sophisticated, or when the material is sufficiently lengthy and difficult, carefully sequenced instruction produces more learning than instruction presented randomly or in some nonoptimal sequence.

Puzzling results have also been obtained in studies comparing typical programs that require learners to respond actively and repeat frames on which they make mistakes with versions of the same programs that require learners merely to read the material without making overt responses. These studies often show no differences or even differences favoring the group that merely reads the material. Such data are not well understood, although the most common interpretation is that the value of active responses and remedial subprograms depends on the length and difficulty of the material for the learners (Tobias, 1973; Abramson & Kagen, 1975). Sophisticated students working on a brief program that they can learn easily may get as much information from reading alone as from responding overtly. In fact, under these circumstances, requiring learners to respond overtly following each brief frame may be more time consuming and irritating than helpful.

Some cognitively oriented theorists have used these puzzling findings to question the very assumptions underlying programmed instruction. They interpret the findings from studies involving scrambling the sequences of programs as evidence that incongruity stimulates discovery learning, and interpret findings showing the superiority of reading over active responding as evidence of the futility of trying to make learners conform to logic imposed by someone else rather than letting them encode and organize material in their own ways. These interpretations may be correct for secondary and college level students who are able to learn efficiently through reading and to tolerate delay of feedback without loss of learning efficiency. However, students in the early grades appear to benefit from the step-by-step sequencing of learning objectives and the frequent opportunities to make overt responses and get immediate feedback that programmed materials feature.

Reviews of the many comparisons that have been made between programmed instruction and conventional instruction indicate mixed results. Studies are about evenly split between those favoring one form and those favoring the other, and differences tend to be small in any case (Bangert, Kulik, & Kulik, 1983; Jamison, Suppes, & Wells, 1974; Kulik, Cohen, & Ebeling, 1980). Consequently, interest in programmed instruction has waned in recent years and shifted toward the newer developments described in subsequent sections of this chapter.

Keller and PSI

Working from principles of operant conditioning, Fred Keller (1968) developed a method of individualizing instruction that he called the Personalized System of Instruction (PSI) and that since has become known as the Keller Plan. The Keller Plan was developed originally for use in a college psychology course, and is presently used in a variety of college courses (McKeachie & Kulik, 1975). Its main features are self-pacing (within limits, students can go as fast or as slow as they choose), mastery orientation (students move on to a new unit only after mastering the preceding unit of criterion), and student control of the examination schedule (students take tests when they decide that they are ready, and may repeat tests as often as necessary until they reach criterion). Following an initial orientation to the course, there are few if any lectures or whole class meetings. Instead, students work individually or with one another to learn from textbooks or programmed materials, and consult with the teacher or with assistants called proctors to get help (Keller & Sherman, 1982; Sherman, 1974).

PSI is popular with college students, or at least with those students who enroll in PSI courses (Kulik, Kulik, & Carmichael, 1974; McKeachie & Kulik, 1975; Robin, 1976). These students enjoy the self-pacing arrangements, the opportunities for individualized tutoring, and the contract options that guarantee particular grades in exchange for particular levels of performance. Also, PSI students typically achieve as well as or better than students in conventional sections of the same courses (Robin, 1976), partly because they tend to put in more time and effort. Born et al. (1972) reported that PSI students averaged 45.5 hours of study time on materials placed in the library for an introductory psychology course, compared to 30.2 hours for students in conventionally taught sections of the same course.

Need for self-discipline

PSI courses work best for students who have the self-discipline and inclination to learn independently (Johnson & Ruskin, 1977). Procrastination and high withdrawal rates are commonly reported in PSI courses, though stiff mastery requirements may minimize the procrastination problem for some students. Robin (1976) reported that students with low grade point averages began studying earlier and studied more often in PSI courses with 100 percent unit mastery criteria than in PSI courses using 50 percent mastery criteria. Many students were not willing to make this effort, though, and ended up withdrawing from the PSI sections. In general, PSI courses demand more self-discipline than many students are willing or able to exert.

Learning Systems

In recent years, several integrated learning systems have been developed for use in elementary and secondary schools (Talmage, 1975). Most of these rely primarily on principles of programmed instruction, although they usually borrow heavily from cognitive principles as well.

Individually Prescribed Instruction

One such system is Individually Prescribed Instruction (IPI), an omnibus learning system for elementary schools (Glaser & Rosner, 1975). IPI converts schooling from a learning situation in which the teacher generally instructs students in groups to one in which students usually learn individually by using programmed packages. IPI is often used in open classroom settings in elementary schools.

In IPI, the teacher's role is shifted from instructor to instructional manager. Teachers decide what programs are appropriate for their students, monitor their progress, and provide individualized help when needed. They do not have to worry about curriculum development (because materials are supplied) or selection (because this is determined by the results of diagnostic tests supplied with the program).

Primary Education Project

The Primary Education Project (PEP) grew out of IPI and was developed as a way to provide individualized instruction in the early elementary grades (Wang, 1974, 1976). PEP allows for more teaching of the class as a whole, and it includes more instruction and support designed to develop students' self-scheduling skills, independent work skills, and other skills for self-management of learning by the students (Wang & Resnick, 1978; Wang, 1981).

Project PLAN

Project PLAN is another packaged program of individualized materials developed for use in the public schools. Like the PEP program, Project PLAN not only identifies learning goals and materials that students are to use in meeting those goals, but also provides students with opportunities to select their own goals and devise their own plans for meeting them (Quirk, 1971; Flanagan et al., 1975).

Individually Guided Education

Individually Guided Education (IGE) is another system devised to help students learn at their own pace through activities suited to their individual needs. However, IGE is a strategy for managing instruction rather than a set of curriculum materials. The IGE model calls for both direct teacher instruction and student work on individualized assignments (including some individualized goal setting and self-managed learning). However, the basic learning goals are specified by local teaching staffs rather than by the program developers, and these local teaching staffs then develop diagnostic tests to use in monitoring progress (Klausmeier, Sorenson, & Quilling, 1971; Schultz, 1974; Klausmeier, Rossmiller, & Saily, 1977).

IGE is distinctive in that it requires major changes in school organization. A typical school will be divided into large multi-age groupings of 100 to 150 pupils, each under the supervision of a unit leader (head teacher), other teachers, and various educational specialists. Teachers use criterion-referenced tests, observation schedules, and work samples to assess achievement levels, learning styles, and motivation levels for the students, and then use this information to identify appropriate instructional objectives and to set up instructional programs for each individual student. Children are grouped according to perceived instructional needs rather than age levels, and movement to new groups or new instructional sequences depends on mastery.

Information about student achievement in these individualized programs at the elementary and secondary levels is hard to evaluate because it is usually confined to scores on criterion-referenced tests that come with the programs. Evaluation data typically show success in meeting the objectives of the program as formulated by the developers, at least in classes where the program is considered to be well implemented. However, such data do not allow conclusions about either the absolute effectiveness or the cost effectiveness of these programs in comparison to traditional approaches (Educational Products Information Exchange, 1974). Reviewers typically report either no differences or very minor differences in the achievement of students in individualized versus traditional programs, with more variation within than between groups (Horak, 1981; Martin & Pavan, 1976).

Computerized Instruction

The ultimate in educational technology is computerized instruction, which offers the computer's information storage and retrieval capacity to enhance the possibilities for branched programming and other individualized instructional features of programmed instruction. In addition, when used in conjunction with videodisc technology, computerized instruction offers opportunities to use modeling, demonstration, and simulation as instructional methods. Work on computerized instruction is one of the most active and exciting areas of contemporary educational research, and as microcomputers continue to become both cheaper and more powerful, the feasibility of their routine use in schools increases (Atkinson & Wilson, 1969; O'Neil, 1981; Taylor, 1980; Lipson & Fisher, 1983).

Computer-assisted instruction

The earliest applications were called computer-assisted instruction (CAI), and involved presenting learners with opportunities to work through programmed packages by interacting with a computer rather than using workbooks or other traditional programmed learning materials. Much early CAI involved nothing more than computerized workbooks, and even today this remains true of most of the drill and practice programs developed for mass distribution. From the standpoint of instructional theory, these CAI programs offer no advantages over traditional programmed instruction, and the need for learners to type in answers and conform to other computer use requirements actually makes CAI less efficient than traditional programmed instruction in many cases. However, the novelty and other mo-

The computer is becoming a more familiar element in the school environment.

tivational features like flashy graphics and game-like elements associated with computerized drill and practice make it worth the trouble for certain learners. Also, because computers are perceived as impersonal and thus more "fair," students may learn to take more responsibility for their own performance under CAI than under teacher-led instruction (Griswold, 1984; Hess et al., 1970).

Computer-managed instruction

Computer-managed instruction (CMI) becomes possible when a powerful computer system is available that can keep track of each student's performance on learning modules and associated tests. The computer can be programmed to direct learners through sequences of modules when they are progressing smoothly, to recycle or branch them through remedial modules when they are having difficulties, and to provide the teacher with records of responses and test results to use in diagnosing the probable source of the problem when special help is needed. CMI eliminates much of the record keeping that is a major burden on teachers attempting to implement individualized learning systems.

Recently, computerized instruction has begun to proliferate as more potential instructional uses of computers have been recognized and more software has become available. Most software is still being produced for individual learners to use, but we should begin to see more programs intended for use by groups of learners working together or for the teacher to use in instructing the class as a whole. Eventually, computers and associated videodisc technology may perform all of the functions presently performed by films, filmstrips, television, overhead projectors, and other media.

Innovations

In the meantime, innovations in computerized instruction are going well beyond electronic workbooks for drill and practice. In courses in science, mathematics, and economics, for example, computerized simulation exercises allow students to apply what they are learning by testing predictions or trying to solve problems under realistic conditions and then getting feedback about the likely outcomes of their decisions (Arons, 1984). The text editing capabilities of microcomputers are now being used in writing classes, where students can edit and revise their compositions by computer and thus bypass the drudgery involved in doing so by hand (Lawlor, 1982; Levin & Boruta, 1983). The graphics capabilities of computers have considerable potential for application in courses in design, art, and architecture. In general, computerized instruction has potential application to just about any grade level or subject matter. What remains to be seen is the degree to which the advantages that computerized instruction brings to a particular situation are sufficient to justify the trouble and expense involved.

Concluding Comments on Educational Technology

From teaching machines through programmed instruction and educational television, new educational technologies have been introduced with great enthusiasm, and predictions have been made that they will revolutionize education in general and replace teachers in particular. Computerized instruction is presently being touted with the same enthusiasm and predictions. So far, most technological innovations have proven useful to some degree in some aspects of education. These innovations have not truly revolutionized education, however. Instead, they have become assimilated into the traditional model of schooling featuring teacher-led group instruction supplemented by recitation, discussion, and individual work on practice and application activities.

We expect that the same will be true of computerized instruction and all other potential technological innovations that depend on the independent learning efforts of the individual student. There are two basic reasons for this prediction. First, under these individualized learning systems, students must be willing and able to maintain concentration, understand and follow directions, and correct and learn from their mistakes while working independently for sustained periods of time. Most students in the early grades and many older students lack the reading comprehension and other independent learning skills required, and many of the students who do have the necessary skills lack the motivation to work on their own in this way for very long. Second, even students who have both the skills and the motivation to learn independently tend to run into trouble if left on their own too long, even when they seem to be progressing nicely. For example, Erlwanger (1975) interviewed bright students who consistently met mastery criteria on unit tests from their individualized mathematics curricula. He found that many of these students had misunderstood the material and developed mathematical concepts that were at least partly incorrect, even though they were able to get the correct answers to the problems intended as application exercises. The students had invented their own rules of thumb, which were useful for solving those particular problems but which would not work, and would leave the students badly confused, later when they encountered different applications of the concepts they were supposed to be learning.

Limitations

Technological innovations can be expected to improve schooling, but as tools that enhance the effectiveness of teachers rather than as replacements for them. So far, it remains to be demonstrated that media and technology provide significant educational benefits in their own right, independent of the quality of the design of the instruction with which they are being used (Clark, 1983).

SUMMARY

Behaviorists approach the study of learning by concentrating on overt behaviors that can be observed and measured, and by seeking to discover general laws that can be used to predict and control such behavior. They discuss behavior primarily in terms of external events that elicit or cue it and that reinforce elicited stimulus-response relationships. Behaviorists have developed principles and techniques designed to induce learning (covered in this chapter) as well as principles and techniques designed to control behavior (covered in Chapter 21).

Early behaviorists studied the conditioning that occurs as associations become established through contiguity and repetition. Pavlov developed the classical conditioning paradigm in which repeated presentation of the conditioned stimulus prior to the appearance of the unconditioned stimulus develops associations between them so that learners begin to produce a conditioned response to the conditioned stimulus that is similar to the unconditioned response that occurs naturally in reaction to the unconditioned stimulus. Conditioned responses built up in this manner can be extinguished by continuing to present the conditioned stimulus but no longer following it with the unconditioned stimulus. Extinguished responses will show spontaneous recovery for a time, but will eventually disappear unless the conditioning paradigm is reinstated. Once conditioned responses are established, they can be expanded through generalization or refined through discrimination if variation is introduced in the range of conditioned stimuli presented and in the consequences that consistently follow these stimuli. Pavlovian or classical conditioning processes are involved in the signal learning or stimulus substitution learning that occurs in school. Much of vocabulary learning occurs this way, for example.

Watson popularized the term behaviorism and showed the application of classical conditioning processes to human emotional development. Thorndike developed the instrumental conditioning paradigm and formulated the law of exercise and the law of effect. Functionalists studied factors that affected the rate or extent of learning, especially the effects of massed versus distributed practice and of continuing practice to overlearning. They popularized learning curves as visual depictions of progress in learning.

Skinner developed the operant conditioning paradigm for shaping behavior through contingent reinforcement. The paradigm can be used to bring behavior under stimulus control by reinforcing responses only when they occur in the presence of the cue stimulus, to develop stimulus discrimination and response discrimination, and to maintain established stimulus-response connections by fading the original 100 percent reinforcement schedule to some partial reinforcement schedule. Partial reinforcement schedules can be based on the time interval between reinforcements or the ratio of responses to be reinforced, and these interval and ratio schedules can be either fixed or variable. Learners adjust to fixed schedules because they allow prediction of reinforcement delivery. Consequently, variable schedules, especially variable ratio schedules, produce steadier and more persistent rates of response.

Skinner advocates applications of operant conditioning principles to education in the classroom, and these principles have been incorporated into behavior modification programs, teaching machines, programmed instruction, and computer-assisted instruction. Over time, however, the emphasis has shifted from reinforcement to programming for continuous progress through small successive approximations as the key to the success of this approach.

Unlike Skinner and traditional behaviorists, social learning theorists include reference to the covert mental activities of the learner in their approach to behavioristic learning theory. Also, in addition to studying learning that occurs through various conditioning paradigms, they study learning that occurs through imitation of models or vicariously experiencing what is happening to models being observed. Bandura distinguishes between the nominal stimulus and the functional stimulus and between imitation and modeling. In the classroom, modeling is an important mechanism not only for demonstrating particular skills but for influencing students' attitudes, beliefs, and behavior.

Meichenbaum and others have developed cognitive behavior modification techniques to develop in learners the capacity for controlling their own behavior through goal setting, planning, self-instruction, self-monitoring, and self-reinforcement. Modeling combined with verbalized self-instruction—where the model surfaces covert mental processes for learners by verbalizing self-talk as he or she models the task—is a particularly powerful method of teaching complex thinking and problem solving to students.

Behaviorists have been prominent in developing educational technology for use in classrooms. Early work on teaching machines evolved into the science and technology of programmed instruction. Programs are designed to move learners in small steps with high rates of success from their initial entry level of skill to the upper level representing the target objective. Linear programs move all learners through a single fixed sequence believed to be effective for teaching everyone, and branched programs include options for skipping certain modules or providing remedial instruction as learner needs dictate. The self-pacing or learner-control aspect of programmed instruction also underscores its status as a form of individualized instruction.

The Keller Plan (also known as the Personalized System of Instruction, or PSI) is a modification of programmed instruction. It features self-pacing, a mastery orientation, and student control of the examination schedule, typically coupled with a contract system for determining grades. Students work individually or with one another to learn from textbooks or programmed materials, get assistance from proctors when they need help, and take examinations when they are ready. Examinations can be repeated, within limits of course, until a particular target grade is achieved. The Keller Plan is used in many college courses. It is popular with students who enjoy learning individually and effective with those students who have the self-discipline to maintain the necessary study schedule.

In recent years, elementary and secondary schools have been using integrated learning systems that combine principles of individualized and programmed instruction with principles drawn from cognitive psychology. Even more recently, computer-assisted instruction and other computerized approaches are being integrated into these learning systems. Despite the high visibility of these technological innovations and the frequent claims that they will revolutionalize education, the research data on them are mixed and there are reasons to doubt the feasibility of approaches that expect students to learn through extensive independent interaction with curriculum materials or computers in the absence of frequent input, guidance, and supervision from teachers.

QUESTIONS AND PROBLEMS

1. Without rereading the text, differentiate between the following terms: extinction, spontaneous recovery, generalization, and discrimination. Most students will have a difficult time defining these terms after simply reading the text one time. Students who have had an introductory psychology course before taking the present course may do better; even so, we suspect that most students will have difficulty defining these terms. Why is this? What are the implications of this for how key terms need to be taught in a course?
2. Without rereading the text, define Thorndike's law of exercise and law of effect. What are the key differences between these two laws? We suspect that you found it easier to remember and differentiate these terms than the terms mentioned in Question 1. Why is this? What is different about the two sets of information that makes one more difficult to learn than the other?
3. Why is massed practice usually less efficient than distributed practice? Cite examples where massed practice would be more efficient than distributed practice.
4. In general, do college instructors encourage massed practice or distributed practice? What about high school instructors?
5. What is partial reinforcement? What are its unique and powerful advantages in a classroom setting?
6. In what way might teacher self-talk that is modeled verbally for students help them to become more reflective and analytical in their classroom responses?
7. Visit a school and determine how microcomputers are being used in classroom instruction. Do all students have equal access to the computers, or do some students have more frequent or different computer experiences than others?
8. In general, characterize the role of microcomputers in the modern classroom. What are the advantages and disadvantages of this technology? Will you use the technology in your own classroom? If so, how?
9. Supporters of programmed instruction and individualized learning systems tout them as solutions to the individualization problem and as escapes from the boredom of lock-step curricula. Critics attack them as ineffective, asocial/mechanistic/dehumanizing, and based on false assumptions about learning. Where do you stand? Why?
10. Would you rather be called a teacher or an instructional manager? Why?
11. How could you determine whether or not students had mastered something to the point of overlearning? What should and could you do if they had?

CASE STUDIES

Lump in the Throat. Cindy Clutch, an otherwise capable and successful student, is having a terrible time in her high school speech class. Each of her first two speeches, although confined to just two minutes each and centered on familiar content that Cindy should have been able to discuss with ease, was a disaster. In each case she started out noticeably nervous and became increasingly so as she went on, turning red, losing her train of thought, stammering uncharacteristically, and in general, showing every sign of acute anxiety. Her speech teacher arranges a private conference to discuss the problem, and after some hemming and hawing, Cindy explains that she has dreaded making speeches in front of the class ever since a traumatic experience occurred in the eighth grade.

As an attractive early maturer, Cindy had been the object of a great deal of attention, both desired and undesired, from the boys. She had handled this well enough during informal contact with the boys in her class, but during this earlier experience, as she stood facing the class while making her presentation, she suddenly became acutely aware that she was wearing a tight sweater and that several of the boys were staring intently at her breasts. She blushed, lost her train of thought, and had difficulty finishing the presentation. She has been anxious in public speaking situations ever since, even though she knows intellectually that she no longer has a reason to be. How does the theory and research on conditioning, especially the classical conditioning paradigm, discussed in this chapter apply to Cindy's problem? What steps might Cindy take to overcome it? How might her speech teacher help?

Conditioning Shank. Karen hurled the frisbee and shouted, "Go get it, Shank!" Shank, a young German shepherd, arched his eyebrows and turned over on his back. Karen grumbled to herself, tramped 50 yards to get the frisbee, and continued to mumble to herself as she returned to the side of her friend Shank, who had meanwhile fallen asleep. Karen shook Shank gently, but said with irritation, "Look at the frisbee." Shank pawed it, then turned over. Karen reached into her jeans and pulled out a handful of dog pellets. As Shank devoured them, Karen said, "Shank, look at the frisbee." Then she hurled the frisbee, yelling, "Go get it, Shank!" Shank ignored her.

What is Karen's training problem? Taking into account the principles of operant conditioning, how would you advise her to change her approach to training Shank? What would you do if you were a teacher who was experiencing problems training a messy and forgetful student to put his things away before he leaves his desk and to keep his area in order?

Practice Makes Boredom. Jim Butkus, a second-grade teacher, walks to Terry Stone's desk. Terry nervously and rapidly stashes a comic book in the desk as Mr. Butkus asks with concern, "Terry, why aren't you practicing your spelling words as I asked?" Terry's face reddens as he shuffles through the book trying to find today's assignment. "It's okay," Mr. Butkus continues reassuringly, "Tell me why you aren't studying?" Terry remains silent for a moment and then quickly blurts out, "I'm tired of spending 15 minutes every day studying spelling words. Practice, practice, practice . . . it's boring!"

Assuming that Terry and his classmates need this spelling practice, how might Mr. Butkus change his approach to spelling instruction so as to provide more interesting or at least more varied ways for the students to get the practice they need? Be specific, and list several examples.

Chapter 8

The Cognitive Structural View of Learning

OBJECTIVES

When you have mastered the material in this chapter you will be able to

1. Describe the cognitive structural approach to learning theory and differentiate it from the behaviorist approach
2. Define the key concepts of gestalt psychology (gestalt, holistic perception, figure-ground relationships, good form, learning through insight) and explain the implications of this approach for classroom instruction
3. Define Bruner's three modes of knowledge representation (enactive, iconic, symbolic) and his concept of the spiral curriculum, and explain his ideas about how teachers can stimulate students' cognitive development
4. Describe the principles of discovery learning built into *Man: A Course of Study* (MACOS)
5. Explain the key ideas underlying three other well known approaches to stimulating learning by discovery (the open education movement, inquiry training, and simulation games)
6. Identify the strengths and weaknesses of discovery learning and the circumstances under which it can and cannot be used effectively
7. Define meaningful reception learning as described by Ausubel
8. Define advance organizers and state their instructional functions
9. Explain Ausubel's ideas about structuring and sequencing instruction so as to ease learning and enhance transfer

In the previous chapter, we described how behaviorists view learning as response to external stimulation controlled through reinforcement. In this and the next chapter, we describe the approaches taken by cognitive theorists who stress the conceptual aspects of learning over its behavioral aspects. Most cognitive theorists concentrate on human learning, especially the meaningful learning of information and intellectual skills that occurs in schools and is mediated through language. They concentrate on understanding these forms of learning and on how to facilitate them through instruction, rather than attempting to formulate general laws of behavior that apply across species.

Cognitive theorists recognize that much learning involves associations established according to the principles of contiguity and repetition. They also acknowledge the importance of reinforcement, although they stress its role in providing feedback about the correctness of responses over its role as a motivator. However, even while accepting such behavioristic concepts, cognitive theorists view learning as involving the acquisition or reorganization of the cognitive structures through which humans process and store information. According to cognitive theorists, intake of information from the environment is active and systematic rather than passive and controlled by cue stimuli, learning involves active cognitive processing of information rather than mere stimulus-response association, and items of information acquired through learning are "sorted," "filed," and "cross-indexed" rather than stored in isolation from one another.

Cognitive structural approach

In this chapter, we discuss the ideas of theorists who stress what we call the cognitive structural approach to learning. This approach holds that meaningful learning involves understanding not only various individual facts and principles, but the relationships between them, and thus building up cognitive structures for retaining this information in an organized way. These theorists approach instruction by concentrating on the key ideas that can be used to organize bodies of information, and then developing ways to teach these key ideas or guide learners to discover them. In the next chapter, we will describe the ideas of cognitive theorists who stress the role of learners' own information processing capabilities in determining their learning, and who approach instruction by developing ways to stimulate learners to use these capabilities to process the information to be learned.

The present chapter begins with discussion of gestalt psychology, which provided the theoretical roots for the cognitive structural approach to learning that eventually developed. It then discusses the two best known approaches that have been developed within the cognitive structural tradition: discovery learning and meaningful reception learning. Discovery learning, as articulated by Jerome Bruner, is stimulated by arranging for students to engage in a series of activities that will guide them toward discovery of basic principles and key ideas. Meaningful reception learning, as described by David Ausubel, is stimulated by presenting these basic principles and key ideas to the students directly so that they can be used as organizers around which to structure larger bodies of related information.

Gestalt Psychology

In the first third of the twentieth century, when behaviorism was dominating American psychology, a variety of approaches were thriving in Europe (Freud in Vienna, Piaget in Geneva, mental measurement work in France and England). In Germany, a movement that came to be called gestalt psychology was developed by Max Wertheimer and his associates Kurt Koffka and Wolfgang Kohler, all of whom later emigrated to the United States to escape the Nazis. The gestalt psychologists were interested in perception as well as in learning, and especially in the fact that perception tends to be organized into meaningful patterns that include the relationships between elements in addition to the elements themselves. "Gestalt" is a German word that corresponds roughly to the English words "pattern" or "configuration." A *gestalt* is an organized, integrated whole that has identity and meaning in its own right and not merely as the sum of its parts. Individual parts can be identified and dealt with as elements, but in addition they are related to one another in gestalten, or configurational patterns, to form larger parts, and ultimately, wholes.

Subjectively organized perception

Gestalt psychologists developed visual illusions and other demonstrations that *perception is both subjective and organized in gestalt fashion*. For example, what do you see when you look at the following?

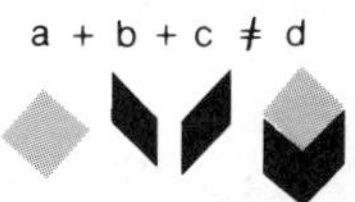

Individually, all you see are three differently shaped two-dimensional figures with four sides each. But when these figures are fitted together, they combine to form the image of a three-dimensional cube that is not merely the sum of its parts. The parts can still be seen unchanged within this new gestalt, and yet the physical properties of the new arrangement tend to make you see a single cube rather than an arrangement of three two-dimensional figures. This illustrates the larger point that human perception tends to be holistic. Typically, we do not take in isolated bits of information and impose meaning on them gradually. Instead, the very act of perception includes the organization of incoming stimuli within meaningful patterns that are recognized instantly if they are familiar patterns.

Figure-ground discrimination

Perception also includes instantaneous figure-ground discrimination, in which we select certain meaningful patterns of input to focus on as figures that stand out from the rest of the input that acts as background. As illustrated in Figure 8.1, these figure-ground relationships often shift, especially when we are processing rich or complex input. Gestalt psychologists used such illustrations to show that we actively impose meaning on the input we receive—different people will see the same input differently.

Figure 8.1 One of Maurits Escher's (1898–1972) well-known lithographs. The forms refuse to "stay still"; they move from background to foreground almost as if they had a life of their own.

Various visual illusions illustrate the same point. A given geometric design can be seen as a stairway going up if looked at one way, but as a stairway going down if looked at another way. The same drawing can be seen as a stylish young woman if looked at one way, but as a sad-eyed older woman if looked at another way (Figure 8.2).

In addition to showing shifts in figure-ground relationships, gestalt psychologists developed demonstrations that figures can be perceived differently depending on how they compare or contrast with other figures or with the background. For example, a gray dot can be made to look lighter by showing it against a dark background, or to look darker by showing it against a light background. Similarly, lines of identical length can be made to look either longer or shorter by adding other lines that are presented near them or in connection with them. Such contrast effects occur with more complex perceptions, as well. For example, teachers grading compositions or essay test responses will tend to grade an average essay higher if it follows several poor essays, but to grade the average essay lower if it follows several well-written essays.

Contrast effects

Explanations for factors governing perception

Based on such demonstrations and various experiments, gestalt psychologists proposed a great number of "laws" to explain some of the factors governing perception and to allow predictions about how particular stimuli would be perceived and remembered. The general organizing principle underlying these laws is the tendency of people to impose good form on stimulus input: To perceive and remember objects and events as conforming to familiar or expected patterns. Even when the input is not simple, regular, or complete enough to justify such perception, we tend to see and remember it as if it were. Elements present in the objective stimulus that conflict with our perceptions are likely to be ignored during the initial perception, and forgotten altogether later when the perception is remembered.

Although gestalt psychology dealt primarily with perception rather than learning, Wertheimer drew on it to formulate guidelines for instruction. He noted, for example, that just as highlighting, framing, contrasting, and other illustration techniques can be used to make particular visual stimuli stand out as figure against the background, parallel techniques for information presentation can be used to make key ideas salient to learners. More generally, Wertheimer stressed the importance of making learners aware of the structure of the content to be learned and the relationships among its elements, so that it could be retained as an organized body of knowledge.

Clarity

Lectures or other verbal presentations to students need to have high signal-to-noise ratios if they are to be heard without difficulty—in other words, a relatively quiet background without distracting noises, and with the speaker talking loudly enough for everyone to hear without straining. Attention to key words can be stimulated by enunciating them more loudly, more slowly, or with exaggerated emphasis. Similar principles hold for reading materials, where space, contrast, letter size and spacing, and other

Figure 8.2

figure-ground considerations can be used to make materials easier to read and to minimize confusion or fatigue. Key words can be stressed through using underlines, boxes, italics, capital letters, or other structuring techniques. At the same time, backgrounds can be kept free from distractors that might pull attention away from the focal stimuli. For example, overliberal use of pictures in introductory reading material sometimes is self-defeating, apparently because children pay more attention to the pictures than to the letters and words they are supposed to be learning.

Some students have difficulty separating figure from ground even when actively trying to do so (see our discussion of field dependent students in Chapter 24). It may be necessary to aid such students by pointing out distinctive features, tracing, showing several examples, or using visual aids. Similarly, it may be necessary to draw some students' attention to contrasts that they might not notice otherwise.

Learning Through Insight

Some gestalt psychologists conducted research on learning. The best known of this work demonstrated that complex learning sometimes occurs rapidly through insight. In a typical experiment, chimpanzees were placed in a situation where food was in sight but could not be reached. After giving up trying to reach it by stretching or jumping, the chimps sometimes would engage in what appeared to be thinking, which culminated in what appeared to be an "aha" experience followed by rapid solution of the problem.

For example, if the food had been suspended from the ceiling so as to be too high to reach, and if the cage contained a box or two, the chimp would usually realize that the food could be reached if the box or boxes were moved under it and used as a platform. In another variation, the food was placed outside of the cage, but a stick was available that could be used to push the food close enough to be grabbed. In a more complex variation, a short stick was available that could be used to gather in a longer stick, and the longer stick could be used to gather the food (Köhler, 1959).

The chimps did not always solve such problems, and sometimes they solved them only when the experimenter arranged conditions to favor discovery of the solution. For example, the problem involving the short stick, the long stick, and the food was unlikely to be solved if these three items were placed far away from one another, but more likely to be solved if the items were lined up in order outside of the cage (first the short stick, then the longer stick, and then the food). In any case, these experiments proved that instrumental learning could occur without trial and error or the shaping of responses through reinforcement. Instead, the chimps "figured out" the solution through deliberate problem-solving efforts, and then demonstrated the solution in a single trial. Furthermore, if placed in the same situation again, they solved the problem immediately without the need to hesitate for thought, indicating that the learning was retained. This was learning by discovery achieved through cognition culminating in insight. It is the same kind of learning that students demonstrate when they intuitively "see"

Learning by discovery

a way to prove a complex geometry theorem. Many educational psychologists believe that such discovery learning should occur regularly in classrooms, and approach instructional questions by asking how conditions can be arranged to guide students toward such discoveries.

Bruner and Discovery Learning

Jerome Bruner (1960, 1966, 1971) is one of the leading cognitive structural theorists. His ideas about how children develop and learn have much in common with those of Piaget. However, he has gone much further than Piaget in making suggestions about how teachers can stimulate learning in the classroom, especially by guiding their students to discover principles and relationships for themselves.

Categorization and Organization of Knowledge

Bruner's ideas begin with his assumptions about human perception and information processing. He notes that we are constantly bombarded with stimulation to all of our senses, much more stimulation than we can consciously attend to and process. Therefore, we attend selectively—we focus on that portion of the stimulus input that is most important or interesting. Furthermore, the input that we attend to is actively perceived and interpreted in an organized fashion, using expectations developed through prior experience. Input processed in this manner is stored in the form of imagery, concepts, and other representational structures, and these are ultimately organized into a grand structure that constitutes the person's model of reality.

Selective attention

In Bruner's view, knowledge is organized into categories that simplify the task of processing and retaining information by allowing us to interpret the new with reference to the familiar. We can recognize specific instances as examples of more general categories of knowledge or events.

Categories of knowledge

Principles of Cognitive Development

Bruner views learning as an ongoing process of developing an increasingly sophisticated cognitive structure for representing and interacting with the world. He describes the process as follows (Bruner, 1966):

1. Growth is characterized by increasing independence of the response from the stimulus (responses learned in particular situations are not merely retained but may become generalized concepts or skills available for use in a variety of situations).
2. Growth is made possible because events are internalized into a "storage system" that amounts to an organized model of the environment (thus children can go beyond merely responding to immediate stimuli because they have a model of the world that they can use to make

predictions about what will happen if they initiate particular kinds of change).

3. Intellectual growth involves an increasing capacity to say to oneself or others, using words or symbols, what one has done or will do. This development gradually frees children from necessary reliance on trial-and-error behavior and enables them to solve problems through logical thinking.
4. Intellectual development is stimulated through systematic and contingent interaction between a tutor and a learner (appropriate instruction stimulates intellectual growth beyond what would occur through spontaneous exploration and discovery).
5. Teaching is greatly facilitated by the medium of language, which provides not only a means of communication but a means for imposing order on our experiences.
6. Intellectual development is marked by the increasing capacity to deal with several alternatives simultaneously, to attend to several sequences during the same time period, and to allocate time and attention in a manner appropriate to these multiple demands.

Modes of Representation of Knowledge

Enactive mode

Bruner identifies three general modes of representation of knowledge, similar to the developmental stages postulated by Piaget. The first, predominant in early childhood but continuing throughout life, is the enactive mode. Knowledge represented in the enactive mode is similar to Piaget's sensorimotor schemas, and reflects Piaget's notion that we know what we do. Enactive mode knowledge is knowledge about how to manipulate the environment through overt behavior. Images, words, symbols, and other purely cognitive processes are not involved to any significant degree. Because both Piaget and Bruner see this kind of knowledge as primary in normal development, many educational theorists assume that all kinds of learning will be most efficient if they begin with some kind of active experience designed to provide a base of enactive mode knowledge on which to build.

Iconic mode

With development, thinking becomes less stimulus bound and dependent on active manipulation of concrete objects. Children become capable of understanding and manipulating knowledge represented in the iconic mode via pictures, images, or memories of previously experienced objects or events. They can begin to think and answer questions about the properties of objects themselves rather than merely about what can be done with these objects; they can perform arithmetic computations without having to count actual objects or use their fingers; they can discuss objects or events based on pictures or stimulated memories; and they can recognize or conserve the constant properties of objects after they have been transformed (a square is still a square if you change its color or size). Although unable to handle completely abstract concepts, children who are able to represent knowledge in the iconic mode can think logically about such knowledge (in the manner of Piaget's concrete operational thinking).

Symbolic mode

Around adolescence, students begin to become able to represent knowledge in the symbolic mode where they can understand and manipulate purely abstract concepts. Students must be able to represent knowledge in the symbolic mode in order to profit from extended verbal instruction in the more formal aspects of subject matter knowledge (higher-order rules and principles expressing relationships among defined concepts).

Importance of variety of experiences

Although Bruner recognizes that students with well-developed abilities to represent knowledge in the symbolic mode are capable of understanding extended expository instruction meaningfully, as far as it goes, at least, he does not recommend this as a way to teach. For one thing, only a portion of the students will become highly skilled in symbolic mode representation. Furthermore, Bruner believes that even these students will not profit much from extended expository instruction about abstract content because this will tend to produce figurative knowledge without corresponding operative knowledge—students will memorize definitions, formulas, or scientific principles without truly understanding them or being able to apply them. Consequently, he stresses the importance of offering students a variety of educational experiences and instructional methods. These would include active "hands on" experiences in addition to verbal explanations and discussions, as well as demonstrations and examples presented in the enactive and iconic modes in addition to explanations in the symbolic mode. He also urges teachers to go beyond effective instruction of particular information by helping students to integrate their knowledge by presenting them with organizing principles, cause-effect explanations, and other aids to help them see how things relate to one another.

The Spiral Curriculum. Bruner is famous and controversial for his statement that any subject matter can be taught in some intellectually honest way to any learner. Some people took this as a claim that anyone can learn anything, and criticized Bruner as a misguided idealist. This is not what Bruner meant, however. The key to his statement is the qualifier "in some intellectually honest way." Bruner believes that at least some aspects of any subject matter can be presented to a particular learner so that the input will be true to the spirit of the subject matter discipline from which the information is drawn (i.e., the information is accurate, organized around useful concepts, and complete in some sense, even though it may be just a small part of a much larger picture from the point of view of a subject matter specialist) and meaningful to the learner (i.e., the learner can relate its content and mode of presentation to his or her existing cognitive categories).

In applying this idea, Bruner recommends what he calls the spiral curriculum—instead of sequencing objectives so that learners move in lockstep fashion through successive steps of increasing difficulty or complexity, learners are brought back to given topics periodically but encouraged to address these topics at different levels of knowledge representation and analysis. This is based on the notion that each time the "spiral" comes around to a particular set of concepts, learners will have broadened and deepened their knowledge about these and related concepts, and therefore will be both able and motivated to undertake newer, deeper explorations into the topic. For example, the ability to recognize and label different animals might be an appropriate initial objective for most students. Then, these students could learn some of the classifications for animals and the similarities and differences among animal types. Later they could learn about the natural habitats and behavior of various animals, and about the differences between wild and domestic animals, or between animals considered edible and those considered inedible. Still later, they could study the same animals in courses in anatomy or physiology.

Thus, Bruner is interested in sequencing, but not the step-by-step sequencing that behaviorists prefer. For one thing, he has little interest in minimizing errors, a principle that is basic to Skinner's approach. Bruner sees errors as being useful for maintaining interest and stimulating hypotheses, if students are not made to feel ashamed of their mistakes or taught with methods that reward speed in "covering the material" rather than success in developing a deep and broad understanding of it. Also, even though he acknowledges the value of organizing and structuring the content to be taught, he notes that often there is no one best way to structure a particular body of content, and that there are limits to what can be accomplished by imposing structure externally. He believes that learners will retain more if allowed to organize material according to their own interests.

Errors as being useful

Discovery Learning

Bruner believes that much learning, and, in particular, learning that is most meaningful to learners, is developed through discoveries that occur during exploration motivated by curiosity. In schools, Bruner would like to maximize the degree to which learners expand their knowledge by developing and testing hypotheses rather than merely reading or listening to verbal presentations of information. Consequently, he advocates instructional methods that encourage and guide students to learn by discovery.

He believes that opportunities to manipulate objects actively and to transform them through direct action are valuable for inducing curiosity, especially with young children. So are activities that encourage students to search, explore, analyze, or otherwise actively process input rather than merely respond to it. In theory, such opportunities not only will increase students' knowledge about the topic at hand, but also will help them to develop generalized learning-to-learn strategies useful for discovering knowledge in other situations.

Man: A Course of Study (MACOS). Bruner's ideas about discovery learning are illustrated in Man: A Course of Study (MACOS), a social studies program developed by Bruner and others for use in elementary schools. The total package includes readings, suggested activities and discussion questions, films, and simulation games. Guidelines for teachers are included, but the developers emphasize that teachers will need to make their own decisions about how much time to spend on various topics and how much simulation to use.

MACOS deals with the varieties of human beings and their habitats, cultures, and behaviors. It relies on features such as novelty, incongruity, and contrast to stimulate students' curiosity and cause them to address the content in an active, inquiry-oriented mode. Rather than routinely presenting information and then moving to application, MACOS frequently introduces topics by presenting students with application problems and inviting them to formulate guiding principles and generate possible solutions on their own before reading further. Thus, the students might be invited to explore questions such as "How does one get through territory where there are strong predators?" before reading information on this topic. Perhaps the classic example is the "fill-in-the-map" exercise in which students are given maps indicating the physical features of an area (temperature, rainfall, elevations, and locations of natural resources and waterways), and invited to speculate about the locations of the capital city and the major seaport, the economic emphases likely to develop in particular regions, or the placement and functions of the major highways or railroads. Later, the students are given more detailed maps indicating the development that actually occurred in the area in question. This feedback will generally confirm the validity and usefulness of the principles of geography being learned, and it will also introduce complexity by showing that exceptions to these principles occur frequently due to unique local factors (capital cities are not always the largest and/or most centrally located cities).

Use of novelty

MACOS uses novelty to stimulate curiosity and thinking by exposing students to unfamiliar people, places, and practices. It also helps students to structure the content by repeatedly calling attention to four kinds of contrast: humans versus animals, humans versus prehistorical evolutionary precursors of *Homo Sapiens*, contemporary humans versus primitive humans, and adults versus children. In general, the program attempts to provide students with models to use in analyzing the social world, to impart respect for the capacities and humanity of man as a continually evolving species, and to develop students' awareness of and confidence in their own thinking and problem-solving abilities.

Evaluation of program

MACOS is difficult to evaluate because little research is available on it and because attention to its pedagogical features and effects has been obscured by the political controversy that surrounds it. Conservatives object to its emphasis on evolution and its depictions of cultural practices that they consider immoral or unsuitable for presentation to children.

MACOS has produced mixed reactions among psychologists and educators. Supporters believe that it is one of the best learning systems available. Others see it as just another social science curriculum, and still others criticize it for depending too much on student initiative and discovery, or conversely, for not going far enough in this direction. Many social studies educators like the processes of discovery and novelty stressed in the program but dislike its content; for example, many feel that there should be more emphasis on modern issues.

Evaluation data on MACOS suggest that students enjoy it and achieve at levels comparable to those of students using more traditional social studies curricula (Cole & Lacefield, 1980; Cort & Peskowitz, 1977). Like most curriculum packages, it probably works better for some teachers and students than for others. Since it is a classical example of the discovery learning approach to teaching, it would be useful for you to examine MACOS if this approach appeals to you. If you are oriented more to the primary grades, you might read *Young Children Reinvent Arithmetic* (Kamii & DeClark, 1985), which describes a discovery learning approach to early mathematics instruction based on Piagetian concepts.

Other Approaches to Discovery Learning

Many other approaches to education have been developed at least in part as efforts to foster learning by discovery (Shulman & Keislar, 1966). Unlike MACOS, these tend to be general approaches rather than curriculum and instruction packages designed for specific courses.

Open Education

During the 1960s, ideas about how children learn drawn from Piaget, Bruner, and other psychologists were combined with ideas about the design and management of schools drawn from the British "infant" schools (elementary schools) to form what became known as the "open education" movement.

The open education movement was a reaction against the traditional model of whole-class instruction featuring expository lecturing, recitation, and individual seatwork. In its place, open education calls for 1) more flexible use of space (replacing anchored desks with light chairs and small tables that can be rearranged easily to create a variety of settings, and using bookcases, area rugs, movable room dividers, and special equipment to create learning centers at different places in the room); 2) planning for a range of small-group or individualized activities to occur simultaneously as students learn through exploration and discovery on their own or with peers; and 3) readiness to respond to students' initiatives and help them to pursue their individual interests. In mathematics and science, for example, students in open education classrooms would receive less textbook-based instruction and spend more time playing mathematical games or working on scientific experiments.

Open-space architecture

The open education philosophy and teaching methods should not be confused with open-space architecture (construction of schools without stationary internal walls so that the space can be used flexibly). The two concepts are distinct: open educational practices can be implemented in self-contained classrooms, and traditional group-based instruction can be

The open classroom allows small-group and individual activities to occur simultaneously.

conducted within schools featuring open-space architecture. In fact, there is only a small correlation between open-space architecture and the use of open education principles (Gump, 1980).

Partially as a result of strong advocacy (see Barth, 1972), the open education philosophy achieved considerable popularity among teacher educators in the 1960s and 1970s and was implemented to some degree in many elementary schools. Many contemporary elementary classrooms are equipped with learning centers offering hands-on experiences, although such learning centers are usually intended to supplement rather than replace traditional group instruction.

The effects of open education are difficult to evaluate. Most studies have been small and poorly controlled, so that any effects observed could have been due to pre-existing teacher differences rather than to the introduction of open education principles, or could have been short-term novelty effects rather than more permanent changes due to the principles themselves. Also, "open education" means different things to different people, so it is difficult to know exactly which dimensions of the philosophy were being implemented in a particular study, and how the results of that study might compare with results of other studies (Marshall, 1981).

Consequently, there has been a great deal of disagreement about the effects of open education. Some reviewers (Horwitz, 1979; Walberg, Schiller, & Haertel, 1979) have concluded that there are no differences between open and traditional education in effects on student achievement, but that open education improves affective outcomes (students' attitudes, self-concepts, curiosity, etc.). However, other reviewers have variously reported no trend at all (Lukasevich & Gray, 1978), minor differences favoring traditional classes on achievement measures but open classes on affective measures (Gage, 1985; Giaconia & Hedges, 1982; Hayes & Day, 1980; Peterson, 1979), or even a significant advantage to traditional classes on affective measures (Rosenshine, 1978). The largest study completed to date (Hayes & Day, 1980), which covered 96 third-grade classrooms in 18 public schools, found no relationship between degree of "openness" and measures of student achievement, self-perceptions, and school attendance. Our impression is that the smaller and less well-controlled studies tend to favor open education (especially on affective measures), but that the larger and better controlled studies tend to favor traditional education (especially on achievement measures).

Combining open with traditional approaches

In any case, it appears that well-planned and coordinated combinations of traditional approaches with open approaches work better than extreme versions of either philosophy. Within such balanced approaches, students receive both expository instruction and opportunities to explore and discover, but most of their discovery learning occurs through exposure to planned series of activities designed to guide them toward particular discoveries. For ideas about implementing open education procedures, see Brown and Precious (1973) or Silberman (1973).

Inquiry Training

Suchman (1962) has developed principles for teaching students the information processing, thinking, and analytic skills associated with active scientific inquiry. Suchman believes that students will not engage in inquiry, especially when it is new to them, unless they are both motivated to do so and taught how to do it. He suggests stimulating curiosity by presenting students with puzzles or discrepancies, helping students to realize that they can pose and attempt to answer questions for themselves, and arming them with the skills for doing so. Such skills include verification (checking facts), experimentation (isolating particular aspects of the problem to be pursued one at a time), and constructuve hypothesis generation (working systematically from the information given rather than guessing randomly).

Phases of inquiry training

Weil and Joyce (1978) identify five phases in inquiry training: 1) presentation of puzzling stimuli, 2) data gathering, 3) experimentation, 4) explaining the problem, and 5) consolidation. The students learn to first establish the facts, then determine relevant questions, and then develop ways to pursue those questions and build explanations for the results they discover. The teacher structures the learning context and supervises the social system, but allows students' ideas to control the intellectual development of work on the problem. Weil and Joyce (1978) suggest the following teacher actions:

1. Encourage students to ask questions that can be answered yes or no (more general questions are harder to verify).

2. When students raise open questions, ask them to rephrase the questions in terms that can be verified.
3. Help students to recognize when they make statements that have not been verified.
4. Use and encourage the use of inquiry language (i.e., calling informed guesses hypotheses, describing students' explanations as theories).
5. Do not approve or reject students' theories, let them test them for themselves.
6. Encourage students to state their theories and assumptions as clearly as possible and to make specific plans for testing them.
7. Encourage interaction among the students.

Results from research on inquiry teaching are mixed, but the approach appears to be beneficial when implemented properly, especially for older or more cognitively mature students who are pursuing complex content. It is one way for teachers to prepare students to explore and discover on their own as opposed to merely encouraging them to do so.

Simulation Games

The works of cognitive theorists, especially Bruner's *Toward a Theory of Instruction* (1966), have been influential in encouraging educators to use simulation activities as vehicles for promoting discovery learning (Boocock & Schild, 1968; Groff & Render, 1983). Some of these are role-playing activities based on actual people and events, such as when social studies students are divided into groups representing various special interests in a state legislature and invited to propose and seek support for budget allocation recommendations, or science students are assigned to groups to work on problems or applications, such as figuring out how to use X-rays to kill cancerous growths without killing the patient.

Students generally respond enthusiastically to simulation games. Cohen (1969), for example, found that 87 percent of the participants in a summer school program for unmotivated junior high students preferred games called "Consumer" and "Democracy" to traditional treatments of the same topics. However, simulation activities do not always enable students to generalize principles that they use in the game to other circumstances (Coleman et al., 1973). It appears that the most helpful simulations are those that include information processing opportunities—chances for students to develop concepts or strategies that can be used in solving a range of problems (Coleman et al., 1973; Case, 1975).

Cohen and Bradley (1978) found that the benefits claimed for simulation games are not convincingly supported by available data. Most studies were brief and confined to just a small part of the school day, so that positive results might have been due to Hawthorne effects or novelty effects. Students who spent most of the day in simulation activities over an extended time might eventually welcome something else.

Cohen and Bradley designed a study to assess more carefully the impact in eight fifth- and sixth-grade classes of a simulation game that included both information processing opportunities and experiential learning. Control group teachers were asked to teach the regular lesson from the textbook on map skills using both facts and concepts. These teachers used normal procedures to teach the lesson in four consecutive 60-minute periods. Experimental teachers played the game "Phantom Submarine." The game assumes that a submarine has been sunk off the coast of Florida and lies 200 feet below the surface, but not on the floor of the ocean. The problem is that the ship carries 200 tons of mercury and is believed to contain a self-triggering device that will cause it to explode if it is entered or brought to the surface. However, because the ship is floating, it may strike an object or self-destruct even if left alone.

John L. Greedy, a treasure hunter, wants to salvage the submarine because the mercury is worth two million dollars. However, if the mercury should be set loose, great damage will be done to fish and plant life. The game builds toward a simulated meeting of the World Pollution Control Committee where students play assigned roles and discuss the problem and try to agree on a solution.

The class is divided into several five-person groups. Groups begin by compiling knowledge about the floor of the ocean, currents, the route of the Gulf Stream, mountain ranges, and so on. Individuals gather this information and share it with the group, and then fill in verbal and graphic material on their own map cards, so that eventually all students in each group have the same information. Then the group decides what to do with the submarine. Finally, the students role play the conference and try to reach a conclusion.

In this study, teachers learned to play the game by playing it and then established a timetable for presenting game and map skills in four 60-minute periods. The periods were used as follows: 1) students were allowed to understand the game's objectives, obtain information, and make individual maps; 2) students determined cause and effect relationships on the basis of available information and discussed their decisions with other groups; 3) students used their knowledge to reach a joint group decision; and 4) students discussed all of the groups' positions.

Both groups were tested immediately following the unit and again two weeks later using the map portion of the Iowa Tests of Basic Skills and a map concept development test. There were no significant differences on the tests administered immediately following the unit. Two weeks later, however, the map skills knowledge of the control students (as measured by the Iowa test) had declined, but that of the experimental students had improved. Concerning the latter students, Cohen and Bradley (1978) write, "Through their previous experience with using information from maps to solve the problem of the submarine, they may have developed a kind of theory about map symbols and usage" (p. 252). They further suggested that because students understood the theory better, they could more easily recognize previous errors, and thus improve their performance over time.

Despite these positive findings, Cohen and Bradley suggest that simulation should not be the only method used in social studies courses, but should be combined with more traditional methods. They contend that simulation activities provide an enjoyable change of pace, and if executed effectively so as to cause students to process information and generalize concepts, they can facilitate student mastery and application of social studies concepts.

Evaluation

For more information about simulation methods, see issues of the journal *Simulation and Games*. For ideas about how to evaluate the potential value and application of proposed simulation activites, see Orbach (1977).

When to Use Discovery Learning

Discovery learning approaches were developed from the premise that learning that occurs through self-motivated, active exploration of areas of personal interest is especially likely to be retained in long-term memory and integrated with previous learning. Despite widespread acceptance of this premise, however, there has not been widespread acceptance of discovery learning principles as the primary approach to instruction in classrooms. Ausubel (1963), Skinner (1968), and others have noted several important limitations on the discovery approach: 1) true discoveries are rare, and most of them are made by the brightest and most motivated students; 2) discovery learning is uncertain and inefficient compared to more direct forms of instruction; 3) it places the teacher in the difficult and unnatural role of withholding information from students who may be experiencing frustration or "discovering" mistaken notions that will have to be "unlearned" later; and 4) it needs careful planning and structuring—providing the students with clear goals, giving them needed basic information or skills, guiding their exploration with cues or questions, and finishing with a review and summary to make sure that what they learned from the experience is complete and accurate.

Limitations of discovery learning

Another problem is that many discovery activities appear to be more trouble than they are worth. For example, inquiry-oriented science curricula often include an experiment calling for comparison of plants grown in sunlight with plants grown in the dark. Teachers often find that this experiment doesn't work because the plants raised in the light fail to thrive for some reason or because the other plants are not sufficiently protected from light or are not left in the dark long enough. Furthermore, even if it does work and the expected differences in plant growth appear, the results are anticlimactic because they are so predictable and because they must be related back to concepts taught several weeks earlier (Eaton, Anderson, & Smith, 1984).

Expository instruction

Even direct comparisons with expository instruction do not always favor discovery learning. First, expository instruction is more efficient than discovery learning in most cases, especially if the material is well organized and sequenced and geared to the students' levels of development. Second, skilled teachers usually can create student motivation to learn about academic topics, even where none existed before. If students are not already interested in the topic, this usually is because they are unfamiliar with it or preoccupied with other things, not because they dislike it. Third, because discovery learning approaches assume a great deal about student motivation, background knowledge, and learning-to-learn skills, they are difficult to implement. This is especially true in the early stages of learning about a topic when students are still working on the basics and cannot yet profitably explore and discover on their own. Thus, total reliance on discovery approaches is rarely if ever feasible.

Uses for discovery learning

On the other hand, although data on the matter are spotty and provide only mixed support (Ausubel & Robinson, 1969; Breaux, 1975; Hermann, 1969; Strike, 1975), discovery learning does appear to be useful, and perhaps optimal, when students have the necessary motivation and skills. Thus, it is wise to build in exploration and discovery opportunities whenever it is important that students develop operative knowledge in addition to figurative knowledge or that they be able to apply and not merely just understand the principles they are learning (Singer, 1977). In addition, discovery learning is essential for objectives involving problem solving or creativity.

Within what is consistent with curriculum objectives, teachers should consider building choice into assignments such as essays, speeches, research papers, or projects. For example, biographical essays might be assigned with the objectives of providing students with opportunities to organize information and conduct relevant research. These objectives could be met without requiring all students to write about the same person. Choices can be built in whenever assignments are intended primarily for enrichment rather than to insure that students master elements of the core curriculum.

Wise teachers also will supplement expository instruction and practice exercises with frequent opportunities for students to discuss what they are learning, apply it in ways that reveal the linkages between abstract principles and concrete experience, and engage in various simulations and inquiry activities. Such teachers will also capitalize on the "teachable moments" that arise when students ask a question or make a comment about a lesson topic. By incorporating such comments into the lesson, and by answering such questions, redirecting them to the class, or arranging to follow-up on them later, teachers can provide their students with information that the students want, when they want it. Significant learning benefits can be expected from these brief departures from lesson plans, and in addition, they encourage active inquiry and are greatly appreciated by students (Flanders, 1970; Evertson, Anderson, Anderson, & Brophy, 1980).

Ausubel and Meaningful Reception Learning

Much school learning involves knowledge or comprehension objectives rather than applications or higher level objectives. For efficiency reasons, most such learning is accomplished through expository instruction rather than discovery methods. In David Ausubel's terms, it involves meaningful reception learning, in which the entire content of what is to be learned is presented to the learner in final form. The teacher's task is to present the material in ways that encourage learners to "make sense" of it by relating it to what they already know and not just to memorize it in rote fashion. Compared to rote learning, such meaningful reception learning will be retained longer, be better integrated with other knowledge, and be more readily available for transfer or application.

Ausubel's affinity with Bruner and other cognitive structuralists is seen in his famous statement that ". . . the most important factor influencing the meaningful learning of any new idea is the state of the individual's existing cognitive structure at the time of learning" (Ausubel & Robinson, 1969, p. 143). Like Bruner, Ausubel emphasizes that school learning should involve organized bodies of knowledge structured around key concepts, not a seemingly random assortment of facts and principles. In contrast to Bruner's emphasis on guiding students to structure the content themselves, however, Ausubel has concentrated on ways that teachers can structure the content for the students through effective expository instruction designed to produce meaningful reception learning (Ausubel, 1963; Ausubel & Robinson, 1969; Ausubel, Novak, & Hanesian, 1978).

Subordinate and superordinate concepts

Ausubel starts with the notion that knowledge is organized into hierarchical structures in which specific details called subordinate concepts are not only related to one another but subsumed under higher level cognitive structures called superordinate concepts. Even if we gradually forget details, we tend to remember key ideas and principles associated with a particular cognitive structure, and to retain the structure itself. The structure provides scaffolding that supports retention of the information as an organized body of knowledge and provides a frame within which to interpret related new knowledge or efficiently relearn forgotten knowledge. Concerning Chapter 6 of this text, for example, even if you do not remember all of the details of Bloom's taxonomy or Gagné's learning hierarchies, you are likely to remember that there are many types and levels of learning, and that these need to be considered in setting objectives, planning instructional activities, and developing evaluation mechanisms.

Signaling

Mayer (1984) has elaborated on Ausubel's ideas for presenting information in an organized fashion by developing techniques for signaling learners by calling their attention to the structural features of presentations. Specifically, signaling techniques refer to the placement within a passage of noncontent words that serve to emphasize the conceptual structure or organization of the passage. Four major types of signals are:

1. Specifications of the structure of relations (cues such as "first," "second," "third," or "the problem is . . . and the solution is."
2. Premature presentations of abstracted or paraphrased statements of key information that will follow ("the main ideas discussed in this paper are. . . .").
3. Summary statements (similar to premature presentations except that they occur at the ends of passages).

4. Point words that indicate the author's perspective or emphasize important information ("more importantly," "unfortunately").

Such signaling helps make the outline structure of a passage more clear and provides a conceptual framework for learners to use in identifying important information and organizing it coherently. Experiments have shown that passages that include such signaling elements are learned better than the same passages without such signaling (Loman & Mayer, 1983; Mayer, Dyck, & Cook, 1984).

Advance Organizers

Ausubel stresses organizing content in logical ways and helping learners to recognize this organization by presenting outlines, noting transitions between parts, and including summaries at the end. In addition, he advocates presenting learners with advance organizers—superordinate concepts within which learners can subsume the new material and relate it to what they already know. Advance organizers differ from conventional previews or summaries that briefly state the main points made in a presentation. Instead, advance organizers characterize the material to be learned at a higher level of abstraction, generality, and inclusiveness. For example, Ausubel (1960) had college students read a 500-word expository organizer before reading a 2,500-word text on the metallurgical properties of carbon steel. The organizer discussed similarities and differences between metals and alloys, and their respective advantages and weaknesses. It presented ideas relevant for understanding the longer passage, but did not include material given in the passage itself. The results of this study showed that students who read the advance organizer retained more of the passage than students who read a 500-word passage on the historical development of methods used for processing iron and steel. Although both the introductory passages were relevant to the general topic of steel, only the advance organizer presented the learners with superordinate concepts within which they could subsume the material in the longer passage (the advance organizer reminded the learners that alloys exist in addition to pure metals and that different alloys have different properties that affect their usefulness for various purposes; then, the longer passage described the properties of a particular alloy—carbon steel).

Advance organizers versus previews or summaries

In describing advance organizers as presenting information at a higher level of abstraction, generality, or inclusiveness than the subsequent text, Ausubel communicates the idea that advance organizers are different from ordinary previews or summaries. Instead of merely summarizing the content of the text in briefer form, advance organizers characterize the general nature of the text (such as by describing its purpose and the approach or line of argument taken to accomplish this purpose) and provide the learner with superordinate concepts within which the text can be subsumed. This should not be taken to mean that advance organizers should be highly abstract or difficult to understand, however. To be useful, the organizers must be stated in terms already familiar to the learner (Ausubel, 1968; Anderson, 1984).

Ausubel believes that advance organizers are especially useful when the material to be learned is not well organized and learners are of limited ability and thus less likely to be able to organize it well for themselves. Research conducted by Ausubel and by numerous other investigators has supported these predictions (Ausubel, 1978; Luiten, Ames, & Ackerson, 1980; Mayer, 1979a, 1979b). Many studies have failed to show an advantage to advance organizers, and reviewers who have simply totaled up positive and negative findings have sometimes questioned their usefulness (Barnes & Clawson, 1975). However, reviewers who first classified the studies according to the learners and the texts used in the research have found that advance organizers as defined by Ausubel do facilitate learning when the text is poorly organized or when the learners lack prerequisite knowledge or abilities (Mayer, 1979a, 1979b). They are especially helpful in enabling learners to transfer what they learn.

Other varieties of organizers

Other research indicates that organizers can facilitate learning when placed either before or after the text (Alexander, Frankiewicz, & Williams, 1979), and that other types of organizers besides the advance organizers described by Ausubel can be effective. These include organizers presented in oral rather than written form (Alexander, Frankiewicz, & Williams, 1979), organizers that present key terms or principles taken from the material to be learned rather than characterizing that material with reference to previous knowledge (Mayer, 1984; Stone, 1982), and organizers that present models or illustrations rather than expository explanations (Mayer, 1984). In general, concrete models, analogies, examples, sets of general higher-order rules, and discussions of main themes in familiar terms are more effective organizers than specific factual prequestions, outlines, summaries, or directions to pay attention to specific key facts or terms (Mayer, 1979b).

Postlesson summaries and review questions

Besides advance organizers, Ausubel has studied postlesson summaries and review questions as devices to facilitate learning and help students to integrate what they learn. His work has provided much support for the advice "Tell them what you are going to tell them; then tell them; then tell them what you told them." For teachers, this would mean the following:

1. Start lessons with advance organizers or at least with previews that include general principles, outlines, or questions that establish a learning set in the students.
2. Briefly describe learning objectives and alert the students to new or key concepts.
3. Present new material in small steps organized logically and sequenced in ways that are easy to follow.
4. Elicit student responses regularly in order to stimulate active learning and insure that each step is mastered before moving to the next.
5. Finish with a review of the main points, stressing general integrative concepts.

6. Follow-up the lesson with questions or assignments that require learners to encode material in their own words and apply or extend it to new contexts.

Linking the New to the Familiar

Various investigators who share Ausubel's concern with structuring content to encourage meaningful learning have studied other factors besides advance organizers and signaling of the organizational structure. These include analogies, metaphors, examples, and concrete models that help learners to link new concepts to familiar ones or to develop concrete referents for abstract concepts.

Analogies

Analogies are often useful ways to link the new to the familiar. Mayer (1984), for example, reports success in explaining the principles of radar by drawing analogies between the reflection of radio waves and the reflection of sound waves that underlies familiar echo phenomena. Royer and Cable (1975) were successful in teaching about the crystalline structure of molecules by drawing analogies to a model constructed from tinker toys. Diagrams or flow charts showing simplified models of biological systems or the workings of complex machines such as engines or computers can make it much easier to learn such information than it would be if the presentation is restricted to verbal information. In general, analogies that help learners link the new to the familiar can be expected to facilitate learning (Mayer, 1975a, 1979a; Hayes & Tierney, 1982), although care must be taken to insure that any potentially misleading aspects of the analogy do not lead to misconceptions in the learners. The same is true for metaphors, models, and other methods of making the abstract more concrete or the strange more familiar.

Teaching for Transfer

In addition to stressing that learning should be meaningful rather than rote and should be retained in an organized fashion rather than forgotten or retained only as isolated bits of knowledge, Ausubel stresses that learning should be available for transfer to new contexts. That is, besides being able to remember and apply learning within the context in which it was originally learned, students should be able to generalize the learning to other relevant contexts and to activate and build on it when extending their learning into new areas. Transfer of existing knowledge to new situations simplifies the task of learning in such new situations.

Vertical transfer

Transfer may be vertical or lateral. Vertical transfer is desired when teaching hierarchically organized skills in which each new level is built on one or more lower levels. To promote vertical transfer, Ausubel recommends following a sequential organization if this applies to the material, making sure that learners have whatever knowledge they need at each step, consolidating learning and insuring mastery before going on to higher steps, stressing general and integrative principles, and following a pattern of progressive differentiation in presenting the content. Where any newly presented material appears to conflict with what has already been taught, it will be important not merely to present the new material but to reconcile the apparent conflicts so that the new material can be integrated within the cognitive structures already developed.

Lateral transfer

Lateral transfer occurs when particular knowledge or skills are used to speed up or simplify learning in some other domain. Although Ausubel recognizes that there are limits on the extent of lateral transfer that can be expected, Ausubel believes that teachers can promote lateral transfer by concentrating on underlying principles and generalizations in teaching content and by giving students opportunities to learn or apply material in realistic situations. In particular, he suggests emphasizing aspects of subject matter content that have the most potential for lateral transfer such as Latin language roots of modern English words or general logic and problem-solving applications of mathematical learning.

Research by Mayer and his colleagues have confirmed many of these ideas. In particular, Bromage and Mayer (1981) found that organizing a technical passage around general principles resulted in better problem-solving transfer performance than by organizing it by topic. Similarly, Mayer (1975b) found that organizing a mathematics lesson so that it moved from familiar prerequisite concepts toward formal definitions and algorithms resulted in better problem-solving transfer performance than organizing the lesson to move from the formal to the familiar. Mayer (1979a) also found that advance organizers and concrete models were especially useful as mechanisms for enhancing recall of conceptual information rather than immediate retention of facts. In general, the text-structuring factors stressed by Ausubel appear to be especially important for insuring that learners grasp the main ideas in a presentation and are able to transfer and apply them later.

In addition to his ideas on structuring content for learners, Ausubel has discussed ways of encouraging learners to use meaningful rather than rote learning strategies for processing information to be learned, and more generally, for activating their existing knowledge and bringing it to bear on new knowledge. However, these topics have been addressed by many other investigators as well and are discussed in detail in Chapters 9 and 10.

SUMMARY

Cognitive structuralists hold that meaningful learning involves not only understanding individual facts and principles, but noting the relationships between them and building up cognitive structures to retain this information in an organized way. These theorists approach instruction by concentrating on the key ideas that can be used to organize bodies of information, and then developing ways to teach these key ideas or guide learners to discover them.

The roots of the cognitive structuralist approach lie in gestalt psychology. Gestalt psychologists note that perception tends to be organized into meaningful patterns structured holistically, rather than built up by combining discrete elements. They produced demonstrations and conducted experiments on such topics as figure-ground discrimination and contrast effects, demonstrated that people tend to impose good form on stimulus input, and demonstrated that learning can occur by discovery achieved through sudden insight. Gestalt psychologists were among the first to advocate guided discovery as an approach to classroom instruction.

Bruner combined ideas from gestalt psychology with ideas from the study of cognitive development, especially perception, memory, and the cognitive organization of information, to develop his approach to education. He noted that humans attend to input selectively and organize it into categories that become increasingly better integrated, differentiated, and mediated by language with development. The earliest knowledge is mostly in the enactive mode, but children later become capable of understanding and manipulating knowledge in the iconic mode via pictures, images, or memories of previously experienced objects or events, and beginning around adolescence, they become able to represent knowledge in the symbolic mode and thus to understand and manipulate abstract concepts.

Bruner believes that any subject matter can be taught to any learners in some intellectually honest way. Thus he advocates the spiral curriculum, in which students are exposed to the same general topic several different times, but in more abstract and sophisticated ways each time. He suggests that teachers instruct by stimulating students' curiosity and guiding them to explore and discover on their own. His approach is illustrated in the social studies program Man: A Course of Study (MACOS) that attempts to stimulate student curiosity through novelty, incongruity, and contrast and invites students to explore and discover by answering questions and conducting experiments.

Discovery learning approaches have also been featured in the open education movement, in Suchman's Inquiry Training approach, and in the simulation games approach to instruction. Discovery learning approaches tend to be enjoyable and useful to students and in some cases are essential for promoting certain higher level objectives, and thus probably should be used to some degree in most classrooms. However, they are time consuming and involve several practical problems and limitations, so that few teachers will be able to use them as the only or even the primary approach to instruction in their classrooms.

Ausubel and others have developed cognitive structuralist approaches to promoting efficient meaningful reception learning through well-structured presentations. Such presentations begin with advance organizers or at least previews that include general principles, outlines, or questions that establish the desired learning set in the students; describe learning objectives and alert the students to new or key concepts; present new material in small steps organized logically and sequenced in ways that are easy to follow; elicit student responses regularly in order to stimulate active learning and insure that each step is mastered before moving to the next; finish with a review of the main points, stressing general integrative concepts; and follow-up the presentation with questions or assignments that require learners to encode the material in their own words and apply or extend it to new contexts. Analogies, metaphors, examples, or concrete models are used to help learners link the new to the familiar, and the instructional plan includes provision for vertical and lateral transfer of what is being learned when this is part of the overall objective.

QUESTIONS AND PROBLEMS

1. Describe in your own words the differences between behavioral and cognitive approaches to learning. In contrast to the first two chapters in this unit, what new emphasis is placed on learning in the present chapter?
2. Define the term gestalt psychology. What is a gestalt? How might the gestalt psychology viewpoint be useful to a classroom instructor?
3. Re-examine the general beliefs of Thorndike, Skinner, and Bruner. Given their beliefs, what would a typical "homework" assignment look like from each point of view? Think about a social studies lesson and about a mathematics lesson and then discuss the role of homework from each of the three theorists' point of view. In particular, what might the length and type of assignments be?
4. Assume that you are going to teach the following three outcomes: Pledge of Allegiance, Bill of Rights, and free-form ice skating. For which of these learning outcomes would a cognitive model be preferable? Could the same learning model be equally appropriate for each outcome? Why or why not? Specifically, if you were teaching the Bill of Rights from a Skinnerian point of view, how would you proceed? What if you were teaching it from the viewpoint of Bruner?
5. Review the material presented about inquiry training. Define in your own terms what inquiry training is and then answer the following question. If you were going to teach students the role of the presidential election in American politics and the importance of Boyle's law in physics, would it be equally important to use inquiry procedures? Why or why not?
6. Think about teaching young children to play either soccer or monopoly. After choosing your teaching context, write five advance organizers that would convey to students the structure of what you would be teaching them.
7. Can students really be taught, or must they learn on their own? Just how much can teachers realistically expect to accomplish?
8. Many behaviorists and others are offended by the tendency of discovery-learning theorists to view themselves as humane rather than mechanistic, so they counter by claiming that it is cruel and inhumane to force students to discover things on their own when you would save them trouble by telling or showing them. Do you agree? Why or why not?
9. Should teachers allow students to make errors or actively attempt to prevent them? Are there circumstances under which it is better for teachers to prevent errors or to allow students to make them? What are some specific examples?
10. Is it literally true that we learn what we do? How would you qualify this assetion, if at all?

CASE STUDIES

An Act of Discovery. Mr. Wilson feels that his American government students are passively accepting and taking notes about whatever he says to them but without carefully evaluating this input or integrating it with their prior knowledge. He wants to find ways to get his students to think more actively and make discoveries on their own. For example, one of the points to be made in the next unit is that most elected officials holding national office are lawyers. How might he arrange for students to discover this fact and the reasons for it on their own?

Just a Game? In his government class, Mr. Johnson uses a simulation game in which the students are assigned to act as state legislators attempting to work out the compromises needed to pass the annual budget. The students are assigned to five groups, each representing a different geographical area of the state with different priorities and interests (the big city, the tourist-oriented counties along the lake, etc.). Each group is assigned goals that would involve earmarking more than its share of the budget for purposes that take high priority in its geographical region. It would take twice as much money as the budget allows to fund all of each group's target goals, so it will be necessary to make compromises and to form coalitions with other groups in order to get as much as one can for one's own group. In other words, the game is quite realistic, simulating what actually goes on in the state legislature.

The game takes place over the course of a week. By Wednesday, Mr. Johnson is pleased in most respects. The students find the game absorbing and challenging, to the point that teams are getting together at lunch time and after school in order to plot strategy, and they are calling up members of other teams at night in an attempt to cut deals. Mr. Johnson is gratified to see this level of motivation and involvement. He is bothered, though, about the degree of personal competitiveness that has crept into the game. The brighter and more assertive students have emerged as the group leaders and are working hard to outsmart one another. Despite Mr. Johnson's efforts to make the simulation as realistic as possible by keeping the students aware that they are role playing state legislators and urging them to make their case based on the benefits to be derived from proposed expenditures, most of the interaction takes place at the level of whether or not Mary Barnett and her group will outfox Greg Richards and his group, rather than at the level of whether or not the farming interests will be able to pursue their agenda at the expense of the big city interests. In short, although the game clearly has great motivational value, Mr. Johnson wonders if it has enough pedagogical value to justify the time spent on it.

What would you tell Mr. Johnson if he were explaining this to you as a fellow teacher? Are his concerns justified? Should he use the game again next year? Should he do anything right now to try to influence how the game is played out during the rest of the week?

Chapter 9

The Information Processing View of Learning

CHAPTER OUTLINE

OBJECTIVES

When you have mastered the material in this chapter you will be able to

1. Describe the information processing approach to learning and explain how it differs from the behaviorist approach and the cognitive structuralist approach
2. Identify similarities and differences between associationist theories and constructivist theories
3. Differentiate semantic memory from episodic memory
4. Define the key concepts in the three-stage information processing model—sensory register, short-term or working memory, rehearsal, chunking, long-term memory, levels of processing—and explain how the model depicts information processing, storage, and retrieval
5. Define the schema concept and explain how schema activation facilitates comprehension
6. Describe the factors known to affect rote learning and explain the nature of their effects: degree of meaningfulness, serial position (primacy and recency effects), stimulus distinctiveness, practice, transfer (positive versus negative, specific versus general), interference (proactive versus reactive), organization of input, levels of processing, state- or context-dependency, and use of mnemonics
7. Describe and give examples of commonly used mnemonics—place method, link method, peg

Student Misconception Effects
Text Organization Effects
Mathemagenic Effects

Current Research on Human Information Processing

Reading Comprehension Research
Expert-Novice Comparisons
Cognitive Simulation and Artificial Intelligence

method, keyword method, elaboration method, pictorial mnemonics, rhymes, acronyms, and visual imagery

8. Describe the factors known to affect meaningful verbal learning—abstraction of the gist of the passage, levels of organization of the passage, activation of schemas and prior knowledge, drawing of inferences, filtering of input through pre-existing misconceptions, responding to structuring and organizational factors built into the text, and generating mathemagenic activities—and explain the nature of their effects
9. Define adjunct questions and state the relative advantages and disadvantages of prequestions and postquestions
10. Describe the major findings of information processing theorists' research on reading, on the behavior of novices and experts, and on cognitive simulation and artificial intelligence

Some cognitive structuralists, described in the previous chapter, emphasize the structure of the content to be learned. For these cognitive structuralists, school learning involves acquiring organized bodies of knowledge, and teaching involves expository instruction or guided discovery designed to call the learners' attention to key ideas and structural features around which the information is organized. Other cognitively oriented theorists (described in the present chapter) accept and use the work of the cognitive structuralists but place more emphasis on the learner than on the content to be learned. For these information processing theorists, learning involves actively processing, storing, and retrieving information, and teaching involves helping learners to develop their information processing skills and apply them systematically when mastering the curriculum. In short, cognitive structuralists emphasize the logical structure of the discipline (subject matter), whereas information processing theorists emphasize cognitive structures built up by the learners themselves. For the most part, the cognitive structural approach and the information processing approach to learning deal with different issues and are complementary rather than competing as elements in a cognitive account of learning and instruction.

Information Processing Theories: Overview

Organization of knowledge

Following the theories of Piaget and others, information processing theorists assume that humans develop increasingly differentiated and integrated cognitive structures that represent and organize their knowledge. Ongoing experience is filtered through these structures: We recognize familiar, meaningful aspects of input, and we interpret the unfamiliar aspects within the contexts established by our perceptions of familiar aspects. Rather than trying to deal with all of the stimuli bombarding our various senses at any given time (which would be impossible in any case), we concentrate on what we see as most interesting or important. It is this focal input that attracts our conscious attention and is most likely to become stored in memory and thus available for retrieval later. Information processing theorists have shown that active intentional learning accomplished through systematic information processing leads to better retention than learning that is less active and systematic.

Interaction between learner and input

Information processing theorists have also shown that the relationships between particular items of input and the learner's larger cognitive structures are surprisingly active and continuous. They believe that, because perception of new experience is filtered through existing cognitive structures, and because new input is almost always open to multiple interpretations, the process of making sense of experience, and thus the process of learning, is best seen as an interaction between the learner and the input, and not as a one-way effect of the input on the learner. Thus, in reading this textbook, you are not merely taking in fully specified information that has only a single set of meanings. Instead, you are interacting with the material by filling in bits of meaning that are inferred but not spelled out explicitly, intepreting the probable meanings when you come across unfamiliar terms, relating the content to your prior experience and knowledge, and making decisions about what content is especially important to remember either for a test or for future reference and application. You and your classmates are all using the same book, and yet each of you will attend to a unique subset of the content as being of focal importance. Even where several of you focus on the same content, each will have a unique interpretation of that content and will associate it with a unique set of prior experiences and related concepts.

Furthermore, your memory of the content itself or your ideas about its meanings and intepretations may change over time if you undergo, which is likely, significant development in key cognitive structures such as your general self-concept, your ideas about what schools should accomplish with students, or your notions about what makes a good teacher. For example, if you are an inexperienced preservice teacher, you may think that the section on classroom management is the most important part of this book, and you may find some of what is said in that section to be surprising or hard to believe, such as the notion that skills for keeping students engaged in well-paced lessons and well-chosen assignments are more important to successful classroom management than skills for handling disruption or defiance. As you gain experience and progress through the developmental stages that new teachers typically go through, however, your ideas probably will change. Chances are that if you should review this text a few years from now, much of the material on classroom management will seem "obvious" and old hat, and much of the material on learning and instruction will seem much more relevant and important than it may seem now. You can illustrate the point by looking backwards, as well: Many of the things that seemed highly complex and of focal importance when you were in high school are routine and taken for granted now (driving, scheduling college courses, balancing your checkbook, etc.).

Theory and research about information processing as it affects learning will be presented in this chapter and the next. The present chapter will discuss methods of promoting rote learning when necessary and promoting meaningful learning whenever possible. Information about more general methods of teaching students to read with comprehension, to study systematically, and to solve problems is presented in Chapter 10.

Associationist and Constructivist Views of Memory

Associationist theories

Most research on human memory has been guided by one of two influential types of theory. Associationist theories were the first to become well established. These theories assume that the retention of new learning depends on the nature and strength of associations between that new learning and previous learning stored in memory, and that forgetting is caused by interference from competing associations. Much of the research supporting associationist theories has involved rote learning of relatively meaningless and disconnected input.

Constructivist theories

Recent research has led to the development of constructivist theories, in which learners are seen as constructing meaning from input by processing it through existing cognitive structures, and then retaining it in long-term memory in ways that leave it open to further processing and possible reconstruction. Constructivists view learning as depending on the degree to which learners can activate existing cognitive structures or construct new ones to subsume the new input. They speak of memory as involving distortion in addition to mere forgetting. Most of the research supporting constructivist theories has involved meaningful learning of connected discourse, typically written prose. The classical work of Ebbinghaus and of Bartlett illustrate these two types of research.

Ebbinghaus

Hermann Ebbinghaus (1885) pioneered what became the associationist approach. He published one of the first treatises on learning and memory that was based on empirical data (records of the outcomes of his own attempts to memorize various types of input under various conditions). Although he worked mostly alone and before the widespread development of scientific psychology, most of his findings have been verified by other researchers using more sophisticated methods. Ebbinghaus wanted to study "pure" memory uncontaminated by previous learning, so he avoided connected discourse and even lists of unconnected words. Instead, he used nonsense syllables (such as *dev* or *lup* in English) that he judged to be free of associations to prior learning. Subsequent work has shown, however, that this is a matter of degree and that nonsense syllables will have at least some associations to meaningful knowledge for most people.

Through his experiments, Ebbinghaus showed that learning improved when the material was rehearsed overtly rather than merely read silently, and that distribution of practice over several shorter trials produced better results than massing of practice into one or a small number of lengthy trials.

Serial position effects

He also discovered serial position effects—when we are trying to memorize something, material at the beginning and the end is learned more quickly than material in the middle. You may have noticed these effects yourself in memorizing poems, literary passages, or even lecture notes. Or, after attending a party, you may remember the names of the first and last people you met, but not those that you met in between, unless there was something special about them that caused you to concentrate on remembering their names.

Ebbinghaus also was among the first to note the relationship between time and learning. He showed that increases in practice time led to increases in performance, although less so as practice time increased and he neared his peak performance level. Graphs illustrating these relationships were among the first learning curves later popularized by functionalists. Ebbinghaus also illustrated forgetting curves—the longer the delay between original learning and the subsequent test, the more that is forgotten, although forgetting is rapid in the early minutes and hours following learning but much slower thereafter.

Forgetting curves

Ebbinghaus adopted the decay theory of forgetting, meaning that memory traces simply fade with time. However, later work caused the decay theory to be replaced by the interference theory, which holds that forgetting is not due to the mere passage of time but instead is due to new learning that interferes with the ability to remember prior learning. This was illustrated, for example, in studies showing that people who memorized a word list before going to bed at night could remember much more of the list after sleeping for eight hours than could people who first learned the original list, then learned several similar lists, and then were tested on the original list only an hour later (McGeoch & McDonald, 1931).

Interference theory

Interference theory still holds up well for rote learning of disconnected material. Here, subsequent learning of similar material is likely to interfere with memory for the original material. The situation is different for the meaningful learning of connected discourse, however. Here, subsequent learning of material that is similar to previously learned material is likely to facilitate memory for both sets of material (i.e., transfer effects rather than interference effects occur), assuming that the previous learning is sufficiently clear, stable, and discriminable from the new learning (Ausubel & Robinson, 1969). The semantic network theory and the schema theory described in the following sections apply better to such meaningful learning than the interference theory does.

Bartlett

Constructivist approach

Bartlett (1932) pioneered what became the constructivist approach. He rejected Ebbinghaus's attempts to study "pure" memory in favor of attempts to study memory as it occurs in ordinary living, and he rejected laboratory tasks and nonsense syllables in favor of more natural stimuli such as human faces, pictures, and connected discourse. In his best known experiments, subjects read brief stories and then produced written versions from memory, first after a delay of 15 minutes and then later at intervals of several weeks or months.

Bartlett's subjects read relatively long stories of 200 to 500 words and had relatively short practice times since they only read each story twice. Consequently, decay theorists such as Ebbinghaus and associationists such as Thorndike would have predicted a great deal of forgetting due to the decay of associative memory traces that were weak to begin with. They would not have predicted significant distortion of the stories, however, because no other stories that might have produced interference effects were interpolated between the original story reading and the subsequent attempt to reproduce the story from memory. Bartlett's results did not confirm these associationist predictions, however.

First, compared to the retention that would be expected for relatively meaningless material of equal length, memory for these stories was quite good. The subjects could remember considerable proportions of the stories, and especially material related to the gist or main idea.

Second, to the extent that the subjects' story reconstructions were less than perfect, they often involved actual distortions and not just omissions or substitutions of one equivalent phrase for another. For example, in one study, British subjects read a story about the cultural practices of certain North American Indians. In recounting the story, the British subjects tended to "normalize" it by substituting thematically similar but culturally more familiar terms and events for those that occurred in the original story. Thus, a seal hunt became a fishing trip, and a canoe became a boat.

"Effort after meaning"

On the basis of such evidence, Bartlett argued that subjects engaged in an "effort after meaning" when they read the stories, seeking to understand them by connecting them to existing cognitive structures that he called schemas. They would use this process to construct a meaning for the story that was plausible and consistent, although it might not be the same meaning intended by the author. Thus, there may be some distortion even in the original learning of the story, especially if the story contains unfamiliar elements that can be understood only partially (by filtering them through more familiar schemas).

Story reconstruction

Bartlett further argued that the stories as originally constructed would undergo reconstruction later if changes occurred in the schemas to which the stories had been connected. Thus, just as immediate memory measures would show distortion from the original story read only 15 minutes earlier, measures taken weeks or months later would show additional distortion from the version produced on the immediate memory test.

Accuracy set

Subsequent research has supported and elaborated most of Bartlett's ideas (Spiro, 1977), although there is much more evidence indicating that activation of relevant schemas affects how material is interpreted and thus encoded in the first place than there is for the notion that later schema change produces significant reconstruction of the originally encoded material (diSibio, 1982). One factor that complicates interpretation here is the degree to which an "accuracy set" is induced in the subjects. Gauld and Stephenson (1967) replicated some of Bartlett's work and showed that subjects who were urged to be strictly accurate and avoid distortions were in fact more accurate than subjects who were instructed simply to "write down the story I've just read to you as exactly as you can." They suggest that Bartlett's work may overemphasize the roles of distortion and reconstruction in memory because his experiments were relatively informal and he did not train his subjects to be strictly accurate. However, bear in mind that Bartlett was interested in studying everyday memory, which usually occurs informally and without benefit of a consciously adopted accuracy set.

Information Processing Models of Learning and Memory

Ebbinghaus and Bartlett contributed work of historical importance, and the contrasts between them illustrate some of the diversity that exists in theory and research on human information processing and memory. A great deal of progress has been made in the 100 years since Ebbinghaus began his work, yet some questions have not received much attention and the questions that have been studied heavily have yielded a range of theory and data that defy integration.

Most research has focused on the intentional learning of material communicated through both oral and written language, partly because so much of formal education involves such intentional verbal learning. Tulving (1972) suggests that memory for such language-based information, which he calls semantic memory, is accomplished through systems of encoding, storage, and retrieval that differ from those used in accomplishing memory for personal experiences, which he calls episodic memory. He argues, for example, that episodic memory tends to be rich in concrete detail and stored in the form of sequences of events occurring in particular places at particular times, whereas semantic memory is more abstract and stored in terms of logically related concepts and principles. This distinction is useful, although the evidence for the larger theory behind it is mixed (Horton & Mills, 1984). Most of what is said in this chapter concerns semantic memory.

Episodic versus semantic memory

The chapter also concentrates on intentional rather than incidental learning. Incidental learning is important and a great deal of it occurs in and out of school, but the factors that determine it are not well understood. Some aspects of experience, such as the timing, frequency, and spatial location of commonly experienced events, appear to be encoded automatically, without intention or apparent effort (Hasher & Zacks, 1984). Consequently, most people can give fairly accurate answers to questions about how many movies they have seen in the last year, where they sat when they last visited a favorite restaurant, or whether there are more lawyers or more tailors in the United States. Other things, such as the fact that paying attention to the organizational structure of a text is useful for learning that text, are learned incidentally by some people but not others, although the latter people can be taught this information and can use it intentionally thereafter.

Intentional versus incidental learning

What Is Encoded?

Many people think of memory as a continuous, sequenced record of previous experience, akin to a videotape that begins with the earliest memory and proceeds linearly through the present. In this view, certain segments may have become faded or even lost due to forgetting, and some may be temporarily unavailable but potentially recoverable through hypnosis, psychotherapy, or encounters with cues such as old photos that cause us to "call

Dormant memories

up" long dormant memories. This view fits many of the known facts about memory. For example, some people appear to have eidetic imagery, popularly known as photographic memory, that allows them to visualize and retrieve previous experience in extreme detail. It is common sensical to believe that everyone else's memory works the same way, but not quite as efficiently. Furthermore, even people with ordinary memories can remember a great many details about important events in their lives or about where they were and what they were doing when they heard the news about Pearl Harbor, John Kennedy, or John Lennon (Brown & Kulick, 1977).

Despite its apparent face validity, this common sense view of memory is not correct (Wickelgren, 1981). First, it applies only to episodic memory, not semantic memory. Even if the episodes in our personal lives were routinely encoded and stored as the equivalent of a running videotape, it would remain true that semantic memory for concepts and principles does not work this way. When we remember a principle, we remember it as a verbally phrased abstraction, not as an image of ourselves reliving the events that occurred when we originally learned the principle. Second, the model is not accurate even for episodic memory. Only certain experiences are encoded as "videotape segments" in the first place, and our memories for even these segments can be distorted, not just weakened, by the effects of later experience (Loftus & Loftus, 1980). Also, our memories typically work with much more speed and much less evidence of sequential processing than the videotape model predicts.

Verbal abstractions

Semantic memory is apparently encoded and stored in the form of verbal abstractions (concept definitions and statements of rules and principles), although there may be associated imagery or linkages to particular prior experiences. You know that $2 + 2 = 4$, for example, and although you can apply this information in concrete situations and can visualize examples of it, it is stored and retrieved primarily as a verbal abstraction—a semantically encoded number fact. Information processing theorists are concerned with how such input gets encoded into semantic memory, and what happens to it after it gets there.

The Three-Stage Information Processing Model

Most learning theorists, however much they disagree on other matters, accept a general three-stage model of human information processing that was developed in the last 20 years using concepts borrowed from computer science. Versions of the model have been proposed by Atkinson and Shiffrin (1968, 1971), Kintsch (1977), Klatzky (1980), and Loftus and Loftus (1976). The model proposes that input first enters a sensory register (also called a sensory store), then is passed along to short-term memory, and then is transferred to long-term memory for storage and potential retrieval. The three stages are seen as integrated subparts of a larger system for coding and transforming raw sensory information into forms that are more permanent and appropriate for integration with previously stored information. All of this is seen as occurring under the executive control of the person, whose allocation of attention determines which aspects of the great range of input available at any moment will be processed through the limited capacity of the system.

Sensory Register. The sensory register receives input from the sensory receivers, primarily the eyes and ears. The neurological processing of this input is very brief, ranging from less than a second for visual sensations to about four seconds for auditory sensations, and then disappears through decay or replacement by new input. Consequently, input that enters the sensory register must be transferred to short-term memory if it is to receive focal attention and further processing. Information entering the sensory register is monitored at a low level of attention so that we are able to attend and respond to it more actively if necessary. If you are driving, for example, and are attending primarily to a conversation you are having with passengers, you nevertheless monitor and respond to traffic signals and to changes in traffic and road conditions. Most of this visual input never enters even your short-term memory, however, so that it decays quickly and is lost permanently.

Short-Term Memory and Rehearsal. Sensory input that the person recognizes as particularly important or interesting in the situation is transferred in the form of meaningful perceptions from the sensory register to short-term memory. This information can be retained longer in short-term memory (up to 15 or 20 seconds without active rehearsal, and indefinitely longer if the person rehearses actively by repeating the information over and over again). However, short-term memory has a very limited capacity. Short-term memory capacity is measured by presenting people with lists of stimuli such as numbers, letters, words, or phrases and then asking them to reproduce the list. Research going back to the work of Ebbinghaus agrees in showing that most people can remember only about seven items without making errors or omissions if these items are unrelated to one another. Thus, even a single phone number may be difficult to remember for even 15 to 20 seconds unless it is repeated continually until dialed or written down.

Chunking

Short-term memory capacity can be increased, however, sometimes dramatically, by chunking the input into subsets that are remembered as single units. For example, the number sequence 149210661984 is difficult to memorize as a string of 12 separate digits. However, it is easily remembered if divided into three chunks corresponding to three famous years (1492, 1066, 1984). Similarly, the words truck, cow, red, train, horse, green, plane, pig, and yellow are remembered much more easily if reorganized into chunks of three vehicles, three animals, and three colors than if memorized in serial order.

George Miller (1956) reviewed a great deal of research and showed that the chunk, and not the individual item, is the real unit determining short-term memory capacity, and that this capacity is remarkably stable across a great range of stimuli. Whatever the stimuli, short-term memory capacity averages about seven chunks of information (plus or minus two, allowing for individual differences). This "7 ± 2" rule holds up well: It is true that any particular chunk of information can be retained indefinitely in short-term memory through active rehearsal, but it is also true that interference effects will cause memory failure once the limited capacity (7 ± 2 chunks) of short-term memory is exceeded.

Working memory

Short-term memory is often called working memory, especially by theorists interested in goal-directed thinking and problem solving. When engaged in such mental work, we can attend to some combination of input from the external environment and information called up from storage in long-term memory, subject to the limit of 7 ± 2 chunks. Because the capacity of working memory is limited, we cannot cope with complex cognitive tasks unless we are able to simplify them. Chunking is one way to simplify by reducing the load on working memory. Another is to break the task into subparts and take on one at a time. Another is to practice certain skills until they become automatic (i.e., they can be exercised with little conscious attention or effort, thus freeing working memory for concentration on tasks that do require such effort). Most of us have learned to walk, eat, and drive automatically, so that we can think or carry on conversations while engaged in these activities. In school, successful students are successful in part because basic skills have become automatic for them. When reading, for example, skilled readers can use most of their working memory capacities for making sense out of what they are reading (comprehension), because basic skills such as decoding words and instantly recognizing the meanings of familiar words have become automatic for them (Chall, 1983; Frederiksen, 1984; Perfetti & Lesgold, 1977). Less skilled readers do not have this luxury—most of their working memory capacity is needed just to decode and understand individual words, so that little is left for "putting it all together." As a result, their comprehension is poor unless they review the passage several times.

Case (1978) has stressed the importance of minimizing the load placed on students' working memory when teaching (especially when teaching young children or teaching complex new material to students at any level). He suggests limiting the number of things that students must attend to at the same time, using familiar terms and cues where possible (familiar input can be processed automatically and thus does not take up limited working memory capacity), and making key cues as salient as possible (if students' attention is cued effectively, they will not have to devote much working memory capacity to the search for cues).

Long-Term Memory and Storage. Information needed for future reference is stored in long-term memory, which theoretically has unlimited capacity and duration, barring senility or other physical malfunction. Some additions to long-term semantic memory are acquired through incidental learning, but many are the intentional results of deliberate efforts. If necessary, you can commit material to long-term memory through "brute force" by actively rehearsing it to the point of overlearning. This approach is inefficient and requires considerable effort and concentration, so it is not the method of choice. However, it may be needed for memorizing such things as phone numbers or lock combinations.

Deeper levels of processing

The more efficient way to intentionally store material in long-term memory is to go beyond mere rehearsal by processing the information at deeper levels (Craik & Lockhart, 1972). Such deeper levels of processing may involve identifying or generating linkages between the new material and other material that is already retained in organized fashion, developing images to supplement the semantic form of the content, thinking about the implications or applications of the material, or answering questions about the material.

Modern theory and research on memory has concentrated on how material gets stored in long-term memory and what happens to it after it gets there. Most theories fit within one of two families: Semantic network theories and schema theories.

Semantic network models (Anderson & Bower, 1973; Collins & Quillian, 1969; Collins & Loftus, 1975; Kintsch, 1974; Rumelhart, Lindsey, & Norman, 1972) are the modern counterparts of early associationist theories. Semantic network theories assume that concepts are stored in long-term memory within hierarchally-organized networks of meaningful association. Some concepts have superordinate-subordinate relationships (animal-dog-collie). Concepts that are part of the same network share some degree of linkage with each other, although the linkages vary from direct and immediate associations (black-white) to more distant relationships sustained only indirectly through linkages to other concepts (black-powder, black-blacksmith).

Within a network, the common attributes of the superordinate concept are stored with that concept, whereas only the particular attributes of each member of the class are stored with the member concept. Thus, the attribute "has wings" is stored with the superordinate concept "bird," but only the attribute "red breast" is stored with the subordinate concept "robin." Because the proximity of concepts stored within the same network is assumed to depend on their degree of meaningful relatedness, semantic network theories predict that the time needed to retrieve information about relationships between two concepts will depend on the distance between them in the network. Thus, it should take less time to decide whether or not all robins are birds than to decide whether or not all robins are animals. Similarly, it should be easier to answer the question "Does a robin have a red breast?" than the question "Does a robin fly?," because memory searches that begin with "robin" move quickly to "red breast." In contrast, the person must move up the hierarchy before encountering "able to fly," because this concept is attached to "bird" rather than "robin."

Most predictions of semantic network theories have been borne out, and in general, semantic network theories provide useful models for the storage of information in semantic memory. Furthermore, because they can be built into computer programs, they have been useful in cognitive simulation research. Here, the construction of models of human information processing and memory can be followed by study of how models respond to new input.

Semantic network theories, however, portray long-term memory as a relatively static storage system that provides the basis for highly routine and predictable access and retrieval. Consequently, such theories have been supplemented in recent years by schema theories. These theories help explain the constructive encoding of input and the reconstruction of stored memories reported by Bartlett and others.

Since Bartlett's groundbreaking work, many investigators have shown that new input is not first understood in some abstract way and only then related to existing knowledge; instead, it is interpreted from the beginning within contexts supplied by that existing knowledge. These collections of related information that provide context for meaningful intepretation of new input are usually called schemas (Rumelhart & Norman, 1978; Anderson, 1984; diSibio, 1982), although very similar concepts have been called plans (Schank & Abelson, 1975), scripts (Schank & Abelson, 1977), or frames (Minsky, 1975; Winograd, 1975).

Even seemingly familiar material may not have much meaning for us unless we can interpret it within relevant schemas. For example, consider the following sentence: "The notes were sour because the seam split" (Bransford & McCarrell, 1974). This sentence contains familiar words arranged according to the rules of English syntax, and you can even recognize it as a causal explanation for an observed event. Yet, the sentence probably will have little meaning for you until you are given the additional clue "bagpipe," and thus are able to interpret it within your "bagpipe playing" schema.

For a more extended example, consider the following paragraph drawn from Dooling and Lachman (1971):

> With hocked gems financing him, our hero bravely defied all scornful laughter that tried to prevent his scheme. "Your eyes deceive," he had said, "an egg not a table correctly typifies this unexplored planet." Now three sturdy sisters sought proof, forging along sometimes through calm vastness, yet more often over turbulent peaks and valleys. Days became weeks as many doubters spread fearful rumors about the edge. At last from nowhere welcome-winged creatures appeared signifying momentous success. (p. 217)

In Dooling and Lachman's experiment, most subjects who read this paragraph without an accompanying title found it relatively meaningless and could not remember much of it later. However, subjects who read the paragraph under the title "Christopher Columbus discovering America" found it entirely meaningful and were able to remember much more of it.

Lest you think that schema activation always leads to a single interpretation or "right answer," consider the following paragraph drawn from Anderson (1984a):

> Tony slowly got up from the mat, planning his escape. He hesitated a moment and thought. Things were not going well. What bothered him most was being held, especially since the charge against him had been weak. He considered his present situation. The

> lock that held him was strong but he thought he could break it. He knew, however, that his timing would have to be perfect. Tony was aware that it was because of his early roughness that he had been penalized so severely—much too severely from his point of view. The situation was becoming frustrating; the pressure had been grinding on him for too long. He was being ridden unmercifully. Tony was getting angry now. He felt he was ready to make his move. He knew that his success or failure would depend on what he did in the next few seconds. (pp. 244–245).

If you are like most people, you thought that this paragraph was about a convict planning to escape from prison, and you had no difficulty interpreting it because you could relate it easily to schemas concerning the thinking of convicts, prison life, and prison escapes. However, if you are familiar with the sport of wrestling, you may have interpreted the paragraph as being about a wrestler trying to escape the hold of an opponent. In this interpretation, the mat is a wrestling mat rather than a prison pallet, the lock is a wrestling hold rather than a piece of hardware, the punishment of roughness involved imposing penalty points for illegal tactics rather than imprisonment for crimes, and the pressure is physical pressure from an opponent rather than psychological pressure from a jailer. Either interpretation is equally valid for this passage, and either yields meaningful interpretation and good memory for the passage.

Although these specially constructed demonstrations are enjoyable and call our attention to the role of schemas in facilitating and determining the nature of text comprehension, the larger point here is that these and other effects of schemas occur routinely, whether we are aware of them or not. How input is encoded and where it is stored in memory will depend on what relevant schemas are activated in interpreting it in the first place, and reconstruction of the input after it is stored may occur later if changes occur in the schemas themselves. These and other factors affecting long-term memory for connected discourse will be discussed later in the chapter, following discussion of factors affecting rote learning.

Factors Affecting Rote Learning

Although most school learning involves meaningful verbal learning of connected discourse, some of it involves primarily rote learning of disconnected verbal material. There are school learning parallels for each of the three major types of learning studied in verbal learning experiments (Mayer, 1982). In serial learning, students are given lists of items to be memorized in order such as the alphabet, or the roster of U.S. presidents. In paired associate learning, students must learn stimulus-response pairs so that they can supply the response item when given the stimulus item such as with states and their capitols, or foreign language synonyms for English words. Finally, in free recall list learning, students are given lists of items that may be recalled in any order such as naming the countries in Europe or listing the thirteen original colonies. Certain well-established facts concerning rote

Serial, paired associate, and free recall list learning

learning of such verbal material include meaningfulness effects, serial position effects, practice effects, transfer effects, interference effects, organizational effects, levels of processing effects, state dependent effects, and mnemonic effects (Mayer, 1982).

Meaningfulness Effects

Highly meaningful words are easier to learn and remember than less meaningful words. This is true whether meaningfulness is measured by the number of associations that the learner has for the word (Palermo & Jenkins, 1964; Cofer, 1971), by the frequency of the word in ordinary printed or spoken language (Deese, 1959; Cofer, 1971), by familiarity with the sequential order of the letters (Underwood & Schultz, 1960), or by the tendency of the word to elicit clear images (Paivio, 1971). An implication here is that retention will be improved to the extent that learners are able to make relatively meaningless material more meaningful by associating it with more familiar material (see the section on mnemonic effects later in this chapter) or by susbstituting familiar, concrete words for unfamiliar, abstract words (Wittrock, Marks, & Doctorow, 1975).

Serial Position Effects

Serial position effects are effects that result from the particular placement of an item within a list. Memory is better for items that are placed at the beginnings (primacy effects) or the ends (recency effects) of lists than for items placed in the middle. An exception to these serial position effects is the distinctiveness effect—an item that is distinctively different from the others, such as a male name among a list of female names, which will be remembered better than the other items regardless of its serial position.

It may be that serial position effects occur because the items at the beginnings and ends of lists serve as "cognitive landmarks" that provide anchors to which the other items may be attached in memory (Mayer, 1982). Other explanations are also possible, however. For example, if the memory test follows immediately after the practice time, recency effects may occur simply because learners are able to hold the last few items of the list in short-term memory long enough to be able to reproduce them first on the recall test. Another theory is that primacy effects occur because the first few items enter an empty short-term memory store, so that more time is available and less interference is encountered in transferring them to long-term memory, compared to what happens with items placed later on the list. Research in support of this theory shows that the recency effect disappears when the recall test is delayed, but the primacy effect is still evident (Craik, 1979). An implication here is that students may remember the beginnings of lessons better than the parts that come afterwards, suggesting the importance of advance organizers and early presentation of key ideas and structuring concepts.

Practice Effects

Active practice or rehearsal improves retention, and distributed practice is usually more effective than massed practice. The advantage to distributed practice is especially noticeable for long lists, fast presentation rates, or unfamiliar stimulus material (Underwood, 1961; Underwood, Kapelak, & Malmi, 1976). The advantage to distributed practice apparently occurs because massed practice allows the learner to associate a word with only a single context, but distributed practice allows association with many different contexts (Glenberg, 1976).

A clear implication here is that practice on tasks such as memorizing poems, spelling words, arithmetic tables, or foreign language vocabulary is most efficient when distributed over a large number of short sessions. If the material is intended to be learned permanently or applied later to other learning, it will be necessary to see that practice continues to the point of overlearning and that sufficient review occurs thereafter to insure that students can retrieve the learning quickly when they need it.

When memorizing verbal material such as poetry or dramatic lines, active, overt practice is likely to be more effective than silent reading. Rehearsing the material aloud is helpful, as are accompanying it with appropriate gestures or even general physical movements such as pacing.

Transfer Effects

Transfer effects are effects of prior learning on the learning of new material. Positive transfer occurs when previous learning makes the new learning easier; negative transfer occurs when it makes the new learning more difficult. The more that two tasks have in common, the more likely that transfer effects will occur.

Specific transfer

Specific transfer occurs when two learning tasks share some components. When the tasks involve similar stimuli and call for making similar responses, positive transfer may be expected. Thus, having learned two-column addition makes it easier to learn three-column addition than it would be if you started from scratch, and having learned ping-pong makes it easier to learn tennis. However, to the extent that tasks involve similar stimuli but call for different responses, negative transfer may occur. Thus, knowledge about adding suffixes to regular words may interfere with handling of irregular words (a child says "runned" instead of "ran"), knowledge about dividing whole numbers may interfere with learning to divide fractions, and knowledge of Spanish may interfere with the learning of Portuguese.

Unfortunately, the majority of specific transfer effects that occur in rote learning are likely to be negative transfer effects rather than positive transfer effects (the opposite is true with meaningful learning). The danger is greatest when the two sets of similar items are being learned at the same time and neither set is well anchored. Less confusion due to negative transfer effects is likely when one set of items has been mastered to overlearning before the second set is encountered (see Chapter 11).

Active practice is a proven aid to memory.

Young children and negative transfer

Problems with negative transfer are especially likely with younger students, so that careful sequencing of material, separation of potentially confusable items, and emphasis on practice to overlearning is especially important in the early grades. Older students and adults can avoid many of these problems through sophisticated information processing, although even here, practice is important to establish and maintain skills.

General transfer

General transfer is transfer that cannot be attributed to shared components among tasks. An example would be general study skills learned in one course and then applied later in other courses on different topics. Such general transfer is discussed later in this chapter and in Chapter 10. Unfortunately, rote learning of specific material offers little or no possibility for positive general transfer, which is one reason why schools should not place much emphasis on it.

Interference Effects

Proactive and retroactive interference

Interference effects occur when memory for particular material is hurt by previous or subsequent learning. Thus, whereas transfer effects occur when learning the new material in the first place, interference effects occur later when trying to remember it. Also, whereas transfer effects can be either positive or negative, interference effects are always negative. Proactive interference occurs when previously learned material impedes ability to remember more recently learned material. For example, most Americans are so accustomed to using the traditional system of weights and measures that they have difficulty remembering and using the Metric system. Retroactive interference occurs when something that is learned more recently interferes with ability to remember something learned previously. Students who first study Latin and then one of the romance languages derived from Latin are likely to forget more of their Latin than students who first study Latin and then study some language that is unrelated to Latin.

Interference effects are the major causes for forgetting of material learned by rote. You can minimize such forgetting by varying the contexts within which practice takes place, seeing that practice continues to overlearning, and, most importantly, encouraging students to process the material in ways that make it meaningful learning rather than rote learning.

Organization Effects

Organization effects occur when learners chunk or categorize the input. Free recall of lists is better when learners organize the items into categories rather than attempting to memorize the lists in serial order (Bower, 1970). Most students will use such chunking strategies on their own when they see opportunities to do so, although learning is likely to be most efficient when teachers organize lists in logical ways and call students' attention to this organization (Bower, Clark, Lesgold, & Winzenz, 1969).

Levels-of-Processing Effects

Craik and Lockhart (1972) argued that words may be processed at several levels ranging from low-level sensory analysis of their physical characteristics to high-level semantic analysis of word meaning. They reviewed literature indicating levels-of-processing effects—the more deeply a word list is processed, the better it will be remembered. In particular, semantic encoding of the content is likely to lead to better memory than nonsemantic encoding. Thus, subjects instructed to note whether or not each word belonged in a certain category remembered more words than subjects instructed to circle every vowel (Jenkins, 1974).

The levels-of-processing notion has held up well as a general principle, although it applies better to some contexts than to others and different investigators do not always agree in classifying particular types of processing as high level or low level (Craik, 1979; Horton & Mills, 1984). Consequently, other investigators prefer different terms such as distinctiveness of encoding, elaboration of encoding, or effort expended during encoding. The common element in these ideas is that memory will be better when learners actively process the information and develop meaningful associations to it (elaborative encoding) than when they merely try to memorize it rotely (maintenance rehearsal).

Elaborative encoding

Stein and Bransford (1979) showed the value of elaborative encoding. Subjects were presented with lists of sentences such as "the bald man read the newspaper" or "the funny man liked the ring," and then were asked memory questions such as "Which man read the newspaper?" Memory for such sentences was improved when the learners were supplied with, or encouraged to generate, elaborations that made the sentences more meaningful by placing the described behaviors within cause-effect contexts (The bald man read the newspaper in order to look for a hat sale. The funny man liked the ring that squirted water.). These elaborations apparently improved memory because they added information that made the described actions meaningful given the nature of the man involved (bald, funny, etc.). This characteristic was essential, because other elaborations that did not provide such significant or relevant information were not successful in improving memory (the bald man read the newspaper while eating breakfast; the funny man liked the ring that he received as a present). Learners actually did worse with the latter types of elaboration than they did with the original short sentences.

Transfer-appropriate processing

Bransford (1979) also speaks of transfer-appropriate processing—what constitutes appropriate processing of particular input will depend on what information the learners need and what they will be expected to do with it. In studying word lists, for example, semantic processing would usually be appropriate because learning will usually be measured with recall tests. However, processing of the physical characteristics of the words would be appropriate if the test was expected to focus on these physical characteristics. Tversky (1973) has shown that learners can adjust their information processing and study strategies according to the kind of test they expect—in this case, a recall test versus a recognition test. More generally, students can be encouraged to remember what they learn by keeping in mind the contexts in which they will need the information and thinking about what they will do with the information when they need it.

State-Dependent Effects

State- or context-dependent effects occur because learning takes place within a specific context and may be most accessible later, at least initially, within that same context. For example, lists are more easily remembered when the test situation is similar to the learning situation, apparently because this maximizes the contextual cues available to aid in retrieving the information (Mayer, 1982). Such state-dependent effects have been shown in many ways, including some unusual ones. For example, Baddeley (1976) has reviewed research showing that lists learned under water are recalled better under water, and lists learned while under the influence of alcohol are recalled best under the same state.

Encoding specificity effects

Of more direct relevance to schooling are the encoding specificity effects demonstrated by Tulving and Thomson (1973): If the word "light" was associated with "head" during learning, it will be easier to remember "light" if the test gives the cue "head" than if the test gives the cue "dark."

At first glance, these state-dependent effects may seem to imply that testing conditions should be kept as similar as possible to learning conditions. This would be true if teaching success were narrowly defined as maximizing scores on tests of memory for specific information. However, given that we usually desire transfer and application rather than mere retention of specific knowledge, the instructional implications here seem to be that the contexts of learning should be varied so that learners can retrieve the information in response to a variety of cues rather than remaining dependent on the cues embedded in a particular context.

Mnemonic Effects

Learners can increase the effectiveness of their rote learning by using mnemonics—strategies for elaborating on relatively meaningless input by associating the input with more meaningful images or semantic context. Four well-known mnemonics methods are the place method, the link method, the peg method, and the keyword method.

The Place Method. The place method (also called the method of loci, after the Latin word for places) involves associating each item on a list with a particular place within a familiar location. For example, you might think of taking a familiar path through the campus or walking through the rooms of your house in a particular order, and encountering each of the items on the list as you pass campus landmarks or move from one room to the next. The familiar sequence involved in "walking" through the campus or house would help you to remember the items on the list in their proper sequence, and the visual imagery involved in "seeing" the items near the landmarks or in the rooms would help you to remember each individual item. The place method has received considerable support in research on human memory (Bower, 1970), and it is usually stressed in memory improvement books written for the general public (Lorayne & Lucas, 1974).

The Link Method. The link method involves forming an image for each item on the list and then linking these items together into an interactive chain. For example, if you need to pick up butter, celery, flour, ground beef, and ice cream at the food store, you might remember these items by imagining preparing a meal in which you first used the flour to make bread, stirring the mixture with the celery as you did so, then used the ground beef to make a meat loaf, and then enjoyed a meal of bread and butter and the meat loaf, with ice cream for dessert. Like the place method, the link method aids memory for specific items by tying the items to images and linking the images into a continuous "story." If the sequence of the items is important, it can be built into the story as well, although this will usually yield more complicated stories.

Often, of course, it will be easier to make a written list than to go to the trouble of using the link method or the other mnemonic devices described here. However, such devices are useful for memorizing lists when writing the list is not possible or permissible, when preparing to deliver a speech that must be given without notes, or when the list will have to be remembered under circumstances in which it is not possible or convenient to take time to consult notes.

The Peg Method. The peg method (also called the hook method) involves using a familiar series or list of items as "pegs" on which newly learned items can be "hung" as they are learned. In the most common example, the pegs are items selected because they are easy to visualize and their names rhyme with the number names (one is a bun, two is a shoe, three is a tree, etc.). To facilitate memory, the items to be learned are then linked to the items on this peg list through imagery. Thus, the first item might be pictured between the halves of a bun, the second item would be linked to the image of a shoe, and so on. The peg method is like the link method in that it relies on imagery to picture items as linked together or interacting in some way. However, whereas the link method involves linking the items to be learned to one another, the peg method involves linking these items to peg items that are easily visualized and already sequenced.

The Keyword Method. The keyword method is a useful mnemonic device for paired associate learning. Originated as a technique for teaching foreign language vocabulary (Atkinson, 1975), the method is also useful for aiding memory for definitions of unfamiliar English words (Pressley, Levin, & Miller, 1982) and technical terms (Jones & Hall, 1982), as well as for linking cities to their products (Pressley & Dennis-Rounds, 1980), states to their capitols (Levin, Shriberg, Miller, McCormick, & Levin, 1980), and proper names to events, accomplishments, or biographical information (Jones & Hall, 1982; McCormick & Levin, 1984; Shriberg, Levin, McCormick, & Pressley, 1982).

The method involves identifying a keyword that helps to maintain the linkage between the items to be associated. For example, the Spanish word "carta" means "letter" in English. A good keyword for "carta" would be "cart," a familiar English word that is easily visualized. The keyword can then be used to link the terms to be associated either through imagery (an image of a shopping cart transporting a letter) or through construction of a meaningful sentence (The cart carries the letter). As another example, the state of Maryland (keyword = marry) can be linked with its capitol of Annapolis (keyword = apple) using an image of two apples getting married (Levin, 1981).

Vocabulary learning

Research indicates that the keyword method substantially improves vocabulary learning, both in foreign language and in one's own language, across the range of grade levels (Pressley, Levin, & Miller, 1982). Furthermore, in several of the vocabulary learning studies, students using the keyword method not only learned more than students left to their own devices, but learned more than students who were using semantically based methods often advocated by reading theorists, such as writing word definitions, using words in sentences, or inferring their meanings from context (Pressley, Levin, Kuiper, Bryant, & Michener, 1982; McDaniel & Pressley, 1984).

The method works best when the keyword is a familiar English word that refers to something easily visualized and that sounds like or is identical to a salient part of the word to be learned. Thus "car" would be a good keyword for the word "carlin," and learners might use the image of an old woman driving a car to help them remember that "carlin" means "old woman."

The keyword method appears to be especially helpful for lower ability students who have not developed efficient methods for learning on their own (McDaniel & Pressley, 1984).

Other Mnemonics. There are many other mnemonic devices in addition to the place, link, peg, and keyword methods (Bellezza, 1981; Lorayne & Lucas, 1974). Bower and Clark (1969) reported success with the elaboration method, where learners who were encouraged to weave together the words on a list into a running story retained more than learners who memorized in the usual way.

Elaboration method

Ehri, Deffner, and Wilce (1984) used pictorial mnemonics to help children remember the sounds that are associated with letters of the alphabet. In teaching about the letter "f," for example, they showed an illustration in which the letter "f" was drawn as the stem of a flower. This visual image helped the children to remember the shape of the letter "f," and the drawing depicted something whose name begins with the "f" sound (flower).

Pictorial mnemonics

Rhymes are often useful mnemonic devices ("*i* before *e* except after *c*," "30 days hath September. . . ."). So are acronyms (YMCA, FBI), especially when they are pronouncable (NATO, UNICEF). You may find it useful to create your own acronyms for special purposes. For example, if you are to give a speech that has five major ideas, it may be helpful to employ a word (e.g., TIGER) whose letters each stand for a key point in the speech (*T* represents the role of transportation in responding to the energy crisis, and so on).

Rhymes and acronyms

Imagery and spatial visualization are often useful mnemonic devices as well. Verbal learning can be assisted by picturing words in the mind, solving problems involving making change can be assisted by visualizing the coins involved, and spatial computations can be assisted by visualizing the rooms or buildings portrayed in the problems. In general, anything that will help learners to process input more deeply, relate it to more familiar material, or supplement the verbal presentation with vivid imagery will help them to learn and remember that material.

Imagery and spatial visualization

Factors Affecting Meaningful Verbal Learning

As we have seen, the main problem facing students trying to learn disconnected material is to find ways to make the material meaningful and thus not have to depend on purely rote learning strategies. Meaningfulness is not a problem, however, for students faced with learning connected discourse unless the material is so unfamiliar or difficult as to make meaningful comprehension impossible. Instead, the problem is coping with the sheer volume of the material by learning it in an organized fashion and retaining it so that it can be retrieved when needed.

Mayer (1982) has identified the following sets of findings from research on learning connected discourse: abstraction effects, levels effects, schema effects, prior knowledge effects, interference effects, text organization ef-

Learning connected discourse

fects, and mathemagenic effects. We will discuss these findings along with those on student misconception effects, a topic that has generated a great deal of recent interest.

Abstraction Effects

Abstraction is the tendency of learners to pay attention to and remember the gist of a passage rather than the specific wording of the sentences. Abstraction effects are seen in experiments in which subjects first read a passage and then later are shown sentences and asked to state whether or not these sentences were included in the passage. In such studies, the subjects tend to recognize sentences that are irrelevant or contradictory to what they have read, but they are unable to distinguish verbatim sentences from similar sentences that carry the same meaning (Sachs, 1967; Bransford & Franks, 1971). In general, to the extent that learners assume that the goal is understanding rather than verbatim memory, and to the extent that the material can be analyzed into main ideas and supportive detail, learners will tend to concentrate on the main ideas and to retain these in semantic forms that are more abstract and generalized than the verbatim sentences included in the passage.

Levels Effects

Levels effects occur when learners believe that some parts of the passage are more important than others. To the extent that the passage is already well-organized or that the learners are able to provide such organization themselves, parts that occupy higher levels in the organization of the passage will be learned better than parts occupying lower levels. Generalizations and key ideas associated with the main theme of the passage will be learned especially well (Kintsch, 1976; Meyer, 1977).

Schema Effects

We have already given several examples ("The notes were sour because the seam split," the paragraph on Christopher Columbus, and the ambiguous prisoner/wrestler story) illustrating how text comprehension is affected by existing schemas. We have also discussed Bartlett's research indicating that memory for previously learned material can become reconstructed over time if the schemas to which it is attached should undergo change themselves. Referring to all of these examples as schema effects reflects our preference for broad use of the term schema and for use of the term schema effects to refer to a collection of more specific effects.

In this regard, Gagné and Dick (1983) suggest that 1) newly learned information is stored by being incorporated into schemas formed on the basis of previous learning; 2) recall of previously learned verbal information is strongly influenced by these schemas, so that remembering is a constructive act; 3) schemas not only aid retention of new material by providing frameworks for storage, but also alter the new information by making it "fit" the expectations built into the schemas; 4) schemas make it possible for learners to make inferences that fill in the gaps in stories or expository prose; 5) schemas are organized not only in terms of figurative verbal knowledge but also in terms of components of intellectual skills (operative knowledge); and 6) ideally, learners will become able not only to process new information efficiently but also to evaluate and modify their own schemas.

Functions of schemas

Similarly, Anderson (1984) identifies the following six functions of schemas: 1) providing ideational scaffolding for assimilation of text information, 2) facilitating selective allocation of attention (concentration on the important aspects of the text), 3) enabling inferential elaboration (inferring details that are implied but not spelled out), 4) allowing orderly memory searches (identifying the kinds of relevant information that will be needed in order to understand the text most efficiently), 5) facilitating editing and summarizing (abstracting the gist or main themes for storage in long-term memory), and 6) permitting inferential reconstruction (filling in gaps in memory later by replacing lost or never-encoded details with inferences based on knowledge of what those details probably were).

Used in a general way, the term schema effects would refer not only to the effects described by Gagné and Dick (1983) and by Anderson (1984), but also to the effects described in the rest of this section and in the later sections on abstraction effects, levels effects, prior knowledge effects, inference effects, and student misconception effects. Mayer (1982), however, uses the term schema effects to refer more specifically to situations in which learners recognize that the text describes a particular instance of a larger class of experiences or events for which they have a well-developed schema, and then use that schema both to process the information (using expectations about the elements to be expected and their probable order and degree of importance) and to aid comprehension by filling in gaps where information is implied rather than stated explicitly. Consider the following paragraph:

> When Mary arrived, the woman at the door greeted her and checked for her name. A few minutes later, she was escorted to her chair and shown the day's menu. The attendant was helpful but brusque, almost to the point of being rude. Later, she paid the woman at the door and left.

Chances are that this paragraph was quite meaningful to you because you recognized that it took place in a restaurant, that Mary had made reservations, that she was seated by the hostess at a table (not merely a chair), that the "attendant" was a waiter, and that the "woman at the door" that Mary paid on the way out was a cashier (probably not the same woman as the hostess who seated her originally). Schank and Abelson (1977) suggest that you could infer all of this information because you possess a schema called a "restaurant script" that includes such slots as "being seated," "ordering," and "paying the check." Theoretically, as soon as you recognized that the paragraph depicted events occurring in a restaurant, you activated your restaurant script and constructed a meaning for the paragraph that included numerous inferences in addition to what was explicitly stated in the text.

Story grammars

Similarly, Rumelhart (1975) and Thorndyke (1977) suggest that people use specialized schemas known as story grammars when reading stories. A story grammar is a set of rules that specify the hierarchical relationships among events or states in a story. The four main slots to be filled in a story are the setting, the theme, the plot, and the resolution. The setting involves a particular time and place, as well as a cast of characters. The theme surrounds an event that the characters are involved in or a goal that they are working toward. The plot involves a series of episodes, each with a goal, behavior directed toward that goal, and the outcome of this behavior. The resolution occurs when the story reaches the climax toward which it has been building and offers some moral or conclusion relating to its theme. Younger children have poorly developed story grammars and thus tend to focus on actions rather than motives and to process stories as if they were relatively disconnected descriptions of events rather than elements woven into a connected story line (Voss & Bisanz, 1982). With age and experience, however, students bring to bear increasingly sophisticated schemas that remind them of the slots they can expect to be filled as they read stories. This knowledge helps them to know what to look for as they read, and is used in organizing their memory for the story. (Setting, theme, plot, and resolution are remembered, perhaps along with some key phrases or quotations. Unimportant details and verbatim phrasing are not.)

Preparing for story reading

Reading comprehension theorists recommend that teachers prepare their students for story reading by telling the students what the story is about and asking them questions designed to activate schemas that they will find useful in comprehending the story. These include schemas relating to the content of the story in addition to story grammars and related schemas concerning the forms and functions of fiction.

Prior Knowledge Effects

Even when the material to be learned does not lend itself to interpretation within a well-developed schema with ready-made slots, prior knowledge effects will still occur to the extent that the learners can use their existing knowledge to establish a context or construct a schema into which the new information can be assimilated (Bransford, 1979). The convict/wrestler paragraph presented earlier is an example. Few people have specific "thinking about breaking a hold" schemas, but people knowledgeable about wrestling are able to use this prior knowledge to interpret the paragraph as being about a wrestler attempting to escape an opponent's hold. Most people, though, see the paragraph as about a prisoner contemplating escape unless they are specifically cued toward the wrestling interpretation.

Providing cues

Learners can exert some control over the perspective they take in interpreting information if cued to do so (Anderson, Pichert, & Shirey, 1983). For example, Pichert and Anderson (1977) had subjects read a passage describing two boys playing in a house. Some were directed to read from the perspective of a home buyer, and others from the perspective of a burglar. These assigned perspectives affected the pattern of details that were remembered later on a recall test. "Home buyers" were more likely to remember that the roof leaked, but "burglars" were more likely to remember the color TV set.

In general, providing cues about what kind of prior knowledge is relevant to understanding a passage is one way for teachers to make vague passages more meaningful to their students. For expository passages, such cuing might involve suggesting analogies or visual imagery that would help link the strange to the familiar. For poetry or fiction, it might involve providing explanations or asking questions designed to alert students to metaphors and other literary devices and to make them aware that the stories or poems can be appreciated on several levels besides the most obvious interpretation.

Inference Effects

Inference effects occur when learners use schemas or other prior knowledge to make inferences about intended meanings that go beyond what is explicitly stated in the text. Three kinds of inferences are case grammar presuppositions, conceptual dependency inferences, and logical deductions.

Case grammar

Fillmore (1968) uses the term case grammar to refer to the assumptions and implications that are built into the use of language. In particular, he notes that declarative sentences typically take a subject-verb-object form, and that the verb implies that the subject took some action on the object. In the context of baseball, for example, the verb "hit" implies a subject (the batter), an object (the ball), and in this case, an instrument for accomplishing an action (the bat). These logical relationships and the imagery associated with them are brought to bear in interpreting statements that are not completely explicit. Thus, people familiar with baseball will infer that the ball has been pitched and the batter has hit a fair ball and reached base safely when they hear "It's a hit," or "He drives a single to left" (Kintsch, 1974; Meyer, 1975).

Conceptual dependency inferences

Conceptual dependency inferences (Schank, 1972) occur when learners recognize cause-effect relationships or other necessary dependencies among ideas in a passage. For example, Kintsch (1976) had students read a story containing the sentences, "A burning cigarette was carelessly discarded. The fire destroyed many acres of virgin forest." Students who read this version of the story easily inferred that the cigarette started the fire, and were just as likely to report this later as students who read a version of the story that spelled this out explicitly.

Logical deductions

Logical deductions occur when readers are given premises that compel certain conclusions. For example, if told that A is taller than B and B is taller than C, they will be able to answer the question "Is A taller than C?" correctly.

Simplification of communication

In addition to providing good demonstrations that meaning is actively constructed from text rather than merely decoded, these various inference effects simplify communication enormously. Instead of having to specify everything that we say in complete detail, we can convey the gist of the information and rely on the listener or reader to infer the rest. In teaching, however, it is wise to be sure that learners get the complete picture when it is important for them to do so. Thus, teachers should ordinarily spell out cause and effect relationships, logical deductions, and the implications of examples or experiments. They should also be alert to the failures of textbooks to be explicit. In recent years, textbook publishers have sought to simplify their texts by substituting shorter words and sentences for longer ones. Ironically, however, the result has often been a reduction in clarity because vague terms were substituted for precise terms and because important logical connectives ("because," "therefore," etc.) were omitted when long sentences were divided into two or more shorter ones (Anderson & Armbruster, 1984).

Student Misconception Effects

So far, our discussion of schema effects, including prior knowledge effects and inference effects, has emphasized the positive by showing how schemas allow us to embed input within meaningful contexts and fill in gaps whenever the message is not complete and explicit. However, there is also a negative side to this process. Schema activation also makes possible the student misconception effects that occur when input is filtered through schemas which are themselves oversimplified, distorted, or just plain incorrect. This happens routinely with young children whose thinking is still in the process of becoming operational, and it happens much more often than you might think with older students and adults, especially when dealing with abstract mathematical and scientific concepts that contrast with naive conceptions about the world built up through concrete experiences.

For example, Eaton, Anderson, and Smith (1984) studied the teaching and learning of a unit on light in fifth-grade science classes. One of the points made repeatedly in the unit is that sunlight reflects off of objects to our eyes, and that it is this reflected sunlight that we are processing when we see. This scientific conception of vision is very different from the naive conception that most people develop; namely, that the sun brightens the objects themselves. There is a test item that shows the sun, a tree, and a boy, and asks the students to show how sunlight enables the boy to see the tree. The correct answer is to draw rays coming from the sun to the tree and then reflecting off the tree to the boy's eyes. On pretests, only about 5 percent of the students were able to answer this item correctly. Of the remaining students who responded at all, the majority drew rays from the sun to the tree, or to the entire landscape, but did not show these rays being reflected to the boy's eyes.

So far, this was unremarkable. However, the students then spent several weeks on the unit, which covered light reflection and vision several times in several different contexts. Yet, post-tests revealed that only 24 percent of the students showed light rays reflecting off the tree to the boy's eyes, and the majority still thought that we see objects because the sun "brightens them up." Replications of this work have yielded similar results, even though conducted in classrooms taught by teachers considered to be generally effective who were using respected and widely adopted curriculum materials.

Inadequate curriculum material

How could this happen? In part, the authors believe, because the curriculum materials were not as clear and explicit as they could have been. More importantly, however, students missed the point here not because they could not understand it, but because they thought they already did understand it and therefore never became aware of the conflict between what the text was saying and what their own misconceptions implied. They read the words, but they did not attend to them that closely or appreciate their full meaning or implications. Consequently, they sailed right through the unit with the same misconceptions that they brought into it.

Mathematics misconceptions

These findings are not unusual. A variety of common misconceptions has been discovered in both mathematics (Davis, 1984) and science (Champagne, Klopfer, & Anderson, 1980; diSessa, 1982), and more are being discovered every day. For example, Davis and McKnight (1980) found that very few third- or fourth-graders solved the following subtraction problem correctly without help the first time they saw it: 7,002 − 25. Furthermore, because of a common misconception about the process of borrowing during subtraction, one particular incorrect answer was common: 5,087. Nor are such misconceptions confined to young children. Matz (1980) includes the following in a list of 33 algebra errors commonly made by high school and college students:

- ☐ Evaluating $4x$ when x equals 6 as 46 or $46x$.
- ☐ Evaluating xy when x equals -3 and y equals -5 as -8.
- ☐ Computing $2x$ divided by $2x$ to be 0.
- ☐ Claiming that one can't multiply by x because "you don't know what x is."

Such misconceptions are common even among professors (Lockhead, 1980; Rosnick & Clement, 1980). Furthermore, they are often highly resistant to change. Investigators studying mathematics misconceptions found that they were difficult to remove even with tutoring, and that they often reasserted themselves even after learners had seemingly mastered the correct concepts.

Eaton, Anderson, and Smith (1984) achieved some success in eliminating student misconceptions about vision, although not easily. They made adjustments in the way that the fifth grade light unit was taught that raised post-test scores on the sun/tree/boy item from 24 percent to 79 percent correct. However, this took both special teacher training (alerting the teachers to probable student misconceptions and ways to confront them) and preparation of special curriculum materials (a revised text that was clearer and more explicit about the difference between the scientific concept and the naive concept, supplemented by specially prepared diagrams and illustrations shown on the overhead projector).

Conceptual change

These and other findings regarding student misconception effects have led to better appreciation of the fact that teaching involves conceptual change rather than infusion of knowledge into a vacuum. Most of the time, students will have at least some background knowledge to bring to bear in processing new input, and often they will have considerable knowledge organized into powerful schemas. Where this is true, the students may process the information primarily by assimilating the new input, or a partial, distorted version of that input, into old schemas, rather than by accommodating the old schemas to take into account the new input. This may be desirable when schemas are complete and accurate, but if they are not, it will lead to student misconception effects. Therefore, in addition to merely explaining material, teachers need to be aware of common misconceptions that their students are likely to hold about the material, and to be prepared to confront these misconceptions directly by making students aware of them and helping them to see how and why the misconceptions are incorrect.

Text Organization Effects

Text organization effects refer to the effects that the degree and type of organization built into a passage have on the degree and type of information that learners encode and remember. We described in the previous chapter the value of structuring elements such as advance organizers, previews, logical sequencing, outline formats, highlighting of main ideas, and summaries. These structuring elements make it possible for learners to retain more of the material by facilitating chunking, subsumption of the material into existing schemas, and by related processes that enable them to encode the passage as an organized body of meaningful knowledge rather than as a list of unrelated items to be memorized.

In addition, text organization elements determine what is learned by cuing the learners as to which aspects of the material are most important and which pre-existing schemas may be relevant. Kintsch and Yarbrough (1982), for example, had groups of subjects read essays that presented the same material in either good or poor rhetorical form. Later tests showed that the two groups were equally good at filling in blanks calling for specific facts, but the subjects who had read the well-organized essays were much better at answering open-ended questions about main points. Thus, a well-organized text or lecture does not merely divide a single lengthy presentation into several shorter subparts; in addition, it sequences the material in a sensible way and helps the learners to encode series of major ideas supported by elaborative details.

Mathemagenic Effects

Rothkopf (1970) coined the term mathemagenic activities to refer to the various things that learners do to prepare and assist their own learning (get ready to concentrate, approach the material with the intention of studying and remembering it, etc.). Wittrock (1974) has discussed learning as a generative process in which learners actively build the to-be-learned material in memory. Mathemagenic effects refer to these effects of active information processing by learners. Mathemagenic activities such as answering adjunct questions or taking notes can significantly enhance intentional learning of meaningful material.

Adjunct Questions. Adjunct questions are questions included within prose passages: prequestions at the beginning, inserted questions within the passage itself, or postquestions added at the end. A great deal of research indicates that students who learn from passages that include these adjunct questions retain more than students who read the same material but without the adjunct questions (Anderson & Biddle, 1975; Andre, 1979; Rickards, 1979; Rothkopf & Bisbicos, 1967; McConkie, 1977; Reynolds & Anderson, 1982; Sagaria & DiVesta, 1978). More specifically, adjunct questions tend to increase intentional learning of material directly related to the questions; they do not improve and may even reduce incidental learning.

Increasing intentional learning

Much of the research on adjunct questions has focused on where such questions should be inserted into the text. Most investigators have concluded that postquestions at the end of the passage or at the ends of subparts are more valuable than prequestions at the beginning of the passage or at the beginnings of subparts. Prequestions are effective in alerting learners to important issues, but they are especially likely to interfere with the learning of material not addressed in the questions (McConkie, 1977; Sagaria & DiVesta, 1978; Klauer, 1984). Similar effects result when specific learning objectives are presented prior to the passage (Gagné & Britton, 1982; Klauer, 1984). Prequestions tend to be most effective when they deal with the most general or important aspects of the passage, and they are most helpful to low-ability learners (Wilhite, 1983).

Position in text

Prequestions

Compared to prequestions, postquestions are less likely to reduce incidental learning by constricting attention to the material addressed in the questions. In addition, they help make learners aware of whether or not they understand the material, and they aid retention by encouraging learners to encode the material in their own words (Sagaria & DiVesta, 1978). Postquestions that direct attention to points that are often misunderstood or missed altogether because of student misconception effects are especially valuable (McConkie, 1977). In general, postquestions facilitate learning by causing learners to review the material systematically (Wixson, 1984), although somewhat different patterns of learning are likely to result depending on whether questions are addressed to material explicitly stated in the passage itself, material that is not explicitly stated but is easily inferred from the passage, or related issues that are not included or implied in the passage itself but can be addressed by activating schemas related to the passage (Wixson, 1983).

Postquestions

Other Mathemagenic Activities. Besides responding to adjunct questions, learners can engage in self-initiated mathemagenic activities that will enhance learning. One of these is notetaking. Notetaking is not helpful when students must learn from a rapidly presented lecture or when they are not given opportunities to review their notes (Faw & Waller, 1976), but it is an effective way to enhance learning from reading text or listening to lectures presented at a slow enough rate to allow both monitoring of the input and writing of notes (Faw & Waller, 1976; Weinstein & Mayer, 1985). Notetaking is likely to be especially effective when students use outline formats and concentrate on main ideas (Mayer, 1984; Carrier & Titus, 1981). Thus teachers are likely to achieve better results when they train their students in effective notetaking than when they merely suggest to the students that they take notes.

Notetaking

Underlining and shadowing

Another useful mathemagenic activity when reading text is underlining, apparently because it helps students to remember key terms and ideas (Rickards & August, 1975). A parallel technique for aiding memory of orally presented material is shadowing: After presenting a key word or phrase, the teacher pauses to let the students repeat it aloud (Mayer & Cook, 1981). Shadowing should be particularly useful in early reading instruction and foreign language instruction.

Mathemagenic activities will be discussed in much more detail in Chapter 10.

Current Research on Human Information Processing

Many of the most exciting advances in contemporary educational psychology are being contributed by investigators studying the information processing aspects of human learning and memory. Many of these involve applications of schema theory (broadly conceived), especially in the areas of reading comprehension, comparisons of novices with experts, and cognitive simulation and artificial intelligence.

Reading Comprehension Research

Reading comprehension (which includes all learning from text, not just what goes on during reading lessons at school) used to be thought of as an information processing activity that proceeded from the "bottom up." That is, readers processed letters and associated the letters with their sounds, then formed these sounds into words, then strung together the words in order to infer meaning from sentences, and so on. It is true that beginning readers do process information this way for a time, as do very poor readers who never become efficient at decoding. Skilled readers, however, process text much more rapidly and are able to use "top down" methods in which the text is filtered through well-formed schemas.

Interaction with text

In effect, skilled readers interact with the text to construct meaning. Comprehension occurs when expectations associated with relevant schemas are fulfilled by specific information in the text. Information that neatly satisfies these expectations is easily encoded into memory so as to "instantiate" the "slots" in the schema. Information that does not fit the schema may not be encoded at all, or may be distorted so that the fit is better. Gaps in the information are filled in by inferences that make the entire meaning gleaned from the passage consistent with the expectations built into the schema. Later, these same expectations that guide the encoding of information in the first place are brought into play again to guide retrieval and reconstruction (Anderson, 1984).

When the material can be assimilated into readily available schemas, reading with comprehension is rapid and relatively effortless. A large portion of the material is processed in the form of already well-organized and meaningful chunks, so that attention and working memory can concentrate on unfamiliar material or elements that do not fit established expectations. However, when no schema is readily available for processing material, it takes much more time and effort to read with comprehension. Even if the words can be decoded with relative ease (as in the paragraph about Christopher Columbus given as an example earlier), it becomes necessary to study them, think about them, and try to imagine what the author is trying to say. If decoding is a problem too, the reader will have to proceed almost on a word-by-word basis, first decoding the words and then coming back to review them later and try to figure out what they might mean. Given the limitations on working memory, the task of reading with comprehension is too difficult to take on all at once under these circumstances.

Importance of phonics

This work has led to renewed appreciation of the importance of instruction in phonics and other decoding strategies, as well as the importance of practicing reading until basic decoding processes become smooth and automatic, because this level of proficiency in decoding is necessary if readers are to have most of their working memory capacity available for understanding and keeping track of the meaning of the text (comprehension). At the same time, however, this work has also led to much greater understanding and appreciation of the strategies that skilled readers use for comprehending text, along with related mathemagenic activities and study skills (see Chapter 10).

Expert-Novice Comparisons

By asking people to think out loud as they solve problems, information processing theorists have been studying how people use their knowledge for thinking about specialized areas such as physics, radiology, or chess (Chi & Glaser, 1982; Chi, Glaser, & Rees, 1981; Larkin, 1981; Newell & Simon, 1972). Often this research involves comparing the thinking of skilled and experienced experts with that of novices in the same field, both to describe in detail "how the experts do it" and to identify the nature and reasons for the problems that the novices experience. Such knowledge can then be used as the basis for instruction designed to move novices toward expert status more quickly by teaching them to think as experts do and by helping them to avoid or at least recover quickly from commonly encountered problems (Greeno, 1980).

Early work in this area was done by deGroot (1965), who compared expert and novice chess players. DeGroot found that if 20 or 25 pieces were arranged randomly on a chess board, experts were no better than novices at reconstructing the arrangement from memory. Both groups averaged about seven pieces correct, as Miller (1956) predicted. However, when the arrangements were recreations of actual chess games, the experts could reconstruct the positions of most or even all of the pieces, whereas the novices could do little better than before.

How can expert chess players reconstruct 25 pieces after seeing them in place for only five or 10 seconds? Apparently, they do it by relying on chunking strategies and by activating familiar chess strategy schemas (Simon, 1979). Instead of trying to keep track of 25 individual pieces, the experts chunk by conceptualizing the play of the game (up to the point shown in the arrangement on the board) in terms of the placement of several groups of pieces (perhaps five or six groups with three to five pieces each). Given what they know about chess strategy, they recognize relationships among the pieces within the groups and relationships of the groups to one another. In addition to enabling them to accurately reconstruct games from memory, this kind of chunking and schema activation by chess experts enables them to play, and usually defeat, a large number of novices at the same time by circulating continuously and taking only a few seconds to decide on a move (Chase and Chi, 1980).

Novice and expert category groupings

Closer to the classroom, Chi, Feltovich, & Glaser (1981) presented expert physicists and novice physics students with a variety of mechanics problems, and asked them to sort these problems into categories and explain their reasoning. They found that novices sorted problems into the same category because they mentioned the same objects (such as pulleys or inclined planes) or the same physics concepts (such as friction). Experts, however, grouped problems together because they involved the same general principle (such as conservation of energy), even though such principles usually were not mentioned in the wording of the problems. Similar findings were reported in mathematics by Schoenfeld and Hermann (1982) and Silver (1979).

These differences in perception and organization of knowledge are paralleled by differences in thinking and problem solving (Shulman & Elstein, 1975; Champagne, Klopfer, & Gunstone, 1982; Newell & Simon, 1972). Here again, novices tend to focus on specific features of problems and try to link them to specific information stored in memory, whereas experts tend to "get the big picture" by identifying problems as particular instances of the application of general principles, and then solving them by activating schemas relevant to these principles and associated problems. Confronted with a mathematics or physics problem, for example, novice students will try to relate the problem to one of the theorems, equations, or formulas that they have memorized. This approach often leads to errors, and even when it leads to the correct answer, the novices may not realize exactly what they have done or why they have done it. In contrast, experts first read and think about the problem as a whole in order to identify its general nature and the principles that apply to it, and only then do they begin to make calculations.

Domain-specific knowledge

In general, experts have much more domain-specific knowledge (knowledge about the issue at hand, like chess or physics, as opposed to more general knowledge), and this knowledge is much better organized hierarchically to allow smooth movement between levels ranging from concrete particulars to abstract generalities.

Experts bring a much broader, deeper, and better organized body of specific knowledge to problems than novices do. In addition, they are more efficient in using the knowledge that they have. They do not consider large numbers of alternatives or work through all logical possibilities when classifying problems or identifying likely solution strategies. Instead, they create a workable problem space (cut the problem down to size) by quickly identifying one or a small number of schemas that probably apply to the problem, and then deal with the problem within the guidelines built into such schemas. There may be some initial checking to make sure that the chosen schema applies (this is why experts tend to analyze the problem first before trying to solve it), but once the problem is properly categorized, experts usually move rapidly toward a successful solution.

Research applied to teachers

The expert-novice comparison approach has recently been used in research on teaching designed to understand how experienced teachers know when to use specific strategies with specific students, and how novice teachers can develop this skill (Fogarty, Wang, & Creek, 1983; Leinhardt, 1983). This research shows that expert teachers, like experts in other fields, are able to use chunking strategies and schema activation in order to keep track of more things at the same time, to recognize (diagnose) student needs or instructional opportunities more quickly and accurately, and to bring to bear a greater variety of strategies with better articulated understanding of why the strategies are appropriate to the situation. As this approach to research on teaching develops, it should begin to yield implications for teacher education.

Interesting research is also being done on the development of expertise in novices. Children's mathematics learning provides several examples. Groen and Parkman (1972) have shown that preschool children typically use a "counting all" method for solving simple addition problems. For 3 + 4, for example, these children will recite "1, 2, 3, 4, 5, 6, 7." However, by first grade, most children use a "choice plus counting on" procedure, in which they first choose the larger of the two numbers to be added and then "count on" the additional numbers. Thus, for 3 + 4, they would recite "5, 6, 7." Most children discover this more sophisticated strategy on their own, without having to be taught explicitly.

"Counting all" method

Shortcuts

They also discover various shortcuts. Fuson (1982), for example, has shown that first-graders are especially fast with addition problems involving "doubles" (2 + 2, 3 + 3, etc.) because they have memorized the answers to these problems and do not need to do any counting at all. Furthermore, they can take advantage of their "doubles" knowledge for solving other problems (i.e., they can convert the problem 5 + 7 into the equivalent of 6 + 6, and solve it that way rather than having to use the "counting on" procedure). Studies of algebra students have shown that, besides being better at recognizing types of problems and associated solution strategies, "expert" students have learned to make "ball park estimates" of what the answers are likely to be, and to check their work as they go along. In combining the expression a/b + c/d, for example, they may substitute numbers for the letters (½ + ¾). By working out the numerical version of the problem, they can check to make sure that they have combined properly (in this case, by first dividing and then adding), something that is not so obvious when just the letters are used (Davis, 1984).

These data suggest several implications for teachers. First, there appear to be no shortcuts to expert knowledge. Detailed domain-specific knowledge is needed, not just a few general principles. Second, learners not only need to acquire knowledge and master strategies; they also need to know when the knowledge is relevant and how to use the strategies in various situations. This implies emphasis on the processes involved in formulating problems and working through solutions, not just on whether learners have used the right formula or gotten the right answer. Third, linkages between the abstract or general and the concrete or particular need to be made explicit. Students should understand why they are working through a geometric proof or conducting a scientific experiment, so that they appreciate the larger meanings of the exercise and come away from it with something more than just the notion that they "got it right." Finally, if students are to become experts, they will need opportunities to apply and synthesize their knowledge. Just listening to lectures and watching demonstrations will not be enough.

Cognitive Simulation and Artificial Intelligence

Many cognitive scientists develop and test models of human information processing using computers. One approach is known as artificial intelligence—applying what is known about knowledge, logic, and communication to the development of computer programs designed to process information and solve problems (Simon, 1981). Computers have been programmed to translate text from one language to another, to interpret pictures, and to "learn" or solve problems by operating on input (using decision and action strategies built into programs). The programs involve such strategies as means-end analysis (comparing the present state to the desired end state in order to identify the nature of the difference and develop ideas about how this difference can be reduced), hypothesize and test (using the available information to develop a hypothesis and then testing this hypothesis), and best-first search (evaluating hypotheses or strategies to identify the one most likely to be correct or successful, and then beginning with this "best" one).

Program strategies

Besides achieving interesting theoretical advances, work in artificial intelligence has produced some impressive practical demonstrations, such as chess programs capable of defeating all but the most expert chess players.

While this specialized computer can defeat its young opponent at chess, it can never play as efficiently as she does.

Limitations in strategic thinking

Yet, ironically, these programs are successful only because of the huge memory capacities and rapid information processing capabilities of computers. They go about strategic thinking in thorough and logical but inefficient ways, more like novices than experts (Waldrop, 1984). Artificial intelligence programs are not good at certain things that human experts do routinely like distinguishing relevant from irrelevant information, responding to situational particulars, and in general, using "common sense." For example, Waldrop (1984) notes Minsky's "dead duck" example: Using rules of logic, computers would be programmed to conclude that Charlie can fly given the information that ducks can fly and that Charlie is a duck. If Charlie is dead, however, he cannot fly. Humans easily accommodate this information, but artificial intelligence programs can do so only with enormous increases in the complexity of programming and the amounts of memory capacity needed, and attempts to build in capacity to deal with all such contingencies that might come up would be prohibitively expensive in time and money.

Simulation of human cognition

For these and other reasons, cognitive scientists have been supplementing work on artificial intelligence with work on the simulation of human cognition. Here, programs are developed on the basis of the actual thinking and behavior of humans engaged in information processing and problem solving, rather than on the basis of purely logical considerations. Many of these are "expert systems" programs developed by modeling the behavior of experts in various fields, although programs have also been developed to model the learning of young children (Klahr & Wallace, 1976) and even to model the buggy algorithms (systematic but erroneous methods) developed by learners for solving mathematics problems (Brown & Burton, 1978). Besides advancing knowledge about human information processing, these simulation approaches are useful for developing efficient methods for teaching particular content and for diagnosing and remediating buggy algorithms and other student misconceptions.

Cognitive simulation procedure

Cognition simulation proceeds according to a bootstrapping procedure in which the scientists first analyze samples of the behavior to be modeled in order to identify what appear to be its essential elements, then they develop a model that includes these elements and build it into a computer program. Next they test the model's ability to "predict" the originally observed samples of behavior, continuing to revise the model until good prediction is achieved, and they then use the model to process new input.

One program of research, for example, began with systematic study of reading specialists attempting to diagnose and prescribe for students encountering reading difficulties. What sorts of information did these reading experts request? Which of this information did they actually use in developing a diagnosis? Which specific diagnoses were used, and what were their critical indicators? What treatments were prescribed for remediating the various reading skill deficiencies diagnosed? No two reading experts handled a given case in exactly the same way, but commonalities could be observed across experts and cases. By building these commonalities into a computer program designed to diagnose reading difficulties, the researchers were able to construct a simulated "consensus expert" that diagnoses and prescribes for reading difficulties more reliably than individual experts do. Furthermore, the model that forms the basis for this computer program has proven useful as a basis for training reading teachers to diagnose, and computer assisted instruction involving applications of the model to actual cases of reading difficulty is being used to train teachers to diagnose such cases (Vinsonhaler, Weinshank, Wagner, & Polin, 1983).

SUMMARY

Information processing theorists concentrate on information processing, storage, and retrieval in their study of human learning. They emphasize cognitive structures built up by learners themselves over the structuring elements that may be inherent in the input or communicated by the teacher. In contrast to the relatively passive and static version of human learning and memory presented by associationist theories, information processing theorists tend to adopt a constructivist view that construes learning as a cognitive representation constructed actively by a learner attempting to make sense out of events or experiences, and sees this cognitive representation as subject to change over time as it interacts with previously stored memories and is affected by newer experiences. The rote memory experiments of Ebbinghaus and the story reconstruction studies by Bartlett are examples of the associationist and constructivist approaches, respectively.

Different experiences are encoded and stored in memory in different ways. Episodes in our personal lives are stored in episodic memory, which features images of ourselves reliving those events. However, intentional learning of material communicated through oral or written language is encoded in semantic memory, which features concept definitions, statements of rules and principles, and other verbal abstractions.

Most information processing theorists accept the three-stage information processing model. According to this model, input first enters the sensory register, then is passed along to short-term or working memory, and then is transferred to long-term memory for storage and potential retrieval. The sensory register has a limited capacity of 7 ± 2 items of information, so that rehearsal and chunking strategies must be used at times when the limited capacity of this working memory is strained by the need to consider many items of input at once. Since the limit is 7 ± 2 chunks rather than individual items, chunking can greatly increase the capacity of working memory to accommodate individual items. Information about concepts and relationships appears to be stored in long-term memory in the form of semantic networks organized hierarchically. Superordinate concepts and their general associated characteristics are stored at higher levels in the networks, and subordinate concepts and their unique associated characteristics are stored at lower levels.

However, input is not merely processed and stored only after it is learned. Instead, the original learning that occurs is an active process of sense making in which the learner activates previously acquired schemas and prior knowledge in order to generate frameworks within which to interpret the new input. In this way, the learner "goes beyond the information given" by filling in gaps, picking up meanings that are implied but not stated directly, and assuming relevant implications.

The learners must rely on rote learning processes when the input is not very meaningful or organized. Besides the level of meaningfulness of the input, rote learning is affected by serial position effects (primacy and recency effects), item distinctiveness, amount and distribution of practice, transfer effects (positive and negative, specific and general), interference effects (proactive and reactive), organization effects, levels of processing effects, state- or context-dependent effects, and mnemonic effects. The place, link, peg, and keyword methods, along with other mnemonics such as the elaboration method and the use of pictures, images, rhymes, and acronyms, all assist the learning of relatively meaningless material by associating it with meaningful and organized material.

The meaningful verbal learning of connected discourse shows abstraction effects, levels effects, schema effects, prior knowledge effects, inference effects, student misconception effects, text organization effects, and mathemagenic effects. Adjunct questions (prequestions, inserted questions, and postquestions) help to elicit mathemagenic effects.

Contemporary contributions of the information processing approach to the study of human learning can be seen in recent research on reading comprehension, on comparisons between novices and experts, and on cognitive simulation and artificial intelligence. These lines of research are important not only for advancing our understanding of sophisticated human cognition in various domains, but for suggesting potential methods of instructing novices so as to move them efficiently toward expert status and the capability for similarly efficient cognition.

QUESTIONS AND PROBLEMS

1. Without re-examining the text or looking at your notes, outline what you remember about human development from what was presented in Chapters 2 through 5. How do you account for the fact that you have remembered some things and forgotten others? Given the models that have been presented in this chapter for how memory works, apply those models to account for your own learning. Compare your outline with that of another student and explain why you have each remembered different things.

2. In your own words, describe what memory is and the conditions under which students are more likely to retain information for future use. How can you as a teacher help students to meaningfully retain information that is presented?
3. When teachers are presenting information in class, can they present too much as well as too little information? Be specific. List conditions under which detailed information may be inappropriate. If you took a behavioral view instead of a cognitive view of learning, would you answer this question differently? Why or why not?
4. In your own words, explain the "7 ± 2" rule. What are the implications of this rule for designing instruction?
5. Re-examine the guidelines that Case (1978) has presented for minimizing the load placed on students' working memory. Assume that you are teaching seventh-grade students the differences between red and white blood cells and their role in helping to maintain a healthy and efficient body. In presenting these distinctions to students, how would you proceed?
6. When presenting information to students, how might encouraging them to ask questions about the material facilitate or inhibit their learning?
7. Differentiate between transfer effects and interference effects. How do these concepts differ from organization and levels-of-processing effects?
8. In your own words explain how *distinctiveness* of encoding, *elaboration* of encoding, and *effort* expended during encoding influence how much information is retained in long-term memory.
9. Given that students can adjust their information processing and study strategies to the kind of test that they anticipate, what are the consequences of this for classroom teaching? To what extent should teachers cue students to the sorts of activities that they will be doing on tests versus keeping this information hidden from them? What are the advantages and disadvantages of sharing information about the type of questions that will be emphasized on an exam?
10. Given extant knowledge about human interests, would we as authors be better to raise questions with you before you read a chapter or afterwards? What are the relative advantages of prequestions and postquestions? Why is this the case?
11. Define in your own terms mathemagenic activities. What are the different types of mathemagenic activities that students can engage in? How can teachers facilitate students' learning and use of such skills?
12. Using the concepts discussed in this chapter, explain why you could not do as well on a high school history test today as you did when you took it. In particular, what was the long-term effect of studying for the test?
13. Have you used mnemonic devices successfully in your own learning? Are there some circumstances in which they seem to work better for you than in other circumstances?
14. As a teacher, how can you help students to learn material so that they will retain it in long-term memory?

CASE STUDIES

Can't Put it All Together. Mrs. Washington is unhappy with her mathematics students' performance on word problems. They solve equations quickly and accurately, and most can complete a page containing 40 problems with no errors.

Yet, as soon as she gives them a few word problems, it's as if they had never heard of algebra. Some can't even begin, others guess the answer without showing any work, and still others represent the problem incorrectly and thus end up solving the wrong equation. Even the students who do manage to get the right answer seem unsure of themselves when questioned.

Even more puzzling and frustrating, the students usually can respond correctly when she guides them through these problems by asking a series of questions. Thus, it is not that they lack the needed knowledge; it's that they don't "get the point" or are unable to "put it all together" when asked to apply this knowledge to problems that are not already formulated algebraically.

Using concepts explained in this chapter such as information storage and retrieval, limited capacity of working memory, or novice versus expert problem solving, develop an explanation for the production deficiency problems that Mrs. Washington's students are experiencing. What can she do to help them overcome these problems?

Two Different Worlds. Mrs. Karo and Mrs. Tapper both teach second grade in school districts that have adopted the Raleigh Company's science curriculum. They are teaching a unit on trees and leaves, and today's lesson focuses on maple trees and on the process of collecting sap to be used in making maple syrup.

Mrs. Tapper teaches in a small town in Michigan. Most of her students are already quite familiar with maple trees because they are surrounded by them and because their parents have taken them on sightseeing drives in the fall when the trees are changing colors. Furthermore, many of them have had first-hand experience with the sap collecting process, either through their own relatives or through attending demonstrations and tasting experiences offered to the public by commercial sap collectors.

Mrs. Karo teaches in inner-city Phoenix. Few of her students have ever been outside of the city, let alone traveled all over the country, so that most of them have never even seen a maple tree. In fact, most of the vegetation with which they are familiar has needles rather than leaves, and none of it looks much like the large trees found in the northern part of the country.

Given what was said in this chapter about how learners activate schemas and prior knowledge when responding to input, what will be the similarities and differences in the responses of Mrs. Tapper's students and Mrs. Karo's students to this science lesson? How meaningful will the information be, and how are they likely to process and store it?

How might the two teachers adapt this lesson to their students? How can Mrs. Tapper work around her students' belief that they "already know that," and see that they learn something? How can Mrs. Karo make the material meaningful and interesting to her students? Which teacher, for example, should do more demonstrating and explaining, and which should allocate more time to discussion?

Part Four

Instructional Applications

Charlie Curvesetter and Frank Frustrated are enrolled in the same American history class. Although they are similar in ability and they devote the same amount of time to studying history, Charlie consistently outperforms Frank on tests and assignments. How can this be?

When working with her class on division of decimals, Mrs. Fitzgerald finds that some of her students learn with little difficulty, some divide the numbers correctly but have trouble placing the decimal point correctly, and a few don't even divide the numbers correctly. Apparently, these latter students never mastered the division skills and associated number facts taught in earlier grades. Clearly, they need systematic remedial instruction—just giving them extra problems to do or requiring them to correct their mistakes will not be enough. How can Mrs. Fitzgerald determine what needs to be included in this instruction, and how might she go about identifying appropriate materials and activities or developing them herself?

Mr. Becker and Mr. Rowe are both active teachers who emphasize teacher-led group instruction featuring lectures, demonstrations, and other presentations to the class, recitation activities, and independent seatwork. Both are quite successful. However, Mr. Becker's presentations tend to last only a few minutes at a time, and observers who spend an hour in his classroom would usually see several short but fast-paced activities. In contrast, Mr. Rowe frequently lectures for 20 or 30 minutes at a time, and observers who visited his classroom for an hour would probably see only two or three relatively slow-paced activities. Given that these two teachers use the same general approach to instruction and achieve similar success, why should their classrooms look so different?

After completing a lecture-demonstration, teacher Susan Melnick moves into a recitation phase of her lesson and begins questioning the students. After calling on volunteers and receiving correct responses to the first of several questions, she decides to call on Terry Tense, an anxious and reticent student. Susan was willing to risk putting Terry "on the spot" in this situation because she was confident that he would be able to answer her question. However, in the seeming eternity since she called out his name, actually only about two seconds, he hasn't taken his eyes off the floor and he has begun to turn red. What should Susan do now?

In Part IV of our text (Chapters 10–13), we discuss some of the instructional applications of the theories, concepts, and research discussed in Part III on learning. We begin in Chapter 10 with information about developing students' skills for learning; specifically, their skills for strategic reading, systematic studying, problem solving, and critical thinking. Among other things, Chapter 10 will explain how differences between Charlie Curvesetter's and Frank Frustrated's notetaking and study skills probably explain the differences in their performance. When listening to lectures, Charlie takes organized notes that outline the presentation and paraphrase the gist of its message. In contrast, Frank's notes are haphazard, seemingly a random selection from the presentation rather than an organized synopsis of it. Also, when studying from the text, Charlie underlines sparingly and uses chunking strategies keyed to the structuring and sequencing devices the author has used in organizing the text, whereas Frank underlines three-fourths of the material and tries, with only limited success, to memorize as much of it as possible. Chapter 10 provides detailed information about how students like Frank can be trained to take notes and study more effectively.

Chapter 11 presents concepts and procedures for systematically conceptualizing the scope and sequence of curricula, establishing sequences of objectives, and designing instruction to meet those objectives efficiently. It explains how Mrs. Fitzgerald would need to do a task analysis of the hierarchy of skills required for successful division of decimals and then work backward from the target objective to her students' present skill levels in order to establish a starting point for remedial instruction. More generally, the chapter discusses systematic approaches to the design of instruction that moves students efficiently from the simple/familiar to the complex/unfamiliar, drawing examples from research on the teaching of concepts.

Chapters 12 and 13 present findings from process-outcome research linking teacher behavior in the classroom to student gain on achievement tests. Chapter 12 reviews research indicating that significant achievement gain is associated with frequent use of teacher-led group instruction and other forms of active teaching in which the teacher carries the content to the students personally rather than relying on the curriculum materials to do so. The chapter also notes, however, that the particulars of the active teaching approach must be adapted to suit the grade level, the subject matter, and the particular needs of the students in the class. This explains the differences between Mr. Becker and Mr. Rowe. Given the descriptions of their classes, it is likely that Mr. Becker teaches in the primary grades and spends most of his time working on basic skills with his students, but that Mr. Rowe teaches at the secondary level in a subject matter (such as history) that emphasizes knowledge more than skills.

Chapter 13 reviews research and offers principles relating to effective performance of two sets of basic instructional skills—making presentations such as lectures, demonstrations, or explanations, and conducting activities that involve questioning and responding to the students such as drill/review, recitation, and discussion. It also offers guidelines for responding to student-initiated questions and comments and for handling seatwork and homework assignments. One of the principles for effectively questioning and responding to students that is discussed in the chapter is that teachers should train their students to respond overtly to questions, and should not allow the students to simply remain silent and wait for their teachers to give the answer or call on someone else. Thus, the chapter argues that Ms. Melnick should simply wait for Terry Tense to respond or perhaps should attempt to help him by rephrasing the question or giving a clue. However, the chapter also notes that there are exceptions to this general rule, and this situation involving Terry may be one of those exceptions, especially if continued waiting yields only further evidence of tension and embarrassment.

Chapter 10

Skills for Learning: Strategic Reading, Systematic Studying, Problem Solving, and Critical Thinking

OBJECTIVES

When you have mastered the material in this chapter you will be able to

1. Define the five general types of learning strategy identified by Weinstein and Mayer—rehearsal, elaboration, organizational, comprehension monitoring, and affective
2. Define the term metacognition and explain why teachers should strive to stimulate students to develop metacognitive awareness of their learning in addition to stimulating the learning itself
3. Describe the strategies used by expert readers that are not used by novice or poor readers
4. Describe the strategy training approach to improving reading skills, and identify the strategies that have been included in successful training experiments
5. Explain and use the SQ3R method for effective studying
6. Describe the deep-level processing and elaboration strategies used by successful studiers
7. Explain and use principles for effective notetaking
8. Describe commonly encountered text patterns that can be used as bases for organizing notes
9. State methods of helping students become strategic learners by reading and studying effectively

10. Define key concepts associated with the information processing approach to human problem solving (well- versus ill-structured problems, algorithms, heuristics, task environment, problem space), and describe the findings of this research indicating that most human problem solving relies on heuristics rather than on the more systematic and logical-deductive mechanisms postulated by classical models
11. Describe the heuristics typically used by expert problem solvers for representing and solving problems, and explain the implications of this information for teaching students to solve problems effectively
12. Explain Ohlsson's enaction theory of human thinking and its implication for teaching thinking skills to students
13. Describe the approaches taken in contemporary programs designed to teach general thinking skills (Philosophy for Children, the CoRT Program and the Instrumental Enrichment Program)

In previous chapters, we noted that the transfer value of learning particular content or skills tends to be limited, and that a great deal of domain-specific knowledge must be accumulated before a novice can become an expert in a particular area. Thus, there appear to be no easy shortcuts to expert functioning.

However, there are certain relatively generic skills which, if mastered thoroughly and used consistently when appropriate, can facilitate learning in a broad range of situations. Reading with speed, accuracy, and comprehension is one such generic skill. Others that have been proposed include logical reasoning, critical thinking, general principles of problem solving, and various mathemagenic behaviors, "learning to learn" skills, and study skills. Ideas about conceptualizing and teaching such skills have been around for a long time, although more on the fringes than in the mainstream of educational psychology. Recently, however, with the emphasis on cognition and human information processing that has come to dominate the field, a great deal of research has been done on the development and functioning of effective strategies for learning, and on how these strategies may be taught to individuals who do not use them spontaneously.

Types of learning strategy

In a review of this work, Weinstein and Mayer (1985) identify the following five general types of learning strategies:

- ☐ *Rehearsal strategies*—These involve actively repeating by either saying or writing the material or focusing attention on key parts of it. For brief rote learning tasks rehearsal may involve nothing more than repeating the material aloud as an aid to memorizing it. For more complex tasks such as learning from lectures or from reading text, rehearsal might involve repeating key terms aloud (shadowing), copying the material, taking selective verbatim notes, or underlining important parts.
- ☐ *Elaboration strategies*—These involve making connections between the new material and more familiar material. For rote learning tasks, elaboration strategies would include forming mental images to associate with the material, generating sentences that relate the times to be learned to one another or to more familiar items, or using various mnemonic devices like the keyword method or the place method. For more complex meaningful learning tasks, elaboration strategies would include paraphrasing, summarizing, creating analogies, taking notes that go beyond verbatim repetition to extend or comment on the material, answering questions (either adjunct questions already included with the text or self-generated questions), and describing how the new information relates to existing knowledge.
- ☐ *Organizational strategies*—These involve imposing structure on the material by subdividing it into parts or clusters and identifying superordinate-subordinate relationships. For simple rote learning tasks, organizational strategies involve breaking lists into subgroups or clusters. Organizational strategies for complex meaningful learning tasks would include outlining the text, creating a hierarchy or network of

concepts, or creating diagrams showing relationships among the concepts.

- ☐ *Comprehension-monitoring strategies*—These involve remaining aware of what one is trying to accomplish during a learning task, keeping track of the strategies one uses and the degree of success achieved with them, and adjusting behavior accordingly. Comprehension-monitoring strategies include noting and taking action when one does not understand something, self-questioning to check understanding, using prequestions or statements of learning objectives to guide study, establishing subgoals and assessing progress in meeting them, and modifying strategies if necessary.
- ☐ *Affective strategies*—These involve eliminating undesirable affect and getting ready to learn. They include establishing and maintaining motivation, focusing attention, maintaining concentration, managing performance anxiety, and managing time effectively.

The remainder of this chapter is devoted to these learning strategies and related cognitive skills that are relatively generic across human learning situations. These skills are not only useful and worth teaching to elementary and secondary school students; you, the reader, should find them helpful in your own learning, including your study of this text. We discuss skills involved in reading for comprehension, studying for retention, problem solving, and thinking.

Strategies for Reading with Comprehension

Production deficiency

In discussing the concept of production deficiency in Chapter 4, we noted that some children continue to rely on rote learning methods for memorizing lists of meaningful words even though they possess superordinate concepts that could be used to group the words into categories and thus simplify the task by using chunking strategies (Flavell, Beach, & Chinsky, 1966). Later work by Flavell and others showed that such production deficiencies in use of clustering strategies for free recall of word lists were special cases of a more general phenomenon: Children's awareness of and ability to use strategies for remembering what they learn emerge gradually and uncertainly, so it is common for them to rely on an inefficient strategy even though they possess knowledge that should enable them to use a more efficient strategy. Their knowledge about deliberate strategies (rehearsal, chunking, etc.) for learning and remembering is spotty and poorly integrated.

Metamemory

Work by Flavell and others on this topic eventually became known as the study of metamemory—the knowledge about how memory works and how to memorize effectively (Flavell & Wellman, 1977; Kail & Hagen, 1982). This work revealed that children only gradually come to learn that certain kinds of material, such as that which is meaningful, organized, or interesting, are easier to learn than other kinds; that recognition tests are easier than recall tests; that paraphrased recall is easier than verbatim recall;

Children who are taught to use efficient reading strategies are better learners.

or that active rehearsal will produce better results than silent reading. Training studies showed that children given metamemory information and strategies usually learned more than control children, although they often reverted to their pretraining behavior soon after the experiment ended unless continually reminded to use the strategies (Kail & Hagen, 1982).

Metacognition

Other research soon revealed similar developmental and individual differences in children's knowledge about cognitive operations other than memory (comprehension, problem solving, etc.). The term metacognition refers to the general topic of knowledge about cognitive processes and how they function, and the term metacognitive awareness refers to a person's conscious monitoring of his or her own cognitive strategies during the process of applying them.

Metacomprehension

A particularly interesting and useful subtopic in research on metacognition is the study of metacomprehension—the strategies that readers use in monitoring, evaluating, and repairing their comprehension of written text during the act of reading it (Paris, Lipson, & Wixson, 1983; Baker & Brown, 1984). Research in this area has shown that children can be taught comprehension monitoring strategies that help them understand what they read and remember it in an organized way. These strategies include generating and responding to questions about the material, making connections between the various parts, identifying relevant background knowledge, drawing inferences from the material, and summarizing and organizing it (Pearson & Gallagher, 1983; Tierney & Cunningham, 1984). Unfortunately, students rarely receive instruction in these comprehension monitoring strategies in typical classrooms (Durkin, 1978–79; Duffy & Mc-

Intyre, 1982; Duffy & Roehler, 1982). Thus, it is important for teachers to be aware of these strategies and to be prepared to teach them to students who do not use them spontaneously. We refer here not merely to teachers of reading at the elementary grades, but to any teachers who expect their students to spend significant amounts of time trying to learn independently from reading text.

Novice versus Expert Readers

A great deal of information about skilled readers' comprehension strategies has been collected by researchers who have traced developmental changes in children or compared good readers with poor readers at the same grade level (Paris, Lipson, & Wixson, 1983). At first, young children tend to concentrate on word recognition and verbatim recall of text, rather than on trying to make sense of what they are reading (Wixson, Bosky, Yochum, & Alvermann, 1984). Only gradually do they learn that studying requires deliberate effort and strategies designed to understand and remember what is being read. Young children presented with memory tasks often fail to generate plans or allocate effort to studying (Kail & Hagen, 1982), and poor readers instructed to study a passage may read it only once, fail to check the difficult parts, and say they are ready for the test without selective studying (Brown, Campione, & Barclay, 1979). Many primary grade children do not realize when directions are inadequate (Markman, 1981) or even when messages are incomprehensible (Flavell, Speer, Green, & August, 1981), although they can detect errors and ambiguities more effectively when explicitly instructed to do so (Markman & Gorin, 1981; Paris & Myers, 1981).

In general, poor readers do not skim, scan, reread, integrate information, plan ahead, take notes, or make inferences as often as skilled readers (Anderson & Armbruster, 1982; Golinkoff, 1976; Ryan, 1981; Sullivan, 1978). They have less plans and are less metacognitively aware when they read, and they have difficulty evaluating a text for its clarity, internal consistency, and compatibility with what they already know (Markman, 1981). They are often unaware that they are experiencing problems in comprehension, and they often fail to take corrective action even when they recognize problems (Brown & Smiley, 1978; Paris & Myers, 1981).

Strategies used by skilled readers

In contrast, skilled readers use strategies that are appropriate for the task at hand (the purpose of the reading), monitor their comprehension as they read, and take corrective actions (use repair strategies) in response to ambiguities and comprehension failures. In particular, they use strategies for: 1) clarifying task demands, 2) identifying important aspects of the message (reading for meaning), 3) focusing on important content rather than minor details (reading for remembering), 4) monitoring their comprehension as they read, 5) checking and reviewing to make sure that goals are being met, 6) taking corrective action when comprehension fails, and 7) recovering from disruptions so that text processing can continue (Brown, 1980).

Strategy Training

Many strategy training experiments have been conducted in which younger or poorer readers were trained to use the strategies employed by more skilled readers, usually with at least some success and sometimes with quite remarkable results. Students trained to use such strategies usually do not function as effectively as students who developed those strategies spontaneously, but they do learn to read with better comprehension than before. Often the training needs to be quite detailed or at least explicit, however; simply giving students a little general information is not enough. Many will need training that includes both operative knowledge (how to use the strategies) and conditional knowledge (when and why to use the strategies) (Paris, Lipson, & Wixson, 1983). We now present a sampling of recent strategy training studies, arranged roughly in order of the grade levels of the students for whom the strategies were designed.

Use of mnemonic aids

Strategy Training in the Primary Grades. Paris, Newman, and McVey (1982) trained seven- and eight-year-olds to use labeling, rehearsal, physical grouping, and self-testing as mnemonic aids in a picture memory task. Half of the children were simply instructed to use these strategies, and the other half were given elaborated instructions that also explained the relations between action and memory and the usefulness of the strategies for helping them to remember. The results showed that all of the children used these strategies more following training, but that those who received the elaborated instructions underscoring the usefulness of the strategies used them the most.

Informed strategies for learning

Paris and his colleagues (Paris, Cross, & Lipson, 1984) developed a training program entitled Informed Strategies for Learning (ISL) designed to increase third- and fifth-graders' awareness and use of effective reading strategies. The program is organized into a set of 14 weekly modules that illustrate the strategies concretely and show students the effort required and the benefits to be expected from their use. For example, a lesson on skimming describes the strategy and shows how to use it and also tells the students when it is useful (as a preview or review technique) and when it is not (during the actual reading for full understanding of the meaning). Students first observe models using the strategies and then practice the strategies themselves along with guidance and feedback from the teacher. Strategies are explained and illlustrated using metaphors familiar to the students. For example, the lesson on evaluating tasks to discover clues to the topic, length, and difficulty of the passage uses the metaphor "Be a Reading Detective." Comprehension-monitoring strategies are made comprehensible by using analogies to traffic signs like the following: "Stop—say the meaning in your own words." "Dead end—go back and reread the parts you don't understand."

The full ISL program includes modules on purposes and skills in reading (Reading is Like a Puzzle), comprehension strategies (A Bag Full of Tricks for Reading), task evaluation (Be a Reading Detective), forming plans (Plan

Your Reading Trip), reading goals and kinds of meaning (What's in the Meaning?), abstracting critical information (Tracking Down the Main Idea), ambiguity and inference (Infer the Hidden Meaning), summarizing main points (Round Up Your Ideas), critical evaluation (Judge Your Reading), comprehension monitoring (The Road to Reading Disaster), resolving comprehension failures (Road Repairs), speed versus accuracy (Skimming Along), and abstracting and highlighting information from text (Focus and Develop the Big Picture). Evaluation data revealed that ISL students made greater gains on cloze tests that require them to supply missing words and error detection tests than control students taught with conventional methods and materials. There were no significant differences on standardized reading comprehension tests, possibly because standardized tests involve answering multiple choice questions about short paragraphs under time constraints, rather than comprehension of longer and more integrated text studied under more normal conditions (Johnston, 1984).

Practice in answering questions

Strategy Training in the Intermediate Grades. Hansen and Pearson (1983) improved fourth-graders' reading comprehension using a program that featured strategy training and practice in answering questions. The strategy training involved story introductions in which the students were asked to relate what they knew from prior knowledge about what to do in circumstances like those the upcoming story characters would experience, predict what the protagonist would do when confronted with these critical situations in the story, then write down their prior knowledge answers on one sheet of paper and their predictions on another, and then weave the two together (to establish the metaphor that reading involves weaving together what one knows with what is in a text). Following these preparations, the students read the story and compared their predictions with what actually occurred.

The other part of the treatment involved changing the nature of the questions asked of the students following story reading. Typically, students are asked about 80 percent literal memory questions and only 20 percent inferential questions. In this study, the literal questions were removed and the students were asked only inference questions. Evaluation data showed that this combination of strategy training with practice in responding to inference questions improved the reading comprehension of the experimental students over that of control students taught in traditional ways. The treatment was especially effective with poor readers.

Text explicit, text implicit, and script implicit questions

Raphael (1984) trained intermediate grade students in strategies for answering questions about a text. Following Pearson and Johnson (1978), she distinguished three types of questions: text explicit, in which the answer is stated explicitly in a sentence in the text; text implicit, in which the information needed to respond is located in the text but requires integration of material found in separate sentences; and script implicit, in which the information must be supplied by the reader through activating scripts (schemas) relevant to the content of the text. Raphael taught the students to identify and respond to these three types of questions, respectively, by noting whether the information was "right there," whether they had to "think and find it," or whether they had to supply it "on my own." Such training was effective in improving students' ability to answer such questions about their reading, especially for low-ability students.

Strategies for low-reading-group students

Duffy, Roehler, and their colleagues (Roehler & Duffy, 1984; Book, Duffy, Roehler, Meloth, & Vavrus, 1985) have trained intermediate-grade teachers to provide explicit, detailed instruction in comprehension strategies to their low-reading-group students. The strategies are the ones typically taught in these grades, such as identifying the main idea, or using a dictionary, but they are taught much more explicitly and thoroughly than usual. Teachers are trained to explain the nature of each skill, tell when and why it is used, model by verbalizing the mental processes that occur when using it, point out sequential aspects and salient featues of the processes involved, and then provide students with opportunities to use the skill and see its effectiveness for themselves. Following instruction, the students are interviewed to see if they can state in their own words what they learned, how one does it, and why it is important to know how to do. Evaluation data reveal modest improvements in standardized reading comprehension test scores and marked improvements in student awareness of how the reading process works and how to use the strategies taught.

Strategies for generating self-questions

Wong and Jones (1982) trained normally achieving sixth-graders and learning-disabled eighth- and ninth-graders in a five-step procedure for generating self-questions designed to help them monitor their understanding of important information in texts. This training substantially improved the learning-disabled students' awareness of important ideas in their reading, their ability to formulate good questions about those ideas, and their performance on comprehension tests on the passages read. The training did not substantially increase the performance of the normally achieving sixth-graders, however, apparently because they had developed their own strategies for accomplishing these goals successfully.

Strategy Training in the Secondary Grades. André and Anderson (1978–79) studied three groups of high school students—a group trained to generate questions about the main points of the text, a group directed to ask such main idea questions but not trained in strategies for doing so, and a group that simply read and reread the material. The data revealed that the trained group outperformed the other groups, and the self-questioning treatment was especially effective with students having low and medium verbal ability.

Singer and Donlan (1982) taught high school students a problem-solving frame based on story grammers as a method of reading fiction analytically. The students learned to note the identity of the leading character in a story, what that character is trying to accomplish, what stands in the way, and so on. The strategy was not immediately effective because students needed time to practice it, but eventually they learned to apply it consistently with corresponding benefits to their comprehension and appreciation of short stories.

Cognitive behavior modification

Meichenbaum and Asarnow (1979) and Fox and Kendall (1983) review research on cognitive behavior modification approaches to strategy training at various levels. These approaches feature modeling combined with verbalized self-instruction. Learners first observe the model, then practice the process themselves while verbalizing self-instructions overtly, and then gradually fade overt verbalizations and transform them into silent self-talk. Skills addressed include identifying the problem (What is it I have to do?), focusing attention and guiding response (Now, carefully stop and repeat the instructions.), self-evaluation and reinforcement (Good, I'm doing fine.), and coping with and correcting mistakes (That's okay; I can take my time until I get it right.).

Bommarito and Meichenbaum (cited by Meichenbaum & Asarnow, 1979) used this approach to teach seventh- and eighth-grade readers having poor comprehension skills methods of monitoring and improving their reading comprehension. The students learned to break the text into manageable units, to determine the skills needed for each step, and to translate these skills into self-statements that could be rehearsed. They suggest that, by the end of the training, the students' internal dialogues would approximate the following:

> Well, I've learned three big things to keep in mind before I read a story and while I read it. One is to ask myself what the main idea of the story is. What is the story about? A second is to learn important details of the story as I go along. The order of the main events or their sequences is an especially important detail. A third is to know how the characters feel and why. So, get the main idea, watch sequences, and learn how the characters feel and why.
>
> While I'm reading, I should pause now and then. I should think of what I'm doing. And I should listen to what I'm saying to myself. Am I saying the right things?
>
> Don't worry about mistakes. Just try again. Keep cool, calm, and relaxed. Be proud of yourself when you succeed. Have a blast! (Meichenbaum & Asarnow, 1979, pp. 17–18)

Using reciprocal teaching

Palincsar and Brown (1984) taught four comprehension-fostering and comprehension-monitoring strategies to seventh-grade poor comprehenders. These strategies included summarizing (self-review), questioning, clarifying, and predicting. They used a reciprocal teaching method, in which the teacher initially did most of the modeling and explaining but then gradually turned over the instructional responsibilities to the students themselves, until eventually they took turns acting as the teacher and leading small group discussions of the texts being read.

When beginning a passage, the teacher would note the title and ask for predictions about the content of the passage. Then the group would read the first segment silently, and the "student teacher" would ask a question about it, summarize it, and then offer a prediction or ask for clarification if appropriate. If necessary, the adult teacher provided guidance to the "student teacher" by prompting, "What questions do you think a teacher might ask here?", instructing, "Remember, a summary is a shortened version; it doesn't include detail.", or modifying the activity, "If you are having a hard time thinking of a question, why don't you summarize first?" The adult teacher also provided feedback and praise concerning the quality and specificity of questions framed, the logic involved in making predictions, and so on.

This treatment produced sizable gains on criterion tests of comprehension, reliable maintenance of these gains over time, generalization to other comprehension tests, and transfer to novel tasks. A follow up study in which ordinary classroom teachers, rather than the experimenters, functioned as instructors produced similarly impressive results.

Goal frame

Armbruster and Anderson (1984) identified frames (organizing structures or schemas) that are frequently used in organizing the material in social studies texts. In history texts, for example, the goal frame is common. This frame has four slots—goal, plan, action, and outcome. These four slots correspond to the main ideas associated with psychological explanations of historical events. The goal is the desired state sought by the person or group; the plan is their strategy for attaining the goal; the action is the overt behavior taken in response to the plan, and the outcome is the consequence of this action, which may or may not satisfy the goal. Armbruster and Anderson suggest that students who are made aware of this goal frame should be able to read history texts with more comprehension and to take better organized notes about historical events to which the frame is applicable (accounts of voyages of discovery, for example). They also identify a problem/solution frame (a variation of the goal frame that applies to accounts of situations in which problems arose during attempts to meet the goal), a compromise frame, and a war frame (both of which apply to accounts of situations in which the goals or plans of two parties are incompatible).

Conclusions about Strategic Reading

Efficient reading with comprehension is strategic: It involves allocation of attention and effort and use of strategies designed to understand the meaning of what is being read and to remember it for future reference (Paris, Lipson, & Wixson, 1983). Specifically, strategic reading involves attending to the implicit and explicit purposes of the reading, activating schemas and relevant background knowledge, allocating attention so as to concentrate on major points rather than trivia, evaluating the content for internal consistency and compatibility with prior knowledge and common sense, monitoring ongoing activities to see if comprehension is occurring by engaging in such activities as periodic review and self-questioning, and drawing and testing of inferences by making interpretations, predictions, and conclusions (Palincsar & Brown, 1984). There is a great variability in the degree to which individuals develop awareness of and reliance on such strategies, and thus in the efficiency with which they read and study. Individuals who do not develop such strategies spontaneously will need instruction in them if they are to develop them at all. Consequently, in addition to becoming a strategic reader yourself, it will be important for you to teach your students to do so, using methods appropriate to their ages and developmental levels.

To learn efficiently from texts, students must be able not only to comprehend what they read, but also to retain and use the information. This requires availability and use of effective strategies for independent studying and learning. Even college students differ considerably in the nature and outcomes of their studying strategies.

This point is illustrated nicely in a study by Van Rossum and Schenk (1984). Their study used a 400-line historical passage as the text. Students first took a pretest on the passage, then read the passage while having the opportunity to study it and take notes, then took post-tests on the passage's content and answered questions about how they studied. About half of the students used a surface-level study approach, which meant attempting to memorize the content. The other half of the students studied used deeper levels of processing. For example, one student first read the text through roughly and tried to form a picture of the content, then read more slowly with attention to the structure of the text while attempting to make connections within and between paragraphs, then went through the material again and tried to repeat to himself without looking at the text and its main lines of information and argument. The surface-level processors were attempting mainly to memorize the material so as to be able to reproduce it, whereas the deeper-level processors were trying to understand the material, develop insights, and think about how it would be used. About two-thirds of the female students used surface-level processing, and about two-thirds of the male students used deep-level processing.

Surface-level versus deep-level processors

When questioned about their conception of the learning process, 33 of the 35 surface-level studiers emphasized memorizing the content, attempting to increase their knowledge, or attempting to acquire facts to be retained or used in practice. Only two of this group described learning as the abstraction of meaning or as an interpretive process aimed at understanding reality. In contrast, 23 of the 34 deep-level studiers emphasized the latter definitions of learning, and only 11 emphasized the former. The surface-level studiers were found to be significantly more nervous in testing situations. (Benjamin, McKeachie, Lin, and Holinger, 1981, also found that highly anxious students tend to rely excessively on repetition and rote memorization rather than more effective study strategies.) These surface-level studiers also reported being disturbed more frequently in some way when studying, and were less likely than the deep-level studiers to report that they enjoyed reading the text.

Evaluation data revealed no difference in responses to factual knowledge questions, but a superior performance by the deep-level studiers on "insight" questions. The free response answers of the surface-level studiers were merely lists of facts with few if any connections made between them. In contrast, the responses of the deep-level processors usually were more coherent, containing main ideas linked to supportive material presented in appropriate sequences following logical lines of argument toward conclusions. Clearly, these differences in conceptualization of learning and approach to studying affected not only how much was learned, but what was learned and how well it was organized.

A great deal has been learned about effective strategies for studying and learning independently, and about how to teach these strategies to students who have not developed them spontaneously. Most of this work has been done recently, although it has its roots in Robinson's SQ3R method (Robinson, 1946, 1970), covered next.

SQ3R Method

Five steps of the SQ3R method

SQ3R is an acronym that stands for the five steps in the SQ3R method—survey, question, read, recite, and review. The first step is to skim or survey the material: Read the title and any introductory material to get a general idea of what the passage is about, note the length and organization of the material to identify the author's general approach, and preview any pictures, charts, or illustrations. Next, question yourself by identifying information that you want or are likely to get from reading the passage. The headings or subheadings are useful in identifying such questions. On encountering the previous heading, for example, you might have asked yourself "What is the SQ3R method?" or "What are the steps in the SQ3R method?"

Then, read the material, paying particular attention to introductory paragraphs and main ideas, rereading difficult passages and looking up unfamiliar words if necessary, while keeping in mind that you are trying to understand and respond to the author's main purpose in writing the material. Next, recite (or recall) the material. Close the book and try to answer in your own words the questions you raised earlier and to state the author's purpose and main ideas in writing the material. Lastly, review by concentrating on passages that you find difficult or have not yet fixed in your mind, and on remembering the main ideas and the linkages between them.

The SQ3R method fits well with the information processing view of human learning (Tadlock, 1978), and it appears to be worth adopting as a systematic "deep-level processing" approach to studying. See Robinson (1970) for more information about SQ3R, and Devine (1981) for information about related methods.

Elaboration Strategies

Weinstein (1982) trained ninth-grade students in elaboration strategies to use during study. These strategies include generating verbal or imaginal elaborators to make material more meaningful, creating analogies to express new material in more familiar terms, drawing implications, and creating relationships through elaborative paraphrasing (relating the material to what is already known while also restating it in one's own words). Five hours of training in which the students were shown how to apply these strategies to a series of school tasks produced better performance on evaluation tests than produced by a control group that practiced those same tasks but did not receive the training in elaboration strategies. Subsequent work by Weinstein has involved training college students to use these strategies in their studies.

Notetaking

In order to retain material for future use, it usually is necessary not only to study it in an active, systematic way, but also to take notes or in some other way preserve key ideas in a form that makes them easy to refer to later. Devine (1981) discusses underlining, marginal notes, summarizing, and outlining as common forms of notetaking.

Underlining

Underlining and related forms of highlighting material believed to be important are among the study techniques used most by college students (Policastro, 1975). Underlining appears to be less effective than other notetaking techniques, however, because it is comparatively passive and has the effect of psychologically deferring the active learning process to some future time. Also, many students use it ineffectively because they underline too much or because they underline before they have absorbed enough of the material to know which parts are important and which are not, so that their underlining is not very helpful in this regard. Thus, underlining may be most useful if done only after reading through the material the first time.

Marginal comments and coding systems

Devine (1981) suggests supplementing underlining with marginal comments or coding systems. Marginal comments might include questions asked of the author, rephrasings of difficult sentences, or definitions of unfamiliar words. Coding systems might include color coding by using markers to indicate main ideas and separate them from supporting evidence, circles around new terms introduced by the author, arrows indicating relationships between ideas, boxes to contain related ideas, marginal numbers to indicate

Learning to take notes efficiently is an essential tool for successful learning.

sequential patterns, stars to indicate the relative importance of ideas to the reader, or question marks to point out unsupported references. If simple underlining is better than passive reading, marginal comments or coding systems are better yet because they involve the reader more actively in the author's presentation.

All of these methods require writing directly in the book, however, and this option is open only to students who own the books and are willing to write in them. Other students will have to rely on outlining, summarizing, and other forms of notetaking. All of these methods are likely to improve learning, although different individuals will prefer or do better with different methods (Rohwer, 1984) and students who learn to take notes systematically will be more successful than those who take notes haphazardly (Carrier & Titus, 1979; Kiewra, 1985a; Ladas, 1980).

Summaries

Notetaking in the form of written summaries is likely to facilitate learning (Doctorow, Wittrock, & Marks, 1978; Taylor, 1982; Brown, Campione, & Day, 1981). Good summaries condense the material and focus on the important ideas. Brown and Day (1980, cited in Armbruster & Brown, 1984) identify six rules essential to effective summarizing: 1) delete trivial material, 2) delete redundant material, 3) substitute a superordinate term for a list of subordinate items when possible, 4) substitute a superordinate event for a list of subordinate actions when possible, 5) select a topic sentence if the author has provided one, and 6) write your own topic sentence if necessary.

Simply telling students these rules was sufficient to improve performance for some students. Others needed training in rules for accomplishing the principles: delete redundant information with red pencil, delete trivial information with blue pencil, write in superordinates for any lists, underline topic sentences if provided, write topic sentences where needed. Students who practiced following these rules and also checked their performance using a checklist gained the most. In any case, following these rules for summarizing should produce both more efficient and higher quality notes.

Notetaking principles

In addition to summarizing, guidelines have been developed for other forms of notetaking. Carrier & Titus (1981), for example, suggest the following general principles for taking notes during lectures: 1) distinguish between superordinate and subordinate information, 2) abbreviate words, 3) paraphrase in your own words, and 4) use an outline format. Kiewra (1985a) suggests that notes that both condense the material and represent a conceptual gathering of main ideas or an integration of new with old information are likely to be more effective than verbatim notes or simple paraphrased lists of information. Notes that elaborate or process information at a deeper level are more likely to be effective than simple recording (Shimmerlick & Nolan, 1976), although verbatim copying and rote studying may be more effective for students who are so anxious as to be unable to use elaborative or deeper-level processing strategies efficiently (Biggs, 1978; Rohwer, 1984).

Using Text Patterns to Organize Notes. In taking notes from a well organized text, the author's own structuring (headings, subheads, etc.) can often be used effectively to organize notes in outline form. In addition or instead, however, it helps to be aware of various text structures (organizing schemas) that are frequently used in expository writing. Devine (1981), for example, identifies six such structures: 1) generalization supported by examples, 2) enumeration (of lists of items), 3) time pattern (in which items or events are placed in chronological order), 4) climax pattern (in which items are arranged from least to most important, from worst to best, from smallest to largest, etc.), 5) compare and contrast pattern, and 6) cause and effect pattern.

Similarly, Meyer (1981) identified the following structures as they appeared in a passage about supertankers: 1) covariance (lack of power and steering in supertankers leads to oil spills), 2) comparison (ground stations for supertankers are like control towers for aircraft), 3) collection (three ways to improve supertanker safety are training of officers, building safer ships, and installing ground control systems), 4) description (oil spills kill wildlife, as indicated by 200,000 sea birds being killed), and 5) response (a solution to the problem that supertankers spill oil is to improve their safety).

Using these text structures when taking notes and studying can improve comprehension (Mayer, 1984; Weinstein & Mayer, 1985). For example, Cook (1982) trained college students to recognize the following five types of structure found in science texts: 1) generalization (the passage explains, clarifies, or extends some main idea), 2) enumeration (the passage lists facts sequentially), 3) sequence (the passage describes a connected series of events or steps in a process, 4) classification (the passage groups material into categories or classes); and 5) compare/contrast (the passage examines the relationship between two or more things). Students taught to recognize these text structures and outline their notes accordingly outperformed control students who were not given this training.

Comprehensive Training Programs

Recently, several investigators have developed comprehensive programs for training students, mainly college students, in learning strategies and study skills (O'Neil, 1978; O'Neil & Spielberger, 1979; Dansereau, 1983; Weinstein & Underwood, 1983; McCombs, 1984; Novak & Gowin, 1984). For example Dansereau and his colleagues (Dansereau, 1983; Dansereau et al., 1979) have developed a comprehensive learning strategy training program that features two primary strategies elaborated by several substrategies and backed by several support strategies. The primary strategy designed to help learners comprehend and retain material is known as first-degree MURDER: set the mood to study, read for understanding by marking important and difficult ideas, recall the material without referring to the text, correct the recall by amplifying and storing the material in order to digest it, expand knowledge through self-inquiry (asking and answering questions), and review mistakes by learning from tests.

Once basic comprehension and retention has been accomplished using first-degree MURDER, learners concentrate on preparing to recall and use the information when it will be needed (when taking a test or on the job) by invoking the second primary strategy known as second-degree MURDER: set the mood, understand the requirements of the task, recall the main ideas relevant to task requirements by using means-ends analysis and planning, detail the main ideas with specific information, expand the information into an outline, and review the adequacy of the final response.

Training in these primary strategies is backed by training in support strategies such as goal setting and scheduling, managing concentration, combating anxiety or other negative emotions, monitoring comprehension, and responding to confusion or mistakes. In addition, the first-degree MURDER strategies are elaborated through various substrategies designed to assist comprehension and encoding processes. Students are taught to paraphrase the material in their own words and generate imagery that will help them to retain it, to identify key ideas, and to note the linkages between these ideas using a notetaking strategy known as networking. Networking involves using codes and symbols to underscore the following six types of linkages: 1) *part link* (the process of wound healing has three parts: the lag phase, the fibroplasia phase, and the construction phase), 2) *type link* (two types of wound are open and closed), 3) *leads to link* (the growth of a scab leads to a scar), 4) *analogy link* (a scab is like a protective bandage, 5) *characteristic link* (an open wound involves a break in the skin), and 6) *evidence link* (an X-ray test can reveal that a bone is broken). Students trained in these learning strategies tend to outperform other students, especially on essay questions. The strategies are especially effective with low achievers who have not developed effective study strategies on their own. The support strategies included in the program make it especially useful for highly anxious students. McCombs (1984) also emphasizes these motivational aspects of learning (in addition to the cognitive aspects) in her program.

Networking

Helping Students Become Strategic Learners

Besides using these learning strategies and study skills yourself and teaching your students about them in general ways, you can stimulate their use by building them into particular academic activities. In preparing your students for a seatwork or homework assignment, you can instruct them to skim the material to get a general overview and note down some questions that they want to get answered before reading the material word for word, provide advance organizers or study guides that call attention to key ideas and structural elements, list key terms and provide definitions or instruct the students to look them up, and encourage students to pay attention to the author's apparent purpose in writing the material and degree of success in achieving it (Devine, 1981).

Partial outlines

Providing students with partial outlines or skeletal notes that they will fill in while listening to a presentation or reading an assignment is particularly helpful (Kiewra, 1985b). It is also helpful to see that students know how to use a textbook—review with them and help them to appreciate the information contained in the title page and preface, the index, the table of contents, the glossary, and the various structuring elements (headings, highlighting, marginal notes) and illustrations (graphs, charts, picture captions). In general, help them to appreciate that learning involves actively making sense of material and organizing it for retention and future use, and that this can be accomplished using a variety of strategies that are usually more effective than the rote learning strategies that many of them continue to rely on.

Problem-Solving Strategies

Besides being able to read with comprehension and study efficiently, students need to learn to solve problems effectively. We refer here not only to problems in mathematics, but to problems in any subject area, or more generally, to any situation in which the person perceives a discrepancy between his or her present state and a desired goal state, and thus desires to take action to eliminate that discrepancy.

Problems differ in the degree to which they are clearly structured (Frederiksen, 1984; Simon, 1978). Well-structured problems present both a clearly defined goal and all of the information needed in order to solve the problem using an appropriate algorithm (a fixed rule or procedure that guarantees a correct answer if applied to appropriate situations and followed precisely). In contrast, ill-structured problems are more difficult to conceptualize or define, let alone solve. The person is aware that a problem exists because the desired goal state is not in effect, but may not be clear about what kind of information will be needed to solve the problem, where this information can be obtained, or how to apply it. There may not even be a single correct answer.

Algorithms

Unlike well-structured problems that can be solved using algorithms, ill-structured problems must be attacked using heuristics (general rules of thumb and procedural guidelines for processing information and solving problems). Heuristics do not guarantee solutions the way algorithms do, but they are applicable to a much broader range of problem situations and allow problem solvers to discover solutions for themselves. Thus, well-structured homework problems in mathematics or science are solved using algorithms based on algebraic operations or Ohm's Law, but ill-structured problems such as predicting the effects of a change in market conditions or attempting to discover cures for diseases require heuristics.

Heuristics

Educational psychologists have long been interested in studying problem solving and identifying ways to teach people to solve problems effectively. Pessimists, impressed by limitations on transfer effects and the need for broad experience and development of a deep fund of domain-specific knowledge in the process of moving from novice to expert status, believe that problem solving cannot be taught directly, although students will benefit from frequent opportunities to develop their problem-solving skills through practice. Optimists, on the other hand, believe that problem-solving skills can be developed more directly by identifying effective problem-solving heuristics and teaching them to students.

Early Views of Problem Solving

Early learning theorists developed contrasting theories about problem solving. Behaviorists such as Thorndike viewed it as an incremental process of trial and error (recall his experiments on cats who discovered how to escape cages by working the latches), whereas gestalt psychologists such as Kohler saw it as a matter of achieving sudden insight following reflection (recall his experiments with chimpanzees induced to discover that available props could be used as tools to reach food). Their debates illuminated interesting issues concerning learning, but did not lead to programs for teaching problem solving.

Wallas (1921) described four stages in the discovery process, based on the study of the behavior of some of the great problem solvers in history. These stages are reminiscent of Kohler's earlier descriptions of the discovery behavior of chimpanzees and are listed as follows:

1. *Preparation*—Learning about the problem and about relevant information that might be useful in solving it.
2. *Incubation*—A period of reflection, analysis, generation of hypotheses, and other thinking about the problem, some of which may be unconscious or may occur during sleep.
3. *Illumination*—The "Aha!" experience that occurs when one suddenly becomes aware of a likely solution.
4. *Verification*—The process of testing the proposed solution to make sure that it does in fact solve the problem.

The discovery stages described by Wallas were merely descriptive rather than prescriptive, but they formed the basis for later prescriptive writings. For example, Polya (1957) offered the following guidelines for problem solving in a famous book entitled *How to Solve It*:

1. *Understand the problem*—Identify what information is given or known, and what is required.
2. *Devise a plan*—Look for connections between the given information and the unknown that might help solve the problem. Does the information seem to fit a general principle or a familiar algorithm? Is the problem analogous to a simple or more familiar problem that might provide guidelines for solving it?
3. *Carry out the plan*—Once a clear plan has been formulated, carry it out step by step, checking to make sure that each step has been included and done correctly.
4. *Look back*—Check the accuracy or usefulness of the obtained result by making sure that it does in fact solve the problem and that it

squares with all of the other information given. If the result checks out, review the result itself and your method of obtaining it for information that may be useful in solving other problems in the future.

John Dewey (1910) was among the first to suggest steps for effective problem solving. His steps are as follows:

1. *Presentation of the problem*—The person must become aware of the problem, or be made aware of it.
2. *Definition of the problem*—The person must define the problem by identifying the present state and the desired goal state, and considering the implications for solution. Sometimes the problem can be defined in different ways with different solution implications.
3. *Development of hypotheses*—Given the problem definition, generate hypotheses for solving the problem.
4. *Testing of hypotheses*—Identify the advantages and disadvantages associated with each proposed solution.
5. *Selection of the best hypothesis*—Identify the solution that offers the most advantages and the fewest disadvantages.

These early approaches to problem solving contain a great deal of good advice and are still influential today. Many modern programs for training or counseling people to solve problems in everyday living follow the steps first proposed by Dewey (Heppner, 1978; Dixon, Heppner, Petersen, & Ronning, 1979). So do many authors' suggestions to students. Clifford (1981), for example, suggests teaching students the following rules for problem solving: 1) clearly define the problem and state the goal, 2) formulate different solutions and state the relative value of each, 3) order the proposed solutions in terms of their potential, 4) try each one in turn until the solution is found, 5) critically evaluate the results of each solution tried, and 6) decide how the process and the product might be used to work out other problems.

Similarly, Bransford and Stein (1985) describe the IDEAL method of problem solving: identify the problem, define it, explore possible strategies for solving it, act on those strategies, and look at the effects of your efforts.

Contemporary Cognitive Views of Problem Solving

Contemporary views of problem solving have been influenced heavily by the human information processing approach to learning and cognition described in the previous chapter, and especially by the research comparing novice with expert problem solvers (Tuma & Reif, 1980; Mayer, 1983). This work shows that expert problem solvers do not proceed in the manner implied by Dewey's stages (in particular, they do not generate a very large number of hypotheses and then test out each one systematically). Instead, they conceptualize the problem by identifying key features and relating them to background knowledge or schemas, and then identify a single hypothesis or a very small number of promising hypotheses for further testing. Phy-

Limiting hypotheses

sicians diagnosing medical problems, for example, do not begin by attempting to list every conceivable source of the patient's symptoms. Instead, they ask questions designed to quickly narrow the search to one or a small number of probable diagnoses, and then pursue these hypotheses (Elstein, Shulman, & Sprafka, 1978). At least when done by experts with sufficient experience and domain-specific knowledge to know what they are doing, this approach is much quicker and easier than the classical approach because it minimizes the time spent, and usually wasted, checking out low-probability hypotheses.

Task environment versus problem space

Newell and Simon (1972) describe such expert problem solvers as relying on heuristics to cut down complex problems to workable size. They differentiate between the task environment and the problem space. The task environment is the large structure of facts, concepts, and their interrelationships within which the problem is embedded. The problem space is the problem solver's mental representation of that task environment. For successful solving of complex problems, the problem space must simplify the task environment sufficiently to allow the person to address the problem within the limits of working memory, and yet be a valid and accurate enough representation to foster effective problem-solving efforts.

Accurate problem representation

Accurate representation of the problem in the first place is the key to the success of this method. If key features of the problem are recognized accurately and related to appropriate background knowledge or problem-solving schemas, the result is likely to be a quick and successful solution. However, if the problem is represented inappropriately, the problem-solving efforts that flow from this problem representation will fail, and the person essentially will have to begin all over again.

In well-structured problems, accurate problem representation may be followed by activation of one or more algorithms that lead directly to solution. In ill-structured problems, however, no such algorithms may be available, and the person may have to rely on heuristics such as reasoning by analogy from more familiar problems, breaking down the problem and working on subparts before dealing with the whole, working backwards from proposed solutions, or testing the most promising hypotheses first (Polya, 1957; Newell & Simon, 1972; Simon, 1980).

Cyert (1980) suggests the following heuristics (drawn from the work of Rubenstein, 1975): 1) keep the big picture in mind without getting lost in details; 2) avoid committing yourself too early to a particular hypothesis when it is just one of several promising hypotheses worth considering; 3) create models to simplify the problem using words, images, symbols, or equations; 4) try to change the representation of the problem if the present one does not seem to be working; 5) use the information to generate questions that you can ask yourself and attempt to answer; 6) be flexible and willing to question the credibility of your premises; 7) try working backwards from possible solutions; 8) keep track of various partial solutions that you may eventually be able to combine; 9) use analogies and metaphors; and 10) talk about the problem.

Various books and courses on problem solving (Polya, 1957; Newell &

Simon, 1972; Wickeigren, 1974; Rubenstein, 1975; Hayes, 1981; Bransford & Stein, 1985) provide instruction in such problem–solving heuristics and opportunities to practice them on "brain teasers" as well as on problems typically found in various academic courses. Reading such books and taking such courses should increase your effectiveness as a problem solver by providing you with the basic heuristic strategies to use systematically and with metacognitive awareness. This may make a great difference, especially for individuals who have not previously been using such strategies systematically. It will not short-circuit the need for experience and domain specific knowledge in particular areas, however. Nor will any other approach yet discovered.

Pattern recognition

One approach that may help accelerate development from novice to expert status, however, is training in pattern recognition as it applies to problem solving within particular domains. In algebra, for example, Mayer (1981) has developed a taxonomy containing over 100 basic problem types. Each general category of problem, such as "motion problem," is represented by different subtypes such as "overtake," "closure," "round-trip," and "speed change." Similarly, Greeno and his colleagues (Greeno, 1980; Riley, Greeno, & Heller, 1982) have identified three types of algebra word problems: cause/change problems (Joe has three marbles, Tom gives him five more. How many marbles does Joe have now?); combination problems (Joe has three marbles. Tom has five marbles. How many marbles do they have altogether?); and comparison problems (Joe has three marbles. Tom has five more marbles than Joe. How many marbles does Tom have?). Although work in this area is just emerging and definitive data are not yet available, it seems reasonable to expect that training students to recognize such problem types would increase their ability to represent problems correctly and link them to appropriate schemas and algorithms.

Numberless problems

Other work in mathematics is designed to reduce novice-like tendencies to over-rely on formulas without genuine understanding and to increase expert-like tendencies to concentrate on conceptualizing the problem accurately before proceeding. One method is to give students numberless problems requiring them to conceptualize the problems and state the strategies that would be used to solve them, but without performing any actual calculations (Good & Grouws, 1979). For example, the students might be asked, "You know the dimensions of a room that you want to paint, the cost of paint per gallon, and the coverage in square feet to be expected from a gallon of paint. How would you calculate the approximate cost of the paint that will be required for the job?"

Strategy training

Bloom and Broder (1950) reported success with strategy training in mathematics problem solving. They worked with college students who had ability and were putting in effort but nevertheless were scoring poorly on examinations. These students were asked to think aloud and pay attention to their own problem-solving processes as they worked through problems, and then to compare these with the processes revealed in transcripts taken from other students who solved the problems more effectively. The students were asked to state in their own words the differences between the model's strategy and those that they used themselves, and to identify implications for changes in their own strategies. Then they would take up a new problem, and again compare and discuss. This training led to clear increases in the experimental students' confidence in problem-solving situations and performance on problem-solving tests. Schoenfeld (1979) reported similar success from a training program involving instructing students in strategies for responding to algebra problems (draw a diagram, try to establish subgoals, consider similar problems with fewer variables, etc.).

Conclusions about Teaching Problem-Solving Strategies

To the extent that you expect your students to be able to apply what they are learning rather than merely to remember it in the form of figurative knowledge, you will need to provide them with frequent application exercises and opportunities to solve problems. Furthermore, you will need to provide most students with instruction in the problem-solving process. The specifics of this instruction will vary with grade level and subject matter, but it should include such heuristics as reading the problem carefully and paraphrasing it into one's own words, identifying the information given and the information desired as well as the possible linkages between these problem elements, separating relevant from irrelevant information, representing the problem clearly and sketching the general plan of attack before attempting to "plug in" formulas or perform calculations, and developing a workable problem space by dividing the problem into a series of subproblems, reasoning by analogy from more familiar problems, working backwards from possible solutions, or substituting specific examples for abstract symbols. Such instruction should include first-person modeling with thinking aloud in addition to typical lecturing, and should proceed to coaching, guided practice, student reflection on and assessment of their strategies, and other activities designed to increase students' metacognitive awareness of the processes involved in solving problems successfully.

Teaching Thinking Skills

In a sense, the entire educational enterprise is an attempt to teach students how to think by first presenting them with important knowledge and skills and then giving them opportunities to apply, analyze, synthesize, or evaluate this input. The developments reviewed previously in this chapter (work on reading comprehension, study skills, and problem solving) can be seen as even more directly designed to stimulate thinking, or at least to stimulate a more thoughtful approach to learning. The most direct approach, however, has been to identify key elements of the thinking process itself and teach these directly to students.

The classical approach to training the mind to think involved curricular emphasis on subjects such as Latin, philosophy, mathematics, and science. Although Thorndike (1924) showed long ago that this approach does not yield generalized improvements in mental functioning, it continues to be emphasized even today.

A more focused variation of this same general approach is to emphasize instruction in thinking skills and tools for developing knowledge. One approach to the teaching of thinking skills is coursework in logic—the use of formal rules of inference to develop conclusions from established premises. Courses in logic teach students to deduce implications from premises and evaluate whether or not conclusions follow from the premises given. For example, given the premises that animals require food and that dogs are animals, it would be logical to deduce that dogs require food, but not to deduce that all animals are dogs.

Logic classes

Critical thinking skills

A related form of instruction is training in critical thinking skills for evaluating the credibility of information. Critical thinking skills include assessing the validity of authors' premises and the soundness of their logic in developing conclusions from those premises, as well as identifying authors' purposes in writing the material (distinguishing attempts to be complete and objective from attempts to sway the reader toward particular conclusions), distinguishing relevant from irrelevant information, recognizing bias and slanted language in the presentation, recognizing and counteracting the effects of rhetorical devices that appeal to emotion rather than evidence (glittering generalities, name calling, testimonials, or "just plain folks" appeals, and stacking the cards by presenting only favorable facts and suppressing unfavorable facts), and distinguishing fact from opinion (Devine, 1981).

Tools for developing knowledge

Instruction in tools for developing knowledge usually emphasizes training in scientific methods. The emphasis here is on scientific rules of inference, and especially on the logic involved in stating questions as formal hypotheses that can be tested using carefully designed empirical experiments.

Deduction theory versus enaction theory

Ohlsson (1983) criticizes these approaches on the ground that they are limited to what he calls the deduction theory of human thinking: They view thinking as systematic application of logical rules of inference. Citing the work on expert-novice comparisons and other contributions stemming from the information-processing approach to the study of human cognition, Ohlsson argues that human thinking is better represented by the enaction theory: The notion that thinking involves mental simulations of real world actions. Instead of using purely verbal methods to draw verbally phrased conclusions from verbally phrased premises, Ohlsson argues, we work with multisensory models of the things or events we are thinking about, and with mental representations of the concrete actions that could be performed on these things or events. For example, ice cubes could be transported, rotated or melted; liquids could be poured, subdivided, or boiled; and algebraic expressions could be rearranged, simplified, or substituted into other expressions. Ohlsson believes that our internal conceptions of the world are more similar to pictures, sculptures, holograms, toy trains, chemical formulas, musical scores, diagrams, or paintings than they are to verbal texts, and that thinking proceeds by application of operators to these mental models under the guidance of heuristics.

Ohlsson believes that traditional approaches to teaching thinking skills will not generalize well because they do not include sufficient attention to the procedural knowledge and heuristics involved in deciding when and why to use a particular procedure. Even if one understands what a theorem says and why it is true, this knowledge is not sufficient to enable one to know when and how to use the theorem. Nor does knowing how the theorem was derived have anything to do with knowing how it can be used in application situations. To teach students to think, Ohlsson argues, teachers should emphasize the processes involved in acquiring and applying disciplinary knowledge. Each field would be thought of as being about the various kinds of change that apply to its subject matter, rather than as a static collection of information and principles. For example, instead of just teaching geographical facts about mountains, continents, forests, and climates, social studies teachers might emphasize mountain formation and erosion, continental drift, deforestation, and changes in average world temperature, and might frequently ask students to predict future situations from current trends or to speculate about what would happen to the ecosystem as a whole if an important change were introduced into one part of it.

Systematic teaching of heuristics

In addition, Ohlsson recommends systematic teaching of heuristics for thinking about and solving problems in particular subject matter areas. For example, students could be given a strategy and asked to apply it to a set of problems, with evaluation concentrating on whether they apply the strategy correctly rather than whether they reach correct answers. Or, students could be asked to solve the same problem using different strategies and to identify the comparative advantages of the different strategies. Or, students could be given an inefficient or partial strategy and asked to improve it. In general, teachers would emphasize the procedural aspects of the content they teach, provide many examples of how this content can be used, and invite students to practice using the content themselves.

Programs for Teaching Thinking Skills

Not content with attempts to build more emphasis on thinking into instruction in traditional subject matter areas, some authors have developed programs of curriculum and instruction designed specifically to develop students' thinking skills. Usually these programs involve combinations of techniques flowing from the deduction theory with techniques flowing from the enaction theory as described by Ohlsson (1983).

Some of these programs involve attempts to teach particular cognitive skills such as Piagetian conservation or the skills stressed by IQ tests (Detterman & Sternberg, 1982), and some place special emphasis on training students to think creatively (see Chapter 24). Three of the more comprehensive "thinking" curricula are described below.

Philosophy for Children. Lipman and his colleagues (Lipman, 1985; Lipman, Sharp, & Oscanyan, 1980) have developed a "philosophy for children" program that introduces preschool and elementary school children to principles of logic and formal inquiry. Using fictional passages as well as questions about philosophical issues as the bases for initiating group discussion, teachers induce their students to exchange views, debate, reason, and in general function as a "community of inquiry" concerning concepts such as fairness, friendship, and truth. The children learn to use language to reason—to assume, suppose, compare, infer, contrast or judge, induce or deduce, classify, describe, explain, define, and inquire. In the process, they learn to recognize and assess chains of logic, deal with syllogisms, recognize fallacies, and in general to develop logical reasoning and critical thinking skills. In addition to the references given above, information about this program and about the general notion of teaching philosophy to children can be found in issues of the journal *Thinking: The Journal of Philosophy for Children*.

The CoRT Program. DeBono (1983, 1985) developed the CoRT program (CoRT is an acronym that stands for Cognitive Research Trust, an organization located in Cambridge, England). This is a program consisting of 60 lessons on thinking intended for nine- to eleven-year olds, although it has been used with both younger and older students as well. The program focuses on thinking skills that will help students to function better in their lives outside of school. Consequently, the content of the lessons avoids both specific school subjects and relatively impractical puzzles and games, in order to concentrate on life events such as deciding on a career, how to spend one's vacation, moving to a new house, or changing to a new job. Instruction focuses on the processes of thinking and decision making.

PMI exercise

For example, the first lesson teaches a scanning tool known as PMI. To introduce PMI, the teacher invites the students to consider the merits of some idea (such as that students should be paid five dollars a week for coming to school or that basic foods should be supplied free to everyone) by thinking about the implications of the idea and categorizing them into three sets labeled: Plus (good points or desirable implications); Minus (bad points or undesirable implications); and Interesting (implications that are neither good nor bad but are nevertheless interesting and worth noting). This method helps students to clarify their thinking about the issue, and to be able to state the reasons underlying the decisions they make.

The PMI exercise is the first of the 60 CoRT lessons. As the program progresses, additional tools for thinking and decision making are added, and students are encouraged to use these tools for thinking about real life decisions rather than merely fanciful ones. In particular, students are encouraged to consider multiple aspects of issues before settling on solutions, and to get input from others through brainstorming and related mechanisms.

In addition to its use by various individual schools and teachers, the CoRT program is being implemented on a grand scale in Venezuela as part of a systematic effort by the government of that country to increase the intelligence of its citizenry by teaching school children to think in addition to teaching them traditional academic content (deBono, 1983; Walsh,

1981). In addition to the CoRT program the Venezuelan efforts include lessons in logic, problem solving, and chess.

The Instrumental Enrichment Program. Feuerstein and his colleagues (Feuerstein, Rand, Hoffman, & Miller, 1980; Feuerstein et al., 1985) have developed the Instrumental Enrichment program for students aged nine or older. The program was originally developed as a special education tool for use with disadvantaged students or students suffering from cognitiive deficiencies or learning disabilities. Its goal was to change the cognitive structures of these students and transform them into autonomous independent thinkers capable of initiating and elaborating ideas. As the program became further developed and better known, it began to be used with normal students as well.

The program encourages cognitive activities such as perceptual organization of information, problem representation, planning, goal analysis, and restructuring of problems when existing plans are not working. It uses a series of progressively more demanding paper and pencil exercises that encourage learners to discover relationships, rules, principles, operations, and strategies. The tasks were designed on the basis of analyses of the processes involved in mental activities, and many of them resemble the tasks used in psychometric tests and laboratory learning experiments. There are some puzzles and brainteasers as well, but in general the program is seen as a bridge between approaches based on thinking within curriculum content domains and approaches that try to develop thinking through content-free exercises.

The exercises range from simple recognition tasks to complex activities involving classification, seeing analogies, and seriation, and they make use of a variety of modalities including numerical, spatial, pictorial, and verbal. Each operation is considered to have input, elaboration, and output phases, and assessment focuses on identifying the phase that is responsible for failure when failure occurs.

Conclusions Regarding Teaching Thinking Skills

The programs just reviewed are one possible response to the criticism that schooling concentrates too much on knowledge and comprehension of specific information and not enough on higher-level cognitive objectives. If their goals and procedures appeal to you, you may wish to investigate them and incorporate them into your teaching. Bear in mind, however, that despite the enthusiasm with which these programs have been received by some educators, their efficacy remains to be demonstrated. Enthusiastic testimonials abound, but there are few systematic data, and the data that do exist suggest positive but limited effects. Also, bear in mind that even when programs are successful in developing certain general thinking or problem-solving skills, possession of such skills will not eliminate the need for broad experience and domain-specific knowledge for functioning as an expert in any particular area of application.

SUMMARY

This chapter concerns development of relatively generic learning skills—strategic reading, systematic studying, problem solving, and critical thinking. Weinstein and Mayer (1985) identify five general types of learning strategies important for efficient learning: rehearsal strategies, elaboration strategies, organizational strategies, comprehension-monitoring strategies, and affective strategies.

Reading comprehension researchers have been studying methods of teaching students to read with metacognitive awareness of their activities, and in particular, with active strategies for metacomprehension (monitoring, evaluating, and repairing comprehension of text during the act of reading it). Strategy training experiments conducted at various grade levels were reviewed, stressing various strategies and yielding various results. The Palincsar and Brown (1984) study is notable for its success in improving reading comprehension by using the reciprocal teaching method to instruct students in the strategies of summarizing, self-questioning, clarifying, and predicting.

Researchers studying learning strategies and study skills have found that some students are surface-level processors who rely primarily on rote learning, whereas more successful students are deeper-level processors who try to understand what they are learning, develop insights, and think about how to use it. Methods have been developed and have achieved success in teaching students to use deeper-level strategies of study. Many of these are variations on the SQ3R method (survey, question, read, recite, review). Others are built around elaboration strategies through which learners generate analogies, imagery, or other linkages relating the new to the familiar.

Teaching students to take better notes is another common strategy. Notes that use an outline format, retain the structuring elements in the presentation, and summarize or paraphrase key elements of the presentation in the learner's own words tend to be more effective than merely underlining or than less complete and organized notes. Calling students' attention to the structuring patterns used to organize presentations will help them to take organized notes.

Comprehensive training programs such as Dansereau's MURDER approach have been developed recently to provide students with systematic training in learning strategies and study skills. Frequently these are offered as courses to college students. The present chapter contains suggestions for how teachers can help their students to study effectively by providing them with relevant information and guidance.

Traditional approaches to teaching problem solving were based on classical models that viewed human problem solving as proceeding systematically and logically from goals through the planning and testing of hypotheses to the development of conclusions from these systematic investigations. More recently, the human information processing approach has shown that many of the problems facing people are ill-structured and thus not well suited to the classical approach, and that they are attacked with heuristics rather than systematic logic and algorithms. Experts tend to cut the complex task environment of a problem down to a convenient problem space by bringing to bear relevant schemas and prior knowledge to develop a useful representation of the problem. Much of their time, in fact, is spent developing an accurate problem representation. If this occurs, solution typically follows quickly and directly. Thus, experts can proceed by quickly identifying one or a small number of highly likely hypotheses, and thus eliminate the need to systematically test all possible hypotheses.

In the absence of such expert knowledge, individuals must rely on heuristics such as working backward from proposed solutions, reasoning by analogy, or dividing the problem into subparts. Various programs designed to develop students' problem-solving skills include instruction in such heuristics and in recognition for various commonly encountered types and patterns of problem.

Traditional approaches to development of thinking skills featured units in logic and critical thinking. Ohlsson criticizes these approaches as being limited to the deduction theory of human thinking, and he argues for approaches representing the enaction theory—emphasis on procedural knowledge and heuristics in addition to figurative knowledge, and subject matter knowledge that emphasizes producing and studying change rather than learning static collections of information and principles. Others have developed comprehensive "thinking" curricula. These include the Philosophy for Children program, the CoRT program, and the Instrumental Enrichment program.

QUESTIONS AND PROBLEMS

1. Are you a strategic learner? That is, do you routinely use the five types of learning strategy described by Weinstein and Mayer (1985)? If not, what things should you be doing that you are not doing now? Draw up a list or a plan for change and use it to guide your studying in the future.
2. Think about the subject matter and grade level that you intend to teach. What strategies will you use to help your students not merely to learn the material, but to learn strategically and with metacognitive awareness of what they are doing and why they are doing it?
3. Do you study differently for an essay test versus a multiple choice test? Differently for material that you expect to use on the job than for material you are learning only for a test? Do these differences make sense given your goals? (If you have difficulty answering these questions, you may need to increase your metacognitive awareness of your studying behavior.)
4. Many teachers of social studies, mathematics, or science take the attitude that they will teach their subject matter and leave reading to the reading teachers. However, many of the students in their classes have difficulty mainly because their skills for learning from texts are not well developed. What, if anything, should such teachers do about this? Discuss this issue with your friends.
5. The Palincsar and Brown (1984) study produced unusually large gains in reading comprehension skills, presumably because of the reciprocal teaching method. What do you think made this method so effective?
6. We discussed the value of noting the frames or structures used to organize texts when reading or taking notes on that text, and we gave examples of text structures commonly used in history and science texts. What structures are commonly used in the texts written for the grade level and subject matter that you intend to teach? What structures commonly appear in the texts you are using now as a student (in your teaching methods text, for example)?
7. What kinds of notetaking do you do (underlining, outlining, summarizing)? Given the guidelines presented in the text, do you see ways to improve your notetaking abilities?
8. Given the grade level and subject matter that you intend to teach, do you expect your students to take notes during times when you are making pres-

entations to the class? If so, what kinds of notes should they take, and what instructions should you give them about notetaking?

9. Do you believe that thinking and problem solving can be taught? Why or why not? If your answer is "yes," do you plan to try to teach thinking and problem solving yourself? If so, how?
10. Teaching has been described as an unusually complex task environment in which it is especially necessary to rely on heuristics in order to create a workable problem space for decision making. What does this mean, and how does it apply to the statement that teaching is partly an art and partly an applied science?
11. If you were to take seriously Ohlsson's suggestion that instruction in a particular field concentrates on the various kinds of change that apply to its subject matter, how would you teach your subject matter differently from the way that it was taught to you?

CASE STUDIES

Preparing for a Test. Sue, complaining to her roommate Suzi, "Oh, I've got to do well on this test or I'm in trouble in this course. I really blew the first test." Suzi said, in a questioning fashion, "Yeah, I wonder what it is about that course that gives you so much trouble. You get practically all As in your other courses, even though you typically do nothing but go to class and then stay up all night before the exam to put it all together." Sue stated with resignation, "The only thing I know is that next week I had better do well or it's curtains." Then she added with excitement, "You know, there is one thing about that course; we have to cover twice as much material as we do in any other class. And the instructor is really interested in facts." How would you suggest that Sue prepare for the exam? Develop a specific study plan.

Nobody Ever Explained it to Me Like That! Gregg is a bright teenager taking demanding honors courses and advanced placement courses. He handles most of his assignments with ease, but occasionally he has difficulty with math problems. At these times, he tends to come to his father, an engineer, for help. In the past, the problems always involved mathematics that the father was familiar with, so he was able to help Gregg after studying the problem for a few minutes. Today, though, Gregg asks for help with a problem of a type that his father has never seen before.

After realizing that he can't figure it out simply by studying it briefly, Gregg's father draws on his own problem-solving heuristics and begins to fire questions at Gregg. Is this the first time that this kind of problem has come up, or has Gregg done similar problems earlier? What does this term mean, and where is it explained in the book? Are there parts of the problem that Gregg recognizes and knows how to handle, and if so, what exactly are the "extra" parts that are causing the difficulty? Has Gregg tried backtracking to the place in the book where this type of problem is introduced so as to review simpler versions of the same type of problem, and then worked forward through increasingly complex versions?

Gregg is initially surprised and displeased by his father's response. He expected an explanation of the problem, not suggestions about how he might solve it himself. Gregg's father is surprised and displeased too, because Gregg's responses to his questions don't go much beyond "I don't know," or "I never thought of that."

Further questioning makes it clear that Gregg has been going through the book problem by problem without getting the big picture. He has never really noticed or thought about the scope and sequencing of the material, has never paid any attention to the table of contents or the chapter outlines, and has never used the index. Nor has he fully appreciated the fact that curriculum strands are organized hierarchically and that exercises occur in an easy-to-difficult sequence, so that reviewing relevant material is a wise strategy when one is stuck on a problem.

As the reality of this sinks in, Gregg's father realizes that Gregg needs more than help with a particular problem—he needs information about how to think about and use a textbook and about heuristics for problem solving in mathematics. If you were Gregg's father, how would you handle this situation? In particular, how could you handle it in such a way as to widen Gregg's overly narrow concentration on getting an answer to this particular problem in order to make him see your message as an eye opening revelation implying that he could be using much more powerful and effective methods of studying and solving problems than he is using now?

Chapter 11

Instructional Design

CHAPTER OUTLINE

OBJECTIVES

When you have mastered the material in this chapter you will be able to

1. Define instructional design and list the steps included in the Gagné and Briggs systems approach
2. Define a curriculum scope and sequence statement and describe the preparation and decision making involved in developing such a statement
3. Describe how curriculum-sequencing decisions are made with the assistance of information processing analysis, task classification, and learning task analysis
4. List the instructional events that Gagné and Briggs believe must be planned for each instructional objective
5. Describe the practical considerations that must be taken into account in developing or selecting materials and media
6. Describe Gropper's ideas for designing an easy-to-difficult sequencing into tasks by manipulating the treatment tools used in teaching the tasks
7. Identify the differences between Skinner's behavioral approach, Gagné's task analysis approach, and Case and Bereiter's cognitive development approach to instructional design
8. Define concepts and concept learning tasks
9. Describe Owen, Blount, and Moscow's model for teaching concepts

10. Distinguish the role of positive examples from the role of negative examples in teaching concepts, and explain how rational sets of examples could be assembled to teach concepts most efficiently
11. Define key concepts in Engelmann and Carnine's approach to concept teaching (faultless communication, juxtaposition of examples, stipulation, interpolation, extrapolation), and explain the procedures they recommend for teaching object concepts, comparative concepts, and transformation sequences

In Chapters 6 through 8 we discussed Gagné's learning hierarchies and his concept of task analysis, the work on programmed instruction with its emphasis on careful sequencing of frames, and the ideas of Ausubel, Bruner, and other cognitive structuralists about the importance of structuring and sequencing information around key concepts. In Chapters 9 and 10, we described the findings of information processing theorists indicating that certain texts are more "considerate" than others because they are organized around structuring devices that provide coherence and flow to the text and thus make it easier to learn. All of these bodies of theory and research suggest that, for a given set of instructional objectives, certain approaches to instruction are likely to be more effective than others.

In particular, these theories imply that instruction will be more efficient and successful when the total collection of knowledge and skills to be learned is divided into units and ultimately individual lessons suited in length and difficulty level to the ages and abilities of the learners, and if both the curriculum as a whole and its individual lessons are structured and sequenced in ways that maximize clarity and ease of learning and minimize the potential for confusion. Instructional design is the art (and applied science) of creating such efficient methods of attaining educational objectives. It includes attention to the materials and activities as well as the methods of instruction, and includes testing and revision cycles in addition to creation of original versions.

The Gagné and Briggs Systems Approach

Gagné and Briggs (1979) state that instructional design is most effective when conducted by means of a systems approach that begins with analysis of needs and goals and proceeds through a series of steps toward eventual demonstration that a developed system of instruction succeeds in meeting the established goals. They outline fourteen stages in the design of complete instructional systems (see Table 11.1).

Instructional system

Gagné and Briggs view an instructional system as an over-arching framework that supplies the necessary means for achieving all of the outcomes called for in a curriculum or course being considered. The systems approach to instructional design accepts whatever goals or outcomes may have been adopted (by the instructional designers themselves or by others empowered to establish instructional objectives), and then draws on the accumulated wisdom contained in teaching models, learning theories, and other relevant sources of information or ideas. The various components included in an instructional system should be internally consistent and mutually reinforcing, but they need not be identical in format nor derived from a single theoretical point of view. Thus, for example, instructional designers might use some approaches to accomplish certain objectives (lecturing and modeling to accomplish knowledge and comprehension objectives), but use other approaches to accomplish other objectives (questioning and discussion followed by application exercises to accomplish application objectives).

Table 11.1 Stages in Designing Instructional Systems

System Level	1. Analysis of needs, goals, and priorities
	2. Analysis of resources, constraints, and alternate delivery systems
	3. Determination of scope and sequence of curriculum and courses; Delivery system design
Course Level	4. Determining course structure and sequence
	5. Analysis of course objectives
Lesson Level	6. Definition of performance objectives
	7. Preparing lesson plans for modules
	8. Developing, selecting materials, media
	9. Assessing student performance (performance measures)
Final System Level	10. Teacher preparation
	11. Formative evaluation
	12. Field testing, revision
	13. Summative evaluation
	14. Installation and diffusion

Source: R. Gagné and L. Briggs (1979). *Principles of Instructional Design* (2nd ed.). New York: Holt, Rinehart and Winston, p. 23

Commercial publishers and other designers of curriculum materials and learning systems should routinely go through all fourteen of the stages shown in Table 11.1, and should continue to recycle through those stages until the system as a whole and each of its component parts have proven their effectiveness in attaining their intended objectives. They seldom do so, however, so that the curricula (including the materials, associated activities, and recommended teaching strategies) that teachers must work with are typically less than ideal and sometimes seriously flawed. Thus, even though most classroom teachers do not become involved in designing learning systems that extend across several grade levels, they nevertheless will need to be familiar with basic principles of instructional design in order to identify the flaws in the learning systems they are given to work with and to be able to adapt or substitute for ineffective components. Furthermore, most teachers will be expected to adapt curricula to the needs of their particular students and to develop remedial programs for students who need them. These activities require the ability to execute the first nine of the stages shown in Table 11.1.

System, course, and lesson level stages

Gagné and Briggs divide their approach into system level stages, course level stages, and lesson level stages. System level stages concern the development of the system as a whole, including all courses or other subdivisions that may exist within it. In developing an elementary school mathematics curriculum, for example, work to be done at the systems level would include deciding what should be taught, sequencing these objectives and the activities associated with them, and then assigning a portion of the sequence to each of the grade levels to be included (such as grades one through six). Provision would be made for review at the beginning of each year and when introducing new topics that build on knowledge or skills taught earlier, but in general, both within and across years, overlearned material would be phased out and new or more difficult material phased in. Some system level stages (1–3) concern initial planning prior to the development of lessons and materials, but others (stages 10–14) concern the testing, revision, and dissemination that should follow such development. Course level stages concern the development of particular courses within the larger system, and lesson level stages concern the development of individual lessons within these courses.

Initial System Level Stages

Stage 1: Analysis of needs, goals, and priorities. Instructional systems are designed to meet perceived needs, so planning begins with establishing consensus on the nature of these needs, setting priorities among them, and stating their implications in terms of instructional objectives. In military or industrial training or other specialized educational settings, it is possible and often necessary to be quite precise in specifying and prioritizing needs. There is more leeway for decision making in designing instruction for the schools, however, at least in the United States (some nations with highly centralized educational systems control curricula to the extent that all students in a given grade are working on the same assignments from the same pages in the same book on any given day). Each state has its own guidelines and requirements, but these tend to be quite general references to the numbers of courses required in various subject matter areas, without details about exactly what will be taught in these courses or how it will be taught. Commercial publishers use these legal guidelines along with the pronouncements of national councils representing various subject matter specialties and the content included on standardized tests for guidance in setting curriculum objectives. Local developers (individual teachers or committees representing schools or school districts) may also be guided by objectives standards adopted by their local school boards or school curriculum committees, although they usually exercise considerable autonomy in making curriculum decisions (Schwille et al., 1983).

In any case, instructional designers need to make decisions about what knowledge and skills are to be taught, to what levels of depth and mastery, to what students, and in what sequence. Systematic design of instruction cannot begin until consensus is reached on these decisions. At that point, the designers are in a position to develop a curriculum scope and sequence statement that provides a detailed listing of the objectives to be included, in the order in which they are to be taught.

Stage 2: Analysis of resources, constraints, and alternative delivery systems. Given the intended curriculum scope and sequence, the designers now need to consider how each of the objectives can be accomplished efficiently. What methods are known or believed to be effective for teaching these objectives? What materials will be needed, and what kinds of activities will the students engage in?

These questions will have to be addressed within the context of whatever financial or other constraints apply. Some activities or equipment that would be ideal for teaching particular objectives are too expensive, bulky, noisy, dangerous, or otherwise unfeasible for routine use in typical school settings. Similarly, some activities do not lend themselves to implementation within the physical setting of the typical classroom, and some are not feasible for use by a single teacher who must work with 25 or 30 students. Consequently, compromises will have to be made, and certain objectives may even have to be dropped or reduced in priority. In any case, the work of Stage 2 should culminate in plans that include consensus not only about the objectives to be taught but also about the appropriateness and feasibility of the anticipated methods for teaching these objectives to the anticipated students under anticipated constraints.

Stage 3: Determination of scope and sequence of curriculum and courses; delivery system design. At this stage, the designers elaborate the curriculum scope and sequence statement by assigning different sequences of objectives to different courses, stating objectives in terms of learner performance, and clarifying the details of the delivery system to be developed. Gagné and Briggs stress the importance of stating objectives in terms of learner performance (rather than in terms of what the materials present or what the teacher does) so that measures of performance can be developed and used later when evaluating the system. Clarifying the details of the delivery system to be developed involves identifying the types and amounts of materials that will have to be purchased or developed, the equipment and media forms that will be needed, the activities that will be involved, and the manuals and procedures that will be required for training teachers. Once this stage of system level planning has been completed, the focus shifts to course and lesson level work.

Course Level Stages

Target and enabling objectives

Stage 4: Determining course structure and sequence. Gagné and Briggs distinguish between target objectives (major objectives to be reached only by the end of the course) and enabling objectives (objectives that are smaller in scope and represent steps toward the attainment of target objectives). At this stage of instructional design, the target objectives of the course are clustered into units of instruction that will each require perhaps one to three weeks of study to complete. The sequencing of instruction is then considered, first for the sequencing of the units themselves and then for the sequencing of objectives within units.

Sequencing

Sequencing may or may not be crucial. In designing a course to teach a hierarchically ordered series of mathematics skills, it would be essential to begin with the simplest skills and proceed in an orderly fashion up the hierarchy. In designing a social studies course on western Europe, however, units on Germany, France, and Great Britain might be presented in any order with equally satisfactory results. Sometimes the content lends itself to presentation in two or more different sequences that offer different advantages and disadvantages depending on the specific objectives to be pursued or the personal preferences of the instructor. For example, courses in history or in developmental psychology can be organized either chronologically (beginning with the first developmental stage or historical period, then proceeding to the next, and then the next, embedding coverage of each major topic within the presentations on each of the periods) or topically (treating each topic separately and embedding discussion of change over time within these topical units). The chronological approach has the advantage of highlighting "the big picture" and showing how it changes over time, but it results in fragmented discussion of particular topics. The topical approach has the opposite characteristics.

In situations where there are no hierarchical relationships or logical dependencies dictating that objectives be taken up in particular sequences, instructional designers may even want to deliberately modularize their units (make them self-contained and usable in any order) so as to provide instructors with choice and flexibility. This strategy has been followed in preparing the present text. The present unit on instructional applications assumes mastery of the previous unit on learning, but otherwise, the units have been prepared as modules that can stand on their own without depending on prior mastery of material in other units. They can be taken up in almost any order, not just the order in which they appear in the text. The book has been prepared this way because some instructors will not have enough time to cover everything in the book, and some will want to omit certain material (child development, measurement and evaluation) because their students will be taking an entire course on that topic in addition to a course in educational psychology. Instructors differ in what material they want to include or emphasize in teaching educational psychology, and in their preferences for sequencing that material. The modular organization of the present text accommodates these contingencies by making it easier for instructors to omit certain units or to reorder them into the sequence they prefer.

Preparing units as modules

Stage 5: Analysis of course objectives. At this stage, the instructional designer performs detailed analyses of the target objectives of the course. Gagné and Briggs recommend three kinds of analysis at this point: information processing analysis to reveal the sequence of the mental operations required to perform the objective, task classification to categorize learning outcomes and identify the conditions of learning that will have to be established, and learning task analysis to identify the enabling objectives that will need to be taught prior to teaching target objectives.

Information processing analysis identifies the sequence of steps involved in a target performance. Gagné and Briggs advocate using flow charts to depict these steps. Figure 11.1 shows an information processing analysis of the process of subtracting two-place numbers. In the flow chart system used in the figure, trapezoids are used to represent inputs, rectangles to represent actions, and diamonds to represent choices or decisions.

Use of flow charts

Figure 11.1 An Information Processing Analysis of the Subtraction of Two-place Numbers

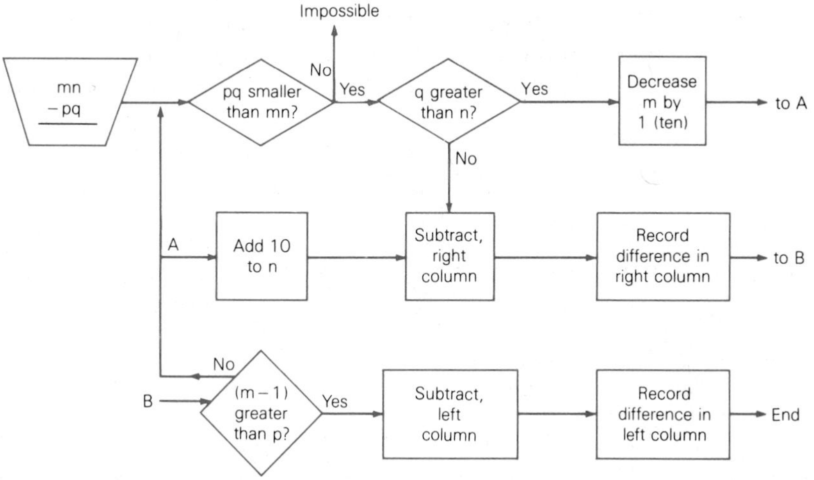

From R. Gagné, (1977). "Analysis of Objectives," in L. J. Briggs (Ed.), *Instructional Design*. Englewood Cliffs, N.J.: Educational Technology Publications. Copyright © 1977. Reproduced by permission of the copyright owner.

Uses for information processing analysis

Gagné and Briggs note two primary uses for such information processing analyses. First, they provide especially clear descriptions of the target objectives and thus help sharpen one's planning for both instruction and measurement of the objective. Second, the detailed analysis often reveals steps in the process that might not have been recognized otherwise. Concerning the subtraction skill illustrated in Figure 11.1, for example, it becomes clear that the learners must be able to distinguish the larger from the smaller of two numbers before carrying out the process of subtraction. If the learners do not already possess this capability, it will have to be taught as an enabling objective that supports progress toward the target objective of subtracting two-place numbers.

Task classification

Task classification involves categorizing course objectives into task categories that imply different conditions of learning. In the Gagné and Briggs system, tasks are categorized as involving intellectual skills, cognitive strategies, information, attitudes, or motor skills, and intellectual skills are further categorized into discriminations, concrete concepts, defined concepts, rules, and higher-order rules. Different conditions of learning are associated with each of these categories and subcategories (see Chapter 6), so that awareness of task type is helpful in planning instruction.

Learning task analysis

Learning task analysis involves identifying the prerequisites for learning both target and enabling objectives. In the case of intellectual skills, this analysis will produce a formal learning hierarchy that begins with discriminations and proceeds systematically up through concrete concepts, defined concepts, rules, and higher-order rules. Other categories of learning objectives (verbal information, cognitive strategies, motor skills, attitudes) do not relate to one another in the manner implied by formal learning hierarchies, but it is often possible to identify certain of these skills that are logically prerequisite to other ones, and to use this information in sequencing instruction. For example, in teaching a mnemonic device (i.e., a cognitive strategy) to help learners remember a list of rules, it makes sense

Figure 11.2 A Learning Hierarchy for Subtracting Whole Numbers

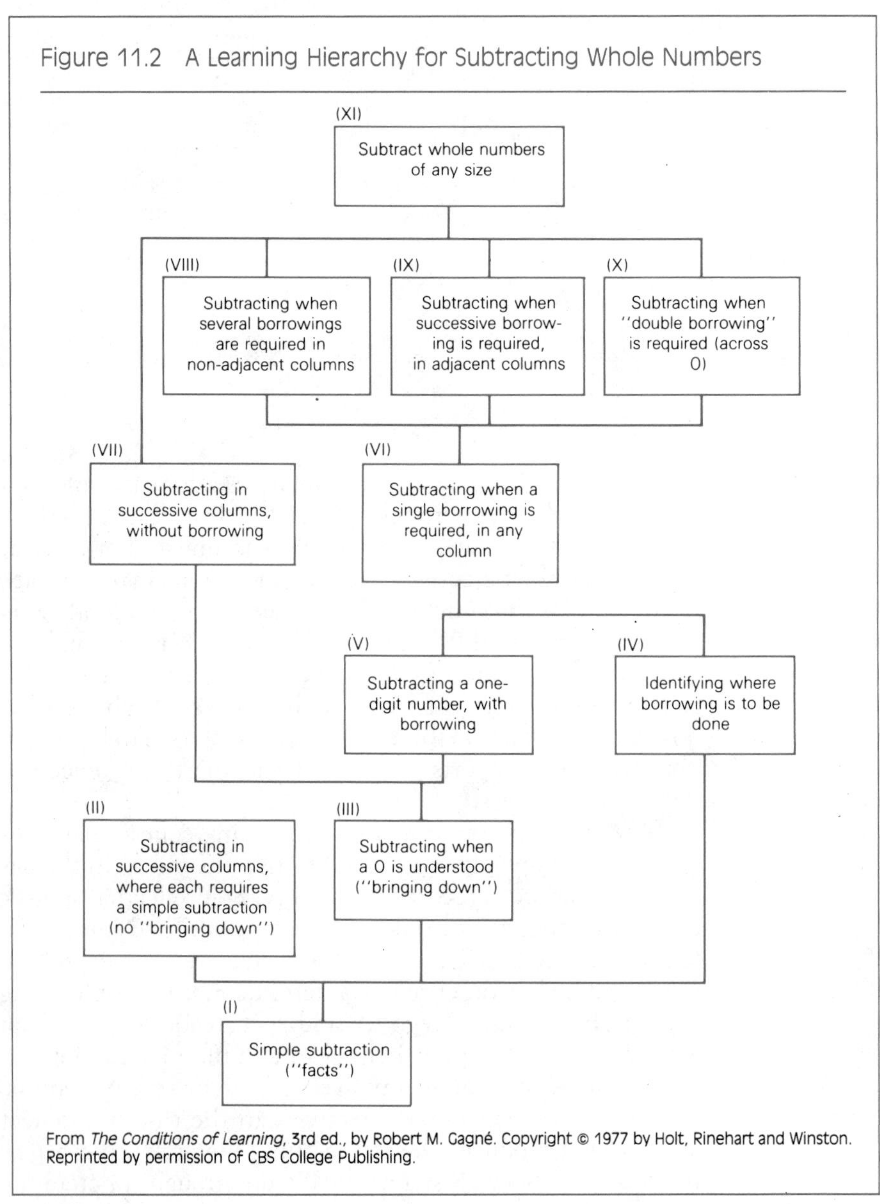

From *The Conditions of Learning*, 3rd ed., by Robert M. Gagné. Copyright © 1977 by Holt, Rinehart and Winston. Reprinted by permission of CBS College Publishing.

to teach the list of rules first so that the learners have a better understanding of the meaning and usefulness of the mnemonic device when they learn it.

A learning hierarchy for subtraction of whole numbers is shown in Figure 11.2. Such a hierarchy, in combination with more detailed information processing analyses such as those shown in Figure 11.1, are helpful in identifying which skills need to be taught and in what order.

Lesson Level Stages

Stage 6: Definition of performance objectives. At this stage, specific objectives are written for each lesson to be included in the course. These objectives will be used to guide development of both the instruction (including the materials and activities in addition to the content to be presented) included in the lesson and the evaluation devices to be used to assess the effectiveness of that instruction.

Stage 7: Preparing lesson plans (or modules). The nature of these plans will depend on the nature of the instruction anticipated. For teacher-led, group-based instruction, the lesson plan is mainly a guide for use by the teacher. If individualized, self-paced learning modules are to be developed, the plan will include a statement of objectives, a list of materials to be read, a guide to activities to be performed, a self-check test, and instructions about presenting completed work and arranging for tests by the teacher (Gagné & Briggs, 1979). In this text, we will concentrate on planning for teacher-led group instruction.

For each lesson objective, a plan needs to be developed that includes the following steps: 1) listing the instructional events to be brought into

Table 11.2 Events of Instruction and Their Relations to Processes of Learning

Instructional Event	Relation to Learning Process
1. Gaining attention	*Reception* of patterns of neural impulses
2. Informing the learner of the objective	Activating a process of *executive control*
3. Stimulating recall of prerequisite learnings	*Retrieval* to working memory
4. Presenting the stimulus material	Emphasizing features for *selective perception*
5. Providing "learning guidance"	*Semantic encoding*
6. Eliciting the performance	Activating a *response organization*
7. Providing feedback about performance correctness	Establishing *reinforcement*
8. Assessing the performance	Activating *retrieval*; making *reinforcement* possible
9. Enhancing retention and transfer	Providing cues and strategies for *retrieval*

Source: R. Gagné and L. Briggs (1979). *Principles of Instructional Design* (2nd ed.). New York: Holt, Rinehart and Winston, p. 157

Table 11.3 Instructional Events and the Conditions of Learning They Imply for Five Types of Learned Capabilities

	Type of Capability				
Instructional Event	*Intellectual Skill*	*Cognitive Strategy*	*Information*	*Attitude*	*Motor Skill*
1. Gaining attention	Introduce stimulus change: variations in sensory mode				
2. Informing learner of objective	Provide description and example of the performance to be expected	Clarify the general nature of the solution expected	Indicate the kind of verbal question to be answered	Provide example of the kind of action choice aimed for	Provide a demonstration of the performance to be expected
3. Stimulating recall of prerequisites	Stimulate recall of subordinate concepts and rules	Stimulate recall of task strategies and associated intellectual skills	Stimulate recall of context of organ-ized information	Stimulate recall of relevant information skills and human model identification	Stimulate recall of executive subroutine and part skills
4. Presenting the stimulus material	Present examples of concept or rule	Present novel problems	Present information in propositional form	Present human model demonstrating choice of personal action	Provide external stimuli for performance including tools or implements
5. Providing learning guidance	Provide verbal cues to proper combin-ing sequence	Provide prompts and hints to novel solution	Provide verbal links to a larger meaningful context	Provide for observation of model's choice of action, and of reinforcement received by model	Provide practice with feedback of performance achievement
6. Eliciting the performance	Ask learner to apply rule or concept to new examples	Ask for problem solution	Ask for information in paraphrase, or in learner's own words	Ask learner to indicate choices of action in real or simulated situations	Ask for execution of the performance
7. Providing feedback	Confirm correctness of rule or concept application	Confirm originality of problem solution	Confirm correctness of statement of information	Provide direct or vicarious reinforcement of action choice	Provide feedback on degree of accuracy and timing of performance
8. Assessing performance	Learner demonstrates application of concept or rule	Learner originates a novel solution	Learner restates information in paraphrased form	Learner makes desired choice of personal action in real or simulated situation	Learner executes performance of total skill
9. Enhancing retention and transfer	Provide spaced reviews, including a variety of examples	Provide occasions for a variety of novel problem solutions	Provide verbal links to additional complexes of information	Provide additional varied situations for selected choice of action	Learner continues skill practice

Source: R. Gagné and L. Briggs (1979). *Principles of Instructional Design* (2nd ed.). New York: Holt, Rinehart and Winston, p. 166. Copyright © 1979 by Holt, Rinehart and Winston. Reprinted by permission of CBS College Publishing.

play to accomplish the objective; 2) determining the materials, media, or agents to be employed for making each of these instructional events possible; 3) Designing or planning learning activities, including plans for how media and materials are to be used; and 4) previewing the selected media and materials to plan the roles or events that the teacher needs to accomplish for the lesson.

The instructional events mentioned by Gagné and Briggs are the words and actions of the teacher that present input to the students and help them to process and respond to this input in ways that will move them toward accomplishing the objective. Gagné and Briggs have identified nine instructional events that would be included in a complete plan for teaching a particular objective. These nine instructional events are shown in Table 11.2, along with the information processing activities that they are supposed to engender in the learner. In addition, Table 11.3 shows the different forms that these instructional events take depending on whether one is teaching intellectual skills, cognitive strategies, information, attitudes, or motor skills.

It is here and in the next stage that the instructional planner's creativity, knowledge of the subject matter and how to teach it, and knowledge of the learners' needs and interests come into play. Even given various constraints that rule out some options, there usually will be a great many different ways to approach teaching a particular objective. The instructional designer will have to decide what information to present and at what level of difficulty and redundancy, what examples or demonstrations to use, what media or materials may be essential (or if not essential, important enough to successful instruction to justify the trouble and expense involved in including them), and what kinds of practice and application activities will be needed.

Gaining attention

Gaining attention, for example, can be accomplished simply by saying "Look here." However, the lesson will probably be more successful if the teacher begins by saying or doing something to arouse the students' curiosity or interest in the content. This might be done by posing an interesting question that the lesson will answer, by showing an interesting prop or performing a demonstration, or by underscoring the importance of the knowledge or skills to be taught by telling students why they will need them or where they will use them. Depending on the learning objective, the students, and other factors, some methods of gaining attention will be more effective than others. The same is true of other instructional events such as stimulating recall of prerequisite capabilities (Can these merely be mentioned or elicited through questioning, or will it be necessary to lead the students through a series of review exercises?), presenting the stimulus material (Which examples would be helpful, and which might be misleading? In what order should the helpful examples be presented?), or providing learning guidance (When and how should the teacher instruct didactically? Attempt to elicit insights through questioning? Assign activities designed to stimulate discovery learning?).

Stage 8: Developing or selecting materials and media. Some of the planned instructional events will require particular media or materials. It may be possible to select or adapt these from existing sources, although if this is done it will be important for the instructional designer to preview these media or materials and make sure that they are appropriate before including them in the lesson. Where plans call for materials that cannot be obtained elsewhere, it will be necessary to design them. Besides effectiveness in helping students to accomplish lesson objectives, materials and media need to be assessed with an eye toward such practical factors as: the size of the group with whom the activity can be used on a single occasion; how easily the media can be interrupted for discussion or response to questions; the probable affective impact on the learners; the degree to which teachers may need special training for using the medium; the time and trouble required to set it up; and the costs involved in purchasing, storing, and maintaining the media (Briggs, 1970). Besides being costly, many of the special materials and media proposed for use in schools have proven to be overly time consuming, difficult to use, or otherwise problematic according to these practical criteria (Clark, 1983), which is why relatively inexpensive and convenient print materials continue to be relied on heavily despite developments in audiovisual technology and computers.

Stage 9: Assessing student performance (performance measures). Gagné and Briggs have included this stage to underscore their point that lesson design includes not only preparation of instructional materials and methods, but also preparation of performance measures capable of determining whether or not students have achieved the lesson's objective. Instructional planning is not complete without such assessment, and instructional development is not complete until the lesson succeeds in achieving the objective.

Final System Level Stages

Stages 10 through 14 in the Gagné and Briggs scheme apply only to the designers of comprehensive learning systems, and will not be considered in detail here (see Table 11.1). They involve designing methods for training teachers to use the new system, conducting formative evaluation by pilot testing courses or individual lessons on a small number of classes and identifying revision needs (Dick, 1977), field testing the system as a whole in a few sites and making further revisions, conducting summative evaluation in which the revised (and presumably complete) system is implemented in enough sites to allow statistical analysis of its effectiveness in meeting its objectives, and developing methods for diffusing information about the presumably proven system and installing it in new sites.

Other General Approaches to Instructional Design

The Gagné and Briggs (1979) treatment is perhaps the best known and most widely used approach to instructional design, but it is just one of many such approaches (for reviews and information, see Andrews & Goodson,

1980; Braden & Sachs, 1983; Dick & Carey, 1978; Gagné & Dick, 1983; Reigeluth, 1983; and the various issues of the *Journal of Instructional Development*). Many of these other approaches are very similar to the Gagné and Briggs approach, differing only in terminology and degree of elaboration of particular points. Some differ in more substantial ways, however, and a few differ considerably because they envision a different kind of instruction from the didactic approach stressed by Gagné and Briggs.

Gropper

Treatment tools

Gropper (1983) outlines a behavioral approach to instructional design that uses Skinnerian terminology and focuses on skills instruction but otherwise is similar in most respects to the Gagné and Briggs approach. However, Gropper goes into detail in discussing what he calls the treatment tools for use in designing practice tasks: the degree of cuing provided, the size of the unit of behavior that is practiced, the mode of stimulus and response required, the variety built into tasks, the content built into tasks, and the frequency with which the task is practiced. In particular, he provides guidelines for variations in the use of these treatment tools at different stages in the instructional sequence.

Cuing

Cuing, for example, would be frequent and specific early in a unit, but would be faded gradually as mastery develops. In teaching penmanship, students might first be provided with model script to trace over, then expected to copy (but not trace over) model script, and then to write on their own without visual cues available. In teaching French, students might first be asked to imitate French being spoken on tape, then to read French from printed text, and then to speak it in conversation.

The size of the unit of behavior to be practiced would also vary across the sequence of instruction. Practice might begin with isolated subskills (estimating how many places in a dividend a divisor will go or punctuating sentences), proceed to intermediate combinations of steps (doing long division problems one step at a time or writing sentences or paragraphs), and then proceed toward final practice (doing entire long division problems or writing short essays). In addition to varying the sheer size of the task, the designer can vary the task complexity (driving in empty parking lots versus driving on the streets in light traffic) or the standards for acceptable performance (gradual increase in the standards of acceptable penmanship or decrease in the numbers of errors acceptable in typing).

Size and complexity of task

Response and stimulus modes

Variations in response mode can also be used to gradually increase the level of demand on the learners. Initial practice examples might require only recognition of the correct answer (by selecting it from several alternatives), whereas intermediate practice might call for editing (correcting the answer if it is incorrect), and final practice might call for production (supplying the answer in the absence of any cues at all). Similarly, the stimulus mode of presentations can be varied by beginning with concrete examples and moving toward more technical or abstract definitions, or beginning with procedures before introducing general principles.

Variety

A variety of examples could be planned to promote generalization and transfer. Within this variety, examples would be sequenced from easy to difficult according to the degree to which they were familiar to the students, similar to previously encountered examples, and salient in their defining characteristics. Thus, students would practice forming plurals for regular nouns before taking on irregular nouns, and would design experiments involving only one variable before moving to designs involving multiple interacting variables.

Varying content

The content of practice tasks can also be varied. Early in a sequence, for example, critical features of examples can be exaggerated in order to call attention to them and help prepare the students to note more subtle variations on those same dimensions to be presented later. Also, for certain objectives it may be helpful to promote the practice of errors (usually one wants to minimize this, but sometimes it is helpful to call students' attention to certain common errors and help them discriminate correct from incorrect performance) or to alter the typical sequence of behaviors (to disassemble something or work backward from an end state before attempting to assemble or work forward toward the end state).

Varying frequency

Finally, the frequency of practice can be varied. Typically, a great deal of distributed practice (however much it takes to produce mastery) would be programmed following introduction of a new skill, with fading of practice to a maintenance level thereafter.

Gropper's ideas help supplement those of Gagné and Briggs by showing how an easy-to-difficult sequencing can be designed into instruction not only by making sure that objectives are sequenced in an appropriate order, but also by manipulating the treatment tools used to teach each individual objective.

Case and Bereiter

Case and Bereiter (1984) credit Gagné for moving instructional design from behaviorism to cognitive behaviorism, but argue that the field needs to develop further toward what they call "cognitive development." Following Skinner (1954), they argue that the behavioral approach to instructional design includes the following steps:

1. Identify the potential reinforcers that are available and effective for the learners in question.
2. Identify and objectively describe the desired behavior.
3. Describe the initial or "entering" behavior of the learner.
4. Define a series of behaviors, starting with the entering behavior and leading to the desired terminal behavior, such that each successive behavior represents a small modification of the previous one.
5. Move students through the sequence of behaviors using demonstrations and instructions coupled with positive reinforcements of behavioral variations that are in the desired direction.
6. Insure, through reinforced practice, that each behavior is thoroughly learned before advancing to the next step.

Case and Bereiter credit Gagné with correcting three important weaknesses in Skinner's approach. First, Skinner emphasized reinforcement and the issue of *how* to change behavior, but Gagné showed that the more typical problem is identifying in sufficient detail *what* needs to be taught. Gagné shifted the focus of attention from the how to the what of behavior change by shifting focus from reinforcement to the nature of the behaviors themselves. A second problem was that behavioral theory dealt exclusively with observable behaviors and thus was difficult to apply to school learning. Gagné recognized different types of learning, and in particular emphasized the intellectual skills taught in school. The third and most important weakness in the behavioral approach was failure to specify how to carry out Step 4—identifying behaviors that are steps in the direction of the terminal behavior and determining that these steps are small enough to be negotiated successfully by the learner. Gagné's notions of learning hierarchies and task analysis provided such guidance.

In contrast to these steps in the behavioral approach, Case and Bereiter suggest that the following steps characterize Gagné's approach:

1. Identify the intellectual skill that the instructional program is intended to teach, and develop a measure to assess its presence.
2. Using the technique of hierarchical task analysis, identify successively lower level skills until a level has been reached such that all students are expected to possess the skills on entry into the program.
3. Develop assessment devices for each skill and subskill and use them to determine the individual student's entering competence.
4. Present instruction that progresses from the student's existing skills to skills at successively higher levels in the hierarchy.
5. Before beginning to teach any new skill, make sure that the student has mastered all the lower-level skills that it depends on.

Limitations of Gagné approach

Case and Bereiter argue that the Gagné approach works well for a great range of instructional situations, but not for all such situations, and suggest that its failures are typically due to one of two common problems. First, with highly difficult tasks, it sometimes yields instruction that is too difficult because students have to consider so many components in progressing through the hierarchy that the task exceeds the limits of their working memories. Second, the hierarchies yielded by a purely logical analysis of tasks do not always correspond to the developmental order in which components of the task are mastered naturally, and this natural order may be more appropriate for instruction than the order based on logical analysis. Furthermore, students at particular levels of cognitive development will have particular concepts and preconceptions about the task, such that instruction may have to begin with these familiar concepts and may have to take into account these preconceptions. In the case of preconceptions that seem valid to the students but happen to be incorrect, it will be necessary to show the inadequacies of the preconceptions in order to make the students willing and able to fully appreciate the instruction and make the necessary changes in their present thinking. Combining these considerations, Case and Bereiter (1984) suggest that a "cognitive development" approach to instructional design should include the following steps:

1. Identify the task to be taught and develop a measure for assessing students' success or failure with it.
2. Develop a procedure for assessing the strategy that students employ on the measure.
3. Use this procedure to assess the strategies that students use at a variety of ages, including both ages where success is not achieved by current methods and ages where it is.

4a. Devise an instructional sequence for "recapitulating development" (i.e., for bringing students from one level to the next in the course of instruction).

4b. Keep the working memory load at each step within reasonable limits.

5. Once students' performance at one level becomes relatively automatic, move on to the next.

Collins and Stevens

Questioning and inquiry teaching strategies

Collins and Stevens (1983) present an approach to instructional design that is different from most other approaches because it focuses on the use of questioning and inquiry teaching strategies to bring about higher-level cognitive objectives and discovery learning. They describe ten instructional strategies: 1) selecting positive and negative examples, 2) varying case studies systematically, 3) selecting counterexamples, 4) generating hypothetical cases, 5) forming hypotheses, 6) testing hypotheses, 7) considering alternative predictions, 8) entrapping students, 9) tracing consequences to a contradiction, and 10) questioning authority.

Creating dissonance or curiosity

The first three of these strategies are similar to those appearing in didactic approaches, except that Collins and Stevens focus on selecting and sequencing examples so as to create dissonance or curiosity in students and thus set the stage for inquiry-oriented discussion, rather than focusing on using examples so as to teach concepts through efficient didactic instruction. The strategy of generating hypothetical cases is used to challenge students' reasoning or force them to take into account factors that they are presently ignoring.

In this inquiry approach, students are challenged to form and evaluate hypotheses rather than given rules or principles, and are prodded to consider alternative predictions whenever they tend to jump to conclusions without adequate consideration of alternatives. The strategy of entrapping students is used to reveal the inadequacies of erroneous preconceptions. Entrapment involves using the students' own thinking to show how it leads to incorrect predictions or conclusions. Tracing consequences to a contradiction is a similar strategy. Finally, the strategy of questioning authority involves training students to think for themselves rather than rely on the teacher or the book for correct answers.

In addition to discussing these instructional strategies, Collins and Stevens (1983) present rules for structuring and sequencing dialogues with students designed to achieve particular objectives. We mention their work briefly here not to explain it in detail but to underscore the point that thoughtful instructional design is just as important for discovery and inquiry-oriented approaches as it is for other approaches to teaching.

Power and Limits of Systematic Instructional Design

The principles articulated by Gagné and Briggs (1979) and other instructional design theorists can be quite helpful in planning effective instruction. They underscore the need to clarify instructional objectives and keep these in mind when designing and evaluating instruction, and they remind us that certain sequences, instructional methods, examples, or activities may be more helpful than others for accomplishing those objectives. On the other hand, these theories have yet to be tested scientifically or supported with much scientific research (Mayer, 1985). Furthermore, despite the progress in this regard noted by Case and Bereiter (1984), instructional design theories are still of limited value for developing ideas about how particular objectives can be taught most effectively. Task analysis and related procedures are helpful, but instructional developers still have to rely primarily on their own knowledge of content and pedagogy, and especially on their knowledge of what students of particular ages or cognitive development levels know about the topic, and how this knowledge can be profitably expanded. To illustrate some of the complexities involved, we will review research on the learning and teaching of concepts.

Concept Learning

Concept and concept learning

Educational psychologists have accumulated a great deal of information about concept learning to inform instructional designers who are working in developing methods to teach concepts. Following Tennyson and Park (1980), we define a concept as a set of specific objects, symbols, or events that share common characteristics (defining attributes) and thus can be referenced by a particular name or symbol. Thus, concept learning involves the identification of these defining attributes of concepts that can be generalized to new examples and can be used to discriminate valid examples of the concept from nonexamples.

Early work on concept learning presented experimental subjects with carefully prepared series of stimuli and asked them to state whether each stimulus was or was not an example of the concept. For example, Bruner, Goodnow, and Austin (1956) used a series of 81 cards that presented stimulus combinations varying along four dimensions that had three values for each: shapes of objects shown (squares, circles, or crosses), color of objects shown (red, green, or black), number of objects shown (one, two, or three), and number of borders around these objects (one, two, or three). In a typical experiment, subjects were shown a chart illustrating all of the cards and asked to select one that they thought might illustrate the concept to be learned (such as that any card containing at least one red object was an instance of the concept, and all other cards were not). The subject would be given feedback about his or her choice, and then allowed to select another example. This would continue until the subject was able to verbalize the concept correctly.

Cue salience

Such experiments revealed several factors that influence concept learning. One is cue salience: Certain cues are noticed and used to discriminate stimuli more easily than others. For example, Trabasso and Bower (1968) used flower designs that varied in color of flower, number and shape of leaves, and angle of branches. They found that students learned much more quickly when concepts were based on color than when they were based on angle of branch.

Task variables that influence learning

There are also several task variables that influence learning (Bourne, Ekstrand, & Dominowski, 1971; Mayer, 1982). One of these is the nature of the rule defining the concept. Rules involving only a single attribute (choose the red object) are easier than rules involving more than one attribute (such as color and shape). Furthermore, among rules involving more than one attribute, conjunctive rules (choose red squares) are easier to learn than disjunctive rules (choose any card that contains either a red object or a square or both). Also, when rules involve more than one attribute, increasing the number of relevant dimensions leads to quicker solution, but increasing the number of irrelevant dimensions makes learning more difficult. Finally, subjects usually learn faster from positive instances than from negative instances.

Limitations

Such findings were interesting but subject to important limitations that minimized their usefulness in developing guidelines for instruction. For one thing, the "instruction" was restricted to presentation of examples, so that learners were forced to rely on guesswork and reasoning to build up a definition of the concept. Other research suggests that concept learning is more efficient when accomplished through didactic instruction rather than discovery learning, and when it includes direct statements of rules and definitions in addition to presentation of examples (Francis, 1975; Clark, 1971; Klausmeier, Ghatala, & Frayer, 1974; Woodson, 1974).

Model for teaching concepts

The latter research suggests the following model for teaching concepts (Owen, Blount, & Moscow, 1978):

1. Present a concept definition that includes the concept label and the concept's defining attributes.
2. Present positive examples of the concept, emphasizing the defining attributes.
3. Present negative examples of the concept that help distinguish defining attributes from irrelevant attributes.
4. Present positive and negative examples of the concept. Ask the student to identify the positive examples. Then ask why the negative examples are not examples of the concept.
5. Provide feedback. Give specific reasons for errors, rather than leaving it up to students to figure out why they were wrong.

Later research also revealed a second limitation in the early work on concept learning: Many of the concepts used were arbitrary or artificial, and the stimuli were limited to examples that clearly were or were not instances of the concepts being taught. For example, squares, circles, and crosses are completely different from one another, as are red, green, and black colors. Under more normal learning conditions, however, stimuli often differ by degrees rather than so starkly, and concepts sometimes merge into one another in ways that make them difficult to define and discriminate without ambiguity.

Fuzziness of natural categories

For example, Rosch (1978) and her colleagues have shown that natural categories learned through real world experience (bird, furniture, student) are fuzzy in the sense that the boundary lines between them are not firm. Unlike conjunctive concepts defined by a specific list of critical attributes that are all present in any example of the concept, natural categories are not so clear cut. Instead, they are fuzzy concepts defined by the fact that all of their members share a family resemblance based on a basic core of features (Rosch & Mervis, 1975). Any given instance of the category contains some of these features, but usually not all of them. Thus, for example, "singing," "flying," and "smallness" are all attributes that help define the natural category "birds," even though many birds do not have all of these attributes, and some, like the ostrich, have none of them. People can rate the degree to which examples show "goodness of fit" to natural categories ("pillow" is a poor example of "furniture," "lamp" is a better example, and "chair" is an excellent example). Furthermore, they are able to answer questions about typical examples (Is a chair a piece of furniture?) more quickly than they can answer questions about atypical examples (Is a pillow a piece of furniture?).

Children's use of basic level categories

Of most direct relevance to instructional design, Rosch and her colleagues have shown that children first learn to classify and label objects using basic level categories (chair, table) rather than superordinate level categories (furniture) or subordinate level categories (easy chair, kitchen table). Furthermore, even adults are better able to use basic level categories for thinking and reasoning purposes than they are able to use superordinate or subordinate level categories (Rosch et al., 1976; Rosch & Lloyd, 1978). Such data suggest that concept teaching might sometimes proceed most efficiently by starting with concepts of medium generality or complexity (if these happen to be basic level categories) rather than by starting with the simplest or most specific and building systematically toward the most complex or general.

Teaching Concepts

We have seen that instructional designers typically call for sequencing material from the simple to the complex, and that research on concept learning suggests first stating the concept definition and identifying its defining attributes, next presenting positive examples of the concept, and then presenting negative examples. These are useful general principles, but there are exceptions. Case and Bereiter (1984) note the need to begin with relevant concepts and preconceptions that learners harbor at the moment (and in the case of misconceptions, to confront these directly), and the work of Rosch and her colleagues (Rosch & Lloyd, 1978) suggests beginning with basic level categories (start with the most typical or familiar and then work both upwards and downwards from there) rather than with simpler concepts that represent subordinate level categories. Other investigators who have sought to identify the most efficient ways to teach concepts also have suggested qualifications and elaborations of these general principles.

Positive-introductory examples

Clark (1971) reviewed the concept teaching literature and concluded that instruction should begin with positive-introductory examples, then move to positive-confirmatory examples, and then move to negative examples. Positive-introductory examples illustrate the defining attributes and are as free as possible of irrelevant attributes. They are used to call learners' attention to the defining attributes of the concept with as little confusion or distraction as possible. In teaching the concept of "square" for example, defining attributes would include: a) four sides, b) all sides are of equal length, and c) all corners are right angles. Irrelevant attributes would include how a square is oriented in space and the size of the square. The squares shown as positive-introductory examples would all be the same size and constructed from horizontal and vertical lines.

Positive-confirmatory examples

Positive-confirmatory examples also contain all of the defining attributes, but in addition display one or more irrelevant attributes. Thus, positive-confirmatory examples for the "square" concept would include squares of varying sizes and spatial rotation, as long as they are constructed of four equal sides joined at right angles.

Negative examples

Finally, negative examples lack one or more of the defining attributes and thus are not instances of the concept. These range from stimuli that are not the same dimensions as the concept (a picture of an elephant) through those that share certain similarities but none of the defining attributes (geometric figures with more or fewer than four sides, and where the sides are of unequal length) to stimuli that share one or more defining attributes but are still negative examples (rectangles that are almost square). Ordinarily, negative examples would be confined to those sharing the same conceptual class with positive examples of the concept (in this case, geometric figures). Within this restriction, however, an increasing variety of both positive examples and negative examples would be displayed as instruction progressed, in order to make learners aware of both the degree to which the concept generalizes (illustrated by the range of positive examples) and the limits beyond which it cannot be stretched (illustrated by negative examples, especially those that share several defining attributes and thus are "near misses").

Merrill and Tennyson

Merrill and Tennyson (1977; see also Tennyson & Park, 1980) suggest similar guidelines. Their model includes a definition of the concept expressed in terms of its defining attributes, an expository presentation using rational sets of examples, and a practice phase in which students are required to differentiate between examples and nonexamples of the concept and to justify their choices with reference to its defining attributes.

Rational sets

Rational sets of examples are sets selected to call students' attention to defining attributes and minimize errors due to overgeneralization, undergeneralization, or misconception. Such rational sets include examples that are diverse in form and ordered from easy to difficult, and they are selected for their value in illustrating particular points. For example, undergeneralization errors (identifying examples as nonexamples) can be minimized by making sure that the set of examples includes the full range of variation that occurs in the defining attributes (squares come in a great range of sizes and spatial rotations). Overgeneralization errors (identifying nonexamples as examples) can be minimized by making sure that the nonexample set includes typical "near misses" (rectangles that are almost square).

Matched pairs

To focus learners on the attributes of interest, it is often helpful to use matched pairs of examples and nonexamples that differ on one or more defining attributes but do not differ in their irrelevant attributes. The presence or absence of irrelevant attributes must be varied from one set of examples to the next, however, in order to avoid inducing misconceptions in the learners. For example, if all examples shown are constructed of horizontal and vertical lines, learners might develop the misconception that this spatial orientation is essental to the definition of a square.

Engelmann and Carnine

Faultless communication

Engelmann and Carnine (1982) provide detailed suggestions about the selection and juxtaposition of examples when teaching different kinds of concepts. They believe that instruction should be designed to accomplish faultless communication–instruction that communicates exactly what is intended, and nothing else. A faultless communication admits of only one interpretation. If tryout produces only the expected response, the instruction is considered faultless and is retained (although some pruning of unnecessary redundancy may still be needed). If tryout produces unexpected responses, the instruction is faulted and needs revision (different selection or sequencing of examples or of the accompanying explanation).

Communications are judged faultless if they meet the following requirements:

1. They present a set of examples that are "the same" with respect to one and only one distinguishing quality–the quality that is to serve as the basis for generalization.
2. They provide two signals—one to identify every example that possesses the quality to be generalized ("square") and a second to identify every example that does not have this quality ("not square").
3. They demonstrate a range of variation among positive examples that will encourage learners to induce a rule that is appropriate for clas-

sifying new examples on the basis of "sameness" (the defining attributes).

4. They show the limits of permissible variation by presenting negative examples.
5. They provide a test of generalization that involves new examples that fall within the range of variation within defining attributes demonstrated earlier.

Sameness is demonstrated through positive examples, selected and juxtaposed not merely to show the most typical or easily observed examples of the concept, but to show the entire range of examples to which the concept applies. (Or if this would be too much for the learner to handle, to show that portion of the range that the instructor expects the learner to be able to master).

Juxtaposition rules

The basic juxtaposition rules are as follows: To show sameness, juxtapose examples that are greatly different and treat each example in the same way; to show difference, juxtapose examples that are only minimally different and treat them differently. In teaching the concept of "truck," for example, the instructor would include pictures of a variety of trucks such as panel trucks, tankers, or moving vans in order to be sure that the examples do not inadvertently stipulate that the term "truck" applies only to a particular type of truck. Furthermore, to help clarify the limits of the concept, negative examples would concentrate on objects that are just minimally different from trucks, like cars, trains, or pushcarts, rather than objects that are drastically different, like apples or roses.

Including the full range of variation among the positive examples allows the learner to *interpolate*—to recognize that the concept applies to all examples that fall in between these extremes. Also, concentrating the negative examples on objects that are just minimally different from the concept to be generalized allows the learner to *extrapolate*—to recognize that the concept does not apply to objects that are even more different than these negative examples are.

Different concepts call for different approaches to instruction. Object concepts (nouns) are usually taught best by beginning with positive examples. However, noncomparative single-dimension concepts (between, over, curved, running, pointed) are usually taught most efficiently by beginning with negative examples and then showing positive examples. Both approaches work equally well for certain types of concepts, and sometimes certain subtypes do not follow the rules that hold for other subtypes. The authors believe that the most effective way to teach any particular concept must ultimately be determined empirically through systematic tryout and revision based on formative evaluation data.

Object Concepts (Nouns). In teaching the word "vehicle" (a noun standing for a class of objects), for example, Engelmann and Carnine recommend the following sequence (using pictures to illustrate the examples):

Example	*Teacher Wording*
1. Rowboat	This is a vehicle.
2. Train	This is a vehicle.
3. Car	This is a vehicle.
4. Truck	This is a vehicle.
5. Swing set	This is not a vehicle.
6. Power lawn mower	This is not a vehicle.
7. Tractor	Is this a vehicle?
8. Rowboat with motor	Is this a vehicle?
9. Electric drill	Is this a vehicle?
10. Treadmill	Is this a vehicle?
11. Car	Is this a vehicle?

The first four examples establish that a vehicle is something that one gets into for the purposes of transportation. The diversity of positive examples illustrates that this includes transportation on water as well as on land, and includes muscle powered as well as motor powered means of transportation. The two negative examples are selected to rule out likely misinterpretations. The swing set rules out the notion that sitting and moving is sufficient for something to be called a vehicle, and the lawn mower rules out the possibility that moving and being motor powered makes something a vehicle. These negative examples were selected to be minimally different from the positive examples. Presumably, learners will extrapolate from these examples in order to conclude that other things that are even less like vehicles (such as the electric drill and the treadmill in the test segment) are not vehicles, either. Note also that the test segment contains positive examples not encountered previously (tractor, rowboat with motor). These examples fall within the range of extremes already illustrated in the first four positive examples. By interpolating the information given in those first examples, learners should be able to realize that the later positive examples are also vehicles.

If the presentation had been confined to positive examples, learners might have overgeneralized the concept of vehicles to include anything that moves or anything that accommodates a person in a sitting position. By showing negative examples that include these features but still are not vehicles, the sequence illustrates that these features by themselves are not sufficient to define a vehicle. The two negative examples included in the teaching sequence are especially well chosen because they each have not one but two features that might be confused in identifying vehicles (the power mower has both a motor and movement; the swing has both movement and the capacity to accommodate a person in a sitting position). The same information could have been conveyed using other examples, of course, but less efficiently (more examples would have been needed). One must be careful not to include questionable examples among the "near misses," however. Thus, one probably should not use pictures of a person on roller skates or on a pogo stick, because at least some definitions of vehicle would include these as positive examples. This illustrates the point made earlier that most concepts, especially those reflecting natural categories encountered in real world experience, are fuzzy sets based on family resemblances rather than firmly bounded sets identified by clear presence of defining attributes.

Comparative Concepts. In contrast to the positive-examples-first sequence used in teaching nouns, Engelmann and Carnine suggest that instruction in comparative single-dimension concepts should begin with negative examples. The sequence below would be used for teaching the concept "getting heavier." The student's hand would be placed palm up on a table or flat surface, and the teacher would exert downward pressure against the student's palm to create the sensation of the finger getting heavier or not heavier (the hand would be placed on a surface rather than held out in the air so that it could not move down and perhaps stimulate the misrule that "getting heavier" means moving further down). In the following example, the numbers indicate the degree of pressure exerted, with 1 representing the least pressure and 10 representing the most pressure:

Example	*Teacher Wording*
Starting point: Pressure 3	Feel this
1. Pressure 2	It didn't get heavier.
2. Pressure 2	It didn't get heavier.
3. Pressure 3	It got heavier.
4. Pressure 7	It got heaiver
5. Pressure 9	Did it get heavier?
6. Pressure 9	Did it get heavier?
7. Pressure 5	Did it get heavier?
8. Pressure 6	Did it get heavier?
9. Pressure 3	Did it get heavier?
10. Pressure 4	Did it get heavier?
11. Pressure 2	Did it get heavier?
12. Pressure 5	Did it get heavier?
13. Pressure 10	Did it get heavier?

Since "getting heavier" is a comparative concept along a dimension (in this case, the dimension of pressure on the palm), the sequence begins with a starting point that establishes the dimension (the teacher exerts pressure and says, "Feel this"). Then come two negative examples that are minimally different from the concept to be taught. One involves a slight decrease in pressure, and the other involves no change at all. The learner is now set up to attend to the "pressure on the palm" dimension and to anticipate a change that does involve "getting heavier." Then come two positive examples, one showing a small change and the other showing a large change. The examples are chosen to illustrate that any increase in pressure, and not an identical increase each time or a progressively greater increase each time, is "getting heavier." This sequence should have established the concept: Examples 5 through 13 are test items to insure that it did. Note that these examples include another "no change" item as well as a variety of positive and negative changes, including some that the learner has not seen yet. Note also that the sequence as a whole and certain examples in particular are designed to focus the learner on change from one state to the next (getting heavier), rather than on a particular state (lightness or heaviness). At Example 6, for example, the teacher exerts heavy pressure on the student's palm, but nevertheless this is not an example of "getting heavier" because it represents no change from Example 5.

Transformation Sequences. The previous examples involving juxtaposition of positive and negative instances are used when teaching simple concepts and requiring learners to recognize examples of those concepts and discriminate them from nonexamples. Transformation sequences are more complicated because instead of simply teaching learners to apply a single response (the term for the concept) to a range of examples, we teach learners to produce different responses to different examples. Transformation sequences have no negative examples; instead, learners produce different responses to different positive examples. Much of what is learned in school, especially the manipulation of symbols, involves transformation sequences.

Consider teaching students to recognize and be able to state the subject of a sentence. Engelmann and Carnine suggest beginning with typical examples that differ in only minor ways (Fast runners went to the park; A runner went to the park; Five runners went to the park; That runner sat in the park). Then, introducing examples that illustrate the range of the concepts to be taught while minimizing potential confusion due to variation on other factors (Henry's dog ran in the park; Those pigeons flew over the park; He wanted to go to the park). Finally, introducing examples that include variation in both the concept to be taught (the subject of the sentence) and other elements (A dog and five men sat on the hill; The yellow pencil and the white pencil are on the desk; Phone books are very useful).

Although recognizing the advantages of presenting examples in an easy-to-hard sequence, Engelmann and Carnine argue the need for a variety of examples planned to minimize undesirable stipulations by learners. For example, if given nothing but examples in which the subject of the sentence consisted of a noun modified by an adjective (fast runners, a runner, five runners, etc.), students might infer that all sentence subjects took this form, and might be confused by other forms (pronouns, unmodified nouns, compound subjects, etc).

In addition to providing a great deal more information about the concepts discussed briefly here, Engelmann and Carnine (1982) discuss instructional strategies (including example selection and juxtaposition) for more complex concepts and for cognitive operations and behavioral skills. Their book is especially useful for those interested in designing instruction for the elementary grades.

Conclusion

Systematically designed instruction is likely to be more effective than more haphazardly designed instruction, and sources on instructional design are helpful in this regard. However, so far there has been more theory development than research in this area, and there are exceptions to even seemingly obvious principles (sometimes it is more efficient to start with the most typical or familar concepts in a hierarchy rather than with the simplest ones; in order to avoid undesirable stipulations, it appears important to introduce a broad range of positive examples early in a sequence, rather than proceeding systematically from easy to hard examples or from regular to atypical examples). The principles described in this chapter will be helpful, but ultimately there is no substitute for systematic tryouts followed by revision based on formative and summative evaluation data.

Assessing curricula

In assessing curricula being considered for potential adoption, be sure to assess the degree to which the developers have taken the trouble to conduct such evaluation and revision before publishing. Are claims based on substantial field testing with impressive results, or merely on unsupported assertions and testimonials? Is the content divided and sequenced in appropriate ways? Are the clarity of exposition and the selection and juxtaposition of examples for particular lessons effective in creating what Engelmann and Carnine call faultless communication? Curricula that fail to meet these and other criteria implied in this chapter probably should be avoided, and even curricula that do measure up will probably need to be supplemented or adapted in response to local needs.

SUMMARY

Instructional design is the art (and applied science) of creating efficient methods for attaining educational objectives. Gagné and Briggs recommend a systems approach containing system level stages, course level stages, and lesson level stages. The initial system level stages involve analyzing needs, goals, and priorities and then considering resources, constraints, and potential delivery systems in order to develop a curriculum scope and sequence statement that specifies the objectives to be taught, sequences them in a sensible order, and identifies the delivery system to be used for instruction.

Course level stages involve dividing the content into courses organized around target objectives and their respective enabling objectives and sequenced logically. To accomplish this, instructional developers would perform information processing analyses (perhaps using flow charts to depict the results visually), task classifications (with attention to the particular conditions of learning associated with each type of task), and learning task analyses (including identification of relevant learning hierarchies for instruction in intellectual skills).

Lesson level stages involve identification of the specific instructional objectives for each lesson and planning of the particular instructional events (including attention to media and materials and to evaluation) to be used to accomplish these objectives. It is here that instructional designers bring to bear their creativity,

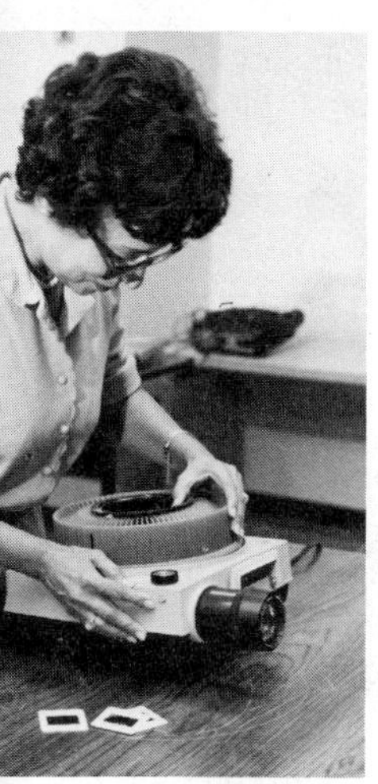

Visual aids should be integrated into the overall teaching strategy.

knowledge of the subject matter, and knowledge of the students in deciding what information to present, what examples or demonstrations to use, what media or materials to use, and what kinds of practice and application activities will be needed.

The final system level stages in the Gagné and Briggs approach involve evaluating, field testing, and diffusing information about the developed learning system.

Gropper presents a behavioral approach to instructional design that contains useful ideas on how to structure practice activities in an easy-to-difficult sequence by manipulating the treatment tools of degree of cuing provided, size of unit of behavior practiced, mode of stimulus and response required, variety built into the tasks, content built into the tasks, and frequency of practice. Case and Bereiter explain how Gagné's approach to instructional design was an advance over Skinner's because it shifted emphasis from reinforcement to the nature of the skills to be taught, recognized different kinds of learning, and offered learning hierarchies and task analysis as methods for sequencing the instruction. They also argue, however, that Gagné's approach needs to be modified to take into account limitations on learners' working memories and to teach steps in the order in which they tend to be learned naturally rather than necessarily in the subordinate-to-superordinate order suggested by logical analysis.

Collins and Stevens present instructional design ideas for guided discovery and inquiry approaches. Here, the emphasis is on selecting and sequencing examples so as to create dissonance or curiosity, to stimulate students to make predictions and consider alternative possibilities, and eventually to arrive at the target objective through a process of exploration and discovery.

The systems approach to instructional design is a useful one, but it is limited by the fact that the best ways to teach something are rarely obvious and must be established through experimentation. Some of these complexities are illustrated in a review of research on concept learning and teaching in the second part of the chapter. Early work on concept learning viewed it as a matter of logical deduction from clear cut positive and negative instances. However, Rosch and others have shown that the natural categories involved in most of the concept learning that occurs through natural experience are not so clear cut; instead, they are fuzzy sets based on family resemblances. Frequently, such learning begins with basic level categories (chair) before it proceeds to either superordinate level categories (furniture) or subordinate level categories (easy chair).

Most advice concerning concept teaching stresses beginning with clear definitions of the concept that state its defining attributes, proceeding to display positive examples, and then moving to negative examples and discrimination exercises. Merrill and Tennyson, for example, discuss presenting rational sets of examples selected to call students' attention to the defining attributes and minimize errors due to overgeneralization, undergeneralization, or misconception. They recommend sequencing examples from easy to difficult and making sure that the positive examples include the full range of variation that occurs in the defining attributes and that the negative examples include "near misses."

Engelmann and Carnine argue the importance of designing instruction to achieve faultless communication and note that this is not always achieved by beginning with positive examples or by proceeding in an easy-to-difficult sequence. Unlike object concepts, comparative concepts are usually taught more efficiently by beginning with negative examples. Also, whatever the type of concept being taught, the instructional designer needs to select and juxtapose examples in ways that will not only communicate the range of variation and limits of application of the concept, but also prevent learners from developing inappropriate stipulations—beliefs that the concept applies only to a particular subset of the actual range of application.

QUESTIONS AND PROBLEMS

1. Compare the scope and sequence statements for two or more curricula designed to teach the same subject matter at the same grade level. You will probably notice that each curriculum includes objectives not included in the other and the objectives shared in common are not always taught in the same order. Study these differences. Are they merely matters of taste, or is one curriculum notably better than the other in its selection or sequencing of objectives?
2. Study a curriculum developed for the grade level and subject matter you intend to teach. Would you use it as is, or can you see places where you would want to omit certain objectives and associated activities or supplement by bringing in or developing additional ones? If possible, compare notes with experienced teachers who have used this curriculum.
3. Given your choice, would you prefer to select objectives and develop curriculum materials and activities yourself or have this done for you by policy makers and commercial publishers? If the former, how will you respond to administrative and parental pressures to emphasize certain objectives, and how will you evaluate and perfect the materials and activities you develop? If the latter, what will you do if you find that the adopted curriculum package is not well suited to the needs of your students, or if some students appear to need remedial work that the adopted curriculum package does not provide?
4. Select an objective commonly taught in the grade level and subject matter you intend to teach. Perform an information processing analysis to identify the sequence of steps leading to the target performance and construct a flow chart to depict this information visually. What does this information tell you about where instruction should begin and about what steps should be included and in what order?
5. The list of instructional events shown in Table 11.2 was composed with didactic instruction in mind. How might this list be changed for lessons designed to achieve higher-level cognitive objectives? For lessons that relied on inquiry procedures or discovery learning?
6. Given that special materials or media may bring important added dimensions to teaching but also may be impractical for various reasons, what special materials and media do you foresee using in your own teaching? What advantages do these bring that make them worth the trouble?
7. For a given objective that you are likely to teach, describe how an easy-to-difficult sequence can be designed into a series of practice tasks by manipulating the treatment tools described by Gropper.
8. Gagné advocates using learning hierarchies and other tools for sequencing tasks on a logical basis, whereas Case and Bereiter advocate sequencing tasks according to the order in which their components are typically developed through ordinary experience. What kinds of student and task do Gagné's ideas fit best, and what kinds of student and task do Case and Bereiter's ideas fit best? Why?
9. Select two concepts from the subject matter you are likely to teach and design instruction for each of these concepts that includes a clear definition of the concept that specifies its defining attributes and a rational set of examples that

illustrates both the range and the limits of application of the concept. Check your examples to make sure that you have not inadvertently confined your positive examples to a subset that would cause the learners to stipulate inappropriately. Also, be sure that your positive examples are not all confounded with an irrelevant attribute, and thus likely to cause learners to believe that this irrelevant attribute is a defining attribute.

10. Engelmann and Carnine have found that object concepts are generally taught most efficiently by beginning with positive examples, but comparative concepts are generally taught most easily by beginning with negative examples. Why should this be? Can you formulate a more general rule about when to begin with positive examples and when to begin with negative examples? Compare notes with your friends.

CASE STUDIES

Tinkering. Ed Anderson is not very pleased with the new science curriculum adopted by his school district. The general objectives make sense—he is pleased with what is taught and with the order in which the lessons are sequenced. However, he has found that many of the lessons just don't work very well. Sometimes the materials or methods are inadequate or overly cumbersome, and sometimes the suggested activities and exercises seem pointless. Therefore, he decides to stick with the objectives but to find or develop better ways to accomplish them in the case of about half of the lessons.

Should teachers make wholesale changes like this? Why or why not? What steps could Ed take to ensure that the new media, materials, and activities that he introduces actually succeed in meeting the objectives and are improvements over the ones that came with the curriculum?

Better Sequencing and Examples? Ed Sikes is generally pleased with his course in educational psychology, but he is aware of certain repeated failures. Each time he teaches the course, it seems that many students confuse Piaget's terms assimilation and accommodation, confuse negative reinforcement with punishment, confuse cognitive level with difficulty level, and have trouble describing the differences in mental functioning to be expected between a bright six-year-old and a dull fourteen-year-old.

What may be causing these problems, and what might Dr. Sikes do to eliminate them? In particular, what changes might he make in the sequencing of his instruction and in the number and kinds of examples he uses to illustrate concepts?

Chapter 12

Approaches to Classroom Instruction

CHAPTER OUTLINE

OBJECTIVES

When you have mastered the material in this chapter you will be able to

1. Define process-outcome research and describe the relationships with achievement gain that such research has established for the following five sets of variables: Opportunity to learn/content covered, role definition/expectations/time allocation, classroom management/student engaged time, consistent success/academic learning time, and active teaching
2. Identify teacher behaviors known to be associated with positive student attitudes
3. Define ethnographic methods of classroom research and identify the classroom process variables found associated with achievement gain in the ethnographic study reported by Tikunoff, Berliner, and Rist (1975)
4. Describe the models of active teaching used in experiments by Good and Grouws (1979) and by Anderson, Evertson, and Brophy (1979)
5. Describe the uses and limits of teacher-led, group-based instruction
6. Explain and give examples of the concept of functionally equivalent paths to the same levels of achievement
7. Describe how effective active instruction differs between the early grades and the upper grades and between low SES and high SES settings

8. Describe how effective active teaching would be adapted to accommodate differences in students' individual characteristics (aptitude, developmental stage, reading level, personality, work mode preference, and general work habits)
9. Identify the similarities and differences in the guidelines suggested by Good and Power (1976) for adapting effective active instruction to the needs of five types of student (successful, social, dependent, alienated, and phantom students)

Teachers have to process a great deal of information in order to make intelligent decisions about how to instruct their students. Even in the abstract, instruction is a complex topic. We noted in Chapter 6 that different types of learning (cognitive strategies, intellectual skills, information, motor skills, attitudes) require different types of instruction, and in Chapters 7 through 9 we reviewed three major lines of theory and research on learning (behaviorist, cognitive structuralist, and information processing) and reviewed a variety of approaches to instruction that each has spawned.

Models of teaching

Other approaches could have been presented in addition to these. For example, Joyce and Weil (1980) describe 23 different models of teaching, classified into four types (information processing, social interaction, focus on the individual person, and behavior modification). Information processing models concentrate on presenting material in ways that learners can process and retain most easily, and on trying to foster information processing skills in the learners. Social interaction models stress the group-living aspects of schooling and arrange instruction so that students interact with and learn from one another as well as the teacher. These approaches emphasize fostering good group relations in addition to mastery of the formal curriculum. Personal models apply principles of humanistic psychology in an attempt to promote both intellectual and emotional development in individuals (self-actualization, mental health, creativity). Finally, behavior modification models stress the sequencing of activities to promote efficient learning and the shaping and control of behavior through reinforcement.

Each of these models has something worthwhile to offer, and each stresses certain things at the expense of others. Even if we ignore personal and social development for the moment and confine our attention to instruction in the formal academic curriculum, it is obvious that teachers face choices about what to teach and how to teach it, and that their decisions will affect what their students learn. Furthermore, the instructional decisions facing teachers are much more complex than those facing curriculum designers and textbook writers. Teachers do not have the luxury of being able to take the time to revise and perfect instruction intended for individual learners. Instead, they must find ways to both manage and instruct classes of 20 to 40 students, while working almost continuously in public and responding to the multidimensionality, simultaneity, immediacy, unpredictability, and other pressures of classrooms as described in Chapter 1. Consequently, teachers are seldom able to sustain instruction that is ideal according to some theoretical model or combination of models. Instead, they must make do with compromises that enable them to accomplish the most progress possible with the most students possible under the prevailing constraints.

Theories of learning and models of teaching provide useful input to teachers facing these complexities. So does research on teaching, especially research that establishes linkages between classroom processes (teacher behaviors, teacher-student interaction) and the products or outcomes of instruction (gains in achievement, changes in students' attitudes or in their self concepts as learners). Research designed to develop information about these linkages is known as process-outcome (or process-product) research.

Until about 1970, not much process-outcome research was available, and what there was had produced confusing and often contradictory findings. Great strides have been made in this area since then, however, especially in linking teacher behavior to student achievement.

Process-Outcome Research

In a typical process-outcome study, each teacher in the sample is observed for several hours (ranging from three or four hours to 20 hours or more, depending on the study) under specified conditions (subject matter, time of day, size of group being taught) by observers trained to use systematic data collection methods. Some of these are high inference methods that require the observer to exercise judgment (rate the clarity of the teacher's explanations on a five-point scale: 1 = very low, 2 = low, 3 = medium, 4 = high, 5 = very high). Others are low inference checklists or category systems used to record the presence/absence or frequency of occurrence of prespecified events (each time the teacher asks a question, the observer notes whether the student answered it correctly, and if so, whether the teacher praised the student's answer). Once observations are completed, the data for each teacher are aggregated and used to develop averages or other scores representing the teacher's behavior (average clarity rating; average number of student answers praised per hour; percentage of correct student answers that were praised). These process measures are then correlated with measures, typically standardized tests, of student achievement, adjusted for class differences in achievement at entry, or measures of affective outcomes.

Teacher Behavior and Student Achievement

Several large scale field studies have been conducted using these methods in the last 15 to 20 years (Brophy & Evertson, 1976; Evertson et al., 1980; Fisher et al., 1980; Flanders, 1970; Good & Grouws, 1977; McDonald, 1977; Soar & Soar, 1979; Stallings, 1975; Stallings et al., 1977, 1978; Tikunoff, Berliner, & Rist, 1975). These large-scale studies, along with several smaller ones by other investigators, have established a small but growing and well-replicated body of knowledge about the relationships between teacher behavior and student achievement. Furthermore, some of these correlational relationships have been established as causal through experimental studies (Anderson, Evertson, & Brophy, 1979; Clark et al., 1979; Good & Grouws, 1979; Good, Grouws, & Ebmeier, 1983; Stallings, 1980).

Brophy and Good (1985) have recently published a comprehensive review of this body of research (for briefer reviews see Brophy, 1979; Denham & Lieberman, 1980; Good, 1979; Rosenshine & Berliner, 1978; or Rosenshine & Stevens, 1984). These reviews agree in identifying certain classroom events and teacher behaviors as consistent correlates of student achievement gain. The evidence is strongest and most consistent for the following five sets of variables.

Opportunity to learn/content covered. Amount learned is related to opportunity to learn, whether this is measured in terms of the number of pages of curriculum covered (Good, Grouws, & Beckerman, 1978; Borg, 1979) or the percentage of test items that were taught through lecture or recitation activities in class (Arehart, 1979; Armento, 1977; Cooley & Leinhardt, 1980; Dunkin & Doenau, 1980; Nuthall & Church, 1973; Smith, 1979). Student opportunity to learn is determined in part by the length of the school day and the school year, and in part by the following four variables.

Role definition/expectations/time allocation. Achievement is maximized when teachers define instructing students in the formal academic curriculum as basic to their roles as teachers, expect their students to master the curriculum, and allocate most of the available time to activities designed to promote such mastery (Brophy & Evertson, 1976; Fisher et al., 1980; Stallings, 1975). Observers describe such teachers as business-like and task oriented, and report that most of the available classroom time is allocated to activities with academic objectives rather than to activities with other types of objectives (personal adjustment, group dynamics) or no clear objectives at all ("free time," student choice of games or pastimes).

Classroom management/student engaged time. Not all time allocated to academic activities is actually spent engaged in these activities. Students' engagement rates depend on the teacher's ability to organize and manage the classroom as an efficient learning environment where academic activities run smoothly, transitions are brief and orderly, and little time is spent getting organized or dealing with inattention or resistance. High-task engagement rates attained through such successful classroom management are among the most frequent and powerful correlates of student achievement (Brophy & Evertson, 1976; Coker, Medley, & Soar, 1980; Fisher et al., 1980; Good & Grouws, 1977; Soar & Soar, 1979; Stallings, 1975; Stallings et al., 1977, 1978). The classroom management strategies that produce these high rates of student engaged time are discussed in Chapter 20.

Consistent success/academic learning time. To learn efficiently, students must be engaged in activities that are appropriate in difficulty level and otherwise suited to their current achievement levels and needs. Thus, it is important not only to maximize content covered by pacing students briskly through the curriculum, but also to see that they make continuous progress all along the way, moving through small steps with high or at least moderate rates of success and minimal confusion or frustration (Brophy & Evertson, 1976; Fisher et al., 1980). High success rates of 90 to 100 percent are especially desirable when students must work independently for extended periods of time without teacher supervision or the opportunity to get help immediately if they should become confused. Lower (although still relatively high) success rates are acceptable and sometimes desirable when the teacher is present to provide guidance and immediate corrective feedback. In general, however, to the extent that teachers present students with inappropriate assignments, they tend to err on the side of presenting overly difficult work for which the students are not prepared rather than overly repetitive or pointless busywork (Jorgenson, 1977; Rosenshine, 1980).

To point up the importance of high rates of success, the authors of Phase III–B of the Beginning Teacher Evaluation Study (Fisher et al., 1980) coined the term academic learning time (ALT), which they define as the time that students spend engaged in academic tasks that they can perform with high rates of success. These authors would characterize students as enjoying high levels of success on a task when they understand what they are supposed to do and are able to do it correctly without errors, except for occasional errors due to carelessness or miscalculation. In their study, ALT consistently showed significant positive correlations with achievement.

Academic learning time

Three additional points should be made about success rates. First, as Bennett et al., (1981) have pointed out, we need to consider not only the frequency of errors but their timing and quality. Early in a unit, when new learning is taking place, relatively frequent errors may be expected. Later, however, when mastery levels are supposed to have been achieved, errors should be minimal. Also, some errors occur because students have the right general idea but make a minor miscalculation, or because they involve sound logic that is based on assumptions that are plausible but happen to be faulty. Such "high quality" errors are understandable and may even generate useful "teachable moments," but errors suggesting inattention, hopeless confusion, or alienation from the content are undesirable.

Error frequency timing, and quality

Second, in speaking of the desirability of high rates of success, we do not mean to imply that such success is always attained quickly or easily. The high success rates described are construed to result from effort and thought, not mere "automatic" application of already overlearned algorithms.

High success rates

Third, bear in mind that success rates on a particular task will depend not only on the inherent difficulty level of the task itself but also on the degree to which the teacher has effectively prepared the students for the task by explaining key concepts, reviewing the directions, and working through examples. In other words, a task that might be too difficult if presented with little or no preparation might be just right if introduced with sufficient structure and implemented with sufficient provision for guidance and feedback to the students. Thus, nothing in these findings contradicts Vygotsky's notion (Vygotsky, 1978; Rogoff & Wertsch, 1984) that instruction should focus on the students' zone of proximal development (i.e., should focus on what the student is able to learn with help rather than on what the student already is able to do independently). The research does, however, caution against creating undue frustration or confusion by trying to move too far too fast, and against placing undue strain on students' working memories by trying to get them to transfer or apply knowledge or skills that they have not yet mastered thoroughly.

Student preparation for task

Active teaching. Students achieve more in classes where they spend most of their time being taught or supervised by their teachers than when working on their own or not working at all (Arehart, 1979; Brophy & Evertson,

Student achievement is increased when the teacher actively supervises work through lecture and demonstration.

1976; Good & Grouws, 1977; Stallings, 1975; Stallings et al., 1977, 1978). Such classes include frequent lessons (whole class or small group, depending on grade level and subject matter) in which the teacher presents information and develops concepts through lecture and demonstration, elaborates this information in the feedback given following responses to recitation or discussion questions, prepares the students for follow-up assignments by giving instructions and going through practice examples, monitors progress on those assignments after releasing the students to work on them independently, and follows up with appropriate feedback and reteaching when necessary. The teachers in such classes carry the content to the students personally rather than leaving it to the curriculum materials to do so, although they usually convey information in brief presentations followed by recitation or application opportunities. There is a great deal of teacher talk in these classes, but most of it is academic rather than procedural or managerial, and much of it involves asking questions and giving feedback rather than extended lecturing.

Research findings

Taken together, the findings on these five variables indicate that teachers who systematically pursue academic objectives elicit higher achievement from their students than teachers who fail to pursue any clear objectives at all, who try to pursue academic objectives but are unable to do so for lack of effective classroom management skills, or who concentrate on various affective objectives more than on teaching the academic curriculum. The data also indicate that teachers who use traditional group-based instructional methods and carry the content to their students personally through active instruction get better results than teachers who rely on individualized learning modules and other materials-based approaches. Although the latter approaches have been shown to work under some circumstances, they typically do not work well in the ordinary classroom where one teacher must work with 20 to 40 students. As noted in Chapter 7, most students are not prepared to learn efficiently through independent reading and direction following—they need explanation, supervision, guidance, and feedback from the teacher. Thus, despite its well-known limitations, the traditional method of teacher-led group instruction may be the optimal solution in the typical classroom to the challenge of maximizing the achievement of the class as a whole while working within the constraints imposed (in particular, the high student-teacher ratio).

Teacher Behavior and Student Affect

A few studies have linked classroom processes to affective outcomes in addition to achievement outcomes (Evertson et al., 1980; Flanders, 1970; Stallings, 1975). These studies indicate that student attitudes are linked most closely to measures of teacher warmth and student orientation—praise, use of student ideas, willingness to listen to students and respect their contributions, and socializing with students in addition to instructing them. These teacher behaviors are mostly just different from rather than either similar to or contradictory to the teacher behaviors associated with achievement. Thus, the two sets of behaviors are compatible to an extent, but beyond some point, further efforts devoted toward pursuit of one set of objectives will come at the expense of opportunities to pursue other objectives. Thus, even ideal teaching will involve trade-offs rather than optimizing in an absolute sense (Clark, 1982; Evertson, 1979; Peterson, 1979; Schofield, 1981).

Teacher warmth

Soar and Soar (1979) have helped to clarify the relationships between the cognitive aspects and the affective aspects of teacher-student interaction by showing that there is a disordinal relationship between emotional climate indicators and achievement gain indicators. That is, negative emotional climate indicators (teacher criticism of students, negative affect displayed by teacher or pupils, pupil resistance to the teacher) usually show significant negative correlations with achievement, whereas positive emotional climate indicators (teacher praise of students, positive affect displayed by teacher or pupils) usually do *not* show significant positive correlations. Thus, it appears that efficient learning in the classroom does not require a notably warm emotional climate. It is true that negative climates are disfunctional, but neutral or mildly warm climates appear to be at least as supportive of achievement as more clearly warm climates. In short, student achievement gain depends primarily on the amount and quality of the instruction received from the teacher. Teacher warmth will make a good classroom climate and pupils will like the teacher; but by itself this climate will not produce achievement.

Relationship between emotional climate indicators and achievement gain indicators

Some Examples from Research

To provide a more concrete picture of the kind of instruction that is associated with high achievement gain, we will provide examples from three lines of research.

Tikunoff, Berliner and Rist (1975) studied second- and fifth-grade classrooms during reading and mathematics instruction. The 40 teachers selected for observation were drawn from a larger sample of 200 teachers who had previously been observed teaching specially prepared two-week units of instruction. The 40 teachers selected for further observation included the ten at each grade who had elicited the largest adjusted achievement gains from their students, and the ten at each grade who had elicited the smallest gains.

For the second study, these 40 teachers were visited during reading and mathematics instruction lessons by observers trained in the ethnographic methods of data collection developed by anthropologists. That is, instead of using rating scales or coding systems designed to draw attention to particular events and develop data on previously specified dimensions, these ethnographers took detailed field notes describing and attempting to make sense of events as they unfolded. Later, transcripts of these field notes were read to identify dimensions on which they could be rated, and ratings were eventually done on 61 such dimensions. For 21 of these dimensions (shown in Table 12.1), significant differences were observed between the more effective and less effective classes at both grade levels and in both subject matter areas.

Effective teaching and structure

Note that the differences summarized in Table 12.1 do not support simple statements about effective and ineffective teaching. Effective teachers were found to encourage their students to work on their own, but they also monitored the students' work and provided a great deal of structure. Similarly, the more effective teachers showed more spontaneity in their teaching, even though their lessons were quite structured; for instance they had frequent reviews and clear objectives. To allow more focused examination of the behaviors found generally effective in their study, Tikunoff, Berliner, and Rist rearranged the list into the following clusters:

Classroom Climate

conviviality	(more)
engagement	(more)
defiance	(less)
cooperation	(more)
promoting self-sufficiency	(more)
adult involvement	(more)

Teacher Instructional Moves

attending	(more)
monitoring learning	(more)
structuring	(more)
spontaneity	(more)
pacing	(sensitive to individual differences in students)
abruptness	(less)
filling time	(less)
illogical statements	(less)

Table 12.1 Behaviors That Separated More and Less Effective Mathematics and Reading Teachers at Both Second and Fifth Grade

Teacher (T) or Student (S)	More (+) or Less (−) Frequently a Descriptor of Effectiveness	Behavioral Variable and Definition
T	−	*abruptness:* unanticipated switching by teacher, e.g., from instruction to classroom management, to behavior management, to instruction, to behavior management.
T	+	*accepting:* teacher reacts constructively (overt, verbal, nonverbal) to students' feelings and attitudes.
T	+	*adult involvement:* adults other than the teacher are allowed to instruct.
T	+	*attending:* teacher listens actively to what a student is saying, reading, reciting.
T	−	*belittling:* teacher berates child in front of others.
T	+	*consistency of message* (control): teacher gives a direction or a threat and follows through with it.
T & S	+	*conviviality:* warmth, familylike quality to classroom interaction; good feelings between teacher-students, students-students.
S	+	*cooperation:* students cooperate with other students, teacher; willingness on part of students to help each other.
S	−	*defiance:* a student's open resistance to teacher's direction; refuses to comply.
S	+	*engagement:* students express eagerness to participate, appear actively, productively involved in learning activities.
T	−	*filling time:* teacher fills "empty" time periods with busy work.
T	−	*illogical statements:* teacher makes a statement whose consequences would be ridiculous if carried out.
T	+	*knowledge of subject:* teacher seems confident in teaching a given subject, and demonstrates a grasp of it.
T	+	*monitoring of learning:* teacher checks on student's progress regularly and adjusts instruction accordingly.
T	−	*oneness:* teacher treats whole group as "one" in order to maintain peer climate.
T	+	*optimism:* teacher expresses positive, pleasant, optimistic attitudes and feelings.
T	+	*pacing:* teacher appears to perceive learning rate of students and adjusts teaching pace accordingly.
T	+	*promoting self-sufficiency:* teacher encourages students to take responsibility for their own classwork.
T	−	*recognition seeking:* teacher calls attention to self for no apparent instructional purpose.
T	+	*spontaneity:* teacher capitalizes instructionally on unexpected incidents that arise during class time.
T	+	*structuring:* teacher prepares students for lesson by reviewing, outlining, explaining objectives, summarizing.

Source: Drawn (with slight alteration) from W. Tikunoff, D. Berliner, & R. Rist (1975). An ethnographic study of the forty classrooms of the Beginning Teacher Evaluation Study known sample. Technical Report No. 75-10-5, San Francisco: Far West Laboratory.

Teacher Behavior-Control Moves	
consistency of message	(more)
belittling	(less)
oneness	(less)
Teacher Characteristics	
accepting	(more)
optimistic	(more)
knowledge of subject	(more)
recognition seeking	(less)

The following two examples come from experimental studies done as follow-ups to correlational process-product work. In each study, teachers were trained to use instructional principles that earlier correlational work had suggested were correlated with gain in student achievement. Then, classrooms were observed to assess teacher implementation of the principles, and students were tested to assess learning outcomes. Each study found that experimental teachers implemented the recommended principles more systematically than control teachers, who used whatever methods they had been taught previously or had developed on their own, and that the experimental teachers produced significantly greater achievement gain than the control teachers.

Good and Grouws (1979) developed the instructional model shown in Table 12.2 for fourth-grade mathematics classes. The model is similar to traditional fourth-grade mathematics instruction in many ways, although it is more systematic. It includes guidelines for time allocation to insure that mathematics is taught for about 45 minutes each day, and calls for supplementing this instruction with homework assignments. Note that although the model calls for students to work primarily individually on seatwork and homework assignments, it also calls for a great deal of active instruction by the teacher. New concepts are presented in detail during the development portion of the lesson, and the teacher both makes sure that students know how to do the assignment before releasing them to work individually and reviews the assignment with them the next day. This rich schedule of instruction, opportunity to practice, and feedback, along with frequent testing, helps to insure continuous progress.

Anderson, Evertson, and Brophy (1979) developed a more lengthy set of guidelines for first-grade teachers to use during small-group reading instruction. Most of these were supported by their findings, although the data indicated that a few principles should be dropped and that others should be subdivided, elaborated, or otherwise revised. The revised set of principles (Anderson, Evertson, & Brophy, 1982) is shown in Table 12.3.

The model is similar to that of Good and Grouws in that it includes time allocation guidelines and an emphasis on active instruction by the teacher followed by opportunities to practice and receive feedback. However, there are several important differences due to subject matter and grade level. For one, first-grade reading is typically taught in small groups to better accommodate the slow pacing associated with taking turns reading aloud

Table 12.2 Summary of Key Instructional Behaviors

Daily Review (First 8 minutes except Mondays)
1. Review the concepts and skills associated with the homework
2. Collect and deal with homework assignments
3. Ask several mental computation exercises

Development (About 20 minutes)
1. Briefly focus on prerequisite skills and concepts
2. Focus on meaning and promoting student understanding by using lively explanations, demonstrations, process explanations, illustrations, and so on.
3. Assess student comprehension by
   a. Using process/product questions (active interaction)
   b. Using controlled practice
4. Repeat and elaborate on the meaning portion as necessary

Seatwork (About 15 minutes)
1. Provide uninterrupted successful practice
2. Momentum—keep the ball rolling—get everyone involved, then sustain involvement
3. Alerting—let students know their work will be checked at the end of the period
4. Accountability—check the students' work

Homework Assignment
1. Assign on a regular basis at the end of each math class except Fridays
2. Should involve about 15 minutes of work to be done at home
3. Should include one or two review problems

Special Reviews
1. Weekly Review/Maintenance
   a. Conduct during the first 20 minutes each Monday
   b. Focus on skills and concepts covered during the previous week
2. Monthly Review/Maintenance
   a. Conduct every fourth Monday
   b. Focus on skills and concepts covered since last monthly review

Source: Good, T., Grouws, D., and Ebermeier, H., *Active Mathematics Teaching.* Copyright © 1983 Longman Inc.

from the readers, so the principles were developed with this instructional format in mind. Second, because first-graders are still learning the student role and teachers must be concerned about maintaining their attention and controlling the timing and nature of their contributions to the lesson, the principles shown in Table 12.3 include reference to the organization and management of the group, not just to instruction in the content. Third, the principles focus on the teacher's interactions with individual students, even though the instruction takes place in a group context, because much of first-grade reading group instruction involves a series of interactions with individual students more than instruction to the group as such. In contrast, mathematics instruction to the whole class at the fourth-grade level is directed mostly at the group, and dealings with individuals are mostly minor variations on the main themes established in statements to the class as a whole.

Table 12.3 Guidelines for First-Grade Teachers

General Principles
1. Reading groups should be organized for efficient, sustained focus on the content.
2. All students should be not merely attentive but actively involved in the lesson.
3. The difficulty level of questions and tasks should be easy enough to allow the lesson to move along at a brisk pace and the students to experience consistent success.
4. Students should receive frequent opportunities to read and respond to questions and should get clear feedback about the correctness of their performance.
5. Skills should be mastered to overlearning, with new ones gradually phased in while old ones are being mastered.
6. Although instruction takes place in the group setting, monitor each individual and provide whatever instruction, feedback, or opportunities to practice that he or she requires.

Specific Principles
Programming for Continuous Progress
1. *Time.* Across the year, reading groups should average 25–30 minutes each. The length will depend on student attention level, which varies with time of year, student ability level, and the skills being taught.
2. *Academic focus.* Successful reading instruction includes not only organization and management of the reading group itself (discussed below), but also effective management of the students who are working independently. Provide these students with: appropriate assignments; rules and routines to follow when they need help or information (to minimize their needs to interrupt you as you work with your reading group); and activity options available when they finish their work (so they have something else to do).
3. *Pace.* Both progress through the curriculum and pacing within specific activities should be brisk, producing continuous progress achieved with relative ease (small steps, high success rate).
4. *Error rate.* Expect to get correct answers to about 80 percent of your questions in reading groups. More errors can be expected when students are working on new skills (perhaps 20–30 percent). Continue with practice and review until smooth, rapid, correct performance is achieved. Review responses should be almost completely (perhaps 95 percent) correct.
Organizing the Group
1. *Seating.* Arrange seating so that you can both work with the reading group and monitor the rest of the class at the same time.
2. *Transitions.* Teach the students to respond immediately to a signal to move into the reading group (bringing their books or other materials) and to make quick, orderly transitions between activities.
3. *Getting started.* Start lessons quickly once the students are in the group (have your materials prepared beforehand).
Introducing Lessons and Activities
1. *Overviews.* Begin with an overview to provide students with a mental set and help them anticipate what they will be learning.
2. *New words.* When presenting new words, do not merely say the word and move on. Usually, you should show the word and offer phonetic clues to help students learn to decode.

Table 12.3 (*continued*)

Specific Principles

3. *Work assignments.* Be sure that students know what to do and how to do it. Before releasing them to work on activities independently, have them demonstrate how they will accomplish these activities.

Insuring Everyone's Participation

1. *Ask questions.* In addition to having the students read, ask them questions about the words and materials. This helps keep students attentive during classmates' reading turns and allows you to call their attention to key concepts or meanings.
2. *Ordered turns.* Use a system, such as going in order around the group, to select students for reading or answering questions. This insures that all students have opportunities to participate and it simplifies group management by eliminating handwaving and other attempts by students to get you to call on them.
3. *Minimize call-outs.* In general, minimize student call-outs and emphasize that students must wait their turns and respect the turns of others. Occasionally, you may want to allow call-outs, to pick up the pace or encourage interest, especially with low-achievers or students who do not normally volunteer. If so, give clear instructions or devise a signal to indicate that you intend to allow call-outs at these times.
4. *Monitor individuals.* Be sure that everyone, but especially slow students, is checked, receives feedback, and achieves mastery. Ordinarily this will require questioning each individual student and not relying on choral responses.

Teacher Questions and Student Answers

1. *Academic focus.* Concentrate your questions on the academic content; do not overdo questions about personal experiences. Most questions should be about word recognition or sentence or story comprehension.
2. *Word attack questions.* Include word attack questions that require students to decode words or identify sounds within words.
3. *Wait for answers.* In general, wait for an answer if the student is still thinking about the question and may be able to respond. However, do not continue waiting if the student seems lost or is becoming embarrassed, or if you are losing the other students' attention.
4. *Give needed help.* If you think the student cannot respond without help but may be able to reason out the correct answer if you do help, provide help by simplifying the question, rephrasing the question, or giving clues.
5. *Give the answer when necessary.* When the student is unable to respond, give the answer or call on someone else. In general, focus the attention of the group on the answer and not on the failure to respond.
6. *Explain the answer when necessary.* If the question requires one to develop a response by applying a chain of reasoning or step-by-step problem solving, explain the steps one goes through to arrive at the answer in addition to giving the answer itself.

When the Student Responds Correctly

1. *Acknowledge correctness (unless it is obvious).* Briefly acknowledge the correctness of responses (nod positively, repeat the answer, say "right," etc.), unless it is obvious to the students that their answers are correct (such as during fast-paced drills reviewing old material).

Table 12.3 (*continued*)

Specific Principles

2. *Explain the answer when necessary.* Even after correct answers, feedback that emphasizes the methods used to get answers will often be appropriate. Onlookers may need this information to understand why the answer is correct.
3. *Follow-up questions.* Occasionally, you may want to address one or more follow-up questions to the same student. Such series of related questions can help the student to integrate relevant information. Or you may want to extend a line of questioning to its logical conclusion.

Praise and Criticism

1. *Praise in moderation.* Praise only occasionally (no more than perhaps 10 percent of correct responses). Frequent praise, especially if nonspecific, is probably less useful than more informative feedback.
2. *Specify what is praised.* When you do praise, specify what is being praised, if this is not obvious to the student and the onlookers.
3. *Correction, not criticism.* Routinely inform students whenever they respond incorrectly, but in ways that focus on the academic content and include corrective feedback. When it is necessary to criticize (typically only about 1 percent of the time when students fail to respond correctly), be specific about what is being criticized and about desired alternative behaviors.

Source: L. Anderson, C. Evertson, and J. Brophy (1982). *Principles of small-group instruction in elementary reading.* East Lansing, MI: Institute for Research on Teaching, Michigan State University (Occasional Paper No. 58), pp. 2-10.

Adapting instruction to each situation

These examples illustrate how even within the domain of basic skills instruction in the elementary grades, instruction must be adapted to the subject matter, the students, and other context factors. Classroom research continues to develop support for instructional principles of varying generality, but there appear to be no specific instructional behaviors that are ideal for all types of students and situations. Different instructional objectives (mastering well-defined knowledge or skills versus applying them to complex problem solving or creativity, for example) require different instructional methods, and progress toward other kinds of objectives (promoting the personal development of the students or the social development of the class as a whole) requires still other methods. Process-outcome research can inform teachers about the relationships between teacher behavior and student outcomes, but teachers must decide for themselves what outcomes they wish to promote and in what order of priority.

Uses of Group-Based Instruction

Teachers make a difference

The success of process-product research in recent years is gratifying for several reasons. First, such research has reaffirmed what should have been obvious all along but what some had tried to deny or minimize—the fact that teachers make a difference. Such research has shown clearly that some teachers elicit more achievement from their students than others do, and it has begun to identify the classroom management and instructional behaviors associated with such success in eliciting student achievement gain. It helps move the field beyond testimonials and unsupported claims toward scientific statements based on credible data. Finally, it is gratifying to most teachers because it validates, for the most part, the principles of practice that they developed intuitively or through their own experimentation.

For example, Hunter (1984) has developed what she calls "templates" to be used in describing, interpreting, and evaluating the quality of teaching. One such template suggests that effective lessons contain the following elements:

Effective lessons

1. Anticipatory set (something said or done to prepare the students to learn in general and to focus on key stimuli in particular).
2. Objective and purpose (tell students the purpose of the lesson).
3. Input (new information).
4. Modeling (demonstrations of skills or procedures).
5. Checking for understanding (through questions or requests for performance).
6. Guided practice (under direct teacher supervision).
7. Independent practice (once students know what to do and how to do it).

The process-product research findings reviewed in this and the next chapter fit well with and provide support for Hunter's notions about effective teaching.

Along with the points made earlier about what it is reasonable to expect teachers to accomplish while working within the constraints that they typically face, these findings suggest that most teachers will use the traditional method of teacher-led, group-based instruction as their basic approach. This is especially true if they are concentrating on instruction in basic skills, or on instruction in knowledge, comprehension, and most application objectives in almost any subject matter area. Compared to the feasible alternatives, teacher-led, group-based instruction appears to be an effective approach for classroom teaching of any body of knowledge or set of skills that has been sufficiently well-organized and analyzed so that it can be presented (explained, modeled) systematically and then practiced or applied during activities that call for student performance that can be evaluated for quality and, where incorrect or imperfect, given corrective feedback.

Effectiveness of teacher-led group-based instruction

Limits of Group-Based Instruction

Limitations on use

This type of instruction covers a lot of what most teachers will attempt to accomplish, but it also excludes a lot. It excludes activities with analysis, synthesis, or evaluation objectives, such as units on creative writing, projects involving conducting and reporting research, or creating a product of considerable complexity that requires diverse skills, that are accomplished more effectively using inquiry or guided discovery methods. It also excludes activities designed primarily to develop attitudes rather than knowledge or skills, like art or music appreciation units and many units in English, social studies, and physical education. Thus, teacher-led, group-based instruction may not be the primary approach used in certain courses, and even where it is the primary approach, it would ordinarily be a base to work from rather than the only method used. The teacher would shift to other methods for particular units or activities. Even here, however, the teacher would continue to monitor and interact with the students, rather than do paperwork or engage in other noninteractive activity.

Active instruction

Because of the complexities mentioned in the previous paragraph, we prefer the term "active instruction" to the term "teacher-led, group-based instruction" and its synonyms. This is because, even though we expect most lessons to be structured and led by the teacher and most instruction to be delivered to groups rather than individuals, we also expect teachers to depart from these general tendencies as instructional objectives or situational circumstances dictate. Even during these departures, however, we would expect teachers to be engaged in planned, systematic activities designed to accomplish particular objectives, and thus to be actively interacting with students while monitoring and responding to their performance on assigned tasks (see Good, 1979, for more on this point).

Different Paths to Success

We have already noted that the forms of active teaching that are most commonly associated with success in producing achievement gains on standardized tests are not necessarily appropriate for teaching the kinds of objectives that are not well measured by such tests. We now want to add a second caution: These commonly observed methods, although successful, are not necessarily the only or even the best way to achieve knowledge, comprehension, or application objectives. There may be different but functionally equivalent paths to the same levels of achievement. For example, it may make no significant difference whether the three main points of a presentation are summarized at the beginning or the end, so long as they are summarized, or whether a mathematics computation review is done with flash cards during a lesson or through a seatwork assignment afterwards.

Checking for student understanding

Rosenshine (1983) elaborates on this point in arguing that there are certain teaching functions that must be accomplished one way or another to insure efficient achievement gain, but that a variety of different methods may be available for accomplishing these functions. For example, one such function is checking for student understanding after presenting new information. He notes that this might be accomplished through: 1) a recitation activity in which the teacher asks the students a great many questions on the material, 2) having students write answers to written questions on paper or a chalkboard while the teacher circulates, 3) having students write answers on paper and then check them with a neighbor, or 4) assigning students to discuss the main points of the presentation in small groups and prepare a summary for presentation to the class.

Similarly, Good and Power (1976) have discussed common teaching tasks

Table 12.4 Multiple Ways to Accomplish Common Teaching Tasks

Teaching Task	Behavioral Resolution
1. Task differentiation	A. material assigned or made available in the classroom B. grouping students C. teacher questions that vary in cognitive demand
2. Maintaining task involvement	A. highly interesting tasks B. tasks that lead to student mastery C. insulation from interruption of fellow students
3. Review	A. distribution of printed teacher summary B. students prepare their own written summary C. teacher or student oral summary D. supervised board work
4. Accountability	A. oral questions B. call for show of hands during group work followed by random check of hand raisers C. group discussions followed by student written responses to discussion questions
5. Making time for teacher to work with individual students	A. peer tutoring B. learning centers C. independent work

Source: T. Good and C. Power, "Designing Successful Classroom Environments for Different Types of Students." *Journal of Curriculum Studies*, 8 (1976): 45–60.

that can be accomplished through several different approaches. Five such tasks and some of the alternative methods of accomplishing them are shown in Table 12.4.

Two Successful Classrooms

Comparable success using different approaches

Given that particular teaching functions can be accomplished using different methods and that these in turn can be combined in different configurations, we can expect different teachers to achieve comparable levels of success using different approaches, even if they work at the same grade level and teach to the same objectives. Ralph Kinderstone and Judith Blondell are two such teachers.

Ralph Kinderstone has taught fourth grade at Grandview Elementary School for the past three years. After graduating from the state university, he successfully completed his first year in law school. However, while working part-time for a law firm, he realized that he would not enjoy the day-to-day roles that lawyers perform. So, he went back to school, obtained his teaching certificate, and became a teacher, which he has found to be demanding but satisfying work.

Judith Blondell has taught in the fourth grade for three years at Golden West Elementary School. She had always wanted to be a teacher, so she majored in education and then moved directly into the profession. Although it has proven to be more demanding than she originally expected, she likes her job and plans to continue teaching indefinitely.

Ralph and Judith have at least three things in common: they teach fourth grade, they enjoy teaching, and they are successful. The fifth- and sixth-grade teachers at their schools are happy to get their students because they have good study habits and have mastered basic knowledge and skills. Their students do better on standardized achievement tests than students of similar aptitude and background, and both students and parents speak favorably of them. There are both similarities and differences in the ways that they achieve this success. Let us take a brief look at how they teach mathematics.

Ralph Kinderstone. Ralph Kinderstone basically teaches the class as a whole group, although a few faster students are working a couple of units ahead of the class. His presentations and demonstrations are well done. After he gives a demonstration, he may request one or two students to repeat it, but he seldom calls on more than two. He expects students to listen, and they do. He also listens carefully to the students and demonstrates genuine respect for their responses.

When he makes presentations (development work on a concept or a review of skills), he will also ask several questions. He is careful not to let students call out answers without permission, and he insists that they listen carefully to one another's responses. When students answer incorrectly, as they do about 30 percent of the time, he tends to ask another student or provides process feedback (explaining why the answer was wrong), but this is done briefly. The pace of the discussion is brief.

Before assigning independent seatwork he has all students work a couple of problems and he inspects the work of several students to ensure that they understand the task that they are to do independently or in small groups. If students do poorly, he repeats the demonstration and explains the concepts and skills that are needed to complete the seatwork.

Typically, about half of a 40-to-50 minute period is spent reviewing completed homework and introducing new assignments. After the initial presentation, students are allowed to work individually or in small teams, whichever they choose, on assigned problems. The assigned work is sufficiently difficult that no more than 20 percent of the class will finish it before the mathematics period ends. Those students who finish may choose from a series of interesting mathematics tasks that vary widely in difficulty. Students who do not complete the assignment complete it as homework. If students apply themselves in class, they seldom have more than 15 to 20 minutes of homework.

After Mr. Kinderstone assigns seatwork, he stands at the front of the class, scanning the room for a minute or so, and then he goes to those few students who seem confused or have difficulty in settling themselves down. After quickly engaging these students in the assigned task, he retires to his

When a student has difficulty with an assignment, the teacher should be available to answer questions and provide assistance.

desk and, depending on the circumstances, he either visits with individual students (reviewing their work, helping them to set goals) or works demandingly, but genuinely, with the students who are ahead of the class. However, he is available at all times for students who have tried to do the work but encounter difficulty (early in the year he consistently encouraged students to seek him out when they had difficulty). When students come to him, they receive immediate, brief, and task-relevant feedback. He rarely circles the room looking at students' work. When students want help, they seek him out.

Things move quickly in this classroom. Students drill a couple of minutes each day on important skills, and occasionally, Mr. Kinderstone will conduct a general review. However, the students are regularly learning new material and proceed through the text rapidly. He tests students with brief 15-minute tests at least once or twice a week. Student progress in the course is graphed by their test scores, and monthly, he allows students to see their own graphs privately. Students whose work reaches a high plateau (stated and known to students) and students who show sufficient improvement over the year have been promised a gift of a math game that everybody enjoys playing.

Once every two weeks, or so, a math period will be devoted to team games in which matched teams are pitted against one another. The tournaments are always unannounced but are "alleged" to be contingent on good student performance or tests or homework—students believe that good work leads to tournament play. Peers will sometimes criticize a student who is not doing assigned work so that they can all have team play.

When minor misbehavior occurs, Mr. Kinderstone ignores it or corrects it with a nod of his head. If it is impossible to use such techniques, or if they go unheeded by students, he is quick to stop the behavior by reminding students of the rules and the effect of their conduct on other students. He is more likely to warn students than to punish them, but if he does promise a punishment he invariably carries it through.

Judith Blondell. Judith Blondell's instructional program in mathematics is quite different from Ralph Kinderstone's. She teaches math twice a day—20 to 30 minutes in the morning and 20 to 30 minutes in the afternoon—rather than once a day in a long block.

The pace in her class is slower than the pace in Mr. Kinderstone's class. The same types of problems are worked on for several consecutive days. However, math periods often end with a few minutes of drill time via participation in an instructional game that allows some of the drill to come in a game atmosphere. She supervises this activity by watching some of the students closely and by having students keep written records of the errors they make in drill games.

She is very active in the classroom. Much of her time is spent demonstrating mathematics skills and carefully watching as many students perform the same task or a similar one in front of the class. She works hard to get participation and will accept (respond to the student's answer, praise effort, and so on) virtually any academically relevant response that a student makes, whether or not the student has permission to speak.

In general, her students, in contrast to those in Mr. Kinderstone's class, respond with wrong answers less frequently (15 to 20 percent of the time). When a student responds inappropriately to a question, she typically waits for the student to correct the response, provides a clue, or repeats the question. She actively encourages student responses.

Mrs. Blondell's students spend only 15 to 20 percent of their time on individual seatwork. Early in the year they spent only 10 percent of their time on individual assignments. In contrast, students in Mr. Kinderstone's class spend 50 percent of their time working independently of the teacher.

Early in the year, Mrs. Blondell rarely used nonverbal techniques to control students. Now she uses eye contact and will ignore minor misbehavior. She still reacts quickly, consistently, and firmly when moderate misbehavior occurs, but she is not loud or punitive.

Teaching Effectively in Different Contexts

Some of the differences between Mr. Kinderstone and Mrs. Blondell occur simply because of differences in personal preference, and merely provide additional illustrations that particular teaching functions can be accomplished in a variety of ways. However, several of the illustrated differences occur because these teachers work with very different types of students. Mr. Kinderstone's school is located in the nicest part of a university town. The parents of his students tend to be university professors, lawyers, physicians, business executives, and others of high socioeconomic status (SES). Within the range to be expected at the fourth grade level, his students have very well-developed skills for reading, following directions, and working independently. In contrast, Mrs. Blondell's school is located in an inner-city neighborhood and serves students from low-SES families in which most parents are either unemployed or working in low-paying unskilled occupations. Her students do not have very well-developed independent study skills.

Matching teaching style with SES background

These two teachers are both effective because they each have molded an instructional system that meets the needs of the students that they teach. In other words, they are not merely successful even though they teach differently; they are successful *because* they teach differently. If they were to exchange classrooms, they would not be nearly as successful unless they changed their teaching styles.

Both teachers are effective classroom managers who maximize the time that their students spend engaged in appropriate academic activities, and both are active teachers who carry the content to their students rather than depend on curriculum materials to do so. In addition to these similarities, however, the two teachers reveal several differences that illustrate additional findings from process-product research (reviewed in Brophy & Good, 1985) concerning teacher behaviors that promote achievement gain in low-SES versus high-SES classrooms.

In high-SES elementary school settings, teachers have to be concerned with overcompetitiveness among their students, whereas in low-SES classrooms, they have to be more concerned about fear of failure and general anxiety. Consequently, Mr. Kinderstone works to make sure that his students do not overcompete for public response opportunities: He does not allow students to call out answers, and he encourages the students to listen to one another. He does use competitive games, but he does not announce these in advance and he rotates the teams regularly to minimize possible negative consequences of such competition.

In contrast, Mrs. Blondell encourages her students to participate actively in academic activities, because most of them tend to be reticent, at least in public response settings. She asks simpler questions than Mr. Kinderstone does–her students answer about 80 percent of her questions correctly, whereas his answer only about 70 percent correctly. Furthermore, if her students do not respond or respond incorrectly, she will usually stay with them and try to elicit an improved response by giving them more time or by providing help by rephrasing the question or giving clues. Mr. Kinderstone does not need to provide such support or assistance nearly as often, because his students are usually eager to respond and will speak up if they know the answer or have a likely guess.

Most of Mr. Kinderstone's students achieve well above grade level. Because they can read assignments, have mastered the math concepts they need, and are motivated to perform, it makes sense to allow them to spend time in independent work or in small group activities. It also makes sense to allow them to come to him and seek feedback when they need it. In contrast, Mrs. Blondell's students need much more direct instruction in the content, and more teacher structuring and supervision when working on assignments. Consequently, it makes more sense for her to divide mathematics instruction into two shorter segments rather than use one longer one, and to circulate around the room during seatwork time rather than wait for students to come to her for help.

There are some similarities in the two teaching styles. Both teachers are very consistent and follow through on what they say, both in managerial and in instructional situations. Also, both are nonevaluative. That is, rather than reacting with praise or criticism to students as individual persons, they give feedback that focuses on the content of the students' answers or the correctness of their work, although Mrs. Blondell's students are more in need of and respond better to encouragement than Mr. Kinderstone's students, so it is useful for her to provide more praise than he does.

Both teachers basically teach the class as a whole group and regularly present structured lessons followed by assignments with clear expectations about what is to be accomplished. In both classrooms, mastery of mathematics concepts and facts is the major goal. Mr. Kinderstone allows the students to work in groups as a social outlet, but he expects that time to be spent on the work, and he holds individual students accountable for mastery via his frequent quizzes.

Context variables

Student SES is just one of many variables that must be taken into account in adapting instruction to the context. Other context variables include grade level, subject matter, time (of year, week, or day), the specific objectives of the activity and its place within the curriculum as a whole, the status characteristics of the students (sex, race, ethnicity, language dominance), and the heterogeneity of the group. Research information is available regarding some of these context variables. We will discuss some of it here and some in a later section on individual differences.

In their review, Brophy and Good (1985) found several sets of interaction effects that appear repeatedly in process-product research and suggest that different kinds of treatment are needed to maximize achievement for different kinds of students.

Grade level. In the early grades, students need a great deal of instruction in and opportunity to practice classroom management routines and procedures in addition to instruction in the curriculum. Less of this instruction in routines and procedures is needed in the intermediate and secondary grades, but here it becomes especially important to be clear about expectations and to follow up on accountability demands. Also, in the early grades, the lessons involve instruction in basic skills and are often conducted in small groups, and it is important that each student participates overtly and often. In the later grades, lessons typically are with the whole class and involve applications of basic skills or consideration of more abstract content. Here, the overt participation of each student is less important than factors such as teachers' structuring of the content, clarity of statements and questions, and enthusiasm. Finally, praise and symbolic rewards are common in the early grades but give way to the more impersonal and academically centered instruction common in the later grades. Older students do not respond as positively to praise, especially public praise, as do younger students, although it is important that teachers treat their contributions with interest and respect.

Student SES/ability/affect. SES is a "proxy" for a complex of correlated cognitive and affective differences between subgroups of students. The cognitive differences involve IQ, ability, and achievement levels. Process-product data indicate that, compared to high-SES/high-achieving students, low-SES/low-achieving students need more control and structuring from their teachers: More active instruction and feedback, more redundancy, and smaller steps with higher success rates. This will mean more review, drill, and practice, and thus more lower-level questions. Across the school year, it will mean exposure to less material, but with emphasis on mastery of the material that is taught and on moving students through the curriculum as briskly as they are able to progress.

Affective correlates of SES include the degree to which students feel secure and confident versus anxious or alienated in the classroom. High-SES students are more likely to be confident, eager to participate, and responsive to challenge. They want respect and require feedback, but usually do not require a great deal of encouragement or praise. They thrive in an atmosphere that is academically stimulating and somewhat demanding. In contrast, low-SES students are more likely to require warmth and support from their teachers in addition to good instruction, and to need more encouragement for their efforts and praise for their successes. Also, it is especially important to teach them to respond overtly rather than remain passive when asked a question, and to be accepting of their (relevant) call-outs and other academic initiations when they do occur.

Teacher's intentions/objectives. To the extent that students need new information, they are likely to need group lessons featuring information presentation by the teacher followed by recitation or discussion opportunities. The appropriateness of follow-up practice or application opportunities would depend on the objective. When it is sufficient that students be able to reproduce knowledge on cue, routine seatwork assignments and tests might suffice. However, if students are expected to integrate broad patterns of learning or apply them to their everyday lives, it will be necessary to schedule activities that involve problem solving, decision making, essay composition, preparation of research reports, or construction of some product.

Adapting Instruction to Students' Individual Characteristics

Even when working from teacher-led group instruction as a base, teachers can introduce some degree of differentiation in their treatment of individual students designed to accommodate those students' personal characteristics. Some of the more important such characteristics are as follows:

1. General competence and aptitude (Does the student process and com-

prehend information rapidly? What is the cognitive style of individual learners?).

2. General developmental level (Is the student preoperational?).
3. Student reading ability (Probably closely related to aptitude, but not always).
4. General personality adjustment (Is the student peer-oriented? Anxious? Dependent?).
5. Work mode preference and general work habits (Do students prefer to work alone, with the whole class, or in small groups? Do they prefer written or verbal performances?).

Aptitude

Aptitude makes a difference. Brighter students can process information quickly; less capable students need more time to assimilate and integrate material. Fast students can watch a demonstration and perform; slow students need to manipulate objects themselves and need several examples. Similarly, bright students often enjoy difficult assignments; less capable students like easy assignments.

Developmental stage

The developmental stage of students has important instructional implications. Younger children's attention spans are shorter than those of older students, and they generally need relatively short lessons and frequent review. Very young children need rest periods built into the school day. Older students can benefit from longer assignments, more complex choices, and more independent work. Preoperational students need numerous concrete examples; students beyond this stage can work with abstractions and learn propositionally. Students at certain developmental stages avoid members of the opposite sex, but a few years later the opportunity to work with members of the opposite sex in small group work may be highly motivating for some learning tasks, such as those that are not overcomplex and do not demand total attention. Young students generally want to please adults; subsequently, peer expectations and influences rival adult influences.

Reading level

Reading level may seem to be an obvious consideration, yet many teachers with students who vary considerably in reading ability try to implement individualized programs with reading assignments that represent the same level of difficulty. In such instances, the material will be much too demanding for some students and too easy for others. Teachers who employ many individual assignments where students have to read material, directions, and so forth on their own need to be especially alert to the need for materials that vary in reading difficulty. Teachers who use individual assignments must also consider students' general abilities and desires to work independently.

Students' individual personality

The general personality of a student is also a major consideration in assessing whether or not a learning environment is successful for him or her. Dependent students will seek teacher structure and support; independent students will want little of either. Some students want to be with peers; others are more introverted and prefer more solitude. A student's personality also influences the degree, frequency, and type of feedback that is needed or preferred.

Preference for work mode

Preference for work mode depends to some extent on student personality (dependent students prefer to be with the teacher), but some work styles are independent of personality and cognitive aptitude or style. For example, some students enjoy writing reports and stories but dislike answering questions; other students have the opposite preference. Some students prefer a variety of working assignments; other students really like only one mode (whole class, individual, and so forth).

Work habits

Work habits are also important considerations. Some students are very careless and poorly organized. Other students are enthusiastic bookkeepers but somehow cannot put together all the associated facts and other data they collect. If teachers want to alter such work habits, their choice of learning activities will have to be designed with this in mind. In the meantime, such activities will have to be minimized and carefully monitored.

Five Student Types and Their Instructional Needs

Good and Power (1976) discuss the instructional needs of the following five types of students that can be found in most classrooms and that have been discussed in classroom research:

1. *Successful students*—These students are task oriented and academically successful. They participate in lessons, turn in assignments on time (almost always complete and correct), and create few if any discipline problems. Teachers are likely to direct difficult questions to them because they get most of them right. Successful students like school and tend to be liked by both teachers and peers.
2. *Social students*—Social students are more person oriented than task oriented. They have the ability to achieve but value socializing with friends more than working on assignments. They are likely to be called on fairly often by teachers, both to keep them involved in lessons and because they are able to answer easy questions. Social students tend to have many friends and be popular in the peer group, but are usually not well liked by their teachers because their frequent socializing creates management problems.
3. *Dependent students*—Dependent students frequently look to the teacher for support and encouragement, and often ask for additional directions and help. They are frequent hand-raisers. In secondary schools, most dependent students achieve at a low level. Teachers generally express concern about the academic progress of dependent students and do what they can to assist them. Peers often reject dependent students because they tend to be socially immature.
4. *Alienated students*—Alienated students are reluctant learners and potential dropouts. In the extreme, they reject the school and everything that it stands for. This rejection may take one of two forms: open hostility or withdrawal into cynicism and passivity. The hostile alienated students create serious disruptions through their aggression and defiance, whereas the passive alienated students withdraw to the

fringes of the classroom and may be ignored by their teachers and most of their peers. Teacher attitudes toward alienated students typically range between indifference and rejection.

5. *Phantom students*—Phantom students are those that seem to fade into the background because they are rarely noticed or heard from. They tend to be average in everything but involvement in public settings. Some are shy, nervous students, while others are quiet, independent workers of average ability. They work steadily on assignments, but are rarely involved actively in group activities because they never volunteer, and are rarely involved in managerial interchanges because they never create disruption. Typically, neither teachers nor peers know these students very well or think about or interact with them very often. Teachers are likely to have difficulty remembering these students if asked to list everyone in the class.

Good and Power surveyed the literature on these five types of students and developed lists of suggestions about how teachers might accommodate their contrasting preferences and needs. Some of their suggestions are shown in Table 12.5.

Accommodating to students' preferences

Although based partly on research, the suggestions given in Table 12.5 should be considered speculative hypotheses rather than proven guidelines for two reasons. First, accommodating to students' preferences may not be the same as meeting their needs. Several studies have shown that allowing students to choose their own learning methods or arranging to teach them in the ways that they prefer to be taught will produce *less* achievement gain than teaching them in some other way (Clark, 1982; Schofield, 1981; Solomon & Kendall, 1979). Second, accommodating to particular personal qualities of students often has the effect of reinforcing those qualities, and sometimes these are qualities that the teacher will want to change if possible. It would be easy, for example, to respond reciprocally to the behavior of phantom students and passive-withdrawn alienated students by minimizing interaction with them—never calling on them unless they indicate a need for help. This might even maximize the comfort of both the teacher and the students involved. However, it probably would not be in the students' best interests.

Individualizing instruction

Even though these complexities must be kept in mind, the suggestions in Table 12.5 offer ideas about how teachers can introduce a degree of individualization into their instruction even while basically teaching the class as a group. Some of these suggestions can be incorporated with relative ease—those that merely involve interacting more often or more affectively with certain students than with others. Other suggestions would be more difficult and time consuming to implement (those that call for preparing different activities or assignments for different subgroups). Even where it is not possible to introduce such variation into the activities and assignments planned for a particular day, however, these guidelines are useful for judging the appropriateness of the variety built into the activities and assignments planned for a week or a unit. There should be enough balance to deliver

Table 12.5 Suggestions for Meeting the Needs of Five Different Types of Students

	Success	Social	Dependent	Alienated	Phantom
I. Type of Input Needed from Teacher					
A. Substantive Explanation of Content	very high	very high	high	high	high
B. Procedural Directions	low	low	high	moderate-high	moderate-low
C. Socializing, Emotional Support, Humor	very low	low-moderate	moderate	moderate (establish private rapport)	low
II. Type of Task Needed					
A. Reading Skills Required	high	high	low	low	moderate
B. Task Difficulty Level	very high	high	low-moderate	low-moderate	moderate
C. Abstractness Level	high	moderate	low initially	low initially	moderate
D. Cognitive Level	high	moderate	low-moderate	low-moderate	moderate
E. Degree of Structure (Specificity about what to do and how to do it)	low	moderate	high	high	moderate
F. Opportunity to Make Active, Overt Responses	not important	high	high	high	moderate
G. Opportunity to Make Choices	moderate (stress on enrichment)	moderate (stress on choices to work with others)	low	moderate (stress on relevance)	low
H. Interest Value of Task to Student	not important	moderate	low	high	low
I. Length of Task	long	short	moderate	moderate	long
III. Type of Response Demanded					
A. Written	high	low	high	moderate	high
B. Oral	low	high	low	low	low
C. Physical	low	moderate	moderate	high	low
IV. Individual vs. Group Settings					
A. Individual	high	low	high	high	high
B. Group	low	moderate	low	low-moderate	low
V. Emphasis on Competition	high	moderate	low-initially	low	moderate
VI. Type of Feedback from Teacher					
A. Personal Praise	low	low	moderate	moderate (private)	low
B. Personal Criticism	low	low	low	very low	low
C. Praise of Good Work	low	moderate	moderate	moderate (private)	low-moderate
D. Criticism of Poor Work	moderate	moderate	low	low (but communicate demand)	low-moderate

Source: Condensed and adapted from T. Good and C. Power "Designing Successful Classroom Environments for Different Types of Students." *Journal of Curriculum Studies*, 8 (1976): 45–60.

something for everyone, rather than a restriction of plans to activities and assignments that are well matched to the needs of one or two subgroups but poorly matched to the needs of the others.

The suggestions are also useful for identifying the basic approach that is most likely to be successful for particular classrooms (depending on the mix of students in those classrooms). For example, Ralph Kinderstone's approach was well suited to his classroom because of its high percentage of successful students, whereas Judith Blondell's approach was well suited to her classroom because of its high percentages of dependent and alienated students. Most classes are less extreme and easily characterized than the two example classes, of course, but the examples are useful for illustrating how teachers will need to tailor the specifics of their approach to active whole-class instruction to the needs of their students.

SUMMARY

Process-outcome research links classroom processes, particularly teacher behaviors, to their cognitive (achievement) or affective (attitudes) outcomes. Such research has shown that gains in student achievement are associated with five sets of variables concerning the quantity of instruction that students receive from their teachers: opportunity to learn/content covered, role definition/expectations/time allocation, classroom management/student engaged time, consistent success/academic learning time, and active teaching. It also has shown that positive student attitudes are associated with measures of teacher warmth and student orientation (praise, use of student ideas, willingness to listen to students and respect their contributions, time spent socializing with students in addition to instructing them). Negative affect and negative classroom climates are associated with poor achievement gain, but good achievement gain is at least as likely in neutral or mildly warm climates as in more clearly warm climates.

The correlational findings from the ethnographic data collected by Tikunoff, Berliner, and Rist (1975) and the teacher behavior guidelines developed from earlier correlational work and used in experimental studies by Good and Grouws (1979) and by Anderson, Evertson, and Brophy (1979) were reviewed as examples of the kind of active teaching that process-outcome research has shown to be associated with achievement gain. The authors suggest that most teachers will use this active instruction approach as their basic method of instruction, because compared to the feasible alternatives, it is effective for teaching any body of knowledge or set of skills that has been sufficiently well organized and analyzed so that it can be presented (explained, modeled) systematically and then practiced or applied during activities that call for student performance that can be evaluated for quality and (where incorrect or imperfect) given corrective feedback. Instructional objectives that do not fit this characterization will require different methods.

Few if any specific instructional behaviors are appropriate in all teaching contexts. Furthermore, there may be several different but functionally equivalent paths to the same levels of achievement. Thus, it makes more sense to think in terms of instructional functions that need to be accomplished rather than in terms of specific behaviors to be labeled as appropriate or inappropriate. Furthermore, even within the general method of active teaching that appears to be an appropriate base for most teachers, the specifics of application will vary with grade level, subject matter, and the nature of the students. Ralph Kinderstone and Judith Blondell provide examples of such variation.

Guidelines are given for how instruction can be expected to vary with grade level, student SES/ability/affect, and teachers' intentions/objectives, as well as for how teachers can adapt instruction to students' individual characteristics. In particular, Good and Power (1976) present suggestions for adapting whole class instruction to take into account the particular needs and preferences of successful students, social students, dependent students, alienated students, and phantom students.

QUESTIONS AND PROBLEMS

1. Were you under the impression (or have you been taught) that effective teaching is simply a matter of mastering a few "crucial" behaviors? What is wrong with that statement? What would be a more accurate description of effective teaching?
2. Do the differential suggestions made for teaching different student types make sense to you? If so, can you see ways to do all of these things simultaneously (remember, most if not all of these student types will exist in any given classroom)? List some of the ways.
3. Most process-outcome research has used standardized tests for measuring achievement gain. In what ways might this make the results of such research limited or misleading? Compare notes with your friends.
4. Suppose a process-outcome study were to eliminate differences in quantity of instruction by limiting the sample to experienced teachers who were effective classroom managers committed to active teaching toward the same set of objectives. Under these conditions, any differences in success would be due to quality rather than quantity of teaching. What qualitative factors do you think would make for differences in how much or how well the students learned? How could you measure these quality indicators?
5. As a teacher, you will have considerable autonomy in allocating classroom time to particular objectives. What would you see as your responsibilities and options in the following three situations: a) The adopted curriculum contains a unit on some topic that you do not consider very important, but there is no particular pressure on you to teach it; b) You do not consider the unit very important, but it is part of the official curriculum mandated by your school district; c) You recognize that the unit is important but for some reason do not feel competent to teach it effectively or do not enjoy teaching it. Would you omit the unit or reduce the time allocated to it under these circumstances? Why or why not? Compare notes with your friends.
6. How can you both move students through the curriculum at a brisk pace and program for consistent success and minimal frustration? Write down some specific strategies for responding to this dilemma. In particular, what should you do when 80 percent of the students have clearly mastered the objectives of a lesson but 20 percent have not?
7. Should school districts evaluate teachers according to whether or not they display behaviors that process-outcome research has shown are correlated with student achievement gain? Why or why not?
8. If Ralph Kinderstone and Judith Blondell were to trade places, which of their present teaching strategies could they retain and which would they have to change?

9. What does it mean to say that SES is a "proxy" standing for a complex of correlated cognitive and affective differences between subgroups of students? What are the advantages and disadvantages of using such "proxy" variables? In particular, how can we use such "proxy" variables in ways that will help teachers to differentiate in their treatment of students in ways that meet those students' needs effectively, but at the same time minimize the degree to which we create undesirable biases and stereotyped expectations in teachers?
10. What does it mean to say that accommodating students' preferences is not the same as meeting their needs? How should teachers define "meeting their students' needs," and how can they evaluate their degree of success in doing so?

CASE STUDIES

Read each of the following descriptions of how a teacher conducts his or her class, and using the material presented in this chapter, critique the teacher's approach.

A Mixed Class. Laura Stemard teaches fourth-grade mathematics. Her students are distributed fairly equally among the top, middle, and lower ranges of social class background. She has two students who are being mainstreamed.

Laura works with the entire class for 20 to 30 minutes a day (only the two students being mainstreamed work on individual assignments). In general she spends 15 minutes reviewing homework and discussing the assignment. Questions she asks are very easy (90 percent are answered correctly), and if students miss a question she simply goes on. The last 15 minutes of each day are spent completing assigned seatwork. She circles the room, providing detailed feedback to students who are not finished. When students finish they are expected to find something to do (although nothing explicit is provided) and not to bother others.

An Elite Group. "Pack" Wilson runs his algebra class as smoothly as he ran the high school football team 15 years earlier. All his students are college-bound, but, as he puts it, he likes to "let the good horses run." The top 5 to 8 students in each class are taught as a separate group and receive special assignments.

Classroom discussion involves application of concepts and infrequent review. He tests twice a week, and students have one hour of homework daily. He spends roughly half of each period with each of the two groups.

When he works with one group, the other group works on assigned seatwork individually. The assignments are clear but difficult. Students rarely misbehave in his class. The small group of top students in each class is moving through curriculum material 25 percent faster than other students. He almost never talks to individual students during class about their work, and actively discourages average students from approaching him unless they are totally stuck.

An Inner-City Speech Class. Toni Frick teaches a high school speech course in an inner-city school. Although the course is an elective, most students take it. Each day in the class is a bit different, although there is a general sense of purposefulness. On the average, three days a week are spent in oral speech (teacher demonstrating technique, student practice, and so on). Toni has two goals for the students: (1) to be able to write and deliver an interesting and informative speech, and (2) to be able to talk extemporaneously.

During most oral presentations she divides the class into outliners (these students attempt to chart the flow of the speech), critics (students who attempt to note the weakest part of the speech), and helpers (who focus upon the especially good parts of the speech). Sometimes the criticism and support are aimed at particular parts of the speech; at other times—especially later in the year—students can choose from any part of the speech.

In addition to writing down comments relevant to their roles, students fill out general evaluations (how interesting, how clear, and so on) and may be called upon by the teacher to present and defend their critiques. After presenting a speech students listen to the public evaluations carefully, because each speech is typically repeated once and major criticism must be accommodated.

The remaining two days of each week are reserved for an analysis of written speeches (Who would have written this speech? What content is avoided? Is it found emotional? How would a black audience react? Why?) and to practicing speech writing. In such activities the teacher attempts to match the complexity of the task to the students' level of mastery, although most of this work is done individually.

Chapter 13

Basic Instructional Skills

CHAPTER OUTLINE

OBJECTIVES

When you have mastered the material in this chapter you will be able to

1. List the strengths and weaknesses of the lecture method and identify situations in which the lecture method is appropriate
2. Describe the steps to be taken and the decisions to be made in planning effective lectures
3. List factors that enhance and detract from the clarity and organization of teachers' presentations
4. List factors that enhance and detract from the effectiveness of such presentations in gaining students' interest and holding their attention
5. Differentiate between types of activity that involve questioning and responding to students (drills, reviews, recitations, discussions) and describe the purposes and uses of each
6. List the strengths and weaknesses of recitation activities as classroom instruction devices
7. State the findings of process-outcome research on difficulty level of question and cognitive level of question as they relate to student achievement gain
8. List criteria for judging the quality of teachers' questions
9. State the findings of research on the length of time that teachers wait before calling on a student to answer a question
10. Explain how pacing and wait time should be expected to vary with the objectives of recitation activities

11. Describe the factors to be considered in deciding which student to call on to respond to a question
12. State guidelines for reacting when students fail to respond, when they respond incorrectly, when they give an incomplete or only partially correct response, and when they give a correct response
13. State guidelines for responding to relevant and irrelevant student questions and comments
14. Describe the differences between the teacher's role in conducting drill and recitation activities and the teacher's role in conducting discussions
15. List criteria for identifying effective discussions and alternatives to questioning that teachers can use for producing lengthy and insightful student responses during discussions
16. List criteria for judging the effectiveness of seatwork and homework assignments and guidelines for handling seatwork and homework effectively

Whatever their grade level, subject matter, or approach to instruction, most teachers will need to rely on two basic sets of instructional skills more or less continuously in their interactions with their students: the skills involved in making presentations (lecturing on content, demonstrating skills or procedures, elaborating on the text), and the skills involved in questioning and responding to students (conducting recitations, drills, and discussions). These skills are basic to the concept of active teaching as described in Chapter 12, as well as to the ordinary person's notion of what it means to teach.

Making Presentations: Lecturing

We have noted that teachers who stimulate sizable achievement gain in their students tend to carry the content to their students personally rather than rely on the curriculum materials to do so. This means that such teachers frequently make presentations in the form of lectures, explanations, or demonstrations to the whole class or to small groups. Sometimes, especially in advanced subjects at the secondary level, these presentations are similar to the lengthy lectures or lecture-discussions seen commonly in college classes. This is not the norm, however. More typically, presentations by elementary and secondary teachers are short (5 to 20 minutes) and followed by some practice or application activity, or if longer, are broken into segments with periods of questioning or discussion in between (Good & Grouws, 1977; Arehart, 1979).

In this chapter, we will use the term lecture to refer to extended presentations; the term explanation to refer to brief explications of a particular concept; and the term demonstration to refer to the modeling of skills or procedures. Explanations and demonstrations may be embedded within lectures or delivered in isolation. The term presentation will be used as a more general term that includes lectures, explanations, and demonstrations.

Popularity and criticisms of method

Lecturing is a commonly used teaching technique, because it is efficient (in a brief time, the teacher can expose students to a body of content that might take them a long time to find and absorb on their own), it can be used with groups or entire classes rather than just with individuals, it gives the teacher control over the content to be taught, it can easily be combined with other methods and adjusted to fit the available time, the physical environment, and other situational constraints. Also, many teachers enjoy it because it gives them an opportunity to display their knowledge and "perform" for their students. For these reasons the lecture method has retained popularity with teachers, even though it has been criticized as limiting students to a passive learner role, denying students the opportunity to practice social skills, relying on the usually false assumption that all students need the same information, wasting students' time by telling them things that they could read for themselves, focusing on the lowest level of cognition, or going on too long to the point of boring or confusing students (Henson, 1980; McLeish, 1976). Although we have all suffered through lectures that had these undesirable effects, it should be noted that most of these problems are caused by overuse or inappropriate use of the lecture method, and are not inherent in the method itself (McMann, 1979).

Nor do empirical data suggest that lecturing is inappropriate in any general sense. Reviews summarizing studies comparing lecture versus discussion or other methods of learning typically conclude that about half of the studies favor the lecture approach and half do not (Dubin & Taveggia, 1968; Voth, 1975). Such "no difference" findings are to be expected when data are aggregated without taking into account factors such as the quality of the instruction or the objectives to which it is directed. Thus, the real question is not "Is the lecture method better than other alternatives?" but "For what purposes is the lecture method appropriate?" McKeachie and Kulik (1975), for example, reviewed studies separately according to whether the criteria of learning focused on facts, higher-level thinking, or attitudes and motivation. They reported tendencies for lecture to be superior to discussion for promoting factual learning, but for discussion to be superior to lecture for promoting higher-level thinking and attitudes and motivation.

Appropriate use

Various authors (Davis & Alexander, 1977; Gage & Berliner, 1984; Henson, 1980; Hoover, 1968; McMann, 1979) have suggested that the lecture method is appropriate in the following situations:

1. When the objective is to present information.
2. When the information is not available in a textbook or some other readily accessible source.
3. When the material must be organized and presented in a particular way for the students.
4. When it is necessary to arouse interest in the subject.
5. When it is necessary to provide an introduction to a topic that the students will then read about on their own, or to provide instructions about learning a task.
6. When the information is original or must be integrated from a number of different sources.
7. When material needs to be summarized or synthesized (following a discussion or inquiry process).
8. When the text or curriculum materials need updating or other elaboration.
9. When the teacher wants to present alternate points of view or interpretations, or to clarify issues in preparation for discussion or debate.
10. When the teacher wants to provide supplementary explanations of material that students are likely to have difficulty learning on their own.

The lecture method probably will be an appropriate teaching device if used for one or more of these purposes. Just how effective it will be will depend on the care and skill with which the lecture is prepared and delivered. Guidelines for preparing effective lectures are now presented, based on the advice of experts and the findings of process-outcome research on classroom teaching.

Preparing the Lecture

Elements of effective lessons

In Chapter 8, we suggested that effective lessons would: 1) start with advance organizers or previews that include general principles, outlines, or questions that establish a learning set; 2) briefly describe the objectives and alert the students to new or key concepts; 3) present new material in small steps organized logically and sequenced in ways that are easy to follow; 4) elicit student response regularly in order to stimulate active learning and insure that each step is mastered before moving to the next; 5) finish with a review of the main points, stressing general integrative concepts; and 6) follow up the presentation with questions or assignments that require students to encode the material in their own words and apply or extend it to new contexts.

Davis and Alexander (1977) offer similar criteria for good presentations, and also note the importance of motivating the students at the beginning of the presentation, stimulating attention periodically, and following principles of effective delivery like maintaining eye contact, avoiding distracting behaviors, modulating voice pitch and volume, and using appropriate gestures. They also suggest that the portion of the lecture devoted to one-way communication be limited to 20 to 30 minutes (this norm was intended for lectures to adults; correspondingly shorter norms would be appropriate for correspondingly younger students).

Insofar as it goes, process-product research supports these guidelines. Teachers' ability to structure subject matter for their students is associated with student achievement gain (Tikunoff, Berliner, & Rist, 1975). In particular, achievement is maximized when teachers not only actively present material but structure it by beginning with overviews, advance organizers, or review of objectives; outlining the content and signaling transitions between lesson parts; calling attention to main ideas; summarizing subparts of the lesson as it proceeds; and reviewing main ideas at the end (Alexander, Frankiewicz, & Williams, 1979; Armento, 1977; Clark et al., 1979; Fisher et al., 1980; Fortune, 1967; Gage et al., 1968; Rosenshine, 1968; Schuck, 1981; Smith & Sanders, 1981; Wright & Nuthall, 1970). Also, achievement is higher when presentations are rated as high in clarity (Good & Grouws, 1977; McConnell, 1977; Smith & Land, 1981) and delivered with enthusiasm (Armento, 1977; McConnell, 1977) and appropriate gestures and movements (Rosenshine, 1968). Presentations should be planned to incorporate these features.

Instructional objectives

Planning begins with instructional objectives—what information is to be conveyed to students, and what they will be expected to do with it. Effective lectures are presented with specific objectives in mind; they are not rambling, "off the top of the head" discourses that merely take up classroom time. The lecture should supplement, not merely duplicate, the input that students get from reading textbooks and completing assignments.

Given appropriate objectives, good planning proceeds to consideration of practical matters. Do the students possess needed knowledge and skills? Does the teacher possess the needed information? Are needed materials and equipment available? Can the objectives be accomplished within the available time?

Once these practical matters are worked out, Davis and Alexander (1977) suggest preparing an outline by listing two or three key points to be made, ordered logically, and identifying interesting and relevant examples, illustrations, anecdotes, or experiments that will help make these points. The next step is to develop a more comprehensive instructional plan that includes attention not only to the presentation of the content but to listing appropriate questions that might be asked during or after the presentation, planning any demonstrations that will be needed, preparing overhead transparencies or other audiovisual aids, preparing handouts to be distributed to the students, and preparing follow-up activities or assignments. Handouts might include diagrams or illustrations, definitions of key terms, outlines of the presentation (including partial outlines intended to be used as guides to notetaking), or study guides designed to help students get the most out of the presentation and the subsequent activities or assignments.

Comprehensive instructional plan

Planning should include attention to motivational elements as well as to the academic content. Unless the students are already highly motivated to learn the information to be presented, it is wise to begin the presentation by posing a provocative question, presenting a powerful epigram or quotation, telling an interesting related anecdote, mentioning puzzling or paradoxical facts, or using some of the other techniques for arousing student interest and curiosity described in Chapters 14 through 18.

Motivational elements

Delivering the Lecture

Successful lectures typically begin with establishment of a learning set, proceed to presentation of information structured and sequenced for clarity and delivered with enthusiasm and appropriate gestures, and end with review of integration of the material.

Establishing a Learning Set. Besides stimulating student interest or curiosity, teachers should begin lectures by establishing an appropriate learning set in their students. Thus, the introduction to the lecture should include advance organizers or previews that cue students as to the nature of the content and the schemas or prior knowledge they will need to bring to bear in understanding it, as well as mention of the objectives to be accomplished. If the teacher wants the students to pay particular attention to certain content or to take particular kinds of notes, such instructions should be presented and clarified at this time. If the information is going to be applied in some way later, the students should be alerted to this so that they can attend to the lecture with the subsequent application in mind. In general, a good introduction leaves the students not only motivated to attend actively to the lecture, but also well informed about its contents and about how they are expected to respond to or use the information.

Clarity of Presentation. Ideally, lectures are clear and easy to follow. But what makes for clarity? At minimum, clear presentations are free of what Hiller, Fisher, and Kaess (1969) called vagueness terms. These authors have identified the following nine categories of such vagueness terms:

Vagueness terms

1. Ambiguous designation (somehow, somewhere, conditions, other).
2. Approximation (about, almost, kind of, pretty much, sort of).
3. "Bluffing" and recovery (actually, and so forth, anyway, as you know, basically, in other words, to make a long story short).
4. Error admission (excuse me, I'm sorry, I guess, I'm not sure).
5. Indeterminate quantification (a bunch, a couple, a few, a lot, a little, some, several).
6. Negated intensifiers (not many, not very).
7. Multiplicity (aspects, kinds of, sort of, type of).
8. Possibility (chances are, could be, maybe, perhaps).
9. Probability (frequently, generally, often, probably, sometimes, usually).

Smith and Land (1981) review research indicating that presentations containing such vagueness terms are less clear than presentations that are free of vagueness terms. In the following example, the vagueness terms are italicized.

> This mathematics lesson *might* enable you to understand *a little more* about *some things* we *usually* call number patterns. *Maybe* before we get to *probably* the main idea of the lesson, you should review *a few* prerequisite concepts. *Actually*, the first concept you need to review is positive integers. *As you know*, a positive integer is any whole number greater than zero. (Smith and Land, 1981, p. 38)

Smith and Land also note that clarity can be reduced by *mazes*—false starts or halts in speech, redundantly spoken words, or tangles of words. Mazes are italicized in the following example.

> This mathematics lesson *will enab . . .* will get you to understand *number, uh,* number patterns. Before we get to the *main idea of the,* main idea of the lesson, you need to review *four conc . . .* four prerequisite concepts. The first *idea, I mean, uh,* concept you need to review is positive integers. A positive *number . . .* integer is any whole *integer, uh,* number greater than zero. (Smith and Land, 1981, p. 38)

Discontinuity

A third element that can detract from clarity is discontinuity, in which the teacher interrupts the flow of the lecture by interjecting irrelevant content or mentioning relevant content at inappropriate times. Repeatedly saying "uh" is another detractor from clarity.

Clarity of presentation

Other research has attempted to specify indicators of clarity in more positive terms. Smith and Sanders (1981) showed that presentations were easier to follow when highly structured. Following Anderson (1969), they defined structure in terms of linear redundancy in the appearance of key concepts. In well-structured presentations, key concepts tend to be repeated from one sentence to the next, although new ones are gradually phased in and old ones phased out. This structure is typical of prose that moves systematically through a series of related statements. In poorly structured presentations, the content is more jumbled. Key concepts are repeated just as often, but not in contiguous sentences. As a result, even if the same sentences are included in each version, the well-structured presentations are clearly recognizable as organized sequences of related facts, but the poorly structured presentations sound more like lists of unrelated facts.

Rule-example-rule pattern

Rosenshine (1968) reviews research indicating that clarity of presentation is associated with appropriate gestures and movements, rule-example-rule patterns of discourse, and frequent use of explaining links. In the rule-example-rule pattern, the teacher first presents a general rule, then a series of examples, and finally a restatement of the general rule. This contrasts with patterns in which teachers either never state the rule or state it only once rather than giving it both before and after the examples. Explaining links are words that denote cause, means, or purpose (because, in order to, if . . . then, therefore, consequently, and so on). Use of such explaining links makes explicit the causal linkages between phrases or sentences in ways that might not be clear without such language. For example, consider the following sentences:

Explaining links

1. Chicago became the major city in the midwest and the hub of the nation's railroad transportation system.
2. Because of its central location, Chicago became the hub of the nation's railroad transportation system.

The first example presents the relevant facts but does not make explicit the linkage between them, as the second example does. If asked, "Why did Chicago become the hub of the railroad transportation system," most students taught with the second example would respond, "Because of its central location." However, many students taught with the first example would respond, "Because it is a big city," or would answer in some other way that indicated failure to appreciate the linkage between a city's geographical location and the role that it plays in a nation's transportation system.

Other guidelines about clarity in lecturing can be inferred from the work on text structuring described in Chapters 9 and 10 and the work on selection and juxtaposition of examples and concepts described in Chapter 11. Students are likely to find a presentation easier to follow to the extent that the teacher has used a logical organizing structure and has made this structure explicit to them, and they are likely to comprehend concepts to the extent that the teacher presents them with rational sets of examples that both indicate the nature and range of defining attributes through positive examples and show the limits of application through negative examples.

Perrott (1982) suggests that clear presentations feature continuity, sim-

Judging clarity factors

plicity, and explicitness. She suggests the following criteria for judging these clarity factors:

Continuity

1. *Sequence of discourse*—The lesson should follow a planned sequence that is made obvious to the students. Diversions from this structure should be kept to a minimum, and where they do occur (usually in response to student questions or comments), it should be made clear to the students that they are diversions.
2. *Fluency*—The teacher should speak in easily intelligible grammatical sentences, seldom leaving sentences unfinished or having to interrupt in order to reformulate a statement.

Simplicity

1. *Avoid grammatical complexity*—The teacher should keep sentences short, minimize multiple qualifying clauses, and use visual means such as diagrams, tables, and models to communicate complex relationships that are difficult to understand from a verbal presentation.
2. *Vocabulary*—The teacher should use simple language that is within the students' normal vocabulary for effective communication. Only those technical terms needed for adequate comprehension of the material should be introduced during the lecture, and these should be defined or explained adequately.

Explicitness

1. *Inclusion of all the elements of an explanation*—Explanations should include both identification of the components (objects, events, processes) to be related, and specific description of the relationship between these components (causal, justifying, interpreting, etc.).
2. *Explicit explanation statements*—The teacher should include explaining links that clarify the causal or logical relationships between the components being related.

Use of chunking strategies

If the lecture is lengthy, the teacher can help the students use chunking strategies by explicitly noting its subparts and the transitions between them, and by including internal summaries at the end of each subpart. If the continuity of the presentation has been broken by student questions or discussion, the teacher can help re-establish the desired learning set by restructuring the presentation before continuing with it by reminding the students of the overall structure of the presentation and of the place at which it is being resumed.

Pacing, Gestures, and Enthusiasm. Although there is no substitute for appropriately selected and well-structured content, the success of a lecture will also depend on the lecturer's communication skills.

Pacing

Pacing is one crucial component. An overly slow pace will induce boredom and cause many students to tune out, and an overly rapid pace will leave many students frustrated and confused. The pace is often too slow in many classrooms, and experiments involving increasing the tempo of presentations have sometimes increased student achievement (Rippey, 1975; Carnine, 1976). Thus, at least for material that is relatively familiar and easy to learn, brisk pacing may be ideal. On the other hand, experiments in science classes involving presentations of abstract or complex content have shown increased achievement in classrooms where teachers were taught to slow down their pacing by waiting 3 to 5 seconds following each statement (Tobin, 1980; Tobin & Capie, 1982). Thus, relatively familiar, easy, or low-level content may be taught best with brisk pacing, but relatively unfamiliar, difficult, or high-level content requires slower pacing, possibly considerably slower than normal in some situations.

Gestures and movements

Gestures and movements can also enhance the effectiveness of a lecture. Gestures, facial expressions, pointing, and appropriate movements can increase comprehension if they supplement the oral communication effectively and are not overly theatrical or otherwise distracting. The stimulus variations introduced through such gestures and movements are especially likely to enhance the comprehension of secondary students (Wyckoff, 1973).

Enthusiasm

Finally, teacher enthusiasm during lecturing is likely to affect both student achievement and student attitudes (Rosenshine, 1970; Abrami, Leventhal, & Perry, 1982). There is no need for histrionics, especially for teachers who are not comfortable "performing" for their students, but it should be clear from the presentation that the teacher finds the content meaningful and interesting, and expects the students to do so too.

Concluding the Lecture. Rather than simply coming to a stop, lectures should end with planned conclusions designed to accomplish particular objectives. Most typically, the conclusion will involve review of the main points that the teacher wants the students to remember, presented with emphasis on the structuring elements that tie these points together. Following this review, the teacher would ordinarily shift from lecture to some other mode of instructional interaction with the students, such as inviting questions, initiating discussion, or shifting to a follow-up assignment or some other activity.

Questioning and Responding to Students

Along with making effective presentations, basic instructional skills include structuring effective reviews, recitations, and discussions through well-planned sequences of questions and responding effectively to the answers that these questions elicit from students. Theoretical sources suggest that such questioning is important to provide teachers with feedback about the effectiveness of their instruction and to provide students with opportunities to practice and receive feedback about their progress in meeting knowledge and comprehension objectives and with opportunities to pursue higher-level objectives by applying, analyzing, synthesizing, or evaluating what they are learning. Furthermore, process-outcome research (reviewed in Brophy &

Responding to student questions with attention and interest helps to establish a good learning environment.

Good, 1985) indicates a positive relationship between frequency of academic questions addressed to students and size of gain in student achievement. Along with frequent presentations of academic content, frequent questioning and responding to students during public lessons are also part of the pattern of active teaching that is associated with success in eliciting student achievement gain.

Drills, recitations, and discussions

Activities involving questioning and responding to students range from drills or reviews designed to test or reinforce students' knowledge of specific facts taught and practiced previously (where the emphasis is on obtaining "right answers" and moving at a brisk pace), to discussions designed to stimulate students to respond diversely and at higher cognitive levels to what they have been learning (where the pace is slower, the emphasis is on developing insights and implications, and where there may be many acceptable answers to a given question, and no single "right answer"). In between are various recitation activities that vary in pace and cognitive level of question. These include the questioning and response segments that occur in between presentation segments of extended lessons, as well as most activities that teachers refer to as "going over the material" or "elaborating on the text." Board work in mathematics and the questioning that occurs in the process of preparing students for assignments would also be included here.

Recitation method

Educational critics working from a theoretical rather than an empirical base often speak warmly of discussion but criticize drill and most forms of recitation as boring, unnecessarily teacher-dominant, restricted to low-level objectives, or designed to make students passive and oriented toward producing right answers rather than to thinking. Yet, like the criticisms of the lecture method, these criticisms are directed mostly to the overuse or inappropriate use of the recitation method rather than to weaknesses inherent in the method itself. Furthermore, like the lecture method, the recitation method persists as a frequently used approach to classroom instruction (Dillon, 1982; Durkin, 1978–79; Gall, 1970; Hoetker & Ahlbrand, 1969; Sirotnik, 1983; Stodolsky, Ferguson, & Wimpelberg, 1981). Apparently, this is because recitation is well suited to the task of instructing students in the classroom context. It allows the teacher to work with the whole class or a significant subgroup rather than with individuals; it provides students with opportunities to learn from one another as well as from the teacher; it is an efficient way for teachers to respond to students' common needs for opportunities to practice and receive immediate feedback on their learning of new content; it provides a quick and convenient way for teachers to check on the effectiveness of their instruction before moving on to additional instruction or a follow-up assignment; and it brings managerial advantages in the form of greater student attention and easier teacher monitoring of the class than is typical in individualized learning situations. Thus, for most teachers the question is not whether to use recitation, but when to use it and how to use it effectively.

We will review expert advice and findings from process-outcome research concerning the nature and sequencing of the type of questions to ask and the processes of questioning the students, eliciting responses, and reacting to those responses with feedback or additional questioning.

Preparing Sequences of Questions

Much of the advice to teachers about questioning, as well as much of the research on the topic, concerns the issue of level of question. Actually this issue subsumes two separate topics—difficulty level of question and cognitive level of question.

Difficulty Level of Question. The difficulty level of a question is determined by whether or not the students will be able to answer it. Whatever the cognitive level of the response that the question demands, the question is easy if most students can answer it correctly and difficult if most students cannot.

Process-outcome data indicate that the highest achievement gains are seen in classes where most, perhaps 75 percent, of the teachers' questions are answered correctly, and most of the rest yield partially correct or incorrect answers rather than no responses at all. Brophy and Evertson (1976) found that the optimal percentage varied according to the socioeconomic status of the students. Achievement gain was maximized in high-SES classes when about 70 percent of the questions were answered correctly, but achievement was maximized in low-SES classes when about 80 percent of the questions were answered correctly. Thus, students appear to learn efficiently when they can answer most of their teacher's questions correctly, although high-SES students profit from a somewhat greater level of challenge than the level that is optimal for low-SES students.

Accuracy of response

Although the 75-percent norm is a useful rule of thumb, bear in mind that it represents an average calculated by aggregating data from various question-and-answer settings. We would expect success rates to be lower than 70 percent when teachers first present new material to students and begin to question them about it, but to be up closer to 100 percent for a drill on familiar material that is supposed to have been mastered. Furthermore, since the 75-percent norm applies only when answers can be characterized as either right or wrong, it is irrelevant to discussions on matters of taste, value, or opinion.

Cognitive Level of Question. Cognitive level of question is determined by scoring the nature of the response that the question demands according to the Bloom taxonomy (knowledge, comprehension, application, analysis, synthesis, evaluation) or related typologies (fact versus thought question; product versus process versus opinion question). Reviews of research on teacher-questioning behavior agree in finding that most, perhaps 80 percent or more, of teachers' questions are low-level knowledge or comprehension questions rather than high-level questions (Dunkin & Biddle, 1974; Gall, 1970; Rosenshine, 1971; Wilen, 1984; Winne, 1979; Hare & Pulliam, 1980). Educational critics typically take this as evidence that teachers ask too many low-level questions and not enough high-level questions, but the empirical research on this issue is mixed.

High-level questions

Higher-order questions do tend to elicit higher-order responses from students (Martin, 1979; Lamb, 1976), although many students' responses will be at a lower cognitive level than the question called for (Dillon, 1982; Mills et al., 1980; Willson, 1973). Furthermore, many process-outcome studies on the topic have revealed positive relationships between the number or percentage of higher-level questions asked by teachers and student achievement, especially achievement of higher-level objectives (Redfield & Rousseau, 1981). However, several studies reported positive relationships between achievement gain and lower-level questions by teachers, coupled with negative relationships or absence of significant relationships for higher-level questions. Most of these were correlational field studies done in primary grade classrooms in schools serving primarily low-SES populations (Soar & Soar, 1979; Brophy & Evertson, 1976; Stallings, 1975; Good & Grouws, 1977), but some such studies involved middle class students at higher grade levels (Clark et al., 1979; Clasen, 1983). Also, some experimental studies seem to show that lower-level questions are at least as effective as higher-level questions for promoting achievement of both lower-level and higher-level objectives (Clark et al., 1979; Dillon, 1981a; Gall et al., 1978; Ryan, 1973, 1974).

Given such conflicting findings, it is not surprising that some reviewers are either unable to identify a clear trend in the data (Dunkin & Biddle, 1974; Rosenshine, 1971) or draw conflicting conclusions (Redfield & Rousseau, 1981; Winne, 1979).

What conclusions can be drawn? First, the data refute the simplistic but frequently assumed notion that higher-level questions are categorically better than lower-level questions. Several studies indicate that lower-level questions can facilitate learning, even learning of higher-level objectives.

Second, even when the percentage of higher-level questions correlates positively with achievement gain, the numbers on which these correlations are based typically show that only about 25 percent of the questions asked were classified as higher level. Thus, as a rule of thumb, we should expect teachers to ask more lower-level than higher-level questions, even when dealing with higher-level content and seeking to promote higher-level objectives.

These are just frequency norms, however. In order to develop more useful information about cognitive level of question, researchers will have to develop more complex ways of coding that take into account teachers' goals (it seems obvious that different kinds of questions are appropriate for different goals), the quality of the questions (clarity, relevance, etc.), and their timing and appropriateness given the flow of the lesson. Also, such research will have to shift from the individual question to the question sequence as the unit of analysis. Teachers do not plan in terms of asking a certain percentage of lower-level questions and a complementary percentage of higher-level questions. Instead, they plan sequences of questions designed to accomplish particular objectives. For some purposes such as asking students to suggest a possible application of an idea, and then probing for details about how the suggested application might work, a sequence that begins with a higher-level question and then proceeds through several lower-level follow-up questions would be appropriate. A different purpose, such as trying to call students' attention to relevant facts and then stimulate them to integrate these facts and draw a conclusion, would call for a series of lower-level questions followed by a higher-level question.

Question sequence

If question sequences are carefully planned to accomplish particular objectives that in turn are integral parts of a well-designed unit of instruction, issues surrounding the cognitive level of questions will tend to take care of themselves. That is, if the objectives of an activity make sense and the planned sequence of questions is suited to those objectives, then the sequence makes sense. On the other hand, if the activity is supposed to stimulate students to analyze or synthesize what they have been learning but the questions are all at the knowledge and comprehension level, the plans will need to be revised. The same is true if the questions appear to be a random selection of test items rather than one or more planned sequences designed to accomplish particular objectives.

Quality of Questions

Aside from difficulty level and cognitive level, process-outcome research does not have much to say about the quality of effective questions. Wright and Nuthall (1970) did find that teachers who asked one question at a time elicited higher achievement gain than teachers who tended to ask two or more questions consecutively before stopping to give students a chance to respond. Presumably, the latter teachers were not well prepared for their recitation or discussion activities, so that many of their initial questions were poorly formulated and had to be rephrased one or more times.

Questions in a question-and-answer session should be clear, brief, purposeful, and directed to the level of the class.

Groisser (1964) suggests that good questions are clear, purposeful, brief, natural and adaptable to the level of the class, and thought provoking. Clear questions precisely describe the specific points to which students are to respond. In contrast, vague questions can be responded to in too many ways and their ambiguous nature confuses students. Thus, "What tense is used in this clause?" (written on the board) is better than "What do you see here?" and "Should 18-year-olds be allowed to buy beer?" is better than "What about beer?"

Purposeful questions are planned and sequenced with particular objectives in mind. Brief questions tend to be preferable to longer ones because they usually are more clear and to the point. If several points have to be made in order to set up a final question, this is usually best done through a series of questions that move toward the final question one step at a time rather than by asking a single long, involved question preceded by several dependent clauses.

Questions ordinarily should be phrased in natural language adapted to the level of the class. If students do not understand the question, they cannot respond along the lines desired by the teacher. Finally, good questions are thought provoking, especially in discussions. They arouse student curiosity and interest and help them to clarify their ideas and to analyze or synthesize facts in addition to merely listing them. This aspect of question quality is especially important as students move into the upper elementary and secondary grades.

Thought-provoking questions

Groisser (1964) cautions against frequent use of four types of questions that often lead to unproductive student responses: Yes-no questions, tugging questions, guessing questions, and leading questions. Yes-no questions are often used merely as warm-ups to other questions. For example, the teacher asks "Was Grant a good general?" After the student answers, the teacher

Yes-no questions

asks "Why?" or says "Explain your reason." Groisser believes that these yes-no questions merely confuse the lesson focus and waste time, so that it is better to ask the real question in the first place. We see two additional problems with these yes-no questions and with all questions that involve a simple choice between two alternatives ("When water freezes, does it expand or contract?"). First, such questions encourage guessing, because students will be right 50 percent of the time even if they have no idea of the correct answer. Second, such questions have low diagnostic power. One of the important advantages to questioning the students is that it gives the teacher feedback about whether or not they know the material and about the nature of any confusion they may be experiencing. However, because of the guess work and the lack of elaboration involved in responding to yes-no and simple-choice questions, student responses to such questions do not carry nearly as much useful information as responses to more substantive questions do.

Tugging questions

Tugging questions typically follow halting or incomplete student responses ("Well . . . ?" "Yes . . . ?"). Essentially, tugging questions say "Tell me more." They provide no help to students who are stuck for a response, and they may be perceived as nagging or bullying. Instead of asking such tugging questions, teachers are usually better off simply remaining silent or else providing help by rephrasing the question or giving clues.

Guessing questions

Guessing questions require students to guess the answer because they do not possess the facts that would be needed to allow them to deduce it systematically. Guessing questions can be useful as methods of arousing interest in a topic, and they may have instructional value if they are designed to stimulate students to think logically rather than merely guess randomly (estimation exercises in mathematics and various inquiry approaches to science would be included here). However, guessing questions asked for no particular purpose usually just waste time and may encourage students to respond to questions thoughtlessly rather than rationally.

Rhetorical questions

Leading or rhetorical questions ("Don't you agree?") are undesirable because they reinforce student dependence on the teacher and undercut attempts to condition students to expect that teacher questions call for serious thought and formulation of responses.

Addressing entire class

Other suggestions about good questioning procedure, drawn from Loughlin (1961), Groisser (1964), and Good and Brophy (1984), are as follows: First, most questions should be addressed to the entire class rather than to an individual student. That is, the teacher would first ask the question, then give the class time to think, and then call on someone to respond. This way, everyone in the class is responsible for the answer. If the teacher were to name a student to respond before asking the question, only that student would be held responsible for answering. The other students would be less likely to try to answer it in their own minds. However, there are times when a teacher might want to call on a student before asking a question such as when the teacher wants to draw an inattentive student back into the lesson, when the teacher wants to ask a follow-up question of a student who has just answered, or when the teacher plans to call on a shy student who may be "shocked" if called on without warning. Questions ordinarily should be distributed widely among the students rather than addressed primarily to the same few students who provide most of the answers. This will keep most students attentive and accountable for answering the questions, and will provide everyone with opportunities to respond and get feedback.

Questions should be asked in a normal conversational tone of voice rather than in a more formal tone that connotes testing. Typically, they should be asked one at a time and should not be repeated, to condition students to the notion that each teacher question calls for an answer. Multiple questions or continually revised questions are signs of poor preparation and disorganized thinking, and repeating questions merely distracts students.

In summary, a good question is clear in identifying the issue on which the students are to focus and the nature of the response desired, demands a substantive, thoughtful response from students, and is followed by a pause during which students are given time to think and formulate such a response.

Waiting for a Response

Rowe (1974) reported data which at the time seemed remarkable, even hard to believe: After asking questions, the teachers she observed tended to wait less than one second before calling on someone to respond. Furthermore, even after calling on a student, they tended to wait only about a second for the student to give the answer before supplying it themselves, calling on someone else, or attempting to help by rephrasing the question or giving clues. Such findings do not seem to make sense, because they suggest that the teachers were undercutting the value of their questions by failing to give them time to have the desired effect on student thinking.

Results of increasing wait-time

Rowe followed up these observations by training teachers to see what would happen if they extended their wait-times from less than one second to three to five seconds. Surprisingly, most of the teachers found this difficult to do, and some never did succeed. However, in the classrooms where the teachers did extend their wait-times to three to five seconds, the following desirable changes occurred:

1. Increase in the average length of student responses.
2. Increase in the frequency of unsolicited but appropriate student responses.
3. Decrease in failures to respond.
4. Increase in the incidence of speculative responses.
5. Increase in the incidence of student-to-student comparisons of data.
6. Increase in the incidence of statements that involved drawing inferences from evidence.
7. Increase in the frequency of student-initiated questions.
8. Increase in the variety of verbal contributions to lessons by students.

In short, Rowe found that longer wait-times led to more active participation in lessons by a larger percentage of the students, coupled with an increase in the quality of this participation. Subsequent research (reviewed in Tobin, 1983a, 1983b) has replicated and extended these findings. In particular, this research verifies that increasing wait-time leads to longer and higher quality student responses to teacher questions and participation by a greater percentage of the students in the class (Fagan, Hassler, & Szabo, 1981; Rice, 1977; Swift & Gooding, 1983; Tobin, 1980; Tobin & Capie, 1982). These effects are most notable on the less able students in the class.

Problems in extending wait-time

Subsequent research has also verified Rowe's finding that many teachers experience difficulty in attempting to extend their wait-times. For example, in DeTure's (1979) study, even after training, no teacher attained an average wait-time longer than 1.8 seconds. Why should this be? The matter has not been studied systematically, but it seems likely that the answer lies in the pressures on teachers to maintain lesson pacing and student attention. Some teachers may be reluctant to extend their wait-times because they fear, with justification in some cases, that they may lose student attention or even lose control of the class if they do. This is one of many illustrations of how good classroom management and good instruction are mutually dependent and supportive of each other, and it also illustrates one of the continuing dilemmas that require teacher decision making and adjustment to the immediate situation. Wait-times of 3 to 5 seconds are generally preferable to shorter wait-times because they allow more thinking by more students, but the teacher may have to move to shorter wait-times when the class is restive or when time is running out and it is necessary to finish the lesson quickly.

Even without training, most teachers will adjust wait-times at least to some degree according to the type of question asked. They are likely to wait longer, for example, following higher-level questions (especially analysis and synthesis questions) than following lower-level questions (Arnold, Atwood, & Rogers, 1974). Furthermore, the causal linkages between question level and wait-time seem to work in both directions. In addition to noting effects on students, some of the investigators who trained teachers to increase wait-times noted that this change also led to interaction patterns in which the teachers asked fewer questions per time-unit than before, but more questions at higher cognitive levels (Rice, 1977; Fagan, Hassler, & Szabo, 1981).

Thus, in general, we should expect interactions featuring mostly lower-level questions to move at a quicker pace with shorter wait-times, compared to interactions featuring higher-level questions. The appropriateness of these pacing and wait-time factors will depend on the objectives of the activity. Thus, while it is true that most studies in which teachers were trained to slow the pace and extend wait-time have produced positive outcomes, it is also true that these studies have tended to be done in intermediate- and upper-grade levels and in the context of teaching abstract or difficult material. Anshutz (1975) reported no science achievement differences between short and long wait-time for students in grades 3 and 4, and Riley (1980) reported interaction effects on science achievement in grades 1 through 5. A decrease in achievement occurred when wait-time was extended from medium to long for low-level questions, whereas an increase in achievement was noted when wait-time was extended for high and mixed cognitive level questions.

Matching pacing and wait-time to questions

The basic principle here is that pacing and wait-time should be suited to the questions being asked, and ultimately, to the objectives these questions are designed to accomplish. A fast pace and short wait-times are appropriate for drill or review activities covering specific facts. However, to the extent that questions are intended to stimulate students to think about the material and formulate original responses rather than merely retrieve responses from memory, it will be important to give time for these effects to occur. This is especially true for complex or involved questions, where students may need several seconds merely to process the question before they can even begin to formulate a response to it. When a slow pace and thoughtful responding are desired, teachers should not only adjust their wait-times but make their objectives clear to the students. Unless cued, some students may not realize that they are supposed to formulate an original response rather than remember something taught to them explicitly, and some may think that the teacher is looking for speed rather than quality of response.

Selecting a Respondent

As noted previously, it is usually best to address the question to the whole class, pause to give the students time to think, and then call on one of them to respond rather than to identify the respondent before even asking the question. Given that the question has been asked, however, whom should the teacher call on? A student likely to know the answer? A volunteer? A student who has not participated lately? Little research is available on this isssue.

Teachers are often advised to be random or at least unpredictable in calling on students to respond to questions, because this will make all students accountable for being prepared to answer the questions and thus will help maintain student attention to the lesson. Research on classroom management does suggest that attention is better when teachers are unpredictable rather than predictable in their patterns of calling on students (Kounin, 1970; Smith, 1980). Thus, it probably is wise to distribute questions in such a way that students know that they may be called on at any time.

Brophy and Evertson (1976) and Anderson, Evertson, and Brophy (1979) observed an exception to the "unpredictable" guideline in their studies of small group instruction (mostly in reading) in the primary grades. In these studies, teachers who elicited the most achievement from their students used a predictable, patterned method of allocating reading turns and response opportunities in these small group interactions. Rather than skip around unpredictably, they would start at a particular place in the group and then proceed systematically around the group, moving from one student to the next. There appear to be several reasons why the patterned-turns method was appropriate in this setting. For one, it insured that all students participated often and roughly equally. This is important in the early grades, when students need opportunities to practice overtly and get feedback from the teacher. Unless teachers use the patterned method or some other method of making sure that response opportunities are distributed equally, they tend to call on the brighter and more assertive students more often than the other students. Also, given the age levels of the students, the structure and predictability that the patterned-turns method imposed on these small group lessons probably was supportive of learning. In low-SES settings, such structure probably helped anxious and alienated students follow and concentrate on the lessons, and in high-SES settings, it cut down on the students' tendencies to compete for response opportunities because the students knew that everyone would get a turn.

Patterned-turns method

The patterned-turns method would ordinarily be inappropriate in whole class settings, however, because it tends to slow pacing in unhelpful ways and because its lack of flexibility creates mismatches between the nature of a question and the readiness of a particular student to respond. Furthermore, it is not advisable even in small group settings with older students who may be tempted to look ahead and attempt to predict and practice material that they expect to be questioned about later, thus tuning out most of the discussion that occurs in the meantime. Thus, the suggestion that teachers be unpredictable in distributing response opportunities is good advice for most teaching situations.

Need for involvement of everyone

This leaves the issue of whom to call on. A good rule of thumb is to try to keep everyone involved while accommodating individual needs and preferences. As students move through the grades, they become progressively more capable of learning from monitoring classroom interaction, and consequently progressively less in need of responding overtly at frequent intervals. Thus, calling more often on "phantom" students who pay attention to lessons but seldom volunteer to respond to questions will not necessarily increase their achievement (Hughes, 1973; Good & Brophy, 1974). Even so, it probably is a good idea to call on these students, and on any students who seldom volunteer, when opportunities arise, both to develop their confidence and willingness to participate and to reinforce the perception that academic questions and interactions are intended for the class as a whole, not just for the subset of students who volunteer routinely.

Nonvolunteers

Thus, students who do not volunteer often probably should be called on whenever they do volunteer, and in addition, should sometimes be called on as nonvolunteers. Process-outcome research suggests that calling on nonvolunteers is not harmful, and sometimes is advisable, so long as the students who are called on are able to respond correctly most of the time. Thus, it is a good idea for teachers to call on nonvolunteers when they are confident that these students will be able to respond correctly, but it is not a good idea to embarrass them by requiring them to respond to questions that they cannot handle. Even when calling on nonvolunteers, teachers should maintain a conversational tone and an atmosphere suggestive of common exploration of the subject matter, rather than an ordeal in which the teacher is going to find out who knows the answers and who doesn't.

Setting guidelines

Teachers may sometimes wish to invite or at least allow students to call out answers without first seeking and getting permission to respond, especially if the students are typically anxious or reticent. Even so, it is important that teachers retain control over response opportunities by socializing their students to follow desired guidelines. If teachers fail to do this and instead allow themselves to be conditioned by the students, a small subgroup of assertive students will co-opt most response opportunities for themselves and another subgroup will cease active attention to lessons.

Reacting to Student Responses

Teachers' reactions to student responses will depend to some extent on the nature of the question asked and the nature of the student called on, but mostly they will depend on the nature of the student's response. Possibilities include failure to respond at all, responding incorrectly, giving a response that is partly correct or incomplete, and responding correctly.

When the Student Fails to Respond. Sometimes students make no overt response at all. They remain silent, possibly thinking about the question and formulating a response, or possibly simply waiting for the teacher to do something. Process-outcome research indicates that teachers who sustain the interaction in these situations by waiting for a response or eliciting a response through additional questioning get higher achievement from their students than teachers who terminate the interaction by giving the answer or calling on someone else. Apparently, this is another situation where it is important for teachers to socialize their students rather than allow themselves to be conditioned by the students. In particular, teachers should train their students to respond overtly to questions, even if only to say "I don't know."

Waiting for the response

Thus, the initial strategy here is simply to wait for the student either to begin to answer the question or to say that he or she does not know how to respond. The teacher should be willing to wait patiently in these situations, and should caution the other students to remain quiet and give the designated respondent a chance to formulate an answer, rather than waving their hands or calling out answers. When teachers do this routinely, their students are likely to respect one another's response opportunities and the designated respondent is likely to say something before long. If waiting does not elicit a response, the teacher should probe ("Do you have an idea?") in an attempt to elicit a response.

Simplifying the question

If there is still no response, the teacher should simplify by rephrasing the question or giving clues. This should continue until the teacher elicits a substantive response, either correct, partly correct, or incorrect, at which point the feedback reactions described in the following sections can be used.

If it is necessary to give the answer, it may be advisable to have the student repeat this answer, in order to give the student practice in responding overtly and in order to end the interaction on a positive note.

Failure to respond at all is likely to be a problem only with very young students. See Blank (1973) for suggestions about methods of simplifying response demand to levels that will allow such students to respond overtly.

Teacher persistance in seeking improved responses in failure situations, especially when there is no initial response at all, is part of the pattern of positive teacher expectations (Brophy & Evertson, 1976) and sense of personal efficacy as an instructor (Gibson & Dembo, 1984) that is associated with success in eliciting student achievement gain.

When the Student Responds Incorrectly. When students make a substantive response that happens to be incorrect, teachers usually should begin by indicating that the response was not correct. Perhaps 99 percent of the time, this negative feedback should be confined to simple negation of the correctness of the response and should not include personal criticism of the student. However, such criticism may occasionally be appropriate for students who have been persistently inattentive or unprepared.

Acknowledging incorrect answers

The teacher should note explicitly but in a matter-of-fact way that the response was incorrect, because the respondent and some of the onlookers may not realize this unless told. Thus, teachers should not leave the matter ambiguous, or worse, treat the answer as if it had been correct. This will only confuse the students who do not know what is going on and communicate a low opinion of the respondent's intelligence to those who do. It may sometimes be appropriate to try to encourage the respondent by praising the effort or good thinking involved in deriving the answer, but this should be done in a way that leaves both the respondent and the onlookers clearly aware that the answer was incorrect.

Eliciting an improved response

Following the initial negative feedback, teachers usually should try to elicit an improved response by rephrasing the question or giving clues. This is especially advisable when the question is a complex one that lends itself to simplification. Again, the idea here is to sustain the interaction with the original respondent and attempt to elicit an improved response and thus end the interaction on a positive note. However, if the question calls for a specific fact that one either knows or does not know, if the sustained questioning appears to be creating significant anxiety or embarrassment in the respondent, or if for some other reason the teacher believes that further questioning would amount to pointless pumping, it may be preferable to terminate the interaction by giving the answer or calling on someone else.

Giving extended explanations

If it becomes necessary to give the answer, it may be advisable to elaborate by giving a more extended explanation of why the answer is correct or how it can be determined from the information given. Such extended explanation should be included in the feedback whenever the respondent or some of the onlookers might not get the point from hearing the answer alone, as well as at times when a review or internal summary is needed.

When the Response is Incomplete or Only Partially Correct. Frequently, especially in response to complex questions, students offer responses that are partially correct and partially incorrect or are correct as far as they go but less complete than the teacher desires. Here, the teacher's reaction should begin with affirmation of the correctness of that part of the response that is correct. In the case of incomplete responses, this would be followed by additional questioning designed to elicit the part that the student left out. In the case of partly correct and partly incorrect responses, the initial affirmative feedback would be followed by negative feedback or additional questioning designed to call attention to the error and help the respondent to correct it.

When the student's response is too vague or ambiguous to allow the teacher to be sure whether or not it is correct, or whenever the teacher simply wants the respondent to elaborate on the original answer for the benefit of the rest of the class, the teacher's initial reaction might be a call for clarification or elaboration such as, "Tell me more about that" or "Could you elaborate on that for me?"

If the respondent's answer is "correct but not desired" because it will have the effect of moving the discussion away from the topic at hand, the teacher can acknowledge its correctness but then refocus the discussion by asking a follow-up question like, "Okay, but how does that relate to . . . ?"

When the Student Responds Correctly. Correct answers should be explicitly acknowledged as such, unless this information is obvious without an explicit statement from the teacher (which it might be, for example, if the students understand that an answer is correct whenever the teacher simply moves on without commenting on it). Perhaps 90 percent of the time such acknowledgement should be limited to brief head nods or short affirmation statements, and thus should not include more intense or personal praise of the respondent. Such praise is often intrusive and distracting, and it may even embarrass the recipient, especially if the accomplishment was not especially praiseworthy in the first place.

Student achievement and teacher praise

These guidelines are suggested by process-outcome research indicating that teachers who maximize their students' achievement gains are sparing rather than effusive in praising correct answers. They tend to keep attention focused on the academic content of the lesson rather than on the success or failure of individuals in responding to their questions. When such teachers do praise, the praise tends to be spontaneous admiration of genuinely noteworthy accomplishment rather than premeditated application of "praise technique" (see Chapter 16 for suggestions about praising effectively).

Although it is not especially important that teachers praise students' answers frequently, it is important, especially in the upper elementary and secondary grades, that teachers treat students' contributions with interest and respect. Older students tend to feel especially encouraged and reinforced when teachers use their ideas by incorporating them into the lesson (Flanders, 1970; Evertson et al., 1980; Edwards & Surma, 1980).

Another useful response, both for encouraging the respondent and for moving the activity along in desired directions, is to ask one or more follow-up questions or invite the respondent to elaborate on his or her original correct answer.

Finally, in the case of opinion questions or other questions that do not have correct answers or have many potentially correct answers, the teacher can accept a response by writing it on the board and then redirect the question to the class in order to elicit additional answers from additional respondents. Questions about the possible motives for a fictional character's actions or about factors that led up to World War I, for example, could be redirected to the class following each of several acceptable responses.

Responding to Student Questions and Comments

Relevant student questions

Besides reacting to student responses to teacher questions, teachers must react to student-initiated comments and questions. Process-outcome research indicates that teachers who elicit high achievement gain from their students tend to ignore or reject irrelevant student questions and comments that intrude into the activity or suggest failure to pay attention or take it seriously, but tend to be receptive to relevant questions and comments. This is not surprising, because relevant student questions indicate a need for clarification or a desire to know more about the subject, and relevant student comments suggest that students are actively thinking about the material and relating it to their experiences and knowledge. Thus, such questions and comments present "teachable moments" that teachers would be foolish not to take advantage of.

Teacher receptiveness

Yet, some teachers not only fail to be receptive to such questions and comments and to respond to them effectively, but cut them off with irritation or in some other way respond in a manner that makes the students sorry that they asked the question or made the comment in the first place. Research on this topic indicates that embarrassment or humiliation due to a teacher's response to one's question or comment is a frequent experience among students, and that many students have simply stopped asking questions because of it (Dillon, 1981a). Thus, although response to such questions or comments may occasionally have to be kept very brief or delayed until after class because time is short or because a more complete response would move the lesson too far away from its intended focus, teachers should continually make it clear to their students that they welcome such questions and comments, and when possible, should respond to them fully or incorporate them into the ongoing lesson.

Conducting Discussions

Although drill and recitation are frequent in classrooms, true group discussion is rare (Dillon, 1984). Even activities that teachers call "discussion" tend to be recitations in which teachers ask questions and students respond by reciting what they already know or are presently learning. Relatively few such activities are actual discussions in which the teacher and students, working as a group, share opinions in order to clarify issues, relate new input to their prior knowledge or experience, or attempt to resolve some question or solve some problem.

In order to structure and conduct such discussions, teachers must adopt a different role from the role they play in drill and recitation activities. Instead of acting as the primary source of information and the authority figure who determines whether answers are correct or incorrect, the teacher acts as a discussion leader who structures the activity to the extent of establishing its focus, setting boundaries, and facilitating interaction, but otherwise assumes a less dominant and less judgmental role. The discussion may begin in a question-and-answer format, but it should gradually evolve into an exchange of views in which students respond to one another as well as to the teacher, and respond to statements as well as to questions.

Discussion leader role

If ideas are being collected, the teacher should record them by listing them on the board or on the overhead projector, for example, but should not evaluate them as good or bad, right or wrong. Once the discussion gets going, the teacher may wish to intrude into it periodically in order to make connections between ideas, point out similarities or contrasts, request clarification or elaboration, invite students to respond to one another, summarize progress achieved so far, or suggest and test for possible consensus as it develops. However, the teacher does not attempt to push the group toward some previously determined set of conclusions (if the teacher were to do this, the activity would be a guided discovery lesson rather than a discussion).

Discussion pace

Compared to recitation activities, the pace of discussions will be notably slower, with longer periods of silence between bursts of speech. These will provide the participants with opportunities to process what has been said and to formulate responses to it.

Dillon (1981b) has shown that teacher statements can be just as effective as questions for producing lengthy and insightful responses during such discussions. He has also noted (Dillon, 1978) that questions may impede discussions at times, especially if they are closed-ended questions that call for brief responses or are perceived as attempts to test the students rather than to solicit their ideas. To avoid this problem, Dillon (1979) lists six alternatives to questioning that teachers can use to sustain discussions:

Alternatives to questions

1. *Declarative statements*—In discussing the effects of war on the domestic economy, the teacher might respond to a student's statement by thinking "When the war broke out, unemployment dropped." The teacher could introduce this thought into the discussion by stating it directly rather than putting it into the form of a question such as "What happens to the unemployment rate in war time?" or "What causes a drop in unemployment?" The statement provides information that the student will have to accommodate and respond to, but compared to a question, it invites longer and more varied responses.
2. *Declarative restatements*—Teachers can show students that they have

attended to and understood what the students have said by occasionally summarizing. Such summarizing may be useful to the class as a whole, and in addition, psychotherapists using nondirective counseling techniques have found that reflecting people's statements to them tends to stimulate additional and deeper responding.

3. *Indirect questions*—When a direct question might sound challenging or rejecting, the teacher can make a statement like "I wonder what makes you think that" or "I was just thinking about whether that would make any difference or not." Such indirect questions might stimulate further thinking without generating anxiety.
4. *Imperatives*—Similarly, statements such as "Tell us more about that" or "Perhaps you could give some examples" are less threatening than direct requests for the same information.
5. *Student questions*—Rather than do all of the questioning themselves, teachers can encourage students to ask questions in response to statements made by their classmates.
6. *Deliberate silence*—Sometimes the best response to a statement is to remain silent for several seconds in order to allow time for students to absorb the content and formulate follow-up questions or comments.

In general, if teachers expect an activity to involve genuine discussion and not merely recitation, they will have to make this fact clear to the students and alter their own role and questioning behavior accordingly.

Seatwork and Homework Assignments

If homework is to successfully reinforce classroom instruction, the teacher needs to carefully monitor the results.

In addition to questioning and responding to students orally during lessons, teachers provide opportunities for practice and application through seatwork and homework assignments and provide feedback to students when going over or returning those assignments. Not much research is available on seatwork and homework assignments, even though students typically spend half to three-fourths of their time in school working independently (Fisher et al., 1980). Similarly, although most studies on the topic indicate that homework provides a useful supplement to classroom instruction and increases student achievement (Good & Grouws, 1979; Rickards, 1982; Strother, 1984), little is known about how much or what kind of homework should be assigned.

Process-outcome research suggests that independent seatwork is probably overused and is not an adequate substitute either for active teacher instruction or for drill/recitation/discussion opportunities. However, seatwork and homework assignments provide needed practice and application opportunities, and thus should be used to some degree. Ideally, such assignments should be varied and interesting enough to motivate student engagement, new or challenging enough to constitute meaningful learning experiences rather than pointless busywork, and yet easy enough to allow high rates of success with reasonable effort.

Effective seatwork guidelines

Student success rates, and the effectiveness of seatwork assignments generally, are enhanced when teachers explain the work and go over practice examples with the students before releasing them to work independently. Furthermore, once the students are released, the work goes more smoothly if the teachers circulate to monitor progress and provide help when needed. If the work has been well chosen and explained, most of these "helping" interactions will be brief, and at any given time, most students will be progressing smoothly through the assignment rather than waiting for help.

Performance should be monitored for completion and accuracy, and students should receive timely and specific feedback. Where the whole class or group has the same assignment, review of the assignment can be part of the next day's lesson. Other assignments will require more individualized feedback. Where performance is poor, teachers should provide not only feedback but reteaching and follow-up assignments designed to insure that the material is mastered.

Need for stating objectives

Anderson (1981, 1984) showed that students often did not understand the purpose of seatwork assignments, and tended to think about assignments primarily in terms of finishing them rather than in terms of learning what they were supposed to be learning. Observations of the teachers in these classrooms suggested why this was so. When presenting the assignments in the first place, these teachers tended to concentrate on what to do and how to do it, but seldom included statements about the objectives of the assignments. When they circulated among the students as they worked on the assignments, the teachers tended to comment more on looking busy and finishing the work than on the quality of response or level of understanding displayed by the students. They seldom talked about cognitive strategies for doing the work (checking for accuracy and meaningfulness, identifying difficulty areas, applying general strategies to particular tasks). Instead, most of their explanations were procedural, such as "Read the sentence and circle the word that goes in the blank" without explaining how to select the appropriate word. Anderson's work suggests that if teachers want their students to view seatwork and homework assignments as learning experiences rather than merely as routine chores that have to be done for no particular purpose, they will have to provide appropriate modeling and instructions to the students.

Unsuccessful seatwork tasks

Although most of the seatwork that teachers assign their students appears to be intended to appropriately extend or deepen student knowledge rather than merely to keep them busy (Rosenshine, 1980), critical analyses of seatwork suggest that much of it is defective and unlikely to succeed in meeting its intended objectives. Furthermore, this is just as true of the workbooks and other seatwork assignments provided with published curricula as it is of seatwork that teachers design themselves (Osborn, 1982, 1984). These tasks are frequently either too easy or too difficult for most of the students, poorly coordinated with what is being taught during group lessons at the time, or designed in such a way as to be more likely to confuse or mislead the students than to teach them the target concepts. Osborn suggests the following guidelines for seatwork and workbook tasks:

1. A sufficient proportion of these tasks should be relevant to the instruction that is going on in the rest of the unit or lesson.
2. Another portion of these tasks should provide for a systematic and cumulative review of what has already been taught.
3. These tasks should reflect the most important, and thus seatwork-appropriate, aspects of what is being taught in the larger curriculum. Less important tasks should be used only as voluntary activities.
4. Extra tasks should be available for students who need extra practice.
5. The vocabulary and concept level of the task should relate to that used in the rest of the program and used by the students working with the program.
6. The language used in the tasks should be consistent with that used in the rest of the lesson and in similar seatwork tasks.
7. Instructions should be brief, clear, unambiguous, and easy to follow.
8. The layout of pages should combine attractiveness with utility.
9. Tasks should contain enough content so that students doing them are likely to *learn* rather than merely be *exposed.*
10. Tasks that require students to make discriminations should be preceded by sufficient practice on the components of these discriminations.
11. The content should be accurate and precise; seatwork tasks should not present wrong information or perpetuate misrules.
12. Some of the assigned tasks should be fun and have an obvious payoff to the students.
13. Most student response modes called for in these tasks should be consistent from task to task.
14. Student response modes should be as close as possible to actual reading and writing (as opposed to circling, underlining, drawing arrows from one word to another, etc.).
15. The instructional design of individual tasks and of task sequences should be carefully planned.
16. There should be a finite number of task types and forms.
17. The art that appears on the pages should be consistent with the prose of the task.
18. Cute, nonfunctional, space- and time-consuming tasks should be avoided.
19. Tasks should be accompanied by brief explanations of purpose.
20. English-major humor should be avoided.

Workbooks accompanying published curricula

The very basic nature of these guidelines and the light touch with which Osborn has written them may tempt the reader to think that these notions are obvious and thus not very important. However, critical inspection of the workbooks that accompany most published curricula will reveal that many of the tasks included in them violate one or more (usually several) of these guidelines. The directions are frequently long and complex or so brief and ambiguous that they cannot be understood by most of the students, so that guesswork or copying result. Sometimes the response procedures called for are so complex as to be confusing and to cause students to lose sight of the ostensible academic purpose of the assignment (draw a red circle around present-tense verbs, draw a black line under past-tense verbs, and draw green parentheses around future-tense verbs). Many tasks have no real instructional value because they do not develop skills but instead call for students to exercise some skill for no particularly useful purpose (count the prime numbers in a number series or the pronouns in a paragraph).

In summary, then, teachers should keep Osborn's guidelines in mind not only when creating their own seatwork assignments but when inspecting the workbooks that come with published curricula and deciding which assignments to use. Wise teachers will inspect such assignments to see if they have pedagogical value in the first place, and even if they do, will follow up by working the assignments themselves in order to identify inadequate or misleading instructions, erroneous examples, printing errors, and other complications that students should be made aware of.

Homework assignments

The same general guidelines apply to homework assignments, but with the additional constraint that the assignment should be realistic in length and difficulty given the students' abilities to work independently without supervision and feedback from the teacher. Thus, 5 to 10 minutes might be appropriate for fourth-graders, whereas 30 to 60 minutes might be appropriate for college-bound high school students.

Need for monitoring homework assignments

Another important point is that homework performance must be monitored. Voluntary homework might be of some use to that proportion of the students who do it conscientiously, but if homework is to have systematic instructional value for the class as a whole, it will be necessary to set up accountability systems to make sure that homework is completed and turned in on time, to review or grade the work the next day or as soon as possible thereafter, to provide students with feedback, and to take corrective action, such as by requiring students to correct all mistakes and then turn in the work again, or by providing reteaching and follow-up remedial work when necessary.

SUMMARY

All teachers are likely to rely regularly on two basic sets of instructional skills—the skills involved in making presentations (lecturing, demonstrating, explaining), and the skills involved in questioning and responding to students (conducting drills, recitations, and discussions).

Presentations tend to be short and sandwiched between other activities in the early grades, but more extended lectures become frequent in the upper grades. Even at the secondary level, however, lecturing should not ordinarily extend beyond 20 to 30 minutes. Although it has limitations, the lecture method also has important strengths and versatility, and can be used appropriately in certain situations, such as when the objective is to present information, especially information that is not found in the desired form in the textbook or some other readily accessible source. Like all instructional design, preparation for lectures begins with consideration of the objectives and of the constraints and practical considerations that may apply.

This should be followed by development of an outline listing key points to be made, and then a comprehensive plan that includes attention to questions that might be asked during or after the lecture, demonstrations and visual aids to be included, handouts to be distributed, and follow-up activities or assignments. The planning should include a beginning that will attract student attention and interest and induce the appropriate learning set, and an ending that will review key points, tie things together, and bring the presentation to closure.

The lecture should be clear and easy to follow. This will be accomplished if the teacher avoids vague terms, mazes, discontinuity, and other problems that detract from clarity, as well as enhances clarity by structuring and sequencing the material appropriately, beginning with advance organizers, using rule-example-rule patterns, and including explaining links that make explicit the causal or logical connections between elements. Attention to and comprehension of the lecture will also be enhanced if it is delivered with appropriate pacing, gestures, and communication of enthusiasm about the content.

Like lecturing, activities involving questioning and responding to students have both strengths and limitations that make them more useful for some purposes than for others. The two major purposes of such activities are to provide opportunities for the teacher to assess student understanding of what has been presented and to provide opportunities for the students to process and respond more actively to the material than they are likely to do when merely listening to a presentation. In general, such activities have greater pedagogical value and generate a better response from the students when the emphasis is more clearly on providing the students with opportunities to process and respond to input than on finding out who knows the answers and who does not.

Questioning activities range from fast-paced drills and reviews of specific factual knowledge to slow-paced discussions designed to stimulate students to respond diversely and at high cognitive levels. Either of these extremes, as well as the range of recitation activities that lie in between, may be appropriate for accomplishing particular instructional objectives. Teachers have been criticized for conducting too much drill and recitation and not enough discussion, and this may be true in many classrooms. However, in such cases the problem is a lack of balance between different instructional objectives and their associated activities, and not something inherently inappropriate with drill or recitation activities.

Process-outcome research suggests that achievement gains are maximized when teachers elicit correct responses to about 75 percent of their questions and elicit substantive (partially correct or incorrect) answers rather than no responses at all to the rest of their questions. High-SES classes appear to respond to a somewhat greater level of challenge than low-SES classes, but even here, perhaps 70 percent of the questions should be answered correctly. Within these general rules of thumb, we should expect lower success rates on questions about material just being introduced and considerably higher success rates on review questions covering material that has supposedly been mastered.

Process-outcome research on the cognitive level of teacher questions has produced confusing and contradictory results. There is no support for the simplistic conclusion that higher-level questions are good and lower-level questions are bad, or even for the notion that there should be more higher-level questions than lower-level questions. However, it is difficult to develop more positive or prescriptive guidelines from this body of research. The problem is that research has used the individual question rather than the sequence of questions as the unit of analysis, when it is the sequence that needs attention. Assuming the appropriateness of the instructional objective in the first place, the real issue is the degree to which a planned sequence of questions makes sense as a way to accomplish that objective.

Research and expert opinion suggest that good questions are clear, purposeful, brief, natural and adapted to the level of the class, thought-provoking, addressed initially to the entire class rather than to an individual student, distributed widely among the students, asked one at a time, and asked in a normal conversational tone of voice. After asking the question, the teacher should wait long enough for students to process the question and formulate responses to it. This wait-time may be very brief, perhaps a second or less, following factual questions during fast-paced reviews, but it should be 3 to 5 seconds or longer during slower-paced discussions or during activities designed to get students to analyze or synthesize their knowledge. Experiments in which teachers have been trained to increase their wait-times have revealed that longer wait-times produce more active participation in lessons by a larger percentage of the students, coupled with an increase in the quality and length of their responses.

For accountability reasons, it is usually wise to distribute questions in such a way that students know that they may be called on at any time. Although research on primary-grade reading groups has shown that the patterned-turns method is more effective than a random or unpredictable method of calling on students in this particular setting, it seems advisable that teachers try to be unpredictable in their selection of respondents to questions when teaching in whole class settings or at higher grade levels. It is important that each student respond overtly and frequently in the early grades when basic skills are being taught, but this becomes less important as students become capable of learning by attending to lessons without having to respond overtly themselves. Thus, it is less essential, at least for producing achievement gain, that teachers in the upper elementary and secondary grades distribute response opportunities roughly equally among their students. However, both to provide all students with opportunities to respond in public and to avoid having classroom recitations evolve into interchanges between the teacher and just a few assertive students, it is wise to try to keep everyone involved and to call on nonvolunteers as well as volunteers. The nonvolunteers should be able to answer most of the questions they are asked correctly, however.

Guidelines are given for reacting to students in four situations: when they fail to respond at all, when they respond incorrectly, when they give an incomplete or partially correct response, and when they give a correct response. In general, it is best for teachers to sustain the interaction with the original respondent and attempt to elicit an improved response rather than to terminate the interaction by giving the answer or calling on someone else. Teachers should train their students to respond overtly, even if to say "I don't know", rather than to remain silent when called on. If the student needs help, the teacher can simplify or rephrase the question or give clues. Which techniques to use and how long to persist in attempting to elicit improved responses will depend on the nature of the question asked, the psychological state of the respondent, and external factors such as time availability and the attention and patience of the rest of the class.

Students who answer correctly need to know that their answer has been correct, as do the onlookers, but this is usually best accomplished with simple affirmative feedback rather than with more extended or intense praise. Except for spontaneous expressions of admiration of outstanding answers, teacher praise of correct responses in public situations tends to be intrusive and distracting, and may even embarrass certain students. On the other hand, it is important to treat students' contributions with interest and respect, and to use their ideas by incorporating them into the lesson whenever possible. It is also important to be receptive to relevant questions and comments by the students.

In order to conduct effective discussions, teachers must adopt a discussion-leader role that differs from the role that they play in drill and recitation activities. Although they structure the discussion and keep it on track, they act more as a collector and clarifier of opinions than as a judge of their correctness. A good discussion will proceed at a slower pace than the typical recitation activity, and although it may begin with questions and answers, it should gradually evolve into an exchange of views in which students respond to one another as well as the teacher and respond to statements as well as questions. Dillon suggets six alternatives to questioning that teachers can use to elicit lengthy and thoughtful student responses during discussions.

Independent seatwork and homework assignments are desirable elements of balanced instructional approaches for most classrooms, even though some teachers overuse the seatwork method. Ideally, seatwork and homework assignments will be interesting enough to engage student attention, new or challenging enough to constitute worthwhile learning experiences or practice/application opportunities, and yet easy enough to allow high success with reasonable effort. Their effectiveness is likely to depend on the degree to which teachers go over the assignments with the students before releasing them to work independently, monitor performance for completion and accuracy, supply timely and specific feedback, and follow up with appropriate remedial instruction where necessary. Osborn presents guidelines for judging the effectiveness of seatwork and workbook activities. Guidelines concerning homework assignments are similar to those for seatwork assignments, but with the additional constraint that such homework must be realistic in length and difficulty for the students involved.

QUESTIONS AND PROBLEMS

1. Pay close attention to the presentations made by instructors in your various classes. In your judgment, what makes for differences in the interest value, clarity, and all around usefulness of these presentations? Can you identify criteria beyond those included in this chapter?
2. What types of presentation are used most typically in the grade level and subject matter you expect to teach? Are there extended lectures, or just briefer presentations preceding or sandwiched in between other activities?
3. Given that students will have textbooks, films, and other sources of input, what do you foresee as the role of your presentations to them as a teacher? How will these presentations complement or supplement these other sources?
4. How can you check on the effectiveness of your presentation during or immediately following it? Is it enough to say "Any questions?" If not, what should you do?
5. Using the guidelines presented in this chapter, develop a comprehensive plan for a presentation at the grade level and in the subject matter you intend to teach. Include attention to props, media, and follow-up questions and activities in addition to the selection and organization of the content. If possible, get your plan critiqued, revise it, and then try out the presentation in the classroom setting and revise once more if necessary.

6. If possible, audiotape or, preferably, videotape yourself making a presentation and then analyze the content for organization, sequencing, and clarity, and the delivery for pacing, gestures, and enthusiasm.
7. What types of drill/review, recitation, and discussion activities do you expect to use in your own teaching? Are these expectations realistic given the grade level and subject matter?
8. Why do you think it is that, even when pursuing higher-level cognitive objectives, teachers are likely to ask more lower-level questions than higher-level questions?
9. Why is it more profitable to plan in terms of question sequences rather than individual questions?
10. If you expect your questions to generate cognitive activity in your students rather than merely to provide an opportunity to test their knowledge, what does this imply about pacing, wait-time, and distribution of response opportunities to different individuals in the class?
11. Do you think that you might become one of those teachers whose wait-times are counterproductively short? If so, why? What steps could you take to inhibit your impulsiveness and increase your tolerance for the periods of silence associated with longer wait-times?
12. Some students are quite successful in that they understand what they are learning, turn in assignments correctly and on time, and earn high grades. Yet, they seldom volunteer to answer questions and in general prefer to watch and listen rather than to contribute to classroom activities. Should you accommodate these students by mostly leaving them alone, or should you frequently call on them as nonvolunteers in order to force them to participate? Compare notes on this issue with your friends.
13. How should you handle students who feel pressured and embarrassed in public response situations when they cannot supply the correct answer immediately? Should these students be considered exceptions to the general rule that teachers should sustain the interaction and try to elicit an improved response in these situations?
14. How should you respond if a student asks a question that from one point of view is an excellent question that sets up a "teachable moment" that may have value in extending the content for the class, but that you suspect has been asked as a ploy to put off an expected quiz until tomorrow rather than because the student really wants the information?
15. If you really want students to ask questions when they feel the need for information, what are some dos and don'ts concerning your response to those questions?
16. Are you prepared to adopt the change in role that is required if teachers are to stimulate genuine discussion among their students? How should you respond when a student or even the class as a group expresses opinions that differ from yours? How should you respond when a student offers an opinion that is sincere but immature or socially naive, thus producing snickering by classmates?
17. What kinds of seatwork assignments do you expect to use, and for what purposes? What accountability procedures and mechanisms for providing assessment and feedback will you use?
18. Will you assign homework? If so, for what purposes? How will you assess whether these purposes are being met?

Too Many Questions. Ms. Kane had been teaching for two weeks at Bayside Jr. High School. This was her first teaching job and she had looked forward to it. However, she was already discouraged and beginning to feel that she had made a poor choice of career. In particular, she was bothered by the fact that after about five minutes of lecturing, she would notice a number of confused student faces, inevitably followed by what to her were a series of irritating questions (Why are you telling us this? Do we have to remember all of this? Didn't we do this yesterday?). If Ms. Kane asked you for advice about how she might improve the introductory aspects of her lesson presentations, what would you suggest?

Oh, Shut Up! Mr. Moderator likes to include a lot of discussion in his social studies classes. He particularly likes to pose some problem, invite student opinions on how it might be solved, and then probe the pros and cons of these suggestions in a discussion in which the students respond to one another as well as to him. This approach has worked successfully in the past. Even though some students participated more than others, there was wide participation and the students found the discussions stimulating and educational.

This year, though, the discussions have increasingly been dominated by two students who particularly enjoy both hearing themselves talk and arguing with each other. This makes for useful interchange at times, but often the two of them seem to be arguing just for the sake of arguing, and both Mr. Moderator and the rest of the class are getting pretty tired of listening to them day after day. What can Mr. Moderator do about this? List possible options and order them in terms of their probable effectiveness in solving the problem.

Part Five

Motivation

Sandra noticed that her heart was beating rapidly while she listened to a classmate make an extemporaneous speech. "Four more speakers, and then it's my turn," she moaned softly to herself. "Why do I always get so nervous when I have to speak in front of a group?" Her heart pounded so loudly she could hear it. "I hate this class and this pressure!" she thought.

Sam flung the box against the wall. "Helen!" he screamed, "This space cruiser kit is driving me crazy! The directions say a child can assemble it in 15 minutes, but I've been working on the thing for over an hour. Don't you ever again buy a toy for me to assemble on Christmas Eve!"

Jane confidently walked into the professor's office and without being asked, sat down in the chair beside her desk. "Jane," the professor said, "I've been very pleased with the writing you have done in this course. Not only are your themes interesting, but you support your beliefs quite well." Jane looked her professor in the eye, smiled brightly, and said, "I'm glad to hear this. I've really worked on writing and rewriting and I had reached a point at which I was satisfied with my work. However, I am glad that your evaluation matched my own."

Mr. Robbins, the tenth-grade chemistry instructor, said to the class, "This is a critical experiment. The procedures we used to verify this process will be used again and again in the next three weeks. If there are any questions about the process, why we're doing it, or alternative procedures that could be used, please ask them now." Although no student was completely certain of the process that had just been demonstrated and many students were confused, no one raised his or her hand to get additional clarification.

"Look, Sally, I know that Rick is going to raise hell with you, but we can make it worth your while to take the overseas job. After all, it's not going to be a lifetime there, just two or three years. When you come back you can expect a big promotion." Sally listed several personal objections—the same arguments she had used during the preceding 45-minute conversation with her supervisor. After another five minutes the supervisor said, "Sally, there's one thing I haven't told you. In addition to all the other advantages I mentioned, your salary would jump from $25,000 to $36,000." Within a few minutes, Sally agreed to the assignment.

These vignettes illustrate important themes in motivation. The first vignette shows how anxiety associated with performing in a classroom can interfere with that performance. Minor stress associated with interest and wanting to do well is probably appropriate; however, too much stress undermines performance.

The second vignette is central to classroom motivation. Many students have learned to blame themselves when things go wrong, even though they may not be at fault. Frustration and failure in school predictably lead to self-castigation and eventually will erode student performance.

The third vignette depicts a student who is responding capably and with intrinsic motivation. That is, the student has defined the task and evaluated her performance. She is interested in getting feedback from others, but is not overly dependent on their evaluation. One goal for classroom teachers is to help students to develop such initiative and confidence in tackling school assignments.

The fourth vignette depicts a common but unfortunate situation. In too many classrooms, students have learned that it is better to "look good" than to get academic information when they need it.

The fifth vignette shows that external rewards, in some cases, influence behavior. In this chapter, we will discuss the role of external rewards in motivating classroom behavior.

In the chapters that follow, we discuss major issues in the study of motivation, present recent theories, and illustrate how these theories apply to classroom practice. Many practical ideas are discussed; however, at the outset we need to acknowledge that enhancing student motivation is not an easy task because students bring different levels of interest, energy, and ability to the classroom and thus vary widely in their responses to learning opportunities.

Chapter 14 presents some major distinctions and defines central terms that are needed in the study of motivational concepts. Here we show the evolution of motivational theory by discussing key historical concepts and theorists. Chapter 15 provides extensive coverage of modern cognitive theories and some of the research evidence on which these emerging perspectives are based.

Chapter 16 focuses on application of motivational principles to classroom settings. The chapter stresses the need for teachers to function as decision makers and tailor their motivational strategies to the particular students they teach. The chapter presents a series of ideas that, if applied intelligently, have rich potential for enhancing student motivation.

Chapter 17 discusses the relationship between teachers' performance expectations for individual students and the ways that teachers interact with, group, and select curriculum assignments for these students. The chapter summarizes extant research on teacher expectation effects and presents detailed guidelines that teachers can apply to enhance the communication of positive, appropriate expectations.

Chapter 18 discusses approaches to motivation that emphasize non-cognitive student outcomes like prosocial behavior and self-efficacy. This chapter describes some of the problems of the traditional classroom as viewed from the humanistic perspective. Chapter 18 also presents examples of humanistic approaches useful for teachers who want to pursue affective goals.

Chapter 14

Basic Concepts of Motivation

OBJECTIVES

When you have mastered the material in this chapter you will be able to

1. Define the concept of motivation from both the behavioristic and cognitive theoretical perspectives
2. Explain how needs and drives develop and how their satisfaction affects students' motivation to learn
3. Discuss the practical application of Maslow's need hierarchy to the motivation of classroom learning
4. Explain the concept of intrinsic motivation and its relationship to student effort and performance
5. Explain how cognitive dissonance is created and can be used to motivate belief changes
6. Discuss the difference between high and low levels of achievement motivation in children and its implications for teaching

As the warm Nevada sun fills the room, Professor John Wilson glances at the clock that reads 6:05 A.M. and moves quietly in order not to disturb his wife, Helen. Happily, he takes his coffee pot to his den and sits down by the typewriter. This was the day he had been waiting for. Final exam week was over. "Now," he says to himself, "I can finish the chapter on motivation that I've been wanting to write for three months." Two hours later, Doug, a friend, calls and invites John to play tennis, stating, "After all, John, the students are gone, and it will be one of the few times we can get a court without waiting an hour or two." John gives in and agrees to play tennis. How can we explain why John's hands ended up around a tennis racket rather than on typewriter keys?

Predicting behavior

Perhaps a more difficult question is, "Could we have predicted John Wilson's behavior in advance?" To predict his response, what would we need to know about John, the writing assignment, and his friend Doug? Some of the many questions we might ask include the following: Does John like the actual process of writing? Does he enjoy writing about motivation, or is it just a necessary part of the book? Does he know the subject matter? Does he want to say more about the topic than room permits? If the book is completed by a specific date is there a monetary reward? Similarly, we might ask a series of questions about his friend Doug: Is he a professional friend? Is he John's department chairman? How does John usually feel after playing with Doug—does he come home relaxed and ready for work or is their game typically filled with quarrelsome debates over line calls so that John returns in an irritated state?

We could continue listing relevant factors, but in a particular instance none of these factors listed may prove to be important. The decision may depend on such events as "All my tennis clothes are dirty" or "I don't have any tennis balls or money to buy them." Predicting behavior in a single instance is risky business, and attempts to do so will often result in error. We might, if given enough information about John, his perceived needs, interests, and abilities (particularly his writing ability and skill at playing tennis), be able to predict the amount of time he would choose to write or to play tennis each week. But predicting his behavior at a given moment is hazardous.

At one time or another all of us have made resolutions, only to have a phone call or knock at the door dissolve the commitment we made to ourselves. Some of us are more likely to respond to certain stimuli in particular situations than are others, and these differences provide the basis for making predictions. Hence, predictions are more accurate for explaining general proclivities such as prefering to work alone on math problems and in a group on social study problems, than for making specific predictions, such as which instructional mode or subject matter a student will prefer at a given point in time.

Motivation Defined

Definition of motivation

We define motivation as a hypothetical construct to explain the initiation, direction, intensity, and persistence of goal-directed behavior. Motivational theorists explain motivation as including all or some of the following concepts: need for achievement ("I want to do well on the final." "I want to play winning tennis."); need for affiliation ("I want to work with my friends."); incentives (reward or punishment); habit ("I never take a study break until 11:00 P.M." "I only play tennis in late afternoon."); discrepancy ("How could I, a moral person, have lied about such a trivial matter?") and innate curiosity ("That seems to work, but I wonder why?").

However, such concepts are usually studied in isolation. All are useful ways of looking at human behavior, but no single concept provides an adequate explanation for motivation. The concepts just listed provide a way to think about behavior and ideas about theoretical frameworks for designing classroom environments, but they do not yield prescriptions that can be applied independent of particular settings (Ball, 1984; Good & Tom, in press).

Factors that influence behavior

Theoretical frameworks provide more comprehensive ways of looking at and predicting behavior than do individual concepts. Different schools of psychologists have looked at "why" questions (an analysis of factors that influence behavior) from different perspectives and have offered varying explanations. Behaviorists feel that behavior is determined by reinforcement contingencies, so they seek to explain motivation by identifying the cues that elicit behavior and the reinforcement that sustains it. Cognitive psychologists believe that people decide what they want to achieve, and that their thought processes control behavior. Hence, cognitive theorists are most concerned with how people process information and interpret personal meanings in particular situations. Humanists also believe that people act on their environments and make choices about what to do, but they are more concerned with the general course of personal development, the actualization of potential, and the removal of obstacles to personal growth. In this chapter we will stress the cognitive approach to motivation. Most aspects of the behavioral approach have already been outlined (in Chapter 7) and the humanistic or affective perspective will be presented in Chapter 18.

Behavioristic Theory

Behavior analysis suggests that behavior is initiated by the occurrence of an external or internal stimulus, and that the direction of behavior is then determined by mechanistic stimulus-response bonds, or habits, built up through reinforcement.

The behavioristic point of view can be explained as follows: The human infant is born with certain biological drives such as hunger that motivate behavior. Through basic conditioning processes, certain behavior patterns that become associated with the reduction of primary biological drives eventually acquire motivating powers of their own and function as secondary drives (such as dependence, social affiliation, aggression). Behavior that satisfies these secondary drives will be reinforced and thus repeated. A long history of consistent reinforcement will produce strong response tendencies. For example, if a student studies during weekends and is rewarded by higher grades she will continue this practice even though attractive alternatives are available. Different reinforcement histories will lead to different interests and ultimately to different abilities. For instance, a person who is consistently rewarded for playing the piano and develops a strong interest in doing so will, in time, outperform others who initially had similar talent but did not receive reinforcement in this area.

Behavioristic versus cognitive approach

Distinctions between the behavioristic and the cognitive approaches to motivation gradually have become blurred as behaviorists have expanded what is included in the list of potential secondary drives (e.g., curiosity, competence) and secondary reinforcements (e.g., children's symbolic behavior in the form of internal statements like "I was right! It works!" is the only reward obtained in some situations). In general, however, behaviorists place more emphasis on external rewards and the systematic arrangement of reinforcement contingencies, whereas cognitive theorists place more emphasis on internal rewards and related cognitive processes.

Expectancy-Value Theory of Motivation

Some theorists (e.g., Atkinson, 1954, 1964; Vroom, 1964) have articulated expectancy-value theories of motivation. They assert that behavior is, in large part, determined by a multiplicative relation between one's expectation about attaining a goal and the valence or attractiveness of the goal. Hence, expectancy-value theorists like Atkinson and Vroom recognized that one's belief about whether a goal could be achieved and the attractiveness of a goal to the individual mediate between stimuli and response. (Atkinson's work will be discussed in more detail later in the chapter.)

Bandura: A Modern Behavioral Viewpoint

Bandura's (1977) social learning theory is a modern behaviorial theory in that it is based largely on the rewards and consequences of specific behavior, yet also considers how students interpret past events and set goals for themselves. According to Bandura, there are two major sources of motivation.

Predicting outcomes

One source deals with predicting outcomes of behavior: If I study hard, will I pass? Can I make the team? Will my speech be well received? Based on the consequences of past actions, the person tries to predict what future consequences will be.

Setting goals

A second source of motivation is actively setting goals that become personal standards for evaluating performance. We tend to continue our efforts until we meet the standard that we have set. While working toward goals, we imagine the positive things that will occur if we succeed and the negative things that will occur if we fail. Upon reaching a goal, we are satisfied for a period of time, but then we begin to identify new goals or to increase the standards that we have for our performance.

Efficacy expectations

Clinical data suggest that efficacy expectations, beliefs about one's ability to succeed, determine how much effort people will expend and how long they will persist in the face of obstacles (Bandura, 1977). According to Bandura, goals that are specific, moderately difficult, and likely to be reached in the not too distant future are most likely to enhance general persistence and effort, and to lead to increased efficacy expectations if reached successfully. Specific goals provide unambiguous standards for judging performance. Goals of moderate difficulty provide a realistic challenge; success in reaching such goals reinforces confidence in one's own abilities and thus increases efficacy perceptions.

Applying Social Learning Theory to Classroom Motivation

If goals for individual students are to be specific and obtainable, different students will need different goals. What is a moderately difficult goal for one student may be a very difficult goal for another. If students can be motivated to adopt externally set learning goals as their own objectives, they will become more self-motivated to achieve. According to the social learning position that Bandura and others articulate, students are more likely to value goals set by the teacher if such goals are clear, specific, reasonable, moderately challenging, and reachable in a relatively short time.

Because people vary in their ability to set goals, evaluate their performance, and reinforce themselves for success, it is likely that many students will need help in these areas. Social learning theory suggests that teachers can provide such help through modeling, cuing, and reinforcing ("That's a good list of goals to accomplish during study hall. Last week you were still trying to do too much. You should be able to complete all of these things today. Good thinking.").

Need Theories

One of the earliest motivational concepts was the concept of need. Many theorists explain human behavior in terms of personal needs. We discuss the theories of Henry A. Murray and A. H. Maslow in this section.

Murray

Murray (1938) was one of the first to explore the need concept. He defined need as a construct (a convenient fiction or hypothetical concept) that stands for a force that influences one's perception and behavior in the attempt to change an unsatisfying situation. A need is a tension that leads an organism to move in the direction of a goal. The goal state is an event capable of releasing the felt tension.

Table 14.1 Murray's Psychogenic Need System

1. Abasement—to surrender . . .
2. Achievement—to overcome obstacles . . .
3. Affiliation—to form friendships and associations . . .
4. Aggression—to assault or injure . . .
5. Autonomy—to resist influence or coercion . . .
6. Counteraction—proudly to refuse admission of defeat . . .
7. Deference—to admire and willingly follow . . .
8. Defendance—to defend oneself against blame or belittlement . . .
9. Dominance—to influence or control others . . .
10. Exhibition—to attract attention to one's person . . .
11. Harmavoidance—to avoid pain, physical injury . . .
12. Infavoidance—to avoid failure, shame, humiliation . . .
13. Nurturance—to nourish, aid or protect . . .
14. Order—to arrange, organize . . .
15. Play—to relax, amuse oneself . . .
16. Rejection—to snub, ignore or exclude . . .
17. Sentience—to seek and enjoy sensuous impressions . . .
18. Sex—to form and further an erotic relationship . . .
19. Succorance—to seek aid, protection or sympathy . . .
20. Understanding—to analyze experience . . .

Murray's concept of need was based on an exhaustive study of a small number of "normal" humans. Table 14.1 contains a list of the twenty social needs Murray found in his studies. These twenty social motives are called psychogenic, or secondary, needs because they are "learned" needs and to some extent dependent on a particular cultural experience.

Psychogenic needs

Viscerogenic needs

In addition to secondary needs, Murray postulated viscerogenic, or primary, needs, which are common to all humans. If these physical needs are not met, the organism dies. Murray noted that needs can also be classified as positive or negative. Positive needs force the organism in a positive way toward other objects, and negative needs such as pain force the organism to withdraw from other objects.

Effective press

According to Murray, a need is typically triggered by an effective press (external determinant of behavior), and these two forces combine to form a pattern of behavior, or theme. Murray's theoretical view suggests that a need may become established by the frequent occurrence of a specific press. For example, a small child may develop a need to achieve in the face of an effective press, such as when parents challenge a child at an early age, expect the child to meet these challenges, and reinforce his or her achievement.

Many of the needs Murray identifies are not evidenced in all cultures. A need develops and motivates behavior only if an individual is exposed to a certain press. A person belonging to a social group that frowns on competition is unlikely to develop a driving need to compete. Children who are reared within the same culture but who live in contrasting social-class settings are exposed to different presses and will come to school with different needs.

Murray's view suggests that behavior is usually an attempt to avoid or release unpleasant tensions. Early events are seen as especially important because once a need is created, it tends to perpetuate itself. For example, the child who is taught to compete may always need to demonstrate competitiveness, even when placed in situations that do not call for it. Furthermore, Murray suggests that once an individual learns how to satisfy his or her needs, behavior within that context is likely to become habitual. Presumably, it is easier to teach someone new behavior in a new context than in one in which he or she has functioned for a long period of time.

Given the above views, it is possible to modify personality or behavior patterns of an individual to some extent so that teachers potentially can have some effect on students' motivation. However, Murray's viewpoint implies that change gets more difficult as children get older. Unless the school effort is systematic and sustained, it is likely to have little permanent effect. (As we shall see, other theoretical viewpoints are more hopeful.)

Few psychologists today believe that all human behavior is a release from or avoidance of unpleasant tensions. Still, Murray's perspective is interesting; our needs often compel us to act in certain ways. We are all familiar with people who must achieve, or who must dominate. Within Murray's framework, all behavior is viewed as purposeful, as it is an attempt to satisfy a need or accomplish a goal. However, Murray makes it clear that needs vary. Some individuals have more need for power, whereas others have more need for achievement or for harmonious social relations. No classroom activity can satisfy the needs of all students simultaneously.

Applying Murray's Theory

Teachers familiar with the individual needs of their students can use their knowledge to motivate learning efforts. Teachers who identify ways to present material to meet the needs of their students will help make the material interesting to the students.

Differential interests

Differential interests may emerge in the same ways as differential personalities and coping styles. Consider two preschoolers, Sam and Bill, who both have abusive, hypercritical parents. Bill finds that when he buries himself in a hobby or looks at pictures in magazines and stays away from his parents he rarely gets into trouble with them. It would not be surprising if Bill enjoys looking at pictures and is able to absorb himself in reading primers by the time he enters kindergarten. Sam, on the other hand, finds that a "passive-withdrawal" reaction (to a similar press) is maladaptive. His absorption in solitary play generally, and any behavior associated with "reading-like" activities specifically, brings a negative response from his parents. Sam is highly unlikely to exhibit much interest in solitary learning tasks

The successful teacher finds a strategy to meet each child's needs.

when he enters kindergarten. Although children seldom develop interest in achievement as a response to abusive parents, it does happen. We include this example here to illustrate that interests may develop in response to nonobvious need/press factors.

Murray's conceptualization reminds us that individuals differ in need patterns. In terms of classroom practice, this implies that effective instruction requires varied organizational structures, lesson approaches, and incentives.

Maslow

The concept of human need is also central to A. H. Maslow's theory that unsatisfied needs create tension that directs behavior toward goals that the individual perceives as rewarding—in other words, goals that reduce tension.

Hierarchy of needs

Maslow (1962) conceptualized a hierarchy of needs arranged in the following order of priority:

1. Physiological needs (sleep, thirst)
2. Safety needs (freedom from danger, anxiety, or psychological threat)
3. Love needs (acceptance from parents, teachers, peers)
4. Esteem needs (mastery experiences, confidence in one's ability)
5. Need for self-actualization (creative self-expression, attempt to satisfy one's curiosity)

Maslow suggests that unless lower needs are satisfied, it is difficult for higher needs to be appreciated, let alone satisfied. The well rested, psychologically secure student may seek to master academic skills and even generate questions to pursue independently, but the exhausted student will have little energy for such activity. Physiological needs are necessary for maintaining life; if they are not met, other needs will disappear or be forced

Physiological needs

into the background. When physiological needs are satisfied, however, progressively higher needs become more powerful.

Maslow suggests that even if all needs were met, a new discontent would soon develop. A musician must make music; a writer must write. But Maslow suggests that if individuals are to seek actively what they are and must be, they must first resolve lower needs. There are temporary exceptions to the order in which needs are fulfilled. For example, you, no doubt, have deprived yourself of a "prepotent" need like sleep in order to prepare for an exam, in the hope of mastering the material (an esteem need). However, Maslow feels that people generally respond to the more basic of two needs.

Resolution of lower needs

Maslow's view recognizes the influence of environmental pushes and pulls, but offers hope that people will respond in thoughtful and productive ways to external presses. However, our search for self-actualization can be influenced by external forces. Students who give up sleep or miss a meal to do well on an exam may be prompted by forces other than their own needs for esteem. This may be the case for Jim, a student at Difficult University, who received the following letter from his father:

> Dear Son:
>
> The receipt of your midterm grades has made it necessary that I write. Your mother and I assure you of our continuing love and affection, for we know you are trying. However, we feel that you are trying more to test our patience than to apply yourself to school demands. Rest assured that the money source that supplies your physiological needs (fraternity house bill, warm clothes, money for food, and so forth) will be terminated at the end of the semester if your grades are not significantly improved. Love as always, your father,
>
> T. L. Motivator

Applying Maslow's Theory

Several implications of Maslow's theory are obvious. A child who comes to class hungry or tired is likely to seek physical rest and to withdraw psychologically from academic pressures. Similarly, a student who comes from a poorly structured home environment may not respond well to lengthy independent work assignments.

Addressing higher needs prematurely

Sometimes teachers err in their motivational attempts because they address higher needs too soon. It is better that students feel secure in the classroom, achieve limited but real mastery, and learn to work with other students before they address higher needs. Most young children do not have a built-in capacity for completely autonomous direction; to force them to shoulder such responsibility prematurely is to ask for poor progress.

Building a base

Building a base for future growth takes time. How can adults help students to look at their actions, think about them, and plan for (rather than hide and fear) evaluation? Maslow (1954) states that the most stable and healthy self-esteem is based on deserved respect from others rather than unwarranted adulation. To allow for growth, it is necessary that a student experience mastery.

Cognitive Theories

Cognitive theories of motivation emphasize that how people *think* about what is happening to them is as important a determinant of subsequent behavior as the objective reality of what takes place. For example, our reaction to a test score is based in part on our past performance and the past performance of others, but also on our feelings about how hard we have worked, how fair the test was, and so on.

Cognitive perceptions influencing behavior

Weiner (1966) conducted a study that illustrates how cognitive perceptions influence behavior. He began with the finding that students with high anxiety levels do better on certain experimental tasks when they have initially experienced success. If they do not do well on the first task, their performance on the second task declines. Conversely, with low-anxiety students, failure facilitates and success depresses subsequent performance on such tasks. Behaviorists interpret such results to mean that some students need more drive than others, depending on the difficulty of the task.

In the original research done from a behavioristic perspective, experimenters initially assigned subjects to either easy tasks (to insure success) or difficult tasks (to insure failure) and then had all subjects work on tasks of comparable difficulty. In contrast, Weiner (1966), in his study, manipulated the naturally occurring relations between easy tasks and success and difficult tasks and failure. Subjects who were actually working on difficult tasks were given information that led them to believe they were doing well, and subjects working on easy tasks were led to believe that they were doing poorly. Under these conditions, low-anxiety students did better (learned after fewer attempts) on the easy tasks, but high-anxiety students did better on the difficult tasks, presumably because they thought they were making progress. The normal reactions of these students to failure had been reversed! The motivational consequences that stemmed from perceived task success or failure, rather than from the individual's drive level, were the determinants of performance in this study. These results are difficult to explain from a behavioristic stance and illustrate one of the critical differences between the behaviorial and the cognitive frameworks: the extent to which perception of events is seen as a determinant of behavior.

Intrinsic Motivation

The evolution of motivational theory, based on comparison of Murray's theory with Maslow's, shows progressively more belief in the view that individuals can control their behavior. The statement that follows, from Edward J. Murray (1964), connects Maslow's thoughts on motivation with more recently developed cognitive theories that emphasize individual perception of external events and intrinsic motivation:

> In the past, the field of motivation and emotion was dominated by two theories—the classical Freudian and the classical behaviorist. The Freudian image of man was that of a creature driven by inherited, unconscious sexual and destructive instincts constantly

seeking release in a frustrating social environment. The behaviorist view was that of a creature quietly metabolizing in the shade, occasionally goaded into action by the hot sun and the lure of a cold glass of beer. Man is not simply warding off noxious stimuli and seeking the peace of death or Nirvana. He actively interacts with the environment. He is curious, playful, and creative. He conceives great ideas, seeks meaning, and envisions new social goals. (p. 119)

Deci

According to Edward Deci (1975), intrinsically motivated behaviors are those in which one engages in order to feel competent and self-determining. He hypothesizes that intrinsic motivation depends on the perception that one's behavior results from internal causes rather than external pressures. A related hypothesis is that there will be a decrease in intrinsic motivation if a person's feelings of competence and self-determination are reduced.

Deci contends that every reward, including feedback, has two parts—a controlling element and an informational element. If the controlling element is most salient, the actor is likely to perceive the locus of causality of his or her behavior as external. If the informational element dominates, the actor will tend to attribute his or her behavior to internal causes—to be intrinsically motivated. An implication here is that incentives and rewards may control behavior but erode intrinsic motivation unless they are used in informational as opposed to controlling ways. Although the theoretical arguments and the associated empirical evidence are complex and in some instances contradictory (see for example, Bates, 1979), most recent evidence has illustrated the utility of distinguishing between control and information elements (see, Lepper & Greene, 1978).

Types of intrinsically motivated behavior

Deci (1975) argues that there are two types of intrinsically motivated behavior. One type occurs when there is no stimulation and the person is motivated to find stimulation. The other type of intrinsically motivated behavior involves mastering challenges or reducing incongruity (or dissonance). Deci argues that people feel competence and self-determination only when they are able to master challenges and reduce dissonance. To feel satisfied, they must be able to find pleasurable stimulation and deal effectively with over-stimulation. People in general, and especially students, seem to seek and and master challenges that are optimal for them.

Applying Deci's Theory

Clearly, Deci's definition of intrinsic motivation sets a challenging task for the classroom teacher. First, the teacher must realize that a task that is interesting for one student may be uninteresting to the others. Furthermore, even if two students are interested in the same topic or task, the level of involvement needed before saturation is reached may vary considerably between the two students. What is appropriate for one student may be over-stimulation for another.

Part of the difficulty in applying Deci's framework is that perception (for example, a student's interpretation of teacher behavior) is as important as what actually occurs (e.g., the teacher's behavior itself). In any case, it seems important that teachers who use extrinsic feedback and rewards make them informational (helping students to see themselves as fulfilling their own goals) as opposed to controlling (causing students to see themselves as responding to teacher demands).

Hunt

J. McVicker Hunt (1960) challenges both the assumption that all behavior is motivated and the notion that the human organism is inactive unless stimulated by need, painful stimulation, or habit. He summarizes a variety of animal and human studies that suggest that play is most frequently observed when young animals or children are in a "satisfied" state. These conclusions coincide well with Maslow's view that only satisfied individuals are likely to seek new needs and experiences.

Hunt maintains that if activity is intrinsic in living organisms, it is not necessary to see all behavior as intended to reduce or avoid stimulation. He also suggests that an incongruity, a discrepancy between what is known and what is perceived or presented, will initiate action. As an illustration of incongruity Hunt writes, "The temperature at which the thermostat is set supplies a standard against which the temperature of the room is continually being tested. If the room temperature falls below this standard, the test yields an incongruity which starts the furnace to 'operate'." Hunt believes that an optimum of incongruity exists for each individual and that only the individual can choose a source of input that provides this optimum.

Applying Hunt's Theory

Incongruity as motivation

Hunt's notion suggests that the teacher, by carefully controlling the amount of new material presented and its level of difficulty, can capitalize on incongruity as a source of motivation. Materials that present a challenge, assuming that students can use information they possess to meet the challenge, may arouse students to reduce the incongruity. The student who has learned two views of why the American Constitution was written as it was may be curious to explore yet a third view. The student who has not yet studied the Constitution may find it impossible to examine three detailed and conflicting views at the same time. There appear to be relationships among the student's capacity for incongruity, the information he or she possesses, past success as a learner, and so on, such that for most learners too wide a gap will be frustrating and too small a gap will be boring.

Dissonance Theory

Cognitive dissonance theory elaborates on the tension reduction aspects of intrinsic motivation. Dissonance, as Leon Festinger (1957) first pointed out, is tension that arises when two psychologically inconsistent cognitions, such as opinions, attitudes, or beliefs, occur simultaneously. He hypothesized that cognitive dissonance occurs when one becomes aware of stimuli (for example, information, behavior) that are contrary to one's beliefs about oneself. Presumably the two psychologically inconsistent cognitions will create tension, or dissonance, that is unpleasant. This dissonance motivates the person to take action to reduce it.

People as rationalizing agents

As Aronson (1972) points out, the theory of cognitive dissonance sees us as rationalizing rather than as rational: People are more motivated to believe that they are right than they are to be right. Hence, much of our motivation is to justify our own behavior and to correct actions and information that threaten our self-definitions. However, dissonance does not necessarily have to be viewed as a negative press. Deci (1975) argues that dissonance may lead to positive (e.g., curiosity) motivation in some individuals. Still, most experts on the subject characterize dissonance as a negative, unpleasant state.

Cognitive dissonance theory suggests that we may selectively "cover our tracks" after making a decision. Before people make a decision to buy a new TV or dishwasher, they often seek comparative information about the desirability of different brands. However, after the purchase is made, they may begin to read advertisements selectively (reading ads only about the TV they purchased), to guarantee that they will be reassured about the brand they selected.

External justification

Often we can justify our behavior externally. Fred wants to know if you liked his presentation in speech class. Your response, "It was pretty good; I enjoyed it" may be at odds with your covert evaluation, "It was dull and I could not understand it," and your perception of yourself as an honest person. Here the dissonance would probably be minimal because you could justify your behavior on "obvious" grounds (I didn't want to hurt his feelings and I had no constructive suggestions). You would not be motivated to change your opinion of Fred's speech or examine your own motives for saying what you said. Dissonance occurs only if we felt that we should have been honest.

Threat to self-concept

To account for this phenomenon, Aronson (1972) states that dissonance is most powerful in situations where the self-concept is threatened. He argues, "This formulation is based upon the assumption that most individuals like to think of themselves as decent people who wouldn't ordinarily mislead someone unless there was good reason for it—especially if, in misleading that person, the consequences for him could be disastrous." If people believe that their statements will have serious behavioral consequences for those who listen, they are considerably more likely to experience dissonance, because their self-concept is directly threatened (How can I, a good person, behave this way?). Dissonance, as Aronson feels, is most likely to occur when an individual's behavior is different from his or her personal definition of self—as when people who view themselves as intelligent do something stupid.

Dissonance theory has various classroom applications. Through the careful use of materials and assignments, students can be taught that first impulses are often erroneous, and if we act on them we will behave foolishly. Systematic teaching of the need to re-examine assignments periodically and to form our own opinions rather than to accept the reports of others or our own first impressions would be valuable.

Role playing

Students who have rigid and inappropriate role definitions and attitudes toward self or others can perhaps be helped to change those beliefs by role playing more appropriate behaviors. Dissonance theory suggests that if people behave contrary to their real beliefs, they will tend to reduce dissonance by changing their beliefs if they cannot find an easy way to justify their behavior.

Corno and Rohrkemper: Self-Regulated Learning

SRL strategies

Corno and Rohrkemper (in press) deal with intrinsic motivation by stressing self-regulated learning (SRL), a form of student cognitive processing at its most complex and integrative level. These authors argue that self-regulated learning consists of specific cognitive activities, including deliberate planning and monitoring, which learners use as they encounter and attempt to solve academic tasks. They believe that learning is less self-regulated when some of these processes are taken over by classroom teachers or other students. Their emphasis in determining whether self-regulated learning is occurring is whether or not the task is accomplished in a particular fashion, not whether or not it is accomplished per se. Simply put, students engaged in self-regulated learning take more active mental approaches to academic tasks. They think and actively attempt to use internal resources to solve problems rather than relying on teachers or other students to accomplish tasks for them.

Cognitive functioning at this level allows a student to develop a more positive self-concept and presumably to become more confident and productive in the academic environment. Corno and Rohrkemper argue in favor of arranging classroom conditions so that they will aid in fostering this kind of self-actualized learning. They maintain that students will recognize conditions under which they can employ SRL strategies and processes, and will develop a "schema" by which they organize SRL processes into an easily-invoked format.

Social versus independent instructional situations

The authors feel that social instructional conditions best lend themselves to SRL applications, in contrast to independent instructional situations. These social instructional conditions (e.g., noisy classroom atmosphere, inability to concentrate, frequent comparisons of one's work with that of others) however, can also be detrimental to SRL. One of the advantages of SRL is that it enables the students to work independently as greater demands are placed on the teacher's time and instruction thus becomes less complete. In addition, Corno and Rohrkemper state that SRL can improve student achievement, because most students do not know how to learn and therefore have not experienced the rewards and virtues of learning for its own sake. SRL is also reported to more likely be used by successful rather than unsuccessful students.

The authors attempt to place SRL within a larger and more integrated framework of classroom instruction. They advocate an interaction between classroom context (e.g., instruction, task, content, management variables and other process variables) and the level of a students' self-appraisal and self-regulation. What needs to be further explored are how factors such as students' locus of control or self-presentational styles affect intrinsic motivation, and the cognitive processes by which students develop SRL behaviors and attitudes.

Applying SRL

Corno and Rohrkemper feel that teachers need to obtain different types of information from students than most teachers presently do. For example, teachers might have students write out questions about an assignment that they have read in order to assess the student's interest and level of cognitive processing in relation to the assignment. Teachers also might make more systematic efforts to raise questions about the processes that students are using. They might ask students not only for answers, but how they derived their answers, what alternative answers that they considered and rejected, and the reasons they rejected those answers. Teachers might try to discover why students read some books but not others and why they select particular themes or research topics.

Achievement Motivation Theory

Another type of cognitive theory that has been used to explain behavior is achievement motivation theory. Some persons achieve more than others. In some cases it is easy to understand achievement differences—some people are just more intelligent or are physically stronger than others. However, persons of similar aptitude and physical characteristics often achieve in dramatically different ways. Some psychologists argue that differential achievement among individuals of similar potential occurs because some individuals need to achieve more than others. Achievement becomes a dominant part of their lives and they organize their time and talent in order to pursue achievement goals rather than pursue affiliative needs or other goals.

McClelland

Thematic Apperception Test (TAT)

David McClelland (1976) was greatly influenced by the work of Henry Murray (discussed in this chapter) and has used the Thematic Apperception Test (TAT) as a measure of the need for achievement. The TAT is a series of pictures that subjects are asked to use as a basis for telling stories, and these stories are believed to be related to the subjects' needs. Although it is beyond our purpose here to review the literature dealing with this test, there is some reason to believe that those who score high in achievement motivation on the TAT by having their stories exhibit positive goal anticipation, achievement striving, and success seeking also exhibit more achievement-related behavior than those who score lower.

Atkinson

Building on work with McClelland, Atkinson (1964) formulated a comprehensive theory of achievement motivation and behavior. He postulated that the tendency to approach an achievement goal (T_s) is a product of three factors: the need for achievement or the motive for success (M_s); the probability of success (P_s); and the incentive value of success (I_s). However, fear of failure can also be aroused in an achievement-related situation. Thus, there is also a tendency to avoid failure (T_{af}), which is the product of three factors: the motive to avoid failure (M_{af}); the probability of failure (P_f); and the incentive value of failure ($-I_f$). M_s is conceptualized as the capacity to experience pride in task achievement and T_{af} is the capacity to experience embarrassment or shame in the face of task failure.

Achievement versus avoidance

According to Atkinson's theory, a person's achievement motivation for any particular task is the strength of the tendency to approach the task minus the strength of the tendency to avoid failure. Thus a person is high in resultant achievement motivation when M_s exceeds M_{af} ($M_s > M_{af}$). As Weiner (1972) points out, for subjects low in resultant achievement motivation, all achievement tasks are somewhat aversive and elicit fear. However, tasks that are very easy or very difficult are comparatively less aversive than are tasks of intermediate difficulty. For students with high resultant achievement motivation ($M_s > M_{af}$), tasks of intermediate difficulty are conducive to maximum motivation.

Atkinson and Litwin (1960) have presented data to show that subjects high in resultant achievement motivation are much more likely to choose tasks of intermediate difficulty than are subjects low in resultant achievement motivation. These data provide empirical support for Atkinson's theory.

The subjects in this experiment played a ring toss game. The goal (in the subjects' eyes) was to toss the ring over the peg. Subjects were free to stand wherever they wished within a range of one to fifteen feet from the target. Presumably the subjective probability of success was high at one foot and low at fifteen feet. The incentive value of success was assumed to increase as subjects stood further from the peg. However, the incentive value of failure decreased as subjects stood farther away. A successful toss from about twelve feet no doubt would be perceived as a demonstration of competence, and failure from this distance as "no big deal." But a successful toss from about two feet would be only a minor accomplishment, and a miss from that distance would be disappointing and perhaps embarrassing. As predicted, subjects with high achievement motivation (a high tendency to approach success and a low tendency to avoid failure) tossed their rings much more frequently from the moderate-risk distances of between nine to eleven feet than did subjects low in achievement motivation. The latter

Incentive values of success and failure

subjects generally made close tosses of between one to six feet or distant tosses of between twelve to fifteen feet, avoiding intermediate distances of seven to eleven feet.

An interesting test of Atkinson's theory of achievement motivation involves task choice following success or failure. In the theory, $M_{\underline{s}}$ (I want to achieve) and $M_{\underline{af}}$ (I don't want to fail) are viewed as relatively stable personality factors, and the incentive values of a goal depend on the subject's perception of the probability of success ($P_{\underline{s}}$).

The general trends in the literature on the effects of success and failure on motivation as Weiner (1972) summarizes them, are:

1. Motivation is enhanced following failure among individuals high in resultant achievement motivation (they want to do better).
2. Motivation is inhibited following failure among individuals low in resultant achievement motivation (they are "turned off").
3. Motivation is decreased following success among individuals high in resultant achievement motivation (they have proven their skills and have no need to continue to do so).
4. Motivation is enhanced following success among individuals low in resultant achievement motivation (they are relieved to find that they are successful and want to continue with this safe, rewarding activity).

Applying Achievement Theory

Students with high achievement needs but equally high failure fears are likely to select relatively easy, clearly manageable tasks. Students with high achievement motivation and little fear of failure are more likely to select tasks that test their limits more fully. Teachers can help students engage in goal-relevant tasks by reducing their fear of failure, by helping them to develop positive achievement motivation, and by manipulating task incentives.

Two additional comments that stem from achievement motivation research are worth examining, especially since they appear to have value in educational settings.

Realism in vocational aspiration

First, there is some evidence that more realism in vocational aspiration is exhibited by students who are high in resultant achievement motivation than by students who are low. Individuals low in achievement motivation do not appear to have adequate self-knowledge to make realistic vocational choices. Data suggest that these individuals are relatively inaccurate in estimating their abilities.

Second, the difficulty of class assignments may have major effects on student performance. Too often task difficulty is fixed for the entire class and is a compromise that does not stimulate any group of students maximally. For example, students in a math class are told that they will get an A if they do 90 percent of their math problems correctly. For some of the students this is comparable to tossing a ring from two feet, but for others it is more like tossing from twenty feet.

Work done by Atkinson and others on achievement motivation is helpful in making predictions at a given point in time. However, one may ask why some individuals take risks and others avoid them.

Stipek (1984) analyzes antecedent conditions of achievement motivation. She emphasizes developmental issues that are related to achievement motivation, with particular attention to changes in cognitions related to achievement, such as performance expectations, self-perceptions of ability, or perceptions of causes of achievement outcomes, and in cognitive processes like information processing that underlie changes in these cognitions. She stresses the development of several emotions related to achievement—how children value achievement outcomes, their attitude towards school, and their emotional responses to certain achievement outcomes.

Failure-avoidance behavior

Stipek's own observations indicate that preschoolers focus on tasks rather than outcomes. First grade is a structured environment, but students are still task-focused. In later grades, however, school becomes more competitive, and in their attempts to avoid failure, students begin to demonstrate behaviors such as learned helplessness. Generally, the higher the grade level, the higher the occurrence of failure-avoidance behavior (Miller, 1982; Rholes, Blackwell, Jordan, & Walters, 1980; Weisz, 1979).

Performance expectancy

Stipek also discusses developmental changes in children's cognitions that could account for changes in students' achievement behavior. One cognition related to achievement behavior is performance expectancy. This is generally high until second or third grade, and thereafter decreases through sixth grade (Stipek, in press). Self-perceptions of competence in children also generally decrease during the elementary grades. Starting in second grade, children's ability estimates correlate increasingly with objective performance feedback they receive from teachers (Eshel & Klein, 1981). Research also indicates a substantial drop in self-perceptions after students enter junior high school (Parsons, Midgely, & Adler, in press).

Values

Academic achievement

Young children confuse achievement with good conduct (Stipek, 1981; Stipek & Tannatt, in press) and see the classroom as primarily social rather than academic. A study by Brophy and Evertson (1981) indicates that achievement concerns become increasingly important over the elementary years. For adolescents, peer approval and physical competence are salient, and academic achievement assumes less value for some students, especially those who have a history of academic failure. Other teenagers may begin to value achievement more as they start to consider careers or while they are attending college.

Affect Theory

Research on affect related to school generally shows less positive evaluations as grade level increases (Parsons et al., in press), with an especially steep decrease in junior high (Haladyna & Thomas, 1979). There is little research on students' emotional responses in achievement contexts or to specific achievement outcomes. One study showed that fourth and fifth grade students generally described their classroom-related emotions negatively (Weiner, Anderson, & Prawat, 1982).

Younger children are more likely to say they engage in achievement behavior to master tasks (intrinsic motivation), while older children more often report extrinsic reasons such as grades (Blumenfeld & Pintrich, 1982; deCharms, 1980). Again, this change is especially noticeable at the junior high level (Parsons, et al., in press).

Performance Feedback

Performance evaluations

In seeking explanations for changes in achievement-motivation characteristics, Stipek focuses on teachers' performance evaluations, which also change with grade level, as well as on students' reactions to teacher feedback.

Social Evaluative Feedback

Research shows that young children focus on social reinforcement (praise or criticism) rather than objective (I usually get all problems correct in math), symbolic (I usually get an A in math), or normative (I usually do better than everyone else) feedback about their performance. Older students tend to consider both objective and social feedback in their expectations for future performance.

Stipek believes that young children emphasize social reinforcement in part because they perceive their teacher's role as being similar to that of their parents, and because young children view adults as moral authorities and are especially concerned with pleasing them. Stipek also observes that kindergarten and first-grade teachers frequently use social feedback and rarely criticize the results of students' efforts. Brophy (1981) points out that teachers in early elementary grades frequently praise students after they make mistakes and that students view this praise as a positive reflection of their ability. Older students, however, interpret praise following failure as an indication of low ability.

The amount of positive feedback students receive from teachers also seems to decrease with age. This may be due to variations in the classroom structure; that is, younger students are more likely to receive feedback because they are taught in small groups more often than older students.

Symbolic Feedback

Symbolic feedback includes such things as grades, smiling faces, the giving of metallic paper stars, etc. Children in kindergarten and first grade often associate these symbols with social approval. Grades begin to affect students' self-concept of ability and they begin to value grades for their own sake at

Students compare their work with that of their classmates.

about third grade (Eshel & Klein, 1981). Also, older children come to value grades because they allow a comparison of their performance with that of their peers.

Objective Feedback

Objective feedback conveys information only about the correctness of a student's response. Such feedback has different implications for younger pupils and for older pupils, with feedback becoming a more important influence on students' achievement-related cognitions over time. Stipek suggests cognitive processing and wishful thinking as two reasons for these developmental differences.

Integration of objective failure information

Because young children generally expect to succeed and have high self-perceptions of ability even after failures, it appears that they cannot cognitively process and integrate information about multiple failure experiences. Even if they were able to do so, they seem not to view ability as a stable attribute, and they equate ability with effort until age 10 or 11 (Dweck, in press).

Stipek notes that recent research suggests that young children between the ages of 4 and 8 can process objective information about past failures (Stipek, Roberts, & Sanborn, 1983), especially when making predictions about the future performance levels of their peers. Another study (Stipek & Hoffman, 1980) showed that pupils' predictions of their own future performance levels were more accurate when they received external rewards for accuracy of prediction.

Wishful thinking

Another factor that might explain why young children don't use objective failure information, even when they are capable of processing such information, is wishful thinking, the tendency to deny information that is contradictory to their desire to succeed, and to believe that the mere wish to succeed can lead to success (Piaget, 1925, 1930).

Normative Feedback

Most children do not compare their performance to that of others until second grade, therefore, their self-evaluations are largely unaffected by information about the performance of others (Boggiano & Ruble, 1979). Stipek and Tannatt (in press) found that children in second and third grade were more likely to explain competency ratings of self and others in terms of relative performance and task difficulty than were younger children. Again, Stipek believes that these developmental differences are due largely to changes in classroom organization. That is, classrooms tend to become more formal and structured in the upper grades (Arlin, 1976), with more whole-class instruction and public response opportunities (Brophy & Evertson, 1981). Parsons et al. (in press) found that more students were ability grouped for math in the upper grades. Furthermore, teachers in these grades used letter grades more often (Gronlund, 1974), and were more likely to describe a student as a good example to the class (Brophy & Evertson, 1981). Normative feedback becomes particularly salient at the junior-high level (Brophy & Evertson, 1978). Thus, the amount of normative feedback as well as the chances for social comparisons increase with grade level.

Developmental Change in Values, Affects, and Goals

Most children learn to define academic success in relation to the performance of others. However, such a view of performance means that many children will fail in their own eyes. By sixth grade most students view ability as being stable and increased effort as being of little use. This may account for the negative feelings that many junior-high school students have toward school and for the sharp decrease in students' self-perceptions of ability that occurs at this age. Stipek feels that, along with these achievement-related cognitions, students show corresponding negative emotions related to achievement (like anxiety, fear, shame, or embarrassment).

Stipek speculates that the increase in performance feedback in upper grades is also associated with an increasing emphasis on external reward for achievement. Older students achieve less for the sake of mastering a task than for symbolic rewards such as grades.

Stipek concludes that changes in the educational environment can help but that they would not likely be as successful with older students as with younger ones. This is because older students practice strategies to "avoid learning" and to enhance their self-presentation.

SUMMARY

Motivation has been discussed in terms of needs, affiliation, incentives, habit, discrepancy, and innate curiosity. All of these concepts are useful, but no single one provides an adequate explanation for motivation. Theoretical frameworks are needed to link various concepts and improve predictions. Behaviorists have focused on past reinforcement and present contingencies, while cognitive psychologists believe that people decide what they want to achieve and that perceptions, understanding, information processing, and curiosity are important.

The behavioristic point of view begins with the assumption that the drive to fulfill biological needs motivates behavior. Through attempts to satisfy biological drives, secondary drives such as dependence or aggression are learned. If reinforced, behavior associated with them is repeated; if not, it disappears. Murray postulated that both positive and negative needs interact with environmental pressure to form a pattern of behavior, or theme. Once created, needs tend to perpetuate themselves, so early experiences are especially important. Murray's theory can be used to identify student interests and predict how students might react to given classroom circumstances. Maslow also used the concept of needs and arranged them into a hierarchy. He believed that unfulfilled basic needs interfere with learning.

Cognitive explanations emphasize individuals' perceptions of events and their influences on behavior. Murray and Maslow, for example, both stress individuals' control over their own behavior. Hunt observes that play and other behavior in the young occurs most frequently when needs are satisfied, and suggests that incongruity may serve as motivation. Deci argues that intrinsic motivation is a goal that classroom teachers need to promote. Aronson proposes that cognitive dissonance serves to motivate, and can be used to bring about constructive changes in student behavior. Atkinson has formulated a comprehensive theory of achievement behavior involving both individual and situational variables. Stipek has reviewed extant work about how students' need for achievement develops and how various classroom conditions influence students' motivation. She stresses the need for primary school teachers to help students develop appropriate achievement expectations at an early age.

QUESTIONS AND PROBLEMS

1. Human motivation has been debated for centuries. Pessimists believe that people must be pushed by motivational pressures, which include direct, or at least implied, threats of punishment for noncompliance. Optimists believe that negative push is unnecessary and the same degree of motivation can be accomplished through the pull of positive incentives. Those who are still more optimistic do not believe that any incentives at all are necessary, holding that positive and prosocial motives are basic to human nature. Where do you stand on these issues? Why? What does your stance imply concerning your approach to classroom motivation?
2. If Maslow is taken seriously, one implication is that students will not be very motivated to learn in school unless more basic needs are met. However, teachers rarely are in a position to meet basic needs that are not being met at home. Does this mean that teachers have no hope of motivating such students? Why or why not?
3. Individual differences in students' motivational needs are problematic for teachers because the same teacher behavior that might motivate certain students might simultaneously turn off other students. What can be done about this?
4. If you have selected teaching as your vocation you probably are favorably disposed toward education. Chances are that you found and continue to find learning rewarding for its own sake, in addition to whatever other motives may

be involved. However, as a teacher you will encounter many students who are apathetic toward learning, anxious and fearful when tested or placed in testlike situations, or even completely negative toward school and teachers. What can you do to develop a better understanding of these students and to help prepare yourself for dealing with them effectively?

5. Given that students require different types of homework and seatwork assignments because of their varying abilities, how could you make differential assignments without implying that one student is less capable than another?
6. Corno and Rohrkemper studied the concept of self-regulated learning, which we covered in this chapter. Define this concept in your own words. What is the value of this concept? Why would it be important for teachers not only to provide students with some choice in curriculum assignments but also to determine why students make those selections?

CASE STUDIES

Judy's Dilemma. Judy enjoys mathematics and works hard both at school and at home. Her mathematics class is an individualized program and, within limits, she can proceed through the material at her own pace. From time to time she has to wait until a few other students are at her level so that the teacher can begin another unit. However, even when she has to wait to begin a new topic, Judy enjoys mathematics class. The teacher has arranged several options that students can select during "delay" times. Some of these topics involve straightforward review, but other problems are "tricky" and involve novel application of concepts. Moreover, there are also choice units that present historical material about people who have discovered various mathematical principles and the unusual or interesting situations in which these discoveries were made. Also, there are materials that illustrate the way in which mathematics is used in the "real world."

Judy, however, hates history. Every week is the same: Monday and Tuesday the teacher lectures (*BORING!*) and Wednesday, Thursday, and Friday are devoted to small-group work. She dislikes listening to the same students who always talk although they have little to say and she dislikes answering a set of questions that the teacher prepares daily. She often thinks to herself "How can one person so consistently ask the most banal questions and turn an interesting subject into a bore?"

Using a motivational framework, how would you explain Judy's differential reaction to the two subjects? Is it the subjects per se, the way that the teachers present the subjects, or Judy's individual needs that are most important? If you were the history teacher, what could you do to make the course more interesting to Judy? Are there students who have needs/interests that are different from Judy's who might be "hurt" by the changes you propose? If so, what types of students?

Despondent Dick. Dick's face flushed. He desperately attempted to recall what he was going to say next. His knees became weak, and he was embarrassed. Finally, he said, "Ms. Townsend, I can't remember what I was going to say. I'd better stop." She said, "That's okay, Dick, but look at your notes, and after Judy answers the next proof I want you to explain your proof." Later Dick gave an acceptable explanation. After the class Dick approached Ms. Townsend and said, "Look, it's getting tougher and tougher for me in geometry. Everybody's so much better than I am. I feel like an idiot." If you were Ms. Townsend what would you say and do?

Chapter 15

Cognitive Viewpoints

CHAPTER OUTLINE

OBJECTIVES

When you have mastered the material in this chapter you will be able to

1. Discuss how attribution theory explains achievement motivation and the motivational tasks for the teacher
2. Define task-endogenous motivation and explain its role in the classroom
3. Be able to differentiate between task-involvement and ego-involvement and explain their respective motivational roles in the classroom
4. Define learned helplessness and describe how teachers can help students with this problem to overcome it
5. Discuss deCharms' theory of personal causation and its application to the classroom
6. Differentiate between origins and pawns
7. Discuss motivation from the standpoint of direction, persistence, continuing motivation, activity, and performance

Recent cognitive views of motivation are discussed in this chapter. The chapter begins with a discussion of attribution theory, which has evolved from achievement theory and is presently one of the most popular theories for explaining classroom motivation. This chapter also discusses recent motivational work that distinguishes between task- and ego-involvement motivation and between teacher-controlled and student-controlled learning environments. Furthermore, the chapter discusses the relationship between students' perceptions of self-worth and their classroom motivation and describes a general theory that suggests enhancing students' perceptions of personal causation. Finally, the chapter discusses teacher socialization efforts in helping to enhance students' motivation to learn.

Attribution Theory

Attribution theory has evolved from achievement motivation theory. This cognitive theory of motivation deals with perceived causes of success and failure in achievement situations: ability, effort, task difficulty, luck, and failure to use the right "approach" or "strategy" for the problem. This is not an exhaustive list of all the ways in which a person might account for success or failure but it does cover the major ways in which success and failure are "explained" (Frieze et al., 1983; Weiner, 1984). Although there are many possible explanations for why one could fail, effort and ability are the most likely causes that students report. When students explain their achievement results, individuals attach the most significance to how they perceive their ability and how hard they try (Graham, 1984).

The cognitive and behavioral aspects of attribution theory are presented in Figure 15.1. In Stage 1 the pupil first perceives the achievement task and makes causal attributions (How difficult does the task appear? Will my performance on it depend on ability, effort, or luck?). Having perceived the task and made a causal attribution, the student estimates his or her probable success or failure at the task and develops an affective anticipation: hope of success, fear of failure.

Causal factors

Casual factors vary in stability. One's perception of one's general ability is stable over time and one's perception of the difficulty of a given task is reasonably stable. However, the amount of effort we put out at a particular time varies, as does luck. Causal factors also vary in controllability. Luck is something that we do not control, but effort is within our control. Similarly, ability is an aspect of internal control that the subject carries with him or her, whereas the task and its difficulty are set by the experimenter and are external to the subject.

A person brings to a task a given level of ability and may or may not put forth effort, but the nature of the task and luck, or the lack of it, are beyond the person's immediate control. Hence, in addition to looking at the four reasons a person may use to explain performance, it is possible to divide these explanations further on the basis of stability and locus of control. Such a division is presented in Table 15.1.

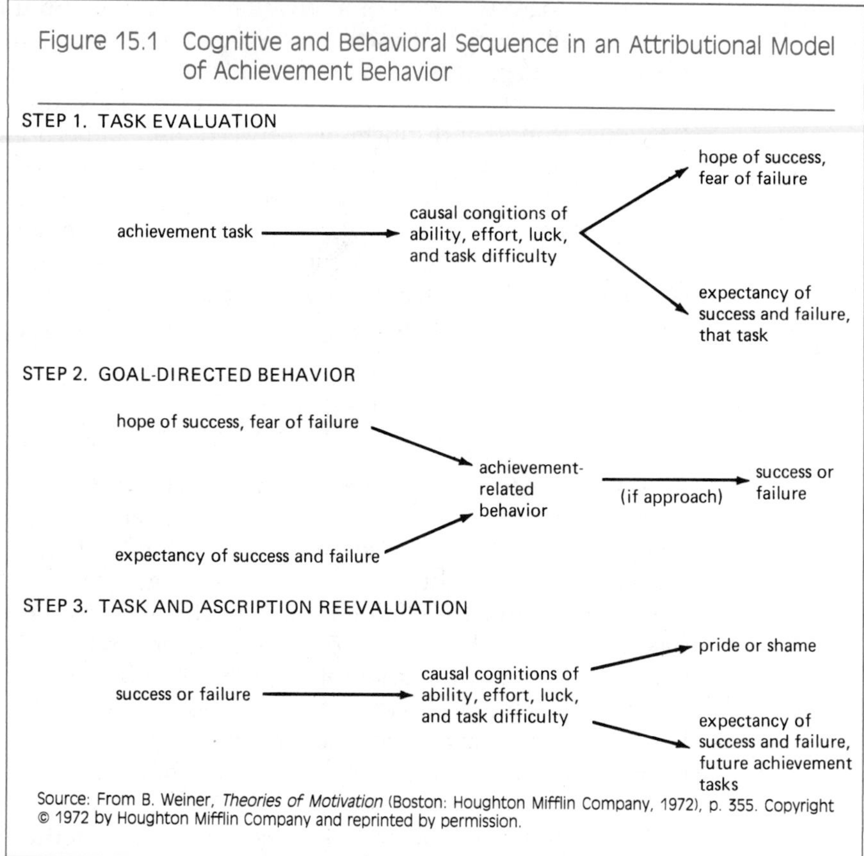

Figure 15.1 Cognitive and Behavioral Sequence in an Attributional Model of Achievement Behavior

Source: From B. Weiner, *Theories of Motivation* (Boston: Houghton Mifflin Company, 1972), p. 355. Copyright © 1972 by Houghton Mifflin Company and reprinted by permission.

Locus of control

The term *locus of control* was first introduced by Rotter (1954) and refers to how individuals tend to explain their successes and failures. Those who perceive an external locus of control see their behavior as being caused by external events (I succeeded because I was lucky. I failed because the teacher doesn't like me). Individuals with an internal locus of control feel that they are responsible for their successes and failures (I was successful because I'm bright. I failed because I didn't try).

Internality versus externality

The distinction between internality and externality is useful because research by Rotter (1966) and others suggests that changes in one's expectations of success and failure are more frequent and pronounced in skill than in chance situations. Individuals with an internal locus of control prefer and perform better under conditions where skill determines the outcome, while those with an external locus of control prefer and perform better under chance conditions (Lefcourt, 1966).

It is important to stress that locus of control is a learned "state of perception" and can be altered, although change, especially in naturalistic settings, does not necessarily occur rapidly. If a task appears to call for a

Table 15.1 Determinants of Achievement Behavior

Locus of Control	Stability: *Stable*	*Unstable*
Internal	ability	effort
External	task difficulty	luck

general level of ability, immediate success or failure on it will not change one's perception of personal ability. In general, though, one's level of performance on a task affects one's beliefs about one's ability on that task and others like it. The causality attributed to one's performance will influence the extent to which one is likely to change estimates of his or her ability. Again, tasks that are perceived to be influenced by internal characteristics are more likely to motivate attitude change than are those tasks that the person perceives as externally controlled.

From a cognitive point of view, motivation depends on what the person thinks about the task (Weiner, 1983; deCharms, 1984). If a student feels that a classroom game is "rigged," little can be done to influence his or her efforts until that attitude is changed. However, as we have shown previously, the way one thinks about a task, especially a novel task, can be modified.

An Attribution Theory of Student Motivation: Weiner

Weiner, an influential theorist in the attribution tradition, summarizes (from the point of view of attribution theory) the salient characteristics of students high in achievement motivation this way. Students high in achievement motivation:

1. Prefer situations in which the consequences of their actions can be ascribed to the person (hypothesized).
2. Have learned to attribute outcome to effort (demonstrated).
3. Are sensitive and reactive to cues indicating the importance of effort expenditure (demonstrated).

Weiner (1979) is now attempting to broaden attribution theory arguments into a general theory of motivation. His general framework of motivational influences is presented in Figure 15.2. Many of the linkages seem plausible, but systematic research is just beginning on many parts of the model (on "other consequences" in particular).

According to Weiner (1984), a theory of student motivation that accurately reflects the complexity of classroom life must include three general principles. First, it should incorporate the full range of cognitive processes,

Figure 15.2 Partial Representation of an Attributional Theory of Motivation

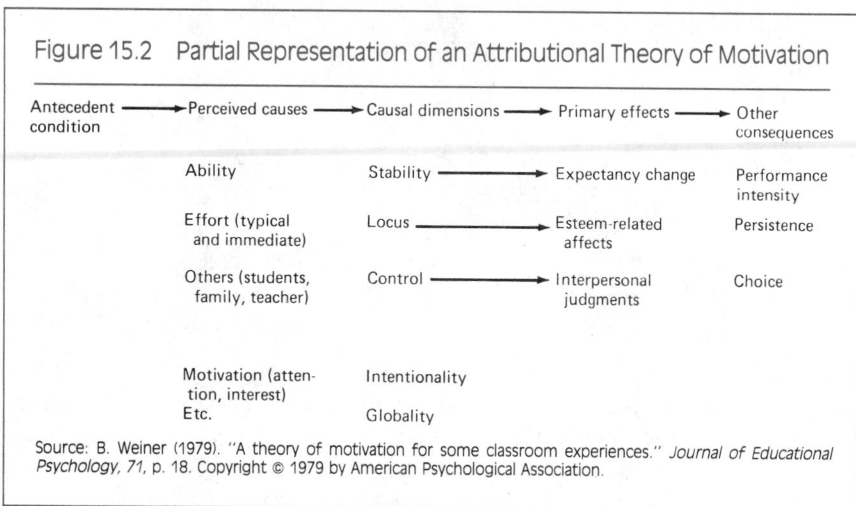

Source: B. Weiner (1979). "A theory of motivation for some classroom experiences." *Journal of Educational Psychology, 71*, p. 18. Copyright © 1979 by American Psychological Association.

including information search and retrieval, attention, memory, categorization, judgment, and decision making. The theory must emphasize the conscious thoughts that accompany mental events and behavior, particularly students' concern with self.

Second, a theory of motivation should include the full range of emotions. Previous theorists have tended only to involve the broad pleasure–pain principle, and not to distinguish among various emotions within these two categories.

Third, a theory of motivation must explain both rational actions (such as when students use strategies to deal with anxiety), and nonrational actions (such as when students fail to attribute failure to themselves) with identical concepts. Thus to reflect classroom life a theory must include many concepts as well as their interrelationships (e.g., reinforcement, self-worth, achievement, power).

Weiner (1984) asserts that the basic principle of attribution theory is that persons attempt to understand *why* events occur and to search for causes. These searches serve multiple functions, such as reducing surprise and uncertainty or promoting future goal attainment, and they occur in all areas of motivation. The number of potential causes of events is almost unlimited, and is strongly related to the activity in question, whether it involves educational achievement, noneducational achievement, or interpersonal success or failure. Weiner presents the following classifications of causes.

Causal Dimensions of Weiner's Attribution Theory

Locus

The first dimension of causality, locus, distinguishes between internal causes that are located within a person such as intelligence, effort, or physical attractiveness, and causes that are *external* like task difficulty or luck.

Consistency

A second dimension of causality, consistency, includes temporal stability and globality. Stability distinguishes causes according to their stability over time. For example, ability is perceived as relatively lasting, as opposed to effort, which can vary considerably within a short time. Thus, prior outcomes perceived as due to ability predict the future more accurately than outcomes ascribed to effort. Globality refers to differences among causes in cross-situational generality, or whether a cause is specific (failing a math test due to low math aptitude) or general (failing because of low intelligence).

Responsibility

A third dimension, responsibility, consists of controllability and intentionality and is strongly related to evaluative consequences of behavior. Controllability refers to how much control the actor has over his or her behavior. A person is assumed to have more control over effort than over ability, which is an inherited characteristic. Similarly, failure due to a lack of effort is perceived as more intentional, and would result in greater punishment, than failure due to improper use of a strategy.

Antecedents of Causal Attribution

Informational cues

There are numerous determinants of causal attributions. For example, informational cues such as present performance on a task in addition to a person's past performance on the same task or a similar task can partly determine attributions for current success and failure. Other examples of informational cues are the pattern and randomness of performance, task characteristics, and persistence of behavior.

Causal schemata

Psychological structures, or causal schemata, also affect causal attributions. One such structure involves attentional factors. Studies reveal that actors (the people performing the actions) tend to make situation attributions, but observers (people who observe the actors) tend to make trait (general across situations) attributions. This finding is explained by the actor's attention to the environment and the observer's focus on the actor. For example, at a college football game the general performance of a player (actor) or the occurrence of a particular event may be seen in different ways by a player and by a fan (observer). The fan tends to explain the event by attributions to a player's traits (attentiveness, lack of desire), whereas the player uses situational explanations (it was a hard tackle). Similarly a principal watching a teacher may explain a poor lesson by making attribution to teacher traits like poor organization or poor delivery, whereas a teacher tends to see particular situational factors like having had inadequate preparation for this particular lesson or a student's failure to read the assignment as the cause of the poor lesson.

Consequences of Causal Attribution

Expectancy of success

Attribution theory proposes that changes in expectancy for success after attainment or nonattainment of a goal depend on the perceived constancy of the cause of the performance. For example, success with math that is attributed to math aptitude will likely result in higher expectations for future success in math than will success that is ascribed to a lucky guess or to help from other students.

Attribution Retraining Programs

If the success expectancy proposal is correct, then change in a student's causal perceptions should lead to change in the student's behavior. Attributional change programs thus attempt to alter persons' perceived causes of failure in order to increase their achievement-related behavior. Such programs try to change the attributions of students who attribute their academic failures to low ability, by training them to attribute failure to internal, controllable causes like having made insufficient effort or having used the wrong strategy.

Attributions and Affect

There are many affective consequences to success or failure. Studies show that success at achievement-related activities results in happiness, regardless of the cause of success. Other, more specific attribution-emotion relationships are ability-competence, long-term effort-relaxation, help from others-gratitude, and luck-surprise/happiness. Of course, contrasting affective responses follow attributions for failure (e.g., low ability—humiliation; hindrance from others—anger).

Causal dimensions as determinants of emotions

Casual dimensions also are important determinants of emotions: pride or self-esteem (attribution of success to self), anger (attribution of failure to factors controllable by others), gratitude (attribution of success to positive internal factors or to help from others), guilt (attribution of failure to one's own negative traits), pity (attribution of others' troubles to factors beyond their control), and hopelessness (attribution of a negative outcome to stable factors).

Affect as a motivator of action

Studies support an attribution-emotion-action sequence. For example, people are more likely to pity and subsequently to offer help to an individual who is in need because of factors they perceive to be beyond his or her control than to a person they perceive as in need due to controllable factors. Research further shows that emotions rather than causal perceptions seem to be the immediate motivators of action.

Emotions can also indirectly cause behavior because they are important precursors of causal thinking. For instance, pity from an observer indicates to the actor that the cause of his or her problem is stable and uncontrollable. Thus, the actor will likely infer that action would be useless. Conversely, anger would communicate that the actor could alter behavior, because the anger indicates that the observer perceives the actor's problem to be under the actor's control.

According to Weiner (1984), this theory meets three requirements for a theory of student motivation. Future studies need to determine the number of and relationships among the causal dimensions, develop new methods

Students should learn to use teacher feedback in assessing their efforts to complete a task successfully.

for measuring emotions and causal thinking, specify the relationship of expectancy and affect to action, and increase the theory's generalizability.

Applying Attribution Theory

In contrast to alternative ways of looking at and predicting human behavior, attribution theory suggests a different interpretation of the teacher's motivational task. Like Hunt's emphasis on incongruity (the match between ability and task), attribution theory recommends tasks that are of appropriate difficulty. However, it places considerably more emphasis on helping students to perceive the relationship between effort and success. Many students explain their successes or failures on the basis of habitual ways that they have learned to view their behavior, rather than on the basis of the actual causal factors operating in the situation—such as saying "I failed because I'm dumb," rather than "I failed because I got frustrated and gave up quickly instead of persisting or getting help." From an attribution theory perspective the teacher's major role is to help students develop the capacity for using feedback appropriately. We shall return to this important teaching task in Chapter 16.

Nicholls: Task Involvement Theory

Nicholls (1984) discusses two contrasting psychological states associated with mastering a task. Task-involvement is the desire to master a task primarily in order to learn or develop ability in that particular task. Ego-involvement refers to a concern with demonstrating high capacity to self or others, involving a comparison of one's effort and performance with that of others.

Ego-involvement

Generally, when people are working on skills tasks, their tendency to use the more complex definition of ability (to become ego-involved) increases in relation to factors that heighten their concerns about the evaluation of their ability. Thus, when a teacher announces a test of important skills, students are likely to view their ability as capacity, and their ego-involvement should increase.

Nicholls cites several studies that support these predictions. Generally, test-like or competitive conditions and public self-awareness tend to cause participants to view ability as capacity (Jagacinski & Nicholls, 1982; Ames, Ames, & Felker, 1977). Furthermore, these ego-involving conditions increase external attributions and reduce interest in the task (Ryan, 1982; Deci, Schwartz, Sheinman, & Ryan, 1981).

Task difficulty preference and performance

Task Difficulty Preference and Performance

Nicholls' (1984) theory assumes that people will attempt to demonstrate high ability. In order to ascertain what behavior will best demonstrate high ability, it is necessary to specify the relationship between peoples' expectations for demonstrating ability and two other factors—task difficulty and performance feedback.

Task-Involvement Preferences

The theory predicts that students who are task-involved, regardless of their self-perceptions of ability, will view tasks that appear to require moderate to high effort as offering them the best chance to perform well and demonstrate their ability. They will not select tasks on which either success or failure seems certain. Likewise, task-involved persons who are assigned tasks will show higher effort on moderately challenging tasks, that is, on tasks they perceive as requiring effort to show high ability. This is an ideal situation for learning, because learning is an end in itself.

Ego-Involvement Preferences

Ego-involved persons' expectations for demonstrating ability will depend on how well others perform or expect to perform, as well as on their own expectations for success. To demonstrate high ability, they believe they must perform above average. Persons who are ego-involved and believe their capacity is low (those that have given up the attempt to demonstrate high ability) will avoid moderately difficult tasks or "realistic" challenges and will not perform well on such tasks because they believe that their best effort is not good enough. Rather, such individuals tend to choose easy tasks, where effort will result in success. Those who have a low self-concept of ability but still desire to demonstrate high ability to others will choose extremely difficult tasks, on which their failure does not necessarily indicate a lack of ability.

Conversely, individuals who believe that they have high capacities are not threatened by ego-involving situations. They expect effort to result in success, and thus expect to perform best on moderately difficult tasks. These persons also expect to do well on difficult tasks, but may relax on tasks they perceive as easy and thus perform poorly. For these persons, academic tasks are chances to demonstrate high capacity rather than chances to learn or develop their skills.

Educational Implications

Nicholls (1984) argues that the idea that task-involvement is superior to ego-involvement is supported not only by theory, but also by a values position that holds that the purpose of education is for each student to develop his or her intellectual potential to the fullest extent. Thus, if teachers can promote optimal motivation for intellectual development in all students, they can achieve educational equity (Nicholls, 1979). However, ego-involving classes will hinder the learning of students with low perceived ability.

On the other hand, if the major purpose of education is viewed as preparing students for work in our capitalistic economic system, where self-worth and income depend on status, one would view ego-involving competitive classrooms more favorably. Even those who hold this view, however, would not want lower-ability students to become too ego-involved and thus to give up on learning, until they had mastered the basic skills.

In fact, Nicholls argues that developmental changes in children's concept of ability, coupled with grade level differences in teaching practices, lead most students to attain minimum competence before they become ego-involved. Preschool children tend to have high performance expectations and will attempt almost anything. In the early school years, however, as ability begins to mean performing better than others, many children are likely to feel incompetent (Nicholls & Miller, 1983). Because success is more meaningful when few others succeed, students become more concerned with performing well in comparison to others, and thus become more ego-involved. In adolescence, when students view ability as capacity, low self-perceptions of ability threaten self-esteem and hinder performance in ego-involving situations. It is also harder for teachers to praise an older student's effort and improvement without implying that he or she has low ability (Meyer et al., 1979).

Unfortunately, as grade level increases, teaching practices that promote ego-involvement generally increase (Eccles, Midgley, & Adler, 1983). Researchers have identified techniques that promote task-involvement, but according to Nicholls, most teachers do not use them.

deCharms: Personal Causation Theory/Origin Training

According to deCharms (1984), there are three general ways to consider teaching and learning: (1) the teacher demonstrates and the learner imitates; (2) the teacher provides information to the learner, who is a passive recipient; and (3) the learner is an active agent who interacts with the environment. deCharms believes that the key to *enhancing* motivation involves adopting the third view.

Theoretical Framework

deCharms (1984) defines personal causation as "doing something intentionally to produce a change," and agency as "the reasonable use of knowledge and habits [learned responses] to produce desirable changes" (p. 276). When agency is successful, a person causes a desired change and believes that he or she originated it. When agency fails, the person does not cause the change (some other person or object has inhibited change), and the agent believes that he or she is a pawn. The result of a successful change is a reinforcer, though deCharms points out that the concept of a reinforcer as it is commonly used is too broad. For example, failure often increases a person's attempts to succeed, and reinforcement is not always observable. deCharms prefers to think of personal causation rather than reinforcement as the key to understanding behavior, though he emphasizes that the concept cannot be demonstrated empirically. He believes, however, that educators can develop activities that improve or inhibit students' sense of personal causation and can study the effects of these activities.

deCharms and colleagues have broadened the concept of origin to include choice, which implies a degree of freedom and responsibility, and encourages the actor to feel ownership of behavior. deCharms points out, though, that an "origin-enhancing" environment is not a classroom in which students are allowed to do as they please, and that the terms "origin" and "pawn" are relative.

Hidden cost of rewards

deCharms (1968) refers to the negative effects of extrinsic rewards on intrinsic motivation as "the hidden costs of rewards." Thus, if a person independently decides to behave in a specific manner but later finds that someone else values the behavior enough to reward it, the person may not continue to feel freedom, ownership, and choice. Instead, the person may begin to produce the behavior only to get the reward, and the behavior may disappear when the reinforcer is not present. There is considerable research support for this effect (Deci, 1975, 1980; Lepper and Greene, 1978) that indirectly illustrates the importance of student choice and the way reinforcement is used in the classroom.

Classroom structure and pupil motivation

deCharms (1984) points out the curvilinear relationship between classroom structure and pupil motivation; that is, both overly structured and very unstructured classrooms are likely to inhibit students' motivation. In discussing structure, two key variables are number of choices students have and degree of teacher dominance (Lewin, Lippitt, & White, 1939; Perlmuter & Monty, 1979). deCharms proposes that dominance and choice are negatively related, and points out that two negatively related variables often have a curvilinear relationship to a third variable, in this case, motivation.

This theory of the relationship between teacher dominance and pupil choice was the basis of and was affected by a large research program conducted by deCharms and colleagues (the Carnegie Project) which showed that teachers could enhance students' motivation.

Research Evidence: The Carnegie Project

The Carnegie Project began in 1967 with a four-year study in grades 4 through 8 of low-income black students whose sixth- and seventh-grade teachers were trained to use motivation-enhancing exercises in their classrooms. These exercises focused on self-concept, achievement motivation, realistic goal setting, and the origin-pawn concept (deCharms, 1976). Activities related to each concept were emphasized for 10 weeks, for about 100 minutes each week.

Results on the origin-pawn variable were measured through coding of imaginative stories written by both the control and the experimental students. Analyses of the stories showed that after training, the experimental group's story characters more frequently set their own goals, determined their own directed activity, were more realistic, took more personal responsibility for their actions, and were more self-confident.

Concerning achievement, the training significantly improved students' Iowa Test Scores in grades 6 and 7. The treatment had a greater effect on boys than girls, and affected language skills more than math skills. Reading scores were least affected. Further, both absences and tardiness were reduced in the experimental classes, and the reverse was true in the control group. Results also showed that after training, experimental group students took more moderate risks in a spelling game.

Applying Personal Causation Theory

deCharms states that the most important way that teachers can enhance motivation is to believe that they themselves are origins and that all of their students can be origins too (this belief is related to notions of self-fulfilling prophecies, which we discuss in Chapter 17). Teachers can also establish the right amount of structure for the class as a whole and for individual students within it by allowing students some choices and by encouraging positive pupil influence attempts and independent activity.

Students should not be allowed too many or too few choices. Students must understand alternatives they are to choose from, and beginning choices must be simple and short-range. The choice should be personal if possible, and the alternatives should be moderately challenging.

Covington: Self-Worth Theory

Self-worth motive

Covington (1984) refers to a person's tendency to present a positive self-image as the self-worth motive. Research on the self-worth motive in achievement situations indicates that individuals tend to attribute their successes to themselves and their failures to external conditions.

In the classroom, the self-worth motive is reflected primarily in self-perceptions of competency. Because our society tends to equate achievement with human value, students view ability as important to academic success, and they want others to attribute their success to ability rather than effort (Nicholls, 1976). Teachers also value ability. However, because in schools students compete for a limited number of rewards, few students can have much success. Furthermore, this competition over-emphasizes the role of ability in achievement (Ames & Ames, 1984), and this causes students who fail to feel inadequate. Thus, students are likely to involve strategies designed to avoid failure and save face.

Strategies to Avoid Failure

The most direct way students can avoid failure is not to participate. For example, they may feign attention or appear eager to answer a question, hoping the teacher will call on someone who appears less certain or involved.

When students are forced to participate, yet expect to fail, students may attempt to blame failure on factors other than ability. Examples of this strategy are setting unrealistically high goals, delaying work until the last minute, or expending little or no effort to complete a task (underachievement).

A third type of strategy to avoid failure involves insuring success. Students who use this strategy prefer very simple tasks that are well below their abilities. This strategy could also involve setting low goals; for example, a student may announce that he or she will be satisfied with a grade of C.

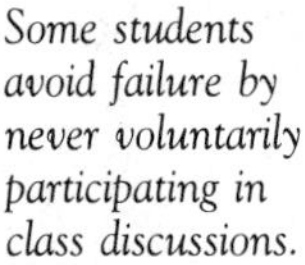

Some students avoid failure by never voluntarily participating in class discussions.

However, because students who set low goals frequently experience success, success loses its value as a reinforcer.

Failure-avoidance strategies

All of these failure-avoidance strategies ultimately lead to failure, and students who use the strategies are labelled as failure-prone. According to Covington, the problem is not one of low ability, but of basing one's self-concept on achievement, combined with setting unrealistically high standards for academic performance. Evidence shows that some students use failure-avoidance strategies as a result of early home experiences (e.g., Coopersmith, 1967), while others develop these strategies later as a result of competitive classroom environments.

The Role of Effort and Excuses

Failure dynamics

Student manipulation of effort expenditure is important in avoiding the threat of failure because failure despite high effort implies low ability and results in shame. For example, Covington and Beery (1976) found that self-estimates of effort expenditures were low following failure. Furthermore, describing a task as very difficult improves the performance of persons who frequently worry about failure, suggesting that in this situation threat to self-esteem is reduced because failure can be attributed to external causes rather than to one's skill deficiencies. Although expending little effort in failure situations may preserve one's self-perceptions of ability, Covington, Spratt, and Omelich (1980) found that low effort also caused students to label themselves negatively as being either unmotivated or lazy.

Success dynamics

Covington and Omelich (1979a) demonstrated that, at least under hypothetical conditions, increases in college students' perceived effort enhanced their pride in success and offset the negative effects of low ability estimates. Because successful performance increases self-perceptions of ability, there is little need for the biased, egocentric reports of reduced effort that people often give in failure situations. Most students are willing to accept public acknowledgment of effort that leads to success, though some pupils attempt to minimize the role of effort even when they are successful.

The desire to learn probably depends as much on the certainty of an individual's self-concept of ability and the discrepancy between a positive, publicly-held image and a negative, privately held image, as it does on the level of self-concept. Thus, as long as students are somewhat uncertain of the causes of their failures, even when the uncertainty results from their defensive tactics, they may respond well to praise and success.

Teacher Rewards and Punishment

Several studies show that although the primary determinant of teacher rewards is high achievement, teachers also reward effort (Blumenfeld, et al., 1977; Eswara, 1972). Students whom teachers see as having tried hard are rewarded more for success and punished less for failure. Students must thus balance the implications that high effort means low ability if they fail, but obvious lack of effort leads to punishment from the teacher. Excuses seem to enable them to do this. Covington and Omelich (1979b) thus characterize effort as a double-edged sword.

Covington and Omelich asked college students to state how teachers would respond and how they as students would respond following four kinds of test failure: low effort/excuse; high effort; little effort/excuse; and little effort. Results showed that college students feel that teachers would punish students who fail without making an effort more than those who try. Students and teachers had conflicting reactions to effort. For example, in the failure under high effort condition, teachers punished students least, but students in this category felt most incompetent and experienced the most personal dissatisfaction and shame. Although low effort reduced students' negative feelings, it resulted in more punishment by the teacher, unless the student had a plausible excuse for the low effort. In the case of success, there was little evidence of conflict between student and teacher values.

Attributional Factors

Successful students tend to attribute their successes to skill and effort, and their failures to lack of effort. Students who accept failure, however, attribute their successes to external factors such as luck, and their failures to lack of ability (Ames, 1978). In its extremes, failure-acceptance results in learned helplessness, a situation in which people do not even try to obtain reinforcement because they believe that their efforts cannot succeed (Abramson, Seligman, & Teasdale, 1978). However, a series of experiments by Snyder and colleages indicates that intervening ability attributions are an important contributor to learned helplessness, in addition to the conclusion that effort does not pay off.

Learned helplessness

Demoralization

Little is known about the process by which frequent failure leads to demoralization, except that self-perceptions of low ability, effort, and the availability of excuses are critical factors. A study by Covington and Omelich (1981) shows the role of these three factors. The study concerned repeated test-taking failures that occurred naturally among college students in a large, mastery-based psychology course. Students could take several similar forms of the same test and could study in between tests in order to obtain what they considered an acceptable grade. However, many students never achieved a grade that was even minimally acceptable to them, and thus experienced repeated failure. The results showed that such repeated failure not only lowered self-perceptions of ability, but because of their increasing importance as an explanation for failure, increased the role of low ability perceptions as causes of grief and hopelessness. This process occurred more rapidly for students who initially had low self-concepts; self-confident students tended to attribute their failures to external causes. Thus, one of the important factors mitigating against low self-perceptions of ability in the face of failure is the availability of plausible external explanations.

However, as failure becomes more frequent, it is harder for a person to utilize plausible self-serving explanations, and one's public image becomes more like the negative private one. Both self-presentation and self-consistency needs (the tendency to reduce inconsistencies between one's self-perceptions, one's behavior, and others' perceptions of the behavior) occur simultaneously, but which need dominates depends on how effectively a person is able to cope with failure.

Self-Worth Theory: Instructional Guidelines

Research points to the need for teachers to increase the number of rewards available to students in order to reduce competition, so that students do not have to concentrate on avoiding failure because they have no chance to succeed. Teachers can use techniques such as absolute standards for excellence, self-competition, and cooperative learning.

Teachers should demonstrate to students that effort and outcome are strongly related. For example, students should be taught to divide a complex classroom task into more manageable parts, a process that may allow success without requiring students to set lower goals. Teachers also should emphasize reasons for failure that students can control: incorrect task analysis, overly high expectations, and low effort.

Effort-affect linkage

Teachers also need to promote a positive effort-affect linkage by emphasizing effort and improvement over prior accomplishments, instead of ability, when they evaluate student performance. Assuming that the task was of appropriate difficulty level, this will enhance the likelihood that students' self-praise following success will depend more on their effort, and that failure will be attributed to low effort. If failure threatens students' self-perceptions of ability, however, shame results and students are not likely to be task-involved. Pride in ability will only continue as long as students are successful.

Covington emphasized that teachers must carefully consider the advantages and disadvantages of implementing these guidelines. For example, in a classroom where the teacher emphasizes effort rather than ability as important to rewards, will students value good grades as much as they would in a competitive environment? According to Covington, a thorough analysis of classroom learning structures is a crucial next step in research on achievement behavior.

Covington concludes that teachers must design curricula so as to promote both students' self-validation and self-accuracy. Teachers should not devalue the role of ability in achievement, but they must ensure that students do not associate personal worth with ability or performance. To avoid this perception, students must come to view ability as a repertoire of skills that increases continuously throughout their lives, rather than as a stable trait.

Maehr: Toward a Theory of Personal Investment

Though the study of motivation in academic settings has focused on theories of achievement motivation, Maehr (1984) points out that teachers and students have other goals as well. For example, some children may complete their homework because their parents will not let them play until they do so, and some older students who are not motivated to achieve in school may practice very hard in order to make the basketball team. Maehr believes that researchers, and especially practitioners, would benefit from a broader view of motivation. To this end, he proposes a theory of personal investment that is based on achievement research as well as on the study of other social motives.

Motivation and Behavior

According to Maehr (1984), past study of motivation has been concerned largely with internal processes such as attribution or competence. However, we make inferences about a person's motivation on the basis of his or her observed behavior. Most discussion of motivation in academic settings involves five overlapping types of behavior patterns: direction, persistence, continuing motivation, activity, and performance.

Direction refers to the choices that individuals make between alternative behaviors. A student may decide to play tennis rather than study, or to write a biology paper rather than do math homework. We infer choice on the part of a person who does one thing when other options are available.

Persistence is the attention an individual gives a task or event over a period of time. Persistence can also be viewed as an instance of direction in which the person repeatedly chooses the same behavioral alternative.

Continuing motivation is the voluntary, self-initiated return (after an interruption) to a task or task area that one had worked on previously. Continuing motivation is an important educational outcome for many educators (Maehr, 1976).

Activity level refers to the fact that some persons do more things than others. However, activity level is in many ways a more complex and less reliable indicator of motivation than choice, persistence, and continuing motivation. For example, physiological factors are likely to affect activity more than the other three factors. Furthermore, in some classroom situations, the predominant motivational pattern is one of direction rather than activity.

Finally, variation in *performance* is another behavioral pattern that we use to infer motivation, if the variation cannot be explained by competence, skill, or physiological factors. Performance level is determined by several factors, including a combination of the four other motivational patterns. As such, it is not a refined measure of motivation, but it nevertheless is often the basis of inferences about motivation.

According to Maehr, though these five patterns are not comprehensive, and although they involve judgments about behavior, they do represent what teachers talk about when they want to motivate students.

The Concept of Personal Investment

In order to integrate the five behavior patterns, Maehr uses the concept of personal investment (PI), or the idea that when one observes all five mo-

Using personal resources

tivational behavior patterns in a person, that person is investing his or her personal resources in a specific way. Personal resources include time, talent, and energy. Maehr states that the emphasis is on a person distributing resources rather than the availability of resources. Maehr's model thus stresses qualitative differences in motivation rather than the presence or absence of motivation, though the model assumes that different persons may have different levels of motivation.

Sources of Personal Investment

The Role of Meaning. Maehr believes that the meaning of a situation to a person is the primary determinant of personal investment. For example, though a person may appear to an observer to have succeeded or failed, the person may not feel that he or she has succeeded or failed. People perceive success and failure differently because they have varied standards for performance, and also because they may judge the value of a task differently. The latter phenomenon may be important in explaining cross-cultural differences in achievement motivation. Thus, when people achieve goals or participate in activities that they value, they are more likely to feel successful.

There are three basic, interrelated aspects of meaning that are important in determining personal investment in a particular situation: (1) beliefs about self; (2) perceived goals of behavior; and (3) perceived alternatives for pursuing these goals, or action possibilities. In some form or another, these three factors are important aspects of all theories of motivation.

Beliefs about self

Judgments of self-competence, or subjective judgments of ability to perform effectively in a situation, are an important facet of one's sense of self (see other related views, especially Nicholls). Individuals who feel competent in an area are more likely to make preferences and choices for tasks that enhance the development of talent and ability in that area (Kukla, 1978; Maehr, 1983; Nicholls, 1983).

Goals

Maehr feels that individuals' definitions of goals will vary by how they define success and failure in a situation. The goal is what a person expects to derive from his or her performance, and this will depend on the value of the activity to the person.

Types of goals

Based on his research, Maehr focuses on four goal possibilities: task, ego, social solidarity, and extrinsic rewards. In the task goal category there are two purposes for behavior. A person can be completely involved in a task, or an individual can be attempting to demonstrate competence. Ego goals involve trying to do better than a socially defined standard, especially relative to the performance of others. Social solidarity goals involve attempts to please significant others or to gain social approval. To persons with these goals, demonstrating good intentions is more important than showing competence, performing better than others, or enjoying oneself. Extrinsic rewards refer to goals such as money, prizes, or grades that are not intrinsically related to the performance of a task.

Goals and behavior

Goals affect behavior. Under extrinsic reward, goal behavior is directed towards external evaluation and reward. To develop the independent, self-initiated learning pattern that is the goal of many educators, a task-goal orientation must be encouraged. If a student is primarily interested in performing a task rather than in how others evaluate his or her performance, the student is likely to continue performing, even when no one is evaluating performance.

In many classrooms, however, the prevailing goal structure is the ego-condition. Research shows that students differ substantially in their response to competitive situations. Maehr (1983) attributes this variation to differences in the sense of competence each individual has. Thus, students who feel competent are confident in competitive situations, and the reverse is true for students with low self-concepts.

Challenge-seeking behavior

On the basis of Atkinson's theory and research, Maehr hypothesizes how the four goal conditions might affect a person's challenge-seeking behavior. Under task-goal conditions all persons will show choice-performance patterns similar to those of persons with high achievement motivation. In ego conditions, however, self-perceptions of competence mediate challenge seeking. Persons confident of their ability seek challenge; those who lack confidence avoid challenge. Motivation is fairly high in the social solidarity condition and does not vary according to the subjective probability of success or the level of challenge. In the extrinsic rewards condition, individuals tend to maximize their rewards. Given a choice between an assured means to obtaining an extrinsic reward and a less certain one, a person will choose the certain one.

Action possibilities

Action possibilities are the behaviors a person perceives as available in a situation. They are determined by what the person perceives as possible as well as what the individual views as appropriate in terms of sociocultural norms. Thus, a person may have considerable information about the violin and violin playing, but may not be interested in learning to play the violin if this behavior is not encouraged or rewarded by reference groups (i.e., friends, family).

Antecedents of Meaning. Maehr focuses on four types of antecedent, external factors that are critical in determining the meaning that activities have for persons: personal experience, the teaching-learning situation, information, and sociocultural factors. Also, different external factors will differentially affect the four components of meaning discussed above.

Personal experience

Individuals usually bring a set of meanings based on their past experiences to each new situation. A student's sense of competence in a particular subject is thus significantly affected by past successes and failures in that area.

Teaching-learning situation

Two important aspects of the teaching-learning situation that affect the meaning the situation holds for a person are social expectations and task design. In the classroom, social expectations frequently take the form of peer expectations for the achievement-related behavior of individual students. These group expectations pressure students to attempt certain goals and to behave in specific ways. Several features of a task can also affect the meaning of the task to a student. First, some tasks are inherently more motivating; that is, they have ideal levels of uncertainty and unpredictability (Deci, 1975). The manner in which performance on a task is evaluated can also affect motivation. External evaluation tends to reduce students' intrinsic interest in a task (Maehr, 1976), so that they are less likely to continue working on the task on their own. Another feature associated with the task is the amount of choice students are allowed when they perform a task. More freedom of choice promotes task goals, and more external control enhances extrinsic goals.

Information

Though information affects all aspects of meaning that determine personal investment, its greatest impact is probably on behavioral options. For example, vocational information can play an important role in choices that students make in order to reach certain career goals.

Sociocultural factors

One's social-cultural group(s) play a significant role in making certain behaviors more acceptable or valued than others. Research shows that culture affects achievement by defining what success and failure mean (Maehr & Nicholls, 1980) and by specifying how one should obtain success and avoid failure (Fyans et al., 1983).

Teacher Socialization as a Mechanism for Developing Student Motivation to Learn

Brophy (1985) and Brophy and Kher (in press) review research related to how student motivation to learn can be developed through teacher modeling and socialization behavior. This work has both important theoretical and practical implications.

Definition of Motivation to Learn

The authors view motivation to learn as both a general trait where students value learning for its own sake and a situation-specific state where students engage purposefully in classroom tasks in order to master certain concepts and skills. Brophy and Kher argue that students who are motivated to learn will not necessarily find classroom tasks intensely exciting, but they will take them seriously, find them meaningful, and attempt to get the intended benefit from them. This definition emphasizes the cognitive processes that accompany learning rather than the demonstration of skills or knowledge through performance or the student's attempts to achieve certain standards of excellence such as in obtaining good grades. Important concepts of motivation are illustrated in Table 15.2.

Optimizing Student Motivation to Learn

In order for students to develop positive motivation, the negative attitudes, etc., depicted in the top of Table 15.2 must be eliminated. Brophy and Kher state that the following conditions are required, but are not sufficient,

Table 15.2 Qualitative Aspects of Students' Motivation Related to Specific Academic Tasks

Direction of Attitude	Task Endogenous Motivation		Task Exogenous Motivation	
	Task Value Focus	*Performance Outcome Focus*	*Task Value Focus*	*Performance Outcome Focus*
Negative	*Affect*: Anger or dread. Student dislikes the task, which is in effect a punishment.	*Affect*: Anxiety, embarrassment, fear of failure.	*Affect*: Alienation, resistance. Student doesn't want to acquire this knowledge or skill.	*Affect*: Apathy, resignation, resentment.
	Cognition: Task focus is "invaded" by resentment, awareness of being coerced into unpleasant or pointless activity.	*Cognition*: Task focus is "invaded" by perception of confusion, failure, helplessness. Attribution of (poor) performance to insufficient ability.	*Cognition*: Perceptions of conflict between what this task represents and one's self concept, sex role identification, etc. Anticipation of undesirable consequences to involvement in such tasks.	*Cognition*: Perception that one cannot "win," that one has no realistic chance to earn desired rewards, satisfactory grades, etc.
Neutral	Neutral attitude toward task; open minded (if new) or indifferent (if familiar).	No particular expectations; neither success nor failure are salient concerns.	Neutral; the knowledge or skills developed by the task elicit neither avoidance nor excitement.	No extrinsic consequences are expected; performance will neither be rewarded nor punished.
Positive	*Affect*: Enjoyment, pleasure. Engagement in this task is a reward in its own right.	*Affect*: Satisfaction (perhaps occasional excitement) as skills or insights develop. Pride in craftsmanship, successful performance.	*Affect*: Energized, eager to learn this knowledge or skill (for its instrumental value).	*Affect*: Excitement, happy anticipation of reward.
	Cognition: Relaxed concentration on the processes involved in doing the task. "Flow." Metacognitive awareness of what the task requires and how one is responding to it. Focus on the academic content when learning, and on the quality of the product when performing.	*Cognition*: Perception of progress toward goals, achieved with relative ease. Attribution of (successful) performance to (sufficient) ability plus (reasonable) effort. Focus on one's developing knowledge and skills.	*Cognition*: Recognition that the task is a subgoal related to attainment of important future goals (often as a "ticket" to social advancement). Focus on the "relevant" aspects of learning.	*Cognition*: Recognition that one can attain desired rewards with relative ease. Focus on meeting stated performance criteria.

Source: This table is reprinted from J. Brophy and N. Kher "Teacher socialization as a mechanism for developing student motivation to learn." In R. Feldman (ed.), *Social Psychology Applied to Education* (Cambridge: Cambridge University Press, in press).

for students to develop positive task-endogenous motivation to learn: (1) a patient, encouraging teacher who supports learning efforts; (2) an appropriate match between student ability and task difficulty; (3) tasks that are sufficiently varied and interesting; and (4) a teacher who generally presents tasks as learning opportunities with which he or she will assist students rather than as ordeals to be endured to get good grades or to please the teacher. However, these conditions will only insure a minimal level of motivation. Brophy and Kher believe students' motivation to learn is optimized when it has the characteristics associated with positive, task-endogenous motivation, depicted in the lower left sections of Table 15.2.

Research suggests that the tendency to be absorbed in tasks seems to be a trait that is developed in different persons through experience, or socialization (Graef, Csikszentmihalyi, & Gianinno, 1981). The application value of Brophy's work on socializing student motivation to learn will be discussed in detail in Chapter 16.

SUMMARY

We have stressed the cognitive view of motivation in this chapter. Cognitive explanations emphasize individuals' perceptions of events and the influences of these perceptions on behavior. Weiner discusses attribution theory and the four perceived causes of success and failure—ability, effort, task difficulty, and luck—to explain achievement behavior. Weiner also discusses the role of affect in the motivational process.

Nicholls distinguishes between mastering a task to show ability per se (task-involvement) and mastering a task to demonstrate ability in comparison to another person (ego-involvement). Nicholls suggests that how students define a task influences what tasks they select (e.g., do they prefer high or low risk tasks) and how they interpret success or failure on tasks. He believes that a more general orientation to tasks (ego versus task involvement) may influence students' attributions about performance.

deCharms argues that the most important way that teachers can enhance motivation is to believe that pupils can be origins. An origin is one who acts on the environment and who can plan and assume responsibility for success. deCharms notes that "origin-enhancing" classrooms are not classrooms in which students are allowed to do as they please and that the term "origin" is relative. The concept of origin includes choice, which implies a degree of freedom and responsibility, and encourages the actor to feel ownership of behavior.

Cognitive theorists believe that individuals are motivated to present a positive self-image; Covington refers to this as the self-worth motive. In the classroom, the self-worth motive is reflected primarily in self-perceptions of academic competency. Covington argues that some students spend time developing strategies to avoid failure, such as nonparticipation, blaming failure on others or insuring success by attempting easy or trivial tasks. Such strategies are ultimately self-defeating. Covington concludes that teachers must design curricula so as to promote both students' self-validation and self-accuracy.

Maehr notes that the study of motivation focuses primarily on theories of achievement motivation. He contends, however, that students and teachers have other important goals as well. According to Maehr, recent motivational discussions emphasize internal processes such as attribution; still, he contends that we tend to make inferences about the motivation of individuals on the basis of their observed behavior. Maehr presents five behavior patterns: direction, persistence, continuing motivation, activity, and performance, as well as the concept of personal investment as ways of exploring motivation.

QUESTIONS AND PROBLEMS

1. What difference does it make if students feel that they get an "A" because of luck or because of hard work? How might such a perception or attribution influence the way students prepare for the next exam in a course?
2. What are the major differences between achievement theory (presented in Chapter 14) and attribution theory (discussed in this chapter)?
3. In your own words define task-involvement and ego-involvement motivation. Assume that you are introducing a particular unit in some class (e.g., during a second-grade spelling lesson, during a tenth-grade biology lesson). Specify what you would do to make it more likely that students would complete their work with a task-involvement motivational perspective.
4. Think about the college courses that you are now taking from the perspective of task- and ego-involvement. What percent of the class assignments you receive produce task-involvement? Why is this the case?
5. In terms of this text's descriptions of origin- and pawn-like classrooms, compare your elementary and high school classrooms. Did you receive more opportunities for autonomy and decision making as you progressed through the educational system? If not, why do you suppose this was the case?
6. How would you characterize your coursework in college with regard to origin and pawn characteristics? Can a classroom involve too much decision making and too little teacher structure? What is the difference between a laissez-faire environment and one that is appropriately open-ended?
7. Given that too much structure for one student may be too little structure for another, how can teachers apply theories of personal causation in the classroom? Considering that the motivational needs of individual students vary widely and that often what one student needs may be counterproductive for another student, how can teachers apply the ideas presented in this chapter?
8. Discuss strategies to avoid failure that were presented in this chapter. Summarize the implications of this work in your own words. Have you ever used these or other strategies in the classroom? How can a teacher prevent or at least lessen the likelihood that students will learn to develop strategies for avoiding failure (in the sense in which the term was used in this chapter)?
9. Think about the mastery learning study that took place in a large introductory psychology classroom at the University of California-Berkeley that was described in this chapter. Would you like to receive most of your coursework in an environment like that? If not, why not, and if so, why?
10. Discuss the implications for you as a future classroom teacher. How might you begin and end lessons in order to improve their motivational value? Do you think that it is possible for a teacher to utilize these strategies too frequently or too seldom? From your understanding of this literature, which is most likely to be the greater problem?

Middle of the Road. Clara Glick is a tenth-grade speech teacher at Crestview High School. Crestview serves an upper middle-class population in a small, but affluent community dominated by a large state university. Clara's class is distinguished by minimum student involvement and infrequent disturbances. Students pay attention but do not seem to be greatly interested in the various activities that take place during the speech class.

Although the topics vary from time to time, each class period usually involves three or four students presenting speeches, with each speech followed by a couple of minutes of general critique. The type of speech being presented varies from month to month (e.g., an extemporaneous speech, a prepared sales speech, an expository speech). In general, Clara emphasizes talking about historical topics, such as why Wall Street collapsed as opposed to speaking about a trivial event like having one's new dress accidentally rip.

The course is well-organized and Clara has prepared several examples of speeches that students could present during class. Furthermore, she provides exhaustive reading lists and complete examples of successful speeches that students can study. She has prepared evaluation sheets that are adapted to each of the different types of speeches that students give. Thus, when students give expository speeches they utilize the form that Clara has prepared. In her evaluation sheets, she emphasizes the correct format of speeches rather than their content (e.g., are all parts of the expository speech there? Is too much time spent on any one part? Is the delivery of the speech acceptable for the type of audience?).

Unlike some speech classes, few students in Clara Glick's class dread giving their speeches or feel embarrassed about the feedback they get from other students. Clara emphasizes that students should be very positive and gracious in their responses. Accordingly, students often gush when they give feedback to classmates. In general, they view the course as "soft" but somewhat interesting.

What type of students are most likely to benefit from this speech class? Explain your reasoning. What might Clara do to improve the course so that it is more meaningful to all types of students?

Playing it Safe. Although Frank spends an hour and a half each night studying for Spanish class, he pretends to his friends that he never studies. Furthermore, Frank works hard to get the teacher's attention early in the lesson because he wants to answer easy questions. When he takes part in the conversational part of the lesson (he participates in this part of the lesson only when called on by his teacher), he is careful to use words that are easy to pronounce. How would you characterize Frank's problem? What, if anything, should a classroom teacher do about it?

Chapter 16

General Guidelines for Classroom Motivation

OBJECTIVES

When you have mastered the material in this chapter you will be able to

1. Define *classroom motivation* and discuss how extrinsic and intrinsic rewards interact to affect it
2. Discuss research relating time spent on learning tasks to achievement
3. List the four motivational tasks teachers must perform and explain how they can accomplish these tasks
4. Explain the value accommodating student interest and allowing choice in learning activities have for classroom motivation
5. Discuss three ways to individualize instruction and motivate learning that do not require hiring additional teachers or aides
6. Contrast the motivational effects of competitive versus cooperative learning situations
7. Discuss Brophy's teaching strategies for increasing students' motivation to learn
8. Discuss Keller's motivational model in terms of interest, relevance, expectancy, and satisfaction

The previous chapter offered several different theories that explain why people initiate and maintain behavior. These theories provide rich input and assist the teacher in classroom decision making. At present, no theory is able to predict completely how teachers should behave or structure their classrooms to guarantee that all students will be optimally stimulated. That is, it is impossible to say that if teachers behave in a specified way, all students, or even certain types of students, will be motivated to expend effort on assigned tasks.

School instruction and learning take place in a group context. A pupil's behavior in private (e.g., an experimental setting) may be different from that in the presence of classmates. For example, certain adolescent girls may reveal high achievement needs and exhibit competitive behavior in an experimental setting, but remain relatively inactive in the classroom because of their perceived female role expectations for compliant behavior.

We believe that experimental findings have relevancy for classroom teaching but should not be interpreted literally. Students will benefit from classroom tasks that are moderately stimulating, but despite a high level of need achievement, there are few students who want to work on tasks continuously when they only have a 50 percent chance of success. Fortunately, educators and psychologists are beginning to test motivational ideas more frequently in classrooms (see, for example, Arkin and Maruyama, 1979), and in time more specific and directly applicable findings will be available. This qualification is not presented to discourage teachers from applying the results of research, but rather to remind teachers that when they attempt to influence behavior it will be in a social setting. Because most motivational research has occurred in laboratory settings, teachers need to view motivational principles as means for interpreting classroom events and behavior, but not as prescriptive "answers" for all classrooms.

In this chapter we discuss some general ideas for motivating and enhancing student performance. We also discuss some common assumptions that are inappropriate, and thus interfere with the effectiveness of teachers who try to apply them.

Task Motivation

Task motivation refers to the levels of task involvement and persistence that students exhibit, regardless of who designs or sets the task. We use this definition because, despite popular sentiment that surrounds terms such as "student choice," "student-initiated ideas," and so on, we do not believe that a student definition of the learning situation is always more motivating than appropriately made teacher assignments. Both teacher- and student-structured learning assignments can be useful.

As we have noted in the previous chapter, psychologists define motivation as the process of arousing, directing, and maintaining behavior. Here we focus more on the apparent classroom behavior of students, because this is the best source for teachers to use when making educated guesses about

Classroom behavior

whether students are motivated. We believe that students probably are motivated when they spend a great deal of time attending to lessons and working on assignments or self-selected academic tasks. However, as Ball (1977) points out: "Definitions of 'motivated' and 'unmotivated' depend, in part, upon who does the observing." He notes that two teachers who observe a student work for a long period of time might reach different conclusions about the student's motivation—one teacher may feel that the student is highly motivated and another may feel the student is persistent but works only because the teacher has set the task. The interpretation of motivation is a subjective process. We prefer a simple initial question: Is the student engaged in assigned work?

The problem for the classroom teacher is to align students' motives and classwork. Teachers attempt to do this by trying to influence their students' motives and by selecting content that matches their interests, or else by letting students help identify relevant content.

Motivational and instructional problems

In this context, we need to distinguish whether or not a student's poor performance is a motivational or a general instructional problem. When a student can do the assigned work but fails to do so for whatever reason, a motivational problem exists. Teachers who regularly assign material that is much too difficult will eventually erode student interest in performing well. In time, instructional ineptness (the continual assignment of material that is too difficult) will generate motivational problems where students give up trying. In the short run, this problem is basically instructional, not motivational.

Instructional and motivational problems coexist in the classroom, and it is difficult to separate them except for purposes of discussion and emphasis. When we discuss task difficulty in this chapter, the emphasis is on student perception of task difficulty; in our discussion of learning, we stressed the match between task demands and students' cognitive skills. Students' perceptions of their failure or success at a task vary widely and are often erroneous. Despite the fact that students' perceptions may be wrong, if students believe they cannot do the work or that the teacher does not reward effort, their effort will be reduced. The teacher's job is to select appropriate tasks—tasks that are instructionally important and able to be done by the student—and to convince students that if they make an appropriate effort, progress will follow.

Extrinsic rewards

Extrinsic rewards are also an important factor in motivation. Indeed, we suspect that, given the vast number of hours students spend in schools, external rewards such as giving free time or a chance to play games can be defended on the grounds that they make school life more pleasant, even if improved learning does not follow. Still, we suspect that if students do not perceive their work assignments as challenging or at least appropriate, anything the teacher does will be of considerably lower value.

Intrinsic rewards

There is much debate concerning which source of reward, extrinsic or intrinsic, is best. For example, Deci (1975) argues that people often engage in activities for which there is no clear reward; that is, they do things because

After completing a challenging assignment, these students are enjoying recess and an opportunity to relax.

of intrinsic motivation (e.g., it is fun or stimulating). There is research to illustrate that when individuals are rewarded externally for an activity they had been engaging in for its intrinsic value, their intrinsic interest in that activity decreases. However, other research indicates that under some conditions, external rewards can increase activity levels and intrinsic motivation (Bandura, 1977). We believe that both extrinsic and intrinsic rewards or sources of motivation have a role in the classroom, and that the more appropriate question is, "How does each type of reward influence students' perceptions and behavior?"

Both Deci (1975) and Bandura (1977) note that many students do not come to school with intrinsic motivation for school tasks, and it may be useful for teachers to use rewards like giving verbal praise or offering the opportunity to play games to help students become involved in school subjects.

Teacher praise

Brophy (1981) has noted that teacher praise is sometimes used in a way that interferes with the development of intrinsic motivation. He has developed a set of guidelines for delivering praise in a way that emphasizes informational rather than controlling feedback. These guidelines are presented in Table 16.1.

The most direct way to increase student motivation is to make learning tasks as interesting as possible. If rewards make tasks more attractive and interesting and encourage students to expend more effort, then they are useful, at least in the short run. One drawback when external rewards are used excessively is that they are frequently employed in a way that makes students more dependent on the teacher or on other external support. Therefore, external rewards should not be used excessively. As Bandura (1977) points out, excessive use of rewards presents difficulties when the time comes to eliminate them.

Table 16.1 Guidelines for Effective Praise

Effective Praise	Ineffective Praise
1. is delivered contingently	1. is delivered randomly or unsystematically
2. specifies the particulars of the accomplishment	2. is restricted to global positive reactions
3. shows spontaneity, variety, and other signs of credibility; suggests attention to the student's accomplishment	3. shows a bland uniformity that suggests a conditioned response made with minimal attention
4. rewards attainment of specified performance criteria (which can include effort criteria, however	4. rewards mere participation, without consideration of performance processes or outcomes.
5. provides information to students about their competence and the value of their accomplishments	5. provides no information at all or gives students no information about their status
6. orients students toward better appreciation of their own task-related behavior and thinking about problem solving	6. orients students toward comparing themselves with others and thinking about competing
7. uses own prior accomplishments as the context for describing present accomplishments	7. uses the accomplishments of peers as the context for describing students' present accomplishments
8. is given in recognition of noteworthy effort or success at difficult tasks (for *this* student)	8. is given without regard to the effort expended or the meaning of the accomplishment
9. attributes success to effort and ability, implying that similar successes can be expected in the future	9. attributes success to ability alone or to external factors such as luck or task difficulty
10. fosters endogenous attributions (students believe that they expend effort on the task because they enjoy the task and/or want to develop task-relevant skills)	10. fosters exogenous attributions—students believe that they expend effort on the task for external reasons like pleasing the teacher or winning a competition or reward
11. focuses students' attention on their own task-relevant behavior	11. focuses students' attention on the teacher as an external authority figure who is manipulating them
12. fosters appreciation of and desirable attributions about task-relevant behavior after the process is completed	12. intrudes into the ongoing process, distracting attention from task-relevant behavior

Source: Jere E. Brophy, "Teacher praise: A functional analysis," *Review of Educational Research,* (Spring 1981): 5–32. Copyright 1981, American Educational Research Association, Washington, D.C.

Student Task Involvement: A Proxy for Student Motivation

It is reasonable to predict that students who do relatively well in school will do assigned seatwork, listen carefully to classroom conversations, raise their hands to answer questions, and concentrate on assigned tasks when working on group projects. Many studies demonstrate a relationship between such behaviors and academic achievement (see McKinney, Mason, Perkerson, & Clifford, 1975). On the other hand, some students spend considerable time walking around the room, talking to neighbors about nontask events, searching for unnecessary materials, and generally wasting time.

Time spent on tasks

Students also vary widely in the amount of time they spend on tasks in open settings and in individualized settings where materials have presumably been adjusted to meet individual differences in students' cognitive abilities. Lack of student time on a task is more likely to be a motivational than an instructional problem in individualized settings—students are not off task because they cannot do the work. Shimron (1973) examined the extent to which slow and fast students spent differential time on curriculum tasks. All students were in the same classroom in an Individually Prescribed Instruction (IPI) program. In this curriculum, students follow a predetermined sequence of tasks but proceed at their own pace. Each of the target students was observed for five twenty-minute periods. Four students were called "fast" because they had mastered the most curriculum tasks. Four students were labeled "slow" because they had mastered the fewest units prior to observation. Virtually no peer-peer, work-related contacts took place in this individualized program. Differences between the fast and slow students included: (1) fast students spent twice as much time working on assignments; (2) slower students spent twice as much time in off-task behavior; and (3) student-teacher interaction occurred at a much higher rate for faster students. Shimron suggests that the lows may have spent less time on curriculum tasks because: (1) they needed more gradual sequencing; (2) they may not have fully mastered some prerequisite task; and (3) the units may not have interested them.

Low achievers are easily diverted from concentrating on classroom assignments.

Differences between high and low achievers

Other research supports the finding that high achievers spend more time on task than low achievers (see Good & Beckerman, 1978). There is also evidence that the differences in measured work involvement between highs and lows may be underestimated. In a small but comprehensive case study of two high- and low-achieving students, King (1979) notes that lows report more preoccupation with thoughts about personal failure, possible teacher reactions, and so on. That is, even while apparently working on assigned tasks, lows are less focused on task demands.

Because low achievers spend less time working and thinking about classroom assignments, it seems likely that the achievement differences between highs and lows will widen with time. To make the situation more difficult, it is likely that as lows fall farther behind they will feel worse about their classroom status and put forth even less effort.

We believe that motivation is as responsible as student ability for poor student performance. If task involvement for low-achieving students can be increased, or if lows can be given more time to complete assigned work, perhaps the achievement differences between highs and lows would not widen as sharply over time as they do at present. Fortunately, there are data that illustrate that the poor performance of lows can be enhanced, and that appropriate motivation and instruction can help low-aptitude students to do better.

Variation in Time Usage

Data collected in the Beginning Teacher Evaluation Study (see Denham & Lieberman, 1980) show that the amount of time allocated to a particular topic varies considerably from school to school and from classroom to classroom. Furthermore, once instruction in a subject has begun, the actual time spent on instruction varies according to such factors as grouping practices, instructional techniques, class size, student ability distribution, number and length of interruptions, and the ability of the teacher to manage the classroom. Estimates differ, but studies basically indicate that only about 50 to 60 percent of the school day is actually used for instruction.

On-task behavior

A more refined measure of learning time is student engagement, or on-task behavior. Recent observational studies suggest that pupils are on task about 70 to 75 percent of the time. In the BTES study (Fisher et al., 1980) it was found that classes vary as much as 40 percent in rates of attentiveness. However, although variations in amount of time on task occur across days, students, and classrooms, little research has attempted to ascertain the sources of this variation as being due to student factors, classroom teaching practices, or day-to-day fluctuations. It is clear from a variety of studies, though, that teachers' beliefs and behaviors are strongly related to time utilization (e.g., Arlin, 1982; Schmidt & Buchmann, 1983). Teachers who believe that learning the curriculum is the top priority in the classroom allocate more time to instruction than teachers who value other objectives more highly. It is also the case that student factors influence the amount of engaged time observed. Research has indicated that high-ability and female students have higher rates of on-task behavior.

Finally, it is worth noting that some areas of the curriculum appear to receive little instructional time. In a study of 75 teachers in grades 2 through 6, Ebmeier and Ziomek (1983) found that an average of only 15 minutes per week was spent on science in second-grade classes. By fifth grade, this average had only increased to 43 minutes. Furthermore, the time spent on science in most classes was considerably lower than what the district recommended.

Mode of instruction

Mode of instruction is a manipulable variable that has been shown to be related to engagement. Using the BTES data, Rosenshine (1980) found that engagement averaged 70 percent during unsupervised seatwork and 84 percent during teacher-led discussion. These differences were important because the students spent about 70 percent of classroom time doing seatwork, a practice necessitated by grouping. Whether whole- or small-group instruction is better depends on whether the losses in time through grouping are compensated for by increased quality of group instruction such as appropriate seatwork tasks or instruction that is better matched to students' ability. However, most empirical evidence suggests that too often classroom designs that call for large amounts of student seatwork are marked by insufficient procedural details and tasks that are poorly matched with student ability (Anderson, 1981; Doyle, 1982).

Studies of Time and Learning

Most recent studies of time and learning involve engaged time, reflecting the opinion of many persons that an indisputable relationship has been established between engaged time and amount of learning (Harnischfeger & Wiley, 1976; Borg, 1980; Sirotnik, 1982). However, others are more qualified in their support of this relationship (Kepler, 1980; Husen, 1967; Karweit, 1976).

Karweit (1983) concludes from her review of eight studies of engagement rates that the relationship between time and learning is "weak and inconsistent." Still, an examination of studies included in her review shows that low to moderate correlations between attention and learning existed (.09–.43), even when ability was statistically controlled.

Problems with Time Research

In many studies, time measures have been taken independently of measures of instructional behavior (what and how well are teachers teaching), classroom organization, and curriculum task. The early emphasis on time measures per se (independent of context) was understandable, but given extant knowledge and our increased capacity for studying time (i.e., methodological advances in the BTES study) it is now necessary to become more integrative and comprehensive in our research. Clearly, the work by Berliner (1979) shows that more refined measures of time usage that include consideration of task appropriateness and student engagement are more strongly associated with student achievement than are measures that consider only the amount of time allocated to particular subject matter.

Implications of Research on Time on Task

Time on task studies yield suggestions that can stimulate teachers' thinking about instructional strategies (see Wynne & Stuck, 1982; Good & Brophy, 1984). Some of these strategies are straightforward (e.g., begin and end lessons on time; minimize confusing distractions), but recent research is suggesting that the most important factors in increasing engagement rates and achievement may be teacher behaviors related to classroom organization, quality of instruction, and students' perceptions of tasks and directions. To gather the latter information, teachers will not only have to observe but question and talk to their students to discover things like their interests and their task preferences.

It now seems clear that the same amount of learning time can have dramatically different consequences, depending on classroom and individual student factors. It is also clear that learning depends on both student attention and appropriate instruction. Theories of classroom learning, and subsequent studies of time and learning, should be based more on accommodating student diversity in ability and on quality of instruction rather than on allocated time per se. This dynamic view of learning assumes that factors affecting classroom learning like student interest and instructional pace vary over time and that on-going events in classrooms like composition factors and specific subject matter assignments affect this variation. Time spent on academic tasks is important, but quality of the time expenditure is more important. For an excellent review of instructional time studies see Fisher and Berliner (1985).

Quality of time expenditure

Mastery learning

Mastery learning is an instructional strategy that allows students to study material until they master it. Bloom (1976) argues that if students are allowed the time to master material instead of being pushed ahead prematurely and if tasks are sequentially ordered in appropriate ways, it is possible for almost all students to master most of the material in present school curricula. In motivational terms, the increased time to learn material up to the point of mastery helps students to experience success. In time, frequent success experiences and the knowledge that students acquire will enable them to exert more effort and to experience more success on subsequent curriculum tasks (Covington, 1984). Bloom (1976) presents data to suggest that 80 percent of students reach an achievement level that fewer than 20 percent of these students would attain under nonmastery conditions.

It is beyond our present purpose to review the extensive body of mastery-learning research that has been conducted at a variety of grade levels, and in several countries. For an extended explanation of mastery learning and a critical analysis of this instructional strategy see Bloom (1976), Greeno (1978), and Block (1984). However, we should note in closing that mastery learning is great in theory and appears to work well in secondary schools and especially at the college level. However, it sometimes does not work well in elementary schools when, in practice, it means that students spend a great deal of their time trying to learn independently from curriculum materials.

Motivational Tasks for the Teacher

We now turn from a discussion of general issues to specific motivational strategies. We believe that the motivational tasks of the teacher can be broken down into four general areas: starting assignments; maintaining task involvement; maintaining motivation over the school year; and building or enhancing students' capacity for self-evaluation.

Starting Assignments

Creating stimulating and appropriate assignments

The first step in teaching students is the assignment of tasks that provide some stimulation and are appropriate in the sense that they are moderately difficult relative to the students' ability levels. The context in which pupils work and their interest in the task also set limits on the difficulty of the assignment. For example, if students are to work independently, tasks need to be somewhat easier than when students have access to immediate feedback.

Creating student interest

A second aspect of starting assignments is to capture students' attention. Teachers should relate a topic to students' interests or attempt to create interest in the topic. Task interest can be created by allowing students to choose whenever possible. Choice can also provide useful information for students and teachers alike. For instance, teachers might have students provide a brief written statement to explain the reasons for their choices. Such feedback might help the teacher and student, in time, to understand personal preferences and interests. Unfortunately, because of time restrictions, limited resources, or importance of content, it is sometimes not feasible to provide choice.

Creating clear learning goals

Another prerequisite for starting the lesson is to be sure that learning goals are clear. Students are often exposed to a topic without being provided with a specific focus. For example, in a study unit on India, students could learn about standard of living, social class (caste) differences, the historical form of government, and so on. For any topic there are many possible outcomes, and teachers and students often fail to focus their attention on the same aspects. Some students work hard but perform poorly on tests because they study the wrong material. Such conditions teach students that a relationship between effort and outcome does not exist, and undermine student motivation.

Maintaining Task Involvement During Seatwork

After starting the assignment, teachers need to be certain that they maintain student task involvement. For some students the hardest aspect of doing seatwork is getting started; once they begin a task they tend to work reasonably well. Hence, after teachers establish interest in an assignment they should be careful to see that students begin work immediately. The teacher who has been working with the entire class and then makes a seatwork assignment will find it profitable to monitor the whole class for a couple of minutes and not become immediately involved with one student or become absorbed in paperwork at the desk until all students are engaged in work.

Demanding attention to the task

Teachers can create conditions for maintaining involvement in several specific ways. They can demand attention to the task. If students are going to work for fifteen minutes on an assignment, the teacher might remind them that some of their work will be checked and feedback will be given at the end of that period. Why should students begin work immediately if their work won't be checked until the next day, or not at all? Research shows that knowledge of results is a key aspect in maintaining student interest and performance (Waller & Gaa, 1974).

Teachers need to monitor seatwork carefully, paying attention to the quality of work as well as to student behavior.

Despite the fact that students in some classes spend 70 percent of the instructional day doing seatwork (i.e., reading or written tasks completed without direct teacher supervision), little formal study of seatwork has been completed. This is surprising, since effective management practices such as accountability for completed seatwork increase student involvement in assigned work (Emmer & Evertson, 1980).

Anderson (1984) conducted one of the few studies of seatwork designed to examine in depth what students do during seatwork and how they attempt to understand and complete assignments. Results showed that students spend from 30 to 60 percent of time allocated to reading instruction doing some aspect of seatwork. Furthermore, an average of 50 percent, but in some classes virtually 100 percent, of seatwork assignments utilized commercial products such as workbooks, dittos, and reading materials. In many cases, these materials were all from the same basal series.

Although there were some differences from class to class, seatwork assignments within each class were very similar across time, with the same form of assignment often used two to five times a week (e.g., Read a sentence and then choose one of three pictures that represents the meaning of the sentence).

In six of the eight classes Anderson studied, over half of the seatwork assignments were given to the whole class. Thus, despite the fact that the students were assigned to different groups, they still completed the same seatwork assignment. Overall, the typical pattern of seatwork within a class involved common assignments, with workbooks and dittos used for practice in reading skills.

Teacher Directions and Explanations. Anderson found that teacher instruction related to seatwork assignments seldom included statements about what would be learned. Anderson suggests that most students would benefit from more specific content-related explanations and feedback than students in the classes in this study received.

Seatwork for Low Achievers. Anderson (1984) reports that the researchers were especially aware of the inappropriateness of many seatwork assignments that low achievers received. These students frequently did poorly on their assignments and often derived answers by using strategies that allowed them to complete tasks without understanding what they were supposed to be learning. Anderson suggests that poor seatwork habits developed in first grade may contribute to the subsequent development of a passive learning style. Low achievers, who often work on assignments they do not understand, may come to believe that schoolwork does not have to make sense, and that, consequently, they do not need to obtain additional information or assistance. In contrast, Anderson notes that because high-achieving students seldom have difficulty with seatwork, any problems they do have are likely to motivate them to take steps to reduce confusion and to obtain additional appropriate information.

Maintaining Motivation Over the School Year

All of us grow tired of doing the same thing day after day. The school year is very long and, all other things being equal, the younger the student, the more slowly the time appears to pass. In general, teachers need to focus on learning tasks and to attempt to elicit the most attention possible from students. However, teachers have to relax the system from time to time if student interest is to be maintained at a reasonable level.

Creating special events

One way to maintain interest is occasionally to schedule an enjoyable change of pace. Nothing excites students so much as the chance to do something that is both unexpected and pleasurable. Special events can even be related to academic goals. For example, students of all ages can benefit from preparing a classroom newspaper or constructing a new learning center, and they can be assigned responsibilities that are fun and suited to their individual abilities and interests (e.g., writing a creative essay, interviewing students, writing up sports results).

There are good reasons for making special events relevant to previous academic assignments. Once students complete a unit they often do not encounter the material again, but the use of previous learning in novel ways encourages student motivation on daily assignments. Enjoyable assignments that incorporate previous learning help students to see that the material they study will benefit them in the future. Knowing that the material will reappear in later units encourages student retention and integration.

Although the value of an instructional technique depends on curriculum content and learning goals, some variety in learning mode and task assignment is useful in motivating more students. Each learning activity has a built-in structure that tends to favor some students.

Student motivation is enhanced by participation in special events that relate to individual interests and abilities.

Building Student Self-Evaluation

Teachers need to expand their students' abilities so that they can develop their own academic interests and can maintain and evaluate their progress toward academic goals. Some students, young children in particular, have limited capacity for such self-direction, and certain students of all ages have little interest in planning and evaluating their academic performance. Teachers need to be aware of these limitations and should not attempt to go too far too quickly.

Benefit of feedback

All students will benefit from feedback about their academic performance. This information can be used in such a way as to help students set realistic goals and evaluate their performance. Students who have such opportunities to an extent appropriate for their age level are well on their way to self-management.

When asked to evaluate their performance, many students may find it difficult to respond. With training and specific focus, however, students can become better critics of their own work. Students who have criteria (e.g., does each paragraph have one topic sentence?) can evaluate their progress over time. Similarly, students can be trained to make better estimates of how long it will take them to complete various assignments and to identify the type of work that truly interests them. Students will gain self-evaluative skills only if the teacher works toward this goal by, perhaps, requiring students to decide when their work is carefully done, helping students to identify criteria for making such an evaluation and by providing emotional support.

Teacher Strategies of Influence

Teachers can manipulate four major conditions in the classroom: the tasks students are assigned; students' perceptions of these tasks; their rapport with the class generally and with individual students specifically; and the reward structures they introduce.

Teachers can manipulate the design of a task (teacher, student, both), its nature (content, difficulty, abstractness, length), the mode (whole-class, groups, individual), and the time allowed for completion. Furthermore, teachers can alter the frequency of feedback, the type of feedback (conference, written), and the percentage of time students work on assigned or selected tasks. The possible combination of factors is large. For example, teachers can use student-selected assignments that are not related to student interests, and teacher-assigned tasks that are, or vice versa. The point is that teachers who match learning tasks to students' cognitive abilities and interest levels have taken a major step in establishing the conditions necessary for learning.

Matching tasks to cognitive abilities and interest levels

Teachers can also manipulate students' perceptions of tasks. Here the task remains constant, but the teacher helps the student to change his or her attitude toward the task.

Teacher's relationship to students

A third way of viewing the teacher's motivational role is to examine his or her relationship to the students. Students who listen intently to every word teachers utter are ready to perform, teachers have only to tell them how. Teachers will have to encourage such students to depend more on themselves for direction. Students who are suspicious of adults represent a different motivational problem. Teachers must develop a personal relationship with these students if they are to make a difference in their classroom achievement.

Reward mechanism

A fourth major way of viewing the teacher's motivational role is through the reward mechanism established in the classroom. Can all students be successful? Or does the way in which assignments are structured and evaluated guarantee that the success of some students will necessarily lower the success rate for others? Teachers who set high standards and individual goals are mainly helping those students who are ready to compete, and are maximizing student mastery of cognitive material. Teachers who place students in groups, grade group performance, and reward effort, are helping students who are unable to compete as well as promoting prosocial and general affective growth. In the long run, informal evaluations given by teachers probably affect student behavior as much as formal evaluations and reward procedures like grades.

In actual practice it is difficult to separate these sources of influence. For example, the teacher who manipulates task demand by allowing two students to work together may affect the reward structure as well. However, the four levels of influence we discussed may encourage teachers to consider using a variety of strategies, not just, for example, curriculum changes or talks with students.

In the remainder of this chapter we shall discuss several specific recommendations made by educators and psychologists as ways teachers can enhance motivation. Potential problems in applying these methods are also discussed.

Student Interest

In general, we suggest that when important skills are involved such as reading or computation, teachers must see that their students master the material. However, in situations when basic skills are not being learned, and when inadequate student performance is primarily motivational in nature, teachers should take a careful look at their instructional goals. Most appropriate instructional goals involve the acquisition and use of processes, rather than rote learning of specific content, especially in secondary schools. Usually there is no single way to learn the material most efficiently; however, some teachers present the curriculum in a "one-road-to-learning" fashion, trying to force all students to learn the content in the same way.

For example, why should seventh-grade students who resist oral music classes because they cannot sing well be forced to attend and to sing? Such a rigid approach to curriculum probably will only succeed in causing students

In appreciation subjects, assignments need not be arbitrary. In this art class, students may choose the subjects of their pictures.

to internalize their resistance to music so that they will never enjoy it. Why not allow these students to spend time in appreciation courses, sampling a variety of musical expressions and developing their own musical tastes? Using student ideas does not mean watering down the curriculum by pursuing nonsubstantive topics. The suggestion is that student interests can be incorporated to involve the student in a meaningful endeavor.

Student Choice in Assignments

Effect of student choice on learning

Assuming that the options teachers provide are equally appropriate, student choice of task may have some important effects on learning. Fisher, Blackwell, Garcia, and Greene (1974) conducted a study on teaching fourth- and fifth-grade students from low-income families fundamental arithmetic skills through use of computer-assisted instruction (CAI). These researchers found that the control subjects, who did not get to choose what problems they did, worked more problems on the computer than did the choice group. However, choice subjects had more task involvement in the problems they worked on, although the mean differences in task involvement between the two groups were small. Perhaps, as the authors speculate, the higher engagement level (real interest in each problem) slowed down the speed of the choice students. The ultimate value of working more problems, as the control students did, versus the benefit from more attention to task, which the choice students appeared to have, remains to be demonstrated.

Student engagement and task difficulty

A third result of this study was that as task difficulty increased, student engagement decreased. The potential theoretical value of such a finding, if replicated in future research, is considerable. One would predict from Hunt's theory of the cognitive match (1961, 1965) that task engagement is highest when students work on problems similar to their achievement levels. The investigators noted that seeking optimal stimulation by matching skill and problem difficulty was more common to some student choice patterns than to others. However, as Maslow and other theorists point out, students are unlikely to seek cognitive stimulation unless other needs have been met. Some students no doubt did not perceive the task as a chance to test skills, but rather were responding to the need to move through the curriculum as fast as possible, to look good, to avoid failure, and so on. It is clear that under self-selection conditions, some students will not pick tasks that match their present cognitive skills.

Other data also suggest that students working on tasks with self-regulated levels of difficulty may set inappropriate goals. Felixbrod and O'Leary (1974) report that in the absence of teacher surveillance, and in the presence of high rewards, many children will select lenient standards in order to maximize their rewards. As deCharms (1984) has argued, the level of choice and personal freedom can be either too limited or too overwhelming for students (see Chapter 15).

Variations in Value of Student Choices

The value of providing students with "choice points" depends on the developmental levels of the students, the reward structure associated with the task, the general climate of cooperation-competition in the classroom, the extent to which students have been prepared to make choices, and the nature of the task itself.

Part of the problem in motivational research is that most laboratory and classroom investigators of motivation focus on one dimension (choice; reward; students who have received achievement motivation training versus those who have not; and so on). The Felixbrod and O'Leary (1974) study suggests that in the presence of strong external rewards, self-selection of appropriate learning standards may be undermined. To put it another way, if the teacher rewards poor choices (from the viewpoint of optimizing learning gains), does not reward good choices, and does not prepare students for free-choice activities, it seems unlikely that student choice will enhance motivation or achievement.

Satisfying personal interests

If used appropriately, choice allows students a chance to satisfy personal interests while completing learning tasks. In addition, there is reason to believe that students in classrooms that allow opportunity for choice are more likely to believe that they, not the teacher or other external forces, are responsible for their own learning (Ames, 1984; deCharms, 1984).

Student choice is also a way in which teachers can express directly their trust in students and the positive expectation that students can design and control many aspects of their educational lives. However, even this process can go too far. One of the authors has a friend who teaches at a high school that allows students to drop a course any day prior to taking the final exam. We think that the attitude such a policy communicates is that the school staff does not care about student learning. We argue that student choice should be combined with real commitments to learning.

Opportunities for Individualization and Teacher-Student Contact

Teachers need to interact individually with students. Teachers who meet with individual students are in a good position to assess student interests and needs, as well as to help students adjust their expectations appropriately. How can the teacher who does not have an aide or other resources find the time to do this? We now discuss instructional techniques that not only motivate students, but also provide teachers with time for conferences with individual pupils.

Learning Centers

Teachers can obtain time to meet with individuals or with small groups through the effective use of independent learning assignments—work done at a special place in the room, such as a learning center. Such assignments are ideal ways to provide for student choices and interests and are a convenient method for both elementary and secondary school teachers to individualize certain aspects of instruction. Individual assignments also function as an effective backup system when students finish their work. Unfortunately, bright students are often penalized by the delegation of needless busywork when they finish their assignments prematurely. Teachers might set up in the classroom one or two activity centers where students complete assigned tasks on a predetermined schedule, or to which students go when they finish other work assignments.

The number of teacher-prepared assignments that might be used at a learning center is endless. Some involve elaborate equipment or sequences of material, while other equally useful assignments do not need concrete materials. Older students can even help prepare their own learning stations. Figures 16.1 and 16.2 illustrate different activities that could be used.

Using the Entire Class as a Laboratory

Hands-on experience

Use of the classroom as a laboratory for active involvement of students in "hands-on" experience has become a popular technique. Students actually measure and construct, rather than deal with only paper-and-pencil problems. To accomplish such work, the class can be divided into learning stations, each with sufficient manipulable equipment to accommodate a few students and allow them to perform and experiment directly, rather than merely to watch the teacher and one or two other students demonstrate. The advantage of dividing the class into stations, in addition to having the opportunity for direct manipulation, is that some relatively complex learning assignments can be completed that would simply be impossible to set up at each student's desk.

If appropriately designed, classroom space that provides students with direct manipulative practice also allows the teacher the chance to observe their performances directly. If they are not overused, such activities add

Figure 16.1 A Card from *Project Mathematics Activity Kit, K-3*

Dimes and Pennies

1. Use dimes and pennies to show these numbers.

36 15 47 28
50 22 30 13

Rule: Use as many dimes as you can before you use any pennies.

Source: *Project Mathematics Activity Kit, K-3*. Copyright © by Holt, Rinehart and Winston of Canada, Ltd.

variety and may spark student interest. High school teachers need to be aware that not all students are functioning at Piaget's highest level of formal operations, and that some students at the concrete level of operations may well need to perform manipulations in order to learn the concepts being taught.

Microcomputer Use

Another way to structure more time for teachers to interact with individuals or small groups of students can be provided by the appropriate use of mi-

Figure 16.2 Examples of Series and Parallel Activities

Mathematical Topic—Multiplication

Progressive Interpretations of Multiplication

I Union of Equivalent Disjoint Sets

II Cartesian Product

III Algorithmic

Series and Parallel arrangements within the above interpretations.

I. Ia Join 3 sets of 2 buttons each

Ib Equal jumps on number line i.e. 0 2 4 6

Ic Rectangular arrays i.e. 3 by 2 array depicted as
0 0
0 0
0 0

Id If 3 persons each have 2 shoes, how many shoes in all?

II. IIa Problem: I have 3 kinds of ice cream (vanilla, chocolate, strawberry) and 2 kinds of topping (Pistachio and Blueberry). If a sundae is made of 1 kind of ice cream and 1 kind of topping, how many different kinds of sundaes can I make?

IIb If Nicole has 3 blouses and 2 skirts how many blouse-skirt combinations can she make?

IIc How many ways can I pair a letter with a number using the following sets: Set A = (a,b,c); Set B = (1,2).

IId If Set A has 3 members and Set B has 2 members, how many elements are there in AXB? (AXB is the symbol used to denote the Cartesian Product of Set A and Set B.)

III. IIIa $3 \cdot 17$ interpreted as 10 + 7 (each multiplied by 3)

$$\begin{array}{r} 10 + 7 \\ 3 \\ \hline 30 + 21 = 51 \end{array}$$

IIIb* $3 \cdot 7$ interpreted as $3(10 + 7) = 3 \cdot 10 + 3 \cdot 7 = 30 + 21 = 51$

IIIc $3 \cdot 17$ interpreted as

$$\begin{array}{r} 17 \\ \underline{3} \\ 21 \\ \underline{30} \\ 51 \end{array}$$

IIId $3 \cdot 17$ interpreted as

$$\begin{array}{r} 17 \\ \underline{3} \\ 51 \end{array}$$

Source: R. Reys and T. Post, *The Mathematics Laboratory: Theory to Practice* (Boston: Prindle, Weber, and Schmidt, 1973). Reprinted by permission of the authors.

crocomputers in the class. Everything just mentioned in terms of learning stations can be accomplished with microcomputers. Both traditional station approaches and microcomputer stations are appropriate and the variety possible of different types of work stations is important for maintaining student motivation. Microcomputers can be used not only to facilitate the cognitive learning of individual students, but also to facilitate social interactions in small-group assignments. Webb (1984), in a study of students 11 and 14 years old, provides evidence to illustrate that learning computer programming can be accomplished successfully in group settings. This empirical evidence supports the many anecdotal reports that microcomputers can be used to increase communication among students. For example, Rubin (1980, 1982) reports informal evidence that microcomputers can be used to help students share ideas when writing a story or working on shared tasks such as classroom newsletters, polls, and so on. (For more information about educational computer programs, see Vockell and Rivers, 1984.)

Peer Tutoring

Peer tutoring can be a useful strategy for helping the teacher individualize instruction, possibly motivating student behavior, and allowing students to become responsible for assisting other students. Both the student who receives help and the student who provides it can benefit (see Good & Brophy, 1984). Furthermore, the teacher who engages a large percentage of the class in peer or individual work can use this time for sustained effort with individual students.

Thomas (1970) presents some particularly interesting data. He examined the behavior of fifth- and sixth-grade tutors and college tutors who were all tutoring second-grade students in reading. The elementary students appeared to be as effective as the college tutors! However, there were some notable differences in the style of elementary-age and college-age tutors. The elementary-age tutors were generally direct and businesslike. They accepted the fact that younger students were having problems and used the time period to help them. College students were much more indirect. They seemed to feel it was necessary to get the tutees to like them, to enjoy the story, and so on. Hence, under certain conditions, student tutors may be more effective than an actual teacher or adult aide when direct instruction is called for, when a simple vocabulary is sufficient and when students remember their own difficulties and can use those experiences in the teaching situation.

Tutoring styles

Added gains for tutors

Tutors often gain as much as the students being tutored. The extra review of material they teach and the additional practice they get while tutoring are likely to increase their knowledge or skills in the subject matter. Furthermore, data suggest that when students are trained for their roles, they are more likely to be effective. Thus, if the tutoring focuses on cognitive skills that are important rather than on exercises that just kill time, and if the tutor and tutee know and understand their roles (e.g., if the teacher has role-played tutoring techniques in the classroom), tutoring can be a valuable instructional and motivational aid.

Strategies such as peer tutoring and learning stations are helpful in part because they bring variety and the opportunity to meet different needs to the classroom. However they are also useful because they free the teacher to talk to students. If teachers are to create task involvement rather than ego involvement (see Nicholls, 1984, and Chapter 15), they need time to talk to students and to understand their perspectives.

The Influence of Cooperation and Competition on Motivation

Johnson and Johnson (1974, in press) argue that one of the myths concerning competition is that achievement, success, and general motivation depend on competing successfully with other persons. These researchers point out that achievement motivation theory emphasizes the challenge of moderate risk of failure, and that such risk taking is based on realistic assessment of the difficulty of the task with regard to one's own ability level, not the ability levels of other individuals.

Cooperative, competitive and individualistic structures

Johnson and Johnson (in press) suggest that there are three basic structures in which learning can proceed: cooperative, competitive, and individualistic. They note that virtually no research has been carried out to compare the effects of individualistic structures with cooperative or competitive structures. This is an important research question, with more and more curricula being designed for individualized learning. On common sense grounds, they argue that social development will be facilitated further by cooperative than by individualistic goal structures. After reviewing a variety of research studies, they suggest that most instructional activities should take place within a cooperative goal structure.

Shared tasks

We tend to agree with Johnson and Johnson's basic argument, but along with deCharms (1984), we would qualify it somewhat in the sense that there can be too much or the wrong type of cooperation as well as too little. Furthermore, following Corno and Rohrkemper (in press), if the goal is to help students use their personal resources to learn, it is not clear that shared tasks are always the best procedures to use. Some students respond well to rigorous task demands. These students should receive such challenges from time to time in written work or in group work with similar students. The work of Johnson and Ahlgren (1976) suggests that a student's attitudes toward cooperativeness and competitiveness may be independent; that is, a given individual can be high or low on both dimensions. Hence, teachers who attempt to vary motivational strategies need to be aware that some students enjoy both competitive and cooperative activities, or don't enjoy either, whereas other students have a distinct preference for one or the other (Ames, 1984). We should point out, however, that public tasks, as a general rule, should be marked by cooperation or manageable competition. For related discussion see Ames and Ames (1984, in press).

Increasing Achievement Motivation

The concept of need achievement was discussed in the previous chapter, and we now return to the topic in order to examine its classroom application at a more specific level. Increasing achievement motivation involves teaching the relationship between risk-taking behavior and accomplishment, and using feedback to modify goals. Easy goals are not the answer, because they provide little satisfaction and little or no mastery of new material. There is not much long-term benefit in continually providing students with easy tasks, although initial success may help them to become aware of the fact that they *can* achieve, as can be seen in the success of mastery learning programs. Difficult goals provide minimal hope for academic accomplishment and typically lead to failure, frustration, and eventual task withdrawal. Students low in achievement motivation have learned to set either unrealistically high or low goals, making it difficult for them to function as independent learners. Helping students to develop more realistic goals and predictions partly involves helping them to understand the advantages of setting moderately difficult goals.

Easy versus difficult goals

In practical terms, there are many ways in which students can be taught to work toward realistic goals. Several academic games display a close relationship between effort and success. In the "Business Game" (used in many need-achievement courses) students must assemble models out of tinker toys. The models can be sold for profit. However, participants must "buy" the raw materials for the models that they build. Within the time allowed, and using their own skills such as speed of assembly, participants must decide how much raw material to buy. If they underbuy they end up with time left but no raw materials, and profits will not be maximized. Students will also fail if they overbuy and have more material than time to assemble the product. Such games are designed to force participants to carefully analyze the risks involved in setting goals.

Setting realistic goals

The use of feedback to establish realistic goals becomes critical after students become aware of the need for and the advantages of setting moderately difficult goals. Obviously, if students are to set moderate goals, they need some way to calculate the relative difficulty of the task. Feedback records describing past performances on similar types of work and other informational sources (teachers may have a variety of assignments at learning centers that are coded according to degree of difficulty) are especially important when students are first attempting to set realistic goals.

Using feedback

As Alschuler, Tabor, and McIntyre (1971) point out, students need to focus initially on "doable" assignments as well as on assignments that are linked to personal involvement, so that success or failure will have real meaning. Tasks like "finish my history project," suggest a dull, "have to do it" orientation rather than personal striving and interest. Goals that are related to academic excellence and reflect personal involvement are preferable ("I want to give a better class presentation than I did last time; I want to keep everybody tuned in and even teach the teacher something new.").

A related teacher objective is to help students identify problems that prevent them from successfully completing tasks. Another objective is to help students translate long-range assignments and responsibilities into smaller, more manageable units. In time, if students see the advantages of moderate risk taking and possess feedback to use in establishing realistic goals, they may begin to seek out activities that require personal effort, and begin to strive for academic success.

Training for Need Achievement: Possible Harmful Effects

Essentially, these techniques are attempts to teach students how to increase their desire to achieve, their interest in striving for excellence. One can reasonably question how far the process should go, and even whether students' basic achievement motivation should be tampered with at all. Emphasis on self-reliance and taking calculated risks is probably appropriate, but a heavy commitment to achievement per se is a value question that is difficult to resolve. We all know persons who must achieve and whose identities are related to achievement. Such individuals are driven. Teachers need to be aware that too much or too little achievement drive can exert an undesirable influence on student behavior. The key is probably to help students of all ability levels to set realistic achievement goals in the context of achieving other developmental social goals.

Motivational Design of Instruction: Keller

Keller (1983) summarizes many theories of motivation and synthesizes extant knowledge to form a model for application. He discusses four major dimensions of motivation: (1) *interest*, which refers to the learner's curiosity and the extent to which curiosity is aroused and sustained adequately over time; (2) *relevance*, or the learner's perception that instruction is related to personal needs or personal goals; (3) *expectancy*, which involves the learner's perceived likelihood of success and the extent to which he or she perceives success as being under personal control; and (4) *satisfaction*, which refers to the learner's intrinsic motivations and his or her reactions to extrinsic rewards. An advantage of Keller's model is that it provides four reasonably specific categories that can be used to synthesize many approaches to motivation. The model is therefore a valuable heuristic for thinking about the design of instruction in classroom settings.

Interest

As Keller notes, practically every theory of learning includes some assumptions about interest. Clearly, one must pay attention to a stimulus for learning to occur. Interest is more likely to be maintained if curiosity is stimulated and if students have the opportunity to engage in activities that allow them to act on their curiosity by exploring and manipulating various objects. Unfortunately, in too many instructional settings, students are given little encouragement or opportunity to explore either physically or intellectually. Keller presents the following five strategies for stimulating and maintaining student interest and curiosity in lessons:

1. Use novel, incongruous, conflictual, and paradoxical events. Attention is aroused when there is an abrupt change in the status quo.
2. Use anecdotes and other devices to inject a personal, emotional element into otherwise purely intellectual or procedural material.
3. Give students the opportunity to learn more about things they already know about or believe in, but also give them moderate doses of the unfamiliar and unexpected.
4. Use analogies to make the strange familiar and the familiar strange.
5. Guide students into a process of question generation and inquiry.

Conflict in strategies

As Keller notes, there are no simple rules for applying these strategies in classrooms. On the surface, some of the strategies seem to conflict with one another. For example, Strategy 1 encourages teachers to use novel situations, but Strategy 3 encourages them to give individuals the opportunity to learn about the things that they are already interested in. Obviously, people want to learn more about things that they are already interested in and for this reason they join clubs, attend dinners with friends more than with strangers, and so forth. However, as Keller notes, the inclusion of unusual or exotic material from time to time can help initiate or maintain curiosity in a group.

What might create optimal interest in one student may be too much for another student. That is, if a student is already interested in a topic, attempts on the part of the teacher to create interest may only irritate the student, who merely wants basic information about the topic. In general, though, Keller assumes that students are more likely to be understimulated than overstimulated.

Relevance

Keller argues that personal motivation will increase when individuals perceive that an instructional task will satisfy a basic need, motive, or value. Keller's strategies for increasing personal motivation are intended to: (1) enhance achievement striving behavior and provide opportunities to achieve standards of excellence under conditions of moderate risk; (2) make instruction responsive to the power motive, provide opportunities for choice, responsibility, and interpersonal influence; and (3) satisfy the need for affiliation, establish trust, and provide opportunities for no-risk, cooperative interaction. The concept of relevance can be traced to the need theorists that were discussed in Chapter 14. In particular, relevance is associated with individuals achieving personal needs or goals, and three important considerations are needs for: achievement (e.g., content mastery), affiliation (e.g., close personal relationships), and power (e.g., need to influence other persons).

Strategies

It is important to realize that these three objectives cannot be met simultaneously in a classroom setting. Keller's first set of strategies responds to need for achievement, where moderate levels of competition and individual contracting may be most appropriate. The second set of strategies is related to helping individuals fulfill power needs. It is important to give students positions of genuine authority and assign classroom activities that allow them to satisfy power needs, such as exhibited in debating or in argumentative essays. The third set of strategies would help students to initiate and maintain close working relationships with other students. A variety of cooperative activities would be important if these needs are to be met in the classroom (see Chapter 18 for an extended discussion of some of these strategies).

These three needs cannot be met at the same time by a single instructional strategy, just as no experience in life will satisfy all three of these motives simultaneously. Self-study may be highly motivating for students with high need achievement, but it may be unsatisfactory for persons with high needs for affiliation or power.

Expectancy

The expectancy factor refers to the idea that a person's expectations for success or failure can affect performance. In Chapters 14 and 15 we noted several concepts that are related to people's expectations for their own performance. Among the concepts that are important for the study of self-expectancy are locus of control, attributions, personal causation, and learned helplessness. Keller offers four strategies for increasing expectancy for success: (1) increase experiences with success (on meaningful tasks—not on trivial or easy tasks); (2) use instructional-design strategies that indicate requirements for success; (3) use techniques that offer personal control over success; and (4) use attributional feedback and other devices that help students relate success to personal effort and ability.

In Chapter 17 we discuss at length teacher expectations for student performance and the way in which they influence student behavior. In the present chapter, and preceding ones, we have focused on students' own perceptions of success. Clearly, an important motivational task for teachers is to help their students see themselves in a positive, "can do" fashion.

Outcomes

Outcomes refer to the satisfaction of goal accomplishment and the motivation for performance on similar tasks in the future. How do teacher reinforcement and feedback influence students' subsequent performance? As Keller notes, research findings in this area are complex and at times contradictory. This is partially because the objective behavior of teachers, which can be seen and described, is often not as powerful as students' covert interpretations of teacher behavior, which can only be inferred. That is, teachers' attempts to provide informational feedback may be interpreted by students as controlling feedback (see the discussion of intrinsic motivation in Chapter 15). Acknowledging these difficulties and the tentativeness of the framework, Keller provides several strategies for increasing the appropriateness of outcomes for maintaining intrinsic satisfaction with instruction. His chief recommendations are to use task-endogenous rather than task-exogenous rewards and to use verbal praise and informative feedback rather than threats, surveillance, or external performance evaluation.

Endogenous rewards

In theory, endogenous rewards do not tend to be perceived as having a controlling influence and are customarily ones that naturally follow from a task, like an increase in skills following practice. Keller argues that if intrinsic motivation is the goal, then it is useful to create a positive but noncontrolling environment (see the discussion of Deci in Chapter 14). In general, students will benefit from receiving feedback and information that has pleasurable consequences rather than aversive ones and will enjoy the opportunity to make decisions and to occasionally be rewarded for tasks that they are at least partially responsible for selecting and developing.

Despite the attractive features of this model and its potential to influence the design of motivational aspects of classroom instruction, Keller notes that the model does not yield specific, prescriptive strategies. Nor does research on motivation result in such strategies. A strategy that works one day, for example, may not work the next day because it loses its effect or because what was once stimulating and challenging is now too easy for students. Although motivational research yields important concepts and findings that can be used in thinking about classroom behavior, every classroom strategy has an optimal level with respect to its influence on behavior. Specifically, too low a level of motivation as well as too high a level of motivation can reduce performance. The goal for teachers is to achieve a reasonable match between learners' curiosity, learners' achievement motivation, and the academic requirements of the subject matter.

List of Motivation Strategies

In this chapter we discussed some important ideas in detail that we feel have important implications for classroom practice. In the remainder of the chapter, we would like to present a comprehensive, but brief summary of most motivational ideas that have been discussed in the literature.

Review of the literature suggests this list of strategies that classroom teachers can use to motivate their students to engage themselves productively in academic activities. This list begins with a discussion of basic assumptions that underlie its use and then presents 40 motivational strategies divided into five major groupings.

Jere Brophy is presently conducting a series of studies of student motivation and is synthesizing relevant literature about teacher effects in student motivation. The work on student motivation is based on conceptual papers on the general topic of motivation (Brophy 1983a, 1983b). This particular list of strategies is drawn from Brophy (1985).

Basic Assumptions

We assume that the following conditions will be in effect in the classrooms under discussion. The list is not intended for application to classrooms where these assumptions do not hold.

1. *Fixed Academic Objectives*—This list is intended to apply to situations in which the teacher intends to involve the students in academic activities such as lessons, tasks, or assignments, selected with particular academic objectives in mind. Such activities are part of the formal program of curriculum and instruction and are not recreational activities or enrichment activities that lack specific academic objectives.
2. *Task Appropriateness*—We assume that the activity is appropriately difficult for all students. If the task is so familiar or easy that it constitutes nothing more than busy work, and especially if the task is so unfamiliar or difficult that students cannot succeed on it even if they apply reasonable effort, no strategies for inducing student motivation to learn are likely to succeed.
3. *Moderation/Optimal Use*—We assume that an optimal level exists for the effective use of particular strategies. Strategies used too frequently or routinely may lose their effectiveness, and even a single use of a particular strategy can become counterproductive if it goes on too long or gets carried to extremes.
4. *Supportive Environment*—We assume that the teacher employs classroom organization and management skills successfully to establish the classroom as an effective learning environment, and is a patient, encouraging individual who makes the students feel comfortable during academic activities and supports their learning efforts. Anxious or alienated students are unlikely to develop motivation to learn academic content.

Task Design and Selection Strategies

The strategies in this section involve capitalizing on students' existing intrinsic motivation by selecting or designing tasks that they will find attractive or enjoyable. These strategies should produce heightened task engagement sustained by the fact that the students enjoy the actual processes involved in doing the task. Because these effects are based mostly on affective (liking for the task) rather than cognitive (cognitions concerning the task) mechanisms, they do not directly stimulate student motivation to learn. Still, given equal task feasibility and effectiveness in helping students accomplish curricular objectives, tasks that students find interesting or enjoyable are preferable to tasks that they find boring or irritating. These strategies are as follows:

1. *Optimal Challenge/Difficulty Level*—The task should provide some challenge to students but should offer the prospect of success with reasonable effort.

2. *Novelty/Variety*—The academic content, the form of the task, the media involved, or the nature of the responses demanded from the students should be new to the students or at least different from what they have been working on recently.
3. *Autonomy*—To the extent that they are capable of doing so, students should be allowed to exercise autonomy in deciding how to organize their time and effort in order to meet task requirements.
4. *Choice*—Within the constraints imposed by academic objectives, the students should be offered choices of alternative tasks or alternative ways to meet requirements.
5. *Adapt Tasks to Students' Interests*—Basic skills should be practiced within the context of many different content areas (for example, by allowing students to select their own topics for required compositions), and tasks should be designed to focus on content known to be of interest to the students.
6. *Activity/Manipulation Opportunities*—The task should allow students to interact with the teacher or with one another, to manipulate materials, or in some other way to respond actively rather than merely to listen or read. Ideally, these opportunities will often go beyond the simple question-answer formats seen in typical recitation and seatwork activities in order to include projects, experiments, discussions, role play, simulations, and creative applications.
7. *Feedback Features*—The task should not only allow students to respond actively, but should be designed so that their responses trigger immediate feedback that they can use to guide subsequent responses. So-called "self correcting" materials have these feedback features built in. Teachers can build them into more typical classroom activities by leading the group in going through the activity, circulating to provide feedback during independent seatwork times, or arranging for students to get feedback from answer keys or from discussing the work with one another.
8. *Creation of Finished Products*—The task should have meaning or integrity in its own right rather than be merely a subpart of some larger entity, so that students experience a satisfying sense of completion or accomplishment when they finish it. Ideally, task completion should yield a finished product that the student can use or display.
9. *Fantasy/Simulation*—Where more direct application is not feasible, fantasy or imagination elements should be introduced that engage students' emotions or allow them to experience events vicariously (i.e., invite them to imagine that they are Abraham Lincoln and have just received the news from Fort Sumter), or set up role play or simulation activities that allow students to identify with various characters or to deal with the content in direct, personalized ways. Ideally, such fantasy/simulation will confront students with problems that they need to solve by drawing on the knowledge and skills that they have been learning.
10. *Game-like Features*—Practice and application exercises for almost

any kind of content could be presented as games or could be structured to include features typically associated with games or recreational pastimes: "test yourself" challenges, puzzles and problem-solving activities, and the like. Some such activities involve clear goals but require the student to solve problems, avoid traps, or overcome obstacles in order to reach the goals. Others challenge students to "find the problem" (i.e., to identify the goal itself in addition to developing a method of reaching it). Others involve elements of suspense or hidden information that emerge as the activity is completed, like puzzles that convey some message or provide the answer to some question once they are filled in. Still others involve a degree of randomness or some other method for inducing uncertainty about what the outcome of one's performance is likely to be on any given trial. Ideally, such game-like elements will complement, and not detract from, the academic benefits of the activity.

Strategies that Involve Imposing Task Exogenous Contingencies

The strategies in this section tie task engagement or performance to rewards, punishments, or other factors exogenous to the task itself. They do not change either the task itself or students' task endogenous values or expectations. Consequently, they do not directly stimulate the development or activation of student motivation to learn. Instead, they provide extrinsic motivation by linking task performance to delivery of consequences that the students value. These strategies include the following:

1. *Offer Rewards as Incentives for Good Performance*—Teachers can motivate students to try to do their best by offering rewards for success in meeting stated performance criteria. Ideally, these performance criteria will be individualized so that each student is capable of earning the reward if he or she puts forth reasonable effort on the task.
2. *Portray Knowledge and Skills as Means Toward Attainment of Life Goals*—If the knowledge or skills developed by a task have immediate application in students' lives or will be important for their future success in society, make students aware of these consequences of task mastery. Teachers can make these linkages concrete by citing personal experiences or examples involving individuals who are role models to the students.
3. *Goal Setting/Self Challenge*—Encourage students to set specific goals that are difficult yet realistic, to commit themselves to striving to attain these goals, and to take satisfaction (reinforce themselves) when they succeed in meeting these goals. Such goal setting should be individualized so that target performance levels are phrased in terms of improvement over the student's previous accomplishments and not in terms of comparison with the accomplishments of other students.
4. *Interpersonal Competition*—The chance to compete for prizes or recognition can add incentive to classroom activities. However, such

competition will be motivating only to those who have a good or at least an equal chance of winning. To insure this, it will be necessary to use team competition in which the teams are balanced by ability profiles or individual competition in which a handicapping system is in effect that equalizes everyone's opportunity to win. Ideally, competition will be depersonalized so that emphasis is placed on the content learned rather than on who won or lost.

5. *Interpersonal Cooperation*—Students, especially those oriented toward social affiliation, may prefer activities done as part of a group engaging in individualized forms of the same activities. Teachers can capitalize on this by arranging for students to work together cooperatively in pairs or groups. Ideally, these activities will be structured so that everyone in the group has an active and preferably unique role to perform, so that one or two students do not dominate the interaction and leave the remaining students to function merely as onlookers.
6. *Combinations of Cooperation with Competition*—Student-team competition can be designed so that there is a great deal of cooperation within teams in addition to competition between teams. Also, debates or other activities intended to produce controlled conflict between students with different points of view can be designed so that students ultimately focus on resolving issues rationally and achieving consensus rather than on defeating opponents.

Strategies Designed to Induce Student Motivation to Learn

The strategies described in this section should directly stimulate or activate student motivation to learn. They involve changing the ways in which students view and approach tasks rather than changing the tasks themselves. Although these strategies should induce positive affect (liking for tasks) to some degree, they are oriented primarily toward inducing the cognitions associated with motivation to learn (i.e., the information-processing and problem-solving strategies involved in high quality task engagement).

1. *General Modeling*—Model interest in learning routinely: let the students see that you value learning as a rewarding, self-actualizing activity that produces personal satisfaction and enrichment. Share your interests in current events and items of general knowledge and, most especially, in aspects of the subject matter that you teach. Call attention to current books, articles, television programs, or movies on the subject.
2. *General Communication of Expectations*—In addition to modeling your own motivation to learn, consistently project attitudes, beliefs, expectations, and attributions that imply that your students share, or are learning to share, such motivation to learn. If you treat your students as if they already are eager learners, they will be more likely to become eager learners. Let your students know that you expect them to be curious, to want to learn facts and understand principles

clearly, and to develop their skills and do a good job on assignments and projects.

3. *Induce Students to Value Specific Activities*—When presenting particular tasks to students, induce them to anticipate valuing the task by sharing your perceptions of how interesting or informative it is, how important the skills that the task teaches are, and so on. Give specific reasons or examples.
4. *Model the Process of Engaging in Specific Activities with Motivation to Learn*—In teaching particular content or skills, include examples that clearly demonstrate the information-processing and problem-solving strategies that you used during the activity. Rather than merely telling students what to do, show them how to do it by thinking out loud as you demonstrate.
5. *State Learning Objectives and Provide Advance Organizers*—When introducing a task, call students' attention to the academic benefits that they should receive from engaging in it. This will help them to establish a learning set to guide their approach to the task.
6. *Induce Curiosity/Interest*—Stimulate curiosity or interest in an activity by making students feel the need to resolve some ambiguity or obtain more information about a topic. Show students that their existing knowledge is not complete enough to enable them to accomplish some valued objective, that it is internally inconsistent or inconsistent with certain new information, or that the knowledge they presently possess in scattered form can be organized around certain general principles or powerful ideas. In general, put the students into an active information-processing or problem-solving mode by posing questions or problems for them.
7. *Induce Dissonance/Cognitive Conflict*—Ask questions or make statements that point up unexpected, incongruous, or paradoxical aspects of the content to be learned. Counter any tendency of the students to think that they already know everything there is to know about a topic by pointing out unusual or exotic aspects, noting exceptions to general rules, or challenging students to solve the "mystery" that underlies a paradox.
8. *Structure Academic Activities as Learning Experiences, Not Performance Tests*—Make clear separations between instruction/practice activities and tests. Treat recitation questions and practice exercises as opportunities to work with and apply the material rather than as testing devices designed to see who knows the material and who doesn't. In general, encourage students to engage in academic activities with motivation to learn, free from anxiety or premature concern about performance adequacy.
9. *Induce Students to Generate Their Own Motivation to Learn*—Besides stimulating motivation to learn by using the strategies described above, it is possible to induce students to generate such motivation for themselves. Ask them to identify questions that they would like to get answered in relation to the topic, to list their own interests

in the topic, to note things that they find to be surprising, and so on.

10. *Induce Metacognitive Awareness of Learning Efforts*—Train students to remain aware of their goals during task engagement and to monitor the strategies they use in pursuing these goals, the effects of the strategies as they are used, and their own responses to these events as they unfold. In particular, train the students to respond to errors as cues for analysis and concentrated efforts, rather than as cues for becoming frustrated and giving up.
11. *Provide Informative Feedback*—Give students feedback about their progress in understanding content or mastering skills. Where such feedback does not occur automatically in the process of engaging in a task, supply it by monitoring and correcting performance, providing answer keys, allowing students to give feedback to one another, or some other method. Ideally, such feedback should occur during or as soon as possible following response so that students do not develop and practice erroneous concepts or strategies; it should be clear, specific, and constructive; it should be presented in ways that encourage and provide guidance for continued learning efforts; it should include recognition of progress made or partial successes achieved; and it should help in attributing difficulties not to lack of sufficient ability on the part of the student but to lack of effort, if that is clearly the case, or more likely, to confusion about what to do or reliance on an inappropriate strategy for doing it. This type of feedback should be private rather than public.

Strategies Designed to Induce Desirable Expectations Concerning Performance Outcomes

The strategies in this section are designed to induce students to develop positive expectations about performance outcomes by making them aware that they have the ability to succeed if they apply reasonable effort. Whereas the strategies in the previous section encourage students to value the tasks they work on, strategies here encourage them to believe that they can meet task demands successfully if they apply themselves. These strategies assume that the task is appropriate in difficulty level and that the students will receive timely and informative feedback about the accuracy of their responses and the progress they are making toward ultimate objectives. Where these assumptions do not hold, the strategies cannot work effectively.

1. *Program for Success*—The simplest way to insure that students expect success is to make sure that they achieve success consistently. Program them for success by beginning at their level, moving in small steps, and preparing them sufficiently for each new step so that they can adjust to it without much confusion or frustration.
2. *Help Students to Recognize that They Can Succeed if They Apply Reasonable Effort*—Make sure that students develop the following per-

ceptions and attibutional inferences: (a) effort/outcome covariation (the levels of success they achieve will depend on the levels of effort they put forth); (b) internal locus of control (the potential for controlling success or failure lies within themselves rather than in external factors that they cannot control); (c) personal causation (origin) concepts (students can act as origins in bringing about desirable outcomes through their own behavior, rather than having to act as pawns whose fate is determined by factors beyond their control); (d) sense of efficacy/competence (students should recognize that they have the abilities to succeed in academic tasks if they choose to use them); (e) desirable performance expectations and attributions (students should learn to attribute their success to a combination of sufficient ability and reasonable effort and to attribute their failures to insufficient effort, confusion, or use of inappropriate strategies); (f) incremental concept of ability (students learn to think of ability as potential that is developed continually through learning activities, rather than as a fixed level of capacity that predetermines and limits their potential for success). These perceptions and attributional concepts can be fostered through modeling, socialization and feedback, helping students to think of effort as an investment rather than a risk, helping students to recognize that success on particular tasks depends not so much on general abilities as on task-specific knowledge and skills developed through instruction and practice, and helping students to focus on task mastery by stressing high quality task engagement and continuous progress through the curriculum rather than comparisons with norms or with peers.

3. *Self-Monitoring and Reinforcement Training*—Train students to monitor their performance progress in meeting short-term goals and to reinforce themselves for meeting these goals and for making progress toward long-term goals. For cumulative skill-development tasks, encourage students to compare performance samples taken at different points in time or to keep personal diaries, logs, graphs, or progress charts.

Strategies Designed to Induce Active Learning with Metacognitive Awareness

The strategies in this section are designed to teach students to process input actively by concentrating their attention, making sure that they understand, integrating the new information with existing knowledge, and encoding and storing it in a form that will allow them to remember and use it later.

1. *Actively Preparing to Learn*—Teach your students to mobilize their resources and approach academic tasks in thoughtful, proactive ways by establishing a learning set (eliminating distractions, focusing concentration) and previewing and planning tasks before beginning them.

2. *Committing Material to Memory*—Teach students mnemonics, note taking, underlining, and related devices for assisting memory.
3. *Encoding or Elaborating on the Information Presented*—Teach students to encode information in their own words through paraphrasing and summarizing, to relate it to what they already know by identifying analogies with familiar concepts or examples of how the new material applies to familiar concepts or situations, and to assess their understanding by trying to explain the material in their own words or answer questions about the material.
4. *Organizing and Structuring the Content*—Teach students to structure content by dividing it into sequences or superordinate-subordinate relationship clusters. Teach outlining, identification of main idea and sequence, and recognition of various structuring devices (whole-part, rule-example, question-answer, structure-function, generalization-elaboration).
5. *Monitoring Comprehension*—Teach students to monitor their own comprehension routinely by remaining aware of the goals they are working toward, the strategies they select, the relative success of those strategies, and the remediation efforts undertaken when those strategies have not been effective. Teach strategies for checking work, detecting errors, and responding to errors by backing up and rereading, looking up definitions, identifying previous places in the text where the confusing point is introduced or discussed, searching the recent progression of topics or problems for clues to information that has been missed or misunderstood, taking note of what information is given and what information is required in a problem, retracing steps to see if the strategy might be inappropriate or incomplete, and generalizing possible alternative strategies.
6. *Maintaining Appropriate Affect*—Model and instruct students in desirable ways of approaching academic activities—being relaxed but alert and ready to concentrate or being ready to derive enjoyment or at least to take satisfaction from engaging in the task—but not in undesirable ways such as with anger or anxiety. In particular, model coping with failure or frustration by generating reassuring self-talk and refocusing attention on coping with the task rather than on negative affect, evaluations, or attributions associated with learned helplessness.

SUMMARY

Motivation, the process of arousing, directing, and maintaining behavior, is heavily influenced by context and multiple stimuli. Classroom teachers must adjust research findings and theoretical positions to specific individuals in given settings, and use both extrinsic and intrinsic rewards to motivate learning. High achievers spend more time on task-related behaviors than low achievers, and the gap widens over time. Bloom argues that mastery learning would make it possible for all students to succeed, since additional instructional time permits low achievers to master material also.

In the area of starting assignments, teachers can foster motivation by providing stimulating and appropriate assignments, capturing student attention, allowing student choices, and setting clear learning goals. They can maintain task involvement during seatwork by allowing students to work without interruption, demanding attention to the tasks, and providing knowledge of results. Maintaining motivation over the year involves scheduling a change of pace occasionally, making special events relevant, breaking up the day with special brief assignments that are enjoyable, and providing feedback about academic performance.

Teachers can manipulate four major motivation-related conditions in the classroom: tasks students are assigned, student perceptions of tasks, teacher rapport with students, and the reward structure. They can employ such techniques as using student preferences, student choices, individualization, learning centers, "hands-on" experience, peer tutoring, games or simulations, and other variations of "standard" practices. These techniques should be used with due regard for student needs and motives, as outlined by Murray and others.

Keller (1983) summarizes many theories of motivation and synthesizes extant knowledge to form a model for application. Keller's model provides four reasonably specific categories that can be used to think about classroom motivation. The four dimensions he uses are: (1) interest (learner's curiosity); (2) relevance (learner's perception that task relates to personal need); (3) expectancy (learner's perceived likelihood of success); and (4) satisfaction (learner's intrinsic motivation or reaction to external rewards).

Brophy provides a comprehensive and practical list of the various ideas that classroom teachers can use to motivate students to engage productivity in academic activities. In particular, the list offers ways to encourage students to value learning and academic content per se.

QUESTIONS AND PROBLEMS

1. Summarize in your own words Keller's motivational model. Think about your own experience as a student and describe the classrooms that most and least approximated this model. What do these experiences suggest about the value of Keller's model and about strategies for motivating students?
2. Review and think about the suggestions that Brophy makes and then determine how many classrooms you have been in where 70 percent or so of the recommendations have been followed. Does your answer surprise you? How do you account for this?
3. Prior to listing motivational strategies, Brophy presents four major assumptions about classrooms where these ideas will apply. In your opinion, why does he make these assumptions? Have you been in classrooms where these assumptions did not pertain? If so, describe one such class.
4. Do you include student motivation in your definition of teaching success? That is, are you satisfied so long as students learn the material, or do you believe that they also must become enthusiastic about you and the subject matter? What difference does it make? Can one goal get in the way of the other goal? How?
5. Think about your own teachers. Which ones stand out in your mind as especially good or bad? How did they attempt to motivate students in general and you in particular? What does this imply about how you define motivation?
6. Do you find it intuitively obvious or perhaps seriously confusing that students with notably poor motivation may be won over by teachers who concentrate

mostly on instruction and only secondarily on motivation? Can you see why teachers who try to improve students' self-concepts without making demands or providing success experiences would be perceived as patronizing bleeding hearts by such students? Explain.

7. What is your position on the intrinsic versus extrinsic motivation issue? Most people say that intrinsic motivation is much more essential for students than extrinsic motivation. Some find extrinsic motivation to be unacceptable for a variety of reasons. However, both research and simple observation reveal that intrinsic motivation is not observable in certain students, and that extrinsic methods seem to work quite well under most circumstances. What does all of this suggest about human nature? About motivation? About your views on teaching and learning?
8. Once you have led a horse to water, can you make it drink, or not? Why? Are there students whom no teacher could motivate? If so, what does motivate these students?

CASE STUDIES

Test Review. The bell rings, students make a mad dash for seats, and interesting conversations are left dangling in mid-sentence. The bell transforms the excited buzz of informal exchange to a formal, passive, "heavy" silence. Marge Hiebert audibly sighs and starts the class. "Last Friday we had an exam so I guess I should give back your papers and tell you what you did wrong. The geography proofs were poorly done. Let me show you the really bad, silly mistakes on the test. Pay attention because you have to learn this stuff . . . it's going to be on the mid-term exam and I don't want to see these same mistakes." How effective is the teacher feedback going to be in motivating student behavior? Why? What would be a more effective strategy?

A Poor Follow-Up. Helen finished the experiment and walked around the class with the beaker in front of her so that all the students could see the chemical reaction. Then she carefully placed the beaker on a lab table and returned to the front of the room. She smiled and confidently asked, "Now, are there any questions?" She paused and waited 15 seconds and then said, "Okay, then go to your lab table and do the follow-up experiment."

At first students at the tables buzzed with talk and activity; however, after a couple of minutes, Helen noticed that purposeful activity was occurring at only one of the five tables. She was puzzled because she knew that the students had followed her example and that the follow-up experiment was simple. How could she find out what the problem was? What should she say?

Hostile Bill? Mr. Baker hesitated to call on Bill Maddi, a large boy who sat with a sullen look on his face in the rear of the sixth-grade classroom, because Bill acted in a distant, hostile way all day, even though nothing had transpired between him and Bill on this, the opening day of school. Finally, he decided that he had to interact with Bill and he said, with some uncertainty, "Bill, would you read the directions for the next set of exercises?" Bill retorted loudly and quickly, "No, I'm not interested in this stupid stuff." After quieting the class, Mr. Baker called on another student to respond, and the period continued.

During the rest of the week several similar incidents occurred. In each case, when Bill was asked to read he refused to do so, sometimes gracefully or humorously, but generally with belligerence or hostility; however, when Bill was asked to make an oral response he usually did so. Finally, Mr. Baker put two and two together and concluded that Bill could not read well and was embarrassed to do so in front of the class. How could Mr. Baker verify his hypothesis during an interview with Bill? What should he say and do? If he is correct that Bill cannot read well, what should he do about it? Specifically, what type of instructional tasks should Bill be assigned? What would a typical school day be like for Bill?

Chapter 17

Teacher Expectations as Self-Fulfilling Prophecies

OBJECTIVES

When you have mastered the material in this chapter you will be able to

1. Explain, with examples, the process by which teacher expectations become self-fulfilling prophecies
2. Discuss ways in which teachers communicate low or self-defeating expectations
3. Discuss the effects of high- versus low-ability grouping on students' expectations and performance
4. Differentiate among proactive, reactive, and overreactive teachers and discuss some reasons why the latter two types may produce undesirable self-fulfilling prophecy effects
5. List and explain things a teacher can do to develop more accurate expectations of all students, and to help low-achieving students develop more realistic expectations for themselves
6. Explain how success or failure experiences affect student self-concept
7. Discuss techniques a teacher can use to help students perceive the relationship between success and personal effort
8. Explain the role of student perceptions in classroom expectation effects

General motivational concepts that teachers might use in the classroom were discussed in the previous chapter. In this chapter we want to stress ways in which classroom teachers might inadvertently undermine the efforts of low-achieving students, and how these problems can be avoided.

A few years ago an experiment conducted by Rosenthal and Jacobson (1968) proved to be one of the most exciting and controversial reports to appear in the history of educational research. These investigators presented data to suggest that teachers' experimentally induced expectations for student performance were related to actual levels of student performance. Students who were expected to do better even though there was no real basis for this expectation did do better.

After all students had been given a test of general ability at the beginning of the year, randomly selected students were described to their teachers as "late bloomers" who would probably make very large gains. The information presented to teachers was not based on student test performance. Except for the expectations that had been created in the teachers by the experimenters, there was no reason to predict increased performance by these late bloomers. At the end of the year, the same test of general ability was readministered to all students, and the data indicated that the experimental students did outgain their classmates, although the difference was due mainly to large differences in grades one and two. The classes in grades three to six showed no differences. Experimental students in grades one and two also outperformed their classmates in reading achievement, and teachers described them as more likely to succeed in the future, more interesting, happier, and more intellectually curious than students who were not labeled as late bloomers.

Unfortunately, secondary sources describing the study made exaggerated claims that went far beyond those made by Rosenthal and Jacobson, and the study captured the imagination of the general public. For example, an ad in the *Reader's Digest* was titled "Self-Fulfilling Prophecy—A Key to Success." The ad itself read: "Actual experiments prove this mysterious force can heighten your intelligence, your competitive ability, and your will to succeed. The secret: Just make a prediction! Read how it works."

Some attempts to replicate Rosenthal and Jacobson's data (e.g., Claiborn, 1969) have been unsuccessful. However, in the past few years work by a large number of investigators using a variety of methods has established unequivocally that teachers' expectations can and do affect classroom behavior. (For extended reviews of this research see Marshall & Weinstein, 1984; Cooper & Good, 1983; Brophy, 1983; Braun, 1976; Braun, Neilsen, & Dykstra, 1975; Brophy & Good, 1974; Dusek, 1975; Finn, 1972.)

Teacher Expectations: A Definition

Teacher expectations are defined here as inferences that teachers make about present and future academic achievement and general classroom behavior of students. Teacher expectations may concern either the entire class or specific individuals. General expectations include teachers' beliefs about the changeability versus the rigidity of students' abilities, the students' potential for benefiting from instruction, the appropriate difficulty level of material for students in general or for a particular subgroup, and whether the class should be taught as a group or individually. Individual teachers vary greatly in these general beliefs. Some teachers believe that student behavior can be changed. Others are more likely to feel that they have to adjust to student behavior because it is unlikely to change (Brophy & Rohrkemper, 1981).

Bases for expectations

Expectations for individual students may be based on student record information (intelligence and achievement test data, past grades, comments by previous teachers, or knowledge about the student's family) or on initial contact with students in the classroom (apparent motivation, willingness to comply with school rules, general work habits).

Negative expectations

Some schools have become so sensitive to possible expectation effects that cumulative records are not kept for fear that teachers will read them and develop negative expectations. When the file records are available, some teachers avoid them to prevent the formation of expectations. We understand such reactions, and the motivation behind them is laudable; however, the reaction is not constructive. All of us form expectations naturally on meeting and interacting with students. Relevant information accurately collected and recorded may help us to form more realistic expectations.

Willis (1972) has shown that contact with students in the classroom leads to differential expectations within a few days after the school year begins, even if teachers try to avoid forming opinions. Her study illustrates that the formation of expectations is normal and is inherently neither good nor bad. The critical issue is the accuracy of the expectations and the flexibility with which they are held. Inaccurate expectations will do damage if teachers are unwilling to reexamine them and if instructional decisions are based on them.

Inaccurate expectations

As we have noted elsewhere (Brophy & Good, 1974), expectations tend to be self-sustaining. They affect both perception, by causing teachers to be alert for what they expect and less likely to notice what they do not expect, and interpretation, by causing teachers to interpret and perhaps distort what they see so that it is consistent with their expectations. Some expectations persist even though they do not coincide with the facts.

Self-Fulfilling Prophecy

Teachers form and hold expectations for student behavior. However, our use of the term "self-fulfilling prophecy" describes situations in which teachers' expectations influence the teachers' behavior and, subsequently, the students' behavior. When a teacher's initial perceptions of students' ability and motivation are inaccurate, the teacher may treat students as if they were different from what they actually are. In time, such teacher behavior may move students in the direction of the original, and erroneous, expectation. The following is an example of a self-fulfilling prophecy:

Jan Getty, an average first-grader, is the daughter of a well-known artist. The teacher knows that the artist is bright and creative. She attributes these same qualities to Jan even though Jan rarely exhibits any behavior that others would call creative. In general, Jan's day-to-day behavior is routine and marked by a dependency on others for direction. The teacher consistently encourages Jan "to do her own thing." She accepts Jan's work, but demands that Jan express her own thoughts. At the end of the school year, Jan is among the most original thinkers in the room. She can characteristically project five or six alternative and plausible endings for the stories that appear in her reader. The endings are quite creative and go far beyond the basic format of the story.

Concrete behaviors

The process we have described in this example is not magical. To the extent that teacher expectations function as self-fulfilling prophecies, this is because of concrete behaviors. Teacher expectations do not influence student behavior directly. If student behavior is influenced, expectations must be communicated to the student either directly or indirectly, through teacher behavior or classroom arrangements (the type of assignment the student receives, the type of group he or she is placed in, and so on).

Consider another example. Bill Burt, the son of a former All-American basketball player, is 6′5″ tall and weighs 225 pounds as a sophomore in high school. Quin Chase, a high school basketball coach, has been waiting impatiently for three or four years for Bill to become eligible for varsity basketball. During practice, Coach Chase works Bill as hard as any other player. He acknowledges his success on the floor, but he is also quick to point out his mistakes, just as he does for other players on the team. Eventually Bill earns a starting berth on the team, wins All-State honors as a sophomore, and leads his team to a second-place finish in the state tournament. Despite the fact that Bill developed as a star and the team did very well, as Coach Chase had originally expected, this is not an example of a self-fulfilling prophecy. Coach Chase did not treat Bill differently from any of the other players. A self-fulfilling prophecy refers to a situation in which differential expectations (high or low expectations for student performance) are followed by differential behavior.

Let us take a look at a situation that does reflect a self-fulfilling prophecy. Early in the year, Coach Chase realizes that Bill, even as a sophomore, is going to be outstanding. However, the coach doesn't think that Bill can make All-State or be as good as he might be unless he puts considerable pressure on Bill and works out publicity gimmicks to sell Bill to "voters" in the state. Examples of pushing Bill include almost demanding Bill to practice on Saturdays and part of Sundays to the possible neglect of his studies, asking him to engage in separate body-building and conditioning exercises beyond the normal procedures prescribed for other team members, and arranging for Bill to work on selected weaknesses in his game by scrimmaging against accomplished college players. Examples of publicity gimmicks might include emphasizing Bill and his talents rather than the team during pre- and postgame discussions with the local and visiting press; allowing Bill to guard the weakest player on the opponent's team so that he can concentrate on his offense and not have to worry about playing defense; and leaving Bill in games that the team has won in order to allow him to build up his scoring statistics.

Factors for a self-fulfilling prophecy

When we talk about a self-fulfilling prophecy we expect three factors to be present. First, there is an original expectation. Second, there will be the presence of behaviors that consistently communicate that expectation. Finally, there will be evidence that the original expectation has been confirmed. In the case of Jan Getty's teacher we saw the expectation work subconsciously; in the example of Bill Burt it worked as an explicit strategy. Self-fulfilling prophecies may occur with or without teachers' awareness that their behavior is being systematically influenced by their attitudes. In summary, a self-fulfilling prophecy occurs when an erroneous belief leads to behavior that makes the originally false belief become true.

Sustaining Expectations

Self-fulfilling prophecies are the most dramatic form of teacher expectation effects because they involve changes in student behavior (Cooper & Good, 1983). Cooper and Good use the term sustaining expectations to refer to situations in which teachers fail to see student potential and hence do not respond in ways that encourage the students to fulfill their potential. In summary, self-fulfilling expectations bring about a change in student performance, whereas sustaining expectations prevent change. As Cooper and Good have noted, sustaining expectations are subtle but probably occur more frequently, whereas self-fulfilling expectations are more dramatic but occur less frequently. Both types of teacher expectations are important concepts and provide a way of examining classroom events. In this chapter we will organize information presented around the concept of self-fulfilling prophecies, but both forms of expectation are important.

Teacher Expectations: A Model

Below is a model that we have presented elsewhere (Good & Brophy, 1984) to describe how self-fulfilling prophecies may affect classroom behavior:

1. The teacher expects specific behavior and achievement from particular students.
2. Because of these expectations, the teacher behaves differently toward different students.
3. This treatment by the teacher tells each student what behavior and achievement the teacher expects from him or her and affects the student's self-concept, achievement motivation, and level of aspiration.
4. If this teacher treatment is consistent over time, and if the student does not actively resist or change it in some way, it will shape his or

her achievement and behavior. High-expectation students will be led to achieve at high levels, but the achievement of low-expectation students will decline.

5. With time, the student's achievement and behavior will conform more and more closely to that originally expected from him or her.

"Other-directed" subjects

Teacher expectations are not automatically self-fulfilling. Students may prevent expectations from becoming fulfilled by resisting them in ways that force teachers to change their original expectations. Frank (1963) summarized the personality traits of patients who were most responsive (i.e., were highly suggestible) to placebo treatments in medical research and noted that dependent, "other-directed" subjects were especially susceptible to expectation effects. Johnson (1970), extending this work, has suggested that students who are dependent, adult-oriented, and generally other-directed would be especially vulnerable to expectation effects.

Communication of Inappropriate Expectations

What are some of the ways in which teachers communicate low, self-defeating expectations to students? The following are some of the more common ways in which low expectations might be expressed (Good & Brophy, 1984):

1. Waiting less time for low-achieving students to answer: Teachers have been observed to provide more time for high-achieving students to respond than for low-achieving students.

A teacher's attitude sometimes reflects preconceived expectations concerning the students abilities.

2. Not staying with lows in failure situations: In addition to waiting less time for lows to begin their responses, teachers have been found to respond to lows' (more so than highs') incorrect answers by giving them the answer or calling on another student to answer the question instead of trying to elicit the answers from them.
3. Rewarding inappropriate behavior of lows: In some studies teachers have inappropriately praised marginal or inaccurate student responses. Praising incorrect responses when peers know the answers may only emphasize the academic weakness of such students.
4. Criticizing lows more frequently than highs: Somewhat at odds with the above finding is the observation that in some studies teachers have been found to criticize lows proportionately more frequently than highs when they provide wrong answers. Such teacher behavior is likely to reduce the risk-taking behavior and general initiative of lows. (The seeming discrepancy between variables 3 and 4 may reside in differing teacher personalities. Teachers who praise inappropriate answers from lows may be mired in sympathy for these students, whereas hypercritical teachers may be irritated at them for delaying the class or providing evidence that the teaching has not been completely successful.)
5. Praising lows less frequently than highs: Also in contrast to 3 above, some research has shown that when lows provide correct answers they are less likely to be praised than highs, even though they provide fewer correct responses.
6. Not giving feedback to public responses of lows: Teachers in some studies responded to lows' answers, especially correct answers, by calling on another student to respond. Failure to confirm their answers seems undesirable in that these students more than others may be unsure of the adequacy of their responses.
7. Paying less attention to lows: Studies have shown that certain teachers attend more closely (smile more often and maintain greater eye contact) to highs than lows.
8. Calling on lows less often: Teachers have been found to call on high-achieving students more frequently than low-achieving students. The difference in public participation rates appears to become more sharply differentiated with increased grade level.
9. Differing interaction patterns with highs and lows: Interestingly, contact patterns between teachers and lows appear to be different in elementary and secondary classrooms. In elementary classrooms highs dominate public response opportunities, but highs and lows receive roughly the same number of private teacher contacts. In secondary classrooms highs become even more dominant in public settings, but lows receive more private conferences. At this grade level private conferences with teachers may be a sign of inadequacy and a source of embarrassment, especially if the teacher does not initiate many private contacts with highs.
10. Demanding less from lows: Several studies have suggested that this

is a relevant variable. It can be seen as an extension of the more focused "giving up" variable discussed in 2 above. This is a broader concept suggesting such activities as giving these students easier tests and letting the students know it or simply not asking the students to do academic work.

11. Other variables that have demonstrated differential teacher interaction with high- and low-achieving students include: (a) seating lows farther from the teacher; (b) interacting with lows more privately than publicly and monitoring and structuring their activities more closely; (c) differential administration or grading of tests and assignments in which highs but not lows are given the benefit of the doubt in borderline cases; (d) less friendly interactions with lows, including less smiling and fewer other nonverbal indicators of support; (e) briefer and less informative feedback to the questions of lows; (f) less eye contact and other nonverbal communication of attention and responsiveness; (g) less use of effective but time-consuming methods with lows when time is limited; (h) giving longer reading assignments, providing more time for discussion of the story, and generally demanding more from high than low reading groups; (i) interrupting lows more often when they make reading mistakes; (j) asking low groups higher-level comprehension questions less often.

Grouping Effects

We have seen that teachers often engage in different types of behavior with high- and low-achieving students or with high and low groups of students. Other studies suggest that teachers behave differently and have varied effects on the performance of students who are assigned to different ability groups in the same classroom. Weinstein (1976) noted in a study of three first-grade classrooms that the reading group to which students were assigned contributed a significant increment of 25 percent to the prediction of mid-year achievement over what could be predicted on the basis of students' initial readiness scores. Weinstein did not, however, find differences in teaching behavior that would account for the differential effects of group assignment. Still, it appears that group placement may represent an expectation effect that influences student achievement indirectly by decreasing or increasing motivation, or directly by exposing students to poor or good reading models for example.

Assignment to groups

Reading groups

Eder (1981) also studied first-grade reading groups and found that students who were likely to have difficulty in learning to read generally were assigned to groups where social context was not conducive to learning. In part this was because assignments to first-grade reading groups were based on kindergarten teachers' recommendations, and a major criterion of placement was the maturity of the students not just their perceived ability.

Most of the students in Eder's study had similar academic abilities and were all from middle-class backgrounds. None of the students could read prior to entering first grade; however, there were probably some important differences with respect to various reading readiness skills. Still, their progress in reading could plausibly be related to the reading instruction they received in first grade. Despite the relative homogeneity of these pupils, the first-grade teacher still grouped them for reading instruction.

Because the most immature, inattentive students were assigned to low groups, it was almost certain that these groups would cause more managerial problems than others, especially early in the year. In the low group, the teacher was often distracted from the student reader because of the need to manage other students in the group. Peers, therefore, often provided the correct word for the student who was reading. Readers were not allowed time to ascertain words on their own, even though less than a third of the students interviewed reported that they liked to be helped and most thought this help interfered with their learning. Eder found that low students had less time than highs to correct their mistakes before other students or the teacher intervened.

Eder also found that students in the low group spent 40 percent of their listening time not attending to the lesson (versus 22 percent in the high group). Low students frequently read out of turn, adding to the general confusion. Eder reported twice as many teacher "managerial acts" in the low group as in the high group (157 versus 61) and found that turn interruption increased over the course of the year. Due to management problems, frequent interruptions, and less serious teaching, low students may inadvertently have been encouraged to respond to social and procedural aspects of the reading group rather than to academic tasks.

McDermott (1976) found that good readers spent more time reading to the teacher than did low students. However, like Weinstein, he found that teachers did not differ in the amount of time that they worked with the high and low reading groups. Hunter (1978) did find differences between high and low groups in allocated reading time in two second-grade classes. She also reported that low reading groups were interrupted more often than high groups. One of the reasons low groups received less time for reading was that their reading groups were often interrupted by other students who needed help or information from the teacher. Such interruptions did not occur when the teacher worked with the high group.

Differences in Teacher Behavior Toward High and Low Groups

As Hiebert (1983) and Borko and Eisenhart (in press) note, reading lessons for high-ability and low-ability students often show marked contrasts. For highs, the reading lesson is a loosely structured event with opportunities to read aloud or silently, give multiple answers, interpret reading passages, and answer meaningful questions. In contrast, low-ability students experience a more highly structured format in which decoding skills, short specific answers, and appropriate behavior are stressed. In a study of a single elementary school, Hart (1982) noted that reading for low-ability students was a group experience in which these students met at an earlier time, were part of a smaller group, had more special arrangements, and more extra helpers. With lows, teachers emphasized decoding rather than understanding language. In general, low students were kept busy during reading group, while highs had more fun and more often attempted to understand what they read.

Emphasis on decoding in low groups

In a small but intensive study of teacher behavior toward high and low reading groups in second-grade classrooms, Borko and Eisenhart (in press) found that in low groups, the ability to decode words was most frequently emphasized and was often the basis for evaluation of reading skills. They note that typical activities for these students included sight reading, trying to sound out words in a sentence, and picking out letters to complete words. Low-group students were also asked frequently to provide rules for sounding out vowels and consonant blends and to provide other decoding rules. Low-group students have fewer opportunities than highs to demonstrate comprehension.

In contrast, high-group students spent more time extracting the meaning from their text in public, shared activities than they did on decoding. Although these students worked on skills such as vowel sounds, these activities constituted a smaller part of reading group time than in the low group. Borko and Eisenhart also found that teachers allowed high-group students to work on word skills on their own and saved public time in reading groups for answering questions based on the stories that had been read silently. During these activities, success was indicated by students' ability to recall information from the stories, to draw inferences from the stories, and to relate the stories to personal experiences or opinions.

Certain qualifications in these data need to be acknowledged. For example, some of the differences in teacher behavior may be student effects on the teacher (i.e., some students in low groups may be more attentive and some differences in teacher behavior may be appropriate (i.e., lows may need more work on skills). Still, we believe that students placed in lower groups often receive less serious instruction.

These studies illustrate that both the extent to which and the way in which teacher expectations are communicated in classrooms vary widely. However, although the particulars vary, at a general level there is a tendency in some classrooms for low students to be treated in ways that differ from how students believed to be more capable are treated. Good and Weinstein (in press) define these general differences in Table 17.1.

Variations in Communication of Expectations

The ways in which teacher expectations are communicated in classrooms vary widely. There is no single way to illustrate how individual teachers differ toward highs and lows. When considering discrepancies in research findings, it is useful to consider the following points. First, to bring about a self-fulfilling prophecy, it would not appear necessary for teachers to exhibit all, or even many, of the variables cited previously as indices of low

Table 17.1 Central Dimensions of Teachers' Communication of Differential Expectations

Students Believed to be More Capable Have	Students Believed to be Less Capable Have
more opportunity to perform publically on meaningful tasks	less opportunity to perform publically, especially on meaningful tasks
more autonomy (e.g., more choice in assignment, fewer interruptions)	less autonomy (frequent teacher monitoring of work, frequent interruption)
more assignments that deal with comprehension, understanding	less choice of curriculum assignments but more opportunity to work in drill-like assignments
more opportunity to think	less opportunity to think and analyze since much work is aimed at practice
more opportunity for self-evaluation	less opportunity for self-evaluation
more honest/contingent feedback	less honest/more gratuitous feedback
more respect for the learner as an individual with unique interests and needs	less respect for the learner as an individual with unique interests and needs

Source: This table is taken from T. Good and R. Weinstein (in press). "Classroom expectations: One framework for exploring classrooms." In K. Kepler-Zumwalt (ed.), *Theory into Practice: 1986 ASCD Yearbook.* Reprinted by permission of Association for Supervision and Curriculum Development, Alexandria, VA.

expectations. If teachers assign lows considerably less content than they can handle, that variable alone could reduce student learning, even if teachers call on lows frequently. Similarly, if teachers give low students less time to practice reading or allow allocated time to be interrupted frequently, this could be a sufficient condition for reducing student achievement. Third, some of the teaching differences identified by the observational research collected in the attempt to verify self-fulfilling effects seem to be illogical and/or inappropriate (e.g., less reading time for lows, noncontingent praise), whether or not the occurrence of the behavior is due to teacher expectations. Fourth, naturalistic studies prohibit inferences about causality, but teacher expectations, at a minimum, provide a rich conceptual heuristic for looking at classroom behavior.

We hope that our discussion of the self-fulfilling prophecy literature has provided you with a way of looking at direct and indirect ways in which teachers behave toward high- and low-achieving students. There are no automatic conclusions from these data, since they are largely correlational. For example, we do not know if low groups will achieve at higher levels when they have fewer interruptions. There are, nevertheless, some data to illustrate that changes in teacher expectations and teacher behavior can produce changes in student achievement.

Changing Expectations

Many of the ideas discussed by Good and Brophy (1973) about differences in teacher behavior toward high and low achievers were incorporated in an extensive three-year project sponsored by the Los Angeles County school system (Martin, 1973). Mary Martin and Sam Kerman directed the "Equal Opportunity in the Classroom" project, with the goal of sensitizing teachers to the possible damaging effects of their behavior toward low-achieving students. Their second goal was to present teachers with a variety of skills to use with these students.

The project showed that teachers did change their behavior toward low students by calling on them more often, and so on, and that low students in the classrooms of teachers who received the training showed a marked increase in achievement in contrast with lows in control or comparison classrooms. Furthermore, the gains of the low students did not result in an achievement decrement for high students. It thus appears possible to improve the progress of low students by changing teaching behavior, and these changes in teaching behavior do not necessarily affect other students in the class adversely.

Individual Differences Among Teachers

Before attempting to pursue the problem of teacher expectations by offering suggestions about how teachers might react to low achievers, it is important to note that many teachers do not reflect self-fulfilling prophecies in their behavior. Let us consider what motivates teacher behavior. Why do teachers treat high- and low-achieving students differently?

Expectation Effects Are Not Universal

Not all teachers have been found to treat low-achieving students in detrimental ways. Some teachers, even though they are aware that some students are low achievers and even though they have relatively low expectations for these students in comparison with other students in the classroom, do not treat these students detrimentally. From a series of naturalistic classroom studies (Brophy & Good, 1974), it is possible to describe at least three types of teachers.

Proactive teachers

Proactive teachers do not allow their expectations for low-achieving students to undermine their instructional activities. If anything, these teachers spend more time interacting with low-achieving students than with relatively high achievers. Furthermore, these teachers structure their classrooms and learning activities so that high-achieving pupils do not suffer because of the teachers' increased awareness of low-achieving students and the attention they direct toward them.

Reactive teachers

The second group of teachers appears to be *reactive* in their classroom style. These teachers allow existing differences between high and low students to unfold so that high-achieving students, due to their own initiative and ability, come to dominate public classroom life. High-achieving students receive more response opportunities in such classrooms, but that is simply because they raise their hands more frequently and thus answer more questions.

Overreactive teachers

The third group of teachers is *overreactive*. They characteristically overemphasize student differences and supply qualitatively and quantitatively better treatment to high-achieving students than to low-achieving students. Such differences in teacher behavior exaggerate and extend initial differences between these two student groups.

Why Self-Fulfilling Prophecies Operate in the Classroom

Teacher unawareness

Given that most teachers want to be effective in the classroom, why is it that some behave in obviously inappropriate ways toward low-achievers? There are several possible explanations, the most basic being that teachers are unaware of much of their classroom behavior.

Ehman (1970) compared teachers', students', and classroom observers' reports of classroom events and found that students and classroom observers were in general agreement, but that the reports of neither of these two groups corresponded very closely to teachers' reports. Presumably, teachers were too busy teaching to be aware of what their pupils were doing. Emmer (1967) found that teachers underestimated the amount of time that they talked in the classroom. Although Cooper and Good (1983) found teachers to be reasonably aware of some behavior in the classroom, in some instances teachers' perceptions differed from those of observers and students.

Ego-protective behavior

A second possible explanation is defensive or ego-protective behavior on the part of teachers. Wolfson and Nash (1968), observed discrepancies between what teachers did and what teachers believed they did in the classroom and found that teachers, when pressed to describe events outside of their awareness, tend to describe themselves in the most favorable light. Beckman (1970) found that teachers in a lab setting assumed personal credit for success when students succeeded but explained failures by blaming students or other factors.

A slightly different interpretation can be made from the data that Ames (1975) presented. They had teachers teach short lessons to small groups of children. Teacher self-report data did not reveal ego defensiveness on the part of these teachers; they did not take personal credit for success or blame students for failure. Both success and failure were explained by the teachers in terms of student characteristics (primarily high or low student motivation), not their own teaching behavior. Observers were also present at this study, but their explanations differed dramatically from that of the teachers. The observers attributed success and failure to good and poor teaching.

Teacher orientation

What do these differences mean? They suggest that teachers tend to be oriented toward presenting material and the apparent success of their students in mastering it. These data again illustrate that it is difficult for teachers to monitor their own behavior during the act of teaching, not only because the classroom is so busy, but also because their focus is on presenting material.

The data presented by Ames and Ames do not necessarily indicate a more wholesome teacher perspective. Teachers who attribute success and failure exclusively to student characteristics may also be unwilling to examine their own behavior as a possible factor that may interfere in the learning process. We suspect that student, environmental, and teacher-school factors are all involved and must be examined when failure occurs.

Teacher behavior conditioned by students

We have considered two reasons to explain why teachers behave differently toward students. A third factor is that students condition teacher behavior (see Winne & Marx, 1977). Several experiments have indicated that teachers' behavior changes as a function of student behavior; thus, differential behavior may be the result of a bidirectional feedback loop in which high-achieving students reinforce teacher behavior and the subsequent teacher behavior reinforces student behavior. Klein (1971) examined the behavior of guest lecturers in college classrooms and found lecturers to be much more indirect (asking questions, praising, using students' ideas) during periods of positive student support than during periods of apparent student disinterest. It is likely that the facial expressions and body postures of students, and so on, control teacher behavior under normal teaching circumstances as well. The student who maintains eye contact with the teacher is more likely to have the teacher repeat or rephrase the question than the student who looks embarrassed and stares at the floor, thus conditioning the teacher to give the answers or call on someone else.

High achievers may attract more teacher attention because they reward teachers. Their classroom performance is qualitatively superior to that of low achievers, and hence provides the teacher with more feedback that his or her efforts have been successful.

Rewarding student contact

Teachers may spend more time with highs not because they are unconcerned about lows, but because they enjoy contact with highs. Rewarding contacts may subtly condition and reinforce teacher behavior so that teachers tend to seek them out more often. This is more likely to occur as children become older. Students in secondary classrooms who provide their teachers with novel explanations will probably receive additional teacher questioning and interest, unless the teacher is threatened by the quality of a student's explanation. Also, as Cooper (1979) has noted, teachers perceive the classroom behavior of highs as more controllable and predictable than that of lows. Hence highs may reward teachers not only by performing better but also by presenting them with fewer problems. Cooper, Hinkel, and Good (1980) have found that there appears to be some relationship between teachers' perceptions of control and classroom behavior. For example, it was noted that students over whom teachers perceived less control more frequently received no teacher feedback to their classroom responses compared to students over whom teachers perceived more control.

Other Explanations for Differential Teacher Behavior

Why is it that some teachers noticeably differentiate their behavior toward high- and low-achieving students and others show only minimal differences in their behavior? Following the work of Dweck and Elliott (1983), Marshall and Weinstein (1984) contend that teachers' beliefs about the nature of intelligence may influence their classroom behavior. Some teachers view intelligence as an entity and thus see it as relatively stable and singular in nature. In contrast, other teachers view intelligence as incremental, as a repertoire of skills and knowledge that can be increased.

Nature of intelligence

Teachers who hold an entity view of intelligence would be more likely to place students in a stable heirarchy according to performance expectations and to treat these students differently on the basis of these expectations. Marshall and Weinstein argue that low achievers in the classrooms of these teachers may use performance information to make detrimental social comparisons. That is, when students perceive that they are treated differently according to their ability they may use this information to compare themselves with other students and may see themselves as less capable and expect less of themselves. However, in classrooms where teachers hold an incremental view of intelligence, teacher statements and curriculum assignments communicate the belief that each student has the ability to improve regardless of current status, that individual differences in rates and modes of learning are normal, and that students can learn from those who have already acquired certain skills.

Differential teacher behavior

Good (1983) argues that a basic cause of differential teacher behavior is that classrooms are very busy and complex environments that make it difficult for teachers to assess accurately the frequency and quality of their interactions with individual students. A second explanation involves the fact that much classroom behavior has to be interpreted before it has meaning. Research (e.g., Anderson-Levitt, in press) suggests that once a teacher develops an expectation about a student, such as a particular student is not capable of learning, the teacher interprets subsequent ambiguous behavior or events in a way consistent with the original expectation. It is clear that most classroom behavior is ambiguous and subject to multiple interpretations both from the standpoint of the teacher as well as that of students. Thus, teachers who have developed ways to monitor classroom behavior more systematically and more accurately and who are willing to examine classroom behavior from multiple viewpoints may be more likely to communicate appropriate expectations to all students.

Causality

According to Good (1983), a third reason why teachers differentiate more or less in their behavior toward high- and low-achieving students involves causality. Some teachers believe that they can and will influence student learning (for example, see Brophy & Evertson, 1976). Such teachers may interpret student failure as a need for more instruction, more clarification, and eventually increased opportunity to learn. Other teachers, because they assign blame rather than assume partial responsibility for student failure, may interpret failure as a need to provide less challenge and fewer opportunities to learn. This is similar to the entity and incremental view of intelligence that Marshall and Weinstein advance; however, this view also considers teachers' self-efficacy views as well. Teachers who have doubts about their ability to instruct certain types of students or to teach certain subject matter may communicate low expectations to students, just as teachers who hold low expectations for students may communicate these expectations.

Manner of student presentation

A fourth explanation for differential teacher behavior involves the way in which students present themselves to the teacher. Because of linguistic deficiencies or lack of awareness of social cues, some students may have much more difficulty convincing teachers that they know the material than will other students. Thus, there are different reasons why teachers may hold and communicate low expectations and each of these explanations applies in certain contexts.

Obviously, these influences are dynamic and often occur in combination. For example, in a recent observational study Confrey and Good (1981) note that in one class students were placed in either a high or a low mathematics group on the basis of their teacher's interpretation of the students' performances during the first weeks of mathematics class. The assignment of students to the high group was based in part on the speed with which they performed mathematics tasks. Ironically, a week of observation indicated that students in the low group often watched what the teacher was doing in the high group, and in interview sessions they indicated that they observed the highs because they wanted to get a step ahead and learn what the high group was learning. Unfortunately, because the teacher was interested in speed of performance and because lows spent time watching the other group rather than doing their own seatwork, their incomplete seatwork assignments reinforced the teacher's original expectations and supported the belief that the assignments to high and low groups were correct.

Student interpretation of roles

Students' interpretations of their classroom roles and their behavior influenced and maintained teacher expectations and behaviors.

Finally, we should note that some self-fulfilling effects occur in the classroom because teachers and students are culturally conditioned to expect certain types of responses from girls or boys or from minority students.

Cultural expectations

Cultural expectations exert pressure not only in estimating the achievement potential of students, but in defining the curriculum and general purposes of schooling.

Developing Appropriate Expectations

The invidious effects of low expectations and the reasons why some teachers may communicate them have been reviewed. Now we want to emphasize two expectations that we do not want to convey to the reader: equal expectations for all or high expectations for all.

First, we do not suggest that all students should receive equal (in the

Mistake of identical treatment

sense of identical) classroom treatment. Some students will learn more quickly than others. Some will be relatively reticent but will learn mostly by listening and actively, but covertly, evaluating what they hear. Paradoxically, the pressure for equal student performance is the source of invidious and self-defeating comparisons that eventually erode the confidence and motivation of many students. Any strategy or expectation that is aimed at all students will insure failure for many. Sameness is inappropriate as an expectation and self-defeating as a strategy.

Need for realistic expectations

High expectations for all students will not magically help slower students reach new plateaus. In hopes of motivating student performance, a teacher might announce: "This story is so simple and interesting that all of you should finish it in half an hour." If some students need an hour to read the story because they do not know the vocabulary or do not find the story interesting, they are left with two basic choices: they can pretend to finish the assignment and hope they are not "found out," or they can continue to read while the teacher or their peers make remarks about their slowness or the delay they are causing. The student will feel bad either way, and if such events are repeated regularly, the slow students will tend either to accept their inferior status or to blame the teacher and school. High performance expectations that are consistently impossible for students to reach will erode student effort.

Awareness of classroom behavior

Teachers are human and will make many errors in assessing students' needs. As we have argued before, the most basic way to reduce errors is by obtaining information about classroom behavior. Teachers need to become more aware of their classroom behavior in general, as well as their interactions with students they perceive to be low achievers in particular. As a starting point, teachers could review their behavior with an eye toward the results of studies previously reported in this book. Relevant questions include the following:

- ☐ Do I praise or encourage lows when they initiate comments?
- ☐ Do I stay with lows in failure situations?
- ☐ Do I stay with lows in success situations?
- ☐ Do I avoid calling on lows in public situations?
- ☐ How often do lows have positive success experiences in public situations?
- ☐ Are lows needlessly criticized for wrong answers or failures to respond?
- ☐ Are lows placed in a "low group" and treated as group members rather than as individuals?
- ☐ Do I ignore the minor inappropriate behavior of lows, or do mild violations of classroom rules bring on strong reprimands?
- ☐ How often do lows get to select a study topic?
- ☐ How frequently do lows have a chance to evaluate their own work and to make important decisions?
- ☐ What are the work preferences of individual students—do they like to listen or to work in pairs—and how often are those work preferences honored?

Skill Development Through Meaningful Practice

Skill work and task motivation

Teachers sometimes overrespond to low achievers' basic skill deficiencies. At first glance, this seems to be reasonable behavior. If students don't have word attack skills, then they need to develop such skills if they are to become more independent readers. Up to a point, teachers' emphasis on skill development is good, but if students work constantly on skills, their general task motivation may be eroded.

Need for practicing skills

Earlier in this chapter material was presented to illustrate that reading-group work for low achievers in some classrooms is more fragmented than is the case for more capable readers. Teachers who constantly interrupt low students when they are reading may compound the problem by allowing even less time to directly practice reading. If students are to derive personal satisfaction from any task, they must have opportunity for meaningful and successful practice. Students who have low reading ability need to have the chance to practice the act of reading. It is amazing to see how little time low achievers have for reading in some classrooms. Too often they are drowned in a sea of drill work and constant reminders of inadequate performance. Although reading attack skills need to be developed, students also need the chance to actually read. Teachers need to balance their demands for drill work with the opportunity for students to read for meaning and pleasure. Similar problems are seen in other curriculum areas.

Erosion of student motivation

Student motivation can be eroded in other ways. How would you feel if everything that you did was done better and faster by someone else? This is the situation that poor readers often face. They hear the teacher discuss a story with other students long before they have a chance to read it. If this experience is repeated daily, it is apt to lower their interest in the reading material because these students have heard others discuss the story and because they know that others have already accomplished the task.

Some teachers think that by dividing a class into smaller groups, it is easier to meet the different learning speeds of students.

Furthermore, it would be hard to believe that all teachers could bring the same degree of enthusiasm to the third or fourth discussion of a story. Teacher motivation may thus influence student reaction. Teachers may inadvertently focus more on the mechanics of reading than on general comprehension by the time they read the story with low achievers.

Variation of assignment

One way to break out of this joint trap for teachers and poor readers would be periodically to assign different stories to the low reading group. New stories would provide a chance for these students to reach their own conclusions and insights. It would also be possible to reduce motivational problems by allowing low-achieving students to work with a different reading system. However, the use of a different system might inadvertently increase the perceived difference in reading ability among students.

Problems with using special materials

There are other problems associated with using special materials. For example, a colleague of ours, Dr. Bob Germain, has noticed that some of the more structured curriculum materials have unanticipated and undesirable consequences for student learning. In an analysis of social studies materials, he noted that in an attempt to provide low achievers with help in processing content materials, too much structure was provided. As a case in point, he suggests that telling poor readers where the answers to comprehension questions can be found will probably discourage them from reading and thinking. Hence, students with comparatively few reading skills are *rewarded* for not reading.

If the spread of student ability in a classroom is extremely wide, it may be necessary to use different curriculum content. However, periodic insertion of new stories or new tasks is a better teacher response than using different curricula unless the spread in student ability is too great to accommodate.

Challenge higher students

Another way that teachers can address the motivational problem of lows is to challenge higher students appropriately. If teachers are exposing high students to material of appropriate difficulty, then they too will be making mistakes from time to time. Teachers will have to review word-attack and interpretive skills with these students as well. The fact that *all* students have to exert effort will not be lost on the low achievers.

Unequal opportunities

The low-ability student frequently gets to do an activity only after more capable students have performed the task. In elementary schools, teachers often allow students free work time after assigned tasks are completed. In high school chemistry classrooms, more complex experiments are performed only after simpler experiments have been completed successfully. Opportunities for independent study are often available only after certain work has been completed.

There are times when a fixed sequence has to be followed, for example, all students need to master safety procedures in the lab; however, if teachers analyze the situation carefully, it is often possible to assign tasks so that students who move through the curriculum more slowly do not always just repeat the same experience as the others. Logic may dictate the necessity of having students perform simpler experiments or do independent studies with more restricted scopes before they perform more complex ones. But often there are not good reasons for having all students complete the same experiments. Pupils who move through material more slowly could be asked to perform relatively simple but different experiments. Indeed, when slower students are doing such work, more advanced students might be referred to them to learn about the outcomes of experiments that they themselves did not perform.

Treating Low Achievers as Individuals

Teachers too often group and treat all low-achievers as though they were one student. It is especially vital to learn about the unique needs and interests of students who may view school as irrelevant or as a punishment. Paradoxically, when teachers visit informally with students, it is rarely with lows. The contradiction lies in the fact that most of these students want teacher contact but do not know how to obtain it, and in general are convinced that teachers like them less than other students and do not want to be bothered with them.

Recognizing coping strategy

Student behaviors that have been institutionalized through practice and reward are difficult to change. The first step is to recognize the coping strategy that the student uses and then systematically reward competing (e.g., answering versus not answering) responses. But to be able to do this, it is necessary for teachers to know individual students.

Students who are victimized by low expectations and who receive inappropriate classroom treatment may be entirely correct when they attribute their task success to external factors. If teachers do not feel that increased student effort will enhance performance and if they do not reward effort, it is unlikely that students will perceive the relationship between personal effort and task success. Indeed, a case study by King (1979) in one classroom found that low achievers were not being rewarded for their effort, despite the fact that these students were generally on task and working hard.

Student Perceptions

We have presented data in this chapter to illustrate that some teachers treat their high- and low-achieving students differently. It also appears that students perceive that teachers react differently to high and low achievers (Weinstein & Middlestadt, 1979). Hence, on the basis of these differing interaction patterns, students may infer different levels of teacher affect. If teachers take the time to talk to low achievers in private, they may begin to reduce these students' beliefs that no one cares about them, and may learn valuable clues about how these students see classroom events.

Student perceptions of differential treatment

However, as Good and Weinstein (in press) note, while these studies demonstrate agreement among students in their perceptions of differential treatment by the teacher, other studies suggest important differences in individual students' interpretations of classroom behavior. Obviously, these variations in interpretation influence the way in which students think about and react to classroom opportunities. In interviews of junior high students,

Good (1981) found that some students believed that the teacher called on students in order to evaluate their understanding of assigned materials; other students believed that the teacher called on students in order to use up available instructional time. Changing teacher behaviors like call-ons and wait time may not alter students' behavior so much as it will change students' perceptions of what these teacher behaviors mean. Also, changing teachers' behaviors may be insufficient unless students' perceptions change as well.

Changing Students' Low Expectations

If teachers are to help students change their self-perceptions, they must perceive and understand students' self-perceptions in addition to examining their own expectations.

Many students do poorly in school because they are hesitant and fear failure. Students with poor self-concepts may give up hope and expect mediocrity or worse as inevitable. There are some empirical data to support this argument. Kagan and Moss (1962) report high correlations (.70 or better) between children's expectations of failure in a problem situation and withdrawal from the task. Hence, on school tasks and in general nonschool activities, persons with low self-concepts may be inclined to withdraw or give up in the face of pressure or stress.

Expectations and withdrawal

As one would predict, a negative self-concept appears to hinder initial school adjustment and academic progress (Mussen, Conger, & Kagan, 1974). Numerous studies show that a low self-concept is associated with poor school performance (e.g., see Brookover, Paterson, & Thomas, 1962; Purkey, 1970).

The precise way in which a teacher can help children or adolescents to improve their self-views varies with the individual student and the teaching situation. The difficulty of changing self-views probably increases as the age of the student increases. However, two general strategies are noncontingent acceptance and honest feedback.

Noncontingent acceptance and honest feedback

McCandless and Evans (1973) stress the importance of noncontingent acceptance (of sincere effort) and the provision of sensitive but realistic and honest feedback. Too often, teachers and other adults overlook low-achieving students' problems or provide them with unrealistic feedback. Despite the good intentions behind it, such behavior has invidious, detrimental effects upon students. The maladaptive effects of inappropriate praise are aptly summarized in the following:

> First, the child who realizes that his product or performance is lacking may become confused by the discrepancy between his own judgment and the feedback he is receiving. He may then alter his own judgment and standards to coincide with the feedback he has received, or he may become distrustful of the adult and discount his future pronouncements. . . . Another possible consequence of excessive praise is the establishment of the child's image of himself as infallible. The child who is lavishly approved or rewarded for any performance may have difficulty at a later time accepting the harsh reality that he, too, sometimes fails. Faced with failure, the child may become defensive and refuse

> to admit that his performance is lacking. He may possibly be overwhelmed by the failure and magnify it out of proportion so that it becomes incapacitating. In either event, this child will have difficulty coping with failure and turning it to his advantage as a learning experience. (Nardine, 1971, pp. 342–343)

Success, Failure, and Feedback

If teachers are to provide students with more appropriate feedback, they must understand how low achievers are apt to react to teacher feedback. In general, success raises a student's level of aspiration (his or her hopes for performance on similar tasks). However, the student's previous experience influences the immediate effects of task failure and task success. Sears (1940) studied this problem by choosing three groups of fourth-, fifth-, and sixth-grade students: a successful group that had always received good school grades; a failure group that had consistently performed poorly in school; and a mixed group that had a successful history in reading but an unsuccessful history in arithmetic.

Success and aspiration

Influence of background on predictions

Each student was exposed to a number of typical reading and arithmetic tasks and asked to estimate the time it would take to complete each task that followed. Students with previous failure histories were extremely variable in their predictions—sometimes they overestimated; sometimes they underestimated. Students with a background of success set much more realistic time goals. Interestingly, the mixed group was more variable (about as variable as the failure group) than success students in arithmetic, but as good as the success group in predicting their times in reading, the subject in which they had done well. The data provide strong evidence that perception of task difficulty (how long it will take to complete the task) is related to success experiences, and that poor achievement is partly a function of inability to use feedback appropriately. The time it took failure students to complete the task they had just finished did not greatly affect their prediction for the next task. Again, we see why it is difficult to discuss teacher motivational influence strategies separately. Objective task difficulty and student perception of task difficulty are inseparable in classroom life.

The students were then asked to complete similar tasks, but were given false information about their performance on the previous tasks. Half of the students in each group were told that they had performed well, and half were told that they had performed poorly. The chief finding was that failure feedback tended to make the estimates of all groups more variable.

Aspirations and expectations

In general, success leads to high but realistic aspirations, whereas failure leads either to unrealistically low expectations or unrealistically high aspirations. In failure situations, the aspirations are not genuine expectations, at least in the case of students who verbalize unrealistically high ones. Such students do not genuinely expect to achieve their stated goals, in contrast to the more successful students who aspire to high but realistic performance that is within their grasp.

Repeated failure experiences in school will cause students to develop an inability or unwillingness to use task feedback appropriately. If they begin to experience success, their past history of failure may still lead them to under- or overreact to their performance and continue to make unrealistic predictions for subsequent task performance. They may need time to get accustomed to success, and this success will have to be on realistic tasks. Sometimes teachers with the best intentions can inadvertently undermine student initiative by making assignments obviously easy or by using too much praise. Teachers who can help students to achieve success on tasks that they perceive as relevant will have taken a major step in helping students to develop appropriate, positive learner expectations.

Increasing Student Motivation

A key teacher task in increasing student motivation is to help students perceive the relationship between success and personal effort. As a starting point, teachers might ask students to discuss tasks on which they have done poorly and have students explain why their performances were poor. Teachers also need to assess students' ability to determine the amount of time and effort necessary for completing tasks successfully. For example, teachers might ask students to estimate the amount of time necessary to complete a particular task, collect follow-up information, and provide this information to students during conferences. Teachers might also help students to distinguish between tasks they can and cannot do. Similarly, teachers could check on the general accuracy of students' perceptions by asking them to indicate the extent to which they felt they had correctly or incorrectly answered various examination questions.

Assessing students' predictive ability

Such assessment should be followed by active attempts to help the learner distinguish between tasks that he or she really can do and those that are beyond his or her control. The critical factor is that some practical pay-off follows. The student needs to see what happens when one does apply oneself to an academic task. Thus, the next step is to create a series of tasks that are clearly tied to the student's work effort so that, proportionately, the greater the student effort, the greater the success on the task. It is now necessary to provide the student with feedback about his or her progress on the task. Such feedback should focus on the process, that is, the relationship between effort and success.

Helping students make realistic predictions

After demonstrating that the student's effort is related to task performance, it would be useful to let the student know through individual conferences that the teacher regularly assigns tasks that the student can do, and that anytime the student cannot find information or does not know how to proceed, he or she should ask for help. In addition to letting students know that assigned work will be at an appropriate difficulty level, it is also useful to stress to students that tasks are assigned to facilitate student understanding and ability and not just to fill time. The teacher should create the expectation that assigned tasks, although appropriately difficult and challenging, can be completed if the student wants to do so. A teacher who can do this has established the minimum conditions for helping stu-

Assisting students in pursuit of academic goals

dents expend energy in pursuit of academic goals. From dissonance theory we know that once a student sees that his or her personal efforts are related to task success, it will be difficult for the student to explain away failure. The incongruity between poor performance and knowledge that the student can accomplish the task may exert subtle pressure on the student to expend more time and effort on subsequent activities.

Allowing students to win

Making it possible for students to "win" in the classroom is an important motivational concept. Too often classrooms are "rigged" so that some students invariably will lose. Some teachers allow students to pursue their own individual interests if they have finished their assignments. However, some students never finish their assignments and, therefore, they never get to participate in free-time activity.

Rewarding student effort

If teachers want to use external incentives like free-time periods or concrete rewards to spark student effort, they should be careful to guarantee that student effort, and not student aptitude, is being rewarded. The student should be rewarded for completing a task within a reasonable amount of time based on past level of achievement and not because of his or her learning speed. To put it another way, when teachers use incentives to improve student performance, low and high achievers should receive assignments that would take them roughly equal amounts of time to complete assuming good use of available time. If teachers follow this procedure, students are rewarded for their effort. Thus, we have outlined a strategy that is consistent with the cognitive viewpoint presented in Chapter 16. If students are to assume personal responsibility for their classroom assignments, they must see tasks as relevant and they must see a relationship between personal effort and classroom success.

Emphasizing Instructional Help, Not Sympathy

As we have noted elsewhere (Brophy & Good, 1974), sympathy alone is misplaced and self-defeating. Teachers who give easier tests to lows, who always ask them elementary questions, or who give up on them in public-response situations do not help, and often worsen, their plight.

Kleinfeld (1972) presented a penetrating ethnographic analysis of teacher behavior with Indian and Eskimo students who were experiencing culture shock on moving from their native rural schools to urban, integrated schools, showing that sympathy alone was not enough to help these students. She found that the most effective teachers were those who took a personal interest in students, engaged in informal conversations with them, adapted instruction to their different backgrounds and achievement levels, were highly supportive of their attempts to learn, and avoided use of criticism. From her observations, the most effective teachers first established rapport with the students and then communicated an "active demand" to them:

> The essence of the instructional style which elicits a high level of intellectual performance from village Indian and Eskimo students is to create an extremely warm personal relationship and to actively demand a level of academic work which the student does

not suspect he can attain. Village students thus interpret the teacher's demandingness not as bossiness or hostility, but rather as another expression of his personal concern, and meeting the teacher's academic standards becomes their reciprocal obligation in an intensely personal relationship. (Kleinfeld, 1972, p. 34)

Creating an Appropriate Classroom Climate

Teachers have to legitimize the aid they provide to lows, or else the lows and their other students as well will interpret increased teacher attention as a sign that they are inferior. Kleinfeld (1972), for example, argued that one way to reduce the debilitating effects of special attention to lows is to individualize much of classroom instruction so that teachers are able to have periodic individual contact with all students. In such environments, more frequent and extended contact with lows seems less out of place.

Individual contact with students

In the early grades, the teacher may be able to influence students' self-views and achievements by dealing with the individual student more appropriately. As the student becomes older, the problem increases in difficulty. At older age levels, the student's behavior is controlled in part by peer expectations. Students who expect poor performance from a peer may behave in ways that make it more likely that the student will fail. When a low student goes to the board to do a math problem, he may be accompanied by a chorus of hushed but audible giggles. The shy, reticent student who does not respond immediately when called on may automatically receive reactions of irritation from classmates.

Peer expectations

Teachers can help lows gain more self-respect and respect from classmates if they allow them to achieve notable public success from time to time. Doing this successfully involves much planning and work, for trivial or unsuccessful exposure of lows may deepen the problem. However, public success is important and worth planning for. As we have noted, most of the successes of lows are private although many of their failures occur in public.

Helping lows gain respect

Often teachers can use unique talents that students already possess or can capitalize on the life styles of individual students. Kleinfeld (1972), for example, reported that some teachers were able to increase the prestige of village students and reduce hostility toward them by making their skills, such as "surviving in the wilderness," public knowledge. At other times, teachers need to work with students for long periods of time to help them learn skills like teaching a fifth-grade student how to run a projector, or allowing him or her to make a movie. Once a student has learned a skill, he or she should be allowed to demonstrate it publicly. Repeated public successes involving such skills, especially those deemed important by the peer group, will do much to raise the esteem with which lows are regarded by their classmates.

Appropriate Use of Praise

Brophy (1981) argues that feedback—knowledge of results—is helpful and promotes effective learning. However, he notes that students, or at least many students, do not *need* praise. He has documented the fact that teachers not only fail to praise contingently (reward only quality performance) but often praise students for low-quality work or even incorrect answers. This is done by teachers to encourage effort, not to reinforce quality performance. However, if students recognize that this is what the teacher is doing, the result is most likely to produce embarrassment or discouragement. If praise is to be used effectively, especially on low achievers, it must be used only after adequate performance on a genuine assignment. Furthermore, as Brophy argues, if praise is to be effective, it must be used for informational rather than controlling reasons (see Chapter 16 for specific recommendations about how to praise effectively).

SUMMARY

Teacher expectations—the inferences that teachers make about present and future achievements and behaviors of students—can undermine the efforts of low-achieving students. Since Rosenthal and Jacobson published their well-known study in 1968, there has been great interest in such effects and the processes by which expectations form. Factors involved in the self-fulfilling prophecy seem to be: (1) the originial expectation; (2) behaviors that communicate that expectation; and (3) evidence confirming the original expectation. There is evidence of a wide variety of common ways in which low expectations are expressed to low-achieving students, including verbal feedback, grouping, wait-time, attention, seating, and other subtle teacher communications.

Attempts to reduce the negative impact of low expectations include sensitizing teachers to the potentially damaging effects of such attitudes, increasing awareness of their own classroom behavior, and providing better feedback and support to teachers dealing with low achievers. It has been found that proactive teachers are less likely to allow low expectations to influence their interactions with students than are reactive or overreactive teachers. Also, teachers who have realistic expectations of all their students and base differential treatments on such expectations are likely to foster better growth than those whose expectations for students are unrealistic.

In general, it seems that dealing with students as individuals and giving them challenges and opportunities appropriate to their existing levels of development will provide the kind of setting in which healthy self-concepts, levels of aspiration, and motivation will thrive best. However, to be successful, teachers have to find time for face-to-face contacts with certain individual learners and become sensitive to the way students define and perceive classroom tasks.

QUESTIONS AND PROBLEMS

1. In your own words, explain the difference between sustaining and self-fulfilling expectations.
2. Marshall and Weinstein differentiate between viewing intelligence as entity or incremental. What is the importance of this distinction?
3. Consider the concepts of origin and pawn that were presented in Chapter 16 and discuss the concepts in terms of teacher expectations.

4. Consider the concepts task-involvement and ego-involvement (see Chapter 16) and explain their relationship to expectation effects. What types of tasks are most likely to be assigned to students who are viewed as more or less capable? Why is this the case?
5. In this chapter stress has been placed on inappropriate expectations that teachers communicate to individuals or groups of students believed to be less capable. Think of some positive and appropriate expectations that teachers could express to the entire class. Using your own ideas as well as those of Brophy (see also Chapter 16), write out statements that teachers could make at the beginning or end of a lesson to encourage the performance of all, or at least most, students in the class.
6. There probably are certain topics or broad subject matter areas that you will be required to teach even though you find them uninteresting or distasteful. What are some of these in your case? What can you do to reduce the danger that you will create the same kinds of negative attitudes in your students?
7. A great many suggestions about motivating students were made in this chapter, probably more than most teachers could, or would want to use. Which of the ideas seemed more relevant and likely to be useful for you? In answering this question, bear in mind that the optimal motivation techniques for your use in the classroom are not necessarily the ones that you prefer as a student, but the ones that will be most successful with the students you teach.
8. We have stressed the importance of success experiences, and for good reasons. However, students will need to be corrected when they have made mistakes, and guided when they are confused. How can this be accomplished in ways that will not damage motivation? Can it be accomplished in ways that actually will increase motivation? How?
9. Differentiate between teachers' appropriate and inappropriate use of praise in the classroom. Can praise be harmful?

CASE STUDIES

A Student Conference. Mr. Morgan has graded the first set of history papers and sees that Jim Kline has done a terrible job. In a vague way he remembers Jim. Jim is a student in the third-period class, sits in the back of the room, and as far as Mr. Morgan remembers, has never spoken in class. He appears well dressed but uninterested.

Mr. Morgan decides that he wants to have a conference with Jim to discuss the exam specifically and the class generally. He wants to "pull the trigger" on Jim's performance and let him know that it was poor, but he also wants to let Jim know that he accepts him and wants to work out a way in which Jim can increase his performance. What would you do in this conference? How would you start? Write out a few lines of dialogue to show how you would begin.

An Instructional Dilemma. Jane Stoverink teaches with two other teachers in a unit composed of 62 students in the elementary school. (In terms of a traditional organization, most of the students are fifth- and sixth-graders, although a few very bright fourth-graders are in the room.) Unfortunately, the weakest students in the unit are mostly minority students. How can Jane and the other two teachers group students for regular instruction and special activities in a way that will motivate students and yet provide a good chance for high and low achievers to interact regularly? Describe and defend your plan in detail.

Avoiding Confrontation. Jim, a first-year science teacher, left the fall teacher orientation wondering how he was going to survive attendance registers, purchasing, what to do with the Baker boys who evidently cause trouble, and many other things. In the first month of teaching he worked constantly on organizing the classroom, learning his students' names, preparing lesson plans, and so on. One afternoon he asked one of his students, Mark, to collect the matches they had been using in the introduction to the Bunsen burner experiment. Mark was larger than the rest of his class and had showed that he enjoyed this slight responsibility. While supervising this process, Jim was matching first and last names of his students when the name Mark Baker clicked in his mind for the first time. "Is he one of those Baker boys the principal has warned us about?" he wondered. During his preparation period, Jim stopped for a brief chat with the school counselor and verified that this was so. Mark was the youngest of the Baker boys. Soon Jim could hear himself finding fault with Mark and demanding behavior he had not required previously. A confrontation soon occurred, Mark said some words Jim felt were uncalled for, and Mark was sent to the principal for discipline. What role did teacher expectations have in Mark's involvement in a disciplinary situation? How could Jim have prevented this confrontation?

Reading Drill. Mary, a second-year teacher, teaches first grade in a neighborhood school in an affluent section of town. Earlier in the year, she divided the class into five equal-sized reading groups. By May, the top reading group, the Cardinals, is discussing stories they read on their own and are tape recording their own stories and listening to stories recorded by other students in their group. Mary worked hard with the lowest group, the Cubs, because she wanted them to make progress. She spent a little more time with the Cubs each day than the other groups and she carefully examined their oral reading and emphasized correct pronunciation and reading expression. She discourages word substitution because she wants students to learn to pay attention to detail—to be careful readers. How many of these differences in teacher behavior do you believe to be appropriate and necessary? Should a teacher teach the low group the same way he or she teaches the high group? Defend your answer.

Chapter 18

From the Humanistic Perspective

OBJECTIVES

When you have mastered the material in this chapter you will be able to

1. Contrast the goals for learning and motivation of humanistic teachers, psychologists, and educators with those who hold more cognitive positions
2. List and explain the parental and teacher behaviors associated with high self-esteem and affective growth
3. Discuss the affective taxonomy and the three dimensions of affect as ways to integrate affective goals into the curriculum
4. Discuss the relationships of class scheduling, structure, and nonacademic potential to the enhancement of students' personal development
5. Define individualized and open education and the effect of these innovations on cognitive and affective measures of student performance
6. Define prosocial behavior and tell how teachers can promote it through cooperative learning activities
7. Discuss extant research on cooperative and affective programs
8. Discuss the three important characteristics of humanistic teachers and the value decisions involved in teaching for humanistic goals

Psychologists in the humanist tradition, similar to cognitive psychologists, emphasize the importance of perception and awareness as major forces that determine human behavior. However, humanistic psychologists are interested in the impact of schooling on emotional and affective development of students as well as on their cognitive growth. In brief, humanists are somewhat more interested in affect, or how people feel about their perceptions, whereas cognitive psychologists are somewhat more interested in how individuals conceptualize, or think about, an event.

Humanists Have Different Perspectives

Many humanists support the view that people need to be sensitive to their personal growth and interests. It would be misleading to suggest that humanists represent a single viewpoint. Combs et al. (1974) summarizes one humanistic perspective in the following statement:

> To understand humans . . . it is necessary to understand the behaver's perceptual world, how things seem from his point of view. This calls for a different understanding of what the "facts" are that we need in order to deal with human behavior; it is not the external facts that are important in understanding behavior, but the meaning of the facts to the behaver. (p. 15)

Self-perceptions and potential

Obviously, the concern for an individual's feelings and self-perceptions is similar to the cognitive motivational point of view. However, humanists' interest in self-perceptions is not limited to improving attitudes toward school and achievement. Humanists emphasize the importance of understanding a student's perceptual world in order to help the individual fulfill his or her basic potential (Rogers, 1983). The following quote captures some of the spirit of becoming "more human."

> If I had my life to live over, I'd try to make more mistakes next time. I would relax, I would limber up, I would be crazier than I've been on this trip, I know very few things I'd take seriously any more. I'd certainly be less hygenic. I would take more chances, I would take more trips, I would scale more mountains, I would swim more rivers, and I would watch more sunsets. I would eat more ice cream and fewer beans. I would have more actual troubles and fewer imaginary ones. You see . . . I was one of these people who lives prophylactically and sensibly and sanely, hour after hour and day after day. Oh, I've had my moments and if I had it to do all over again, I'd have many more of them. In fact, I'd try not to have anything else, just moments, one after another instead of living so many years ahead of my day. I've been one of these people who never went anywhere without a thermometer, a hot water bottle, a gargle, a raincoat, and a parachute. If I had it to do all over again, I'd travel lighter, much lighter than I have. I would start barefoot earlier in the spring, and I'd stay that way later in the fall. And I would ride more merry-go-rounds, and catch more gold rings, and greet more people, and pick more flowers, and dance more often. If I had it to do all over again—But you see, I don't.

Although the concern for developing human potential is present in the writing of all humanists, the importance attached to particular outcomes varies widely. Some argue that humanistic approaches enhance cognitive performance and mastery of school subjects. Other humanists state that they do not know if humanistic teaching improves general school performance. Yet others state that they do not care if humanistic teaching relates to general school performance because personal development is an important objective of schooling per se.

The Problem of Schooling from a Humanistic Perspective

Individual humanists, of course, emphasize different aspects of schooling as particularly problematic from their point of view. However, in the following list, Rogers (1983) describes many of the issues of schooling that generally bother humanists. He claims that too many students have learned the following:

1. There is no place for restless energy in class.
2. One conforms or suffers unpleasant consequences.
3. Submission to rules is expected.
4. Making a mistake is bad.
5. Punishment for a mistake is humiliating.
6. Spontaneous interest does not belong in school.
7. Teacher and disciplinarian are synonymous.
8. School on the whole is unpleasant.
9. Most textbooks are boring.
10. It is not safe to differ with the teacher.
11. There are many ways to get by without studying.
12. It is okay to cheat.
13. Daydreams and fantasy can make the day pass more quickly.
14. Studying hard to get good grades is behavior frowned upon by one's peers.
15. Most of the learning relevant to life occurs outside of school.
16. Original ideas have no place in school.
17. Exams and grades are the most important aspects of education.
18. Most teachers are, at least in class, impersonal and boring.

This list provides a viewpoint that can be used for thinking about school reform. However, it should be clearly noted that climate conditions vary from school to school. Some schools are much more attractive from both an affective and cognitive viewpoint than are other schools (see Purkey & Smith, 1985). Although the list presented above forcefully presents a view, it is a view that does not represent all schools or classrooms.

There is, however, overall agreement on the general motivational process that underlies meaningful growth. Carl Rogers has been one of the most prolific and widely read proponents of humanistic education. Rogers (1969, 1983) has presented ten humanistic learning principles:

Humanistic learning principles

1. Human beings have a natural potentiality for learning.

2. Significant learning takes place when students perceive the subject matter as relevant to their own purposes.
3. Learning that involves a change in self-organization—in the perception of oneself—is threatening and tends to be resisted.
4. Those learnings that are threatening to the self are more easily perceived and assimilated when external threats are at a minimum.
5. When threat to the self is low, experience can be perceived in differentiated fashion and learning can proceed.
6. Much significant learning is acquired through doing.
7. Learning is facilitated when the student participates responsibly in the learning process.
8. Self-initiated learning that involves the whole person of the learner—feelings as well as intellect—is the most lasting and pervasive.
9. Independence, creativity, and self-reliance are all facilitated when self-criticism and self-evaluation are basic and evaluation by others is of secondary importance.
10. The most socially useful learning in the modern world is the learning of the process of learning, a continuing openness to experience and incorporation into oneself of the process of change.

The meaning of most of these principles of learning appears obvious at first glance. However, applying the principles in the classroom when attempting to motivate students is most difficult. For example, what are the best ways to encourage constructive self-criticism, and are certain types of "learnings" impossible or impractical to learn by doing? In any event, these ten principles suggest that students are best motivated on an intrinsic basis and that much individualization of the curriculum is needed if basic needs are to be fulfilled.

Again, it should be emphasized that a teacher can generally accept the ten principles and still be very interested, or only moderately interested, in subject matter achievement. How teachers behave and structure classroom learning will vary depending on their beliefs about what is important in teaching as well as their attitudes about how to motivate students. The classroom strategies of teachers who want primarily to promote cognitive gain will differ from those of teachers who are more concerned about students learning about themselves and others. In this chapter a variety of ways for integrating humanistic perspectives into the curriculum will be explored.

Affective and Cognitive Development

It appears that the process of affective development—how we feel about ourselves, about others, and about specific subject matter—is similar to cognitive development. The critical difference is the content that is emphasized. If one wants students to develop more differentiated views toward self and others at school, then content must be presented to allow students to feel and think about self and others in more complex and systematic ways. Initially we learn about ourselves through concrete experiences and feedback from others. Gradually we form a concept of who we are, what we can and cannot do, and ultimately, about our general worth. The initial self-view is highly dependent on the quality of early life experiences.

Antecedents of Affect

Parent behaviors

Several researchers who studied the home conditions that produce children who feel good about themselves and others have reached highly similar conclusions. The following parent behaviors appear important: (1) completely accepting the child as a person, although not all of the child's behavior; (2) setting clear standards and expectations for the child; and (3) offering respect and giving latitude for child initiative within defined limits (see, e.g., Coopersmith, 1967; White & Watts, 1973).

A reasonable hypothesis, at least for the preschool and early elementary school years, is that behaviors similar to those observed in parents of high self-esteem children will be most conducive to growth in school. Individualization that allows for structured progress and warm teacher-child relationships appear to be prerequisites for both affective and cognitive growth.

In addition, affective growth, like cognitive growth, depends on a sensible match between an individual's ability and new learning tasks that are assigned. Few teachers would assign a story demanding seventh-grade reading ability to a child reading at the second-grade level. However, teachers often provide students with too much or too little structure in learning assignments.

Interchangeable teacher comment

An example of a variable that appears central to both positive self-concept development and achievement is the interchangeable teacher comment (see Aspy, 1973; Rogers, 1983). An interchangeable teacher comment is a statement following a student's expression of affect that lets the student know that he or she has been heard. Hearing what students have to say and expressing interest is no doubt a direct way of telling them that they are accepted, and acceptance by others appears to be a fundamental prerequisite to self-acceptance. Furthermore, interchangeable teacher comments have been found to have favorable effects on student achievement. There is indirect evidence that such teacher behavior may be related to student attitudes as well. Students in experimental settings, deCharms (1984) found, had more positive attitudes toward teachers who incorporated student suggestions.

More is known about how teachers can assist students' cognitive growth than about how they can facilitate affective development. However, there is much indirect evidence (e.g., from studies of parent-child interaction) that teachers can make a difference in affective development. Some of the most promising programs for influencing the affective development of students are presented later in the chapter.

A Taxonomy for Affective Education

Affect refers to how we feel about something. Figure 18.1, which presents a taxonomy for classifying affective goals, was developed by Krathwohl, Bloom, and Masia (1964). Ringness (1975) suggests that the taxonomy might help teachers clarify their understanding of how they can teach in a way that promotes students' affective development. Ringness notes that if a teacher were conducting a unit on pollution, for example, it would be useful to realize that when students become aware of pollution they are not necessarily willing to take action. However, the teacher's goals may be only to make students more willing to listen, and to read about the topic.

Student response

Higher levels of the taxonomy suggest that students can develop more commitment to a topic or belief. Some teachers are primarily interested in having students respond to a topic. Initially students may only verbalize the teacher's position (acquiescence). In time students may become willing to state and defend their positions publicly. At higher levels of the taxonomy (the third level) students begin to internalize their own beliefs (e.g., a student may accept the need to manage the environment). In certain areas the opinions of others do not control the behavior of a student who has reached the third level of affective integration. Ringness (1975) notes that students subsequently may integrate their beliefs about the environment with other beliefs and might even generalize further by becoming involved in a related concern or by voluntarily devoting time to environmental issues.

Key questions concern the extent to which classroom experiences should help students to build a cohesive value structure, what topics should be subjected to such value examination, and how much curriculum time should be utilized in this way. Relatively little curriculum time is needed to accomplish receiving or responding goals; considerably more time may be necessary to reach higher levels of the taxonomy.

Krathwohl et al.'s model provides a useful conceptual reference that suggests how various levels of student affect might be associated with curriculum content. The taxonomy also includes many of the principles of Rogers (1983) that were noted earlier in the chapter, such as helping students to generate more internal beliefs.

Limitations of the taxonomy

Patterson (1973) has criticized this affective taxonomy because, from his perspective, it deals with only a small part of personal or emotional development. He writes:

> Affective education is concerned with the development of self-awareness. This development requires first that the individual be permitted and be able to express and disclose himself, so that he can see or perceive himself as he is. This requires that he feel free to be himself, to be open and honest, in his expression of himself. Second, the individual must be able to explore, look at, and evaluate himself. Part of this process includes feedback from others on how he is perceived by them.

Patterson is probably correct in stating that the taxonomy is limited in terms of dealing with some of the more dynamic aspects of personal development and insight that might be pursued in affective or humanistic

Figure 18.1 The Range of Meaning Typical of Commonly Used Affective Terms Measured Against the *Taxonomy* Continuum

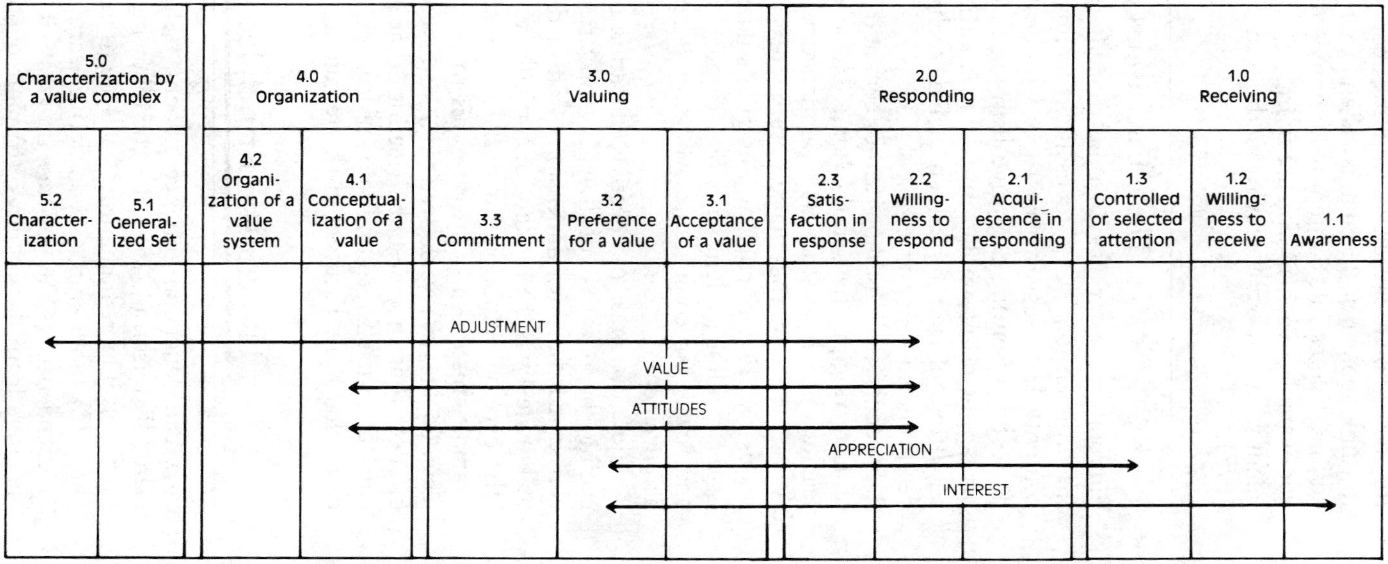

5.0 Characterization by a value complex		4.0 Organization		3.0 Valuing			2.0 Responding			1.0 Receiving		
5.2 Characterization	5.1 Generalized Set	4.2 Organization of a value system	4.1 Conceptualization of a value	3.3 Commitment	3.2 Preference for a value	3.1 Acceptance of a value	2.3 Satisfaction in response	2.2 Willingness to respond	2.1 Acquiescence in responding	1.3 Controlled or selected attention	1.2 Willingness to receive	1.1 Awareness

ADJUSTMENT

VALUE

ATTITUDES

APPRECIATION

INTEREST

Source: D. Krathwohl, B. Bloom, and B. Masia. *Taxonomy of Education Objectives: Book 2 Affective Domain*, p. 37. Copyright © 1964 Longman Inc.

education. Still, we think that the taxonomy provides useful information that can stimulate teachers' thinking about affect. It provides specific ways to think about instructional goals and thus allows teachers to select methods, procedures, and content to help students to achieve affective outcomes. For example, teachers who are trying to help students to internalize beliefs might wish to use role-playing methods in the classroom (see Weil & Joyce, 1978).

Three Dimensions of Affect

Curriculum content

Simpson and Gray (1976) note that affect in humanistic education has three dimensions. One focus is on feelings that grow out of curriculum content. They suggest that those who deal with this dimension of affect do so by presenting cognitive learning in an exciting and personal way, perhaps by using simulation games. Another dimension concerns the preconditions of learning, which include feelings of competence that help to determine student success.

Enhancing self-esteem

Students' feelings about self-esteem and self-adequacy are influenced by child-rearing practices in the home. However, as Simpson and Gray argue, teachers can help students to enhance self-esteem in a variety of ways. Among the ways they suggest are: increasing teacher awareness of unconscious rejection of students; helping students to cope with interpersonal issues; building student autonomy through the assignment of responsibility; and rewarding competence wherever it appears, not just subject matter achievement.

Making feelings the content of curriculum

These two areas of affective education have been discussed in the preceding chapters that dealt with motivation. However, we have not yet considered the third dimension of affect discussed by Simpson and Gray: making feelings the content of curricula; to use the words of these authors, "the personal, emotional material that a student brings to class from, for example, his dreams, his reactions to people or situations, knowledge of fears, doubts, or joys derived from introspection" (p. 2). The three aspects of affect that they describe (feelings that grow out of the content of the curriculum itself, preconditions of learning, and feelings as the content of curriculum) are discussed in the remainder of this chapter.

Humanistic Principles in Application

How can education enhance students' self-insight and personal development? Patterson (1973) notes the following changes that need to be made in schools if more humanistic goals are to be pursued: (1) more open scheduling; (2) more emphasis on active learning; (3) more stress on student independence; (4) more stress on creativity; (5) more opportunity for cooperative learning activities; (6) more opportunity for self-evaluation; and (7) greater emphasis on personal integrity, nonacademic potential, and an intrinsic curriculum.

Open Scheduling

Too often classroom learning is bounded by arbitrary time limits. Humanists would like to see more open schedules that relate better to the needs of students. The possibilities for increased flexibility are limitless. For example, increasing numbers of high school students are assuming part-time jobs. The school could adapt to these students' needs by providing more flexible class schedules or course credit for work experiences. However, some studies suggest that many high school students work primarily to support their cars and recreational activities. Hence, the call here is for flexibility but a firm willingness to encourage student academic growth . . . not to submerge educational values with youth culture values.

In presenting basic subject matter, it is easy to identify ways in which a routine time schedule interferes with learning. For example, to illustrate certain chemical reactions it would be useful to have students for a two- or three-hour block of time. Why couldn't the schedule be modified so that students could occasionally spend extended time periods in particular subjects when the nature of the learning experience suggests that more time is desirable?

"Beating the system" behavior

Two of Patterson's terms need explanation. He contrasts personal integrity with "beating the system" behavior. He notes that school experiences often encourage students to be passive recipients of knowledge. Students learn to do whatever is necessary in order to get good grades, even if that includes feigning attention or even cheating. Patterson writes: "The school system stifles self-expression, causing feelings of resentment, alienation, and self-hate, and leads to conforming behavior. Clearly, such effects are inconsistent with self-actualizing behavior or responsible citizenship" (p. 90). Teachers who encourage students to state their own learning objectives, to evaluate their own learning, and to challenge the evidence on which texts or the teachers themselves base their conclusions will help students respond openly and effectively.

Schools may inadvertently reinforce the tendency of some students to "beat the system" by stressing only academic competence. Students may be encouraged to do whatever they can to obtain school rewards for academic achievement, including misrepresenting their own views, and to ignore any nonacademic talents they might possess. If schools placed more emphasis on recognizing nonacademic potential there would be fewer inappropriate academic pressures on many students because more students would be seen as talented (Marshall & Weinstein, 1984).

Nonacademic potential

Student Independence

How far should teachers go in reducing structure or letting students set goals? deCharms (1972, 1984) described two types of motivational states. "Origin" refers to the condition in which one works for one's own goals; "pawns," in contrast, work for someone else. deCharms (1972) notes that he modified some of his early thoughts about how to help students develop self-initiated behavior intended to make a change in the environment after working with students. He writes:

> A romantic view of an Origin as a free spirit untrammeled by pressure from others and society is popular with many college students in the United States. In this view, the person bears no responsibility to established authorities. We have become more and more skeptical of such a view. . . . Not to push people around is a beginning in treating people as Origins, but we soon found that letting them do anything they wanted to do was *not* treating them as Origins either. (p. 83)

In conducting research, deCharms has seen the necessity for teachers to impose certain limits and to encourage students to assume responsibility within manageable limits. Teachers who wish to aid students in being more like Origins fulfill their role by helping students to set realistic goals, become aware of strengths and weaknesses, make concrete plans for reaching goals, and examine continuously their efforts to see if they are making progress toward personal goals (see also the discussion of deCharms in Chapter 15).

Individualized and Open Education

Traditionally, the self-contained classroom was the basic organizational plan of elementary schools. Students received the same instruction at the same time, despite the fact that their abilities and interests for particular school tasks varied widely. Although many institutions have departed from the self-contained plan, it is still frequently used in elementary schools and is dominant in secondary schools.

In the past few years schools have experimented with individualized education, especially in elementary schools and college instruction, and open education, especially in elementary schools. This is an attempt to make school learning more suited to the individual needs of students by allowing students to proceed through the curriculum at their own pace, to choose some of their learning tasks, and so on. However, it is obvious that if teachers allow students more time to work at their own rate and on topics of unique interest, there is less opportunity for cooperative learning with other students. Individualized education has been criticized on other grounds as well. Lipson (1974) notes that whole-class instruction and performance in front of a large group have some distinct motivational advantages. He suggests that large-group work may enhance the perceived importance of the learning task.

Suiting learning to individual needs

In terms of a more immediate and direct goal—helping students to master subject matter—individualized education is useful for many types of students. But data indicating that individualization leads to more favorable affective responses are contradictory, and there is no evidence for prosocial gains. Peterson (1979) provides a good review of much of the research on open and individualized classrooms, and she reports that individualized programs foster some, but not all, affective goals.

Evaluation problems

Part of the problem in evaluating individualized and open education is that the terms mean different things to different people. Hence, one in-

The value of open classrooms is still open to debate.

dividualized program might appear to have more favorable effects on affect than do other individualized programs. Still, the affective gains in these programs are not that large, and they are not consistently superior to the affective responses of students in self-contained classrooms.

Open classrooms

The effects of open classrooms on student affect are similar to those found in comparisons of individualized and self-contained classrooms. Although the meaning of open education depends on how it is put into practice at a particular school, it is clear that those interested in open education have considerable interest in improving certain affective states. There are many comparisons of open and traditional classrooms in the research literature. For example, Wright (1975) matched fifth-grade students from traditional and open classes on variables like SES, ability, and past achievement, and compared students' cognitive and affective outcomes. He found that, more than two years after they had been in the school program, students' affective outcomes were the same in open and traditional classrooms; however, students in traditional classrooms scored higher on cognitive measures.

Student anxiety

One variable that tends to be negatively influenced by open education is student anxiety. Several studies comparing student responses in open and more traditional classrooms indicate that students in open classrooms report higher levels of anxiety. A negative interpretation of this finding is that students are given too little structure and find the number and types of decisions they have to make unmanageable. When open education programs fail, it may be because they have not fully responded to all of the ten principles that Rogers sees as critical determinants of learning. Students may be threatened by too many choices, especially if they have not been taught how to engage in self-evaluation. This is not intended as a general criticism against all open education programs, because some of them have worked well. But many such programs have attempted to produce affective changes too quickly and have not provided the structure necessary to support cognitive as well as affective growth. As Friedlander (1975) puts it:

> It is a gross oversight of available knowledge in psychology to assume that looser structure in the environment of the classroom is of some benefit for all children, just because it is a great benefit for some children. It is predictable that children who have a low tolerance for ambiguity and uncertainty would find an open classroom that operates very successfully for some children extremely threatening and anxiety provoking. (p. 467)

Noncognitive gains

Some reviewers have reached conclusions more optimistic than ours about the effects of open classrooms (e.g., Horwitz, 1979). However, it should be clear that noncognitive gains (self-concept, creativity, and so on) have not been impressive in any educational setting. Even programs designed explicitly to improve noncognitive performance have found it difficult to produce consistent and large gains. For example, Mansfield, Busse, and Krepelka (1978) note that the results of creativity training programs are inconsistent in terms of both performance and attitudes, although these programs may be justified on the grounds that they are enjoyable activities.

Quality versus form

It also must be emphasized that the quality with which an organizational form is implemented is more important than the form itself. For example, more students may be doing different tasks in an "individualized" classroom than in most traditional classrooms, but this is an illusory gain if individual students do not have appropriate tasks to perform. Marshall and Weinstein (1984) report that there is considerable variation within the categories of open and traditional classes in how classes actually operate. Despite the fact that open classrooms can define more areas as important and thus potentially allow more students to be successful in different areas, competition and traditional areas of mastery still dominate in some open classrooms. However, in theory there are many reasons why more open and individualized classrooms could be helpful in facilitating achievement and cognitive gains. In practice, gains are not automatic and there can be too little structure or the wrong kind of structure as well as too much.

As we have seen, studies on "open" and traditional classrooms yield different findings. In large measure this is because open classrooms vary considerably as do traditional classrooms. In a careful, comprehensive study of over 150 classrooms, Giaconia and Hedges (1982) concluded that open classrooms made no difference in achievement and were, on average, slightly inferior to achievement gains in more traditional classrooms. However, "open" education was associated with more creativity and independence. As Gage (1985) notes, open education, when done appropriately, can enhance some important affective outcomes without seriously depressing achievement scores.

Task and Social Relationships

Activity structures

Bossert (1977), in a study of four elementary school classrooms, found that the type of activity structure influenced how the classroom would be managed by the teacher. Three activity structures were used frequently: recitation (teacher-led discussion), class tasks (task assigned to the entire class), and multi-tasks (e.g., independent or small group work). He found that the percent of time that teachers used each of these activity structures varied widely. Furthermore, the amount of free time that teachers allowed students varied from 3.6 to 17.2 percent.

Bossert was impressed by the fact that lesson formats tended to force teachers to manage lessons in particular ways. In the recitation format, all participants are highly visible and all interactions are public. Hence, teachers must rely more on commands than on personal influence in controlling students. In other formats, teachers could use more private control techniques.

Classroom instruction organization and pupil achievement

Bossert notes that there are two possible effects of classroom instruction organization on pupil achievement. First, pupil achievement may be influenced by the effect task organization has on the frequency of individualized teacher contacts with students. Because one of the most important aspects of a teacher's skill is the ability to handle individual differences in students' responses to instruction, a teacher must be able to allocate time for individual assistance when pupils need specific help. Bossert argues that teachers who use multi-task activities are better able to provide individual assistance when necessary. This activity structure frees the teacher from constant control over instructional activities and allows him or her to give more assistance to pupils who need help. In contrast, recitation gives a teacher fewer opportunities to provide individual assistance, and when assistance is given, high-achieving students tend to receive a disproportionately high share of teacher contact. Thus, the task organization of a classroom may limit a teacher's ability to supply special individual assistance, at least to some pupils.

Teacher authority

Bossert contends that a second way in which task organization may influence pupil achievement is in its effect on teacher authority. Teachers who rely primarily on the exercise of formal authority are less likely to be able to develop affective bonds that promote willing cooperation, an interest in learning, and achievement among pupils. Affective relationships are diminished in the recitation format because this format places the teacher in full, public control over the activity. When a given teacher is in charge of supervising the activity, it is difficult for the teacher to become involved in the activity as a participant with small groups of students. Multi-task structures, then, may allow teachers more frequent individual contacts with students as well as more opportunity to share and discuss material with students in a more cooperative way.

Bossert contends that socialization is basically a process of social interaction and that the nature of recurring task activity shapes the way in which students view interpersonal relationships, especially with authority figures. If teachers are always in charge, it is less likely that students will have the opportunity to develop self-regulation and/or the ability to work socially with other students.

Classroom Environment

Marshall and Weinstein (1984) provide a complex model specifying how classroom environment variables may reflect different teacher performance expectations that in turn influence students' own expectations and performance. Two of these general variables are discussed here: locus of responsibility for learning and evaluation, and motivational variables.

Responsibility and Choice. Teachers control the locus of responsibility for learning and evaluation in the classroom, and they can share that responsibility to varying degrees with individual students. Marshall and Weinstein argue that the amount of responsibility students have may affect their susceptibility to teachers' expectations. Research has shown that students perceive that teachers offer more choices to high achievers than to low achievers and give more directions to low achievers. It may be that when teachers allow high-achieving students to plan their own goals and projects, the goals that these students select and the procedures they follow may show more variety and thus diminish the comparability of the products that they are working on (Rosenholtz & Rosenholtz, 1981). It appears that in some classrooms high achievers benefit from having more choices. First, their work is less open to comparison with others in their group. Second, the freedom to pursue to some extent their own learning activities may motivate high achievers to work harder than they would if they had to follow a simple set of directions, as low-achieving students must often do.

Responsibility and Evaluation. Shared responsibility for evaluation is not a part of many classrooms. Teachers generally do most of the evaluation, and when students do have the opportunity to check answers it is usually against an answer sheet that the teacher has prepared. When the teacher is the evaluator, students are dependent on the teacher for judgments about their ability, and their performance is more susceptible to teacher expectations. In contrast, when the teacher encourages students to evaluate their own performance and to develop their own standards and criteria, evaluation may be more private and may be based on criteria that are more realistic and understandable to students. Thus, students may be less vulnerable to external evaluation pressures. For example, being called on as frequently as other students to make public responses may be less important in a classroom in which students spend considerable time setting their own learning goals and engaging in self-evaluation. Clearly, the locus of responsibility for learning and evaluation will mediate grouping effects and the individual response opportunities that students receive.

Self-Evaluation. It seems ironic to us that in some sixth-grade classrooms there are fewer opportunities for learners to make choices and to evaluate their own work than in most first-grade classrooms. We suspect that if teachers placed more emphasis on helping learners to develop the capacity for self-direction and self-evaluation, many of students' invidious comparisons of their work to the work of others would disappear.

We believe that one important outcome of schooling should be to help students to develop greater capacity for self-direction and independent learning. Though students should be able to do as their teachers request and feel some pride when they accomplish external goals, in time they should learn to determine when and how well they have completed a task without external feedback from the teacher or other sources. Further, we believe that students must also learn to determine task direction, to engage in task evaluation, and to integrate self- and other-directed work.

As part of affective education, students can interview each other concerning a controversial issue.

Affective Curricula

There are many ways to build affective education into the curriculum. Issues of modern science and medicine could be topics for affective instruction. Virtually any social study issue contains subject matter that can be approached from an affective viewpoint as well as with a cognitive or conceptual emphasis. Material about American explorers might touch on what they thought about when exploring new frontiers as well as the details of their achievements. Students could be encouraged to relate the feelings identified to their own experiences.

Confluent education

Brown (1971) uses the term "confluent education" to reflect the integration of affect into subject matter. He suggests numerous concrete exercises for doing this when teaching English and social studies. However, there is no reason for affect to be limited to reactions to text material. For example, students could be requested to keep a personal log in order to note how they feel about topics such as life in school or a presidential campaign. Similarly, they could be encouraged to interview other students about their feelings, or could be given the opportunity to interview productive elderly people or persons actively involved in societal issues.

As we noted previously, some humanists urge that affect be studied directly, not just in relation to traditional school topics. It is beyond the scope of this chapter to review such curricula in detail (for a good review of some available programs, see Simpson & Gray, 1976); however, we provide a few examples of how affect can become a part of the curriculum.

Magic Circle exercise

As an example of an exercise that would work well in elementary schools, Simpson and Gray cite the Magic Circle (based on the Human Development Program developed by Harold Bessell and Uvaldo Palomares). Students have a chance to give and receive information with other students. To increase awareness students can discuss topics such as: something I like about you; something I like about myself; or if I could do anything I wanted it would be ________.

"Something I like about you" exercise

The "something I like about you" exercise allows students to hear positive comments about themselves from other students. They also have a chance to experience the feeling of someone's saying something nice about them, and the chance to verbalize that feeling. Through such activities students can progressively consider the events that keep them from doing as they wish, and look at their behavior as it affects other people.

Trumpet March exercise

At the secondary level, one activity Simpson anad Gray describe is the Trumpet March: Diagram and Details (developed at the Center for Humanistic Education at the University of Massachusetts). In this activity students have a chance to gather and evaluate data about their own behavior and that of others. Table 18.1 illustrates some of the questions on which students are asked to reflect.

Values-clarification activities

Another major way in which affect has become part of the school curriculum in some classrooms is through values-clarification activities. Simon, Howe, and Kirschenbaum (1972) argue that many persons do not clearly understand their values. To facilitate self-insight, these authors prepared 79 values-clarification activities. One activity asks the participants to list 10 to 15 things that provide them pleasure or joy. Then they are asked to write after each item the date that they last experienced it. Participants are then asked to place a dollar sign by each item that costs money, a P by those items that require planning, an S by those items done with someone else, and an A by those things done alone. Finally, they are asked to study the list and to contemplate what it reflects about their values.

Some teachers might be interested in helping students to understand the needs and interests of others who differ from themselves in important ways. For example, students who learn about the varied interests of aged citizens may not only gain more understanding and empathy toward the aged, but may also become increasingly aware of the naturalness of aging in the human growth process.

Children's attitudes toward the elderly

Jantz, Seefeldt, Galper, and Serock (1976), at the Center on Aging at the University of Maryland, have produced a curriculum guide on children's attitudes toward the elderly. Included in their material are films and books to which children might react, as well as concrete experiences to share with elderly individuals. This curriculum offers children accurate information about the elderly, a chance to see the behaviors of different elderly people in a variety of roles, and the opportunity to develop positive feelings about growing old.

Women's role in society

There are many curriculum materials that help to describe the nature and importance of women's roles in society. Teachers could use such information profitably in discussions about discrimination and related issues. One particularly good set of materials is a series of pamphlets entitled, *Cracking the Glass Slipper: PEER's Guide to Ending Sex Bias in Your Schools.* PEER is a project of the NOW (National Organization for Women) Legal Defense and Education Fund and is supported by the Ford Foundation, the Carnegie Foundation, and the Rockefeller Family Fund. Its goals are to monitor enforcement progress under federal law forbidding sex discrimination in education, and to assist groups working for sexual equality in education in their local schools.

Aesthetic education

Yet another way in which more affective material might be taught to students is through aesthetic education. In the past few years some have argued that students should become sensitive to the aesthetic aspects of

Table 18.1 Examples of Questions Associated with the Trumpet March

Step One: Experience Confrontations
I interact with a situation that generates data; and

Step Two: Inventory Responses
How did I respond? What was unique? What common?

a. What did you just do? Describe your behavior.
b. What were you aware of?
c. At what points did you feel comfortable or uncomfortable?
d. At point X, how did you think or feel?
e. Where in your body did you feel something?
f. What sentences did you say to yourself? Were these *should, can't,* or *won't* sentences?

Step Three: Recognize Patterns
What is typical of me?

a. Did you do anything that surprised you?
b. Did you do anything different from what you usually do?
c. How do you usually respond in similar situations? Can you think of a similar situation where you've responded the same?
d. How often have you thought, felt, or acted like this? In what circumstances?

Step Four: Own Patterns
What function does this pattern serve for me?

a. How does it serve you?
b. How does your pattern make you feel good?
c. What does it protect you from?
d. What kinds of freedom does it give you?

Step Five: Consider Consequences
What does happen or could happen in my life because of this pattern?

a. What price do you have to pay?
b. How much does it cost you?

Step Six: Allow Alternatives
Will I allow myself any additional patterns of response?

a. What are the first steps you could take to change?
b. What are the options you have?
c. Using each alternative, go through the trumpet again.

Step Seven: Choose

Source: From Simpson and Grey, *Humanistic Education: and Interprepation.* Copyright © 1976 by The Ford Foundation. Reprinted with permisson from Ballinger Publishing Company.

experience (see, e.g., *Coming to Our Senses: The Significance of the Arts for American Education*). The interest here is not necessarily in improving students' ability to perform, but in making them more aware of aesthetic issues. How does one react to art, music, and objects of beauty? How does one evaluate a theatrical performance? By direct involvement and teaching, aesthetic education programs help students to develop and understand criteria for responding to aesthetic experiences. In short, the goal of such training is to make students better consumers of such experiences.

Evaluation of Affective Programs

As Baskin and Hess (1980) note, deliberate efforts to alter the emotional and social behavior of students are a part of the curricula of many schools. Though according to these authors there has been little serious evaluation of the programs, they summarize extant information. They used three criteria to select program evaluations for their analysis. Programs were included if they used affective curricula to achieve affective goals, if the curriculum included a specific time during the school day for specific affective activities, and if acceptable evaluation data were available.

The programs accepted for inclusion by Baskin anad Hess (1980) were: (1) A Cognitive Approach to Solving Real Life Problems; (2) Developing Understanding of Self and Others (DUSO); (3) Human Development Program (HDP); (4) interpersonal skills training project; (5) AWARE; (6) Schools Without Failure (SWF); and (7) Teacher Effectiveness Training (T.E.T.).

Baskin and Hess note that these affective programs differ in what topics they emphasize. They classify these seven programs in three areas: internal-emotional, cognitive, and overt-behavioral. The internal-emotional dimension includes feelings, emotions, self-perceptions, and attitudes toward school. The cognitive dimension refers to pupils' understanding of principles of social causation and their ability to generate alternative solutions to hypothetical social situations. The behavioral dimension involves observable interpersonal behavior such as effective interactions with peers or adults. The goals are summarized in Table 18.2. Baskin and Hess indicate that effectiveness of programs varied with objectives. However, they suggest that these data, although incomplete in many respects, do show that affective programs can positively influence both cognitive outcomes and overt behavior. However, they call for more extensive evaluation of affective programs.

Others, too, have lamented the lack of research on affective programs. For example, Elardo and Elardo (1976) argue that it is important for schools to focus on outcomes other than cognitive ability. They argue that social and emotional development also occur as part of the learning process and it should be an important consideration in examining the success of schooling. In summarizing information about programs dealing with social development, they examined and critiqued four programs that have been implemented in many elementary schools: Ojemann's (1959) Causal Ap-

Focusing on outcomes other than cognitive ability

Table 18.2 Curriculum Objectives of Seven Affective Education Programs

Goals	Affective Education Programs						
	CA[a]	DUSO	HDP	IST[b]	PA[c]	SWI	T.E.T.
Internal Emotional Area							
Raising student self esteem		X[d]	X	X	X	X	
Accepting self responsibility	X	X				X	
Encouraging positive attitudes toward school						X	
Developing a success identity						X	
Cognitive Area							
Understanding social causation	X		X		X		
Generating alternative solutions	X				X		
Generating alternative consequences	X				X		
Developing self knowledge	X	X	X	X[e]	X		
Gaining ability to talk about emotions	X	X	X		X		
Overt Behaviorial Area							
Developing better interpersonal relationships	X						
Developing respect for others				X[e]	X		X[e]
Increasing communication skills	X			X[e]			X[e]
Increasing interpersonal effectiveness	X	X	X	X[e]	X		X[e]
Decreasing discipline problems	X					X	X
Developing role taking skills					X		
Using "I messages"							X[e]
Using active listening							X[e]
Using "Method III" problem solving							X[e]
Increasing academic achievement		X		X			

[a] A Cognitive Approach to Solving Real Life Problems
[b] Interpersonal Skills Training
[c] Project AWARE
[d] An "X" indicates that the affective program states the mediating outcome as one of the objectives of the program. This objective was not necessarily assessed in the evaluations reviewed.
[e] These objectives apply to teachers rather than to students.

Source: Excerpted from E. Baskin and R. Hess. "Does affective education work: A review of seven programs. *Journal of School Psychology* 18 (1), 1980. Reprinted by permission of Human Sciences Press.

proach to Human Behavior; the Human Development Program; Reality Therapy/Schools Without Failure; and Developing Understanding of Self and Others (DUSO). They concluded that these four programs are the major attempts to humanize education during the early and middle childhood years, and that they provide examples of ways in which the traditional school curriculum can be expanded.

However, these programs were disappointing in several respects. Elardo and Elardo report that the program descriptions did not contain clear statements regarding the mechanisms by which human understanding develops. It is therefore difficult to determine on what basis the curriculum planners sequenced materials, and the four programs are not well integrated into current child development research and theory. Each program expressed much concern for developing self-esteem; however, there was little focus on students' relations with others. The authors argue the need to move beyond individualism, to look at the group and the classroom needs of students, and to consider prosocial behavior.

Hudgins (1979) argues that educators have long extolled the virtues of thrift, respect, and dependability. He further notes that in modern times there has been growing concern with students' development of positive self-concepts and increasing attempts to make classrooms more responsive to affective outcomes. Although affective educational programs are important, Hudgins notes that there are relatively few data to evaluate resultant affective gains.

TAD program

Hudgins presents data from a study he conducted to test the effects of the Toward Affective Development (TAD) program. He points out that there were no significant effects of this program on students' self-concepts or social adjustment. He notes that there is considerable anecdotal praise of such affective programs in the literature, but few data to support such advocacy. Furthermore, he states that the strong intuitive appeal of affective education for some people may cause them to support a program without further research on its effectiveness.

Noncognitive Outcomes of Cooperative Learning

Affective goals through cooperative learning

Many affective goals may be achieved without the use of affective curricula. For example, recently there has been considerable interest in allowing students to work together to learn cognitive, subject-matter material (e.g., mathematical story problems). Here affective topics are not taught directly or systematically, but students may "learn" them in the process of studying together and generally sharing information. In the 1970s many humanistic educators attempted to make major changes in the curriculum to achieve affective goals. Although many educators in the 1980s still advocate an affective curriculum, many now pursue affective goals indirectly through cooperative learning.

Though most roles adults assume involve cooperation, traditional classrooms actually discourage cooperative behaviors. Students are generally not allowed to help each other. Schools promote competition among students for grades and the idea that those who do not excel are not worthy and that students have responsibility only for themselves.

Encouraging cooperation

Slavin (1984) reviewed studies of instructional programs that encourage and reward students for cooperating. These programs in which students work in small groups to learn academic content are called Cooperative Learning. The positive effects on achievement of such programs as Student Teams-Achievement Divisions (Slavin, 1978), Teams-Games-Tournaments (DeVries & Slavin, 1978), and Jigsaw Teaching (Lucker, Rosenfield, Sikes, & Aronson, 1976) are well established. However, what has attracted most attention to these methods is their positive effects on such noncognitive outcomes as intergroup relations, self-esteem, and peer norms concerning achievement.

Though there are a variety of cooperative learning strategies, most have the following characteristics:

1. Students work in small teams (4 to 6 members) where membership remains stable for many weeks.
2. Students are encouraged to help other group members learn academic material or perform a group task.
3. Students receive rewards based on group performance.

In other respects, however, cooperative learning methods vary widely: whether the teacher assigns students to teams or students choose their own teams; whether or not the reward is explicit; how much individual students are accountable for their contributions; how much autonomy students are allowed within their teams; and the actual content studied.

Classroom Cooperative Learning Techniques

Most research on cooperative learning techniques concerns the three models mentioned above, as well as Group-Investigation (Sharan & Sharan, 1976). These programs have been extensively studied in classrooms and are comparatively easy to implement because books have been written describing important procedural details.

Teams-Games-Tournaments (TGT). In TGT, four- to five-member teams (students are assigned so as to maximize variability within teams of ability, sex, and race) prepare for a tournament. After a teacher presentation, teams complete worksheets, study together, and quiz one another on material to be covered in the tournament (competitive quiz), which is held once a week. Students represent their teams in academic games at three-person tournament tables, to which they are assigned according to past performance. Because students are always competing against peers of similar ability, the low achievers have just as much chance to earn points for their teams as the high achievers do. A newsletter publicizes successful teams and first-place scorers. Team membership is stable, but table assignments can change.

Student Teams-Achievement Divisions (STAD). The teams in this program are similar to those in TGT, except that it uses 15-minute quizzes instead of games and tournaments after students study. In early studies of STAD, scores of the highest six students (based on past performance) were compared, with the winner earning the most points for his or her group, the second place person fewer points, etc. In more recent studies an "improvement score" has been used.

Jigsaw Teaching. Jigsaw students are also assigned to small heterogeneous teams. Academic material is subdivided into as many sections as there are team members, and students study their sections with members of other teams who have the same sections. Next they go back to their groups and teach their sections to team members. Then, all team members are quizzed on the entire unit. Scores are recorded only as grades for individual students, however, and there is no team score. This method is thus high in task interdependence and low in reward interdependence. In a modification of Jigsaw, called Jigsaw II, quiz scores are used to form team scores.

Group Investigation. In this program students form their own teams and teams choose subtopics from a unit the whole class is studying. Then team members break their team's subtopic into individual tasks that must be completed to achieve their group goal. Each group then makes a presentation about its subtopic to the class. Rewards are not specified.

Research Studies: Noncognitive Outcomes

Cooperation. Several studies clearly show that cooperative experiences increase students' cooperative and altruistic behaviors more than competitive or individualistic experiences. For example, Kagan and Madsen (1971) found that students who had cooperative experiences allocated more rewards to peers than to themselves. Wheeler and Ryan (1973) found that cooperative classroom experiences positively affected students' attitudes toward cooperation. A study by Bridgeman (1977) showed that students who had used the Jigsaw technique could take the perspective of another person better than control students. Though these studies and others suggest that cooperative learning can promote behaviors that enable students to get along with others, Slavin points out that the effects may be due in part to social desirability; that is, to students' desire to do what they think is correct. Long-term assessments of attitude change are needed, as well as actual measures of cooperative behavior.

Mutual Concern. One of the most researched and well-supported findings is that cooperative learning increases students' liking of others (Johnson & Johnson, 1974; Slavin, 1977a). There is also considerable evidence for positive effects on mutual concern, but the findings are somewhat inconsistent (DeVries & Slavin, 1978; Slavin & Karweit, in press). In particular, some studies with younger students show no effects, in part because their attitudes are difficult to measure reliably and tend to be generally positive.

Race Relations. Research has shown that students in desegregated schools tend to segregate themselves into racial and ethnic groups. Studies of cooperative learning illustrate that this technique can improve race relations, though again, results are inconsistent. Three STAD studies that measured the number of cross-race (black-white) choices students made on a sociometric instrument yielded the strongest and most consistent effects (Slavin,

1977b, 1979; Slavin & Oickle, 1981). Slavin (1979) conducted a nine-month follow-up and found that even though experimental students had different teachers and classmates, they still named more friends of the other race than students in the control group. Three of four studies of TGT in desegregated schools also found positive effects on race relations (DeVries, Edwards, & Slavin, 1978). Effects were not as strong or consistent with the Jigsaw and Group-Investigation methods as with the other two programs. According to Slavin, this may be due to the fact that in the STAD and TGT programs, the scoring system gives each pupil an equal chance to contribute maximum points to the team. Thus, it is unlikely that any team member will be seen negatively by teammates; that is, as lowering the team score. Slavin advocates further research to study how much cross-race classroom friendships generalize to other school settings and to out-of-school settings, and the effects of cooperative learning on prejudice and on preventing interracial or interethnic conflict. Most research has investigated black-white relations; other races need to be studied as well.

Mainstreaming. Research has shown that when low-achieving students are mainstreamed into regular classrooms, they are not well accepted by other students. However, Ballard, Corman, Gottlieb, and Kaufman (1977) found that when average and mainstreamed pupils worked cooperatively on group projects, the average students accepted the learning-disabled pupils more than average students in control classes. Madden and Slavin (1980) found that STAD decreased the number of learning-disabled students rejected by normal-progress peers, but did not increase the number of learning-disabled students chosen as friends or workmates. In this same study, STAD significantly increased achievement and self-esteem for all students. Slavin advocates research that examines effects of cooperative learning on mainstreaming of physically handicapped and emotionally disturbed students in addition to the existing research on slow learners. Activities of regular and special education teachers also need to be coordinated.

Liking of School. The effects of cooperative learning on liking of school are also mixed. DeVries and Slavin (1978) measured satisfaction in eight studies and found positive effects in three. In many cases, however, the lack of significant effects occurred with elementary students, who generally express positive attitudes even prior to cooperative learning. This is also a problem in STAD research. Effects of Jigsaw on student liking of school are also mixed. According to Slavin, these inconsistent findings are likely due to how students' attitudes are measured. For example, Madden and Slavin (1980) found that measures of general satisfaction with school (such as TGT and STAD studies used) showed no effects after cooperative learning, but when students were asked specific questions about the cooperative learning method they used, the researchers obtained strong differences between experimental and control groups.

Self-Esteem. Jigsaw is the method that focuses most on improving self-esteem, since students have key information that makes them important to their groups. Two studies showed positive effects of this technique on self-esteem, but a third did not. TGT and STAD have also been shown to affect self-esteem, though results are inconsistent (DeVries, Lucasse, & Shackman, 1979; Madden & Slavin, 1980; Oickle, 1980). Effects are generally positive, but somewhat inconsistent, showing various changes in general, social, and academic self-esteem.

Pro-Academic Norms. Slavin (1977c) argues that cooperative learning strategies affect students' academic performance because they encourage students to be concerned about how much their peers are learning, since students must get their groupmates to learn if their group is to succeed. Studies generally support this relationship (Hulten & DeVries, 1976; Slavin, 1978; Madden & Slavin, 1980).

Locus of Control. Gonzales (1979), Johnson, Johnson, and Scott (1978), Slavin (1978), and Wheeler and Ryan (1973) all found significant positive effects of various cooperative learning strategies on locus of control, or how much students believe their outcomes depend on their efforts. Slavin believes these effects are due to the fact that cooperative learning involves very clear tasks that students must accomplish to obtain success. Also, cooperative learning may give students success experiences they have not had previously, and persons tend to attribute success to their own efforts and failure to other factors.

In summary, several cooperative learning methods have been shown to affect a variety of noncognitive outcomes in similar ways. According to Slavin (1984), what actually occurs in cooperative classrooms needs to be examined in future research. Long-term field study of how various outcomes occur is also necessary. That is, cooperative learning changes many classroom variables, and researchers need to identify which changes affect cognitive and noncognitive variables. Researchers must also expand and refine the classroom programs so that they can be implemented more thoroughly and more widely.

Prosocial Behavior

It is impossible to discuss the many noncognitive outcomes that various writers argue are the responsibility of the schools to foster. However, we do want to discuss one such variable in order to illustrate areas that some humanistic educators advocate as legitimate and important aspects of schooling. Many people who are concerned about the increasing need for dependence on others dictated by modern society and about what they see as moral deterioration argue that schools must encourage the development of prosocial behavior (i.e., becoming more considerate, helping, and altruistic toward others).

Mussen and Eisenberg-Berg (1977) define prosocial behavior as ". . . actions that are intended to aid or benefit another person or group of people without the actor's anticipation of external rewards. Such actions often entail some cost, self-sacrifice, or risk on the part of the actor" (pp. 3–4). Very little is known about personality characteristics or the nature of day-to-day experiences that make people more motivated to express generosity, sympathy, or help to others. Individuals who write about prosocial behavior often suggest that self-rewards—increased feelings of self-satisfaction that follow a helping act—or internalized needs or motives influence prosocial behavior, but there is little empirical evidence to support this contention (Mussen & Eisenberg-Berg, 1977).

Parents whose children exhibit prosocial behaviors generally assign manageable responsibility to children at an early age, encourage children to reflect upon their feelings and those of others, and explain the reasons behind rules of conduct. Teachers can reward prosocial behavior when it occurs and model prosocial behavior themselves directly in the classroom by, for example, behaving in kind ways toward teacher aides, student teachers, fellow teachers, and most importantly, toward students.

Degree of emphasis

Teachers must decide how much emphasis to place on prosocial learning. Should teachers merely reward cooperative behavior when it occurs, or should they structure classroom activities so that opportunities for prosocial action are increased? Teachers can choose to support prosocial behavior while presenting the traditional curriculum, or they can include prosocialization in the curriculum as a major goal. For example, students can be assigned to work together on a committee report in such a way that the report is the major goal of the activity and cooperation is an indirect benefit. Alternatively, the same activity can be structured so that prosocial behavior is the major goal and the report is the indirect benefit. Teachers can also explore prosocial topics directly.

Integrating prosocial principles into the classroom

A study by Aronson et al. (1975), shows how prosocial principles can be integrated into the classroom, with cooperation as a major goal. In a project concerned with eliminating prejudice toward minorities, these investigators had teachers make use of learning teams in a way that not only demanded general cooperation among team members, but that forced students to listen to each team member. Each team member was given a critical piece of information needed by fellow members to write a biographical story. Hence, it was important that students listen to each group member because this was the only way they could get the information. Although these investigators found that general views toward students of other races were not altered, students' attitudes toward minority individuals who were fellow team members improved considerably. Presumably, more time and additional techniques might prove successful in altering more general prejudices. At any rate, the data suggest that prejudices held toward specific individuals can be improved by structured group work that demands shared participation. These activities take time, but are worth the effort. Readers who are interested in applying this technique should review a book devoted to it as well as the curriculum topics that could be used in the classroom (Aronson et al., 1978).

Aronson (1977) suggests that the strategy works because: (1) the technique makes all students more active; (2) it forces students to pay attention to others, especially to low achievers; (3) students feel gratitude for the help they receive; (4) students find it gratifying to see their positive effects on others; (5) the experience creates dissonance (Why would I put out efforts for others if I didn't like them?); and (6) the experience increases self-esteem (People are not paying attention to me; when I do better, people pay more attention to me).

When teachers make individual assignments or assign students to learning teams, they may also be influencing the type of affect that students are likely to experience, as well as students' attitudes toward other students and their learning rates. For example, if certain students learn frequently with others, they are more likely to experience anger as well as gratitude, depending on how well the learning goes, than when they work on individual assignments. (For more discussion on the role of student affect in learning, see Graham, 1984.)

The Humanistic Teacher

Who is the humanistic teacher? The question is apt to provoke a wide range of responses. Any question about teacher effectiveness is difficult to answer. Patterson (1973) cites three important dimensions that are commonly mentioned by other writers who attempt to define the humanistic teacher. He notes that humanistic teachers are genuine. They do not fear the students they teach nor hide behind a facade. They are willing to share their views openly. Patterson writes: "He doesn't feel one thing and say another. He isn't likely to be able to conceal his real feelings completely or consistently, but in his expression of his feelings he recognizes and accepts them as *his* feelings. He does not project blame for his feelings and reactions onto the students. He accepts responsibility for his own behavior. He says, 'I'm irritated,' 'I'm angry . . .'" (pp. 103–104).

Expression of feelings

Patterson does not condone the frequent expression of anger or other personal feelings that might harm students, but he does note that teachers who are aware of their feelings and those of their students can prevent disruption by acknowledging such anger openly. Speaking to the issue of anger, Patterson writes: "He recognizes it as his feelings and accepts responsibility for his behavior. If a child's behavior angers him, he makes it clear that it is the behavior, not the child, which does so."

A second characteristic of the humanistic teacher cited by Patterson is respect for the child as a person. Basically, respect is shown by accepting the student for what he or she is. It involves caring actively about the opinions and feelings that students possess. In Patterson's words, "There is an acceptance of imperfections, mistakes, and errors, changes in mood and motivation, etc., as aspects of being human. There is confidence in the basic goodness of each individual, in the capacity of the individual to grow and to develop, to actualize his potential in an appropriate environment" (p. 107).

Respect for child

Empathic understanding

Empathic understanding is a third characteristic of the humanistic teacher. This is understanding that goes further than the type of information a teacher can obtain by reading students' cumulative records or through informal observation of students in the classroom. Empathic understanding involves an active attempt by teachers to place themselves in their students' positions and to become sensitive to their perceptions and feelings. It is an effort to understand the unique perceptions of individual students. Humanistic writers believe that empathic understanding is rare and that if teachers could express, even occasionally, that they see, understand, and accept students, much potential would be unlocked. The call is for more nonevaluative feedback that illustrates to students that teachers understand the feelings that students verbalize. Aspy (1972) presents data that illustrate that teachers can learn to express more respect for students' ideas and responses when they interact with students, and that in such classrooms students begin to initiate more interaction.

There have been several attempts to develop scales that measure students' perceptions of teachers' empathic understanding, genuineness, and openness. Barrett-Lennard (1959; 1962) developed a way to measure such variables by asking students to respond to 64 questions on a six-point scale (from "yes, I strongly feel it is true" to "no, I strongly feel it is false"). Some of the questions from that instrument follow:

- ☐ She wants me to think that she likes me or understands me more than she really does.
- ☐ She cares for me.
- ☐ She realizes what I mean even when I have difficulty in saying it.
- ☐ She just takes no notice of some things that I think or feel.
- ☐ She is impatient with me.
- ☐ She nearly always knows exactly what I mean.

Research Evidence

Empathy toward students

Although there has been little research on affective programs per se, there has been research on certain affective behaviors of teachers. Rogers (1983) reviews some of the research on facilitative teachers (high empathy), much of it drawn from work by the National Consortium for Humanizing Education (NCHE). A good deal of this research was conducted by David Aspy and Flora Roebuck. The central premise of these studies is that students learn more and engage in more appropriate classroom behavior when they receive high levels of understanding, caring, and genuineness from their classroom teachers. In the NCHE model interpersonal behaviors consistent with Rogers' facilitative conditions of empathy and positive regard were explored. In one study, Aspy and Roebuck report that students in classes of teachers who had high levels of empathy had higher achievement and self-concept gains, among other variables, than students in low-empathy classrooms.

This program of research found that teachers who provided high levels

In high-empathy classrooms, students are encourged to create special projects and reports.

High- versus low-empathy classrooms

of empathy also exhibited the following other behaviors: (1) more response to student feeling, (2) more use of student ideas and ongoing instructional interactions, (3) more discussion with students, (4) more praise of students, (5) more congruent teacher talk (more authentic, less ritualistic), and (6) more tailoring of content to individual students. In addition, in comparison to low-empathy classrooms, the classroom activities in high-empathy classrooms exhibited more of the following characteristics: (1) the learning goals are derived from cooperative planning between teacher and student, (2) the classroom is individualized, (3) there are more projects and displays created by students—more active involvement of students, (4) more freedom from time limits—fewer deadlines, more flexibility, and (5) more emphasis on productivity and creativity than on evaluation.

In addition, Rogers (1983) reviewed similar research on instructing teachers how to become more empathic and presents summaries of several important programs that have attempted to implement these ideas. Also, Rogers includes a thorough discussion of the politics of education and outlines some of the problems that classroom teachers who attempt to implement humanistic philosophy will encounter.

Cognitive Versus Affective Goals

Numerous studies illustrate the point that affective and cognitive gains do not necessarily occur at the same time. A brief review of one study may illustrate more forcefully that the teacher cannot be all things to all people. Ligon, Hester, Baenen, and Matuszek (1977) conducted a massive study of the relationship between affective and achievement growth in elementary and secondary schools. Their data showed that there was not a clear linear relationship between affect and achievement. They write:

> Raising a child's self-concept or improving his attitude toward school does not ensure an increase in his achievement level. . . . Compensatory education programs which

claim that activities designed to improve a child's self-concept or attitude toward school will in turn improve the child's achievement may be well advised either to address improvement in achievement more directly or to set up affective objectives separate from achievement objectives. (p. 1)

Number of teaching tasks

Part of the dilemma that teachers in American classrooms face is that they are expected to respond to a variety of issues (Good, Biddle, & Brophy, 1975). Their teaching tasks are so numerous—including health education, sex education, subject-matter mastery, self-concept development, citizenship, prosocial behavior—that it is impossible for them to meet all demands.

Teachers then have to make *value* decisions about their personal instructional goals and how to pursue them. Tradeoffs are involved so that progress in some areas does come at the expense of progress in other areas. As Aspy (1972; 1977) notes, teachers have to balance interpersonal relationships with and between students with the traditional substantive responsibilities of schooling.

Prawat and Nickerson: Study of Affective Teachers

We have talked about affect as though it had a standard or common definition, but psychologists or educators often mean different things when they speak of affect. In an attempt to define the way teachers perceive affect, Prawat and Nickerson (1985) asked teachers to describe the affective or noncognitive behavior of students by writing about five classroom events that had actually occurred. The task was relatively open-ended in order to allow teachers to express their own meanings. Interestingly, it was found that teachers most frequently reported incidents that represent interpersonal affect. Teachers seemed less concerned about students' attitudes toward self and seldom reported incidents that reflected their affect toward subject matter.

Affective student outcomes

Prawat and Nickerson (1985) note that few studies have examined the relationship between teacher thought and action and student affective outcomes. Of a sample of 40 teachers, these investigators selected 10 teachers for focused interviews. These 10 teachers were selected to represent three distinct clusters of teachers, each reflecting a particular goal orientation: affective, cognitive, or mixed (a balance of cognitive and affective goals). The study sought to determine whether or not teachers with more affective orientations behave in ways that stimulate more or better affective outcomes in their students.

Prawat and Nickerson found that positive affect was *not* more evident in classrooms of teachers who placed higher priority on affective outcomes than it was in classrooms in which teachers stressed more traditional cognitive outcomes. Indeed, these investigators found that high-affective teachers were less successful than mixed teachers in promoting affective outcomes. The authors argue that valuing affect to the exclusion of cognitions may be counterproductive for both affective and cognitive student progress. Interestingly, the study showed that successful cooperative behavior tended to occur more often in formal contexts as opposed to informal settings. That is, in contexts where teachers indicated the work that was to be done and who was to work together, there tended to be more cooperative student behavior.

Small-group, cooperative work was not incompatible with teacher direction and teacher supervision. In fact, Prawat and Nickerson found that teacher supervision appeared to enhance the quality of the interpersonal interaction that took place in the classroom. They speculate that teachers who frequently use small groups and who provide a great deal of structure and guidance may place equal emphasis on cognitive and affective goals. It may be that when students work together to reach important academic goals, shared cooperative behavior that involves high motivation and high engagement rates follow. These data, although based on a small sample, are consistent with the viewpoint that we have expressed previously in this chapter—that there can be too much or too little emphasis on most instructional goals. Prawat and Nickerson's findings suggest that a balance of goals may be associated with more optimal levels of student motivation and more progress on cognitive and affective goals.

Balance of goals

SUMMARY

Because humanists are interested in emotional and affective development as well as the cognitive variables of perception and awareness, their theories stress self-perceptions and potential. Although there is great diversity within the field, the affective and noncognitive outcomes of schooling are of greater concern to humanists than behaviorists or cognitivists. In the area of motivation, humanists focus on intrinsic rather than extrinsic variables, as exemplified by the theories of Abraham Maslow and Carl Rogers.

Good attitudes toward self and others appear to develop in homes where there are complete acceptance of the child, clear standards and expectations, respect and latitude for the child within defined limits. Either too much or too little structure seems to inhibit affective growth, but teacher recognition and acceptance appear central to positive self-concept development and achievement. Patterson and others argue that humanistic goals require the following changes in schools: (1) more open scheduling, (2) more emphasis on active learning, (3) more stress on student independence, (4) more stress on creativity, (5) more opportunity for cooperative learning activities, (6) more opportunity for internal evaluation, and (7) greater emphasis on personal integrity, nonacademic potential, and an intrinsic curriculum.

deCharms described two types of motivational states. "Origin" is the condition in which one works for one's own goals, while "pawns" work for someone else. The open classroom has been widely touted as a means for suiting learning to individual needs, but Wright and others have failed to find clear evidence of greater cognitive gains in open than in structured programs. Many kinds of activities have been developed to integrate affect into subject matter, including consciousness-raising experiences, the study of social problems, and aesthetic education. Prosocial behavior also has been advanced as an important goal, and some success has been reported in experimental programs. In general, it appears that the teacher who is genuine in relating to students, displays respect for them, and shows empathic understanding will help to further humanistic goals.

QUESTIONS AND PROBLEMS

1. To what extent should schools and teachers be responsible for helping students develop increased understanding of individuals who differ from them, such as the elderly? To what degree should such goals be pursued during school time?
2. What does the term "humanistic teaching" mean to you? Have some of your teachers fulfilled this definition? Were they more successful than the average teacher in presenting basic subject matter material?
3. What does the term interchangeable teacher comment mean? Write a one-page dialogue that provides specific and appropriate uses of interchangeable comments.
4. How would humanistic elementary school teachers differ from humanistic college teachers? How would they be the same?
5. If teachers emphasize prosocial cooperative learning, is it possible that students will have to suppress their individual academic interests so that group interests can be fulfilled?
6. Assume that you want to emphasize affective goals in the class you teach. What are the implications of the Prawat and Nickerson study for how you design classroom tasks? Should affective tasks be taught independent of cognitive tasks?
7. Summarize in your own words the value of cooperative learning programs as summarized in the Slavin review.

CASE STUDIES

The Year Begins. Sally Jones opens the door and walks confidently into Room 203 at Bayside Junior High. She smiles and says, "I'm Ms. Jones, your English teacher. There are four or five important things we are going to do in the first two months of school. First, everyone is going to write critical reports on a movie and a book."

Ted, with a slight whine in his voice: "A book *and* a movie?" Sally, with warmth but finality: "Yes, both. In a few minutes I'll tell you the form for your report, but now I want to give you a general feel for what's happening in this course so that you can begin to plan your work for class assignments. The important thing in writing the two critical reports is to present your genuine reactions in such a way that others can understand your feelings. There will also be two group assignments due during the first two months. You'll be assigned one, and the other you can select yourself on the basis of the stories that interest you. These assignments will involve rewriting the last few pages of stories that we read. On a sheet that I'll pass out in a few minutes you'll see a long list of 300 books grouped into 30 smaller divisions of topical interest. For example, sports, cars, classics, and romance are all topics included in the list."

What expectations does Sally communicate to the class? In general, what strengths or weaknesses does her introduction have with regard to motivation variables? What other things might she have done? Rewrite "The Year Begins" from the perspective of a teacher who wants to introduce affective topics into the curriculum or from the viewpoint of the teacher who believes that affect is a major aspect of the curriculum.

Classroom Daydream. Tim Blanton is a third-year biology teacher at Rockhurst High School. Jane Myer is a sophomore at Rockhurst and a reluctant biology student in Mr. Blanton's class. The class period seems endless to Jane who stares out the window and wonders about whether she will make the "cut" on the basketball team this afternoon. The coach said this would be the day the squad would be announced. Mr. Blanton kindly but directly says, "Jane what else can we see about cell structure on the slide?" Jane says, "Oh, ah, I'm sorry but I wasn't paying attention. I'm preoccupied and my mind was wandering." Several kids wink and snicker. Helen blurts out, "Yeah the subject is so boring I can see why you are falling asleep. This lab doesn't seem important to me." Jane turns red and Mr. Blanton turns pale. Seeing the effect of her comments on Mr. Blanton, Helen looks apprehensively at the floor. What should Mr. Blanton say or do now?

Part Six

Classroom Management

As Mr. Floden turns his back and heads to his desk, Huey launches a massive wad of paper that rises majestically in the air and then hits Mr. Floden squarely in the back. The class breaks out with loud, spontaneous laughter.

Judy Griffin explains the assignment carefully; as soon as she finishes several hands are waving frantically in the air. Before Judy can call on any of the students, Tim blurts out, "Do we have to do this by next Monday? Why not next Friday? This is a lot of work." The class buzzes with excitement and there is constant haggling with the teacher for the next ten minutes over the number of pages that they have to do as well as the format in which the paper must be written.

Bill Roundtree curtly announces to his sales staff, "I want biweekly reports on your sales progress; we need to get sales up by 12 percent. This is important and I expect to have good progress immediately. Some of you are going to get big rewards out of this; however, others may be in trouble and you may be looking for other jobs if you don't get that sales performance up."

Helen answers the phone, and at the same time nods toward the empty chair in the corner as a visitor sits down. As she continues to listen on the phone, she hands an application form to the visitor to fill out. She glances at her appointment calendar and buzzes Mr. Wilson on the office intercom to let him know that it is time for him to leave for his 10:00 meeting in the board room.

These vignettes involve different aspects of classroom and societal management that teachers and students must deal with. The first vignette deals with public misbehavior, a significant aspect of classroom life that teachers must address. However, although the episode in Mr. Floden's class would be a significant, threatening event for any teacher, most classroom management issues are less dramatic than this. Still, teachers do need to develop strategies for handling direct threats to their authority.

The second vignette illustrates another difficulty that teachers face in managing classrooms. Not only do teachers have to have careful, well-laid out plans, they need to be able to convince students to become engaged in learning activities. Although rules and procedures are an important part of classroom management, there is growing evidence that a major part of success as a classroom manager is the ability to elicit student cooperation in classroom learning goals (Doyle, 1985).

The third example illustrates two principles that often are part of management systems—alerting and accountability. Teachers need to alert students that certain performances are important and will be examined. Teachers also need to hold students accountable—to actually check their work in order to determine the extent to which students have mastered important skills and concepts. Unlike managers in certain businesses, teachers do not have the authority, except under extraordinary circumstances, to "fire" students or assign them to other teachers. Thus, the incentives and motivational systems that teachers can use depend more on logic and the ability to solicit student cooperation than they do on external rewards and incentives. As will be seen in the material that follows, teachers can engage in too much alerting as well as too little, and can overstructure or understructure their classrooms.

The fourth vignette describes the essence of a successful teacher. Teachers have to do many things at the same time and do each of those things well. The executive secretary in this story is able to perform three tasks simultaneously. Successful teachers, especially in elementary schools, must be able to initiate, maintain, and supervise several different learning activities at the same time.

Successful classrooms do not just happen. They are created, maintained, and restored (when necessary) by teachers who exhibit certain personal qualities, spend time planning and preparing, and use effective techniques. Because they are effective managers, they will avoid most serious problems, but they know how to handle such problems when necessary. They also know how to structure and use the physical space and equipment in ways that work for their students.

Classroom management is usually the major concern of beginning teachers (Fuller, 1969; Doyle, 1985), and for good reason. It is basic to success in meeting both cognitive and affective objectives, and principals and supervisors stress it in rating teachers. Teachers who have serious management problems cannot do much teaching because they spend so much time reacting to these problems. In addition, students apparently have little respect or liking for such teachers.

Despite differences in number, type, and severity of problems, the basic principles for sound classroom management are the same for all teachers. Differences are mostly in the time and energy that teachers must devote to management. In ideal situations, management is a minimal concern that primarily involves preventing problems by individualizing instruction to meet students' needs. At the opposite extreme, a teacher faced with five separate classes of unruly preadolescents may have to spend more time and energy on management than on all other aspects of teaching combined.

Prospective teachers, therefore, need to consider how their personal qualities and preferences affect their teaching roles, both in general and in regard to specific grade levels and classroom settings. Our treatment of classroom management will begin in Chapter 19 with a discussion of some personal characteristics that are desirable in all teachers, and the factors that individual teachers must take into account in deciding on the particular teaching roles they will play.

In Chapter 20 we discuss the basic skills involved in creating and maintaining an effective learning environment. In Chapters 21 and 22 we turn our attention to techniques for dealing with students who require more individualized instruction. Chapter 21 reviews behavioristic approaches to coping with students' behavior problems, and Chapter 22 presents humanistic approaches.

Several basic ideas underlie this entire section on classroom management. First, successful classroom managers must have certain personal qualities. Without them, teachers are unlikely to succeed, no matter what specific techniques they use. Second, the keys to success lie in good planning and effective prevention of problems rather than in being able to handle problems after they occur. Third, no single approach will equip a teacher to handle all classroom management tasks successfully. As Doyle (1985) notes, maintaining a good management system requires some attention each day. However, it is possible to build an effective, comprehensive, and internally consistent system by combining elements from different approaches that complement one another. Finally, each teacher must discover what approaches work best for him or her; teachers are not likely to successfully use approaches that conflict with their beliefs or personal predispositions.

Chapter 19

Overview of Classroom Management

CHAPTER OUTLINE

OBJECTIVES

When you have mastered the material in this chapter you will be able to

1. Discuss the relative importance of group and individual student differences for classroom management
2. Differentiate between a socialization orientation to teaching and an instructional orientation to teaching
3. Match teaching a given grade level with either the socialization or the instructional teaching role and give a rationale for the match
4. Discuss the problems and rewards of choosing a socialization orientation to teaching
5. List and explain the expectations and responsibilities of teachers as authority figures
6. Describe five characteristics of teachers who are successful socialization agents
7. Describe six characteristics of successful parents, showing the relevance of each for teaching
8. Explain the relationship between school size/class size and student activity, achievement, and attitudes
9. Diagram and explain a classroom design that would foster individualized instruction in an open-space school

Expectations and knowledge

To manage classrooms effectively, teachers need both clear expectations about how students should spend their time and knowledge about what to do when their expectations are not being met. Expectations define classroom management goals and guide decisions about creating, maintaining, and restoring desirable student behavior. Teachers who have clear expectations about what their students should be doing can organize the classroom and plan activities accordingly, articulate these expectations clearly to students, and recognize when discrepancies between expectations and actual student behavior are unacceptably large. Such discrepancies indicate a need for action, at which point the teacher must call on knowledge of general principles, and of the needs and characteristics of the particular students involved, to decide what to do.

Student role

Taken together, teachers' expectations about appropriate student activities and behavior can be called the student role. Elements that make up the student role include: (1) mastery of basic skills; (2) development of interest in and knowledge about the topics included in the formal curriculum; and (3) participation, usually as a member of a group, in extracurricular experiences. Extracurricular experiences like assemblies or fire drills are considered necessary for efficient institutional functioning. Most, however, are designed to support either the program of instruction, like field trips or music programs, or to develop qualities believed important for all citizens, like physical education and the pledge of allegiance.

As Jackson (1968) and Doyle (1985) have noted, the following are identified with the student role: regimentation of activity, restriction of movement, and subordination of individual desires to the personal authority of the teacher and the less personal but often restrictive school and classroom rules. The rules help provide for an orderly and reasonably satisfactory group living experience within an institutional setting, but they do so at a price. Behavior considered natural and appropriate elsewhere like boisterous talk and play is forbidden at schools; to help a friend is sometimes considered cheating in school, but to fail to help a friend in a social setting is treachery!

Implications for Classroom Management

We shall approach classroom management with a kind of cost/benefit analysis, considering techniques with an eye toward what they are designed to accomplish, what they do in fact accomplish, and what side effects they may have. Certain practices like requiring students to remain absolutely silent at all times unless addressed by the teacher are seen as inappropriate because they are not essential to any worthwhile goal or because their positive effects are outweighed by negative ones (persistent authoritarian and punitive techniques, for example).

In our discussion of management we will stress problem prevention; however, we will also provide strategies for dealing with misbehavior when it does occur. Furthermore, we will discuss how teachers can manage classroom groups as well as helping individual students (Doyle, 1985).

Individual and Group Differences

Individual and group differences among students have implications for classroom management. Differences in age, sex, and ethnicity come readily to mind, along with variables such as maturity and responsibility. If anything, these variables are probably given too much weight, leading to overly polarized differential prescriptions for boys versus girls or black students versus white students. Actually, except for age or developmental differences, there is little evidence indicating that different types of students require very different techniques (Kounin & Obradovic, 1968; Good & Stipek, 1983). Most recommendations for differential treatment involve minor qualifications on major themes rather than clear-cut contrasts. Even so, certain group and individual differences among students do merit consideration by teachers trying to optimize their classroom management.

Sex differences

For example, well-established sex differences (Maccoby & Jacklin, 1974) indicate that boys are more physically active than girls, at least during childhood, so that tight restrictions on movement are more difficult for them. The combination of sustained attention and physical immobility is especially difficult for younger students, regardless of sex. This does not imply that physical restrictions should be abandoned; all students can adjust to some degree. Before specifying implications, we must ask: (1) Is the instructional model used in the classroom appropriate for the students? (2) If so, what physical restrictions are really necessary? (3) Are there multiple ways to accomplish objectives so that teachers can allow students to use the methods most preferred by them?

Adjusting to restrictions

Once restrictions are minimized, teachers can ease students' difficulty in adjusting to them. Activities can be scheduled so that sustained concentration is required when students seem most able to handle it. Recess and less demanding activity can occur at other times. Students who need more physical activity can be given opportunities to obtain it in a great many ways that still accomplish instructional goals, or at least do not conflict with them. In general, the optimal approach is one that establishes the desired learning environment while simultaneously imposing the fewest restrictions on the teacher and the students (Brophy & Putnam, 1979).

Cultural characteristics

Characteristics that vary across groups or cultures may have implications for classroom management. Many adolescents resent being touched in any way. Many teachers have angered students by taking away or otherwise overreacting to articles of clothing, combs, or other highly valued possessions. Middle-class teachers accustomed to forbidding physical aggression or vulgar language usually become more tolerant of these behaviors if they are assigned to work with lower-class students (Metz, 1978). Such teachers need to be sensitive about the danger of worsening existing conflicts between themselves and their students. Monitor roles should not place students in conflict with the peer group, and appointments to peer leadership positions will require the support of the existing peer leaders (Roberts, 1970; Reissman, 1962).

Eye contact

Middle-class teachers typically expect students to maintain eye contact with them during disciplinary contacts, to indicate both attention and respect. However, certain minority groups are taught to avert their eyes in such situations. For them, maintaining eye contact may connote defiance, not respectful attention. It is important for teachers to be aware of such cultural differences.

Need for tolerance

More generally, teachers must be open-minded and tolerant in dealing with students from different cultural backgrounds. This does not necessarily mean catering to student preferences or reinforcing their expectations. Students accustomed to authoritarian treatment or brutality need acceptance and warmth from their teachers. Furthermore, it is clear that some students function more as origins (assume responsibility for their own learning, make appropriate demands on the teachers), whereas other students behave more like pawns (deCharms, 1984). Classroom management strategies may have to be adjusted so that "pawn" students assume more self-control (see related discussion in Chapter 15). Minority-group students who are alienated from school learning and discriminated against by the majority of the student body require a combination of warmth and determination from the teacher in demanding achievement efforts and enforcing conduct limits (Kleinfeld, 1975).

Student Behavior Problems

Most of the "problems" teachers deal with are essentially trivial. Loud talking, noisy movements, and similar disruptions are considered normal and appropriate outside the classroom. However, some students present more enduring and serious problems. About one student in ten has moderate to severe adjustment problems, and the rate climbs to three in ten if mild problems are included (Clarizio & McCoy, 1976). About three boys for every girl have moderate to severe problems, so the rates are about 15 percent in boys and 5 percent in girls. About two-thirds of these childhood disturbances are related to specific external stress factors and are likely to show significant improvement within a year or two, even without professional treatment (Clarizio & McCoy, 1976).

Dealing with offenders

Many teachers will strike tacit bargains with persistent offenders, minimizing educational demands and even interactions with them in return for a degree of compliance (Hargreaves, Hester, & Mellor, 1975). This tactic can backfire, however. Teachers often will not intervene with such students when their misbehavior is relatively mild, but then will overreact when they do intervene, thus reinforcing the students' perceptions that the teacher is picking on them. In general, indirect methods that try to avoid dealing with problems or pretend that they do not exist are more likely to reinforce than to extinguish the problem behavior. While it is true that teachers may have to be more tolerant of the misbehavior of disturbed students, and may need to spend a great deal of time working with them individually, the general principles of classroom management to be discussed here hold for disturbed students just as for other students (Kounin & Obradovic, 1968; Hewett & Watson, 1979).

Choosing Your Role

As students progress through school grades they undergo personal and social development that affects the role of the teacher and the goals and techniques of classroom management. Brophy and Evertson (1978) identified four stages:

1. *Kindergarten and the early elementary grades*—Here students are being socialized into the role of student and instructed in basic skills. Most are still oriented to adults as authority figures, predisposed to do what they are told, and likely to feel gratified when they please teachers and upset when they do not. They turn to teachers for directions, encouragement, solace, assistance, and personalized attention. Serious disturbances usually are not yet present. Consequently, teachers function primarily as instructors and trainers. The emphasis is on teaching students what to do rather than on getting them to comply with familiar rules. These instructional or socialization aspects of classroom management are basic to the teacher's job in the early grades; indeed, it probably is not possible to teach young children effectively without spending considerable time on these tasks.
2. *The middle elementary grades*—Time spent handling classroom management concerns is reduced and teachers are able to concentrate on instructing students in the formal curriculum. This stage starts when basic socialization to the student role is completed and continues as long as most students remain adult oriented and relatively compliant. Students are familiar with most school routines, and the serious disturbances seen frequently in later years have not yet become common. Creating and maintaining an appropriate learning environment remains central to teaching success, but this task consumes less teacher time.
3. *The upper elementary and lower high school grades*—As more and more students switch orientation from pleasing teachers to pleasing the peer group, teachers begin to be resented when they act as authority figures, and maintaining control of the class can be difficult at times. Certain students become more disturbed and harder to control than they used to be. As a result, classroom management again becomes a prominent part of the teacher role, perhaps even more important than teaching the formal curriculum. Students have mastered tool skills and can manage much of their learning on their own. The teacher's primary problem now is motivating them to behave as they know they are supposed to, not instructing them in how to do it, as in the first stage.
4. *The upper high school grades*—As many of the most alienated students drop out of school and the rest of the students become intellectually and socially more mature, classrooms once again assume an academic focus. Classroom management requires even less time than it did during the second stage, because students assume almost complete

responsibility for managing their movements and activities at school. Teaching at these higher levels is mostly a matter of instructing students in the formal curriculum. Classroom management remains important but requires little time, except in the first few class meetings, and student socialization conducted with the group almost disappears. The socialization that does occur is mostly informal, conducted during out-of-class contacts with individuals, mostly within the school setting, however.

Grade-level choice

These developmental aspects of classroom management should be considered when one is preparing to teach at particular grade levels. Teachers who enjoy working with young children, who like to provide nurturant socialization as well as instruction, and who have the patience and skills needed for socializing young children into the student role would be especially well placed in the primary grades. Elementary teachers who want to concentrate mostly on instruction would be best placed in the middle grades. Grades seven to ten would be best for teachers who enjoy or at least are not bothered by the provocative behavior of adolescents, and who see themselves as socialization agents and models at least as much as instructors. The upper high school grades are best for teachers who want to function mostly as subject-matter specialists.

Handling serious problems

There has been much debate, but little research and certainly no ironclad findings, about how to handle the most serious problems: racial and other group tensions; severe withdrawal and refusal to communicate; hostile, antisocial acting out; truancy; refusal to work or obey; vandalism; and severe behavioral disorders or criminality. Psychotherapists have not achieved much success in dealing with behavior disorders, and neither they nor correctional institutions have achieved even modest success in dealing with severe delinquency and criminality. Yet teachers typically are asked to cope with such problems, while at the same time coping with the problems of thirty or more other students (five times as many in junior high and high school); instructing all these students in the school's curriculum; and dealing with the conflicting pressures presented by the school district, the principal,

Teenagers display a wide range of conduct in the classroom setting.

other teachers, the students themselves, the parents, and their own personal lives. Some teachers respond to this with determination to solve whatever problems come along. We hope that their energy and optimism hold out indefinitely. If so, they probably will succeed.

Other teachers respond by concluding that it is better to concentrate on a few tasks and perform them well than to try to do all of them. We find this position quite understandable. A teacher with little interest or appetite for pupil socialization, who recognizes this predisposition and chooses to teach at grades where socialization is a minimal problem and to concentrate on becoming highly skilled at putting across subject matter, probably is making a wise decision.

Recognizing limitations

The same is true for teachers who choose to teach grades where socialization is of extreme importance (especially the junior high grades). Such teachers, who recognize their own limitations and work within them will have different effects on students than will teachers who deal with the entire spectrum of responsibilities. Their effects will tend to be positive and probably greater in the long run than they would have been if these teachers had tried to do everything and ended up doing nothing very well.

Teachers who choose to minimize socialization activities can do so, although they cannot eliminate them entirely. If they are content with a primarily instructional role, they can get by with classroom management strategies that are effective for maintaining an orderly classroom but not for changing severely disturbed students. Such teachers can legitimately take the position that changing such students is not their job, and can let school counselors or other treatment experts assume this function, confining their own efforts with such students to instructional activities.

The Teacher as a Socialization Agent

Teacher commitment

Teachers who want to have important socialization effects on students can accomplish this goal, but they will need to understand the commitment involved in this decision and the frustrations to be encountered because of rules and regulations, uncooperative school officials or parents, and students who fail to respond to their best and most persistent efforts. A teacher who makes a commitment to deal with student problems in addition to providing instruction in the formal curriculum also may need:

- ☐ To invest time and energy to cultivate close personal relationships with students that go far beyond those necessary for purely instructional purposes.
- ☐ To spend a lot of time outside regular school hours dealing with students and their families, perhaps to even be "on call" as a counselor to students who have no one else to turn to.
- ☐ To receive no extra financial compensation for such efforts, and perhaps even some opposition from school officials.
- ☐ To deal with the wrath of a student's parents or another person who may be involved in the situation.

A teacher who is committed to helping problem students must be willing to spend time with parents.

- ☐ To deal with complex problems that have developed over a period of years, along with the additional handicap of having to deal with the student in group situations while within the role of an authority figure responsible for upholding school rules.

Difficulties of Socialization

Teachers typically do not have special training in methods of dealing with serious personality or behavior disorders. Neither do they have the luxury of being able to interact with students by taking a friendly, nonauthoritarian therapist's role. Instead, they have to find ways to reach disturbed students while still playing authority figure, and while dealing with them every day in class in addition to contacting them individually. As a result, even the most energetic, determined, and skilled teachers will have only limited success. This is not bad in itself because the success rates even of professionally trained therapists are not impressive. However, it does mean that, in addition to possessing all the qualities listed above, teachers who commit themselves to socialization functions must be able to simultaneously expect the best and yet be prepared for the worst. Teachers who expect to succeed consistently or to be rewarded with expressions of love and gratitude will be disappointed. Rewarding experiences occur, but so do frustrations. Many students will not respond at all, despite continued and appropriate attempts to reach them. Others will respond and make initial progress only to regress and end up worse than they started. Furthermore, relatively few "success cases" will respond with overt gratitude or other direct reinforcement of the teacher.

Limited success rates

Even the most talented and determined teachers can work successfully with only so many students at one time. Overcommitment will cause diminishing returns. Therefore, teachers will have to be selective about their "caseloads," holding them within a manageable limit, if they are to expect success.

Overcommitment

If you think that you can try to reach students persistently despite a steady diet of frustrations, you probably have a good chance to be a successful socialization agent. In fact, if you find the prospect exciting and challenging rather than dismal, you might consider teaching any of the grades between fifth to tenth grade, where student socialization needs are most frequent and intense.

Teachers' Advantages as Socializers

Teachers have some advantages over therapists and other specialists. First, they see students every day and under a variety of conditions; thus they have more and better information; therapists usually must rely on what clients choose to tell them. Their authority-figure role has advantages, too. Teachers can interact with students in a variety of realistic situations, and they are in a position to provide either rewards or punishments to selected student behavior. Teachers who want to act as socialization agents can achieve reasonable success and satisfaction if they approach the task with realistic expectations and attitudes in addition to having the ability to diagnose problems and respond to them effectively.

The Teacher as Authority Figure

Student attitudes and expectations

Students expect teachers to manage their classrooms effectively. Nash (1976) found six main themes in elementary students' attitudes and expectations concerning teachers: (1) keeping order (strict rather than soft punishes if necessary); (2) teaching (keeps you busy); (3) explaining (can be understood, gives help if you need it); (4) interesting (provides variety, not boring); (5) treating fairly (consistent, does not play favorites or pick on anyone); and (6) acting friendly (kind or nice, talks gently rather than shouts, can laugh when appropriate).

Metz (1978) found similar attitudes among high school students. Students in high tracks expected mastery of the field and continuous intellectual challenge from their teachers. They seldom rebelled, but they often challenged teachers on academic grounds. Students in low tracks were more concerned about teachers' personal qualities such as whether he or she is not mean, does not shout, treats everyone alike and does not play favorites, accuses only when justified, explains material so it can be understood. These students often tested teachers by disobeying rules and causing disruptions. However, they did not question the teacher's right to exert authority, even though they sometimes resisted that authority.

In general, all students expect the teacher to act as the classroom authority figure, and desire a predictable structure in each classroom. They accept a variety of leadership styles from different teachers, so long as each individual teacher is consistent. However, they have little sympathy for teachers who cannot or will not control their classrooms, taking the attitude that such teachers deserve all the grief they get.

Suppression of unacceptable behavior

Regardless of the teaching role you see as ideal, some suppression of unacceptable behavior will be necessary. Behavior that is disruptive to instruction or harmonious group living will have to be stopped, forcibly if necessary. Violence, weapons, and destruction, among other things, cannot be allowed (Feldhusen, 1979). These "nonnegotiables" will have to be presented to students when necessary or appropriate as absolutely forbidden. Violence will be punished, weapons will be confiscated, and property destruction will require restitution. Students or parents who refuse to accept this should be politely referred to the police.

Positive approach

Of course, we speak here of situations where serious unacceptable behavior is widespread and essentially out of control. Problems such as these should not even be mentioned when they do not exist. Where they exist in mild and limited forms, they should be approached in positive ways designed not only to eliminate the undesirable behavior but also to solve the underlying problems and channel the students into more appropriate activities. Everyone involved must understand that individuals are responsible for their own behavior; students who cause trouble despite repeated warnings will be required to take the consequences (Glasser, 1977).

Attempting to protect students by insulating them from the consequences of their own behavior, or to minimize the seriousness of crimes such as assault and battery or mugging that occurred on the school campus between students rather than on the street between strangers, is self-defeating, even if well meant. The result usually is an escalation of problems, as the more antisocial students come to see that they can get away with more and other students realize that they cannot rely on school authorities to accept responsibility for controlling the situation.

Need to suppress misbehavior

Thus, no matter where you stand on the issue of the degree to which the teacher has a responsibility to solve student problems rather than merely to suppress unacceptable behavior, you must be prepared to forcibly suppress misbehavior by students who leave you no other alternative. This is a serious problem that must be emotionally resolved by those of you who care deeply about students as individuals in the broader sense, and not merely as learners in the narrower sense. Almost every school exhibits continuing and inescapable problems with which every teacher must be prepared to deal at some level.

Research on Teacher Role Orientations

Responsibility for student outcomes

Teachers' classroom behavior is affected by the way they perceive their role and abilities as teachers (Ames, 1983; Clark & Peterson, 1985). Ames (1983) contends that teachers arrive at attributions about their teaching effectiveness through a belief system organized around personal values, and that their causal attributions for student performance affect whether or not they see a need to change their teaching behavior. He assumes that some teachers perceive their teaching acts to be strongly related to student outcomes. This belief that positive efforts can lead to positive outcomes from students is derived from these teachers' more general value orientation that they are responsible for student outcomes.

More explicitly, Ames organizes the chain of beliefs as follows: (1) teaching is important; (2) teachers engage in intentional acts to produce positive outcomes; (3) achieving success with students is generally feasible, given situational aids and constraints. He presents results from an empirical study to support this conceptualization. He found that teachers who valued competence and believed that teaching was important were more likely to consider their own behavior as a possible source of influence than were teachers who did not believe that teachers were responsible for student learning.

Teachers' perceptions

There is also evidence that teachers' perceptions of students, and more specifically, of reasons for students' misbehavior, influence how teachers respond when behavior problems occur. Rohrkemper and Brophy (1983) have theorized that teachers' attributions about student performance affect their ideas concerning their teaching roles, which in turn affect their responses to students. Teachers who had been identified either as outstanding or as average teachers by their principals were asked to read vignettes depicting various student problems and to describe what they would say and do if these problems occurred in their own classrooms. The types of problems presented to teachers appear in Table 19.1.

Disruptive behavior cannot be allowed to interfere with instruction.

Based on distinctions made by Gordon (1974), these researchers included in the vignettes: (1) teacher-owned problems (student behavior interfering with the teacher's meeting his or her own needs); (2) teacher-student shared problems (the teacher and student interfering with each other's need satisfaction); and (3) student-owned problems (not caused by the teacher). Their results indicate that teachers' attributions of students' problems to causes, as well as their beliefs about their own potential impact on students, varied across the three levels of problem ownership. Their results for teacher-owned problems are particularly thought provoking. Teachers' descriptions of their intentions in such situations were characterized by a higher frequency of punishment, restricted language, and emphasis on short-term control attempts. Such teacher actions would appear to be self-defeating and would simply maintain inappropriate behavior of students. Presumably, because teachers' prognoses for long-term change were poor, they chose to respond to specific problems without attempting to eradicate or to change their underlying causes.

Rohrkemper and Brophy have provided a useful strategy for relating teacher attributions to potential sequences of classroom behavior. More specifically, they have illustrated how an attributional framework can be utilized for describing and understanding teachers' reactions to particular problem situations. Their work illustrates that attributional inferences are necessary but potentially harmful, particularly in the case of teacher-owned problems. Their classification of student problems provides some important distinctions that teachers could use to think about their behavior when they interact with problem students in the classroom.

Attributional inferences

The implications of this research for classroom practice are important. That teachers make these attributional interpretations and related emotional responses to student behavior is understandable; however, teachers are the professional adults in the situation and must be prepared to control these emotions and give students what they need. Those presenting student-

Table 19.1 Problem Student Types

1. *Failure Syndrome.* These children are convinced that they cannot do the work. They often avoid starting or give up easily. They expect to fail, even after succeeding. Signs: easily frustrated; gives up easily; says "I can't do it."
2. *Perfectionist.* These children are unduly anxious about making mistakes. Their self-imposed standards are unrealistically high, so that they are never satisfied with their work (when they should be). Signs: too much of a "perfectionist"; often anxious/fearful/frustrated about quality of work; holds back from class participation unless sure of self.
3. *Underachiever.* These children do a minimum to just "get by." They do not value schoolwork. Signs: indifferent to schoolwork; minimum work output; not challenged by schoolwork; poorly motivated.
4. *Low Achiever.* These children have difficulty, even though they may be willing to work. Their problem is low potential or lack of readiness rather than poor motivation. Signs: difficulty following directions; difficulty completing work; poor retention; progresses slowly.
5. *Hostile Aggressive.* These children express hostility through direct, intense behaviors. They are not easily controlled. Signs: intimidates and threatens; hits and pushes; damages property; antagonizes; hostile; easily angered.
6. *Passive Aggressive.* These children express opposition and resistance to the teacher, but indirectly. It often is hard to tell whether they are resisting deliberately or not. Signs: subtly oppositional and stubborn; tries to control; borderline compliance with rules; mars property rather than damages; disrupts surreptitiously; drags feet.
7. *Defiant.* These children resist authority and carry on a power struggle with the teacher. They want to have their way and not be told what to do. Signs: (1) resists verbally; (a) "You can't make me. . ."; (b) "You can't tell me what to do. . ."; (c) makes derogatory statements about teacher to others; (2) resists nonverbally; (a) frowns, grimaces, mimics teacher; (b) arms folded, hands on hips, foot stomping; (c) looks away when being spoken to; (d) laughs at inappropriate times; (e) may be physically violent toward teacher; (f) deliberately does what teacher says not to do.
8. *Hyperactive.* These children show excessive and almost constant movement, even when sitting. Often their movements appear to be without purpose. Signs: squirms, wiggles, jiggles, scratches; easily excitable; blurts out answers and comments; often out of seat; bothers other children with noises, movements; energetic but poorly directed; excessively touches objects or people.
9. *Short Attention Span/Distractible.* These children have short attention spans. They seem unable to sustain attention and concentration. Easily distracted by sounds, sights, or speech. Signs: has difficulty adjusting to changes; rarely completes tasks; easily distracted.
10. *Immature.* These children are immature. They have poorly developed emotional stability, self control, self care abilities, social skills, and/or responsibility. Signs: often exhibits behavior normal for younger children; may cry easily; loses belongings; frequently appears helpless, incompetent, and/or dependent.
11. *Rejected by Peers.* These children seek peer interaction but are rejected, ignored, or excluded. Signs: forced to work and play alone; lacks social skills; often picked on or teased.
12. *Shy/Withdrawn.* These children avoid personal interaction, are quiet and unobtrusive, and do not respond well to others. Signs: quiet and sober; does not initiate or volunteer; does not call attention to self.

Source: J. M. Levine and M. C. Wang, *Teacher and Student Perceptions: Implications for Learning*, Hillsdale, N.J.: Lawrence Erlbaum Associates, 1983.

owned problems need to learn to cope effectively—teacher sympathy is not enough. Those presenting teacher-owned problems could use a little sympathy or at least concern, as well as information about how to behave differently—anger and punitive responses will not help the situation in any fundamental way.

Teacher responses as typical human responses

The more general point here is that these teacher responses are typical human responses: We tend to respond with sympathy to people we see as victims but to respond with anger to people we see as intentionally causing us problems. However, effective professionals get beyond these immediate emotional reactions in two ways: (1) by suppressing or controlling the emotions and especially the typical response to those emotions; and (2) by trying to help the person gain insight into his or her behavior and develop more effective coping mechanisms.

Managerial style and classroom behavior

There are data to show that in some instances teachers' managerial style influences how students think about classroom behavior. Rohrkemper (1984) has argued that students whose teachers use a behavior modification style, in contrast to students whose teachers use a more inductive style, develop sophistication about behavioral action-reaction linkage but not about the motives and intentions that underlie these behaviors. Teachers who emphasize only rules and consequences may elicit conformity but fail to develop understanding and self-guidance in their students, compared to teachers who make sure that their students understand the reasons for rules.

Ideal Attitudes and Behavior

Importance of liking one's teacher

Teachers should be liked by their students. Characteristics important here are the same ones for making anyone well liked—having a cheerful disposition, being friendly, having emotional maturity, sincerity, trustworthiness, and other qualities indicating good mental health and personal adjustment. These general qualities apply to all aspects of the teacher role. In addition, certain qualities are essential when teachers function in the role of classroom authority figure. Many of these involve "ego strength" (an underlying self-confidence that enables teachers to remain calm in a crisis)—the ability to listen actively without becoming defensive or authoritarian, avoiding win-lose conflicts, and maintaining a problem-solving orientation rather than resorting to withdrawal, blame, hysteria, or other emotional overreactions. Teachers with serious problems in these areas will not be successful classroom managers, no matter what techniques they use.

Characteristics of successful socializers

More specifically, teachers who achieve the greatest success as student socializers tend to have the following characteristics (Brophy & Putnam, 1979):

1. They have realistic perceptions of themselves and of their students—This means seeing themselves and their students for who they are, without letting their perceptions become clouded by romanticism, guilt, hostility, personal problems, fear, anxiety, or other emotional reactions that can reduce reality contact.

2. They enjoy their students, but within a teacher-student relationship—This means they enjoy spending time talking to and interacting with students and getting to know them as individuals, while maintaining an identity as an adult, a teacher, an occasional authority figure, and so on. Such a teacher is friendly without being overfamiliar, and comfortable with a group without being a group member.
3. They clearly see their roles and are comfortable with them—To be consistent in their interactions with students, teachers need to be clear about their own roles in relationship to students and about the types of behavior that they do and do not value and will or will not tolerate. Once they achieve this clarity, teachers will know exactly what they want, will be able to explain it coherently to their students, and will be comfortable with it in their own minds.
4. They have positive attitudes toward being challenged and tested—Teachers who are comfortable in such situations can approach them as games of one-upmanship. This can be enjoyable as well as useful for impressing students, providing that the teacher "wins" in ways that inspire admiration rather than resentment. For example, students who try to get away with something by finding and citing loopholes in classroom rules can be complimented for their cleverness but firmly refused. This will soften the effect of refusal. In contrast, getting angry or punishing such students would only make things worse.
5. They exhibit patience and determination—Some students will persist with misbehavior despite continued punishment because they have learned that eventually they will get their way if they keep at it long enough. Such behavior is difficult to extinguish, but it can be done. The teacher's task is to convince students that there will be no giving up and no such thing as getting away with misbehavior without paying a price.

Qualities of Effective Socialization

Other qualities that probably affect teachers' socialization of students can be inferred from what is known about effective parental behavior. The following traits characterize parents who are successful in getting their children to adopt their ideals and internalize their standards for behavior (Brophy, 1977; Martin, 1975; Hoffman, 1977).

Acceptance. Children who are accepted unconditionally for what they are tend to develop a sense of security, a positive self-concept, and a prosocial attitude toward other people (Coopersmith, 1967). In contrast, children who are rejected because of characteristics that their parents find unacceptable and children who are accepted only conditionally when they do things that please the parents have problems in these areas. Depending on the degree of rejection, they may feel threatened by others and hostile toward them, have low self-esteem and other self-concept problems, or be generally antisocial.

Since teacher acceptance or rejection presumably will have similar effects on students, it is important for teachers to project acceptance and unconditional positive regard (Rogers, 1969, 1983) to each individual student.

Firm But Flexible Limits. Successful parents state clear limits and enforce them firmly. However, they keep limits flexible and negotiable. Rules are liberalized as children assume more independence and responsibility. Parents who err in either direction are likely to have problems. Those who have few limits or none at all tend to end up with children lacking in self-discipline and self-control, while the children of those whose limits are too numerous and rigid tend to be either overconforming, dependent, and uncreative, or rebellious and resentful (Baumrind, 1971).

The implication here is that successful classroom managers will impose clear-cut classroom rules and enforce them consistently, but keep them to a minimum and flexible enough to allow for individual differences and changes over time. Students can become more and more involved in the rule-setting process as they become more mature.

Positive Expectations. Children tend to acquire their parents' expectations and attitudes, and to use them both for defining what is "normal" and for deciding what expectations and attitudes apply to themselves. One result is the self-fulfilling prophecy, or Pygmalion effect: Regardless of whether expectations originally were accurate, children are likely to fulfill them if adults consistently expect them to have certain qualities and treat them accordingly.

Self-fulfilling prophecy

In the school setting, teachers who expect students to succeed and treat them accordingly are likely to see them succeed, insofar as they can, while teachers who expect them to fail and treat them accordingly are likely to see them fail (Good & Brophy, 1984). Self-fulfilling prophecy effects are not confined to student achievement; they apply with equal force to student conduct. Students treated as basically good people who want to do the right thing, whose lapses are treated as being due to ignorance or forgetfulness, are likely to become the prosocial people they are expected to become (Grusec, Kuczynski, Rushton, & Simutis, 1978; Miller, Brickman, & Bolen, 1975). Students treated as if they are inherently evil or under the control of powerful antisocial impulses, whose lapses are taken as evidence of immorality rather than as isolated mistakes, probably will turn out to be antisocial, just as expected.

Thus it is important for teachers to project positive expectations in their interactions with students, treating them as if they already are or are at least trying to be the kind of people that they as teachers want them to be. Admonitions such as "John, be careful with that microscope—we wouldn't want to break it," or saying in private, "Mary, I was surprised to hear you ridiculing Jean when you were talking to Mary Ann today—how about trying to understand her better rather than just running her down?" illustrate these principles. The teacher should treat the student as a responsible person, or at least as someone who will be responsible in this regard in the future, and provide prescriptive information rather than personal criticism. In contrast, consider comments such as "I don't know why you can't sit still," "Do you think it's funny to make noises like that?" or "You are going to have to find some other way to take out your frustrations—we'll have no hitting in the classroom." These criticisms do not provide positive guidance; they also imply that no change in the student's behavior is really expected.

Supplementing demands with explanations

Rationales and Explanations. Parents tend to be more successful when they supplement their socialization demands with explanations. This means not only telling children what to do, but also telling them why it is important to do it. Explanations of this sort tend to help children see that rules and demands are imposed for good reasons rather than as arbitrary exercises of adult power, and to be aware of the implications of their behavior for themselves and others (Hess, 1970; Hoffman, 1977; Good & Brophy, 1984).

Ability to see implications

This ability to see implications or "take the role of the other" is necessary for the development of a prosocial moral orientation, a tendency to live by the "golden rule"—treating others the way one would like to be treated oneself. Furthermore, if people do not understand the reasons underlying a demand, they are unlikely to adopt it in guiding their own behavior, following it only if they will be punished when they do not. This information can be communicated to individual students during private contacts, but it also can be developed in teacher-led discussions with the class (Good & Brophy, 1984; Glasser, 1969; Gordon, 1974).

Moral development

Research on moral development shows that children progress to successively higher levels of moral knowledge as they grow older (Brophy & Willis, 1981; Lickona, 1975; Kohlberg, 1980; Mosher, 1980). Young children tend to have a hedonistic or punishment-avoidance orientation. Their behavior responds more to their own desires and fears of punishment than to an intellectual moral system. By the time they reach elementary school, children have developed moral codes. However, these tend to be in the form of overgeneralized rules acquired from adults—a list of dos and don'ts followed without any real understanding. Some children never really develop much past this stage, so that even as adults, their moral thinking is mostly confined to a set of overgeneralized, rigid rules.

Where conditions for moral development are more favorable, schoolchildren gradually develop a higher level of moral knowledge. Rules become less rigid as the child learns to take into account situational factors and to separate motives, intentions, and actions. By adolescence, these rules usually are organized into a coherent, general moral system, so that the student not only can identify the most just or moral way of behaving in a given situation, but also can explain his or her choice by relating it to general principles of morality.

Although the situations producing good inner self-control and a highly developed moral sense are complex and not completely understood, at least two things appear to be important. Children must see ideal behavior patterns modeled by the adults around them, and they must come to see that rules are supported by rationales based on logic and consideration of the general welfare of people. Rules should not be seen as arbitrary demands to be followed only because they may be enforced by a powerful authority figure.

Consistency in Rule Enforcement. Inconsistency is confusing. Even if they are willing, it is difficult for people to learn rules if the rules are unclear or keep changing. It also is frustrating, producing resentment and the feeling that the authority figure is arbitrary or undependable if things that were all right yesterday are punished today, or vice versa. This encourages deliberate disobedience (usually called "testing") designed to see if a verbalized rule will really be enforced.

Inconsistency in the ways that different individuals are treated produces resentful feelings of favoritism and being picked on. This is perfectly understandable. If we see authority figures allow others to do something but then we are punished for doing the same thing ourselves, we resent it.

Modeling. This is a special aspect of consistency. It comes down to practicing what you preach. Authority figures usually cannot have a double standard, one for themselves and one for others. Unless they can explain any exceptions satisfactorily, they will have to live up to their own ideals and rules if they expect others to do so. Anything short of this is hypocrisy.

Studies of children's reactions in situations where adults verbalize an ideal but then do not practice it show that children tend to do what they see and not what they hear; that is, they tend to do what they are expected to do. If adults' true expectations differ from their verbalizations, children will tend to conform to the true expectations. The implication of this is clear: teachers must model and generally live up to ideals that they verbalize if they expect their students to follow suit. In areas such as politeness and good manners, friendliness and helpfulness toward others, and consideration for the rights and feelings of others, teachers who do not practice what they preach by modeling it in their own behavior will be perceived as hypocrites or worse, and will not be respected or obeyed (Bryan & Walbek, 1970; Lickona, 1975).

Physical Design of Classrooms

After making basic decisions about their roles, teachers must design a classroom management system (rules, behavior, self-discipline), a social system, and a physical environment that support their instructional and management plans. We will discuss the social and management systems in chapters that follow. Here we stress that teachers' management systems are influenced by the size of the schools in which they teach, the size of their classes, and how they manage physical space. We stress that good management involves the prevention of problems; a carefully laid out physical environment can reduce or eliminate a number of potential problems.

Figure 19.1 Desk Arrangements

A = rows

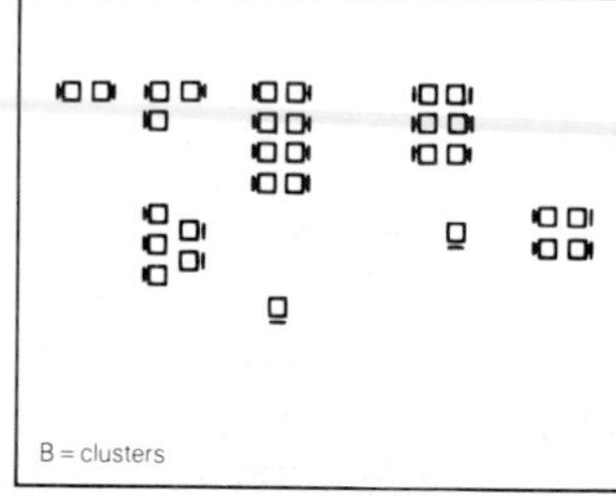

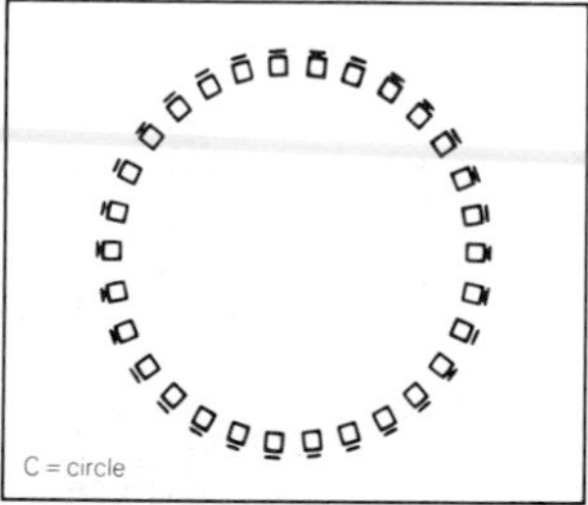

Source: Rosenfield, P., Lambert, N., and Black, A. (1985). Desk arrangement effects on pupil classroom behavior. *Journal of Educational Psychology, 77*(1), 101–108.

Desk arrangement

The effects of physical settings on students are of interest because classroom arrangement influences student involvement and participation rates, and because the use of physical space is not always congruent with intended objectives (Gump and Good, 1976). The physical setting of the classroom can influence student behavior either directly or indirectly through teacher behavior (Arlin, 1979) and through different types of task structure (Doyle, 1985).

As a case in point, Rosenfield, Lambert, and Black (1985) provide clear evidence that desk arrangement influences student behavior. Students were observed during a lesson in which they were brainstorming about ideas for writing assignments. Students who were seated in circles did much better than students who were seated in rows or clusters. Presumably the enhanced visibility made it easier for students to participate and to be monitored (see Figure 19.1). Thus, it is clear that a variety of teachers' decisions, even

The arrangement of desks in a circle can improve student performance.

decisions about how to seat students, can have important influences on student behavior.

Size of School

Barker and Gump (1964) present data to show that as school size increases, individual students' participation in all types of high school activities decreases. Students in small schools are necessarily involved in school life, since the setting itself forces the behavior, more intimately than the average student in a larger school. To achieve the advantages of smaller schools, some larger schools have devised alternative structures such as house plans to give students a greater identity with part of the school.

Though Barker and Gump's data suggest that richness and variability of experience are most likely to occur in the small school, they also show that large schools offer students more opportunities for specialization. Hence, the relative advantages of a school depend on the goals one wants to achieve in the school setting. The nature of the setting obviously makes some goals easier to reach than others. However, as Barker and Gump suggest, it may be easier to bring variety (e.g., TV classes, self-instructional materials) to smaller schools than it is to raise the level of individual participation in large schools.

Much experimental research indicates the undesirable effects of high spatial density. Prerost and Brewer (1975) review research showing that anxiety and irritability increase in crowds and self-evaluation decreases. Their own data show that even humor can be negatively affected by crowded conditions. Large numbers of students, regardless of available space (density), may exert a negative influence on student activity.

Density, though, does not always have undesirable effects. Krantz and Risley (1977) report that some of the undesirable effects of density can be reduced without markedly increasing physical space. They compared the attentiveness of kindergarten children when the children were allowed to crowd in front of the teacher for story time with a condition in which each child sat on a marked and separate floor space. Children's attention was found to be higher in the marked space condition. As Houseman (1972) suggests, clarity of one's physical space helps to reduce conflict.

Size of Class

An intriguing area of educational research concerns the effects of class size on learning. How many students should be in a first-grade classroom, where they will learn to read? Can sixth- or twelfth-grade classes have more students than first-grade classes without reducing their effectiveness? Unfortunately, these and many other questions about class size do not have direct answers, despite their obvious bearing on educational policy.

The largest observational study examining class size and student achievement involved 18,500 classrooms (Olson, 1971). Observers' ratings of individualization, interpersonal regard, group activity, and amount of creativity present in classrooms decreased as class size became greater. Although there are numerous studies showing that smaller class size is not always associated with student achievement gains, Sitku (1968) stresses that there are twice as many studies that favor smaller over larger classes.

A meta-analysis of research on class size conducted by Glass and Smith (1978) shows that on average, smaller classes achieve higher achievement scores than larger classes, and that the advantage of reducing classes is not strong until class size goes below 15 students. However, as Figure 19.2 shows, the expected difference in student achievement between a class with 25 pupils and one with 30 pupils is much smaller than when the reduction goes from 15 to 10 pupils.

In another review of the literature, Smith and Glass (1979) studied the impact of class size on teaching process, teacher satisfaction, and pupil attitude. Teachers appear to have much higher satisfaction scores in smaller classes and students also report somewhat more favorable attitudes. Also, smaller class size was associated with more individualization and more student participation.

Cahen, Filby, McCutcheon, and Kyle (1983) hypothesized that a reduction in class size would increase the amount of time students were actively involved in academic work, increase the frequency of teacher contact with individual pupils, enhance teacher knowledge of students' needs, and increase the quality of instruction. To test these beliefs Cahen et al. reduced the class size of four primary-grade classrooms in two different sites. In one site, class size was reduced from 20 to 13 and in the other site from 35 to 22. They found that students were more involved in work, spent less time

Figure 19.2 The Glass-Smith Curve

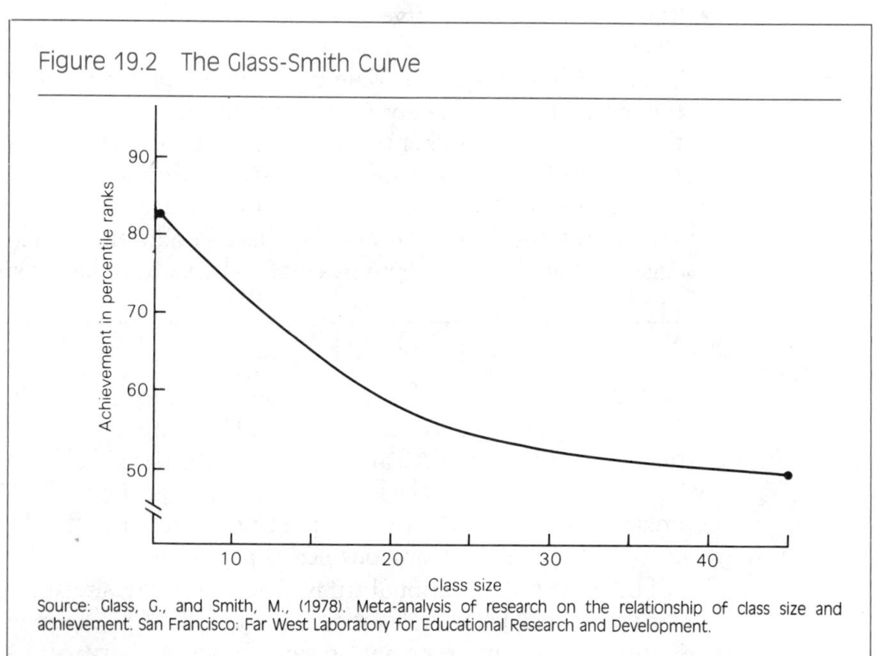

Source: Glass, G., and Smith, M., (1978). Meta-analysis of research on the relationship of class size and achievement. San Francisco: Far West Laboratory for Educational Research and Development.

waiting for teacher feedback when they had a specific problem, were off-task less frequently, and waited less frequently because they had no assignment.

Thus, Cahen et al. found that changes did occur in classroom process; however, the overall pattern of classroom instruction remained the same despite a substantial reduction in classroom size. They note that the classroom program functioned more effectively but the basic program remained the same. Thus, with a smaller class size, teachers did the same thing but with fewer students—fewer students made the management task easier but did not alter the instructional task. They further note in the results of their field study of class size that teachers and students were generally happier and more productive in smaller classes, and achievement was higher. However, they state, "The machinery functioned more smoothly, but the design of the machine remained the same. For those with a different vision of education, this result may be discouraging" (p. 201).

Desirable changes do not occur automatically when class size is reduced. One study concluded that university students were likely to rate large classes as favorably as small classes (Marsh, Overall, & Kesler, 1979). Fox (1967) found that a reduction in class size did not improve learning because teachers taught smaller classes the same way they had taught larger classes.

Minimizing difference in achievement

The importance of the teacher is clearly represented in research conducted by Evertson (1982). Evertson's case studies show how teachers minimize the difference in achievement between large and small classes by working much harder in the larger classes, but at the cost of more regimentation, less individualized contact, and cutting out the important "extras" that may not raise standardized achievement test scores but improve quality of life in classrooms.

The effects of reducing class size are *not* automatic. A smaller class size creates a more favorable environment but the potential gains are mediated by how the teacher uses the opportunity. Teachers who are willing to individualize instruction can use the opportunities created by smaller classes to increase student performance in important ways.

Teacher's management skills

The effects of class size on learning depend on many factors. Particularly important are a teacher's general management skills. Teachers who are poor managers of thirty-two children will probably manage twenty-two children poorly. However, a similar reduction in class size might help an average classroom teacher to become a better manager, and a good teacher to become an excellent one.

Setting up smaller units

Usefulness of Reductions in Size. Although teachers typically cannot directly affect the size of their classes, they can divide their classes into smaller units for some instruction. By using parent volunteers and teacher aides, teachers can increase the amount of time they supervise individual and group work. As we have seen, the very presence of teachers, as well as the feedback they provide, can enhance student involvement. By using different organizational strategies like learning centers or peer tutoring, teachers can also reduce the size of their instructional groups.

If we accept the fact that small groups or small classes may have positive effects on learning or the conditions under which learning takes place, it is important to question why a reduction in size makes a difference. Why should students learn more in small groups as opposed to large groups or whole classes? Students and teachers both may benefit from working in small groups for one or more of the following reasons:

1. Instruction can be geared to the specific needs of the students in the group.
2. The teacher can directly monitor the work of the students and provide corrective feedback immediately.
3. Students may feel more comfortable asking questions in small groups. This may be especially important for shy or slow students.
4. Students may pay more attention and apply themselves to a task a greater percentage of the time because they are under the direct supervision of the teacher.
5. Students may feel more responsible for completion of a task in small groups.

There are limits to the size and range of a group that a teacher can instruct effectively, although we believe that students should come into contact with a variety of learners in school settings. If the variance in learner aptitude in a class is too great, the teacher cannot accommodate it optimally and academic goals suffer. In large classes (more than twenty-five pupils) we hypothesize that teachers who emphasize independent activities are more likely to benefit high-aptitude students. Conversely, teachers in such classes who emphasize large-group instruction are more likely to benefit middle- and low-ability students. In large classes it is probably easier to accommodate differences in learner ability by gearing most activities to low and middle students and supplementing instruction for high-ability students with carefully planned independent work.

Improving Classroom Physical Environments

One of the authors observed an enthusiastic fourth-grade teacher presenting a creative writing assignment. The teacher began by asking students to describe what interesting things they could do with a gigantic box that stood in the front of the room. She wrote suggestions on the board and gave appreciative responses to students who presented ideas. Students were on the edges of their seats, waving their arms with excitement as their ideas were solicited. Eventually, with students participating enthusiastically, the teacher wrote on the board a paragraph combining several ideas.

Then the teacher said, "Now I want you to write your own original story. Tell me the fun things you could do with a giant frog that is bigger than you are! Think and be creative. Take your time. We have half an hour." Five minutes after this request was made, only two or three students had started to work on their stories. The transition from public discussion to private composition was difficult, largely because of the way the teacher had arranged the room. Individual desks had been placed together in groups of six to form rectangular tables. At each cluster, a student had three students sitting directly opposite and one or two students sitting directly beside him or her. If students looked up they were almost guaranteed eye contact with someone sitting close to them.

Students quietly but incessantly continued to exchange ideas for two or three minutes about what they could do with a big box or a big frog. Finally the teacher announced with frustration, "Look, when you finish the paper you can climb up on the chair and put it in the big box!"

The race was on. The room was completely quiet except for the sound of pencils moving rapidly across paper and the occasional ripping of paper as it was torn from a pad. Within seven minutes all students in the class had finished and had climbed the magic chair to drop their stories in the big box. Students were motivated to produce quickly but not to think or to use their imaginations. Unfortunately, a seating arrangement that would have been conducive to small-group work turned out to be inappropriate for private composition.

This story illustrates that other learning stimuli—in this case, motivation—may be more powerful than physical setting variables. At the same time, physical setting variables exert important effects on the learning situation. The teacher's comment inviting students to put their finished papers in the big box had a powerful, negative influence on student behavior. However, in part it was the seating arrangement that produced the lack of student task involvement and led to the teacher's frustration and thoughtless statement.

Match Between Physical Design and Program Activity

Physical seating variables

Some ecological psychologists (e.g., Ross, 1984) use the term synomorphy to refer to the compatibility between the program of action in an activity and the physical aspects of the setting. From the perspective of order, one can easily see how furniture arrangements and types of desks and other equipment can affect the density of students, opportunities for interaction, and the extent to which teachers can observe on-going behavior.

Weinstein (1979) recently reviewed research on the effects of physical features of class environments. She notes that different spatial arrangements appear to have little effect on student achievement but do affect students' attitudes and conduct. In particular, it seems important to clearly separate areas serving different purposes and to design classroom traffic avenues carefully. Density appears to increase dissatisfaction and aggression and to decrease student attentiveness and involvement in assigned activities.

Synomorphy

As classroom functions change, seating patterns must be altered. Despite the fact that many classrooms are equipped with movable desks, some teachers use one seating arrangement exclusively.

Altering room arrangements

The room in Figure 19.3 is arranged for students to listen to individual reports given by three students. This arrangement is acceptable for this purpose, but not ideal. It is adequate because most students can see the

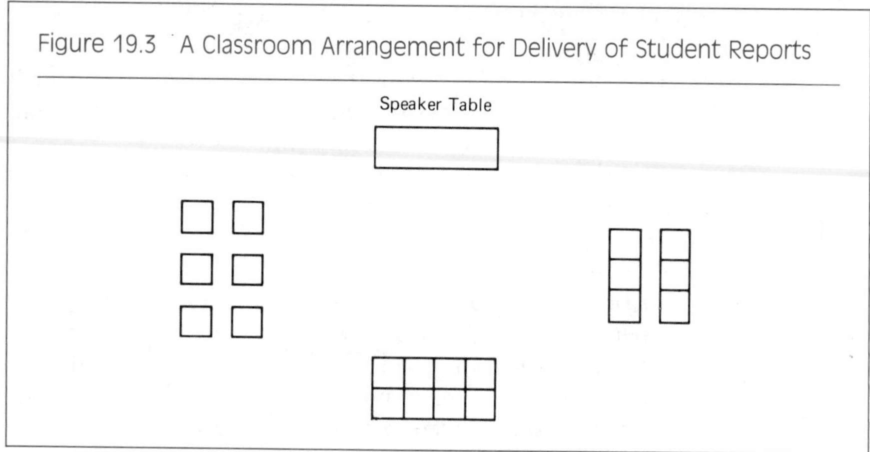

Figure 19.3 A Classroom Arrangement for Delivery of Student Reports

speaker if the speaker stands, although pupils who have inside seats will face away from their desks and may have a difficult time taking notes. If students need to pass out material or demonstrate a procedure, the clustering of students and the open space will facilitate either of these needs. What makes this plan an effective design is the fact that the teacher plans to follow the three five-minute presentations with a half hour of related small-group work. The arrangement is fine for small-group activity and students can begin to work as soon as the presentations end. Furthermore, the groups are arranged so that the teacher, by selecting an appropriate position while working with one group, can also monitor the other groups easily. The teacher could sit in the middle of the open-space area and allow students to come to him or her as they need information or clarification. However, with young children, or early in the year, it is more profitable for the teacher to rotate from group to group.

Figure 19.4 illustrates several different seating arrangements. Again we make the point that there is no single ideal arrangement. Some seating patterns support certain types of behavior and activities better than others.

Space Utilization

Physical environment and behavior

Some research suggests that minor changes in the physical environment can lead to important changes in behavior. For example, Weinstein (1977) found that additional shelving, increased space for individual work, and more partitions around certain areas encouraged more frequent use of individual work areas in open classrooms. After these physical changes had been made, management problems decreased and task-relevant behaviors increased.

Evans and Lovell, used sound-absorbent partitions of varying height that were placed so that traffic was directed away from certain class areas and that made class area boundaries more salient, resulting in several small areas

Figure 19.4 Several Classroom Seating Arrangements

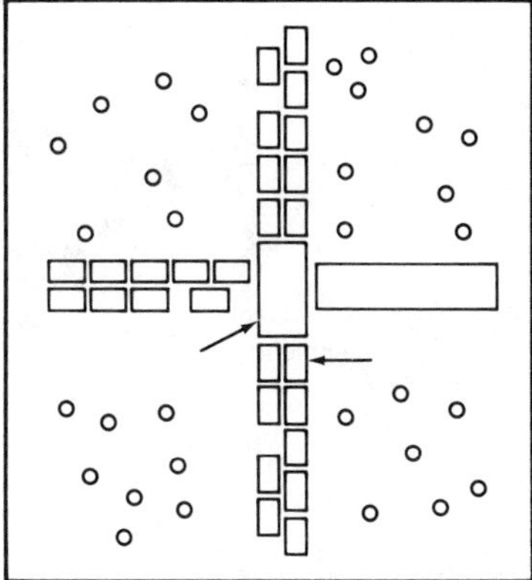

This "cross plan" creates more floor space. The open areas can be used when exploring a variety of different activities.

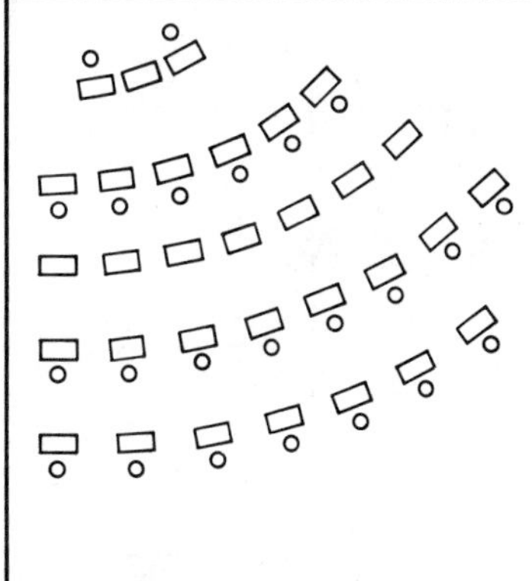

The class directs its attention to one or two people in front of the group. This arrangement can be used to prepare for a lesson or to summarize and evaluate a recently completed activity.

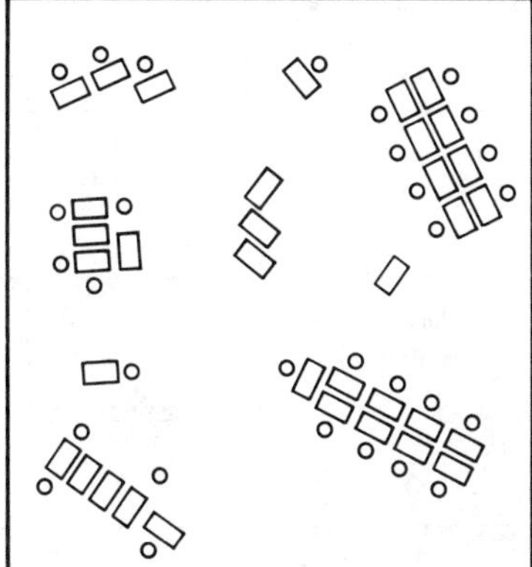

This arrangement allows pupils to work in small group activities and move freely from one work area to another.

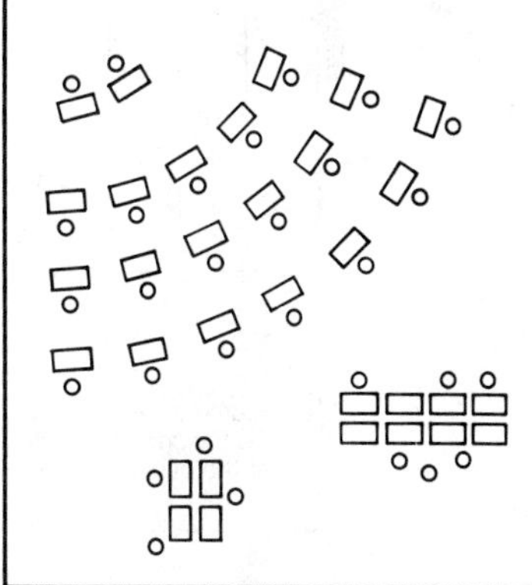

This plan provides for a large group activity while two smaller groups work on projects elsewhere in the room. To minimize distractions, children in the large group face away from the work areas.

Source: Reproduced by permission from Reys, R., and Post, T. (1973). *The Mathematics Laboratory: Theory to Practice*. Boston: Prindle, Weber, and Schmidt.

Figure 19.5 An Experimental Floor Plan Before the Intervention

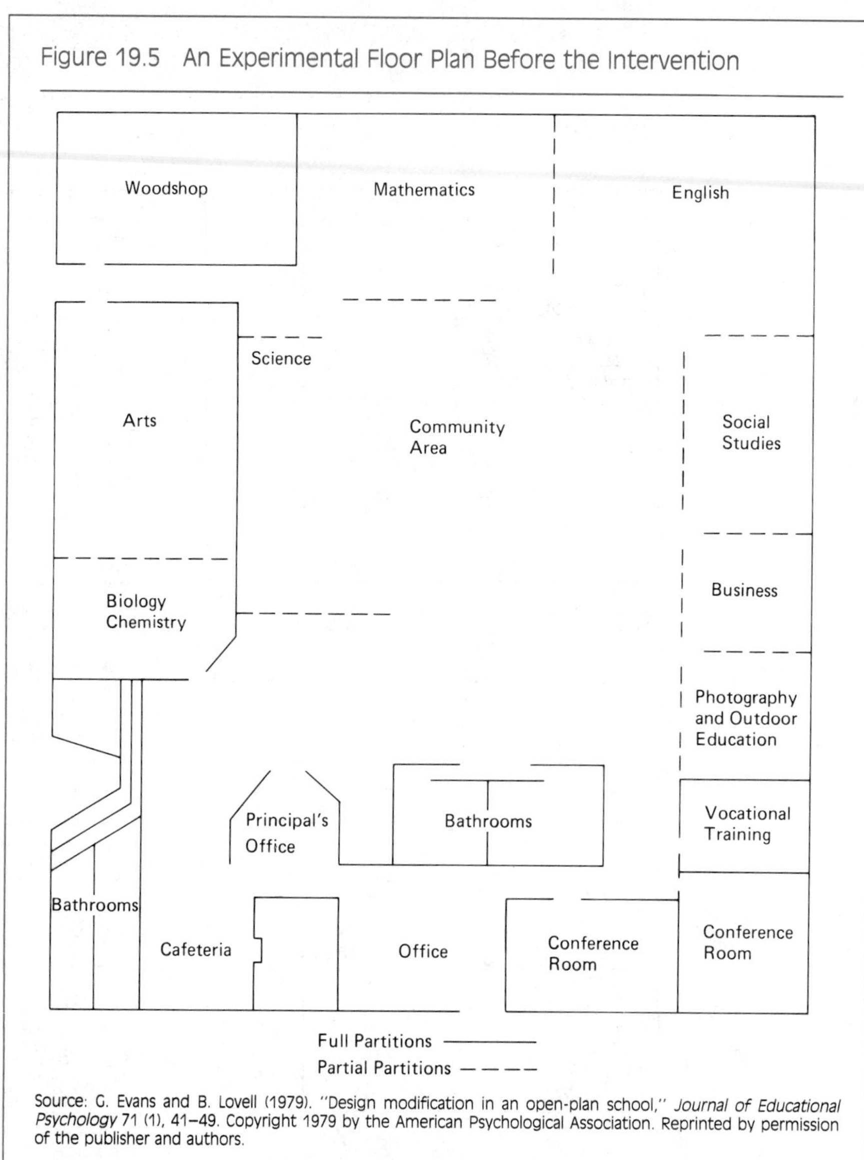

Source: G. Evans and B. Lovell (1979). "Design modification in an open-plan school," *Journal of Educational Psychology* 71 (1), 41–49. Copyright 1979 by the American Psychological Association. Reprinted by permission of the publisher and authors.

that provided more opportunity for private work. Both the control and the experimental schools were alternative high schools with similar philosophies. The physical arrangement in the experimental school before and after the modification is shown in Figures 19.5 and 19.6. Observations were made in both the experimental and control schools before and after the design changes in the experimental school. Results showed that classroom interruptions decreased and that the number of content questions increased. Hence, the design changes in the open-plan high school were associated with desirable changes in classroom behavior.

Glaser (1977) notes that the physical design of the classroom must support the psychological requirements of the learning model being used if instruction is to be effective. In an open classroom using both individual and group instruction, it is important that the classroom boundaries be very distinct to prevent one group of students or activities from interfering with another group. Although this is simply common sense, it is amazing how often a classroom's physical arrangement does not support on-going instructional activities.

Wang (1973) provides useful advice about designing classrooms for individualized instruction in the early elementary school years. Her design for a first-grade classroom is shown in Figure 19.7.

As Glaser notes, there are several distinctive aspects to this physical arrangement. He identifies the following features:

Figure 19.6 An Experimental Floor Plan After the Intervention

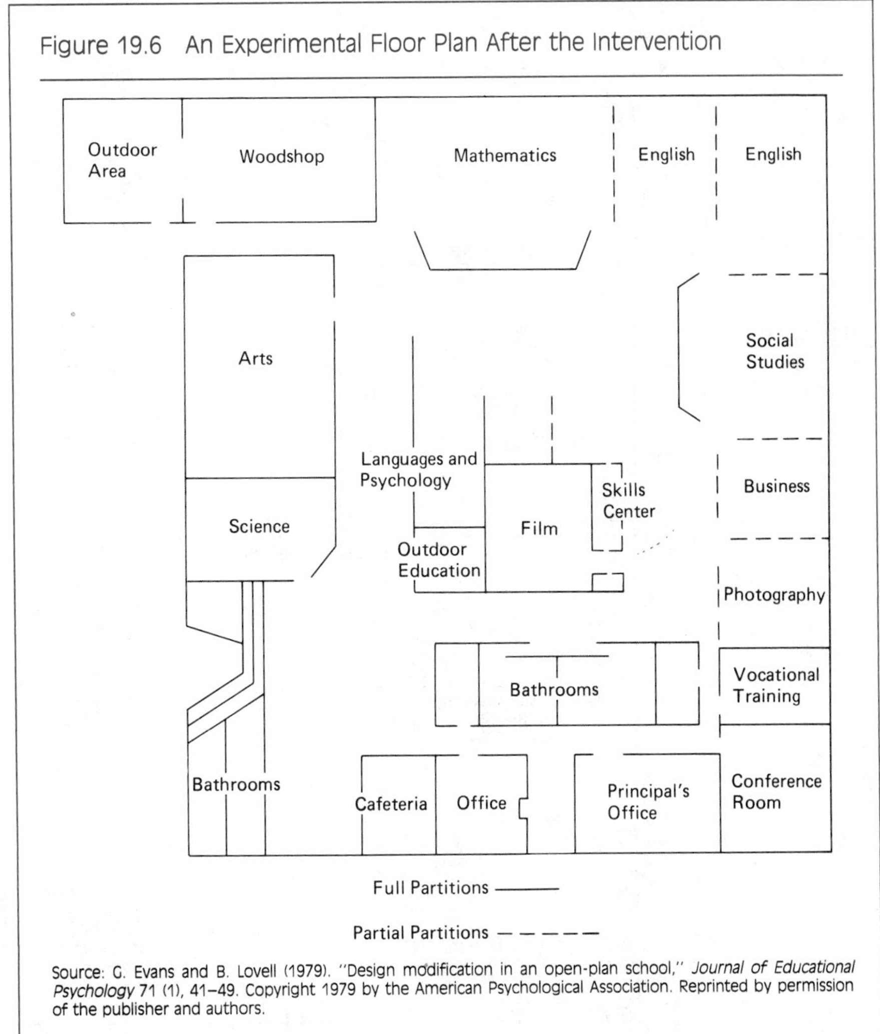

Source: G. Evans and B. Lovell (1979). "Design modification in an open-plan school," *Journal of Educational Psychology* 71 (1), 41–49. Copyright 1979 by the American Psychological Association. Reprinted by permission of the publisher and authors.

Figure 19.7 A Recommended First-Grade Classroom

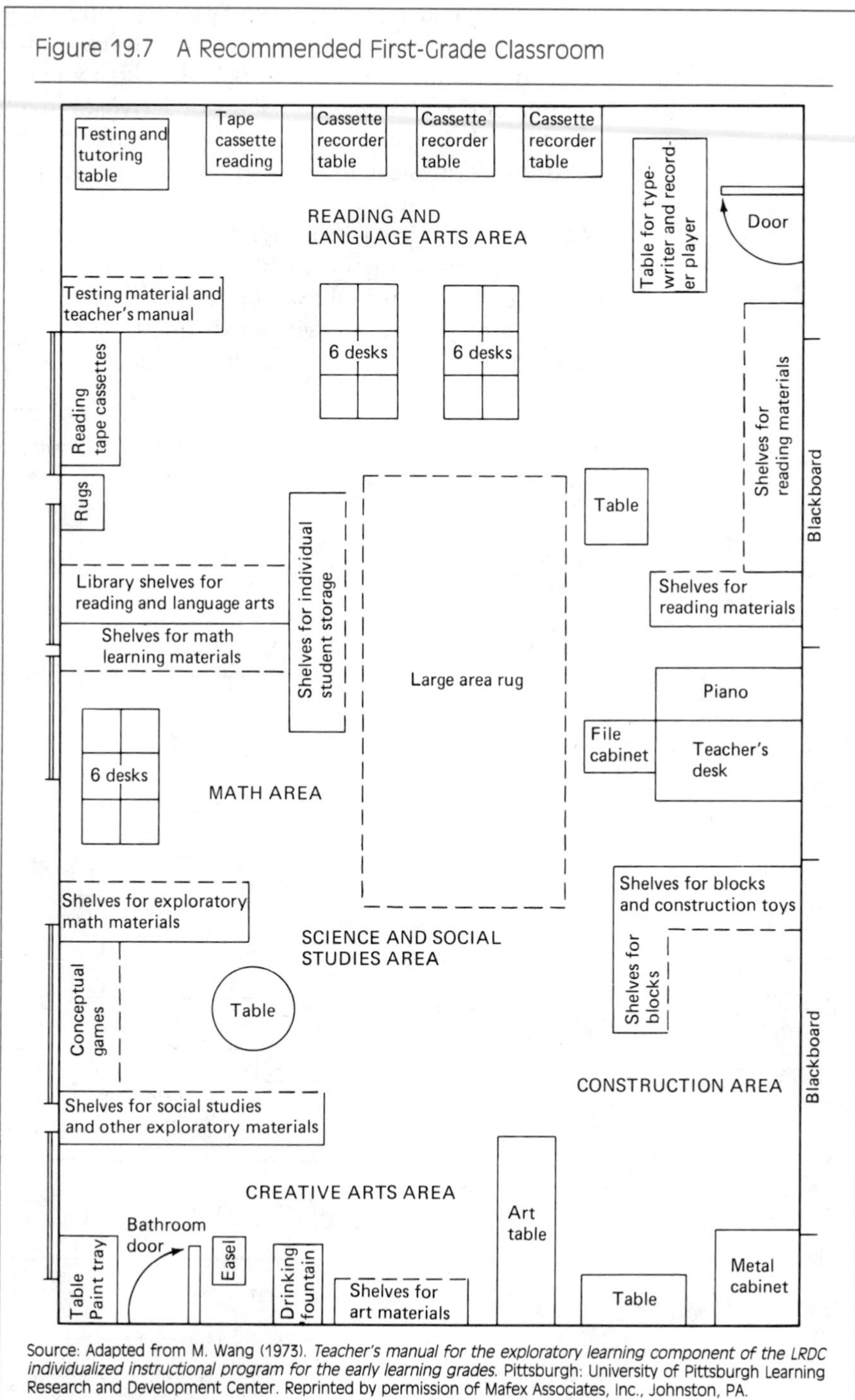

Source: Adapted from M. Wang (1973). *Teacher's manual for the exploratory learning component of the LRDC individualized instructional program for the early learning grades.* Pittsburgh: University of Pittsburgh Learning Research and Development Center. Reprinted by permission of Mafex Associates, Inc., Johnston, PA.

1. The rows of desks are gone. There are places for individual work, and places for group work and interaction.
2. Each work area is clearly defined.
3. There is storage space in each area so that material needed in that area can be obtained easily.
4. The physical areas are arranged in order to encourage integration of activities and sharing of equipment (e.g., math and science areas are adjacent).
5. The open space encourages movement and flexibility.

If space is not used effectively, the advantages of small-group instruction can easily be lost. It is better to instruct thirty students in a large group than to allow small groups to work under conditions that prohibit concentration.

SUMMARY

Effective classroom management involves both clear expectations about student behavior and knowledge about what to do when expectations are not met. Although age, sex, and ethnic differences play a role, common basic principles seem to apply. Thus, teachers who are friendly, mature, sincere, trustworthy, and who have sufficient ego strength to deal fairly and constructively with students can use a variety of techniques effectively. Such teachers will consider the characteristics of various developmental stages along with sex, ethnicity, and past experiences in dealing with students.

The role of socialization agent is a difficult one with many constraints and powerful forces opposing it. However, teachers have some advantages over therapists and other specialists because of their frequency of contact with students and student expectations that they will maintain authority over classroom behavior. To be successful, teachers must be consistent, positive in their approach, and determined in their suppression of unacceptable behavior. They must have realistic perceptions of themselves and of students, enjoy students within the confines of the relationship, be clear and comfortable in role portrayal, exhibit positive attitudes toward tests and challenges, and display patience and determination in dealing with persistent misbehavior.

Like parents, teachers must project acceptance and unconditional positive regard for students, set firm but flexible limits, uphold the positive expectations that lead to success and responsible behavior, provide explanations for socialization demands, be consistent in rule enforcement, and model desired behaviors that they expect students to exhibit.

Classroom environments generally can be improved by carefully considering stimuli affecting student behavior, including those originating from peers, teacher, space, furniture, and displays. Glaser emphasizes the need to make physical design supportive of the psychological requirements for learning. That is especially important if the advantages of small-group instruction are to be realized, since student task-orientation and accountability can be either supported or disrupted by the physical setting.

QUESTIONS AND PROBLEMS

1. Do you fit Fuller's (1969) interpretation of developmental stages in the process of becoming a teacher? Are you concerned primarily about "survival" and classroom management right now?
2. A prospective teacher from a white, middle-class, suburban home is faced with the prospect of teaching in an inner-city school with lower-class, urban, minority students. What should this person do to prepare? What should a new teacher in the process of escaping urban slum life do to prepare for teaching in a "silk stocking" district?
3. What is your preferred role in the balance between instructional and managerial/counseling activities with students?
4. How can teachers be "overly" sympathetic to disturbed students?
5. What kinds of students are especially appealing to you and thus likely to receive favoritism if you are not careful? What kinds turn you off and will be especially hard for you to treat impartially and with positive attitudes and expectations?
6. Do you have strong preferences concerning seating arrangements or classroom groupings? What implications do these have for your teaching?

CASE STUDIES

Pranksters. Jim Knipp, an algebra teacher at Willow High School, sits down at his desk and immediately springs to his feet. A quick glance confirms his guess that he had sat down on a melted candy bar. The class resounds with the howl of laughter. What should Jim do now?

Talkative Margery. Jim Heald, a first-year teacher, watched with interest as three attractive girls burst into the room, glanced at him, and headed for the back of the class. As the period wore on, he became progressively more irritated with the girls. They talked incessantly during his presentation. Finally in frustration he called on Margery, the loudest of the three. "Margery, I've been trying to explain the goals of our physics class. You've been talking for the past 20 minutes. Apparently, you know what our goals are here. Would you please summarize them for me?" She looked at him, and half laughed as she said, "No, I think I'd better listen."

Would you have responded to Margery in the same way that Jim Heald did? If not, why not? In general, should students be allowed to choose their seats in high school classes? Why, or why not? Do elementary school students need more or less choice than secondary students?

Chapter 20

Establishing and Maintaining A Good Learning Environment

CHAPTER OUTLINE

Preparing the Physical Environment
- Overall Monitoring
- Seating Arrangements
- Traffic, Bottlenecks, and Lines
- Student Independence and Responsibility
- Backup Activities
- Supplies and Equipment

General Principles of Group Leadership
- Group Structure
- Leadership Style
- Teacher Image
- Reasonable Rules and Limits
- Minimal and Flexible Rules
- Getting Off to a Good Start
- Research on Management Early in the School Year
- Why Proactive Management Works: Toward a Theory
- Student Control
- Research into Practice

Specific Group Management Techniques
- Other Studies of Group Management

Maintaining Attention During Lessons

Maintaining Engagement in Seatwork

OBJECTIVES

When you have mastered the material in this chapter you will be able to

1. Describe what a teacher can do to make the classroom an environment that promotes learning, independence, and responsibility
2. Differentiate authoritarian, democratic, and laissez-faire leadership styles
3. Describe authoritative leadership and its effects, and differentiate it from democratic leadership
4. Discuss things a teacher can do to build personal trust and credibility with students
5. List and explain at least four characteristics of classroom rules that assist classroom management
6. Discuss these group management skills of successful teachers: preparedness, maintaining student involvement, "withitness," overlapping, and group alerting
7. Explain at least three techniques to engage and maintain students' attention during lessons or seatwork

In this chapter we first discuss the advance preparation that contributes to effective classroom management, especially the need to arrange the physical environment for efficient functioning and to develop a workable set of classroom rules. This discussion builds on the research evidence presented in the preceding chapter on the effect of the physical environment on student behavior. The previous discussion stressed the importance of a match between the teacher's goals and the physical arrangement of the classroom. Here we emphasize practical ways for preparing effective classroom environments. Finally, we will review theory and research on group leadership styles and techniques and discuss specific classroom practices that follow from this research.

Preparing the Physical Environment

Effective classroom management begins with preparation of the classroom itself. What can be done to make it an attractive and efficient learning environment? Regardless of how good or bad the available space and equipment may be, some arrangements are going to be better than others. There may be several arrangements that are appropriate, if the teacher is going to be dealing with different classes that vary in size or other important ways, or if the class is going to involve diverse activities.

Overall Monitoring

High priority should be given to arranging the classroom so that the teacher can monitor all areas at all times. Teachers should plan to sit or stand so that they are facing the class, and should keep this in mind when identifying areas of the room that will be used for the whole class or for small group lessons. Students should be seated facing the teacher when attention to the teacher is expected. This will make it easier for the teacher to monitor the class and will minimize the degree to which students distract one another.

Seating Arrangements

Students' seats should be located in ways that will facilitate attention and minimize disruption. Usually this will mean keeping desks or tables in reasonably neat arrangements, with students seated facing the teacher. However, other arrangements will be optimal when students are assigned to work in groups. The groups can then be arranged in small circles or ovals, facilitating small-group communication. If several groups are meeting simultaneously, they should be spread out so as to minimize interference and distraction. Assuming that they act responsibly without supervision, perhaps they can be allowed to meet outside the classroom, so as not to disturb the rest of the class.

Traffic, Bottlenecks, and Lines

Heavily traveled traffic routes should be free of obstacles and wide enough to accommodate the flow. This will make for smooth, efficient movement around the classroom and will minimize the problems that occur when students bump into furniture or one another.

Minimize waiting time

Problems are likely to develop when students are standing in lines, whether these are deliberately formed by the teacher or are the result of bottlenecks. Teachers can do many things to minimize the time students spend standing and waiting. One is to delegate authority or use monitors to handle time-consuming housekeeping tasks such as passing out books or papers, checking out supplies, taking attendance, and making collections. Activities like using the toilet or drinking fountain can be left to individual initiative within whatever limits are necessary, instead of requiring large groups to go at one time or using some other regimented approach.

Students enjoy serving as monitors.

Supplies like scissors or paste should be dispensed from several places around the room so students do not have to line up and wait their turn at a single source. Checking worksheets can be accomplished as a group activity, by asking students to indicate a need for checking when they are ready or when they think they need help, or by the teacher circulating around the room. Necessarily repetitive activities like "show and tell" or having students give brief speeches can be staggered across several days to avoid the boredom that sets in when everyone takes a turn in a single session.

Student Independence and Responsibility

Helping students handle routine tasks

Too much time is often spent supervising students in meeting their personal needs and everyday housekeeping tasks. Interruptions for these purposes are a major source of discontinuity in academic activities. Teachers can minimize these interruptions by preparing the classroom and the students so that students can handle most routine tasks on their own. This is especially important in the early grades when a student's ability to handle everyday tasks may depend on the degree to which the teacher has anticipated his or her needs. Young students can handle most of their own belongings with the help of coat hooks and cubbyholes or lockers, but these should be within easy reach and should be assigned individually. Color codes, pictures, and labels can be affixed to storage areas to help students locate what they are looking for and remember where to return the items when they are finished. Everyday equipment should be stored where it can be reached and removed easily, and small items should be stored in containers that will not break and that can be opened and closed without difficulty. Notices giving instructions or rule reminders can be displayed prominently in activity centers so that students who need help will not always have to come to the teacher.

Backup Activities

Effective classroom managers have contingency plans for what to do when scheduled activities are canceled or bad weather precludes outdoor recess. They prepare for these times as they would for lessons. Any needed props are handy, and the teacher is ready to conduct the activity smoothly. Even more important is the development of a system of backup activities, preferably including options to allow for individual choice, to make available to students when they finish independent work assignments. These options should include a number of attractive individual and small-group learning activities and pastimes. The students should know what their options are and what rules govern them, and should be able to exercise these options on their own initiative without having to get directions from the teacher.

Options for individual choice

Preventive preparation of this kind will cut down the time teachers need to spend handling routine classroom management problems, thus making the task much easier.

Supplies and Equipment

In order to reduce managerial squabbles that result when students try to borrow or take one another's supplies, teachers should keep in a handy but safe place a supply of commonly used materials and equipment that students are expected to bring on their own but occasionally lose or forget. Agreements and regulations will be required to see that this extra equipment supply continues to fulfill its original purpose and does not become abused by students who desire to keep "borrowed" items, or who deliberately "forget" things in order to get extra attention from the teacher.

General Principles of Group Leadership

In addition to organizing the physical environment, teachers must organize the individuals assigned to the class into a cohesive group that functions effectively under their leadership. Several general principles are involved here, as well as numerous specific techniques for specific situations.

Group Structure

Effective groups show cohesiveness and positive attitudes. Less effective groups are divided into conflicting subgroups or into a dominant ingroup and a collection of isolated individuals in the outgroup. As the classroom leaders, teachers can promote group cohesiveness by arranging for cooperative experiences, minimizing competition, promoting prosocial behaviors, and helping each member of the class to identify with the class as a whole. They should avoid such behaviors as playing favorites, picking on scapegoats, fostering inappropriate competition, or refusing to allow students to work together or help one another (Johnson, 1970; Johnson & Johnson, 1975; Stanford, 1977; Slavin et al., 1985).

Promoting group cohesiveness

Gaining confidence of peer leaders

Where students have been together for some years and constitute an intact group with well-established peer leadership, teachers probably will need to gain the confidence and cooperation of the peer leaders, and avoid coming into direct conflict with them or causing them to lose face before the group.

Leadership Style

Authoritarian, democratic, and laissez-faire leadership

Lewin, Lippitt, and White (1939) conducted a classic field experiment in which adults working with groups of ten-year-old boys were trained to act consistently authoritarian, democratic, or laissez-faire. Authoritarian leaders gave orders without much explanation, telling everyone what to do and with whom. Democratic leaders took time to solicit opinions and achieve some consensus about what to do and how to do it, and allowed some choice of work companions. Laissez-faire leaders did not really lead at all, giving only vague directions and sketchy answers to questions. The three leadership styles were evaluated both for group productivity (Were the groups efficient in carrying out assigned tasks?) and group affect (Did the boys enjoy the experience?).

Boys in democratic-led groups developed warm feelings for one another and for the leader, and enjoyed their experience. These affective benefits were achieved with only a slight cost in efficiency—the productivity of the democratic-led groups was not quite as good as that of the authoritarian-led groups. The authoritarian-led groups were the most efficient because the leaders kept everyone working at a good pace. However, the boys in these groups showed tension and generally negative feelings toward one another and toward the leader. Laissez-faire leadership did not succeed by either criterion. The ostensible freedom experienced by these boys did not make up for the lack of leadership, so they spent much time working at cross purposes, produced very little, and had negative reactions to the experience.

Later studies of group leadership have produced similar results. Laissez-faire leadership is generally ineffective; authoritarian leadership is efficient but otherwise unattractive; and democratic leadership produces positive attitudes and good group relations, although at some cost in efficiency. This implies that democratic leadership is best as an overall style, although more structured leadership may be required when efficiency is important.

Authoritative leadership

Baumrind's (1971) research on child rearing provides some perspective for these findings on group leadership styles. Baumrind classified parents as authoritarian, authoritative, or laissez-faire. These classifications are similar to those used by Lewin, Lippitt, and White (1939), except that "authoritative" replaces "democratic." As Baumrind (1971) notes, "democratic" leadership is not really democratic at all because decisions are not made by majority vote. It is "authoritative" in the sense that the leader has a position of authority and responsibility, speaks as an experienced and mature adult, and retains ultimate decision-making power. However, rather than act in an authoritarian manner, authoritative leaders solicit input, seek consensus, and take care to see that everyone understands the rationales for decisions as well as the decisions themselves. Baumrind reports that children of authoritative parents show the most advanced levels of autonomy and independence for their ages, and have greater confidence and healthier self-concepts.

There are two reasons for stressing Baumrind's work in discussing classroom management. First, the term authoritative is preferable to the term democratic because it retains the notion that the teacher has the ultimate responsibility for classroom leadership. The idea that decisions should be made by majority vote was not intended and is not supported by the research of Lewin, Lippitt, and White (1939), despite their use of the term democratic. Nor does other research support the notion of truly democratic classroom leadership, although this style is often recommended on a philosophical basis (e.g., Glasser, 1969; Gordon, 1974).

Second, this research provides a more convincing and data-based argument to support authoritative over authoritarian and laissez-faire methods. Authoritative methods are not merely better perceived; they are more effective in building the cognitive structures and behavioral control mechanisms within children that enable them to become both independent and responsible in managing their affairs. Authoritative teacher behavior in the classroom should help students to see and internalize the rationales that underlie classroom rules, and to learn to operate within the rules on their own initiative. Authoritarian approaches based on external pressure do not encourage the development of internal control mechanisms. Instead, they generate conflict and tension even when they succeed in controlling behavior (Hoffman, 1977).

Teacher Image

Teachers must establish themselves in the eyes of students as likeable, knowledgeable, respectable, credible, trustworthy, and generally attractive individuals. The specifics of this will vary with each teacher's unique personality and style, but certain common themes are important. One way or another, teachers should get across ideas such as the following:

- ☐ That they enjoy both the personal interaction and the instructional aspects of teaching.
- ☐ That they look forward to knowing each student individually and are willing to help students however they can, not just with the subject matter.
- ☐ That they expect to teach the subject matter successfully to all students and are prepared to help each individual progress as far as he or she can.
- ☐ That they view themselves as teachers and resource persons, not as disciplinarians. Certain behavior is expected and insisted on, and other kinds of behavior are forbidden, but the teacher will not make an issue of these matters unless a student does.

Student testing of teachers

Students will test teachers on these and other matters, and teachers need to respond in ways consistent with what they have led the students to expect. This builds trust and credibility, and minimizes misbehavior that occurs for no other reason than to find out if teachers mean what they say.

Reasonable Rules and Limits

Setting rules

Teachers must decide for themselves what are reasonable rules and limits based on circumstances. The "circumstances" include the teacher's own role definition and values, the ages and number of students involved, the length of interaction with students (keeping the same ones all day long versus changing classes every fifty or sixty minutes), the general levels of student conformity versus rebelliousness, and the regulations of the principal and the school district. It is not possible to state a simple set of rules that can be used by all teachers.

For example, a kindergarten or first-grade teacher usually will have to take personal charge of tasks such as passing out paper or worksheets, although some children can help in monitor roles. Fifth- or sixth-grade teachers will not need to perform this job. The students themselves will already have most items, and they can simply be instructed to pick up supplies distributed in class. Supply distribution rules generally are not needed in high school, but teachers should develop efficient ways to distribute materials so that time is not wasted or disruptions encouraged.

Supply distribution

Similarly, in the early grades teachers may have to insist that no one respond to questions or make comments without first being called on (Anderson, Evertson, & Brophy, 1979). However, as students get older and more able to participate in group discussions, teachers can and probably should be more flexible (Evertson, Anderson, & Brophy, 1978). Flat prohibitions against calling out should be abandoned in favor of rules such as "Feel free to contribute your ideas to the discussion, but wait until the person who is speaking has finished." When several want to talk at once, the teacher can keep track of the order informally and intervene if necessary, but there is no need for the kind of rules used in first grade.

Student responses

Minimal and Flexible Rules

Some general guidelines can be put forward. First, rules should be minimized, should refer to the general qualitative aspects of behavior rather than to specific dos and don'ts, and should be flexible and open to change as situations dictate. Minimizing the number of rules helps make it easy for all students to remember them and makes accepting them easier than if a long and demoralizing list were involved.

Rules such as "We will treat one another with courtesy and respect" or "We will keep the classroom clean and neat" cover a great number of specific behaviors and eliminate the need for long lists of specifics. Such rules are broad, but still prescriptive enough for most of the specifics to be obvious.

Furthermore, they are phrased in positive ways that make them easier to explain in a manner likely to motivate students toward acceptance.

Maintaining flexibility

Maintaining flexibility is important because many behaviors are appropriate or at least tolerable under some circumstances, but not others. For example, quiet talking might be allowed for those who have finished assignments. If this gets too loud, the teacher can simply say so and ask the students to quiet down—there is no need to demand total silence or to revoke the talking privileges. This avoids two problems that frequently cause conflict between teachers and students: unreasonable enforcement of a rule, or, conversely, loss of teacher credibility resulting from inconsistency, which students perceive as teacher confusion or hypocrisy rather than reasonable adjustment to situational differences.

Certain behavioristic approaches include the notion that rules should be extremely specific in order to avoid confusion and spell out the consequences of violations. We believe, however, that any gains in avoidance of misunderstanding that might come with a large number of overly specific rules would be canceled by the communication of negative expectations and needless regimentation.

Getting Off to a Good Start

A good student response must be earned; it cannot be taken for granted. In fact, in classrooms where conflict with authority figures in general and teachers in particular is typical, getting the year off to a good start by establishing the right expectations and relationships is crucial (Doyle, 1985; Moskowitz & Hayman, 1976). This may mean that several days or even weeks must be devoted more to getting organized and socialized than to teaching the curriculum, but time spent this way is well worth it in the long run (Evertson & Anderson, 1979). In the early grades, teachers will need to conduct actual lessons, including instruction, practice with feedback, and review, to show students how to handle daily routines such as moving from a reading group to seatwork, using the pencil sharpener, or managing the equipment in a learning center. Older students may not need such detailed instruction, but teacher expectations should be made explicit enough to prevent students from becoming involved in a game of "What rules apply here?" (Evertson & Anderson, 1978).

Research on Management Early in the School Year

Until recently there had been relatively little examination of how teachers organize and manage classrooms at the beginning of the year. Fortunately, in the past few years there has been important research in this area—research that is especially useful to beginning teachers.

To collect evidence related to classroom management at the beginning of the school year, Emmer, Evertson, and Anderson (1980) intensively observed in 27 third-grade classrooms during the first three weeks of the school year and at three- or four-week intervals throughout the year. Using these data, they then identified teachers who had comparable classes at the beginning of the year but differed in their management effectiveness (degree of student involvement in lessons) during the year. Comparisons of these teachers revealed that successful classroom managers devoted much of the first day and the first few weeks to establishing classroom procedures and rules, beginning with those of most immediate interest to the students (bathroom, storage, lunch, recess, and so on).

The first few academic activities introduced were simple, enjoyable, and likely to produce success. The teachers usually worked with the whole class and stayed with and personally supervised the students the entire time, putting off grouping and sustained independent work until basic procedures and routines were established. They monitored students carefully so that they could move quickly when instructional help or behavioral intervention were needed. They told students precisely what they wanted them to do, and then supervised them while they did it. In general, they established their credibility by following through on their statements so that the students learned that they meant what they said.

Importance of advanced planning

The successful managers also revealed evidence of advanced planning and preparation. They had arranged their rooms to make the best of whatever resources they were given to work with, often making changes in anticipation of problems with existing arrangements. They had thought about their rules and expectations so they could describe them to students in specific terms. They handled most housekeeping and paperwork before students arrived at school or after they went home, so that most classroom time was spent instructing the class. In general, they were better prepared and organized, not only for managing student conduct, but for instruction as well. In contrast, the least effective classroom managers created problems for themselves practically from the moment students arrived because they were unclear or inconsistent about stating what they wanted, or because they failed to follow through.

Based on the results of this classroom organization study and related classroom management research, Evertson, Emmer, Sanford, and Clements (1983) wrote *Improving Classroom Management: An Experiment in Elementary School Classrooms*, a manual summarizing management principles and guidelines for starting the school year. The manual is organized around eleven guidelines for classroom organization, and contains case studies, checklists, and detailed explanations for each guideline. The eleven guidelines appear in Table 20.1.

In a related study, experimental teachers received the manual and attended two three-hour workshops. Twenty-three elementary school teachers (Grades 1 through 6) received the training and 18 others served as control teachers—they agreed to be observed but had no information about the eleven good management practices.

Observational data indicated that treatment teachers used more of the recommended behaviors than control teachers, though some of the control teachers were good managers. In addition, there were significantly fewer inappropriate student behaviors, lower proportions of students off-task, and

Table 20.1 Classroom Guidelines for Organization and Management

1. *Readying the classroom.*—Be certain your classroom space and materials are ready for the beginning of the year.
2. *Planning rules and procedures.*—Think about what procedures students must follow to function effectively in your classroom and in the school environment; decide what behaviors are acceptable; develop a list of procedures and rules.
3. *Consequences.*—Decide ahead of time consequences for appropriate and inappropriate behavior in your classroom, and communicate them to your students; follow through consistently.
4. *Teaching rules and procedures.*—Teach students rules and procedures systematically; include in your lesson plans for the beginning of school sequences for teaching rules and procedures, when and how they will be taught, and when practice and review will occur.
5. *Beginning-of-school activities.*—Develop activities for the first few days of school that will involve students readily and maintain a whole-group focus.
6. *Strategies for potential problems.*—Plan strategies to deal with potential problems that could upset your classroom organization and management.
7. *Monitoring.*—Monitor student behavior closely.
8. *Stopping inappropriate behavior.*—Handle inappropriate and disruptive behavior promptly and consistently.
9. *Organizing instruction.*—Organize instruction to provide learning activities at suitable levels for all students in your class.
10. *Student accountability.*—Develop procedures that keep the students responsible for their work.
11. *Instructional clarity.*—Be clear when you present information and give directions to your students.

Source: From "Improving Classroom Management: An Experiment in Elementary School Classrooms" by C. M. Evertson, E. T. Emmer, J. P. Sanford, and B. S. Clements, 1983. *Elementary School Journal, 84*(2).

greater proportions of students engaged in appropriate tasks in the treatment classes than in the control classes.

These same researchers also wrote a manual for junior high school management and have examined the effects of good training at that level as well. They note that junior high teachers did not need to do as much instruction concerning basic classroom routines, but they needed to be very clear and consistent in following up on accountability procedures concerning seatwork.

Importance of teaching routines and procedures early

In another study, Evertson and Anderson (1979) found that effective managers spent more time at the beginning of the year helping students to behave appropriately. These teachers had carefully thought out general standards for classroom conduct and procedures concerning how students could get assistance, line up, and turn work in, and they communicated this information to students. Some teachers had to "teach" these skills daily, but effective managers taught them systematically only at the beginning of the school year. Although it seems a small point, it is amazing how much time teachers can save by teaching simple routines and procedural expectations to students early in the year.

Importance of dealing quickly with misbehavior

Evertson and Anderson report that better managers were also more careful monitors of student behavior and dealt with misbehavior more quickly than less effective managers. More effective managers alerted students to the behavior they expected and held students accountable. To the extent that students internalized these rules, they could monitor their own behavior more continuously (e.g., they knew when and how to get help from other students about missed assignments).

In a study that compared how beginning teachers started the year with the procedures used by a group of more experienced teachers nominated as "best" teachers by their students, Moskowitz and Hayman (1976) found that experienced teachers spent more time setting expectations and establishing behavior patterns on the first day than the beginning teachers did. Even so, the experienced teachers were also more willing to accept and use student ideas. Hence, teachers who are successful managers are not necessarily stern and rigid. They do appear to be skillful in stating expectations and listening to and working with students to be sure that workable rules are established and enforced (workable and shared expectations are probably more important conditions than who initiates the rules). Simply put, these instructors teach norms for appropriate classroom behavior.

Why Proactive Management Works: Toward a Theory

Teachers who are successful managers start the year by establishing rules and procedures (either announced or negotiated) and by communicating desired classroom behavior. Other teachers who are ambiguous about their behavioral expectations spend much time attempting to clarify. Students in these teachers' classes may spend considerable time wondering, and sometimes justly so, whether their behavior is inappropriate or not. In effective managers' rooms it is thus easier to know what is expected, and it is easier for students and teachers to monitor classroom behavior because they can distinguish appropriate from inappropriate behavior (Good & Hinkel, 1982).

New teachers sometimes are advised to "clamp down" early in the year to show that they mean business. This advice can backfire if taken the wrong way. Consistency and follow-through concerning classroom rules are important, but teachers who set themselves up as "the enemy" by alienating students through vindictive behavior are in for a year-long conflict.

Avoiding alienation

It is important that teachers who establish rules actively monitor and deal with inappropriate behavior, especially serious misbehavior. Effective managers may therefore sanction more behavior during the first three or four days of the year than do other teachers. Because students eventually engage in fewer off-task behaviors, it soon becomes even easier for the teacher to monitor the class and to sanction behavior appropriately (e.g., correct the right student for his or her misbehavior). Failure to follow up on inattentive, disruptive behavior suggests to students that the teacher is

Dealing with inappropriate behavior

not serious about maintaining rules, and such behavior encourages students to do as they please. Similarly, teachers who consistently reprimand the wrong student or a student who joined but did not initiate the misbehavior indicate to students that they do not have the skills to maintain a management system.

If teachers exhibit a lack of purpose or a lack of interest in maintaining a management system, it is likely that students will ignore them and their classroom rules much of the time. Teachers should establish reasonable and workable rules, expect compliance, monitor the class, and insist on appropriate behavior when necessary, and students will understand teachers' seriousness and purposefulness about classroom management and will begin to internalize classroom rules, expectations, and procedures.

Necessity of completing curriculum tasks

In addition to establishing procedural and behavioral expectations, teachers must also demand that students use their time to complete curriculum tasks. Effective managers assume that students will complete assignments and hold students accountable for work. Students know what to do when they finish assignments and do not waste time trying to determine the next step. That is, effective managers construct classroom environments in which expectations for student behavior are continuous.

Ambiguous classroom roles

In some classrooms teachers make it difficult for students, as well as themselves, to monitor their own behavior. For example, following a demonstration lesson such teachers might assign seatwork but say, "If you work now, you won't have homework." Such statements and expectations make students' classroom role ambiguous. Presumably, students can do the work now or later. Hence, when students choose not to do seatwork it is difficult to tell whether or not their behavior is appropriate. Furthermore, there is the question of what these students will do while their classmates are engaged in seatwork.

In contrast, more effective managers are likely to make a transition from demonstration to seatwork in the following way: "Now do problems 15 through 30 at your desks. In ten minutes we will check to see what progress you have made and correct any problems we encounter. If you have difficulty with a problem, do the next one and I'll be around to help you. Get started now."

Total management

As Good and Hinkel (1982) emphasize, *all* of these aspects of management must operate for the system to work. For example, even teachers who establish credibility with students during the first few days of school, who daily establish explicit learning goals, and who build in continuous criteria so that students know what is expected of them at any given moment will soon lose students if their students' work is not checked on a regular basis.

Accountability

Doyle (1982) argues that accountability drives the task system and that students tend to take seriously only that work for which they are held accountable. Teachers need to learn the importance of the accountability factor and explore ways in which it can be handled creatively and constructively.

In essence, a good management system announces clear intentions and makes it possible to monitor teacher and student behavior to see whether progress is being made toward shared goals. For students who are intrinsically motivated by school tasks and teachers, it tells how to proceed and do well in the classroom. For students without these orientations, it helps to establish conditions to enable them to learn self-control and to engage in academic tasks. These students come to understand that rewards and privileges are associated with personal progress on assigned tasks.

Student Control

Our discussion of effective management does not necessarily imply heavy or total teacher control, although good management in the early school years may involve much teacher monitoring and frequent feedback. As Doyle (1985) notes, classroom order does not necessarily mean passivity or rigid conformity to rules; it simply means that students are following the program of action necessary for instructional objectives to be accomplished at a given time. As students become older, there should be less need for teachers to remind them of what behavior is appropriate. Still, students at all ages should understand what constitutes appropriate work and behavior.

Importance of feedback

Students also need feedback about their progress on self-chosen goals as well as information on goals established by the teacher. After students have developed appropriate learning expectations and independent work skills, then teachers can reasonably require students to work more independently and assign them more complex tasks (Good & Hinkel, 1982).

Management skills and student achievement

Good management skills provide a necessary, but not sufficient structure for active classroom learning. Poorly managed classes inhibit students' involvement in the instructional program and negatively affect learning outcomes. The correlational evidence relating the management behaviors reviewed here to student achievement is very consistent and the obtained relationships are typically moderate (Brophy, 1983; Doyle, 1985). Furthermore, there is increasing experimental evidence that the managerial principles discussed above can be taught to teachers, who can use them to improve student attention to assigned work (e.g., Anderson et al., 1979; Brophy, 1983; Good, Grouws, & Ebmeier, 1983).

Research into Practice

Effective managers in the research reviewed appeared to be good decision makers who understood their students' perceptions and needs and adjusted their teaching accordingly (Emmer et al., 1980). That is, in contrast to other teachers, effective managers first teach students about rules related to their most immediate needs. Effective managers are also more likely to appropriately consider the following factors in relation to lesson design: (a) attention span of students, (b) relation of lesson content to students' interests, (c) appropriate work standards, and (d) assurance of reasonably high levels of student success. It thus seems that in addition to an understanding of management techniques, teachers must also possess a keen understanding of how students learn and develop. Having presented these qualifications on the research, we now discuss practical management strategies suggested by this research.

Specific Group Management Techniques

Easily the most important work on group management is a series of investigations conducted by Kounin (1970) and his colleagues. Kounin approached the topic by contrasting the videotaped classroom behavior of teachers known to be successful classroom managers with the behavior of teachers who had continuing and severe management problems. The idea was to see what differentiated the two groups of teachers in their handling of student disruptions. This approach was clear and simple, but it failed. It did not yield a single variable that differentiated consistently between teachers who handled problems successfully and those who did not. When faced with a classroom disruption, the most successful teachers acted similarly to the teachers whose classrooms were chaotic and out of control!

Problem prevention

Fortunately, the researchers did not give up in frustration. In observing the tapes, they developed hunches about variables that *would* differentiate the two types of teachers. Systematic follow-up that involved coding these variables paid off by revealing how the successful teachers did it. Their success lay in their ability to prevent problems rather than in their ability to deal with problems once they occurred. They were no more successful than other teachers in *dealing* with serious problems, but they were considerably more adept at *avoiding* them. That is, good classroom managers are not sharply differentiated in terms of how they react to student misbehavior. Rather, the key behaviors that distinguish good classroom managers are techniques that prevent misbehavior by eliciting student cooperation and involvement in assigned work.

Effective versus ineffective managers

Kounin (1970) identifies several variables that differentiate effective and ineffective managers. We emphasize seven of these concepts: "withitness," overlapping, smoothness, momentum, alerting, accountability, and seatwork variety. Brief definitions of these terms follow; later we discuss these findings more fully.

"Withitness"

"Withitness" refers to the extent to which a teacher communicates awareness of student behavior. One basic operational definition used by Kounin for measuring withitness was the ratio of the number of times the teacher stopped misbehavior appropriately (e.g., sanctioned the right student or stopped the misbehavior before it became more serious) to the total number of teacher attempts to stop misbehavior.

Overlapping

"Overlapping" refers to a teacher's ability to deal with two or more issues at the same time. Kounin found that some teachers could deal with multiple events simultaneously, whereas other teachers became too involved in one activity and neglected the other.

Smoothness

"Smoothness" is the teacher's ability to move through an instructional sequence without interrupting academic work by providing irrelevant information to students or by overresponding to classroom behavior that is not interfering with classroom work. A negative example of smoothness would be a teacher's request for a student to pick up a piece of trash during a public lesson, thereby delaying all students and breaking their concentration on the lesson.

Momentum

"Momentum" refers to avoiding behavior that slows down a lesson unnecessarily. Teachers who continue to complain about a student's behavior after he or she is back on task, who slowly pass out worksheets to the class one at a time, or who dwell on an academic topic longer than is necessary for student understanding illustrate poor momentum.

Alerting

"Alerting" behaviors are teachers' attempts to keep students engaged in tasks by telling students that their work will be examined or checked. Examples of alerting during recitation lessons include teachers calling on students randomly or reminding students that they may be asked to comment on responses of other students. During individual seatwork, the teacher may alert students by telling them that their work will be checked in a few minutes.

"Accountability" is defined as the extent to which teachers follow up on their alerting behaviors. Do teachers actually ask students to respond to the answers of other students, after alerting students to that possibility? From Kounin's standpoint, the purpose of alerting behaviors is to keep students involved (e.g., to remind students to listen even though another student is responding), whereas accountability behaviors assess students' performance (e.g., to find out if they listened).

Variety of seatwork

"Variety of seatwork" assigned was associated with more student effort and less misbehavior.

More recently, Kounin and Gump (1974) studied 596 videotaped lessons and found that the teachers of lessons that had higher student involvement provided continuous, explicit cues for appropriate behavior and insulated students from external intrusions.

Teacher Preparedness. First, the successful teachers were well organized and prepared for teaching during lessons and for assigning and monitoring seatwork. They wasted little time in making transitions from one activity to another. Less successful classroom managers frequently had long, awkward transitions that led to student restlessness. During lessons, the successful teachers maintained interest at high level and kept up a lively pace. They knew where they were going and how they intended to get there. Less successful teachers continually confused the students and interrupted pacing by stopping to get something that should have been prepared in advance, stopping to check something because they were not sure what to do next, repeating themselves for no good reason or because they were vague the first time, and vacillating or even contradicting themselves.

Maintaining Student Involvement. The successful teachers also maintained high involvement in lessons by arousing motivation directly and by holding students accountable for remaining attentive to what was going on by such devices as asking a lot of questions or otherwise getting student response, or being unpredictable in questioning patterns. The less successful teachers did this much less often. These differences resulted in briskly paced lessons with high student involvement in the former case, and slowly paced or disjointed lessons with student confusion and low involvement in the latter.

Similar differences were observed during seatwork periods. The more successful teachers had prepared seatwork assignments that provided variety for the students and allowed for individual student differences by varying level of difficulty. Their seatwork assignments were challenging as well as instructive, while the seatwork assignments of the less successful teachers were boring or ill-suited to the interests and abilities of the students. Again, the result was student boredom and restlessness, leading to disruptions and other misbehavior.

Continuous monitoring of the whole classroom

Teacher "Withitness." A more general teacher characteristic, important in both lesson and seatwork contexts, was what the authors called "withitness." This term refers to the degree to which the teacher is aware of and continually monitoring what is going on in all parts of the classrooom, and is thus able to take action to stop a developing disruption before it becomes really serious. Successful classroom managers had this quality. The less successful ones became so wrapped up in what they were doing that they were unaware of other parts of the room. This made them slower to recognize and to react to disruptions, and likely to make many more mistakes in their reactions than the more "with it" teachers. Mistakes included timing errors (waiting too long to respond, so that what should have been a minor problem developed into a major one), target errors (not knowing the actual culprits, and sometimes failing to notice all students who were involved, or even blaming some who were not involved), and overreactions (shouting,

A teacher may choose to discuss a problem with a student in private.

becoming hysterical, or otherwise overreacting emotionally when the situation called for calm control).

Reaction errors

Each type of error led to increased problems. Timing errors allowed routine horseplay and similar disruptions to develop into arguments and fights. Target errors minimized student accountability by allowing culprits to get away with something and harmed teacher-student relationships when teachers mistakenly blamed the wrong students. Seeing classmates get away with misbehavior probably encouraged others to try to do the same. Finally, emotional overreactions produced student resentment and sometimes led to what Kounin and his colleagues called "ripple effects." This refers to the rise in levels of tension and distraction that often occurs when teachers respond in strongly negative and punitive ways to student misbehavior. Sometimes this sort of reaction causes the frequency and intensity of disruptions to increase as well.

Ripple effects

Experimental studies of punishment would not predict these "ripple effects." In theory, seeing others being punished should reduce the likelihood of misbehavior by observers, who presumably experience the punishment vicariously (Bandura, 1969). Typically, however, experiments testing this thesis involve brief experiences with strangers. In the classroom, teacher behavior is predictable after the first few days or weeks. It is likely that explosions of anger by frustrated teachers have a cathartic effect, reducing the likelihood of similar explosions in the immediate future. Where this is the situation, alert students are likely to take advantage of it.

Thus, ironically, teachers who react explosively in dealing with immediate problems may be setting themselves up for additional problems in the future. This does not always happen, because many students apparently are not affected by such overreactions. However, in combination with the many other negative results that occur when teachers lose their tempers and become unnecessarily punitive, this factor again underscores the need for teachers to use positive approaches to classroom management.

Overlapping Activities. Another important key to successful classroom management, related both to smooth pacing and to "withitness," is what Kounin and his colleagues called "overlapping." This is the ability to do two or more things at once, such as responding to students who come for help or direction without having to break the pace of a small group lesson. Overlapping appears to be a product of preparation, ability to anticipate needs, and ability to pay attention to and deal with more than one thing at a time. Overlapping helps keep students engaged in productive activities by minimizing the time they spend waiting for the teacher to respond to a demand or to tell them what to do.

Smooth Transitions. Another important variable noted by Kounin was smoothness of transitions between and within activities. This involves consistent teacher behavior, combined with training students to follow daily routines that promote efficiency in changing activities. This is supplemented by brief but clear and complete instructions to the group concerning matters specific to that day or activity. Teachers should not allow themselves to be repeatedly distracted by the questions or actions of individuals, give out too many and too specific instructions, repeat themselves unnecessarily, interrupt everyone to ask if previous instructions have been carried out yet, or confuse students who are trying to carry out previous instructions by giving new ones that may or may not be meant for them (Evertson & Anderson, 1978).

Transitions within activities are often lengthy and confusing because teachers are not prepared. This leads to false starts in which orders are given and then retracted, or to interruption of movement into the new activity because something omitted from the previous one is now remembered.

Group Alerting. Yet another aspect of effective management noted by Kounin is "group alerting," which refers to teacher behavior designated to maintain or reestablish attention during lessons. In the positive sense, group alerting involves things that teachers do to keep the rest of the group attentive while any one member is reciting. These include looking around the group before calling on someone to recite, keeping the students in suspense as to who will be called on next by selecting randomly, getting around to everyone frequently, interspersing choral responses with individual responses, asking for volunteers to raise their hands, throwing out challenges by declaring that the next question is difficult or tricky, calling on listeners to comment on or correct a response, and presenting novel or interesting material.

Negative aspects of group alerting include overconcentration on the student doing the reciting to the point that the rest of the group is not monitored, directing new questions only to the reciter, picking the reciter before a question is even stated, and having reciters perform in a predetermined order.

Accountability. In addition to these group alerting techniques, Kounin identified several techniques that maximize student accountability for paying attention. Teachers can hold students accountable by requiring them to hold up props, show their answers, or otherwise indicate attention to the lesson, having them recite in unison while monitoring carefully, asking listeners to comment on recitations, asking for volunteers, circulating and checking performance, and calling on individuals. Many of the techniques that Kounin lists under "accountability" are similar to those listed under "group alerting."

Other Studies of Group Management

Subsequent research by others supports most, but not all, of Kounin's recommendations. In a correlational study of second- and third-grade classes (Brophy & Evertson, 1976) and in an experimental study of first-grade reading groups (Anderson, Evertson, & Brophy, 1979), withitness, overlapping, and smoothness of lesson pacing and transitions all were associated

Random selection of students to recite

not only with better management, but with better learning. However, these studies did not support some of the group alerting and accountability techniques, especially the notion of being unpredictable in calling on students to recite. The teachers who were more successful went around the group in order, seldom calling for volunteers and not allowing students to call out answers. Good and Grouws (1975) found that group alerting was positively related to student learning of fourth-grade mathematics, but accountability was related curvilinearly—teachers who used a moderate amount were more successful than those who used too much or too little.

Choral responses

Research findings are also mixed concerning the value of choral responses. Such responses do allow all members of the group to respond more often, and they provide variety. However, unless the group is small and the teacher is very attentive to each individual, a chorus of correct responses from a majority of the group can easily drown out mistakes and cover up failures to respond. This is especially a problem with students in the early grades, who need individualized opportunities to respond and get feedback from the teacher (Anderson, Evertson, & Brophy, 1979; Blank, 1973).

Eliciting and maintaining student attention

In general, the major management objectives during lessons involve eliciting and maintaining student attention, including times when students are supposed "just" to watch and listen. This is done primarily by making sure that lesson content is interesting and challenging and that the teacher is prepared well enough to conduct the lesson smoothly. This should be sufficient for most students. For the others, group alerting and accountability techniques may be required periodically.

Techniques drawn from Kounin and other sources are integrated in the next sections, which present guidelines for group management in the two most typical classroom contexts—group lessons and seatwork periods.

Maintaining Attention During Lessons

Some inattention and minor misbehavior can be expected during most lessons. This routine misbehavior is dealt with most successfully through a combination of careful monitoring of students (Kounin's "withitness"), modeling expected behavior, reinforcing expected behavior, and extinguishing undesirable behavior.

Successful monitoring

One requirement for successful monitoring is being able to see each student and to make eye contact if necessary. A second is to form the habit of continuously scanning the group or class. Students who know that the teacher can see them and regularly keeps an eye on what is going on are much less likely to misbehave than students who know they have a good chance of getting away with something.

It is not enough just to see that students give the appearance of remaining attentive to and understanding a lesson, because most students can do this without actually following the lesson (Brophy & Evertson, 1976). Both to insure accountability and to sample student comprehension as a guide to lesson pacing, it is important to ask a question or require the student to periodically make some kind of response. Such questions usually have the greatest managerial value when students have no way of knowing in advance when the teacher might ask them to respond or whom the teacher might call on next.

Hazards in maintaining accountability

Maintaining student accountability through such questions will be successful only if the teacher avoids three potential hazards. First, care should be taken not to upset or put on the spot a student who regularly shows anxiety and fear of failure. When students like these are not paying attention, it is usually better to stimulate attention in more direct ways, such as by calling for it or by giving advance warning ("John, listen carefully to Ralph, because I want to ask you about his comments.").

Second, teachers must concentrate on involving everyone rather than on catching the inattentive. Observations of teachers who thought they were questioning randomly typically reveal that they call on certain students often and certain others rarely or never. The students they call on are high-achieving students who are expected to know the answers, while the students not frequently called on or never called on usually are low achievers who the teacher does not feel can answer, or students the teacher does not like and thus attempts to avoid (Good, 1970; Brophy & Good, 1974).

Third, the greatest danger in maintaining student accountability through unpredictable questioning or response demands is that the technique will be overused and become obvious to the students. Teachers can counteract this by occasionally explaining the rationale for calling on a variety of students. For example, they could say, "I want to call on most of you today, so that I can find out if we know most of the key concepts, or if we have to work on them some more."

Demanding student attention

We have been focusing on conditioning attention through relatively impersonal and indirect methods. When inattention is prolonged or disruptive, a direct call for attention may be required. The best way to demand student attention is to do so briefly and perfunctorily (O'Leary, Kaufman, Kass, & Drabman, 1970).

If eye contact can be made with the student, a demand for attention can be accomplished nonverbally through looks, expressions, or gestures. If verbalization is required, it should be confined to a simple directive like "Pay attention, John," delivered quickly, concisely, and with the expectation that it will be followed. The teacher should pause just long enough to make sure that the student has heard, and then go on with the lesson. This minimizes the interruption of the lesson flow and thus the likelihood that other students will become distracted.

Other effective ways of putting a stop to minor misbehavior include humorous or other responses that tell the student to change behavior, but do so in a benign and generally positive way. For example, if a student has been teasing a fellow student, making faces or noises, or doing something that he or she knows is inappropriate, there is no need to pause and explain the nature of the misbehavior. The teacher needs only to indicate that it must stop, using some comment such as "That's enough, John," or pleasantly saying, "Very funny, John, but now I want you to pay attention."

Maintaining Engagement in Seatwork

Appropriate difficulty level

Each student should have a seatwork assignment that is appropriate in difficulty level and is as interesting as curriculum demands allow. By preparing the necessary materials and explaining regulations to students, teachers should set up mechanisms that enable students to know exactly what to do if they have difficulty with their assignments and what to do when they finish them. Situations in which trouble starts because a student has given up on an assignment that is too difficult or has finished an easy assignment and has nothing to do simply should not exist. Preparation here includes not only the seatwork itself but options for other activities open to students who complete their assignments.

General techniques

Techniques for maintaining student engagement in seatwork, assuming that the seatwork is interesting and appropriate, are similar to those for maintaining attention to lessons. The major difference is that during lessons students tend to be seated facing the teacher so that eye contact is established more frequently and easily and monitoring is much simpler. It is easier for students to appear to be working on seatwork assignments when they are not than it is for them to appear to be following lessons when they are not. Nevertheless, the same general principles apply: monitor as continuously as possible, set up and explain rules, communicate positive expectations, condition through a combination of modeling, reinforcement, and extinction, and intervene only when necessary and with as little disruption as possible.

Moving around the classroom

Unless they are tied down elsewhere by, perhaps, teaching a small group, it is a good idea for teachers to move around the room during seatwork times, keeping a general check on everyone's progress and stopping to give corrections. Teachers should position themselves so that they can see all or at least the majority of the class, keep moving around, be unpredictable

Students need reinforcement and feedback during seatwork.

in their movements, and avoid becoming so absorbed with an individual student that they forget to monitor what is going on elsewhere.

The need for the teacher to monitor the whole class seems especially important during the early part of the school year while students are still learning the work system. In an intensive analysis of narrative records from junior high school English classes, Doyle (1984) found that successful managers establish an activity system early in the year and closely supervise the system, ushering it along and protecting it from intrusion or disruption. During seatwork for the first three weeks, for example, contacts with individual students were brief and the teacher circulated around the room maintaining a whole-group perspective. In classes that began with frequent inappropriate and disruptive student behavior, successful managers tended to push the curriculum and talk about work rather than misbehavior. Less successful managers, on the other hand, tended to focus public attention on misbehavior by their frequent reprimands so that eventually all work ceased. By November of the school year, observations indicated that if a work system was established effectively, a successful teacher often spent less time orchestrating the total group and more time with individual students. By this point, the work system itself seemed to be carrying the burden of order and the teacher was free to attend more to particular aspects of classroom events.

Establishing a work system

Problems can often be prevented or stopped simply by moving close to students who are goofing off, particularly when the students know exactly what they should be doing and realize that they are not doing it. Under these circumstances, there usually is no need for the teacher to say anything, and also good reason not to, since it will distract those students who are working.

Brief interventions

Finally, interventions with students during seatwork times should be brief, rather than prolonged tutoring attempts (Brophy & Evertson, 1976; Evertson, Anderson, & Brophy, 1979), and should be confined to students who really need help or direction. Teachers who are overly intrusive and verbal when making rounds during seatwork often interrupt students needlessly, and may even create anxiety or other undesirable reactions.

SUMMARY

Effective classroom management begins with preparation of the physical environment. Classrooms should be arranged so that the teacher can monitor all areas at all times, attention can be facilitated and disruption minimized, supplies are readily accessible, and there are no obstacles to the flow of traffic. Students should be taught to handle routine tasks with minimal supervision, and contingency plans should be prepared for times when regularly scheduled activities cannot take place. Preventive preparation reduces management problems dramatically.

Students should also be organized into cohesive groups having positive attitudes and constructive goals. Gaining the confidence of leaders is an important step, as is developing a leadership style that promotes interaction. Lewin, Lippitt, and White found that a democratic style was better than an authoritarian or laissez-faire style, while Baumrind stressed the advantages of authoritative leadership over authoritarian or laissez-faire. The teacher with a positive image, who sets reasonable rules, and permits students to respond freely, will experience minimal problems.

Kounin and others have found that successful classroom managers prevent discipline problems from emerging. They appear to do this by being well organized and prepared, maintaining student involvement, recognizing and stopping disruptions promptly, overlapping multiple activities, and maintaining accountability on the part of the entire group. Monitoring of all students, frequent eye contact, requests for overt responses, humor, movement about the room, brief interventions, and appropriate difficulty levels all help to maintain student involvement in learning tasks.

QUESTIONS AND PROBLEMS

1. The authors stressed the need to get off to a good start, but said that setting yourself up as "the enemy" is not the way to do so. What is?
2. Considering the grade level at which you intend to teach, what are the classroom procedures in which you should plan to provide your students with instruction and practice?
3. Why do you believe good managers have a few general rules rather than many specific ones?
4. What is the difference between reactive and proactive management?
5. Why is it that teachers who frequently use Kounin's group accountability techniques tend to have management problems, even though these techniques do return attention to the lesson?
6. Considering the grade level at which you intend to teach, can you state clearly the types and difficulty levels of seatwork assignments that will meet Kounin's criteria of variety and challenge?
7. How might the principles discussed in this chapter be modified for teachers working in the following situations: team teaching, open classroom teaching, or individualized, self-paced instruction.

CASE STUDIES

An Inattentive Group. Ruth Miller is distracted by two boys' inattentiveness in the back of the room. She continues to present information to the whole class, but as she does so she notices that a third student has joined the discussion at the back of the room, and that another is watching the three. If you were Ruth Miller, what would you do now? Does it make any difference if it is a second-grade or twelfth-grade class? If so, how?

Start of the Year. Jed Kemper, a history teacher in an affluent suburban high school, is teaching for the first time. Given that his students have been in school for several years, what should Jed say about classroom management? Be specific in your response. Outline a role-play situation of your comments made to your first class.

Chapter 21

Principles and Techniques of Behavior Modification

OBJECTIVES

When you have mastered the material in this chapter you will be able to

1. Define modeling and its effects on observers, list three characteristics of good models, and explain how modeling can be used to teach thinking and self-control
2. Discuss the role of cues in controlling behavior
3. Distinguish with illustrative examples (a) direct versus vicarious reinforcement; and (b) positive versus negative reinforcement
4. Explain how a teacher can teach and then maintain increasingly complex academic and social behavior using reinforcement techniques
5. Discuss the drawbacks of teacher praise and other external reinforcement systems
6. Define satiation and extinction techniques to stop undesirable behavior and explain when their use is appropriate
7. State how the effects of negative reinforcement and punishment differ and how punishment can be used most effectively

Previous chapters describe the personal qualities of teachers that are basic to successful classroom management and they review principles for establishing an effective learning environment and for managing everyday group activities. Although we stress the role of the individual teacher in managing student behavior, we recognize that school level policies and support are also important.

The principles stressed in the two previous chapters are sufficient for handling most management concerns. However, some students require special, individualized treatment. This may involve behavior modification techniques, covered in this chapter, or various humanistic approaches to counseling, covered in Chapter 22.

Behavior modification techniques are especially useful in dealing with such routine problems as persistent inattention, daydreaming or fooling around instead of working, calling out answers or unwanted comments, trying to get attention by making faces or noises, showing off items forbidden by the school, changing seats, or moving around the room without permission.

Techniques for establishing and maintaining desired behavior include modeling, cuing, and reinforcement. Methods for stopping undesirable behavior include satiation, extinction, negative reinforcement, and punishment. We now cover techniques for establishing and maintaining desired behavior.

Modeling

We acquire a great deal of learning vicariously as we observe the behavior of other people (models) and its consequences for them. Learning through modeling goes on whenever we observe others with whom we can identify, so that much learning is unplanned and unsystematic.

Conscious and systematic modeling

Teachers can accomplish much in the classroom by influencing student behavior through modeling, especially if they learn to model consciously and systematically. Bandura (1969) identifies three broad classes of effects that models can have on the behavior of observers:

1. *Observational learning/modeling effects*—Observers acquire new response patterns that did not previously exist in their behavioral repertoires, for example, in observing a demonstration of laboratory equipment.
2. *Inhibitory/disinhibitory effects*—Existing response patterns in observers are inhibited when models are punished for similar behavior or disinhibited when models are reinforced for similar behavior. For example, students' tendencies to call out cruel or obscene comments about one another are affected by whether or not peers who do this are reinforced or punished by the teacher or their classmates.
3. *Response facilitation effects*—The behavior of the model in a particular situation cues observers to follow suit, even though they probably would have behaved differently without such modeling. For instance,

students are likely to imitate teacher behavior in response to the principal's announcements (paying respectful attention rather than ignoring).

Modeling can be a powerful instructional tool and behavior management technique for teachers. Our definition of modeling includes nonverbal behavior, verbalizations made in carrying out the behavior, and instructions and explanations given before, during, or after the behavior. These verbalizations help define the meaning of the behavior and shape observers' reactions to it.

Characteristics of Models Who Are Imitated

Teachers who form personal relationships with their students and become the kinds of individuals that the students look up to and want to be like are more apt to be imitated than teachers who remain at a distance or stress the contrasts between themselves and their students. Another factor is the degree to which the model's behavior is rewarded. Teachers who are respected and who accomplish their goals are more likely to be imitated than teachers who are not successful.

High-prestige models are more likely to be imitated than low-prestige models, particularly when the prestige is based on qualities that potential imitators would like to possess. This implies that teachers must retain students' respect and perhaps also a degree of professional distance, but still be friendly and attractive enough to make students want to be like them.

Modeling and Classroom Management

Everyday modeling relevant to classroom management includes such things as listening attentively when students recite or answer questions, handling

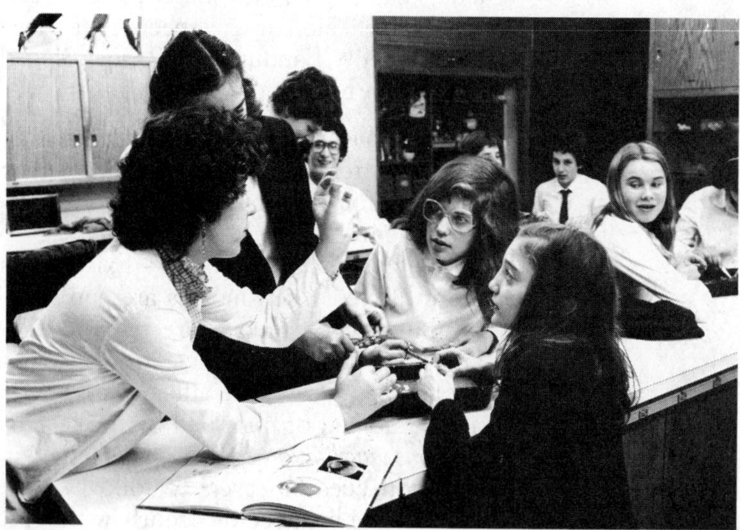

Teachers can maintain professional distance from students, but still create a friendly atmosphere.

equipment carefully and replacing it properly, and remaining conspicuously quiet during times for concentrated thinking.

Teacher modeling

Similarly, teacher modeling is important for developing rational control of behavior by acting on well thought-out decisions, not impulses; developing respect for others by treating them as worthwhile, valued people; developing good group climate by not making hostile criticism or scapegoating, not playing favorites, and by exhibiting emotional control by being able to accept adversity or criticism without becoming upset or angry; and responding with rational attempts to diagnose and solve problems.

Teachers can often instruct students in various classroom routines most efficiently through modeling—showing how to use the pencil sharpener or how to operate audio-visual equipment, for example. They can also use modeling to teach thinking and problem solving, especially when combined with verbalized self-instructions and other techniques of cognitive behavior modification (Meichenbaum, 1977).

Building Self-Control

Cognitive behavior modification

Cognitive behavior modification stresses the development of self-control rather than the imposition of external control. It emphasizes thinking and subjective experience more than overt behavior, and goal setting, planning, and self-instruction rather than reinforcement. For example, if a teacher and a student discuss a plan of action and the student writes out the plan, then student behavior, classroom conduct, and academic performance become more explicit and hence potentially more controllable by the student. Such a technique also allows teachers to individualize arrangements with students, and it places more emphasis on student self-control, self-management, and self-instruction and less on one-to-one relationships between specific behaviors and rewards. Contracts can be helpful in dealing with students who are poorly motivated, easily distracted, or resistant to schoolwork or the teacher.

Goal setting

Experience with some of the elements involved in contingency contracting such as goal setting and self-monitoring of behavior revealed that these elements could have positive effects of their own, independent of reinforcement. For example, inducing students to set goals for themselves can lead to performance increases, especially if those goals are specific and difficult rather than vague or too easy (Rosswork, 1977). Apparently, setting goals not only provides students with specific objectives to pursue, but it leads them to concentrate their efforts and monitor their performances more closely. The process does not always work, however. Sagotsky, Patterson, and Lepper (1978) found that exposure to goal-setting procedures had no significant effect on students' study behavior or academic achievement, largely because many of the students did not follow through by actually using the goal-setting procedures they had been shown.

Self-monitoring

The same study did show the effectiveness of self-monitoring procedures, however. Students taught to monitor and maintain daily records of their study behavior did show significant improvement in both the study behavior and tested achievement. This is only one of many studies illustrating the effectiveness of procedures designed to help students monitor their classroom behavior more closely and control it more effectively (Glynn, Thomas, & Shee, 1973; McLaughlin, 1976; O'Leary & Dubey, 1979; Rosenbaum & Drabman, 1979).

These procedures designed to develop self-control in students have two potential advantages over earlier procedures that depended on external control by the teacher. First, teachers cannot continuously monitor all of the students and reinforce them appropriately. When responsibility for monitoring, and perhaps reinforcing, performance is shifted from the teacher to the students, this difficulty is removed. Second, behavior modification methods that depend on the reinforcing activity of the teacher tend not to generalize to other settings nor persist beyond the term or school year. If students can learn to monitor and control their own behavior, they may also be able to apply these self-control skills to other classrooms or even to nonschool settings.

Verbalized Self-Instructions

Teaching self-control skills

Self-control skills are typically taught using procedures that Meichenbaum (1977) calls cognitive behavior modification. One technique combines modeling with verbalized self-instructions. Rather than just telling students what to do, the model (teacher) demonstrates the process. The demonstration includes not only the physical motions involved but verbalization of the thoughts and other self-talk (self-instructions, self-monitoring, self-reinforcement) that should accompany the physical motions.

Modeling combined with verbalized self-instructions

Modeling combined with verbalized self-instructions (as well as various related role-play approaches) can be helpful with a variety of student problems. Meichenbaum (1977) describes five stages of this approach: (1) an adult models a task while speaking aloud (cognitive modeling), (2) the child performs the task under the model's instruction (overt, external guidance), (3) the child performs the task while verbalizing self-instructions aloud (overt self-guidance), (4) the child whispers self-instructions while doing the task (faded overt self-guidance), and (5) the child performs the task under self-guidance via private speech (covert self-instruction). Variations of this approach not only have been used to teach cognitively impulsive students to approach tasks more effectively but also have been used to help social isolates learn to initiate activities with their peers, to teach students to be more creative in problem solving, to help aggressive students learn to control their anger and respond more effectively to frustration, and to help frustrated and defeated students to cope with failure and respond to mistakes with problem-solving efforts rather than withdrawal or resignation.

"Turtle" technique and "Think Aloud" program

Recent applications of this approach include the "turtle" technique of Robin, Schneider, and Dolnick (1976), in which teachers teach impulsive and aggressive students to assume the "turtle" position when upset. The students learn to place their heads on their desks, close their eyes, and clench their fists. This gives them an immediate response to use in anger-provoking situations and thus enables them to delay inappropriate behavior and to think about constructive solutions to the problem. The turtle position is actually not essential; the key is training children to delay impulsive responding while they gradually relax and think about constructive alternatives. However, it is a gimmick that many younger students find enjoyable, and it may also serve as a crutch to children who might otherwise not be able to delay successfully. Similarly, the "Think Aloud" program of Camp and Bash (1981) is designed to teach children to use cognitive skills to guide their social behavior and to learn to cope with social problems. It is useful with students in the early grades, especially those prone to paranoid interpretations of peer behavior or aggressive acting out as a response to frustration.

Generalization of skills taught through cognitive interventions has not yet been demonstrated convincingly (Pressley, 1979). However, approaches featuring modeling, verbalized self-instructions, and other aspects of self-monitoring and self-control training appear to be very promising for use in classrooms, both as instructional techniques for all students and as remediation techniques for students with emotional or behavioral problems (McLaughlin, 1976; O'Leary & Dubey, 1979; Rosenbaum & Drabman, 1979).

Cuing

When students have difficulty remembering to perform certain behaviors, teachers can help by cuing—providing a brief direction or reminder to cue the students' attention and behavior. To be effective, cues must occur before the action occurs (Krumboltz & Krumboltz, 1972) and they should be delivered only when needed; otherwise, they begin to resemble nagging.

Repeated problem behavior

Cues are especially useful for problem behavior that occurs repeatedly in specific situations, such as when students get into squabbles while sharing equipment in a learning center. If the teacher is able to analyze the situation and identify the timing and reasons for trouble, problems can be short-circuited through cuing: "Your group will be going to the learning center next period. Remember, no more than three to a learning center at one time, and everyone is to share the equipment."

Advance reminders and coaching

Cuing through advance reminders and coaching is especially useful because providing cues during the activity itself might be embarrassing or might interrupt the flow of classroom activities. Students can be prepared through discussions of how to handle the upcoming situations and by including many examples of what to do and what to avoid. Such discussions might also include modeling with verbalized self-instructions as well as more typical explanations, or perhaps even role-play exercises to give students an opportunity to practice the expected behaviors. Verbal cuing can be supplemented with supports, such as posting instruction sheets or rule reminders in learning centers or on equipment, using arrows to indicate direction of movement, or labeling shelves to show where equipment belongs. Students who have special problems managing their time independently or remembering what they are supposed to do can be helped by assigning peers to remind or supervise them, or by preparing checklists for them to use themselves.

Discrimination

Cuing may be particularly useful when a problem involves discrimination—certain behavior is appropriate under some circumstances but not others. Here the student needs to learn to recognize the cues indicating whether or not the behavior is appropriate, rather than how to perform the behavior itself. Explanations of the rationales for the differences are important, as are multiple examples: no shouting or shrieking at any time; quiet conversational talk in designated areas is allowed among students who have completed assignments; talk during work time is confined to getting help from designated persons and within designated limits; talk is not allowed during recitations and discussions except when you have the floor; talk is not allowed during tests. Students must make similar discriminations about when and how to move around the room, approach the teacher with an individual problem, or call out comments and suggestions. Teachers working with younger students, and all teachers in the first few days or weeks of school, will have to do a lot of this kind of cuing. However, cuing should be reduced, both in frequency and specificity, as students begin to behave appropriately on their own.

Cuing combined with other techniques

Many aspects of cognitive behavior modification combine cuing with several other features (Glynn, Thomas, & Shee, 1973; McLaughlin, 1976). Examples include self-assessment (student evaluates own performance relative to goals), self-recording (student keeps records of own relevant behaviors), self-determination of reinforcement (student establishes own contingencies between own behaviors and types or amount of reinforcement), and self-administration of reinforcement (student reinforces self upon performing contracted behaviors).

Self-reinforcement

Self-reinforcement may be helpful for students who are deficient in achievement motivation or who make inappropriate attributions about the reasons for their successes. The self-reinforcement process calls students' attention to their specific accomplishments and encourages them to verbalize statements of satisfaction and praise to themselves for having achieved goals. It may also help them to attribute their accomplishments to their own efforts rather than to external factors.

Self-monitoring and self-evaluation

Self-monitoring and self-evaluation can often be aided with checklists, scoring keys, periodic progress reports, or other devices that help students to assess systematically what they have and have not accomplished with respect to schoolwork and behavior goals. These techniques place the responsibility for monitoring and managing student behavior on the students themselves, but in ways likely to be informative and attractive to them.

Academic survival skills and prosocial personal skills

Recent extensions of these techniques include training in academic survival skills such as attending, following directions, and volunteering to answer questions (Cobb & Hops, 1973), as well as training in prosocial personal skills such as initiating interactions, helping, and sharing (Cartledge & Milburn, 1978). A combination of modeling and instructions is used to teach the skill, and self-monitoring and reinforcement procedures can be added to insure that it will be maintained.

Reinforcement

Behavioristic psychologists stress reinforcement as the primary mechanism for establishing and maintaining behavior. There are difficulties in defining reinforcers. Some people are not reinforced by things that most others find rewarding, and some things commonly seen as punishments are experienced as rewards by some individuals. This has led behavioristic psychologists to use a circular definition of a reinforcer as being anything that increases or maintains the frequency of behavior when it is made contingent on performances of that behavior. That is, if a particular consequence increases or maintains the frequency of a behavior, it is a reinforcer; if it does not affect the behavior, it is not a reinforcer.

Premack Principle

This basic idea has many applications in school settings, especially Premack's (1965) formulation of it. The "Premack Principle" states that opportunities to engage in behavior that is performed spontaneously at a high rate can be used as rewards for increasing the frequencies of behaviors performed spontaneously at lower rates. For example, students who are not completing assignments can be motivated to do so by informing them that they will not be allowed to do something they want to do until they turn in the assignments. The Premack Principle provides flexibility, allowing teachers to develop reward systems suited to each individual, and to get around the problem that no single "reward" will be motivating for everyone.

Positive Reinforcement or Reward

Reinforcers are either positive or negative. Positive reinforcers correspond roughly to what we usually call rewards. They include material rewards

Students interpret a break as a reward for classwork.

(food, money, prizes, or tokens that can be exchanged for something desired), social rewards (praise, grades, honors, status symbols, attention from the teacher or peers), and activity rewards (opportunities to choose and engage in desired activities, use special equipment, or play games).

Negative Reinforcement

Negative reinforcement involves increasing the rate of a desired behavior by freeing the person from some unpleasant state when the behavior is performed. For example, students can be allowed to escape failing grades through makeup work that allows them to master material they should have mastered earlier. Although negative reinforcement technically involves reinforcing desirable behavior, it also involves withholding reinforcement from students who do not meet performance demands. Typically, these students are behaving in some undesirable way, not merely failing to produce desired behavior. Consequently, negative reinforcement is discussed in more detail in a later section of the chapter dealing with techniques for stopping undesirable behavior.

Vicarious Reinforcement

Reinforcement may motivate not only the student who receives it, but also, through modeling effects, other students who observe it. In theory, a teacher can motivate a student to work carefully not only by praising his or her careful work, but also by praising careful work performed by others, especially friends or peers with whom the student identifies. However, teachers cannot assume vicarious motivating effects because not all students find the same consequences reinforcing. Teacher praise of a peer will vicariously motivate students who also want such praise, but not those who do not value teacher praise.

Using Reinforcement in the Classroom

Teachers can strengthen desirable student behavior by reinforcing that behavior after it occurs. The behavior can be something minor such as raising one's hand and waiting to be recognized rather than calling out an answer during a lesson, or something more substantial such as turning in completed and carefully done seatwork assignments for a week. The reinforcer can be anything that the student values and is willing to work for.

When conditioning the behavior of animals, it is important to reinforce immediately after performance of the behavior, so that the animal can make the connection between performance and reinforcement. This is not as essential for humans, because this connection can be explained verbally. Language can also be used to describe the particulars of the desired behavior, thus eliminating guesswork as to what is being reinforced, and to link reinforcement to a series of behaviors performed over time, as in the example just mentioned concerning seatwork performance during an entire week.

Fading of reinforcement

In the early stages of trying to establish a new behavior, it may be important to reinforce often, even 100 percent of the time, and perhaps to also reinforce immediately after performance of the behavior. As the behavior becomes more established, it is possible to delay reinforcement as well as to reduce its ratio or increase the intervals between deliveries. This fading of reinforcement can continue until one reaches the minimal level needed for sustaining the behavior.

Social and symbolic rewards

In addition to reducing the frequency of reinforcement as behavior becomes established, the teacher may want to change the nature of the reinforcers, especially if they are expensive or require too much teacher time or effort. This requires substituting social and symbolic rewards for tangible reinforcers like candy or prizes. Sometimes, of course, students will not value social or symbolic rewards, so the teacher will have to take action to build the capacity of these rewards to function as reinforcers. Krumboltz and Krumboltz (1972) suggest accomplishing this by using the principle of substitution—if a person does not value a potential reward, begin presenting it immediately before presenting a reward that is valued. This should strengthen the association of the nonvalued reward with the valued reward, so that ultimately the nonvalued reward becomes valued in its own right. For example, students who do not turn in assignments regularly might be given a weekly report summarizing their successes and failures in this regard. Access to a valued reward such as the opportunity to go on a special outing could be made contingent on earning positive reports. Over time, the presentation of a positive report should in itself become reinforcing to such students.

To the extent that students do respond to social and symbolic rewards, they can also be weaned from dependence on teacher reinforcement by being taught to reinforce themselves. Students can be encouraged not only to note errors, but to grade themselves and perhaps reinforce themselves for success with stars, smiling faces, or positive comments. Students who have been making progress in meeting conduct goals can learn to reinforce themselves with the help of graphs or charts.

Shaping Behavior Through Successive Approximations

Subgoals

For reinforcement to be effective, successful performance must be elicited often enough to be reinforced frequently. When bad habits are deeply ingrained, or when students have not yet established reliable cognitive control of their own behavior, it may take some time before the desired behavior occurs, even if the motivation to change exists. Teachers can still use reinforcement to shape behavior, however, if they analyze the total tasks facing students and divide them into subgoals that can be organized sequentially in order of difficulty. Students can then obtain success and be reinforced regularly as they approach the ultimate goals one step at a time. For example, hyperactive students who tend to leave their seats and roam the room or bother other students when they are supposed to be doing seatwork could be reinforced in the following way. First, the teacher could concentrate on getting them to stay in their seats, perhaps beginning by reinforcing them for remaining in their seats for five minutes at a time. As success is achieved, the teacher can increase the time periods gradually until they cover the entire seatwork period. When students can remain in their seats, the teacher can add prohibitions against making noises or bothering other students. Initially, reinforcement for not bothering others might be provided separately from that dealing with staying in the seat, although eventually the two sets of criteria could be combined. If problems include careless work in addition to leaving the seat and bothering others, the teacher could begin to phase in expectations for careful work. Ultimately, reinforcement is based not only on staying in the seat and not bothering others, but also on careful and sustained application to the seatwork assignment itself.

Simple behaviors like staying in the seat can be measured in time units for successive shaping: first five minutes, then ten minutes, and so on. Meeting each successive subgoal requires the student only to persist longer with the same kind of behavior. With more complex tasks, such as a series of subgoals that leads to successful completion of seatwork assignments, meeting successive subgoals often involves more complex behaviors, or more complex combinations of behaviors formerly reinforced separately. This means periodic changes in the specifications of what behaviors qualify for reinforcement. The teacher must handle this carefully to insure that students do not believe that the teacher is not keeping promises. The key here is to help students recognize and appreciate the progress they have made, and thus to see that higher expectations are now appropriate. Many teachers find contingency contracting systems to be effective in communicating these perceptions.

Changes in specifications

Contingency contracting combines rewarding and extinguishing methods and applies them in a formalized way. After the teacher explains the method and outlines alternatives, the teacher and student jointly draw up a contract specifying in precise terms the behavior the student will be expected to show and the contingent rewards that will be earned once the contract is fulfilled. A contract can be purely oral, although it is customary to formalize it by having the student write down the specific details of the agreement (see Figure 21.1). In instructional areas, such contracts call for students to complete a certain amount of work at a certain level of proficiency to obtain a reward. Behavior management contracts describe specific criteria of improvement that must be met.

The main advantage of contingency contracts is that they insure that students see the relationship between behavior and its consequences. Furthermore, when students are required to draw up the contract themselves, they make personal commitments that are real and meaningful to them

Figure 21.1 A Sample Contingency Contract

Contract for week of April 3-7

I, John Richardson, agree to work carefully on my seatwork assignments and complete them to the best of my ability before leaving my seat to go to the game center. I further agree to redo work done incorrectly after it is returned to me and after I have received any additional instructions or help that I need. I understand that I am free to go to the game center during any seatwork period as soon as I have completed my work assignments as described above.

Signed John Richardson, Student

Agreed Sidney Weaver, Teacher

because they express them in their own words rather than merely agree to demands that the teacher makes.

Providing structure

Contracts can provide needed structure for students who are distractible. Initially contracts can be confined to short time periods and a limited number of tasks and can be displayed on or near students' desks so that students can refer to them for reminders or instruction. Contracts can also be useful for students who are poorly motivated or resistant to schoolwork or the teacher. With these students, teachers can include a period of negotiation prior to the finalizing of contracts in which students have the opportunity to make suggestions and state whether or not they think the demands are reasonable.

Uses of contingency contracting

Teachers can use contingency contracting to control behavior during lessons and group activities, although it probably is best suited to motivating students to work carefully on seatwork assignments. Most misbehavior occurring during lessons is relatively minor; making it the object of a contingency contract tends to call too much attention to it. However, contingency contracting is useful for minimizing or eliminating lesson disruptions if the disruptions are serious and if they can be clearly defined (e.g., leaving one's seat or calling out insults). A contract for seatwork can state that a student must get a specific number of problems correct within a certain amount of time in order to fulfill his or her obligation.

Contingency contracting will not work if the contracts are unreasonable. Teachers must individualize contracts, requiring different things from various students according to their relative abilities to complete assignments and cope with the behavioral demands of school.

Goal Setting

Helping students to set and meet personal goals enables them to obtain reinforcement from school activities. Rosswork (1977) found that setting goals, especially specific, difficult goals, was more effective than offering monetary incentives to produce high levels of performance. Goal setting was also more effective than nonspecific encouragement. Extrinsic incentives may be necessary when a task is not meaningful to students, but goals and goal setting probably are more relevant to meaningful tasks (Rosswork, 1977).

Ranking rewards

The high school students studied by Ware (1978) also stressed the importance of meeting personal goals. From a list of fifteen potential rewards, students were asked to rank rewards for desirability and effectiveness. They ranked the opportunity to reach a personal goal first, followed by school scholarships; compliments and encouragement from friends; being accepted as a person or having their opinions sought; trophies, certificates, medals, or ribbons; job-related physical rewards such as raises and vacations; special privileges or responsibilities; formal letters of recognition or appreciation; having their names printed in the newspaper or repeated on a loud speaker; teacher or employer compliments and encouragement; money for specific accomplishments; parties, picnics, trips, or banquets; election to office; being chosen to be on special programs; and being the winner in a contest. Thus, not only did students rank personal goal attainment first, but they valued rewards such as peer esteem and symbolic recognition more than teacher praise and several types of concrete rewards.

Teachers did not predict students' rankings of rewards. When asked to rank the same list, teachers placed reaching personal goals and winning school scholarships at the bottom, while overrating getting names printed in the newspaper or repeated on a loud speaker, obtaining special privileges or responsibilities, and winning a contest. Interestingly, teachers ranked praise from a teacher or employer even lower than students did, demonstrating awareness that their praise is not very reinforcing compared with other potential rewards.

Social Reinforcement

Teacher praise

Theorists of virtually every persuasion stress the importance of teacher praise. However, functional analyses of teacher praise in the classroom typically indicate that it often is not reinforcing. Many students are not motivated by it at all, and praise is embarrassing for some students or makes them otherwise uncomfortable so that it actually functions as punishment (Brophy & Evertson, 1976; Good & Grouws, 1975; Thompson & Hunnicutt, 1944). Even for teachers who have the potential to use praise as reinforcement, good intentions alone are not enough. Praise is unlikely to reinforce effectively unless it is (1) sincere (ideally, spontaneous); (2) adapted in form and intensity to the specific accomplishments in question (no gushing over trivia); (3) related to the preferences of the individual (some students cringe in response to public praise but appreciate sentiments expressed privately); and (4) specifically descriptive of what the student did that was praiseworthy (Good & Brophy, 1978, 1984; O'Leary & O'Leary, 1977).

Much "praise" commonly given in the classroom does not satisfy these criteria (Anderson, Evertson, & Brophy, 1979; Weinstein, 1976; Brophy, 1981). For example, many teachers praise students who are behaving appropriately, and simultaneously try to ignore others who are behaving inappropriately, thus trying to take advantage of the vicarious reinforcement principle. This teacher behavior is rarely reinforcing in practice. First, the praise involved is seldom praise at all. It is not spontaneous, and the target behaviors are not really praiseworthy—typically they involve being quiet or standing in line. Even when sincerely intended by the teacher, such praise often causes embarrassment, even humiliation, to the students singled out for attention.

Vicarious reinforcement principle

Another common class of misguided reinforcement attempts involves praise of inhibited students who hesitate to contribute to discussions. It is important to make the experience rewarding when these students do contribute (e.g., by smiling and showing interest in their contribution), but it is not wise to call attention to them with comments like, "See, you can speak up when you want to!"

Failure to be specific

Failure to be specific is a common problem in the praise attempts of teachers. For example, Anderson, Evertson, and Brophy (1979) found that fewer than 10 percent of the praise statements made by twenty first-grade teachers specified what was being praised. This low rate held even though ten of the teachers were in an experimental group that had been advised to specify the praiseworthy aspects of student behavior whenever they praised.

Student attributes

The effects of praise and criticism interact with certain student attributes. For example, praise and encouragement are especially reinforcing for students who are introverted, inhibited, low in self-esteem, and accustomed to failure. Students who are self-confident and accustomed to success are not as responsive to such attempts at reinforcement.

Rewards as reinforcers

These considerations serve as reminders that teachers need to perform functional analyses of their own behavior and their students' responses to make sure that assumed "rewards" actually function as such. Praise or symbolic rewards such as stars and smiling faces may be effective, but if they are not, teachers need to use other reinforcers. In addition to the commonly mentioned material rewards, reinforcers can include such things as the opportunity to be first in the lunch line, use of the library, performance of tasks that students enjoy, the chance to make choices that students consider to be important, and a great many other things not often thought of as reinforcers for good conduct or good academic work.

Reinforcer Satiation

Even rewards that function as reinforcers may not continue to do so indefinitely. Typically, satiation sets in if students are rewarded with the same thing again and again. Even if the reward was highly prized initially, it is likely to lose some of its attraction and power as a reinforcer as students become accustomed to it. Therefore, teachers must not only make sure that the rewards they offer to particular students function as reinforcement for those students, but they must also change reinforcers periodically or, preferably, arrange for the students to select from a variety of reinforcements (Safer & Allen, 1976).

For teachers who rely heavily on reinforcement techniques applied to the class as a whole (as opposed to using them sparingly on individual students), individualizing reinforcers and combating reinforcer satiation involve extensive recordkeeping and other time demands.

Token Reinforcement Systems

Token reinforcement systems provide one way to handle these problems. Such systems include instructions to students about the behaviors to be reinforced, a means of making potentially reinforcing stimuli (tokens) contingent on student behavior, and rules governing the exchange of these tokens for other privileges (O'Leary & O'Leary, 1977). Students are awarded points (paid in the form of tokens, punches on a punch card, checkmarks, or some other symbol entered in a book) and then allowed to spend these points on reinforcers they select from the menu. Points are awarded for both behavioral and academic goals (individualized, at least to some degree), and the "prices" of reinforcement selections vary according to demand. For instance, twenty minutes in the library or twenty minutes talking quietly with friends in the classroom might cost thirty points, whereas participation in a special field trip or other special event might cost five hundred points.

Token reinforcement systems began in hospitals and other treatment institutions, but they have also been used successfully in schools (Thompson et al., 1974; Safer & Allen, 1976). Most typical classroom teachers find these systems to be more trouble than they are worth, but they are popular with teachers conducting special remedial classes or working in programs that emphasize individualized learning packages.

Reinforcement and Intrinsic Motivation

Humanists and others who see reinforcement approaches as mechanistic and manipulative oppose them. Instead of bribing students, these critics argue, teachers should develop students' intrinsic motivation through such methods as building novelty and interest into the curriculum, modeling enjoyment of learning and achievement motivation, and helping them to appreciate their own growth in knowledge and skills. Such thinking has recently acquired some empirical support. Deci (1975, 1985) and many others have shown that the introduction of extrinsic rewards for performance of a particular behavior reduces intrinsic motivation to perform that same behavior, so that sustained performance in the future becomes dependent upon extrinsic reinforcement. However, as Deci notes, behavior modifiers call for the introduction of reinforcers only if the desired behavior does not presently exist, presumably for lack of sufficient motivation, intrinsic or otherwise. Also, behavior modifiers would build fading programs into the treatment to reduce the required frequency and intensity of reinforcement, and switch from concrete or immediately consumable reinforcers to more symbolic ones. Delivery of reinforcement using the principles outlined in Chapter 16 will also reduce the danger of eroding intrinsic motivation.

Eden (1975) proposes a theory of motivation that helps explain why extrinsic reinforcement may be appropriate despite the findings of Deci (1975) and others. He notes that the motivational effects of behavioral consequences depend on the relevance of those consequences to the motive operating at the time. In theory, reinforcers congruent with operating motivational systems will have a strong positive effect on net motivation, but other reinforcers will have a slightly negative effect. Thus, teacher praise for careful work will motivate students who want that social reinforcement but will have a slightly negative effect on the motivation of students who find the task intrinsically motivating or who are working toward some material reward, such as a prize.

This concludes our discussion of techniques for increasing and maintaining desired behavior. We now turn to methods for stopping undesirable behavior.

Satiation

A simple technique for dealing with certain minor misbehaviors is to let them run their course by allowing, or requiring, if necessary, students to repeat the behaviors until fatigue and boredom set in. According to Krumboltz and Krumboltz (1972), satiation is effective when the behavior does not lead to powerful rewards (if it does, extinction will be necessary), the behavior is counterproductive and the student can see this, and the behavior is not harmful. Such behaviors include throwing spitballs, making faces or noises, or almost any type of classroom clowning that is silly rather than really funny. Inviting students to continue to do such things allows them to get it out of their systems and takes away the novelty and desire, at least for the present.

Limited use of satiation

Satiation is probably most effective if used sparingly and with a minimum of fanfare. If used too often, it can become an enjoyable ritual in itself, particularly if the teacher makes it an enjoyable experience, or a bone of contention between the teacher and students who feel picked on, if the teacher humiliates them.

Extinction

Undesirable behavior that leads to reinforcement will not decrease through satiation, unless the student becomes satiated with the reinforcement it produces. Therefore, teachers must handle such behavior with other techniques. The major means for reducing it (not merely controlling it) is extinction through nonreinforcement. To extinguish effectively, the teacher, who must control the reinforcements that maintain the behavior, assures that performance of the behavior no longer leads to the expected reinforcement.

Ignoring undesirable behavior

The most common nonreinforcement technique in the classroom is simply ignoring and getting peers to ignore the behavior that appears to be motivated by a desire for attention. Some students find attention, even negative attention involving disapproval, to be reinforcing and will repeat any behavior that brings them the attention they desire.

Limits on use of extinction

Extinction is not always feasible in the classroom. Certain misbehaviors are too disruptive or dangerous to be ignored, and some students assume that anything not explicitly disapproved is acceptable. Open defiance, obscenities, hostility directed specifically at the teacher, or similarly provocative behaviors demand response. Attempts to ignore such behaviors will confuse students or leave them with the impression that the teacher is not aware of what is going on, is unable to cope with it, or just doesn't care.

Reinforcement plus extinction

Even when feasible, ignoring is never effective by itself; it must be coupled with reinforcement of desired behavior (O'Leary & O'Leary, 1977). Used in combination, teacher reinforcement and extinction can be effective, but only for students whose behaviors are under the control of reinforcement from the teacher in the first place. Ignoring misbehaving students will have no effect on behaviors that peers reinforce.

Tanner (1978) suggests four criteria for determining when ignoring is appropriate: when the problem is momentary, when it is not serious or dangerous, when drawing attention to it would disrupt the class, and when the student involved is usually well behaved. These criteria, along with the findings of Kounin (1970), leave little room for the systematic use of ignoring in an attempt to extinguish misbehavior that is disruptive and persistent. Kounin's work suggests that some comment or signal to the inattentive student is necessary whenever the problem seems likely to escalate.

Negative consequences

Ignoring can also have negative consequences. Students who do not realize that they are being ignored deliberately, or who do not know why they are being ignored, may increase their efforts to get attention by becoming more and more disruptive. Brief explanations to such students probably are much more effective than waiting for them to become conditioned through repeated frustration.

Negative Reinforcement

Like modeling, cuing, and positive reinforcement, negative reinforcement is a technique for increasing desired behavior. It is discussed here among techniques for stopping misbehavior, however, because teachers should only use it when students have been misbehaving persistently despite more positive attempts to get them to change.

Termination of aversive experiences

Negative reinforcement occurs when improved behavior brings about the termination of an aversive experience. For ethical reasons, teachers are not advised to place students deliberately in aversive situations so that teachers can use negative reinforcement by releasing students when they behave well. However, the natural consequences of many forms of misbehavior are aversive, and teachers can often arrange to let students escape some of these consequences by improving their behavior.

Makeup exams and extra credit assignments, for example, allow students to avoid low grades by improving their mastery of material. Unruly classes can be kept after school until they become more cooperative. Students who have not been controlling themselves can be required to take time out from classroom activities until they regain control.

Negative reinforcement is not punishment

Notice that negative reinforcement is not punishment—students do not suffer aversive consequences or lose rewards as a result of misbehavior (see Table 21.1). Instead, reinforcement is withheld pending performance of desired behavior. The aversive condition persists solely because the students have not behaved appropriately, and they can terminate it at any time by changing their behavior. Negative reinforcement is most effective when the teacher warns students in advance, to underscore that the students themselves are responsible if reinforcement is not forthcoming. Ideally, such warnings stress the call for improved behavior rather than the withholding of reinforcement like, for example, "Class, I know you don't like to get out late, but you're going to stay until you settle down and pay attention to this announcement."

Punishment

Punishment controls undesirable behavior by making aversive consequences contingent on such behavior.

Stopgap measure

The use of punishment should be minimized because it is a stopgap measure at best. To the extent that it is effective at all, punishment only

Table 21.1 Reinforcing and Punishing Effects of Consequences of Behavior

	Desirable Consequences	Undesirable Consequences
Application of consequences following behavior	Positive reinforcement: behavior leads to reward. Increases rate of behavior.	Punishment: behavior leads to aversive consequences. Decreases rate of behavior.
Removal of consequences following behavior	Punishment: behavior leads to loss of reward. Decreases rate of behavior.	Negative reinforcement: behavior leads to escape from aversive consequences. Increases rate of behavior.

suppresses the overt performance of undesirable behaviors, but even here the effects usually are situational and temporary. In any case, punishment does not change students' underlying desires to misbehave or the reasons why those desires exist; it does not provide guidance to students by indicating what they should do instead; and it causes problems of its own by engendering resentment.

In general, effective punishment is mild rather than severe, informative rather than merely punitive, and tailored to the specific misbehavior in ways likely to help the student see why the misbehavior is inappropriate.

Optimal moment for punishment

Redl (1966) suggests that teachers wait for the optimal moment rather than try to punish immediately, especially when students are emotionally upset. Punishing students while they are aroused and angry may only increase their alienation, while waiting until they are calm enough to listen but still concerned about the problem might be much more effective.

Ineffective Forms of Punishment

Suspension

Certain forms of punishment almost never work. Suspension from school is probably the most obvious. It does remove disruptive students from class, but many of them welcome the time off from school. Even if suspension does function as punishment, the students lose class time and fall behind in work, and most will be resentful rather than contrite. Thus, except in extreme cases such as those discussed in the next chapter, school suspension is a mistake.

Extra classwork

The same is true of punishing students by forcing them to do extra classwork. By assigning schoolwork as punishment, the teacher conveys that the work is unpleasant.

Physical punishment

Physical punishment is also generally ineffective. Many teachers and school administrators realize this but favor maintaining physical punishment as an option (where it is legal), intending to rely on its value as a threat without actually using it frequently. Others, including many parents, object to physical punishment on philosophical grounds. There is a simpler objection, however: Physical punishment does not work except in unusual situations. The best examples of its failure are antisocial delinquents and criminals, who almost always come from homes in which adults relied on physical punishment to socialize children. It keeps them under control to a degree while they are still young and afraid, but it builds anger and resentment that emerge as children get older (Feshbach, 1970).

Physical punishment is a direct attack on the student, and as such it almost invariably creates anger and resentment. Furthermore, these emotions usually will be much stronger than any feelings of fear or contrition, so the punishment does not reduce the tendency for the student to misbehave. It will not help to make the physical punishment as mild as possible, either. Slaps on the wrist and light paddling do not inspire much fear, especially in students accustomed to harsher treatment. Such students may even enjoy mild physical punishment because it gets them attention from peers.

Group punishment

Another technique that we do not recommend is group punishment, in which contingencies are arranged so that an entire class or group is punished because of the misbehavior of an individual. Some writers recommend this technique for extreme cases, because the peer pressure generated can be very powerful. Like physical punishment, however, it is difficult to use effectively, and the undesirable side effects are likely to outweigh any advantages. For one thing, this technique forces students to choose between the teacher and one of their classmates. Many students will choose the classmate, uniting in sullen defiance of the teacher and refusing to blame the classmate if group punishment is applied. Even if students do go along with the teacher and pressure the classmate, the technique engenders unhealthy attitudes in the target student and perhaps in the other students as well.

Guidelines for Effective Punishment

When misbehavior persists despite repeated, positive attempts to stop it, mild forms of punishment may be necessary. Threat of punishment is usually even more effective than punishment itself, particularly when phrased in a way that reminds students that it will be their own fault if punishment results.

Punishments should be flexible and tailored to the specific situation. Fear of unknown consequences usually functions as a punishment, while expectation of known consequences frequently does not. Other guidelines are listed below:

- ☐ Punishment should be threatened before it is actually used. This should be done in a way that makes clear to students that the teacher hopes it will not have to be used and that the students will be fully responsible if it is used.
- ☐ When punishment is used, it should be a deliberate, systematic method for suppressing misbehavior, not an involuntary emotional reaction, a way to get revenge, or a spontaneous reaction to provocation.
- ☐ The punishment should be as short and mild as possible, but unpleasant enough to motivate students to change their behavior.
- ☐ The punishment should be combined with positive statements of expectations and rules, focusing more on what the students should be doing than on what they should not be doing. The teacher should make clear to students why the rule exists, why their misbehavior cannot be tolerated, why they have left no alternative other than punishment.
- ☐ Ideally, punishment should be combined with negative reinforcement, so that students must do something positive to show good faith and escape punishment (e.g., stating that students will lose some privilege for a specific time probably is less effective than stating that they will lose the privilege until behavior improves sufficiently to warrant removal of the punishment).

Effective punishment

Some of the most effective punishments are very mild, at least from a teacher's perspective. For example, merely keeping students after class for a few minutes to discuss problems can have a punishing effect, especially if it prevents them from doing something they want to do immediately. A delay of even a few minutes may cause a student to have to go to the end of the lunch line or to go home alone instead of with friends. These may be more effective punishments for most students than being sent to an isolation area, sent to the principal, or physically punished.

Teachers do not have to present punishment explicitly as such, nor does it have to be something that we usually think of as shameful or painful. For example, if property destruction is involved, the punishment should require that the students fix or replace what they have broken. If this is not possible, punishment might involve some other kind of service such as cleaning up the school grounds or performing some similar chore that requires them to make restitution. In general, destructiveness is often handled best with overcorrection methods—the student must not only change behavior but must make restitution by fixing or replacing damaged items.

Overcorrection methods

Students who are upset, angry, or out of control as a result of a particular situation, and hyperactive or aggressive students who are having bad days, may respond well to time out from regular classroom activities. Teachers can ask them to move to an isolated part of the room, a desk in the hall, or perhaps the principal's office, until they can collect themselves and behave appropriately. Time out usually works best if presented not as a punishment, but as an opportunity for students to solve their own problems.

Time out

Response cost

Abuse of privileges usually is eliminated best with response cost—making it clear that costs will be attached to certain unacceptable behaviors, and that students who do not heed fair warnings will have to pay those costs. Ideally, costs are logically related to the offenses; students who abuse library privileges will have them suspended, students who are persistently destructive with certain equipment will not get to use the equipment for a time, or students who start fights at recess will have to stay in or play alone.

Detention

Students who refuse to work on assignments usually are best handled by in-school or after-school detention during which they are required to work

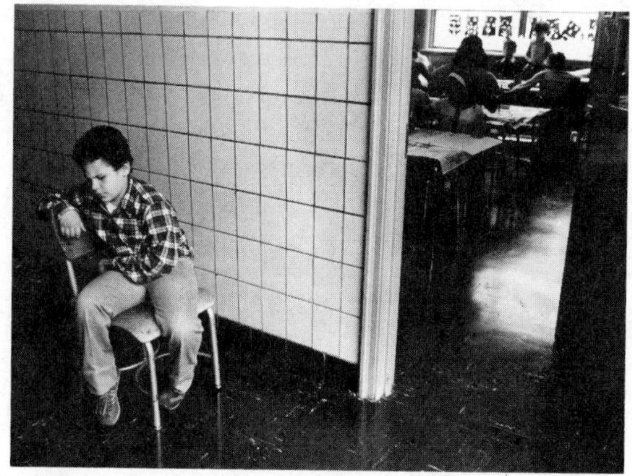

Isolating a student is an extreme form of punishment.

on assignments. This shows them that attempts to escape assignments by refusing to work or creating diversions will only result in their having to spend extra time in school.

Teachers can best manage provocations and attention-getting behaviors by gentle and humorous put-downs. If these behaviors persist, punishment should be designed to frustrate students' intended goals completely. For example, students who persist in shouting out obscenities can be required to copy these repeatedly during free time until they are satiated.

Truly effective punishment does not leave students with revengeful attitudes. Instead, it provides them with feelings of guilt, shame, frustration, or embarrassment. They realize that they have gotten into trouble because of their own failures to respond to earlier, more positive attempts to curb their misbehavior.

Using Techniques Systematically

Behavior modification techniques must be used correctly and consistently with one another. For example, Dasho (1978) reports that a teacher tried the following techniques over a short period for dealing with a disobedient boy: firmly reminding the boy about the rules; moving his desk to isolate him from the class; depriving him of recess; positive reinforcement; and finally ignoring him. More generally, Dasho reports that teachers commonly vacillated among calm appeal to rationality, threatening punishment, and ignoring. Such unsystematic combining of techniques is unlikely to succeed for any length of time.

Even teachers who try to implement principles of behavior modification more systematically often have trouble at first. For example, Harris and Kapche (1978) list twenty-six different errors that such teachers commonly commit. Therefore, if you intend to use these techniques systematically, carefully study sources such as Krumboltz and Krumboltz (1972) and O'Leary and O'Leary (1977) to master concepts, and try to arrange for help in the form of observation and feedback as you work on techniques in class.

SUMMARY

A variety of minor but annoying student misbehaviors require teacher command of the principles of behavior modification in order to shape more constructive behavior. Techniques for establishing and maintaining desired behavior include modeling, cuing, and reinforcement; methods for stopping undesirable behavior include satiation, extinction, and punishment.

Modeling is a powerful influence on behavior if teachers use it systematically. Students tend to imitate most the behaviors of high-prestige models, especially when they can identify with the models and see that the models' desirable behaviors are rewarded. Modeling can foster a wide range of desired behaviors, especially when coupled with verbalized self-instruction to achieve self-control.

Cues for appropriate behavior can be of help when dealing with repeated problem behavior. Advance reminders, coaching, and similar supports are especially useful when students have trouble discriminating between appropriate and inappropriate times for talking, moving about, and the like. This technique can be combined with self-assessment, self-recording, and self-reinforcement.

Reinforcement is the primary behavioristic mechanism for establishing and maintaining behavior. When used in the form of the Premack Principle with appropriate schedules of reinforcement, it is applicable to classroom situations. Contingency contracting clarifies relationships between behavior and consequences, provides structure, and motivates students. Also, social reinforcement and various token reinforcement systems can support behavior.

Teachers can reduce undesirable behaviors through satiation, extinction, negative reinforcement, and punishment. All of these techniques require careful management to avoid undesirable side effects. It is especially important when using punishment to remain alert to the possibility of undesired and unintended consequences.

QUESTIONS AND PROBLEMS

1. Does using reinforcement in the classroom amount just to bribing students to learn? Explain why or why not, and discuss your answer with friends.
2. Have you ever used modeling combined with verbalized self-instruction as a teaching device? What are its advantages and disadvantages compared to ordinary lecture/demonstration?
3. How a message is phrased is often at least as important as the content of the message itself. What principles apply to the following situations: praise that is reinforcing to students and not condescending or patronizing, and cuing that involves helpful pointers or reminders and not nagging.
4. If you use contracts, tokens, or other formalized reinforcement systems in your class, you will probably want to do so only with a few students who seem to need such extra structuring/incentives. How will you explain the situation so that you do not create either self-concept problems in the few students singled out for special treatment or jealousy in the rest of the class?

CASE STUDIES

Mr. Knight Loses His Cool. Jim Dell, a sixth-grade student, heads for the pencil sharpener. Mr. Knight says, almost yelling, "Jim, go back to your seat! That's the fifth time I've had to tell you to get in your seat! Stay there!" Moments later Jim wanders out of his seat, sits on Wanda's desk, and begins a conversation with her. "Jim," Mr. Knight yells, "What's wrong with you? Can't you do anything right?" Jim's face muscles tighten as he stares at the floor sullenly. How would you have reacted to Jim's desk-sitting behavior? What should Mr. Knight do now? In general, how would you deal with Jim's out-of-seat behavior?

In Search of Self-Monitoring Skills. Jan Barnes is a tenth-grade English teacher. She bemoans the fact that when she assigns a brief research/essay paper of between four to five pages, containing 20 references, students ask endless questions. How can she develop a management system for helping students to assume more responsibility for finding their own references and making independent decisions about what to include in the paper?

Chapter 22

Humanistic Approaches to Counseling Disturbed Students

OBJECTIVES

When you have mastered the material in this chapter you will be able to

1. Discuss four common background experiences of students who show severe or chronic behavior problems in school
2. Explain how Rudolf Dreikurs theoretically analyzes student misbehavior and what practical advice he gives for the handling of student problems
3. Define and discuss the techniques of the life space interview for dealing with misbehavior problems
4. List and explain Glasser's ten-step approach to dealing with problem students and the rationale that underlies it
5. Explain the philosophy behind Gordon's Teacher Effectiveness Training (TET), his concept of problem ownership, and the TET techniques that facilitate teacher-student communication (e.g., active listening and "I" messages)
6. Discuss Gordon's six-step "no lose" method for solving student-teacher conflict
7. Explain the two key elements of the authors' integrated eclectic approach to problem solving and identify the elements in a real-life illustration of problem solving

The classroom management principles discussed in the previous three chapters will enable teachers to establish and maintain an effective learning environment, manage the class as a group, and deal with routine school adjustment problems that individual students present. Certain students, however, will show chronic, severe problems that make it difficult for the teacher to reach them or that require frequent reliance on negative reinforcement or punishment to exert control. In this chapter, we shall discuss some characteristics of these students and some of the techniques for dealing with them that humanistic approaches to psychology and psychotherapy suggest.

Paths to Distorted Development

Disturbed parents

The life history of each seriously distorted individual is unique, but several themes are common. First, most come from homes in which one or both parents are seriously disturbed. These need not be broken homes; many children would be better off if their parents were divorced instead of fighting continuously while remaining married. In any case, students reared in homes featuring parental strife, modeling of low frustration tolerance, verbal and physical violence, and socialization based on threats and punishment are likely to mistrust adults, particularly authority figures. They are likely to have well-developed antisocial tendencies and poor self-control.

Cycles of failure

A different type of distorted development involves cycles of failure, feelings of inadequacy, and attempts to compensate for failure or cover up by acting out. This kind of misbehavior often occurs primarily in school situations. Typically, problems start when students are in the early grades and suffer blame and rejection (usually real, but sometimes only perceived) because of school failure. Students like these often develop rigid self-concepts of hopeless inadequacy in relation to school tasks. This sets in motion a series of self-fulfilling prophecy effects, since students who expect failure and rejection are likely to experience failure and rejection. By acting hopelessly inept and alienated, they condition teachers to perceive and treat them as such (Dreikurs, 1968; Covington, 1983). Teachers often give up on students who are unresponsive, impulsive, wrapped up in fantasy, or virtually certain to say or do something silly if they do respond (Brophy, Evertson, Anderson, Baum, & Crawford, 1976).

Alienation from learning

Teachers often overlook students who are alienated from learning and who are also passive. These pupils may continue to become more withdrawn and depressed if teachers do not intervene. This means changing both students' behavior and self-perceptions by helping them to learn and to realize that they are capable of learning (Purkey, 1970; Deci, 1985; Covington, 1983).

Demands for attention

Students who do not receive enough of the right kind of attention and respect from parents, teachers, or peers may strive to obtain it through clowning or disruptive behavior. Others come to be regarded as disruptive at school because of indulgence in tobacco or marijuana, pills or other drugs, drinking, obscene language, or sexual activity. Except for involvement with hard drugs like heroin, such behavior is typical of students, especially secondary students, who are relatively bright and well adjusted, compared to the kinds of disturbed students described previously.

Dealing with existing conditions

Many problems, however, can be handled successfully without a full understanding of how they develop. In most cases it is more important to understand and deal with people as they are now rather than to delve into their past histories. This point is worth stressing, for at least two reasons. First, there is a tendency to cite poor home backgrounds both to explain disordered behavior and to justify failure to do anything about this behavior. It is true that the more disturbed individuals are, and the longer they have been disturbed, the more difficult it will be to change them. However, this is very different from saying that nothing can or should be done. Second, partly as a holdover from early psychoanalysis, teachers frequently believe that classroom misbehavior that is part of a general pattern of disorder must be handled through psychotherapy. At one level, this is true. Even when they want to, teachers probably should not even attempt to solve a student's overall adjustment problems if they are serious. But it is also true that teachers must take action to change misbehavior in their classrooms if they expect to stop it.

Counseling Techniques

Personality theory and techniques of counseling and psychotherapy are natural sources for classroom teachers to draw on in developing methods for dealing with problem students, but early attempts were not very successful. Most techniques of psychoanalysis and other early forms of intensive individual psychotherapy were not suitable for use with children, and teachers, who were busy dealing with entire classes, did not have adequate time to use them.

As counseling and psychotherapy became more diversified, new techniques that were more humanistic and behavioral were developed. These are more limited but also more specific in intent, and more immediate in their effects. Classroom teachers can use many of these techniques effectively.

Dreikurs

Although the writings of Rudolf Dreikurs (1968) are psychoanalytic (Adlerian), they are intended for teachers and applicable in the classroom.

Importance of family dynamics

Predictably, Dreikurs stresses the importance of early family dynamics, tracing problems to such sources such as parental overambition or overprotectiveness and sibling relationships that make certain children feel discouraged or inadequate. Dreikurs sees children as reacting to these central themes in their lives, compensating for feelings of inferiority by developing a style of life designed to protect self-esteem and avoid danger areas. He believes that children who have not worked out a satisfactory personal adjustment and place in the peer group will seek one of the following four goals (listed in increasing order of disturbance): (1) attention, (2) power, (3) revenge, or (4) display of inferiority (to get special service or attention).

Analysis of behavior

The first step for teachers is to analyze problem behavior and determine what goals students are pursuing. For example, attention seekers are disruptive and provocative, but will not openly defy or challenge as will power seekers, who in turn will not seek to hurt or torment, as will revenge seekers. Persistent dependency and the seeking of help will differ in quality and purpose, depending on whether students merely want attention or have given up attempts to cope and have opted to display inferiority and helplessness.

Explaining the problem to students

Dreikurs advises teachers to observe problem students, diagnose the meaning of their behavior, and then explain this diagnosis to the students in private. The teacher should make the students understand the goals of their own behavior, rather than speculating about presumed causes. If the teacher is not sure about these goals, it can be helpful to speculate about them to see whether or not this strikes a responsive note in students ("I wonder if you do that just to get attention.").

Dreikurs opposes artificial punishment, but stresses the value of allowing the natural consequences of maladaptive behavior to occur. He stresses the linkage between maladaptive behavior and unwanted consequences as part of the attempt to develop insight and build a willingness to abandon self-defeating goals and make commitments to more productive ones.

Life Space Interviews

Improving life conditions

Morse (1971), describes the goal of a life space interview as fostering adjustment and obtaining a degree of behavioral compliance by providing life space relief (improving the life conditions of the student, especially in the classroom). Incidents of defiance or serious misbehavior often provide the impetus. In this type of interview, the teacher talks to students privately, trying to obtain their perceptions of the incident and the events that led up to it. This provides an opportunity for students to experience catharsis and ventilation, and for teachers to express a desire to help.

Acceptance of student's feelings

As the interview proceeds, the teacher seeks to obtain an accurate and detailed description of what happened and an indication of the meaning of the event to the student. Students may be upset by different events—one student may be concerned about being picked on by peers, while another may be upset about being blamed by the teacher. The teacher tries to communicate acceptance of the feelings the student conveys without necessarily accepting the student's actions.

Working with the student

Once this balance is accomplished, discussion can move toward deciding what must be done. This involves analysis to identify places where relief can be provided or changes made. The teacher offers to work together with the student to find ways to prevent repetition of the problem. How can the problems that led up to the incident be eliminated or reduced? What will happen if there is a repetition of the incident? The teacher avoids moralizing and empty threats, confining discussion of consequences to those that the teacher seriously intends to use in the future if there should be a repetition of the behavior.

Within this general model, teachers should provide the following additional help that particular students need:

1. Teachers should help students see and accept reality and abandon defensive distortions.
2. Teachers should show students how their inappropriate behavior is self-defeating.
3. Teachers should clarify values.
4. Where necessary, teachers should suggest means that will help students deal with problems more effectively.
5. Teachers should help students think for themselves and avoid being led into trouble by others.
6. Teachers should help students release anger by expressing sympathy and understanding.
7. Teachers should help students deal with emotions like panic, rage, or guilt following emotional explosions.
8. Teachers should maintain open communication.
9. Teachers should provide friendly reminders.
10. Teachers should help clarify thinking and facilitate decision making.

Glasser and Reality Therapy

In suggesting applications of what he calls "reality therapy" to the classroom, William Glasser provides guidelines for general classroom management and for problem solving with individual students. He has a wide following among teachers, and survey data indicate that systematic implementation of his program is associated with reductions in referrals to the office, fighting, and suspensions (Glasser, 1977). More rigorous tests of his methods are not available (nor are they for other approaches described in this chapter).

Facilitative school atmosphere

The book *Schools Without Failure* (1969) illustrates Glasser's interest in creating a generally facilitative atmosphere in schools, not just facilitative teacher-student relationships. He stresses that schools and classrooms be as humanistic as possible—they should be cheerful and courteous, communal, open to student input and communication generally, and staffed by people who believe that students are capable of exercising responsibility.

Jointly established rules

Glasser advocates that teachers and students jointly establish rules during classroom meetings, and that they hold additional meetings to adjust the rules or develop new ones that apply to novel situations. Teachers adopt the role of discussion leaders and not authority figures during these meetings, setting limits only with respect to what is possible within the law and the rules of the school. Decisions are to be made by vote rather than negotiation. This part of Glasser's approach is not as well accepted as his problem-solving steps, because many teachers oppose student self-government on principle, and others find it overly cumbersome.

Ten-step method

Glasser's ten-step method of dealing with problem students does not require use of his classroom meetings approach to rule setting, although Glasser himself stresses the latter and, in any case, insists that everyone must recognize rules as reasonable and beneficial if they are to be effective. Glasser describes his approach to discipline as no-nonsense, but also as constructive and nonpunitive. It involves making clear to students that they can and must control themselves and follow school rules if they expect to stay in school.

Glasser's first step is to select a student for concentrated attention and elicit typical teacher reactions to the student's disruptive behavior. Second, analyze Glasser's list of problem-solving techniques to see which ones do and do not work, resolving not to repeat those that fail. Third, personal relations with the student should be improved. Extra encouragement should be provided by asking the student to perform special errands, or by taking other initiatives to show concern and imply that things are going to improve.

This method continues indefinitely. If the problem behavior reappears, whereupon a new approach is added at the fourth step. Instead of repeating past mistakes, the teacher simply should ask students to describe what they are doing. This causes students to analyze their behavior, perhaps for the first time, and to begin to see their own responsibility for it, although they may try to rationalize. In any case, once students describe their own behavior accurately, the teacher simply should ask them to stop it.

The fifth step is used if the problem persists. The teacher should call a short conference and again ask students to describe the behavior, and to state whether or not it is against the rules or recognized informal expectations. The teacher also should ask the students what they should be doing instead of what they have been doing. All this is done in a warm and supportive way, but with insistence that students both express the inappropriateness of their own behavior and describe what they should be doing instead.

If this does not work, the sixth step also involves calling conferences and getting students to focus on their misbehavior, but includes announcing that a plan is needed to solve the problem. The plan must be more than a simple agreement to stop misbehaving, because this has not been honored in the past.

If the sixth step does not work, Glasser's seventh step calls for isolating the students or using time-out procedures. During their periods of isolation, students should be charged with devising plans for insuring that they follow the rules in the future. Isolation will continue until the students have devised such a plan, have had it approved, and have made a commitment to follow it.

If this doesn't work, the eighth step is in-school suspension. This should be announced to the students firmly but matter-of-factly. Suspended students will now have to deal with the principal or someone else other than the teacher, but this other person will repeat earlier steps in the sequence and press the students to come up with a plan that is acceptable.

If disruptive conduct persists, stop the lesson and call a short conference with the troublemakers.

The ninth step applies only to students who remain out of control during in-school suspension. Glasser recommends calling their parents to take them home, and then starting over with them the next day. The tenth step is removal from school and referral to another agency.

Glasser's ten-step approach is attractive to a great many teachers because it clearly is applicable in the classroom and because it provides a sequence of specific steps for dealing with problems that have not responded to normal methods. It also illustrates features common to several approaches, including the behavioristic, that seem to be converging. One is insistence on minimal standards of behavior, specifically behavior in school, regardless of students' personal backgrounds. All students must follow reasonable rules of behavior.

Responsibility for behavior

A related notion is that students are responsible for their own behavior and will be held to that responsibility. Teachers will do whatever they can to help students solve their problems, but these are the students' problems and not the teacher's. This approach may seem harsh, but it assumes that rules are reasonable and fairly administered, and that teachers try to be helpful, cooperate with students in making feasible adjustments, and, in general, maintain a positive, problem-solving stance. Where these assumptions do not hold, Glasser's methods, like any others, can be destructive. For instance, an authoritarian teacher can concentrate more on building a case against problem students than on trying to help them.

Gordon and Teacher Effectiveness Training

Glasser's ideas were widely disseminated and adopted in the late 1960s and early 1970s. Many teachers use them today, and interest in reality therapy workshops remains high. The same is true for workshops on behavior modification approaches. However, the approach being disseminated most vigorously now is Thomas Gordon's (1974) Teacher Effectiveness Training (TET).

"No lose" arrangements

Gordon's philosophy stresses freedom, responsibility, and abandonment of power and authority in favor of negotiation of "no lose" arrangements. He advises teachers to be open and caring toward their students, but also to maintain their individuality or separateness. He urges minimizing authoritative control over students, replacing this with teacher-student interdependence and mutual meeting of needs.

Problem ownership

Problem solving starts with identification of problem ownership. Some problems are owned strictly by teachers, some strictly by students, and others by both teachers and students. Solutions to problems are facilitated if all parties involved recognize problem ownership accurately and respond accordingly.

Student-owned problems

Student-owned problems include anxiety, inhibition, and poor self-concept. For these problems Gordon recommends passive listening (showing that you hear and understand what students are saying), door openers (invitations for students to talk), and especially, active listening. Active listening goes beyond simply paying attention and showing that you understand; it includes providing feedback to students that responds to the underlying meanings of their messages.

In short, Gordon recommends an updated form of Carl Rogers's nondirective counseling (Rogers, 1951, 1983) for such students, and he rejects as ineffective responses those that contain what he calls "the language of unacceptance." This is any response to the students' expressed fears or anxieties that does not take them seriously. This obviously includes flat contradictions or scoffing, but also takes in well-meaning attempts to cheer students up by praising or distracting them.

Language of unacceptance

Active listening

Gordon recommends active listening as an instructional technique during class discussions as well as a management technique to use on individuals. It helps students dissipate their feelings before getting down to work when something upsetting has happened and it helps promote smooth parent-teacher conferences. Through active listening, teachers help students, not by trying to assume responsibility for their problems, but by helping them to find their own solutions and become more independent, confident, and self-reliant.

Teacher-owned problems

Teacher-owned problems occur when students behave in ways that make teachers frustrated or angry. They require a different set of techniques from those used when students own the problem. In the latter case it is important for students to communicate and for the teacher to be a listener and counselor. When the teacher owns the problem, the teacher does the communicating, sending messages to students and trying to influence them to change.

"I" and "You" Messages. Gordon lists a number of ineffective techniques for trying to change students. These include confrontations that backfire, "solution" messages that students resent and that induce only dependent and artificial compliance even when they do work, put-down messages that breed resentment without bringing about constructive changes, and indirect messages that may hurt the teacher's credibility. Gordon notes that most of these ineffective messages are "you" messages, used when the situation calls for "I" messages. It is the teacher in such cases who has the problem and thus the teacher who must do the communicating. "I" messages reveal feelings and vulnerabilities, but in ways that pay off by fostering intimacy and describing the problem without imputing unfortunate motives to the students.

"I" messages have three major parts. The first part indicates the specific behavior that leads to the problem ("When I get interrupted. . . ."). The second specifies the effect on the teacher (". . . I have to start over and repeat things unnecessarily. . . ."). This shows students that their behavior is causing the teacher real problems, and this message alone will be sufficient to motivate most students to want to change. The third part specifies the feelings generated within the teacher because of the problem (". . . and I become frustrated.") Taken together, the three parts link specific student behavior as the cause of a specific effect on the teacher, which in turn produces undesirable feelings in the teacher.

"No Lose" Method of Problem Solving. Gordon maintains that combinations of environmental manipulation, active listening, and communication through "I" messages will solve most problems. However, sometimes the needs motivating unacceptable student behavior are very strong or the relationship with the teacher is very poor, and conflict will continue. Genuine conflict involves problems owned by both students and teachers. It must be approached in ways that avoid winning or losing and that meet the needs of all parties involved. Gordon's "no lose" method is a process of searching until such a solution is found.

Conflict resolution

Prerequisites for use of the method include active listening (students must believe that their needs will be accepted if they are expected to risk serious negotiation), use of good "I" messages to state teacher needs clearly and honestly, and communication to students that this is a new and different approach (for teachers who have not been using it regularly). There are six steps to be followed in this approach: (1) define the problem, (2) generate possible solutions, (3) evaluate these solutions, (4) decide which solution is best, (5) determine how to implement the solution, and (6) assess how well the solution is solving the problem.

Defining the problem

Defining the problem properly includes accuracy about problem ownership and identification of only those people who are really part of the problem. This continues until everyone is agreed. For this purpose, it is vital that the problem be described in terms of conflicting needs, not competing solutions.

Generating solutions

When generating solutions, it is important simply to list them and not to evaluate them prematurely. Once evaluation starts, solutions that are objectionable to anyone for any reason should be eliminated. Deciding which solution is best involves persistent search for consensus rather than a resort to voting. Proposed solutions can be tested by imagining the consequences. When agreement is reached, specific implementation plans and responsibilities are drawn up, including plans for later assessment. The result should be a "no lose" agreement with which everyone explicitly states satisfaction and readiness to honor.

Broken agreements

Not all agreements are honored, however. Agreements may be broken when students do not perceive the conflict in the first place, seeing only the teacher's problem; do not believe that their needs are heard and understood by the teacher (this can happen even when the solution meets their needs); or agree to the solution because of peer or teacher pressure. Gordon warns teachers against using power when students break agreements. Instead, he suggests that they send strong "I" messages to communicate disappointment and indicate that now they share a new problem.

Assertion of power

Gordon clearly does not like the idea of power assertion by teachers under any circumstances, but he admits that it may be necessary when there is danger involved, when students do not understand the logic of the teacher's position, or when there is insufficient time for more leisurely problem solving.

Value conflicts

Gordon also notes that certain conflicts involve competing value systems (dress code, use of drugs, personal grooming, language and manners, morality, patriotism, religion) for which no mutually acceptable solutions are possible. "I" messages are not effective in such cases because the teacher's logic does not make sense to the students. Value conflicts should be labeled as such, and not as conflicts of personal needs. Gordon still recommends self-disclosure and "I" messages to show students where teachers stand and to open the door for possible discussion and behavior change, but that is all. He advises dropping the matter if the first "I" message does not produce any positive response from students. Teacher persistence at this point is seen as irritating preaching or nagging.

Evaluation of Humanistic Approaches

There are many similarities among the recommendations of humanistic theorists. Many of their ideas are essentially identical, and most of the rest are complementary. Glasser is probably the most realistic, recognizing explicitly that power assertion sometimes will be necessary because of persistent student irresponsibility, not just because of pressures, dangers, or value conflicts. Even his approach may assume too much; some students will resist making commitments because their misbehavior is too rewarding, and some will require stronger sanctions than social encouragement (Clarizio & McCoy, 1976).

Research Evidence

Brophy and Rohrkemper (1981) examined how 98 elementary teachers interpreted and stated how they would cope with twelve chronic student problem types. Problem types included failure syndrome, perfectionist, underachiever, low achiever, hostile aggressive, passive aggressive, defiant, hyperactive, distractible, immature, rejected by peers, and shy-withdrawn. The teachers who were studied had been nominated by their principals as either outstanding or average in their ability to cope with problem students (for more complete descriptions of problem types, see Chapter 17).

Following Gordon (1974), Brophy and Rohrkemper (1981) classified problems as: (1) teacher-owned, where the students' behavior interferes with the teachers' needs or agenda, (2) student-owned, where the students' needs or agenda is frustrated by people or events other than the teacher, and (3) shared problems, where students' behavior does not directly challenge the teacher but has consequences for classroom management and control. The teachers saw students who presented teacher-owned problems as acting intentionally, and thus as blameworthy for their misbehavior. Those with student-owned problems, in contrast, were seen as victims of circumstances beyond their control.

Brophy and Rohrkemper noted that teachers in this sample appeared to have limited knowledge and skill in the various treatment models available for these problem types and did not always feel that solving these problems was a part of their duties as classroom teachers. They were pessimistic about changing students who presented teacher-owned problems, and focused on immediate control strategies rather than long-run problem-solving strategies in responding to these students. They saw students with student-owned problems as difficult to change, but they were motivated to try to do so through long-term remediation programs.

Teacher responsibility for solving problems

Teachers believed to be effective managers behaved in ways generally consistent with the principles advocated by Glasser and Gordon. They noted that teachers rated as effective by their principals and by classroom observers were willing to assume responsibility for solving problems. They worked with problem students themselves instead of or in addition to referring them to the principal or a counselor and they used long-term solution-oriented approaches. In contrast, less effective teachers focused on controlling misbehavior in the immediate situation, often by using threat or punishment. Effective teachers concentrated on helping their students to understand and cope with the problems that caused their symptomatic behavior.

An Integrated Approach

There is so much in common among the theories of Dreikurs, Redl, Morse, Glasser, and Gordon that teachers can draw on all of them to develop an integrated, eclectic approach to problem solving. Key elements include gathering complete and accurate information and seeking genuine solutions, not just stopgap suppression measures.

Gathering Information

Most people realize that one should not make decisions or take action without complete and accurate information. However, many people are not aware that undesirable outcomes can result when authority figures behave as if they were seeking information when no information is needed or obtained. For example, if a student should call out a provocative remark or create a disturbance, there may be no need for questioning. Unless it is so serious as to require a conference, the situation should be handled with a brief or even humorous response such as "Cool it, John." The teacher should not interrupt instruction to ask unnecessary and essentially meaningless and rhetorical questions like "John, how many times do I have to tell you not to do that?"

Unnecessary questions

Avoid student loss of face

When it is necessary to gather information, do so in ways that avoid causing any student to lose face. Investigations should be conducted in private, to minimize students' needs to save face, to refuse to back down no matter what, or to defy the teacher. It is also helpful to state that everything said during the discussion will be held in confidence unless some explicit agreement to the contrary is made. Insist that students keep quiet while classmates speak, reassure them that they will have a chance to give their versions later, and proceed toward the truth gradually by asking questions and pointing out discrepancies in different versions. Questions should concentrate on establishing exactly what happened and on trying to determine the motives behind the actions. The motives are important because students often misread one another's behavior—for example, by interpreting accidents as deliberate provocations or minor teasing as serious insults.

Recognize rationalizations

When questioning students, it is important not to be taken in by their rationalizations or attempts to project responsibility for their own behavior onto others. Students who get into regular scrapes with authority figures are usually masters of rationalization. When they cannot successfully deny or evade responsibility for their behavior, they will attempt to excuse or condone it by giving reasons such as "He started it"; "People who leave money lying around like that *should* have it stolen"; and "He looked at me funny." For detailed and fascinating analyses of these kinds of rationalization, see *Children Who Hate* (Redl & Wineman, 1951).

Withholding information

Investigations occasionally reach an impasse because one or more students are lying or withholding part of the truth. It usually is best to acknowledge this openly and express both disappointment that the whole truth is presently not being told and the expectation that it will be told. If persistent efforts along this line still do not succeed, the teacher must decide whether or not the discussion itself will end the matter or whether some form of punishment is required.

Finding Solutions

Positive solutions

Once all needed information is collected, the next step is to work out a solution. The solution should be perceived as positive, not punitive, in intent and effect and as acceptable to everyone, not just the majority. The teacher may have to limit the range of possible solutions by stating clearly that certain things cannot be done because they are not possible or are outside school rules.

At this stage, attention should focus on the future and on solving the problems that led to the conflict, not the conflict itself. Attempts to rehash points already gone over in the investigation phase should be cut short, and students should be reminded that since everyone understands the problem, it is time to work out a solution. Solutions do not have to be permanent or irrevocable; they can be explicitly tentative and subject to review at a designated future date.

Teacher suggestions

If the students are unable to come up with realistic suggestions, teachers will have to make the suggestions themselves. These should be tentative and open to comment and evaluation. If students endorse a proposed solution, the teacher should ask them to think carefully before making final agreements, again emphasizing that students must make the decision and will be responsible for abiding by it. Students should not be allowed to come away with the idea that the teacher foisted a demand on them to which they really did not agree.

Problem-Solving Vignette. Many of these problem-solving principles are exemplified in the following vignette. Vera Wise is a teacher who is concerned about an increase in the frequency and seriousness of attention-getting behavior among her students over the last few weeks. The problem is worse in the last hour or so of school. Increasing numbers of students have been involved, fooling around and calling out remarks instead of working on their assignments. The primary instigators seem to be Bill, Jim, David, and Paul, four boys who sit close together and are part of a clique both in and out of school.

Vera has tried talking individually to each of these boys, as well as to other students, but the problem has worsened. The boys promise to improve their behavior, but they don't. The problem came to a head this afternoon, when one of the boys (Vera is not sure which) said something obscene and embarrassing to Mary, an attractive girl who is physically well developed and is the object of much interest and discussion among the boys. Most of the class heard the remark and passed it along to the few who didn't hear the first time. Vera responded by warning the class sharply that this kind of behavior had gone far enough, and by telling Bill, Jim, David, and Paul to stay after class to see her about it. Jim started to protest that he hadn't said it, but Vera cut him off with the statement that she wanted to see all four boys and would explain why later. During the remainder of the period, Vera decided that this particular incident was not as important as the more general problem. Consequently, she decided to concentrate on changing the behavior of all four boys rather than on trying to find out who made the remark to Mary.

At the end of the period, as classmates prepared to leave, Jim and Paul looked surly, while Bill and David looked sheepish. The others were snickering at them and making guesses about what was going to happen. A few tried to hang around to find out, but Vera made a point of getting rid of them and closing the door before beginning the meeting. The meeting went as follows:

TEACHER: As I said in class, the remark made about Mary today was out of line, and it was just the latest of a number of things like that that have been going on recently. I think the time has come to put a stop to it, and I have kept you boys here because you four seem to be responsible for most of it.

The teacher begins by making it clear that she wants to talk about the general issue, not just what happened today, and that she considers all four boys to be responsible. Her behavior throughout the meeting is consistent with this opening statement.

JIM: Like I said before, I didn't do it. Besides, I can't stay because I have to go to practice and coach wants us there five minutes after the bell.

PAUL: Yeah, I didn't do it either, and I have to go home and mow the lawn today.

TEACHER: Let's get a couple of things straight. First, I'm not especially interested in finding out which one of you embarrassed Mary today. I'm interested in discussing the larger problem of putting an end to this kind of thing. You four are here because you all do it more than anyone else. Furthermore, we're all going to stay here until we settle the problem for good. That includes everyone. Jim, if you like, I will call the coach and explain. Paul, if you want, I will call your home, but you are both going to stay here until we get finished. (Both Jim and Paul indicate that they don't want the teacher to make any calls.)

Jim and Paul both try to get off by making excuses. The teacher offers to call and "explain," but this offer is refused. Although the offer was genuine in the sense that the teacher would have followed through if either boy had asked her to, she knew that this was unlikely because both boys probably knew that they would only compound their troubles if the teacher called the coach or a parent. With this response, the teacher both cuts off further attempts to escape the meeting and makes it clear that she intends to keep everyone there until she is satisfied. She also makes it specifically clear to Jim again that she is not interested in finding out who insulted Mary but instead is interested in the larger problem.

JIM: Well, David did it, not me. Besides, he does it a lot more than anyone else. When I do it, it's usually because he gets me started. (David glares but says nothing.)

Now Jim tries to blame it on David. The teacher again points out that she is interested in the larger issue and she makes it clear that Jim is both guilty of numerous instances of similar behavior

TEACHER: No good, Jim. David probably does do it more, but you are responsible for your own behavior, and you can't use him for an excuse. If you didn't do it yourself a lot, you wouldn't be here now. (Jim glumly remains silent at this point.) David, if you did do it, I think you should apologize to Mary. She was very embarrassed, and whoever is responsible owes her an apology. But, as I said, I don't want to talk about what happened today; I want to talk about what's been going on over the last several weeks, and all four of you have been thickly involved in it.

recently and responsible for his own behavior regardless of what other students do. Her suggestion that David apologize is left simply as a suggestion with no attempt to follow up. This is appropriate, because a forced apology in front of the class would only further embarrass Mary and enrage David. The teacher has nothing to lose by suggesting this, and everyone might gain something if David follows through and does apologize to Mary sometime in the future. This statement also is consistent with the teacher's later statement that obscenity as such is not as important as respecting other peoples' rights and feelings. Also, by giving minimal time and attention to the information that David was responsible for today's problem, the teacher again reinforces her earlier statement that she wants to talk about the larger problem and about all four of the boys.

PAUL: Well, we won't do it anymore. (Jim and David immediately nod and say "yes," while Bill nods solemnly.)

TEACHER: Sorry, but that's not good enough, either. I've talked to all of you, sometimes more than once. Every time you said that you wouldn't do it again, but you've kept doing it. So I'm afraid I can't take your word on it and let it go at that. We're going to have to discuss this some more and come to some kind of agreement that I can accept.

Under other circumstances, it probably would have been best for the teacher to take the boys at their word, perhaps ending the discussion on a more positive note, stressing happiness that they have seen the problem and are willing to respond to it in a mature fashion. However, given that these boys have pledged to change in the past and have not done so, it is perfectly appropriate for the teacher to refuse to accept their pledges to change and to point out her reasons why. Furthermore, she now makes it clear that this discussion is going to continue until a real solution is reached.

PAUL: Well, what's the big deal anyway? Words that people think are "dirty" don't hurt anybody, and besides, everyone knows what they mean.

TEACHER: In the first place, Paul, while it is true that there is nothing

Paul now takes the tack of trying to make the teacher feel guilty for being unreasonable. She counters nicely by acknowledging that his argument is valid up to a point, but then noting that it ignores certain factors in the larger context that make it impossible for schools to allow this kind of disruptive behavior.

really wrong with these words, they are out of place in the classroom. More importantly, though, it's not just the words. It's the other things that go with them. For example, today Mary was terribly embarrassed, and no one had the right to do that to her. Also, you are distracting the whole class from their work, and let's not forget that you're supposed to be here at school to learn, not to goof off. But you're not doing your work. You know that I allow students to talk when they finish their assignments, but you four have been fooling around and making loud remarks instead of working on your assignments and then talking quietly after you finish.

She then goes on to make the even more important point that she is more concerned about students' mutual respect for one another than about mere obscenity. The boys are much more likely to feel guilt or shame about having embarrassed Mary than they are about having used obscene language. Finally, the teacher makes the additional point that the disruptive behavior of these students is interfering with their own work and that of their classmates. This is done in a way that points out implicitly that the teacher's rules are reasonable but that these four boys are abusing them.

JIM: Well, I can't help it. I say things without thinking, or else because David or somebody else gets me started. I've tried to stop, but I can't. Besides, it's not natural to try to stop from saying things that pop into your head at times like that.

TEACHER: Really! Well, suppose I invited your mother to sit in here for a few days? Do you think you might control yourself then? (Jim's expression changes from surly self-confidence to confusion and anxiety.)

TEACHER: You don't have to answer the question. You all know the answer; you don't use that kind of language around your mothers, and you don't have any trouble controlling yourself, either. So why don't we drop the lame excuses and start by recognizing that you can and will stop if you make the effort to do so.

At this point, Jim again tries to evade responsibility. In addition to blaming others for "getting him started," he goes on to suggest that the teacher is asking something unreasonable and unnatural. The teacher wastes no time in dismissing this specious argument, pointing out that self-control is not a problem when the student is sufficiently motivated to show it. Her choice of an example here is particularly apt—students who use obscene language, particularly boys, almost always shrink at the thought of using it in the presence of their own mothers. The teacher closes this exchange a little roughly, characterizing what the boys have been saying as "lame excuses." However, under the circumstances, she is quite justified, because this is an accurate description of what has been happening. Also, she stresses personal responsibility for actions. Ultimately, she is not responsible for controlling these boys; they are responsible for controlling themselves.

PAUL: Yeah, but what are we supposed to do then? Sit there and keep our mouths shut?

TEACHER: No. I'm not asking you to do anything special, I'm only asking you to follow the rule that applies to everyone in the class: work on your assignment until you finish it. If you have time left over, then you can talk quietly, but without disrupting others.

Paul now takes a new approach, no longer attempting to rationalize the misbehavior but attacking the reasonableness of the teacher's request. She counters this by again repeating the rule, which is clearly reasonable, and also by making a point of the fact that she is only asking these boys to keep the same rule that applies to everyone else; she is not picking on them or asking them to do anything unusual.

PAUL: But I already said I would do that.

TEACHER: Yes, and I already said that all four of you have failed to keep your word on that. So what are we going to do? I don't want to make this into a big deal. In fact, I think it's silly to have to discuss something like this with students like yourselves, who should know better. But the problem is serious and is getting worse, and I am going to see that it stops before it gets out of hand. If I have to, I'll punish you all severely, but I don't want to do that. I asked you here to lay out the problem and to see if you had any suggestions about how it could be solved. Are there ways I could help by making some changes?

Paul now goes back to repeating his pledge of reform and the teacher again points out that he has made this pledge and has broken it in the past. She then pulls together a few statements to make the situation clear to the boys: they have created the problem through their own misbehavior; she doesn't even want to discuss it but they have forced it on her; the problem is serious enough that it is going to be stopped one way or another; she is inviting them to make suggestions and expressing willingness to follow them if they are feasible and have a chance of improving the situation (even though she could simply make a decision on her own about what to do and present it to the boys with no opportunity for discussion).

DAVID: Like what kind of changes?

TEACHER: Well, I could change your seats and separate you from one another. I could give you extra work or other things to do so that you wouldn't have time to goof off. I could try to arrange to have some of you transferred to other classes. (These suggestions yield negative reactions, except that Jim agrees to change seats and move away from David.)

In suggesting changes here, the teacher knows that they are unlikely to be acceptable to the boys. This is one way of informing them of possible negative consequences that will result if the problem is not stopped, without actually threatening such consequences. The fact that Jim agrees to change his seat is mildly surprising; it probably results from his own need to try to show that he was serious in his earlier claim that David tends to get him in trouble. In any case, it gives the teacher an op-

TEACHER: Okay, Jim, we'll arrange that. I hope it helps. Are there any other suggestions as to how we can solve this problem? (Long silence.)

portunity to agree with a suggestion, thus showing good will on her part.

PAUL: All I can think of is what I said before—I won't do it anymore, and this time I mean it. (The others nod.)

TEACHER: Well, I have to admit that I can't think of anything else other than punishment, and as I said, I don't want that. However, let me warn you right now that if any of you breaks his word this time, I will have to punish you. At the very least, you will have to stay after school for several days, and if there's any repeat of the kind of obscenity that went on today, I may have to contact your parents. I mention this because I want you to understand just how serious this problem is, and I want you to know that your word won't be any good in the future if you break it this time.

When the boys offer no more suggestions, the teacher changes from refusal to accept pledges of reform to a conditional acceptance. This is the appropriate time to make this switch, because the boys now have ceased their belligerence and rationalization, realizing that they are going to have to change their behavior and begin serious discussion of what might be appropriate in the future. As a hedge against failure to keep the pledge, the teacher threatens punishment in the future. However, she does it in a way that does not suggest that she expects to have to use it. Also, the kinds of punishment she mentions help underscore her seriousness about this issue.

TEACHER: What about your workbooks? I know that all of you are behind, that the work you did in the last few weeks contains a lot of sloppy errors because of your fooling around. I want those workbooks brought up to date, the errors corrected, and the books turned in to me for checking shortly. How about Friday? (Today is Wednesday.)

JIM: (Dejectedly) I'm way behind, and I have practice again tomorrow and a game Friday night. I'm not sure I can get it in by Friday.

TEACHER: All right, what about Monday? That will give you all the rest of the week plus the weekend. (All nod agreement.) All right,

In closing the discussion, the teacher turns to the problem of incomplete and sloppy work in the workbooks. She requires the students to make this up, although she agrees to a delay when a reasonable excuse is given for it. Although this will have a punishing effect in the technical sense, it is not the kind of behavior students typically perceive as punishment. The teacher merely is requiring them to do the same things that she requires of other students. The fact that it will cost them extra time and trouble in the next few days is their fault, not hers. This aspect of the discussion also underscores the point made earlier, that failure to do work is one of her concerns, not just hearing obscene words spoken in the classroom.

then, we'll make it Monday. Remember, I want you not only to catch up, but to review your work over the last three weeks or so and correct any errors you made because you weren't paying close attention to what you were doing. Work as far as the end of page 128. Okay? (All agree.) Is there anything else that any of you wants to add? (After a brief silence, all shrug or shake their heads negatively.)

TEACHER: Well, there is still the question of what to say in class tomorrow. You four are not the only ones who have been fooling around and making remarks. Tomorrow I intend to tell the class that we discussed the situation and agreed that certain things need to stop, and I intend to remind everyone about the rules. I probably also will stress some of the other things I've pointed out to you, but I don't want to say anything more about our discussion. For your own good, I suggest that you say as little as possible about it yourselves. Perhaps just say that we had a talk and made some agreements.

Finally, in closing the discussion, the teacher explicitly brings up the question of what is to be said to the class the next day. She makes it clear that she is going to make a statement, but also pledges not to embarrass the four boys or divulge any details of this discussion. This again underscores her intention to solve the problem rather than to punish the boys, and reiterates her earlier remarks about avoiding embarrassment of students.

TEACHER: Also, I would appreciate it if you urged some of your classmates to follow the rules, too, so that I don't have to hold any more sessions like this with anyone else. Anyway, I won't embarrass you or give any details about what we have said and done here, but I think some brief statement needs to be made, because everyone in the class is going to be wondering. Is this plan acceptable? (All nod agreement.) Is there anything else? (All shake their heads negatively.) O.K., get going, and let's have no more of this.

Note, too, that she tries to enlist the help of the boys in this endeavor, suggesting that they minimize discussion about what went on and that they encourage their classmates to follow the rules. They may or may not do this, and she makes no attempt to check up on them. However, she has nothing to lose with this request, and it emphasizes that the boys share the problem and that they are responsible for solving it.

Note that throughout the discussion Paul and Jim have been vocal and occasionally belligerent. Under other circumstances David might have been too, but since he was guilty of the incident that led to the discussion, he apparently has chosen to remain quiet and avoid getting into further trouble. Bill said nothing throughout the discussion, except to agree on occasion when the group agreed in unison. This may be because he is very embarrassed and remorseful, or it may be that he regularly reacts to such discussions with sullenness and nonresponsiveness. If the latter is the case, it is important for the teacher to see that he agrees explicitly to what has transpired, so that he will not claim later that he never consented to it. In this case, the teacher judges that Bill has reacted as have the other boys and has made the same commitment, even though he did not at any time speak out for himself.

SUMMARY

Disturbed students frequently come from homes in which they have experienced cycles of failure and feelings of inadequacy, often leading them to attempt to compensate by acting out. Even if not actively aggressive, they may be alienated from learning and demand attention through clowning or disruptive behavior.

Dreikurs believes that attention, power, revenge, and displays of inadequacy (listed in increasing order of disturbance) are the four goals of student misbehavior. He advises teachers to diagnose the goal of misbehavior and attempt to reveal it to students in a nonthreatening, private interview. Redl, another psychoanalytic theorist, recommends the life-space interview as a means for crisis intervention.

Glasser's theory, which he calls " reality therapy," is based on humanistic principles involving the creation of a facilitative school atmosphere. His ten-step method is designed to be constructive and nonpunitive, with minimal but graduated responses to persistent misbehavior, and self-control as the desired end result. Gordon's "teacher effectiveness training" (TET) is very similar, stressing freedom and responsibility rather than authority and power. Active listening is a method he recommends for helping students find their own solutions to their behavior problems.

Since the ideas of Dreikurs, Redl, Morse, Glasser, and Gordon have much in common, teachers can draw on all of them to form an integrated eclectic approach to problem solving, which will be illustrated in the case study that appears at the end of this chapter.

QUESTIONS AND PROBLEMS

1. Why do we insist that classroom problems be dealt with in the classroom when we acknowledge that they may be merely part of a much broader personality disturbance?
2. How realistic are your expectations regarding students' attitudes and behavior toward you as a teacher? Are you prepared to handle irrational hostility or defiance effectively?

3. How can teachers maintain humanistic values in harmony with their role as an authority figure? Are you prepared to punish effectively when (*when*, not *if*) you have to?
4. What should Vera Wise, the teacher in the vignette, have done if one or more of the boys blatantly failed to keep his promises? Write out your responses and analyze why certain teacher statements are desirable in dealing with blatant misbehavior.

CASE STUDY

Laura Simpson's Problems. Laura Simpson teaches English in a junior high school that draws 85 percent of its students from five nearby elementary schools. The remaining 15 percent of the population are black students bused in from a predominantly black neighborhood in another part of town. As a group, the black students are of lower socioeconomic status (SES) than the white students, so they provide proportionately fewer high achievers and proportionately more low achievers. The students, as a group, have a wide range of ability, achievement, and personal attitudes toward the school.

Laura is a very dedicated English teacher. She spends much of her time preparing both group and individualized activities, but the range of student abilities and interests with which she must cope creates many problems. Partly to accomplish desegregation and partly to avoid the elitism and other problems that usually accompany ability grouping by class, the school has a firm policy of heterogeneous grouping. Thus, each of Laura's five classes contains students ranging from functional illiterates to very bright high achievers capable of handling class activities such as drama or written assignments that involve composing poems or fiction. This makes it difficult to find activities with enough common ground to be interesting and worthwhile for everyone. Laura keeps searching for such activities and occasionally succeeds in finding them, but more often than not she must treat students differently.

She feels guilty about this sometimes, because it seems to contradict school policy and because it segregates the students by ability groups and, to a degree, by social class and race. However, the high achievers seem to need and want the challenge of difficult and complex assignments, and they become understandably bored and restless when Laura tries to conduct general lessons on things they learned long ago. This almost always causes some problems of student disruption. These are occasionally fairly serious, such as the time that one of her brighter students caused a near-riot by publicly complaining that Laura was wasting everyone's time by trying to teach "those dummies who don't want to learn and couldn't learn even if they did."

On the other hand, when Laura attempts to involve everyone in a high-level activity such as a dramatic reading of a play, the activity is almost always ruined by the disruptive behavior of the low achievers in the class. The reading skills of some students are so limited that they can only be assigned the most simple parts. Thus their main role is to keep quiet and listen.

As if all this were not bad enough, the students are at "that age." Almost every day and in almost every class, Laura must deal more or less continually with such adolescent behavior as attention-getting, defiance of authority, flirting, deliberate noise making, obscene or funny gestures and sounds, and wisecracks. In addition to these merely routine problems, occasionally there are really serious ones, such as fights between students or open defiance directed at her. Laura can usually handle whatever comes up, but it takes a lot of energy, and it often leaves her wondering whether she is a teacher or a warden.

Laura sees about 150 students each day for about 55 minutes each. Ten students present serious problems that Laura has been unable to solve. Let us look at these "problem" students.

Mary is bright and comes from a high-status home. In fact, her father is on the school board, and both her parents are among the town's leading citizens. However, Mary apparently dislikes both school in general and Laura in particular. She goes out of her way to show it by affecting boredom and disdain. When Laura attempts to deal with her, she responds in a way perhaps best described as "snotty." She often states that school is a drag, strictly for squares, and has even threatened Laura with trouble, presumably through her father's position on the school board, although Mary is too smart to say this directly.

Ben and Leon are two black students bused to the school. Both are alienated from school and hostile and aggressive toward peers in general and whites in particular. They have been suspended in the past for racial incidents and have been sent to detention repeatedly for refusing to turn in work. Their mere presence, individually and especially together, puts everyone on edge. They are likely to overreact to even minor incidents, to complain loudly that they are being picked on, and to use any excuse for picking a fight.

George, Joan, and Marie have all made it clear that they do not like Laura, and frankly, Laura does not like them. Although George and Joan seem to do all right in other teachers' classes, and although Laura generally gets along quite well with most students, there is something about these three that bug her, and apparently something about her that bugs them. As a result, they take every opportunity to embarrass or provoke her, and she finds herself responding with uncharacteristic defensiveness and anger.

Nancy provokes problems because she needs constant monitoring and protection. She has limited ability in the first place, and this problem is compounded by learning disabilities that have left her hopelessly unable to cope with the seventh-grade curriculum. She is immature, dependent, anxious, unhappy, and generally lost at school. Furthermore, unlike others in similar situations who often evoke sympathy or protectiveness from their peers, Nancy has been rejected and is often picked on or ridiculed by classmates. Laura has succeeded in stopping this for the most part, but she realizes that she has not solved the more fundamental problems involved. Students' tendencies to ridicule Nancy merely have been driven underground rather than eliminated.

Pete is both bright and attractive, maybe too attractive for his own good. He rarely causes serious problems, but he does not apply himself to his studies. Instead, he works at being "cool," trying to impress the other boys and charm the girls. He is often inattentive because he is busy "goofing off" with his friends or flirting with the girls. He is pleasant and outwardly cooperative when Laura tries to reach him, but he never really changes his behavior.

Art is commonly referred to as a juvenile delinquent, and in his case this is an understatement. He has frequently been suspended from school for activities such as extorting money through threats and carrying and brandishing weapons. He is part of a gang composed primarily of boys who have been thrown out or who have dropped out of school, and the word is that they spend much of their time stealing, getting drunk, using drugs, and generally engaging in petty crimes and teenage gang activities. Art is just marking time until he can drop out or succeed in getting himself kicked out.

Finally, Jim causes little trouble, but he seems to be deeply disturbed psychologically. In fact, he shows signs of developing schizophrenia: he is withdrawn, introverted to the point where he is usually not even aware of what is going on around him, and lacks friends or apparent interests. Morbid and depressing themes are predominant in his conversation, reading, and selection of research topics for assignments. Almost all the students say he is "weird," and they call him "Psycho" behind his back.

Laura has virtually given up serious attempts to change the fundamental problems of these ten students. She finds herself more and more often merely minimizing the disruptions they cause, even if it means excluding them from class, sending them to detention, or taking other measures that are likely to worsen their problems in the long run. At least, she reflects ruefully, this gets them out of her hair for a short time.

Laura Simpson is dedicated and generally successful, but her success requires constant energy and skill, and it is not total. There are some students she does not reach at all, and many others that she succeeds with only partially, often because of constraints beyond her control. If you were in Laura's position, how would you try to change this generally unsatisfactory situation?

Part Seven

Individual Differences

Helen, Jim, Ricky, and Ruth were assigned to conduct an experiment in chemistry class. They were good friends and had been in school together for several years. They worked well as a team. Jim prepared the equipment for the basic experiment while Ricky sorted the chemicals and made the measurements so that they would be ready when Jim had the apparatus set up. Helen read in her notebook about the "cautions" and made directive comments to Ricky or Jim from time to time. Ruth started to outline the group report and she finished the purpose and procedures section just as Ricky and Jim finished their tasks.

This part is about individual differences. It is clear that individuals think about what happens to them and interpret events in terms of their experiences, abilities, self-concepts, and interests. Hence, students perceive, interpret, and evaluate the same event in different ways.

In the example presented above, students have automatically started to play roles they have learned in the classroom. In this instance, the roles reflect traditional sex roles. The male students are setting up and conducting the experiment, while the females are observing and writing about it. In this example the teacher did not assign tasks; students simply assumed roles they had learned.

Teachers must deal with such individual differences in learning styles and personalities that students bring to the classroom, as well as with inequalities that may be created by schooling itself (i.e., elementary school science instruction encouraged boys to participate more in science activities). Each student is an individual and must be treated as such. This principle is clear, even simple, in the abstract, but it involves overwhelming complexities when teachers try to put it into practice. What are the important characteristics on which students differ, and what are the implications of these differences for individualized treatment?

To deal with these complexities, educators and researchers have developed labels and associated measurement methods that describe students with respect to social class, IQ, cognitive styles, and creativity. Other labels describe various types of exceptional students who are deemed to require "special education." These labels and their implications for education will be considered in this section.

There has been much opposition to labeling in recent years because many labels are demeaning and appear to produce undesirable self-fulfilling-prophecy effects. This is a real danger, especially if the labeling of students is not accompanied by remedial instruction or other treatment designed to eliminate or compensate for their problems.

When students are described with specific labels, it is helpful to ask "So what?" If the labels are meaningful and helpful, the question should be answerable with statements like "Therefore, they need treatment X," or "Therefore, they will benefit more from treatment X than from treatments Y or Z." This is clearly the case with a label like "myopic" (nearsighted): the student is fitted with corrective glasses or contact lenses. Linkages between clear-cut remedial procedures and labels such as low IQ, disadvantaged, learning disabled, or emotionally disturbed are not so clear, however. Thus, the value of labels, even so-called "diagnostic" ones, depends not only on their accuracy but on the degree to which they provide guidance for remediating the implied problems.

In Chapter 23, we discuss socioeconomic status and IQ, two of the individual difference variables used most frequently to describe students and in some cases to justify decisions about them, and differences in sex role expectations. In Chapter 24, we discuss students' cognitive styles and creativity, and consider how teachers can foster development in these areas. Finally, in Chapter 25 we consider the instruction of students whose handicaps or special needs often caused them to be labeled as abnormal and to be segregated from the educational mainstream in the past, but who now are being returned to it as a result of Public Law 94-142.

Chapter 23

Socioeconomic Status, IQ, and Gender Differences Among Students

OBJECTIVES

When you have mastered the material in this chapter you will be able to

1. Distinguish differences between high- and low-SES families and tell how the cognitive environment of a high-SES home encourages learning
2. Criticize five common but incorrect assumptions about IQ tests, showing how the theoretical concept "intelligence" differs from the term "IQ"
3. Tell how IQ test scores can be interrelated and used properly in teaching situations
4. Define and discuss Level I versus Level II skills and their implications for IQ improvement
5. Discuss how the academic performance of both males and females is affected by cultural expectations
6. Show how cultural expectations and learning are relatively more important than biological expectations in determining differences between males and females in reading and mathematics performance
7. Explain how teacher praise and criticism differentially affect males and females and the implications of research in this area for improving classroom performance of both groups

Socioeconomic Status

Among individual difference variables that are used to describe particular students or even entire school populations, the most important may be socioeconomic status (SES) and social class. The two terms are often used interchangeably, but they are defined and measured differently. SES is a cold, impersonal statistic compiled from indices such as type of occupation, years of education, size of income, quality of housing, and desirability of neighborhood. Social class usually is defined in a more personal way that expresses local prestige and respectability. In effect, one's social class is determined by the perceptions of others. Persons are high in social class to the extent that people in a community describe them or their families as being respectable, influential, or prestigious (Warner, Meeker, & Eells, 1949; Hess, 1970).

Both SES and social class are "proxy" variables that represent a complex of intercorrelated attributes that partially describe people. They are useful for making educated guesses about individuals, but they do not substitute for detailed information about a person. We prefer to use the term SES in this book because SES is more objectively measured, although we usually use it to refer to lifestyle variables associated more closely with the term "social class" than to variables such as income.

All of the variables mentioned above, along with race, ethnicity, and various religious, political, and social customs, tend to correlate together into clusters (Yando, Seitz, & Zigler, 1979; Blau, 1981). No single SES variable causes all of the others in any simple way, but the educational level of parents is probably the most basic, in the sense that the other variables lose all or most of their power for predicting such things as student achievement once the educational level of the parents is statistically controlled (Hess, 1970; Stevenson et al., 1978). In any case, parental education level is especially important to teachers because it is linked to parental interest in and attitudes toward education (Shipman et al., 1976; Laosa, 1982).

Well-educated parents

Parents who are well educated generally value education and expect their children to become well educated. They usually show interest in their children's progress and in meeting and collaborating with teachers, and they typically volunteer in school functions, participate in PTA and fund-raising activities, and help supervise field trips.

Low SES parents

The situation is different with low-SES parents. Many quit or were expelled before finishing high school, and most of the rest ended their schooling at high school graduation. Most of these parents know the value of education and want their children to go as far as possible (Hess, 1970). However, few are knowledgeable about schools or accustomed to dealing with them. Many are awed or even afraid when faced with the prospect of talking to teachers. They tend to be both grateful and cooperative if teachers establish themselves as people devoted to low-SES students' best interests, and not as authority figures threatening to expel their children.

Parents who value education are often active in the PTA.

The Disadvantaged

People at the lowest SES levels are often referred to as "the disadvantaged." In our view, there has been too much emphasis on the problems and difficulties of these people (which are clearly real and not likely to go away in the immediate future), and not enough on their potential and how they can learn to achieve it (which also is real but relatively unfulfilled as yet). Too often, being labeled as disadvantaged causes students to be written off as lost causes rather than to receive special, effective treatment likely to enable them to succeed at school.

Identification of disadvantaged

It is worth noting who the disadvantaged are and how they got to be that way. According to economic indicators, about 20 percent of the population are disadvantaged because they are on welfare or have inadequate incomes. Depending on where you draw the line, this percentage could go much higher. In terms of race and urban versus rural status, the majority of disadvantaged families are white and a large proportion are rural. So much attention has been focused on urban blacks that many people think terms like "disadvantaged" refer primarily to this group. It is true that a greater percentage of blacks than whites is disadvantaged, but it also is true that this percentage is a minority of the total number of disadvantaged. About 80 percent of the disadvantaged are white.

Elimination of SES differences

For a time, it was thought that SES differences could be eliminated entirely through educational enrichment. Influenced by Hunt (1961) and Bloom (1964) in particular, psychologists and educators began to believe that the problem could be solved if children had certain crucial experiences during the first few years of life. A few writers still take this position (White, 1975), but most experts do not believe that SES differences can be eliminated through any quick and easy method. Thus, Project Head Start, Project Follow Through, and other programs aimed at the disadvantaged no longer are seriously expected to eliminate SES differences in IQ, although these programs are believed to be helpful because of their health and nutrition benefits, and because they facilitate school achievement and ultimate educational attainment (Lazar & Darling, 1982; Miller & Bizzell, 1983; Zigler & Valentine, 1979; Lazar et al., 1977; Clarke & Clarke, 1976; Gray, Ramsey, & Klaus, 1982).

The disadvantaged are often stereotyped as having values and attitudes contrary to "middle-class values," although this is not the case. Disadvantaged parents do not do anything in particular, deliberately or otherwise, to impair their children's intellectual development or mental health. Typically they mean well, and usually want the same things for their children that other parents want. The major difference between disadvantaged and advantaged parents is that the former lack the knowledge that would enable them to obtain things they want (Hess, 1970).

Cognitive environment

Furthermore, it is relevant knowledge and experience, not financial resources, that seem to be the keys to the quality of the cognitive environment a home provides (Hess, 1970; Hess, Holloway, Dickson, & Price, 1984; Gottfried, 1984; Shipman et al., 1976; Deutsch, 1973; Marjoribanks, 1972; Trotman, 1977; Wolf, 1966; Moore, 1968; Freeberg & Payne, 1967; Bradley, Caldwell, & Elardo, 1977; Clark, 1983; Sigel, 1985). That is, children's cognitive development depends more on the modeling and intellectual stimulation they get from their parents than on the mere presence of material possessions. Parents who provide a rich cognitive environment interact with their children often and not just when they need to, frequently at length, and in ways likely to stimulate thinking (Hess, 1970; Brophy, 1970; Laosa, 1978; Hess & Shipman, 1965; Hess & McDevitt, 1984; Steward & Steward, 1974). They label objects and events, explain causal relationships, discuss future activities in advance, and accompany discipline with instructions containing information as well as demands. They also answer children's questions, encourage their exploratory efforts, and, in general, provide them with a rich context of meaning within which to understand and assimilate

A head start class helps preschool children adjust to the classroom environment.

each new experience. More generally, they model intellectual activity and verbal communication in everyday activities by reading newspapers and books for both information and pleasure, by watching educational as well as purely entertaining television programs and discussing their content, by stimulating mealtime conversations about daily events, by participating in social and political organizations, and by visiting zoos, museums, and other educational settings.

Reaching the truly disadvantaged

Children who are truly disadvantaged do not get much of this kind of stimulation. Often, their parents are not even aware of their own roles in providing a cognitive environment in the home, and even when they are, they often lack knowledge about what to do and how to do it (Hess, Shipman, Brophy, & Bear, 1968; Hess, 1970). Meeting the needs of these people effectively will require action by many social institutions besides the schools. Disadvantaged parents need information about health, nutrition, and occupational options, as well as legal counseling and other assistance in coping with complex modern society. Meanwhile, their children attend the public schools, where they often progress slowly and sometimes become alienated. In general, these students need instruction that follows the same general principles outlined in the rest of this book, not something that differs clearly from what is effective with other students. However, they do especially well with teachers who share warm, personal interactions with them but also hold high expectations for their academic progress; require them to perform up to their capacities; and move them along at the most rapid pace possible. In short, effective teachers break through social-class differences and other potential barriers to communication in order to form close relationships with disadvantaged students, but they use these relationships to maximize students' academic progress, not merely to provide friendship or sympathy (Brophy & Evertson, 1976; Kleinfeld, 1975; St. John, 1971).

Intelligence Quotient (IQ)

Teachers form impressions, usually accurate, of their students' academic abilities very quickly, even if they do not have access to home background information and cumulative record files (Brophy & Good, 1974; Willis, 1972). They use such cues as general signs of alertness and comprehension, quality of questions and comments, and, of course, performance on academic tasks.

Origin of IQ test

This assessment process, which teachers have always carried out informally, has become formalized over the last 65 years through the use of standardized tests of intelligence and achievement. This movement began with the work of Alfred Binet in the early 1900s in France. Binet was not trying to design a test of intelligence, but to identify children likely to have difficulty in school. He began by analyzing the abilities that seemed necessary for school success, and then worked backwards to develop tests to measure these abilities. He was looking for tests that discriminated adequately between children within a grade level—tests that were too easy or too hard were not very useful because everyone either passed or failed. This meant that different tests were needed for various grade levels. Besides the ability to discriminate, Binet's primary criterion for including a test in his battery was the degree to which the test correlated with or predicted later school success. Note that this is very different from a criterion such as the degree to which a test measures some ability believed to be part of what we call "intelligence."

Binet's tests were very successful and were quickly adopted in England and America. However, British and American psychologists who adopted them did more than just translate the tests into English and use them to screen children. First, they referred to the tests as "intelligence tests," abandoning the detailed profiles of performance across a variety of measures that Binet relied on in favor of a single index that came to be called the "Intelligence Quotient" or IQ. Then psychologists elaborated the notion of intelligence testing and the concept of IQ with the following idea about the tests and what they measure:

1. The tests are more than mere indicators of school success; they measure fundamental intellectual abilities.
2. Underlying these abilities is a generalized factor (usually called "g"). This factor is general intelligence.
3. General intelligence is transmitted genetically and thus is fixed at conception. Repeated measures may produce slightly different scores because of situational factors or measurement errors, but, theoretically, perfect measurement would yield precisely the same IQ every time for any individual.
4. Both individual and group differences are fixed and unchangeable. Differences in educational experiences or opportunities might affect the degree to which intelligence is expressed, but will not affect intelligence itself.
5. Intelligence is more than simply a statistical predictor of academic achievement. It is a *cause*, usually by far the most important cause. So, when students do not achieve as highly as their measured IQs lead us to expect, they are underachievers who are not working up to their abilities.

These statements combine nicely to form a consistent theory. However, not one of them is correct, at least in the extreme form in which each is stated. It is clear that humans possess a great many different intellectual abilities, even though many of these abilities correlate highly with one another. Also, even though IQ tests can be constructed to yield a single score, they do not measure a single ability. There is no correspondence between an IQ score and the size or functioning efficiency of the brain or any particular part of it, and there is no single ability that we can call "intelligence."

Diverse conceptions of intellectual abilities

Diverse conceptions of intellectual abilities can be seen in the variety of tasks included on "intelligence tests." The revised Stanford-Binet Intelligence Scale measures verbal reasoning, quantitative reasoning, abstract-

Table 23.1 An Outline of the Content Included on the Revised Stanford-Binet Intelligence Scale

I. Crystallized Abilities
  A. Verbal Reasoning Area Score
    1. Vocabulary: age 2–18+
    2. Comprehension: age 2–18+
    3. Absurdities: age 2–9
    4. Verbal Relations: age 9–18+
  B. Quantitative Reasoning Area Score
    1. Quantitative: age 2–18+
    2. Number Series: age 5–18+
    3. Equation Building: age 8–18+
II. Fluid-Analytic Abilities
  C. Abstract/Visual Reasoning Area Score
    1. Pattern Analysis: age 2–18+
    2. Copying: age 2–9
    3. Matrices: age 5–18+
    4. Paper Folding and Cutting: age 8–18+
III. Short-Term Memory
  D. Short-Term Memory Area Score
    1. Bead Memory: age 2–18+
    2. Memory for Sentences: age 2–18+
    3. Memory for Digits: age 5–18+
    4. Memory for Objects: age 5–18+

This material is reprinted with permission from Thorndike, R. L., Hagen, E., & Sattler, J. (1986). *Stanford-Binet Intelligence Scale* (4th ed.). Chicago: Riverside Publishing Co.

visual reasoning, and short-term memory (see Table 23.1). The Wechsler Preschool and Primary Scales of Intelligence (WPPSI), the Wechsler Intelligence Scale for Children, Revised (WISC-R), and the Wechsler Adult Intelligence Scale (WAIS) also contain a variety of tasks, although not as many as the Stanford-Binet. These tests are divided into subscales composed of verbal tasks (general information items, vocabulary words, series of digits to memorize both forward and backward, arithmetic word problems, items calling for statements of similarities between objects or concepts, and comprehension items asking how one should respond to problems such as finding a stamped, addressed, and sealed letter in the street or discovering a fire in a crowded theater) and performance tasks (finding the missing parts in incomplete drawings, unscrambling cartoon panels to get them into the right order, assembling jigsaw puzzles, and completing coding tasks in which each of 10 digits is each paired with a simple geometric symbol that must be written under the digit whenever it appears).

The Stanford-Binet and the Wechsler scales are the most reliable and best validated of the intelligence tests in wide use, but it is clear that they do not measure a single, easily definable ability. Scores from the various tasks and subscales do correlate at least moderately (often very highly) however, and the variety of content apparently helps ensure test reliability.

Short-form tests

There are many short-form "IQ tests" devised for group administration. These usually focus on just a few tasks or even only one (typically vocabulary). However, group tests are notably less reliable than the individually administered batteries (Hopkins & Brach, 1975). In any case, even when IQ is measured reliably, it does not represent a single, clear-cut ability.

Changes in IQs

IQs are not fixed at conception, either. Honzik, McFarlane, and Allen (1948) found more change than stability in a longitudinal study of middle-class children across childhood and adolescence. A majority of these children changed at least 15 points in IQ, and a third changed 20 points or more. McCall, Appelbaum, and Hogarty (1973) report similar findings in another longitudinal study spanning ages two and one-half to 17. Changes in Stanford-Binet scores between these ages averaged 28.5 points, and a seventh of the changes were 40 points or more. Furthermore, the changes were not random. High-SES children tended to maintain or gain in IQ, but low SES children tended to drop. Gainers were described as independent and competitive in their preschool years, and as independent, scholastically competitive, self-initiating, and problem solving during elementary school. Their parents were described as providing encouragement and stimulation of cognitive activities in the home, and as using rational rather than fear-oriented approaches to childrearing.

Much other research (reviewed in Willerman, 1979) confirms that certain children predictably maintain or gain in IQ over time, and others tend to lose. In particular, high-SES children typically maintain or gain, and low-SES children usually lose (this is the familiar "cultural disadvantage" phenomenon). Also, curious, persistent children are likely to gain, but passive, dependent children are likely to lose. Jensen (1969) and others interpret these data as being due to the influence of genetic IQ on personal traits as well as academic performance, but we believe that they are better interpreted as evidence of the influence of socialization (including both parental child rearing practices and education at school) on intellectual development.

Genetic component

Human intellectual functioning clearly has a strong genetic component, but it is probably not nearly as strong as Jensen and others argue (Loehlin, Lindzey, & Spuhler, 1975; Willerman, 1979). There is increasing evidence that the IQs of different social classes or racial groups can be influenced by changes in the environment (Mackenzie, 1984). For example, Schiff, Duyme, Dumaret, and Tomkiewicz (1982) report that children of unskilled workers adopted as infants into high-SES families had IQs averaging 14 points higher than those of their siblings who were reared by their natural parents.

Reaction ranges

The present consensus of genetics experts is that a reaction range of about 25 points is to be expected for IQ scores. That is, assuming that they have similar genes, the difference in ultimate IQs between individuals growing up in a minimally stimulating environment versus those growing up in a maximally stimulating environment is likely to be about 25 points (Scarr-Salapatek, 1975). It so happens that high-SES children typically average about 110–115 on IQ tests when they are four years old and have similar or slightly higher averages when they are adults (Tyler, 1965); urban disadvantaged children average about 95 on IQ tests when they are four years old but drop gradually to about 80 or 85 as adults. However, urban disadvantaged children in successful intervention programs maintain average IQs of about 100–105.

This difference is quite close to the 25-point difference predicted by geneticists. However, this is a crucial difference, because adults with IQs in the 80–85 range are usually functionally illiterate school dropouts who tend to be unemployable or only marginally employable. Many end up on welfare or in prison. In contrast, adults with IQs in the 100–105 range are likely to at least graduate from high school, secure reasonable employment, and, in general, to participate fully and productively in society.

Intelligence Test Data and Teaching

Intelligence testing has been controversial since its inception (Kamin, 1974). Lately it has been under attack by those who believe that it simply labels students without doing them any good, and by those who hold that intelligence tests are inherently biased in favor of white, middle-class students and against students from lower-class backgrounds and minority groups (Mercer, 1973; see also Oakland, 1977).

Group differences

The latter claim does not hold up very well. Existing group differences in IQ are real, and do not disappear when attempts are made to improve rapport with the examiner, to improve comfort in testing situations, or to use only "culture fair" tests, although these factors may improve scores somewhat (Jensen, 1969; Loehlin, Lindzey, & Spuhler, 1975; Samuel, 1977; Duncan, Featherman, & Duncan 1972). Though intelligence tests do not measure any single, fixed general mental ability, they do measure important abilities such as understanding and following instructions, reasoning and drawing conclusions, and solving problems. They also measure vocabulary, reading comprehension, arithmetic computation, and other skills taught in schools.

Most people recognize these abilities as general cognitive skills important for everyone, and not as specialized knowledge reflecting the cultural traditions or bias of middle-class whites or any other particular group (Ebel, 1975). IQ tests are not perfectly objective, however. Certain vocabulary items include words that have gone out of style or are typically used only in cities or only in rural areas, and the scoring of a few items dealing with general information or comprehension occasionally is questionable. The percentage of such items on widely used IQ tests has always been low, however, and most of them have been removed in recent revisions. Thus, content analysis of the IQ tests in wide use today does not support charges of rampant cultural bias. Perhaps more importantly, studies that compare IQ tests with other sources of information about students do not indicate any such bias. If anything, omnibus individualized tests like the Stanford-Binet may overestimate rather than underestimate the academic abilities of lower-class and minority-group students, assuming that they are monolingual English speakers (Messe, Crano, Messe, & Rice, 1979; Cleary, 1968; Cleary et al., 1975; Hartlage & Steele, 1977; Jensen, 1974, 1976). Students whose English is limited because they are learning it as a second language cannot be tested reliably with IQ tests, or, for that matter, any tests that are entirely in English.

Predictors of achievement

Furthermore, despite controversy and criticism, IQ tests remain the most reliable predictors of school achievement and, to a degree, of student potential, particularly in the elementary grades. If used to measure students' potential and not as mechanisms to label or restrict them, IQ tests can enable teachers to make decisions that will optimize instruction. This is especially true of students who are deficient in reading, writing, and test-taking skills, because ordinary school tests underestimate the knowledge and abilities of these students. IQ tests can also be reliable indicators of the capacity of students who are unfamiliar with the English language, if they are tested with so-called "culture-fair" or nonverbal IQ tests that eliminate the need for verbal instructions and responses.

Verbal deficiencies

IQ tests can identify students who are bright but score poorly on typical tests due to their verbal deficiencies. Presumably, these students will achieve at much higher levels than they do now if their verbal deficiencies are eliminated through effective remedial instruction in basic skills. If testing reveals poor nonverbal skills in addition to low verbal skills, poor performance is not due solely to verbal deficiency. Remediation will require much more intensive and individualized treatment.

Uses and misuses of IQ test

Thus, even though there is a real danger of misuse of IQ tests by harmfully labeling students, and even though IQ tests have limited diagnostic usefulness because they rarely point to specific things that teachers need to do to remediate problems, they do have some uses, and banning them altogether, which has been done in certain school districts, probably is a mistake.

The key is to distinguish between different kinds of IQ tests. Group-administered tests that depend heavily on reading and test-taking skills are of minimal value. Most of them are essentially vocabulary tests and do not add anything of value to the information gotten from standardized achievement tests. On the other hand, individually administered omnibus IQ tests like the Stanford-Binet or the Wechsler scales provide information about a variety of abilities, and "culture-fair" tests can reveal hidden abilities among disadvantaged students or students who speak English as a second language.

Types of Intellectual Abilities

Investigators interested in psychometric testing have conducted many logical and statistical analyses of intelligence test data to try to identify what Thurstone (1938) called "primary mental abilities." Some, like Cattell (1971) and Guilford (1967), developed very complex models involving large numbers of specific abilities. Even models like these are limited, however, because they are based on IQ test data that come only from verbal and pencil and paper tests and thus do not include such intellectual attributes as curiosity or social intelligence (Neisser, 1976).

The distinctions between intellectual abilities that have been most useful to date are simple ones, such as the difference between associative learning and memory and higher levels of abstract thinking and reasoning. Jensen's (1969) distinction between Level I and Level II skills is perhaps the most useful formulation of this dimension.

Level I skills

Level I skills include association learning and rote memory and are required for such tasks as committing specific material to memory, learning to use an alphabetic code that transforms the letters of the English alphabet into a new set of symbols, or learning to communicate in a new language. Such tasks require little or no reasoning or problem solving, although they do demand concentrated effort, and even cognitive strain if the demands on attention and memory are great enough. Thus, tasks requiring only Level I skills are not necessarily easy, and some are beyond the abilities of most people. Examples of such skills could be memorizing *Moby Dick*, learning to type 200 words a minute, or producing accurate, instantaneous translations for the United Nations. Level I abilities are primarily involved in mastering the basic skills taught in the early grades of school and in learning factual information.

Level II skills

Level II skills include the information-processing activities involved in perceiving stimuli and the abstract thinking and reasoning needed to solve problems, especially problems not encountered previously. Level II abilities are measured in IQ test items that require respondents to state similarities or differences (How are an elephant and a whale alike?), supply meaningful analogies (Train is to track as automobile is to ______.), or solve abstract problems (Supply the next number: 1, 4, 9, 16, __.). Level II skills are required to succeed in school tasks such as reading comprehension (understanding the connections between events in a story and drawing correct inferences about their implications, not just remembering the events themselves), solving most word problems in math, or understanding and being able to use abstract principles in any subject matter.

Although there are individual differences, there do not appear to be important social class or other group differences in Level I skills, and development of Level I skills appears to be closely related to the quality and amount of schooling an individual receives. Schools are less successful in developing students' Level II skills, however. In part, this is because Level II skills have a much stronger genetic component than Level I skills (Jensen 1969, 1970, 1973; Jensen & Figueroa, 1975; Vernon, 1981).

Also, it is much more difficult to provide direct instruction in Level II skills. That is, we can present students with tables containing the basic facts of addition, subtraction, multiplication, and division, and can help students commit these facts to memory. We can also immediately judge any particular factual answer to be right or wrong, and can show why it is wrong if necessary. However, the Level II skills involved in mathematical problem solving cannot be taught so directly. We can of course have students practice by requiring them to solve problems, and we can even instruct them in "learning to learn" or problem-solving skills such as carefully reading the problem, systematically identifying the information given and separating it from the information required, and generating and testing hypotheses. However, these efforts typically meet with only limited success and do not generalize to problem situations that are very different from the ones students have practiced, even though they involve the same problem-solving principles.

Increasing IQ scores

This is why it is now generally recognized that continuously increasing the IQs of students is not an appropriate objective for schools or teachers. Small initial increases (an average of 5–10 points across the first few grades) can be expected for disadvantaged students whose Level I skills have not been well developed at home. Few if any such gains will be seen among children whose Level I skills are already well developed before they get to school, and generalized gains in Level II abilities are not to be expected at all. These statements refer to group averages, however, and individual students may well gain or lose considerably.

Of course, lack of gain in average IQ does not mean that children are not learning or developing their cognitive abilities. Students with IQs averaging 110 are much more knowledgeable and intellectually competent at age ten than they were at age eight, even though their average IQ has not changed and even though they are in the same Piagetian stage of concrete operations. This is because IQ is a relative index of one's intellectual abilities compared to those of other individuals the same age.

Consistent IQ scores

The point here is that a lack of change in IQ scores over time does not mean that nothing has happened or that the children possess the same skills they possessed earlier. Instead, it means that their intellectual abilities have developed at a pace that allows them to maintain the same general position, compared to other children, that they maintained earlier. Once children reach school age, schooling is the most important single factor affecting the rate of development of intellectual abilities (Goulet, Williams, & Hay, 1974), even though continuously raising students' IQs is not a school goal. Schools will be very successful if they merely maintain the group IQ levels (or the averages on standardized achievement tests, for that matter) from year to year. The IQs of disadvantaged students, however, often slip a little from year to year. This is especially true of older elementary students who must rely more on independent reading and learning.

Types of intelligence

Gardner (1983) contends that there are many types of intelligence and that too often we pay attention to only one type of intelligence—verbal proficiency. The types of intelligence that Gardner recognizes include: (1) linguistic intelligence, (2) musical intelligence, (3) logical/mathematical intelligence, (4) spatial intelligence, (5) bodily-kinesthetic intelligence, and (6) personal/social intelligence. It is important for teachers to recognize that individuals grow in many different areas and that intelligence is not a single, all-or-nothing phenomenon. Too often teachers do not recognize and encourage the strengths and skills that low-status or disadvantaged students bring to the classroom. Others have also noted that there are multiple ways to define and assess potential and have urged teachers to look for various expressions of ability in classrooms (e.g., Marshall & Weinstein, 1984; Sternberg, 1984).

Gender Differences

Historically, men and women have received different and unequal opportunities for professional development. Subtle gender biases pervade all of American education (Anderson, 1972). Distinctions in language and social conventions continue to differentiate men and women and to unnecessarily exaggerate gender differences. Fortunately, Americans are becoming more sensitive to distinctions made between the sexes, and some progress has been made toward a more equitable distribution of resources and opportunities between men and women.

Persistence of sexism

Despite signs of progress, it is still easy to document sexism in American culture. Some inequities are due to past practices, but a number of beliefs and practices continue to limit the contributions of women. As a case in point, the Women's Educational Equity Communication Network Newsletter (Spring, 1979) points out that the average 12-month salary for male college faculty members far exceeds the average salary for women faculty members. Furthermore, women represent only 9.5 percent of full professors in American colleges, but 50.6 percent of instructors are women, although some of this difference can be explained by the fact that male faculty have generally been teaching longer than women. Despite the fact that recent data indicate that workplace salaries have improved for women, there is still sufficient evidence to contend that men, as a group, receive higher salaries than women for seemingly comparable work.

Societal attitudes

As an illustration of differential societal attitudes toward men and women, Mischel (1974) reports that boys, men, girls, and women all tend to devalue work when it is labeled as a woman's job. Thorne and Henley (1975) note that women are more likely to be called by first name only than are men and that in mixed-gender conversations men are more likely to interrupt women than vice versa. The media have perpetuated a restrictive view of women as well, for example, in the types of stories published in newspapers and magazines. Even cartoons in women's magazines reflect a consistent bias; Kramer (1974) notes in a selective survey that men were twice as likely as women to speak in cartoon caricatures.

Such consistently presented societal expectations are obviously internalized to some extent and limit the self-expectations of women. Cultural expectations may also influence the performance of males. Although schools have not created such attitudes, they have helped to maintain them. Helping both male and female students to become aware of restrictive language, roles, and practices that limit their potential is the most direct way that teachers can help to reduce exaggerated sex differentiation.

Sexism in Books for Children

Britton (1975) examined 16 reading series to determine the extent to which women were placed in noncareer roles. Her examination revealed that males played a major role 58 percent of the time. In marked contrast, women played a major role in only 14 percent of the stories. (In some stories there was no dominant male or female character.) Despite the fact that females comprise approximately one-half of the work force, males were placed in career roles much more frequently.

Stewig and Knipfel (1975) analyzed 100 children's books published between 1972 and 1974 to determine whether or not the books represented the variety of roles that women fulfill. They note that there was major improvement over books examined in an earlier study (Stewig & Higgs, 1973), but that women's roles were still not represented accurately. Children's readers continued to feature women less often and to place them disproportionately in dull, passive roles. Marten and Matlin (1976) reached a similar conclusion.

Garrett-Schau and Scott (1984) contend that about 90 percent of pupils' school learning time is spent using instructional materials like textbooks, literature, films, tapes, and software. They note that students also spend considerable time reading from similar materials outside of school, and that these materials, including the manner in which they depict gender characteristics, have tremendous potential to influence students.

Sexist material

In classifying materials according to gender characteristics, the authors determined that some materials are sex-biased (sexist). In these materials females appear as main characters less often than males and are portrayed in more minor roles than are males. In contrast, sex-equitable materials reflect the reality of the presence of females in the world and note their contributions.

Gender Differences in Intellectual Functioning

Maccoby (1966) and Maccoby and Jacklin (1974) carefully review the literature on gender differences in intellectual functioning (e.g., general intelligence, number ability, verbal ability, spatial ability, problem solving) and report that research does not reveal consistent differences. There is thus no reason to believe that boys and girls cannot succeed equally well in different school subjects or in subsequent vocational fields.

Hyde (1981) applied meta-analysis review techniques to the studies that Maccoby and Jacklin examined and found that the general differences between males and females in all of the abilities were very small. She stresses that even the "well-established" differences are in fact trivial, and hence there is little basis for arguing that either men or women have superior intellectual abilities in certain areas.

Achievement differences

However, as we shall see below, boys and girls do achieve in somewhat different ways. Considering the evidence Maccoby and Jacklin present and Hyde's clarification of these data, it seems unreasonable to explain this differential achievement on the basis of innate biological differences. Rather, performance differences between the sexes are for the most part learned behaviors that are induced by societal expectations, the behavior of adults, and so forth.

Personality. Gender differences in personality are reported consistently. Boys and girls behave in different ways, as do adult men and women. In fact, some argue that it is partially because of these differences in expressive style (as opposed to intellectual ability) that boys do not perform as well in school as girls and that women hold proportionately fewer high-salaried professional jobs than men.

Cultural expectations

However, we suspect that cultural expectations are a more plausible explanation for gender differences in achievement than are behavioral styles. We believe this in part because Maccoby and Jacklin's (1974) review suggests that even on those few personality measures where stable differences appear there is considerable overlap between boys and girls. For example, assertiveness training is often believed to be especially important for women, but Kirkland (1978) found that many adolescent boys needed training to correct problems such as shyness.

Role of socialization

Considering the significant overlap between boys and girls on most behavioral and personality measures, it seems likely that personality structure is influenced more heavily by socialization than by biological differences. Bem (1974, 1975) notes that people tend to view behavior as masculine (assertive, bold) or feminine (tender, passive). However, her research suggests that many effective, well-functioning individuals exhibit both types of characteristics. Bem (1975) argues that such individuals may "some day come to define a new and more human standard of psychological health" (p. 643).

Societal expectations

Reading Performance. To illustrate that boys as well as girls may be victims of societal expectations, and that students of both genders can do well in the same subject, we shall explore differences in reading achievement. Young girls in this country, on the average, consistently outperform boys on a variety of verbal performance measures (Maccoby & Jacklin, 1974). Johnson (1976) notes that despite the lack of agreement on the cause of the problem, there is a consensus that girls read better than boys. In addition, boys are more likely to suffer severe reading problems than are girls. For example, Mumpower (1970) reports a ratio of seven boys to three girls among students referred to reading clinics with severe reading disabilities.

Recent research suggests, however, that boys do show superior reading ability in some cultures. Comparing fourth- and sixth-grade students in Germany and in the United States, Preston (1962) found that German boys outperformed girls in both reading comprehension and speed. Johnson's (1976) study of second-, fourth-, and sixth-graders' reading performance in four countries (Canada, England, Nigeria, and the United States) supports Preston's conclusions. His comparisons show a strong gender x culture interaction (either boys or girls tend to perform better, depending on the culture). In the United States, 16 of 18 comparisons (six tests at three grade levels) favored girls, and girls outperformed boys on 14 of 18 comparisons in Canada. These findings were reversed in England and Nigeria. In England, 11 of 18 comparisons favored boys, and in Nigeria 15 of 18 comparisons favored boys. Such data make it difficult to explain differential reading progress between boys and girls with biological arguments.

Other data also contradict the argument that boys cannot read as well as girls because they mature more slowly. Stanchfield (1973) reports that a reading series with content of high interest to first-grade boys (principal characters were intelligent, daring males) eliminated reading differences between boys and girls. Thus, although the stories that males read in schools appear to project males in more interesting and more dominant leadership roles (e.g., Marten & Matlin, 1976), it appears that such "socialization" stories do not necessarily lead to better reading achievement among boys. Ironically, the level and content of stories may be more appropriate for girls. Thus, it seems that the content of textbooks needs to be adjusted to improve both the interest level and the societal roles projected for males and females.

Textbook content

Asher and Markell (1974) found that when fifth-grade boys read a story drawn from a high-interest area, they read as well as fifth-grade girls (who also read high-interest material). In contrast, boys were significantly poorer readers of low-interest material than were girls. Whether reading content was of high or low interest, girls read well. It is important to note that the teachers who used the Stanchfield materials successfully were all women. This study is a strong retort to many critics who argue that boys do poorly in school because most teachers are female and insist upon a "feminine culture" (passivity, order, dependence) that boys rebel against, to the short-term detriment of their achievement.

Effect of teacher's sex

Other data also refute this contention, showing that the effects of male teachers on boys' school achievement are relatively unimportant. Literature reviews consistently find no differences between male and female teachers' classroom behavior (see Brophy & Good, 1974; Lahaderne, 1976). Vroegh (1976) found in only two of 15 studies that male teachers had a favorable but minor influence on boys. Lahaderne (1976) reviewed eight studies and reports no notable favorable effects of male teachers on boys.

That male teachers have little, if any, differential influence on boys' achievement is explained by the fact that male teachers interact with both boys and girls in the same general way that female teachers do. For example, in a comprehensive assessment of classroom interaction, Good, Sikes, and Brophy (1973) found only one significant relationship of teacher gender to student gender in 62 comparisons.

Apparently, the reading performance of American boys is more susceptible to motivational variables than is girls' performance. This may be because girls view reading as an activity that has personal significance for them, whereas boys attach somewhat less value to reading per se. Presumably, then, because of culturally induced sex-role socialization, girls come to attach more value to reading than do boys.

Girls' avoidance of math courses

Mathematics Performance. Questions similar to those raised above can be asked about the mathematics performance of girls. However, less research has been done in this area. Available evidence does suggest that the situation for girls in mathematics is similar to that for boys in reading. Indeed, the differential achievement of males and females in mathematics appears to be due more to the fact that young females tend to bypass elective courses in mathematics than it is that they perform less well in them. Girls' achievement motivation is affected when the stories in their readers inadvertently reinforce very narrow professional career aspirations. The deleterious effects occur later when girls decide not to take elective courses in mathematics and/or to compete academically, thus limiting the possibility for certain professional training in college. Fennema and Sherman (1977) found no evidence of male superiority in mathematics achievement when affective variables and exposure to math courses were controlled.

Marshall (1984) analyzed the responses of approximately 300,000 sixth-grade children who had taken the Survey of Basic Skills, Grade Six, as part of a California Assessment Program. He found differences in sixth-grade boys' and girls' responses to computation and story problems. Boys did somewhat better than girls on story problems and girls tended to perform better than boys on computations.

Pattison and Grieve (1984) found that girls in Grades 10 and 12 perform better than boys on logical and relatively abstract mathematics problems. This evidence illustrates that young girls' generally poorer performance on story problems is less a function of their ability to reason logically and abstractly than of the way in which they are encouraged to think about and to do mathematics. It should be noted that Pattison and Grieve found that boys did relatively better in mastering problems of proportionality and three-dimensional problems (Maccoby & Jacklin, 1974) than did girls. This is consistent with the findings presented earlier—that boys have a slight tendency to do better on spatial relation problems than do girls. Again, these are relatively small differences, and some girls outperform most males. We believe that teachers should teach all types of mathematics to both boys and girls, because evidence suggests that all students can learn.

Motivational conditions

When appropriate motivational conditions are present, girls generally do as well as boys in mathematics at all levels. Christoplos and Borden (1978) demonstrated that the performance of pupils of both sexes on a mathematics test is influenced to some extent by the interest level of the problems that students are asked to solve. Hence, it could be argued that school materials that interest boys may not optimally stimulate girls' performance.

Motivation appears to be a major problem in females' performance in science as well as mathematics. Steinkamp and Maehr (1984) reviewed the literature comparing girls' and boys' motivation and achievement in science. They found that gender differences in both motivation and achievement are smaller than is generally assumed; however, differences do occur, and they generally favor males, who show better attitudes and greater achievement in science. These findings suggest that an important goal for classroom teachers, especially elementary teachers, is to generate more achievement motivation for girls to perform better in science.

On the basis of their examination of fourth-grade mathematics classrooms, Peterson and Fennema (in press) recommend that teachers (1) provide girls as much opportunity to solve high-level math problems as boys; (2) extend positive feedback to girls, particularly for effort and for using the appropriate mathematics strategy; (3) encourage divergent thinking by girls; and (4) stimulate independence (e.g., not give the answer to low-level mathematics problems that girls should be able to answer themselves).

The Relation of Gender Role to Student Role

Changes in relationship between sex role and student role

Despite girls' advantage over boys in the elementary grades, as girls get older their achievement falls progressively farther behind that of boys. The main reason for this is the gradual change in the relationship between gender role and student role. As boys get older and move into high school and college, the conflict that once existed between the student role and the male sex role disappears, and achievement in school becomes perceived as a stepping-stone toward later achievement. An occupation becomes a basic part of the sex-role expectation. In contrast, the harmony between the student role and the female role that exists when young girls are in the first few grades of elementary school gradually lessens, so that by high school and college girls experience conflict between the demands of the student role (compete for grades and prepare yourself for a full-time occupation) and traditional female roles (avoid competition for grades and other activities that might make you unattractive or threatening to boys, and prepare yourself to be a wife and mother).

Classroom interaction data from several studies show the behavioral correlates of these phenomena. Girls are usually less assertive than boys, so that boys have most of the interactions with teachers and make most of the contributions to discussions (despite the fact that teachers criticize boys more frequently). In seeking approval, girls are much more likely than boys to use withdrawal and other avoidance-oriented strategies rather than more direct techniques (Lahaderne & Jackson, 1970).

Differential Effects of Praise and Criticism

Although most educational writers have questioned the appropriateness of teacher behavior for boys (e.g., the passive school environment), Bank, Biddle, and Good (1980) note that general classroom interaction patterns may be as detrimental for girls as boys. They suggest that a discrimination model assumes that adverse teacher behavior such as a lack of attention or criticism has negative effects on the students at whom it is directed.

However, it is possible to argue that seemingly negative treatment by teachers may have positive effects in the long run. Dweck et al. (1978) also make such an argument, suggesting that it is the quality, not the quantity, of teacher criticism that determines its effects. Although they found that boys received more criticism from teachers than did girls, they also noted that much of this criticism was directed at boys' lack of effort. Thus, the criticism did not threaten boys' sense of personal ability. Although girls were less likely to be criticized, the criticism they did receive was more likely to involve the quality of their academic performance. According to Dweck et al., teachers who behave in such ways inadvertently increase the probability that boys will blame their failure on inadequate effort, and that girls will attribute their failure to a lack of ability—with possible long-term, negative effects on their self-confidence. However, it should be noted that Eccles et al. (1983) and other investigators have not found this difference in teacher criticism. Thus, Dweck et al.'s findings may not be generalizable.

The implications that Dweck et al. suggest for their findings, however, draw support from research on intrinsic motivation conducted by Deci (1975). He found that college-age female subjects were more affected by verbal praise than were male subjects. Positive feedback increased the intrinsic motivation of males but decreased the intrinsic motivation of females. This effect occurred whether the experimenter was male or female. Deci explains the differential effect of verbal praise on males and females in the following way: "For females the change in perceived locus of causality process was initiated, whereas for males the change in feelings of competence and self-determination was initiated." This may imply that the controlling aspect of positive feedback for females is more salient than the informational aspect, whereas for males the informational aspect is more salient. And, indeed, that implication seems very plausible if one considers the traditional socialization process in our culture.

Positive feedback

Girls are taught that they are to be more dependent than boys, and more sensitive to interpersonal matters. Such seemingly insignificant matters as frequent trading of compliments about clothing, and so on, may make girls more attuned to feedback from others. Women frequently define themselves in terms of men. They usually assume their husbands' names and even if they work, their professional roles are often secondary to their husbands'.

Socialization and autonomy

Deci argues that because men are socialized to be more independent, they are less inclined to respond to the controlling aspects of feedback (I'm doing this because someone else wants me to.) and are more likely to respond to the informational aspects of feedback (Am I becoming more proficient or competent?). Deci believes that if verbal praise is to enhance intrinsic motivation, especially for females, it should focus on information, not control.

Further research will show whether Deci's and Dweck et al.'s conclusion, that young girls have less inclination toward autonomous achievement and receive little encouragement in school to develop such an interest, is valid. Fortunately, broader socialization practices are emerging, and the school behavior of girls is beginning to change in identifiable ways (see Duke, 1978).

Sexism in the Classroom

Sadker and Sadker (1985) note that there is still a marked degree of sexism in American classrooms. They make the following observations, based on their general review of the literature and a three-year study:

1. When girls begin school they are generally ahead of boys in reading and basic mathematics computation, but by the time they graduate from high school, boys have higher SAT scores in both areas than do girls.
2. It still appears that during high school some girls become less committed to careers, although their grades and achievement test scores are just as good as boys'.
3. Girls are less likely to take advanced math and science courses even though they have the ability to be successful in these areas.
4. Girls are much more likely than boys to attribute academic failure to internal factors such as ability rather than to external factors such as task difficulty.

In accounting for these differences, Sadker and Sadker point to some of the following characteristics of society that may help to explain this differential use of talent.

1. Men speak more often and frequently interrupt women.
2. Listeners appear to pay more attention to male speakers, even when male and female speakers use similar styles and make similar, if not identical, points.
3. Women participate less actively in conversation. That is, they do more gazing and are more often passive bystanders in social conversations among peers.
4. Women often transform declarative statements into more tentative ones (This is a good restaurant, isn't it?). Such statements may lessen women's ability to influence others in conversations.

One's gender too often inappropriately though subtly affects the classroom teaching one receives. Few teachers dramatically discriminate in the extent to which they call on boys and girls; however, many teachers condone existing differences that students bring to the classroom. For example, if students are assigned to small, four- or five-person learning teams in science, girls tend to assume passive roles (being the recorder for the group), whereas boys are more likely to take assertive, active roles (performing the experiment). Teachers need to be more sensitive to these subtle but extremely important differences in socialization that in the long run can dramatically affect the extent to which a student is interested in science or mathematics as a career.

Teacher contact

It is important to realize that some of the advantages of more contact with the teacher that girls enjoy, at least in the early elementary grades, may be more apparent than real. Research by Grant (1984) helps to explain why girls in elementary school seem to have all the advantages and yet do not do so well later in school. Grant's examination of the quality of interactions that young girls share with the teacher suggests that teachers socialize girls to be responsible and conforming rather than competent or creative.

Improving Classrooms for Boys and Girls

Developing new sex roles

The process of socialization to the newer, less restrictive sex roles and to the women's liberation phenomenon that we are presently experiencing should begin early. As we have pointed out previously (Brophy & Good, 1974), teachers at all levels can probably be helpful to girls by encouraging them to be more active in the classroom and by making systematic efforts to observe and get to know each girl as an individual. We speak of making a systematic effort because this is what will be required. If teachers merely passively react to students, they will spend most of their time with boys. Many girls will not come to the teacher; the teacher must go to the girls. We believe that this effort is worthwhile, however, because society cannot afford to allow overrestrictive sex-role expectations to pressure girls into hiding their abilities or talents. Teachers can help by encouraging girls to speak their minds, by calling on them to participate if they do not volunteer, by assigning them to leadership roles for group projects, and by taking similar actions that encourage girls to be less passive.

Broadening perspectives for girls

Teachers can also broaden the perspectives of young girls by noting that girls can become doctors, scientists, lawyers, and so on. In the past, if you asked preschool and early elementary schoolgirls what they would like to be when they grew up, they almost always mentioned mother, teacher, stewardess, movie star, nurse, and secretary and practically never mentioned professions that traditionally have been dominated by males but increasingly are open to females. Teachers should deliberately suggest these alternatives to girls and use learning experiences such as stories involving females in leadership positions, compositions or discussions about the work of female scientists, and so on. There are many books that detail the accomplishments of women, and these should be available in classrooms. Teachers can also help by encouraging girls to take advanced courses in areas such as mathematics as early as possible.

As we note elsewhere (Brophy & Good, 1974), several studies show that teachers tend to overestimate the achievement potential and intelligence of girls and underestimate that of boys, and have higher expectations for girls than for boys of equal ability. In addition, teachers have more negative attitudes toward boys, particularly regarding their school motivation and their potential to disturb classrooms and present management problems. There is an additional complication: teachers' expectations and attitudes usually interact with boys' achievement levels much more than with the achievement levels of girls. Although boys are generally more prominent in the classroom, high-achieving boys tend not only to be more salient, but to be seen as active, well-adjusted, successful, and generally positive in the eyes of the teacher. Low-achieving boys are also more prominent, but teachers tend to see them as lazy, immature, maladjusted, and troublesome. Hence, low-achieving males are especially likely to receive criticism from teachers and to experience school difficulty. Teachers must therefore be sensitive to their perceptions of the behavior of males and not attempt to socialize them into passive students.

SUMMARY

Many differences among students are relevant to teachers' instructional decisions, but two of the most important are SES and social class. These factors correlate with other variables such as race, ethnicity, and various religious, political, and social customs into clusters of characteristics that teachers should take into account in their planning. For example, well-educated parents are likely to be more interested in school activities and other aspects of the education of their children than are low-SES parents, many of whom have had limited educations and disappointing associations with schools. Though teachers must deal with the problems disadvantaged students present, they must also consider these students' needs for relevant knowledge, experience, and cognitive stimulation.

Informal teacher assessments of students' academic aptitudes have been increasingly supplemented by standardized intelligence and achievement tests. Although Binet developed his tests to measure various abilities related to school success, American and British psychologists altered Binet's ideas by establishing the notion of a single IQ score based on a number of questionable assumptions. The Stanford-Binet and Wechsler scales are currently the most reliable and best validated instruments, but they do not measure any single, easily definable ability. Further, even though there is a strong genetic component, scores vary with time and other variables over a considerable range.

Gender roles and gender differences in performance are topics that have long been of interest to educators and researchers. Maccoby and Jacklin carefully reviewed the research and concluded that most differences relate to experiences rather than to biological factors. Girls tend to read better than boys, but tend to avoid mathematics. In both cases, differences appear to be due to motivational factors relating to social expectations and experiences. As Deaux (1984) notes, it is time to shift our view of gender as a static category to a more dynamic process. That is, behavior is influenced to some extent by biological gender, but also is heavily influenced by individual choices, situational pressures, and the types of persons an individual regularly meets in social situations. Teachers need to realize that each student is a unique learner who must be dealt with as an individual.

QUESTIONS AND PROBLEMS

1. It is not uncommon for persons promoted to supervisory positions in business and industry to refuse promotion or to resign their new jobs after a few weeks. They prefer to remain ordinary workers, at lower salaries, and without administrative titles. Why?
2. Many Americans resist terms such as socioeconomic status or social class because they seem inconsistent with our traditional values of individualism and equality. If you feel this way, try to keep those feelings from biasing your responses when

answering the following questions: (a) What is your own SES background? (b) How has it affected your development to date by influencing the experiences you have had? (c) Have you undergone changes in beliefs, attitudes, or behavior due to a change in SES? (d) How might your SES affect your interactions with students of various backgrounds?

3. How can schools and teachers simultaneously accomplish both of the following: (a) realistically take into account differences in SES, IQ, and other variables that can affect students' interest in or readiness for various courses or activities, and (b) promote equal opportunity and quality education for all?
4. Under what circumstances, if any, would you request IQ testing for your students? Why? How would you use the results?
5. A student can achieve quite well at school for several years, showing impressive gains on standardized achievement tests, and yet show no gain at all in IQ. Explain.
6. Sex-role socialization is so much a part of our society that we are all affected by it to some degree. There are differences among people in the degree to which they have experienced the effects of gender stereotyping and in the awareness of such effects. In what ways have you been affected by sex-role socialization? What steps can you take to find out?
7. If you are male, are you reluctant to show affection or emotions or to do things traditionally associated with a woman's role? If you are female, are you inhibited about asserting yourself, exercising leadership and authority, competing, or doing things that are traditionally associated with men?
8. How do you react to men who have characteristics traditionally labeled as feminine or to women who have characteristics traditionally labeled as masculine? What does this mean for you as a teacher?
9. As a teacher, how would you deal with a situation in which girls assume a passive role in teamwork while boys assume more active roles. How could you change students' attitudes and beliefs as well as their behavior?

CASE STUDIES

Language Barrier. Tran Van Do is a recent Vietnamese immigrant assigned to Jo Cornell's class. Although he is the same age as the other students, Tran cannot participate much in class activities or do many assignments because he knows very little English. Jo arranges to have him tested, and he is given the parts of the WISC-R that do not require language facility. Tran's performance on these subtests would translate into an IQ of 115 if matched by equivalent performance on the verbal subtests that he cannot take at the moment. What, if anything, does this tell Jo about how to plan instruction for Tran?

Exploration in Sexism. Janet Trumbower and Henry Marshall team teach in the sixth grade in an open-plan school. They have decided to examine curriculum content and interaction—including student-student dialogue, teacher-teacher interaction, and teacher-student conversations—and to assess the degree of sexism present in their social studies classroom. They intend to involve students in the process. How might they proceed in order to make this a valuable learning experience for everyone? In what ways could they collect evidence (what would be looked at and by whom)? Are there things that they should be careful to avoid in this process? List some of your reservations.

Chapter 24

Cognitive Style and Creativity

CHAPTER OUTLINE

OBJECTIVES

When you have mastered the material in this chapter you will be able to

1. Define the cognitive style called conceptual tempo, distinguishing it from simple response speed
2. Explain how differences in conceptual tempo are related to school learning and problem solving, and how conceptual tempo is most effectively modified
3. Define and discuss the characteristics of field-dependent versus field-independent persons
4. Explain how the field-dependence/independence cognitive style affects students' preferred learning modes and teachers' preferred instructional patterns in the classroom
5. Discuss how creativity is measured and how it relates to IQ
6. Discuss the two general criteria of creative responses and the value of creativity measures to education
7. Describe several techniques for fostering creativity in classroom learning

Most individual difference variables relevant to education can be classified easily as either intellectual abilities or personality traits. This is not true, however, for cognitive style and creativity, which involve elements of both cognition and personality. People who differ systematically in cognitive style or creativity differ mostly in amount and patterns of intellectual abilities, but they also differ on a variety of personality variables. These variations show up in classrooms, both in teachers' instruction and in the learning styles of students.

Cognitive Style

Cognitive style variables

Cognitive style refers to the way that people process information they perceive and to various strategies they use when responding to tasks. A variety of cognitive styles has been identified and studied (see Sigel & Coop, 1974), including the following variables:

- ☐ Attention to the global features of stimuli versus fine details
- ☐ Discrimination of stimuli into a few large categories versus many small categories
- ☐ Tendency to classify items on the basis of observable characteristics versus similarities in function, time, or space versus common possession of some abstract attribute
- ☐ Quick, impulsive versus slow, painstaking problem-solving behavior
- ☐ Intuitive, inductive versus logical, deductive thinking
- ☐ Tendency to impose one's own structure on what is perceived versus allowing perceptions to be structured by the specific features of the focal stimulus, influences from the background or context in which the focal stimulus is embedded, or other external sources

Inspection of this list reveals why cognitive style variables are called styles rather than abilities. They refer to *how* people process information and solve problems, not *how well*. They sometimes do affect the quality of performance, however, because each style is helpful in performing certain tasks but not others.

Conceptual Tempo

Differences in conceptual tempo

Conceptual tempo is a cognitive style dimension referring to the degree to which people are cognitively impulsive versus reflective in deciding upon a response when two or more alternatives are plausible. Differences in conceptual tempo are most obvious and are measured in matching-to-sample tasks, where people are shown a drawing of an object or figure and are asked to indicate which of a number of other drawings is exactly the same as the sample. The other drawings are all similar to the sample in varying degrees, but only one is exactly like it. Cognitively impulsive people respond by inspecting the alternatives briefly and then quickly selecting the one they believe to be correct. They have short response latencies—they respond quickly—but they make a lot of errors because they do not take the time to compare carefully. Often they do not even inspect all of the alternatives (Kagan & Kogan, 1970), responding instead as soon as they come to a response alternative that is not obviously wrong. Cognitively reflective people deliberate before responding, carefully considering each alternative. They take longer to respond, but they make fewer errors.

When conceptual tempo was first described (Kagan et al., 1964), the emphasis was on speed of response (response latency) and not on other qualitative characteristics that might affect accuracy. Since then, it has become clear that these other characteristics must be considered. First, in addition to those who are either fast and inaccurate or slow and accurate, some people are both fast and accurate or slow and inaccurate. Thus, some people respond quickly because they are very skillful and efficient at a task, rather than impulsive in their problem-solving behavior.

Fast responders, even fast/inaccurate responders, are not necessarily impulsive in any general sense. Research by many investigators (reviewed in Block et al., 1974; Huston-Stein et al., 1976; Bentler & McClain, 1976) shows that speed of response in matching-to-sample tasks does not correlate consistently with personal traits other than speed of response in other problem-solving situations where more than one plausible alternative is available. Specifically, fast responders are not especially likely to be hyperactive, unable to delay gratification, or otherwise impulsive in the classroom or in everyday life. Thus, the term "cognitively impulsive" is misleading because of its connotation of general behavioral impulsivity. If anything, individuals who are both fast and inaccurate in problem solving can be described as anxious rather than impulsive (Block et al., 1974). That is, they behave as they do in problem-solving situations not because they are carefree and unconcerned about making mistakes, but because they are anxious and vulnerable, and tend to respond "impulsively" in an attempt to cope with, and to escape from, stressful problem-solving situations.

Characteristics of fast responders

Conceptual tempo is important to education because it is related to early reading progress (Kagan & Kogan, 1970; Sunshine & DiVesta, 1976) and to performance on other tasks commonly encountered at school. This is not surprising, because many school tasks require careful discrimination of similar yet different stimuli (*p* versus *q*, *if* versus *it*). Students predisposed to notice such fine differences in detail and to withhold interpretation until first impressions are verified are likely to read more accurately than other students.

Reading progress

Differences in conceptual tempo are believed to be shaped by modeling and socialization in the home, although Kagan, Pearson, and Welch (1966) and others have shown that conceptual tempo can be socialized in school as well. They found that cognitively impulsive boys who spent a school year in the classroom of a very reflective teacher became notably more reflective themselves. This does not have clear implications for teachers, however, because not all teachers are cognitively reflective, and also because a reflective conceptual tempo is not always superior to an impulsive one. Rollins and Genser (1977) found that a reflective tempo was superior for problem solving in tasks that were relatively simple, with only a few plausible response alternatives. However, in very complex tasks involving many different dimensions and a great many possible response alternatives, the impulsive responders who moved immediately to consideration of the more likely solutions generally solved tasks faster and with fewer errors than extreme reflectives who tested out each possible solution systematically, thus wasting a lot of time examining unlikely solutions.

Strategy use and demands of a task

The point is that success in problem solving is determined not by speed of response or some other simple variable, but by the match between the strategy that a person uses and the demands of a task. This can be seen in results of studies in which investigators attempted to modify conceptual tempo. The earliest intervention studies concentrated on slowing down the speed of response, and not on changing children's information processing or problem-solving strategies. Cognitively impulsive children were cautioned to take their time, and perhaps exposed to a model who responded slowly. They were warned to pay attention but were not directed to attend to anything specific. Typically, the children learned quickly and began to respond much more slowly. However, they made just as many errors as before!

Problem-solving training

Investigators who trained children to use more efficient problem-solving skills obtained much better results (Heider, 1971; Egeland, 1974; Ridberg, Parke, & Hetherington, 1971; Meichenbaum & Goodman, 1971). For example, Meichenbaum and Goodman (1971) used a cognitive behavior modification approach involving modeling and verbalized self-instructions. Theorizing that fast/inaccurate responders had inadequate verbal control over their own motor behaviors, they developed methods to train these children to talk to themselves to provide guidance during problem solving. First, the experimenter performed the task while talking aloud. This provided modeling not only of problem-solving behavior but of the self-instructional behavior that facilitates accuracy. Then the children performed the task while the experimenter instructed them aloud, and as they achieved consistent success, verbalization of self-instructions was reduced to whispering and finally to silent (inner) speech (cf. Vygotsky, 1962). The experimenter's modeling stressed not only the importance of responding slowly and carefully, but also the actual response process:

> I have to remember to go slowly to get it right. Look carefully at this one (the standard). Now look at these carefully (the response alternatives). Is this one different? Yes, it has an extra leaf. Good, I can eliminate this one. Now, let's look at this one (another response alternative). I think it's this one, but let me first check the others. Good, I am going slowly and carefully. OK, I think it's this one.

The modeling also included errors and how to cope with them, a feature that probably was especially valuable, considering that fast/inaccurate responders tend to be anxious in problem-solving situations: "It's OK, just be careful. I should have looked more carefully. Follow the plan to check each one. Good, I am going slowly."

Even this kind of explicit modeling, however, was not enough by itself.

Meichenbaum and Goodman found that children exposed only to the modeling did learn to respond more slowly but did not improve their accuracy. Only the children who received self-instructional training in addition to modeling became more accurate problem solvers. This seems to have clear implications for teachers, not only in dealing with fast/inaccurate responders, but for dealing with any students whose information processing strategies or strategies for solving particular types of problems are inappropriate and ineffective. Self-instructional training may be especially useful for students who seem anxious and thus less likely to solve problems calmly and rationally on their own. For these pupils, teacher demonstrations or even extensive modeling may not be enough; they may need opportunities to role play successful problem-solving strategies by verbalizing self-talk out loud and getting any necessary correction or feedback.

Self-instructional training

Psychological Differentiation

Field-dependent versus field-independent people

A second cognitive style dimension with implications for education is called psychological differentiation, also known as field dependence versus field independence or as global versus analytic perceptual style (Witkin et al., 1977). People who are low in psychological differentiation (those who can be called field dependent or global) have difficulty differentiating stimuli from the contexts in which they are embedded, so that their perceptions are easily affected by manipulations of the surrounding contexts. People who are high in psychological differentiation (those who can be called field independent or articulate) perceive more analytically. They separate stimuli from background or context, so that they change their perceptions less when changes in context are introduced.

Examples of psychological differentiation

Psychological differentiation is exhibited in a remarkable variety of situations. One of the most basic is when the stimulus in question is the person's own body. Witkin et al. (1962) observed persons who were seated in specially constructed chairs in rooms that made use of optical illusions to confuse them about directionality and the force of gravity. Field-dependent people were very confused by these situations and did not do well when asked to estimate the degree to which their bodily positions differed from the vertical upright or when requested to change positions so that they would be upright. Some people were off as much as 45°, so that they literally did not know which way was up. Field-independent people were less affected by these manipulations.

Rod and frame tests

Similar results were obtained with the "rod and frame" test. Here, people in a darkened room are presented with a luminous rod that can be tilted in any direction and are asked to adjust the rod until it is vertical. The task is made much more difficult than it would otherwise be because the rod is surrounded by a luminous square frame that also can be tilted in any direction. Certain tilts produce optical illusions much like those in the "tilted rooms" at amusement parks. Here, too, field-independent people are more successful than field-dependent people in adjusting the rod to the true vertical and resisting optical illusions.

Embedded figure tests

Psychological differentiation also occurs in cognitive tasks such as embedded figure tests, where familiar stimuli are embedded in more complex configurations that mask them, such as finding five animals in a picture. Field-independent people are good at these kinds of tasks, but field-dependent people have trouble with them. More generally, field-independent people are likely to overcome the existing organization of the perceptual field, or even to restructure it, but field-dependent people tend to adhere to the existing structure. This is true for social perceptions as well as for perceptions of the physical world. Field-dependent people's perceptions and opinions are strongly affected by those of other people, whereas field-independent people are more likely to resist social pressures and make up their minds on the basis of their own perceptions.

Social dimensions of cognitive style

These are not merely IQ or ability differences, but true contrasts in perceptual style. This is most easily seen in social situations, especially ambiguous ones. Here, field-dependent people are likely to be attentive to and to make more use of prevailing social frames of reference, to look at the faces of others more frequently for cues as to what they are thinking and feeling, to attend more to verbal messages with social content, to take greater account of external social referents in defining their attitudes and feelings, to be physically closer to and to interact more with other people, and, in general, to prefer to be with people in social situations (Witkin et al., 1977). In this regard, it is not surprising that field-dependent people tend to be better liked by others, to be perceived as warm, tactful, considerate, socially outgoing, and affectionate, and to know and be known to more people than are field-independent people. The latter have a more abstract, theoretical, analytic, and impersonal orientation. This makes them more able to resist external pressures toward conformity, but it also makes them more likely to be perceived as cold, distant, or insensitive.

Sex differences in cognitive style

Of course, these statements apply to people who are at the extremes of the dimension of psychological differentiation. Most people are not nearly so extreme, although they may tend more toward one set of attributes than the other. Also, neither cognitive style preference is superior to the other in all situations. Field-independent people are better equipped to deal with situations that call for impersonal analysis, but field-dependent people are better equipped for situations that place a premium on social perceptiveness and interpersonal skills. In view of these differences, it should not be surprising that psychological differentiation is related to gender—males are more likely to be field independent and females to be field dependent. This group difference is reliable and significant, beginning in the adolescent years, at least, but it is small in comparison to the range of differences observed within genders (Maccoby & Jacklin, 1974; Witkin et al., 1977). Furthermore, it is associated with childrearing practices such as training children to be independent thinkers and problem solvers versus overprotecting them and keeping them dependent (Dyk & Witkin, 1965).

Classroom Implications. Psychological differentiation affects students' preference for and response to different kinds of learning content and teach-

Group work versus independent study

ing methods (Witkin et al., 1977). Field-dependent students tend to prefer to learn in groups and to interact frequently with one another and with the teacher, whereas field-independent students may respond better to more independent and more individualized approaches such as contract systems (especially those that allow considerable student choice of what to do and when and how to do it) or individual research projects. Field-independent students are more likely to have self-defined goals and to respond to intrinsic reinforcement, but field-dependent students may require more extrinsic reinforcement and more structuring by the teacher as to what to do and how to do it. Field-dependent students will work to please the teacher and will be more motivated by praise and encouragement than field-independent students, who tend to pursue their own goals.

Field-independent students not only prefer to structure their own learning and, to a degree, develop their own learning strategies, but apparently are better at doing so in most cases. Field-dependent students may need more explicit instruction in problem-solving strategies or more exact definitions of performance outcomes (Witkin et al., 1977).

Subject matter preferences

There are few if any overall achievement differences between students who differ in their cognitive style, but there are differences in preferences for and achievement in various subjects. Field-independent students prefer and generally do better in math and science, whereas field-dependent people generally prefer and do better in the humanities and social studies. Field-independent people tend to be found in occupations that place a premium on theoretical and analytic interests—mathematician, chemist, biologist, engineer, physician, production manager, carpenter, mechanic, or artist. Field-dependent students are oriented toward occupations that stress social skills—social worker, counselor, teacher, administrator, or politician. Even within the same general field, differences in cognitive style can be seen in choices of subfield—experimental versus clinical psychology, surgical versus psychiatric nursing, production manager versus personnel director (Witkin et al., 1977).

Psychological differentiation among teachers

Psychological differentiation is an important variable among teachers as well. From what has been said so far, you will not be surprised to learn that a relative emphasis on field independence rather than field dependence is likely among math, science, and industrial arts teachers compared to social studies, humanities, or general elementary school teachers.

Field-independent teachers prefer impersonal teaching situations and emphasize the more cognitive or theoretical aspects of teaching, whereas field-dependent teachers prefer frequent interaction with students and tend to stress class discussion (Witkin et al., 1977). Field-independent teachers have been found to use questions mostly as instructional tools to be asked when introducing topics and following student answers, whereas field-dependent teachers use questions primarily to check on student learning following instruction (Moore, 1973). Field-independent teachers tend to emphasize their own standards and to formulate principles themselves when explaining material to students, but field-dependent teachers tend to involve students more in organizing the content and sequencing the teaching-learning process and encourage them to formulate their own principles (Gordon & Gross, 1978; Witkin et al., 1977). Field-independent teachers are more likely to inform students when they are incorrect, to tell them why they are incorrect, and to express displeasure with students who are performing below capacity. Field-dependent teachers are less likely to express critical feedback.

Learning outcomes

In view of the range of teacher and student variables affected by psychological differentiation, it is not surprising that this cognitive style dimension is associated with learning outcomes. For example, field independence has been found to be associated with mathematics and spatial abilities even when general intelligence is controlled (Satterly, 1976). More generally, students tend to achieve more in subject matter areas that they prefer, and tend to do better when matched in cognitive style with their teachers (Witkin et al., 1977; Packer & Bain, 1978).

Even so, it is not clear that students or even teachers would be better off if matched in ways likely to reinforce their existing preferences, especially if they lie at the extremes of this psychological differentiation dimension. Extreme field independents have social adjustment problems, and extreme field dependents conform to the point that they seem to lack a mind of their own. Such individuals might be better off in the long run if they could learn to appreciate and function more frequently in their nonpreferred orientation.

Need for teacher awareness

It is important that teachers learn to recognize and respect both orientations, to build on students' existing strengths, and to avoid letting stylistic differences lead to discriminatory practices or personality clashes. Field-independent teachers can help meet the needs of field-dependent students by structuring their learning experiences sufficiently for them to be able to cope effectively, by providing encouragement and praise for success, by remaining objective and supportive when criticizing mistakes, and, in general, by developing a positive personal relationship with them. Field-dependent instructors accustomed to indirect communication that depends on perception of subtle social cues will need to be more direct when dealing with field-independent students. Such students may not recognize critical feedback unless it is presented explicitly, nor are they likely to resent or become upset by such criticism. Also, field-independent students are not likely to respond strongly or even positively to warmth or praise from a teacher, nor should a teacher feel rejected when this occurs. Finally, it is important that field-dependent teachers respect field-independent students' needs for privacy and distance, and that they avoid penalizing the students unreasonably for low social participation.

The value of teacher awareness and consideration of students' cognitive styles is shown in a study by Doebler and Eicke (1979). Fifth-grade teachers in the experimental group were given information about their students' field dependence-independence, along with suggestions about teaching strategies likely to be successful with each type. Compared to students in control classes whose teachers were not given this information, the experimental students showed better self-concepts and attitudes toward school.

Frank (1984) argues that the typical classroom procedure in which the teacher lectures and students take notes may favor the performance of field-independent students. To reduce this effect, Frank suggests that teachers consider providing students with external aids such as outlines on the board or handouts that organize the presentation that may help the performance of field-dependent students without detracting from the performance of field-independent students.

Roberge and Flexer (1984) found that the degree of field dependence-independence did not affect the reading achievement of sixth-, seventh-, and eighth-grade students. Although field dependence versus field independence is an important construct, there may be many areas in which the dimension is less important to classroom performance. For example, reading and comprehending written texts may be less related to this dimension than to the social organization of classroom tasks, such as those that follow the reading assignment.

In summary, it is clear that cognitive style is an important dimension on which teachers can anticipate and plan for individual differences in the classroom. However, teachers need to use cognitive style information as stimulation for thinking about individual students rather than as a basis for treating students as groups (Messick, 1984; Good & Stipek, 1984).

Creativity

Creativity is something that most of us value and recognize when we encounter it, however, it is very difficult to define and measure it. Many writers argue that it is part of or the same as general intelligence, but contrasts in the creative achievements of people with similar IQs seem to dispute this (MacKinnon, 1962). Thus, creativity is associated with IQ, but IQ tests apparently do not measure it directly.

Attempts to define and measure creativity began with J. P. Guilford's presidential address to the American Psychological Association in 1950. Guilford introduced a model representing mental abilities and claimed that these abilities collectively form a map or structure of intelligence. Included in the model is a list of mental operations, one of which is called divergent production and is basic to what some investigators mean by the creative process.

Convergent and divergent production

Guilford contended that information retrieval from memory storage can involve two kinds of operations—convergent production or divergent production. Convergent production involves searching for specific information to solve a problem that requires a single, logically necessary, correct answer (If Mary is taller than Sally and Sally is taller then Gwen, who is the tallest?). In contrast, divergent production is required for problems that have no single correct solution but can be answered in many different and equally acceptable ways (What can we do with a pencil besides use it for writing?).

Traits needed for creativity

Pursuing creativity further, Guilford (1959) determined that it involves divergent thinking with respect to the traits of fluency, flexibility, and originality of thought processes. Individuals high in ideational fluency can produce a great many ideas or concepts relevant to some problem in a short time. Those high in flexibility are able to shift from the direction of thinking or problem solving they have been using if new problems or conditions call for new approaches. Individuals high in originality can, in addition to noting the obvious or commonplace, make unusual or even unique observations. Thus, highly creative individuals can generate ideas at a rapid rate (fluency), "break set" in order to attack problems from a new perspective (flexibility), and generate new and genuinely different ideas (originality).

Measures of Creativity

Torrance (1962, 1966, 1972) has developed a variety of tests for measuring divergent thinking. The tests include generating unusual uses for a box or a brick, completing an ambiguous partial sketch by turning it into an interesting picture, or suggesting how a stuffed animal might be improved in such a way that it might be more interesting or fun to play with. Using an approach similar to Guilford's, responses to these tasks are scored for fluency, flexibility, and originality (see Figure 24.1).

Relationship to IQ

These tests show low but significant correlations with IQ, averaging about .20 (Torrance, 1975). Other investigators report similar correlations (see Andrews, 1975). In general, there is a closer relationship between divergent production ability and IQ at the lower levels of the IQ range than at the higher levels. That is, individuals with low IQs generally do not score well on divergent production tests. People having high scores on such tests usually have at least average IQs, but a high IQ does not guarantee high divergent production ability.

Wallach and Kogan (1965) discovered that the relationship between IQ and so-called creativity test scores varies with the types of test used. Moderate or even high correlations with IQ can be expected if a so-called creativity test has a time limit and includes convergent production tasks that call for a particular correct answer, in addition to divergent production tasks. On the other hand, if the "creativity" test battery is confined to divergent production tasks, and if testing is conducted under relaxed or playful conditions, the relationships between fluency, flexibility, and originality scores and IQs drop almost to zero.

Getzels and Jackson (1962) were early leaders in exploring the relationship between divergent thinking, intelligence, and creative performance. They also noted a positive but low correlation between creativity test performance and IQ, using a sample composed primarily of extremely bright students. Among these bright students, they noted some striking differences between those highest in IQ but lower in creativity (low-divergent) and those highest in creativity (high-divergent) but lower in IQ. The following excerpts are responses from a low-divergent student and a high-divergent

Figure 24.1 Guilford's Model of the Structure of the Intellect

Guilford identifies five basic mental operations: cognition, memory, divergent thinking, convergent thinking, and evaluation. Each of these operations can process each of four kinds of content (behavioral, semantic, symbolic, and figural), and each of these twenty combinations of mental operations with content categories can produce any of six kinds of mental products: units, classes, relations, systems, transformations, and implications. Creativity tests call for divergent thinking, usually to produce transformation of figural or symbolic content.

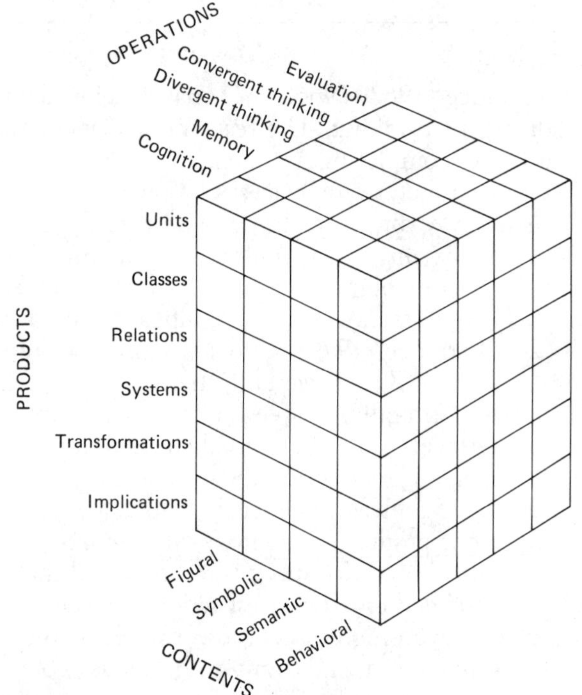

Source: From J. Guilford, "Three Faces of Intellect." *American Psychologist,* 1959, *14,* 469–479. Copyright © 1959 by the American Psychological Association. Reprinted by permission of the publisher and author.

student to two different stimulus cards. The first card was perceived most often as a man seated in an airplane, and the second as a man working either very late or very early in an office.

The low-divergent thinking subject: "Mr. Smith is on his way home from a successful business trip. He is very happy and he is thinking about his wonderful family and how glad he will be to see them again. He can picture it, about an hour from now, his plane landing at the airport and Mrs. Smith and their three children all there welcoming him home again."

The high-divergent thinking subject: "This man is flying back from Reno where he has won a divorce from his wife. He couldn't stand to live with her anymore, he told the judge, because she wore so much cold cream on her face at night that her head would skid across the pillow. He's now contemplating a new skid-proof face cream."

The low-divergent thinking subject: "There's ambitious Bob down at the office at 6:30 in the morning. Every morning it's the same. He's trying to show his boss how energetic he is. Now, thinks Bob, maybe the boss will give me a raise for all my extra work. The trouble is that Bob has been doing this for the last three years, and the boss still hasn't given him a raise. He'll come in at 9:00, not even noticing that Bob had been there so long, and poor Bob won't get his raise."

The high-divergent thinking subject: "This man has just broken into this office of a new cereal company. He is a private eye employed by a competitive firm to find out the formula that makes the cereal bend, sag, and sway. After a thorough search of the office he comes upon what he thinks is the current formula. It turns out that it is the wrong formula and the competitor's factory blows up. Poetic justice!" (Getzels & Jackson, 1962, pp. 39–40).

In discussing these findings, Getzels and Csikszentmihalyi (1975) stress that the high-divergent group were able to free themselves from the stimulus, but the low-divergent group focused on it. "For the low-divergent students the problem was essentially one of following up on what others had given them. If the picture stimulus is of a man in an airplane, he tells a story about travel. . . . For the high-divergent thinking subject, the problem was one of constructing something that he wants to give. The picture may be of a man in an airplane, but the story he wants to tell is about a divorce . . . ." (p. 99). Differences such as these eventually led Getzels and Csikszentmihalyi to view creativity as problem finding more than as problem solving.

Validation of Creativity Tests

Torrance, Tan, and Allman (1970) report that undergraduate teacher trainees who scored higher on situational tests of creativity demonstrated more creative teaching behavior in the classroom six years later. Torrance (1972) reviewed thirteen predictive validity studies of his creativity tests. The data are supportive but not decisive. It is interesting that the battery predicted achievement better in areas such as writing than in other fields such as business (Torrance, 1975). Perhaps this is because the test battery in its present form best measures verbal fluency.

Situational creativity

As Getzels (1975) notes, not many data exist, and there is still a need for more research on predictive validity to support the belief that situational creativity measures are related to creative and original performance later in life. At present, it appears that such measures do not predict creative performance among adult professionals, although they usually correlate positively but weakly with indicators of creativity in "amateur" or nonprofessional endeavors (Mansfield, Busse, & Krepelka, 1978).

Novelty and value as creative standards

What, then, is creativity? Although there is no universally accepted definition, two criteria are widely accepted. First, a product must be novel if it is to be called creative. The second criterion is value. A creative product must reflect value by being judged correct (a technical solution works) or good (the music is satisfying).

Our interest in creativity tests is based in part on their ability to sensitize educators to the fact that intelligence is broader than present measures indicate. Even now, creativity tests can identify students whose considerable talent would otherwise go unnoticed.

Fostering Creativity in the Classroom

Valuing creativity in students

How can teachers foster creativity in the classroom? Probably the first step is to learn to value it! Nearly everyone values the concept of creativity, of course, but student creativity in the classroom can be irritating, disruptive, or even threatening to teachers. Getzels and Jackson (1962) found that teachers preferred students low in divergent thinking to those higher in divergent thinking, even though all of the students were bright and the divergent thinkers produced more imaginative and original responses. This is not really surprising. Schools are inherently rule-bound and conservative institutions, which is both necessary and appropriate, at least to a degree, so that much student creativity is likely to contrast or even conflict with what is routine, familiar, expected, and "correct." If students are urged to think and act creatively, some of their responses will be both novel and valuable; however, others will be novel but silly, obscene, outrageous, or bizarre. Teachers who intend to foster creativity will have to accept this fact.

Reis and Renzulli (1984) reviewed outstanding programs for gifted students and noted that although the unique qualities of the people who administer a particular program are important, effective programs still have many of the following characteristics in common:

1. They open doors to all interested participants as enrichment experiences are planned.
2. They provide a basis for students to work hard and to pursue individual interests intensively.
3. They provide mechanisms for students to display excellence and share it with others, thereby challenging other students both within the program or in regular classes to emulate it.
4. They motivate nonidentified students to participate without the constraints of predetermined IQ or achievement cut-off scores.
5. They allow all teachers and students to share their interests and expertise with other interested students and teachers.
6. They relieve students of the burden of repetitious, boring tasks and assignments that are often used to fill the typical school day.

Importance of childhood experiences

Clues about factors that may foster creativity have been gathered in retrospective reports of the childhood experiences of creative adults. In general, highly creative adults report having been exposed to a rich variety of experiences as children, and remember having been encouraged to ask questions and to test out their ideas through active experimentation. Such adults were usually encouraged to pursue their interests through collections, hobbies, development of specialized knowledge, or pursuit of talents or skills (Wallach, 1971).

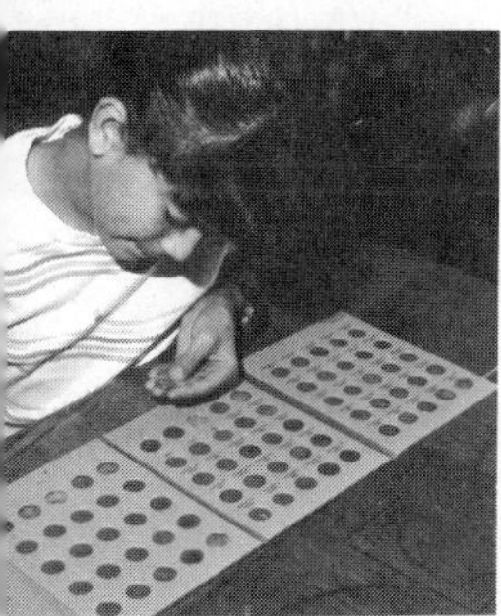

Children enjoy pursuing interests through collections and hobbies.

Torrance (1962) includes such ideas in his recommendations for developing creativity in the classroom, and adds several others: encourage manipulation of objects and ideas; teach students to test out their ideas systematically; teach students to value creative thinking; caution against premature or unwarranted dismissal of "wild" ideas; teach students that everyone has creative potential and that it is not something possessed only by a few; and induce creative thinking by asking students to generate alternative solutions to problems, to speculate on what might have happened if historical events had been different, to suggest worthwhile inventions or improvements, or to solve other problems that call on their divergent production abilities.

Encouraging creativity

Note that most of these suggestions can be incorporated into everyday teaching of the regular school curriculum without having special materials or scheduling special "creativity time." Teachers can learn to do many of these things automatically by habitually asking themselves, when planning activities and assignments, "Have I included opportunities for students to think and to solve problems in connection with this topic? . . . Have I included opportunities for them to use their divergent production abilities?" In addition to incorporating the above suggestions into the curriculum, it would be beneficial to also add assignments involving poetry, fiction, or other creative writing; action projects requiring research and development leading to a creative product; and the like.

Special programs

Special programs designed to facilitate divergent thinking or other aspects of creativity are available for teachers not content merely with establishing an encouraging classroom atmosphere and seeking to foster creativity within the context of teaching the regular curriculum. The Productive Thinking Program (Covington, Crutchfield, Davies, & Olton, 1974) is a self-instructional program for fifth and sixth graders. It attempts to develop creative problem-solving abilities and favorable attitudes toward problem solving through booklets that teach problem-solving skills in a cartoon format. Many of the problems involve convergent thinking, but some involve divergent thinking as well. Evaluations of the program provide some evidence that it improves student performance on tests of divergent thinking, although best results are obtained when teachers adapt the materials and instruct the students themselves rather than distribute the materials for students to use in a self-instructional program, as the program developers originally intended (Mansfield, Busse, & Krepelka, 1978).

Brainstorming

Parnes (1967) developed a program that includes a variety of divergent production activities but emphasizes a technique that he calls brainstorming. Brainstorming involves generating ideas, usually in a group setting, in response to some question or problem. Students are encouraged to volunteer whatever ideas occur to them, regardless of whether or not the ideas seem reasonable or correct. Ideas are recorded for later evaluation, but no criticism is permitted until everyone's ideas have been contributed. The Parnes program is used mostly in college and high school courses, where it has been generally successful in increasing divergent thinking scores. Myers and Torrance (1966) developed sets of workbooks designed to foster creativity in elementary school children. Like other approaches, this one involves teaching students to value creative thinking and provides practice in a variety of divergent production tasks. It may be useful in improving divergent thinking ability, especially when teachers guide students in the use of the workbooks, although no clear data are yet available (Mansfield, Busse, & Krepelka, 1978).

Teaching creative thinking

Davis (1976) and his colleagues have developed a variety of methods for teaching students to think creatively. In one study, college students were asked to think of changes and/or improvements for a doorknob. Three methods of encouraging creative thinking were tested, two of which proved effective. The first involved providing students with a list of seventy-three possible ways to make changes. This method was not very effective, apparently because students did not really try to think creatively but instead simply worked their way through the list.

A second group of students received lists containing only seven suggestions: add and/or subtract something; change color; change the material; change by rearranging the parts; change shapes; change size; and change design or style. This method effectively stimulated creative thinking in that the students with the short list produced about twice as many ideas as the students with the long list or students who received no suggestions at all. The list was long and specific enough to stimulate a variety of ideas, but not so complete as to inhibit creativity.

The students who produced the most ideas, however, were those who used the matrix or checkerboard technique. This involved analyzing the stimulus in question into its various dimensions and then combining the values of these dimensions into new arrangements. For example, on a problem involving new solutions to the energy crisis, one axis of a two-dimensional checkerboard matrix could be the source of power (wind, solar, ocean tides, geothermal, and so on). Each of these power sources could be combined with ideas arranged along another axis indicating uses for the power (heating homes, transportation, cooking, manufacturing). Cross referencing these two lists produces certain interesting and novel combinations that stimulate creative thinking. In this vein, ideas about changing doorknobs might be stimulated by combining considerations of placement of the knob on the door (listing various possible places in terms of horizontal and vertical distance from the edge of the door) with various lock arrangements (dead bolt versus spring lock versus no lock at all; key versus no key).

Results of creativity training programs

We have mentioned only a few of many varied creativity training programs and materials available, and new ones appear regularly. Most programs have at least some value in that students usually enjoy them and find them stimulating. However, it is questionable whether such programs actually produce any genuine, lasting, or generalizable improvements in creative thinking abilities. Results are mixed at best, and even supportive results involve scores on tests of divergent production rather than more rigorous criteria such as evidence of increased creativity in schoolwork or in everyday life. Furthermore, higher creativity scores can be a result of increased persistence on criterion tests by students who have been specially trained and know that they are expected to perform well, of the advantages provided by training that involves tasks very similar to those on the criterion tests, or even of improved attitudes or confidence.

The last factor may be the most important of all. Manske and Davis (1968) found that students gave much more original responses when they were instructed to be original, and much more practical responses when they were instructed to be practical, when responding to the same problems. Wallach and Kogan (1965) concluded that students who were intelligent but not highly creative were merely disinclined rather than unable to use their imaginations. Many students' barriers to creative thinking reside solely in their own minds due to factors such as social inhibition, fear of failure, lack of confidence, or even the belief that they lack creativity (Davis, 1976). If this is true, it seems likely that student creativity will be fostered most effectively not by special training programs, although these may be useful, but by teachers who model and encourage creativity in their everyday interactions with students and who create a classroom atmosphere and intellectual climate that value originality and playful consideration of ideas at least as much as mastery of organized knowledge.

Overcoming barriers to creativity

As Sigel (1984) notes, there is increased interest in helping students to become more productive and creative, and to become independent thinkers. This is ironic in the sense that helping students to think better should be the key task of schooling so that learning becomes a life-long process. In the past, educators emphasized helping gifted students to develop their creative talents more fully. Recently, there has been increased understanding of and interest in the need for *all* students to become more creative and independent in their approach to classroom learning activities.

Metacognitive strategies

One area that has received special attention involves enabling students to develop metacognitive strategies for monitoring their own learning. In Chapter 14 we discussed the need for students to become more autonomous learners (Corno & Rohrkemper, in press). Similarly, Chapter 10 emphasized student learning strategies (e.g., Weinstein & Mayer, 1985). Here we want to remind readers that although creativity has for a long time been treated as a special topic, more recent research focuses on creativity as a general process. Costa (1984) recommends the following twelve strategies that teachers can use across a variety of grade levels and subject areas to increase students' capacity for metacognition:

1. *Planning strategy*—Teachers can help students think about the decisions they are going to make and the rules they will follow in completing an assignment. Students can be encouraged to plan ahead and to outline the tasks they will need to complete.
2. *Generating questions*—It is important for students to be able to raise questions about material they read and think about. Too often textbooks simply present a series of questions at the end of a reading passage and teachers routinely check students' answers to these ques-

tions. It seems much more important for students to develop questions about the material and propose some of their own learning activities. Such thinking should help students develop self-awareness and take more control of their learning.

3. *Choosing conscientiously*—Costa contends that teachers can promote metacognition in students by helping students explore the consequences of their choices and decisions prior to, during, and after the act of deciding. For example, questions that challenge students to consider the number of references that might be available on a particular topic are useful in getting students to think through whether or not a paper topic will generate new questions that should be examined or whether it merely summarizes a topic on which considerable research has already been conducted.
4. *Evaluating multiple criteria*—Students can be encouraged to think about their responses from a variety of viewpoints and to consider how persons representing various groups might react differently to a statement or report that students have prepared. Rather than simply coming up with a label like "A" or "Well Done," teachers should encourage students to think about the relative strengths and weaknesses of their work and the work of other students.
5. *Taking credit*—Students can be encouraged to identify with what they have done and to invite feedback from peers in the spirit of making their products better. The teacher can routinely describe publicly the things that students have done well and help students identify their strengths.
6. *Outlawing "I can't"*—Costa encourages teachers to consciously inform students that excuses such as "I don't know how to" or "I'm too slow" are unacceptable. Teachers can encourage students to identify what information they require, what materials they need, and what skills they lack in performing assigned or self-chosen work.
7. *Paraphrasing or reflecting students' ideas*—Inviting students to translate, compare, and paraphrase the teacher's ideas or those of other students stimulates them to become better listeners to the ideas of others as well as their own.
8. *Labeling students' behaviors*—The teacher can help students develop better awareness of their own cognitive processes by labeling students' behaviors as they occur in the classroom. For example, "What you are doing is called an experiment. That is hypothetical thinking. I can see that you've made at least two inferences in that assumption. What I see you doing is making a plan of action."
9. *Clarifying students' terminology*—Teachers can help students become more active thinkers by encouraging them to extend their thinking when they use vague, nonspecific terminology. For example, students might say "It's not fair" or "That's lousy." Teachers need to help students clarify these values by asking questions such as "What would be more fair?" or "In what sense is it lousy?" Similarly, students can be encouraged to examine the processes through which

they generate answers. Students often do assigned work without thinking about the processes involved.

10. *Role playing and simulations*—Costa contends that role playing can stimulate metacognition because when students assume the role of another person, they assume the thinking and attributes of that person. This can be an important step in helping students become more hypothetical in their thinking.
11. *Journal keeping*—Writing personal thoughts in a diary or log can help students synthesize thoughts and actions and translate them in a more general way. Such a written record also provides an opportunity to revisit initial perceptions and beliefs about assigned work.
12. *Modeling*—Costa maintains that modeling and thinking out loud are an excellent means by which teachers can influence student behavior. Teachers who demonstrate metacognition can probably help some students to think in similar ways.

Costa's recommendations are relevant for teachers who are trying to teach general higher-order skills. These strategies are especially helpful when teachers use these twelve principles to encourage students to develop original solutions and new ways to state problems.

Although there has been some research on teaching thinking skills, many related recommendations are only tentative, and subsequent research must verify which strategies are most useful for certain students or content areas. Still, it seems safe to say that student thinking and creativity has been a neglected area and the recent emphasis on improving students' skills in these areas is important. (For a review of some suggestions for teaching thinking and creativity, see Falkof & Moss, 1984; Grennon, 1984; Sigel, 1984; Brooks, 1984; Olson, 1984; Gall, 1984; Dillon, 1984; Edwards & Marland, 1984; Martin, 1984.)

SUMMARY

Cognitive style and creativity appear to involve elements of both cognition and personality. They refer to how people process information and solve problems, not how well they do so. Conceptual tempo is a cognitive style dimension dealing with impulsivity versus reflectivity in responding to two or more plausible alternatives. Psychological differentiation is a second dimension involving field dependence versus field independence, or global versus analytical perceptual style. Both dimensions have implications for teachers in terms of students' preferences for and responses to different learning situations, as well as their approaches to teaching.

Creativity is a variable of interest to educators, but one that is difficult to define or measure. It is associated with IQ, but IQ tests do not measure it directly. Elements such as divergent production, fluency, flexibility, and originality are involved. Talented researchers such as Guilford, Torrance, and Getzels and Jackson have done extensive work in the area, but valid and reliable tests of creativity that have compelling social significance have yet to be developed.

Teachers can foster student creativity in several ways. Valuing creativity and accepting divergent thinking are critical, as is the provision of a wide variety of experiences and opportunities for students to use creative talents. Activities such as brainstorming, searching for novel solutions to problems, and dealing with several dimensions of a problem simultaneously appear to have value as well.

QUESTIONS AND PROBLEMS

1. As a teacher, when should you teach to a student's strength in a way that matches the student's cognitive style and when should you teach in a way that forces a student to develop new skills, such as by forcing a field-independent student to work in a group?
2. Some students who have problems learning to read will make many errors because of cognitive impulsivity; others will make many errors because of more serious deficiencies in perception or memory. How can teachers distinguish between these two types of students?
3. Why is it not enough for a teacher to teach cognitively impulsive students to slow down and take their time before responding?
4. Should participation in class discussions be taken into account when grading in addition to scores on tests and assignments? Why or why not? Can you and your classmates reach a consensus on this question?
5. Although psychologists are unable to define and measure creativity satisfactorily, they, as well as people in general, seem to think that they know what the word means and that they can recognize creativity when they see it. How do you define creativity? What are some of the things that indicate creativity?
6. Do you think of creativity as a programmed genetic trait, as an ability that is learned but not teachable, or as something that is teachable? What implications does this have for your teaching?
7. Would you supplement the regular curriculum with special activities designed to foster creativity? Why or why not?
8. Take the twelve principles Costa offers for enhancing metacognition and apply them to a unit you plan to teach. Discuss how you would use these principles in your teaching.
9. Summarize in your own words how field-dependent students differ from field-independent students. What are the three or four most important differences between these two types of students that a teacher must consider?

CASE STUDIES

Drill. Royal Grind wants to make sure that his junior high English students know their grammar, so most class time is devoted to workbook exercises like underlining the right word, crossing out the wrong word, and correcting the misspelled words as well as diagramming sentences. Students work on the exercises individually, and Royal spends much of his time correcting their papers. What changes could he introduce that would still allow him to stress grammar but would introduce elements that would be more appealing to field-dependent students and more likely to allow all of the students to use their creativity?

Mental Mathematics and Estimation. Jane Keystone is a sixth-grade mathematics teacher in Middleview Elementary School. Because she works in a large, departmentalized school, she teaches only math, five periods a day. In class she stresses individual problem solving and estimation that is done mentally without pen and paper or calculators. She stresses that mathematics does not merely involve obtaining correct answers, but is also a way to organize information quantitatively so that decisions can be made. Every day Jane takes 15 minutes for mental mathematics and work on estimation. The rest of her instruction is similar to that of other teachers. Which students are most likely to benefit from Jane's teaching? Why? How can Jane adjust instruction so that more students can benefit?

Chapter 25

Educating Students with Special Needs

CHAPTER OUTLINE

OBJECTIVES

When you have mastered the material in this chapter you will be able to

1. Discuss three problems associated with the placement and education of children with special needs in special settings and programs
2. Explain how Public Law 94-142 attempts to remedy the problems of special education through mainstreaming within the least restrictive environment
3. Discuss the ways teachers can prepare themselves and their students to deal effectively with handicapped students
4. Define the handicaps of visual and hearing impairment, and tell how teachers can assist students with these handicaps
5. Define the handicaps of speech impairment and stuttering, and tell how teachers can assist students with these handicaps
6. Define and differentiate the handicaps of learning disabilities, mild retardation, and behavior disorders, and tell how teachers can assist handicapped students
7. Explain what an Individual Educational Program (IEP) is, how one is written, and how it attempts to ensure due process for the handicapped

Theoretically, our national policy of free public education for all means that public schools are available to any student who wishes to enroll. This has not been the case in practice, however. For much of our history, black students either received no public school education at all or were required to attend segregated black schools. More recently, schools in the southwestern states have attempted to disclaim responsibility for teaching the children of illegal aliens who reside within their districts. Even among students initially considered appropriate for admission to public schoools, some may be excluded or expelled from regular school programs because they are judged to disrupt normal classroom procedures. Courts have upheld such exclusion on the basis of mental and physical deficiencies, health, pregnancy, flagrant or willful misbehavior, and even unconventional clothes or personal appearance (Flowers & Bolmeier, 1964).

The Traditional Emphasis on Special Placement

Special placement within public schools

Recent court decisions have struck down most of the above mentioned exclusion criteria so that attendance in regular public school programs is now more clearly established as a universal right in practice as well as in theory. The majority of students affected by these changes are those who have special educational needs because of handicaps such as impairments in vision, hearing, speech, or physical mobility; crippling diseases; mental retardation; emotional disturbances; and learning disabilities. Until recently, many of these students were placed in institutions such as schools specifically for the blind or the deaf. Those with less extreme handicaps usually were accepted by the public school system but often were segregated from the rest of the students for all or at least part of the day. They attended "special education classes" or spent much of their time in "resource rooms" where instructors who were not always specially trained could provide them with more individual attention and specialized help.

In theory, the following approach made good sense: identify those students who have special needs by using screening procedures and follow up with diagnostic test batteries where indicated; follow up diagnosis with needs assessment to identify precisely which specialized services and forms of instruction each individual student required; and then place the student in a setting in which this treatment could be received from a special teacher prepared to provide it. Unfortunately, this is not what usually happened in practice. Disenchantment set in, and sentiment gradually switched from special placement procedures to retaining special students in the regular classroom. Chaffin (1974) cites the following four major reasons for this switch:

1. The equivocal results of research on the effectiveness of special classes for the mildly retarded.
2. The recognition that many of the diagnostic instruments used for identifying retardation were culturally biased, resulting in frequent inappropriate diagnosis and placement.

3. The realization that the problems of being labeled and segregated into special settings might be greater than those involved in coping with handicaps in normal settings.
4. Court litigation that took the above problems into account and stressed the rights of all children to appropriate educational treatment over the rights of schools to choose their clients.

Problems Regarding Special Placement

Concerning the first problem Chaffin cites, it should be noted that the data on the effectiveness of special settings and programs are unimpressive. Special programs for the deaf seem to work reasonably well: deaf students in special schools show higher achievement than comparable deaf children in regular schools. Beyond this, however, it is not at all clear that specialized programs and settings provide benefits that handicapped students are unable to get in regular classrooms.

Biases in diagnosis

The data on diagnosis are equally discouraging. First, the problem of cultural bias is serious (Oakland, 1977; Cleary, Humphreys, Kendrick, & Wesman, 1975) and may be compounded if students are tested in English when English is not their primary language. This has led to the misclassification of a great many children of low socioeconomic status, especially if they are members of racial or ethnic minority groups, as mentally retarded when this label is not justified (Mercer, 1973).

Misuse of diagnostic testing

Diagnostic testing has been misused. Often the classroom teacher must request such testing. Many teachers request testing more out of a desire to get rid of students who present personality or behavior problems than out of concern about meeting these students' special educational needs. In some districts, special classrooms became dumping grounds for problem students, while peers with similiar abilities, test profiles, and achievement levels were kept in regular classrooms because they got along better with their teachers.

Validity of diagnoses

In addition to problems with the instruments themselves and with the reasons for their use, there are also questions about the reliability and validity of special-education diagnoses and of the presumed linkages between diagnoses and treatments. Research on the diagnostic activities of well-trained and highly regarded specialists in such fields as learning disabilities and reading problems reveals that they show very poor agreement with one another, and even with themselves, when they encounter the same case twice (Gil, Vinsonhaler, & Wagner, 1979). Also, diagnoses often are not linked systematically to proposed treatments. Instead of recommending specific treatments for each diagnosis, specialists prescribe the same general kinds of treatments regardless of the diagnosis (Weinshank, 1978). Data such as these indicate that although the concept of specialized diagnosis and treatment seems sensible, it does not currently function effectively in practice.

Negative effects of labeling

The third problem Chaffin discusses concerns the negative effects of labeling and segregation. Psychologists and sociologists have long recognized that being labeled as different can produce social stigma, damage the self-concept, and, in general, initiate a series of negative self-fulfilling prophecy effects. The process is exaggerated if the stigma results in segregation of the "different" from the "normal."

Recognition of these problems by educators led to a change of attitudes in the early 1970s. For example, MacMillan, Jones, and Meyers (1976) estimate that between 11,000 and 18,000 EMR (educable mentally retarded) students were returned from special to regular classrooms in California alone between 1969 and 1972. Court litigation gradually began to speed up this process, as a variety of decisions, mostly at the local and state levels, supported the rights of handicapped students (Cohen & DeYoung, 1973; Collings, 1973; Gilhool, 1973; Vaughn, 1973). This legal activity culminated on a national scale with the passage of Public Law 94–142.

Legal changes

The Impact of Public Law 94-142

Public Law 94-142, The Education for All Handicapped Children Act, was signed by the president in 1975 but did not become effective until Fall 1977. The law called for a number of sweeping changes, although its implementation was left primarily to individual states, and there has been considerable variation among states. Briefly, the law sets forth the following requirements:

> Public schools are mandated to search out and enroll every handicapped child, no matter how profound the handicap, in an educational program that is "appropriate" to the child.
>
> Schools are required to write an individualized educational plan (IEP) for each such child. This requires forming teams of school personnel to assess a student's educational needs and specify in writing the goals, objectives, schedules, placements, and plans for evaluation and review.
>
> Schools must bring needed special services to pupils whenever this is feasible, rather than move the pupils to special sites. This procedure removes many of the barriers between regular and special education, and redefines the roles of regular and special education teachers in relation to one another and to students.
>
> Finally, the schools must seek the participation of the parents of handicapped children in making these plans and decisions. The parents must be given full access to all records on their children, and the schools must take care to observe the children's and parent's rights to due process in the event of disagreement. (Reynolds, 1978)

Mainstreaming

In short, this law commits the nation to a policy of mainstreaming handicapped students by placing them in the least restrictive environment in which they will be able to function and still have their special needs met.

There is increasing resistance to removing students from regular classrooms unless there is a clear need for a special program. Messick (1984) suggests that before a student is removed from a regular classroom and placed in a special education class, a two-phase aptitude assessment ought to be utilized. The first assessment should attempt to verify whether or not the student is able to learn under well-conceived, regular classroom instruction and to assess whether or not the regular teacher has attempted to alter the classroom environment in order to respond more effectively to the learner's needs. Is it possible that a different teacher or special curricular materials might help keep the student in a regular classroom?

Only after it has been established that the regular classroom teacher presented plausible instruction to the student should special testing and placement in a special group be considered because of the possible stigma involved for the child.

Snow (1984) notes that EMR students are not a homogeneous group; they differ from one another in as many ways as other students differ from one another. He stresses that educators need to identify these pupils' particular strengths as well as their weaknesses, and to prescribe treatment accordingly.

According to Snow, some special education programs simply establish generally lower expectations for students instead of adapting instruction to individual differences in order to achieve as many common goals as possible. He notes that such programs do not reflect special education in the best sense of the word, and are actually dead-end placements where common goals have been dropped altogether.

Least Restrictive Environment Principle. Least restrictive environment implies that special students are not to be classified by handicap and given permanent special placement on the basis of their classification, but instead are to be moved to special stations only if they require it and only for as long as necessary. The following continuum of educational environments proceeds from most to least restrictive (Reynolds, 1978):

- ☐ Full-time residential school
- ☐ Full-time special day school
- ☐ Full-time special class
- ☐ Regular classroom plus part-time special class
- ☐ Regular classroom plus resource room help
- ☐ Regular classroom with assistance by itinerant specialists
- ☐ Regular classroom with consultative assistance
- ☐ Regular classroom only

The principle of least restrictive environment calls for students to be placed in settings as far down this list as possible. Profoundly deaf children, for example, usually will require full-time special schools or special classes, but children with less severe hearing problems and children with a variety of vision problems can spend part or even all of their time in regular classrooms, although probably with some assistance from consultants or itinerant specialists. As another example, emotionally disturbed students who periodically become withdrawn and uncommunicative might be able to spend most of their time in regular classrooms but receive temporary special treatment or special placement in another setting during periods of severe withdrawal.

Increased interaction between professionals

These examples illustrate how P.L. 94-142 has loosened the boundaries between regular and special education and led to much more interaction between regular classroom teachers, special education teachers, and other specialists such as school psychologists and diagnosticians. Most teachers now need training in methods of meeting the needs of special students in addition to the traditional preparation for teaching.

These additional demands on regular classroom teachers should not be minimized, neither should they be exaggerated. When P.L. 94-142 was passed, some people thought that it called for all handicapped students to be placed in regular classrooms, regardless of type or severity of handicap. This mistake was understandable, because the bill's language emphasized correcting past injustices as well as the right of all handicapped children to an appropriate education. The key term here is "appropriate," which is defined in terms of the least restrictive environment. Thus, the law does not eliminate special educational settings or require that all students be placed in regular classrooms.

State program requirements

Implementation Procedures. Public Law 94-142 does not fully spell out its implementation. This will be determined gradually by court decisions, state laws, and local practices (Hansen, 1976). The law does place six major requirements on state programs as a condition for obtaining federal support:

1. Handicapped students must be educated to the maximum extent appropriate, in the least restrictive environment.
2. Nondiscriminatory, culture-free testing in the native language of the student is necessary prior to placement in special programs.
3. Prior consultation with parents must take place before special placement.
4. An individualized educational program (IEP) must be prepared specifically for each handicapped student.
5. Public school programs must serve nonpublic school students if they are handicapped and require services that the federal government funds.
6. Staff development programs must be conducted in every school district.

Note that these guidelines concentrate on ensuring due process, provision of services to the public, and availability of staff development programs to teachers, but they do not mandate the content of the programs. This is determined primarily at the school district level. At present, there is essentially no research-based knowledge about how to implement mainstreaming optimally (Dunn, 1973; MacMillan, Jones, & Meyers, 1976), so that local specialists will likely determine implementation in a given school district.

Current experimentation

There is much experimentation currently going on, both concerning what kinds of students can and should be placed in regular classrooms, and what special arrangements, if any, their regular teachers will have to make. Under this new experimentation, teachers will get materials and help from itinerant special-education teachers or other consultants, as well as guidelines from inservice activities and from the individualized educational plan (IEP) written for each student.

Teaching Special Students: General Considerations

When preparing to work with handicapped students, teachers need to shed any stereotypes they may have developed because of past labeling and segregation of these students. Handicapped students are not qualitatively different from other students. Their handicaps limit what they can do, but they are not different from other students in any other respect. They develop and learn according to the same general principles, respond to the same kinds of incentives, and develop the same kinds of motivational systems. For the most part, then, the principles described throughout this book apply as much to handicapped students as to other students (Larrivee, 1985). This is true even for those who are labeled "emotionally disturbed" (Kounin & Obradovic, 1968).

Teachers can prepare to deal with students with special needs by reading and taking courses in special education and by consulting with specialists. Perhaps more importantly, they can observe in classrooms where handicapped students are mainstreamed, both to learn about the techniques the teachers are using and about the students themselves. It is always helpful to analyze classroom events from the perspective of students (Doyle, 1978), but especially so from the perspective of handicapped students where questions can be answered such as: What classroom tasks can they accomplish as well as other students without any special provisions or help? What additional tasks might they accomplish with assistance? In the case of tasks that cannot be completed, even with assistance, are there other approaches that might allow these students to get the same benefits?

These questions illustrate a major consideration to keep in mind in dealing with special students—instead of concentrating on their handicaps, capitalize on their strengths in order to compensate for their deficiencies. Certain goals and objectives may have to be reduced for some special stu-

Capitalizing on strengths

A handicapped student can successfully attend a regular class.

dents, and some may have to be reached in unusual ways, but by and large these students should pursue the same objectives as other students. This principle is easy to understand when we think about blind students whom, since they cannot see, we teach through their other senses, but it applies to other special students as well.

Need for positive attitudes

There is some evidence that some teachers hold inappropriate expectations for teaching handicapped students. For example, Hannah and Pilner (1983) contend that teachers, like many citizens, do not have positive attitudes toward the handicapped. Although there is some variation in attitudes toward particular handicapping conditions, in general many teachers have negative beliefs and feelings toward these students and are somewhat reluctant to enter into teaching relationships with them.

As a future teacher you need to work on developing appropriate positive expectations for teaching mainstreamed students. If you do not hold appropriate expectations it is unlikely that your students will develop favorable attitudes toward handicapped peers.

Preparing the Class for Mainstreamed Students

Teachers involved in mainstreaming will be most effective if they structure not only their own expectations and behavior but also those of their students. What and how much to tell a class will depend on the nature of incoming mainstreamed students' handicaps, and on what the students can and cannot do without assistance. If a student's handicap is not obvious, it may be best to say nothing at all about it to other students and to let the mainstreamed student enter the class as any other newcomer would.

This would not be possible, of course, in the case of obvious handicaps that require a wheelchair or a prosthetic device, or that include noticeable deficiencies in vision or hearing. In such a case, other students in the class should be told what to expect and how to act. The teacher should obtain students' cooperation in welcoming new students and in helping them to participate as much as they possibly can as regular members of the class.

Handicaps should be described directly and matter-of-factly, without dramatics or attempts to generate exaggerated sympathy or pity, as in this example:

> Class, tomorrow we are going to be joined by a new member named Linda Johnson. We are going to need to rearrange the room a little bit to get ready for Linda because she uses a wheelchair. She needs the wheelchair because several years ago she had an accident that left her paralyzed from the waist down, so she can't walk. She hasn't let this stop her from keeping up with her studies and participating in most activities outside the classroom, however. You'll see for yourself starting tomorrow. Meanwhile, though, I want to make sure that she can get in and out of the classroom easily. I was thinking that she could park her wheelchair right up in front of this row here. There is a nice clear path between here and the door. She won't need a regular desk but she will need some place to keep things while she is with us, so I was thinking that we could move that bookcase up next to where her wheelchair will be parked, and let her use part of it to keep her things in.

The teacher can go on to ask if there are any questions, answering any that can be answered at present, and indicating that the others will be worked out at the time Linda joins the class. A few of the students might be assigned as a welcoming committee to make a point of getting to know Linda and "showing her the ropes," as well as providing her with any special help she may need. Peer tutoring is often valuable for meeting the needs of mainstreamed students. Beyond this, the new student can request additional forms of assistance, if needed.

Modeling and structuring of expectations

With this kind of modeling and structuring of expectations and behavior, most students adjust to new, handicapped classmates as they would adjust to any new classmates. Older students will typically take this in stride. Younger students who are unfamiliar with wheelchairs or prosthetic devices are naturally curious and ask questions, and teachers should answer these questions matter-of-factly, or have the handicapped students answer and demonstrate. There is no need to protect handicapped students from these questions; they get them all the time.

In general, then, teachers can prepare for mainstreaming by gaining information about, observing, and interacting with handicapped students, especially those being mainstreamed in other classrooms, and then by establishing appropriate expectations and behavior in their own classrooms.

Meeting Special Needs

It is not yet clear how many students are likely to be mainstreamed. Egbert (1978) estimates that the various types of handicapped students eligible for mainstreaming constitute about 12 percent of the total school age population. Statistics from the Bureau of the Handicapped indicate the following percentages: visually impaired, 0.1 percent; hearing impaired, 0.6 to 0.8 percent; speech impaired, 3.5 to 5.0 percent; crippled and health impaired, 0.5 percent; emotionally retarded, 2.5 to 3.0 percent; mentally retarded, 2.5 to 3.0 percent; and learning disabilities, 2.0 to 4.0 percent.

Many types of handicapped students have been taught successfully in regular classrooms all along, such as those students who have allergies, asthma, arthritis, diabetes, epilepsy, cerebral palsy, muscular dystrophy, as well as those who have had amputations. Health disabilities will not be discussed here because of their great variety; for further information, see Safford (1978), Dunn (1973), or Gearheart and Weishahn (1976).

Visual Impairment

Blind and partially seeing students

Two major distinctions are often made within the larger category of visual impairment. Blind students are those who have central vision acuity of 20/200 or less in the better eye after correction. Students whose visual fields are restricted to 20 degrees (tunnel vision) are usually classified as blind as well. Partially seeing students have visual limitations that interfere with

Teachers should look for signs of visual and other impairments that require special attention.

their learning to the extent that they require special teaching services and aids if they are to perform up to their potential.

Ways in Which the Teacher Can Assist

1. Referral to an eye specialist for complete evaluation.
2. Acquire special learning aids (large-print texts, Braille texts, tape-recorded learning exercises).
3. Help visually impaired students to develop self-care skills (e.g., by taking students on a playground tour and helping them to note potential hazards).
4. Foster conceptual development by using senses such as touch and smell to help students differentiate objects they cannot see.
5. Encourage students to express their thoughts and to communicate in the classroom.
6. Encourage students to use what vision they do have.
7. Remember that reading Braille takes twice as long as reading visually.
8. Seating these students on the window side of the classroom, not facing the light, and giving them desks with a dull surface.

Hearing Impairment

Deaf and partially hearing students

There are two major types of hearing impairments. Deaf students develop a severe hearing loss at birth or prior to age two or three that prevents them from learning to speak. Partially hearing students are those whose hearing losses are not severe enough to prevent the development of spoken language, or who develop a hearing loss after they learn to talk.

Ways in Which the Teacher Can Assist

1. Referral to a specialist for complete evaluation.
2. If the loss is slight (20–40 decibels), the student may benefit from a hearing aid and from extra help with new vocabulary. Favorable seating and lighting and speech-reading instruction may be needed as well.

3. Students with moderate (41–55 decibels) hearing losses can hear conversational speech at a distance of 3–5 feet but may miss as much as 50 percent of class discussion if they cannot see the lips of speakers or if speakers' voices are weak. Hence, teachers need to make visual cues available (the teacher shouldn't turn away from the student when talking, should speak clearly, shouldn't stand between the student and the window).
4. If the hearing loss is marked (56–70 decibels), teacher talk and conversation must be very loud in order to be understood. Also, the student will have difficulty participating in group discussion and is likely to have problems with vocabulary (language usage and comprehension). Listening is hard work for such students, so they may become fatigued during activities that involve prolonged listening.
5. The teacher needs to learn how hearing aids function and how to maintain them.

Speech Impairment

Articulation disorders

Students with speech impairments either cannot comprehend the spoken language of others or cannot express themselves meaningfully with spoken words. The most frequent problems that public school teachers deal with are articulation disorders. There are four common articulation disorders: omissions (at for that): substitutions (that for than); distortions (shled for shed); and additions (puhlease for please). Other problems include voice disorders (e.g., too loud, too soft, pitch too high) and stuttering.

Ways in Which the Teacher Can Assist

1. Refer students to a speech therapist for complete evaluation.
2. Help students pronounce sounds correctly.
3. Help students to *hear* their spoken errors.
4. Encourage students to use new words frequently once they can pronounce the words correctly.
5. Help students to rehearse oral skills, such as by introducing someone, and allow them to practice their skills publicly.

Stuttering. Stuttering is still poorly understood. No one really knows what causes it, despite a variety of explanations. Thus, advice on how to help students who stutter varies widely. However, the following suggestions for dealing with stutterers are frequently made:

1. Cue these students before calling on them.
2. Focus on the content of what they say, not how they say it.
3. Do not label them as stutterers.
4. Do not allow them to use stuttering as a crutch to avoid schoolwork. If the stuttering prohibits participation in an activity, be sure to have them do an additional written assignment or some other substitute activity.

5. Many students stutter in one situation (e.g., when called to answer) but not another (e.g., reading aloud). If so, continue to give them plenty of oral practice in those situations that do not create problems in order to build confidence that may generalize to problem situations.

Mildly Mentally Handicapped

Learning disabled and mildly retarded students are the largest groups of special students with which the regular classroom teachers work. Mental retardation refers to subaverage general intellectual functioning *with* accompanying deficits in adaptive behavior. To be classified as retarded, then, a child must have both a low IQ and difficulty adapting to social situations. In general, only mildly retarded children (IQ 50–70) are likely to be mainstreamed, not students with more severe mental limitations.

Ways in Which the Teacher Can Assist

1. Focus on a few basic skills. Be sure that assignments are highly relevant.
2. Provide concrete learning experiences as frequently as possible.
3. Present instruction in brief periods (5 to 10 minutes).
4. Provide frequent feedback and review.
5. Give simple, step-by-step directions.
6. Try to eliminate possible distractions.
7. Use curriculum materials that are appropriate to students' interests and reading levels.
8. Be alert to the fact that these students need more time to learn the same material.
9. After students have learned something, provide many practice/recall opportunities.
10. Do not repeatedly do things for these students that they should learn to do for themselves.

Behavior Disorders

A behaviorally disturbed student shows one or more of the following characteristics to a marked extent over a period of time:

1. Inability to learn that cannot be explained by intellectual inabilities or health problems.
2. Difficulty relating to peers and teachers.
3. Extreme behavioral reactions to normal events.
4. General moodiness or depression.
5. Frequent physical symptoms or fear associated with school problems.

Ways in Which the Teacher Can Assist

1. Verbalize to students the problems they present to the teacher or to other students (i.e., tell them gently but honestly why others react to them negatively).

2. Help students to dispel the delusion of uniqueness.
3. Model appropriate expression of emotions.
4. Stop misbehavior or emotionality before it becomes traumatic.
5. Develop firm behavioral expectations and clear managerial guidelines.
6. Provide praise when warranted and specify the praiseworthy behavior.
7. Set up places where these students can occasionally work alone.
8. Don't expect quick results or give up because you see little progress. These students' maladaptive behaviors were established over a long time period. It takes time to resocialize inappropriate behavior.

Orthopedic Handicaps

Orthopedic handicaps include defects of structure or function of bones, joints, and muscles. Such handicaps limit movement, but in the absence of other handicapping conditions, these students can learn the same material that nonhandicapped students of similar aptitude learn.

Ways in Which the Teacher Can Assist

1. Allow these students to do whatever they can for themselves.
2. Where necessary, allow them to leave the room a couple of minutes early to avoid crowded hallways.
3. Be alert to the fact that orthopedic shoes and other equipment are heavy and that it is hard work to move heavy equipment.
4. If the student is wearing orthopedic equipment, learn how it works and how to assist when simple malfunctions occur.
5. Be alert for safety problems (e.g., bad brakes on wheelchairs, worn crutch tips that will not provide stability on a slippery floor).

Learning Disabilities

The concept of learning disability is relatively new; learning disability programs were only introduced in the late 1960s. Students with learning disabilities have learning problems (usually language usage) that do *not* involve emotional disturbance, mental retardation, or visual or hearing impairment to a significant degree. Hence, the definition is somewhat ambiguous and circular. For a learning disability to be present, there must be a serious discrepancy between potential and actual performance, and *no other* impairment substantially associated with the deficit. For an illustration of how a learning disability might be manifested, see the case study presented in Table 25.1.

Ways in Which the Teacher Can Assist

1. Recognize that each student with a learning disability is likely to have unique problems.
2. Teach at the readiness level initially (not to the potential level).
3. Structure assignments that allow for immediate success.
4. Make brief assignments.

Table 25.1 Jim and Mark: A Study of Similarities and Differences

Jim	*Mark*
Age: 9 years	Age: 9 years
Grade: 3	Grade: 3
Years in school: 4½	Years in school: 4½
Reading achievement: 1.6 (grade equivalent)	Reading achievement: 1.6 (grade equivalent)
Group IQ score: 75	Group IQ score: 75

The preceding descriptions of Jim and Mark are obviously identical. However, their IQ scores, as indicated by an *individual* test of intelligence, are quite divergent:

Jim	Mark
Full-scale WISC IQ: 68	Full-scale WISC IQ: 102

The test indicates that Jim is very likely borderline EMR, and that Mark is probably learning disabled. Additional data are then gathered.

Jim	Mark
Arithmetic: 1.8 (grade equivalent)	Arithmetic: 3.2 (grade equivalent)

Generally, EMR students have basic skills in mathematics that are at about the same level as their reading skills, although sometimes they are higher if they mainly involve rote memory. In contrast, many learning disabled students who have severe problems in reading may do near grade-level work in mathematics as long as reading is not required. The reverse may also be true of learning disabled students; they may do satisfactory work in reading but have significant problems in mathematics. It is the inconsistency in performance among various academic areas and various types of activities that characterizes learning disabled students.

Additional information about the boys' abilities in classroom interaction, apparent ability to learn from peers, and ability to conceptualize follows:

Jim	Mark
In classroom interaction regarding relationships of planets and the sun, Jim had real difficulty following the idea of relative movement. He can follow class discussion as long as concepts are simple, but has difficulty making generalizations. Jim's speaking vocabulary is better than his reading vocabulary, but it is still far below the class average.	In classroom interaction regarding relationships of planets and the sun, Mark was one of the first in the class to understand. In most topics related to science, if no classroom reading is involved, Mark does very well. On a verbal level, he conceptualizes and generalizes well. Mark's reading vocabulary (words he can recognize in print) is no better than Jim's; however, his spoken vocabulary is up to the class average in all respects and is above-average in science areas.

Many learning disabled students have a performance profile (in such areas as reading achievement, arithmetic achievement, vocabulary, ability to generalize, and ability to conceptualize) that is characterized by many ups and downs. They sometimes (or in some academic areas) seem average or perhaps above average, but in some areas they may be even less able than some EMR students. It is possible for a learning disabled student to be low in *all* areas of achievement and class interaction, but this is unusual. In contrast, the performance profiles of EMR students are usually relatively flat.

Source: From B. Gearheart and M. Weishahn. *The Exceptional Student in the Regular Classroom,* 3rd ed. (St. Louis: Times Mirror/Mosby College Publishing, 1984). Copyright © 1984 Times Mirror/Mosby College Publishing. Reprinted by permission of Charles E. Merrill Publishing Company, Columbus, Ohio.

5. Review work with students frequently.
6. Observe closely and attempt to determine how each student learns best. Direct experiences and manipulative materials typically work well.
7. Frequently assess students' understanding to diagnose inappropriate

assignments as soon as possible (What was the story about? Tell me what you've read in your own words).

8. Give students plenty of time to respond. Processing information and searching for items in memory are usually difficult for learning disabled students. Typically, it is best to ask students a question and wait silently for a response. Repeating or rephrasing the question confuses such students.
9. If a student is on medication, find out the effects of the medication. If it causes excessive drowsiness or stimulation, see if the dosage can be adjusted.

Teaching Learning Disabled Students in the Secondary School

Many secondary teachers will teach students with learning disabilities. At the elementary school level, learning disability programs focus on remediation and building basic academic skills, especially in reading and mathematics. When possible, teachers also emphasize higher-order thinking skills, especially in the upper-elementary grades.

This trend should continue as students with learning disabilities move into secondary programs (Gearheart & Weishahn, 1984). Although some secondary students still need basic skill instruction, many will benefit from instruction that requires them to synthesize, generalize, and to apply information to everyday problems. Recognizing student differences in potential, Gearheart and Weishahn (1984) make the following recommendations for secondary teachers who work with learning disabled students:

Recommendations for working with students

1. For students who can express themselves orally but are unable to prepare orderly, well-conceived written reports, a carefully taped response to an assignment might be permitted.
2. If taped reports cannot be accepted, the teacher could agree to address the content of reports without regard to mechanics. Some sort of grading or evaluation system may be devised that, in effect, does not lead to failure because of mechanics but is based on the student's understanding of subject content. Students and their parents must understand and agree to such an arrangement and be told, preferably in writing, that the writing skills that the students do not have are deliberately not being evaluated. This should help prevent later claims by the student or parent that the student did not receive an effective education.
3. Peer tutors may be used in many ways and in a wide variety of subject areas.
4. Study-skill classes or sessions may be organized to help students explore alternate ways to identify, analyze, categorize, and recall information (Sheinker & Sheinker, 1982). Since some students have been exposed to only one major method of learning, and since the

learning disabled student is likely to require different learning styles and techniques, this method may pay big dividends.

5. Although by the secondary level it may be too late to emphasize basic reading skills (word attack skills and the like), it is not too late to teach students the need for different reading rates for different types of materials.
6. Other skills, such as preparing for tests, taking notes, and outlining, may be emphasized (Sheinker & Sheinker, 1982). The teacher may agree to provide a student with an outline of material to be learned in advance as a framework within which to organize study.
7. The teacher can provide the student and the resource room teacher with lists of critical new vocabulary words in advance so that the student may study them before presentation in class.
8. The teacher can notify the learning disabilities resource teacher of areas in which the student is falling behind, particularly those that will be essential in future learning (sequential or cumulative skills and information areas).

Keeping Handicaps in Perspective

Need for flexibility

We have just given a brief listing of some of the characteristics of handicapped students and the things teachers can do to help these students succeed in regular classrooms. It is worth stressing however, that one should not take these lists, or any other information about handicaps too literally or rigidly.

Remember, the characteristics listed for various types of handicapped students concern their *relative* abilities compared to other students and not absolute deficiencies or limitations. Also, few students who fit a particular handicap label have all or even most of the listed characteristics. A mildly mentally handicapped student, for example, may have generalized academic difficulty but not necessarily any problems with coordination, frustration tolerance, attention span, or social immaturity. In effect, then, such a student is no different from any other student who has difficulty keeping up with the class, except for the label "mildly mentally handicapped."

Neither should one overreact to the lists of ways that teachers can help. These are just a few representative suggestions, not a blueprint for solving special students' problems. The point here is that special students probably are best served if teachers view them essentially as regular students with special needs. The following suggestions for dealing with students with visual handicaps illustrate this point (Dunn, 1973):

1. Be alert to the behavioral signs and physical symptoms of visual difficulties in all students. Be sure that proper referrals are made and that everything possible is done to correct or ameliorate the problems.
2. Accept and provide for a wide range of individual differences on many dimensions, of which vision is just one.

3. View visual limitation as only one difficulty, and not the most important characteristic of the student. Do not let the handicap become the central focus in the student's life. Do not allow handicapped students to exploit their visual limitations to get inappropriate special treatment, and do not exploit them by "showing them off" to classroom visitors. As much as possible, treat them the same as you treat other students.
4. Make visually limited students "your own" as much as other students. Do not consider them as belonging to the residential school, the resource teacher, or the itinerant teacher. Get help from these special resource people, but do not expect them to reteach what should have been taught in the regular classroom, and do not let the student play one teacher against another.
5. When in doubt, regular classroom teachers should do what they would consider to be best for any student.

Individual Educational Programs

Public Law 94-142 requires that an Individual Educational Program (IEP) be designed to meet each handicapped student's unique needs. The IEP should describe the student's present educational performance, short-term learning goals, and annual learning goals. It also should specify the amount of time the student will spend in the regular classroom, which teacher is responsible for which objectives, and how the student's progress will be evaluated. Once a student has been formally referred for special education services, a placement committee is formed to write the initial IEP and to continue to supervise the student's progress for as long as special education services are provided. The membership of such committees varies from state to state, but the core committee is likely to include the teachers who will instruct the student, the principal, the person who evaluates the student (a school psychologist or social worker), and when possible or feasible, a parent and the student.

Responsibilities of IEP committee

The committee typically has the following responsibilities: (1) obtaining information about the student, (2) assessing the student's needs for special education, (3) developing the IEP, (4) evaluating the special services, and (5) making sure that prescribed procedures are followed to protect the rights of students and their parents. The latter includes ensuring due process with regard to keeping the parents and the student fully informed about and included in decision making, assurance of confidentiality about records, recognition of the student's right to be represented by a parent or guardian, assessment with nondiscriminatory instruments presented in the student's native language, and commitment to the principle of placing the student in the least restrictive environment feasible under the circumstances.

Assessment procedure

The assessment procedures used by the placement committee should be complete and wide-ranging, with input from several sources. This is a major departure from previous procedures in which a diagnostician administered a few tests, wrote a report, and made recommendations on the basis of the results. Table 25.2 shows the variety of information sources that can be drawn upon and the rationale for their use.

Table 25.2 Sources and Uses of Information

Source	Rationale for Use
1. Referral Forms	Information contained on referral forms, if well stated, can be used to form hypotheses concerning what other kinds of information may be needed, the criteria for acceptable performance, and the perspective of the person(s) making the referral.
2. School Records	Inspection of cumulative and other available records can be helpful in determining whether or not there are factors that might help to account for the reason for referral, whether or not there seem to be any trends in problem growth, and whether other areas seem to be in need of closer evaluation.
3. Standardized Tests	Standardized tests may be used to obtain information on how one child compares with other children. In many cases, standardized tests are required for determination of eligibility. These types of tests cover such areas as intelligence, achievement, and personality.
4. Developmental Scales	These scales compare areas of child development within the child and as compared with other children. They are especially useful with younger or more severely handicapped children, pinpointing both strengths and weaknesses.
5. Criterion-Referenced Tests	This type of test places the child at a certain level in some area of skill development. It is especially helpful for planning purposes because criterion statements can be used as goals for instruction.
6. Observation	Observational data can focus on a very specific child characteristic, such as a child's interaction with other children, and can point out areas in need of further evaluation and confirm or disconfirm other information. Observations may be formal or informal and include such things as anecdotal records, interaction analysis, checklists, and rating scales. These observations may take place in any setting, including the home. Observational data are best obtained by those who are close to the child in his/her normal environment.
7. Interviews	Interviews with the parent, the child, and/or the teacher yield information which lends perspective to other kinds of information. They also pinpoint areas that may be priority needs or strengths.
8. Work Samples	Work samples are similar to criterion-referenced testing; they provide information concerning the level of the child in some area of skill development. They are useful in planning intervention in academic areas.
9. Consultants	Consultants may provide information that is not usually available to an educational planner. This may include medical, therapeutic, and family information and may be used to plan services in related areas, define limitations on other planning, or identify areas of major need.

Evaluation and integration of recommendations

The placement committee is charged not merely with following recommendations but with evaluating and integrating them. Student evaluations and reports are to be judged on such criteria as the following:

- ☐ Is the report written in understandable language?
- ☐ Are the tools or processes used for evaluation identified?
- ☐ Is the setting described in which the evaluation occurred?
- ☐ Does the evaluation contain concise statements of specific results?
- ☐ Are problem areas identified by the evaluation procedure specified?
- ☐ Are problem areas identified by behavioral observations specified?
- ☐ Does the report contain concise statements of strengths and weaknesses?
- ☐ Is the information relevant to educational planning?
- ☐ Does the report describe conditions that influence ability to perform tasks?

Thus, the committee evaluates the source and quality of available information in addition to taking the information into account in trying to decide what is best for the student. Only after assessing all of this information and integrating it with input from the participants does the placement committee prepare the actual IEP.

Early experience with placement committees indicated that they were usually composed of the individuals who were supposed to be involved, but that most of the activity was initiated by school administrators, school psychologists, or other specialists. Classroom teachers, parents, and students usually played more passive roles. This will probably change as the procedures become more familiar and as teachers become more confident of their own abilities to judge what is best for special students. For example, Ysseldyke, Algozzine, and Allen (1981) found that classroom teachers' participation in special education team meetings varied considerably (it averaged 27 percent, but the range was from 3 percent to 82 percent). After studying team decision making, they concluded that the approach teams take should become more formalized and standardized. They recommend that team meetings follow these steps:

Team meetings

1. The purpose of the meeting should be stated at the beginning and a statement should be made expressing the value and need for alternative opinions and data.
2. An agenda should be prepared and followed.
3. Information regarding the problem should be solicited from each team member. It should be expected that corroborative evidence will be sought and that teachers' perceptions of students' strengths and weaknesses in the classroom are as useful as psychometric data.
4. Any decision should represent a consensus of team members.

Developing a successful IEP

Figure 25.1 illustrates an IEP that follows both the spirit and the letter of the law and seems likely to help in organizing school resources to meet the needs of the student appropriately. As you first examine the program, it may seem deceptively simple, but bear in mind that the development of

Figure 25.1 A Typical Individual Education Program

INDIVIDUAL EDUCATION PROGRAM

Child's Name Frank West **Date Referred to Committee** March 2

School Crescent Point High School

SUMMARY OF PRESENT LEVELS OF PERFORMANCE

Frank wants to stay in school. He recognizes that his reading ability is low and he wants to learn to read. Teacher observations and test scores indicate that he has a basic understanding of the concepts and operations of fundamental mathematics. He has the ability to follow through on assignments which interest him. He experiences the most difficulty when he is asked to do school work which he doesn't understand or is presently incapable of doing. He is extremely unhappy in the self-contained classroom and does not associate with his classmates. He looked forward to being placed in a "regular" classroom but he has trouble controlling his anger when he can't do the required work. He does independent reading (e.g., newspapers and sports books). Teachers and school personnel often view his behavior as inappropriate for school. This has resulted in numerous suspensions.

PRIORITIZED LONG-TERM GOALS

(1) Frank will improve in his reading ability.
(2) Frank will experience success in the regular classroom.
(3) Frank will be given the opportunity to explore a range of career alternatives.
(4) Frank will develop positive relationships with peers and teachers.
(5) Frank will become more of a participant and less of a spectator in areas of interest.

(Continued on next page)

Figure 25.1 (continued)

Short-Term Objectives	Special Education and Related Services	Person Responsible	Beginning and Ending Dates	Review Date
(1) Design a reading program building on Frank's areas of interest:				
A. Develop sightword vocabulary builders using the newspaper and sports books.	EMR teacher/ support from remedial reading teacher/ supplemental materials	EMR teacher	March 7 June 1	May 1
OBJECTIVE: improve Frank's sight word vocabulary by 25%				
B. Using math word problems designed to incorporate new vocabulary words. Frank will improve in his ability to deal with math word problems.	EMR teacher/ supplemental materials	math teacher	March 7 June 1	May 1
C. An independent reading list based on occupational opportunities will be developed. Frank will read and discuss such materials.				
D. Frank will be encouraged to report on independent reading to his teacher–later to his peers.	EMR teacher	EMR teacher	March 15 June 1	May 15
(2) Frank will remain in the regular math class.				
A. Teacher will design sequential math materials building on Frank's strengths.	math teacher/ math supervisor	math teacher	March 7 June 1	May 15
OBJECTIVE: Frank will experience academic success.				
B. Shop teacher will design math problems in that content area. Frank will be allowed to experience finishing a project from the conceptual stage through completion.		shop teacher	March 7 June 1	May 15
C. Frank will be enrolled in an intramural or PE program.	P.E.	P.E. instructor	March 7 June 1	May 15

(3) Frank will spend two hours per week for three weeks with the vocational counselor discussing his readings in job opportunities.	EMR teacher	vocational counselor	March 30 June 1	April 20
(4) Frank will assume increasing amounts of responsibility for his own learning as evidenced by his willingness to complete required projects and seek help from teachers.	EMR teacher	all of Frank's teachers	March 7 June 1	May 15

PLACEMENT DECISIONS

Frank will remain in EMR class for reading and language arts. He will attend a regular math class, shop class, and be enrolled in a P.E. class.

PERCENT OF TIME IN REGULAR CLASSROOM
50%

FOR THE COMMITTEE, RECOMMENDATIONS FOR SPECIFIC PROCEDURES/TECHNIQUES, MATERIALS, INFORMATION ABOUT LEARNING STYLE, ETC.

Frank's basic strength lies in the fact that he recognizes his weakness in reading and that he wants to stay in school. It is extremely important that he be allowed to experience success in an academic setting.

CRITERIA FOR EVALUATION OF ANNUAL GOALS

(1) Reading and math will be evaluated on the basis of teacher test and standardized test.
(2) Social behavior will be based on staff observations and Frank's observations as well as suspensions.
(3) Relations with teachers and peers (most likely dependent upon academic success) will be based on observations.

Committee Members Present

____
____
____
____
____

Dates of Meetings

____
____
____

a successful plan involves a great deal of data gathering, resolution of differences in opinion and interpretation, compromise, and careful planning. Note the array of specific recommendations, each of which includes identification of the person responsible, specification of the time required, and provision for review and possible revision of the recommendation if it does not seem to be appropriate.

Research on Mainstreaming

In the past few years there have been numerous studies and reviews of the effects of mainstreaming children. We will discuss some of this research here.

Thompson, White, and Morgan (1982) studied teacher-student interaction patterns in 12 third-grade mainstreamed classrooms, focusing their observations on four groups of students: (1) nonhandicapped high achievers, (2) nonhandicapped low achievers, (3) learning disabled students, and (4) behaviorally handicapped students.

Thompson et al. conducted this study because mainstreaming programs had been implemented throughout the United States without an adequate data base describing how teachers and handicapped students interact in such settings. Many individuals had predicted that students would be hurt rather than helped by mainstreaming. For example, some special educators were concerned that mainstreamed students might be ignored in the classroom, or face more criticism, or receive less serious teaching. Thus, these students' social comparisons to other students would be negative in that handicapped students would be less likely to develop positive self-concepts and to achieve in the classroom (see, for example, Larsen, 1975).

Teacher-student interaction patterns

Thompson et al. found that teacher-student interaction patterns did vary among the four groups observed; however, they found no strong evidence that general preferential treatment or treatment likely to result in better educational gain was consistently provided to any single group of students. They did find that behaviorally handicapped students in mainstreamed settings received a larger proportion of teacher time than did other students.

Voeltz (1982) reports data showing that the acceptance of regular-education pupils in Grades 4 through 6 of peers with severe handicaps can be positively affected by direct experiences with severely handicapped students, especially when regular students receive social interaction training that enables them to interact more sensitively and knowledgeably with handicapped peers.

Leinhardt (1980) studied the effects of assigning poor-prognosis first-grade students to separate transition classrooms, and compared the effects of this strategy with giving similar children instruction in regular classrooms. She also examined the effectiveness of an individualized reading program (NRS) for instructing low-performance students in beginning reading skills.

Her data suggest that low-performance students learn to read better in regular instructional settings and under the NRS program. She argues that these results are most likely due to two factors. First, the individualized program provided teachers with strategies and tools for teaching heterogeneous students. Second, students in regular classroom settings received substantially more reading instruction than their counterparts in transition rooms.

Stipek and Sanborn (1983) observed teacher-child interactions in two preschool programs. In particular, they noted the interactions of teachers with mainstreamed handicapped children and children perceived by their teachers as "high risk" academic problems. Stipek and Sanborn found that teachers offered unrequested assistance and praise to the handicapped and high-risk children more than to nonhandicapped children.

These authors suggest that the frequency of teacher-initiated interactions with handicapped and high-risk children may have important implications for these children's socialization into a formal achievement setting. By initiating the majority of interactions with these children, teachers established a relationship in which the teachers controlled and structured the environment, and the children perhaps learned to play a passive role. That is, the students did not need to seek information or assistance because teachers offered it to them.

Teachers who teach mainstreamed students need to guard against being overly critical and demanding of the students because they have some difficulty in learning, but they also need to realize that they can do too much for these students. Students have to initiate and learn on their own as well as respond to teacher structuring.

Madden and Slavin (1983) reviewed research on the effects of placing students with mild academic handicaps in full-time special education classrooms, in part-time regular classes with resource support, or in full-time regular classes. They conclude that research favors placement in regular classrooms using individualized instruction or regular instruction supplemented by well-designed resource programs to improve the achievement, self-esteem, behavior, and emotional adjustment of academically handicapped students. They found no consistent benefits of full-time special education for important outcomes.

Need for needs of all students to be met

Madden and Slavin contend that the effects of mainstreamed classrooms on nonhandicapped students need to be assessed. It would be counterproductive to improve the achievement or social emotional adjustment of academically handicapped students at the expense of the achievement of nonhandicapped students or vice versa. They conclude that available evidence suggests that methods that are effective for mildly academically handicapped students are at least as effective as traditional methods for teaching nonhandicapped students. They argue that the most effective mainstreaming approaches are those that recognize that all students are special and have unique social and academic needs and that classroom organization must be responsive to the needs of all students.

SUMMARY

In the past, students with special needs were placed in special institutions or classes. However, data on the effectiveness of special settings and programs are unimpressive, so the current trend is toward retaining special students in regular classrooms. Problems in diagnosis, the reliability and validity of classifications and their treatment implications, the negative effects of labeling, and various legal changes have all contributed to this trend. Public Law 94-142, which became effective in the Fall of 1977, commits the nation to a policy of mainstreaming handicapped students.

Teachers working with special students need to shed their stereotypes and recognize the many similarities of these students to their peers. They should prepare themselves to capitalize on special students' strengths, prepare other students to interact constructively with them, deal realistically and matter-of-factly with handicaps, and establish appropriate positive expectations.

Data indicate the presence in the school age population of the following percentages of handicapped students: visually impaired, 0.1; hearing impaired, 0.6 to 0.8; speech impaired, 3.5 to 5.0; crippled and health impaired, 0.5; emotionally retarded, 2.5 to 3.0; mentally retarded, 2.5 to 3.0; and learning disabilities, 2.0 to 4.0. Pupils in each category have special needs with important implications for teachers. The law requires that an Individual Education Program (IEP) designed to meet a student's unique needs be planned for each handicapped student. The program should describe present educational performance, short-term learning goals, and annual learning goals.

QUESTIONS AND PROBLEMS

1. How far can ordinary public schools go in striving to meet the ideal of free public education for all? Specifically, what categories of students, if any, should be excluded from public schools? Why? How? Who should decide, and on what basis?
2. Considering the grade level and subject matter you expect to teach, what special provisions will you need to make for handicapped students (special teaching techniques, substitute assignments, special tests)? For blind students? Deaf students? Paraplegics?
3. How can conflict or disagreements among participants in an IEP meeting (principal, diagnostician, special-education teacher, classroom teachers, parents) be resolved in the best interests of the student? What should be done if there is no consensus?
4. What, if anything, should a teacher say about mainstreamed students to classroom visitors like parent volunteers, observers from a college of education, PTA representatives, and so on?
5. The need for special provisions for the physically handicapped is usually obvious to everyone. But what about students with emotional or behavioral disorders? Should these students sometimes be exempted from demands or given special privileges? If so, how should this be explained to classmates?
6. What are the advantages for regular students of having mainstreamed students in the classroom?

Special Teaching Techniques. Dan Jones and Don Martin are the two most disruptive students in Joyce Putnam's class. Both are often out of their seats, are unable to concentrate on their work for long, frequently get into fights and arguments with classmates, and resist Joyce's authority. Dan has been diagnosed as hyperactive and takes Ritalin. Don does not take medication, but he has been diagnosed as emotionally disturbed, with poor impulse control and frequent inappropriate affect. How should Joyce deal with these two boys? Specifically, what special techniques or procedures should she use? Should her approach be essentially the same with both boys, or are there things she should do with one but not the other?

Moving Forward. Sam had done terribly during the first two weeks of school. His work was poor, especially his seatwork. At times, it seemed like Sam was doing an assignment other than the one that Ms. Murphy had put on the board. Yesterday Sam had gotten into trouble several times for talking with Molly, the attractive girl seated next to him. Today he had done all his seatwork perfectly. Ms. Murphy wondered if the move to the front of the room near her had helped Sam. What are possible reasons for Sam's improved performance? What should Ms. Murphy do to confirm her diagnosis?

Part Eight

Measurement and Evaluation

There is presently a great deal of interest in improving school and teacher performance through more testing of both teachers and students. In some states teachers must pass exams before they are certified. More and more states are requiring students at selected grade levels to pass achievement tests mandated by the state. Tests can be important indicants of performance and can be very helpful in improving the quality of instruction. However, as Frederiksen (1984) argues, tests influence teacher and student performance. Furthermore, most tests (e.g., multiple-choice tests) assess knowledge that is easy to measure and do not measure more complex and perhaps more important cognitive abilities. As a classroom teacher, you will likely face increasing pressure to test students in the next few years, and part of your success as a teacher will depend on your ability to determine whether or not a test is related to important instructional goals. You must not allow testing to dictate the curriculum in inappropriate ways.

Although there has long been an interest in evaluating student achievement, teacher evaluation is relatively new. For an unusually detailed discussion of the techniques of teacher evaluation and some of the issues involved, see the *Handbook of Teacher Evaluation* (Millman, 1981).

Measuring and evaluating student performance is an important part of a teacher's professional responsibility. Let us assume that you are a teacher who has decided to state your grading criteria at the beginning of the school year. You pass out a sheet listing a group of tests, totaling 500 credit points. Everyone who gets 450 points (90 percent) or more will get an "A," those getting between 400 and 449 points will get a "B," and so on down the scale.

This plan seems fair and sensible, but what if at the end of the term you find that test scores are extremely high? If so, you face one of two possible results:

1. If you follow your plan, over 50 percent of the students will get an

"A." However, you now realize your tests were much too easy. You are sure, based on questions and comments and on class discussion, that many of the students with more than 450 points did not really learn much of the material.

2. Over 50 percent of your students should get an "A." In this case students' grades match your other information. The tests were of an appropriate level of difficulty and measured mastery of key concepts and skills. Student behavior in the classroom indicated general interest in and knowledge about the subject matter, and there was no evidence of cheating or other reasons for artificially high grades.

What might you do in these situations, and what implications might there be for you and your students? What about the opposite situation, with point totals discouragingly low, where more than 50 percent of your students will get "Fs"?

1. You realize that your expectations were unrealistic, and your test questions were too difficult or too tricky. Even your best students, who gave every evidence of interest and understanding in class discussions and activities, had difficulty with the tests. You discounted student complaints that the tests were difficult. But the tests were given, and the scores are recorded. Now what?
2. In a contrasting situation, scores are very low, but this time you have no reason to question test difficulty. The questions were drawn directly from classroom presentations and assigned readings, and there were no tricky questions. You have every reason to believe that your tests were fair and valid, but your students nevertheless did poorly. Your observations suggest that lack of motivation was the reason. Students were not studying very hard, if at all, and did not learn much. Now what?

Information that will help you to avoid such dilemmas is presented in the following chapters on basic measurement (Chapter 26), statistical concepts (Chapter 27), and sound test construction (Chapter 28). Finally, in Chapter 29 we discuss principles for grading students fairly, even when the information available is less than ideal.

Chapter 26

Principles of Educational Measurement

OBJECTIVES

When you have mastered the material in this chapter you will be able to

1. Explain the concept of measurement error, and how the standard error of measurement can be used to interpret and accurately report test scores
2. Define test reliability and explain how one can use correlation coefficients or the standard error of measurement to express test reliability
3. Discuss the importance of high test reliability and the factors that can affect the reliability of a test
4. Explain content and criterion validity of tests, and the factors that can decrease test validity
5. Define norm-referenced and criterion-referenced tests and explain how to distinguish them
6. Explain how questions for norm-referenced tests are selected, how such tests are "normed," and their usefulness to both teachers and students
7. State principles for the selection and effective use of standardized, norm-referenced achievement tests

Assessment and evaluation of students' progress in mastering the curriculum are basic tasks of teaching. Most teachers must collect some systematic achievement data to provide a basis for grading, but even teachers who are not required to assign formal grades still need to assess student achievement in order to gather feedback about the effectiveness of their own teaching, to identify topics and individual students that require additional instruction, and to provide guidance for planning new instruction.

Informal assessment

Teachers do much of this assessment informally in the process of observing students' attention to lessons and engagement in assignments, monitoring their answers to questions during class activities, and correcting their written assignments. This kind of informal assessment is very important, but it is subjective and thus open to the influences of teacher expectations and attitudes and other biasing sources. It also is usually unsystematic: teachers monitor certain students much more closely than others (e.g., see Marshall & Weinstein, 1984); some students have learned to "look good" during class activities and to get help with their written assignments, so that they appear to have mastered much more material than they really have; some will make generally good progress but consistently make certain kinds of mistakes because they do not know a key concept or lack a skill, deficiencies that are not obvious from casual daily observation. Consequently, it is important to supplement informal monitoring with formal assessment that measures student achievement under standardized conditions.

Curricula are composed of strands or sequences that build toward terminal objectives describing the knowledge or skills that students are expected to master. Occasionally these objectives are limited and specific, as in the requirement that the student be able to name all the letters of the alphabet without error or run a hundred meters within a time limit. Usually, however, objectives are more sweeping and ambitious—we want students to be able to express their thoughts in acceptable prose (spelling, grammar, and other mechanics; good paragraphing and organization generally) or to apply basic mathematical principles and facts in everyday situations (computing the best bargain, estimating how much wallpaper to purchase for a room). Here it is not feasible to test students on every possible application of what they have learned, or even to test them on everything they have been taught. This is unnecessary, and too time consuming in any case. Therefore, we sample students' knowledge or skills by requiring them to perform a few tasks selected from among the key terminal objectives in the curriculum sequences recently taught.

Errors of Measurement

Formal measurement

Formal measurement situations involve standardized conditions. Students are required to respond to the same set of questions or tasks, or to equivalent forms that measure the same items of knowledge or skills. Ideally, all students are measured under standard conditions: they are instructed in the same ways (in general, but with individual attention as needed) and tested at the same time and under the same conditions (time limits, permission to use a book or other aids such as calculators). In general, everything is arranged to ensure that each student's score accurately represents his or her level of mastery.

Inaccuracy of test scores

In practice, of course, test scores are not so accurate. First, recall that the test itself is just a sample of the full range of things that students have been taught. Any particular test favors certain students because of differences in what they learned originally or in what they emphasized in preparing for the test. Second, a great variety of situational factors affects the performance of individual students. Those who are well prepared, well rested, and able to concentrate on the test will do their best. Others, however, will lose points because of factors that may be beyond their control: they did not get a good night's sleep, they were physically ill or emotionally stressed on the day of the exam or when they were studying for it, and so on.

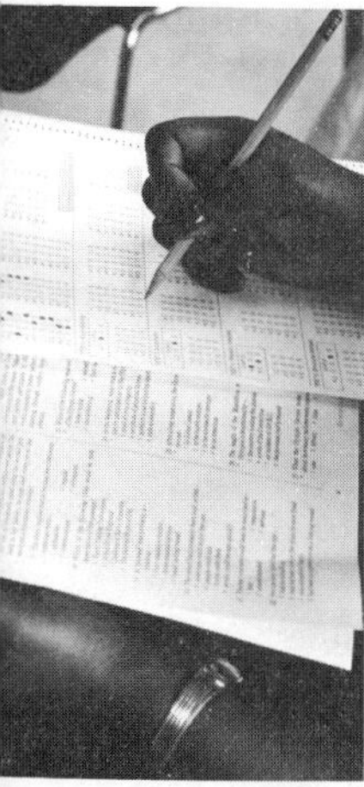

al measurement of g skills.

Because of such factors, test scores are just estimates of students' true levels of mastery. They can be thought of as composed of two parts: true level of mastery and an artificial increment or decrement reflecting sampling errors (a different set of items would have yielded a different score) or situational factors (a student would have scored differently if tested at another time or under other circumstances). Along with other factors to be described later, these sampling errors and situational factors contribute to the measurement error that exists to some degree in almost any set of test scores. This is represented in the following equation:

$$\text{Test score} = \text{true score plus or minus measurement error}$$

The degree of measurement error distorting any particular student's test score cannot be determined precisely, but the measurement error associated with any particular test or measurement device can at least be estimated from information about the test's reliability (the concept of reliability is discussed below). This estimate for any particular test is called the test's standard error of measurement. The higher the standard error, the less accurate the test. The degree of error in educational measurement is usually larger than it is for measurement of height, weight, or other physical factors, because educational measurement is less direct, relies on less precise instruments, and applies to knowledge and skills that are themselves less stable than physical factors (Mehrens & Lehmann, 1978).

Standard error of measurement

For most IQ tests, the standard error is about 5 points. Therefore, if a students gets a score of 105, we can be reasonably confident that the true IQ is somewhere between 100 and 110 (assuming that there is such a thing as a true IQ score), but we cannot assume that it is exactly 105. Nor can we confidently assume that the student has more aptitude than another who scores 102 or less than one who scores 108. The test is just not that precise. Similar considerations apply to interpreting a standardized achievement score that "places" a student at a "grade level" of 6.8 or implies that the student has achieved more than precisely 63 percent of all the students at the same grade level.

Distribution of standard error

Errors of measurement are assumed to be distributed randomly with respect to individuals' true scores, so that repeated measurements theoretically would yield a normal curve distributed on either side of the true score (the normal curve is explained in detail in the next chapter). Use of the probability statistics associated with normal curves allows us to use band interpretation of test scores when we know a test's standard error of measurement. Thus, in the example above, we can say that we are 68 percent certain that the student who scored 105 has a true IQ between 100 and 110 (plus or minus one standard error from the obtained score of 105), and 95 percent certain that the true IQ is between 95 and 115 (plus or minus two standard errors).

Test Reliability

A test's standard error of measurement varies inversely with its reliability: reliable tests have low standard errors and thus allow more precise measurement and more confident interpretation. Reliability refers to the stability or consistency of test scores across repeated measurements. A reliable test should yield similar results when administered two or more times during a short period (a few weeks) to the same students. Students who obtain high scores the first time should obtain similar scores the second time, and so on.

Correlation Coefficients

Reliability is estimated using correlation methods, and expressed numerically with correlation coefficients that vary from −1.00 through zero to +1.00. There are several kinds of correlation coefficients computed with various formulas that will not be reviewed here (for detailed discussions of reliability, see Kubiszyn & Borich, 1984; Mehrens & Lehmann, 1978; Cronbach et al., 1972; or Stanley, 1971). All of them, however, vary from −1.00 to +1.00, and indicate the direction and strength of the relationship, if any, between two sets of scores.

The symbol *r*

The symbol *r* stands for the correlation coefficient. When *r* is positive, there is a positive correlation between the two sets of scores, so that individuals high on one measure are likely to be high on the other. When *r* is negative, there is an inverse relation (negative correlation) between the two sets of scores, and individuals high on one measure are likely to be low on the other. When *r* is zero, there is no correlation at all between the two sets of scores, so individuals' scores on the first measure give us no information at all about their probable scores on the second measure. Some typical correlations illustrating these relationships are shown below.

Measures	r
Two equivalent forms of the same test	.95
IQ subtest score and total IQ score	.70
Adult heights and weights	.60
High school and college grade point average	.50
Socioeconomic status and IQ	.35
Height and IQ	.05
Date of appearance of first tooth and college grade point average	.00
Family size and school achievement	−.30
Frequency of serious classroom disruptions and student achievement	−.40
Scores on a test of achievement and a checklist of learning deficiencies	−.80

The correlation coefficients expressing a test's reliability must be quite high (at least .70 and preferably over .90) for the test to be reliable enough to be useful for confident measurement and decision making. Figure 26.1 shows scatterplots of hypothetical students' scores on two administrations of the same ten-item test. Notice that where there is a perfect positive relationship (r = 1.00), each student gets the same score on both occasions. However, where r = .75, most scores vary a point or two, and many vary by three or even four points. Where r = .50, there are more frequent and larger differences, which severely limit the usefulness of the test. Reliability is low, the standard error of measurement is high, and scores cannot be interpreted with much precision. Differences of four or five points between students are probably real, but differences of a point or two are probably just measurement error.

Importance of Reliability

Unreliable tests are not only imprecise, they are unfair to students. When scores vary like those shown in Figure 26.1, where r = .50, or worse yet, where r = .35 or .00, there is probably something wrong with most of the items, and students' answers are shaped by factors other than the knowledge or skills presumably being tested. Items probably are ambiguous, misleading, unrelated to what was taught, or otherwise inappropriate.

Item level reliability

A highly reliable test is reliable even at the item level, not just for total scores (see Baker, 1977, or Kubiszyn & Borich, 1984, for detailed information about item analysis). Thus, if John Smith got the first seven items and items nine and ten correct the first time, but missed item eight and items eleven through fifteen, he should have the same or a very similar pattern of correct and incorrect answers the second time he takes the test. This assumes, of course, that John has not received any additional instruction between testings, and that he has not sought answers to the questions he missed.

Reliability in the sense of consistency of scores across long time periods when the same students are retested with the same test is not of particular importance in education. This is because education by its very nature in-

Figure 26.1 Scattergrams of Correlations of Various Sizes Between Sets of Scores on the Same Ten-Item Test (N = 50 students)

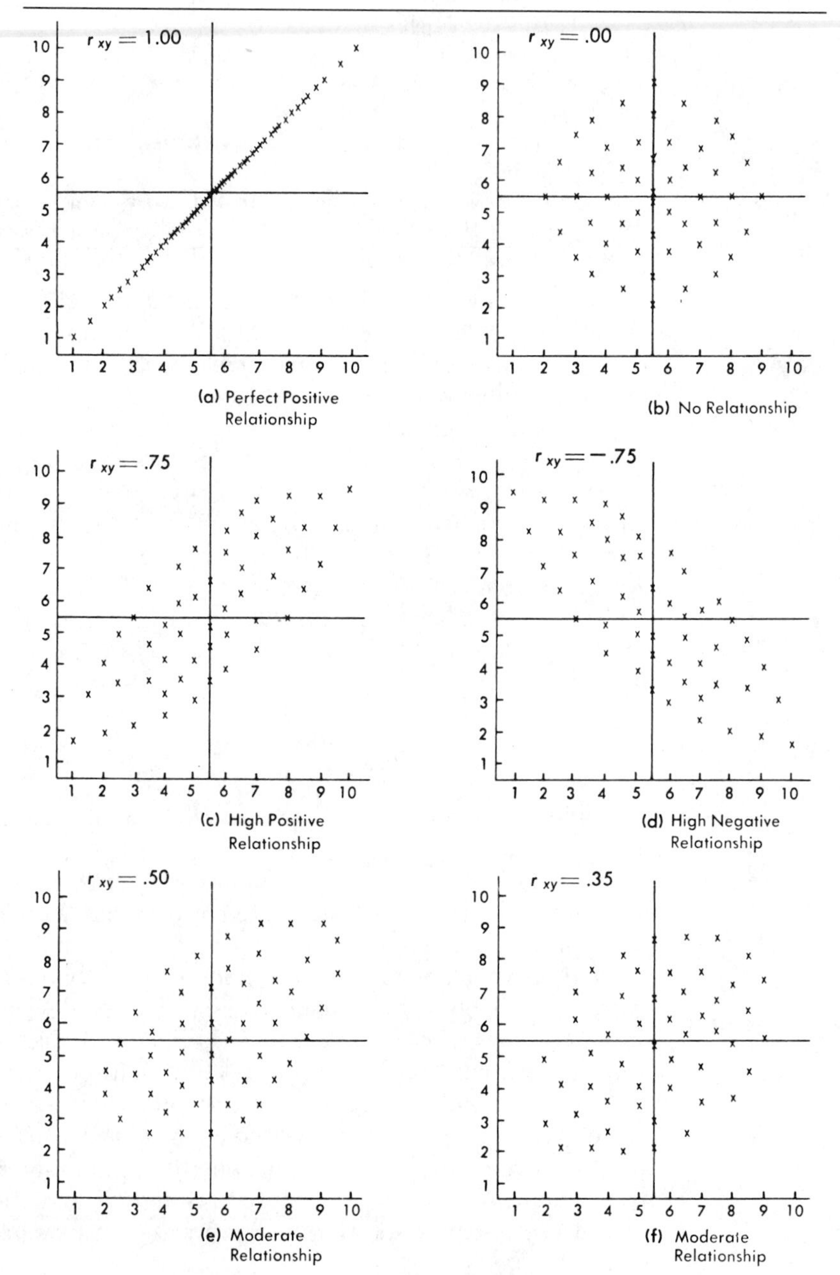

Source: W. Mehrens and I. Lehmann, *Measurement and Evaluation in Education and Psychology*, 2nd ed. (New York: Holt, Rinehart and Winston, 1978), p. 84. Copyright © 1978 by Holt, Rinehart, and Winston. Reprinted by permission of CBS College Publishing.

volves change, specifically the attempt to increase students' knowledge and skills. Thus, over a long period, we ordinarily do not expect reliability for repeated performance on the same test.

However, good tests should have the kind of short-term reliability that comes with well-constructed test items. Other factors that affect reliability include (Mehrens & Lehmann, 1978; Kubiszyn & Borich, 1984):

1. *Test length*—Other things being equal, a longer test is more reliable than a shorter one because it involves a larger sample of the knowledge or skill objectives taught.
2. *Heterogeneity of the student group*—Reliability tends to be higher when scores are spread out over a large range because measurement errors are small in comparison to the range of differences between true scores.
3. *Item difficulty*—Reliability is higher when most items are of medium difficulty for the group tested because this spreads the scores out over a greater range, in comparison to scores that would be obtained if most items were either too easy or too hard.
4. *Objectivity of scoring*—The reliability of tests that can be scored objectively tends to be higher because with subjective scoring, equivalent student performance might be scored differently because of differences in scorers' judgments at various times, even if the scorer is the same person.

Reliability is only one of the attributes of a good test, however. An even more basic attribute is validity. Reliability is a precondition for validity in the sense that a test cannot be valid if it is not reliable. However, validity involves several considerations in addition to reliability.

Test Validity

At the most basic level, a test is said to be valid if it measures what it is supposed to measure. Some tests are not valid for anything, because they are composed of items that are poorly constructed or completely inappropriate for the student population. Other tests are valid for some purposes but not for others. For example, a very good test of mastery of the spelling curriculum in a particular fourth-grade spelling program is less valid for measuring fourth-grade spelling mastery by students taught with a different curriculum, still less valid for measuring spelling mastery by students in adjacent grades, and invalid for measuring student mastery of curriculum areas other than spelling.

Specialists in test construction talk about many different kinds of validity, but of these, content validity and criterion validity are the most important for teachers. Content validity concerns the degree to which test content is drawn from the specific curriculum being tested. Except for special situations, such as tests of creative ability or of the degree to which skills

Content validity

learned in a specific context will generalize, test content should be limited to knowledge and skills actually taught to the students.

Tests that are valid in other ways but lack content validity usually are described as "unfair." This means that the results may be accurate, that is, the students' scores reflect their relative mastery of the content of the test, but misleading. If the test is composed of many items dealing with matters not taught in school, but learned unsystematically in other experiences, it will measure neither student ability nor student achievement. Instead, it probably measures combinations of things like student SES, test-taking and guessing abilities, and differences in reading rates and preferences.

Criterion validity

Criterion validity is the degree to which scores on a test predict (correlate with) performance on other criteria, particularly behavioral ones. Criterion validity becomes more important as attention shifts from mastery of specific knowledge and skills toward attempts to measure probable success in generalizing or applying these skills. In a driver-education course, it is important that students show mastery of the knowledge taught in the course by scoring well on knowledge tests, but it is even more important that they apply this knowledge when they actually drive.

Even tests that have good reliability and content validity may have poor criterion validity. In fact, this is one of the implications of recent investigations of fundamental skills in the population at large, studied in national assessment research sponsored by the government as well as in several smaller research projects. These studies indicate that many high school students cannot apply basic language arts and math skills, even though they can pass certain tests or seatwork exercises that measure knowledge of these skills in isolation from one another. For example, many students have difficulty communicating clearly even in short essays. Run-on sentences and spelling, capitalization, and punctuation errors are common.

Similarly, many high school students had difficulty with such seemingly simple math tasks as computing the cost of items on a grocery list, determining the amount of change that should be returned to a shopper, or converting decimals to percentages. Paragraphs explaining in simple language the gist of laws protecting consumers against impulse buying were a mystery to most readers sampled, and only a small percentage could follow the kinds of complex instructions involved in filling out income tax forms. Students do appear to be making progress in some areas but tests show that there are still some major problems. (For an especially good review of mathematical areas where students do well and poorly, see Carpenter, et al., 1984.)

Competency in basic skills

These and other data have led increasing numbers of people to conclude that schools are doing a poor job of teaching basic "life" skills. If criterion validity is given primary weight in judging education, and if preparing students to perform practical, everyday tasks is a basic criterion, this negative conclusion is justified. Student scores on a variety of national assessment measures kept slipping throughout the 1960s and 1970s (see, for example, Harnischfeger & Wiley, 1976), although there is some evidence to suggest that test performance has started to increase again. Still, the number of high school graduates who are unable to apply fundamental math and language concepts seems unreasonably large, and average student performance on standardized measures is less than it was a decade ago (Stedman & Smith, 1983). Such performance has led to the imposition of competency tests (performance criteria) that must be passed as a condition of awarding high school diplomas in several states. Students who cannot pass these tests after several tries are given a certificate of attendance, but not a diploma that indicates successful completion of requirements.

Threats to Validity

The validity of a test is reduced by anything that reduces the degree to which the test measures what it is supposed to measure. This is most obvious in the case of lack of content validity. Tests are unfair and inappropriate to the extent that they include material that was not taught or assigned. However, even tests with content validity can be invalid for other reasons.

One large category of threats to test validity includes test-taking skills, writing skills, ability to work efficiently under time pressure, and related individual differences. These skills are not specific to the subject matter, but they affect test scores. For example, except where speed is one criterion for success, tests either should have no time limits at all or generous limits that will minimize the effects of ability to work under time pressure (versus degree of mastery of the material). The result will be what is called a power test, a test that probes students' mastery (their "power") over the material. Similarly, unless language arts skills like capitalization, spelling, punctuation, and writing organization are considered part of the criterion for successful performance on a test in history or science, these tests should be scored strictly for completeness and correct responses with no extra credit for good writing or deduction for poor writing.

Power test

Notice that we qualify these statements. This is because there is disagreement about what should be the criteria for success in various subject areas. Some teachers believe that speed is important for certain skills or that language arts skills should be taken into account in grading tests in other subject areas, while other teachers strongly believe otherwise. There is no simple answer here. Considering the national assessment data mentioned previously, we see some merit in the argument that answers to essay questions should be written and organized coherently as well as be correct in other respects. However, it is not difficult to find exceptions. For example, teachers working with students who speak English as a second language may want students to develop functional competence in English as an ultimate goal, but it would be silly for them to try to assess competence in math with a word-problem test constructed in English if most of the students cannot read English functionally.

Other threats to validity concern the content of the test or types of items that compose it. Written tests are fine for assessing knowledge and comprehension, but behavioral skill objectives may require behavioral tests for valid assessment.

Test Varieties

Tests are classified in many different ways. One of the most important distinctions is between norm-referenced tests and criterion-referenced tests. Norm-referenced tests usually are prepared for use on a national scale by professional test developers. Standardized instructions and test items are developed in a series of pilot testings, and scoring norms are developed on the basis of responses by a large and presumably representative sample of students. These norms then are converted into standardized scores, grade-level equivalent scores, IQ equivalent scores, or other scores that enable test users to compare data on their students with "national norms."

Norm-referenced tests

A method called stratified random sampling is used in norming these tests. It is the same method that opinion polls and TV rating services use. The key to accuracy here is the identification of a representative sample. In theory, this means "representative of the nation at large," although in practice blacks and other minority groups often are excluded from such samples. Samples are stratified by making sure that certain percentages (corresponding to the percentages in the population of interest) of identifiable groups are included. Gender, SES, and geographical area are typical variables used for stratification. Within these stratification limits, sampling is supposed to be random.

Stratified random sampling

For example, if a male third grader from a middle-class background who attends an urban school in the Southeast is needed, the boy selected for inclusion in the norming sample should be chosen randomly from a large list of boys who fit these classifications. Such randomizing is done partly because many of the statistics used in connection with norm-referenced tests assume random sampling, and partly to guard against systematic biases that would creep in if random sampling were not used. For example, if the sample were selected primarily from among friends of the test makers, it is likely that students' motivation to do well on the test and students' rapport with the tester would be unusually high.

Appropriate stratified random sampling can produce remarkably accurate results even when the sample includes only a fraction of the total population. TV networks are able to generate precise predictions of final vote totals through computerized extrapolation from key precincts. However, this system has certain weaknesses, because the behavior of one individual in the sample is taken as representative of thousands of others in the same category. Nevertheless, the norms that come with standardized tests are usually reasonably accurate. They provide information about local performance compared to expectations or averages for the nation at large.

Criterion-referenced tests

Criterion-referenced tests are keyed to the learning objectives taught to the specific students who take the tests. The purpose is not to compare the students to other students, but to determine the degree to which they have mastered these objectives. This kind of information is more useful than information from norm-referenced tests for identifying objectives that have been taught successfully or that need to be retaught. Thus, criterion-referenced tests give teachers useful information for planning future teaching. However, such tests usually give little or no useful information for comparing local students with national norms. (For detailed information about criterion-referenced tests, see Kubiszyn & Borich, 1984; Gronlund, 1985; Glaser & Nitko, 1971; Popham, 1972; or Hambleton, Swaminathan, Algina, & Coulson, 1978.)

Criterion-referenced versus norm-referenced tests

The different rationales and goals of criterion-referenced tests versus norm-referenced tests require that different kinds of items be included in them. Selection of items for criterion-referenced tests is straightforward. Content is confined to material actually taught to students, and the tests include either all objectives that students are supposed to have mastered or a sample of them. Samples typically stress the final or highest objectives toward which related lessons were built. Criterion-referenced tests often must be individualized, especially if they are used in programs that allow students to proceed at their own paces. Different students work on various objectives at any given time, and they will require different tests when they finish instructional sequences. Although they can be used for grading, criterion-referenced tests focus attention on the degree to which individual students have mastered specific objectives.

Norm-referenced tests, however, are concerned primarily with discriminating students from one another. This means that items are included on the basis of power to discriminate in addition to content validity. However, content validity is also important, especially if the tests are intended to assess students on "universal" objectives. Norm-referenced tests do this well when curriculum content is relatively homogeneous (such as reading and math in the early grades), but are not as reliable when there is little universal content (such as social studies at any grade level and most subjects at higher grade levels).

Regardless of the popularity or prestige of a norm-referenced test, it is a poor evaluation device if its items do not correspond well with the curriculum. Sometimes substantial differences in scores between classes or schools occur simply because the groups used different curriculum packages, and one of them included many more objectives assessed by the test than the other one did (see Pidgeon, 1970).

More recently, an examination of what is included in mathematics textbooks and what is measured on particular standardized achievement tests revealed that the degree of overlap between texts and tests varies widely. Teachers may do an excellent job teaching, but student performance on a standardized test will not reflect it if the test is a poor measure of what was taught. Specifically, Freeman et al. (1983) examined three widely used curricula and five standardized tests and found that some tests would be appropriate for use with a particular curriculum but the use of other achievement tests would seriously underestimate how much students had learned.

Discriminating between students

In addition to the problem of content validity, developers of norm-referenced tests are interested in discriminating between students. They have no interest in items that are so easy that everyone answers them correctly or so difficult that no one does, because such items contribute nothing to variance in test scores. Variance comes from items that some students pass and others fail. Theoretically, ideal items are those that half the students pass and the other half fail, because such items discriminate similar students most clearly, producing a normal distribution of scores that also have a wide range. However, because of differences in the achievement levels of students in the same grade, it is necessary to include a range of item difficulty in order to discriminate between students at different achievement levels.

The easiest items do not discriminate between high achievers and are only minimally useful for discriminating between average students. However, they will discriminate the lowest 5–10 percent from the next 5–10 percent. Similarly, very difficult items do not differentiate among most students (who will fail them), but can discriminate the top 5–10 percent from the next 5–10 percent.

Combining these considerations, developers of norm-referenced tests usually first screen items for content validity, seeking items that are as universal as possible in the curricula used in schools, and then construct a test designed to discriminate as well as possible among students at each grade. This is accomplished by having the greatest number of items of moderate difficulty with decreasing numbers of easier and harder items. Because of this distribution of the difficulty of items on norm-referenced tests, these instruments typically discriminate most reliably and meaningfully among students in the middle two-thirds or so of the distribution.

Distribution extremes

As one moves toward the extremes of the distribution, score differences are less meaningful. At the extremes (the lowest and highest 2–3 percent), even seemingly large differences may be essentially meaningless. Thus, a student who scores five grades behind grade level probably is no worse off than a student who is four grades behind grade level. The same is true of IQ tests. Below about 70 or above about 130, differences in IQ scores are not useful for predicting school success, at least in normal schools.

In some schools, norm-referenced tests are administered to gain information about the performances and abilities of students. To the extent that these tests measure skills and knowledge relevant to a school's instructional program, they can provide useful information about the strengths and weaknesses of the program and the progress of individual students. The norm-referenced tests of most interest to teachers are standardized tests of achievement available from commercial test publishers.

Standardized Achievement Tests

Standardized achievement tests are most useful in the lower grades, because content validity is less of a problem. There is more agreement about the core curriculum for language arts and mathematics in the early grades, and the same basic skills are taught using different curriculum packages and various methods. Consequently, although they are highly correlated with IQ scores, standardized achievement tests for the early grades are relatively valid methods of assessing student progress in achieving basic skills such as letter identification and discrimination, matching, copying, spelling, knowledge of letter-sound relationships (phonics), vocabulary, reading comprehension, and basic mathematical computations.

Interpreting data correctly

However, standardized test data must be interpreted carefully if they are to be used appropriately. Relatively few schools have student populations comparable to the students used to develop norms for the test, so that test norms are inappropriate in most cases. Schools populated by students whose home backgrounds and IQ scores are clearly higher than average can and should exceed "expectations" based on standardized tests. Depending on the nature of the school, it might be appropriate to expect 60, 80, or even 95 percent of the students to score "above grade level," even though theoretically many of the students should score at grade level and half of the rest should score above it and half below it. Similarly, in a school populated primarily by students from disadvantaged backgrounds who have lower than average IQs, it might be appropriate to expect that only 40, 20, or even 5 percent would score "above grade level."

Comparisons across classes should be minimized. They are most meaningful if confined to the same grade in the same school (assuming that these classes are not ability grouped or otherwise organized so that some would be expected to do better than others). Comparisons across years should be made cautiously.

Value of subtests

As with IQ test results, teachers will find feedback from standardized tests most useful if it is broken down by subtests, so that they can see patterns of strengths and weaknesses. For example, two teachers might have similar class averages for total scores on a standardized achievement test, but one might obtain notably better results in language arts, while the other teacher's class might do better in math.

Norm-Referenced Tests at Higher Grade Levels

In general, as one measures aspects of the curriculum other than basic skill areas and at upper grade levels, norm-referenced tests become less valid as measures of quality of instruction. They become more like IQ tests rather than criterion-referenced achievement tests because they contain relatively small proportions of items testing material that was specifically taught by a given teacher. For instance, second-grade arithmetic is pretty standard around the country, but seventh-grade social studies is not. A "standardized" test of seventh-grade social studies is more likely to be a test of general knowledge than a test of specific knowledge learned in a particular seventh-grade social studies class.

Teachers attempting to interpret scores from a norm-referenced test should obtain a copy of the test and identify the degree to which it measures knowledge of the material they actually teach.

Teachers' Use of Norm-Referenced Tests

In summary, teachers are likely to find norm-referenced tests useful if they have content validity (that is, if most items measure knowledge and skills

Students are very concerned about performance on tests.

actually taught by the teacher, and if they are not culturally biased) and if local students' scores can be compared meaningfully with those of the norming sample. When this is the case, and when teachers carefully follow instructions concerning time limits, standardized directions, and other aspects of test administration and scoring, valid results can be expected.

Information about the norming sample and about testing and scoring procedures should be included in the test manual. If not, such information can be found in the various mental measurement yearbooks edited by Buros (cf. Buros, 1972, 1978). In addition, the Buros yearbooks contain detailed reviews of most standardized tests, information about their general validity and reliability, and, in many cases, additional norms or other information useful for interpreting tests when they are administered to specialized samples. Levy and Goldstein (1984) have also prepared an extensive review of available tests.

Diagnostic and Prescriptive Tests

IQ tests and norm-referenced achievement tests do not provide much diagnostic or prescriptive information to teachers, but certain criterion-referenced tests do. Many of these are standardized diagnostic tests developed by individuals interested in special-education students. They are designed to identify specific problems in perceiving or responding, and they can be useful for identifying the precise nature of the underlying problem when a student has persistent difficulty with particular work. They include tests of color blindness; difficulty in perceiving boundaries or in separating figure from ground; other problems in visual perception; hearing problems; difficulties in sound or sound-pattern recognition; other problems in auditory perception; physical factors that interfere with proper speech; poor motor functioning in areas such as eye-hand coordination; understanding of directional relationships; perseveration (difficulty in stopping or inhibiting a motor response once it has begun); and various coordination problems.

Tests of this sort are numerous, and they will continue to accumulate as new information about the nature and causes of learning disabilities is discovered. Teachers should keep informed of diagnostic tests of this kind in areas related to their teaching specialties. Even though the present reliability of specialists in using such tests for diagnosis and prescription is low (Gil, Vinsonhaler, & Wagner, 1979; Weinshank, 1978), the tests may be used to identify specific learning disabilities and to develop treatments to help students overcome them.

SUMMARY

Informal assessment of student performance is important, but it is also subjective and thus open to bias. It is therefore important to supplement informal monitoring with formal assessment under standardized conditions. Even then, test scores are only estimates of students' true levels of mastery. The standard error of measurement provides an estimate of the degree of measurement error associated with a particular test or measurement device. It varies inversely with reliability—highly reliable tests have low standard errors and thus allow more precise estimates of student performance.

A test is said to be valid if it measures what it is supposed to measure. Content validity refers to the match between test content and curriculum content. Criterion validity refers to the degree to which scores on a test correlate with performance on criterion measures, often expressed in terms of behavioral criteria. Validity is threatened when content is inappropriate, when time plays an undue role in performance, when test-taking skills influence scores, or other extraneous factors influence test outcomes.

Tests are classified in many different ways. An important distinction is between norm-referenced versus criterion-referenced tests. The former compares students with other students whereas the latter compares each student's performance with stated criteria. Norm-referenced tests are useful to teachers if they have content validity, are not culturally biased, and if students' scores can be compared meaningfully with the norming sample. Criterion-referenced tests are keyed to the learning objectives of a course and provide information about the degree to which students have mastered such objectives. When used for diagnosis and prescription, such tests can help identify specific learning disabilities and treatments that could enable students to overcome them.

QUESTIONS AND PROBLEMS

1. Bear in mind that IQ tests and standardized achievement tests are carefully constructed to produce a normal distribution of scores when administered to a large and heterogeneous population. However, students in a single class are a small and often homogeneous population. What do their "standardized" test scores mean?
2. Why is high test reliability necessary but not sufficient to insure good test validity?
3. Depending on the purpose of a test, the degree to which an item discriminates between the students (about half of them pass it and about half of them fail it) might be extremely important or not important at all. When is such discrimination at the item level important, and when is it unimportant?
4. What kinds of standardized tests and statistics would you use in teaching? Why?
5. Under what circumstances, if any, is it appropriate for teachers to use anything other than pure power tests?
6. Some states are beginning to test teachers' knowledge of subject matter and professional teaching skills. How appropriate is it to compare your knowledge and skills with those of teachers from other schools or from other states?
7. Students sometimes say, "I got an 'A' on the test but I didn't learn anything." Can this really happen? Do tests measure learning or performance?
8. In your own words, define the term "true score." Why do tests seldom reflect a precise, true score?

CASE STUDIES

An Unfair Test? Carol Kewig states to her principal, "It's not fair to use that standardized achievement test as part of my evaluation. The students are learning and I am doing a better than adequate job. That test is just irrelevant. It may be useful for looking at social studies programs in some secondary schools, but not in ours!"

In what specific ways could Carol and her principal determine whether or not the test, or part of it, could provide appropriate feedback? From your point of view, how should an elementary or secondary school teacher be evaluated?

A Research Finding. Rapidly but with full attention Bill Boswell read an article in the prestigious journal, *Schoolhouse Research*. Later he discussed the article with Helen. "You know, that article was very important. The authors, Akers and Silverman, contend that teachers wait less time for low achievers to respond than for high achievers. But," he went on excitedly, "the important thing is that when teachers did wait for low achievers to respond, they were more likely to give an answer and to give longer answers! That's neat. Waiting behavior on the teacher's part correlates positively with the frequency and length of low achievers' answers."

In what ways has Bill overresponded to the article he read? How would you use these results in your own teaching? What evidence would you need in order to assume a definite relationship between any teacher behavior and student behavior?

Chapter 27

Statistical Concepts

CHAPTER OUTLINE

OBJECTIVES

When you have mastered the material in this chapter you will be able to

1. Explain in general terms the meaning and use of descriptive statistics called central tendency and dispersion measures
2. Define and contrast the mean, the median, and the mode
3. Explain the meaning of skewed distributions and why it is often better to use the median, rather than the mean, with skewed distributions
4. Compare and explain the range and the variance/standard deviation measures of a distribution of scores
5. Define and discuss the uses of percentiles and percentages
6. Explain the properties of the normal distribution and its meaning for education
7. Define standard scores and explain how they relate to the normal distribution

When a test or other measuring device is administered to a class, each student earns a score. If the teacher's only concern is to evaluate or grade students according to absolute pass-fail criteria, each score can be considered individually. However, the teacher may want to "grade on a curve" by assigning grades that reflect students' performances relative to the rest of the class rather than relative to an absolute standard. Also, for the teacher's own information or for the school records, it may be necessary to obtain information about the performance of the class as a group.

Descriptive statistics

Information about the performance of an entire class requires calculation of descriptive statistics. These are numerical indices indicating where on the scale of possible scores a class's actual scores are clustered (averages, or measures of central tendency), and the degree to which the class's scores are clustered closely around the average score versus distributed widely along the range of possible scores (measures of range, variance, or dispersion). These statistics are described in the first part of the chapter.

Normal curve

The second part of the chapter considers statistics associated with the concept of the normal curve. These statistics are used to estimate the degree of measurement error expected in a set of test scores. They are useful in judging which test scores are essentially equivalent and which represent a genuine difference in knowledge or skill mastery (Is there a real difference between a student who scores 85 and another student who scores 78 on a test, or is this difference well within the expected measurement error and thus likely due to chance factors?).

Descriptive Statistics

Measures of central tendency and dispersion

Descriptive statistics describe distributions of scores, such as the scores of a class of students on a spelling test. Typically, descriptive statistics are divided into measures of central tendency (average, mean, median, mode) and measures of dispersion (range, variance, standard deviation).

Averages

Averages, particularly means, are more familiar to most people than measures of the dispersion of scores in a distribution. However, in many ways, dispersion data provide more information than averages. This is es-

While grading papers, a teacher receives feedback on student performance and teacher effectiveness.

pecially true when scores are extremely variable and no score occurs frequently. In this case, the average has little meaning, even though it is possible to compute it. For example, it makes little sense to state that the average animal weighs twenty pounds, because the very concept of an "average animal" makes little sense in the first place. In discussing sizes and weights of animals, distribution statistics indicating the percentages of animals at different weight levels are much more informative than an average.

Score distribution

A simple score distribution and some of the statistics associated with it are shown in Table 27.1. This is a tally of student scores on a ten-item spelling test. The statistics reveal that the test was moderately difficult for the students. This may be obvious to you at a glance, but in case it is not, take a look at each of the statistics that we can compute from this score distribution and at some of the information we can infer from studying the tallies.

First, note that thirty students took the test, so there are thirty scores. In statistical terminology this is $N = 30$. The tallies indicate the number of students who earned each of the possible scores between zero and 10. They indicate that two students got scores of 10, three got scores of 9, three got scores of 8, and so on. This tally is called a frequency distribution. It shows the frequency with which each possible score appeared in the actual distribution. Note that no student scored zero or 2, even though these scores were possible.

Frequency distribution

This distribution provides much useful information, even without the computation of any additional statistics. For example, if we were to look

Table 27.1 Frequency Distribution of Scores on a Ten-Item Test Taken by Thirty Students

Score	Number of Students: Tally	Number of Students: Total
10	II	2
9	III	3
8	III	3
7	~~IIII~~ III	8
6	IIII	4
5	IIII	4
4	III	3
3	II	2
2		0
1	I	1
0		0
		$N = 30$

$$\text{Mean} = \frac{\text{Sum of scores}}{\text{Number of scores}} = \frac{190}{30} = 6.33$$

Median = Middle score = 7

Mode = Most frequent score = 7

Range = 1 to 10 (possible range = 0–10)

N = Number of scores = 30

only at the measures of central tendency and notice that the scores average 6 to 7, we might conclude that the test was too difficult, considering that 10 was perfect. However, the scores are spread out well, or to put it another way, the test discriminates between the students well. This means that the test items were at various difficulty levels. Consequently, the results can be viewed with some confidence, assuming that the test has content validity.

Contrast this with test results that have similar central tendency scores but a very narrow distribution (for example, 10 students score 7, and the other 20 score 6). This score distribution would also have an *N* of 30, and a mean of 6.33, but it might provide less information about teaching success or student learning. There probably is little meaningful difference between the students who scored 7 and those who scored 6, so that the test does not discriminate between the students. Furthermore, the scores pile up in the center instead of at the bottom or top of the possible range. Unless the class is extremely homogeneous, something probably is wrong with the test.

If the scores pile up at the top, this means that the test is too easy or that the students have learned the material thoroughly. If most of the scores are at the bottom, the test is too hard or the students were not prepared for it. However, a concentration of scores somewhere in the middle is puzzling. Such a score distribution might mean that seven of the items are easy ones that most students got correct, and that three items are unreasonably difficult, ambiguous in their wording, not relevant to the material the students were supposed to have mastered, or otherwise inappropriate, so that few students got them correct.

Concentration of middle-range scores

To investigate the problem, you would need to make a frequency distribution of scores. In this case, you would need a distribution for each item, not just for the whole test (see Table 27.2). Frequency distributions like these should be made routinely, to obtain information for interpreting averages. They also facilitate computation of central tendency measures.

Central Tendency Statistics

The mean

The most common measures of central tendency are the mean, the median, and the mode. Of these, the mean corresponds most clearly to the more familiar term, "average." The mean is computed simply by adding the scores and dividing the total by the number of scores (*N*). Thus, for the distribution shown in Table 27.1, the 30 scores total 190 points. The mean is computed by dividing this 190 by 30 (the number of students) to arrive at a mean of 6.33 (rounded to two decimals).

In the distribution shown in Table 27.2, twenty students scored 6, and ten students scored 7. The score total would be 190, or $(20 \times 6) + (10 \times 7)$, so that the mean would be 190 divided by 30, or 6.33.

For most statistical purposes, the mean is the preferred measure of central tendency. Many consider it to be the most representative measure, because it takes into account each individual score, producing a weighted average. Students who score 10 on the test contribute 10 points to the total used

Table 27.2 Frequency Distribution of Scores on a Ten-Item Test Taken by Thirty Students

Students	1	2	3	4	5	6	7	8	9	10	Total
1. Aaron	1	1	0	1	1	0	1	0	1	1	7
2. Alfred	0	1	0	1	1	0	1	0	1	1	6
3. Alice	1	1	0	1	0	0	1	0	1	1	6
4. Beth	0	1	0	1	1	0	1	0	1	1	6
5. Bonnie	1	1	0	0	1	0	1	0	1	1	6
6. Clark	1	1	0	1	1	0	1	0	1	0	6
7. Cuthbert	1	1	0	1	1	0	1	0	1	1	7
8. Dahlia	1	1	0	1	1	0	1	0	1	1	7
9. David	1	1	0	1	0	0	1	0	1	1	6
10. Douglas	1	1	0	1	1	0	1	0	1	0	6
11. Felicia	1	1	0	0	1	0	1	0	1	1	6
12. Frank	1	1	0	0	1	0	1	0	1	1	6
13. George	1	0	0	1	1	0	1	0	1	1	6
14. Helen	1	1	0	1	1	0	1	0	1	1	7
15. John L.	1	1	1	1	1	0	1	0	0	1	7
16. John R.	1	1	0	1	1	0	0	0	1	1	6
17. June	1	1	0	1	1	0	1	0	0	1	6
18. Karen	1	1	0	1	1	0	1	0	1	1	7
19. Karl	1	0	0	1	1	0	1	0	1	1	6
20. Missy	1	1	0	1	1	0	1	0	0	1	6
21. Nancy	1	1	0	1	1	0	1	0	1	1	7
22. Patricia	1	1	0	1	1	0	0	1	1	1	7
23. Raymond	1	1	0	1	1	0	1	0	1	1	7
24. Rosa	1	1	0	1	1	0	1	0	0	1	6
25. Ruby	0	1	0	1	1	0	1	0	1	1	6
26. Sam	1	1	0	0	1	0	1	0	1	1	6
27. Seth	1	1	0	1	1	0	1	0	1	1	7
28. Thomas	1	1	0	1	1	0	0	0	1	1	6
29. Vera	1	1	0	1	1	0	1	0	1	0	6
30. Walter	1	1	0	1	1	0	0	0	1	1	6
Totals	27	28	1	26	28	0	26	1	26	27	190

Scores	Tally	Total		
6	卌 卌	20	Mean = 190/30 = 6.33	Range = 6–7
	卌 卌	10	Median = 6	Possible range = 0–10
7	卌 卌	30	Mode = 6	N = 30

in computing the mean, and students who score 1 contribute only 1 point to this total. In addition, the mean is related to several other statistics used in certain complex analyses, whereas the median and mode are not. Statisticians prefer it because its mathematical properties allow them to do more with it than they can do with the other two measures of central tendency.

The median

The median is simply the middle score—half of the scores are above it and half are below it. In the example in Table 27.1, the median score is

7, which is the most frequent score as well. The same is true in Table 27.2, where the median is 6, and 6 is also the most frequent score. However, this was purely accidental. In a distribution in which the scores of thirty students were spread out so that three students got each of the scores between 1 and 10, the median would be 5.5. This is because fifteen students would have scores between 6 and 10, and fifteen would have scores between 1 and 5. In situations like this, where no score represents the median of the distribution, a common practice is to split the difference between the two scores that come closest to it. In this example, these scores are 5 and 6, so the median is 5.5.

The mode

The mode is the most frequent score. The mode is 7 in Table 27.1 and 6 in Table 27.2. The mode is less useful and meaningful than the mean or median. Sometimes it is impossible to identify, as in the distribution mentioned previously, in which exactly three students scored at each of the 10 scores possible. In this case, there is no mode. In other cases, there is more than one mode. This would happen, for example, if ten students scored 6, ten students scored 7, and the remaining ten students were dispersed over several other score categories.

Bimodal distributions

Bimodal distributions have two modes, like the distribution shown in Table 27.3. Bimodal distributions are of interest because they suggest that the scores may come from two qualitatively different groups. Bimodal distributions like those shown in Table 27.3 are found most often when the same test is given to groups of students who differ in some important way. For example, such a distribution might represent vocabulary scores on a test given to a combined group of second and fourth graders. Some second graders would do better than some fourth graders, but in general, the second

Table 27.3 A Bimodal Distribution

Score	Number of Students: *Tally*	Number of Students: *Total*
10	III	3
9	III	3
8	~~IIII~~ I	6
7	III	3
6	I	1
5	II	2
4	III	3
3	~~IIII~~ I	6
2	I	1
1	I	1
0	I	1

$$\text{Mean} = \frac{\text{Sum of scores}}{\text{Number of scores}} = \frac{175}{30} = 5.83$$

Median = Middle score = 6.5

Modes(s) = Most frequent scores(s) = 3, 8

Range = 0 to 10 (Same as possible range)

N = Number of scores = 30

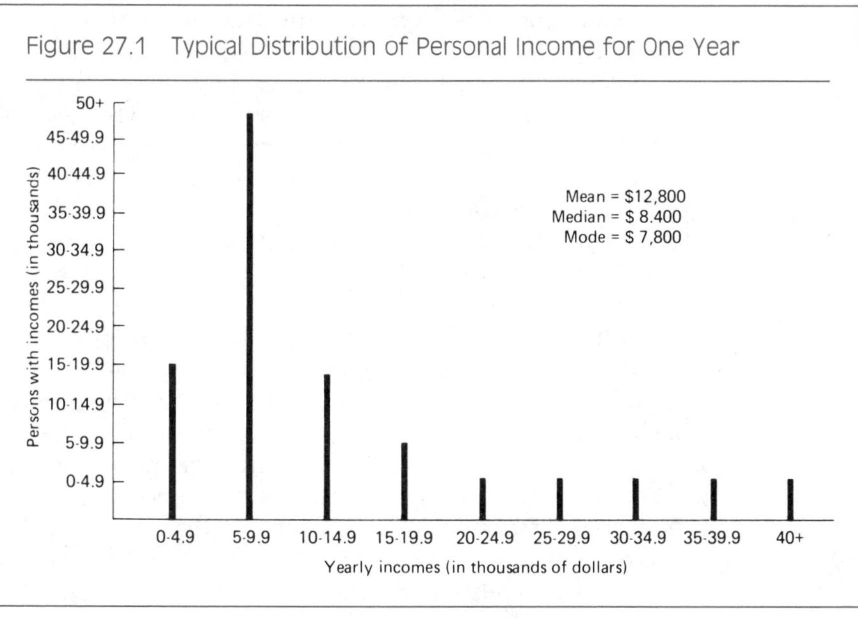

Figure 27.1 Typical Distribution of Personal Income for One Year

graders would cluster around the lower mode (3), while the fourth graders would cluster around the higher mode (8).

The mean and median usually are equally good measures of central tendency, even though statisticians usually prefer the mean because of its mathematical relationships to other statistics. Sometimes the mean and median are considerably different, however. When this occurs, the median usually is more meaningful. The difference usually occurs because the distribution is very unusual and the effects of a few individuals with extreme scores distort the mean. The classical example of this is income distributions, where the median is much more meaningful than the mean.

Skewed distributions

Distributions of income by individuals or by families are seriously skewed. This term refers to distributions in which the scores are concentrated at one end of the possible range, so that the mean has many more scores on one side of it than on the other. This can be seen in Figure 27.1, which shows a distribution of personal incomes that is fictional but typical of a distribution that might occur for a city that has about 100,000 wage earners. Note that the vast majority of wage earners are concentrated in the range between zero and $15,000 per year. These salary figures are low because part-time wage earners are also included in the distribution (i.e., teenagers who work at a fast food restaurant only in the summer). The distribution is seriously skewed: the mean is $12,800, but incomes range from zero to above $40,000 per year. In fact, this skew is even more extreme than the figure shows, because the last group includes several millionaires and many others making considerably more than $40,000 a year. The incomes of these few individuals are included in the calculation of the mean, so that the mean becomes an unrealistically high estimate of the average income in the community. By contrast, the median is much more realistic and meaningful.

Mean versus median

The median is more meaningful and reliable than the mean, because it is not sensitive to unusually high scores at the extremes of the distribution. For example, if the income of everyone in the community were to rise exactly $1,000 in the following year, both the mean and the median would go up exactly $1,000. However, suppose that two millionaires moved into town. This would cause a notable increase in the mean, falsely implying that the town as a whole was improving economically. In contrast, these two individuals would have little or no effect on the median. The opposite would be the case if two or three of the town's present millionaires were to move outside its limits. Again, the median would be unaffected, but the mean would drop notably, giving the false impression that the town was having economic difficulties. These examples show why the median is preferred over the mean as an index of average income. More generally, they illustrate how the mean is especially sensitive to extreme scores, particularly in skewed distributions. To the extent that situations like this occur in your own testing, you probably should use the median rather than the mean as an index of central tendency. This might be necessary, for example, if you were teaching in a class made up of generally low-ability students except for two or three with extremely high abilities, or vice versa.

Distribution Statistics

Where feasible, often the simplest way to get information about score distributions is to tally them, individually (as in Table 27.1) or in groups (as in Figure 27.1). However, sometimes certain statistics describing distributions are needed for other purposes. Just as there are several statistics that describe the central tendencies of distributions, there are several others that describe the dispersion of scores.

Range

The simplest statistic, the range, that describes the dispersion of scores has already been mentioned. The range of scores in a distribution extends from the lowest score through the highest score. Sometimes the observed range extends across the complete possible range (see Table 27.4), but not always (see Table 27.1). Taken in conjunction with a measure of central tendency, the range provides important information for interpreting descriptive statistics.

For example, two classes could have mean IQs of 100. However, the classes would be very different if the first class ranged from 65 to 147, while the second class ranged only from 89 to 108. The latter class is quite homogeneous in ability compared to the former class, where the range of student ability is so great that some form of grouping or individualization seems needed.

Sometimes the range alone does not provide enough information about the distribution, because it reflects only the two most extreme scores. For example, in the heterogeneous class mentioned above, we stated that the highest IQ was 147. The composition of this class and the implications for

Table 27.4 Conversion of Raw Test Scores to Percentages and Rank-Order Scores in Order to Combine Data into a Single Score Distribution

	Raw Scores			Percentages $\left(\frac{\text{Score}}{\text{Perfect Score}}\right)$		
Students	*Test 1*	*Test 2*	*Test 3*	*Test 1*	*Test 2*	*Test 3*
1. Art	48	42	96	96	84	96
2. Bill	36	30	74	72	60	74
3. Debra	47	45	94	94	90	94
4. Fran	32	33	76	64	66	76
5. George	32	29	71	64	58	71
6. Ida	33	31	63	66	62	63
7. Jill	48	40	95	96	80	95
8. Robert	46	42	93	92	84	93
9. Sam	40	37	86	80	74	86
10. Susie	41	39	88	82	78	88
Actual range	32–48	29–45	63–96			
Perfect score	50	50	100			

Rank				
Test 1	*Test 2*	*Test 3*	*Mean %*	*Mean Rank*
1.5	2.5	1	92	1.7
7	9	8	69	8.0
3	1	3	93	2.3
9.5	7	7	69	7.8
9.5	10	9	64	9.5
8	8	10	64	8.7
1.5	4	2	90	2.5
4	2.5	4	90	3.8
6	6	6	80	6.0
5	5	5	83	5.0

Outlier

the teacher are very different if IQ scores are gradually and normally distributed between the two extremes instead of one of the extremes being an outlier (a single case that is notably lower or higher than all the rest of the scores). Two classes in which the highest IQs were 147 would be very different if in one class there were a dozen or so students with IQs between 110 and 147, and if the second highest IQ in the other class was 116. The first class contains many bright students, and the one with the IQ of 147 is not significantly brighter than several other students in the class. However, a student with an IQ of 147 in a class were the next highest IQ was 116 would be an outlier, considerably brighter than the rest.

To guard against problems like this, it is sometimes useful to go beyond specification of the range of scores by using other distribution statistics. Among the more familiar of these are percentiles. Conversion of raw scores into percentile scores involves computing the percentage of scores in the total distribution that are lower than a particular score. For example, the fiftieth percentile is roughly equivalent to the median. Fifty percent of the scores in the distribution are higher than this score and 49 percent are below it. A score that is at the seventy-fifth percentile is lower than only 25 percent of the scores in the distribution, and higher than 74 percent of the scores.

Percentiles

Conversion of raw scores into percentages is useful for many purposes, but especially when one wants to average scores across tests with different numbers of items in them and to weight the tests equally. Scores from each test can be converted into percentages of the total possible score, and then averaged. Both percentiles and percentages can be used to rank students. Simple percentages are easier to compute (see Table 27.4) and thus most appropriate if they give the information needed. However, percentile scores not only allow the ranking of students, but also provide more specific information about the exact placement of a given student relative to other students and to the range of scores as a whole.

Percentages

An even simpler way to differentiate students is to rank them. This may be all that teachers need for most purposes. However, when standardized test data are being used, simple ranking can allow only for comparisons within the classroom. In order to make comparisons with the norms that come with the test, it will be necessary to transform raw scores into percentile scores or some other form of standardized score. Some tests allow only for specification of quartiles (fourths), deciles (tenths), or other simplifications of percentile score conversions.

Ranking

Other distribution statistics that teachers need to be familiar with, even though they are unlikely to have to compute them, are the variance and standard deviation. The two are related; the standard deviation is the square root of the variance.

Variance

The variance is the average of the squares of the differences between each of the individual scores and the mean of the distribution. It can be computed by first computing the mean score for the distribution, then computing the difference between each individual's score and the mean, then squaring each of these difference scores, then summing these squared difference scores, and then dividing this sum by the number of scores (N). Distributions with small variances and standard deviations have many scores close to the mean (as in Table 27.2), while distributions with large variances and standard deviations have many scores that vary considerably from the mean (as in Table 27.1). As does the mean, the variance and standard deviation both have certain statistical properties that allow them to be used in calculations that cannot be computed otherwise.

The size of the variance depends directly on the percentage of scores that differ from the mean and the size of these differences. The more such scores, and the more different from the mean they are, the larger the variance. The same is true for the standard deviation, because it is simply the square root of the variance. Thus, to repeat and summarize: variance and standard deviation are both measures of the degree to which scores are dispersed from the mean rather than similar to it. The larger the variance and standard deviation, the greater the degree of dispersion of scores away from the mean.

Standard deviation

The Normal Curve

Figure 27.2 shows two estimates of the probable results of repeated experiments designed to estimate frequencies or probabilities in a population from data on small samples. For example, if we did not know that the probability of getting "heads" when coin tossing was .50, we could estimate it by taking samples of ten coin tosses. The most likely result of such an experiment would be five heads and five tails. However, sometimes we would get four or six heads due to random sampling error. Less often, we would get three or seven, and still less often we would get either fewer or more heads. The probability is only about .001 that we would get either no heads or all heads in ten tosses.

These probabilities can be estimated precisely because we know in advance that the probability of heads on a random toss is .50. The bar graph shown in Figure 27.2 is one case of what is called the binomial distribution. This distribution can be used to compute the exact probabilities of errors in samples of ten measurements when the attribute being measured is either present or absent with a 50 percent probability, as in drawing black cards from a deck, tossing a coin, or drawing the shorter of two straws.

Binomial distribution

The normal distribution and the normal curve associated with it (which is superimposed upon the binomial bar graph in Figure 27.2) are used for most statistical purposes, because most things are distributed normally (rather than binomially). This is easiest to see with variables like height. If the heights of all adult males in the country were plotted in a frequency distribution like that shown in Figure 27.2, they would form a normal curve with the same statistical properties as the normal curve shown in the figure. The only difference is that this normal curve would be somewhat flatter and more extended, because height is distributed more smoothly and with greater variability than bimodal variables that fit the binomial distribution.

Normal distribution

The mean height is about 70 inches, but the range of normality extends several inches in each direction from the mean. Furthermore, even individuals a foot or so above or below the mean are still biologically normal, though they are statistically unusual.

Note that certain biologically abnormal individuals do not fit expectations based upon the normal curve. This is because they are not from the same population (that is, the population of biologically normal adult males). Men who are genetic midgets or dwarfs or who have glandular abnormalities

Figure 27.2 Binomial and Normal Distributions of Ten Coin Tosses Showing Numbers of heads Expected*

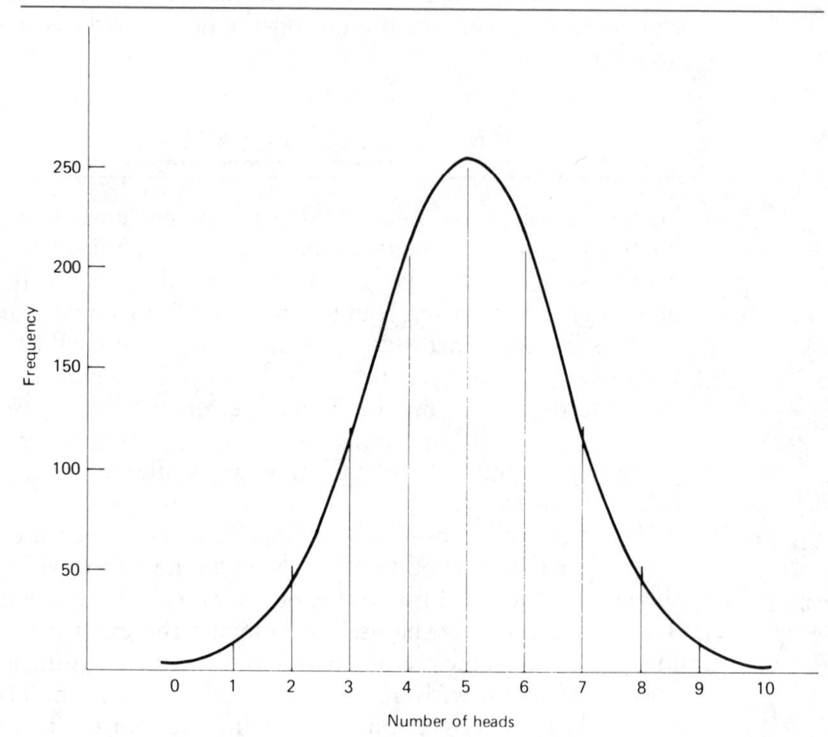

Score (heads)	Frequencies: Binomial	Frequencies: Normal	Cumulative proportions: Binomial	Cumulative proportions: Normal
10	1	1.8	1.000	1.000
9	10	10.5	.999	.998
8	45	42.5	.989	.988
7	120	116.1	.945	.946
6	210	211.6	.828	.833
5	252	258.5	.623	.626
4	210	211.6	.377	.374
3	120	116.1	.172	.167
2	45	42.5	.055	.054
1	10	10.5	.011	.012
0	1	1.8	.001	.002
Sum	1,024	1,023.5		

* The binomial distribution is shown by the bar graph, the normal distribution is shown by the curve.

that cause them to be physical giants are qualitatively different, not merely statistically different, from normal men. They represent altogether separate populations.

The same kind of thing happens in education, where most student measures are known or assumed to be distributed normally except for certain individuals who form separate populations. For example, distributions of IQ scores follow the normal curve except for a "bump" at the low end that indicates a greater number of individuals with low IQs than are expected by chance (Jensen, 1969). They exist because of biological abnormalities that make them qualitatively different from the majority who are biologically normal. Low IQ scores are found, for example, among Downs Syndrome children, hydrocephalics, and individuals who suffered brain damage at birth due to oxygen deprivation.

Similarly, distributions of achievement scores in particular schools or classrooms will depart significantly from normality if "the population" really is two populations, such as in a majority speaking English as a first language and reading it with varying degrees of fluency, and a minority speaking English as a second language and unable to read it functionally at all. Thus, if a trait is really distributed normally in the population, repeated samples designed to estimate the mean and distribution of the trait should approximate normal curves. If more than one mode appears, or if the curve departs significantly from normality, it probably means that two qualitatively different populations are involved.

Kinds of normal curves

Any curve that fits a complex mathematical definition (that we will not explain here) is a normal curve, so that there are a great many kinds of normal curves. If the attribute to be measured is constant, so that any differences in repeated samplings are due only to measurement error, and if the measurement instrument is reliable and valid, normal curves representing repeated measurements will show scores clustered at the real population mean, with little dispersion in either direction, as in Figure 27.3. This is the sort of curve that would be obtained if the height of the same individual were measured repeatedly and rounded off to the nearest quarter inch.

On the other hand, if the attribute is distributed widely in the population and does not cluster around any particular average, or if the measurement methods used in estimating it are unreliable, normal curves that look like the one in Figure 27.4 will result. Both types of curves can be used to estimate means, but estimation is much more precise in the case illustrated by Figure 27.3, because the standard deviation and variance are very low. As a result, it can be stated with a high degree of confidence that the true population mean lies within a very narrow range. In contrast, in situations like those illustrated in Figure 27.4, the considerable variation in repeated measurements does not allow a very precise or confident estimation of the population mean.

Normal curves have many properties that make them particularly useful in education and psychology. First, if an attribute being measured is distributed normally in the population (and most are), repeated measurements

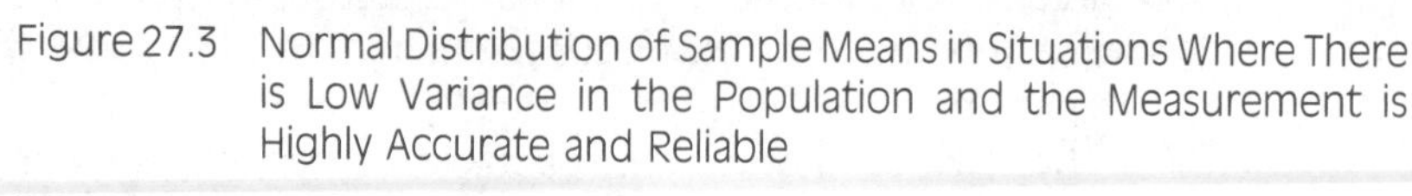

Figure 27.3 Normal Distribution of Sample Means in Situations Where There is Low Variance in the Population and the Measurement is Highly Accurate and Reliable

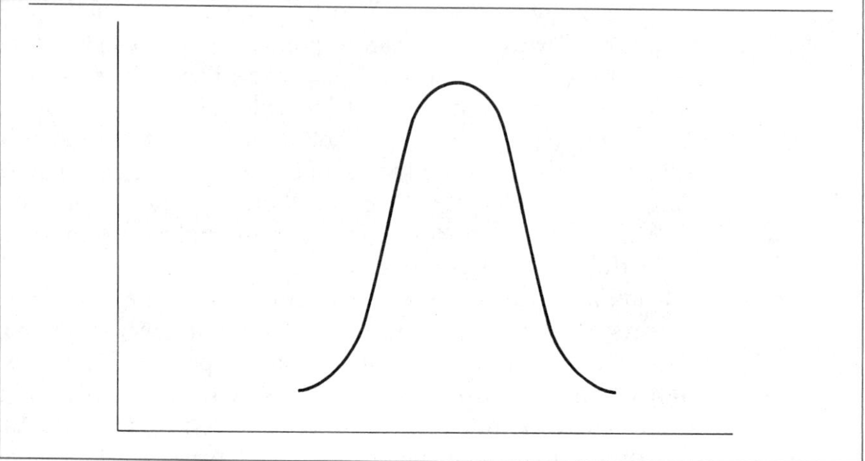

from small samples will approximate the normal curve in their statistical properties. They also will approximate the real population distribution in their means and standard deviations (assuming adequate measurements). The mean, the median, and the mode will all be located at or near the real mean of the population, and errors in estimating the mean and the standard deviation can be calculated to specified probability levels. This leads to statements such as "with 95 percent confidence, the population mean is estimated to lie between 98 and 102." A statement like this might result from repeated measurements of IQ, where the mean for the population at large is 100.

Figure 27.4 Normal Distribution of Sample Means in Situations Where There is High Variance in the Population and the Measurement is Unreliable

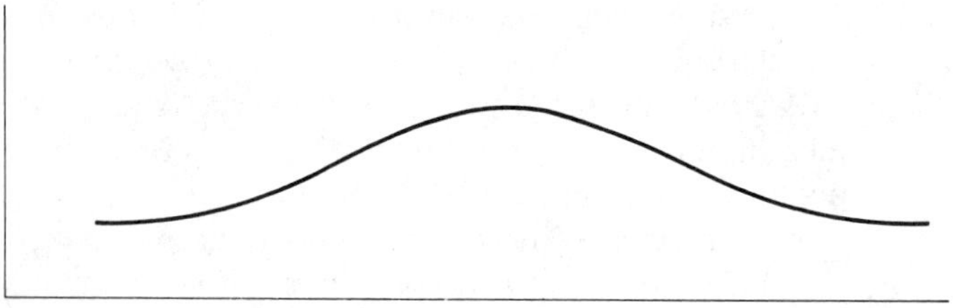

Figure 27.5 The Relationship of Several Common Scoring Scales

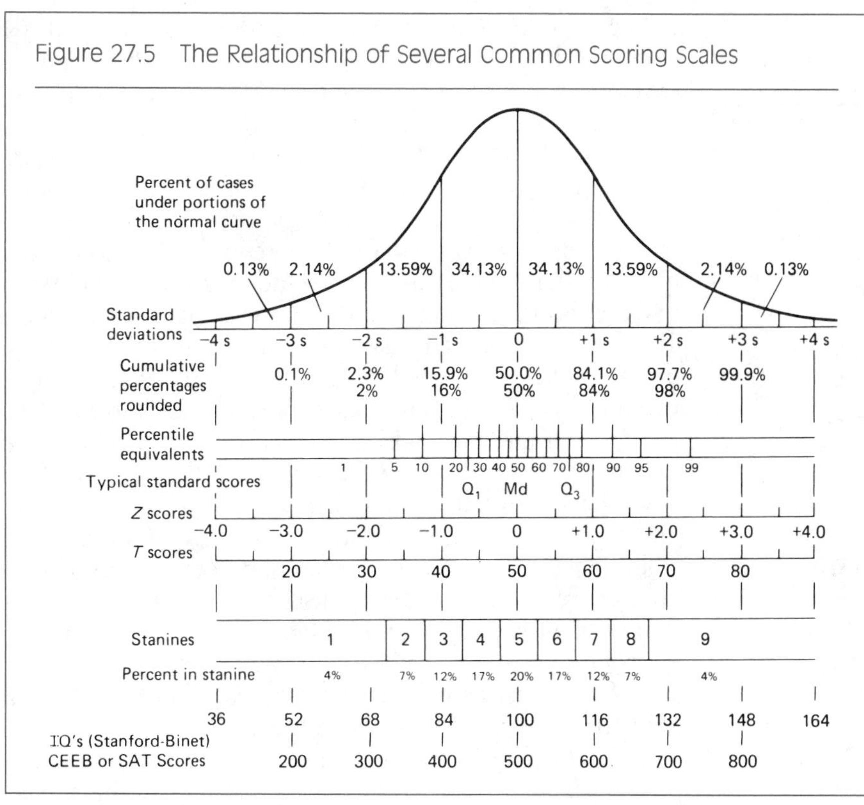

The normal curve also has other useful properties. For example, for complex statistical reasons we will not attempt to explain here, the relationships between the standard deviations of scores distributed normally and the percentage distributions of these scores are known and can be specified. About 68 percent of the scores will fall between −1 and +1 standard deviations from the mean, and about 95 percent will fall between −2 and +2 standard deviations. This is true of all normal curves, regardless of their means or standard deivations. This is illustrated in Figure 27.5. Thus, the chance of a score being more than two standard deviations away from the mean is only about 5 percent. This fact is used in drawing inferences about whether or not differences between observed means are "statistically significant."

z-scores

Figure 27.5 illustrates some of the relationships between different measures of central tendency and dispersion and the relationship of these measures to the properties of the normal curve. First, it can be seen that any scores can be transformed into z-scores, which are standard deviation units or standard deviation scores. A score that is one standard deviation above the mean would have a z-score of +1.0 and a score of two standard deviations below the mean would have a z-score of −2.0.

Typically, z-scores are fitted to a normal distribution with a mean of zero and a standard deviation of 1.0. All that is required to calculate z-scores is to compute the mean and standard deviation of a distribution of scores, compute the differences between scores and the mean, and convert these differences into standard deviation units. For example, if a score is 15 points above the mean and the standard deviation is 10, the z-score would be +1.5 (15 ÷ 10 = 1.50). Transformation of raw scores into z-scores allows the use of the normal curve for statistical estimation and significance testing.

T-scores

Some tests provide for transformation of raw scores into standard scores, or T-scores. This is similar to z-score transformation, except that it gets rid of minus signs. Many different standard score distributions have been used, but the most common one uses a mean of 50 and a standard deviation of 10. For this type of transformation, a raw score that was at the original mean would be assigned a value of 50 and would still be at the mean of the new distribution. A raw score that was one standard deviation below the original mean would be assigned a score of 40 (one standard deviation below the new mean), and a raw score that was one and a half standard deviations above the original mean would be assigned a score of 65 (one and a half standard deviations above the new mean).

IQ scores

IQs are standard scores. In computing them, raw scores from the IQ tests are transformed into a normal distribution with a mean of 100 and a standard deviation of either 15 or 16, depending on the test. Thus, students who get total raw scores equal to the mean for students their age are assigned IQs of 100, while students who get total raw scores two standard deviations above the mean are assigned IQs of 130 or 132, depending on the test.

The rationale for this procedure is that IQ tests measure something called "intelligence," which is distributed normally in the population. As we have seen, there is little justification for this assumption. Nevertheless, IQ tests continue to be used widely, and the method of converting raw scores into transformed scores with a normal distribution and a mean of 100 continues to be common practice.

Other useful information about normal curves is illustrated in Figure 27.5. Note that regardless of the mean and standard deviation involved, the following relationships are constant in all normal distributions:

1. Scores one standard deviation below the mean are at about the 16th percentile ($z = -1.0$, or $T = 40$).
2. Scores one standard deviation above the mean are at about the 84th percentile ($z = +1.0$, or $T = 60$).
3. Scores two standard deviations below the mean are between the 2nd and 3rd percentiles.
4. Scores two standard deviations above the mean are between the 97th and 98th percentiles.
5. In general, once raw scores are fitted to some kind of normal distribution, relationships between raw scores, standard scores, z-scores, and percentiles can be stated easily.
6. The farther apart two scores are, the more likely it is that the difference between them is real rather than due to chance measurement error.

7. By combining information about the differences between raw scores with information about the number of scores in the distribution and the standard deviation of the distribution, it is possible to develop precise estimates of the probability that two scores differ by chance. Where this probability is low (below .05, for example), the difference is said to be statistically significant.

SUMMARY

In order to use test scores to evaluate the performance of a group of students, teachers must calculate statistics that describe the characteristics of the distributions of scores. These are usually divided into measures of central tendency (mean, median, mode) and measures of dispersion (range, variance, standard deviation). Taken together, these data reveal typical or average performance for the class as a whole and the spread of scores around that average.

The mean is found by adding all of the scores and dividing by the number of scores, the median is the middle score in any array, and the mode is the most frequently occurring score. The range is the difference between the lowest and the highest scores in an array, while the variance is found by squaring the difference between each score and the mean, adding together these squared differences, and dividing by the number of scores. The standard deviation is the square root of the variance.

The normal curve represents the distribution of many kinds of variables in a normal population. It is a useful construct in testing because it provides a basis for examining test scores or other measures in relationship to each other, and estimating the percentile ranks of the scores. Also, if the scores are normally distributed, it is possible to transform raw scores into standard scores such as *z*-scores or T-scores. This allows the use of the normal curve for statistical estimation and significance testing.

QUESTIONS AND PROBLEMS

1. Why use statistics at all? That is, why not merely report the results of tests and be done with it?
2. Transformation of raw scores into standardized scores does absolutely nothing to change the relative placement of any individual's score in comparison to those of the rest of the class. However, transformation into scores that are forced into a normal distribution *will* change the relative placement of scores with reference to one another. Do you understand this difference? What are some of its implications?
3. Ordinarily, teachers use the class mean whenever they need to express class performance on a test in a single score. Sometimes, though, the mean is misleading. When would the median be more appropriate? The mode?
4. Which indicates the best performance—a percentile equivalent score of 75, a *z*-score of +1.0, a T-score of 62 (where the mean = 50 and the standard deviation = 10)?
5. What problems would you have in trying to explain a T-score to a parent?

CASE STUDY

Differences Among Three Math Classes. Ms. Lanier teaches general math to three classes of ninth graders. The classes are supposed to be formed randomly from among the ninth graders at Holt School who do not qualify for more advanced math courses. During the first week of school, Ms. Lanier gives each class the same twenty-item review/pretest. The test data are shown in the accompanying table. For each class, identify or compute the number of students and the mean, median, mode, range, and (optionally) variance and standard deviation. What do these statistics reveal about the three classes?

Score	Class 1	Class 2	Class 3
20	0	0	0
19	0	0	0
18	0	0	1
17	0	1	0
16	0	2	0
15	1	2	1
14	1	5	0
13	2	3	1
12	3	1	0
11	5	1	1
10	6	0	1
9	4	1	1
8	4	2	0
7	2	2	3
6	1	5	2
5	1	3	6
4	0	1	5
3	0	1	3
2	0	0	3
1	0	0	2
0	0	0	0

Chapter 28

Test Construction

OBJECTIVES

When you have mastered the material in this chapter you will be able to

1. Explain the importance of representative sampling of content and test length
2. Explain the six levels of Bloom's taxonomy of educational objectives and how the taxonomy is used in test construction
3. List the three steps involved in writing an instructional objective, and discuss the advantages and disadvantages of using instructional objectives in teaching
4. Discuss the six suggestions for writing good essay questions, and explain how essays should be graded to minimize teacher bias and error
5. Discuss the guidelines for writing objective test questions, and contrast their advantages and disadvantages with those of essay questions
6. Define criterion-referenced and norm-referenced tests, explain how they differ, and tell when each is best used

So far, we have presented some fundamental principles of educational measurement and some of the statistics useful for describing and making decisions about the score distributions that such measurement generates. We now turn to the construction of the actual measurement devices themselves.

Test Length and Content Coverage

Typically, tests cover only a small sample of the content and objectives taught, and decisions have to be made about what to include. This problem is most serious for final exams given at the end of the term or school year, but it is relevant to unit and weekly tests as well.

We have already mentioned one criterion—a test ordinarily should stress the terminal objectives of sequences of instruction within a content area, because these usually are the instructional objectives in the first place, and because mastery of these terminal objectives usually means mastery of lower-level objectives as well. It is also helpful to sample from the full range of content taught, and to include enough items to allow reliable measurement.

Sampling from content taught

Sampling from the full range of content taught will help ensure that the teacher recognizes areas of weakness, that students are accountable for learning all of the material, and that students will view the test as fair. Students may not perceive the test as fair if it emphasizes only a few areas, especially if these are areas the students thought were unimportant. For example, a fifteen-item objective test on comparative political systems might ask several questions about evolutionary forces and key individuals who shaped the development of those systems, only a couple of questions about how the systems presently operate and about the practical implications of similarities and differences between countries, and no questions at all about probable future trends.

Let us examine how such a test could have biased effects. Table 28.1 shows the percentage of time that eight students of comparable ability spent studying for the test. The student victimized the most by the test is Ruth, who spent only 20 percent of her time reviewing historical development, which turned out to be 80 percent of the exam, and 60 percent of her time studying future trends, which were not included on the exam at all. In contrast, Judy did well on the test. She spent 75 percent of her time preparing for the first part, and the remainder of her time studying material tested on the second part. Other students made different choices and scored differently on the basis of their choices.

Table 28.2 presents the distribution of scores that students might have made on such a test. It can be seen that the distribution of scores is not directly related to the percentage of time spent studying for key parts of the exam, but it does correspond closely.

In any test situation many factors operate. For example, Bill may have scored lower than Joan because he was absent during a class discussion that dealt with material needed to answer three of the exam questions (a longer

Table 28.1 Distribution of Test Items and Percentage of Time Students Spent Studying Three Areas of Comparative Politics

Test	Historical Development (in percent) 80 (12 items)	Present Functioning (in percent) 20 (3 items)	Future Trends (in percent) 0
		Students' Study Times (in percent)	
Alice	33	33	33
Jane	33	33	33
Bill	25	50	25
Ted	50	25	25
Joan	50	50	0
Judy	75	25	0
Ruth	20	20	60
Tom	33	33	33

test makes such effects less likely). However, Joan may score higher because she has better test-taking skills (for example, she notices subtle clues in two poorly written test questions that give the answers away). Alice may have scored lower than Jane or Tom because she spent too much time thinking about the first few questions and did not have a chance to respond to the last questions.

Measurement errors

The point is that some error of measurement is going to occur in any test. A test that unfairly samples content will exacerbate minor problems into major ones. As can be seen in Tables 28.1 and 28.2, the test on comparative politics is not fair. It has a systematic tendency to favor some students who guessed correctly about how to spend their study time.

Test length

Some of these problems may be connected with the length of the test. As a rule of thumb, test reliability increases with test length, so that a thirty-item test is ordinarily more reliable than a fifteen-item test. However,

Table 28.2 Students' Scores on the Classroom Test in Comparative Politics

Alice	8	Joan	12
Jane	10	Judy	14
Bill	7	Ruth	7
Ted	11	Tom	10

this assumes that the test equally samples each of the major content areas addressed. If this is not the case, adding to the length of the test may not improve its reliability or its fairness.

For example, if we increase our fifteen-item comparative political systems test to thirty items, but ask twenty-three questions on the first part, seven questions on the second part, and none at all on the third part, the problems illustrated above will still exist. The test is a more reliable measure of student mastery of the first and second parts, but it still gives no information at all about mastery of the third part, and it is still unfair to students who concentrated their study time on the third part.

Even when a test does sample evenly from different aspects of the content taught, test items still might favor certain students over others. Suppose we want to test students' abilities to read quickly and comprehend material. This requires students to read paragraphs, and these paragraphs have to be concerned with some type of content. For example, Sally might be knowledgeable about and interested in baseball, and Ted may not. If some material on the test deals with baseball, Sally may be able to read it more quickly and remember more of it because she is more familiar with specialized terms, even though she may be no better than Ted in terms of general reading ability and comprehension. However, if students must read several paragraphs dealing with various topics, these individual differences in knowledge and interest will balance out. This is the major reason why longer tests tend to be more reliable than shorter ones, other things being equal.

Cognitive Levels of Test Content

Bloom's taxonomy

Besides sampling from the full range of topics covered, we might also wish to sample various levels of understanding of the material. The *Taxonomy of Educational Objectives* (Bloom et al., 1956) may be used in thinking about various cognitive demands that different kinds of test items make on students. The following taxonomy contains six levels, ordered from simplest to most complex (see Chapter 6 for more details about this taxonomy):

- ☐ *Knowledge*—To remember and to recall information. (Who were the first five presidents of the United States? Recite the alphabet. What author wrote Hamlet?)
- ☐ *Comprehension*—To understand the relations between facts or concepts. (Translate a French sentence into English. Predict the probability of rain when given key facts. Determine the relative size of a standard deviation by looking at a distribution of scores.)
- ☐ *Application*—To use information and procedures that are comprehended. (Given a set of student scores, compute the mean and standard deviation. Write sentences that are grammatically correct.)
- ☐ *Analysis*—To break down an idea into its parts. (Diagram sentences. Identify the setting, plot, and climax of a novel.)
- ☐ *Synthesis*—To rearrange parts to form a new whole. (Write a class play. Watch a film of one's teaching and plan a better strategy.)

☐ *Evaluation*—To know the value of methods for given purposes. (Was the play credible, well paced? Was the teaching more effective?)

To the extent that all these levels of content mastery were included as instructional goals for the curriculum sequences being tested, we might want to sample from each level. This will help get a balanced view of each student's learning as well (some students are good at understanding and remembering discrete facts but have trouble synthesizing them, integrating them with general principles, and applying their knowledge in problem-solving situations; other students have the opposite pattern of strengths and weaknesses). Table 28.3 illustrates a plan for a test that samples both the range of topics taught and a variety of levels of cognitive demand. For simplicity, the six cognitive level categories from the taxonomy are combined to form two categories. The first (terms, facts, principles) represents the first two levels of the taxonomy (knowledge and comprehension).

Table 28.3 also summarizes the teacher's plans for three different units. The first unit on weather indicates that the largest percentage of instruction will focus on application of concepts to predict weather. Hence, the exam should emphasize this information, and students should know that when they prepare for the test.

Table 28.3 Three Plans for Classroom Tests with Specification of Content and Cognitive Emphasis

Content	Cognitive Objectives		
	Terms, Facts, Principles	*Applications*	*Total Percentage*
Unit 1: Weather			
A. Atmosphere	20	0	20
B. Air masses and fronts	15	5	20
C. Causes of precipitation	0	15	15
D. Predicting	0	40	40
E. Control	5	0	5
Unit 2: Weights and Measures			
A. Length	10	0	10
B. Weight mass	10	0	10
C. Time	10	0	10
D. Standard measures			
1. Metric system	60	0	60
2. GCS	5	0	5
3. KMS	5	0	5
Unit 3: Comparative Politics			
A. Historical development	80	0	80
B. Present function	0	20	20
C. Future trends	0	0	0

The second plan indicates that understanding general facts and principles of the metric system is a key instructional goal. (Perhaps an application unit will follow this one.) Such an outline of goals helps teachers to make instructional decisions (how much time to spend in class, the type of homework to assign) and to write appropriate tests. Unfortunately, many teachers fail to provide students with this information; typically, teachers erroneously confuse general knowledge of test expectations with knowledge of specific questions.

Instructional Objectives

We have discussed test construction as if all content topics and all instructional objectives included in a unit were equal. However, teachers often want to stress certain topics or objectives they consider to be especially important. In this case, it may make sense for the teacher not only to emphasize these key goals during instruction but to emphasize them in constructing tests and in making suggestions to students about how to allocate their preparation time.

In general, instruction is more effective to the extent that teachers have specific plans and communicate clear expectations to students about what they are to learn. These shared expectations about what course content is important and about what types of test will be used can help improve the reliability of teacher-made tests. Test construction experts contend that teachers must resolve three questions if they are to teach effectively: (1) What will I teach? (2) How will I know when students have learned it?, and (3) What materials and activities will be necessary? These three questions represent the three parts that compose an instructional objective. Three steps are involved in writing these objectives (Mager, 1962; Gronlund, 1985).

1. Name the terminal behavior—what proof would you accept that the learner has achieved your goal (Must the student swim a lap or a mile, design a blueprint, or build a garage?).
2. Specify the conditions under which the behavior will be demonstrated (Will students write essay questions or deliver a speech; will answers be picked from a list or from memory; will students evaluate a live debate or analyze written material?).
3. Announce the criteria for acceptable performance (15 out of 20 for an A; run a mile in less than 8 minutes for a B; write a theme with no grammatical errors to pass the grammar unit review).

In Chapter 6, we summarized the general advantages and disadvantages of instructional objectives. Some of these arguments are presented below, as they apply to evaluation issues. However, even before reading the list it is useful to note that neither advocates of instructional objectives nor their opponents have a correct view. The value of instructional objectives depends on how teachers use them.

Teachers should give clear instructions concerning expectations and format before administering tests.

Advantages of Instructional Objectives

1. They increase teacher awareness of what students should be working on and lead to more optimal planning. A wider range of objectives is included.
2. They provide a basis for assessing continuous progress (allowing students to proceed at their own rates) because instruction focuses on specific skills.
3. Students have a better blueprint for guiding their learning activity; hence, they learn more.
4. After reaching a criterion, students have more time to work on their own learning activities.

Disadvantages of Instructional Objectives

1. They increase teacher control at the expense of students' control of objectives.
2. They unduly emphasize things that can be measured; only low-level objectives are likely to be measured.
3. Once established (the teacher invests the time to write objectives and set up a measurement system), the system perpetuates itself; objectives remain the same; spontaneity is reduced.
4. A great deal of instructor time is used in writing instructional objectives; such time could be better used in other ways, such as in one-to-one conferences.

Our only major concern with instructional objectives is that at times teachers apply them too specifically, or apply them to content for which they are inappropriate.

Communicating Expectations to Students

It may be useful for students to know that their themes will be graded on the basis of ideas, organization, mechanics, and sentence structure. Table 28.4 shows that such knowledge has practical consequences for students.

In Ms. James's class students know they should spend most of their time generating ideas; however, they also realize that they should polish their general language and grammar. In contrast, students in Ms. Wilson's class should concentrate on developing major ideas. If she wishes to assess students' use of correct grammar, she will do so with separate, focused tests. Mr. Adkins's students know that they should spend about half of the time available for composition by carefully examining sentence structure, grammar, and so on. Mr. Adkins believes that the only proof of knowledge of grammar is in its application in written composition. Different expectations are reflected in Ms. Stanford's objectives. She stresses organization, especially paragraphing, more than the other teachers; however, students' grammatical mistakes do not affect their scores. In the margin, she puts an X by any sentence that contains a grammatical error and gives students five minutes to correct their errors. Grades are lowered slightly if students cannot find their mistakes.

Communicating teacher expectations

Teachers' performance expectations vary widely, and teachers should communicate their expectations to students prior to examinations. However, too much information may lock both teachers and students into unproductive patterns of behavior. If Mr. Adkins were to define every conceivable organizational, grammatical, and sentence-structure error and assign points in advance (minus points: 4, inappropriate use of colon or semicolon; 2, inappropriate use of comma; 5, sentence without subject; and so forth) he might inadvertently constrict student behavior. His students could learn to write three or four short paragraphs, using very simple sentences and words. If students were left at this level, it would be an unfortunate loss.

Table 28.4 Criteria for Grading Students' Papers in Four Different Classrooms

Teacher	Ideas	Organization	Mechanics	Sentence Structure
Ms. James	70	10	10	10
Ms. Wilson	85	15	0	0
Mr. Adkins	50	10	25	15
Ms. Stanford	50	50	0	0*

* Assumes that all student errors are corrected by students when papers are handed back.

Facts Versus Concepts

Test blueprints

What does a good test blueprint look like? What percentage of questions should be factual? What percentage should cover application or evaluation? There is no formula for a good plan. A plan should clarify instructional goals, assist in planning instruction, and help the teacher to prepare a test that measures intended goals. Sometimes it makes sense to have a little application and much orientation to basic facts. At other times balance between application and facts is more appropriate, and sometimes it makes sense to stress application. The teacher should know content and cognitive goals prior to instruction and should match the exam to the instructional emphases. It is simply not fair to students, nor is it effective evaluation, to lead them to expect one type of test and present another.

Types of Test Items

We have discussed the need for reliable tests and have noted that a test must sufficiently cover assigned content if it is to produce an interpretable score. Equally important is the need for questions that measure objectives appropriately. In this section, we describe two types of questions that teachers can utilize on classroom tests and we examine some of the strengths and weaknesses of these questions.

Writing the Essay Question

Teachers who use the following measurement guidelines for writing essay exams can improve their ability to measure student performance rather than teacher bias (Thorndike & Hagen, 1977; Tenbrink, 1974; Kubiszyn & Borich, 1984):

1. Know the mental processes you want students to use before starting to write test questions.
2. Write essay questions so that students have clear tasks. (Are students to recognize biased presentations? Are they to distinguish verifiable from unverifiable facts?)
3. Be sure essay questions require students to do more than reproduce information.
4. Be sure that questions are not too numerous or too lengthy.
5. Include questions that vary in difficulty.
6. Provide students with clear directions for essay tests. (Students need to know if the answer is to be outlined or written out completely, the point value of each question on the test, and the criteria the teacher will use to evaluate their answers.)

Often teachers write essay questions that only call for factual information. To assess factual information given in response to an essay question is a waste of time. Knowledge and comprehension can be assessed more efficiently and reliably by objective tests. Teachers must decide which cognitive level they want to test prior to writing questions, because this decision determines the type of test they should construct. Teachers should then tell students precisely what type of response is desired.

Vague questions

Too often essay questions merely tell students to discuss an issue and they force students to guess what the teacher really wants. Imagine yourself answering the following exam question in a teacher-education course: "Discuss the factors that contribute to student learning." Does the teacher simply want a list of all factors that relate to student learning? Should you discuss the importance of each factor or the role of each factor? This question does not indicate what type of answer the teacher wants.

The question is vague in other ways as well. What is meant by the term "factors?" If you apply a literal definition, then hundreds of factors are involved (quality of prenatal care, and so on). An example of a clearer question would be: "Illustrate how a teacher could hypothetically improve the performance of an anxious but capable (IQ 115) student in a speech class. Be sure that your response illustrates the use of dissonance, feedback, reward, and success in public and private classroom situations."

Essay questions, if used correctly, should require students to do more than reproduce information. Questions that ask students to predict or to write their own examples are generally better than questions that require students to merely present facts.

Problem-solving questions

Asking students to solve problems is an especially good way to use essay questions. For example: "The first paragraph that follows describes the academic problems of Ted Jenkins. The following three paragraphs describe a teacher's attempt to deal with the problems. Compare and contrast the three solutions, with special consideration to the short-term and long-term effects of the plans on Ted's general dependency, class achievement, and peer status." This question forces students to do more than simply reproduce information.

Appropriate number of questions

Some teachers, perhaps because they feel uncomfortable asking so few questions and neglecting so much content, ask too many essay questions and undermine the unique role that an essay question can play. Essay exams are useful to the extent that they provide students with an opportunity to demonstrate their ability to recall, organize, and apply facts and principles. However, to rush students through ten essay questions in fifty minutes is self-defeating.

Arrangement by difficulty level

However, it is possible to ask a few essay questions (four or so) in fifty minutes, and it is useful to vary the difficulty of these questions. If the questions are all simple, students with average mastery will not be differentiated from students with excellent mastery. Similarly, if all the essay questions are very difficult, the test will not differentiate students with minimal mastery from students with average mastery. It is generally desirable to arrange test items in order of expected difficulty, to prevent some students from giving up on initially reading the most difficult or detailed questions.

Necessity for complete directions

It is also important to provide students with complete directions. For example, teachers may occasionally prefer that students outline their answers rather than write them out. (Teachers may not want to penalize students who write poorly, or may think that it is important to ask a few extra questions.) Such expectations should be clearly communicated to students. It is especially important to specify how many points each question is worth. Without such knowledge, students cannot effectively plan how much time to spend on various questions.

The Essay Test. Read the two answers that appear below in response to the question: "Compare the powers and organization of the central government under the Articles of Confederation with the powers and organization of our central government today." Which student deserves the higher grade? What grade should Student A receive? Student B? Which answer is better written? Which conveys more knowledge? More comprehension?

Student A

Our government today has a president, a house of representatives, and a senate. Each state has two senators, but the number of representatives is different for each state. This is because of compromise at the Constitutional Convention. The Articles of Confederation had only a Congress and each state had delegates in it and had one vote. This Congress couldn't do much of anything because all the states had to say it was alright. Back then Congress couldn't make people obey the law and there wasn't no supreme court to make people obey the law. The Articles of the Confederation let Congress declare war, make treaties, and borrow money and Congress can do these things today. But Congress then really didn't have any power, it had to ask the states for everything. Today Congress can tell the states what to do and tax people to raise money they don't have to ask the states to give them money. Once each state could print its own money if it wanted to but today only the U.S. Mint can make money.

Student B

There is a very unique difference between the Central Government under the Articles of Confederation and the National Government of today. The Confederation could not tax directly where as the National Government can. The government of today has three different bodies—Legislative, Judicial, and Executive branches. The Confederation had only one branch which had limited powers. The confederate government could not tax the states directly or an individual either. The government of today, however, has the power to tax anyone directly and if they don't respond, the government has the right to put this person in jail until they are willing to pay the taxes. The confederation government was not run nearly as efficiently as the government of today. While they could pass laws (providing most of the states voted with them) the confederate government could not enforce these laws, (something which the present day can and does do) they could only hope and urge the states to enforce the laws.

How hard is it for you to *quantify* the differences between the two responses? How much better is the response you rate higher? How do you think the grades you assigned compare to those your classmates gave? We suspect that the ratings of the two responses will vary widely in your class.

Thorndike and Hagen (1969) presented these two answers (along with three others) to two groups of graduate students taking a course in tests and measurement. They asked the groups to assign a maximum of 25 points to the questions, provided them with a model answer, and stressed that the grade should be based on completeness and accuracy, not grammar or spelling. The papers received a wide variety of scores from the two groups of raters. Student A's paper received scores ranging from 5 to 25 points, and Student B's paper was scored as low as 3 and as high as 25. The ratings of the papers depended on who rated them.

These findings indicate that it is important for teachers who use essay tests to develop objective criteria for scoring such tests. Is the paper assigned a 20 or 21 really inferior to the paper assigned a 24 or 25? To put it another way, the teacher must be sure that the scores reflect demonstrated student performances, not teacher biases. Some techniques for accomplishing this follow.

Sorting method

Scoring Essay Exams. Green (1975) notes that there are two generally acceptable techniques for grading an essay—the point-score method and the sorting method. The sorting method is easier to use than the point-score method, and, although not as reliable, it can be used fairly. The steps involved in sorting are: (1) quickly read all the papers, sort papers into piles (A, B, C, pass, fail), and place borderline papers into the higher category with a question mark on them; (2) read the responses again, paying special attention to borderline papers; (3) assign a grade to each paper on the basis of the pile it ends up in.

Point-score method

The point-score procedure calls for the following: (1) a grading key that includes features that should be present in student answers for full credit (partial credit for each part of the response should be determined in advance); (2) reading all responses to the same question consecutively and assigning the number of earned points to each question as it is read; (3) reading all responses to the next question; and (4) when all questions have been read, totaling the points and assigning a grade.

Halo effect

In general, the point-score method is the best way to grade essay tests because it uses a fixed standard (an answer key) and guards against halo effects that interfere with effective grading. A halo effect refers to the tendency to rate or evaluate a person or performance on the basis of a global impression rather than according to a specific trait or performance. The sorting method also yields generally reliable scores, however, and teachers who test frequently and often use essay tests may have to rely on this technique.

Need to read papers anonymously

Both methods of grading essay questions require that teachers read papers anonymously. This can be done by telling students to put their names on the backs of their papers. It is easy to read something extra into an answer by a good student, and it is equally easy to demand more from a student we believe to be marginal (demand more proof that the student really deserves full credit). An advantage of the point-score method is that the teacher reads answers to the same question consecutively in all papers. Students who write poor responses to the first question are not as likely to be inadvertently penalized when the teacher reads the second question as they could be if the teacher read responses to the two questions one after another.

However, if the teacher writes the point value at the bottom of the first question (where the teacher cannot avoid seeing it when he or she begins to grade the second question), the usefulness of this procedure is reduced somewhat. Similarly, if the teacher repeatedly grades student B's responses immediately after student A's, student B's score might be systematically influenced (Follman, Lowe, & Miller, 1971; Hales & Tokar, 1975). If student A is among the best in the class, the contrast between the two papers might be sufficiently glaring for B's score to suffer. Similarly, B's score might look better than it actually is if it repeatedly follows a low scorer's paper. For this reason teachers should shuffle papers after reading all responses to a particular question.

Constructing model answers

Mehrens and Lehmann (1978) recommend that teachers construct model answers to essay questions as they write the questions, not after the test is given. This procedure calls attention to faulty wording, inadequate time allotment, inappropriate difficulty level, and similar problems early enough for teachers to correct them prior to test administration.

Writing Objective Test Items

We agree with Thorndike and Hagen (1977) and Kubiszyn and Borich (1984) who contend that multiple-choice items can measure the same aspects of an educational objective as any other pen and paper test, except written expression and originality. Analysis, synthesis, and all other levels of cognitive processing can be tested with multiple-choice items. The multiple-choice format is the most versatile form of an objective test item. The item has two parts: the *stem* which represents the problem, and three or more possible correct answers, one of which is the correct answer and the others are *distractors*. Consider the following illustration:

A major conclusion from the Brophy-Evertson (1976) and the Good-Grouws (1975) studies is:

a. Individual learning is the most effective overall learning mode in elementary schools.

b. Varying the pace of instruction accommodates the learning needs of most elementary school pupils.

c. Different patterns of teaching behavior may be important for different types of learners.

d. Subgroup teaching is more effective than whole-class teaching.

The answer to this question is c, and choices a, b, and d are designed to be distractors—plausible alternatives for students who do not know the answer.

How can one write or recognize a good question? We know that a good test question must ask the student to respond to important content, but what other criteria are there? Thorndike and Hagen (1977) provide a number of guidelines for writing multiple-choice items:

Guidelines

1. The stem must present a problem.
2. Include most of the item in the stem and keep options short.
3. Keep the stem as short as possible.

4. Use the negative infrequently in the stem but make it noticeable by underlining the not when it is included.
5. Use new material in stem problems and attempt to measure application.
6. Include only one correct or clearly best answer.
7. Try to make all options plausible.
8. Do not cue the answer (by making it longer than the others or using predictable patterns—B, C, D, A, B, C, D, A, and so on).

The first four suggestions are all related to helping students know precisely the question they are answering. If a stem does not present a problem, the student has to spend valuable time trying to figure out what the problem is. Similarly, lengthy questions make it more difficult to identify the problem. Since the purpose of the test is to assess knowledge and not reading ability, a clear presentation of the problem is desirable. Using "not" in the stem is acceptable if the student is aware that it is there. When students read stems rapidly they may miss the word. If the word "not" is used it should be underlined.

Which of the following is not typical of successful students?
- a. essentially task oriented
- b. tend to be liked by peers
- *c. more person than task oriented
- d. cooperative in class

As noted, the correct answer to this question is c. The "not" is emphasized in this question, the stem presents the problem, and both the stem and the answer choices are relatively brief.

Although it is not essential to present novel material in the stem, such material may help teachers to ask questions that require students to do more than just memorize facts. For example, rather than ask students "Which of the following is not recommended by Thorndike and Hagen. . . ?" it is possible to present a series of ten objective questions and ask students to indicate how many test construction principles are violated in each item.

Advantage of objective test

The primary advantage of the objective test, when properly constructed, is that it provides a relatively unbiased assessment of student performance. The inclusion of partially correct answers reduces the objectivity of the test because judgments have to made about the degree of correctness, and if answer choices are not plausible, the chances that a student will guess the answer are increased. Often test questions give away answers (the right answer is often longer, the stem provides a grammatical clue, the answer has to begin with a "not," verb tense, or the teacher may have a habit of placing the right answer in the same position). When test answers can be guessed the test measures students' ability to take tests, not their knowledge.

Other Forms of Objective Questions

We emphasize the multiple-choice question because it is the most versatile form of objective test. However, there are other forms of objective tests, and each has distinct advantages and limitations. Three other popular objective test formats are true-false, completion, and matching tests.

True-false tests

In general, true-false questions can be constructed much more quickly than multiple-choice items. Unlike multiple-choice questions, the true-false format forces students to choose between two alternatives rather than between four or five. For example, true or false: assimilation occurs when the child integrates a new idea into a scheme he or she already has.

Brown (1976) notes that true-false questions can be used to good advantage with young children, especially when only a general estimate of student performance is necessary. A major problem that limits the general use of true-false questions is that some content is very difficult to express in a true-false form. Furthermore, students will be correct fifty percent of the time by guessing; hence, the diagnostic power of true-false questions is low.

Short-answer and completion tests

Short-answer and completion items require students to finish a statement from recall rather than recognition. On a multiple-choice test students select (recognize) the best answer from a series of choices. In contrast, in a short-answer format students provide their own answers. It is considerably more difficult to construct a multiple-choice item that presents four or five carefully written and plausible alternatives than it is to write a stem and to allow students to provide their own answers.

Consider this question: "Motivation can be defined as ______ ?" Obviously, it takes considerably more time to present this question in a multiple-choice format than to write the question in its present form. However, the ease of scoring multiple-choice questions typically compensates for the time needed to construct the items and often yields more reliable scores than those obtained from a completion test. Indeed, some forms of completion test possess some of the same scoring problems as essay tests. For example, for questions like the one presented above, many responses can be partially or wholly correct. Teachers must invariably use their judgment in scoring some responses to completion questions.

Short-answer and completion items are especially useful in math and science courses, where formulas or equations can be requested, and for testing spelling and language, where specific bits of information often are required. In any subject matter, they are good for testing knowledge of definitions and technical terms (Mehrens & Lehmann, 1978).

Matching exercises

Matching exercises require students to link items in one column with corresponding items in another column:

Column A	*Column B*
____ 1. Intelligence tests	A. Freud
____ 2. Cognitive development	B. Skinner
____ 3. Trust vs. mistrust	C. Erikson
____ 4. Reinforcement	D. Piaget
____ 5. Modeling	E. Kounin
____ 6. Formal operations	F. Binet
	G. None of the above

In this example, students would receive credit for answering F, D, C, B,

G, and D for items 1–6, respectively. Matching exercises are useful for testing memory of specific facts: terms, definitions, dates, events, etc. They are easy to construct and score, as long as each item has just one clearly correct answer. To avoid cuing correct answers, it is helpful to have more response alternatives (Column B in the example) than items (Column A), or to include response alternatives that may be used more than once (D in the example).

Types of Test Items: Summary

No particular type of test or test item is best in all circumstances. Advocates sometimes claim that essay tests are better for measuring higher-level objectives and that objective tests are better for measuring factual recall or other low-level objectives. However, this is not the case. Essay tests can be used purely to grade low-level skills (punctuation, capitalization, spelling), with no attention whatsoever to the degree of creativity put into the essay, or they can be used to test factors such as sentence structure, paragraph structure, or story theme. Similarly, multiple-choice tests can measure learning objectives at almost any level of difficulty or sophistication. Multiple-choice tests are not necessarily restricted to low-level objectives. Thus, classifications such as subjective versus objective or essay versus multiple choice are not very useful.

Other differences between test items are more a matter of teacher or student preference than of necessity. For example, essay tests allow students to organize their answers and to integrate material. However, to students with above-average writing skills, they provide an advantage not directly relevant to the course, but relevant to success on essay tests. Essay tests are confined to a relatively small portion of the material covered, they are time-consuming to grade, and the grading is notoriously subjective.

Multiple-choice and other objective tests present different advantages and disadvantages. Advantages include speed and objectivity of scoring, sampling a much larger number of objectives in the same amount of time, quicker feedback to students, and collecting a broader-based set of data on how well students have mastered a wide range of course objectives. However, some students have test-taking skills that give them a particular advantage on this kind of test, independent of subject content. The items are structured completely by the teacher, so that the test provides little opportunity for students to integrate material or to discuss it in their own words.

Using a variety of testing methods

Because there are advantages and disadvantages to different kinds of tests, perhaps the best solution is to use a variety of tests and assignments (essays or term papers, for example). This procedure enables teachers to balance differential student test-taking abilities with different kinds of tests, and to achieve a balance between the kinds of learning strategies and content mastery that various tests foster.

Criterion-Referenced and Norm-Referenced Measurement

The distinction between criterion-referenced and norm-referenced measurement does not affect the type of item that one includes on exams, but influences why a particular item is selected.

Gronlund (1985) contends that criterion-referenced tests are especially helpful in measuring the minimum knowledge or skills to be obtained from an instructional program and that norm-referenced tests are most appropriate for estimating progress toward higher-level, complex learning outcomes when continuous development is possible as is typically the case in higher-level cognitive goals. Mastery or criterion-level measurement is not appropriate for this purpose. However, as Gronlund notes, it is possible to use criterion- and norm-referenced strategies simultaneously. For example, one could describe a student's behavior in terms of both percentage correct (Alice found 10 of 14 errors) and percentage of students surpassed (75 percent).

Difficulty of questions

In both criterion-referenced and norm-referenced testing, teachers should communicate general objectives to students and must use an adequate and appropriate sample of test questions. The major difference between the two types of measurement lies in the difficulty of questions.

Again, teachers can employ both criterion- and norm-referenced techniques as the subject matter dictates. In general, if important and universal objectives can be identified as in the early elementary school grades, it appears more reasonable to stress criterion-referenced measurement and to report student progress in terms of measured objectives. In secondary settings, where there are less clear goals, norm-referenced measurement (perhaps combined with minimum performance levels and criterion-referenced measurement where possible) is a viable assessment strategy.

Additional Assessment Procedures

We have discussed written tests and how they can be constructed and used appropriately. However, teachers measure student learning in many other ways. Any assessment procedure a teacher uses must be valid and reliable if it is to be useful. We now discuss assessment procedures other than pen-and-paper tests.

Performance Tests

A performance test demands that an individual, or sometimes a group of individuals, make a decision, solve a problem, or perform some prescribed behavior like delivering a speech. Some contend that student behavior—

not student knowledge as shown on pen-and-paper tests—is the critical variable in determining whether students have mastered material or developed social maturity. Indeed, many teacher-education programs use student performance as a part of assessment. Similarly, several states have now adopted beginning teacher evaluation programs in which teachers have to demonstrate classroom competency before they are allowed to become fully certified.

Obviously, many performance measures that could be obtained are not worth the effort necessary to do so. A third-grade classroom teacher could call students individually to the front of the class and ask them to find selected countries on the globe. However, the same information can be obtained more reliably and quickly by asking students to pencil in the names of a variety of countries on a dittoed, blank map.

Advantage of performance measures

Most knowledge can be assessed through pen-and-paper measures. However, if behaviors are critically important they can be assessed with rating scales and checklists by having individuals perform. The advantage of performance measures is that they provide direct evidence that a student can perform a specific skill. The disadvantage is that the process of observing the performance of individuals is time consuming for both students and teachers.

Brown (1976) lists the following examples of skills that one might want to measure directly: painting a watercolor, typing 40 words per minute, conducting an opinion poll, conducting a counseling interview, programming a computer, making a souffle, or assembling a carburetor.

To obtain reliable scores on performance tests, as on pen-and-paper tests, students need to know precisely what they are to demonstrate and the criteria by which their performance will be judged. Similarly, teachers should prepare checklists and rating scales that adequately describe student performance.

Teachers may use performance tests or oral presentations as part of their assessment programs. The general procedure teachers follow is the same as that for construction of classroom tests: (1) identify general instructional objectives (content and cognitive skill), (2) plan instructional activities, and (3) assess student learning and the instructional program.

Green (1975) notes that the content of an industrial arts course might include:

1. Common hand tools and their use
2. Common power tools and their use
3. Qualities of various types of hard and soft wood
4. Safety rules
5. Joints: butt, miter, dowel, and mortise
6. Fasteners: screws, nails, staples, corrugated fasteners, and glue
7. Finishes: oil, wax, paint, varnish, shellac, lacquer, glass, and plastics
8. Project selection and construction

From this type of content list teachers make decisions about the importance of each objective (objectives 1, 2, and 3 may be 75 percent of the course), and the evidence they will accept as proof of mastery (pen-and-paper test, performance).

Immediate evaluation

In many performance-testing situations teachers must evaluate performance as it occurs (to tape speeches or to film a student cutting with a power tool is unwieldy). An example of a checklist that could be used to describe a student's observation of safety rules appears in Table 28.5. This scale allows one to mark whether or not a specific behavior occurs.

Rating Scales. A rating scale does more than record the presence or absence of behavior; it forces the rater to judge the quality of the performance. An example of a rating scale appears in Table 28.6. In general, it is easier for errors to occur when using rating forms than checklists. Yet a rating is often necessary to estimate quality.

Improving reliability

Several steps can be taken to improve the reliability of ratings. The first and most important one is to obtain several ratings on different days. All of us vary from day to day and from situation to situation. The more ratings we have the more likely we will be to describe typical, not atypical, behavior. Second, make a separate rating for each separate performance element. For example, teachers using the rating scale presented in Table 28.6 can note a student's inability to follow a plan without losing sight of the fact that the student used tools properly.

Too often teachers do not rate performance dimensions separately. Use of overgeneralized rating scales may result in a single behavior unduly hurt-

Table 28.5 Checklist for Evaluating Pupil's Compliance with Safety Regulations in Use of Circular Saw

DIRECTIONS: As each pupil uses the circular saw, observe his procedure and place a check mark in the blank preceding each safety regulation with which he fails to comply.

_____	1.	He makes adjustments to the saw only when the power is turned off.
_____	2.	He uses the guard, kickback device, and spreader for all cuts except such special cuts as dadoes, etc.
_____	3.	He uses a pusher stick when ripping small pieces of stock.
_____	4.	He uses the ripping fence to guide the work when ripping stock.
_____	5.	He uses the crosscut gauge when crosscutting stock.
_____	6.	He never attempts to clear away scraps from the table top with his fingers while the saw is on.
_____	7.	He removes the ripping fence when crosscutting long pieces of stock.
_____	8.	He does not reach over and in back of the saw to pull pieces through.
_____	9.	He does not let tools and scrap stockpile up on the saw table.
_____	10.	He checks the stock before cutting to see that there are no nails, screws, or grit present in the wood.
_____	11.	He raises the saw blade no more than $\frac{1}{8}$ inch above the stock being cut.
_____	12.	He asks the instructor to inspect special setups before beginning the cutting operation.

Source: From John A. Green, *Teacher-Made Tests,* 2nd ed. New York: Harper & Row, 1975. Adapted from Frank Pexton Lumber Co., "Safety Rules for the Safe Operation of Power Wordworking Tools," Denver, CO: pp. 8–9. By permission.

Table 28.6 Rating Scale for Projects in Industrial Arts

DIRECTIONS: Rate each item in the scale on the basis of 4 points for outstanding quality of performance. 3 points for better than average, 2 points for average, 1 point for inferior, and 0 for unsatisfactory or failure. Encircle the appropriate number to indicate your rating, and enter the total of these numbers at the bottom of the sheet. If an item does not apply, draw a horizontal line through the item so that it will not be included in the total score.

Procedure Scale

	Item	Rating
1.	To what extent did he follow the detailed steps of his plan?	0 1 2 3 4
2.	To what extent did he avoid having to do work over because of failure to follow his plan?	0 1 2 3 4
3.	To what extent did he refrain from spoiling materials by working accurately and carefully?	0 1 2 3 4
4.	To what extent did he follow approved procedures in performing specific operations?	0 1 2 3 4
5.	To what extent did he exhibit skill in the use of:	0 1 2 3 4
	a. layout and measuring tools?	
	b. cutting edge tools?	0 1 2 3 4
	c. boring and drilling tools?	0 1 2 3 4
6.	To what extent did he show improvement in the use of tools?	0 1 2 3 4
7.	Did he select the proper tool for each operation?	0 1 2 3 4
8.	Did he use all tools properly?	0 1 2 3 4
9.	To what extent did he exhibit initiative in revising his plan as required by changing conditions?	0 1 2 3 4
10.	Did he practice difficult operations to minimize material spoilage and poor workmanship?	0 1 2 3 4
11.	To what extent did he keep profitably employed? Busy?	0 1 2 3 4
12.	To what extent did he maintain a fair balance between quality of work performed and time consumed?	0 1 2 3 4
13.	To what extent was he able to do his own work without assistance from instructor or other students?	0 1 2 3 4

Product Scale

	Item	Rating
1.	To what extent is the finished product an embodiment of the original plan?	0 1 2 3 4
2.	Does the general appearance of the project reflect neat, orderly work?	0 1 2 3 4
3.	Are the dimensions of the actual project the same as those on the drawing, within reasonable tolerances?	0 1 2 3 4
4.	How do angular measurements check with those specified?	0 1 2 3 4
5.	Of what quality is the finish?	0 1 2 3 4
6.	To what extent were materials used to advantage?	0 1 2 3 4
7.	Do all joints fit properly?	0 1 2 3 4
8.	Are all margins uniform, curved and irregular lines properly executed, etc?	0 1 2 3 4

Source: From John A. Green, *Feature-Made Test*, 2/E (New York: Harper and Row, 1975). Copyright 1963, 1975 by John A. Green. (After *Measuring Educational Achievement*, by William J. Micheals and R. Ray Karnes, McGraw-Hill, 1950). Reprinted by permission of Harper & Row, Publishers, Inc.

ing or helping a student. For example, a speech teacher who likes an enthusiastic beginning may penalize a student too much for a slow start (unless this behavior is in a separate category), even though other parts of the speech such as eye contact, clear voice, and purpose are good.

Halo effects

Teachers must guard against halo effects when they use rating forms. It is easy for a student's previous record of performance to influence the present rating, partly because the identity of the student cannot be masked, as it can be with written papers, and because the rating must be made immediately. Thus, the teacher may not rate students who typically give good speeches as critically as he or she rates other students.

Teachers sometimes use rating scales inappropriately because they break tasks down into too many small steps and fail to obtain a general rating of a project or presentation. Sometimes poor performance on one aspect does not negatively affect total performance (a low score in inappropriate hand usage may not hurt the speech, while poor eye contact may make it totally ineffective). However, teachers should make considerable effort to include major criteria in the rating form itself. Green (1975) offers the following criteria for evaluating a student's oral presentation.

Criteria for evaluation

1. Rapport with audience
2. Enthusiastic presentation
3. Effective organization
4. Clarity
5. Correct grammar
6. Good word choice
7. Adequate knowledge of subject
8. Significance of material
9. Stage presence
10. Appropriate gestures

Grading performance and progress is difficult, and errors will occur. Use of observation checklists and rating forms are two ways in which tests can be given more fairly. Remember that ratings are judgments, not facts. Another important factor to keep in mind is that the form used for rating will influence student behavior. If the criteria do not reward descriptive speech and penalize mispronounciation, predictable behavior will follow.

Similar concerns have been raised about the effects of rating scales that are used to rate teaching effectiveness or teachers' classroom behavior and decisions. If items are on the checklist (e.g., does the teacher use simulations, does the teacher involve students in small-group discussions), these items may influence teachers to overuse these aspects of teaching.

Informal Assessment

Formal testing is only one way that teachers can get information, and not always the best way. In addition to formal testing or rating, teachers can collect information by observing, by questioning, or by inspecting the work their students perform.

Oral tests

In addition to this regular, informal monitoring, teachers may wish to conduct oral tests by calling on students to answer questions or recite individually. Records of this performance can be kept and used as feedback to guide instructional decisions and as information to be used in grading, just as with student performance on written assignments. Teachers who conduct oral tests should be sure to include everyone or else to randomize questions. If they only call on students who volunteer, they will overestimate student understanding, and if they only call on nonvolunteers, they will underestimate this understanding and put certain students on the spot continuously.

If everyone is to be questioned, the teacher may wish to proceed in a pattern, calling on students alphabetically or in rows. If so, the teacher probably should let the students know this, cautioning them to pay attention and think about how they would answer each question, but to do so silently without calling out answers or raising their hands. This will minimize confusion and help insure that students will get the most out of listening to exchanges between the teacher and other students.

Observing seatwork

Much useful information also can be obtained from observing and correcting students while they work on seatwork assignments. In subject areas such as elementary language arts or English composition, and in mathematics at almost any level, seatwork is as good or better than formal tests for monitoring progress, although teachers may wish to test for other reasons.

Classroom Assessment: Some Summary Suggestions

Each teacher and testing situation is unique, however, these general guidelines can be offered:

1. If you consider testing important, it is probably a good idea for you to test frequently over short time spans, using criterion-referenced tests when possible so that you can use your test data for reteaching and individualized instruction, as well as for grading.
2. Be clear about learning objectives. If you are, you are unlikely to run into problems such as lack of content validity, and you will not create tests that measure content that was taught but do not measure the objectives that you want to measure.
3. Take care that you allow students ample time to finish a test unless time is a relevant factor.
4. If you intend to test over the entire course content, be sure that your test samples equally from different parts of the course.
5. On the other hand, if you wish to stress certain content, alert students to this so that they can adjust their preparation plans accordingly. In fact, if you are extremely clear about objectives, you can give students a number of potential test questions and inform them that the test will be composed of a subset of these questions. This will ensure that the students study all the material that you consider important.

6. Try to maintain some balance between essay tests (or essay-type assignments) and objective tests, because certain students do notably better on one type of test than the other, independent of course content. Also, as pointed out previously, different kinds of tests promote various kinds of learning. A balance between test types is usually preferable to reliance on only one.

Test-Taking Skills

Even a carefully constructed test, under certain circumstances, can yield unreliable results. One of the biggest threats to obtaining accurate information about student performance is the fact that some students can take tests better than other students. Unfortunately, some students experience debilitating anxiety during testing or evaluation situations and thus underperform. As Hill and Wigfield (1984) note, several recent educational trends may serve to increase this problem further. Minimal competency testing, the increased use of test scores to evaluate educational programs, and greater public pressure for high levels of skill learning and achievement in schools are some of the many reasons why some students may do poorly in evaluative situations (for a review of the degree of impact of anxiety on student performance, see Hill & Wigfield, 1984).

Improving student skills

Hill and Wigfield argue that teachers may want to help students to understand testing and to develop more adequate skills for taking both teacher-made and standardized tests. To this end they have developed an in service training model to help prepare students for testing situations. These authors feel that allowing students to practice with test formats, respond to difficult material, and learn good test-taking strategies will help to improve student effort, motivation, and performance in test situations. Evaluative data show that the in service training program has been associated with improved student test performance, particularly in the language arts area. An outline of the skills and motivational dispositions follows.

Examples of Test-Taking Skills and Motivational Dispositions

1. General test skills and knowledge:
   a. Be comfortable and sit where you can write easily.
   b. Pay attention to the teacher when she or he talks.
   c. The teacher can help you understand how to work on the test, but can't tell you the answer to a problem on the test.
   d. Taking tests is something we learn to do in school.
2. Positive motivation—do your best:
   a. All I ask is that you do your best. I will be really pleased if you try to do your best.
   b. If you finish a section before time is up, go back and check your answers. Don't disturb others; instead, work quietly at your desk.
   c. Before we begin, remember to carefully listen to me, be quiet, take a deep breath, and feel relaxed.

3. Positive motivation—expectancy reassurance:
   a. Some tests have some very hard problems. Don't worry if you can't do some problems.
   b. It's okay if you aren't sure what the right answer is. Choose the answer you think is best. It's okay to guess.
   c. If you work hard but don't finish a test, don't worry about it! The most important thing to me is that you try hard and do as well as you can. I know you'll do a good job if you try!
4. Test strategy and problem-solving skills:
   a. There is only *one* best answer.
   b. Do what you know first. If you can't answer a problem or it's taking a lot of time, move on to the next one. You can come back later if you have time.
   c. Don't rush. If you work *too fast*, you can make careless errors. You have to work carefully.
   d. Don't work too slowly. Do the problems at a moderate rate.
   e. Pay close attention to your work.
   f. Keep track of where you are working on the page by keeping one hand on this spot.

SUMMARY

Construction of tests involves consideration of a number of issues such as content coverage, test length, item types, weighting, and various related matters. Since tests only sample mastery of the content taught in a course, it is important to sample from the full range of content and to include enough items to allow reliable measurement. Otherwise a test may yield biased results and the errors of measurement are likely to be increased. Generally, test reliability increases with test length, so errors of measurement can be reduced by adding items if content coverage and other important qualities are carefully considered.

In addition to content coverage, it is important to consider the levels of understanding involved in test items. The six levels of Bloom's taxonomy provide a convenient reference for planning test items that measure different cognitive levels. Simultaneous examination of content and level permits planning of tests that will cover the instructional objectives of a course adequately. Item type is another critical factor, since essay items can be used to assess higher levels in the cognitive domain more easily than objective items. However, it is frequently more difficult to sample a wide range of content with essay than with objective items.

Teachers can use various means of assessment other than written tests. Performance tests can be used if actual performance on a task, rather than knowledge, is the essential factor. Rating scales provide a basis for estimating the quality of performance directly. Informal assessments, perhaps based on observation supplemented by oral tests, can be used along with more formal assessments like written tests in evaluating student performance.

Student test-taking skills can be improved by helping them to understand the reasons for testing and by helping them to develop appropriate skills for taking tests. Test-taking skill training can help to improve the reliability and validity of classroom tests.

QUESTIONS AND PROBLEMS

1. What would you do if students correctly pointed out to you that your tests concentrated on only a quarter or so of the assigned material, thus benefiting those who studied this part of the material thoroughly and penalizing those who studied all of the material?
2. Some students clearly do better on objective tests than on essay tests, or vice versa. What implication, if any, does this fact have for your testing and grading practices?
3. Is it better to test frequently but briefly, or infrequently but exhaustively?
4. What types of tests do you like and dislike as a student? How might these likes and dislikes affect your behavior later as a teacher? Are your biases appropriate for the subject matter, grade level, and types of students that you expect to teach?
5. Considering the grade level and subject matter you expect to teach, how can you evaluate the progress of students who do not read or write English efficiently?
6. Prepare a model essay test on the functions of the Supreme Court for sixth-grade students and another for eleventh-grade students. How would the two tests vary? Compare your two essay tests with those of classmates.

CASE STUDIES

A Lesson on the American Revolution. Read the following material describing the American Revolution. As you read it, identify concepts and facts that you would want students to learn. Take notes as you read in order to:

1. Write four instructional objectives that will tell students what they should learn.
2. Prepare a test blueprint.
3. Write four multiple-choice items that measure objectives in your blueprint.

The American Revolution and Its Meaning. The American Revolution grew largely out of change in Britain's colonial purposes and methods. In 1763 the American colonists seemed content with their status. If Great Britain had not attempted to tighten the loosely knit empire and to make more money out of it, the break between Britain and the colonies would probably not have come when it did or as it did.

But once the break took place changes came fast in the Americans' attitudes toward Great Britain and toward their own society. The fears, hopes, dreams, and material pressures caused by war produced some major changes in American life. Nevertheless, America after the war years looked remarkably like colonial America. The conservative nature of the American Revolution was caused largely by two circumstances. The first is that the colonists began fighting in an effort to preserve what they already had, rather than to create a new order. The second is that the war did little damage to agriculture, the basis of American economy.

Reconstructing the Empire. After the French and Indian War, the British decided that they could no longer afford to neglect their American colonies. The government issued a series of laws and decrees aimed at establishing more effective control over the colonies.

With French power eliminated in America after 1763, colonists moved west and provoked a new Indian war, the Pontiac Conspiracy. To quiet the Indians and to gain time to organize the territory acquired from France, Parliament issued the Proclamation of 1753. This act forbade the colonists to settle west of the Appalachian Mountains. Then, in 1764, Parliament passed the Sugar Act. This act placed new duties on sugar, coffee, wine, and certain other imported products, reduced the tax on molasses, and provided ways to collect all duties more effectively.

There were only scattered protests to these first measures. But a major crisis over taxation quickly followed. In 1765, Parliament passed the Stamp Act. Colonial resistance took a number of forms. Colonial leaders refused to do any business requiring the use of stamps to show that the tax had been paid. Trade came to a halt, and courts of justice closed since virtually all legal papers needed stamps. Politicians organized bands of patriots, largely workingmen, who called themselves Sons of Liberty. They pressured reluctant business people to support the boycott and forced Stamp Act officials to resign by their use of threats and violence.

Even more significant was a meeting in New York of delegates from nine colonies. This Stamp Act Congress was the first really effective act of political cooperation among so many colonies. It adopted a series of resolutions protesting the new tax law and other new policies, such as the trials of accused smugglers by military courts. British business people hurt by the colonial boycott persuaded Parliament to repeal the Stamp Act in 1766. At the time, Parliament restated its right to pass laws for the colonies.

Parliament continued to pass new and unpopular laws that caused the division between the colonists and Great Britain to grow larger. Occasional brawls between the colonists and the British soldiers quartered in Boston finally ended in the Boston Massacre in 1770. British soldiers shot five members of an unarmed mob. Similar brawls between soldiers and colonists occurred in New York and added to the growing dislike and fear between the colonists and the British.

The Lull and the Storm. In the spring of 1770, British-colonial relations took a marked turn for the better. The British soldiers in Boston withdrew to the fort in the harbor to prevent further incidents. A new Parliamentary ministry took office. Its leader, Lord Frederick North, had all of the Townshed duties repealed except that on tea. North allowed the Quartering Act to expire and also promised that no new taxes would be imposed on the colonies. There was rejoicing in the colonies, and for more than two years there seemed to be a real reconciliation.

Then a series of episodes produced serious conflicts that finally led to independence. The first took place in June 1772, when a group of Rhode Islanders raided and burned the *Gaspée*, a customs vessel. The British decision to try the offenders in England, assuming they could be identified, alarmed the colonists, who saw this decision as yet another blow to the right of trial by jury. The colonists organized Committees of Correspondence to keep each other informed about local conflicts between colonial and British authority and to circulate propaganda against British rule.

In 1773, the tea crisis speeded up the final break with Great Britain. The colonists saw the British East India Company's monopoly on the sale of tea as another example of colonial exploitation for British profits. The colonists prevented the sale of tea up and down the Atlantic coast. In Boston, the center of colonial protest, a band of citizens destroyed the cargo of tea ships.

Parliament responded angrily in 1774 with the Coercive Acts, labeled the Intolerable Acts by the colonists. At the same time, Parliament passed the Quebec Act, which was not intended as a colonial punishment, but which the colonists interpreted as one.

With the Intolerable Acts, Parliament showed that it intended to enforce British authority, regardless of the cost to trade and remaining colonial good will. All the colonies united firmly in support of Massachusetts. The Committees of Correspondence organized a Congress, which met in Philadelphia in September 1774 to deal with the mounting crisis. The fifty-five delegates from twelve colonies (Georgia was not represented) voted to support Massachusetts, to denounce Parliament's legislation for the colonies since 1763, and to form a Continental Association to enforce a complete boycott of trade with Britain.

By the spring of 1776, it became clear to most members of the Congress that reconciliation between the colonies and Great Britain was impossible without completely surrendering the colonial position. In all thirteen colonies, the Americans had removed the royal officials. The colonists were disillusioned with the king, who had stoutly supported Parliament. And their position was strengthened by Thomas Paine's bitter attack in *Common Sense* on monarchy in general and on the king in particular. The Continental Congress responded to the events of the year by adopting the Declaration of Independence.

The War and Its Strategy. The Americans' victory in the War of Independence had a number of reasons. First, they fought on home ground. Second, they received considerable help from France and Spain. And third, their commander, George Washington, realized that time was on the American side if he could avoid an early defeat.

The British met with serious difficulties in using their superior strength on the distant rebellion. The war against the colonies was unpopular with many merchants, some members of Parliament, and even some generals. The British did not have the manpower needed to put down the revolt so they had to hire thirty thousand mercenary soldiers from Germany. In addition, the British navy was in bad shape . . . [Material describing the war is omitted].

The Revolution at Home. After the revolution against Britain, relatively few changes occurred in American institutions. State governments were established under new constitutions, beginning in 1776, but they resembled the colonial governments they replaced. Under the new constitutions, the representative assemblies held most political power. Voters in most states elected their governors, whose power was reduced. In most of the colonies, the right to vote had depended on possession of some property. During the war, nearly all property qualifications for voting and officeholding were either lowered or dropped.

The new states guarded their powers jealously. They gave some authority to the new government of the United States formed under the Articles of the Confederation in 1781. But they kept all authority relating to local government. The central government, which itself lacked an effective executive office, directed the army and conducted foreign relations. But it could not regulate commerce, nor did it have the authority to tax citizens directly. It had the right to request money from the states, but could not enforce its requests.

Merchants and other creditors suffered from the interruption of commerce during the war. But farmers and debtors benefitted from the demand for food stuffs and the creation of a vast supply of paper money by the revolutionary government to pay its debts. Much property owned by Loyalists was confiscated. In most cases, it went to property holders rather than to landless people. Stimulated by war, democratic ideas affected some social relationships. Perhaps the most striking examples were the decisions of several northern states to abolish slavery. Some southern states simplified the process of freeing slaves. The numbers of freed slaves increased substantially. Most states prohibited the slave trade during the Revolution. Thus, Americans emerged from their War for Independence with a working national political system and a society and economy that were not deeply divided.

Test Plan, American Revolution: Three-Day Unit. Assume that the test plan below has been given to students to guide their study of the unit on the American Revolution. How will the plan influence student behavior? Discuss the value of this blueprint. Is it good or bad? Defend your answer.

	Cognitive Objectives		
	Terms, Facts, Principles	*Application*	*Total Percent*
A. *Causes*			
1. In England	10	0	10
2. In the colonies	10	0	10
B. *Battle Strategy*			
1. General attitude–Motivation of soldiers	20	0	20
2. Specific battles	0	0	0
C. *Consequences of the War*			
1. Relationship with England	0	5	5
2. Relationship with world	0	5	5
3. Life in the colonies	0	50	50

Chapter 29

Assigning Grades

OBJECTIVES

When you have mastered the material in this chapter you will be able to

1. Discuss the educational and practical purposes of grading versus evaluating students, and provide reasons why strict "grading on a curve" is not appropriate
2. Explain how the three basic methods of grading work
3. Describe the advantages and disadvantages of fixed-standard versus norm-referenced grading systems
4. List and explain the four considerations a teacher might use in adjusting grades
5. Describe individualized contracts for grades and tell when and how contracts are appropriate to use
6. Discuss the relationship between different grading methods and student motivation and perception of success
7. Make recommendations for setting up a grading system that will minimize both teacher and student anxiety about the process

You are probably familiar with the term "grading on the curve." Originally, this method assumed that student mastery of course material would be distributed normally, so that grades would also follow a normal distribution: 2 percent "A," 14 percent "B," 68 percent "C," 14 percent "D," and 2 percent "F." This notion did not last long, however, because it involves several faulty assumptions.

First, even if students' efforts were equal, the distribution of content mastery would not ordinarily be normal, because the distribution of students' aptitudes is not typically normal in any classroom. Second, students' efforts usually are not equal, and many teachers want grades to reflect effort as well as objective achievement. Third, even if both effort and achievement were distributed normally, this in itself would not necessarily mean that grades should be distributed normally. The "ideal" distribution of grades varies with their intended purpose or function: to motivate/reward effort, document progress, measure achievement relative to absolute standards or individualized expectations, or qualify students for advancement or certification, among others.

Function of grades

Most teachers intend their grades to perform several functions, typically including motivation/reward and documentation of progress. As a compromise between grading purely on the basis of effort or only according to absolute achievement, they adjust grades based on achievement to take into account effort. In addition, teachers may try to grade as highly as the facts seem to justify, believing that this will maximize the motivational value of the grades and minimize damage to students' self-concepts. The result often is a method called grading on the curve, although it does not involve using the normal curve as just described. Instead, the teacher determines in advance that the class will receive a certain percentage of each of the grades to be assigned (for example, 30 percent "A," 30 percent "B," 30 percent "C," and 10 percent "D" or "F"). This assures that grades will be distributed in a way that seems to make sense, assuming that differences in student performance correspond roughly to the percentages assigned.

Grading on the curve

But does it? If the class as a whole does well on the test, adhering rigidly to this grading plan means that many students who answered better than 90 percent of the items correctly will get a grade of "C," despite their good performance and despite the fact that the differences between them and the students who get an "A" are trivial. Thus, grading on a curve is not always appropriate. Under what conditions would it be a fair and appropriate way to grade?

Ambiguous questions

Another point to consider is that teacher-made tests often include questions that seem straightforward to teachers but turn out to be ambiguous to students. Sometimes more than one alternative answer is correct or at least justifiable. Should you credit only the answer you considered to be correct in the first place? Should you credit only the answer you consider to be the best answer? Should you credit all answers that are justifiable? Does it make any difference? If your answer to the last question was "No," consider the probability that students who receive no credit under one procedure but would have under another may be outraged, especially if their final grades are affected. Sometimes, due to poor phrasing or typographical omissions, none of the response alternatives are correct. What should you do about these items when you grade the test? Should you ignore these items? Give everyone credit for them?

Thinking about these hypothetical situations probably has made you realize some of the complexities involved in grading. The simplest solution, and the one that many persons favor, is to abolish grading altogether. This is a realistic solution up to a point, but not a complete one.

Grading versus evaluation

It is important to make a distinction between grading and evaluation. Grading may not be necessary, but evaluation is. Teachers must evaluate both their own behavior and their students' progress regularly if they are to function efficiently. Failure to do so represents only avoidance of an uncomfortable problem, not a solution to it.

Most necessary evaluation can be accomplished without formal grading, although the complexities involved in testing apply in varying degrees to other methods as well. Student progress can be assessed through a variety of evaluation methods besides tests. Questions and comments in class, the ability to answer questions about content, performance on special assignments and projects, and written work all can help a teacher monitor student progress. Where tests are used, there is no need to return them with letter grades or percentage scores. In addition, or even instead, teachers can return tests with detailed comments about the strengths and weaknesses of students' efforts, focusing on progress and on ways to improve rather than on how students did in comparison to one another.

Ultimately, though, students will have to take relatively objective tests so that their performances can be compared not only with one another, but with the achievement of students in the country at large. External pressures for test data of this kind come from citizens and state educational agencies interested in school quality. Also, colleges and universities use such information to make decisions about admissions and course advisement.

Uses for test data

Many employers require information about the basic literacy and mathematical skills of prospective employees. Most desirable jobs have minimal

For tests to have value, teachers should review them in detail with students.

Need for accurate assessment

educational requirements. Furthermore, employers have become wary of grades because they have seen too many people with high school or college degrees who do not have the skills expected of such graduates. Consequently, in examining transcripts, many employers pay much more attention to scores on standardized tests than to grades. If no such scores are available, they are likely to test prospective employees themselves before offering to hire them. Thus, due to external pressures of this sort, instructors who refuse to grade or who systematically assign very high grades to everyone regardless of performance do not do their students any favors in the long run. They are leaving to someone else the unpleasant task of making it clear to certain students that they are deficient in basic skills and will be handicapped because of this unless they obtain remedial help.

Grading

We have just stressed the need for accurate assessment and have noted that teachers can assess student progress through formal tests and ratings as well as informal monitoring. Ultimately, this information has to be turned into a description of student progress or a grade.

Many instructional programs, especially at the elementary school level, now stress continuous monitoring of student performance, which enables teachers to keep specific records of student progress. Often schools using such systems do not assign grades in the first few school years. Instead, student progress is reported in terms of skills expected and skills mastered.

Individual standard method

When teachers do assign grades, there are three basic methods they can use. The individual standard is based on a student's progress in relation to his or her capacity. A bright student must master more material to get an A than a slower student. Such a method demands careful testing at the beginning of the year, and students must be informed of the relative performance levels they must obtain in order to get specified grades. The individual standard method is difficult to implement. For example, if two students score 49 and 60 on a 100-item pretest, how does one set fair standards for what these students must do to earn an A, B, C, or D in the course? How can effort be graded? Furthermore, most people, including employers and parents, want to know how much students learned or what they can do, not how their performance compares with their ability or potential. However, some teachers can and do grade on the basis of an individual standard, or at least assign grades partly on the basis of such information.

Fixed standard method

Most teachers in American classrooms use a fixed standard to assign grades—criterion-referenced tests are based on fixed standards. The teacher assigns a level of performance to correspond with different grades on the basis of how students have performed previously. Establishing a standard of performance is very difficult for the beginning teacher, who may want to obtain tests used by teachers who have taught similar students in order to begin building realistic expectations. The "fixed" standard varies from teacher to teacher. A 70 on Mr. Marx's algebra exams equals a C; in Mrs. Thomas's room it's a D. Still, when a teacher uses fixed standards, students know what performance levels correspond to different grades.

Teachers who know that some parts of a course are more difficult than others may vary their standards from exam to exam. It is best to explain the current standard to students when they are ready to take the exam: "I know this material is tough, and students in the past have had more trouble on it than any other unit. Thus, on this test, any score above 80 percent will be an A." Similarly, teachers who recognize that a group of students is better or worse than the typical class they teach may alter their standards in order to prevent giving an excessive number of high or low marks.

Norm-referenced grading

Norm-referenced grading compares a student's achievement with the performance of the class rather than with a fixed standard of subject-matter mastery. A student's grade depends on how well other students do. If a student scores 90 on an exam, but all other students score above 90, he or she has done poorly. Conversely, if a student scores 70, but all other students score below 70, he or she has done well. Teachers who use norm-referenced grading often assign grades using the mean and standard deviation of the class. However, achievement is not distributed on a normal curve. Some classes, even though comparable in ability to other classes, will put out less effort, and so forth. Hence, teachers who use a normal curve for grading will unfairly penalize some students. For example, students who perform "well" in an exceptionally capable and hard-working class would be downgraded.

A Class Grading Example

Consider the record of student performance presented in Table 29.1. Assume that there are 30 students in the class and that each student in the table represents two other students who performed identically. We can see that Heather and Jeff have earned the most points in the course. Heather, for example, received 27 out of 30 possible points on her class presentation and was the highest performer in the class on this task (rank 1). Jeff received 26 of 30 points and tied with Sandra as the second highest scorer on this assignment (since Sandra and Jeff are tied for second and third, they receive a rank of 2.5).

How can we assign grades using the three methods just discussed? To use an individual standard we would have to have information about student ability. Assume that the students as they appear in Table 29.1 are ranked in terms of course aptitude (Heather has the most; Terrill has the least). Using such criteria, we might decide that Sandra deserves an A (she had a relatively low aptitude but high performance), and that Jeff's and Heather's performances warrant a B (high aptitude, high performance). However, Heather and Jeff have scored 90, and how high a level can we demand? In part, the criteria would be determined by the differences in students' aptitudes. If the IQ difference between Heather and Terrill was 115–108, it would be inappropriate to expect much, if any, extra performance from

Table 29.1 Summary of Student Performance on Five Course Assignments

	Class Presentation (30%)		Assigned Paper (10%)		Exam I (25%)		Exam II (25%)		Homework (10%)			
	Raw	*Rank*	*Raw*	*Rank*	*Raw*	*Rank*	*Raw*	*Rank*	*Raw*	*Rank*	*Total*	*Rank*
Heather	27/30	1.0	10	1.5	20/25	5.5	24/25	1	9/10	6.5	90	1.5
James	24/30	8.5	2	8.5	19/25	8.0	12/25	8	9/10	6.5	66	10.0
Jeff	26/30	2.5	10	1.5	24/25	1.0	20/25	4	10/10	2.5	90	1.5
Jill	25/30	5.5	6	5.5	18/25	9.0	18/25	6	10/10	2.5	77	5.0
Pat	25/30	5.5	6	5.5	20/25	5.5	21/25	2	9/10	6.5	81	4.0
Peggy	24/30	8.5	3	7.0	20/25	5.5	14/25	7	8/10	9.5	69	8.0
Sam	23/30	10.0	9	3.0	16/25	10.0	10/25	10	9/10	6.5	67	9.0
Sandra	26/30	2.5	8	4.0	22/25	2.5	20/25	4	10/10	2.5	86	3.0
Skip	25/30	5.5	2	8.5	22/25	2.5	11/25	9	10/10	2.5	70	7.0
Terrill	25/30	5.5	1	10.0	20/25	5.5	20/25	4	8/10	9.5	74	6.0

Heather. A difference of 140–85 would be a different case. However, the practical difficulties in implementing an individual standard are overwhelming, and this method typically creates more misunderstanding and arbitrariness than it resolves.

A fixed standard provides a clear basis for assigning grades. It is easy to use, although it may take a great deal of time and thought to establish initial standards. Teachers using a fixed standard assign students grades on the basis of announced standards, but it is important to realize that the distribution of grades will vary as a result of the standards. Consider the three standards presented below. All would look realistic to teachers and students at the beginning of a course.

Fixed Standard A	Fixed Standard B	Fixed Standard C
A = 94% or above	A = 90% or above	A = 93% or above
B = 85–93%	B = 80–89%	B = 85–92%
C = 75–84%	C = 70–79%	C = 78–84%
D = 60–74%	D = 60–69%	D = 70–77%
F = below 60%	F = below 60%	F = below 70%

However, if these three standards are applied to the students in Table 29.2, different grades will be assigned. In general, standards A and C are higher than B, although standard A is more liberal in the "D" range than is standard C. Standard B establishes lower cut-off points for the assignment of As, Bs, and Cs than do standards A and C.

Table 29.2 is an expanded version of Table 29.1, and represents the distribution of thirty students (assuming that the performance of each student in Table 29.1 is typical of two other students in the class). An examination of Table 29.2 and the standards proposed above indicates that no students would have received As if fixed standards A and C were used in the course. Standard A would have resulted in the assignment of 15 Ds, while in both standards B and C only 9 Ds would have been assigned. Furthermore, standard C would have resulted in the assignment of 9 Fs, but none would have been assigned using standards A or B. It should be clear that shifting standards by even small percentages can result in different distributions.

Yet another way to assign grades is by norm-referenced standards; that is, by inspecting the distribution of grades within a class and allowing natural breaks in the distribution of scores to determine the assignment of letter grades. Whenever there are no explicit standards for judging student performance, as is typically the case in secondary schools, we recommend such norm-referenced comparisons.

Recommendations for Grading

Grading should implement the philosophy of the school and the teacher as fairly as possible. Decisions about grades have to be made on the basis of one's particular situation; you may teach in a school that has fixed grading

Table 29.2 Student Scores and the Assignment of Grades Using Three Fixed Standards and a Norm-Referenced Comparison

Student Score	Standard A	Standard B	Standard C	Norm-Referenced Comparisons
90	B	A	B	A
90	B	A	B	A
90	B	A	B	A
90	B	A	B	A
90	B	A	B	A
90	B	A	B	A
86	B	B	B	B
86	B	B	B	B
86	B	B	B	B
81	C	B	C	B
81	C	B	C	B
81	C	B	C	B
77	C	C	D	C
77	C	C	D	C
77	C	C	D	C
74	D	C	D	C
74	D	C	D	C
74	D	C	D	C
70	D	C	D	C− D+ ?
70	D	C	D	C− D+ ?
70	D	C	D	C− D+ ?
69	D	D	F	D
69	D	D	F	D
69	D	D	F	D
67	D	D	F	D
67	D	D	F	D
67	D	D	F	D
66	D	D	F	D
66	D	D	F	D
66	D	D	F	D

guidelines, or you may have complete freedom to set your own standards. In general, we recommend that grades not be assigned on the basis of individual standards (evaluating an individual's performance in terms of his or her ability). The establishment of individual standards makes most sense in a nongraded system characterized by continuous assessment. If individual standards are used in grading, they should be applied after the major decisions are made, when the teacher is choosing between two close alternatives (is the grade C− or D+?).

Fixed standard

Fixed standards make most sense when teachers have a firm notion of what students can do and when they can set standards based on realistic expectations (as in criterion-referenced grading). In some areas such standards are readily available (the student needs to make at least 15 out of 20 free throws over three consecutive testings to earn an A), but in other areas it may take some time to establish realistic expectations (to earn an A should a student spell correctly, on the average, 90 or 95 percent of the assigned vocabulary?).

Teachers who use fixed standards must be careful that a single poor performance does not preclude a student obtaining a reasonably high mark. They can do this by allowing students to drop their lowest score, assuming of course that the teacher tests frequently. The procedure of allowing students to drop one of only two or three scores can cause as many problems as it solves. (For example, consider the situation where Ted has a 50, 70, 90; and Jim has an 80, 70, and 70.)

Dropping lowest scores

Teachers who are willing to take the extra time necessary to prepare and grade "make-up" exams can help students to continue to make effort to learn material. That is, teachers can allow students to retake one or two exams instead of dropping their lowest test score. Retesting has the obvious disadvantage of creating more work for the teacher but it does encourage new effort by students.

Retesting

By now you realize that there is no totally fair way to grade students. Each decision is really a hypothesis about how to help students perform as well as they can. Individual students are always affected differently by "class" rules. In the example just presented, we can see that Ted will be hurt if one test score is not eliminated; however, if a test score is dropped, Jim will be hurt in comparison to Ted (in terms of total class average).

We recommend that beginning teachers use a combination of norm-referenced standards and common sense, unless they are teaching in a non-graded situation or a criterion-referenced system (most teachers from fourth grade through high school, however, do assign grades). As teachers gain more experience and have expectations about what students can do, they can shift to fixed standards.

The chief advantage of the fixed system is that it puts the control of grades in students' hands. If the standards are appropriately fixed, students who work hard can earn good grades. However, if the standards are too low, students are not challenged; if the standards are too high, students will give up.

The major disadvantage to norm-referenced comparisons is that they interpret performance not in terms of some absolute standard (15 out of 20 free throws), but in terms of how a student performs in comparison to other students. (If the class average is 10, 15 may be excellent, but a 15 may be poor if the class average is 18). However, when teachers do not have firm expectations about how students will perform, standards broadly imposed by the collective performance of all students will probably be fairer than fixed standards.

Adjusting Grades

Teachers do not have to rely totally on fixed standards or norm-referenced comparisons. Four possible considerations that a teacher might wish to use in making grade adjustments are: (1) consistency of performance, (2) performance on major course objectives, (3) special credit work, and (4) contract work. However, if teachers use any or all of these considerations they should explain to students how they will be used and what influence they will have on grades early in the course.

After examining the distribution of scores in Table 29.2, we could use consistency of performance as a criterion in borderline cases. For example, Skip, a student with a 70 (see Table 29.1), falls short of the C cutoff. His grade is hurt by his score on the assigned paper and his performance on Exam II. However, his performance on Exam I is excellent. Here the criterion of consistency does not help us. If his total score was influenced by one low score, we might give him the higher grade, but his performance is inconsistent and therefore difficult to describe with a single grade.

A second criterion that might help us is the importance of particular objectives. For example, Skip's total course performance is heavily influenced by his performance on a minor task, the assigned paper. If the teacher found the paper difficult to grade or if the assignment was accompanied by consistent student complaints (e.g., not enough time to write), the teacher might assign Skip a higher grade on this basis. However, Skip also did poorly on the second exam, and unless the teacher has absolutely no confidence in the grade on the assigned paper, there is no basis for giving Skip a higher mark.

Although the criteria of consistency and importance of objectives may be helpful in making minor adjustments, they sometimes provide no help at all. For this reason teachers sometimes allow students to raise their final grades by doing special-credit work or by fulfilling contracts. Assignments that call for mastery and effort are viable ways of assessing student performance and extending teacher flexibility in grading. Credit for such assignments should be given after norm comparisons have been made. Hence, a teacher might have one or two extra assignments worth a few points during a grading period. Borderline students who earn enough extra credit points would be assigned a higher grade.

Special-credit work

Contracting for Specific Grades. Where individualized contracts are used, it is possible to allow students some choice concerning the degree and types of effort they will expend. This is done by explicitly promising specific grades in exchange for specific levels of accomplishment on various tasks. For example, an A might require both earning 90 percent on a test and doing a project, a B might call for only earning 90 percent on the test, a C earning 80 percent on the test, and so on. Minimal requirements can be established for those who only wish to receive a passing grade and progressively more difficult standards can be set for earning higher grades.

With this plan, students know exactly what they will need to do in order to get a particular grade, and they can lower their effort if they are willing to take a lower grade. In addition to providing students some choice and making a clear connection between level of effort and assigned grades, contracting allows the teacher to establish requirements that ensure that students master the objectives considered most important or essential to the course.

This system works very well where all students in the course are capable of achieving the highest grade, although some will require more time and effort to do so than others. Often such arrangements involve the Keller plan for personalized, self-paced instruction (Keller, 1968). In this plan, students not only can choose the effort they want to expend and the resulting grade, but are given as much time as they need to complete their work (see Chapter 7).

Keller plan

This type of plan is usually not feasible in the elementary and middle school grades, partly because relatively few students have the maturity needed to exercise choices appropriately and follow through with independent work, and also because the range of individual differences is often so large that common or standard requirements for everyone in the class may not be practical. However, less formalized variations of the same general ideas can be developed by making agreements or contracts with individual students, adjusting the requirements so that they are matched appropriately to student abilities and present levels of achievement. Teachers must explain this process to their classes, however, because students understandably will want to know why there are different standards for different students. For a discussion of some experimental work on related programs at the college level, see Covington (1984) and the motivation unit in this textbook.

Grades and Student Success

We have argued that success is necessary if students are to maintain positive self-views and involvement in assigned schoolwork. A grading system based on absolute standards, but standards that some students cannot attain, guarantees that these students will give up and expend only minimal effort in pursuing coursework. Norm-referenced comparisons will also ensure that some students reduce their time and effort in the course; for example, those who do poorly on a first exam and have no hope of improving their relative positions in the future.

However, we have also argued that students do not respond to gratuitous, empty praise and that when students perceive assignments as easy they will attribute good performance not to their own efforts, but instead to external causes like luck or easy assignments. Hence, students' task persistence, confidence, and so on will not be maximized by easy standards.

Teachers who use grades are caught in the middle. If they assign them too leniently or too restrictively, they will not motivate students as much as they could. We encourage teachers who must use grades to set standards that allow every student to obtain at least a grade of C, or whatever grade indicates satisfactory completion of general course expectations. This does not mean that every student will achieve at least a C, but it does mean

Students comparing report cards.

that conditions should be arranged (by offering extra work, for example) so that students who work productively can earn an acceptable mark.

Grading: A Summary

Grade inflation

We mentioned previously that grading is probably the most unpleasant aspect of teaching for most teachers, but that it remains a necessary one despite suggestions from some persons that it be eliminated. It may be helpful to point out that much teacher concern about grading is unnecessary, because low grades are not nearly as traumatic for students as most teachers think they are. First, students are very realistic about their own performances, both absolutely and in comparison to classmates, so that students' expectations concerning grades are likely to conform fairly closely to the actual grades they receive. Second, grades assigned are often higher than those that students expect, especially in this recent period of "grade inflation." Grade inflation is not necessarily good—in fact, it seems unlikely to motivate students positively. Also, some students are irritated when they see classmates who have accomplished much less than they have still receive the same grades.

Developing and clearly communicating evaluation methods

The keys to satisfactory grading are developing clearly valid methods to assess learning (they involve measuring knowledge directly related to the content of the course, as opposed to general information, test-taking skills, or other student individual differences that are unrelated to course content), and communicating these evaluation methods and criteria precisely to students. The latter aspect is important, because many students become unnecessarily anxious if they do not know the basis on which grades will be assigned, and virtually all students want some assurance that grading will be reasonable and fair. One of the most common complaints against instructors that keeps appearing in studies of student evaluations of teaching is that they fail to specify the bases for grading, or that they assign grades in an arbitrary manner or on the basis of insufficient information.

The "insufficient information" problem usually refers to grades that are assigned on the basis of a single final examination or an assignment that covers only a small fraction of course content. In the case of grading on the basis of term papers rather than tests, the objection is that the grade may have little or nothing to do with the degree to which the student learned material taught in the course. Unless notified otherwise, students generally expect to be held responsible for material presented in class and in assigned readings, and they usually prefer several tests or short assignments to one or two large tests or long assignments. These preferences are understandable and for the most part appropriate, and they seem compatible with most teaching goals, including goals involving integration of all material covered in a course. The latter objective can be accomplished by testing periodically during the course for content mastery and then giving a final exam that poses more integrative questions. For more information about marking systems (e.g., grade inflation, effects on motivating students, percentage grading, pass-fail grading, etc.), see the fifth edition of the *Encyclopedia of Educational Research* (Mitzel, 1984).

Teacher Evaluation Standards

The reader interested in more advanced information about how teacher evaluative standards and testing practices influence student effort could profitably consult Natriello and Dornbusch (1985). These researchers hypothesize that students will respond more favorably to evaluations and to the teachers who administer them when they see those evaluations as: (1) addressed to central rather than peripheral aspects of the task at hand, (2) influential in evaluating their progress or mastery, (3) soundly based, and (4) reliable.

Natriello and Dornbusch (1985) also offer a six-stage model for evaluation designed to improve student effort and performance. Their work provides detailed information about: (1) attention to the processes of task assignment, (2) criteria setting, (3) sampling, (4) appraisal, (5) feedback, and (6) improvement. Especially interesting is their stress on the need to teach students how to interpret and evaluate data reliably. Simply put, these authors contend not only that appraisals need to be technically fair (reliable, valid), but that students need to perceive them that way.

Microcomputers and Classroom Testing

As Kubiszyn and Borich (1984) note, there will soon be software packages available to help teachers with many of the technical tasks of measuring student performance that we have discussed in these four chapters. The microcomputer will be a powerful clerical aid for managing classroom instruction. Teachers will be able to use it to identify potential instructional objectives (i.e., what do other fifth-grade social studies teachers emphasize), to develop test items, to analyze the effectiveness of each test item, and to analyze grade distributions.

Statistical software programs will enable teachers to keep comprehensive records of student performance over several consecutive years, thus allowing them to analyze their tests systematically without spending the considerable time now necessary to obtain information and perform calculations (Gage & Berliner, 1979). Such programs could help teachers become more adept at analyzing their behavior over time. For example, when the teacher makes a major change in the assignments in a course, what effect does this have on student performance? Microcomputers thus make it possible for teachers to evaluate the effects of new instructional techniques or test performance, and make it easy to study issues like grade inflation or declines in achievement over time (Kubiszyn & Borich, 1984).

Successful teachers are good decision makers who have clear and appropriate learning plans, can communicate these goals to students, and can establish appropriate classroom conditions in which students can work cooperatively and productively to achieve those goals. Microcomputers will not change the basic conditions of teaching. However, the microcomputer will provide many teachers with relief from clerical and record-keeping burdens.

SUMMARY

The practice of assigning grades according to a normal distribution has become less popular in recent years because it fails to take into account the fact that student aptitudes often are not normally distributed in a given classroom. Also, teachers often want grades to reflect effort as well as aptitude, since they use them for motivation/reward as well as for documentation of progress. The result is a modified system that is still called "grading on the curve," but does not follow the distribution of the normal curve.

Grading involves many complexities, but some form of evaluation of student performance is essential. It may involve alternatives to grading, such as progress reports or ratings, but the need for accurate and realistic information about progress is essential. When grades are used, teachers can choose the individual standard, which examines a student's progress in relation to capacity; the fixed standard, which uses established criteria; or the norm-referenced system, which compares each student's performance with the performance of the entire class. Each system has advantages and disadvantages, but in most classes there are no explicit standards and norm-referenced comparisons seem most practical.

Grading should implement the philosophy of the school and the teacher as fairly as possible. Since grades may affect motivation and general performance, it is important to examine the implications of all decisions carefully. Grade adjustments can be made on the basis of consistency, performance on major objectives, special credit work, or contract work. Caution must be used, since grades assigned either too leniently or too restrictively will inhibit motivation and performance.

QUESTIONS AND PROBLEMS

1. The assumption that grading cannot be avoided pervades this chapter. Do you agree with this assumption? If not, what would you propose as a realistic alternative?
2. It is possible to be clear and consistent in grading by announcing your intentions to students and then following through on them. But is it possible to be fair? Does the concept of fair grading make any sense at all? If so, define it. If not, why not?
3. No matter where you draw the line between grades, some students with the highest marks in a grade range will ask if they can earn extra credit or if you would extend the range down one more point so that they can get a higher grade. How will you respond to these students?
4. Some students, independent of their ability (high- and low-achievement students, male and female students, and so forth), develop what is called "fear of success." Among other things, this may include an aversion to high grades, or at least grades that are "too high." Is this their problem, or is there something that you as a teacher should try to do about it? If so, what? If you see it as "their" problem, explain your point of view.
5. How should teachers grade highly competent students who consistently do just enough to qualify for a B, even though they could do A-level work with below-average effort? Under what circumstances, if any, might it be appropriate and perhaps helpful to such students to give them less than a B grade?

CASE STUDY

Grading Test Results. Examine the four mathematics test scores that students have earned (each test is worth 100 points). (1) How consistent is student performance across the four tests? What problems are caused by inconsistent student performances? (2) If you were assigning grades using norm comparisons and your common sense, what would be the cutoffs for A, B, C, and D? Defend your choices for borderline students.

	Test 1 (25%)	Test 2 (25%)	Test 3 (25%)	Test 4 (25%)	Total Points
Alan	80	85	90	96	351
Candy	85	70	65	60	280
Cheri	98	92	100	90	380
Debbie	100	75	90	74	339
Ed	70	90	65	70	295
Frank	90	95	74	90	349
Gene	82	83	82	80	327
Joe	90	91	93	94	368
Karen	70	75	70	69	284

(continued)

	Test 1 (25%)	Test 2 (25%)	Test 3 (25%)	Test 4 (25%)	Total Points
Linda	65	60	60	60	245
Owen	70	75	70	69	284
Peter	69	78	65	70	282
Ralph	60	60	70	60	250
Reggie	65	85	60	60	270
Renee	70	70	70	70	280
Rita	90	90	90	90	360
Sandra	93	100	85	80	358
Stan	76	72	73	71	292
Stephen	100	85	90	89	364
Warren	50	60	72	80	262

References

Abrami, P., Leventhal, L., & Perry, R. (1982). Educational seduction. *Review of Educational Research, 52,* 446–464.

Abramson, L., Seligman, M., & Teasdale, J. (1978). Learned helplessness in humans: Critique and reformulation. *Journal of Abnormal Psychology, 87,* 49–74.

Abramson, T., & Kagen, E. (1975). Familiarization of content and different response modes in programmed instruction. *Journal of Educational Psychology, 67,* 83–88.

Adams, J. (1977). Motor learning and retention. In M. Marx & M. Bunch (Eds.), *Fundamentals and applications of learning.* New York: Macmillan.

Adams, R., & Biddle, B. (1970). *Realities of teaching: Explorations with videotape.* New York: Holt, Rinehart and Winston.

Ahern, F., Johnson, R., Wilson, J., McClearn, G., & Vandenberg, S. (1982). Family resemblences in personality. *Behavior Genetics, 12,* 261–280.

Alderman, M. (1984). Essential motivation for the preservice teacher: Achievement motivation. Paper presented at the annual meeting of the American Educational Research Association, New Orleans.

Alexander, L., Frankiewicz, R., & Williams, R. (1979). Facilitation of learning and retention of oral instruction using advance and post organizers. *Journal of Educational Psychology, 71,* 701–707.

Alhajri, A. (1981). Effect of seat position on school performance of Kuwaiti students. An unpublished dissertation, University of Missouri—Columbia.

Alschuler, A., Tabor, D., & McIntyre, J. (1971). *Teaching achievement motivation.* Middletown, CT: Educational Ventures Inc.

American Institutes for Research. (1976). *Impact of educational innovation on student performance: Project, methods, and findings for three cohorts.* Project LONGSTEP Final Report, Vol. 1. Palo Alto: American Institutes for Research.

Ames, C. (1978). Children's achievement attributions and self-reinforcement: Effects of self-concept and competitive reward structure. *Journal of Educational Psychology, 70,* 345–355.

Ames, C., & Ames, R. (1981). Competitive versus individualistic goal structures: The salience of past performance information for causal attributions and affect. *Journal of Educational Psychology, 73,* 411–418.

Ames, C., & Ames, R. (1984). *Research on motivation in education,* Vol. 1. New York: Academic Press.

Ames, C., & Ames, R. (in press). *Research on motivation in education,* Vol. 2, New York: Academic Press.

Ames, C., Ames, R., & Felker, D. (1977). Effects of competitive reward structure and valence of outcome on children's achievement attributions. *Journal of Educational Psychology, 69,* 1–8.

Ames, C., & Felker, D. (1979). Effects of self-concept on children's causal attributions and self-reinforcement. *Journal of Educational Psychology, 71,* 613–619.

Ames, R. (1975). Teachers' attributions of responsibility: Some unexpected nondefensive effects. *Journal of Educational Psychology, 67,* 668–676.

Ames, R. (1983). Teachers' attributions for their own teaching. In J. Levine & M. Wang (Eds.), *Teacher and student perceptions: Implications for learning.* Hillsdale, NJ: Erlbaum.

Ames, R. (1984). Help-seeking and achievement orientation: Perspectives from attribution theory. In B. DePaulo, A. Nadler, & J. Fisher (Eds.), *New directions in helping.* New York: Academic Press.

Anderson, C. (1983). The causal structure of situations: The generation of plausible causal attributions as a function of type of event situation. *Journal of Experimental Social Psychology, 19,* 185–203.

Anderson, G., & Walberg, H. (1974). Learning environments. In H. Walberg (Ed.), *Evaluating educational performance. A sourcebook of methods, instruments, and examples.* Berkeley, CA: McCutchan.

Anderson, J., & Bower, G. (1973). *Human associative memory.* New York: Wiley.

Anderson, L. (1981). Student responses to seatwork: Implications for the study of students' cognitive processing. Paper presented at the annual meeting of the American Educational Research Association, Los Angeles.

Anderson, L. (1981). Short-term student responses to classroom instruction. *Elementary School Journal, 82,* 97–108.

Anderson, L. (1984). The environment of instruction: The function of seatwork in a commercially developed curriculum. In G. Duffy, L. Roehler, & J. Mason (Eds.), *Comprehension instruction: Perspectives and suggestions.* New York: Longman.

Anderson, L., Evertson, C., & Brophy, J. (1979). An experimental study of effective teaching in first-grade reading groups. *Elementary School Journal, 79,* 193–223.

Anderson, L., Evertson, C., & Brophy, J. (1982). *Principles of small-group instruction in elementary reading.* East Lansing, MI: Institute for Research on Teaching, Michigan State University (Occasional Paper No. 58).

Anderson, O. (1969). *Structure in teaching: Theory and analysis.* New York: Teachers College Press.

Anderson, R. (1984a). Role of the reader's schema in comprehension, learning, and memory. In R. Anderson, J. Osborn, & R. Tierney (Eds.), *Learning to read in American schools: Basal readers and content texts.* Hillsdale, NJ: Erlbaum.

Anderson, R. (1984b). Some reflections on the acquisition of knowledge. *Educational Researcher, 13,* 5–10.

Anderson, R., & Biddle, W. (1975). On asking people questions about what they read. In G. Bower (Ed.), *Psychology of learning and motivation,* (Vol. 9). New York: Academic Press.

Anderson, R., Hiebert, E., Scott, J., & Wilkinson, I. (1985). *Becoming a nation of readers: The Report of the Commission on Reading.* Washington, DC: National Institute of Education.

Anderson, R., Pichert, J., & Shirey, L. (1983). Effects of the reader's schema at different points in time. *Journal of Educational Psychology, 75,* 271–279.

Anderson, R., Reynolds, R., Schallert, D., & Goetz, E. (1977). Frameworks for comprehending discourse. *American Educational Research Journal, 14,* 367–381.

Anderson, S. (1972). *Sex differences and discrimination in education.* Worthington, OH: Charles A. Jones Publishing Co.

Anderson, T., & Armbruster, B. (1982). Reader and text studying strategies. In W. Otto & S. White (Eds.), *Reading expository material.* New York: Academic Press.

Anderson, T., & Armbruster, B. (1984). Content area textbooks. In R. Anderson, J. Osborn, & R. Tierney (Eds.), *Learning to read in American schools: Basal readers and content texts.* Hillsdale, NJ: Erlbaum.

Anderson-Levitt, K. (in press). Teachers' interpretations of student behavior: A case study and a model. *Elementary School Journal.*

André, M., & Anderson, T. (1978–79). The development and evaluation of a self-questioning study technique. *Reading Research Quarterly, 14,* 605–623.

André, T. (1979). Does answering higher-level questions while reading facilitate productive learning? *Review of Educational Research, 49,* 280–318.

Andrews, F. (1975). Social and psychological factors which influence the creative process. In I. Taylor & J. Getzels (Eds.), *Perspectives in creativity.* Chicago: Aldine.

Andrews, G., & Goodson, L. (1980). A comparative analysis of models of instructional design. *Journal of Instructional Development, 3*(4), 2–16.

Anshutz, R. (1975). An investigation of wait-time and questioning techniques as an instructional variable for science methods students microteaching elementary school children.

(Doctoral dissertation, University of Kansas, 1973). *Dissertation Abstracts International, 35*, 5978A.

Archer, S. (1982). The lower age boundaries of identity development. *Child Development, 53*, 1551–1556.

Arehart, J. (1979). Student opportunity to learn related to student achievement of objectives in a probability unit. *Journal of Educational Research, 72*, 253–269.

Arkin, R., & Maruyama, H. (1979). Attribution affect and college exam performance. *Journal of Educational Psychology, 71*, 85–93.

Arlin, M. (1976). Open education and pupils' attitudes. *Elementary School Journal, 76*, 219–228.

Arlin, M. (1979). Teacher transitions can disrupt time flow in classrooms. *American Educational Research Journal, 16*, 42–56.

Arlin, M. (1982). Teacher responses to student time differences in mastery learning. *American Journal of Education, 90*, 334–352.

Arlin, P. (1975). Cognitive development in adulthood: A fifth stage? *Developmental Psychology, 11*, 602–606.

Arlin, P. (1981). Piagetian tasks as predictors of reading and math readiness in grades K–1. *Journal of Educational Psychology, 73*, 712–721.

Armbruster, B., & Anderson, T. (1984). Structures of explanations in history textbooks or so what if Governor Stanford missed the spike and hit the rail? *Journal of Curriculum Studies, 16*, 181–194.

Armbruster, B., & Brown, A. (1984). Learning from reading: The role of metacognition. In R. Anderson, J. Osborn, & R. Tierney (Eds.), *Learning to read in American schools: Basal readers and content texts.* Hillsdale, NJ: Erlbaum.

Armento, B. (1977). Teacher behaviors related to student achievement on a social science concept test. *Journal of Teacher Education, 28*, 46–52.

Arnold, D., Atwood, R., & Rogers, V. (1974). Question and response levels and lapse time intervals. *Journal of Experimental Education, 43*, 11–15.

Arons, A. (1984). Computer-based instructional dialogs in science courses. *Science, 224*, 1051–1056.

Aronson, E. (1972), *The social animal.* San Francisco: Freeman.

Aronson, E., Blaney, N., Sikes, J., Stephan, C., & Snapp, M. (1975). Busing and racial tension: The jigsaw route to learning and liking. *Psychology Today, 8*, 43–50.

Aronson, E., Blaney, N., Stephan, C., Sikes, J., & Snapp, M. (1978). *The jigsaw classroom.* Beverly Hills, CA: Sage.

Asher, S., & Markell, R. (1974). Sex differences in comprehension of high- and low-interest reading material. *Journal of Educational Psychology, 66*, 680–687.

Ashton, P., & Webb, R. (in press). *Teacher efficacy.* White Plains, NY: Longman.

Aspy, D. (1972). *Toward a technology for humanizing education.* Champaign, IL: Research Press.

Aspy, D. (1973). A discussion of the relationship between selected student behavior and the teacher's use of interchangeable responses. Paper presented at the annual meeting of the American Educational Research Association, New Orleans.

Aspy, D. (1977). An interpersonal approach to humanizing education. In R. Weller (Ed.), *Humanistic education.* Berkeley, CA: McCutchan.

Atkinson, J. (1954). Explorations using imaginative thought to assess the strength of human motives. In M. Jones (Ed.), *Nebraska symposium on motivation* (Vol. 2). Lincoln: University of Nebraska Press.

Atkinson, J. (1964). *An introduction to motivation.* Princeton, NJ: Van Nostrand.

Atkinson, J. W., & Litwin, G. H. (1960). Achievement motive and test anxiety as motives to approach success and avoid failure. *Journal of Abnormal and Social Psychology, 60*, 52–63.

Atkinson, R. (1975). Mnemotechnics in second-language learning. *American Psychologist, 30*, 821–828.

Atkinson, R., & Shiffrin, R. (1968). Human memory: A proposed system and its control processes. In K. Spence & J. Spence (Eds.), *The psychology of learning and motivation.* New York: Academic Press.

Atkinson, R., & Shiffrin, R. (1971). The control of short-term memory. *Scientific American, 225*, 82–90.

Atkinson, R., & Wilson, H. (Eds.). (1969). *Computer assisted instruction: A book of readings.* New York: Academic Press.

Ausubel, D. (1960). The use of advance organizers in the learning and retention of meaningful verbal material. *Journal of Educational Psychology, 51*, 267–272.

Ausubel, D. (1963). *The psychology of meaningful verbal learning: An introduction to school learning.* New York: Grune & Stratton.

Ausubel, D. (1968). *Educational psychology: A cognitive view.* New York: Holt, Rinehart and Winston.

Ausubel, D. (1978). In defense of advance organizers: A reply to the critics. *Review of Educational Research,* 48, 251–257.

Ausubel, D., Montemayor, R., & Svajian, P. (1977). *Theory and problems of adolescent development* (2nd ed.). New York: Grune & Stratton.

Ausubel, D., Novak, J., & Hanesian, H. (1978). *Educational psychology: A cognitive view.* New York: Holt, Rinehart and Winston.

Ausubel, D., & Robinson, F. (1969). *School learning: An introduction to educational psychology.* New York: Holt, Rinehart and Winston.

Ausubel, D., & Sullivan, E. (1970). *Theory and problems of child development,* (2nd ed.). New York: Grune & Stratton.

Baddeley, A. (1976). *The psychology of memory.* New York: Basic Books.

Behnke, G., Bennett, J., Chase, C., Day, J., Lazar, C., & Mittleholtz, D. (1979). Coping with classroom distractions: The formal research study. Report IR & DT 79-2, San Francisco: Far West Laboratory for Educational Research and Development.

Baker, F. (1977). Advances in item analysis. *Review of Educational Research, 47,* 151–178.

Baker, F., & Brown, A. (1984). Metacognitive skills and reading. In P. Pearson, M. Camil, R. Barr, & P. Mosenthal (Eds.), *Handbook of Reading Research.* New York: Longman.

Ball, S. (1977). *Motivation in education.* New York: Academic Press.

Ball, S. (1984). Student motivation: Some reflections and projections. In R. Ames & C. Ames (Eds.), *Research on motivation in education.* Orlando, FL: Academic Press.

Ballard, M., Corman, L., Gottlieb, J., & Kaufman, M. (1977). Improving the social status of mainstreamed retarded children. *Journal of Educational Psychology,* 69, 605–611.

Bandura, A. (1969). *Principles of behavior modification.* New York: Holt, Rinehart and Winston.

Bandura, A. (1977). *Social learning theory.* Englewood Cliffs, NJ: Prentice-Hall.

Bangert, R., Kulik, J., & Kulik, C. (1983). Individualized systems of instruction in secondary schools. *Review of Educational Research, 53,* 143–158.

Bank, B., Biddle, B., & Good, T. (1980). Sex roles, classroom instruction, and reading achievement. *Journal of Educational Psychology, 72,* 119–132.

Barker, R., & Gump, P. (1964). *Big school, small school.* Stanford, CA: Stanford University Press.

Barnes, B., & Clawson, E. (1975). Do advance organizers facilitate learning? *Review of Educational Research, 45,* 637–659.

Barrett, D., Radke-Yarrow, M., & Klein, R. (1982). Chronic malnutrition and child behavior: Effects of early caloric supplementation on social and emotional functioning at school age. *Developmental Psychology, 18,* 541–556.

Barrett-Lennard, G. (1959). Dimensions of the client's experience of his therapist associated with personality change. Unpublished doctoral dissertation, University of Chicago.

Barrett-Lennard, G. (1962). Dimensions of therapist response as causal factors in therapeutic change. *Psychological Monographs,* 76(3), Whole No. 562.

Barth, R. (1972). *Open education and the American school.* New York: Agathon.

Bartlett, F. (1932). *Remembering.* Cambridge: Cambridge University Press.

Baskin, E., & Hess, R. (1980). Does affective education work: A review of seven programs. *Journal of School Psychology, 18*(1), 40–50.

Bates, J. (1979). Extrinsic rewards and intrinsic motivation: A review with implications for the classroom. *Review of Educational Research,* 49, 557–576.

Baumrind, D. (1971). Current patterns of parental authority. *Developmental Psychology Monograph, 4* (No. 1, Part 2).

Bear, G., & Richards, H. (1981). Moral reasoning and conduct problems in the classroom. *Journal of Educational Psychology, 73,* 644–670.

Beckman, L. (1970). Effects of students' performance on teachers' and observers' attributions of causality. *Journal of Educational Psychology, 61*, 76–82.

Behnke, G., Bennett, J., Chase, C., Day, J., Lazer, C., & Mittleholtz, D. (1979). Coping with classroom distractions: The formal research study. Report IR & DT 79-2. San Francisco: Far West Laboratory for Educational Research and Development.

Bell, R. (1971). Stimulus control of parent or caretaker behavior by offspring. *Developmental Psychology, 4*, 61–72.

Bellezza, F. (1981). Mnemonic devices: Classification, characteristics, and criteria. *Review of Educational Research, 51*, 247–275.

Bellugi, U., & Klima, E. (1972). The roots of language in the sign talk of the deaf. *Psychology Today, 6*, 661–664.

Bem, S. (1974). The measurement of psychological androgyny. *Journal of Consulting and Clinical Psychology, 42*, 155–162.

Bem, S. (1975). Sex role adaptability: One consequence of psychological androgyny. *Journal of Personality and Social Psychology, 31*, 634–643.

Bem, S. (1981). Gender schema theory: A cognitive account of sex typing. *Psychological Review, 88*, 354–364.

Benjamin, M., McKeachie, W., Lin, Y., & Holinger, D. (1981). Test anxiety: Deficits in information processing. *Journal of Educational Psychology, 73*, 816–824.

Bennett, N., Desforges, C., Cockburn, A., & Wilkinson, B. (1981). *The quality of pupil learning experiences: Interim report.* Lancaster, England: Centre for Educational Research and Development, University of Lancaster.

Bentler, P., & McClain, J. (1976). A multitrait-multimethod analysis of reflection-impulsivity. *Child Development, 47*, 218–226.

Bergmann, C., Bernath, L., Hohmann, I., Krieger, R., Mendel, G., & Theobald, G. (1976). *Schwierigkeiten junger Lehrer in der Berufspraxis.* Giessen: Zentrum fur Lehrerausbildung der Justus Liegig-Universitat.

Berliner, D. (1979). Tempus educare. In P. Peterson & H. Walberg (Eds.), *Research on teaching: Concepts, findings, and implications.* Berkeley, CA: McCutchan.

Berliner, D. (1982). Executive functions of teaching. Paper presented at the annual meeting of the American Educational Research Association, New York.

Berliner, D. (1983). The executive who manages classrooms. In B. Fraser (Ed.), *Classroom management.* Bentley, Australia: Western Australian Institute of Technology.

Berndt, T. (1982). The features and effects of friendship in early adolescence. *Child Development, 53*, 1447–1460.

Biggs, J. (1978). Individual and group differences in study processes. *British Journal of Educational Psychology, 48*, 266–279.

Blank, M. (1973). *Teaching learning in the preschool: A dialogue approach.* Columbus, Ohio: Merrill.

Blasi, A. (1980). Bridging moral cognition and moral action: A critical review of the literature. *Psychological Bulletin, 88*, 1–45.

Blau, Z. (1981). *Black children/white children: Competence, socialization, and social structure.* New York: Free Press.

Block, J. (1982). Assimilation, accommodation, and the dynamics of personality development. *Child Development, 53*, 281–295.

Block, J. (1984). Making school learning activities more playlike: Flow and mastery learning. *Elementary School Journal, 85*, 65–76.

Block, J., Block, J., & Harrington, D. (1974). Some misgivings about the Matching Familiar Figures Test as a measure of reflection-impulsivity. *Developmental Psychology, 10*, 611–632.

Bloom, B. (1964). *Stability and change in human characteristics.* New York: Wiley.

Bloom, B. (1976). *Human characteristics and school learning.* New York: McGraw-Hill.

Bloom, B., & Broder, L. (1950). *Problem-solving processes of college students.* Chicago: University of Chicago Press.

Bloom, B., Englehart, M., Furst, E., Hill, W., & Krathwohl, D. (1956). *Taxomony of educational objectives: The classification of educational goals. Handbook I: Cognitive domain.* New York: Longmans Green.

Blumenfeld, P., Hamilton, V., Bossert, S., Wessels, K., & Meece, J. (1977). Teacher talk and student thought: Socialization into the student role. In J. Levine & M. Wang (Eds.), *Teacher and student perceptions: Implications for learning.* Hillsdale, NJ: Erlbaum.

Blumenfeld, P. C., & Pintrich, P. R. (1982). *Children's perceptions of school and schoolwork: Age, sex, social class, individual and classroom differences.* Paper presented at the annual American Educational Research Association Meeting, New York.

Bogen, J. (1977). Some educational implications of hemispheric specialization. In M. Wittrock (Ed.), *The human brain.* Englewood Cliffs, NJ: Prentice-Hall.

Boggiano, A., & Ruble, D. (1979). Competence and the overjustification effect: A developmental study. *Journal of Personality and Social Psychology, 37,* 1462–1468.

Bogin, B., & MacVean, R. (1983). The relationship of socioeconomic status and sex to body size, skeletal maturation, and cognitive status of Guatemala City school children. *Child Development, 54,* 115–128.

Boocock, S., & Schild, E. (1968). *Simulation games in learning.* Beverly Hills, CA: Sage.

Book, C., Duffy, G., Roehler, L., Meloth, M., & Vavrus, L. (1985). A study of the relationships between teacher explanation and student metacognitive awareness during reading instruction. *Communication Education, 34,* 29–36.

Borg, W. (1977). Changing teacher and pupil performance with protocols. *Journal of Experimental Education,* 45, 9–18.

Borg, W. (1979). Teacher coverage of academic content and pupil achievement. *Journal of Educational Psychology, 71,* 635–645.

Borg, W. (1980). Time and school learning. In C. Denham & A. Lieberman (Eds.), *Time to learn.* Washington, DC: National Institute of Education.

Borg, W., Kelley, M., Langer, P., & Gall, M. (1970). *The Minicourse: A micro-teaching approach to teacher education.* Beverly Hills, CA: Macmillan Educational Services.

Borko, H., & Eisenhart, M. (in press). Students' conceptions of reading and their experiences in school. *Elementary School Journal.*

Born, D., Davis, M., Whelan, D., & Jackson, D. (1972). College student study behavior in a personalized instruction course and a lecture course. Paper presented at the Kansas Conference on Behavior Analysis in Education, Lawrence, KS.

Boshier, R., & Thom, E. (1973). Do conservative parents nurture conservative children? *Social Behavior and Personality, 1,* 108–110.

Bossert, S. (1977). Tasks, group management, and teacher control behavior: A study of classroom organization and teacher style. *School Review, 85,* 552–565.

Botvin, G., & Murray, F. (1975). The efficacy of peer modeling and social conflict in the acquisition of conservation. *Child Development,* 46, 796–799.

Bourne, L., Ekstrand, B., & Dominowski, R. (1971). *The psychology of thinking.* Englewood Cliffs, NJ: Prentice–Hall.

Bower, G. (1970). Organizational factors in memory. *Journal of Cognitive Psychology, 1,* 18–46.

Bower, G. (1979). Analysis of a mnemonic device. *American Psychologist, 58,* 496–510.

Bower, G., & Clark, M. (1969). Narrative stories as mediators for serial learning. *Psychonomic Science, 14,* 181–182.

Bower, G., Clark, M., Lesgold, A., & Winzenz, D. (1969). Hierarchical retrieval schemes in recall of categorized word lists. *Journal of Verbal Learning and Verbal Behavior, 8,* 323–343.

Bradbard, M., & Endsley, R. (1983). The effects of sex-typed labeling on preschool children's information-seeking and retention. *Sex Roles,* 9, 247–260.

Braden, R., & Sachs, S. (1983). The most recommended books on instructional development. *Educational Technology, 23* (2), 24–28.

Bradley, R., Caldwell, B., & Elardo, R. (1977). Home environment, social status, and mental test performance. *Journal of Educational Psychology,* 69, 697–701.

Brainerd, C. (1977). Feedback, rule knowledge and conservation learning. *Child Development,* 48, 404–411.

Bransford, J. (1979). *Human cognition.* Belmont, CA: Wadsworth.

Bransford, J., & Franks, J. (1971). The abstraction of linguistic ideas. *Cognitive Psychology, 2,* 331–350.

Bransford, J., & McCarrell, N. (1974). A sketch of a cognitive approach to comprehension: Some thoughts about understanding what it means to comprehend. In W. Weimer & D. Palermo (Eds.), *Cognition and the symbolic processes.* Hillsdale, NJ: Erlbaum.

Bransford, J., & Stein, B. (1985). *The IDEAL problem solver.* San Francisco: Freeman.
Braun, C. (1976). Teacher expectation: Sociopsychological dynamics. *Review of Educational Research, 46,* 185–213.
Braun, C., Neilsen, A., & Dykstra, R. (1975). Teacher's expectations: Prime mover or inhibitor? *Elementary School Journal, 76,* 181–187.
Breaux, R. (1975). Effects of induction versus deduction and discovery versus utilization on transfer of information. *Journal of Educational Psychology, 67,* 828–832.
Briars, D., & Siegler, R. (1984). A featural analysis of preschoolers' counting knowledge. *Developmental Psychology, 20,* 607–618.
Bridgeman, D. (1977). *The influence of cooperative, interdependent learning on role taking and moral reasoning: A theoretical and empirical field study with fifth-grade students.* Unpublished doctoral dissertation, Santa Cruz: University of California.
Briggs, L. (1970). *Handbook of procedures for the design of instruction.* Pittsburgh: American Institutes for Research.
Brislin, R. (1983). Cross-cultural research in psychology. In M. Rosenzweig & L. Porter (Eds.), *Annual Review of Psychology,* Vol. 34. Palo Alto: Annual Reviews, Inc.
Britton, G. (1975). Sex stereotyping and career roles. In P. Insel & L. Jacobson (Eds.), *What do you expect?* Menlo Park, CA: Cummings Publishing Company.
Broeders, A. (1980). *Beginnende leerkrachten: Werksituatie en arbeidssatisfactie.* Doctoraalscriptie, Instituut voor Onderwijskunde, K. U. Nijmegen.
Bromage, B., & Mayer, R. (1981). Relationship between what is remembered and creative problem-solving performance in science learning. *Journal of Educational Psychology, 73,* 451–461.
Bromme, R., & Brophy, J. (1983). Teachers' cognitive activity. A paper prepared for the BACOMET Project (Basic Components of Mathematics Education for Teachers). East Lansing: Michigan State University.
Brookover, W., Paterson, A., & Thomas, S. (1962). Self-concept of ability and school achievement. Final report of Cooperative Research Project No. 845, U. S. Department of Health, Education and Welfare, Office of Education. East Lansing: Michigan State University.
Brooks, M., Fusco, E., & Grennon, J. (1983). Cognitive levels matching. *Educational Leadership,* 40(8), 4–8.
Brooks-Gunn, J., & Matthews, W. (1979). *He & she: How children develop their sex-role identity.* Englewood Cliffs, NJ: Prentice-Hall.
Brooks-Gunn, J., & Peterson, A. (Eds.). (1983). *Girls at puberty.* New York: Plenum.
Brophy, J. (1970). Mothers as teachers of their own preschool children: The influence of socioeconomic status and task structure on teaching specificity. *Child Development, 41,* 79–94.
Brophy, J. (1977). *Child development and socialization.* Chicago: Science Research Associates.
Brophy, J. (1979). Teacher behavior and its effects. *Journal of Educational Psychology, 71,* 733–750.
Brophy, J. (1981). Teacher praise: A functional analysis. *Review of Educational Research, 51,* 5–32.
Brophy, J. (1983a). Conceptualizing student motivation. *Educational Psychologist, 18,* 200–215.
Brophy, J. (1983b). Fostering student learning and motivation in the elementary school classroom. In S. Paris, G. Olson, & H. Stevenson (Eds.), *Learning and motivation in the classroom.* Hillsdale, NJ: Erlbaum.
Brophy, J. (1983c). Classroom organization and management. *Elementary School Journal, 83,* 265–285.
Brophy, J. (1985). Classroom strategy research. Progress Report for the period from October 1, 1984–March, 1985. East Lansing: Institute for Research on Teaching, Michigan State University.
Brophy, J., & Evertson, C. (1976). *Learning from teaching: A developmental perspective.* Boston: Allyn & Bacon.
Brophy, J., & Evertson, C. (1978). Context variables in teaching. *Educational Psychologist, 12,* 310–316.
Brophy, J., & Evertson, C. (1981). *Student characteristics and teaching.* New York: Longman.
Brophy, J., Evertson, C., Anderson, L., Baum, M., & Crawford, J. (1976). The student attribute study: Preliminary report (abbreviated version). Report #4037, Research and De-

velopment Center for Teacher Education, University of Texas, Austin, TX.

Brophy, J., & Good, T. (1974). *Teacher-student relationships: Causes and consequences.* New York: Holt, Rinehart and Winston.

Brophy, J., & Good, T. (1985). Teacher effects. In M. Wittrock (Ed.), *Third handbook of research on teaching.* New York: Macmillan.

Brophy, J., & Kher, N. (in press). Teacher socialization as a mechanism for developing student motivation to learn. In R. Feldman (Ed.), *Social psychology applied to education.* Cambridge: Cambridge University Press.

Brophy, J., & Putnam, J. (1979). Classroom management in the elementary grades. In D. Duke (Ed.), *Classroom management.* The seventy-eighth yearbook of the National Society for the Study of Education, Part II. Chicago: University of Chicago Press.

Brophy, J., & Rohrkemper, M. (1981). The influence of problem ownership on teachers' perceptions of and strategies for coping with problem students. *Journal of Educational Psychology, 73,* 295–311.

Brophy, J., & Willis, S. (1981). *Human development and behavior.* New York: St. Martin's Press.

Brown, A. (1980). Metacognitive development and reading. In R. Spiro, B. Bruce, & W. Brewer (Eds.), *Theoretical issues in reading comprehension.* Hillsdale, NJ: Erlbaum.

Brown, A., Campione, J., & Barclay, C. (1979). Training self-checking routines for estimating test readiness: Generalization from list learning to prose recall. *Child Development, 30,* 501–512.

Brown, A., Campione, J., & Day, J. (1981). Learning to learn: On training students to learn from texts. *Educational Researcher, 10,* 14–21.

Brown, A., & Day, J. (1980). Strategies and knowledge for summarizing texts: The development of expertise. (Unpublished manuscript). Urbana: University of Illinois.

Brown, A., & Smiley, S. (1978). The development of strategies for studying texts. *Child Development, 49,* 1076–1088.

Brown, F. (1976). *Principles of educational and psychological testing* (2nd ed.). New York: Holt, Rinehart and Winston.

Brown, G. (1971). *Human teaching for human learning.* New York: Viking.

Brown, J., & Burton, R. (1978). Diagnostic models for procedural bugs in basic mathematical skills. *Cognitive Science, 2,* 155–192.

Brown, M., & Precious, N. (1973). *The integrated day in the primary school.* New York: Ballantine.

Brown, R., & Kulick, J. (1977). Flashbulb memories. *Cognition, 5,* 73–99.

Brozek, J. (1978). Nutrition, malnutrition, and behavior. *Annual Review of Psychology, 29,* 157–177.

Bruch, H. (1958). Psychological aspects of obesity in adolescence. *American Journal of Public Health, 48,* 1349–1353.

Bruner, J. (1960). *The process of education.* Cambridge, MA: Harvard University Press.

Bruner, J. (1964). The course of cognitive growth. *American Psychologist, 19,* 1–15.

Bruner, J. (1966). *Toward a theory of instruction.* Cambridge, MA: Harvard University Press.

Bruner, J. (1971). *The relevance of education.* New York: Norton.

Bruner, J., Goodnow, J., & Austin, G. (1956). *A study of thinking.* New York: Wiley.

Bryan, J., & Walbek, N. (1970). Preaching and practicing generosity: Children's action and reactions. *Child Development, 41,* 329–353.

Bryant, B., & Crockenberg, S. (1974). Cooperative and competitive classroom environments. *Catalogue of Selected Documents in Psychology, 4,* 53.

Bullough, V. (1981). Age at menarche: A misunderstanding. *Science, 213,* 365–366.

Burkhart, R. (Ed.). (1969). *The assessment revolution: New viewpoints for teaching evaluation.* National Symposium on Evaluation in Education. New York State Education Department, Buffalo State University College.

Burling, R. (1973). *English in black and white.* New York: Holt, Rinehart and Winston.

Buros, O. (Ed.). (1972). *The seventh mental measurement yearbook.* Highland Park, NJ: Gryphon Press.

Buros, O. (Ed.). (1978). *The eighth mental measurement yearbook.* Highland Park, NJ: Gryphon Press.

Bybee, R., & Sund, R. (1982). *Piaget for educators,* (2nd ed.) Columbus: Merrill.

Cahen, L., Filby, N., McCutcheon, G., & Kyle, D. (1983). *Class size and instruction.* New York: Longman.

Camp, B., & Bash, M. (1981). *Think aloud: Increasing social and cognitive skills—a problem-solving program for children, primary level.* Champaign, IL: Research Press.

Capon, N., & Kuhn, D. (1979). Logical reasoning in the supermarket: Adult females' use of a proportional reasoning strategy in an everyday context. *Developmental Psychology, 15,* 450–452.

Carnine, D. (1976). Effects of two teacher presentation rates on off-task behavior, answering correctly, and participation. *Journal of Applied Behavior Analysis, 9,* 199–206.

Carpenter, T., Matthews, W., Lindquist, M., & Silver, E. (1984). Achievement in mathematics: Results from the National Assessment. *Elementary School Journal, 84,* 485–496.

Carrier, C., & Titus, A. (1979). The effects of notetaking: A review of studies. *Contemporary Educational Psychology, 4,* 299–314.

Carrier, C., & Titus, A. (1981). Effects of notetaking pretraining and test mode expectations on learning from lectures. *American Educational Research Journal, 18,* 385–397.

Carter, R., Hohenegger, M., & Satz, P. (1982). Aphasia and speech organization in children. *Science, 218,* 797–799.

Cartledge, G., & Milburn, L. (1978). The case for teaching social skills in the classroom: A review. *Review of Educational Research, 48,* 133–156.

Case, R. (1975). Gearing the demands of instruction to the developmental capacities of the learner. *Review of Educational Research, 45,* 59–88.

Case, R. (1978). A developmentally based theory and technology of instruction. *Review of Educational Research, 48,* 439–463.

Case, R., & Bereiter, C. (1984). From behaviourism to cognitive behaviourism to cognitive development: Steps in the evolution of instructional design. *Instructional Science, 13,* 141–158.

Cattell, R. (1971). *Abilities: Their structure, growth, and action.* Boston: Houghton-Mifflin.

Chaffin, J. (1974). Will the real "mainstreaming" program please stand up! (or . . . should Dunn have done it?). *Focus on Exceptional Children, 6,* 1–18.

Chall, J. (1983). Literacy: Trends and explanations. *Educational Researcher, 12,* 3–8.

Champagne, A., Klopfer, L., & Anderson, J. (1980). Factors influencing the learning of classical mechanics. *American Journal of Physics, 48,* 1074–1079.

Champagne, A., Klopfer, L., & Gunstone, R. (1982). Cognitive research and the design of science instruction. *Educational Psychologist, 17,* 31–53.

Chase, W., & Chi, M. (1980). Cognitive skill: Implications for spatial skill in large-scale environments. In J. Harvey (Ed.), *Cognition, social behavior, and the environment.* Hillsdale, NJ: Erlbaum.

Chi, M., Feltovich, P., & Glaser, R. (1981). Categorization and representation of physics problems by experts and novices. *Cognitive Science, 5,* 121–152.

Chi, M., & Glaser, R. (1982). *Final report: Knowledge and skill differences in novices and experts.* Technical Report No. 7. Pittsburgh: Learning Research and Development Center, University of Pittsburgh.

Chi, M., Glaser, R., & Rees, E. (1981). Expertise in problem solving. In R. Sternberg (Ed.), *Advances in the psychology of human intelligence,* (Vol. 1). Hillsdale, NJ: Erlbaum.

Chomsky, N. (1965). *Aspects of the theory of syntax.* Cambridge, MA: M.I.T. Press.

Christoplos, F., & Borden, J. (1978). Sexism in elementary school mathematics. *Elementary School Journal, 78,* 275–277.

Claiborn, W. (1969). Expectancy effects in the classroom: A failure to replicate. *Journal of Educational Psychology, 60,* 377–383.

Clair, M., & Snyder, C. (1979). Effects of instructor-delivered sequential evaluative feedback upon students' subsequent classroom-related performance and instruction ratings. *Journal of Educational Psychology, 71,* 50–57.

Clarizio, H., & McCoy, G. (1976). *Behavior disorders in children* (2nd ed.). New York: Crowell.

Clark, C., Gage, N., Marx, R., Peterson, P., Stayrook, N., & Winne, P. (1979). A factorial experiment on teacher structuring, soliciting, and reacting. *Journal of Educational Psychology, 71*, 534–552.

Clark, C., & Peterson, P. (1985). Teachers' thought processes. In M. Wittrock (Ed.), *Handbook of research on teaching* (3d ed.). New York: Macmillan.

Clark, C., & Yinger, R. (1979). Teachers' thinking. In P. Peterson & H. Walberg (Eds.), *Research on teaching*. Berkeley, CA: McCutchan.

Clark, D. C. (1971). Teaching concepts in the classroom: A set of teaching prescriptions derived from experimental research. *Journal of Educational Psychology, 62*, 253–278.

Clark, R. (1982). Antagonism between achievement and enjoyment in ATI studies. *Educational Psychology, 17*, 92–101.

Clark, R. (1983). *Family life and school achievement: Why poor black children succeed or fail*. Chicago: University of Chicago Press.

Clark, R. (1983). Reconsidering research on learning from media. *Review of Educational Research, 53*, 445–459.

Clarke, A., & Clarke, A. (Eds.). (1976). *Early experience: Myth and evidence*. New York: Free Press.

Clarke, A., & Ruble, D. (1978). Young adolescents' beliefs concerning menstruation. *Child Development, 49*, 231–234.

Clasen, D. (1983). The effect of four different instructional strategies on the achievement of gifted seventh grade students. Paper presented at the annual meeting of the American Educational Research Association, Montreal.

Clausen, J. (1975). The social meaning of differential physical and sexual maturation. In S. Dragastin & G. Elder (Eds.), *Adolescence in the life cycle: Psychological change and social context*. Washington, DC: Hemisphere.

Cleary, T. (1968). Test bias: Prediction of grades of Negro and white students in integrated colleges. *Journal of Educational Measurement, 5*, 115–124.

Cleary, T., Humphreys, L., Kendrick, S., & Wesman, A. (1975). Educational uses of tests with disadvantaged students. *American Psychologist, 30*, 15–41.

Clements, D. (1984). Training effects on the development and generalization of Piagetian logical operations and knowledge of number. *Journal of Educational Psychology, 76*, 766–776.

Clifford, M. (1981). *Practicing educational psychology*, Boston: Houghton-Mifflin.

Cobb, J., & Hops, H. (1973). Effects of academic survival skill training on low achieving first graders. *Journal of Educational Research, 67*, 108–113.

Cofer, C. (1971). Properties of verbal materials and verbal learning. In J. Kling & L. Riggs (Eds.), *Woodworth and Schlosberg's experimental psychology*. New York: Holt, Rinehart and Winston.

Cohen, J., & DeYoung, H. (1973). The role of litigation in the improvement of programming for the handicapped. In L. Mann & D. Sabatino (Eds.), *A first review of special education* (Vol. 2). Philadelphia: J.S.E. Press with Buttonwood Farms.

Cohen, K. (1969). The effects of two simulation games on the opinions and attitudes of selected sixth, seventh, and eighth grade students. Educational Resources Information Center, Document ED 031 766.

Cohen, M. (1979). *Student influence in the classroom*. Unpublished doctoral dissertation, Washington University, St. Louis, MO.

Cohen, R., & Bradley, R. (1978). Simulation games, learning, and retention. *Elementary School Journal, 78*, 247–253.

Coker, H., Medley, D., & Soar, R. (1980). How valid are expert opinions about effective teaching? *Phi Delta Kappan, 62*, 131–134, 149.

Colby, A., Kohlberg, L., Gibbs, J., & Lieberman, M. (1983). A longitudinal study of moral judgment. *Monographs of the Society for Research in Child Development, 48*, (No. 1, Serial No. 200).

Cole, H., & Lacefield, W. (1980). MACOS: *Its empirical effects versus its critics*. Education Resources Information Center Document ED 194 397.

Coleman, J. (1961). *The adolescent society*. New York: Free Press.

Coleman, J., Campbell, E., Hobson, C., McPartland, J., Mood, A., Weinfield, F., & York, R. (1966). *Equality of educational opportunity*. Washington, DC: U.S. Government Printing Office.

Coleman, J., Livingston, S., Fennessey, G., Edwards, K., & Kidder, S. (1973). The Hopkins Games Program: Conclusions from seven years of research. *Educational Researcher, 2*, 3–7.

Collings, G. (1973). Case review: Rights of the retarded. *Journal of Special Education, 7,* 27–37.

Collins, A., & Loftus, E. (1975). A spreading activation theory of semantic processing. *Psychological Review, 82,* 407–428.

Collins, A., & Quillian, M. (1969). Retrieval time from semantic memory. *Journal of Verbal Learning and Verbal Behavior, 8,* 240–247.

Collins, A., & Stevens, A. (1983). A cognitive theory of inquiry teaching. In C. Reigeluth (Ed.), *Instructional-design theories and models: An overview of their current status.* Hillsdale, NJ: Erlbaum.

Combs, A., Blume, R., Newman, A., & Wass, H. (1974). *The professional education of teachers* (2nd ed.). Boston: Allyn & Bacon.

Coming to our senses (1977). Report of the Arts, Education and Americans Panel, David Rockefeller, Jr., Chairman. New York: McGraw-Hill, 1977.

Commons, M., Miller, P., & Kuhn, D. (1982). The relation between formal operational reasoning and academic course selection and performance among college freshmen and sophomores. *Journal of Applied Developmental Psychology, 3,* 1–10.

Commons, M., Richards, F., & Kuhn, D. (1982). Systematic and metasystematic reasoning: A case for levels of reasoning beyond Piaget's stage of formal operations. *Child Development, 53,* 1058–1069.

Confrey, J., & Good, T. (1981). Academic progress: Student and teacher perspectives. Research proposal. East Lansing, MI: Michigan State University, Institute for Research on Teaching.

Cook, L. (1982). *The effects of text structure on the comprehension of scientific prose.* (Unpublished doctoral dissertation). Santa Barbara: University of California.

Cooley, W., & Leinhardt, G. (1980). The Instructional Dimensions Study. *Educational Evaluation and Policy Analysis, 2,* 7–25.

Cooper, H. (1979). Pygmalion grows up: A model for teacher expectation communication and performance influence. *Review of Educational Research, 49,* 389–410.

Cooper, H., & Good, T. (1983). *Pygmalion grows up: Studies in the expectation communication process.* New York: Longman.

Cooper, H., Hinkel, G., & Good, T. (1980). Teachers' beliefs about interaction control and their observed behavioral correlates. *Journal of Educational Psychology, 72,* 345–354.

Coopersmith, S. (1967). *The antecedents of self-esteem.* San Francisco: Freeman.

Corno, L., & Rohrkemper, M. (in press). Self-regulated learning. In R. Ames & C. Ames (Eds.), *Research on motivation in education* (Vol. 2). Orlando, FL: Academic Press.

Cort, H., & Peskowitz, N. (1977). *A longitudinal study of man: A course of study. Summary report.* Education Resource Information Center Document ED 151 275.

Costa, A. (1984). Mediating the metacognitive. *Educational Leadership, 42,* 57–62.

Coté, J., & Levine, C. (1983). Marcia and Erikson: The relationships among ego identity status, neuroticism, dogmatism, and purpose in life. *Journal of Youth and Adolescence, 12,* 43–53.

Covington, M. (1983). Motivated cognitions. In S. Paris, G. Olson, & H. Stevenson (Eds.), *Learning and motivation in the classroom.* New York: Erlbaum.

Covington, M. (1984). Strategic thinking and the fear of failure. In J. Segal, S. Chipman, & R. Glaser (Eds.), *Thinking and learning skills: Relating instruction to basic research.* Hillsdale, NJ: Erlbaum.

Covington, M., & Beery, R. (1976). *Self-worth and school learning.* New York: Holt, Rinehart and Winston.

Covington, M., Crutchfield, R., Davies, L., & Olton, R. (1974). *The productive thinking program: A course in learning to think.* Columbus, OH: Merrill.

Covington, M., & Omelich, C. (1979a). It's best to be able and virtuous too: Student and teacher evaluative responses to successful effort. *Journal of Educational Psychology, 71,* 688–700.

Covington, M., & Omelich, C. (1979b). Effort: The double-edged sword in school achievement. *Journal of Educational Psychology, 71,* 169–182.

Covington, M., & Omelich, C. (1981). As failures mount: Affective and cognitive consequences of ability demotion in the classroom. *Journal of Educational Psychology, 73,* 796–808.

Covington, M., Spratt, M., & Omelich, C.

(1980). Is effort enough or does diligence count too? Student and teacher reactions to effort stability in failure. *Journal of Educational Psychology, 72*, 717–729.

Cox, W., & Matz, R. (1982). Comprehension of school prose as a function of reasoning level and instructional prompting. *Journal of Educational Psychology, 74*, 77–84.

Craik, F. (1979). Human memory. In M. Rosenzweig & L. Porter (Eds.), *Annual review of psychology*. Palo Alto, CA: Annual Reviews Inc.

Craik, F., & Lockhart, R. (1972). Levels of processing: A framework for memory research. *Journal of Verbal Learning and Verbal Behavior, 11*, 671–684.

Crain, W. (1980). *Theories of development: Concepts and applications.* Englewood Cliffs, NJ: Prentice-Hall.

Crandall, V., Katkovsky, W., & Crandall, V. (1965). Children's beliefs in their own control of reinforcement in intellectual-academic situations. *Child Development, 36*, 91–109.

Crandall, V., Katkovsky, W., & Preston, A. (1962). Motivational and ability determinants of young children's intellectual achievement behaviors. *Child Development, 33*, 643–661.

Cronbach, L., Gleser, G., Nanda, H., & Rajaratnam, N. (1972). *The dependability of behavioral measurements: Multifacet studies of generalizability*. New York: Wiley.

Cruickshank, D. (1974). The protocol materials movement: An exemplar of effort to wed theory and practice in teacher education. *Journal of Teacher Education, 25*, 300–304.

Cruickshank, D., Kennedy, J., Bush, A., & Myers, B. (1979). Clear teaching: What is it? *British Journal of Teacher Education, 5*, 27–33.

Cuban, L. (1983). Effective schools: A friendly but cautionary note. *Phi Delta Kappan, 64*, 10, 695–696.

Cyert, R. (1980). Problem solving and educational policy. In D. Tuma & F. Reif (Eds.), *Problem solving and education: Issues in teaching and research.* Hillsdale, NJ: Erlbaum.

Damon, W., & Hart, D. (1982). The development of self-understanding from infancy through adolescence. *Child Development, 53*, 841–864.

Damon, W., & Killen, M. (1982). Peer interaction and the process of change in children's moral reasoning. *Merrill-Palmer Quarterly, 28*, 347–367.

Dansereau, D. (1983). Learning strategy research. In J. Segal, S. Chipman, & R. Glaser (Eds.), *Relating instruction to basic research.* Hillsdale, NJ: Erlbaum.

Dansereau, D., Collins, K., McDonald, B., Holley, C., Garland, J., Diekhoff, G., & Evans, S. (1979). Development and evaluation of a learning strategy training program. *Journal of Educational Psychology, 71*, 64–73.

Dasen, P. (1972). Cross-cultural Piagetian research: A summary. *Journal of Cultural Psychology, 3*, 23–39.

Dasho, S. (1978). A communications approach to classroom socialization. Report A-78-12, Effective Teacher Education Program, San Francisco: Far West Laboratory for Educational Research and Development.

Davis, G. (1976). Research and development in training creative thinking. In J. Levin & V. Allen (Eds.), *Cognitive learning in children: Theories and strategies*. New York: Academic Press.

Davis, R. (1984). *Learning mathematics: A cognitive science approach to mathematics education.* London: Croom Helm.

Davis, R., & Alexander, L. (1977). *The lecture method.* East Lansing: Instructional Media Center, Michigan State University.

Davis, R., & McKnight, C. (1980). The influence of semantic content on algorithmic behavior. *Journal of Mathematical Behavior, 3*, 39–87.

Davison, M., Robbins, S., & Swanson, D. (1978). Stage structure in objective moral judgments. *Developmental Psychology, 14*, 137–146.

Deaux, K. (1984). From individual differences to social categories: Analysis of a decade's research on gender. *American Psychologist, 39*, 105–116.

deBono, E. (1983). The direct teaching of thinking as a skill. *Phi Delta Kappan, 64*, 703–708.

deBono, E. (1985). The CoRT thinking program. In J. Segal, S. Chipman, and R. Glaser (Eds.), *Thinking and learning skills, Volume 1: Relating instruction to research.* Hillsdale, NJ: Erlbaum.

deCharms, R. (1968). *Personal causation.* New York: Academic Press.

deCharms, R. (1972). Personal causation training in the schools. *Journal of Applied Social Psychology, 2*, 95–113.

deCharms, R. (1976). *Enhancing motivation: Change in the classroom.* New York: Irvington.

deCharms, R. (1980). The origins of competence and achievement motivation in personal causation. In L. J. Fyans, Jr. (Ed.), *Achievement motivation: Recent trends in theory and research.* New York: Plenum.

deCharms, R. (1984). Motivation enhancement in educational settings. In R. Ames & C. Ames (Eds.), *Research on motivation in education.* Orlando, FL: Academic Press.

Deci, E. (1975). *Intrinsic motivation.* New York: Plenum.

Deci, E. (1980). *The psychology of self-determination.* Lexington, MA: Heath.

Deci, E. (1985). The well-tempered classroom. *Psychology Today*, March, 52–53.

Deci, E., Schwartz, A., Sheinman, L., & Ryan, R. (1981). An instrument to assess adults' orientations toward control versus autonomy with children: Reflections on instrinsic motivation and perceived competence. *Journal of Educational Psychology, 73*, 642–650.

Deese, J. (1959). Influence of inter-item associative strength upon immediate free recall. *Psychological Reports, 5*, 305–312.

deGroot, A. (1965). *Thought and choice in chess.* The Hague: Mouton.

DeLisi, R., & Staudt, J. (1980). Individual differences in college students' performance on formal operations tasks. *Journal of Applied Developmental Psychology, 1*, 201–208.

Dembo, M., & Hillman, S. (1976). An instructional model approach to educational psychology. *Contemporary Educational Psychology, 1*, 116–123.

Denham, C., & Lieberman, A. (Eds.). (1980). *Time to learn.* Washington, DC: U.S. Department of Education.

Detterman, D., & Sternberg, R. (1982). *How and how much can intelligence be increased?* Norwood, NJ: Ablex.

DeTure, L. (1979). Relative effects of modeling on the acquisition of wait-time by preservice elementary teachers and concommitant changes in dialogue patterns. *Journal of Research in Science Teaching, 16*, 553–562.

Deutsch, C. (1973). Social class and child development. In B. Caldwell & H. Ricciuti (Eds.), *Review of child development research* (Vol. 3). Chicago: University of Chicago Press.

Devine, T. (1981). *Teaching study skills: A guide for teachers.* Boston: Allyn & Bacon.

deVoss, G., & Dibella, R. (1981). *Follow-up of 1979–80 graduates at the Ohio State University's College of Education Teacher Certification Program.* Columbus: Ohio State University, College of Education.

DeVries, D., Edwards, K., & Slavin, R. (1978). Biracial learning teams and race relations in the classroom: Four field experiments on Teams-Games-Tournament. *Journal of Educational Psychology, 70*, 356–362.

DeVries, D., Lucasse, P., & Shackman, S. (1979). *Small group versus individualized instruction: A field test of their relative effectiveness.* Paper presented at the annual convention of the American Psychological Association, New York.

DeVries, D., & Slavin, R. (1978). Teams-games-tournaments (TGT): Review of ten classroom experiments. *Journal of Research and Development in Education, 12*, 28–38.

Dewey, J. (1910). *How we think.* Boston: Heath.

Dick, W. (1977). Formative evaluation. In L. Briggs (Ed.), *Instructional design: Principles and applications.* Englewood Cliffs, NJ: Educational Technology Publications.

Dick, W., & Carey, L. (1978). *The systematic design of instruction.* Glenview, IL: Scott, Foresman and Co.

Dillon, J. (1978). Using questions to depress student thought. *School Review, 87*, 50–63.

Dillon, J. (1979). Alternatives to questioning. *High School Journal, 62*, 217–222.

Dillon, J. (1981a). A norm against student questions. *Clearing House, 55*, 136–139.

Dillon, J. (1981b). Duration of response to teacher questions and statements. *Contemporary Educational Psychology, 6*, 1–11.

Dillon, J. (1982). Cognitive correspondence between question/statement and response. *American Educational Research Journal, 19*, 540–551.

Dillon, J. (1984). Research on questioning and discussion. *Educational Leadership, 42*(3), 50–56.

diSessa, A. (1982). Unlearning Aristotelian physics: A study of knowledge-based learning. *Cognitive Science, 6*, 37–75.

diSibio, M. (1982). Memory for connected discourse: A constructivist view. *Review of Educational Research, 52,* 149–174.

Dixon, D., Heppner, P., Petersen, C., & Ronning, R. (1979). Problem solving workshop training. *Journal of Counseling Psychology, 26,* 133–139.

Doctorow, M., Wittrock, M., & Marks, C. (1978). Generative processes in reading comprehension. *Journal of Educational Psychology, 70,* 109–118.

Doebler, L., & Eicke, F. (1979). Effects of teacher awareness of the educational implications of field-dependent/field-independent cognitive style on selected classroom variables. *Journal of Educational Psychology, 71,* 226–232.

Dollar, B. (1972). *Humanizing classroom discipline: A behavioral approach.* New York: Harper and Row.

Dooling, D., & Lachman, R. (1971). Effects of comprehension on retention of prose. *Journal of Experimental Psychology, 88,* 216–222.

Doyle, W. (1978). Task structures and student roles in classrooms. Paper presented at the annual meeting of the American Educational Research Association, Toronto.

Doyle, W. (1982). *Academic work.* Paper prepared for the National Commission on Excellence in Education.

Doyle, W. (1983). How order is achieved in classrooms. Paper presented at the annual meeting of the American Educational Research Association, Montreal, Canada.

Doyle, W. (1984). How order is achieved in classrooms: An interim report. *Journal of Curriculum Studies, 16,* 259–277.

Doyle, W. (1985). Classroom organization and management. In M. Wittrock (Ed.), *Handbook of research on teaching* (3rd ed.). New York: Macmillan.

Dreikurs, R. (1968). *Psychology in the classroom* (2nd. ed.). New York: Harper & Row.

Dubin, R., & Taveggia, T. (1968). *The teacher-learning paradox: A comparative analysis of college teaching methods.* Eugene: Center for the Advanced Study of Educational Administration, University of Oregon.

Duckworth, E. (1979). Either we're too early and they can't learn it or we're too late and they know it already: The dilemma of "applying Piaget." *Harvard Educational Review, 49,* 297–312.

Duffy, G., & McIntyre, L. (1982). A naturalistic study of instructional assistance in primary grade reading. *Elementary School Journal, 83,* 15–23.

Duffy, G., & Roehler, L. (1982). The illusion of instruction. *Reading Research Quarterly, 17,* 438–445.

Duke, D. (1978). The etiology of student misbehavior and the depersonalization of blame. *Review of Educational Research, 48,* 415–438.

Duke, P., Carlsmith, J., Jennings, D., Martin, J., Dornbusch, S., Gross, R., & Siegel-Gorelick, B. (1982). Educational correlates of early and late sexual maturation in adolescence. *Journal of Pediatrics, 100,* 633–637.

Duncan, O., Featherman, D., & Duncan, B. (1972). *Socioeconomic background and achievement.* New York: Seminar Press.

Dunkin, M., & Biddle, B. (1974). *The study of teaching.* New York: Holt, Rinehart and Winston.

Dunkin, M., & Doenau, S. (1980). A replication study of unique and joint contributions to variance in student achievement. *Journal of Educational Psychology, 72,* 394–403.

Dunn, L. (1973). *Exceptional children in the schools: Special education in transition.* New York: Holt, Rinehart and Winston.

Dunn, T. (1984). Learning hierarchies and cognitive psychology: An important link for instructional psychology. *Educational Psychologist, 19,* 75–93.

Durkin, D. (1978–79). What classroom observations reveal about reading comprehension research. *Reading Research Quarterly, 14,* 481–533.

Dusek, J. (1975). Do teachers bias children's learning? *Review of Educational Research, 45,* 661–684.

Dweck, C. (1983). Theories of intelligence and achievement motivation. In S. Paris, G. Olson, & H. Stevenson (Eds.), *Learning and motivation in the classroom.* Hillsdale, NJ: Erlbaum.

Dweck, C., Davidson, W., Nelson, S., & Enna, B. (1978). Sex differences in learned helplessness: II. The contingencies of evaluative feedback in the classroom and III. An experimental analysis. *Developmental Psychology, 14,* 268–276.

Dweck, C. & Elliott, E. (1983). Achievement

motivation. In P. Mussen & E. Hetherington (Eds.), *Handbook of child psychology, IV: Socialization, personality and social development.* New York: Wiley.

Dyk, R., & Witkin, H. (1965). Family experiences related to the development of differentiation in children. *Child Development, 36,* 21–55.

Eaton, J., Anderson, C., & Smith, E. (1984). Students' misconceptions interfere with science learning: Case studies of fifth-grade students. *Elementary School Journal, 84,* 365–379.

Ebbinghaus, H. (1885). *Memory.* (Translated by H. Ruger & C. Bussenius). New York: Dover, 1964 (originally published in Leipzig in 1885).

Ebel, R. (1975). Educational tests: Valid? biased? useful? *Phi Delta Kappan, 58,* 83–88.

Ebmeier, H., & Ziomek, R. (1983). Student academic engagement rates. Final report of the National Institute of Education Grant NIE-G-O-0892, Wheaton, IL Public Schools.

Eccles, J., Midgley, C., & Adler, T. (1983). Age-related environmental changes and their impact on achievement behavior. In J. G. Nicholls (Ed.), *The development of achievement motivation.* Greenwich, CN: JAI Press.

Eden, D. (1975). Intrinsic and extrinsic rewards and motives: Replication and extension with Kibbutz workers. *Journal of Applied Social Psychology, 5,* 348–361.

Eder, D. (1981). Ability grouping as a self-fulfilling prophecy: A micro-analysis of teacher-student interaction. *Sociology of Education, 54,* 151–161.

Edmonds, E., & Bessai, F. (1979). *First class: A survey of Canadian teachers in their first year of service.* Charlottetown: University of Prince Edward Island.

Educational Products Information Exchange (1974). *Evaluating instructional systems: PLAN, IGE, IPI.* (Product Report No. 58). New York: EPIE Institute.

Edwards, C., & Surma, M. (1980). The relationship between type of teacher reinforcement and student inquiry behavior in science. *Journal of Research in Science Teaching, 17,* 337–341.

Edwards, J., & Marland, P. (1984). What are students really thinking? *Educational Leadership, 42,* 63–67.

Edwards, K., DeVries, D., & Snyder, J. (1972). Games and teams: A winning combination. *Simulation and Games, 3,* 247–269.

Egbert, R. (1978). Reflections on the past, present, and future of special education. In J. Grosenick & M. Reynolds (Eds.), *Teacher education: Renegotiating roles for mainstreaming.* Reston, VA: Council for Exceptional Children.

Egeland, B. (1974). Training impulsive children in the use of more efficient scanning techniques. *Child Development, 45,* 165–171.

Ehman, L. (1970). A comparison of three sources of classroom data: Teachers, students, and systematic observation. Paper presented at the annual meeting of the American Educational Research Association.

Ehri, L., Deffner, N., & Wilce, L. (1984). Pictorial mnemonics for phonics. *Journal of Educational Psychology, 76,* 880–893.

Eichhorn, D. (1980). The school. In M. Johnson (Ed.), *Toward adolescence: The middle school years.* Chicago: National Society for the Study of Education.

Eisenberg, N., Lennon, R., & Roth, K. (1983). Prosocial development: A longitudinal study. *Developmental Psychology, 19,* 846–855.

Eisikovits, Z., & Sagi, A. (1982). Moral development and discipline encounter in delinquent and nondelinquent adolescents. *Journal of Youth and Adolescence, 11,* 217–230.

Elardo, P., & Elardo, R. (1976). A critical analysis of social development programs in elementary education. *Journal of School Psychology, 14,* 118–130.

Elstein, A., Shulman, L., & Sprafka, S. (1978). *Medical problem solving: An analysis of clinical reasoning.* Cambridge, MA: Harvard University Press.

Emmer, E. (1967). The effect of teacher use of student ideas on student verbal initiation. Unpublished doctoral dissertation, University of Michigan.

Emmer, E., & Evertson, C. (1980). Synthesis of research on classroom management. *Educational Leadership, 38,* 342–347.

Emmer, E., Evertson, C., & Anderson, L. (1980). Effective management at the beginning of the school year. *Elementary School Journal, 80,* 219–231.

Engelmann, S., & Carnine, D. (1982). *Theory*

of instruction: Principles and applications. New York: Irvington.

Enright, R., Lapsley, D., Harris, D., & Shawver, D. (1983). Moral development interventions in early adolescence. *Theory Into Practice, 22,* 134–144.

Epstein, H. (1978). Growth spurts during brain development: Implications for educational policy and practice. In J. Chall and A. Mirsky (Eds.), *Education and the brain: The 77th Yearbook of the National Society for the Study of Education, Part II.* Chicago: University of Chicago Press.

Erikson, E. (1968). *Identity: Youth and crisis.* New York: Norton.

Erlwanger, S. (1975). Case studies of children's conceptions of mathematics (Part I). *Journal of Children's Mathematical Behavior, 1,* 157–283.

Eshel, Y., & Klein, Z. (1981). Development of academic self-concept of lower-class and middle-class primary school children. *Journal of Educational Psychology, 73,* 287–293.

Eswara, H. (1972). Administration of reward and punishment in relation to ability, effort, and performance. *Journal of Social Psychology, 87,* 137–140.

Evans, G., & Lovell, B. (1979). Design modification in an open-plan school. *Journal of Educational Psychology, 71*(1), 41–49.

Evertson, C. (1979). Teacher behavior, student achievement, and student attitudes: Descriptions of selected classrooms. Austin, TX: Research and Development Center for Teacher Education, University of Texas (Report No. 4063).

Evertson, C. (1982). Differences in instructional activities in higher- and lower-achieving junior high English and math classes. *Elementary School Journal, 82,* 329–350.

Evertson, C., Anderson, C., Anderson, L., & Brophy, J. (1980). Relationships between classroom behaviors and student outcomes in junior high mathematics and English classes. *American Educational Research Journal, 17,* 43–60.

Evertson, C., & Anderson, L. (1979). Beginning school. *Educational Horizons, 57,* 164–168.

Evertson, C., Anderson, L., & Brophy, J. (1978). Texas junior high school study: Final report of process-outcome relationships (Vol. 1). Report No. 4061, Research and Development Center for Teacher Education, University of Texas, Austin, TX.

Evertson, C., Emmer, E., Sanford, J., & Clements, B. (1983). Improving classroom management: An experiment in elementary school classrooms. *Elementary School Journal, 84,* 173–188.

Fagan, E., Hassler, D., & Szabo, M. (1981). Evaluation of questioning strategies in language arts instruction. *Research in Teaching of English, 15,* 267–273.

Falkof, L., & Moss, J. (1984). When teachers tackle thinking skills. *Educational Leadership, 42,* 4–10.

Fanelli, G. (1977). Locus of control. In S. Ball (Ed.), *Motivation in education.* New York: Academic Press.

Faust, M. (1977). Somatic development of adolescent girls. *Monographs of the Society for Research in Child Development, 42*(1) (Serial #169).

Faw, H., & Waller, T. (1976). Mathemagenic behaviors and efficiency in learning from prose. *Review of Educational Research, 46,* 691–720.

Fehrle, C. (1975). Tips on teaching. *Continuing Professional Education, 2, 4.* (University of Missouri—Columbia, College of Education and Extension Division.)

Feiman-Nemser, S., & Floden, R. (1985). The cultures of teaching. In M. Wittrock (Ed.), *Handbook of research on teaching* (3rd ed.). New York: Macmillan.

Feldhusen, J. (1979). Problems of student behavior in secondary schools. In D. Duke (Ed.), *Classroom management. The Seventy-Eighth Yearbook of the National Society for the Study of Education, Part II.* Chicago: University of Chicago Press.

Felixbrod, J., & O'Leary, D. (1974). Self-determination of academic standards by children: Toward freedom from external control. *Journal of Educational Psychology,* 66, 845–850.

Felker, D. (1974). *Building positive self-concepts.* Minneapolis: Burgess.

Fennema, E., & Sherman, J. (1977). Sex-related differences in mathematics achievement, spatial visualization and affective factors. *American Educational Research Journal, 14,* 51–72.

Ferguson, G. (1954). On learning and human ability. *Canadian Journal of Psychology, 8,* 92–112.

Ferguson, G. (1956). On transfer and the abilities of man. *Canadian Journal of Psychology, 10,* 121–131.

Ferster, C. & Skinner, B. (1957). *Schedules of reinforcement.* New York: Appleton.

Feshbach, S. (1970). Aggression. In P. Mussen (Ed.), *Carmichael's manual of child psychology* (3rd ed., Vol. 2). New York: Wiley.

Festinger, L. (1957). *A theory of cognitive dissonance.* Stanford, CA: Stanford University Press.

Feuerstein, R., Rand, Y., Hoffman, M., & Miller, R. (1980). *Instrumental enrichment: An intervention program for cognitive modifiability.* Baltimore: University Park Press.

Feuerstein, R., et al. (1985). Instrumental enrichment, an intervention program for structural cognitive modifiability: Theory and practice. In J. Segal, S. Chipman, & R. Glaser (Eds.), *Thinking and learning skills, Volume 1: Relating instruction to research.* Hillsdale, NJ: Erlbaum.

Fillmore, C. (1968). The case for case. In E. Bach & R. Harms (Eds.), *Universals of linguistic theory.* New York: Holt, Rinehart and Winston.

Finn, J. (1972). Expectations and the educational environment. *Review of Educational Research, 42*(3), 387–410.

Fisher, C., & Berliner, D. (Eds.). (1985). *Perspectives on instructional time.* New York: Longman.

Fisher, C., Berliner, D., Filby, N., Marliave, R., Cahen, L., & Dishaw, M. (1980). Teaching behaviors, academic learning time, and student achievement: An overview. In C. Denham & A. Lieberman (Eds.), *Time to learn.* Washington, DC: National Institute of Education.

Fisher, M., Blackwell, L., Garcia, A., & Greene, J. (1974). Student control and choice: Their effects on student engagement in a CAI arithmetic task in low-income school. Technical Report #41, Stanford Center for Research and Development in Teaching.

Fitch, S., & Adams, G. (1983). Ego identity and intimacy status: Replication and extension. *Developmental Psychology, 19,* 839–845.

Flanagan, J., Shanner, W., Brudner, H., & Marker, R. (1975). An individualized instructional system: PLAN. In H. Talmage (Ed.), *Systems of individualized education.* Berkeley, CA: McCutchan.

Flanders, N. (1970). *Analyzing teacher behavior.* Reading, MA: Addison-Wesley.

Flavell, J., Beach, D., & Chinsky, J. (1966). Spontaneous verbal rehearsal in a memory task as a function of age. *Child Development, 37,* 283–299.

Flavell, J., Botkin, P., Fry, C., Wright, J., & Jarvis, P. (1968). *The development of role-taking and communication skills in children.* New York: Wiley.

Flavell, J., Speer, J., Green, F., & August, D. (1981). The development of comprehension monitoring and knowledge about communication. *Monographs of the Society for Research in Child Development, 46,* No. 192.

Flavell, J., & Wellman, H. (1977). Metamemory. In R. Kail & J. Hagen (Eds.), *Perspectives on the development of memory and cognition.* Hillsdale, NJ: Erlbaum.

Fleetwood, R., & Parish, T. (1976). Relationship between moral development test scores of juvenile delinquents and their inclusion in a moral dilemma discussion group. *Psychological Reports, 39,* 1075–1080.

Flowers, A., & Bolmeier, E. (1964). *Law and pupil control.* Cincinnati: W. H. Anderson Co.

Fogarty, J., Wang, M., & Creek, R. (March, 1982). A descriptive study of experienced and novice teachers' interactive instructional decision processes. Paper presented at the annual meeting of the American Educational Research Association, New York.

Fogarty, J., Wang, M., & Creek, R. (1983). A descriptive study of experienced and novice teachers' interactive instructional thoughts and actions. *Journal of Educational Research, 77,* 22–32.

Follman, J., Lowe, A., & Miller, W. (1971). Graphics variables and reliability and level of essay grades. *American Educational Research Journal, 8,* 365–373.

Ford, C., & Beach, F. (1951). *Patterns of sexual development.* New York: Harper & Row.

Fortune, J. (1967). *A study of the generality of presenting behaviors in teaching preschool children.* Memphis State University (Final Report for

U.S. Office of Education Project No. 6-8468), ERIC ED 016 285.

Fox, D. (1967) *Expansion of the more effective schools' program.* New York: Center for Urban Education. (Evaluation of New York City Title I Educational Projects, 1966–67.)

Fox, D., & Kendall, P. (1983). Thinking through academic problems: Application of cognitive-behavior therapy to learning. In T. Kratochwill (Ed.), *Advances in school psychology,* (Vol. 3). Hillsdale, NJ: Erlbaum.

Francis, E. (1975). Grade level and task difficulty in learning by discovery and verbal reception methods. *Journal of Educational Psychology, 67,* 146–150.

Frank, J. (1963). *Persuasion and healing.* New York: Shocken Books.

Frank, M. (1984). *A comparison between an individual and group goal structure contingency that differed in the behavioral contingency and performance-outcome components.* Unpublished doctoral dissertation, University of Minnesota, Minneapolis.

Frauenglass, M., & Diaz, R. (1985). Self-regulatory functions of children's private speech: A critical analysis of recent challenges to Vygotsky's theory. *Developmental Psychology, 21,* 356–364.

Frederiksen, N. (1984). Implications of cognitive theory for instruction in problem solving. *Review of Educational Research, 54,* 363–407.

Freeberg, N., & Payne, D. (1967). Parental influence on cognitive development in early childhood: A review. *Child Development, 38,* 65–87.

Freeman, D., Kuhs, T., Porter, A., Floden, R., Schmidt, W., & Schwille, J. (1983). Do textbooks and tests define a national curriculum in elementary school mathematics? *Elementary School Journal, 83,* 501–513.

Friedlander, B. (1975). Some remarks upon "open education." *American Educational Research Journal, 12,* 465–468.

Frieze, I., Francis, W., & Hanusa, B. (1983). Defining success in classroom settings. In J. Levine & M. Wang (Eds.), *Teacher and student perceptions: Implications for learning.* Hillsdale, NJ: Erlbaum.

Fuller, F. (1969). Concerns of teachers: A developmental conceptualization. *American Educational Research Journal, 6,* 207–226.

Fuller, F., & Bown, O. (1975). Becoming a teacher. In K. Ryan (Ed.), *Teacher education* (Seventy-fourth Yearbook of the National Society for the Study of Education). Chicago: University of Chicago Press.

Fuller, F., & Manning, B. (1973). Self-confrontation reviewed: A conceptualization for video playback in teacher education. *Review of Educational Research, 43,* 469–528.

Furst, E. (1981). Bloom's taxonomy of educational objectives for the cognitive domain: Philosophical and educational issues. *Review of Educational Research, 51,* 441–453.

Fuson, K. (1982). An analysis of the counting-on solution procedure in addition. In T. Carpenter, J. Moser, & T. Romberg (Eds.), *Addition and subtraction: A cognitive perspective.* Hillsdale, NJ: Erlbaum.

Fuson, K., Secada, W., & Hall, J. (1983). Matching, counting, and conservation of numerical equivalence. *Child Development, 54,* 91–97.

Fyans, L. (1980). *Achievement motivation: Recent trends in theory and research.* New York: Plenum.

Fyans, L., Salili, F., Maehr, M., & Desai, K. (1983). A cross-cultural exploration into the meaning of achievement. *Journal of Personality and Social Psychology, 44,* 1000–1013.

Gage, N. (Ed.). (1963). *Handbook of research on teaching.* Chicago: Rand McNally.

Gage, N. (1985). *Hard gains in the soft sciences: The case of pedagogy.* Bloomington, IN: Phi Delta Kappa.

Gage, N., & Berliner, D. (1979). *Educational psychology* (2nd ed.). Chicago: Rand McNally.

Gage, N., & Berliner, D. (1984). *Educational psychology* (3rd ed.). Boston: Houghton Mifflin.

Gagné, E., & Britton, B. (1982). The role of objectives in guiding the organization of information learned from text. *Contemporary Educational Psychology, 7,* 15–25.

Gagné, E., & Dick, W. (1983). Instructional psychology. In M. Rosenzweig & L. Porter (Eds.), *Annual review of psychology.* Palo Alto, CA: Annual Reviews.

Gagné, R. (1970). *The conditions of learning* (2nd ed.). New York: Holt, Rinehart and Winston.

Gagné, R. (1972). Domains of learning. *Interchange, 3,* 1–8.

Gagné, R. (1977). *The conditions of learning* (3rd ed.). New York: Holt, Rinehart and Winston.

Gagné, R. (1984). Learning outcomes and their effects: Useful categories of human performance. *American Psychologist, 39,* 377–385.

Gagné, R., & Briggs, L. (1979). *Principles of instructional design* (2nd ed.). New York: Holt, Rinehart and Winston.

Gall, M. (1970). The uses of questions in teaching. *Review of Educational Research, 40,* 707–721.

Gall, M. (1984). Synthesis of research on teachers' questioning. *Educational Leadership, 42*(3), 40–47.

Gall, M., Ward, B., Berliner, D., Cahen, L., Winne, P., Elashoff, J., & Stanton, G. (1978). Effects of questioning techniques and recitation on student learning. *American Educational Research Journal, 15,* 175–199.

Gardner, H. (1983). *Frames of mind: The theory of multiple intelligences.* New York: Basic Books.

Garrett-Schau, C., & Scott, K. (1984). Impact of gender characteristics of instructional materials: An integration of the research literature. *Journal of Educational Psychology, 76,* 183–193.

Gauld, A., & Stephenson, G. (1967). Some experiments relating to Bartlett's theory of remembering. *British Journal of Psychology, 58,* 39–49.

Gearheart, B., & Weishahn, M. (1976). *The handicapped child in the regular classroom.* St. Louis, MO: Mosby.

Gearheart, B., & Weishahn, M. (1984). *The exceptional student in the regular classroom* (3rd ed.). St. Louis, MO: Mosby.

Geiger, K., & Turiel, E. (1983). Disruptive school behavior and concepts of social convention in early adolescence. *Journal of Educational Psychology, 75,* 677–685.

Gelman, R. (1980). What young children know about numbers. *Educational Psychologist, 15,* 54–68.

Gelman, R., & Gallistel, C. (1978). *The child's understanding of number.* Cambridge: Harvard University Press.

Gesell, A., & Thompson, H. (1929). Learning and growth in identical infant twins. *Genetic Psychology Monographs, 6,* 1–24.

Getzels, J. (1974). Images of the classroom and visions of the learner. *School Review, 82,* 527–540.

Getzels, J. (1975). Creativity: Prospects and Issues. In I. Taylor & J. Getzels (Eds.), *Perspectives in creativity.* Chicago: Aldine.

Getzels, J., & Csikszentmihalyi, M. (1975). From problem solving to problem finding. In I. Taylor & J. Getzels (Eds.), *Perspectives in creativity.* Chicago: Aldine.

Getzels, J., & Jackson, P. (1962). *Creativity and intelligence: Explorations with gifted students.* New York: Wiley.

Giaconia, R., & Hedges, L. (1982). Identifying features of effective open education. *Review of Educational Research, 52,* 579–602.

Gibbs, J., Arnold, K., & Burkhart, J. (1984). Sex differences in the expression of moral judgment. *Child Development, 55,* 1040–1043.

Gibson, S., & Dembo, M. (1984). Teacher efficacy: A construct validation. *Journal of Educational Psychology, 76,* 569–582.

Gil, D., Vinsonhaler, J., & Wagner, C. (1979). Studies of clinical problem-solving behavior in reading diagnosis. Research Series #42, Institute for Research on Teaching, College of Education, Michigan State University.

Gilhool, T. (1973). Education: An inalienable right. *Exceptional Children, 39,* 597–610.

Gilligan, C. (1982). *In a different voice.* Cambridge: Harvard University Press.

Ginsburg, H., & Opper, S. (1979). *Piaget's theory of intellectual development* (2nd ed.). Englewood Cliffs, NJ: Prentice-Hall.

Glaser, R. (1977). *Adaptive education: Individualized diversity and learning.* New York: Holt, Rinehart and Winston.

Glaser, R., & Nitko, A. (1971). Measurement in learning and instruction. In R. Thorndike (Ed.), *Educational measurement* (2nd ed.). Washington, DC: American Council on Education.

Glaser, R., & Rosner, J. (1975). Adaptive environments for learning: Curriculum aspects. In H. Talmage (Ed.), *Systems of individualized education.* Berkeley, CA: McCutchan.

Glass, G., & Smith, M. (1978). Meta-analysis of research on the relationship of class size and achievement. San Francisco: Far West Laboratory for Educational Research and Development.

Glassberg, S. (April, 1980). A view of the beginning teacher from a developmental perspective. Paper presented at the annual meeting of the American Educational Research Association, Boston.

Glasser, W. (1969). *Schools without failure.* New York: Harper & Row.

Glasser, W. (November–December, 1977). Ten steps to good discipline. *Today's Education,* 66(4), 61–63.

Glenberg, A. (1976). Monotonic and nonmonotonic lag effects in paired-associated and recognition memory paradigms. *Journal of Verbal Learning and Verbal Behavior, 15,* 1–16.

Glick, J. (1975). Cognitive development in cross-cultural perspective. In F. Horowitz (Ed.), *Review of child development research* (Vol. 4). Chicago: University of Chicago Press.

Gliessman, D., & Pugh, R. (1978). Research on the rationale, design, and effectiveness of protocol materials. *Journal of Teacher Education, 29,* 87–91.

Glynn, E., Thomas, J., & Shee, S. (1973). Behavioral self-control of on-task behavior in an elementary classroom. *Journal of Applied Behavior Analysis, 6,* 105–113.

Goffman, E. (1959). *The presentation of self in everyday life.* Garden City, NY: Doubleday.

Golinkoff, R. (1976). A comparison of reading comprehension processes in good and poor comprehenders. *Reading Research Quarterly, 11,* 623–659.

Good, T. (1970). Which pupils do teachers call on? *Elementary School Journal, 70,* 190–198.

Good, T. (1979). Teacher effectiveness in the elementary school: What we know about it now. *Journal of Teacher Education, 30,* 52–64.

Good, T. (1981). Listening to students talk about classrooms. Paper presented at the annual meeting of the American Educational Research Association, Los Angeles.

Good, T. (1983). Recent classroom research: Implications for teacher education. An invited address delivered at the annual meeting of AACTE, Chicago.

Good, T., & Beckerman, T. (1978). An examination of teachers' effect on high, middle, and low aptitude students' performance on a standardized achievement test. *American Educational Research Journal, 15,* 477–482.

Good, T., Biddle, B., & Brophy, J. (1975). *Teachers make a difference.* New York: Holt, Rinehart and Winston.

Good, T., & Brophy, J. (1973). *Looking in classrooms* (1st ed.). New York: Harper & Row.

Good, T., & Brophy, J. (1974). Changing teacher and student behavior: An empirical investigation. *Journal of Educational Psychology, 66,* 390–405.

Good, T., & Brophy, J. (1978). *Looking in classrooms* (2nd ed.). New York: Harper & Row.

Good, T., & Brophy, J. (1984). *Looking in classrooms* (3rd ed.). New York: Harper & Row.

Good, T., & Brophy, J. (1985). School effects. In M. Wittrock (Ed.), *Handbook of research on teaching* (3rd ed.). New York: Macmillan.

Good, T., & Grouws, D. (1975). *Process-product relationships in fourth-grade mathematics classrooms* (Final report of the National Institute of Education Grant NIE-G-00-3-0123). Columbia: University of Missouri.

Good, T., & Grouws, D. (1977). Teaching effects: A process-product study in fourth grade mathematics classrooms. *Journal of Teacher Education, 28,* 49–54.

Good, T., & Grouws, D. (1979). The Missouri Mathematics Effectiveness Project: An experimental study in fourth-grade classrooms. *Journal of Educational Psychology, 71,* 355–362.

Good, T., Grouws, D., & Beckerman, T. (1978). Curriculum pacing: Some empirical data in mathematics. *Journal of Curriculum Studies, 19,* 75–81.

Good, T., Grouws, D., & Ebmeier, H. (1983). *Active mathematics teaching.* New York: Longman.

Good, T., & Hinkel, G. (1982). Schooling in America: Some descriptive and explanatory statements. Paper prepared for the National Commission on Excellence in Education.

Good, T., & Power, C. (1976). Designing successful classroom environments for different types of students. *Journal of Curriculum Studies, 8,* 1–16.

Good, T., Sikes, J., & Brophy, J. (1973). Effects of teacher sex and student sex on classroom interaction. *Journal of Educational Psychology, 65,* 74–87.

Good, T., & Stipek, D. (1984). Individual differences in the classroom: A psychological perspective. In G. Fenstermacher & J. Goodlad (Eds.), *1983 NSSE Yearbook.* Chicago: University of Chicago Press.

Good, T., & Tom, D. (in press). Classroom motivation: A review of four position papers. In R. Ames & C. Ames (Eds.), *Research on motivation in education* (Vol. 2). Orlando, FL: Academic Press.

Good, T., & Weinstein, R. (in press). Classroom expectations: One framework for exploring classrooms. In K. Kepler-Zumwalt (Ed.), *Theory into practice: 1986 ASCD Yearbook.*

Gordon, R., & Gross, R. (1978). An exploration of the interconnecting perspective of teaching style and teacher education. *Journal of Curriculum Studies, 10,* 151–157.

Gordon, T. (1974). *T.E.T.: Teacher effectiveness training.* New York: McKay.

Gorton, R. (1976). *School administration: Challenge and opportunity for leadership.* Dubuque, IA: Wm. C. Brown.

Gottfried, A. (Ed.). (1984). *Home environment and early cognitive development: Longitudinal research.* New York: Academic Press.

Goulet, L., Williams, K., & Hay, C. (1974). Longitudinal changes in intellectual functioning in preschool children: Schooling- and age-related effects. *Journal of Educational Psychology, 66,* 657–662.

Graef, R., Csikszentmihalyi, M., & Gianinno, S. (1981). Measuring intrinsic motivation in everyday life. Paper presented at the annual meeting of the American Psychological Association, Los Angeles.

Graham, S. (1984). Effective spelling instruction. *Elementary School Journal, 83,* 560–568.

Grant, L. (1984). Black females' "place" in desegregated classrooms. *Sociology of Education, 57,* 98–111.

Gray, S., Ramsey, B., & Klaus, R. (1982). *From 3 to 20: The early training project.* Baltimore: University Park Press.

Green, J. (1975). *Teacher made tests* (2nd ed.). New York: Harper & Row.

Greenbowe, T., Herron, J., Lucas, C., Nurrenbern, S., Staver, J., & Ward, C. (1981). Teaching preadolescents to act as scientists: Replication and extension of an earlier study. *Journal of Educational Psychology, 73,* 705–711.

Greeno, J. (1978). Natures of problem-solving abilities. In W. Estes (Ed.), *Handbook of learning and cognitive processes* (Vol. 5). Hillsdale, NJ: Erlbaum.

Greeno, J. (1980a). Some examples of cognitive task analysis with instructional implications. In R. Snow, P. Federico, & W. Montague (Eds.), *Aptitude, learning, and instruction,* (Vol. 2). Hillsdale, NJ: Erlbaum.

Greeno, J. (1980b). Psychology of learning, 1960–1980: One participant's observations. *American Psychologist, 35,* 713–728.

Greer, R. (1983). Contingencies of the science and technology of teaching: Prebehavioristic research practices in education. *Educational Researcher, 12,* 3–9.

Greif, E., & Ulman, K. (1982). The psychological impact of menarche on early adolescent females: A review of the literature. *Child Development, 53,* 1413–1430.

Grennon, J. (1984). Making sense of student thinking. *Educational Leadership, 42,* 10–17.

Griffin, G., Barnes, S., Hughes, R., O'Neal, S., Defino, M., Edwards, S., & Hukill, H. (1983). Clinical preservice teacher education: Final report of a descriptive study. Report No. 9025. Austin, TX: Research and Development Center for Teacher Education.

Griffin, G., Webb, N., & Confrey, J. (1981). Time to learn: Reviews from three perspectives. *Elementary School Journal, 82,* 76–94.

Griswold, P. (1984). Elementary students' attitudes during two years of computer-assisted instruction. *American Educational Research Journal, 21,* 737–754.

Groen, G., & Parkman, J. (1972). A chronometric analysis of simple addition. *Psychological Review, 79,* 329–343.

Groff, E., & Render, G. (1983). The effectiveness of three classroom teaching methods: Programmed instruction, simulation and guided fantasy. *Journal of the Society for Accelerative Learning and Teaching, 8,* 5–13.

Groisser, P. (1964). *How to use the fine art of questioning.* New York: Teachers' Practical Press.

Gronlund, N. (1974). *Improving marking and reporting in classroom instruction: A title in the current topics in classroom instruction series.* New York: Macmillan.

Gronlund, N. (1985). *Stating objectives for classroom instruction* (3rd ed.). New York: Macmillan.

Gropper, G. (1983). A behavioral approach to instructional prescription. In C. Reigeluth (Ed.), *Instructional-design theories and models:*

An overview of their current status. Hillsdale, NJ: Erlbaum.

Grusec, J., Kuczynski, L., Rushton, J., & Simutis, Z. (1978). Modeling, direct instruction, and attributions: Effects on altruism. *Developmental Psychology, 14,* 51–57.

Guilford, J. (1959). Three faces of intellect. *American Psychologist, 14,* 469–479.

Guilford, J. (1967). *The nature of human intelligence.* New York: McGraw-Hill.

Gump, P. (1980). The school as a social situation. In M. Rosenzweig & L. Porter (Eds.), *Annual review of psychology,* (Vol. 31). Palo Alto, CA: Annual Reviews, Inc.

Gump, P., & Good, L. (1976). Environments operating in open space and traditionally designed schools. *Journal of Architectural Research, 5,* 20–27.

Hains, A., & Miller, D. (1980). Moral and cognitive development in delinquent and nondelinquent children and adolescents. *Journal of Genetic Psychology, 137,* 21–35.

Haladyna, T., & Thomas, G. (1979). The attitudes of elementary school children toward school and subject matters. *Journal of Experimental Education, 48,* 18–23.

Hales, L., & Tokar, E. (1975). The effect of quality of preceding responses on the grades assigned to subsequent responses to an essay question. *Journal of Educational Measurement, 12,* 115–117.

Hall, C., & Lindzey, G. (1970). *Theories of personality* (2nd ed.). New York: Wiley.

Hall, P., & Spencer-Hall, D. (1980). *Conditions and processes of problem identification, definition, and resolution in two school systems: Toward a grounded theory.* Final report of the National Institute of Education, Grant NIE-G-78-0042.

Hambleton, R., Swaminathan, H., Algina, J., & Coulson, D. (1978). Criterion-referenced testing and measurement: A review of technical issues and developments. *Review of Educational Research, 48,* 1–47.

Hannah, E., & Pilner, S. (1983). Teacher attitudes toward handicapped students: A review and synthesis. *School Psychology Review, 12,* 12–25.

Hansen, J., & Pearson, P. (1983). An instructional study: Improving the inferential comprehension of fourth-grade good and poor readers. *Journal of Educational Psychology, 75,* 821–829.

Hansen, K. (December, 1976). Implications of P.L. 94-142 for higher education. A paper presented at the Regional Mainstreaming Conference, Kansas City, MO.

Harber, J., & Bryen, D. (1976). Black English and the task of reading. *Review of Educational Research, 46,* 387–405.

Hare, V., & Pulliam, C. (1980). Teacher questioning: A verification and an extension. *Journal of Reading Behavior, 12,* 69–72.

Hargreaves, D., Hester, S., & Mellor, F. (1975). *Deviance in classrooms.* London: Routledge and Kegan Paul.

Harnischfeger, A., & Wiley, D. (1976). Achievement test scores drop: So what? *Educational Researcher, 5,* 5–12.

Harris, A., & Kapche, R. (1978). Problems of quality control in the development and the use of behavior change techniques in public school settings. *Education and Treatment of Children, 1,* 43–51.

Harris, B. (1979). What ever happened to Little Albert? *American Psychologist, 34,* 151–160.

Harrow, A. (1972). *A taxonomy of the psychomotor domain.* New York: David McKay.

Hart, S. (1982). Analyzing the social organization for reading in one elementary school. In G. Spindler (Ed.), *Doing the ethnography of schooling.* New York: Holt, Rinehart and Winston.

Harter, S. (1983). Developmental perspectives on the self-system. In P. Mussen (Ed.), *Handbook of child psychology,* (4th ed., Vol. IV). New York: Wiley.

Hartlage, L., & Steele, C. (1977). WISC and WISC-R correlates of academic achievement. *Psychology in the Schools, 14,* 15–18.

Hartup, W. (1970). Peer interaction and social organization. In P. Mussen (Ed.), *Carmichael's manual of child psychology* (3rd ed., Vol. 2). New York: Wiley.

Hasher, L., & Zacks, R. (1984). Automatic processing of fundamental information: The case of frequency of occurrence. *American Psychologist, 39,* 1372–1388.

Haskins, R., & McKinney, J. (1976). Relative effects of response tempo and accuracy on problem solving and academic achievement. *Child Development, 47,* 690–696.

Hauserman, N., Miller, J., & Bond, F. (1976). A behavioral approach to changing self-concept in elementary school children. *Psychological Record, 26,* 111–116.

Havighurst, R. (1972). *Developmental tasks and education* (3rd ed.). New York: David McKay.

Hayes, D., & Tierney, R. (1982). Developing readers' knowledge through analogy. *Reading Research Quarterly, 17,* 256–280.

Hayes, J. (1981). *The complete problem solver.* Philadelphia: Franklin Institute Press.

Hayes, R., & Day, B. (1980). Classroom openness and the basic skills, the self-perceptions, and the school-attendance records of third-grade pupils. *Elementary School Journal, 81,* 87–96.

Heath, R., & Nielson, M. (1974). The research basis for performance-based teacher education. *Review of Educational Research, 44,* 463–484.

Heider, E. (1971). Information processing and the modification of an "impulsive conceptual tempo." *Child Development, 42,* 1276–1281.

Henderson, R. (Ed.). (1981). *Parent-child interaction: Theory, research, and prospects.* New York: Academic Press.

Henson, K. (1980). What's the use of lecturing? *High School Journal, 64,* 115–119.

Heppner, P. (1978). A review of the problem-solving literature and its relationship to the counseling process. *Journal of Counseling Psychology, 25,* 366–375.

Hermann, G. (1969). Learning by discovery: A critical review of studies. *Journal of Experimental Education, 38,* 58–71.

Hess, R. (1970). Class and ethnic influences upon socialization. In P. Mussen (Ed.), *Carmichael's manual of child psychology* (3rd ed., Vol. 2). New York: Wiley.

Hess, R., Holloway, S., Dickson, W., & Price, G. (1984). Maternal variables as predictors of children's school readiness and later achievement in vocabulary and mathematics in sixth grade. *Child Development, 55,* 1902–1912.

Hess, R., & McDevitt, T. (1984). Some cognitive consequences of maternal intervention techniques: A longitudinal study. *Child Development, 55,* 2017–2030.

Hess, R., & Shipman, V. (1965). Early experience and the socialization of cognitive modes in children. *Child Development, 34,* 869–886.

Hess, R., Shipman, V., Brophy, J., & Bear, R. (1968). *The cognitive environments of urban preschool children.* Chicago: University of Chicago, School of Education.

Hess, R., Tenezakis, M., Smith, I., Brad, R., Spellman, J., Ingle, H., & Oppman, B. (1970). The computer as a socializing agent: Some socioaffective outcomes of CAI (Technical Report No. 13). Stanford, CA: Stanford Center for Research and Development in Teaching, Stanford University.

Hewett, F., & Watson, P. (1979). Classroom management and the exceptional learner. In D. Duke (Ed.), *Classroom management. The Seventy-Eighth Yearbook of the National Society for the Study of Education, Part II.* Chicago: University of Chicago Press.

Hiebert, E. (1983). An examination of ability grouping in reading instruction. *Reading Research Quarterly, 18*(2), 231–255.

Hill, K., & Wigfield, A. (1984). Test anxiety: A major educational problem and what can be done about it. *Elementary School Journal, 85,* 105–126.

Hiller, J., Fisher, G., & Kaess, W. (1969). A computer investigation of verbal characteristics of effective classroom lecturing. *American Educational Research Journal, 6,* 661–675.

Hoetker, J., & Ahlbrand, W. (1969). The persistence of the recitation. *American Educational Research Journal, 6,* 145–167.

Hoffman, M. (1970). Moral development. In P. Mussen (Ed.), *Carmichael's manual of child psychology* (3rd ed., Vol. 2). New York: Wiley.

Hoffman, M. (1977). Personality and social development. In M. Rosenzweig & L. Porter (Eds.), *Annual review of psychology* (Vol. 28). Palo Alto, CA: Annual Reviews.

Hoffman, M. (1979). Development of moral thought, feeling, and behavior. *American Psychologist, 34,* 958–966.

Holt, J. (1964). *How children fail.* New York: Pitman.

Honzik, M., McFarlane, J., & Allen, L. (1948). The stability of mental test performance between 2 and 18 years. *Journal of Experimental Psychology, 4,* 309–324.

Hook, C., & Rosenshine, B. (1979). Accuracy of teacher reports of their classroom behavior. *Review of Educational Research, 49,* 1–12.

Hooper, F., & DeFrain, J. (1980). On delineating distinctly Piagetian contributions to education. *Genetic Psychology Monographs, 101,* 151–181.

Hoover, K. (1968). *Learning and teaching in the secondary school: Improved instruction practice.* Boston: Allyn & Bacon.

Hopkins, K., & Bracht, G. (1975). Ten-year stability of verbal and nonverbal IQ scores. *American Educational Research Journal, 12,* 469–477.

Horak, V. (1981). A meta-analysis of research findings on individualized instruction in mathematics. *Journal of Educational Research, 74,* 249–253.

Horton, D., & Mills, C. (1984). Human learning and memory. In M. Rosenzweig & L. Porter (Eds.), *Annual review of psychology.* Palo Alto, CA: Annual Reviews.

Horwitz, R. (1979). Psychological effects of the "open classroom." *Review of Educational Research, 49,* 71–86.

Houseman, J. (1972). An ecological study of interpersonal conflict among preschool children. Unpublished doctoral dissertation, Wayne State University.

Houston, W., et al., (Eds.). (1973). *Resources for performance-based education.* Albany, NY: State University of New York.

Hudgins, E. (1979). Examining the effectiveness of affective education. *Psychology in the Schools, 16,* 581–585.

Huesmann, L., Eron, L., Lefkowitz, M., & Walder, L. (1984). Stability of aggression over time and generations. *Developmental Psychology, 20,* 1120–1134.

Hughes, D. (1973). An experimental investigation of the effects of pupil responding and teacher reacting on pupil achievement. *American Educational Research Journal, 10,* 21–37.

Hulten, B., & DeVries, D. (1976). *Team competition and group practice: Effects on student achievement and attitudes.* Center Report No. 212. Center for Social Organization of Schools, The Johns Hopkins University.

Hunt, D., & Joyce, B. (1981). Teacher trainee personality and initial teaching style. In B. Joyce, C. Brown, & L. Peck (Eds.), *Flexibility in teaching.* New York: Longman.

Hunt, J. McV. (1960). Experience and the development of motivation: Some reinterpretations. *Child Development, 31,* 489–504.

Hunt, J. McV. (1961). *Intelligence and experience.* New York: Ronald.

Hunt, J. McV. (1965). Intrinsic motivation and its role in psychological development. In D. Levine (Ed.), *Nebraska symposium on motivation* (Vol. 13). Lincoln: University of Nebraska Press.

Hunter, D. (1978). Student on task behavior during reading group meeting. Unpublished doctoral dissertation, University of Missouri-Columbia.

Hunter, M. (1984). Knowing, teaching and supervising. In P. Hosford (Ed.), *Using what we know about teaching.* Alexandria, VA: Association for Supervision and Curriculum Development.

Hurlock, E. (1964). *Child development* (4th ed.). New York: McGraw-Hill.

Husen, T. (Ed.). (1967). *International study of achievement in mathematics: A comparison of twelve countries.* New York: Wiley.

Huston, A. (1983). Sex-typing. In P. Mussen (Ed.), *Handbook of child psychology* (4th ed., Vol. IV). New York: Wiley.

Huston-Stein, A., Sussman, E., & Freidrich, L. (1976). The relationship of cognitive style to social and self-regulatory behaviors in naturalistic settings. Unpublished manuscript, Pennsylvania State University.

Hyde, J. (1981). How large are cognitive gender differences? *American Psychologist, 36,* 292–301.

Hyde, J. (1984). How large are gender differences in aggression? *Developmental Psychology, 20,* 722–736.

Inhelder, B., & Piaget, J. (1958). *The growth of logical thinking from childhood to adolescence.* New York: Basic Books.

Inhelder, B., Sinclair, H., & Bovet, M. (1974). *Learning and the development of cognition.* Cambridge, MA: Harvard University Press.

Jackson, K. (1976). *An assessment of long-term effects of personal causation training.* Unpublished doctoral dissertation, Washington University, St. Louis, MO.

Jackson, P. (1968). *Life in classrooms.* New York: Holt, Rinehart and Winston.

Jackson, S. (1965). The growth of logical thinking in normal and subnormal children. *British Journal of Educational Psychology, 35,* 255–258.

Jagacinski, C., & Nicholls, J. (1982). *Concepts of ability.* Paper presented at the annual meeting of the American Educational Research Association, New York.

Jamison, D., Suppes, P., & Wells, S. (1974). The effectiveness of alternative instructional media: A survey. *Review of Educational Research, 44,* 1–68.

Jantz, R., Seefeldt, C., Galper, A., & Serock, K. (1976). *Curriculum guide: Children's attitudes toward the elderly.* Department of Early Childhood/Elementary Education, College of Education. Center on Aging, Division of Human & Community Resources, University of Maryland.

Jenkins, J. (1974). Remember that old theory of memory? Well, forget it! *American Psychologist, 29,* 785–795.

Jensen, A. (1969). How much can we boost IQ and scholastic achievement? *Harvard Educational Review, 39,* 1–123.

Jensen, A. (1970). Hierarchical theories of mental ability. In B. Dockrell (Ed.), *On intelligence.* Toronto: Ontario Institute for Studies in Education.

Jensen, A. (1973). *Educability and group differences.* New York: Harper & Row.

Jensen, A. (1974). How biased are culture-loaded tests? *Genetic Psychology Monographs, 90,* 185–244.

Jensen, A. (1976). Test bias and construct validity. *Phi Delta Kappan, 58,* 340–346.

Jensen, A., & Figueroa, R. (1975). Forward and backward digit span interaction with race and IQ: Predictions from Jensen's theory. *Journal of Educational Psychology, 67,* 882–893.

Jensen, L., & Murray, M. (1978). Facilitating development of four moral concepts among kindergarten and first-grade children. *Journal of Educational Psychology, 70,* 936–944.

Johnson, D. (1970). *The social psychology of education.* New York: Holt, Rinehart and Winston.

Johnson, D. (1976). Crosscultural perspectives on sex differences in reading. *The Reading Teacher, 29,* 747–752.

Johnson, D., & Ahlgren, A. (1976). Relationship between student attitudes about cooperation and competition and attitudes toward schooling. *Journal of Educational Psychology, 68,* 92–102.

Johnson, D., & Johnson, R. (1974). Instructional goal structure: Cooperative, competitive, or individualistic. *Review of Educational Research, 44,* 213–240.

Johnson, D., & Johnson, R. (1975). *Learning together and alone.* Englewood Cliffs, NJ: Prentice-Hall.

Johnson, D., & Johnson, R. (in press). Cooperative learning. In R. Ames & C. Ames (Eds.), *Research on motivation in education* (Vol. 2). Orlando, FL: Academic Press.

Johnson, J., & Ruskin, R. (1977). *Behavioral instruction: An evaluative review.* Washington, DC: American Psychological Association.

Johnston, G., & Yeakey, C. (1979). The supervision of teacher evaluation: A brief overview. *Journal of Teacher Education, 30,* 17–22.

Johnston, P. (1984). Assessment in reading: The emperor has no clothes. In P. Pearson, M. Camil, R. Barr, & P. Mosenthal (Eds.), *Handbook of reading research.* New York: Longman.

Jones, B., & Hall, J. (1982). School applications of the mnemonic keyword method as a study strategy by eighth graders. *Journal of Educational Psychology, 74,* 230–237.

Jones, L. (1984). White-black achievement differences: The narrowing gap. *American Psychologist, 39,* 1207–1213.

Jones, M. (1957). The later careers of boys who were early or late maturing. *Child Development, 28,* 113–128.

Jorgenson, G. (1977). Relationship of classroom behavior to the accuracy of the match between material difficulty and student ability. *Journal of Educational Psychology, 69,* 24–32.

Joyce, B., & Weil, M. (1980). *Models of teaching* (2nd ed.). Englewood Cliffs, NJ: Prentice-Hall.

Kacerguis, M., & Adams, G. (1980). Erikson stage resolution: The relationship between identity and intimacy. *Journal of Youth and Adolescence, 9,* 117–126.

Kagan, J., & Kogan, N. (1970). Individual variation in cognitive processes. In P. Mussen (Ed.), *Carmichael's manual of child psychology* (3rd ed., Vol. 1). New York: Wiley.

Kagan, J., & Moss, H. (1962). *Birth to maturity: A study in psychological development.* New York: Wiley.

Kagan, J., Pearson, J., & Welch, L. (1966). Modifiability of an impulsive tempo. *Journal of Educational Psychology, 57,* 357–365.

Kagan, J., Rosman, B., Day, D., Albert, J., & Phillips, W. (1964). Information processing and the child: Significance of analytic and reflective attitudes. *Psychological Monographs, 78*(1) (whole number 578).

Kagan, S., & Madsen, M. (1971). Cooperation and competition of Mexican, Mexican-American, and Anglo-American children of two ages under four instructional sets. *Developmental Psychology, 5,* 32–39.

Kail, R., & Hagen, J. (1982). Memory in childhood. In B. Wolman (Ed.), *Handbook of developmental psychology.* Englewood Cliffs, NJ: Prentice-Hall.

Kamii, C., & DeClark (1985). *Young children reinvent arithmetic.* New York: Teachers College Press.

Kamin, L. (1974). *The science and politics of IQ.* Potomac, MD: Erlbaum.

Karweit, N. (1976). Quantity of schooling: A major educational factor? *Educational Researcher, 5,* 15–17.

Karweit, N. (1983). Time-on-task: A research review. Report #332, Center for Social Organization of Schools. The Johns Hopkins University, Baltimore, MD.

Karweit, N., & Slavin, R. (1981). Measurement and modeling choices in studies of time and learning. *American Educational Research Journal, 18,* 157–171.

Keller, F. (1968). Goodbye, teacher! *Journal of Applied Behavior Analysis, 1*(1), 79–88.

Keller, F., & Sherman, J. (1982). *The PSI handbook: Essays on personalized instruction.* Lawrence, KS: TRI.

Keller, J. (1983). Motivational design of instruction. In C. Reigeluth (Ed.), *Instructional-design theories and models: An overview of their current status.* Hillsdale, NJ: Erlbaum.

Kendler, H., & Kendler, T. (1962). Vertical and horizontal processes in problem solving. *Psychological Review, 69,* 1–16.

Kepler, K. (1980). BTES: Implications for preservice education of teachers. In C. Denham & A. Lieberman (Eds.), *Time to learn.* Washington, DC: U.S. Department of Education.

Kiewra, K. (1985a). Investigating notetaking and review: A depth of processing alternative. *Educational Psychologist, 20,* 23–32.

Kiewra, K. (1985b). Providing the instructor's notes: An effective addition to student notetaking. *Educational Psychologist, 20,* 33–39.

Killian, C. (1979). Cognitive development of college freshman. *Journal of Research in Science Teaching, 16,* 347–350.

King, L. (1979). An attributional analysis of student achievement, related behavior and expectancy effect. Doctoral dissertation, University of Alberta.

Kinsbourne, M., & Hiscock, M. (1978). Cerebral lateralization and cognitive development. In J. Chall & A. Mirsky (Eds.), *Education and the brain: The 77th Yearbook of the National Society for the Study of Education, Part II.* Chicago: University of Chicago Press.

Kintsch, W. (1974). *The representation of meaning in memory.* Hillsdale, NJ: Erlbaum.

Kintsch, W. (1976). Memory for prose. In C. Cofer (Ed.), *The structure of human memory.* San Francisco: Freeman.

Kintsch, W. (1977). *Memory and cognition.* New York: Wiley.

Kintsch, W., & Yarbrough, J. (1982). Role of rhetorical structure in text comprehension. *Journal of Educational Psychology, 74,* 828–834.

Kirkland, K. (1978). The effects of group assertion training on the development and maintenance of assertive skills in unassertive adolescents. Unpublished Ph.D. thesis, University of Missouri—Columbia.

Klahr, D., & Wallace, J. (1976). *Cognitive development: An information-processing view.* Hillsdale, NJ: Erlbaum.

Klatzky, R. (1980). *Human memory,* (2nd ed.). San Francisco: Freeman.

Klauer, K. (1984). Intentional and incidental learning with instructional texts: A meta-analysis for 1970–1980. *American Educational Research Journal, 21,* 232–339.

Klausmeier, H. (1976). Instructional design and the teaching of concepts. In J. Levin & V. Allen (Eds.), *Cognitive learning in children: Theories and strategies.* New York: Academic Press.

Klausmeier, H., Ghatala, E., & Frayer, D. (1974). *Conceptual learning and development.* New York: Academic Press.

Klausmeier, H., Rossmiller, R., & Saily, M. (Eds.). (1977). *Individually guided elementary education: Concepts and practices.* New York: Academic Press.

Klausmeier, H., Sorenson, J., & Quilling, M.

(1971). Instructional programming for individual pupils in the multiunit elementary school. *Elementary School Journal, 72,* 88–101.

Klein, S. (1971). Student influence on teacher behavior. *American Educational Research Journal, 8,* 403–421.

Kleinfeld, J. (1972). Instructional style and the intellectual performance of Indian and Eskimo Students. Final Report, Project No. 1-J-027, Office of Education, U.S. Department of Health, Education, and Welfare.

Kleinfeld, J. (1975). Effective teachers of Indian and Eskimo students. *School Review, 83,* 301–344.

Klinger, E., & McNelly, F. (1976). Self-states and performances of pre-adolescent boys carrying out leadership roles inconsistent with their social status. *Child Development, 47,* 126–137.

Koeher, W. (1959). *The mentality of apes.* New York: Vintage.

Koff, E., Rierdan, J., & Jacobson, S. (1981). The personal and interpersonal significance of menarche. *Journal of the American Academy of Child Psychiatry, 20,* 148–158.

Kohlberg, L. (1966). A cognitive-developmental analysis of children's sex-role concepts and attitudes. In E. Maccoby (Ed.), *The development of sex differences.* Stanford, CA: Stanford University Press.

Kohlberg, L. (1969). Stage and sequence: The cognitive-developmental approach to socialization. In D. Goslin (Ed.), *Handbook of socialization theory and research.* Chicago: Rand McNally.

Kohlberg, L. (1978). Revisions in the theory and practice of moral development. In W. Damon (Ed.), *Moral development.* San Francisco: Jossey-Bass.

Kohlberg, L. (1980). A response to Thomas Sobol. *Educational Leadership, 38,* 19–23.

Kohlberg, L. (1981). *The philosophy of moral development.* San Francisco: Harper & Row.

Kohlberg, L., Levine, C., & Hewer, A. (1983). *Moral stages: A current formulation and a response to critics.* New York: Karger.

Kohlberg, L., Yeager, J., & Hjertholm, E. (1967). Private speech: Four studies and a review of theories. *Child Development, 39,* 691–736.

Kohlberg, L., & Zigler, E. (1967). The impact of cognitive maturity upon the development of sex-role attitudes in the years 4 to 8. *Genetic Psychology Monographs, 75,* 84–165.

Köhler, W. (1959). *The mentality of apes.* New York: Vintage.

Kounin, J. (1970). *Discipline and group management in classrooms.* New York: Holt, Rinehart and Winston.

Kounin, J., & Gump, P. (1974). Signal systems of lesson settings and the task-related behavior of preschool children. *Journal of Educational Psychology, 66,* 554–562.

Kounin, J., & Obradovic, S. (1968). Managing emotionally disturbed children in regular classrooms: A replication and extension. *Journal of Special Education, 2,* 129–135.

Kramer, C. (1974). Folk linguistics. *Psychology Today, 8*(6), 82–85.

Krantz, P., & Risley, T. (1977). Behavioral ecology in the classroom. In K. O'Leary & S. O'-Leary (Eds.), *Classroom management: The successful use of behavior modification* (2nd ed.). New York: Pergamon Press.

Krathwohl, D., Bloom, B., & Masia, B. (1964). *Taxonomy of educational objectives. Handbook II: Affective domain.* New York: McKay.

Krogman, W. (1953). Biological growth as it may affect pupils' success. *Merrill-Palmer Quarterly, 1*(1), 90–98.

Krumboltz, J., & Krumboltz, H. (1972). *Changing children's behavior.* Englewood Cliffs, NJ: Prentice-Hall.

Kubiszyn, T., & Borich, G. (1984). *Educational testing and measurement.* Glenview, IL: Scott, Foresman.

Kuhn, D. (1974). Inducing development experimentally: Comments on a research paradigm. *Developmental Psychology, 10,* 590–600.

Kuhn, D. (1976). Short-term longitudinal evidence for the sequentiality of Kohlberg's early stages of moral judgment. *Developmental Psychology, 12,* 162–166.

Kuhn, D. (1979). The application of Piaget's theory of cognitive development to education. *Harvard Educational Review, 49,* 340–360.

Kukla, A. (1978). An attributional theory of choice. In L. Berkowitz (Ed.), *Advances in experimental social psychology* (Vol. II). New York: Academic Press.

Kulhavy, R. (1977). Feedback in written instruction. *Review of Educational Research, 47,* 211–232.

Kulik, J., Cohen, P., & Ebeling, B. (1980). Effectiveness of programmed instruction in higher education: A meta-analysis of findings. *Educational Evaluation and Policy Analysis, 2,* 51–64.

Kulik, J., Kulik, C., & Carmichael, K. (1974). The Keller Plan in science teaching. *Science, 183,* 379–384.

Kunen, S., Cohen, R., & Solman, R. (1981). A levels-of-processing analysis of Bloom's taxonomy. *Journal of Educational Psychology, 73,* 202–211.

Laboratory of Comparative Human Cognition (1983). Culture and cognitive development. In P. Mussen (Ed.), *Handbook of child psychology* (4th ed., Vol. IV). New York: Wiley.

Labov, W. (1972). *Language in the inner-city.* Philadelphia: University of Pennsylvania Press.

Ladas, H. (1980). Summarizing research: A case study. *Review of Educational Research, 50,* 597–624.

Lahaderne, H. (1976). Feminized schools: Unpromising myth to explain boys' reading problem. *Reading Teacher, 29,* 776–786.

Lahaderne, H., & Jackson, P. (1970). Withdrawal in the classroom: A note on some educational correlates of social desirability among school children. *Journal of Educational Psychology, 61,* 97–101.

Lamb, W. (1976). Ask a higher-level question, get a higher-level answer. *Science Teacher, 43,* 22–23.

Laosa, L. (1978). Maternal teaching strategies in Chicano families of varied educational and socioeconomic levels. *Child Development, 49,* 1129–1135.

Laosa, L. (1982). School, occupation, culture, and family: The impact of parental schooling on the parent-child relationship. *Journal of Educational Psychology, 74,* 791–827.

Larkin, J. (1981). Cognition of learning physics. *American Journal of Physics, 49,* 534–541.

Larrivee, B. (1985). *Effective teaching for successful mainstreaming.* New York: Longman.

Larsen, S. (1975). The influence of teacher expectations on the school performance of handicapped children. *Focus on Exceptional Children, 8,* 2–16.

Lawlor, J. (1982). *Computers in composition instruction.* Los Angeles: Southwest Regional Laboratory for Educational Research and Development.

Lawson, A. (1975). Developing formal thought through biology teaching. *American Biology Teacher, 37,* 411–429.

Lawson, A. (1982). The relative responsiveness of concrete operational seventh grade and college students to science instruction. *Journal of Research in Science Teaching, 19,* 63–77.

Lazar, I., & Darling, R. (1982). Lasting effects of early education. *Monographs of the Society for Research in Child Development, 47,* Nos. 2–3, Serial No. 195.

Lazar, I., et al. (1977). *The persistence of preschool effects: A long-term follow-up of fourteen infant and preschool experiments.* Final Report. Denver, CO: Education Commission of the States.

Lefcourt, H. (1966). Internal versus external control of reinforcement: A review. *Psychological Bulletin, 65,* 206–220.

Leinhardt, G. (1980). Transition rooms: Promoting maturation or reducing education? *Journal of Educational Psychology, 72,* 55–61.

Leinhardt, G. (1983). Novice and expert knowledge of individual student's achievement. *Educational Psychologist, 18,* 165–179.

Leinhardt, G., & Smith, D. (April 1984). Expertise in mathematics instruction: Subject matter knowledge. Paper presented at the annual meeting of the American Educational Research Association, New Orleans.

Lenneberg, E. H. (1967). *Biological foundations of language.* New York: Wiley.

Leon, J., & Pepe, H. (1983). Self-instructional training: Cognitive behavior modification for remediating arithmetic deficits. *Exceptional Children, 50,* 54–60.

Lepper, M. (1973). Dissonance, self-perception, and honesty in children. *Journal of Personality and Social Psychology, 25,* 65–74.

Lepper, M., & Greene, D. (1978). *The hidden costs of reward: New perspectives on the psychology of human motivation.* Hillsdale, NJ: Erlbaum.

Lerner, R., & Lerner, J. (1977). Effects of age, sex, and physical attractiveness on child-peer relations, academic performance, and elementary school adjustment. *Developmental Psychology, 13,* 585–590.

Levin, J. (1981). The mnemonic '80s: Keywords in the classroom. *Educational Psychologist, 16,* 65–82.

Levin, J., & Boruta, M. (1983). Writing with computers in the classroom: You get *exactly* the right amount of space! *Theory Into Practice, 22,* 291–295.

Levin, J., Schriberg, L., Miller, C., McCormick, C., & Levin, B. (1980). The keyword method in the classroom: How to remember the states and their capitals. *Elementary School Journal,* 80, 185–191.

Levine, J. M., & Wang, M. C. (1983). *Teacher and student perceptions: Implications for learning.* Hillsdale, NJ: Lawrence Erlbaum Associates.

Levy, P., & Goldstein, H. (1984). *Tests in Education.* Orlando, FL: Academic Press.

Lewin, K., Lippitt, R., & White, R. (1939). Patterns of aggressive behavior in experimentally created social climate. *Journal of Social Psychology, 10,* 271–291.

Lickona, T. (Ed.). (1975). Morality: A handbook of moral behavior. New York: Holt, Rinehart and Winston.

Ligon, G., Hester, J., Baenen, N., & Matuszek, P. (April, 1977). A study of the relationship between affective and achievement measures. Paper presented at the annual meeting of the American Educational Research Association, New York.

Lipman, M. (1985). Thinking skills fostered by Philosophy for Children. In J. Segal, S. Chipman, and R. Glaser (Eds.), *Thinking and learning skills, Volume 1: Relating instruction to research.* Hillsdale, NJ: Erlbaum.

Lipman, M., Sharp, A., & Oscanyan, F. (1980). *Philosophy in the classroom* (2nd ed.). Philadelphia: Temple University Press.

Lipson, J. (March, 1974). IPI Math—An example of what's right and wrong with individualized modular programs. *Learning,* 60–61.

Lipson, J. & Fisher, K. (1983). Technology and the classroom: Promise or threat? *Theory Into Practice, 22,* 253–259.

Little, J. (1981). School success and staff development in urban desegregated schools: A summary of recently completed research. Paper presented at the meetings of the American Educational Research Association, Los Angeles.

Lochhead, J. (1980). Faculty interpretations of simple algebraic statements: The professor's side of the equation. *Journal of Mathematical Behavior, 3,* 29–37.

Lockheed, M. (March, 1982). Sex equity in classroom interaction research. Paper presented at the annual meeting of the American Educational Research Association, New York.

Lockwood, A. (1978). The effects of values clarification and moral development curricula on school-age subjects: A critical review of recent research. *Review of Educational Research, 48,* 325–364.

Loehlin, J., Lindzey, G., & Spuhler, J. (1975). *Race differences in intelligence.* San Francisco: Freeman.

Loftus, E., & Loftus, G. (1980). On the permanence of stored information in the human brain. *American Psychologist, 35,* 409–420.

Loftus, G., & Loftus, E. (1976). *Human memory: The processing of information.* Hillsdale, NJ: Erlbaum.

Loman, N., & Mayer, R. (1983). Signaling techniques that increase the understandability of expository prose. *Journal of Educational Psychology, 75,* 402–412.

Long, H., McCrary, K., & Ackerman, S. (1980). Adult cognitive development: A new look at Piagetian theory. *Journal of Research and Development in Education, 13,* 11–20.

Lorayne, H., & Lucas, J. (1974). *The memory book.* New York: Ballantine.

Loughlin, R. (1961). On questioning. *Educational Forum, 25,* 481–482.

Lucker, G., Rosenfield, D., Sikes, J., & Aronson, E. (1976). Performance in the interdependent classroom: A field study. *American Educational Research Journal, 13,* 115–123.

Luiten, J., Ames, W., & Ackerson, G. (1980). A meta-analysis of the effects of advance organizers on learning and retention. *American Educational Research Journal, 17,* 211–218.

Lukasevich, A., & Gray, R. (1978). Open space, open education, and pupil performance. *Elementary School Journal, 79,* 108–114.

Luria, A. (1976). *Cognitive development: Its cultural and social foundations.* Cambridge, MA: Harvard University Press.

Lynch, M., Norem-Hebeisen, A., & Gergen, K. (1981). *Self-concept: Advances in theory and research.* Cambridge, MA: Ballinger.

Maccoby, E. (1966). Sex differences in intellectual functioning. In E. Maccoby (Ed.), *The development of sex differences.* Stanford, CA: University of California Press.

Maccoby, E. (1980). *Social development: Psychological growth and the parent-child relationship.* New York: Harcourt, Brace Jovanovich.

Maccoby, E., & Jacklin, C. (1974). *The psychology of sex differences.* Stanford: Stanford University Press.

Maccoby, E., & Martin, J. (1983). Socialization in the context of the family: Parent-child interaction. In P. Mussen (Ed.), *Handbook of child psychology,* (4th ed., Vol. IV). New York: Wiley.

MacDonald, F. (1965). *Educational psychology* (2nd ed.). Belmont, CA: Wadsworth.

Mackenzie, B. (1984). Explaining race differences in IQ: The logic, the methodology, and the evidence. *American Psychologist, 39,* 1214–1233.

MacKinnon, D. (1962). The nature and nurture of creative talent. *American Psychologist, 17,* 484–495.

MacMillan, D., Jones, R., & Meyers, C. (1976). Mainstreaming the mildly retarded: Some questions, cautions, and guidelines. *Mental Retardation, 14,* 3–10.

Madden, N., & Slavin, R. (1980). Cooperative learning and social acceptance of mainstreamed academically handicapped students. Paper presented at the annual convention of the American Psychological Association, Montreal.

Madden, N., & Slavin, R. (1983). Mainstreaming students with mild handicaps: Academic and social outcomes. *Review of Educational Research, 53,* 519–569.

Maehr, M. (1976). Continuing motivation: An analysis of a seldom considered educational outcome. *Review of Educational Research, 46,* 443–462.

Maehr, M. (1983). On doing well in science: Why Johnny no longer excels; why Sarah never did. In S. Paris, G. Olson, & H. Stevenson (Eds.), *Learning and motivation in the classroom.* Hillsdale, NJ: Erlbaum.

Maehr, M. (1984). Meaning and motivation: Toward a theory of personal investment. In R. Ames & C. Ames (Eds.), *Research on motivation in education* (Vol. 1). Orlando, FL: Academic Press.

Maehr, M., & Nicholls, J. (1980). Culture and achievement motivation: A second look. In N. Warren (Ed.), *Studies in cross-cultural psychology* (Vol. 2). New York: Academic Press.

Mager, R. (1962). *Preparing instructional objectives.* Palo Alto, CA: Fearon.

Mansfield, R., Busse, T., & Krepelka, E. (1978). The effectiveness of creativity training. *Review of Educational Research, 48,* 517–536.

Manske, M., & Davis, G. (1968). Effects of simple instructional biases upon performance in the unusual uses test. *Journal of General Psychology, 79,* 25–33.

Maracek, J., & Mettee, D. (1972). Avoidance of continued success as a function of self-esteem, level of self-esteem certainty, and responsibility for success. *Journal of Personality and Social Psychology, 22,* 98–107.

Marcia, J. (1980). Identity in adolescence. In J. Adelson (Ed.), *Handbook of adolescent psychology.* New York: Wiley-Interscience.

Marjoribanks, K. (1972). Environment, social class, and mental abilities. *Journal of Educational Psychology, 63,* 103–109.

Markman, E. (1981). Comprehension monitoring. In W. Dickson (Ed.), *Children's oral communication skills.* New York: Academic Press.

Markman, E., & Gorin, L. (1981). Children's ability to adjust their standards for evaluating comprehension. *Journal of Educational Psychology, 83,* 320–325.

Marsh, H., Overall, J., & Kesler, S. (1979). Class size, students' evaluations, and instructional effectiveness. *American Educational Research Journal, 16,* 57–69.

Marshall, H. (1981). Open classrooms: Has the term outlived its usefulness? *Review of Educational Research, 51,* 181–192.

Marshall, H., & Weinstein, R. (April 1984). Classrooms where students perceive high and low amounts of differential teacher treatment. Paper presented at the annual meeting of the American Educational Research Association, New Orleans.

Marshall, S. (1984). Sex differences in children's mathematics achievement: Solving computations and story problems. *Journal of Educational Psychology, 76,* 194–204.

Marten, L., & Matlin, L. (1976). Does sexism in elementary readers still exist? *The Reading Teacher, 29,* 764–767.

Martin, B. (1975). Parent-child relations. In F.

Horowitz (Ed.), *Review of child development research* (Vol. 4). Chicago: University of Chicago Press.

Martin, D. (1984). Infusing cognitive strategies into teacher preparation programs. *Educational Leadership, 42*, 68–72.

Martin, J. (1979). Effects of teacher higher-order questions on student process and product variables in a single-classroom study. *Journal of Educational Research, 72*, 183–187.

Martin, L., & Pavan, B. (1976). Current research on open-space, non-grading, vertical grouping, and team teaching. *Phi Delta Kappan, 57*, 310–315.

Martin, M. (1973). *Equal opportunity in the classroom* (ESEA, Title II: Session A Report). Los Angeles: County Superintendent of Schools, Division of Compensatory and Intergroup Programs.

Martorano, S. (1977). A developmental analysis of performance on Piaget's formal operation tasks. *Developmental Psychology, 13*, 666–672.

Maslow, A. (1954). *Motivation and personality.* New York: Harper & Row.

Maslow, A. (1962). *Toward a psychology of being.* Princeton, NJ: Van Nostrand.

Masters, J., Ford, M., Arend, R., Grotevant, H., & Clark, L. (1979). Modeling and labeling as integrated determinants of children's sex-typed imitative behavior. *Child Development, 50*, 364–371.

Matz, M. (1980). Towards a computational model of algebraic competence. *Journal of Mathematical Behavior, 3*, 93–166.

Mayer, R. (1975a). Different problem-solving competencies established in learning computer programming with and without meaningful models. *Journal of Educational Psychology, 67*, 725–734.

Mayer, R. (1975b). Information processing variables in learning to solve problems. *Review of Educational Research, 45*, 525–541.

Mayer, R. (1979a). Can advance organizers influence meaningful learning? *Review of Educational Research, 49*, 371–383.

Mayer, R. (1979b). Twenty years of research on advance organizers: Assimilation theory is still the best predictor of results. *Instructional Science, 8*, 133–167.

Mayer, R. (1981). Frequency norms and structural analysis of algebraic story problems into families, categories, and templates. *Instructional Science, 10*, 135–175.

Mayer, R. (1982). Learning. In H. Mitzel (Ed.), *Encyclopedia of Educational Research*, (5th ed., Vol. II). New York: The Free Press.

Mayer, R. (1983). *Thinking, problem solving, and cognition.* San Francisco: Freeman.

Mayer, R. (1984). Aids to text comprehension. *Educational Psychologist, 19*, 30–42.

Mayer, R. (1985). Instructional design theories: Building a linking science? *Contemporary Psychology, 30*, 156–157.

Mayer, R., & Cook, L. (1981). Effects of shadowing on prose comprehension and problem solving. *Memory and Cognition, 9*, 101–109.

Mayer, R., Dyck, J., & Cook, L. (1984). Techniques that help readers build mental models from scientific text: Definitions, pretraining and signaling. *Journal of Educational Psychology, 76*, 1089–1105.

McCabe, A., Siegel, L., Spence, I., & Wilkenson, A. (1982). Class-inclusion reasoning: Patterns of performance from three to eight years. *Child Development, 53*, 780–785.

McCall, R., Appelbaum, M., & Hogarty, P. (1973). Developmental changes in mental performance. *Monographs of the Society for Research in Child Development, 38*(3) (Serial #150).

McCandless, B., & Coop, R. (1979). *Adolescents: Behavior and development* (2nd ed.). New York: Holt, Rinehart and Winston.

McCandless, B., & Evans, E. (1973). *Children and youth: Psychosocial development.* Hinsdale, IL: Dryden.

McClelland, D. (1976). *Power: The inner experience.* New York: Irvington.

McConkie, G. (1977). Learning form text. In L. Shulman (Ed.), *Review of research in education*, Vol. 5. Itasca, IL: Peacock.

McConnell, J. (1977). Relationships between selected teacher behaviors and attitudes/achievements of algebra classes. Paper presented at the annual meeting of the American Educational Research Association.

McCormick, C. & Levin, J. (1984). A comparison of different prose-learning variations of the mnemonic keyword method. *American Educational Research Journal, 21*, 379–398.

McDaniel, M. & Pressley, M. (1984). Putting the keyword method in context. *Journal of Educational Psychology*, *76*, 598–609.

McDermott, R. (1976). Kids make sense. Unpublished doctoral dissertation, Stanford University.

McDonald, F. (1977). Research on teaching: Report on Phase II of the Beginning Teacher Evaluation Study. In G. Borich and K. Fenton (Eds.), *The appraisal of teaching: Concepts and process*. Reading, MA: Addison-Wesley.

McDonnell, L. (1985). Implementing low-cost school improvement strategies. *Elementary School Journal*, *85*, 423–438.

McGeoch, J. & McDonald, W. (1931). Meaningful relation and retroactive inhibition. *American Journal of Psychology*, *43*, 579–588.

McGuire, K., & Weisz, J. (1982). Social cognition and behavior correlates of preadolescent chumship. *Child Development*, *53*, 1478–1484.

McKay, H., Sinisterra, L., McKay, A., Gomez, H., & Lloreda, P. (1978). Improving cognitive ability in chronically deprived children. *Science*, *200*, 270–278.

McKeachie, W., & Kulik, J. (1975). Effective college training. In F. Kerlinger (Ed.), *Review of research in education*. Itasca, IL: Peacock.

McKenna, B., & Olson, M. (1975). Class size revisited. *Today's Education*, *64*, 29–31.

McKinney, J., Mason, J., Perkerson, K., & Clifford, M. (1975). Relationship between classroom behavior and academic achievement. *Journal of Educational Psychology*, *67*, 198–203.

McLaughlin, T. (1976). Self-control in the classroom. *Review of Educational Research*, *46*, 631–663.

McLeish, J. (1976). The lecture method. In N. Gage (Ed.), *The psychology of teaching methods (Part I). The Seventy-fifth Yearbook of the National Society for the Study of Education*. Chicago: University of Chicago Press.

McMann, F. (1979). In defense of lecture. *Social Studies*, *70*, 270–274.

McNamee, S. (1978). Moral behavior, moral development and motivation. *Journal of Moral Education*, *7*, 27–31.

Mechanic, A., Daugherty, T., & Arden-Smith, G. (1982). Practical applications of Piagetian observations and Epstein brain growth research in teacher training and sensitization. *The Researcher* (Journal of the Northeastern Educational Research Association), *1*, 9–12.

Meehan, A. (1984). A meta-analysis of sex differences in formal operational thought. *Child Development*, *55*, 1110–1124.

Mehrens, W., & Lehmann, I. (1978). *Measurement and evaluation in education and psychology* (2nd ed.). New York: Holt, Rinehart and Winston.

Meichenbaum, D. (1977). *Cognitive-behavior modification*. New York: Plenum.

Meichenbaum, D., & Asarnow, J. (1979). Cognitive-behavioral modification and metacognitive development: Implications for the classroom. In P. Kendall & S. Hollon (Eds.), *Cognitive-behavioral intervention: Theory, research, and procedures*. New York: Academic Press.

Meichenbaum, D., & Goodman, J. (1971). Training impulsive children to talk to themselves: A means of developing self-control. *Journal of Abnormal Psychology*, *77*, 115–126.

Mercer, J. (1973). *Labeling the mentally retarded*. Berkeley: University of California Press.

Merrill, M., & Tennyson, R. (1977). *Concept teaching: An instructional design guide*. Englewood Cliffs, NJ: Educational Technology.

Messé, L., Crano, W., Messé, S., & Rice, W. (1979). Evaluation of the predictive validity of tests of mental ability for classroom performance in elementary grades. *Journal of Educational Psychology*, *71*, 233–241.

Messer, S. (1972). The relation of internal-external control to academic performance. *Child Development*, *43*, 1456–1462.

Messick, S. (1984). Assessment in context: Appraising student performance in relation to instructional quality. *Educational Researcher*, *13*, 3–8.

Metz, M. (1978). *Classrooms and corridors: The crisis of authority in desegregated secondary schools*. Berkeley: University of California Press.

Meyer, B. (1975). *The organization of prose and its effects on memory*. Amsterdam: North Holland.

Meyer, B. (1977). The structure of prose: Effects on learning and memory and implications for educational practice. In R. Anderson, R. Spiro, & W. Montague (Eds.), *Schooling and the acquisition of knowledge.* Hillsdale, NJ: Erlbaum.

Meyer, B. (1981). Basic research on prose comprehension: A critical review. In D. Fisher & C. Peters (Eds.), *Comprehension and the competent reader.* New York: Praeger.

Meyer, W., Bachmann, M., Biermann, U., Hempelmann, M., Ploger, F., & Spiller, H. (1979). The informational value of evaluative behavior: Influences of praise and blame on perceptions of ability. *Journal of Educational Psychology, 71,* 259–268.

Milak, J. (1980). *A comparison of two approaches of teaching brass instruments to elementary school children.* Unpublished doctoral dissertation, Washington University, St. Louis, MO.

Miller, A. (1982). *Self-recognitory schemes and achievement behavior: A developmental study.* Doctoral dissertation, Purdue University.

Miller, G. (1956). The magical number seven, plus or minus two: Some limits on our capacity for processing information. *Psychological Review,* 63, 81–97.

Miller, L., & Bizzell, R. (1983). Long-term effects of four preschool programs: Sixth, seventh, and eighth grades. *Child Development, 54,* 727–741.

Miller, L., & Dyer, J. (1975). Four preschool programs: Their dimensions and effects. *Monographs of the Society for Research in Child Development,* 40(5–6) (Serial No. 162).

Miller, R., Brickman, P., & Bolen, D. (1975). Attribution versus persuasion as a means for modifying behavior. *Journal of Personality and Social Psychology, 31,* 430–441.

Miller, S., Brownell, C., & Zukier, H. (1977). Cognitive certainty in children: Effects of concept, developmental level, and method of assessment. *Developmental Psychology, 13,* 236–245.

Millman, Jason (Ed.). (1981). *Handbook of teacher evaluation.* Beverly Hills, CA: Sage Publishing, Inc.

Mills, S., Rice, C., Berliner, D., & Rousseau, E. (1980). The correspondence between teacher questions and student answers in classroom discourse. *Journal of Experimental Education,* 48, 194–204.

Minsky, M. (1975). A framework for representing knowledge. In P. Winston (Ed.), *The psychology of computer vision.* New York: McGraw-Hill.

Mischel, H. (1974). Sex bias in the evaluation of professional activity. *Journal of Educational Psychology,* 66, 157–166.

Mitman, A., Mergendollar, J., Packer, M., & Marchman, V. (1984). Scientific literacy in seventh-grade life science: A study of instructional process, task completion, student perceptions and learning outcomes. Final Report. San Francisco: Far West Laboratory.

Mitzel, Harold (Ed.). (1984). *Encyclopedia of Educational Research,* 4 vols. (5th ed.). New York: Macmillan.

Modgil, S., & Modgil, C. (Eds.). (1982). *Jean Piaget: Consensus and controversy.* New York: Praeger.

Moessinger, P. (1978). Piaget on equilibration. *Human Development, 21,* 255–267.

Montagu, A. (1959). *Human heredity.* New York: Harcourt, Brace and World.

Moore, C. (1973). Styles of teacher behavior under simulated teaching conditions. Doctoral dissertation, Stanford University. *Dissertation Abstracts International,* 34, 314A-3150A. (University Microfilms #73-30, 449).

Moore, J. (1968). Cuing for selective note-taking. *Journal of Experimental Education, 36,* 69–72.

Moore, J., & Schaut, J. (1975). An evaluation of the effects of conceptually appropriate feedback on teacher and student behavior. Paper presented at the Association for Teacher Education Conference, New Orleans.

Morse, W. (1971). Worksheet on life space interviewing for teachers. In N. Long, W. Morse, & R. Newman (Eds.), *Conflict in the classroom: The education of children with problems* (2nd ed.). Belmont, CA: Wadsworth.

Mosher, R., (Ed.). (1980). *Moral education: A first generation of research and development.* New York: Praeger.

Moskowitz, G., & Hayman, J. (1974). Interaction patterns of first-year, typical, and "best" teachers in inner-city schools. *Journal of Educational Research,* 67, 224–230.

Moskowitz, G., & Hayman, J. (1976). Success strategies of inner-city teachers: A year-long study. *Journal of Educational Research,* 69, 283–289.

Muir, M. (1977). *Personal responsibility training for elementary school children.* Unpublished doctoral dissertation, Washington University, St. Louis, MO.

Mumpower, P. (1970). Sex ratios found in various types of referred exceptional children. *Exceptional Children, 36,* 621–624.

Murray, E. (1964). *Motivation and emotion.* New York: Prentice-Hall.

Murray, F. (1978). Teaching strategies and conservation training. In A. Lesgold, J. Pellegrino, S. Fokkema, & R. Glaser (Eds.), *Cognitive psychology and instruction.* New York: Plenum.

Murray, F., Ames, G., & Botvin, G. (1977). Acquisition of conservation through cognitive dissonance. *Journal of Educational Psychology, 69,* 519–527.

Murray, H. (1938). *Explorations in Personality.* New York: Oxford University Press.

Mussen, P., Conger, J., & Kagan, J. (1974). *Child development and personality* (4th ed.). New York: Harper & Row.

Mussen, P., & Eisenberg-Berg, N. (1977). *Roots of caring, sharing, and helping.* San Francisco: Freeman.

Mussen, P., & Jones, M. (1957). Self-conceptions, motivations, and interpersonal attitudes of late- and early-maturing boys. *Child Development, 28,* 243–256.

Muuss, R. (1970). Adolescent development and the secular trend. *Adolescence, 5,* 267–284.

Myers, R., & Torrance, E. (1966). *Plots, puzzles, and ploys.* Boston: Ginn.

Nagy, P., & Griffiths, A. (1982). Limitations of recent research relating Piaget's theory to adolescent thought. *Review of Educational Research, 52,* 513–556.

Nardine, F. (1971). The development of competence. In G. S. Lesser (Ed.), *Psychology and educational practice.* Glenview, IL: Scott, Foresman.

Nash, R. (1976). Pupils' expectations of their teachers. In M. Stubbs & S. Delamont (Eds.), *Explorations in classroom observation.* New York: Wiley.

Natriello, G., & Dornbusch, S. (1985). *Teacher evaluative standard and student effort.* New York: Longman.

Neimark, E. (1975). Intellectual development during adolescence. In F. Horowitz (Ed.), *Review of child development research* (Vol. 4). Chicago: University of Chicago Press.

Neimark, E., & Santa, J. (1975). Thinking and concept attainment. In M. Rosenzweig & L. Porter (Eds.), *Annual review of psychology* (Vol. 26). Palo Alto, CA: Annual Reviews.

Neisser, U. (1976). General, academic, and artificial intelligence. In L. Resnick (Ed.), *The nature of intelligence.* Hillsdale, NJ: Erlbaum.

Nelson, K. (1977). Facilitating children's syntax acquisition. *Developmental Psychology, 13,* 101–107.

Newell, A., & Simon, H. (1972). *Human problem solving.* Englewood Cliffs, NJ: Prentice-Hall.

Nicholls, J. (1976). Effort is virtuous, but it's better to have ability: Evaluative responses to perceptions of effort and ability. *Journal of Research in Personality, 10,* 306–315.

Nicholls, J. (1979). Quality and equality in intellectual development: The role of motivation in education. *American Psychologist, 34,* 1071–1083.

Nicholls, J. (1983). Conceptions of ability and achievement motivation: A theory and its implications for education. In S. Paris, G. Olson, & H. Stevenson (Eds.), *Learning and motivation in the classroom.* Hillsdale, NJ: Erlbaum.

Nicholls, J. (1984). Conceptions of ability and achievement motivation. In R. Ames & C. Ames (Eds.), *Research on motivation in education* (Vol. 1). Orlando, FL: Academic Press.

Nicholls, J., & Miller, A. (1983). The differentiation of the concepts of difficulty and ability. *Child Development, 54,* 951–959.

Niemark, E. (1979). Current status of formal operations research. *Human Development, 22,* 60–67.

Nisan, M., & Kohlberg, L. (1982). Universality and variation in moral judgment: A longitudinal and cross-sectional study in Turkey. *Child Development, 53,* 865–876.

Norcini, J., & Snyder, S. (1983). The effects of modeling and cognitive induction on the moral reasoning of adolescents. *Journal of Youth and Adolescence, 12,* 101–115.

Novak, J., & Gowin, D. (1984). *Learning how to learn.* New York: Cambridge University Press.

Nuthall, G., & Church, J. (1973). Experimental studies of teaching behaviour. In G. Chanan

(Ed.), *Toward a science of teaching*. London: National Foundation for Educational Research.

Oakland, T. (Ed.). (1977). *Psychological and educational assessment of minority children*. New York: Brunner/Mazel.

Ohlsson, S. (1983). The enaction theory of thinking and its educational implications. *Scandinavian Journal of Educational Research, 27*, 73–88.

Oickle, E. (1980). *A comparison of individual and team learning*. Unpublished doctoral dissertation, University of Maryland.

Ojemann, R. (1959). The human relations program at the State University of Iowa. *Personnel and Guidance Journal, 37*, 199–207.

O'Leary, K., Kaufman, K., Kass, R., & Drabman, R. (1970). The effects of loud and soft reprimands on the behavior of disruptive students. *Exceptional Children, 27*, 145–155.

O'Leary, K., & O'Leary S. (Eds.). (1977). *Classroom management: The successful use of behavior modification* (2nd ed.). New York: Pergamon.

O'Leary, S., & Dubey, D. (1979). Applications of self-control procedures by children: A review. *Journal of Applied Behavior Analysis, 12*, 449–465.

Olejnik, A. (1980). Adults' moral reasoning with children. *Child Development, 51*, 1285–1288.

Olson, C. (1984). Fostering critical thinking skills through writing. *Educational Leadership, 42*, 28–39.

Olson, M. (1971). Ways to achieve quality in school classrooms: Some definitive answers. *Phi Delta Kappan, 53*, 63–65; 448–450.

O'Neil, H. (Ed.). (1978). *Learning strategies*. New York: Academic Press.

O'Neil, H. (Ed.). (1981). *Computer-based instruction: A state-of-the-art assessment*. New York: Academic Press.

O'Neil, H., & Spielberger, C. (Eds.). (1979). *Cognitive and affective learning strategies*. New York: Academic Press.

Orbach, E. (1977). Some theoretical considerations in the evaluation of instructional games. *Simulation and Games, 8*, 341–360.

Orlofsky, J. (1976). Intimacy status: Relationship to interpersonal perception. *Journal of Youth and Adolescence, 5*, 73–83.

Orlofsky, J., & Ginsburg, S. (1981). Intimacy status: Relationship to affect cognition. *Adolescence, 16*, 91–100.

Orlofsky, J., Marcia, J., & Lesser, I. (1973). Ego identity states and the intimacy vs. isolation crisis of young adulthood. *Journal of Youth and Adolescence, 2*, 211–219.

Osborn, J. (1982). The purposes, uses and contents of workbooks and some guidelines for teachers and publishers. In R. Anderson, J. Osborn, & R. Tierney (Eds.), *Learning to read in American schools: Basal readers and content texts*. Hillsdale, NJ: Erlbaum.

Osborn, J. (1984). Workbooks that accompany basal reading programs. In G. Duffy, L. Roehler, & J. Mason, (Eds.), *Comprehension instruction: Perspectives and suggestions*. New York: Longman.

Osofsky, J. (1976). Neonatal characteristics and mother-infant interaction in two observational situations. *Child Development, 47*, 1138–1147.

Owen, S., Blount, H., & Moscow, H. (1978). *Educational psychology: An introduction*. Boston: Little, Brown and Co.

Packer, J., & Bain, J. (1978). Cognitive style and teacher-student compatibility. *Journal of Educational Psychology, 70*, 864–871.

Page, R. (1981). Longitudinal evidence for the sequentiality of Kohlberg's stages of moral judgment in adolescent males. *Journal of Genetic Psychology, 139*, 3–9.

Paivio, A. (1971). *Imagery and verbal processes*. New York: Holt, Rinehart and Winston.

Palermo, D., & Jenkins, J. (1964). *Word association norms: Grade school through college*. Minneapolis: University of Minnesota Press.

Palincsar, A., & Brown, A. (1984). Reciprocal teaching of comprehension-fostering and comprehension-monitoring activities. *Cognition and Instruction, 1*, 117–175.

Pambookian, H. (1976). Discrepancy between instructor and student evaluation of instruction: Effect on instruction. *Instructional Science, 5*, 63–75.

Parikh, B. (1980). Development of moral judgment and its relation to family environmental factors in Indian and American families. *Child Development, 51*, 1030–1039.

Paris, S., Cross, D., & Lipson, M. (1984). Informed strategies for learning: A program to improve children's reading awareness and comprehension. *Journal of Educational Psychology, 76*, 1239–1252.

Paris, S., Lipson, M., & Wixson, K. (1983). Becoming a strategic reader. *Contemporary Educational Psychology, 8*, 293–316.

Paris, S., & Myers, M. (1981). Comprehension monitoring in good and poor readers. *Journal of Reading Behavior, 13*, 5–22.

Paris, S., Newman, R., & McVey, K. (1982). Learning the functional significance of mnemonic actions: A microgenetic study of strategy acquisition. *Journal of Experimental Child Psychology, 34*, 490–509.

Parnes, S. (1967). *Creative behavior guidebook*. New York: Scribner's.

Parsons, J. (Ed.). (1980). *The psychobiology of sex differences and sex roles*. Washington, DC: Hemisphere.

Parsons, J., Midgely, C., & Adler, T. (in press). Age-related changes in the school environment: Effects on achievement motivation. In J. Nicholls (Ed.), *The development of achievement motivation*. Greenwich, CT: JAI Press.

Patterson, C. (1973). *Humanistic education*. Englewood Cliffs, NJ: Prentice-Hall.

Patterson, G., & Stouthamer-Loeber, M. (1984). The correlation of family management practices and delinquency. *Child Development, 55*, 1299–1307.

Pattison, P., & Grieve, N. (1984). Do spatial skills contribute to sex differences in different types of mathematical problems? *Journal of Educational Psychology, 76*, 678–689.

Pavlov, I. (1927). *Conditional reflexes*. London: Oxford University Press.

Pearson, P., & Gallagher, M. (1983). The instruction of reading comprehension. *Contemporary Educational Psychology, 8*, 317–344.

Pearson, P., & Johnson, D. (1978). *Teaching reading comprehension*. New York: Holt, Rinehart and Winston.

Perfetti, C., & Lesgold, A. (1977). Discourse comprehension and sources of individual differences. In M. Just & P. Carpenter (Eds.), *Cognitive processes and comprehension*. Hillsdale, NJ: Erlbaum.

Perlmuter, L., & Monty, R. (1979). *Choice and perceived control*. Hillsdale, NJ: Erlbaum.

Perrott, E. (1982). *Effective teaching: A practical guide to improving your teaching*. New York: Longman.

Peskin, J. (1980). Female performance and Inhelder and Piaget's tests of formal operations. *Genetic Psychology Monographs, 101*, 245–256.

Peterson, A., & Taylor, B. (1980). Puberty: Biological change and psychological adaptation. In J. Adelson (Ed.), *Handbook of adolescent psychology*. New York: Wiley.

Peterson, P. (1979). Direct instruction reconsidered. In P. Peterson and H. Walberg (Eds.), *Research on teaching: Concepts, findings and implications*. Berkeley, CA: McCutchan.

Peterson, P., & Fennema, E. (in press). Teacher-student interactions and sex-related differences in learning mathematics. *American Educational Research Journal*.

Peterson, P., & Swing, S. (1982). Beyond time on task: Students' reports of their thought processes during classroom instruction. *Elementary School Journal, 82*, 481–491.

Piaget, J. (1925). De quelques formes primitives de causalite chez l' enfant. *L'Année Psychologie, 26*, 31–71.

Piaget, J. (1930). *The child's conception of physical causality*. London: Routledge & Kegan Paul.

Piaget, J. (1932). *The moral judgment of the child*. Translated by M. Worden. New York: Harcourt, Brace, and World.

Piaget, J. (1970). *Science of education and the psychology of the child*. New York: Orion.

Piaget, J. (1973). *The child and reality: Problems of genetic psychology*. New York: Viking.

Piaget, J. (1983). Piaget's theory. In P. Mussen (Ed.), *Handbook of child psychology* (4th ed. Vol. 1). New York: Wiley.

Piaget, J., & Inhelder, B. (1964). *The early growth of logic in the child*. Translated by L. Lunzer & D. Papert. London: Routledge and Kegan Paul.

Piattelli-Palmarini, M. (Ed.). (1980). *Language and learning: The debate between Jean Piaget and Noam Chomsky*. Cambridge: Harvard University Press.

Pichert, J., & Anderson, R. (1977). Taking different perspectives on a story. *Journal of Educational Psychology, 69*, 309–315.

Pidgeon, D. (1970). *Expectation and pupil performance*. Slough, Great Britain: NFER.

Plomin, R., & Foch, T. (1981). Sex differences and individual differences. *Child Development, 52*, 383–385.

Policastro, M. (1975). Notetaking: The key to

college success. *Journal of Reading, 18*, 372–375.

Polya, G. (1957). *How to solve it*, (2nd ed.). Princeton: Princeton University Press.

Popham, W. (1972). *Criterion-referenced measurement*. Englewood Cliffs, NJ: Educational Technology Publications.

Pozner, J., & Saltz, E. (1974). Social class, conditional communication, and egocentric speech. *Developmental Psychology, 10*, 764–771.

Prawat, R., & Nickerson, J. (1985). Relationship between teacher thought and action and student affective outcomes. *Elementary School Journal, 85*, 529–540.

Premack, D. (1965). Reinforcement theory. In D. Levine (Ed.), *Nebraska Symposium on Motivation*, Vol. 13. Lincoln, NE: University of Nebraska Press.

Prerost, F., & Brewer, R. (1975). The effects of high spatial density on the human response. Paper read at the annual meeting of the American Psychological Association, Chicago.

Pressey, S. (1932). A third and fourth contribution toward the coming "industrial revolution" in education. *School and Society, 36*, 668–672.

Pressley, M. (1979). Increasing children's self-control through cognitive interventions. *Review of Educational Research, 49*, 319–370.

Pressley, M., & Dennis-Rounds, J. (1980). Transfer of a mnemonic keyword strategy at two age levels. *Journal of Educational Psychology, 72*, 575–582.

Pressley, M., Levin, J., Kuiper, N., Bryant, S., & Michener, S. (1982). Mnemonic versus nonmnemonic vocabulary-learning strategies: Additional comparisons. *Journal of Educational Psychology, 74*, 693–707.

Pressley, M., Levin, J., & Miller, G. (1982). The keyword method compared to alternative vocabulary-learning strategies. *Contemporary Educational Psychology, 7*, 50–60.

Pressley, M., Reynolds, W., Stark, K., & Gettinger, M. (1983). Cognitive strategy training and children's self-control. In M. Pressley & J. Levin (Eds.), *Cognitive strategy research: Psychological foundations*. New York: Springer-Verlag.

Preston, R. (1962). Reading achievement of German and American children. *School and Society, 90*, 350–354.

Purkey, S. C., & Smith, M. S. (1985). School reform: The district policy implications of effective school literature. *Elementary School Journal, 85*, 353–389.

Purkey, W. (1970). *Self-concept and school achievement*. Englewood Cliffs, NJ: Prentice-Hall.

Purpel, D., & Ryan, K. (Eds.). (1976). *Moral education . . . it comes with the territory*. Berkeley: McCutchan.

Quirk, T. (1971). The student in Project PLAN: A functioning program of individualized education. *Elementary School Journal, 71*, 42–54.

Raphael, T. (1984). Teaching learners about sources of information for answering comprehension questions. *Journal of Reading, 27*, 303–311.

Raths, L., Harmin, M., & Simon, S. (1966). *Values in teaching*. Columbus, OH: Merrill.

Redfield, D., & Rousseau, E. (1981). A meta-analysis of experimental research on teacher questioning behavior. *Review of Educational Research, 51*, 237–245.

Redl, F. (1959). Strategy and techniques of the life space interview. *American Journal of Orthopsychiatry, 29*, 1–18.

Redl, F. (1966). *When we deal with children*. New York: Free Press.

Redl, F., & Wineman, D. (1951) *Children who hate*. New York: Free Press.

Reigeluth, C. (Ed.). (1983). *Instructional-design theories and models: An overview of their current status*. Hillsdale, NJ: Erlbaum.

Reis, S., & Renzulli, J. (1984). Key features of successful programs for the gifted and talented. *Educational Leadership, 41*, 28–34.

Reissman, F. (1962). *The culturally deprived child*. New York: Harper & Row.

Renner, J., Stafford, D., Lawson, A., McKinnon, J., Friot, E., & Kellogg, D. (1976). *Research on teaching and learning with the Piaget model*. Norman: University of Oklahoma Press.

Rest, J. (1974). Developmental psychology as a guide to value education: A review of "Kohlbergian" programs. *Review of Educational Research, 44*, 241–259.

Rest, J., Davison, M., & Robbins, S. (1978). Age trends in judging moral issues: A review of cross-sectional, longitudinal, and sequential studies of the Defining Issues Test. *Child Development, 49*, 263–279.

Reynolds, M. (1978). Some final notes. In J. Grosenick & M. Reynolds (Eds.), *Teacher education: Renegotiating roles for mainstreaming*. Reston, VA: Council for Exceptional Children.

Reynolds, R., & Anderson, R. (1982). Influence of questions on the allocation of attention during reading. *Journal of Educational Psychology, 74*, 623–632.

Reys, R., & Post, T. (1973). *The mathematics laboratory: Theory to practice*. Boston: Prindle, Weber, & Schmidt.

Rholes, W., Blackwell, J., Jordan, C., & Walters, C. (1980). A developmental study of learned helplessness. *Developmental Psychology, 16*, 616–624.

Rice, D. (1977). The effect of question-asking instruction on preservice elementary science teachers. *Journal of Research in Science Teaching, 14*, 353–359.

Rickards, J. (1979). Adjunct postquestions in text: A critical review of methods and processes. *Review of Educational Research, 49*, 181–196.

Rickards, J. (1982). Homework. In H. Mitzel (Ed.), *Encyclopedia of Educational Research* (5th ed.). New York: The Free Press.

Rickards, J., & August, G. (1975). Generative underlining strategies in prose recall. *Journal of Educational Psychology, 67*, 860–865.

Ridberg, E., Parke, R., & Hetherington, E. (1971). Modification of impulsive and reflective cognitive styles through observation of film-mediated models. *Developmental Psychology, 5*, 369–377.

Riegel, K. (1973). Dialectic operations: The final period of cognitive development. *Human Development, 16*, 346–370.

Riley, J. (1980). The effects of teachers' wait-time and cognitive questioning level on pupil science achievement. Paper presented at the annual meeting of the National Association for Research in Science Teaching, Boston.

Riley, M., Greeno, J., & Heller, J. (1982). The development of children's problem solving ability in arithmetic. In H. Ginsberg (Ed.), *The development of mathematical thinking*. New York: Academic Press.

Ringness, T. (1975). *The affective domain in education*. Boston: Little, Brown.

Rippey, R. (1975). Speech compressors for lecture review. *Educational Technology, 15* (November), 58–59.

Roberge, J., & Flexer, B. (1984). Cognitive style, operativity, and reading achievement. *American Educational Research Journal, 21*, 227–236.

Roberts, J. (1970). *Scene of the battle: Group behavior in urban classrooms*. New York: Doubleday.

Robin, A. (1976). Behavioral instruction in the college classroom. *Review of Educational Research, 46*, 313–354.

Robin, A., Schneider, M., & Dolnick, M. (1976). The turtle technique: An extended case study of self-control in the classroom. *Psychology in the Schools, 13*, 449–453.

Robinson, F. (1946). *Effective study*. New York: Harper and Brothers.

Robinson, F. (1970). *Effective study* (4th ed.). New York: Harper & Row.

Roehler, R., & Duffy, G. (1984). Direct explanation of comprehension processes. In G. Duffy, L. Roehler, & J. Mason (Eds.), *Comprehension instruction: Perspectives and suggestions*. New York: Longman.

Rogers, C. (1951). *Client-centered therapy*. Boston: Houghton Mifflin.

Rogers, C. (1969). *Freedom to learn*. Columbus, OH: Merrill.

Rogers, C. (1983). *Freedom to learn: For the 80's*. Columbus, OH: Merrill.

Rogers, C., Smith, M., & Coleman, J. (1978). Social comparison in the classroom: The relationship between academic achievement and self-concept. *Journal of Educational Psychology, 70*, 50–57.

Rogoff, B., & Wertsch, J. (Eds.). (1984). *Children's learning in the "zone" of proximal development*. San Francisco: Jossey-Bass.

Rohner, R., & Nielsen, C. (1978). *Parental acceptance and rejection: A review and annotated bibliography of research and theory*. New Haven, CT: HRAF Press.

Rohrkemper, M. (1982). Teacher self-assessment. In D. Duke (Ed.), *Helping teachers manage classrooms*. Alexandria, VA: Association for Supervision and Curriculum Development.

Rohrkemper, M. (1984). The influence of

teacher socialization style on students' social cognition and reported interpersonal classroom behavior. *Elementary School Journal, 85*, 245–276.

Rohrkemper, M., & Bershon, B. (1984). Elementary school students' reports of the causes and effects of problem difficulty in mathematics. *Elementary School Journal, 85*, 127–147.

Rohrkemper, M., & Brophy, J. (1983). Teachers' thinking about problem students. In J. Levine & M. Wang (Eds.), *Teacher and student perceptions: Implication for learning*. Hillsdale, NJ: Erlbaum.

Rohwer, W. (1984). An invitation to an educational psychology of studying. *Educational Psychology, 19*, 1–14.

Rollins, H., & Genser, L. (1977). Role of cognitive style in a cognitive task: A case favoring the impulsive approach to problem solving. *Journal of Educational Psychology, 69*, 281–287.

Rosch, E. (1978). Principles of categorization. In E. Rosch & B. Lloyd (Eds.), *Cognition and categorization*. Hillsdale, NJ: Erlbaum.

Rosch, E., & Lloyd, B. (Eds.). (1978). *Cognition and categorization*. Hillsdale, NJ: Erlbaum.

Rosch, E., & Mervis, C. (1975). Family resemblances: Studies in the internal structure of categories. *Cognitive Psychology, 7*, 573–605.

Rosch, E., Mervis, C., Gray, W., Johnson, D., & Boyes-Braem, P. (1976). Basic objects in natural categories. *Cognitive Psychology, 8*, 382–439.

Rosenbaum, M., & Drabman, R. (1979). Self-control training in the classroom: A review and critique. *Journal of Applied Behavior Analysis, 12*, 467–485.

Rosenfield, P., Lambert, N., & Black, A. (1985). Desk arrangement effects on pupil classroom behavior. *Journal of Educational Psychology, 77*(1), 101–108.

Rosenholtz, S., & Rosenholtz, S. (1981). Classroom organization and the perception of ability. *Sociology of Education, 54*, 132–140.

Rosenholtz, S., & Smylie, M. (1984). Teacher compensation and career ladders. *Elementary School Journal, 85*, 149–166.

Rosenshine, B. (1970). Enthusiastic teaching: A research review. *School Review, 78*, 499–514.

Rosenshine, B. (1971). *Teaching behaviours and student achievement*. London: National Foundation for Educational Research.

Rosenshine, B. (1976). Classroom instruction. In N. Gage (Ed.), *The psychology of teaching methods*. National Society for the Study of Education, Seventy-seventh Yearbook.

Rosenshine, B. (1978). Review of Teaching styles and pupil progress. *American Educational Research Journal, 15*, 163–169.

Rosenshine, B. (1980). How time is spent in elementary classrooms. In C. Denham & A. Lieberman (Eds.), *Time to learn*. Washington, DC: National Institute of Education.

Rosenshine, B. (1983). Teaching functions in instructional programs. *Elementary School Journal, 83*, 335–351.

Rosenshine, B., & Berliner, D. (1978). Academic engaged time. *British Journal of Teacher Education, 4*, 3–16.

Rosenshine, B., & Stevens, R. (1984). Classroom instruction in reading. In D. Pearson, M. Camil, R. Barr, and P. Mosenthal (Eds.), *Handbook of research on teaching*. New York: Longman.

Rosenshine, R. (1968). To explain: A review of research. *Educational Leadership, 26*, 275–280.

Rosenthal, R., & Jacobson, L. (1968). *Pygmalion in the classroom: Teacher expectation and pupil's intellectual development*. New York: Holt, Rinehart and Winston.

Rosnick, P., & Clement, J. (1980). Learning without understanding: The effect of tutoring strategies on algebra misconceptions. *Journal of Mathematical Behavior, 3*, 3–27.

Ross, R. (1984). Classroom segments: The structuring of school time. In L. Anderson (Ed.), *Time and school learning: Theory research and practice*. London: Croom Helm.

Rosswork, F. (1977). Goalsetting: The effects on an academic task with varying magnitudes of incentive. *Journal of Educational Psychology, 69*, 710–715.

Rothkopf, E. (1970). The concept of mathemagenic activities. *Review of Educational Research, 40*, 325–336.

Rothkopf, E., & Bisbicos, E. (1967). Selective facilitative effects of interspersed questions on learning from written material. *Journal of Educational Psychology, 58*, 56–61.

Rotter, J. (1954). *Social learning and clinical psychology*. Englewood Cliffs, NJ.: Prentice-Hall.

Rotter, J. (1966). Generalized expectancies for internal versus external control of reinforcement. *Psychological Monographs, 80*, 1–28.

Rotter, J. (1980). Interpersonal trust, trustworthiness, and gullibility. *American Psychologist, 35*, 1–7.

Rowe, M. (1974). Wait-time and rewards as instructional variables, their influence on language, logic and fate control: Part I. Wait-time. *Journal of Research in Science Teaching, 11*, 81–94.

Royer, J., & Cable, G. (1975). Facilitated learning in connected discourse. *Journal of Educational Psychology, 67*, 116–123.

Rozin, P., Fallon, A., & Mandell, R. (1984). Family resemblance in attitudes to foods. *Developmental Psychology, 20*, 309–314.

Rubenstein, M. (1980). A decade of experience in teaching an interdisciplinary problem solving course. In D. Tuma & F. Reif (Eds.), *Problem solving and education: Issues in teaching and research.* Hillsdale, NJ: Erlbaum.

Rubenstein, N. (1975). *Patterns of problem solving.* Englewood Cliffs, NJ: Prentice-Hall.

Rubin, A. (1980). Making stories, making sense. *Language Arts, 57*, 285–298.

Rubin, A. (1982). The computer confronts language arts: Cans and shoulds for education. In A. Wilkinson (Ed.), *Classroom computers and cognitive science.* New York: Academic Press.

Ruble, D., & Brooks-Gunn, J. (1982). The experience of menarche. *Child Development, 53*, 1557–1566.

Rumelhart, D. (1975). Notes on a schema for stories. In D. Bobrow & A. Collins (Eds.), *Representation and understanding.* New York: Academic Press.

Rumelhart, D., Lindsay, P., & Norman, D. (1972). A process model for long-term memory. In E. Tulving & W. Donaldson (Eds.), *Organization of memory.* New York: Academic Press.

Rumelhart, D., & Norman, D. (1978). Accretion, tuning, and restructuring: Three modes of learning. In J. Cotton & R. Klatzky (Eds.), *Semantic factors in cognition.* Hillsdale, NJ: Erlbaum.

Rushton, J., & Sorrentino, R. (Eds.). (1981). *Altruism and helping behavior: Social, personality, and developmental perspectives.* Hillsdale, NJ: Erlbaum.

Russell, J. (1982). Cognitive conflict, transmission, and justification: Conservation attainment through dyadic interaction. *Journal of Genetic Psychology, 140*, 283–297.

Rutter, M. (1983). School effects on pupil progress: Research findings and policy implications. In L. Shulman & G. Sykes (Eds.), *Handbook of teaching and policy.* New York: Longman.

Ryan, E. (1981). Identifying and remediating failure in reading comprehension: Toward an instructional approach for poor comprehenders. In T. Waller & G. MacKinnon (Eds.), *Advances in Reading Research.* New York: Academic Press.

Ryan, F. (1973). Differentiated effects of levels of questioning on student achievement. *Elementary School Journal, 41*, 63–67.

Ryan, F. (1974). The effects on social studies achievement of multiple student responding to different levels of questioning. *Journal of Experimental Education, 42*, 71–75.

Ryan, R. (1982). Control and information in the intrapersonal sphere: An extension of cognitive evaluation theory. *Journal of Personality and Social Psychology, 43*, 450–461.

Sachs, J. (1967). Recognition memory for syntactic and semantic aspects of connected discourse. *Perception and Psychophysics, 2*, 437–442.

Sadker, M., & Sadker, D. (March, 1985). *Psychology Today, 19.*

Safer, D., & Allen, R. (1976). *Hyperactive children: Diagnosis and management.* Baltimore: University Park Press.

Safford, P. (1978). *Teaching young children with special needs.* St. Louis, MO: Mosby.

Sagaria, S., & DiVesta, F. (1978). Learner expectations induced by adjunct questions and the retrieval of intentional and incidental information. *Journal of Educational Psychology, 17*, 280–288.

Sagotsky, G., Patterson, C., & Lepper, M. (1978). Training children's self-control: A field experiment in self-monitoring and goal-setting in the classroom. *Journal of Experimental Child Psychology, 25*, 242–253.

Samelson, F. (1980). J. B. Watson's Little Albert, Cyril Burt's twins, and the need for a critical science. *American Psychologist, 35*, 619–625.

Samuel, W. (1977). Observed IQ as a function of test atmosphere, tester expectation, and race of tester: A replication for female subjects. *Journal of Educational Psychology, 69*, 593–604.

Sarason, I., & Sarason, B. (1981). Teaching cognitive and social skills to high school students. *Journal of Consulting and Clinical Psychology, 49*, 908–918.

Satterly, D. (1976). Cognitive styles, spatial ability, and school achievement. *Journal of Educational Psychology, 68*, 36–42.

Savin-Williams, R. (1979). Dominance hierarchies in groups of early adolescents. *Child Development, 50*, 923–935.

Scarr-Salapatek, S. (1975). Genetics and the development of intelligence. In F. Horowitz (Ed.), *Review of research in child development* (Vol. 4). Chicago: University of Chicago Press.

Schaffer, R. (1977). *Mothering*. Cambridge, MA: Cambridge University Press.

Schank, R. (1972). Conceptual dependency: A theory of natural language understanding. *Cognitive Psychology, 3*, 552–631.

Schank, R., & Abelson, R. (1975). Scripts, plans and knowledge. In Proceedings of the Fourth International Joint Conference on Artificial Intelligence, Tbilisi, U.S.S.R.

Schank, R., & Abelson, R. (1977). *Scripts, plans, goals, and understanding*. Hillsdale, NJ: Erlbaum.

Schiedel, D., & Marcia, J. (1985). Ego identity, intimacy, sex role orientation, and gender. *Developmental Psychology, 21*, 149–160.

Schiff, M., Duyme, M., Dumaret, A., & Tomkiewicz, S. (1982). How much *could* we boost scholastic achievement and IQ scores? A direct answer from a French adoption agency. *Cognition, 12*, 165–192.

Schmidt, W., & Buchmann, M., (1983). Six teachers' beliefs and attitudes and their curricular time allocations. *Elementary School Journal, 84*, 162–172.

Schoenfeld, A. (1979). Explicitly heuristic training as a variable in problem solving performance. *Journal for Research in Mathematics Education, 10*, 173–187.

Schoenfeld, A., & Herrmann, D. (1982). Problem perception and knowledge structure in expert and novice mathematical problem solvers. *Journal of Experimental Psychology, 8*, 484–494.

Schofield, H. (1981). Teacher effects on cognitive and affective pupil outcomes in elementary school mathematics. *Journal of Educational Psychology, 73*, 462–471.

Schramm, W. (1964). *Research on programmed instruction: An annotated bibliography* (OE Contract No. 34034). Washington, DC: U.S. Office of Education.

Schriberg, L., Levin, J., McCormick, C., & Pressley, M. (1982). Learning about "famous" people via the keyword method. *Journal of Educational Psychology, 74*, 238–247.

Schuck, R. (1981). The impact of set induction on student achievement and retention. *Journal of Educational Research, 74*, 227–232.

Schultz, K. (1974). *Implementation guide: I/D/E/A change program for individually guided education, ages 5–12*. Dayton, OH: I/D/E/A.

Schwille, J., Porter, A., Belli, G., Floden, R., Freeman, D., Knappen, L., Kuhs, T., & Schmidt, W. (1983). Teachers as policy brokers in the content of elementary school mathematics. In L. Shulman & G. Sykes (Eds.), *Handbook of teaching and policy*. New York: Longman.

Sears, P. S. (1940). Levels of aspiration in relation to some variables of personality: Clinical studies. *Journal of Social Psychology, 14*, 311–336.

Seddon, G. (1978). The properties of Bloom's taxonomy of educational objectives for the cognitive domain. *Review of Educational Research, 48*, 303–323.

Sharan, S., & Sharan, Y. (1976). *Small-group teaching*. Englewood Cliffs, NJ: Educational Technology Publications.

Shavelson, R. (March, 1978). A model of teacher decision making. Paper presented at the annual meeting of the American Educational Research Association, Toronto.

Shavelson, R. (1983). Review of research on teachers' pedagogical judgments, plans, and decisions. *Elementary School Journal, 83*, 392–413.

Shavelson, R., & Stern, P. (1981). Research on teachers' pedagogical thoughts, judgments, decisions, and behavior. *Review of Educational Research, 51*(4), 455–498.

Sheinker, J., & Sheinker, A. (1982). *Study*

strategies: A meta-cognitive approach: Skimming, note taking, summarizing, outlining (four handbooks). Rock Springs, WY: White Mountain Publishing Co.

Sheldon, W. (with the collaboration of S. Stevens). (1942). *The varieties of temperament: A psychology of constitutional differences.* New York: Harper & Row.

Shepard, J. (May, 1973). Lost at C. *Playboy,* 143–144; 192–196.

Sherman, J. (Ed.). (1974). *PSI: Forty-one germinal papers.* Menlo Park, CA: W. A. Benjamin.

Shimmerlick, S., & Nolan, J. (1976). Organization and the recall of prose. *Journal of Educational Psychology,* 68, 779–786.

Shimron, J. (1973). Learning activities in individually prescribed instruction. Paper read at the annual meeting of the American Educational Research Association, New Orleans.

Shipman, V., McKee, J., & Bridgeman, B., with Boroson, M., Butler-Nalin, P., Grant, J., & Mikovsky, M. (1976). Stability and change in family status, situational, and process variables and their relationships to children's cognitive performance. Report PR-75-28, Educational Testing Service, Princeton, NJ.

Shulman, L. (1983). Autonomy and obligation: The remote control of teaching. In L. Shulman & G. Sykes (Eds.), *Handbook of teaching and policy.* New York: Longman.

Shulman, L., & Elstein, A. (1975). Studies of problem solving, judgment, and decision making: Implications for educational research. In R. Kerlinger (Ed.), *Review of research in education.* No. 3. Itasca, IL: Peacock.

Shulman, L., & Keislar, E. (Eds.). (1966). *Learning by discovery.* Chicago: Rand McNally.

Shulman, L. & Sykes, G. (Eds.). (1983). *Handbook of teaching and policy.* New York: Longman.

Sieber, R. (1979). Classmates as workmates: Informal peer activity in the elementary school. *Anthropology and Education Quarterly, 10,* 207–235.

Sigel, I. (1984). A constructivist perspective for teaching and thinking. *Educational Leadership, 42,* 18–21.

Sigel, I. (Ed.). (1985). *Parental belief systems: The psychological consequences for children.* Hillsdale, NJ: Erlbaum.

Sigel, I., Brodzinsky, D., & Golinkoff, R. (Eds.). (1981). *New directions in Piagetian theory and practice.* Hillsdale, NJ: Erlbaum.

Sigel, I., & Coop, R. (1974). Cognitive style and classroom practice. In R. Coop and K. White (Eds.), *Psychological concepts in the classroom.* New York: Harper & Row.

Silberman, C. (Ed.). (1973). *The open classroom reader.* New York: Vintage.

Silver, E. (1979). Student perceptions of relatedness among mathematical verbal problems. *Journal for Research in Mathematics Education, 10,* 195–210.

Simon, A., & Boyer, E. (1967, 1969, & 1970). *Mirrors for behavior: An anthology of classroom observation instruments.* Philadelphia: Humanizing Learning Program, Research for Better Schools, Inc.

Simon, H. (1978). Information-processing theory of human problem solving. In W. Estes (Ed.), *Handbook of learning and cognitive processes. Volume 5. Human information processing.* Hillsdale, NJ: Erlbaum.

Simon, H. (1979). Information processing models of cognition. In M. Rosenzweig & L. Porter (Eds.), *Annual review of psychology.* Palo Alto, CA: Annual Reviews.

Simon, H. (1980). Problem solving and education. In D. Tuma & R. Reif (Eds.), *Problem solving and education: Issues in teaching and research.* Hillsdale, NJ: Erlbaum.

Simon, H. (1981). *The sciences of the artificial.* (2nd ed.). Cambridge, MA: MIT Press.

Simon, S., Howe, L., & Kirschenbaum, H. (1972). *Values clarification: A handbook of practical strategies for teachers and students.* New York: Hart.

Simpson, E., & Gray, M. (1976). *Humanistic education: An interpretation.* Cambridge, MA: Ballenger Publishing Co.

Singer, H., & Donlan, D. (1982). Active comprehension: Problem solving schema with question generation for comprehension of complex short stories. *Reading Research Quarterly,* 5, 228–240.

Singer, R. (1977). To err or not to err: A question for the instruction of psychomotor skills. *Review of Educational Research, 47,* 479–498.

Sirotnik, K. (1982). The contextual correlates of the relative expenditures of classroom time on instruction and behavior: An explanatory study of secondary schools and classes. *American Educational Research Journal, 19*, 275–292.

Sirotnik, K. (1983). What you see is what you get—consistency, persistency, and mediocrity in classrooms. *Harvard Educational Review, 53*, 16–31.

Sitku, E. (1968). The effects of class size: A review of the research. ERIC CED 043 124, EA 003 074. Washington, DC: U.S. Department of Health, Education, and Welfare.

Skinner, B. (1948). *Walden Two*. New York: Macmillan.

Skinner, B. (1954). The science of learning and the art of teaching. *Harvard Educational Review, 24*, 86–97.

Skinner, B. (1958). Teaching machines. *Science, 128*, 969–977.

Skinner, B. (1968). *The technology of teaching*. New York: Appleton-Century-Crofts.

Skinner, B. (1971). *Beyond freedom and dignity*. New York: Knopf.

Skinner, B. (1974). *About behaviorism*. New York: Knopf.

Slavin, R. (1977a). How student learning teams can integrate the desegregated classroom. *Integrated Education, 15*(6), 56–58.

Slavin, R. (1977b). Classroom reward structure: An analytic and practical review. *Review of Educational Research, 47*(4), 633–640.

Slavin, R. (1978). Student teams and comparison among equals: Effects on academic performance and student attitudes. *Journal of Educational Psychology, 70*, 532–538.

Slavin, R. (1979). Effects of biracial learning teams on cross-racial friendships. *Journal of Educational Psychology, 71*, 381–387.

Slavin, R. (1984). Students motivating students to excel: Cooperative incentives, cooperative tasks, and student achievement. *Elementary School Journal, 85*, 53–64.

Slavin, R., & Karweit, N. (in press). Cognitive and affective outcomes of an intensive Student Team Learning experience. *Journal of Experimental Education.*

Slavin, R., Sharan, S., Kagan, S., Lazarowitz, R., Webb, C., & Schmuck, R. (Eds.). (1985). *Learning to cooperate, cooperating to learn*. New York: Plenum.

Slavin, R., & Oickle, E. (1981). Effects of cooperative learning teams on student achievement and race relations: Treatment by race interactions. *Sociology of Education, 54*, 174–180.

Smith, B. (1980). Influence of solicitation pattern, type of practice example, and student response on pupil behavior, commitment to discussion and concept attainment. *Theory and Research in Social Education, 7*, 1–17.

Smith, C. (1982). *Promoting the social development of young children: Strategies and activities*. Palo Alto, CA: Mayfield.

Smith, L. (1979). Task-oriented lessons and student achievement. *Journal of Educational Research, 73*, 16–19.

Smith, L., & Land, M. (1981). Low-inference verbal behaviors related to teacher clarity. *Journal of Classroom Interaction, 17*, 37–42.

Smith, L., & Sanders, K. (1981). The effects on student achievement and studies perception of varying structure in social student content. *Journal of Educational Research, 74*, 333–336.

Smith, M., & Glass, G. (1979). *Relationship of class size to classroom processes, teacher satisfaction and pupil affect: A meta-analysis*. San Francisco: Far West Laboratory for Educational Research and Development.

Snarey, J., Reimer, J., & Kohlberg, L. (1985). Development of social-moral reasoning among kubbutz adolescents: A longitudinal cross-cultural study. *Developmental Psychology, 21*, 3–17.

Snow, R. (1984). Placing children in special education: Some comments. *Educational Researcher, 13*, 12–14.

Snyder, M., Stephan, W., & Rosenfield, D. (1978). Attributional egotism. In J. Harvey, W. Ickes, & R. Kidd (Eds.), *New directions in attribution research*, (Vol. II). New York: Wiley.

Soar, R. (1970–71). *Follow through classroom process measurement and pupil growth*. Final Report. Gainesville, FL: Institute for Development of Human Resources, University of Florida.

Soar, R., & Soar, R. (1972). An empirical analysis of selected Follow-Through programs: An example of a process approach to evaluation. In I. Gordon (Ed.), *Early childhood education*. Chicago: National Society for the Study of Education.

Soar, R., & Soar, R. (1979). Emotional climate and management. In P. Peterson & H. Walberg (Eds.), *Research on teaching: Concepts, findings, and implications*. Berkeley, CA: McCutchan.

Solomon, D., & Kendall, A. (1979). *Children in classrooms: An investigation of person-environment interaction*. New York: Praeger.

Spencer, D. (1984a). The home and school lives of women teachers. *Elementary School Journal, 84*, 283–298.

Spencer, D. (1984b). The home and school lives of women teachers: Implications for staff development. *Elementary School Journal, 84*, 299–314.

Spencer-Hall, D. (1976). A grounded theory of aligning actions in an elementary classroom. Unpublished doctoral dissertation, University of Missouri—Columbia.

Spino, W., Berger, A., Tonjes, M., & Abbott, A. (Eds.). (1972). Florida Center for Teaching Training Materials: FCTTM's annotated catalog of teacher training materials. Coral Gables, FL: Florida Center for Teaching Training Materials, University of Miami.

Spiro, R. (1977). Remembering information from text: Theoretical and empirical issues concerning the "State of Schema" reconstruction hypothesis. In R. Anderson, R. Spiro, & W. Montague (Eds.), *Schooling and the acquisition of knowledge*. Hillsdale, NJ: Erlbaum.

Sprinthall, N., & Thies-Sprinthall, L. (1983). The teacher as an adult learner: A cognitive-developmental view. In G. A. Griffin (Ed.), *Staff development* (Eighty-second Yearbook of the National Society for the Study of Education). Chicago: University of Chicago Press.

St. John, N. (1971). Thirty-six teachers: Their characteristics and outcomes for blacks and white pupils. *American Educational Research Journal, 8*, 635–648.

Staffieri, J. (1967). A study of social stereotypes of body image in children. *Journal of Personality and Social Psychology, 7*, 101–104.

Stallings, J. (1975). Implementation and child effects of teaching practices in Follow-Through classrooms. Monographs of the Society for Research in Child Development, 40, Nos. 7–8 (Serial No. 163).

Stallings, J. (1977). *Learning to look*. Belmont, CA: Wadsworth.

Stallings, J. (1980). Allocated academic learning time revisited, or beyond time on task. *Educational Researcher*, 9(11), 11–16.

Stallings, J., Cory, R., Fairweather, J., & Needels, M. (1977). *Early childhood education classroom evaluation*. Menlo Park, CA: SRI International.

Stallings, J., Cory, R., Fairweather, J., & Needels, M. (1978). *A study of basic reading skills taught in secondary schools*. Menlo Park, CA: SRI International.

Stallings, J., Needels, M., & Stayrook, N. (1979). *How to change the process of teaching basic reading skills in secondary schools: Phase II and Phase III*. Menlo Park, CA: SRI International.

Stanchfield, J. (1973). *Sex differences in learning to read*. Bloomington, IN: Phi Delta Kappa Educational Foundation.

Stanford, G. (1977). *Developing effective classroom groups: A practical guide for teachers*. New York: Hart.

Stanley, J. (1971). Reliability. In R. Thorndike (Ed.), *Educational measurement* (2nd ed.). Washington, DC: American Council on Education.

Staub, E. (1979). *Positive social behavior and morality: Socialization and development*. New York: Academic Press.

Stedman, L., & Smith, M. (1983). Recent reform proposals for American education. *Contemporary Education Review, 2*(2), 85–104.

Stein, B., & Bransford, J. (1979). Constraints on effective elaboration: Effects of precision and subject generation. *Journal of Verbal Learning and Verbal Behavior, 18*, 769–777.

Steinberg, L. (1981). Transformations in family relations at puberty. *Developmental Psychology, 17*, 833–840.

Steinkamp, M., & Maehr, M. (1984). Gender differences in motivational orientations toward achievement in school science: A quantitative synthesis. *American Educational Research Journal, 21*, 39–59.

Steinmetz, S. (1977). *The cycle of violence: Assertive, aggressive, and abusive family interaction*. New York: Praeger.

Sternberg, R. (1984). What should intelligence tests test? Implications of a triarchic theory of intelligence for intelligence testing. *Educational Researcher, 13*, 5–15.

Stevenson, H. (1970). Learning in children. In

P. Mussen (Ed.), *Carmichael's manual of child psychology* (3rd ed., Vol. 1). New York: Wiley.

Stevenson, H., Parker, T., Wilkenson, A., Bonnevaux, B., & Gonzalez, M. (1978). Schooling, environment, and cognitive development: A cross-cultural study. *Monographs of the Society for Research in Child Development, 43,* #3 (Serial #175).

Steward, M., & Steward, D. (1974). Effects of social distance on teaching strategies of Anglo-American and Mexican-American mothers. *Developmental Psychology, 10,* 797–807.

Stewig, J., & Higgs, M. (1973). Girls grow up to be mommies: Sexism in picture books. *School Library Journal, 19,* 44–49.

Stewig, J., & Knipfel, M. (1975). Sexism in picture books: What progress? *Elementary School Journal, 75,* 151–155.

Stipek, D. (1981). Children's perceptions of their own and their classmates' ability. *Journal of Educational Psychology, 73,* 404–410.

Stipek, D. (1984). The development of achievement motivation. In R. Ames & C. Ames (Eds.), *Research on motivation in education* (Vol. 1). Orlando, FL: Academic Press.

Stipek, D. J. (in press). Young children's performance expectations: Logical analysis or wishful thinking? In J. G. Nicholls (Ed.), *The development of achievement motivation.* Greenwich, CT: JAI Press.

Stipek, D., & Hoffman, J. (1980). Development of children's performance-related judgments. *Child Development, 51,* 912–914.

Stipek, D., Roberts, T., & Sanborn, M. (1983). Children's performance expectations for themselves and another child. Unpublished manuscript. Graduate School of Education, UCLA.

Stipek, D., & Sanborn, M. (1983). Preschool teachers' task-related interactions with handicapped and nonhandicapped boys and girls. A paper presented at the American Educational Research Association, Montreal, Canada.

Stipek, D., & Tannatt, L. (in press). Children's judgments of their own and their peers' academic competence. *Journal of Educational Psychology.*

St. John, N. (1971). Thirty-six teachers: Their characteristics and outcomes for black and white pupils. *American Educational Research Journal, 8,* 635–648.

Stodolsky, S., Ferguson, T., & Wimpelberg, K. (1981). The recitation persists, but what does it look like? *Journal of Curriculum Studies, 13,* 121–130.

Stolz, H., & Stolz, L. (1951). *Somatic development of adolescent boys.* New York: Macmillan.

Stone, C. (1982). A meta-analysis of advance organizer studies. Paper presented at the annual meeting of the American Educational Research Association, New York.

Strike, K. (1975). The logic of discovery. *Review of Educational Research, 45,* 461–483.

Strother, D. (1984). Homework: Too much, just right, or not enough? *Phi Delta Kappan, 65,* 423–426.

Suchman, J. (1962). *The elementary school training program in scientific inquiry.* Report to the U.S. Office of Education, Project Title VIII, Project 216. Urbana: University of Illinois.

Sullivan, H. (1953). *The interpersonal theory of psychiatry.* New York: Norton.

Sullivan, J. (1978). Comparing strategies of good and poor comprehenders. *Journal of Reading, 21,* 710–715.

Sunshine, P., & DiVesta, F. (1976). Effects of density and format on letter discrimination by beginning readers with different learning styles. *Journal of Educational Psychology, 68,* 15–19.

Swift, J., & Gooding, C. (1983). Interaction of wait-time feedback and questioning instruction on middle school science teaching. *Journal of Research in Science Teaching, 20,* 721–730.

Tadlock, D. (1978). SQ3R—why it works, based on information processing theory. *Journal of Reading, 22,* 110–112.

Talmage, H. (Ed.). (1975). *Systems of individualized education.* Berkeley, CA: McCutchan.

Tanner, J. (1970). Physical growth. In P. Mussen (Ed.), *Carmichael's manual of child psychology* (3rd ed., Vol. 1). New York: Wiley.

Tanner, J. (1973). Growing up. *Scientific American, 229*(3), 35–43.

Tanner, L. (1978). *Classroom discipline for effective teaching and learning.* New York: Holt, Rinehart and Winston.

Taylor, B. (1982). Text structure and children's comprehension and memory for expository material. *Journal of Educational Psychology, 70,* 323–340.

Taylor, R. (1980). *The computer in the school: Tutor, tool, tutee.* New York: Teachers College Press.

Tenbrink, T. (1974). *Evaluation: A practical guide for teachers.* New York: McGraw-Hill.

Tennyson, R., & Park, O. (1980). The teaching of concepts: A review of instructional design research literature. *Review of Educational Research, 50,* 55–70.

Terman, L., & Merrill, M. (1960). *Stanford-Binet intelligence scale: Manual for the third revision, form L-M.* Boston: Houghton Mifflin.

Thomas, A., & Chess, S. (1970). *Temperament and development.* New York: Brunner/Mazel.

Thomas, J. (1970). *Tutoring strategies and effectiveness: A comparison of elementary age tutors and college tutors.* Unpublished doctoral dissertation, University of Texas at Austin.

Thompson, G., & Hunnicutt, C. (1944). The effect of repeated praise or blame on the work achievement of "introverts" and "extroverts." *Journal of Educational Psychology, 35,* 257–266.

Thompson, H. (1954). Physical growth. In L. Carmichael (Ed.), *Manual of child psychology* (2nd ed.). New York: Wiley.

Thompson, M., Brassell, W., Persons, S., Tucker, R., & Rollins, H. (1974). Contingency management in the schools: How often and how well does it work? *American Educational Research Journal, 11,* 19–28.

Thompson, R., White, K., & Morgan, D. (1982). Teacher-student interaction patterns in classrooms with mainstreamed mildly handicapped students. *American Educational Research Journal, 19,* 220–236.

Thornburg, H. (1982). *Development in adolescence.* (2nd ed.). Monterey: Brooks/Cole.

Thorndike, E. (1913). *The psychology of learning: Educational psychology,* (Vol. 2). New York: Teachers College Press.

Thorndike, E. (1924). Mental discipline in high school studies. *Journal of Educational Psychology, 15,* 1–22, 83–98.

Thorndike, R., & Hagen, E. (1969). *Measurement and evaluation in psychology and education* (3rd ed.). New York: Wiley.

Thorndike, R., & Hagen, E. (1977). *Measurement and evaluation in psychology and education* (4th ed.). New York: Wiley.

Thorndyke, P. (1977). Cognitive structures in comprehension and memory of narrative discourse. *Cognitive Psychology,* 9, 77–110.

Thorne, B., & Henley, N. (Eds.). (1975). *Language and sex: Differences and dominance.* Rowley, MA: Newbury House Publishers.

Thurstone, L. (1938). *Primary mental abilities.* Chicago: University of Chicago Press.

Tierney, R., & Cunningham, J. (1984). Research on teaching reading comprehension. In P. Pearson, M. Camil, R. Barr, & P. Mosenthal (Eds.), *Handbook of reading research.* New York: Longman.

Tikunoff, W., Berliner, D., & Rist, R. (1975). An ethnographic study of the forty classrooms of the Beginning Teacher Evaluation Study known sample. Technical Report No. 75-10-5, San Francisco: Far West Laboratory.

Tisher, R., Fyfield, J., & Taylor, S. (1979). *Beginning to teach: The induction of beginning teachers in Australia* (Vols. 1, 2). Canberra: Australian Government Publishing Service.

Tobias, S. (1973). Review of the response mode issue. *Review of Educational Research, 43,* 193–204.

Tobin, K. (1980). The effect of an extended teacher wait-time on science achievement. *Journal of Research in Science Teaching, 17,* 469–475.

Tobin, K. (1983a). The influence of wait-time on classroom learning. *European Journal of Science Education,* Vol. 5 (No. 1), 35–48.

Tobin, K. (1983b). Management of time in classrooms. In B. Fraser (Ed.), *Classroom management.* Bentley, Australia: Western Australian Institute of Technology.

Tobin, K., & Capie, W. (1982). Relationships between classroom process variables and middle-school science achievement. *Journal of Educational Psychology, 74,* 441–454.

Torrance, E. (1962). *Guiding creative talent.* Englewood Cliffs, NJ: Prentice-Hall.

Torrance, E. (1966). *Torrance Tests of Creative Thinking: Norms-technical manual.* Princeton, NJ: Personnel Press.

Torrance, E. (1972). Predictive validity of the Torrance Tests of Creative Thinking. *Journal of Creative Behavior,* 6, 236–252.

Torrance, E. (1975). Creativity research in education: Still alive. In I. Taylor & J. Getzels (Eds.), *Perspectives in creativity.* Chicago: Aldine.

Torrance, E., Tan, C., & Allman, T. (1970).

Verbal originality and teacher behavior: A predictive validity study. *Journal of Teacher Education, 21*, 335–341.

Towler, J., & Wheatley, G. (1971). Conservation concepts in college students: A replication and critique. *Journal of Genetic Psychology, 118*, 265–270.

Trabasso, T., & Bower, G. (1968). *Attention in learning*. New York: Wiley.

Trachtenberg, D. (1974). Student tasks in text material: What cognitive skills do they tap? *Peabody Journal of Education, 52*, 54–57.

Trotman, R. (1977). Race, IQ, and the middle class. *Journal of Educational Psychology, 69*, 266–273.

Tuddenham, R. (1951). Studies in reputation: III. Correlates of popularity among elementary-school children. *Journal of Educational Psychology, 42*, 257–276.

Tulving, E. (1972). Episodic and semantic memory. In E. Tulving & W. Donaldson (Eds.), *Organization of memory*. New York: Academic Press.

Tulving, E., & Thomson, D. (1973). Encoding specificity and retrieval processes in episodic memory. *Psychological Review, 80*, 352–373.

Tuma, D., & Reif, R. (Eds.), (1980). *Problem solving and education: Issues in teaching and research*. Hillsdale, NJ: Erlbaum.

Tversky, A., & Kahneman, D. (1974). Judgment under uncertainty, heuristics and biases. *Science, 195*, 1124–1134.

Tversky, B. (1973). Encoding processes in recognition and recall. *Cognitive Psychology, 5*, 275–287.

Tyler, L. (1965). *The psychology of human differences* (3rd ed.). New York: Appleton.

Underwood, B. (1961). Ten years of massed practice on distributed practice. *Psychological Review, 68*, 229–247.

Underwood, B., Kapelak, S., & Malmi, R. (1976). The spacing effect: Additions to the theoretical and empirical puzzles. *Memory and Cognition, 4*, 391–400.

Underwood, B., & Schultz, R. (1960). *Meaningfulness and verbal learning*. Philadelphia: Lippincott.

Unger, R. (1979). Toward a redefinition of sex and gender. *American Psychologist, 34*, 1085–1094.

VanRossum, E. & Schenk, S. (1984). The relationship between learning conception, study strategy and learning outcome. *British Journal of Educational Psychology, 54*, 73–83.

Vaughn, R. (1973). Community, courts, and conditions of special education today: Why? *Mental Retardation, 11*, 43–46.

Veenman, S. (1984). Perceived problems of beginning teachers. *Review of Educational Research, 54*(2), 143–178.

Vernon, P. (1981). Level I and Level II: A review. *Educational Psychologist, 16*, 45–64.

Vinsonhaler, J., Weinshank, A., Wagner, C., & Polin, R. (1983). Diagnosing children with educational problems: Characteristics of reading and learning disabilities specialists, and classroom teachers. *Reading Research Quarterly, 18*, 134–164.

Vockell, E., & Rivers, R. (1984). *Instructional computing for today's teachers*. New York: Macmillan.

Voeltz, L. (1982). Effects of structured interactions with severely handicapped peers on children's attitudes. *American Journal of Mental Deficiency, 86*, 38–39.

Voss, J., & Bisanz, G. (1982). Models and methods used in the study of prose comprehension and learning. In S. Black & B. Britton (Eds.), *Expository text*. Hillsdale, NJ: Erlbaum.

Voth, R. (1975). On lecturing. *Social Studies, 66*, 247–248.

Voyat, G. (1982). *Piaget systematized*. Hillsdale, NJ: Erlbaum.

Vroegh, K. (1976). Sex of teacher and academic achievement: A review of research. *Elementary School Journal, 76*, 389–405.

Vroom, V. (1964). *Work and motivation*. New York: Wiley.

Vygotsky, L. (1962). *Thought and language*. Cambridge, MA: M.I.T. Press.

Vygotsky, L. (1978). *Mind in society: The development of higher psychological processes*. (M. Cole, V. John-Steiner, S. Scribner, & E. Souberman, Eds.). Cambridge: Harvard University Press.

Waber, D., Carlson, D., Mann, M., Merola, J., & Moylan, P. (1984). SES-related aspects of neuropsychological performance. *Child Development, 55*, 1878–1886.

Wadsworth, B. (1978). *Piaget for the classroom teacher*. New York: Longman.

Walberg, H., Schiller, D., & Haertel, G. (1979). The quiet revolution in educational research. *Phi Delta Kappan, 61*, 179–183.

Waldrop, M. (1984). The necessity of knowledge. *Science, 223,* 1279–1282.

Walker, L. (1980). Cognitive and perspective-taking prerequisites for moral development. *Child Development, 51,* 131–139.

Walker, L. (1982). The sequentiality of Kohlberg's stages of moral development. *Child Development, 53,* 1330–1336.

Walker, L. (1983). Sources of cognitive conflict for stage transition in moral development. *Developmental Psychology, 19,* 103–110.

Walker, L. (1984). Sex differences in the development of moral reasoning: A critical review. *Child Development, 55,* 677–691.

Wallace, M. (1970). Creativity. In P. Mussen (Ed.), *Carmichael's manual of child psychology* (3rd ed., Vol. 1). New York: Wiley.

Wallach, M. (1971). *The intelligence/creativity distinction.* New York: General Learning Press.

Wallach, M., & Kogan, N. (1965). *Modes of thinking in young children.* New York: Holt, Rinehart and Winston.

Wallas, G. (1921). *The art of thought.* New York: Harcourt, Brace, and World.

Waller, P., & Gaa, J. (1974). Motivation in the classroom. In R. Coop & K. White (Eds.), *Psychological concepts in the classroom.* New York: Harper & Row.

Walsh, J. (1981). A plenipotentiary for human intelligence. *Science, 214,* 640–641.

Wang, M. (1973). *Teacher's manual for the exploratory learning component of the LRDC individualized instructional program for the early learning grades.* Pittsburgh: Learning Research and Development Center, University of Pittsburgh.

Wang, M. (1974). *The rationale and design of the self-schedule system.* Pittsburgh: Learning Research and Development Center, University of Pittsburgh.

Wang, M. (1976). The use of observation data for formative evaluation of an instructional model. *Instructional Science, 5,* 365–389.

Wang, M. (1981). Mainstreaming exceptional children: Some instructional design and implementation considerations. *Elementary School Journal, 18,* 195–221.

Wang, M., & Resnick, L. (1978). *The Primary Education Program.* Johnstown, PA: Mafex Associates.

Ware, B. (1978). What rewards do students want? *Phi Delta Kappan, 59,* 355–356.

Warner, W., Meeker, M., & Eells, K. (1949). *Social class in America.* Chicago: Science Research Associates.

Waterman, A. (1982). Identity development from adolescence to adulthood: An extension of theory and a review of research. *Developmental Psychology, 18,* 341–358.

Watson, J. (1913). Psychology as the behaviorist views it. *Psychological Review, 20,* 158–177.

Watson, J. (1914). *Behavior.* New York: Holt.

Watson, J. (1928). *Psychological care of infant and child.* New York: Norton.

Watson, J., & Rayner, R. (1920). Conditioned emotional reactions. *Journal of Experimental Psychology, 3,* 1–14.

Webb, N. (1984). Microcomputer learning in small groups: Cognitive requirements and group processes. *Journal of Educational Psychology, 76,* 1076–1088.

Weil, M., & Joyce, B. (1978). *Information processing models of teaching.* Englewood Cliffs, NJ: Prentice-Hall.

Weiner, B. (1966). The role of success and failure in the learning of easy and complex tasks. *Journal of Personality and Social Psychology, 3,* 339–343.

Weiner, B. (1972). *Theories of motivation: From mechanism to cognition.* Chicago: McNally.

Weiner, B. (1979). A theory of motivation for some classroom experiences. *Journal of Educational Psychology, 71,* 3–25.

Weiner, B. (1983). Speculations regarding the role of affect in achievement-change programs guided by attributional principles. In M. Levine & M. Wang (Eds.), *Teacher and student perceptions: Implications for learning.* Hillsdale, NJ: Erlbaum.

Weiner, B. (1984). Principles for a theory of student motivation and their application within an attributional framework. In R. Ames & C. Ames (Eds.), *Research on motivation in education* (Vol. 1). Orlando, FL: Academic Press.

Weiner, B., Anderson, A., & Prawat, R. (1982). Affective experience in the classroom. Unpublished manuscript, UCLA.

Weinshank, A. (1978). *The relationship between diagnosis and remediation in reading: A pilot study.* Research Series #37, Institute for Research on Teaching, College of Education, Michigan State University.

Weinstein, C. (1977). Modifying student behavior in an open classroom through changes in the physical design. *American Educational Research Journal, 14*, 249–262.

Weinstein, C. (1982). Training students to use elaboration learning strategies. *Contemporary Educational Psychology, 7*, 301–311.

Weinstein, C., & Mayer, R. (1985). The teaching of learning strategies. In M. Wittrock (Ed.), *Handbook of research on teaching* (3rd ed.). New York: Macmillan.

Weinstein, C., & Underwood, V. (1983). Learning strategies: The *how* of learning. In J. Segal, S. Chipman, & R. Glaser (Eds.), *Relating instruction to basic research*. Hillsdale, NJ: Erlbaum.

Weinstein, R. (1976). Reading group membership in first grade: Teacher behaviors and pupil experience over time. *Journal of Educational Psychology, 68*, 103–116.

Weinstein, R. (1979). Student perceptions of differential teacher treatment. Final report to the National Institute of Education, Grant NIE-G-79-0078, Berkeley, CA.

Weinstein, R., Marshall, H., Brattesani, K., & Middlestadt, S. (1982). Student perceptions of differential teacher treatment in open and traditional classrooms. *Journal of Educational Psychology, 74*, 678–692.

Weinstein, R., & Middlestadt, S. (1979). Student perceptions of teacher interactions with male high and low achievers. *Journal of Educational Psychology, 71*, 421–431.

Weisz, J. (1979). Perceived control and learned helplessness among mentally retarded and nonretarded children: A developmental analysis. *Developmental Psychology, 15*, 311–319.

Wheeler, R., & Ryan, F. (1973). Effects of cooperative and competitive classroom environments on the attitudes and achievement of elementary school students engaged in social studies inquiry activities. *Journal of Educational Psychology, 65*, 402–407.

White, B. (1975). *The first three years of life*. Englewood Cliffs, NJ: Prentice-Hall.

White, B., & Watts, J. (1973). *Experience and environment: Major influences on the development of the young child*. Englewood Cliffs, NJ: Prentice-Hall.

White, C., Bushnell, N., & Regnemer, J. (1978). Moral development in Bahamian school children: A 3-year examination of Kohlberg's stages of moral development. *Developmental Psychology, 14*, 58–65.

White, M. (1977). Social motivation in the classroom. In S. Ball (Ed.), *Motivation in education*. New York: Academic Press.

Whitehurst, G. (1977). Comprehension, selective imitation, and the CIP hypothesis. *Journal of Experimental Child Psychology, 23*, 23–38.

Whorf, B. (1956). *Language, thought, and reality: Selected writings*. Cambridge, MA: Technology Press.

Wickelgren, W. (1974). *How to solve problems: Elements of a theory of problems and problem solving*. San Francisco: Freeman.

Wickelgren, W. (1981). Human learning and memory. In M. Rosenzweig & L. Porter (Eds.), *Annual review of psychology*. Palo Alto, CA: Annual Reviews.

Wilen, W. (1984). Implications of research on questioning for the teacher educator. *Journal of Research and Development in Education, 17*(2), 31–35.

Wilhite, S. (1983). Prepassage questions: The influence of structural importance. *Journal of Educational Psychology, 75*, 234–244.

Willems, E. P. (1967). Sense of obligation to high school activities as related to school size and marginality of student. *Child Development*, 38, 1247–1260.

Willerman, L. (1979). *The psychology of individual and group differences*. San Francisco: Freeman.

Willis, S. (1972). Formation of teachers' expectations of students' academic performance. Unpublished doctoral dissertation, Department of Educational Psychology, University of Texas at Austin.

Willson, I. (1973). Changes in mean levels of thinking in grades 1–8 through use of an interaction analysis system based on Bloom's taxonomy. *Journal of Educational Research*, 66, 423–429.

Wimbey, A., & Lochhead, J. (1980). *Problem solving and comprehension: A short course in analytical reasoning*, (2nd ed.). New York: Franklin Institute Press.

Winne, P. (1979). Experiments relating teachers' use of higher cognitive questions to student achievement. *Review of Educational Research*, 49, 13–50.

Winne, P., & Marx, R. (1977). Reconceptualizing research on teaching. *Journal of Educational Psychology, 69*, 668–678.

Winograd, T. (1975). Frame representations and the declarative/procedural controversy. In B. Bobrow & A. Collins (Eds.), *Representation and understanding*. New York: Academic Press.

Witkin, H., Dyk, R., Faterson, H., Goodenough, D., & Karp, S. (1962). *Psychological differentiation*. New York: Wiley.

Witkin, H., Moore, C., Goodenough, D., & Cox, P. (1977). Field-dependent and field-independent cognitive styles and their educational implications. *Review of Educational Research, 47*, 1–64.

Wittcoff, C. (1980). *Power motivation in the schools*. Unpublished doctoral dissertation, Washington University, St. Louis, MO.

Wittig, M., & Petersen, A. (Eds.). (1979). *Sex-related differences in cognitive functioning: Developmental issues*. New York: Academic Press.

Wittrock, M. (1974). Learning as a generative process. *Educational Psychologist, 11*, 87–95.

Wittrock, M. (Ed.). (1977). *Learning and instruction*. Berkeley, CA: McCutchan.

Wittrock, M. (1978). Education and the cognitive processes of the brain. In J. Chall & A. Mirsky (Eds.), *Education and the brain: The 77th Yearbook of the National Society for the Study of Education, Part II*. Chicago: University of Chicago Press.

Wittrock, M., Marks, C., & Doctorow, M. (1975). Reading as a generative process. *Journal of Educational Psychology, 67*, 484–489.

Wixson, K. (1983). Postreading question-answer interactions and children's learning from text. *Journal of Educational Psychology, 30*, 413–423.

Wixson, K. (1984). Level of importance of postquestions and children's learning from text. *American Educational Research Journal, 21*, 419–433.

Wixson, K., Bosky, A., Yochum, M., & Alvermann, D. (1984). An interview for assessing students' perceptions of classroom reading tasks. *Reading Teacher, 37*, 346–352.

Wolf, R. (1966). The measurement of environments. In A. Anastasi (Ed.), *Testing problems in perspective* (rev. ed.). Washington, DC: Council on Education.

Wolfson, B., & Nash, S. (1968). Perceptions of decision-making in elementary school classrooms. *Elementary School Journal, 69*, 89–93.

Wong, B., & Jones, W. (1982). Increasing metacomprehension in learning disabled and normally achieving students through self-questioning training. *Learning Disability Quarterly, 5*, 228–240.

Woodson, M. (1974). Seven aspects of teaching concepts. *Journal of Educational Psychology, 66*, 184–188.

Wright, C. & Nuthall, G. (1970). Relationships between teacher behaviors and pupil achievement in three experimental elementary science lessons. *American Educational Research Journal, 7*, 477–491.

Wright, I. (1978). Moral reasoning and conduct of selected elementary school students. *Journal of Moral Education, 7*, 199–205.

Wright, R. S. (1975). The affective and cognitive consequences of an open education elementary school. *American Educational Research Journal, 12*, 449–468.

Wyckoff, W. (1973). The effect of stimulus variation on learning from lecture. *Journal of Experimental Education, 41*, 85–90.

Wyne, M., & Stuck, G. (1982). Time and learning: Implications for the classroom teacher. *Elementary School Journal, 83*, 67–75.

Yando, R., Seitz, V., & Zigler, E. (1979). *Intellectual and personality characteristics of children: Social-class and ethnic-group differences*. Hillsdale, NJ: Erlbaum.

Yinger, R. (1977). A study of teacher planning: Description and theory development using ethnographies and information processing methods. Unpublished dissertation. Michigan State University.

Ysseldyke, J., Algozzine, B., & Allen, D. (1981). Participation of regular education teachers in special education team decision making. A naturalistic investigation. *Elementary School Journal, 82*, 160–165.

Zigler, E., & Valentine, J. (Eds.). (1979). *Project Head Start: A legacy of the war on poverty*. New York: Free Press.

Zimet, C. (1976). Reader content and sex differences in achievement. *The Reading Teacher, 29*, 758–763.

Zivin, G. (1979). *The development of self-regulation through private speech*. New York: Wiley.

Name Index

Subject Index